LaunchPad for *How Children Develop*, Fifth Edition

Available August 2017 at launchpadworks.com

Each chapter in LaunchPad for *How Children Develop*, Fifth Edition, features a collection of activities carefully chosen to help master the major concepts. The site serves students as a comprehensive online study guide, available any time, with opportunities for self-quizzing with instant feedback, exam preparation, and further exploration of topics from the textbook. For instructors, all units and activities can be instantly assigned, and students' results and analytics are collected in the Gradebook.

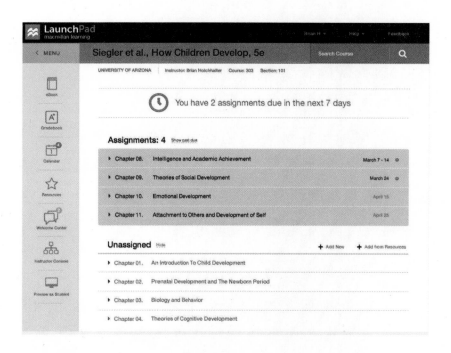

FOR STUDENTS

- Full e-Book of *How Children Develop*, Fifth Edition
- Chapter Summaries
- LearningCurve Quizzing
- Student Video Activities
- Interactive Flashcards
- Research Exercises
- *Scientific American* Newsfeed

FOR INSTRUCTORS

- Gradebook
- Presentation Slides
- Clicker Questions
- Electronic Figures, Photos, and Tables
- Instructor Resources

How Children
DEVELOP

FIFTH EDITION

Robert Siegler
Carnegie Mellon University

Nancy Eisenberg
Arizona State University

Elizabeth Gershoff
The University of Texas at Austin

Jenny R. Saffran
University of
Wisconsin–Madison

Judy DeLoache
University of Virginia

and
Campbell Leaper,
University of California–Santa Cruz,
reviser of Chapter 15: Gender
Development

worth publishers
Macmillan Learning

New York

This is dedicated to the ones we love

Vice President, Editorial, Social Sciences and High School: Charles Linsmeier
Senior Acquisitions Editor: Daniel DeBonis
Development Editor: Andrew Sylvester
Assistant Editor: Katie Pachnos
Executive Marketing Manager: Katherine Nurre
Marketing Assistant: Morgan Ratner
Director of Digital Production: Keri deManigold
Executive Media Editor: Noel Hohnstine
Senior Media Editor: Laura Burden
Media Editorial Assistant: Nik Toner
Director, Content Management Enhancement: Tracey Kuehn
Managing Editor, Sciences and Social Sciences: Lisa Kinne
Senior Project Editor: Vivien Weiss
Media Producer: Elizabeth Dougherty
Senior Photo Editor: Christine Buese
Photo Researcher: Rona Tuccillo
Senior Production Supervisor: Sarah Segal
Director of Design, Content Management: Diana Blume
Senior Design Manager and Cover Designer: Vicki Tomaselli
Interior Design: Tamara Newman
Art Manager: Matthew McAdams
Illustrations: Matthew McAdams; Todd Buck Illustration; Precision Graphics; TSI Graphics, Inc.; MPS Ltd.
Composition: codeMantra U.S. LLC
Printing and Binding: LSC Communications
Cover Art: *Sailboat, Palais Sur Mer*, 2008 (oil on canvas). Andrew Macara/Private Collection/Bridgeman Images

Library of Congress Control Number: 2016956966

ISBN-10: 1-319-01423-2
ISBN-13: 978-1-319-01423-0

Second printing

Worth Publishers
One New York Plaza
Suite 4500
New York, New York 10004-1562
www.macmillanlearning.com

About the Authors

ROBERT SIEGLER is the Teresa Heinz Professor of Cognitive Psychology at Carnegie Mellon University. He is author of the cognitive development textbook *Children's Thinking* and has written or edited several additional books on child development. His books have been translated into Japanese, Chinese, Korean, German, Spanish, French, Greek, Hebrew, and Portuguese. In the past few years, he has presented keynote addresses at the conventions of the Cognitive Development Society, the International Society for the Study of Behavioral Development, the Japanese Psychological Association, the Eastern Psychological Association, the American Psychological Society, and the Conference on Human Development. He also has served as Associate Editor of the journal *Developmental Psychology,* co-edited the cognitive development volume of the 2006 *Handbook of Child Psychology,* and served on the National Mathematics Advisory Panel from 2006 to 2008. Dr. Siegler received the American Psychological Association's Distinguished Scientific Contribution Award in 2005, was elected to the National Academy of Education in 2010, was named Director of the Siegler Center for Innovative Learning at Beijing Normal University in 2012, and was elected to the Society of Experimental Psychologists in 2016.

JENNY R. SAFFRAN is the College of Letters & Science Distinguished Professor of Psychology at the University of Wisconsin–Madison, and is an investigator at the Waisman Center. Her research is focused on learning in infancy and early childhood, with a particular emphasis on language. Dr. Saffran currently holds a MERIT award from the Eunice Kennedy Shriver National Institute of Child Health and Human Development. She has received numerous awards for her research and teaching, including the Boyd McCandless Award from the American Psychological Association for early career contributions to developmental psychology and the Presidential Early Career Award for Scientists and Engineers from the National Science Foundation. In 2015, she was elected to the American Academy of Arts and Sciences.

NANCY EISENBERG is Regents' Professor of Psychology at Arizona State University. Her research interests include social, emotional, and moral development, as well as socialization influences, especially in the areas of self-regulation and adjustment. She has published numerous empirical studies, as well as books and chapters on these topics. She has also been editor of *Psychological Bulletin* and the *Handbook of Child Psychology* and was the founding editor of the Society for Research in Child Development journal *Child Development Perspectives.* Dr. Eisenberg has been a recipient of Research Scientist Development Awards and a Research Scientist Award from the National Institutes of Health (NICHD and NIMH). She has served as President of the Western Psychological Association and of Division 7 of the American Psychological Association and is president-elect of the Association for Psychological Science. She is the 2007 recipient of the Ernest R. Hilgard Award for a Career Contribution to General Psychology, Division 1, American

Psychological Association; the 2008 recipient of the International Society for the Study of Behavioral Development Distinguished Scientific Contribution Award; the 2009 recipient of the G. Stanley Hall Award for Distinguished Contribution to Developmental Psychology, Division 7, American Psychological Association; and the 2011 recipient of the William James Fellow Award for Career Contributions in the Basic Science of Psychology from the Association for Psychological Science.

JUDY DELOACHE is the William R. Kenan Jr. Professor of Psychology at the University of Virginia. She has published extensively on aspects of cognitive development in infants and young children. Dr. DeLoache has served as President of the Developmental Division of the American Psychological Association, as President of the Cognitive Development Society, and as a member of the executive board of the International Society for the Study of Infancy. She has presented major invited addresses at professional meetings, including the Association for Psychological Science and the Society for Research in Child Development. Dr. DeLoache is the holder of a Scientific MERIT Award from the National Institutes of Health, and her research is also funded by the National Science Foundation. She has been a visiting fellow at the Center for Advanced Study in the Behavioral Sciences in Palo Alto, California, and at the Rockefeller Foundation Study Center in Bellagio, Italy. She is a Fellow of the National Academy of Arts and Sciences. In 2013, she received the Distinguished Research Contributions Award from the Society for Research in Child Development and the William James Award for Distinguished Contributions to Research from the Association for Psychological Science.

ELIZABETH GERSHOFF is an Associate Professor of Human Development and Family Sciences at the University of Texas at Austin. Her research focuses on how parental and school discipline affect child and youth development and on how parent education and early education programs, such as the federal Head Start program, can improve the lives of at-risk children. She currently serves as Director of the Interdisciplinary Collaborative on Development in Context and as Associate Director for Faculty Development at the Population Research Center, both at the University of Texas at Austin. Dr. Gershoff has been awarded numerous federal grants from the Centers for Disease Control and Prevention, the National Institute for Child Health and Human Development, the National Institute for Mental Health, and the National Science Foundation to support her research. She was lead author of the volume *Societal Contexts of Child Development,* which won the 2014 Society for Research on Adolescence Social Policy Award for Best Edited Book. She was an Associate Editor at the journal *Developmental Psychology* and served on the executive board of the Developmental Psychology division of the American Psychological Association, the Committee on Policy and Communications at the Society for Research in Child Development, and the convention program committee of the Association for Psychological Science. She is an internationally recognized expert on the effects of physical punishment on children, and her research on the topic has been recognized with a Lifetime Legacy Achievement Award from the Center for the Human Rights of Children at Loyola University Chicago.

Brief Contents

Contents

CHAPTER

2 Prenatal Development and the Newborn Period 43

CHAPTER

3 Biology and Behavior 91

JOSE ORTEGA / ILLUSTRATION SOURCE

TILLY WILLIS / PRIVATE COLLECTION / BRIDGEMAN IMAGES

HERITAGE IMAGES / GETTY IMAGES

PRIVATE COLLECTION / BRIDGEMAN IMAGES

CHRISTIES IMAGES / PRIVATE COLLECTION / BRIDGEMAN IMAGES

ANNA BELLE LEE WASHINGTON / GETTY IMAGES

GEOFFREY CLEMENTS / GETTY IMAGES

FINE ART PHOTOGRAPHIC LIBRARY, LONDON / ART RESOURCE, NY

LAURIE WIGHAM / GETTY IMAGES

SELIGMAN, LINCOLN / LINCOLN SELIGMAN / PRIVATE COLLECTION / BRIDGEMAN IMAGES

Theme 3: Development Is Both Continuous and Discontinuous 687

Theme 4: Mechanisms of Developmental Change 690

Theme 5: The Sociocultural Context Shapes Development 696

Theme 6: Individual Differences 700

Theme 7: Child-Development Research Can Improve Children's Lives 703

Preface

This is an exciting time in the field of child development. The past decade has brought new theories, new ways of thinking, new areas of research, and innumerable new findings to the field. We originally wrote *How Children Develop* to describe this ever-improving body of knowledge of children and their development and to convey our excitement about the progress that is being made in understanding the developmental process. We are pleased to continue this endeavor with the publication of the fifth edition of *How Children Develop*.

As teachers of child development courses, we appreciate the challenge that instructors face in trying to present these advances and discoveries—as well as the major older ideas and findings—in a one-semester course. Therefore, rather than aim at encyclopedic coverage, we have focused on identifying the most important developmental phenomena and describing them in sufficient depth to make them meaningful and memorable to students. In short, our goal has been to write a textbook that makes the child development course coherent and enjoyable for students and teachers alike.

Classic Themes

The basic premise of the book is that all areas of child development are unified by a small set of enduring themes. These themes can be stated in the form of questions that child-development research tries to answer:

1. How do nature and nurture together shape development?
2. How do children shape their own development?
3. In what ways is development continuous and in what ways is it discontinuous?
4. How does change occur?
5. How does the sociocultural context influence development?
6. How do children become so different from one another?
7. How can research promote children's well-being?

These seven themes provide the core structure of the book. They are introduced and illustrated in Chapter 1; highlighted repeatedly, where relevant, in the subsequent fourteen content chapters; and utilized in the final chapter as a framework for integrating findings relevant to each theme from all areas of development. The continuing coverage of these themes allows us to tell a story that has a beginning (the introduction of the themes), a middle (discussion of specific findings relevant to them), and an ending (the overview of what students have learned about the themes). We believe that this thematic emphasis and structure will not only help students understand enduring questions about child development but will also leave them with a greater sense of satisfaction and completion at the end of the course.

Contemporary Perspective

The goal of providing a thoroughly contemporary perspective on how children develop has influenced the organization of our book as well as its contents. Whole new areas and perspectives have emerged that barely existed when most of today's child-development textbooks were originally written. The organization of *How Children Develop* is designed to present these new topics and approaches in the context of the field as it currently stands, rather than trying to shoehorn them into organizations that once fit the field but no longer do.

Consider the case of Piaget's theory and current research relevant to it. Piaget's theory often is presented in its own chapter, most of which describes the theory in full detail and the rest of which offers contemporary research that demonstrates problems with the theory. This approach often leaves students wondering why so much time was spent on Piaget's theory if modern research shows it to be wrong in so many ways.

The fact is that the line of research that began over 45 years ago as an effort to challenge Piaget's theory has emerged since then as a vital area in its own right—the area of conceptual development. Research in conceptual development provides extensive information on children's understanding of such fascinating topics as human beings, plants and animals, and the physical universe. As with other research areas, most studies in this field are aimed primarily at uncovering evidence relevant to current claims, not those of Piaget.

We adapted to this changing intellectual landscape in two ways. First, our chapter "Theories of Cognitive Development" (Chapter 4) describes the fundamental aspects of Piaget's theory in depth and honors his legacy by focusing on the aspects of his work that have proven to be the most enduring. Second, a first-of-its-kind chapter called "Conceptual Development" (Chapter 7) addresses the types of issues that inspired Piaget's theory but concentrates on modern perspectives and findings regarding those issues. This approach allows us to tell students about the numerous intriguing proposals and observations that are being made in this field, without the artificiality of classifying the findings as "pro-Piagetian" or "anti-Piagetian."

The opportunity to create a textbook based on current understanding also led us to assign prominent positions to such rapidly emerging areas as epigenetics, behavioral genetics, brain development, prenatal learning, infant cognition, acquisition of academic skills, emotional development, prosocial behavior, and friendship patterns. All these areas have seen major breakthroughs in recent years, and their growing prominence has led to even greater emphasis on them in this edition.

Getting Right to the Point

Our desire to offer a contemporary, streamlined approach led to other departures from the traditional organization. It is our experience that today's students take child-development courses for a variety of practical reasons and are eager to learn about *children*. Traditionally, however, they have had to wait two or three or even four chapters—on the history of the field, on major theories, on research methods, on genetics—before actually getting to the study of children. We wanted to build on their initial motivation from the start.

Rather than beginning the book, then, with an extensive examination of the history of the field, we include in Chapter 1 a brief overview of the social and intellectual context in which the scientific study of children arose and provide historical background wherever it is pertinent in subsequent chapters. Rather than have an early chapter of "blockbuster" theories that covers all the major cognitive and social theories at once (at a point far removed from the content chapters to which the theories apply), we present a chapter on cognitive developmental theories just before the chapters that focus on specific aspects of cognitive development, and we similarly present a chapter on social developmental theories just before the chapters that focus on specific aspects of social development. Rather than have a separate chapter on genetics, we include basic aspects of genetics as part of Chapter 3, "Biology and Behavior," and then discuss the contributions of genetics to some of the differences among individuals throughout the book. When we originally chose this organization, we hoped that it would allow us, from the first weeks of the course, to kindle students' enthusiasm for finding out how children develop. Judging by the overwhelmingly positive response we have received from students and instructors alike, it has.

Features

The most important feature of this book is the exposition, which we have tried to make as clear and compelling as possible. As in previous editions, we have given extra attention to making it accessible to a broad range of students.

To further enhance the appeal and accessibility of the text, we have retained three types of discussion boxes that explore topics of special interest:

- "Applications" boxes focus on how child-development research can be used to promote children's well-being. Among the applications that are summed up in these boxes are genetic testing, which probes the depths of an individual's genetic makeup; board-game procedures for improving preschoolers' understanding of numbers; the Carolina Abecedarian Project; interventions to reduce child abuse; programs, such as PATHS, for helping rejected children gain acceptance from their peers; and Positive Youth Development and Service Learning Programs, which seek to reduce problem behaviors and increase positive behaviors.

- "Individual Differences" boxes focus on populations that differ from the norm with regard to the specific topic under consideration, or on variations among children in the general population. Some of these boxes highlight developmental problems such as autism, ADHD, dyslexia, specific language impairment, visual impairments, and conduct disorder, whereas others focus on differences in the development of children that center on attachment status, gender, socioeconomic status, and cultural differences.

- "A Closer Look" boxes examine important and interesting research in greater depth than would otherwise be possible: the areas examined range from brain-mapping techniques and the emerging field of social neuroscience to discrepant gender identity to the developmental impact of homelessness and disparities between poverty and health.

In an effort to further engage students, we have added a brief Test Yourself quiz at the end of each chapter. Students can quickly test their comprehension and understanding of the material in preparation for exams or simply as a way to review.

We have also retained a number of other features intended to improve students' learning. These features include boldfacing key terms and supplying definitions both within the immediate text and in marginal glossaries; providing summaries at the end of each major section, as well as summaries for the overall chapter; and, at the end of each chapter, posing critical thinking questions intended to promote deeper consideration of essential topics.

 ## New to the Fifth Edition

We have expanded our coverage of a number of research areas that have become increasingly important in recent years for both the students of child development and the instructors who teach it. In the following paragraphs, we outline some of the highlights of the fifth edition. We hope that you find it to be useful and appealing.

New and Expanded Coverage

In selecting what to cover from among the many new discoveries about child development, we have emphasized the studies that strike us as the most interesting and important. While retaining and thoroughly updating its essential coverage, the fifth edition of *How Children Develop* continues to explore a number of fascinating areas in which there has been great progress in the past few years. Following is a very brief sampling of these many areas:

- The biological and neurobiological basis for developmental processes
- The role of specific gene variants in certain behaviors
- Social, economic, racial and ethnic, and cultural influences on development
- Differences in development in certain special populations
- Brain development and functioning
- The impact of technology and social media
- The expanding role of genetic testing and other gene-based technologies
- Applications of research to education
- The impact of recent cultural and social changes on a child's environment
- Interventions to foster children's social, moral, and emotional adjustment

Attention to these specific areas of research, among other recent developments in the field, has informed the revisions that we have made for the fifth edition. Some of the more significant changes to each chapter include the following:

Chapter 2

- Updated discussion of teratogens to include antidepressant medications and the Zika virus, as well as a brief discussion of the water crisis in Flint, Michigan.
- New coverage of nighttime awakenings for infants and the toll they take on parents, as well as possible interventions.

Chapter 3

- New Box 3.2 on genetic testing and Box 3.4 on poverty and health disparities.
- Box 3.3 has been updated with new mind-mapping and brain-scanning technologies.

- Updated discussions of behavior genetics, including genome-wide association studies, and of molecular genetics, especially genome-wide complex trait analysis.
- New coverage addressing recent research on the brain development of autistic children.
- New section on food neophobia and the development of food preferences.

Chapter 4

- New section on core-knowledge theories, including new coverage in Box 4.3 on educational applications of these theories.

Chapter 5

- Reorganized discussion of perception with greater focus on perceptual narrowing.
- Expanded coverage of cultural differences influencing infant cognitive and perceptual development, from differences in visual perception to differences in motor development.
- New discussion of recent research with touch-screen devices and Skype.

Chapter 6

- New coverage of language mixing and outcomes for bilingualism in Box 6.1, plus updated discussion of language-learning technologies in Box 6.3.
- New box 6.2 on language development and socioeconomic status.
- Expanded discussion of cultural variability in the use of symbols.

Chapter 7

- New Box 7.4 on the development of spatial concepts in blind and visually impaired children.

Chapter 8

- Updated discussion of the influence of environmental factors on the development of intelligence.
- New section on cultural influences in the development of mathematical abilities.

Chapter 9

- Updated coverage of media effects, including the pervasive use of mobile media devices by young children and their parents.
- New Box 9.2 covering developmental social neuroscience.
- Updated material about the effects of child maltreatment.
- Updated material about challenges associated with affluence.

Chapter 10

- New coverage on delayed gratification and implications for long-term development.
- New coverage of emotion display rules and emotion regulation.
- New coverage of internalizing mental disorders, such as depression and anxiety, and their treatment.
- New Box 10.1 on basic emotional expressions in infants, Box 10.2 on emotional intelligence, and Box 10.3 on toxic stress and adverse childhood experiences.

Chapter 11

- Reorganized discussion of the self and identity with greater focus on the interplay between self-esteem, self-concept, and identity.
- New coverage of sexual-minority identity.
- New Box 11.1 on discussing the impact of childcare on attachment, Box 11.2 on interventions to improve attachment, Box 11.3 on developing self-awareness among children with autism, and Box 11.4 on the effect of excessive praise on self-esteem.

Chapter 12

- Reorganized to begin with an introduction to family structure, including the impact of changes in the past few decades.
- Updated coverage of parental discipline and culture.
- Updated coverage of socioeconomic influences on family life.
- New discussions on same-sex parents, extended parents, and grandparents as parents.
- New Box 12.2 on parents' use of spanking and Box 12.4 on family-leave policies.

Chapter 13

- New section on the role of technology and social media in friendships.
- Expanded discussion of bullying and victimization.
- New Box 13.2 on cyberbullying and Box 13.4 on interventions to foster children's peer acceptance.

Chapter 14

- New discussion of peer influences on prosocial behavior.
- Updated Box 14.2 on school-based interventions for promoting prosocial behavior.
- New Box 14.4 on positive youth development and service learning.

Chapter 15

- New discussion of recent neuroscience research and the role of genes as an influence on gender differences in behavioral development.
- New discussion of intersectionality in the context of social identity theory.
- Expanded coverage of gender self-labeling and transgender children.
- Updated discussion of gender discrimination.
- Updated discussion of cultural influences on communication and social behavior.

Supplements

How Children Develop, Fifth Edition, features a wide array of multimedia tools designed for the individual needs of students and teachers. For more information about any of the items below, visit the online catalog at www.macmillanlearning.com.

LaunchPad with LearningCurve Quizzing

A comprehensive web resource for teaching and learning psychology

LaunchPad combines Worth Publishers' award-winning media with an innovative platform for easy navigation. For students, it is the ultimate online study guide with rich interactive tutorials, videos, e-Book, and the LearningCurve adaptive quizzing system. For instructors, LaunchPad is a full course space where class documents can be posted, quizzes are easily assigned and graded, and students' progress can be assessed and recorded. Whether you are looking for the most effective study tools or a robust platform for an online course, LaunchPad is a powerful way to enhance your class.

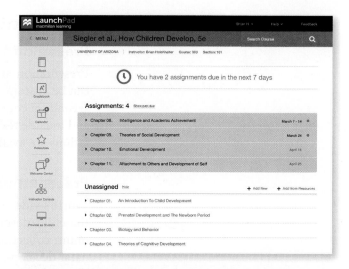

LaunchPad for *How Children Develop*, Fifth Edition, can be previewed and purchased at launchpadworks.com.

How Children Develop, Fifth Edition, and LaunchPad can be ordered together with ISBN-10: 1-319-12343-0 / ISBN-13: 978-1-319-12343-7.

LaunchPad for *How Children Develop*, Fifth Edition, includes the following resources:

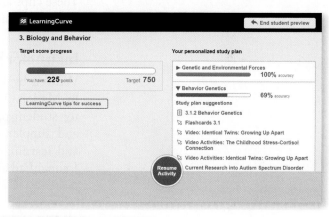

■ The **LearningCurve** quizzing system was designed based on the latest findings from learning and memory research. It combines adaptive question selection, immediate and valuable feedback, and a game-like interface to engage students in a learning experience that is unique to them. Each LearningCurve quiz is fully integrated with other resources in LaunchPad through the Personalized Study Plan, so students will be able to review with Worth's extensive library of videos and activities. And state-of-the-art question analysis reports allow instructors to track the progress of individual students, as well as their class as a whole.

■ **An interactive e-Book** allows students to highlight, bookmark, and make their own notes, just as they would with a printed textbook. Digital enhancements include full-text search and in-text glossary definitions.

■ **Student Video Activities** include more than 100 engaging video modules that instructors can easily assign for student assessment. Videos cover classic experiments, current news footage, and cutting-edge research, all of which are sure to spark discussion and encourage critical thinking.

■ The *Scientific American* **Newsfeed** delivers weekly articles, podcasts, and news briefs on the very latest developments in psychology from the first name in popular science journalism.

■ **Deep integration** is available between LaunchPad products and most learning management systems, including Blackboard, Brightspace by D2L, Canvas, and Moodle. These deep integrations offer educators single sign-on and gradebook sync, now with auto refresh. These best-in-class integrations offer deep linking to all Macmillan digital content at the chapter and asset levels, giving professors maximum flexibility within their LMS.

Presentation and Faculty Support

Presentation Slides

Presentation slides are available in two formats that can be used as they are or can be customized. One set includes all the textbook's illustrations and tables. The second set consists of lecture slides that focus on key themes and terms in the book and include text illustrations and tables. Both of these prebuilt PowerPoint presentations are available through LaunchPad at launchpadworks.com.

Presentation Videos

Worth's video clips for developmental psychology span the full range of topics for the child-development course. With hundreds of clips to choose from, this premium collection includes research and news footage on topics ranging from prenatal development to the experience of child soldiers to empathy in adolescence. These clips are made available to instructors for lecturing in the classroom and also through LaunchPad.

Instructor's Resource Manual

Written by Lynne Baker-Ward of North Carolina State University, and revised by Mallory Malkin, this innovative *Instructor's Resource Manual* includes handouts for student projects, reading lists of journal articles, course-planning suggestions, and supplementary readings, in addition to lecture guides, chapter overviews, and learning objectives. The *Instructor's Resource Manual* can be downloaded in LaunchPad at launchpadworks.com.

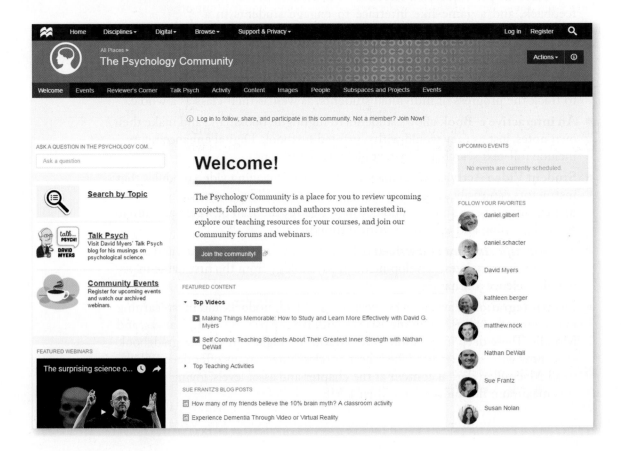

Macmillan Community

Macmillan Community is an online forum where teachers can find and share favorite teaching ideas and materials, including videos, animations, images, PowerPoint slides, news stories, articles, web links, and lecture activities. It is also the home of Worth's abundant social media content, including tweets, blog posts, webinars, and more! Browse the site and share your favorite materials for teaching psychology at https://community.macmillan.com.

Assessment

Test Bank

The Test Bank for *How Children Develop* by Chrysalis Wright of the University of Central Florida and Jill L. Saxon features more than 100 multiple-choice and essay questions for each chapter. Each question is keyed to the textbook by topic, type, and level of difficulty. The Diploma assessment software, available for Windows and Macs, guides instructors through the process of creating a test and allows them to add, edit, and scramble questions; to change formats; and to include pictures, equations, and media links. The Test Bank is available through LaunchPad at launchpadworks.com.

 ## Acknowledgments

So many people have contributed (directly and indirectly) to this textbook that it is impossible to know where to start or where to stop in thanking them. All of us have been given exceptional support by our spouses and significant others—Jerry Clore, Jerry Harris, Xiaodong Lin, Seth Pollak, and Andrew Gershoff—and by our children—Benjamin Clore; Michael Harris; Todd, Beth, and Aaron Siegler; Avianna McGhee; Eli and Nell Pollak; and Noah and Ella Gershoff—as well as by our parents, relatives, friends, and other loved ones. Our advisors in college and graduate school, Richard Aslin, Ann Brown, Les Cohen, Ted Dix, Harry Hake, George Holden, Robert Liebert, Jim Morgan, Paul Mussen, Elissa Newport, and Jim Pate, helped to launch our careers and taught us how to recognize and appreciate good research. We also have all benefited from collaborators who shared our quest for understanding child development and from a great many exceptionally helpful and generous colleagues, including Larry Aber, Karen Adolph, Martha Alibali, Renee Baillargeon, Sharon Carver, Zhe Chen, Robert Crosnoe, Richard Fabes, Cindy Fisher, Aletha Huston, Andrew Grogan-Kaylor, Melanie Jones, David Klahr, Patrick Lemaire, Angeline Lillard, John Opfer, Karl Rosengren, Kristin Shutts, Tracy Spinrad, David Uttal, Carlos Valiente, and Erica Wojcik. We owe special thanks to our assistants, Sheri Towe and Theresa Treasure, who helped in innumerable ways in preparing the book.

We would also like to thank the many reviewers who contributed to this and previous editions: **Daisuke Akiba,** Queens College, City University of New York; **Kimberly Alkins,** Queens College, City University of New York; **Hiram Allen,** College of New Rochelle; **Lynne Baker-Ward,** North Carolina State University; **Hilary Barth,** Wesleyan University; **Christopher Beevers,** University of Texas at Austin; **Martha Bell,** Virginia Tech; **Cynthia Berg,** University of Utah; **Rebecca Bigler,** University of Texas at Austin; **Margaret Borkowski,** Saginaw Valley State University; **Lyn Boulter,** Catawba College; **Renia Brown-Cobb,** Virginia State

University; **Eric Buhs,** University of Nebraska–Lincoln; **G. Leonard Burns,** Washington State University; **Allison Butler,** Bryant University; **Wendy Carlson,** Shenandoah University; **Mel Joseph Ciena,** University of San Francisco; **Kristi Cordell-McNulty,** Angelo State University; **Myra Cox,** Harold Washington College; **Maria Crisafi,** Columbia University; **Emily Davidson,** Texas A&M University–Main Campus; **Peggy DeCooke,** The State University of New York at Purchase; **Ed de St. Aubin,** Marquette University; **Marissa Diener,** University of Utah; **Sharon Eaves,** Shawnee State University; **Jessica Espinosa,** Miami Dade College; **Elisa Esposito,** Widener University; **Urminda Firlan,** Grand Rapids Community College; **Dorothy Fragaszy,** University of Georgia; **Jeffery Gagne,** University of Texas–Arlington; **Jennifer Ganger,** University of Pittsburgh; **Alice Ganzel,** Cornell College; **Catherine Gaze,** Elmhurst College; **Janet Gebelt,** Westfield State University; **Melissa Ghera,** St. John Fisher College; **Susan Graham,** University of Calgary; **Andrea Greenhoot,** University of Kansas; **Frederick Grote,** Western Washington University; **John Gruszkos,** Reynolds University; **Hanna Gustafsson,** University of North Carolina; **Alma Guyse,** Midland College; **Lauren Harris,** Michigan State University; **Sybil Hart,** Texas Tech University; **Karen Hartlep,** California State University–Bakersfield; **Patricia Hawley,** University of Kansas–Main; **Joan Henley,** Arkansas State University; **Susan Hespos,** Northwestern University; **Doris Hiatt,** Monmouth University; **Susan Holt,** Central Connecticut State University; **Lana Karasik,** The College of Staten Island; **Lisa Huffman,** Ball State University; **Kathryn Kipp,** University of Georgia; **Rosemary Krawczyk,** Minnesota State University; **Raymond Krukovsky,** Union County College; **Tara Kuther,** Western Connecticut State University; **Martin Lampert,** Holy Names University; **Richard Lanthier,** George Washington University; **Elida Laski,** Boston College; **Kathryn Lemery,** Arizona State University; **Barbara Licht,** Florida State University; **Angeline Lillard,** University of Virginia; **Lori Markson,** Washington University in St. Louis; **Wayne McMillin,** Northwestern State University; **Martha Mendez-Baldwin,** Manhattan College; **Scott Miller,** University of Florida; **Keith Nelson,** Pennsylvania State University–Main Campus; **Paul Nicodemus,** Austin Peay State University; **Katherine O'Doherty,** Vanderbilt University; **Christin Ogle,** American University; **John Opfer,** The Ohio State University; **Beverly Pead,** Springfield Technical Community College; **Ann Repp,** University of Texas at Austin; **Nicole Rivera,** North Central College; **Sarah Sanborn,** Clemson University; **Leigh Shaw,** Weber State University; **Jennifer Simonds,** Westminster College; **Rebekah Smith,** University of Texas–San Antonio; **Tara Stoppa,** Eastern University; **Mark Strauss,** University of Pittsburgh–Main; **Spencer Thompson,** University of Texas–Permian Basin; **Marisel Torres-Crespo,** Hood College; **Lisa Travis,** University of Illinois Urbana–Champaign; **Roger Webb,** University of Arkansas–Little Rock; **Keri Weed,** University of South Carolina–Aiken; **Sherri Widen,** Boston College; **Fei Xu,** The University of California, Berkeley.

We would especially like to thank Campbell Leaper, University of California–Santa Cruz, for his major contributions to the revision of our chapter on gender development (Chapter 15). We are indebted to Campbell for bringing to the fifth edition his expertise and keen insight in this important area.

Thanks are particularly due to our friends and collaborators at Worth Publishers. As Senior Acquisitions Editor, Daniel DeBonis provided exceptional support and any number of excellent suggestions. We would also like to thank Marge Byers, who nurtured our first edition from its inception and helped us to realize our vision. Peter Deane, our development editor for the first four editions, is in a class by himself in both skill and dedication. Peter's creative thinking and firm understanding of the field enhanced the content of the book in innumerable ways. We are deeply grateful to him. Special thanks go to the development editor for this new edition, Andrew Sylvester, who provided consistently outstanding help throughout the process, as well as to assistant editor Katie Pachnos, senior project editor Vivien Weiss, director of content management enhancement Tracey Kuehn, art manager Matthew McAdams, cover and text designer Vicki Tomaselli, senior photo editor Christine Buese, photo researcher Rona Tuccillo, senior production supervisor Sarah Segal, and compositor codeMantra for their excellent work. They have helped create a book that we hope you will find a pleasure to look at as well as to read. Executive marketing manager Katherine Nurre provided outstanding promotional materials to inform professors about the book. Noel Hohnstine and Laura Burden managed the superb package of ancillary material.

SIR JOHN EVERETT MILLAIS (1829–1896), *Bubbles* (oil on canvas, Britain, 1886)

An Introduction to Child Development

In 1955, a group of child-development researchers began a unique study. Their goal, like that of many developmental researchers, was to find out how biological and environmental factors influence children's intellectual, social, and emotional growth. What made their study unique was that they examined these diverse aspects of development for all 698 children born that year on the Hawaiian island of Kauai and continued studying the children's development for 40 years.

With the parents' consent, the research team, headed by Emmy Werner, collected many types of data about the children. To learn about possible complications during the prenatal period and birth, they examined physicians' records. To learn about family interactions and the children's behavior at home, they arranged for nurses and social workers to observe the families and to interview the children's mothers when the children were 1 year old and again when they were 10 years old. The researchers also interviewed teachers about the children's academic performance and classroom behavior during the elementary school years and examined police, family court, and social service records that involved the children, either as victims or perpetrators. Finally, the researchers administered standardized intelligence and personality tests to the participants when they were 10 and 18 years old and interviewed them at ages 18, 32, and 40 to find out how they saw their own development (Werner, 2005).

Results from this study illustrated some of the many ways in which biological and environmental factors combine to produce child development. For example, children who experienced prenatal or birth complications were more likely than others to develop physical handicaps, mental illness, and learning difficulties. But whether they developed such problems—and if so, to what degree—depended a great deal on their home environment. Parents' income, education, and mental health, together with the quality of the relationship between the parents, especially influenced children's development. By age 2, toddlers who had experienced severe prenatal or birth problems but who lived in harmonious middle-income families were nearly as advanced in language and motor skills as were children who had not experienced such problems. By the time the children were 10-year-olds, prenatal and birth problems were consistently related to psychological difficulties *only* if the children also grew up in poor rearing conditions.

What of children who faced both biological and environmental challenges—prenatal or birth complications *and* adverse family circumstances? The majority of these children developed serious learning or behavior problems by age 10. By age 18, most had acquired a police record, had experienced mental health problems, or had become an unmarried parent. However, one-third of such at-risk children showed impressive resilience, growing up into young adults who, in the words of Werner, "loved well, worked well, and played well" (1989, p. 108D).

Michael was one such resilient child. Born prematurely, with low birth weight, to teenage parents, he spent the first 3 weeks of his life in a hospital, separated from his mother. By his 8th birthday, Michael's parents were divorced, his mother had deserted the family, and he and his three brothers and sisters were being raised by their father, with the help of their elderly grandparents. Yet by age 18, Michael was successful in school, had high self-esteem, was popular with his peers, and was a caring young man with a positive attitude toward life. The fact that there are many children like Michael—children who show great resilience in the face of adversity—is among the most heartening findings of research on child development. Learning about the Michaels of the world inspires child development researchers to conduct further investigations aimed at answering such questions as why individual children differ so much in their response to similar environments, and how to apply research findings to help more children overcome the challenges they face.

Reading this chapter will increase your understanding of these and other basic questions about child development. It will also introduce you to some historical perspectives on these fundamental questions and to the perspectives and methods that modern researchers use to address them. But first, we would like you to consider a basic question for those taking this course: Why study child development?

Reasons to Learn About Child Development

For us, as both parents and researchers, the sheer enjoyment of watching children and trying to understand them is reason enough for studying child development. What could be more fascinating than the development of a child? But there are also practical and intellectual reasons for studying child development. Understanding how children develop can improve child rearing, promote the adoption of wiser social policies regarding children's welfare, and answer intriguing questions about human nature. We examine each of these reasons in the following sections.

Raising Children

Being a good parent is not easy. Among its many challenges are the endless questions it raises over the years. If I drink wine occasionally while I'm pregnant, will it harm my baby even before she's born? Once she's born, is it okay to take her outside in the cold weather? Should my son stay at home for his first few years, or would going to day care be better for his development? Should I try to teach my 3-year-old to read early, or will she learn when she's ready? How can I help my kindergartner deal with her anger? My teenager just started high school, but he seems so lonely and says that no one likes him; how can I help?

Child-development research can help answer such questions. For example, one problem that confronts almost all parents is how to help their children control their anger and other negative emotions. One tempting, and frequent, reaction is to spank children who express anger in inappropriate ways, such as fighting, name-calling, and talking back. In a study involving a representative U.S. sample, 80% of parents of kindergarten children reported having spanked their child on occasion, and 27% reported having spanked their child the previous week (Gershoff et al., 2012). In fact, spanking made the problem worse. The more often parents spanked their kindergartners, the more often the same children argued, fought, and acted inappropriately at school when they were 3rd-graders. This relation held true for Blacks, Whites, Hispanics, and Asians

Will these children be resilient enough to overcome their disadvantaged environment? The answer will depend in large part on how many risk factors they face and on their personal characteristics.

ROBERT NICKELSBERG / GETTY IMAGES

Posters like this are used in the turtle technique to remind children of ways to control anger.

alike, and it held true above and beyond the effects of other relevant factors, such as parents' income and education.

Fortunately, research suggests several effective alternatives to spanking (Denham, 1998, 2006). One is expressing sympathy: when parents respond to their children's distress with sympathy, the children are better able to cope with the situation causing the distress. Another effective approach is helping angry children find positive alternatives to expressing anger. For example, encouraging them to do something they enjoy helps them cope with the hostile feelings.

These strategies and similar ones, such as time-outs, can also be used effectively by others who contribute to raising children, such as day-care personnel and teachers. One demonstration of this was provided by a special curriculum devised for helping preschoolers (3- and 4-year-olds) who were angry and out of control (Denham & Burton, 1996). This curriculum encourages preschool teachers to help children recognize their own and other children's emotions, and to teach children techniques for controlling their anger and peaceably resolving conflicts with other children. One approach that children were taught for coping with anger was the "turtle technique." When children felt themselves becoming angry, they were to move away from other children and retreat into their "turtle shell," where they could think through the situation until they were ready to emerge from the shell. Posters were placed around the classroom to remind children of what to do when they became angry.

The curriculum was quite successful. Children who participated in it became more skillful in recognizing and regulating anger when they experienced it and were generally less negative. For example, one boy, who had regularly gotten into fights when angry, told the teacher after a dispute with another child, "See, I used my words, not my hands" (Denham, 1998, p. 219). The benefits of this program can be long-term. In one test conducted with children in special-education classrooms, positive effects were still evident as long as 4 or 5 years after children completed the curriculum (Greenberg & Kusché, 2006; Jennings & Greenberg, 2009). As this example suggests, knowledge of child-development research can be helpful to everyone involved in the care of children.

Choosing Social Policies

Another reason to learn about child development is to be able to make informed decisions not just about one's own children but also about a wide variety of social-policy questions that affect children in general. For example, does playing violent video games increase aggressive behavior in children and adolescents? How much trust should judges and juries place in preschoolers' testimony in child-abuse cases? Should children who do poorly in school be held back, or should they be promoted to the next grade so that they can be with children of the same age? Child-development research can inform discussion of all of these and many other policy decisions.

Consider the issue of whether playing violent video games makes children and adolescents more aggressive. This issue has been hotly contested by politicians, advocacy groups, and researchers, with some arguing that such games are sufficiently harmful that their sale to minors should be forbidden (e.g., Winter, 2010). In response to this argument, several states, including California, have passed laws regulating the sale of violent video games to minors. However, in 2011, the U.S.

Supreme Court struck down the California law and may do the same to similar laws in other states if similar cases come to trial. The Court's majority opinion indicated that the research introduced as evidence was "unpersuasive."

To provide a more thorough evaluation of the evidence, Ferguson (2015; also see Furuya-Kanamori & Doi, 2016) reviewed findings from 101 studies conducted on the topic. He used a statistical technique known as **meta-analysis,** a method for combining the results from independent studies to reach conclusions based on all of them. This meta-analysis indicated that the effect of playing violent video games on children's and adolescents' aggression was minimal. Minimal is not the same as nonexistent—playing violent video games did appear to increase aggressive behavior by a small amount—but the meta-analysis contradicted claims that violent video games are a major cause of children's and adolescents' aggression (e.g., Strasburger, Jordan, & Donnerstein, 2010). Such quantitative analyses of the impact of various activities on children's behavior are useful evidence in deciding whether the benefits of preventing potentially harmful activities outweigh the costs of impinging on people's freedom to do what they want.

Another issue of social policy in which child-development research has played an important role concerns how much trust to put in preschoolers' courtroom testimony. At present, about 100,000 children testify in legal cases each year (CASA, 2012). Many of these children are very young: more than 40% of children who testify in sexual-abuse trials, for example, are younger than 5 years (Bruck, Ceci, & Principe, 2006; Gray, 1993). The stakes are extremely high in such cases. If juries believe children who falsely testify that they were abused, innocent people may spend years in jail. If juries do not believe children who accurately report abuse, the perpetrators will go free and probably abuse other children. So what can be done to promote reliable testimony from young children and to avoid leading them to report experiences that never occurred?

Psychological research has helped answer such questions. In one experiment, researchers tested whether biased questioning affects the accuracy of young children's memory for events involving touching one's own and other people's bodies. The researchers began by having 3- to 6-year-olds play a game, similar to "Simon Says," in which the children were told to touch various parts of their body and those of other children. A month later, the researchers had a social worker interview the children about their experiences during the game (Ceci & Bruck, 1998). Before the social worker conducted the interviews, she was given a description of each child's experiences. Unknown to her, the description included inaccurate as well as accurate information. For example, she might have been told that a particular child had touched her own stomach and another child's nose, when in fact the child had touched her own stomach and the other child's foot. After receiving the description, the social worker was given instructions much like those in a court case: "Find out what the child remembers."

As it turned out, the version of events that the social worker had heard often influenced her questions. If, for example, a child's account of an event was contrary to what the social worker believed to be the case, she tended to question the child repeatedly about the event ("Are you sure you touched his foot? Is it possible you touched some other part of his body?"). Faced with such repeated questioning, children fairly often changed their responses, with 34% of 3- and 4-year-olds eventually

meta-analysis ■ a method for combining the results from independent studies to reach conclusions based on all of them

In courtrooms such as this one, asking questions that will help children to testify accurately is of the utmost importance.

ST. PETERSBURG TIMES / SCOTT MCINTYRE / THE IMAGE WORKS

BOX 1.1 | a closer look

THE ROMANIAN ADOPTION STUDY

A particularly poignant illustration of the way in which scientific research can increase understanding of human nature comes from studies of how children's ability to overcome the effects of early maltreatment is affected by its timing, that is, by the age at which the maltreatment occurs. This research examines children whose early life was spent in horribly inadequate orphanages in Romania in the late 1980s and early 1990s (McCall et al., 2011; Nelson et al., 2007; Rutter, O'Connor, & The English and Romanian Adoptees Study Team, 2004). Children in these orphanages had almost no contact with any caregiver. For reasons that remain unknown, the brutal Communist dictatorship of that era demanded that staff workers not interact with the children, even when giving them their bottles. Staff members provided the infants with so little physical contact that the crown of many infants' heads became flattened from the babies' lying on their backs for 18 to 20 hours per day.

Shortly after the collapse of Communist rule in Romania, a number of these children were adopted by families in Great Britain. When these children arrived in Britain, most were severely malnourished, with more than half being in the lowest 3% of children their age in terms of height, weight, and head circumference. Most also showed varying degrees of mental retardation and were socially immature. The parents who adopted them knew of their deprived backgrounds and were highly motivated to provide loving homes that would help the children recover from the damaging effects of their early mistreatment.

To evaluate the long-term effects of their early deprivation, the physical, intellectual, and social development of about 150 of the Romanian-born children were examined at age 6 years. To provide a basis of comparison, the researchers also followed the development of a group of British-born children who had been adopted into loving British families before they were 6 months of age. Simply put, the question was whether human nature is sufficiently flexible that the Romanian-born children could overcome the extreme deprivation of their early experience, and if so, would that flexibility decrease with the children's age when they were adopted and with the length of their deprivation.

By age 6 years, the physical development of the Romanian-born children had improved considerably, both in absolute terms and in relation to the British-born comparison group. However, the Romanian children's early experience of deprivation continued to influence their physical development, with the extent of negative effects depending on how long the children had been institutionalized. Romanian-born children who were adopted by British families before age 6 months, and who had therefore spent the smallest portion of their early lives in the orphanages, weighed about the same as British-born children when both were 6-year-olds. However, Romanian-born children adopted between the ages of 6 and 24 months, and who therefore had spent more of their early lives in the orphanages, weighed less; and those adopted between the ages of 24 and 42 months weighed even less (Rutter et al., 2004).

Intellectual development at age 6 years showed a similar pattern. The Romanian-born children who had been adopted before age 6 months demonstrated levels of intellectual competence comparable

corroborating at least one of the social worker's incorrect beliefs. Children were led to "remember" not only plausible events that never happened but also unlikely ones that the social worker had been told about. For instance, some children "recalled" their knee being licked and a marble being inserted in their ear.

Studies of this type have yielded a number of conclusions regarding children's testimony in legal proceedings. One important finding is that when 3- to 5-year-olds are not asked leading questions, their testimony is usually accurate as far as it goes, though they leave out a great deal of information (Bruck et al., 2006; Howe & Courage, 1997). However, when prompted by leading questions, young children's testimony is often inaccurate, especially when the leading questions are asked repeatedly. The younger the children are, the more their recall reflects the biases of the interviewer's questions. In addition, realistic props, such as anatomically correct dolls and drawings, that are often used in judicial cases in the hopes of improving recall of sexual abuse, do not improve recall of events that occurred; they actually increase the number of inaccurate claims, perhaps by blurring the line between fantasy play and reality (Lamb et al., 2008; Poole, Bruck, & Pipe, 2011).

with those of the British-born group. Those who had been adopted between ages 6 and 24 months did somewhat less well, and those adopted between ages 24 and 42 months did even more poorly (Rutter et al., 2004). The intellectual deficits of the Romanian children adopted after age 6 months were just as great when the children were retested at age 11, indicating that the negative effects of the early deprivation persisted for many years after they were adopted into the loving homes (Beckett et al., 2006; Kreppner et al., 2007). Among the enduring intellectual problems were impaired visual memory and attention (Pollak, Nelson et al., 2010).

The early experience in the orphanages had comparably damaging effects on the children's social development (Kreppner et al., 2007). Almost 20% of the Romanian-born children who were adopted after age 6 months showed extremely abnormal social behavior at age 6 years, such as not looking at their parents in anxiety-provoking situations and willingly going off with strangers (versus 3% of the British-born comparison group who did so). Even at age 15 years and in early adulthood, many had difficulty controlling their emotions and forming friendships (Rutter et al., 2009). This atypical social development was accompanied by abnormal brain activity. Brain scans obtained when the children were 8 years old showed that those adopted after living for a substantial period in the orphanages had unusually low levels of neural activity in the **amygdala,** a brain area involved in emotional reactions (Chugani et al., 2001). Subsequent studies have identified similar brain abnormalities among children who spent their early lives in poor-quality orphanages in Russia and East Asia (Nelson et al., 2011; Tottenham et al., 2010).

These findings reflect a basic principle of child development that is relevant to many aspects of human nature and about which nativists and empiricists agree: *The timing of experiences influences their effects.* In the present case, children were sufficiently flexible to overcome the effects of living in the loveless, stultifying institutions if the deprivation ended by age 6 months; living in the institutions until older ages, however, had effects that were rarely overcome, even when children spent many subsequent years in loving and stimulating environments. The adoptive families clearly made a huge positive difference in their children's lives, but the later the age of adoption, the greater the long-term effects of early deprivation.

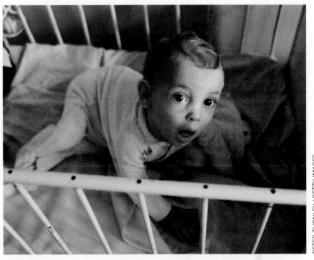

PETER TURNLEY / GETTY IMAGES

This infant is one of the children adopted from a Romanian orphanage in the 1990s. How successfully he develops will depend not only on the quality of caregiving he receives in his adoptive home but also on the amount of time he spent in the orphanage and the age at which he was adopted.

Research on child eyewitness testimony has resulted in many judicial and police agencies revising their procedures for interviewing child witnesses to incorporate the lessons of this research (e.g., State of Michigan, Governor's Task Force, 2011). In addition to helping courts obtain more accurate testimony from young children, such research-based conclusions illustrate how knowledge of child development can inform social policies more generally.

Understanding Human Nature

A third reason to study child development is to better understand human nature. Many of the most intriguing questions regarding human nature concern children. For example, does learning start only after children are born, or can it occur in the womb? Can later upbringing in a loving home overcome the detrimental effects of early rearing in a loveless institutional setting? Do children vary in personality and intellect from the day they are born, or are they similar at birth, with differences arising only because they have different experiences?

amygdala ■ an area of the brain that is involved in emotional reactions

From the time of the ancient Greek civilization of Aristotle, Plato, and Socrates more than 2000 years ago, child development has been viewed as essential to understanding human nature. Studying infants and young children offers an opportunity to learn what people are like before they are affected by the innumerable influences of family and society. One major group of contemporary philosophers and psychologists, known as *nativists,* argues that evolution has created many remarkable capabilities that are present even in early infancy, particularly in areas of special importance, such as understanding basic properties of physical objects, plants and animals, and other people. Another major group of philosophers and psychologists, known as *empiricists,* has argued that infants possess general learning mechanisms that allow them to learn a great deal quite quickly but that infants and young children lack the specialized capabilities that nativists attribute to them.

Until recently, people could only speculate about questions regarding human nature. Now, however, developmental scientists have methods that enable us to observe, describe, and explain the process of development, and thus to deepen our understanding of how we become who we are. Box 1.1 (on page 6) provides one fascinating example of the questions that these methods can address.

Review

There are at least three good reasons to learn about child development: to improve one's own child-rearing practices, to help society promote the well-being of children in general, and to better understand human nature.

Historical Foundations of the Study of Child Development

From ancient Greece to the early years of the twentieth century, a number of profound thinkers observed and wrote about children. Their goals were like those of contemporary researchers: to help people become better parents, to improve children's well-being, and to understand human nature. Unlike contemporary researchers, however, they usually based their conclusions on general philosophical beliefs and informal observations of a few children. Still, the issues they raised are sufficiently important, and their insights sufficiently deep, that their views continue to be of interest.

Early Philosophers' Views of Children's Development

Some of the earliest recorded ideas about children's development were those of Plato and Aristotle. These classic Greek philosophers, who lived in the fourth century B.C., were particularly interested in how children's development is influenced by their nature and by the nurture they receive.

Both Plato and Aristotle believed that the long-term welfare of society depended on the proper raising of children. Careful upbringing was essential because children's basic nature would otherwise lead to their becoming rebellious and unruly. Plato viewed the rearing of boys as a particularly demanding challenge for parents and teachers:

Now of all wild things, a boy is the most difficult to handle. Just because he more than any other has a fount of intelligence in him which has not yet "run clear," he is the craftiest, most mischievous, and unruliest of brutes.

(*The Laws*, bk. 7, 1961, p. 1379)

Consistent with this view, Plato emphasized self-control and discipline as the most important goals of education (Borstelmann, 1983).

Aristotle agreed with Plato that discipline was necessary, but he was more concerned with fitting child rearing to the needs of the individual child. In his words:

It would seem . . . that a study of individual character is the best way of making education perfect, for then each [child] has a better chance of receiving the treatment that suits him.

(*Nicomachean Ethics*, bk. 10, chap. 9, p. 1180)

Plato and Aristotle differed more profoundly in their views of how children acquire knowledge. Plato believed that children have innate knowledge. For example, he believed that children are born with a concept of "animal" that, from birth onward, automatically allows them to recognize that dogs, cats, and other creatures they encounter are animals. In contrast, Aristotle believed that all knowledge comes from experience and that the mind of an infant is like a blackboard on which nothing has yet been written.

Roughly 2000 years later, the English philosopher John Locke (1632–1704) and the French philosopher Jean-Jacques Rousseau (1712–1778) refocused attention on the question of how parents and society in general can best promote children's development. Locke, like Aristotle, viewed the child as a tabula rasa, or blank slate, whose development largely reflects the nurture provided by the child's parents and the broader society. He believed that the most important goal of child-rearing is the growth of character. To build children's character, parents need to set good examples of honesty, stability, and gentleness. They also need to avoid indulging the child, especially early in life. However, once discipline and reason have been instilled, Locke believed that

authority should be relaxed as fast as their age, discretion, and good behavior could allow it. . . . The sooner you treat him as a man, the sooner he will begin to be one.

(Cited in Borstelmann, 1983, p. 20)

In contrast to Locke's advocating discipline before freedom, Rousseau believed that parents and society should give children maximum freedom from the beginning. Rousseau claimed that children learn primarily from their own spontaneous interactions with objects and other people, rather than through instruction by parents or teachers. He even argued that children should not receive any formal education until about age 12, when they reach "the age of reason" and can judge for themselves the worth of what they are told. Before then, they should be allowed the freedom to explore whatever interests them.

Although formulated long ago, these and other philosophical positions continue to underlie many contemporary debates, including whether children should receive direct instruction in desired skills and knowledge or be given maximum freedom to discover the skills and knowledge for themselves, as well as whether parents should build their children's character through explicit instruction or through the implicit guidance provided by the parents' own behavior.

Social Reform Movements

The contemporary field of child psychology also has roots in early social reform movements that were devoted to improving children's lives by changing the conditions in which they lived. During the Industrial Revolution of the 1700s, 1800s, and early 1900s, a great many children in Europe and the United States worked as poorly paid laborers with few if any legal protections. Some were as young as 5 and 6 years; many worked up to 12 hours a day in factories or mines, often in extremely hazardous circumstances. These harsh conditions worried a number of social reformers, who began to study how such circumstances affected the children's development. For example, in a speech before the British House of Commons in 1843, the Earl of Shaftesbury noted that the narrow tunnels where children dug out coal had

> very insufficient drainage [and] are so low that only little boys can work in them, which they do naked, and often in mud and water, dragging sledge-tubs by the girdle and chain. . . . Children of amiable temper and conduct, at 7 years of age, often return next season from the collieries greatly corrupted . . . with most hellish dispositions.
>
> (Quoted in Kessen, 1965, pp. 46–50)

The Earl of Shaftesbury's effort at social reform brought partial success—a law forbidding employment of girls and of boys younger than 10. In addition to bringing about the first child labor laws, this and other early social reform movements established a legacy of research conducted for the benefit of children and provided some of the earliest recorded descriptions of the adverse effects that harsh environments can have on children.

Darwin's Theory of Evolution

Later in the nineteenth century, Charles Darwin's work on evolution inspired a number of scientists to propose that intensive study of children's development might lead to important insights into human nature. Darwin himself was interested in child development, and in 1877 he published an article entitled "A Biographical Sketch of an Infant," which presented his careful observations of the motor, sensory, and emotional growth of his infant son, William. Darwin's "baby biography"—a systematic description of William's day-to-day development—represented one of the first methods for studying children.

Such intensive studies of individual children's growth continue to be a distinctive feature of the modern field of child development. Darwin's evolutionary theory, which employs variation, natural selection, and inheritance as its fundamental concepts, also continues to influence the thinking of modern developmentalists on a wide range of topics: infants' attachment to their mothers (Bowlby, 1969), innate fear of natural dangers such as spiders and snakes (Rakison & Derringer, 2008), sex differences (Geary, 2010), aggression and altruism (Tooby & Cosmides, 2005), and the mechanisms underlying learning (Siegler, 1996).

During the eighteenth, nineteenth, and early twentieth centuries, many young children worked in coal mines and factories. Their hours were long, and the work was often unhealthy and dangerous. Concern over the well-being of such children led to some of the earliest research on child development.

BETTMANN / GETTY IMAGES

The Beginnings of Research-Based Theories of Child Development

In the late 1800s and early 1900s, the first theories of child development that incorporated research findings were formulated. One prominent theory, that of Sigmund Freud, was based in large part on his patients' recollections of their dreams and childhood experiences. Freud's *psychoanalytic theory* proposed that biological drives, especially sexual ones, are a crucial influence on development.

A quite different theory of the same era, that of American psychologist John Watson, was based primarily on the results of experiments that examined learning in animals and children. Watson's *behaviorist theory* argued that children's development is determined by environmental factors, especially the rewards and punishments that follow the children's actions.

By current standards, the research methods on which these theories were based were crude. Nonetheless, these early scientific theories were better grounded in research evidence than were their predecessors, and, as you will see later in the chapter, they inspired more sophisticated ideas about the processes of development and more rigorous research methods for studying how development occurs.

Review

Philosophers such as Plato, Aristotle, Locke, and Rousseau, as well as early scientific theorists such as Darwin, Freud, and Watson, raised many of the deepest issues about child development. These issues included how nature and nurture influence development, how best to raise children, and how knowledge of children's development can be used to advance their welfare.

Enduring Themes in Child Development

The modern study of child development begins with a set of fundamental questions. Everything else—theories, concepts, research methods, data, and so on—is part of the effort to answer these questions. Although experts in the field might choose different particular questions as the most important, there is widespread agreement that the seven questions in Table 1.1 are among the most important. These questions form a set of themes that we will highlight throughout the book as we examine specific aspects of child development. In this section, we introduce and briefly discuss each question and the theme that corresponds to it.

1 *Nature and Nurture:* How Do Nature and Nurture Together Shape Development?

The most basic question about child development is how nature and nurture interact to shape the developmental process. **Nature** refers to our biological endowment, in particular, the genes we receive from our parents. This genetic inheritance influences every aspect of our makeup, from broad characteristics such as physical appearance, personality, intellect, and mental health to specific preferences, such as political attitudes and propensity for thrill-seeking (Plomin et al., 2012). **Nurture** refers to the wide range of environments, both physical and social, that influence our development, including the womb in which we spend the prenatal period, the homes in which we grow up, the schools that we attend, the

TABLE 1.1

Basic Questions About Child Development

1. How do nature and nurture together shape development? *(Nature and nurture)*

2. How do children shape their own development? *(The active child)*

3. In what ways is development continuous, and in what ways is it discontinuous? *(Continuity/discontinuity)*

4. How does change occur? *(Mechanisms of change)*

5. How does the sociocultural context influence development? *(The sociocultural context)*

6. How do children become so different from one another? *(Individual differences)*

7. How can research promote children's well-being? *(Research and children's welfare)*

nature ■ our biological endowment; the genes we receive from our parents

nurture ■ the environments, both physical and social, that influence our development

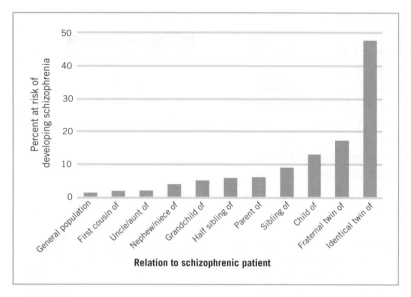

FIGURE 1.1 Genetic relatedness and schizophrenia The closer the biological relation, the stronger the probability that relatives of a person with schizophrenia will have the same mental illness. (Data from Gottesman, 1991)

genome ◼ each person's complete set of hereditary information

epigenetics ◼ the study of stable changes in gene expression that are mediated by the environment

How do you think nature and nurture together led to the son of former Canadian prime minister Pierre Trudeau becoming current Canadian prime minister Justin Trudeau?

broader communities in which we live, and the many people with whom we interact.

Popular depictions often present the nature–nurture question as an either/or proposition: "What determines how a person develops, heredity *or* environment?" However, this either/or phrasing is deeply misleading. All human characteristics—our intellect, our personality, our physical appearance, our emotions—are created through the *joint* workings of nature and nurture, that is, through the constant interaction of our genes and our environment. Accordingly, rather than asking whether nature *or* nurture is more important, developmentalists ask how nature *and* nurture work together to shape development.

That this is the right question to ask is vividly illustrated by findings on the development of schizophrenia. Schizophrenia is a serious mental illness, often characterized by hallucinations, delusions, confusion, and irrational behavior. There is obviously a genetic component to this disease. Children who have a schizophrenic parent have a much higher probability than other children of developing the illness later in life, even when they are adopted as infants and therefore are not exposed to their parents' schizophrenic behavior (Kety et al., 1994). Among identical twins—that is, twins whose genes are identical—if one twin has schizophrenia, the other has a roughly 40% to 50% chance of also having schizophrenia, as opposed to the roughly 0.5% to 1% probability for the general population (Gottesman, 1991; Cardno & Gottesman, 2000; Gejman, Sanders, & Duan, 2010; see Figure 1.1). At the same time, the environment is also clearly influential, since roughly 50% to 60% of children who have an identical twin with schizophrenia do not become schizophrenic themselves; and children who grow up in troubled homes are more likely to become schizophrenic than are children raised in a normal household. Most important, however, is the interaction of genes and environment. A study of adopted children, some of whose biological parents were schizophrenic, indicated that the only children who had any substantial likelihood of becoming schizophrenic were those who had a schizophrenic parent *and* who also were adopted into a troubled family (Tienari, Wahlberg, & Wynne, 2006).

A remarkable recent series of studies has revealed some of the biological mechanisms through which nature and nurture interact. These studies show that just as the **genome**—each person's complete set of hereditary information—influences behaviors and experiences, behaviors and experiences influence the genome (Slavich & Cole, 2013; Meaney, 2010). This might seem impossible, given the well-known fact that each person's DNA is constant throughout life. However, the genome includes not only DNA but also proteins that regulate gene expression by turning gene activity on and off. These proteins change in response to experience and, without structurally altering DNA, can result in enduring changes in cognition, emotion, and behavior. This discovery has given rise to a new field called **epigenetics,** the study of stable changes in gene expression that are mediated by the environment. Stated simply, epigenetics examines how experience gets under the skin.

Evidence for the enduring epigenetic impact of early experiences and behaviors comes from research on **methylation,** a biochemical process that reduces expression of a variety of genes and that is involved in regulating reactions to stress (Lam et al., 2012). One recent study showed that the amount of stress that mothers reported experiencing during their children's infancy was related to the amount of methylation in the children's genomes 15 years later (Essex et al., 2013). Other studies showed increased methylation in the cord-blood DNA of newborns of depressed mothers (Oberlander et al., 2008) and in adults who were abused as children (McGowan et al., 2009), leading researchers to speculate that such children are at heightened risk for depression as adults (Rutten & Mill, 2009).

As these examples illustrate, developmental outcomes emerge from the constant bidirectional interaction of nature *and* nurture. To say that one is more important than the other, or even that the two are equally important, drastically oversimplifies the developmental process.

2 *The Active Child:* How Do Children Shape Their Own Development?

With all the attention that is paid to heredity and environment, many people overlook the ways in which children's own actions contribute to their development. Even in infancy and early childhood, this contribution can be seen in a multitude of areas, including attention, language use, and play.

Children first begin to shape their own development through their selection of what to pay attention to. Even newborns prefer to look at things that move and make sounds. This preference helps them learn about important parts of the world, such as people, other animals, and inanimate moving objects, including cars and trucks. When looking at people, infants' attention is particularly drawn to faces, especially their mother's face; given a choice of looking at a stranger's face or their mother's, even 1-month-olds choose to look at Mom (Bartrip, Morton, & de Schonen, 2001). At first, infants' attention to their mother's face is not accompanied by any visible emotion, but by the end of the 2nd month, infants smile and coo more when focusing intently on their mother's face than at other times. This smiling and cooing by the infant elicits smiling and talking by the mother, which elicits further cooing and smiling by the infant, and so on (Lavelli & Fogel, 2005). In this way, infants' preference for attending to their mother's face leads to social interactions that can strengthen the mother–infant bond.

Once children begin to speak, usually between 9 and 15 months of age, their contribution to their own development becomes more evident. For example, toddlers (1- and 2-year-olds) often talk when they are alone in a room. Only if children were internally motivated to learn language would they practice talking when no one was present to react to what they are saying. Many parents are startled when they hear this "crib speech" and wonder if something is wrong with a baby who would engage in such odd-seeming behavior. However, the activity is entirely normal, and the practice probably helps toddlers improve their speech.

Young children's play provides many other examples of how their internally motivated activity contributes to their development. Children play by themselves for the sheer joy of doing so, but they also learn a great deal in the process. Anyone who has seen a baby bang a spoon against the tray of a high chair or intentionally drop food on the floor would agree that, for the baby, the activity is its own reward. At the same time, the baby is learning about the noises made by

One of the earliest ways children shape their own development is through their choice of where to look. From the first month of life, seeing Mom is a high priority.

methylation ■ A biochemical process that influences behavior by suppressing gene activity and expression

Play contributes to children's development in many ways, including the spatial understanding and attention to detail required to complete puzzles.

continuous development ■ the idea that changes with age occur gradually, in small increments, like that of a pine tree growing taller and taller

discontinuous development ■ the idea that changes with age include occasional large shifts, like the transition from caterpillar to cocoon to butterfly

colliding objects, about the speed at which objects fall, and about the limits of his or her parents' patience.

Young children's fantasy play seems to make an especially large contribution to their knowledge of themselves and other people. Starting at around age 2 years, children sometimes pretend to be different people in make-believe dramas. For example, they may pretend to be superheroes doing battle with monsters or play the role of parents taking care of babies. In addition to being inherently enjoyable, such play appears to teach children valuable lessons, including how to cope with fears and how to interact with others (Howes & Matheson, 1992; Smith, 2003). Older children's play, which typically is more organized and rule-bound, teaches them additional valuable lessons, such as the self-control needed for turn-taking, adhering to rules, and controlling one's emotions in the face of setbacks (Hirsh-Pasek et al., 2009). As we discuss later in the chapter, children's contributions to their own development strengthen and broaden as they grow older and become increasingly able to choose and shape their environments.

3 Continuity/Discontinuity: In What Ways Is Development Continuous, and in What Ways Is It Discontinuous?

Some scientists envision children's development as a **continuous** process of small changes, like that of a pine tree growing taller and taller. Others see the process as a series of occasional, sudden, **discontinuous** changes, like the transition from caterpillar to cocoon to butterfly (Figure 1.2). The debate over which of these views is more accurate has continued for decades.

Researchers who view development as *discontinuous* start from a common observation: children of different ages seem *qualitatively different*. A 4-year-old and a 6-year-old, for example, seem to differ not only in how much they know but in the whole way they think about the world. To appreciate these differences, consider two conversations between Beth, the daughter of one of the authors, and Beth's mother. The first conversation took place when Beth was 4 years old, the second, when she was 6. Both conversations occurred after Beth had watched her mother

FIGURE 1.2 Continuous and discontinuous development Some researchers see development as a continuous, gradual process, akin to a tree's growing taller with each passing year. Others see it as a discontinuous process, involving sudden dramatic changes, such as the transition from caterpillar to cocoon to butterfly. Each view fits some aspects of child development.

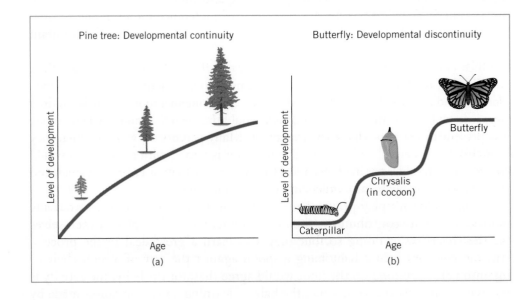

pour all the water from a typical drinking glass into a taller, narrower glass. Here is the conversation that occurred when Beth was 4:

Mother: Is there still the same amount of water?

Beth: No.

Mother: Was there more water before, or is there more now?

Beth: There's more now.

Mother: What makes you think so?

Beth: The water is higher; you can see it's more.

Mother: Now I'll pour the water back into the regular glass. Is there the same amount of water as when the water was in the same glass before?

Beth: Yes.

Mother: Now I'll pour all the water again into the tall thin glass. Does the amount of water stay the same?

Beth: No, I already told you, there's more water when it's in the tall glass.

Two years later, Beth responded to the same problem quite differently:

Mother: Is there still the same amount of water?

Beth: Of course!

What accounts for this change in Beth's thinking? Her everyday observations of liquids being poured cannot have been the reason for it; Beth had seen liquids poured on a great number of occasions before she was 4, yet failed to develop the understanding that the volume remains constant. Experience with the specific task could not explain the change either, because Beth had no further exposure to the task between the first and second conversation. Then why as a 4-year-old would Beth be so confident that pouring the water into the taller, narrower glass increased the amount, and then as a 6-year-old be so confident that it did not?

This conservation-of-liquid-quantity problem is actually a classic technique designed to test children's level of thinking. It has been used with thousands of children around the world, and virtually all the children studied, no matter what their culture, have shown the same type of change in reasoning as Beth did (though usually at somewhat older ages). Furthermore, such age-related differences in understanding pervade children's thinking. Consider two letters to Mr. Rogers, one sent by a 4-year-old and one by a 5-year-old (Rogers, 1996, pp. 10–11):

Dear Mr. Rogers,
I would like to know how you get in the TV.

(Robby, age 4)

Dear Mr. Rogers,
I wish you accidentally stepped out of the TV into my house so I could play with you.

(Josiah, age 5)

Clearly, these are not ideas that an older child would entertain. As with Beth's case, we have to ask, "What is it about 4- and 5-year-olds that leads them to form such improbable beliefs, and what changes occur that make such notions laughable to 6- and 7-year-olds?"

One common approach to answering these questions comes from **stage theories,** which propose that development occurs in a progression of distinct age-related stages, much like the butterfly example in Figure 1.2b. According to these theories, a child's entry into a new stage involves relatively sudden, qualitative changes that affect the child's thinking or behavior in broadly unified ways and move the child from one coherent way of experiencing the world to a different coherent way of experiencing it.

Children's behavior on Piaget's conservation-of-liquid-quantity problem is often used to exemplify the idea that development is discontinuous. The child first sees equal amounts of liquid in similarly shaped glasses and an empty, differently shaped glass. Then, the child sees the liquid from one glass poured into the differently shaped glass. Finally, the child is asked whether the amount of liquid remains the same or whether one glass has more. Young children, like this girl, are unshakable in their belief that the glass with the taller liquid column has more liquid. A year or two later, they are equally unshakable in their belief that the amount of liquid in each glass is the same.

stage theories ■ approaches proposing that development involves a series of large, discontinuous, age-related phases

cognitive development ■ the development of thinking and reasoning

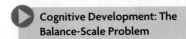

Cognitive Development: The Balance-Scale Problem

FIGURE 1.3 Continuous and discontinuous growth Depending on how it is viewed, changes in height can be regarded as either continuous or discontinuous. (a) Examining a boy's height in absolute terms from birth to 18 years makes the growth look gradual and continuous. (Data from Tanner, 1961) (b) Examining the increases in the same boy's height from one year to the next over the same period shows rapid growth during the first 2½ years, then slower growth, then a growth spurt in adolescence, then a rapid decrease in growth; viewed this way, growth seems discontinuous.

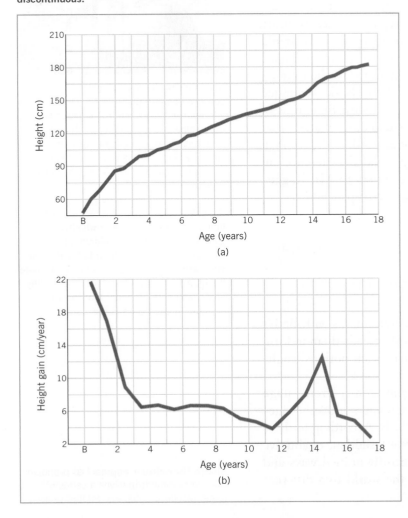

Among the best-known stage theories is Jean Piaget's theory of **cognitive development,** the development of thinking and reasoning. This theory holds that between birth and adolescence, children go through four stages of cognitive growth, each characterized by distinct intellectual abilities and ways of understanding the world. For example, according to Piaget's theory, 2- to 5-year-olds are in a stage of development in which they can focus on only one aspect of an event, or one type of information, at a time. By age 7, children enter a different stage, in which they can simultaneously focus on and coordinate two or more aspects of an event and can do so on many different tasks. According to this view, when confronted with a problem like the one that Beth's mother presented to her, most 4- and 5-year-olds focus on the single dimension of height, and therefore perceive the taller, narrower glass as having more water. In contrast, most 7- and 8-year-olds consider both relevant dimensions of the problem simultaneously. This allows them to realize that although the column of water in the taller glass is higher, the column also is narrower, and the two differences offset each other.

In the course of reading this book, you will encounter a number of other stage theories, including Sigmund Freud's theory of psychosexual development, Erik Erikson's theory of psychosocial development, and Lawrence Kohlberg's theory of moral development. Each of these stage theories proposes that children of a given age show broad similarities across many situations and that children of different ages tend to behave very differently.

Such stage theories have been very influential. In the past 20 years, however, many researchers have concluded that most developmental changes are gradual rather than sudden, and that development occurs skill by skill, task by task, rather than in a broadly unified way (Courage & Howe, 2002; Elman et al., 1996; Thelen & Smith, 2006). This view of development is less dramatic than that of stage theories, but a great deal of evidence supports it. One such piece of evidence is the fact that a child often will behave in accord with one proposed stage on some tasks but in accord with a different proposed stage on other tasks (Fischer & Bidell, 2006). This variable level of reasoning makes it difficult to view the child as being "in" either stage.

Much of the difficulty in deciding whether development is continuous or discontinuous is that the same facts can look very different, depending on one's perspective. Consider the seemingly simple question of whether children's height increases continuously or discontinuously. Figure 1.3a shows a boy's height, measured yearly from birth to age 18 (Tanner, 1961). When one looks at the boy's height at each age, development seems smooth and continuous, with growth occurring rapidly early in life and then slowing down.

However, when you look at Figure 1.3b, a different picture emerges. This graph illustrates the same boy's growth, but it depicts the amount of growth from one year to the next. The boy grew every year, but he grew most during two periods: from birth to age 2½, and from ages 13 to 15. These are the kinds of data that lead people to talk about discontinuous growth and about a separate stage of ado-lescence that includes a physical growth spurt.

So, is development fundamentally continuous or fundamentally discontinuous? The most reasonable answer seems to be, "It depends on how you look at it and how often you look." Imagine the difference between the perspective of an uncle who sees his niece every 2 or 3 years and that of the niece's parents, who see her every day. The uncle will almost always be struck with the huge changes in his niece since he last saw her. The niece will be so different that it will seem that she has progressed to a higher stage of development. In contrast, the parents will most often be struck by the continuity of her development; to them, she usually will just seem to grow up a bit each day. Throughout this book, we will be considering the changes, large and small, sudden and gradual, that have led some researchers to emphasize the continuities in development and others to emphasize the discontinuities.

4 *Mechanisms of Change:* How Does Change Occur?

Perhaps the deepest mystery about children's development is expressed by the question "How does change occur?" In other words, what are the mechanisms that produce the remarkable changes that children undergo with age and experience? How do various forces—such as genetics and experience in the environment—work together to affect development?

One particularly interesting analysis of the mechanisms of developmental change involves the roles of brain activity, genes, and learning experiences in the development of *effortful attention* (e.g., Rothbart, Sheese, & Posner, 2007). Effort-ful attention involves voluntary control of one's emotions and thoughts. It includes processes such as inhibiting impulses (e.g., obeying requests to put all of one's toys away, as opposed to putting some away but then getting distracted and playing with the remaining ones); controlling emotions (e.g., not crying when failing to get one's way); and focusing attention (e.g., concentrating on one's homework despite the inviting sounds of other children playing outside). Difficulty in exerting effort-ful attention is associated with behavioral problems, weak math and reading skills, and mental illness (Blair & Razza, 2007; Diamond & Lee, 2011; Kim et al., 2013).

Studies of the brain activity of people performing tasks that require control of thoughts and emotions show that connections are especially active between the lim-bic area—a part of the brain that plays a large role in emotional reactions—and the anterior cingulate and prefrontal cortex—brain structures involved in setting and attending to goals (Gazzaniga, Ivry, & Mangun, 2013). Connections among these brain areas develop considerably during childhood, and their development appears to be one mechanism that underlies improving effortful attention during childhood (Rothbart et al., 2007). Development of these areas reflects environmental circum-stances as well as genetics. For example, spending one's childhood in poverty has a negative effect on the brain activity needed to suppress negative emotions and improve effortful attention many years later in adulthood (Kim, Evans et al., 2013).

What role do genes and learning experiences play in influencing this mech-anism of effortful attention? Specific genes influence the production of key **neurotransmitters**—chemicals involved in communication among brain cells. Variations among children in these genes are associated with variations in the quality of performance on tasks that require effortful attention (Canli et al., 2005; Diamond et al., 2004; Rueda et al., 2005). These genetic influences do not occur in a vacuum, however. Again, the environment plays a crucial role in these biological

neurotransmitters ■ chemicals involved in communication among brain cells

processes. Infants with a particular form of one of the genes in question show differences in effortful attention related to the quality of parenting they receive, with lower-quality parenting being associated with lower ability to regulate attention (Sheese et al., 2007). Among children who do not have that form of the gene, quality of parenting has less effect on effortful attention.

Learning experiences also can change the wiring of the brain system that produces effortful attention. Rueda and colleagues (2005) presented 6-year-olds with a 5-day training program that used computerized exercises to improve capacity for effortful attention. Examination of electrical activity in the anterior cingulate indicated that those 6-year-olds who had completed the computerized exercises showed improved effortful attention. These children also showed improved performance on intelligence tests, which makes sense given the sustained effortful attention required by such tests. Thus, the experiences that children encounter influence their brain processes and gene expression, just as brain processes and genes influence children's reactions to experiences. More generally, a full understanding of the mechanisms that produce developmental change requires specifying how genes, brain structures and processes, and experiences interact.

Another clear illustration of developmental mechanisms involves the changing role of sleep in promoting learning and generalization (Gómez & Edgin, 2015). Infants spend a great deal of their lives sleeping; for example, 6-month-olds average 14–15 hours of sleep per day (Ohayon et al., 2004). This prolonged sleep serves an important function in promoting learning (Diekelmann & Born, 2010). However, the type of learning that it promotes changes with the maturation of the *hippocampus,* a brain structure that is particularly important for learning and remembering.

During the first 18 months following birth, sleep appears to promote learning of general, frequently encountered patterns, but not learning of the specifics of material only presented once or twice (Gomez, Bootzin, & Nadel, 2006). In contrast, after age 24 months, children tend to show the opposite pattern: when tested shortly after napping, they often better remember the specifics of what they learned than peers who did not nap during that period; but their memory for general patterns is no better than those of peers who did not nap (Kurdziel, Duclos, & Spencer, 2013).

Werchan and Gómez (2014) described mechanisms that could underlie this change from infancy to the preschool period. Their explanation was based on a major theory of memory, called *Active Systems Consolidation Theory* (McClelland, McNaughton, & O'Reilly, 1995), which posits that two interconnected brain areas, the hippocampus and the cortex, simultaneously encode new information during learning (see Figure 1.4). The hippocampus can learn details of new information after one or two experiences; the cortex produces abstraction of general patterns over many experiences. The two brain areas are strongly interconnected, and the theory posits that in older children and adults, hippocampal memories are replayed during sleep, which allows opportunities for the cortex to extract general patterns from the specific memories stored in the hippocampus. The mechanism works in the opposite direction as well; learning general patterns improves the retention of details of new experiences of the same type (Mullally & Maguire, 2014).

These findings and theories led Werchan and Gómez (2014) to hypothesize that the benefits of sleep on infants' memory for general patterns reflect functioning of the cortex, whereas the benefits of sleep on preschoolers' memory for specific experiences reflect functioning of the hippocampus. They proposed that prior to 18 to 24 months of age, the hippocampus is too immature to enable the rapid learning of the details of specific experiences; therefore, sleeping does not benefit memory for these specifics. However, the cortex is mature enough at this age to extract general patterns.

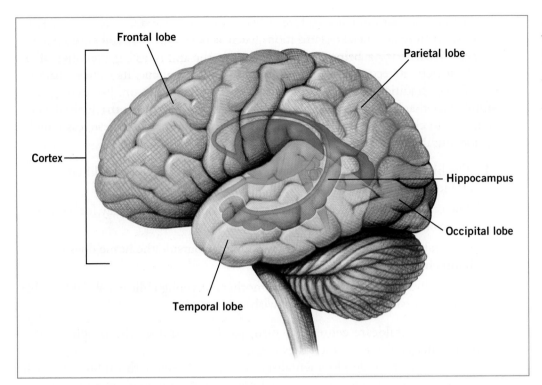

FIGURE 1.4 **The human cortex** The four main lobes of the cortex: frontal, parietal, occipital, and temporal. The hippocampus, which is also shown, is deeper inside the brain than it appears in this figure, whereas the cortex covers outer portions of the brain.

Evidence from numerous studies supports this claim. For example, the number of exposures needed to learn new words decreases considerably between 18 and 24 months (Goldfield & Reznick, 1990). Evidence also indicates that before 18 months, children rarely remember arbitrarily related sequences of events that they have seen only once, but after 24 months, they often do remember these sequences (Bauer et al., 1998). Infants younger than 18 months who hear several unfamiliar words repeatedly just before they nap show a type of brain activity during sleep that is associated with cortical learning processes (Friedrich et al., 2015). Finally, children with known impairments to the hippocampus have a much harder time retaining details of their experiences than do peers without such impairments (Edgin et al., 2015). Thus, sleep is not a waste of time; it is essential for learning and for healthy development in general (Edgin et al., 2015).

5 *The Sociocultural Context:* How Does the Sociocultural Context Influence Development?

Children grow up in a particular set of physical and social environments, in a particular culture, under particular economic circumstances, at a particular time in history. Together, these physical, social, cultural, economic, and historical circumstances interact to constitute the **sociocultural context** of a child's life—which influences every aspect of children's development.

A classic depiction of the components of the sociocultural context is Urie Bronfenbrenner's (1979) bioecological model (discussed in depth in Chapter 9). The most obviously important components of children's sociocultural contexts are the people with whom they interact—parents, grandparents, brothers, sisters, day-care providers, teachers, friends, classmates, and so on—and the physical environment in which they live—their house, day-care center, school, neighborhood, and so on. Another important but less tangible component of the sociocultural context is

 The Wisdom of Generations: Boys' and Girls' Initiations Among the Chokwe and Related People

sociocultural context ■ the physical, social, cultural, economic, and historical circumstances that make up any child's environment the institutions that influence children's lives: educational systems, religious institutions, sports leagues, social organizations (such as boys' and girls' clubs), and so on.

Yet another important set of influences are the general characteristics of the child's society: its economic and technological advancement; its values, attitudes, beliefs, and traditions; its laws and political structure; and so on. For example, the simple fact that most toddlers and preschoolers growing up in the United States today go to childcare outside their homes reflects a number of these less tangible sociocultural factors, including:

1. The historical era (50 years ago, far fewer children in the United States attended childcare centers)
2. The economic structure (there are far more opportunities today for women with young children to work outside the home)
3. Cultural beliefs (e.g., that receiving child care outside the home does not harm children)
4. Cultural values (e.g., the value that mothers of young children should be able to work outside the home if they wish).

Attendance at childcare centers, in turn, partly determines the people children meet and the activities in which they engage.

One method that developmentalists use to understand the influence of the sociocultural context is to compare the lives of children who grow up in different cultures. Such *cross-cultural comparisons* often reveal that practices that are rare or nonexistent in one's own culture, and that may seem strange, are common in other cultures. The following comparison of young children's sleeping arrangements in different societies illustrates the value of such cross-cultural research.

In most families in the United States, newborn infants sleep in their parents' bedroom, either in a crib or in the same bed. However, when infants are 2 to 6 months old, parents usually move them to another bedroom where they sleep alone (Greenfield, Suzuki, & Rothstein-Fisch, 2006). This seems natural to most people raised in the United States, because it is how we and others whom we know were raised. From a worldwide perspective, however, such sleeping arrangements are highly unusual. In most other societies, including economically advanced nations such as Italy, Japan, and South Korea, babies almost always sleep in the same bed as their

In many countries, including Denmark, the country in which this mother and child live, mothers and children sleep together for the first several years of the child's life. This sociocultural pattern is in sharp contrast to the U.S. practice of having infants sleep separately from their parents soon after birth.

OWEN FRANKEN

mother for the first few years, and somewhat older children also sleep in the same room as their mother, sometimes in the same bed (e.g., Nelson, Schiefenhoevel, & Haimerl, 2000; Whiting & Edwards, 1988). Where does this leave the father? In some cultures, the father sleeps in the same bed with mother and baby; in others, he sleeps in a separate bed or in a different room.

How do these differences in sleeping arrangements affect children? To find out, researchers interviewed mothers in middle-class U.S. families in Salt Lake City, Utah, and in rural Mayan families in Guatemala (Morelli et al., 1992). These interviews revealed that by age 6 months, the large majority of the U.S. children had begun sleeping in their own bedroom. As the children grew out of infancy, the nightly separation of child and parents became a complex ritual, surrounded by activities intended to comfort the child, such as telling stories, reading children's books, singing songs, and so on. About half the children were reported as taking a comfort object, such as a blanket or teddy bear, to bed with them.

In contrast, interviews with the Mayan mothers indicated that their children typically slept in the same bed with them until the age of 2 or 3 years and continued to sleep in the same room with them for years thereafter. The children usually went to sleep at the same time as their parents. None of the Mayan parents reported bedtime rituals, and almost none reported their children taking comfort objects, such as dolls or stuffed animals, to bed with them.

Why do sleeping arrangements differ across cultures? Interviews with the Mayan and U.S. parents indicated that the crucial consideration for them in determining sleeping arrangements was cultural values. Mayan culture prizes interdependence among people. The Mayan parents expressed the belief that having a young child sleep with the mother is important for developing a good parent–child relationship, for avoiding the child's becoming distressed at being alone, and for helping parents spot any problems the child is having. They often expressed shock and pity when told that infants in the United States typically sleep separately from their parents (Greenfield et al., 2006). In contrast, U.S. culture prizes independence and self-reliance, and the U.S. mothers expressed the belief that having babies and young children sleep alone promotes these values, as well as allowing intimacy between husbands and wives (Morelli et al., 1992). These differences illustrate both how practices that strike us as natural may differ greatly across cultures and how the simple conventions of everyday life often reflect deeper values.

Contexts of development differ not just between cultures but also within them. In modern multicultural societies, many contextual differences are related to ethnicity, race, and **socioeconomic status** (**SES**)—a measure of social class that is based on income and education. Virtually all aspects of children's lives—from the food they eat to the parental discipline they receive to the games they play—vary with ethnicity, race, and SES.

The socioeconomic context exerts a particularly large influence on children's lives. In economically advanced societies, including the United States, most children grow up in reasonably comfortable circumstances, but millions of other children do not. In 2014, 18% of U.S. families with children had incomes below the poverty line (in that year, $19,096 for a family of three with one adult and two children). In absolute numbers, that translates into more than 16 million children growing up in poverty (U.S. Census Bureau, 2015). As shown in Table 1.2, poverty rates are especially high in Black and Hispanic families and in families of all races that are headed by single mothers. Poverty rates are also very high among the roughly 25% of children in the United States who are either immigrants or children living with immigrant parents—roughly twice as high as among children of native-born parents (DeNavas-Walt & Proctor, 2015).

Children from impoverished families tend to do less well than other children in many ways. In infancy, they are more likely to have serious health problems. Beginning at age 3 years and continuing through at least age 20, their brains, on average, have less surface area, especially in areas that support spoken language, reading, and spatial skills (K. G. Noble, et al., 2015). Throughout childhood and adolescence, they tend to have more emotional problems, smaller vocabularies, lower IQs, and lower math and reading scores on standardized achievement tests (Evans, Li, & Whipple, 2013). In adolescence, they are more likely to have a baby or drop out of school (Penman-Aguilar et al., 2013).

These negative outcomes are not surprising when we consider the huge array of disadvantages that poor children face. Compared with children who grow up in more affluent circumstances, they are more likely to live in dangerous neighborhoods, to attend inferior day-care centers and schools, and to be exposed to high levels of air

socioeconomic status (SES) ■ a measure of social class based on income and education

TABLE 1.2

Percentage of U.S. Families with Children Younger than 18 Living Below Poverty Line in 2014

Group	% in Poverty
Overall U.S. Population	18
White, non-Hispanic	11
Black	32
Hispanic	28
Asian	11
Married Couples	8
White, non-Hispanic	5
Black	11
Hispanic	19
Asian	8
Single Parent: Female Head of Household	40
White, non-Hispanic	32
Black	46
Hispanic	46
Asian	29

Source: U.S. Census Bureau (2015).

cumulative risk ■ the accumulation of disadvantages over years of development

and water pollution (Bell & Ebisu, 2012; G. W. Evans, 2004). In addition, their parents read to them less, talk to them less, provide fewer books in the home, and are less involved in their schooling (Hart & Risley, 2003). Poor children also are more likely than affluent children to grow up in single-parent homes or to be raised by neither biological parent. The accumulation of these disadvantages over years of development, often termed **cumulative risk,** seems to be the greatest obstacle to poor children's successful development (Evans & Cassells, 2014; Morales & Guerra, 2006).

Yet, as we saw in Werner's study of the children of Kauai, described at the beginning of the chapter, many children do overcome the obstacles that poverty presents. Such resilient children are more likely than others to have three characteristics: (1) positive personal qualities, such as high intelligence, an easygoing personality, and an optimistic outlook on the future; (2) a close relationship with at least one parent; and (3) a close relationship with at least one adult other than their parents, such as a grandparent, teacher, coach, or family friend (Chen & Miller, 2012; Masten, 2007). As these characteristics suggest, children's resilience reflects not just their personal qualities but also the interactions they have with other people in their environment (Masten, 2014). Thus, although poverty poses serious obstacles to successful development, many children do surmount the challenges—usually with the help of other people in their lives.

6 Individual Differences: How Do Children Become So Different from One Another?

Anyone who has experience with children is struck by their uniqueness—their differences not only in physical appearance but in everything from activity level and temperament to intelligence, persistence, and emotionality. These differences among children emerge quickly. Some infants in their first year are shy, others outgoing. Some infants play with or look at objects for prolonged periods; others rapidly shift from activity to activity. Even children in the same family often differ substantially, as you probably already know if you have siblings.

Scarr (1992) identified four factors that can lead children from a single family (as well as children from different families) to turn out very different from one another:

1. Genetic differences
2. Differences in treatment by parents and others
3. Differences in reactions to similar experiences
4. Different choices of environments

Different children, even ones within the same family, often react to the same experience, such as this roller coaster ride, in completely different ways.

LOOK DIE BILDAGENTUR DER FOTOGRAFEN GMBH / ALAMY

The most obvious reason for differences among children is that every individual is genetically unique. This is true even of so-called "identical twins." At conception, the genomes of these children are identical, but mutations or copying errors result in several hundred gene differences being present, on average, even before birth (Li et al., 2014). The genomes of all other children are much more different from each other; for example, other siblings, including fraternal twins, differ in 50% of the roughly 25,000 genes in a human being.

A second major source of variation among children is differences in the treatment they receive from parents and other people. This differential treatment is often associated with preexisting differences in the children's characteristics. For instance, parents tend to provide more sensitive care to easygoing infants than to difficult ones; by the second year, parents of difficult children are often angry with them even when the children have done nothing wrong in the immediate situation (van den Boom & Hoeksma, 1994). Teachers, likewise, tend to provide positive attention and encouragement to pupils who are learning well and are well behaved, but with pupils who are doing poorly and are disruptive, they tend to be openly critical and to deny the pupils' requests for special help (Good & Brophy, 1996).

Adolescents who participate in sports and other extracurricular activities are more likely to complete high school, and less likely to get into trouble, than peers who are not engaged in these activities. This is another example of how individuals make choices that influence their development.

In addition to being shaped by objective differences in the treatment they receive, children also are influenced by their subjective interpretations of the treatment. A classic example occurs when each of a pair of siblings feels that their parents favor the other. Siblings also often react differently to events that affect the whole family. In one study, 69% of negative events, such as parents' being laid off or fired, elicited fundamentally different reactions from siblings (Beardsall & Dunn, 1992). Some children were very concerned at a parent's loss of a job; others were sure that everything would be okay.

A fourth major source of differences among children relates to the previously discussed theme of the *active child:* as children grow older, they increasingly choose activities and friends for themselves and thus influence their own subsequent development. They may also accept or choose niches for themselves: within a family, one child may become "the smart one," another "the popular one," another "the naughty one," and so on (Scarr & McCartney, 1983). A child labeled by family members as "the nice one" may strive to live up to the label; so, unfortunately, may a child labeled "the troublemaker."

As discussed in the section on nature and nurture and in the section on mechanisms of development, differences in biology and experience interact in complex ways to create the infinite diversity of human beings. Thus, a study of 11- to 17-year-olds found that the grades of children who were highly engaged with school changed in more positive directions than would have been predicted by their genetic background or family environments alone (Johnson, McGue, & Iacono, 2006). The same study revealed that children of high intelligence were less negatively affected by adverse family environments than were other children. Thus, children's genes, their treatment by other people, their subjective reactions to their experiences, and their choice of environments interact in ways that make each one unique.

7 *Research and Children's Welfare:* How Can Research Promote Children's Well-Being?

Improved research-based understanding of child development often leads to practical benefits. Several examples have already been described, including the program for helping children deal with their anger and the recommendations for fostering valid eyewitness testimony from young children.

Another type of practical benefit arising from child-development research involves educational innovations. Understanding how children reason, remember,

BOX 1.2 | individual differences

CAN CHILDREN LEARN TO BE MORE INTELLIGENT?

Carol Dweck and her colleagues (Dweck, 2006; Dweck & Leggett, 1988) have found that some children (and adults) believe that intelligence is a fixed entity. They see each person as having a certain amount of intelligence that is set at birth and cannot be changed by experience. Other children (and adults) believe that intelligence is a changeable characteristic that increases with learning and that the time and effort people put into learning is the key determinant of their intelligence.

People who believe that intelligence increases with learning tend to react to failure in more effective ways (Dweck, 2006). When they fail to solve a problem, they more often persist on the task and try harder. Such persistence in the face of failure is an important quality. As the great British Prime Minister Winston Churchill once said, "Success is the ability to go from one failure to another with no loss of enthusiasm." In contrast, people who believe that intelligence is a fixed entity tend to give up when they fail, because they think the problem is too hard for them.

Building on this research regarding the relation between beliefs about intelligence and persistence in the face of difficulty, Blackwell, Trzesniewski, and Dweck (2007) devised an effective educational program for middle school students from low-income backgrounds. They presented randomly selected students with research findings about how learning alters the brain in ways that improve subsequent learning and thus "makes you smarter." Other randomly selected students from the same classrooms were presented with research findings about how memory works. The investigators

Screenshot from Brainology, a commercially available educational program based on the findings of Blackwell, Trzesniewski, and Dweck (2007). The software, like the research study, emphasizes that learning makes children smarter by building new connections within the brain.

predicted that the students who were told about the effects that learning has on the brain would change their beliefs about intelligence in ways that would help them persevere in the face of failure. In particular, the changed beliefs were expected to improve students' learning of mathematics, an area in which children often experience initial failure.

The researchers' prediction was borne out. Children who were presented information about how learning changes the brain and enhances intelligence subsequently improved their math grades, whereas the other children did not. Children who initially believed that intelligence was an inborn, unchanging quality but who came to believe that intelligence reflected learning showed especially large improvements. Perhaps most striking, when the children's teachers, who did not know which type of information each child had received, were asked if any of their students had shown unusual

improvement in motivation or performance, the teachers cited more than three times as many students who had been given information about how learning builds intelligence.

Providing children with information about how learning changes the brain and thus builds intelligence is, of course, not the only way to increase their motivation to learn. Another effective method involves presentation of *struggle stories,* which relate how famous or notable people—for example, great scientists such as Albert Einstein and Marie Curie—needed to overcome failures and difficult life circumstances on the way to success. Studies conducted in the United States and in China have shown that hearing such struggle stories improves the science learning of children (Hong & Lin-Siegler, 2012; Lin-Siegler et al., 2016).

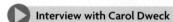 **Interview with Carol Dweck**

form concepts, and solve problems is inherently related to education, and we review many examples of educational applications of child-development research throughout the book, especially in Chapters 4 and 8. One fascinating example comes from studies of children's differing beliefs about intelligence and how those differing beliefs influence their learning (see Box 1.2).

In subsequent chapters, we review many additional examples of how child-development research is being used to promote children's welfare.

Review

The modern field of child development is in large part an attempt to answer a small set of fundamental questions about children. These include:

1. How do nature and nurture jointly contribute to development?
2. How do children contribute to their own development?
3. Is development best viewed as continuous or discontinuous?
4. What mechanisms produce change?
5. How does the sociocultural context influence development?
6. Why are children so different from one another?
7. How can we use research to improve children's welfare?

Methods for Studying Child Development

As illustrated in the preceding section, modern scientific research has advanced the understanding of fundamental questions about child development well beyond that of the historical figures who first raised the questions. This progress reflects the successful application of the scientific method to the study of child development. In this section, we describe the scientific method and examine how its use has advanced understanding of child development.

The Scientific Method

The basic assumption of the **scientific method** is that all beliefs, no matter how probable they seem and no matter how many people share them, may be wrong. Therefore, until beliefs have been repeatedly tested, they must be viewed as **hypotheses,** that is, as testable predictions of the presence or absence of phenomena or relations rather than as truth. If a hypothesis is tested, and the evidence repeatedly does not support it, the hypothesis must be abandoned no matter how reasonable it seems.

Use of the scientific method involves four basic steps:

1. Choosing a question to be answered
2. Formulating a hypothesis regarding the question
3. Developing a method for testing the hypothesis
4. Using the resulting data to draw a conclusion regarding the hypothesis

To illustrate these steps, let's make the *question to be answered* "What abilities predict which children will become good readers?" A reasonable *hypothesis* might be "Kindergartners who can identify the separate sounds within words will become better readers than those who cannot." A straightforward *method* for testing this hypothesis would be to select a group of kindergartners, test their ability to identify the separate sounds within words, and then, several years later, test the reading skills of the same children. Research has, in fact, shown that kindergartners who are aware of the component sounds within words later tend to read more skillfully than their peers who lacked this ability as kindergartners. This pattern holds true regardless of whether the children live in the United States, Australia, Norway, or Sweden (Furnes & Samuelsson, 2011). These results support the *conclusion* that kindergartners' ability to identify sounds within words predicts their later reading skill.

The first, second, and fourth of these steps are not unique to the scientific method. As we have seen, great thinkers of the past also asked questions, formulated

scientific method ■ an approach to testing beliefs that involves choosing a question, formulating a hypothesis, testing the hypothesis, and drawing a conclusion

hypotheses ■ testable predictions of the presence or absence of phenomena or relations hypotheses, and drew conclusions that were reasonable given the evidence available to them. What distinguishes scientific research from nonscientific approaches is the third step: the methods used to test the hypotheses. When rigorously employed, these research methods yield high-quality evidence that allows investigators to progress beyond their initial hypotheses to draw firmly grounded conclusions.

The Importance of Appropriate Measurement

For the scientific method to work, researchers must use measures that are directly relevant to the hypotheses being tested. Even measures that initially seem reasonable sometimes turn out to be less informative than originally thought. For example, a researcher who hypothesized that a supplemental food program would help children suffering from malnutrition might evaluate the program on the basis of weight gain from just before the program to just after it. However, weight is an inadequate measure of nutrition: providing unlimited supplies of potato chips would probably produce weight gain but not improve nutrition; many people who consume large amounts of junk food are obese yet malnourished (Sawaya et al., 1995). Better measures of nutrition would include whether more adequate levels of essential nutrients were present in the children's bloodstreams at the end of the study (Shetty, 2006).

Regardless of the particular measure used, many of the same criteria determine whether a measure is a good one. One key criterion has already been noted—the measure must be directly relevant to the hypothesis. Two other qualities that good measures must possess are *reliability* and *validity*.

Reliability The degree to which independent measurements of a behavior under study are consistent is referred to as **reliability.** One important type of consistency, **interrater reliability,** indicates how much agreement there is in the observations of different raters who witness the same behavior. Sometimes the observations are qualitative, as when raters classify a baby's attachment to her mother as "secure" or "insecure." Other times the observations are quantitative, as when raters score on a scale of 1 to 10 how upset babies become when they are presented with an unfamiliar noisy toy or a boisterous stranger. In both cases, interrater reliability is attained when the raters' evaluations are in close agreement—as when, for example, Baby A in a group being observed for a particular behavior gets a 6 or 7 from all the raters, Baby B gets a 3 or 4 from all of them, Baby C consistently gets an 8 or 9, and so on. Without such close agreement, one cannot have confidence in the research findings because there is no way to tell which (if any) of the ratings was accurate.

A second important type of consistency is **test–retest reliability.** This type of reliability is attained when measures of a child's performance on the same test, administered under the same conditions, are similar on two or more occasions. Suppose, for example, that researchers presented a vocabulary test to a group of children on two occasions one week apart. If the test is reliable, those children who scored highest on the first testing should also score highest on the second, because none of the children's vocabularies would have changed much over such a short period. As in the example of interrater reliability, a lack of test–retest reliability would make it impossible to know which result (if either) accurately reflected each child's status.

Validity The **validity** of a test or experiment refers to the degree to which it measures what it is intended to measure. Researchers strive for two types of validity: internal and external. **Internal validity** refers to whether effects observed within experiments can be attributed with confidence to the factor that the researcher is

reliability ■ the degree to which independent measurements of a given behavior are consistent

interrater reliability ■ the amount of agreement in the observations of different raters who witness the same behavior

test–retest reliability ■ the degree of similarity of a participant's performance on two or more occasions

validity ■ the degree to which a test measures what it is intended to measure

internal validity ■ the degree to which effects observed within experiments can be attributed to the factor that the researcher is testing

TABLE 1.3

Key Properties of Behavioral Measures

Property	Question of Interest
Relevance to hypotheses	Do the hypotheses predict in a straightforward way what should happen on these measures?
Interrater reliability	Do different raters who observe the same behavior classify or score it the same way?
Test–retest reliability	Do children who score higher on a measure at one time also score higher on the measure at other times?
Internal validity	Can effects within the experiment be attributed to the variables that the researcher intentionally manipulated?
External validity	How widely can the findings be generalized to different children in different places at different times?

external validity ■ the degree to which results can be generalized beyond the particulars of the research

structured interview ■ a research procedure in which all participants are asked to answer the same questions

testing. For instance, suppose that a researcher tests the effectiveness of a type of psychotherapy for depression by administering it to a number of depressed adolescents. If three months later many of the adolescents are no longer depressed, can it be concluded that this type of psychotherapy caused the improvement? No, because the students' recovery may have been due to the mere passage of time. Moods fluctuate, and many adolescents who are depressed at any given time will be happier at a later date even without psychotherapy. In this example, the passage of time is a source of internal invalidity, because the factor believed to cause the improvement (the psychotherapy) may have had no effect.

External validity, in contrast, refers to the ability to generalize research findings beyond the particulars of the research in question. Studies of child development are almost never intended to apply only to the particular children and research methods involved in a given study. Rather, the goal is to draw conclusions that apply to children more generally. Thus, the findings of a single experiment are only the first step in determining the external validity of the results. Additional studies with participants from different backgrounds and with research methods that vary in their particulars are invariably needed to establish the external validity of the findings. (Table 1.3 summarizes the key properties of behavioral measures.)

Contexts for Gathering Data About Children

Researchers obtain data about children in three main contexts: *interviews, naturalistic observation,* and *structured observation.* In the following sections, we consider how gathering data in each context can help answer different questions about children.

Interviews and Questionnaires

The most obvious way to collect data about children is to go straight to the source and ask the children themselves about their lives. One type of interview, the **structured interview,** is especially useful when the goal is to collect self-reports on the same topics from everyone being studied. For example, Valeski and Stipek (2001) asked kindergartners and 1st-graders a set of predetermined questions regarding their feelings about school (How much does your teacher care about you? How do you feel when you're at school?) and about their beliefs about their academic competence (How much do you know about numbers? How good are you at reading?). The children's general attitudes toward school and their feelings

One-on-one clinical interviews like this one can elicit unique in-depth information about a child.

about their relationship with their teacher proved to be positively related to their beliefs about their competence in math and reading.

As an alternative to orally administered structured interviews, researchers working with children of reading age will often present the children with printed **questionnaires.** This method often makes it easier for researchers to obtain data from many children simultaneously. With both structured interviews and questionnaires, asking large numbers of children identical questions about their feelings, beliefs, and behaviors—or asking children's parents identical questions about their children's feelings, beliefs, and behaviors—provides a quick and straightforward way for researchers to learn about children.

A second type of interview, the **clinical interview,** is especially useful for obtaining in-depth information about an individual child. In this approach, the interviewer begins with a set of prepared questions, but if the child says something intriguing, the interviewer can depart from the script to follow up on the child's lead.

The usefulness of clinical interviews can be seen in the case of Bobby, a 10-year-old child who was assessed for symptoms of depression (Schwartz & Johnson, 1985). When the interviewer asked him about school, Bobby said that he did not like it because the other children disliked him and he was bad at sports. As he put it, "I'm not really very good at anything" (p. 214). To explore the source of this sad self-description, the interviewer asked Bobby what he would wish for if three wishes could be granted. Bobby replied, "I would wish that I was the type of boy my mother and father want, I would wish that I could have friends, and I would wish that I wouldn't feel sad so much" (p. 214). Such heartrending comments provide a sense of the painful subjective experience of this depressed child, one that would be impossible to obtain from methods that were not tailored to the individual.

As with all contexts for collecting data, interviews have both strengths and weaknesses. On the positive side, they yield a great deal of data quickly and can provide in-depth information about individual children. On the negative side, answers to interview questions often are biased. Children (like adults) often avoid disclosing facts that show them in a bad light, distort the way that events happened, and fail to understand their own motivations (Wilson & Dunn, 2004). These limitations have led many researchers to use observational methods that allow them to witness the behavior of interest for themselves.

questionnaire ■ a method, similar to the structured interview, that allows researchers to gather information from a large number of participants simultaneously by presenting them with a uniform set of questions.

clinical interview ■ a procedure in which questions are adjusted in accord with the answers the interviewee provides

naturalistic observation ■ examination of ongoing behavior in an environment not controlled by the researcher

Naturalistic Observation

When the primary research goal is to describe how children behave in their usual environments—homes, schools, playgrounds, and so on—**naturalistic observation** is the method of choice for gathering data. In this approach, observers try to remain unobtrusively in the background in the chosen setting, allowing them to see the relevant behaviors while minimizing the chances that their presence will influence those behaviors.

A classic example of naturalistic observation is Gerald Patterson's (1982) comparative study of family dynamics in "troubled" and "typical" families. The troubled families were defined by the presence of at least one child who had been labeled "out of control" and referred for treatment by a school, court, or mental health professional. The typical families were defined by the fact that none of the children in them showed signs of serious behavioral difficulties. Income levels and children's ages were the same for the troubled and typical families.

To observe the frequency with which children and parents engaged in negative behaviors—teasing, yelling, whining, criticizing, and so on—research assistants repeatedly observed dinnertime interactions in both troubled and typical homes. To accustom family members to his or her presence, the research assistant for each family made several home visits before beginning to collect data.

The researchers found that the behaviors and attitudes of both parents and children in the troubled families differed strikingly from those of their counterparts in the typical families. Parents in the troubled families were more self-absorbed and less responsive to their children than were parents in the typical households. Children in the troubled families responded to parental punishment by becoming more aggressive, whereas children in the typical households responded to punishment by becoming less aggressive. In the troubled families, interactions often fell into a vicious cycle in which:

- The child acted in a hostile or aggressive manner, for example, by defying a parent's request to clean up his or her room.
- The parent reacted angrily, for example, by shouting at the child to obey.
- The child escalated the level of hostility, for example, by yelling back.
- The parent ratcheted up the aggression even further, perhaps by spanking the child.

As Patterson's study suggests, naturalistic observations are particularly useful for illuminating everyday social interactions, such as those between children and parents.

Although naturalistic observation can yield detailed information about certain aspects of children's everyday lives, it also has important limitations. One is that naturally occurring contexts vary on many dimensions, so it is often hard to know which ones influenced the behavior of interest. For example, it was clear in the Patterson study that the interactions of troubled families differed from those of the more harmonious families, but the interactions and family histories differed in so many ways that it was impossible to specify how the current situation arose. A second limitation of naturalistic studies is that many behaviors of interest occur only occasionally in the everyday environment, which reduces researchers' opportunities to learn about them. A means for overcoming both limitations is the method known as structured observation.

Structured Observation

When using **structured observation,** researchers design a situation that will elicit behavior that is relevant to a hypothesis and then observe how different children behave in that situation. The researchers then relate the observed behaviors to characteristics of the child, such as age, sex, or personality, and to the child's behavior in other situations that are also observed.

In one such study, Kochanska, Coy, and Murray (2001) investigated the links between 2- and 3-year-olds' compliance with their mother's requests to forego appealing activities and their compliance with her requests that they participate in unappealing ones. Mothers brought their

structured observation ■ a method that involves presenting an identical situation to each participant and recording the participant's behavior

Psychologists sometimes observe family interactions around the dinner table, because mealtime comments can evoke strong emotions.

MONKEY BUSINESS IMAGES / DREAMSTIME.COM

COURTESY OF SUWANNA AND DAVID SIEGLER

Temptation is everywhere, but children who are generally compliant with their mother's requests when she is present are also more likely to resist temptation when she is absent (like this boy, the nephew of one of the authors, whose reach, despite appearances, stopped just short of the cake).

toddlers to a laboratory room that had a number of especially attractive toys sitting on a shelf and a great many less attractive toys scattered around the room. The experimenter asked each mother to tell her child that he or she could play with any of the toys *except* the ones on the shelf. Raters observed the children through a one-way mirror over the next few minutes and classified them as complying with their mother's request wholeheartedly, grudgingly, or not at all. Then the experimenter asked the mother to leave the room and observed whether the child played with the "forbidden" toys in the mother's absence.

The researchers found that children who had complied wholeheartedly in the first instance tended to avoid playing with the forbidden toys for a longer time in the second. Moreover, these children were also more likely to comply with their mother's request that they put away the many toys on the floor after she left the room. When retested near their 4th birthday, most children showed the same type of compliance as they had as toddlers. Overall, the results indicated that the quality of young children's compliance with their mother's requests is a somewhat stable, general property of the mother–child relationship.

This type of structured observation offers an important advantage over naturalistic observation: it ensures that all the children being studied encounter identical situations. This allows direct comparisons of different children's behavior in a given situation and, as in the research just discussed, also makes it possible to establish the generality of each child's behavior across different situations. On the other hand, structured observation does not provide as extensive information about individual children's subjective experience as do interviews, nor can it provide the open-ended, everyday kind of data that naturalistic observation can yield.

As these examples suggest, which data-gathering approach is best depends on the goals of the research. (Table 1.4 summarizes the advantages and disadvantages of interviews, naturalistic observation, and structured observation as contexts for gathering data.)

Correlation and Causation

People differ along an infinite number of **variables,** that is, attributes that vary across individuals and situations, such as age, sex, activity level, socioeconomic status, particular experiences, and so on. A major goal of child-development research is to determine how these and other major characteristics of children and influences on them are related to one another, both in terms of associations and in terms of cause–effect relations. In the following sections, we consider the research designs that are used to examine each type of relation.

Correlational Designs

The primary goal of studies that use **correlational designs** is to determine whether children who differ in one variable also differ in predictable ways in other variables. For example, a researcher might examine whether toddlers' aggressiveness is related to the number of hours they spend in day care or whether adolescents' popularity is related to their self-control.

The association between two variables is known as their **correlation.** When variables are strongly correlated, knowing a child's score on either variable allows accurate prediction of the child's score on the other. For example, the number of hours per week that children spend reading correlates highly with their

variables ■ attributes that vary across individuals and situations, such as age, sex, and popularity

correlational designs ■ studies intended to indicate how two variables are related to each other

correlation ■ the association between two variables

TABLE 1.4

Advantages and Disadvantages of Three Contexts for Gathering Data

Data-Gathering Situation	Features	Advantages	Disadvantages
Interview/ questionnaire	Children answer questions asked either in person or on a questionnaire.	Can reveal children's subjective experience. Structured interviews are inexpensive means for collecting in-depth data about individuals. Clinical interviews allow flexibility for following up on unexpected comments.	Reports are often biased to reflect favorably on interviewee. Memories of interviewees are often inaccurate and incomplete. Prediction of future behaviors often is inaccurate.
Naturalistic observation	Children's activities in one or more everyday settings are observed.	Useful for describing behavior in everyday settings. Helps illuminate social interaction processes.	Difficult to know which aspects of situation are most influential. Limited value for studying infrequent behaviors.
Structured observation	Children are brought to laboratory and presented prearranged tasks.	Ensures that all children's behaviors are observed in same context. Allows controlled comparison of children's behavior in different situations.	Context is less natural than in naturalistic observation. Reveals less about subjective experience than interviews.

reading-test scores (Guthrie et al., 1999); this means a child's reading-test score can be accurately predicted if one knows how much time the child spends reading. It also means that the number of hours the child spends reading can be predicted if one knows the child's reading-test score.

Correlations range from 1.00, the strongest positive correlation, to −1.00, the strongest negative correlation. The direction is positive when high values of one variable are associated with high values of the other, and low values of one are associated with low values of the other; the direction is negative when high values of one variable are associated with low values of the other. Thus, the correlation between time spent reading and reading-test scores is positive, because children who spend high amounts of time reading also tend to have high reading-test scores; the correlation between obesity and amount of exercise that a child gets is negative, because more obese children tend to exercise less.

Correlation Does Not Equal Causation

When two variables are strongly correlated and there is a plausible cause–effect relation between them, it often is tempting to infer that one causes the other. However, this inference is not justified, for two reasons. The first is the **direction-of-causation problem:** a correlation does not indicate which variable is the cause and which variable is the effect. In the preceding example of the correlation between time spent reading and reading achievement, greater time spent reading *might* cause increased reading achievement. On the other hand, the cause–effect relation could run in the opposite direction: greater reading skill might cause children to spend more time reading, because reading faster and with greater comprehension makes reading more fun.

The second reason that correlation does not imply causation is the **third-variable problem:** the correlation between two variables may actually be the result of some third, unspecified variable. In the reading example, for instance, rather than greater reading achievement being caused by greater reading time, or vice versa, both of these aspects of reading could be caused by growing up in a family that values knowledge and intelligence.

direction-of-causation problem ■ the concept that a correlation between two variables does not indicate which, if either, variable is the cause of the other

third-variable problem ■ the concept that a correlation between two variables may stem from both being influenced by some third variable

Recognizing that correlation does not imply causation is crucial for interpreting accounts of research. Even findings published in prestigious research journals can easily be misinterpreted. For example, based on a correlation between children younger than 2 years sleeping with a night-light and their later becoming nearsighted, an article in the prestigious journal *Nature* concluded that the light was harmful to visual development (Quinn et al., 1999). Not surprisingly, the claim received considerable publicity in the popular media (e.g., Torassa, 2000). Subsequent research, however, showed that the inference about causation was wrong. What actually seems to have happened is that the nearsighted infants generally had nearsighted parents, and the nearsighted parents, for unknown reasons, more often placed nightlights in their infants' rooms (Gwiazda et al., 2000; Zadnik et al., 2000). As the example illustrates, even seemingly straightforward inferences of causation, based on correlational evidence, frequently prove to be wrong.

If correlation does not imply causation, why do researchers often use correlational designs? One major reason is that the influence of many variables of great interest—age, sex, race, and social class among them—cannot be studied experimentally (see the next section) because researchers cannot manipulate them; that is, they cannot assign participants to one sex or another, to one SES or another, and so on. Consequently, these variables can be studied only through correlational methods. Correlational designs are also of great use when the goal is to describe relations among variables rather than to identify cause–effect relations among them. If, for example, the research goal is to discover how moral reasoning, empathy, anxiety, and popularity are related to one another, correlational designs would almost certainly be employed.

Experimental Designs

If correlational designs are insufficient to indicate cause–effect relations, what type of approach is sufficient? The answer is **experimental designs.** The logic of experimental designs can be summarized quite simply: if children in one group are exposed to a particular experience and subsequently behave differently from a comparable group of children who were not exposed to the experience or were exposed to a different experience, then the subsequent differences in behavior must have resulted from the differing experiences.

Two techniques are crucial to experimental designs: *random assignment* of participants to groups, and *experimental control.* **Random assignment** involves assigning the participants to one experimental group or another according to chance so that the groups are comparable at the outset. This comparability is crucial for being able to infer that it was the varying experiences to which the groups were exposed in the experiment that caused the later differences between them. Otherwise, those differences might have arisen from some preexisting difference between the people in the groups.

Say, for instance, that researchers wanted to compare the effectiveness of two interventions for helping depressed mothers improve their relationship with their infant—providing the mothers with home visits from trained therapists versus providing them with supportive phone calls from such therapists. If the researchers provided the home visits to families in one neighborhood and the supportive phone calls to families in another neighborhood, it would be unclear whether any differences in mother–infant relationships following the experiment were caused by differences between the effectiveness of the two types of support or by differences between the families in the two areas. Depressed mothers in one

experimental designs ■ a group of approaches that allow inferences about causes and effects to be drawn

random assignment ■ a procedure in which each participant has an equal chance of being assigned to each group within an experiment

neighborhood might suffer from less severe forms of depression than mothers in the other, or they might have greater access to other support, such as close families, mental health centers, or parenting programs.

In contrast, when groups are created through random assignment and include a reasonably large number of participants (typically 20 or more per group), initial differences between the groups tend to be minimal. For example, if 40 families with mothers who suffer from depression are divided randomly into two experimental groups, each group is likely to have roughly equal numbers of families from each neighborhood. Similarly, each group is likely to include a few mothers who are extremely depressed, a few with mild forms of depression, and many in between, as well as a few infants who have been severely affected by their mother's depression, a few who have been minimally affected, and many in between. The logic implies that groups created through random assignment should be comparable on all variables except the different treatment that people in the experimental groups encounter during the experiment. Such an experiment was in fact conducted, and it showed that home visits helped depressed mothers more than supportive phone calls did (Van Doesum et al., 2008).

The second essential characteristic of an experimental design, **experimental control,** refers to the ability of the researcher to determine the specific experiences that children in each group encounter during the study. In the simplest experimental design, one with two conditions, the groups are often referred to as the "experimental group" and the "control group." Children in the **experimental group** are presented with the experience of interest; children in the **control group** are treated identically except that they are not presented with the experience of interest or are presented with a different experience that is expected to have less effect on the variables being tested.

The experience that children in the experimental group receive, and that children in the control group do not receive, is referred to as the **independent variable.** The behavior that is hypothesized to be affected by exposure to the independent variable is referred to as the **dependent variable.** Thus, if a researcher hypothesized that showing schoolchildren an anti-bullying film would reduce school bullying, the researcher might randomly assign some children in a school to view the film and other children in the same school to view an equally interesting film about a different topic. In this case, the anti-bullying film would be the independent variable, and the amount of bullying after the children watched it would be the dependent variable. If the independent variable had the predicted effect, children who saw the anti-bullying film would show less bullying after watching it than children who saw the other film.

One illustration of how experimental designs allow researchers to draw conclusions about causes and effects is a study that tested the hypothesis that television shows running in the background lower the quality of infants' and toddlers' play (Schmidt et al., 2008). The independent variable was whether or not a television program was on in the room where the participants were playing; the dependent variables were a variety of measures of children's attention to the television program and of the quality of their play. The television program being played was *Jeopardy!*, which presumably would have been of little interest to the 1- and 2-year-olds in the study. Indeed, the toddlers looked at it an average of only once per minute and only for a few seconds at a time. Nonetheless, the television show disrupted the children's play, reducing the length of play episodes and the children's focus on their play. These findings indicate that there is a causal, and negative, relation between background exposure to television shows and the quality of young children's play.

experimental control ■ the ability of researchers to determine the specific experiences of participants during the course of an experiment

experimental group ■ the group of participants in an experimental design who are presented the experience of interest

control group ■ the group of participants in an experimental design who are not presented the experience of interest but in other ways are treated similarly

independent variable ■ the experience that participants in the experimental group receive and that those in the control group do not receive

dependent variable ■ a behavior that is measured to determine whether it is affected by exposure to the independent variable

Depressed mothers often have difficulty providing sensitive parenting; home visits from trained therapists can help alleviate this problem.

AARON SIEGLER

The quality of infants' and toddlers' play is adversely affected by a television being on in the same room. This is true for even the most precocious children, such as this 1-year-old, the grandson of one of the authors.

cross-sectional design ■ a research method in which participants of different ages are compared on a given behavior or characteristic over a short period

Experimental designs are the method of choice for establishing causal relations, a central goal of scientific research. However, as noted earlier, experimental designs cannot be applied to all issues of interest. For example, hypotheses about why boys tend to be more physically aggressive than girls cannot be tested experimentally because gender cannot be randomly assigned to children. In addition, many experimental studies are conducted in laboratory settings; this improves experimental control but can raise doubts about the external validity of the findings, that is, whether the findings from the lab apply to the outside world. (The advantages and disadvantages of correlational and experimental designs are summarized in Table 1.5.)

Research Designs for Examining Children's Development

A great deal of research on child development focuses on how children change or remain the same as they grow older and gain experience. To study development over time, investigators use three types of research designs: cross-sectional, longitudinal, and microgenetic.

Cross-Sectional Designs

The most common and easiest way to study changes and continuities with age is to use the **cross-sectional** approach. This method compares children of different ages on a given behavior, ability, or characteristic, with all the children being studied once at roughly the same time—for example, within the same month. In one cross-sectional study, Evans, Xu, and Lee (2011) examined the development of lying in Chinese 3-, 4-, and 5-year-olds. The children played a game in which, to win a prize, they needed to guess the type of object hidden under an upside-down paper cup. However, before the child could guess, the experimenter left the room after telling the child not to peek while she was gone. The cup was so fully packed with candies that if the child peeked, some would spill out and it would be virtually impossible for the child to put them all back under the cup.

TABLE 1.5

Advantages and Disadvantages of Correlational and Experimental Designs

Type of Design	Features	Advantages	Disadvantages
Correlational	Comparison of existing groups of children or examination of relations among each child's scores on different variables.	Only way to compare many groups of interest (boys–girls, rich–poor, etc.). Only way to establish relations among many variables of interest (IQ and achievement, popularity and happiness, etc.).	Direction-of-causation problem. Third-variable problem.
Experimental	Random assignment of children to groups and experimental control of procedures presented to each group.	Allows causal inferences because design rules out direction-of-causation and third-variable problems. Allows experimental control over the exact experiences that children encounter.	Need for experimental control often leads to artificial experimental situations. Cannot be used to study many differences and variables of interest, such as age, sex, and temperament.

At all ages, many children peeked and then denied doing so. However, 5-year-olds lied more often, and their lies were more clever. For example, many 5-year-olds explained away the presence of candies on the table by saying that they accidentally knocked over the cup with their elbow; other 5-year-olds destroyed the evidence by eating it. Three-year-olds were the least-skilled fibbers, generating implausible excuses such as that some other child entered the room and knocked over the cup or that the candies came out by themselves.

Cross-sectional designs are useful for revealing similarities and differences between older and younger children. However, they do not yield information about the stability of behavior over time or about the patterns of change shown by individual children. This is where longitudinal approaches are especially valuable.

Being excluded is no fun for anyone. Longitudinal research has been used to determine whether the same children are unpopular year after year or whether popularity changes over time.

Longitudinal Designs

The **longitudinal** approach involves following the same children over a substantial period (usually at least a year) and observing changes and continuities in these children's development at regular intervals during that time. The study at the beginning of this chapter on the development of children in Kauai from before birth to age 40 is one example of a longitudinal study. Another good example of what the longitudinal approach can tell us is Brendgen and colleagues' (2001) examination of children's popularity with classmates. Each child's popularity was examined each year from the time they were 7-year-olds to the time they were 12-year-olds. The popularity of most children proved to be quite stable over this period; a substantial number of children were popular in the large majority of years, and others were unpopular throughout. At the same time, some individuals showed idiosyncratic patterns of change from year to year; the same child might be popular at age 8, unpopular at age 10, and of average popularity at age 12. Such information about the stability of individual differences over time and about individual children's patterns of change could only have been obtained in a longitudinal design.

If longitudinal designs are so useful for revealing stability and change over time, why are cross-sectional designs more common? The reasons are mainly practical. Studying the same children over long periods involves the difficult task of locating the children for each re-examination. Inevitably, some of the children move away or stop participating for other reasons. Such loss of participants may call into question the validity of the findings, because the children who do not continue may differ from those who participate throughout. Another threat to the validity of longitudinal designs is the possible effects of the repeated testing. For example, repeatedly taking IQ tests could familiarize children with the type of items on the tests, thus improving the children's scores. For these reasons, longitudinal designs are used primarily when the main issues are stability and change in individual children over time—issues that can only be studied longitudinally. When the central developmental issue involves age-related changes in typical performance, cross-sectional studies are more commonly used.

Microgenetic Designs

An important limitation of both cross-sectional and longitudinal designs is that they provide only a broad outline of the process of change. **Microgenetic designs,** in contrast, are specifically designed to provide an in-depth depiction of the

longitudinal design ■ a method of study in which the same participants are studied twice or more over a substantial length of time

microgenetic design ■ a method of study in which the same participants are studied repeatedly over a short period

The excitement of discovery is evoked by an insight while this child was trying to solve a problem in the game "Magic C."

Research of Geoffrey Saxe

counting-on strategy ■ counting up from the larger addend the number of times indicated by the smaller addend

processes that produce change (Miller & Coyle, 1999; Siegler, 2006). The basic idea of this approach is to recruit children who are thought to be on the verge of an important developmental change, heighten their exposure to the type of experience that is believed to produce the change, and then intensively study the change *as it is occurring*. Microgenetic designs are like longitudinal ones in repeatedly testing the same children over time. They differ in that microgenetic studies typically include a greater number of sessions presented over a shorter time than in a longitudinal study.

Siegler and Jenkins (1989) used a microgenetic design to study how young children discover the **counting-on strategy** for adding two small numbers. This strategy involves counting up from the larger addend the number of times indicated by the smaller addend; for example, when asked the answer to 3 + 5, a child who was counting-on would start from the addend 5 and say or think "6, 7, 8" before answering "8." Prior to discovering this strategy, children usually solve addition problems by counting from 1. Counting from the larger addend rather than from 1 reduces the amount of counting, producing faster and more accurate solutions.

To observe the discovery process, the researchers selected 4- and 5-year-olds who did not yet use counting-on but who knew how to add by counting from 1. Over an 11-week period, these children received many addition problems—far more than they would normally encounter before entering school—and each child's behavior on every problem was video-recorded. This approach allowed the researchers to identify exactly when each child discovered the counting-on strategy.

Examination of the problems immediately preceding the discovery revealed a surprising fact: necessity is not always the mother of invention. Quite a few children discovered the counting-on strategy while working on easy problems that they previously had solved correctly by counting from 1.

The microgenetic method also revealed that children's very first use of the new strategy often was accompanied by insight and excitement, like that shown by Lauren:

> *Experimenter:* How much is 6 + 3?
> *Lauren: (long pause)* 9.
> *E:* OK, how did you know that?
> *L:* I think I said . . . I think I said . . . oops, um . . . 7 was 1, 8 was 2, 9 was 3.
> *E:* How did you know to do that? Why didn't you count 1, 2, 3, 4, 5, 6, 7, 8, 9?
> *L: (with excitement)* 'Cause then you have to count all those numbers.
>
> (Siegler & Jenkins, 1989, p. 66)

Despite Lauren's insightful explanation of counting-on and her excitement over discovering it, she and most other children only gradually increased their use of the new strategy on subsequent problems, though they eventually used it quite often. Many other microgenetic studies have also shown that generalization of new strategies tends to be slow (Kuhn & Franklin, 2006).

As this example illustrates, microgenetic methods provide insight into the process of change over brief periods. However, unlike standard longitudinal methods, microgenetic designs do not yield information about stability and change over long periods. They therefore are typically used when the basic pattern of age-related change has already been established and the goal becomes to understand

TABLE 1.6

Advantages and Disadvantages of Designs for Studying Development

Design	Features	Advantages	Disadvantages
Cross-sectional	Children of different ages are studied at a single time.	Yields useful data about differences among age groups. Quick and easy to administer.	Uninformative about stability of individual differences over time. Uninformative about similarities and differences in individual children's patterns of change.
Longitudinal	Children are examined repeatedly over a prolonged period.	Indicates the degree of stability of individual differences over long periods. Reveals individual children's patterns of change over long periods.	Difficult to keep all participants in study. Repeatedly testing children can threaten external validity of study.
Microgenetic	Children are observed intensively over a relatively short period while a change is occurring.	Intensive observation of changes while they are occurring can clarify process of change. Reveals individual change patterns over short periods in considerable detail.	Does not provide information about typical patterns of change over long periods. Does not yield data regarding change patterns over long periods.

how the changes occur. (Table 1.6 outlines the strengths and weaknesses of the three approaches to studying changes with age and experience: cross-sectional, longitudinal, and microgenetic designs.)

Ethical Issues in Child-Development Research

All research with human beings raises ethical issues, and this is especially the case when the research involves children. Researchers have a vital responsibility to anticipate potential risks that the children in their studies may encounter, to minimize such risks, and to make sure that the benefits of the research outweigh any potential harm.

The Society for Research on Child Development, an organization devoted to research on children, has formulated a code of ethical conduct for investigators to follow (SRCD Governing Council, 2007). Some of the most important ethical principles in the code are:

■ Be sure that the research does not harm children physically or psychologically.

■ Obtain informed consent for participating in the research, preferably in writing, from parents or other responsible adults and also from children if they are old enough that the research can be explained to them. The experimenter should inform children and relevant adults of all aspects of the research that might influence their willingness to participate and should explain that refusing to participate will not result in any adverse consequences to them.

■ Preserve individual participants' anonymity, and do not use information for purposes other than that for which permission was given.

■ Discuss with parents or guardians any information yielded by the investigation that is important for the child's welfare.

■ Try to counteract any unforeseen negative consequences that arise during the research.

■ Correct any inaccurate impressions that the child may develop in the course of the study. When the research has been completed, explain the main findings to participants at a level they can understand.

Recognizing the importance of such ethical issues, universities and governmental agencies have established institutional review boards made up of independent scientists and sometimes others from the community. These boards evaluate the proposed research to ensure that it does not violate ethics guidelines. However, the individual investigator is in the best position to anticipate potential problems and bears the ultimate responsibility for seeing that his or her study meets high ethical standards.

Review

The scientific method, in which all hypotheses are treated as potentially incorrect, has allowed contemporary understanding of child development to progress well beyond the understanding of even the greatest thinkers of the past. This progress has been built on a base of four types of innovations:

1. Measures that are directly relevant to the main hypotheses of the study
2. Data-gathering situations that yield useful information about children's behavior, such as interviews, naturalistic observations, and structured observations
3. Research contexts that allow identification of associations and cause–effect relations among variables, notably correlational and experimental designs
4. Research designs that allow analysis of the continuities and changes that occur with age and experience, notably cross-sectional, longitudinal, and microgenetic designs

Conducting scientific experiments also requires meeting high ethical standards, including not in any way harming the children who participate; obtaining informed consent for the children's participation in the research; preserving anonymity of all participants; and, after the study, explaining the findings to parents and, when possible, to children, at a level they can understand.

CHAPTER SUMMARY

Reasons to Learn About Child Development

■ Learning about child development is valuable for many reasons: it can help us become better parents, inform our views about social issues that affect children, and improve our understanding of human nature.

Historical Foundations of the Study of Child Development

■ Great thinkers such as Plato, Aristotle, Locke, and Rousseau raised basic questions about child development and proposed interesting hypotheses about them, but they lacked the scientific methods to answer them. Early scientific approaches, such as those of Freud and Watson, began the movement toward modern research-based theories of child development.

Enduring Themes in Child Development

■ The field of child development is an attempt to answer a set of fundamental questions:
  1. How do nature and nurture together shape development?
  2. How do children shape their own development?
  3. In what ways is development continuous, and in what ways is it discontinuous?
  4. How does change occur?
  5. How does the sociocultural context influence development?
  6. How do children become so different from one another?
  7. How can research promote children's well-being?

■ Every aspect of development, from the most specific behavior to the most general trait, reflects both people's biological endowment (their nature) and the experiences that they have had (their nurture).

- Even infants and young children actively contribute to their own development through their patterns of attention, use of language, and choices of activities.

- Many developments can appear either continuous or discontinuous, depending on how often and how closely we look at them.

- The mechanisms that produce developmental changes involve a complex interplay among experiences, genes, and brain structures and activities.

- The contexts that shape development include the people with whom children interact directly, such as family and friends; the institutions in which they participate, such as schools and religious organizations; and societal beliefs and values, such as those related to race, ethnicity, and social class.

- Individual differences, even among siblings, reflect differences in children's genes, in their treatment by other people, in their interpretations of their own experiences, and in their choices of environments.

- Principles, findings, and methods from child-development research are being applied to improve the quality of children's lives.

Methods for Studying Child Development

- The scientific method has made possible great advances in understanding children. It involves choosing a question, formulating a hypothesis relevant to the question, developing a method to test the hypothesis, and using data to decide whether the hypothesis is correct.

- For a measure to be useful, it must be directly relevant to the hypotheses being tested, reliable, and valid. Reliability means that independent observations of a given behavior are consistent. Validity means that a measure assesses what it is intended to measure.

- Among the main situations used to gather data about children are interviews, naturalistic observation, and structured observation. Interviews are especially useful for revealing children's subjective experience. Naturalistic observation is particularly useful when the primary goal is to describe how children behave in their everyday environments. Structured observation is most useful when the main goal is to describe how different children react to the identical situation.

- Correlation does not imply causation. The two differ in that correlations indicate the degree to which two variables are associated, whereas causation indicates that changing the value of one variable will change the value of the other.

- Correlational designs are especially useful when the goal is to describe relations among variables or when the variables of interest cannot be manipulated because of technical or practical considerations.

- Experimental designs are especially valuable for revealing the causes of children's behavior.

- Data about development can be obtained through cross-sectional designs (examining different children of different ages), through longitudinal designs (examining the same children at different ages), or through microgenetic designs (presenting the same children repeated relevant experiences over a relatively short period and analyzing the change process in detail).

- It is vital for researchers to adhere to high ethical standards. Among the most important ethical principles are striving to ensure that the research does not harm children physically or psychologically; obtaining informed consent from parents and, where possible, from children; preserving participants' anonymity; and correcting any inaccurate impressions that children form during the study.

Test Yourself

1. The "turtle shell" technique is an example of a successful intervention that helps preschoolers cope with what?
   a. the sense of isolation
   b. feelings of embarrassment
   c. bullying from peers
   d. their own anger

2. What is meta-analysis?
   a. The reproduction of a past study in order to confirm or debunk the results
   b. A philosophical exploration of an experiment or case study
   c. A method for combining and analyzing the results from several independent studies
   d. A list of all published articles related to a specific area of research

3. Studies have shown that children's testimony is usually accurate when which of the following conditions are met?
   a. The interviewer does not ask leading questions.
   b. One of the child's parents is present.
   c. The child and the interviewer are alone when the testimony is given.
   d. The child is repeatedly prompted during the interview.

4. Sigmund Freud's psychoanalytic theory proposed that development is strongly influenced by biological drives. In contrast, John Watson's behaviorist theory proposed that development is determined by what?
   a. temperament
   b. rewards and punishments
   c. genetic factors
   d. innate mechanisms

JOSE ORTEGA, *Mother and Child*

Prenatal Development and the Newborn Period

Themes

- Nature and Nurture
- The Active Child
- The Sociocultural Context
- Individual Differences
- Continuity/Discontinuity
- Research and Children's Welfare

Picture the following scenario: a developmental psychologist is investigating a very young research participant's perceptual capacities and ability to learn from experience. First, she plays a recording of a nonsense word for the young participant (*tatata*). The participant hears this word multiple times a day, over the course of several months. The psychologist wants to find out whether the participant has learned the novel word, as indexed by brain responses. But before the psychologist can measure the participant's brain waves, something very important has to happen: the participant has to be born!

This scenario is not at all fanciful. Indeed, as you will discover later in this chapter, it is an accurate description of a recent study that is one of many currently revolutionizing the scientific understanding of prenatal development (Partanen et al., 2013). As you will also discover in this chapter, researchers have been asking many questions about the sensory and learning capabilities of fetuses. They have been finding that while in the womb, fetuses can detect a range of stimuli coming from both the outside world and inside the mother's body. Fetuses learn from these experiences and are affected by them after birth.

In this chapter, we will examine the extraordinary course of prenatal development—a time of astonishingly rapid and dramatic change. In addition to discussing the normal processes involved in prenatal development, including fetal learning, we will consider some of the ways in which these processes can be disrupted by environmental hazards. We will also examine the birth process and what the infant experiences during this dramatic turning point, as well as some of the most salient aspects of neonatal behavior. Finally, we will outline issues associated with premature birth.

In our discussion of the earliest periods of development, most of the themes we described in Chapter 1 will play prominent roles. The most notable will be *nature and nurture,* as we emphasize how every aspect of development before birth results from the continual interplay of biological and environmental factors. The *active child* theme will also be featured, because the activity of the fetus contributes in numerous vital ways to its development. In fact, as you will see, normal prenatal development depends on certain fetal behaviors. Another theme we will highlight is the *sociocultural context* of prenatal development and birth. There is substantial cultural variation in how people think about the beginning of life and how they handle the birth process. The theme of *individual differences* comes into play at many points, starting with sex differences in survival rates from conception on. The *continuity/discontinuity* theme is also prominent: despite the dramatic contrast between prenatal and postnatal life, the behavior of newborns shows clear connections to their behavior and experience inside the womb. Finally, the theme of *research and children's welfare* is central to our discussion of how poverty can affect prenatal development and birth outcomes, as well as to our description of intervention programs designed to foster healthy development for preterm infants.

Prenatal Development

▶ The Prenatal Period: Conception to Birth

Hidden from view, the process of prenatal development has always been mysterious and fascinating, and beliefs about the origins of human life and development before birth are an important part of the lore and traditions of all societies.

(Box 2.1 describes one set of cultural beliefs about the beginning of life that is quite unlike those of Western societies.)

When we look back in history, we see great differences in how people have thought about prenatal development. In the fourth century B.C., Aristotle posed the fundamental question about prenatal development that was to underlie Western thought about it for the next 15 centuries: Does prenatal life start with the new individual already preformed, composed of a full set of tiny parts, or do the many parts of the human body develop in succession? Aristotle rejected the idea of preformation in favor of what he termed **epigenesis**—the emergence of new structures and functions during development (we will revisit this idea in Chapter 3 in its more modern form, *epigenetics*). Seeking support for his idea, he took what was then a very unorthodox step: he opened chicken eggs to observe organs in various stages of development. Nevertheless, the idea of preformation persisted long after Aristotle, degenerating into a dispute about whether the miniature, preformed human was lodged inside the mother's egg or the father's sperm (see Figure 2.1).

While the notion of preformation may strike you as simpleminded, our ancient forebears had no way of knowing about the existence of cells, genes, and prenatal development. Many of the mysteries that perplexed our ancestors have now been solved, but as is always true in science, new mysteries have replaced them.

epigenesis ■ the emergence of new structures and functions in the course of development

BOX 2.1 | a closer look

BENG BEGINNINGS

Few topics have generated more intense debate and dispute in the United States in recent years than the issue of when life begins—at the moment of conception, the moment of birth, or sometime in between. The irony is that few who engage in this debate recognize how complex the issue is or the degree to which societies throughout the world have different views on it.

Consider, for example, the perspective of the Beng, a people in the Ivory Coast of West Africa, who believe that every newborn is a reincarnation of an ancestor (Gottlieb, 2004). According to the Beng, in the first weeks after birth, the ancestor's spirit, its *wru,* is not fully committed to an earthly life and therefore maintains a double existence, traveling back and forth between the everyday world and *wrugbe,* or "spirit village." (The term can be roughly translated as "afterlife," but "before-life" might be just as appropriate.) It is only after the umbilical stump has dropped off that the newborn is considered to have emerged from *wrugbe* and to be a person. If the newborn dies before this point, there is no funeral, for the infant's passing is perceived as a return to the *wrugbe.*

These beliefs underlie many aspects of Beng infant-care practices. One is the frequent application of an herbal mixture to the newborn's umbilical stump to hasten its drying out and dropping off. In addition, there is the constant danger that the infant will become homesick for its life in *wrugbe* and decide to leave its earthly existence. To prevent this, parents try to make their babies comfortable and happy so they will want to stay in this life. Among the many recommended procedures is elaborately decorating the infant's face and body to elicit positive attention from others. Sometimes diviners are consulted, especially if the baby seems to be unhappy; a common diagnosis for prolonged crying is that the baby wants a different name—the one from its previous life in *wrugbe.*

So when does life begin for the Beng? In one sense, a Beng individual's life begins well before birth, since he or she is a reincarnation of an ancestor. In another sense, however, life begins sometime after birth, when the individual is considered to have become a person.

 Parenting in Infancy: Beng Caretaking Practices

COURTESY OF ALMA GOTTLIEB

The mother of this Beng baby has spent considerable time painting the baby's face in an elaborate pattern. She does this every day in an effort to make the baby attractive so other people will help keep the baby happy in this world.

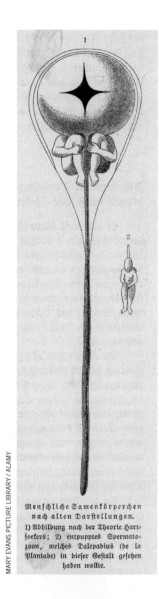

MARY EVANS PICTURE LIBRARY / ALAMY

FIGURE 2.1 **Preformationism** A seventeenth-century drawing of a preformed being inside a sperm. This drawing was based on the claim of committed preformationists that when they looked at samples of semen under the newly invented microscope, they could actually see a tiny figure curled up inside the head of the sperm. They believed that the miniature person would enlarge after entering an egg. As this drawing illustrates, we must always take care not to let our cherished preconceptions so dominate our thinking that we see what we want to see—not what is really there. (From Moore & Persaud, 1993, p. 7).

Conception

Each of us originated as a single cell that resulted from the union of two highly specialized cells—a sperm from our father and an egg from our mother. These **gametes,** or germ cells, are unique not only in their function but also in the fact that each one contains only half the genetic material found in other cells. Gametes are produced through **meiosis,** a special type of cell division in which the eggs and sperm receive only one member from each of the 23 chromosome pairs contained in all other cells of the body. This reduction to 23 chromosomes in each gamete is necessary for reproduction, because the union of egg and sperm must contain the normal amount of genetic material (23 *pairs* of chromosomes). A major difference in the formation of these two types of gametes is the fact that almost all the eggs a woman will ever have are formed during her own prenatal development, whereas men produce vast numbers of new sperm continuously.

The process of reproduction starts with the launching of an egg (the largest cell in the human female body) from one of the woman's ovaries into the adjoining fallopian tube (see Figure 2.2). As the egg moves through the tube toward the uterus, it emits a chemical substance that acts as a sort of beacon, a "come-hither" signal that attracts sperm toward it. If an act of sexual intercourse takes place near the time the egg is released, **conception,** the union of sperm and egg, will be possible. In every ejaculation, as many as 500 million sperm are pumped into the woman's vagina. Each sperm, a streamlined vehicle for delivering the man's genes to the woman's egg, consists of little more than a pointed head packed full of genetic material (the 23 chromosomes) and a long tail that whips around to propel the sperm through the woman's reproductive system.

To be a candidate for initiating conception, a sperm must travel for about 6 hours, journeying 6 to 7 inches from the vagina up through the uterus to the egg-bearing fallopian tube. The rate of attrition on this journey is enormous: of the millions of sperm that enter the vagina, only about 200 ever get near the egg (see Figure 2.3). There are many causes for this high failure rate. Some failures are due to chance: many of the sperm get tangled up with other sperm milling about in the vagina; others wind up in the fallopian tube that does not currently harbor an egg. Other failures have to do with the fact that a substantial portion of the sperm have serious genetic or other defects that prevent them from propelling themselves vigorously enough to reach and fertilize the egg. Thus, any sperm that do get to the egg are relatively likely to be healthy and structurally sound, revealing a Darwinian-type "survival of the fittest" process operating during fertilization. (Box 2.2 describes the consequences of this selection process for the conception of males and females.)

As soon as one sperm's head penetrates the outer membrane of the egg, a chemical reaction seals the membrane, preventing other sperm from entering. The tail of the sperm falls off, the contents of its head gush into the egg, and the nuclei of the two cells merge within hours. The fertilized egg, known as a **zygote,** now has a full complement of human genetic material, 23 chromosomes from the mother and 23 chromosomes from the father. Prenatal development has begun and, if

gametes (germ cells) ■ reproductive cells—egg and sperm—that contain only half the genetic material of all the other cells in the body

meiosis ■ cell division that produces gametes

conception ■ the union of an egg from the mother and a sperm from the father

zygote ■ a fertilized egg cell

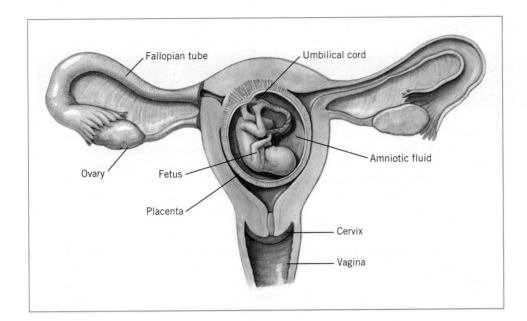

FIGURE 2.2 Female reproductive system A simplified illustration of the female reproductive system, with a fetus developing in the uterus (womb). The umbilical cord runs from the fetus to the placenta, which is burrowed deeply into the wall of the uterus. The fetus is floating in amniotic fluid inside the amniotic sac.

everything proceeds normally, that development will continue for approximately 9 months (on average, 38 weeks or 266 days).

Developmental Processes

Before describing the course of prenatal development, we need to briefly outline four major developmental processes that underlie the transformation of a zygote into an **embryo** and then a **fetus.** The first is *cell division,* known as **mitosis.** Within about 12 hours after fertilization, the zygote divides into two equal parts, each containing a full complement of genetic material. These two cells then divide into four, those four into eight, those eight into sixteen, and so on. Through continued cell division over the course of 38 weeks, the barely visible zygote becomes a newborn consisting of trillions of cells.

embryo ■ the name given to the developing organism from the 3rd to 8th week of prenatal development

fetus ■ the name given to the developing organism from the 9th week to birth

mitosis ■ cell division that results in two identical daughter cells

FIGURE 2.3 (a) Sperm nearing the egg Of the millions of sperm that started out together, only a few ever get near the egg. The egg is the largest human cell (the only one visible to the naked eye), but sperm are among the smallest. **(b) Sperm penetrating the egg** This sperm is whipping its tail around furiously to drill itself through the outer covering of the egg.

(a)

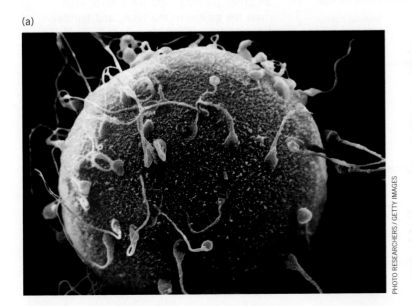

PHOTO RESEARCHERS / GETTY IMAGES

(b)

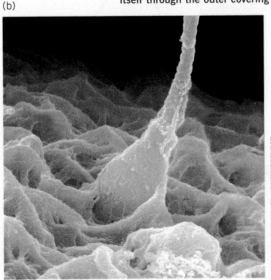

CLOUDS HILL IMAGING LTD. / SCIENCE SOURCE

BOX 2.2 | individual differences

THE FIRST—AND LAST—SEX DIFFERENCES

For decades, scientists thought that at the outset of conception, more male embryos were conceived than female embryos. In fact, there is a slight male bias at birth (51.3%), across generations and around the world. Male fetuses are more susceptible to spontaneous abortion than females in both the 1st week and last several weeks of pregnancy (though it is worth noting that female fetuses are more susceptible in weeks 10–15) (Orzack et al., 2015). Male infants are also more likely to be born at very low birth weights and are less likely to survive than females (e.g., Peacock et al., 2012). The apparent frailty of male fetuses, paired with the male bias at birth, suggested to many researchers that male embryos must significantly outnumber female embryos (Austad, 2015).

However, the results of a recent study suggest that, in fact, conception is equally likely to result in male and female embryos (Orzack et al., 2015). The researchers took advantage of the increased use of reproductive technologies and prenatal genetic tests to determine the sex of nearly 140,000 3- to 6-day-old fetuses. The researchers found almost an exact 50-50 split between male and female at the outset of gestation. Rather than effects of frail male fetuses, it appears that female fetuses are actually less likely to survive early gestation, resulting in the slight male bias at birth.

The girls win the next big competition—survival. During labor and delivery, boys are more likely to experience fetal distress than girls, even when controlling for their larger size and head circumference (DiPietro, Costigan, & Voegtline, 2015). This suggests that, for reasons not well understood, the physiological systems of young males are less able to tolerate the stress of childbirth (DiPietro & Voegtline, 2015). Indeed, for decades, and across many cultural contexts, the infant mortality rates have been higher for boys than for girls (Drevenstedt et al., 2008). This heightened vulnerability is not limited to surviving the immediate postnatal period. Male infants are also more likely than females to die from sudden infant death syndrome (SIDS; Mage & Donner, 2014), discussed in more detail in Box 2.4, and some teratogens appear to disproportionately affect boys. For example, a Canadian study of fetal alcohol spectrum disorder (FASD) found that the incidence rate was 1.4 times higher for boys than for girls (Thanh et al., 2014). Boys also suffer disproportionately from most developmental disorders, including language and learning disorders, dyslexia, attention-deficit disorder, intellectual disabilities, and autism. The greater fragility of males continues throughout life, as reflected in the graph and by the fact that adolescent boys are more impulsive and take more risks than girls; they are also more likely to commit suicide or die violently.

Differential survival is not always left in the hands of nature. In many societies, both historically and currently, male offspring are more highly valued than female offspring, and parents resort to infanticide to avoid having daughters. For example, Inuit families in Alaska traditionally depended on male children to help in the hunt for food, and in former times, Inuit girls were often killed at birth. Until 2015, the Chinese government strictly enforced a "one-child" policy, a measure designed to reduce population growth by forbidding couples to have more than one child. This policy resulted in many parents killing or abandoning their female babies (or giving them up for adoption to Western families) in order to make room for a male child. A more technological approach is currently practiced in some countries that place a premium on male offspring: prenatal tests are used to determine the gender of the fetus, and female fetuses are selectively aborted. These cases dramatically illustrate the sociocultural model of development described in Chapter 1, showing how cultural values, government policy, and available technology all affect developmental outcomes.

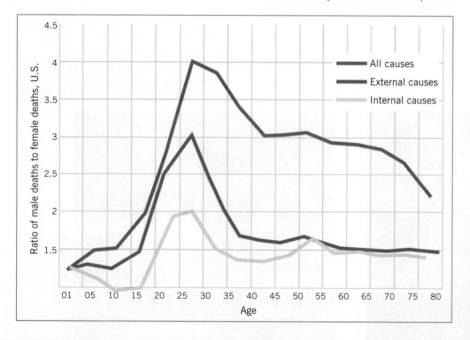

Beginning at birth, the U.S. male-to-female mortality ratio exceeds 1 across the life span. The spike that occurs in adolescence and early adulthood—peaking at 3 male deaths for every female death—is largely the result of external causes, such as accidents, homicide, and suicide.

A second major process, which occurs during the embryonic period, is *cell migration*, the movement of newly formed cells away from their point of origin. Among the many cells that migrate are the neurons that originate deep inside the embryonic brain and then, like pioneers settling new territory, travel to the outer reaches of the developing brain.

The third process in prenatal development is *cell differentiation*. Initially, all of the embryo's cells, referred to as **embryonic stem cells,** are equivalent and interchangeable: none has any fixed fate or function. After several cell divisions, however, these cells start to specialize in terms of both structure and function. In humans, embryonic stem cells develop into roughly 350 different types of cells, which perform particular functions on behalf of the organism. (Because of their developmental flexibility, embryonic stem cells are currently the focus of a great deal of research in regenerative medicine. The hope is that when injected into a person suffering from illness or injury, embryonic stem cells will develop into healthy cells to replace the diseased or damaged ones.)

The process of differentiation is one of the major mysteries of prenatal development. Since all cells in the body have the identical set of genes, what factors determine which type of cell a given stem cell will become? One key determinant is which genes in the cell are "switched on" or expressed. Another is the cell's location, because its future development is influenced by what is going on in neighboring cells.

The initial flexibility and subsequent inflexibility of cells, as well as the importance of location, is vividly illustrated by classic research with frog embryos. If the region of a frog embryo that would normally become an eye is grafted onto its belly area early in fetal development, the transplanted region will develop as a normal part of the belly. Thus, although the cells were initially in the right place to become an eye, they had not yet become specialized. If the transplant is performed later in fetal development, the same operation results in an eye—alone and unseeing—lodged in the frog's belly (Wolpert, 1991).

The fourth developmental process is something you would not normally think of as developmental at all—*death*. The selective death of certain cells is the "almost constant companion" to the other developmental processes we have described (Wolpert, 1991). The role of this genetically programmed "cell suicide," known as **apoptosis,** is readily apparent in hand development: the formation of fingers depends on the death of the cells in between the ridges in the hand plate. In other words, death is preprogrammed for the cells that disappear from the hand plates.

In addition to these four developmental processes, we need to call attention to the influence of hormones on prenatal development. For example, hormones play a crucial role in sexual differentiation. All human fetuses, regardless of the genes they carry, can develop either male or female genitalia. The presence or absence of *androgens*, a class of hormones that includes testosterone, causes development to proceed one way or the other. If androgens are present, male sex organs develop; if they are absent, female genitalia develop. The source of androgens is the male fetus itself. Around the 8th week after conception, the testes begin to produce these hormones, changing the developing organism forever. This is just one of the many ways in which the fetus influences its own development.

We now turn our attention to the general course of prenatal development that results from all the preceding influences, as well as other developmental processes.

embryonic stem cells ■ embryonic cells, which can develop into any type of body cell

apoptosis ■ genetically programmed cell death

identical twins ■ twins that result from the splitting in half of the zygote, resulting in each of the two resulting zygotes having exactly the same set of genes

fraternal twins ■ twins that result when two eggs happen to be released into the fallopian tube at the same time and are fertilized by two different sperm; fraternal twins have only half their genes in common

neural tube ■ a groove formed in the top layer of differentiated cells in the embryo that eventually becomes the brain and spinal cord

amniotic sac ■ a transparent, fluid-filled membrane that surrounds and protects the fetus

placenta ■ a support organ for the fetus; it keeps the circulatory systems of the fetus and mother separate, but as a semipermeable membrane permits the exchange of some materials between them (oxygen and nutrients from mother to fetus and carbon dioxide and waste products from fetus to mother)

FIGURE 2.4 Neural tube In the 4th week, the neural tube begins to develop into the brain and spinal cord. In this photo, the neural groove, which fuses together first at the center and then outward in both directions as if two zippers were being closed, has been "zipped shut" except for one part still open at the top. Spina bifida, a congenital disorder in which the skin over the spinal cord is not fully closed, can originate at this point. After closing, the top of the neural tube will develop into the brain.

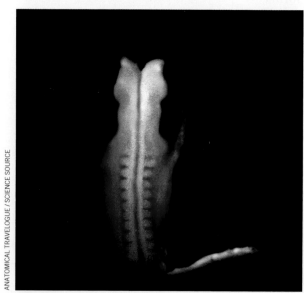

ANATOMICAL TRAVELOGUE / SCIENCE SOURCE

Early Development

On its journey through the fallopian tube to the womb, the zygote doubles its number of cells roughly twice a day. By the 4th day after conception, the cells arrange themselves into a hollow sphere with a bulge of cells, called the *inner cell mass,* on one side.

This is the stage at which **identical twins** most often originate. They result from a splitting in half of the inner cell mass, thus they both have exactly the same genetic makeup. In contrast, **fraternal twins** result when two eggs happen to be released from the ovary into the fallopian tube and both are fertilized. Because they originate from two different eggs and two different sperm, fraternal twins are no more alike genetically than non-twin siblings with the same parents.

By the end of the 1st week following fertilization, if all goes well (which it does for less than half the zygotes that are conceived), a momentous event occurs—implantation, in which the zygote embeds itself in the uterine lining and becomes dependent on the mother for sustenance. Well before the end of the 2nd week, it will be completely embedded within the uterine wall.

After implantation, the embedded ball of cells starts to differentiate. The inner cell mass becomes the embryo, and the rest of the cells become an elaborate support system—including the *amniotic sac* and *placenta*—that enables the embryo to develop. The inner cell mass is initially a single layer thick, but during the 2nd week, it folds itself into three layers, each with a different developmental destiny. The top layer becomes the nervous system, the nails, teeth, inner ear, lens of the eyes, and the outer surface of the skin. The middle layer eventually becomes muscles, bones, the circulatory system, the inner layers of the skin, and other internal organs. The bottom layer develops into the digestive system, lungs, urinary tract, and glands. A few days after the embryo has differentiated into these three layers, a U-shaped groove forms down the center of the top layer. The folds at the top of the groove move together and fuse, creating the **neural tube** (Figure 2.4). One end of the neural tube will swell and develop into the brain, and the rest will become the spinal cord.

The support system that is emerging along with the embryo is elaborate and essential to the embryo's development. One key element of this support system is the **amniotic sac,** a membrane filled with a clear, watery fluid in which the fetus floats. The amniotic fluid operates as a protective buffer for the developing fetus, providing it with a relatively even temperature and cushioning it against jolting. As you will see shortly, because the amniotic fluid keeps the fetus afloat, the fetus can exercise its tiny, weak muscles relatively unhampered by the effects of gravity.

The second key element of the support system, the **placenta,** is a unique organ that permits the exchange of materials carried in the bloodstreams of the fetus and its mother. It is an extraordinarily rich network of blood vessels, including minute ones extending into the tissues of the mother's uterus, with a total surface area of about 10 square yards—approximately the amount of driveway covered by the family car (Vaughan, 1996). Blood vessels running from the placenta to the embryo and back again are contained in the **umbilical cord.**

At the placenta, the blood systems of the mother and fetus come extremely close to each other, but the placenta prevents their blood from actually mixing. However, the placental membrane is semipermeable, meaning that some elements can pass through it but others cannot. Oxygen, nutrients, minerals, and some antibodies—all of which are just as vital to the fetus as they are to you—are transported to the placenta by the mother's circulating blood. They then cross the placenta and enter the fetal blood system. Waste products (e.g., carbon dioxide, urea) from the fetus cross the placenta in the opposite direction and are removed from the mother's bloodstream by her normal excretory processes.

The placental membrane also serves as a defensive barrier against a host of dangerous toxins and infectious agents that can inhabit the mother's body and could be harmful or even fatal to the fetus. Unfortunately, being semipermeable, the placenta is not a perfect barrier, and, as you will see later, a variety of harmful elements can cross it and attack the fetus.

One other function of the placenta is the production of hormones, including *estrogen*, which increases the flow of maternal blood to the uterus, and *progesterone*, which suppresses uterine contractions that could lead to premature birth.

An Illustrated Summary of Prenatal Development

The course of prenatal development from the 4th week on is illustrated in Figures 2.5 through 2.11, and significant milestones are highlighted in the accompanying text. (The fetal behaviors that are mentioned will be discussed in detail in the following section.) Notice that earlier development takes place at a more rapid pace than later development, and that the areas nearer the head develop earlier than those farther away (e.g., head before body, hands before feet)—a general tendency known as **cephalocaudal development.**

Figure 2.5: At 4 weeks after conception, the embryo is curved so tightly that the head and the tail-like structure at the other end are almost touching. Several facial features have their origin in the set of four folds in the front of the embryo's head; the face gradually emerges as a result of these tissues moving and stretching, as parts of them fuse and others separate. The round area near the top of the head is where the eyes will form, and the round gray area near the back of the "neck" is the primordial inner ear. A primitive heart is visible; it is already beating and circulating blood. An arm bud can be seen in the side of the embryo; a leg bud is also present but less distinct.

Figure 2.6: (a) In this 5½-week-old fetus, the nose, mouth, and palate are beginning to differentiate into separate structures. (b) Just 3 weeks later, the nose and mouth are almost fully formed. Cleft palate, one of the most common birth defects worldwide, involves malformations (sometimes minor, sometimes major) of this area. This condition originates sometime between 5½ and 8 weeks prenatally—precisely when these structures are developing.

Figure 2.7: The head of this 9-week-old fetus overwhelms the rest of its body. The bulging forehead reflects the extremely rapid brain growth that has been going on for weeks. Rudimentary eyes and ears are forming. All the internal organs are present, although most must undergo further development. Sexual differentiation has started. Ribs are visible, fingers and toes have emerged, and nails are growing. You can see the umbilical cord connecting the fetus to the placenta. The fetus makes spontaneous movements, but because it is so small and is floating in amniotic fluid, the mother cannot feel them.

Figure 2.8: This image of an 11-week-old fetus clearly shows the heart, which has achieved its basic adult structure. You can also see the developing spine and ribs, as well as the major divisions of the brain.

umbilical cord ■ a tube containing the blood vessels connecting the fetus and placenta

cephalocaudal development ■ the pattern of growth in which areas near the head develop earlier than areas farther from the head

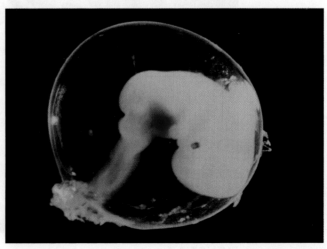

FIGURE 2.5 Embryo at 4 weeks.

BIOPHOTO ASSOCIATES / SCIENCE SOURCE

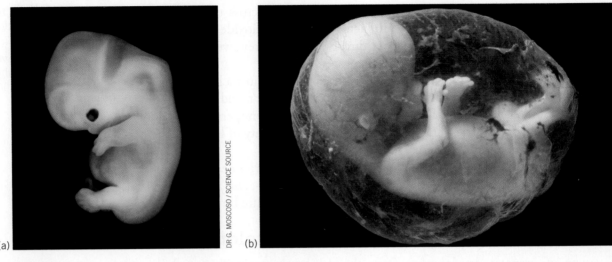

FIGURE 2.6 Face development from (a) 5½ to (b) 8½ weeks.

Figure 2.9: During the last 5 months of prenatal development, the growth of the lower part of the body accelerates. The fetus's movements have increased dramatically: its chest makes breathing movements, and some reflexes—grasping, swallowing, sucking—are present. By 16 weeks, the fetus is capable of intense kicks, although the mother feels them only as a mild "flutter." At this age, the external genitalia are substantially developed, and a different camera angle would have revealed whether this fetus is male or female.

Figure 2.10: This 18-week-old fetus is covered with very fine hair, and a greasy coating protects its skin from its long immersion in liquid. The components of facial expressions are present—the fetus can raise its eyebrows, wrinkle its forehead, and move its mouth. As the fetus rapidly puts on weight, the amniotic sac becomes more cramped, leading to a decrease in fetal movements.

FIGURE 2.7 Fetus at 9 weeks.

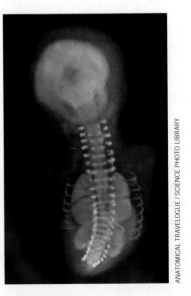

FIGURE 2.8 Fetus at 11 weeks.

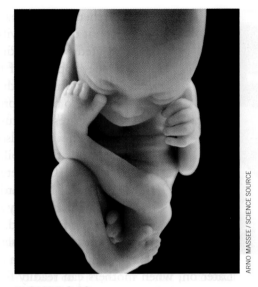

FIGURE 2.9 Fetus at 16 weeks.

FIGURE 2.10 Fetus at 18 weeks.

Figure 2.11: The 28th week marks the point at which the brain and lungs are sufficiently developed that a fetus born at this time would have a chance of surviving on its own, without medical intervention. The eyes can open, and they move, especially during periods of rapid eye movement (REM) sleep. The auditory system is now functioning, and the fetus hears and reacts to a variety of sounds. At this stage of development, the neural activity of the fetus is very similar to that of a newborn. During the last 3 months of prenatal development, the fetus grows dramatically in size, essentially tripling its weight.

The typical result of this 9-month period of rapid and remarkable development is a healthy newborn.

Fetal Behavior

As we have noted, the fetus is an active participant in, and contributor to, its own physical and behavioral development. Indeed, the normal formation of organs and muscles depends on fetal activity, and the fetus rehearses the behavioral repertoire it will need at birth.

Movement

Few mothers realize how early their child started moving in the womb. From 5 or 6 weeks after conception, the fetus moves spontaneously, starting with a simple bending of the head and spine that is followed by the onset of increasingly complex movements over the next weeks (de Vries, Visser, & Prechtl, 1982). One of the earliest distinct patterns of movement to emerge (at around 7 weeks) is, remarkably enough, hiccups. Although the reasons for prenatal hiccups are unknown, one recent theory posits that they are essentially a burping reflex, preparing the fetus for eventual nursing by removing air from the stomach and making more room for milk (Howes, 2012).

The *swallowing* reflex is another particularly important form of fetal movement. The fetus swallows amniotic fluid, which passes through its gastrointestinal system. Most of the fluid is

FIGURE 2.11 Fetus at 28 weeks.

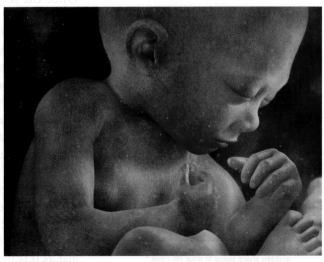

habituation ■ a simple form of learning that involves a decrease in response to repeated or continued stimulation

dishabituation ■ the introduction of a new stimulus rekindles interest following habituation to a repeated stimulus

through her vascular system, her breathing, her swallowing, and various rude noises made by her digestive system. These sounds are not quiet; the noise level in the uterus ranges from about 70–95 decibels (this range spans roughly the sound of a vacuum to the sound of a lawnmower). A particularly prominent and frequent source of sound stimulation is the mother's voice as she talks, with the clearest aspects being the general rhythm and pitch patterns of her speech.

During the last trimester, external noises elicit changes in fetal movements and heart rate, suggesting that the fetus also perceives sounds outside the mother's body (Kisilevsky, Fearon, & Muir, 1998; Lecanuet, Granier-Deferre, & Busnel, 1995; Zimmer et al., 1993). By the time fetuses are at term, changes in heart-rate patterns suggest that they can distinguish between music and speech played near the mother's abdomen (Granier-Deferre et al., 2011). The fetus's heart rate also decelerates briefly when the mother starts speaking (Voegtline et al., 2013). (Transitory heart-rate deceleration is a sign of interest.) The fetus's extensive auditory experience with human voices has some lasting effects, as we discuss in the next section.

Fetal Learning

To this point, we have emphasized the impressive behavioral and sensory capabilities of the fetus in the early stages of development. Even more impressive is the extent to which the fetus learns from many of its experiences in the last 3 months of pregnancy, after the central nervous system is adequately developed to support learning.

Direct evidence for human fetal learning comes from studies of habituation, one of the simplest forms of learning. **Habituation** involves a decrease in response to repeated or continued stimulation (see Figure 2.12). If you shake a rattle beside an infant's head, the baby will likely turn toward it. At the same time, the infant's heart rate may slow momentarily, indicating interest. If you repeatedly shake the rattle, however, the head-turning and heart-rate changes will decrease and eventually stop. This decreased response is evidence of learning and memory: the stimulus loses its novelty (and becomes boring) only if the infant remembers the stimulus from one presentation to the next. When a perceptible change in the stimulus occurs, the infant becomes interested again—a process known as **dishabituation.** Shaking a bell, for example, may reinstate the head-turning and heart-rate responses. (Developmental psychologists have exploited habituation to study a great variety of topics, ranging from speech perception to infant perception of numbers, that you will read about in later chapters.) Fetuses as young as 30 weeks gestation show habituation to both visual and auditory stimuli, indicating that the central nervous system is sufficiently developed at this point for learning and short-term memory to occur (Matuz et al., 2012; Muenssinger et al., 2013).

The mother's voice is probably the most interesting sound frequently available to fetuses. If fetuses can learn something about their mother's voice prenatally, this could provide them with a running start for learning about other aspects of speech after birth. To test this idea, Kisilevsky and colleagues (2003) tested term fetuses in one of two conditions. Half of the fetuses listened to a recording of their mother reading a poem, played through speakers placed on their mother's abdomen. The other half listened

FIGURE 2.12 Habituation Habituation occurs in response to the repeated presentation of a stimulus. As the first stimulus is repeated and becomes familiar, the response to it gradually decreases. When a novel stimulus occurs, the response recovers. The decreased response to the repeated stimulus indicates the formation of memory for it; the increased response to the novel stimulus indicates discrimination of it from the familiar one, as well as a general preference for novelty.

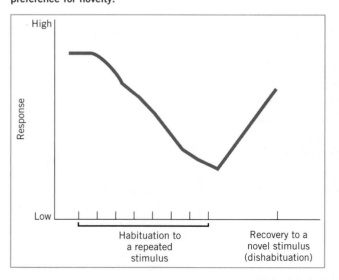

to recordings of the same poem read by another woman. The researchers found that fetal heart rate increased in response to the mother's voice, and decreased in response to the other woman's voice. These findings suggest that the fetuses recognized (and were aroused by) the sound of their own mother's voice relative to a stranger's voice. For this to be the case, fetuses must be learning and remembering the sound of their mother's voice.

After birth, do newborns remember anything about their fetal experience? The answer is a resounding yes! Like the rat pups discussed in Box 2.3, newborn

phylogenetic continuity ■ the idea that because of our common evolutionary history, humans share many characteristics, behaviors, and developmental processes with other animals, especially mammals

---

BOX 2.3 | a closer look

NONHUMAN ANIMAL MODELS OF PRENATAL DEVELOPMENT

Throughout this book, we will use research with nonhuman animals to make points about human development. In doing so, we subscribe to the principle of **phylogenetic continuity**—the idea that because of our common evolutionary history, humans share many characteristics and developmental processes with other living things. Indeed, as we will discuss in Chapter 3, you share most of your genes with your dog, cat, or hamster.

The assumption that nonhuman animal models of behavior and development can be useful and informative for human development underlies a great deal of research. For example, much of our knowledge about the dangers of alcohol consumption by pregnant women comes from research with nonhuman animals. Because scientists suspected that drinking alcohol while pregnant caused the constellation of defects now known as *fetal alcohol spectrum disorder* (page 66), they experimentally exposed fetal mice to alcohol. At birth, these mice had atypical facial features, remarkably similar to the facial anomalies of human children heavily exposed to alcohol in the womb by their mother. This fact increased researchers' confidence that the problems commonly associated with fetal alcohol syndrome are, in fact, caused by alcohol rather than by some other factor.

One of the most fascinating discoveries in recent years, the existence of fetal learning, was first documented on one of comparative psychologists' favorite creatures—the rat. To survive after birth, newborns must find

Scientists interested in human development have learned a great deal by studying maternal behavior in rats.

a milk-producing maternal nipple. How do they know where to go? The answer is that they search for something familiar to them. During the birth process, the nipples on the underside of the mother rat's belly get smeared with amniotic fluid. The scent of the amniotic fluid is familiar to the rat pups from their time in the womb, and it lures the babies to where they need to be—with their noses, and hence their mouths, near a nipple (Blass, 1990).

How was it determined that newborn rats find their mother's nipple by recognizing the scent of amniotic fluid? For one thing, when researchers washed the mother's belly clean of amniotic fluid, her pups failed to

find her nipples; and if only half her nipples were washed, the pups were attracted to the unwashed ones with amniotic fluid still on them (Blass & Teicher, 1980). Even more impressive, when researchers introduced odors or flavors into the amniotic fluid, either by directly injecting them or by adding them to the mother's diet, her pups preferred those odors and tastes after birth (Hepper, 1988; Pedersen & Blass, 1982; Smotherman & Robinson, 1987). These and other demonstrations of fetal learning in rodents inspired developmental psychologists to look for similar processes in human fetuses. As you will see later, they found them.

MELANIE J. SPENCE, THE UNIVERSITY OF TEXAS AT DALLAS

FIGURE 2.13 Prenatal learning This newborn can control what he gets to listen to. His pacifier is hooked up to a computer, which is in turn connected to an audio player. If the baby sucks in one pattern (predetermined by the researchers), he will hear one recording. If he sucks in a different pattern, he will hear a different recording. Researchers have used this technique to investigate many questions about infant abilities, including the influence of fetal experience on newborn preferences.

humans remember the scent of the amniotic fluid in which they lived prenatally. In one set of studies, newborns were presented with two pads, one saturated with their own amniotic fluid and the other saturated with the amniotic fluid of a different baby. With the two pads located on either side of their head, the infants revealed a preference for the scent of their own amniotic fluid by keeping their head oriented longer toward that scent (Marlier, Schaal, & Soussignan, 1998; Varendi, Porter, & Winberg, 2002). These findings extend to specific flavors ingested by the mother. For example, infants whose mothers ate anise (licorice flavor) while they were pregnant preferred the scent of anise at birth, while infants whose mothers did not eat anise showed either a neutral or negative response to its scent (Schaal, Marlier, & Soussignan, 2000).

Experiences in the womb can lead to long-lasting taste preferences. In one study, pregnant women drank carrot juice for three weeks near the end of their pregnancy (Mennella, Jagnow, & Beauchamp, 2001). When tested at around 5½ months of age, their babies reacted more positively to cereal prepared with carrot juice than to the same cereal prepared with water. Thus, the flavor preferences of these babies reflected the influence of their experience in the womb several months earlier. This finding reveals a *persistent* effect of prenatal learning. Furthermore, it may shed light on the origins and strength of cultural food preferences. A child whose mother ate a lot of chili peppers, ginger, and cumin during pregnancy, for example, might be more favorably disposed to Indian food than would a child whose mother's diet lacked those flavors.

Along with flavors, newborns also remember sounds they heard in the womb. In a classic study, DeCasper and Spence (1986) asked pregnant women to read aloud twice a day from *The Cat in the Hat* (or another Dr. Seuss book) during the last 6 weeks of their pregnancy. Thus, the women's fetuses were repeatedly exposed to the same highly rhythmical pattern of speech sounds. The question was whether they would recognize the familiar story after birth. To find out, the researchers tested them as newborns. The infants were fitted with miniature headphones and given a special pacifier to suck on (see Figure 2.13). When the infants sucked in one particular pattern, they heard the familiar story through the headphones, but when they sucked in a different pattern, they heard an unfamiliar story. The babies quickly increased their sucking in the pattern that enabled them to hear the familiar story. Thus, these newborns apparently recognized and preferred the rhythmic patterns from the story they had heard in the womb. As described at the outset of this chapter, infants also remember specific prenatal auditory experiences that were presented externally, via audio speakers adjacent to the mother's abdomen, such as repetitions of a single nonsense word (Partanen et al., 2013).

Newborns exhibit numerous additional auditory preferences based on prenatal experience. To begin with, they prefer to listen to their own mother's voice rather than to the voice of another woman (DeCasper & Fifer, 1980). But how do researchers know that this isn't due to experience in the hours or days after birth? It turns out that newborns prefer to listen to a version of their mother's voice that has been filtered to sound the way it did in the womb (Moon & Fifer, 1990; Spence & Freeman, 1996). Finally, newborns would rather listen to the language they heard in the womb than to another language (Mehler et al., 1988; Moon, Cooper, & Fifer, 1993). Newborns whose mothers speak French prefer listening to French over Russian, for example, and this preference is maintained when the speech is filtered to sound the way it sounded in the womb.

There can be little question that the human fetus is listening and learning. Does this mean that parents-to-be should sign up for programs that promise to "educate your unborn child"? Such programs exhort the mother-to-be to talk to her fetus, read books to it, play music through speakers attached to her abdomen, and so on. Some also urge other family members to speak through a megaphone aimed at the mother's bulging belly in the hope that the newborn will recognize their voices as well as the mother's. Is there any point to such exercises?

Probably not. Although it seems possible that hearing other family members' voices more clearly and more frequently might lead the newborn to prefer them over unfamiliar voices, such a preference develops very quickly after birth anyway. And it is quite clear that some of the advertised advantages of prenatal training would not occur. In the first place, the fetal brain is unlikely to be sufficiently developed to be able to process much about language meaning (after all, even newborn infants can't learn the meanings of words). In addition, the liquid environment in the womb—provided by the amniotic fluid—filters out detailed speech sounds, leaving only pitch contours and rhythmic patterns. Brain development aside, this acoustic environment, along with the fetus's lack of visual access to the external world, would make it impossible for a fetus to learn the meaning of words or any kind of factual knowledge, no matter how much the mother-to-be might read aloud. In short, what the fetus learns about is the mother's voice and the general patterns of her language—not any specific content. We suspect that the current craze for "prenatal education" will go the way of other ill-conceived attempts to shape early development to adult desires.

Review

The most rapid period of development starts at conception, with the union of egg and sperm, and continues for roughly 9 months. The processes through which prenatal development occurs include cell division, cell migration, cell differentiation, and cell death. Every major organ system undergoes all or a substantial part of its development between the 3rd and 8th week following conception, making this a sensitive period for potential damage from environmental hazards.

Scientists have learned an enormous amount about the behavior and experience of the developing organism, which begins to move at 5 to 6 weeks after conception. Some behaviors of the fetus contribute to its development, including swallowing amniotic fluid and making breathing motions. The fetus has relatively rich sensory experience from stimulation both within and outside the womb, and this experience is the basis for fetal learning. Some effects of fetal learning persist long after birth.

Hazards to Prenatal Development

Thus far, our focus has been on the normal course of development before birth. Unfortunately, prenatal development is not always free of error or misfortune. The most dire, and by far the most common, misfortune is spontaneous abortion— commonly referred to as miscarriage. Most miscarriages occur before the woman even knows that she is pregnant. For example, in a Chinese sample, Wang and colleagues (2003) found that approximately one-third of the fetuses did not survive to birth, and that two-thirds of those miscarriages occurred before the pregnancy was clinically detectable. The majority of embryos that are miscarried very early have severe defects, such as a missing chromosome or an extra one, that make further development impossible. In the United States, about 15% of clinically recognized pregnancies end in miscarriage (Rai & Regan, 2006). Across their childbearing

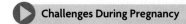
Challenges During Pregnancy

teratogen ■ an external agent that can cause damage or death during prenatal development

sensitive period ■ the period of time during which a developing organism is most sensitive to the effects of external factors; prenatally, the sensitive period is when the fetus is maximally sensitive to the harmful effects of teratogens

years, at least 25% of women—and possibly as many as 50%—experience at least one miscarriage. Few couples realize how common this experience is, making it all the more painful if it happens to them. Yet more agonizing is the experience of the approximately 1% of couples who experience recurrent miscarriages, or the loss of three or more consecutive pregnancies (Rai & Regan, 2006).

For fetuses that survive the danger of miscarriage, there is still a range of factors that can lead to unforeseen negative consequences. Genetic factors, which are the most common, will be discussed in the next chapter. Here, we consider some of the many environmental influences that can have harmful effects on prenatal development.

Teratogens

In the spring of 1956, two sisters were brought to a Japanese hospital, delirious and unable to walk. Their parents and doctors were mystified by their sudden deterioration. The mystery intensified as more children and adults developed nearly identical symptoms. The discovery that all the patients were from the small coastal town of Minamata suggested a common cause: the tons of mercury that had been dumped into Minamata Bay by a local petrochemical and plastics factory. For years, the residents of Minamata had been consuming fish that had absorbed mercury from the polluted waters of the bay. By 1993, more than 2000 children and adults had been diagnosed with what had come to be known as "Minamata disease"—methylmercury poisoning (Harada, 1995). At least 40 children were poisoned prenatally by mercury in the fish eaten by their pregnant mothers and were born with cerebral palsy, intellectual disabilities, and a host of other neurological disorders.

The tragedy of Minamata Bay provided some of the first clear evidence of the seriously detrimental impact that environmental factors can have on prenatal development. As you will see, a vast number of environmental agents, called **teratogens,** have the potential to harm the fetus. The resulting damage ranges from relatively mild and easily corrected problems to fetal death.

A crucial factor in the severity of the effects of potential teratogens is timing (one of the basic developmental principles discussed in Chapter 1). Many teratogens cause damage only if they are present during a **sensitive period** in prenatal development. The major organ systems are most vulnerable to damage at the time when their basic structures are being formed. Because the timing is different for each system, the sensitive periods are different for each system, as shown in Figure 2.14.

There is no more dramatic or straightforward illustration of the importance of timing than the birth outcomes related to the drug thalidomide in the early 1960s. Thalidomide was prescribed to treat morning sickness (among other things) and was considered to be so safe that it was sold over the counter. At the time, it was believed that such medications would not cross the placental barrier. However, many pregnant women who took this new, presumably safe sedative gave birth to babies with major limb deformities; some babies were born with no arms and with flipperlike hands growing out of their shoulders. In a striking illustration of sensitive period effects, serious defects occurred only if the pregnant woman took the drug between the 4th and 6th week after conception, the time when her fetus's limbs were emerging and developing (look again at Figures 2.5 to 2.11). Taking thalidomide either before the limbs started to develop or after they were basically formed had no harmful effect.

Victims of "Minamata disease" include individuals who were exposed to methylmercury prenatally.

BOX 2.4 | applications

SUDDEN INFANT DEATH SYNDROME

For parents, nothing is more terrifying to contemplate than the death of their child. New parents are especially frightened by the specter of **sudden infant death syndrome (SIDS)**. SIDS refers to the sudden, unexpected, and unexplained death of an infant younger than 1 year. The most common SIDS scenario is that an apparently healthy baby, usually between 2 and 5 months of age, is put to bed for the night and found dead in the morning. In the United States, the incidence of SIDS is 56 per 10,000 live births, making it the leading cause of infant mortality between 28 days and 1 year of age (Task Force on Sudden Infant Death Syndrome, 2011). African American and Native American infants are most likely to die from SIDS, whereas Hispanic American and Asian American infants are least likely to die from SIDS. These patterns suggest cultural differences in parenting that might protect some infants from SIDS.

The causes of SIDS are still not well understood. One hypothesis is that SIDS may involve an inadequate reflexive response to respiratory occlusion—that is, an inability to remove or move away from something covering the nose and mouth (Lipsitt, 2003). Infants may be particularly vulnerable to SIDS between 2 and 5 months of age because that is when they are making a transition from neonatal reflexes under the control of lower parts of the brain (the brainstem) to deliberate, learned behaviors mediated by higher brain areas (cerebral cortex). A waning respiratory occlusion reflex during this transition period may make infants less able to effectively pull their head away from a smothering pillow or to push a blanket away from their face.

Despite the lack of certainty about the causes of SIDS, researchers have identified several steps that parents can take to decrease the risk to their baby. The most important one is putting infants to sleep on their back, reducing the possibility of anything obstructing their breathing. Sleeping on the stomach increases the risk of SIDS more than any other single factor

"Face Up to Wake Up." The parents of this infant are following the good advice of the foundation dedicated to lowering the incidence of SIDS worldwide. Since the inauguration of this campaign, SIDS in the United States has declined to half its previous rate (Task Force on Sudden Infant Death Syndrome, 2011).

(e.g., Willinger, 1995). (With respect to the cultural differences in the incidence of SIDS mentioned above, it is significant that Hispanic American parents are the most likely to put their infants to sleep on their back [73%], and African Americans the least likely to do so [53%].) A campaign encouraging parents to put their infants to sleep on their back—the "back to sleep" movement—has contributed to a dramatic reduction in the number of SIDS victims.

Second, to lower the risk of SIDS, parents should not smoke. If they do smoke, they should not smoke around the baby. Infants whose mothers smoke during pregnancy and/or after the baby's birth are more than 3½ times more likely to succumb to SIDS than are babies who are not exposed to smokers in their home (Anderson, Johnson, & Batal, 2005).

Third, babies should sleep on a firm mattress with no pillow or crib bumpers. Soft bedding can trap air around the infant's face, causing the baby to breathe in his or her own carbon dioxide instead of oxygen. Fourth, infants should not be wrapped in lots of blankets or clothes. Being overly warm is associated with SIDS.

Fifth, infants who are breast-fed are less likely to succumb to SIDS (e.g., Hauck et al., 2011). Why would breast-feeding protect infants from SIDS? One possible reason is that breast-fed infants are more easily aroused from sleep than formula-fed infants, and thus may more easily detect when their airflow is interrupted (Horne et al., 2004). Sixth, pacifier use appears to reduce the risk of SIDS (Hauck, Omojokun, & Siadaty, 2005). The reason is likely the same as for breast-fed infants: lower threshold of arousal from sleep. Alternatively, pacifier use might help infants to become more accustomed to breathing when the tongue is in an unusual position.

Finally, room-sharing without bed-sharing is recommended by the American Academy of Pediatrics. By sharing a room, the parent can monitor the baby without the additional risk associated by sharing bedding with an infant (Moon, 2011).

One unanticipated consequence of the "back to sleep" movement has been that North American infants are now beginning to crawl slightly later than those in previous generations, presumably because of reduced opportunity to strengthen their muscles by pushing up off their mattress. Parents are encouraged to give their babies supervised "tummy time" to exercise their muscles during the day.

sudden infant death syndrome (SIDS) ■ the sudden, unexpected death of an infant less than 1 year of age that has no identifiable cause

fetal alcohol spectrum disorder (FASD) ■ the harmful effects of maternal alcohol consumption on a developing fetus. Fetal alcohol syndrome (FAS) involves a range of effects, including facial deformities, mental retardation, attention problems, hyperactivity, and other defects. Fetal alcohol effects (FAE) is a term used for individuals who show some, but not all, of the standard effects of FAS.

college-educated women over 35, reversing the more typical of maternal teratogen exposure, which tends to predominate among less educated expectant mothers, who tend to have fewer economic and social resources.

In the United States, about half of women of childbearing age drink alcohol at least once a month (Tan et al., 2015). Many women continue to consume alcohol in the weeks immediately after becoming pregnant. In part, this is because women often do not discover their pregnancy until after the fourth week of gestation, when they have missed a menstrual cycle. In a study focused on unplanned pregnancies, more than half of the expectant mothers reported using alcohol during the month before they realized they were pregnant (Roberts et al., 2014). Even women who are planning to get pregnant often do not curtail their alcohol consumption; a recent study found that 3 in 4 women who hoped to become pregnant "as soon as possible" continued to consume alcohol (Green et al., 2016). As we have seen, these early weeks of pregnancy are crucial to fetal development.

When a pregnant woman drinks, the alcohol in her blood crosses the placenta into both the fetus's bloodstream and the amniotic fluid. Thus, the fetus gets alcohol both directly—in its bloodstream—and indirectly, by drinking an amniotic-fluid cocktail. Concentrations of alcohol in the blood of mother and fetus quickly equalize, but the fetus has less ability to metabolize and remove alcohol from its blood, so it remains in the fetus's system longer.

Maternal drinking can result in **fetal alcohol spectrum disorder (FASD),** which comprises a continuum of alcohol-related birth defects. Babies born to alcoholic women often exhibit extreme negative outcomes, known as *fetal alcohol syndrome* (FAS) (Jacobson & Jacobson, 2002; Jones & Smith, 1973; Streissguth, 2001; Streissguth et al., 1993). The most obvious symptoms of FAS are facial deformities like those shown in Figure 2.15. Other forms of FAS can include varying degrees of intellectual disability, attention problems, and hyperactivity.

Even moderate drinking during pregnancy (i.e., less than one drink per day) can have both short- and long-term negative effects on development. So can occasional drinking if it involves binge drinking (four drinks or more on a single occasion). Between 2011 and 2013, 3% of pregnant women in the United States reported at least one incident of binge drinking during the previous month (Tan et al., 2015). The negative effects can include low birth weight, increased risk for ADHD, and delays in cognitive development and school achievement (e.g., Behnke et al., 2013).

FIGURE 2.15 Facial features of FAS These two children display the three primary diagnostic facial features of fetal alcohol syndrome: small eyes (as measured across); the absence of, or flattening of, the vertical groove between the nose and the upper lip (smooth philtrum); and a thin upper lip. It appears that the more pronounced these features are in an affected child, the greater the likelihood that the child experienced prenatal brain damage. Roughly 1 in 1000 infants born in the United States has FAS.

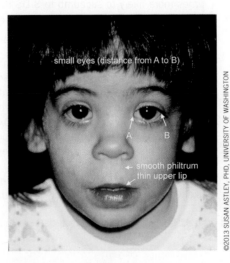

Given the potential outcomes and the fact that no one knows whether there is a safe level of alcohol consumption for a pregnant woman, the best approach for expectant mothers is to avoid alcohol altogether.

Environmental Pollutants

The bodies and bloodstreams of most Americans (including women of childbearing age) contain a noxious mix of toxic metals, synthetic hormones, and various ingredients of plastics, pesticides, and herbicides that can be teratogenic (Moore, 2003). Echoing the story of Minamata disease, evidence has accumulated that mothers whose diet was high in Lake Michigan fish with high levels of polychlorinated biphenyls (PCBs) had newborns with small heads. The children with the highest prenatal exposure to PCBs had slightly lower IQ scores as long as 11 years later (Jacobson & Jacobson, 1996; Jacobson et al., 1992). In China, the rapid modernization that has led to economic success has also taken a toll on health in general and has led to a dramatic increase in pollution-related birth defects due to the unregulated burning of coal, water pollution, and pesticide use (e.g., Ren et al., 2011).

While progress has been made in eradicating some pollutants in the United States, the water crisis in the city of Flint, Michigan, provides clear evidence that environmental hazards continue to pose risks. For example, in an attempt to save money, a policy change in 2014 led to a situation in which water from the Flint River corroded residential pipes, leading to high levels of lead in the local water supply. These increased lead levels disproportionately affected families living in poorer neighborhoods (Hanna-Attisha et al., 2016). Lead is a potent neurotoxin; its effects are most prominently observed on measures of intelligence and academic achievement (Amato et al., 2012), and lead exposure is linked to the development of ADHD symptoms (Nigg et al., 2016). In terms of pregnancy risk, there is a dose–response relationship: higher lead levels in the mother increase the risk of miscarriage, preterm birth, and low birth rate (Ettinger & Wengrovitz, 2010). Incidents like this one highlight the impact that decisions by individuals, groups, and local governments can have on environmental factors, which can in turn have significant and sometimes disastrous consequences on fetal and child development.

Maternal Factors

Because the mother-to-be provides the most immediate environment for her fetus, some of her characteristics can affect prenatal development. These characteristics include age, nutritional status, health, and stress level.

Age

A pregnant woman's age is related to the outcome of her pregnancy. Infants born to girls 15 years or younger are 3 to 4 times more likely to die before their 1st birthday than are those born to mothers who are between 23 and 29 (Phipps, Blume, & DeMonner, 2002). However, the rate of teenage pregnancy has declined substantially in recent years; in 2014, the birth rate for teenagers fell to the lowest recorded level in the United States (24 births per 1000 females younger than 20). While concerns about risk to babies of young moms has abated somewhat in the United States, teen birth rates are still high in other parts of the world, especially less developed nations. For example, in Niger, more than 1 in 5 teenaged girls is a mother (United Nations Population Division, n.d.).

The increasing age at which many women become pregnant is also cause for concern. In recent decades, many women have chosen to wait until their 30s or 40s to have children. At the same time, techniques to treat infertility have continued to improve, increasing the likelihood of conception for older parents. Older mothers are at greater risk for many negative outcomes for themselves and their fetus, including fetal chromosomal abnormalities (see Chapter 3) and birth complications. For instance, children born to older mothers are at heightened risk for autism spectrum disorder (ASD) (e.g., Sandin et al., 2012). Interestingly, the father's age also predicts rates of ASD diagnoses, though not as strongly as the mother's age (Idring et al., 2014). The distinction between mothers' and fathers' ages as predictors suggest that prenatal or birth factors associated with advancing age—limited to the mother—may impact outcomes over and beyond more general effects of having older parents (Idring et al., 2014).

Nutrition

The fetus depends on its mother for all its nutritional requirements. If a pregnant woman has an inadequate diet, her unborn child may also be nutritionally deprived. An inadequate supply of specific nutrients or vitamins can have dramatic consequences. For example, women who get too little folic acid (a form of B vitamin) are at high risk for having an infant with a neural-tube defect such as spina bifida (see Figure 2.4). General malnutrition affects the growth of the fetal brain: newborns who received inadequate nutrients while in the womb tend to have smaller brains containing fewer brain cells than do well-nourished newborns.

Because malnutrition is more common in impoverished families, it often coincides with the host of other risk factors associated with poverty, making it difficult to isolate its effects on prenatal development. However, one unique study of development in very extreme circumstances made it possible to assess certain effects of malnutrition *independent of socioeconomic status*. As we discussed earlier, people of all income and education levels suffered severe famine in parts of the Netherlands during World War II. Children conceived during the Dutch Hunger Winter have since been followed into adulthood. In late middle age, individuals who had experienced malnutrition as fetuses showed impaired performance on attentional tasks, compared with those who had not (de Rooij et al., 2010). These data are consistent with other recent studies that have used sibling pairs to attempt to control for SES and other environmental variables that may be confounded with nutrition. In one large longitudinal study, researchers tracked caloric intake during pregnancy and compared outcomes for siblings in cases where maternal caloric intake differed across pregnancies (Connolly & Beaver, 2015). The results suggested that individual differences in math and reading abilities at age 5 could be predicted by maternal caloric intake during pregnancy.

Disease

Although most maternal illnesses that occur during a pregnancy have no impact on the fetus, some do. For example, if contracted early in pregnancy, rubella (also called the 3-day measles) can have devastating developmental effects, including major malformations, deafness, blindness, and intellectual disabilities. The Centers for Disease Control recommends that women who do not have immunities against rubella be vaccinated before becoming pregnant.

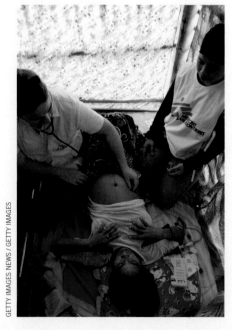

These poor parents in Bolivia are worrying about how they are going to feed their children—a situation all too common throughout the world.

Sexually transmitted infections (STIs) are also quite hazardous to the fetus. Cytomegalovirus, a type of herpes virus that is present in 50% to 70% of women of reproductive age in the United States, is currently the most common cause of congenital infection (affecting 1% to 5% of births; Manicklal, 2013). It can damage the fetus's central nervous system and cause a variety of other serious defects, including hearing loss. Genital herpes can also be very dangerous: if the infant comes into contact with active herpes lesions in the birth canal, blindness or even death can result. HIV infection is sometimes passed to the fetus in the womb or during birth, but the majority of infants born to women who are HIV-positive or have AIDS do not become infected themselves. HIV can also be transmitted through breast milk after birth, but recent research suggests that breast milk contains a carbohydrate that may actually protect infants from HIV infection (Bode et al., 2012).

Evidence has been accumulating for effects of maternal illness on the development of *psychopathology* later in life. For example, the incidence of schizophrenia is 3 times higher for individuals whose mothers had influenza (flu) during the first trimester of pregnancy (Brown et al., 2004). Maternal flu and other types of infections may interact with genetic factors to lead to mental illness. The infections may act on genes that make individuals vulnerable to mental illness risk. Alternatively, genes that are central to the immune system's response to infections may also be involved in brain development, heightening risk for mental illness (e.g., Brown & Derkits, 2010). Of particular note are recent studies suggesting that maternal infections severe enough to warrant hospitalization may be a factor in the development of ASD (Atladóttir et al., 2010; Lee et al., 2015). Maternal infections may later lead to autism in children who are genetically susceptible (as we will see in Chapter 3, ASD is one of the most heritable developmental disorders), potentially due to high levels of cytokines in the developing brain or due to an autoimmune response (e.g., Libbey et al., 2005).

The Zika virus, a mosquito-borne infection, was discovered in 1947 in Uganda and burst onto the world scene in 2016, when it was declared a Public Health Emergency of International Concern by the World Health Organization. While the illness itself is mild and often goes undetected, it can cause a serious birth defect called microcephaly, a condition where the baby's head is much smaller than expected. Depending on the severity of the problem, issues in brain development can range from sensory problems (hearing loss, vision problems) to seizures and intellectual disability. The virus appears to infect fetuses' cortical-neural progenitor cells, resulting in stunted brain growth (Tang et al., 2016). Unlike rubella, many STIs, and the flu, there is no vaccine to protect women against Zika. The only preventative option is to try to avoid mosquito bites in areas where the virus has spread. Women of reproductive age should also take heed of the fact that Zika can be transmitted sexually and might even be transmitted by kissing (D'Ortenzio et al., 2016).

This Brazilian infant suffers from microcephaly, likely due to her mother's Zika infection during pregnancy.

IEJAE / NEWSCOM / XINHUA NEWS AGENCY / RIO DE JANEIRO

Maternal Emotional State

For centuries, people have believed that a woman's emotions can affect her fetus. This hypothesis is difficult to test because of the challenges in measuring maternal distress (DiPietro, 2012). If the mother rates her own emotional state and also provides information about her fetus or infant—that is, the mother provides both the

LAFLOR / GETTY IMAGES

Prenatal exercise classes, as well as yoga or meditation classes, may help reduce pregnancy-related stress.

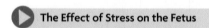

The Effect of Stress on the Fetus

independent and dependent variables—the relationship between these variables may be confounded by the mother's own perspective.

This interpretive issue can be avoided by measuring fetal behavior directly. For example, the fetuses of women who reported higher levels of stress during pregnancy were more physically active throughout their gestation than were the fetuses of women who felt less stressed (DiPietro, Hilton et al., 2002). This increased activity is likely related to hormones, including adrenaline and cortisol, that the mother secretes in response to stress (Relier, 2001). However, it also appears that the fetus itself influences the maternal state; changes in fetal movements and heart rate trigger, moments later, changes in the mother's physiological state, including her own heart rate (DiPietro, Costigan, & Voegtline, 2015).

Such effects can continue after birth. In a study that involved more than 7000 pregnant women and their infants, maternal anxiety and depression during pregnancy were assessed. The higher the level of distress the pregnant women reported, the higher the incidence of behavior problems in their children at 4 years of age—including hyperactivity and inattention in boys, conduct problems in girls, and emotional problems in both boys and girls (O'Connor et al., 2002). Findings such as these, linking prenatal maternal stress to postnatal behavior problems, are likely to also be mediated by increased levels of maternal hormones, such as cortisol, that are elicited by stress (Susman et al., 2001; Susman, 2006). The increased popularity of prenatal yoga and meditation classes may suggest that there are options to reduce pregnancy-related stress, with potential benefits for both mother and fetus.

Like other types of teratogens, it is difficult to tease apart the specific effects of maternal stress from other factors that often co-occur with stress; for instance, expectant mothers who are stressed during pregnancy are likely to still be stressed after giving birth. Genetic factors may also link both maternal stress and postnatal outcomes. One clever study took advantage of the increased use of assistive reproductive technology—*in vitro* fertilization (IVF)—to attempt to tease apart these factors (Rice et al., 2010). In this study, mothers were either genetically related or unrelated to their fetuses. The results revealed effects of maternal stress on birth weight and later antisocial behavior, in both related and unrelated mother–fetus pairs, suggesting that the prenatal environment, not shared genetics, was the strongest predictor of later outcomes. However, for measures of child anxiety, the results suggest that postnatal maternal stress, not prenatal maternal stress, was the strongest predictor of later outcomes.

This study reveals a complex interplay between prenatal and postnatal maternal emotional states. And indeed, we saw a similarly complex relationship in the discussion of perinatal depression earlier in this chapter: women who are depressed during pregnancy are most likely to experience the potentially devastating effects of postpartum depression, which can in turn affect infant development.

Review

Many environmental agents can have a negative impact on prenatal development. The most common teratogens in the United States are cigarette smoking, alcohol consumption, and environmental pollution. Maternal factors (malnutrition, illness, stress, and so forth) can also cause problems for the developing fetus and child. Timing is crucial for exposure to many teratogens; the severity of effects is also related to the amount and length of exposure, as well as to the number of different negative factors with which a fetus has to contend.

The Birth Experience

▶ Birth

Approximately 38 weeks after conception, contractions of the muscles of the uterus begin, initiating the birth of the baby. Typically, the baby has already contributed to the process by rotating itself into the normal head-down position. In addition, the maturing lungs of the fetus may release a protein that triggers the onset of labor. Uterine contractions, as well as the baby's progress through the birth canal, are painful for the mother, so women in labor are often given pain-relieving drugs. Women who self-report a great deal of fear about childbirth earlier in their pregnancies are more likely to choose pain medications, such as epidurals, during the birth process (Haines et al., 2012). These medications are highly effective at reducing pain and do not appear to increase rates of cesarean sections or have negative effects on the newborn infant; however, they can prolong labor and can lead to higher rates of the use of instruments (e.g., forceps) during vaginal births (Anim-Somuah, Smyth, & Jones, 2011).

Is birth as painful for the newborn as for the mother? Actually, there is good reason to believe that birth is not particularly painful for the baby. Compare how much pain you feel when you pinch and pull on a piece of skin on your forearm versus when you wrap your hand around your forearm and squeeze as tightly as you can. The stretching is painful, but the squeezing is not. The mother's pain comes from her tissues being greatly stretched, but the baby experiences squeezing. Hence, the experiences of the two participants are not really comparable (Maurer & Maurer, 1988). Childbirth programs designed to prevent birth from being painful and traumatic for newborns are probably based on faulty premises.

Furthermore, the squeezing that the fetus experiences during birth serves several important functions. First, it temporarily reduces the overall size of the fetus's disproportionately large head, allowing it to pass safely through the mother's pelvic bones. This is possible because the skull is composed of separate plates that can overlap one another slightly during birth (see Figure 2.16). The squeezing of the fetus's head during birth also stimulates the production of hormones that help the fetus withstand mild oxygen deprivation during birth and to regulate breathing after birth. The squeezing of the fetus's body also forces amniotic fluid out of the lungs, in preparation for the newborn's first, crucial gasp of air (Lagercrantz & Slotkin, 1986; Nathanielsz, 1994). This first breath usually comes

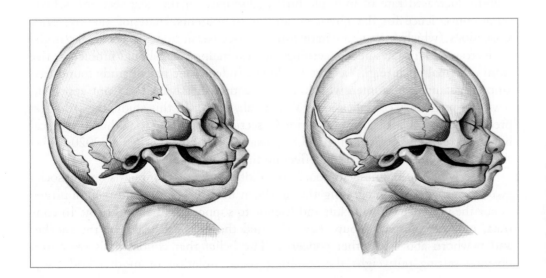

FIGURE 2.16 Head plates Pressure on the head during birth can cause the separate plates of the skull to overlap, resulting in a temporarily misshapen head. Fortunately, the condition rapidly corrects itself after birth. The "soft spot," or fontanel, is simply the temporary space between separate skull plates in the top of the baby's head.

by way of the birth cry, which is a very efficient mechanism for jump-starting respiration: a strong cry not only obtains some essential oxygen but also forces open the small air sacs in the lungs, making subsequent breaths easier. (An important disadvantage of cesarean deliveries is that surgical removal from the womb deprives the fetus of the squeezing action of a normal delivery, increasing the likelihood of its experiencing respiratory problems as a newborn.)

Diversity of Childbirth Practices

Although the biological aspects of birth are pretty much the same everywhere, childbirth practices vary enormously. As with many human behaviors, what is considered a normal and desirable birth custom in one society may seem strange or deviant—or even dangerous—in another.

All cultures pursue the dual goals of safeguarding the *survival and health* of both the mother and the baby and ensuring the *social integration* of the new person. Groups differ, however, regarding the relative importance they give to these goals. An expectant mother on the South Pacific island of Bali assumes that her husband and other kin, along with any children she may already have, will all want to be present at the joyous occasion of the birth of a new child. Her female relatives, as well as a midwife, actively help her throughout the birth, which occurs in her home. Having already been present at many births, the Balinese woman knows what to expect from childbirth, even when it is her first child (Diener, 2000).

A very different scenario has been the tradition in the United States, where the woman in labor usually withdraws almost totally from her everyday life. In most cases, she enters a hospital to give birth, typically attended by a small group of family or close friends. The birth is supervised by a variety of medical personnel, most of whom are strangers. Unlike her Balinese counterpart, the first-time U.S. mother has probably never witnessed a birth, so she may not have very realistic expectations about the birth process. Also, unlike her counterparts in most societies, a U.S. woman in labor has a 32% chance of having a surgical delivery by cesarean (also called C-section)—a rate that is high relative to other countries but has declined in 2014 for the first time in several decades (Martin, Hamilton, & Osterman, 2015).

C-sections are intended to assist infants and mothers facing birth complications, and indeed they have saved untold numbers of lives. However, there are other reasons for the high number of surgical deliveries in the United States, including a vastly increased rate of multiple births (discussed in the next section), scheduling convenience for the physician and/or the parents, maternal obesity, prior C-sections (which may necessitate future C-sections), and physicians' attempts to decrease risk of lawsuits concerning medical malpractice should problems arise from a vaginal birth (e.g., Yang et al., 2009). Indeed, one recent study found that among a sample of women who had a C-section, nearly half did not appear to have any pregnancy complications (Witt et al., 2015). In this study, the strongest predictor of any C-section was a prior C-section, which suggests that as surgical births decrease (a key goal of the U.S. government's Healthy People 2020 initiative), there should be a cascading effect on future surgical births.

Underlying the Balinese approach to childbirth is great emphasis on the social goal of immediately integrating the newborn into the family and community—hence the presence of many kin and friends to support mother and baby. In contrast, modern Western groups have elevated the physical health of the mother and newborn above all other concerns. The belief that childbirth is safer in a hospital setting outweighs the resulting social isolation of mother and baby.

And indeed, while the rates of home births are increasing in the United States (0.9% of all births in 2012; MacDorman, Mathews, & Declerq, 2014), they remain riskier than hospital births. One recent study found that in the United States, infant mortality in hospital births attended by certified midwives was significantly lower than infant mortality in home births attended by certified midwives (Grünebaum et al., 2016). It is worth noting, however, that in Ontario, Canada, where home births are more common (20% of all births) and well integrated into the health care system, the mortality rates for home and hospital births are equivalent, possibly because it is standard practice to transfer home birthing mothers to the hospital when complications arise (as was the case for 25% of home births in this Canadian sample; Hutton et al., 2015).

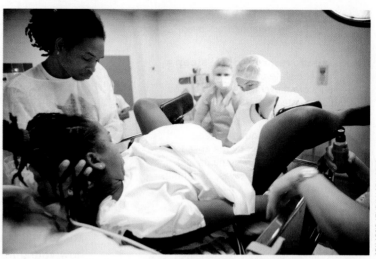

The medical model of childbirth prevails in the United States.

The practices in both the United States and Bali have changed to some degree. In the United States, the social dimensions of birth are increasingly recognized by doctors and hospitals, which often now employ certified nurse-midwives as alternative practitioners for expectant parents who prefer a less medicalized birth plan. As in Bali, various family members—sometimes even including the parents' other children—are encouraged to be present to support the laboring mother and to share a family experience. Another increasingly common practice in the United States is the use of *doulas,* individuals trained to assist women in terms of both emotional and physical comfort during labor and delivery. This shift has been accompanied by more moderate use of delivery drugs, thereby enhancing the woman's participation in childbirth and her ability to interact with her newborn, including engaging in activities such as skin-to-skin contact, which promotes stabilization of physiological processes in the transition from the womb to the outside world (e.g., Rutgers & Meyers, 2015).

In addition, many expectant parents attend childbirth education classes, where they learn some of what their Balinese counterparts pick up through routine attendance at births. Social support is a key component of these programs; the pregnant woman's partner, or some other supportive person, is trained to assist her during the birth. Such childbirth programs are generally beneficial, and obstetricians routinely advise expectant couples to enroll in them. At the same time that these changes are occurring in the United States, Western medical practices are increasingly adopted in traditional, nonindustrialized societies like Bali, in an effort to improve newborn survival rates.

This childbirth in South Sudan is quite different from the norm in the United States. The baby was born at home, with the help of a grandmother, great aunt, and a qualified birth attendant.

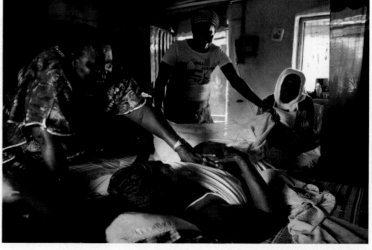

Review

Research on the birth process has revealed that many aspects of the experience of being born, including squeezing in the birth canal, have adaptive value and increase the likelihood of survival for the newborn. Although cultural groups differ in their beliefs and practices related to childbirth, these differences are decreasing as expectant mothers gain access to more diverse birthing options.

state ■ level of arousal and engagement in the environment, ranging from deep sleep to intense activity

rapid eye movement (REM) sleep ■ an active sleep state characterized by quick, jerky eye movements under closed lids and associated with dreaming in adults

non-REM sleep ■ a quiet or deep sleep state characterized by the absence of motor activity or eye movements and more regular, slow brain waves, breathing, and heart rate

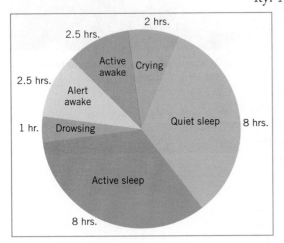

FIGURE 2.17 Newborn states This figure shows the average proportion of time, in a 24-hour day, that Western newborns spend in each of the six states of arousal. There are substantial individual and cultural differences in how much time babies spend in the different states.

FIGURE 2.18 Quiet-alert state The parents of this quiet-alert newborn have a good chance of having a pleasurable interaction with the baby.

The Newborn Infant

A healthy newborn is ready and able to continue the developmental saga in a new environment. The baby begins interacting with that environment right away, exploring and learning about newfound physical and social entities. Newborns' exploration of this uncharted territory is very much influenced by their state of arousal.

State of Arousal

State refers to a continuum of arousal, ranging from deep sleep to intense activity. As you well know, your state dramatically affects your interaction with the environment—with what you notice, do, learn, and think about. It also affects the ability of others to interact with you. State strongly mediates how young infants experience the world around them.

Figure 2.17 depicts the average amount of time in a 24-hour period that newborns typically spend in each of six states, ranging from quiet sleep to crying. Within this general pattern, however, there is a great deal of individual variation. Some infants cry relatively rarely, whereas others cry for hours every day; some babies sleep much more, and others much less, than the 16-hour average shown in the figure. Some infants spend more than the average of 2½ hours in the awake-alert state, in which they are fairly inactive but attentive to the environment. To appreciate how these differences might affect parent–infant interactions, imagine yourself as the parent of a newborn who cries more than the average, sleeps little, and spends less time in the awake-alert state. Now imagine yourself with a baby who cries relatively little, sleeps well, and spends an above-average amount of time quietly attending to you and the rest of his or her environment (see Figure 2.18). Clearly, you would have many more opportunities for pleasurable interactions with the second newborn.

The two newborn states that are of particular concern to parents—sleeping and crying—have both been studied extensively.

Sleep

Figure 2.19 summarizes several important facts about sleep and its development, two of which are of particular importance. First, "sleeping like a baby" means, in part, sleeping a lot; on average, newborns sleep twice as much as young adults do. Total sleep time declines regularly during childhood and continues to decrease, although more slowly, throughout life.

Second, the pattern of two different sleep states—*REM sleep* and *non-REM sleep*—changes dramatically with age. **Rapid eye movement (REM) sleep** is an active sleep state associated with dreaming in adults; it is characterized by quick, jerky eye movements under closed lids, a distinctive pattern of brain activity, body movements, and irregular heart rate and breathing. **Non-REM sleep,** in contrast, is a quiet sleep state characterized by the absence of motor activity or eye movements and more regular, slow brain waves, breathing, and heart rate. As you can see in Figure 2.19, REM sleep constitutes fully 50% of a newborn's total sleep time. The proportion of REM sleep declines quite rapidly to only 20% by 3 or 4 years of age and remains low for the rest of life.

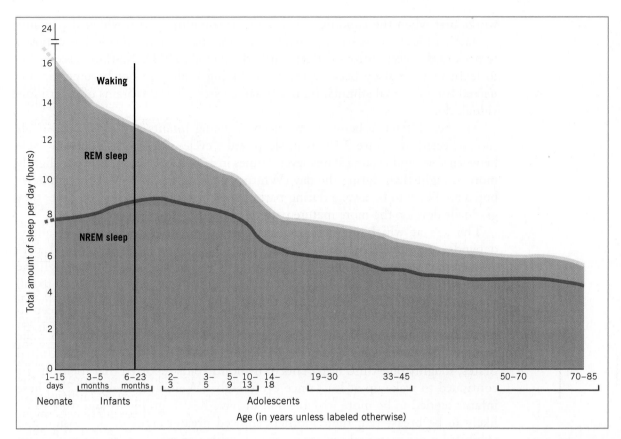

FIGURE 2.19 Total sleep and proportion of REM and non-REM sleep across the life span Newborns average a total of 16 hours of sleep per day, roughly half of it in REM sleep. The total amount of sleep declines sharply throughout early childhood and continues to decline much more slowly throughout life. From adolescence on, REM sleep constitutes only about 20% of total sleep time. (Data from Roffwarg et al., 1966, and from a later revision by these authors)

Why do infants spend so much time in REM sleep? Some researchers believe that it helps develop the infant's visual system. The normal development of the human visual system, including the visual area of the brain, depends on visual stimulation, but relatively little visual stimulation is experienced in the womb (particularly in contrast to fetal auditory stimulation). In addition, the fact that newborns spend so much time asleep means that they do not have much opportunity to amass waking visual experience. The high level of internally generated brain activity that occurs during REM sleep may help to make up for the natural deprivation of visual stimulation, facilitating the early development of the visual system in both fetus and newborn (Roffwarg, Muzio, & Dement, 1966).

Another way in which REM sleep may be adaptive for neonates is that the natural jerking movements (called myoclonic twitching) that occur exclusively during REM sleep may give infants opportunities to build sensorimotor maps (Blumberg, 2015). These twitching movements are most frequent during early development and may help the infant with the difficult problem of linking motor patterns with the specific sensations that they evoke.

Another distinctive feature of sleep in the newborn period is that napping newborns may actually be learning while asleep. In one study that investigated this possibility, infants were exposed to recordings of Finnish vowel sounds while they slumbered in the newborn nursery. When tested in the morning, their brain activity revealed that they recognized the sounds they had heard while asleep (Cheour et al., 2002). Sleeping neonates can also be classically conditioned (Fifer et al., 2010). During the training phase, the newborns were repeatedly presented with a tone just before a puff of air. Given this experience, they quickly learned to expect the air puff after the tone, as evidenced by their making an eye movement in response to the tone alone. Interestingly, newborn sleep conditioning

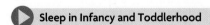 Sleep in Infancy and Toddlerhood

works best when the conditioned stimulus is something with which the infants are familiar: learning is stronger when the stimulus is a human voice, as opposed to backward speech or tones (Reeb-Sutherland et al., 2011). Newborns seem able to learn in their sleep because their slumbering brains do not become disconnected from external stimulation to the same extent that the brains of older individuals do.

Another difference between the sleep of young infants and older individuals (not reflected in Figure 2.19) is in sleep–wake cycles. Newborns generally cycle between sleep and waking states several times in a 24-hour period, sleeping slightly more at night than during the day (Whitney & Thoman, 1994). Although newborns are likely to be awake during part of their parents' normal sleep time, they gradually develop the more mature pattern of sleeping through the night.

The age at which infants' sleep patterns come to match those of adults depends very much on cultural practices and pressures. Indeed, tired parents employ many different strategies to get their infants to sleep through the night—from adopting elaborate, often extended bedtime rituals intended to lull the baby into dreamland to gritting their teeth and letting the baby cry himself or herself to sleep. Over the course of the 1st year of life, nighttime awakenings typically diminish. However, there is a subset of infants who continue to wake regularly. In one large study, with data collected at 10 sites across the United States, roughly one-third of parents of 6-month-olds reported that their infants continued to wake up at least once every night (Weinraub et al., 2012). These infants tended to be more irritable and/or have health problems and were more likely to be breast-fed; their mothers showed greater signs of depression and exhibited more maternal sensitivity than mothers of infants who generally slept through the night.

It is difficult to tease apart the causes and effects from these data. For example, does maternal depression lead to infant sleep problems? Or does lack of sleep lead mothers to become depressed? Regardless of the causal links, this pattern points to a potentially challenging situation in which positive parenting behaviors (breast-feeding, maternal sensitivity), paired with a temperamentally difficult infant, may impact the family's quality of life. Weinraub and her colleagues (2012) suggest that mothers who are generally sensitive may tend to intervene if their

Most American parents want to avoid the 2 A.M. fate of this young father. They regard their baby's sleeping through the night as a developmental triumph—the sooner, the better.

BUBBLES PHOTOLIBRARY / ALAMY

infant has trouble with sleep after the first few months of life. By doing so, caregivers may fail to give the infant the opportunity to learn self-soothing behaviors, as well as potentially reinforce non-sleep behaviors (comforting, nursing).

A number of sleep techniques have been proposed to help parents and infants struggling with sleep, which can take a major toll on all aspects of family life. Some families, however, are reticent to try the methods with the strongest evidence (Mindell et al., 2006): operant conditioning methods, in which the parent either ignores the infant's cries (extinction) or slowly increases their delay in responding (graduated extinction). A recent randomized-control study was designed to determine whether behavioral sleep interventions work and whether they cause undue stress for parents and infants (Gradisar et al., 2016). The results suggest that compared with a sleep-education control group, infants in a graduated-extinction group showed greater improvement in sleep behaviors, with no negative effects on infant stress (cortisol levels) or infant–mother attachment. The study also demonstrated successful effects of another behavioral method, bedtime fading, in which the infant's time in bed is gradually reduced. Both groups showed large decreases in nocturnal wakefulness, with concomitant positive effects on maternal stress.

In contrast with U.S. parents, Kipsigis parents in rural Kenya are relatively unconcerned about their infants' sleep patterns. Kipsigis babies are almost always with their mothers. During the day, infants are often carried on their mother's back as she goes about her daily activities; at night they sleep with her and are allowed to nurse whenever they awaken. As a consequence, these babies distribute their sleeping throughout the night and day for several months (Harkness & Super, 1995; Super & Harkness, 1986). Thus, cultures vary not only in terms of where babies sleep, as you learned in Chapter 1, but also in terms of how strongly parents attempt to influence when their babies sleep.

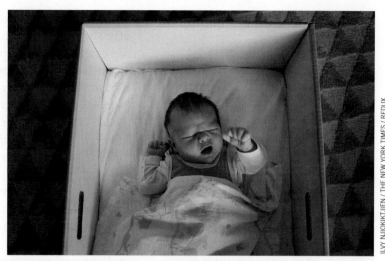

This baby is sleeping in a Finland baby box. Provided by the Finnish government to all expectant mothers who undergo a medical exam in the first 4 months of pregnancy, the baby box comes with additional baby items, including bedding and infant clothes. This practice, as well as other national efforts, has helped decrease Finland's infant mortality rate to one of the lowest in the world (Rosenberg, 2016) This type of room-sharing without bed-sharing is currently recommended, ideally until the infant's 1st birthday, by the American Academy of Pediatrics to prevent SIDS (AAP Task Force on Sudden Infant Death Syndrome, 2016).

Crying

How do you feel when you hear a baby cry? From an evolutionary point of view, adults' strong reactions to infants' crying could have adaptive value. Infants cry for many reasons—including illness, pain, and hunger—that require the attention of caregivers. Parents are likely to attempt to quiet their crying infant by taking care of the infant's needs, thereby promoting the infant's survival. Evolutionary theorists have suggested that across species, mothers are especially attuned to their infants' cries, relative to fathers, because they possess behavioral predispositions and resources (i.e., breast milk) that fathers do not. This view is supported by several studies suggesting that mothers are better than fathers at recognizing when their own infant is crying (e.g., Wiesenfeld, Malatesta, & Deloach, 1981). However, these studies missed an important confounding variable: mothers tend to spend more time with their young infants than fathers. And indeed, when time spent with the infant is taken into consideration, mothers and fathers are equally good at distinguishing their own infant's cries from the cries of unfamiliar infants (Gustafsson et al., 2013). Cry recognition, therefore, appears to be part of the learning process for all caregivers.

swaddling ■ a soothing technique, used in many cultures, that involves wrapping a baby tightly in cloths or a blanket

▶ **Parenting in Infancy and Toddlerhood**

▶ **Never Shake: Preventing Shaken Baby Syndrome**

Carrying infants close to the parent's body results in less crying. Many Western parents are now emulating the traditional carrying methods of other societies around the world.

As unpleasant as it is, crying is a normal behavior. Rather than diminishing over the first few months, as many new parents expect, it actually increases, peaking around 6 to 8 weeks of age. Crying behavior tends to decrease in frequency around 3 to 4 months of age, potentially because, as we will see in our discussion of infant cognitive and motor development in Chapter 5, the infant now has somewhat more control over the environment. During this period, crying bouts tend to increase in the late afternoon and evening, a phenomenon familiar to most caregivers of young infants.

Parents, especially first-timers, are often puzzled and anxious about why their baby is crying, and especially why their infants' crying bouts increase in frequency—and sometimes intensity—over the first two months. The effects of this very normal behavior on parents range from helplessness and guilt to, in extreme cases, a form of child abuse known as shaken baby syndrome, which can result in severe head trauma or death (e.g., Barr et al., 2015). Relatively minimal parental education, developed by the National Center on Shaken Baby Syndrome and provided in hospitals after birth and via public-educational outreach programs, can play an important role in demystifying infant crying. One recent study demonstrated that this informational intervention was highly effective in decreasing emergency room visits based on parental concerns about crying (Barr et al., 2015). Understanding that crying is a normal developmental process can significantly decrease parental stress and—in extreme cases—parent-caused injury to infants.

Soothing What are the best ways to console a crying baby? Most of the traditional standbys—rocking, singing lullabies, holding the baby up to the shoulder, giving the baby a pacifier—work reasonably well (R. Campos, 1989; Korner & Thoman, 1970). Many effective soothing techniques involve moderately intense and continuous or repetitive stimulation. The combination of holding, rocking, and talking or singing relieves an infant's distress better than any one of them alone (Jahromi, Putnam, & Stifter, 2004).

One very common soothing technique is **swaddling,** which involves wrapping a young baby tightly in cloths or a blanket, thereby restricting limb movement. The tight wrapping provides a constant high level of tactile stimulation and warmth. This technique is practiced in cultures as diverse and widespread as those of the Navajo and Hopi in the American Southwest (Chisholm, 1983), the Quechua in Peru (Tronick, Thomas, & Daltabuit, 1994), and rural villagers in Turkey (Delaney, 2000). Another traditional approach, distracting an upset infant with interesting objects or events, can also have a soothing effect, but the distress often resumes as soon as the interesting stimulus is removed (Harman, Rothbart, & Posner, 1997).

Touch can also have a soothing effect on infants. In interactions with an adult, infants fuss and cry less, and they smile and vocalize more, if the adult pats, rubs, or strokes them (Field et al., 1996; Peláez-Nogueras et al., 1996; Stack & Arnold, 1998; Stack & Muir, 1992). Carrying young infants, as is routinely done in many societies around the world, reduces the amount of crying that they do (Hunziker & Barr, 1986). In fact, crying infants show sharper decreases in heart rate, physical movement, and crying when carried about by their mother than when held in her lap. Similar quieting responses are seen in maternal carrying in other species

ANDREY BURKOV / DREAMSTIME

(think of how still lion cubs become when carried by their mother) and are conjectured to be innate cooperative mechanisms that facilitate the mother's carrying efforts (Esposito et al., 2013).

In other laboratory studies, placing a small drop of something sweet on a distressed newborn's tongue has been shown to have a dramatic calming effect (Barr et al., 1994; Blass & Camp, 2003; Smith & Blass, 1996). A taste of sucrose has an equally dramatic effect on pain sensitivity; newborn boys who are given a sweetened pacifier to suck during circumcision cry much less than babies who do not receive this simple intervention (Blass & Hoffmeyer, 1991).

Response to distress One question that often concerns parents is how to respond to their infant's signals of distress. They wonder whether quick and consistent supportive responses will reward the infant for fussing and crying, and hence increase these behaviors, or will instead give the infant a sense of security that leads to less fussing and crying. The literature suggests that both perspectives are valid. In one classic study, Bell and Ainsworth (1972) found that prompt responding to infant cries predicted less crying several months later. Yet in another classic study, Hubbard & van IJzendoorn (1991) found that infants whose cries were ignored during the first 9 weeks cried less during the next 9 weeks.

Colic No matter how or how much their parents try to soothe them, some infants are prone to excessive, inconsolable crying for no apparent reason during the first few months of life, a condition referred to as **colic.** Not only do "colicky" babies cry a lot, but they also tend to have high-pitched, particularly unpleasant cries (Stifter, Bono, & Spinrad, 2003). The causes of colic are unknown and may include allergic responses to their mothers' diets (ingested via breast milk), formula intolerance, immature gut development, and/or excessive gassiness. Unfortunately, colic is not a rare condition: more than 1 in 10 young U.S. infants—and their parents—suffer from it. Fortunately, it typically ends by around 3 months of age and leaves no ill effects (Stifter & Braungart, 1992; St James-Roberts, Conroy, & Wilsher, 1998). One of the best things parents with a colicky infant can do is seek social support, which can provide relief from the stress, frustration, and sense of inadequacy and incompetence they may feel because they are unable to relieve their baby's distress.

Negative Outcomes at Birth

Although most recognized pregnancies in an industrialized society result in the full-term birth of a healthy baby, sometimes the outcome is less positive. The worst result, obviously, is the death of an infant. A much more common negative outcome is low birth weight, which can have long-term consequences.

Infant Mortality

Infant mortality—death during the 1st year after birth—is now relatively rare in the industrialized world, thanks to decades of improvements in public health and general economic levels. In the United States, the 2015 infant mortality rate was 5.87 deaths per 1000 live births, the lowest in U.S. history (Central Intelligence Agency, 2015).

colic ■ excessive, inconsolable crying by a young infant for no apparent reason

infant mortality ■ death during the 1st year after birth

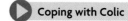 Coping with Colic

low birth weight (LBW) ■ a birth weight of less than 5½ pounds (2500 grams)

premature ■ any child born at 37 weeks after conception or earlier (as opposed to the normal term of 38 weeks)

small for gestational age ■ babies who weigh substantially less than is normal for whatever their gestational age

Although the U.S. infant mortality rate is at an all-time low in absolute terms, it is high compared with that of other industrialized nations. (Table 2.2 shows where the United States' infant mortality rate stood relative to the rates of highest- and lowest-ranked countries in 2015). The *relative* ranking of the United States has generally gotten worse over the past several decades, because the infant mortality rates in many other countries have had a higher rate of improvement.

Why do so many babies die in the United States—the richest country in the world? There are many reasons, most having to do with poverty. For example, many low-income mothers-to-be have no health insurance and thus limited access to good medical and prenatal care—though access for this group has improved with the 2014 passage of the Affordable Care Act (also known as Obamacare). It will be interesting to see whether the removal of some of the obstacles to prenatal care decreases the U.S. infant mortality rate, bringing it up to the level of other countries that guarantee prenatal care at low or minimal cost.

In less developed countries, especially those suffering from a breakdown in social organization due to war, famine, major epidemics, or persistent extreme poverty, the infant mortality rates can be staggering. In countries like Afghanistan, Mali, and Somalia, for example, roughly one of every 10 infants dies before age 1 (Central Intelligence Agency, 2015).

Low Birth Weight

The average newborn in the United States weighs 7½ pounds (most are between 5½ and 10 pounds). Infants who weigh less than 5½ pounds (2500 grams) at birth are considered to be of **low birth weight (LBW).** Some LBW infants are **premature,** or preterm; that is, they are born at 37 weeks after conception or earlier. Other LBW infants are referred to as **small for gestational age:** they may be either preterm or full-term, but they weigh substantially less than is normal for their gestational age, which is based on weeks since conception.

TABLE 2.2

Infant Mortality Rates* for the 10 Highest and 10 Lowest Nations, 2015

Country (Highest)	Infant Mortality Rate	Country (Lowest)	Infant Mortality Rate
Afghanistan	115.08	Monaco	1.82
Mali	102.23	Iceland	2.06
Somalia	98.39	Japan	2.08
Central African Republic	90.63	Singapore	2.48
Guinea-Bissau	89.21	Norway	2.48
Chad	88.69	Bermuda	2.48
Niger	84.59	Finland	2.52
Angola	78.26	Sweden	2.60
Burkina Faso	75.32	Czech Republic	2.63
Nigeria	72.70	Hong Kong	2.73

Note: U.S. infant mortality rate: 5.87

*Infant deaths per 1000 live births

Source: The World Factbook (2015 est.), Country Comparison: Infant Mortality Rate. Central Intelligence Agency. Accessed on June 27, 2016 from https://www.cia.gov/library/publications/the-world-factbook/rankorder/2091rank.html

Afghanistan has the highest infant mortality rate in the world. Among the causes are extreme poverty, poor nutrition, and poor sanitation. The great majority of the population lacks access to clean water, leading to a great many infant deaths related to dysentery, severe diarrhea, and other illnesses.

▶ Low Birth Weight in India

Eight percent of all U.S. newborns are of LBW (Hamilton et al., 2015). As a group, LBW newborns have a heightened level of medical complications, as well as higher rates of neurosensory deficits, more frequent illness, lower IQ scores, and lower educational achievement. Very LBW babies (VLBW; those weighing less than 1500 grams, or 3.3 pounds) are particularly vulnerable; these infants accounted for 1.4% of live births in the United States in 2014 (Hamilton et al., 2015).

There are numerous causes of LBW and prematurity, including several discussed in the section on teratogens: smoking, alcohol, and environmental pollutants such as lead and mercury. In some rapidly developing countries, such as China, high levels of airborne pollution have been linked to both LBW and pre-term birth, likely due to impaired oxygen transport across the placenta (Fleischer et al., 2015). Another cause is the skyrocketing rate of twin, triplet, and other multiple births as a result of the development of increasingly successful treatments for infertility. (The use of fertility drugs typically results in multiple eggs being released during ovulation; the use of in vitro fertilization [IVF] usually involves the placement of multiple laboratory-fertilized embryos in the uterus.) In 1980, 1 in every 53 infants born in the United States was a twin; in 2014, 1 in every 30 infants was a twin (Hamilton et al., 2015). The numbers for higher-order births (triplets and up) have also increased dramatically in recent years. This is a concern because the rates of LBW among multiples are quite high: 55% for twins and higher than 95% for triplets and above (Hamilton et al., 2015).

These newborn quintuplets were born in Albania in 2004. In 2015, 47 quintuplets or higher-order births were born in the United States.

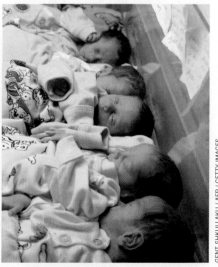

While all new parents have a great deal to learn about caring for their infants, parents of an LBW baby face special challenges from the outset. First, parents have to accept their disappointment over the fact that they do not have the perfect baby they had hoped for, and they may also have to cope with feelings of guilt ("What did I do wrong?"), inadequacy ("How can I possibly take care of such a tiny, fragile baby?"), and fear ("Will my baby survive?"). In addition, caring for an LBW baby can be especially time-consuming, stressful, and, if the infant requires extended treatment, very expensive.

Long-term outcomes What outcome can be expected for LBW newborns who survive? This question becomes increasingly important as newborns of ever-lower birth weights—some weighing less than 1 pound—are kept alive by modern medical technology. The answer includes both bad news and good news.

The bad news is that, as a group, children who were LBW infants have a higher incidence of developmental problems: the lower their birth weight, the more likely they are to have persistent difficulties (e.g., Muraskas, Hasson, & Besinger, 2004). For example, 8-year-old Australian children who were born LBW showed a greater incidence of sensory impairments, poorer academic achievement, and more behavior problems than their term-birth peers (Hutchinson et al., 2013). Other studies suggest links between VLBW and childhood psychiatric issues, especially those involving inattention, anxiety, and social difficulties (e.g., ADHD, autism; Johnson & Marlow, 2011). The hypothesized pathways between LBW and these negative outcomes include white-matter reduction, ventricular enlargement, and other abnormal brain development outcomes.

However, it is important to note that these comparisons often confound SES with birth-weight status. For example, in the aforementioned study by Hutchinson and colleagues (2013), the sample of term-birth families had higher educational attainment and employment status than the preterm sample. Indeed, a German study demonstrated that the strongest predictor of outcomes for VLBW infants is maternal education (Voss et al., 2012). The authors concluded that special services and additional support may be especially important for families of at-risk infants with less educational background.

The good news is that the *majority* of LBW children turn out quite well. The negative effects of their birth status gradually diminish, with children who were slightly to moderately underweight as newborns generally ending up within the normal range on most developmental measures (Kopp & Kaler, 1989; Liaw & Brooks-Gunn, 1993; Meisels & Plunkett, 1988; Vohr & Garcia Coll, 1988). Figure 2.20 depicts a particularly striking example of this fact (Teoh et al., 2006). Indeed, one recent follow-up study of extremely LBW infants (<1000 grams) found that by 18 to 22 months of age, 16% were unimpaired and 22% were only mildly impaired (Gargus et al., 2009).

Intervention programs What can be done to help an LBW infant overcome his or her poor start in life? A variety of intervention programs for LBW newborns offer a prime example of our theme about the role of research in improving the welfare of children. In many of them, parents are active participants, a marked change from past practice. Hospitals formerly did not allow parents to have any contact with their LBW infants, mainly because of fear of infection. Parents are now encouraged to have as much physical contact and social interaction with their hospitalized infant as the baby's condition allows. Indeed, kangaroo care—a variant of the skin-to-skin care discussed earlier, in which parents are used as incubators to help maintain infants' skin temperature and to promote breast-feeding—has been shown to decrease mortality and increase growth, breast-feeding, and attachment (Conde-Agudelo & Díaz-Rossello, 2014).

FIGURE 2.20 Small miracles Rumaisa and Hiba Rahman, shown here shortly after their birth in Chicago in 2004, were born 15 weeks premature. Rumaisa weighed just 9.2 ounces at birth, making her the world's smallest surviving infant. Her sister was slightly heavier, at 1 pound 4.4 ounces. Despite the significant challenges these sisters faced in their early lives, they have both reached appropriate developmental milestones in motor and language abilities, perhaps because they were able to reach 25 weeks in the womb (Rochman, 2011).

PHOTO BY OSCAR IZQUIERDO / LOYOLA UNIV. MEDICAL CENTER VIA GETTY IMAGES

Consistent with skin-to-skin and kangaroo care is the idea that being touched—cuddled, caressed, and carried—is a vital part of a newborn's life. Many LBW infants experience little stimulation of this kind because of the precautions that must be taken with them, including keeping them in special isolettes, hooked up to various life-support machines. To compensate for this lack of everyday touching experience, Field and her colleagues (Field, 2001; Field, Hernandez-Reif, & Freedman, 2004) developed a special therapy that involves massaging LBW babies and flexing their arms and legs (Figure 2.21). LBW babies who receive this therapy are more active and alert and gain weight faster than those who are not massaged. As a consequence, they get to go home earlier. Recent results also suggest that having parents sing to their LBW newborns during their stay in the hospital similarly improves the newborns' health, while also calming parents' fears (Loewy et al., 2013).

When their infant comes home, parents may have to cope with a baby who may be fairly passive and unresponsive, while being careful not to overstimulate the infant in an effort to elicit some response. LBW infants also tend to be fussier than the average baby and more difficult to soothe when they become upset (Greene, Fox, & Lewis, 1983). To compound matters, they often have a high-pitched cry that is particularly unpleasant (Lester et al., 1989).

Another problem for parents is the fact that LBW infants have more trouble falling asleep, waking up, and staying alert than do infants of normal birth weight, and their feeding schedules are less regular (DiVitto & Goldberg, 1979; Meisels & Plunkett, 1988). Thus, it takes longer for the baby to get on a predictable schedule, making the parents' lives more hectic. Parents of a preterm infant also need to understand that their baby's early development will not follow the same timetable as a full-term infant's: developmental milestones will be delayed, often linked more tightly to gestational age at birth than to chronological age after birth. For example, their infant will not begin to smile at them at around 6 weeks of age, the time when full-term infants usually reach this milestone. Instead, they may have to wait several more weeks for their baby to look them in the eye and break into a heart-melting smile. Thus, preterm infants are potentially more challenging to care for while being less rewarding to interact with. One consequence is that children who were born preterm are more likely to be victims of parental child abuse than are full-term infants (e.g., Spencer et al., 2006).

One step that can be helpful to parents of an LBW or preterm infant is learning more about infant development, both during their hospital stay and after returning home. Interventions that provide parents with training in child development, and/or focus on helping parents to become more responsive to their LBW infants, have revealed numerous positive effects, including improved behavioral outcomes, greater weight gain, higher IQs, and myriad other improved outcomes relative to their LBW peers (McCormick et al., 2006; Nordhov et al., 2012; Wassenaer-Leemhuis et al., 2016).

In addition, any parent who is trying to deal with an LBW baby or an infant with other problems would do well to seek social support—from a spouse or partner, other family members, friends, or a formal support group. One of the best-documented phenomena in psychology is that we all cope better with virtually any life problem when we have support from other people. Indeed, one potentially

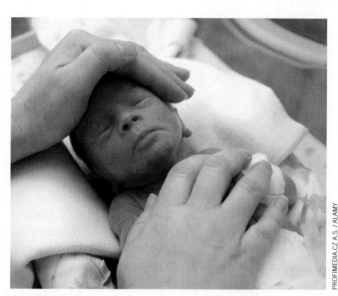

FIGURE 2.21 **Infant massage**
Everybody enjoys a good massage, but hospitalized newborns particularly benefit from extra touching.

important component of successful intervention programs is that they include support sessions, in the hospital and during home visits, designed to encourage parents to talk about their experiences and express their feelings.

It is important to note, however, that while many intervention programs produce gains, often those gains are relatively modest and diminish over time (e.g., McCormick et al., 2006). A second important point is that the success of any intervention depends on the initial health status of the infant. Many programs for LBW babies have been most beneficial to those infants who are less tiny at birth. This fact is cause for concern, as modern medical technology makes it increasingly possible to save the lives of ever-smaller infants who have a high risk of permanent, serious impairment. The third point is the importance of cumulative risk: the more risks the infant endures, the lower the chances of a good outcome. Because this principle is so important for all aspects of development, we examine it in greater detail in the following section.

Multiple-Risk Models

Risk factors tend to occur together. For example, a woman who is so addicted to alcohol, cocaine, or heroin that she continues to abuse the substance even though she is pregnant is likely to be under a great deal of stress and unlikely to eat well, take vitamins, earn a good income, seek prenatal care, have a strong social support network, or take good care of herself in other ways. Furthermore, whatever the cumulative effects of these prenatal risk factors, they will likely be compounded after birth by the mother's continuation of her unhealthy lifestyle and by her resulting inability to provide good care for her child.

As you will see repeatedly throughout this book, a negative developmental outcome—whether in terms of prenatal or later development—is more likely when there are multiple risk factors. In a classic demonstration of this fact, Michael Rutter (1979) reported a heightened incidence of psychiatric problems among English children growing up in families with four or more risk factors (including marital distress, low SES, paternal criminality, and maternal psychiatric disorder) (Figure 2.22). Thus, the likelihood of developing a disorder is slightly elevated for the child of parents who fight a lot; but if the child's family is also poor, the father engages in criminal behavior, and the mother suffers from emotional problems, the child's risk is multiplied nearly tenfold. Across numerous developmental domains, there are cumulative effects of risk factors: the more risk factors, the worse the potential outcomes. These cumulative risk effects impact aspects of child functioning ranging from attachment to language development to well-being (Evans, Li, & Whipple, 2013).

Poverty as a Developmental Hazard

Because it is such an important point, we cannot emphasize enough that the existence of multiple risks is strongly related to SES. Consider some of the factors we have discussed that are known to be dangerous for fetal development: inadequate prenatal care, poor nutrition, illness, emotional stress, cigarette smoking, drug abuse, and exposure to environmental and occupational hazards. All these factors are more likely to be experienced by a woman living below the poverty line than by a middle-class woman. It is no wonder, then, that on the whole, the outcome of pregnancy is less positive for infants of lower-SES parents than for babies born to middle-class parents.

FIGURE 2.22 Multiple risk factors Children who grow up in families with multiple risk factors are more likely to develop psychiatric disorders than are children from families with only one or two problematic characteristics (Rutter, 1979).

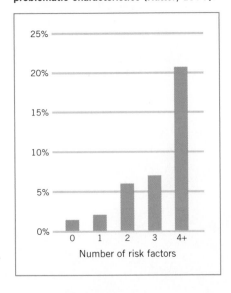

An equally sad fact is that in many countries, including the United States, minority families are overrepresented in the lowest SES levels. According to a study by the National Center for Children in Poverty using data from 2014, 21% of all U.S. children under age 18 live in families whose income places them below the poverty line ($24,008 for a family of four in 2014) (Jiang, Ekono, & Skinner, 2016). However, among African American, Hispanic, and Native American children, the percent living in poverty is 38%, 32%, and 35%, respectively. Thus, children growing up in poverty are disproportionately drawn from racial and ethnic minority groups that have historically faced barriers to economic success.

Resilience

Much of the discussion in this chapter has focused on the many ways in which early developmental processes can go wrong. There are, of course, individuals who, faced with multiple and seemingly overwhelming developmental hazards, nevertheless do well. In studying such children, researchers employ the concept of **developmental resilience** (Garmezy, 1983; Masten, Best, & Garmezy, 1990; Sameroff, 1998). Resilient children—like those in the Kauai study discussed in Chapter 1—often have two factors in their favor: (1) certain personal characteristics, especially intelligence, responsiveness to others, and a sense of being capable of achieving their goals; and (2) responsive care from someone.

In summary, development is highly complex, from the moment of conception to the moment of birth. As you will see throughout this book, that complexity continues over the ensuing years. Although early events and experiences can profoundly affect later development, developmental outcomes are never a foregone conclusion.

developmental resilience ■ successful development in spite of multiple and seemingly overwhelming developmental hazards

Review

The experience of newborn infants is mediated by internal states of arousal, ranging from deep sleep to intense crying, with large individual differences in the amount of time spent in the different states. Newborns spend roughly half their time asleep, but after early infancy, the amount of sleep declines steadily over many years. Researchers believe that the large proportion of sleep time that newborns spend in REM sleep is important for the development of the visual system and brain. Infants' crying is a particularly salient form of behavior for parents, and it generally elicits attention and caretaking. Effective soothing techniques provide moderately intense, continuous, or repetitive stimulation. How parents respond to their young infant's distress is related to later crying.

Negative outcomes of pregnancy are higher for families living in poverty. The United States has higher rates of infant mortality than do many other developed nations. Just more than 8% of all infants born in the United States are LBW. Although most will suffer few lasting effects, the long-term outcome of extremely LBW babies is often problematic. Several large-scale intervention programs have successfully improved the outcome of LBW infants.

According to the multiple-risk model, the more risks that a fetus or child faces, the more likely the child is to suffer from a variety of developmental problems. Low SES is associated with many developmental hazards. Despite facing multiple risks, many children nevertheless show remarkable resiliency and thrive.

CHAPTER SUMMARY

Prenatal Development

■ Nature and nurture combine forces in prenatal development. Much of this development is generated by the fetus itself, making the fetus an active player in its own progress. Substantial continuity exists between what goes on before and after birth in that infants demonstrate the effects of what has happened to them in the womb.

■ Prenatal development begins at the cellular level with conception, the union of an egg from the mother and a sperm from the father to form a single-celled zygote. The zygote multiplies and divides on its way through a fallopian tube.

■ The zygote undergoes the processes of cell division, cell migration, cell differentiation, and cell death. These processes continue throughout prenatal development.

■ When the zygote becomes implanted on the uterine wall, it becomes an embryo. From that point, it is dependent on the mother to obtain nourishment and oxygen and to get rid of waste products through the placenta.

■ Fetal behavior begins 5 or 6 weeks after conception with simple movements, undetected by the mother, that become increasingly complex and organized into patterns. Later, the fetus practices behaviors vital to independent living, including swallowing and a form of intrauterine "breathing."

■ The fetus experiences a wealth of stimulation both from within the womb and from the external environment. The fetus learns from this experience, as demonstrated by studies showing that both fetuses and newborns can discriminate between familiar and novel sounds, especially in speech, and exhibit persistent taste preferences developed in the womb.

Hazards to Prenatal Development

■ There are many hazards to prenatal development. The most common fate of a fertilized egg is spontaneous abortion (miscarriage).

■ A wide range of environmental factors can be hazardous to prenatal development. These include teratogens from the external world and certain maternal characteristics, such as age, nutritional status, physical health, behavior (especially the use of legal or illegal drugs), and emotional state.

The Birth Experience

■ Approximately 38 weeks after conception, the baby is ready to be born. Usually, the behavior of the fetus helps to initiate the birth process.

■ Being squeezed through the birth canal has several beneficial effects on the newborn, including preparing the infant to take his or her first breath.

■ Cultural practices surrounding childbirth vary greatly and are in part related to the goals and values emphasized by the culture.

The Newborn Infant

■ Newborns' states of arousal range from deep sleep to active crying.

■ The amount of time infants spend in the different arousal states varies greatly, both across individuals and across cultures.

■ REM sleep seems to compensate for the lack of visual stimulation that results from the darkness of the womb, and for the fact that newborns spend much of their time with their eyes shut, asleep.

■ The sound of a baby crying can be very aversive, and adults employ many strategies to soothe distressed infants.

■ The infant mortality rate in the United States is high relative to that of other developed countries. It is much higher for babies born to low-SES parents.

■ Infants born weighing less than 5½ pounds (2500 grams) are referred to as being of low birth weight. LBW infants are at risk for a variety of developmental problems, and the lower the birth weight, the greater the risk of lasting difficulties.

■ A variety of intervention programs have been designed to improve the course of development of LBW babies, encompassing both time in the hospital and after the infant returns home.

■ The multiple-risk model refers to the fact that infants with a number of risk factors have a heightened likelihood of continued developmental problems. Poverty is a particularly insidious risk to development, in part because it is associated with numerous negative factors.

■ Some children display resilience even in the face of substantial challenges. Resilience seems to result from certain personal characteristics and from responsive care from someone.

Test Yourself

1. The singular cell that forms when two gametes merge during fertilization is called the
   a. zygote.
   b. ova.
   c. sperm.
   d. embryo.

2. Which process of prenatal development is critical to the specialization of cells?
   a. cell division
   b. synaptogenesis
   c. cell differentiation
   d. apoptosis

3. Harry and Ron are genetically identical twins and are referred to as _____. Althea (a girl) and Stephen (a boy) are also twins, but are clearly _____ twins.
   a. monozygotic; identical
   b. dizygotic; fraternal
   c. dizygotic; monozygotic
   d. monozygotic; dizygotic

4. Which of the following systems protects the developing embryo from dangerous toxins?
   a. amniotic sac
   b. placenta
   c. umbilical cord
   d. neural tube

5. Andrea is 5 months pregnant with her first child. During the sonogram she notices that her child's head is much larger than the rest of its body. Her doctor explains that the disproportionately large head is a result of the normal process of
   a. cephalocaudal development.
   b. proximal-distal development.
   c. lateral development.
   d. bottom-up development.

6. Which of the following senses is the least active while the fetus is in the womb?
   a. hearing
   b. smell
   c. taste
   d. sight

7. Logan's dad is thrilled as Logan laughs each time he shows him a new toy: a monkey that squeaks when he pushes on its belly. After repeated exposure to the squeaking monkey, Logan becomes bored and no longer laughs. This process is known as
   a. habituation.
   b. dishabituation.
   c. classical conditioning.
   d. operant conditioning.

8. The DeCasper and Spence study where pregnant women read aloud twice a day from the same book during their last 6 weeks of pregnancy was designed to assess
   a. fetal attention.
   b. fetal learning.
   c. infant attention.
   d. infant learning.

9. Which of the following does *not* influence the severity of the effect of a teratogen on a developing fetus?
   a. timing of exposure
   b. quantity of exposure
   c. duration of exposure
   d. number of previous pregnancies of the mother

10. Which is *not* a symptom of fetal alcohol syndrome?
    a. facial deformities
    b. intellectual disability
    c. underactivity
    d. attention problems

11. Studies suggest that the squeezing that a fetus experiences during delivery serves several important functions. Which of the following is *not* one of them?
    a. It temporarily reduces the size of the infant's head, allowing it to pass safely through the pelvic bones.
    b. It squeezes fluid from the ear canals, allowing the baby to hear.
    c. It stimulates the production of hormones that help the fetus withstand mild oxygen deprivation.
    d. It forces amniotic fluid out of the lungs, in preparation for the baby's first breaths.

12. Which of the following is a characteristic of non-rapid eye movement (non-REM) sleep?
    a. irregular heart rate
    b. irregular breathing
    c. quick, jerky eye movements
    d. slow brain waves

13. Which of the following describes an infant who is most likely suffering from colic?
    a. Vivian cries for several hours a day for unexplained reasons.
    b. Jeremy cries loudly when he is hungry.
    c. LaTosha cries when she is placed in her crib.
    d. Emelie rarely cries.

14. What intervention program, involving direct skin-to-skin contact, are parents of low-birth-weight infants encouraged to use to support development and promote survival?
    a. swaddling care
    b. massage care
    c. kangaroo care
    d. pouch care

15. What does the multiple-risk model suggest about negative developmental outcomes?
   a. Each risk factor will produce a unique negative outcome.
   b. The presence of one risk factor increases the likelihood that another risk factor will emerge in the future.
   c. The more risk factors that are present, the more likely and worse the potential outcomes will be.
   d. The presence of more risk factors increases the likelihood that a child will develop resilience.

Don't stop now! Research shows that testing yourself is a powerful learning tool. Visit LaunchPad to access the LearningCurve adaptive quizzing system, which gives you a personalized study plan to help build your mastery of the chapter material through videos, activities, and more. **Go to launchpadworks.com.**

Critical Thinking Questions

1. A recent cartoon showed a pregnant woman walking down a street carrying an MP3 player with a set of very large headphones clamped around her protruding abdomen. What point was it making? What research might have provided the basis for the woman's behavior, and what assumptions is she making about what the result might be? If you or your partner were pregnant, do you think you would do something like this?

2. We hear a great deal about the terrible and tragic effects that illegal drugs like cocaine and diseases like AIDS can have on fetal development. In this chapter, tobacco and alcohol use are identified as two of the most common harmful behaviors in the United States. How do the effects of these various substances differ from each other, and should that influence how we as a society perceive their use by pregnant women?

3. Suppose you were in charge of a public-health campaign to improve prenatal development in the United States and you could focus on only one factor. What would you target and why?

4. Pick a country or culture that you are not very familiar with and research the common beliefs and practices with respect to conception, pregnancy, and childbirth. Do their practices appeal to you more than the practices with which you are familiar? Are there beliefs or practices that could be used beneficially with the ones that you are familiar with?

5. Are you more encouraged or more discouraged by the results of infant intervention programs? What would it take to make their gains larger and longer lasting?

6. Speculate on why the infant mortality rate in the United States has steadily gotten worse compared with that of other countries. Suggest some potential policy changes or healthcare initiatives that might help to address these causes.

7. Explain the basic idea of the multiple-risk model and how it relates to poverty in terms of prenatal development and birth outcomes.

Key Terms

amniotic sac, p. 50

apoptosis, p. 49

cephalocaudal development, p. 51

colic, p. 79

conception, p. 46

developmental resilience, p. 85

dishabituation, p. 56

dose–response relation, p. 61

embryo, p. 47

embryonic stem cells, p. 49

epigenesis, p. 45

fetal alcohol spectrum disorder (FASD), p. 66

fetus, p. 47

fraternal twins, p. 50

gametes (germ cells), p. 46

habituation, p. 56

identical twins, p. 50

infant mortality, p. 79

low birth weight (LBW), p. 80

meiosis, p. 46

mitosis, p. 47

neural tube, p. 50

non-REM sleep, p. 74

phylogenetic continuity, p. 57

placenta, p. 50

premature, p. 80

rapid eye movement (REM) sleep, p. 74

sensitive period, p. 60

small for gestational age, p. 80

state, p. 74
sudden infant death syndrome (SIDS), p. 65
swaddling, p. 78
teratogen, p. 60
umbilical cord, p. 50
zygote, p. 46

Student Video Activities

The Prenatal Period: Conception to Birth
Parenting in Infancy: Beng Caretaking Practices
3-D Ultrasound
Challenges During Pregnancy
The Effect of Stress on the Fetus
Birth
Sleep in Infancy and Toddlerhood
Parenting in Infancy and Toddlerhood
Never Shake: Preventing Shaken Baby Syndrome
Coping with Colic
Low Birth Weight in India

Answers to Test Yourself

1. a, **2.** c, **3.** d, **4.** b, **5.** a, **6.** d, **7.** a, **8.** b, **9.** d, **10.** c, **11.** b, **12.** d, **13.** a, **14.** c, **15.** c

TILLY WILLIS, *Waiting* (oil on canvas, 2005)

Biology and Behavior

Themes

- Nature and Nurture
- The Active Child
- Continuity/Discontinuity
- Mechanisms of Change
- Individual Differences
- Research and Children's Welfare

Picture this scene: two children, genetically identical, grow up in different cities and meet each other only as adults. The theme of identical twins reared apart has permeated Western literature since Roman antiquity, culminating in Shakespeare's masterpiece, *The Comedy of Errors*. The dramatic potential of twins separated at birth has continued to fascinate modern audiences, including such classic films as the *Parent Trap*. But what can identical twins who are reared apart tell us about child development? Such situations, while rare, provide a potentially invaluable opportunity to tease apart nature and nurture: same genes, different environments.

Oskar Stohr and Jack Yufa were identical twins separated shortly after their birth in Trinidad in 1933. Oskar was raised by his grandmother in Germany as a Catholic and a Nazi. Jack was raised by his father, in the Caribbean, as a Jew. Despite their very different backgrounds, when the brothers first met as middle-aged men recruited for a research study in Minneapolis, they discovered a remarkable number of similarities between them:

> They like spicy foods and sweet liqueurs, are absent-minded, . . . think it's funny to sneeze in a crowd . . . , flush the toilet before using it, . . . read magazines back to front, dip buttered toast in their coffee. Oskar is domineering toward women and yells at his wife, which Jack did before he was separated.
>
> (Holden, 1980, p. 1324)

Jack and Oskar, who are both now deceased, were participants in the Minnesota Study of Twins Reared Apart, an extensive research project on identical twins separated early in life (Bouchard et al., 1990). More than 100 pairs of such twins were located and brought to Minneapolis to undergo a battery of physiological and psychological tests. Many twin siblings met for the first time since infancy. (The reunited twins in the photo at left showed almost as many striking similarities as did Jack and Oskar, including their having held several very similar jobs and being volunteer firemen.) The Minnesota team of investigators was struck by the extent of the similarities they found in the separated twins; they identified genetic contributions to "almost every behavioral trait so far investigated from reaction time to religiosity" (Bouchard et al., 1990).

As striking as the similarities between separated twins may be, there are several problems with automatically assuming that these similarities are attributable to genetic factors. One issue is that it would be a great oversimplification to suggest that all of the similar traits shared by separated twins are genetic. For example, it would be a stretch to argue that the men in the photograph share a set of genes that predetermined that they both would become firemen. As we will discuss in this chapter, genes code for proteins, not for anything as complex as an occupation (or choice of facial hair). An additional issue is the practice of selective placement: adoption agencies generally try to place children with families of the same general background, so the environments of the separated siblings are often similar in many ways. It is extremely rare for separated twins to be raised like Jack and Oskar, with different languages, religions, and cultures. In fact, the majority of the twins in most behavior genetics studies are from predominantly White, middle-class families in Western countries. New studies focused on emerging populations of separated twins may be able

Identical twins Gerald Levey and Mark Newman were separated at birth and reared separately in middle-class Jewish homes in the New York area. When reunited at the age of 31, they discovered, among many other similarities, that they were both volunteer firemen with droopy moustaches; long sideburns; and a penchant for hunting, fishing, and John Wayne movies. They even drank the same brand of beer, from a can, which they held with their pinkie tucked under the bottom and crushed when they had emptied it.

THOMAS WANSTALL / THE IMAGE WORKS

to address these potential confounds. For example, one prospective longitudinal study is focused on China-born twins separated by international adoption (Segal, Stohs, & Evans, 2011). Other currently ongoing studies are focused on the effects of extreme environment differences, such as a NASA study on the impact of extended periods of space travel on identical twin astronauts Mark and Scott Kelly.

Understanding how genes and environment interact is essential to understanding development at any point in the life span. The focus of this chapter is on the key biological factors that are in play from the moment of conception through adolescence, including the inheritance and influence of genes, the development and early functioning of the brain, and important aspects of physical development and maturation. Every cell in our bodies carries the genetic material that we inherited at our conception and that continues to influence our behavior throughout life. Every behavior we engage in is directed by our brain. Everything we do at every age is mediated by a constantly changing physical body—one that changes very rapidly and dramatically in the first few years of life and in adolescence, but more slowly and subtly at other times.

Several of the themes that were set out in Chapter 1 figure prominently in this chapter. Issues of *nature and nurture,* as well as *individual differences* among children, are central throughout this whole chapter—especially the first section, which focuses on the interaction of genetic and environmental factors in development. *Mechanisms of change* are prominent in our discussions of the developmental role of genetic factors and of the processes involved in the relationship between brain functioning and behavior. *Continuity/discontinuity* in development is also highlighted throughout the chapter. We again emphasize the activity-dependent nature of developmental processes and the role of the *active child* in charting the course of his or her own development. Finally, the theme of *research and children's welfare* is also prominent, especially as we focus on gene-based disorders and on factors that influence healthy physical growth and development.

Identical twins Mark and Scott Kelly have added a unique chapter to the twin studies annals. Both are astronauts and Scott's recent stay of nearly a year aboard the International Space Station while his brother stayed on Earth has provided NASA with the opportunity for a groundbreaking study of the effects of extended space travel, including exposure to radiation, carbon monoxide, and the micro-gravity environment.

Nature and Nurture

Long before there was any understanding of the principles of heredity, people were aware that some traits and characteristics "run in families" and that this tendency was somehow related to procreation. For as long as there have been domesticated animals, for example, farmers have practiced selective breeding to improve certain characteristics of their livestock, such as the size of their horses and the milk yield of their goats, cows, or yaks. People have also long been aware that the environment plays a role in development—that a nutritious diet, for example, is necessary for livestock to produce a good milk supply or fine-quality wool. When scientists first began to investigate the contributions of heredity and environment to development, they generally emphasized one factor or the other as the prime influence—heredity *or* environment, nature *or* nurture. In nineteenth-century England, for example, Francis Galton (1869/1962), a cousin of Charles Darwin, identified men who had achieved "eminence" in a variety of fields and concluded that talent runs in families, because very close relatives of

The phenomenal athletic ability of tennis greats Venus and Serena Williams is almost certainly due to the combination of nature—the genes they inherited from their parents—and nurture—the extensive coaching they received from their father and the tireless emotional support provided by their mother.

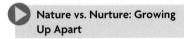

Nature vs. Nurture: Growing Up Apart

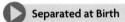

Separated at Birth

genome ■ the complete set of genes of any organism

an eminent man were more likely to be high achievers themselves than were less close relatives.

Among Galton's cases of closely related eminent men were John Stuart Mill and his father, both respected English philosophers. However, Mill himself pointed out that most of Galton's eminent men were members of well-to-do families. In his view, the relation between the achievement of these eminent men and their kinship had less to do with biological ties than with the fact that they were similar in economic well-being, social status, education, and other advantages and opportunities. In short, according to Mill, Galton's subjects rose to eminence more because of environmental factors than hereditary ones.

Our modern understanding of how characteristics are transmitted from parent to offspring originated with insights achieved by Gregor Mendel, a nineteenth-century Austrian monk who observed distinct patterns of inheritance in the pea plants that he cross-bred in his monastery garden. Some aspects of these inheritance patterns were later discovered to occur in all living things, as we will see in the discussion of gene expression later in this chapter (see pages 100–101). A much deeper understanding of how genetic influences operate came in the 1950s with James Watson, Francis Crick, and Rosalind Franklin's identification of the structure of DNA, the basic component of hereditary transmission.

Since that landmark discovery, enormous progress has been made in deciphering the genetic code. Researchers have mapped the entire **genome**—the complete set of an organism's genes—of myriad species of plants and animals, including humans, chickens, mice, chimpanzees, and even several extinct species, including our closest evolutionary relative, Neanderthals (R. E. Green et al., 2010). Indeed, as of 2015, over 250 animal species have had their genomes sequenced (NIH, n.d.). Along with these innovations in gene sequencing have come innovations in gene synthesis: a method for producing DNA. In 2016, scientists announced a plan to synthesize an entire human genome (Boeke et al., 2016), a project with a great deal of potential for scientific and medical advances yet also fraught with ethical concerns (including the theoretical potential to create human life without biological parents).

Comparisons of the genomes of various species have already revealed much about our human genetic endowment—and they have provided numerous surprises. One surprise was the number of genes that humans have: the current estimate of 19,000 protein-coding genes is far fewer than previous estimates, which ranged from 35,000 to more than 100,000 genes (Ezkurdia et al., 2014). A second major surprise was that most of those genes are possessed by all living things. We humans share a large proportion of our genes with bears, barnacles, beans, and bacteria. Most of our genes are devoted, in decreasing order, to making us animals, vertebrates, mammals, primates, and—finally—humans. In the next section, we will look at a third surprise, one that may turn out to be a blockbuster.

As researchers have achieved better understanding of the role of hereditary factors in development, they have also come to appreciate the limits of what these factors can account for on their own. Similarly, as knowledge has grown concerning the influence of experience on development, it has become clear that experience alone rarely provides a satisfactory account. Development results from the close and continual interplay of nature *and* nurture—of genes *and* experience—and this interplay is the focus of the following section.

Genetic and Environmental Forces

The interplay of genes and experience is exceedingly complex. To simplify our discussion of interactions among genetic and environmental factors, we will organize it around the model of hereditary and environmental influences shown in Figure 3.1. Three key elements of the model are the **genotype**—the genetic material an individual inherits; the **phenotype**—the observable expression of the genotype, including *both* body characteristics and behavior; and the **environment**—every aspect of the individual and his or her surroundings (including prenatal experience) other than the genes themselves.

"We think it has something to do with your genome."

These three elements are involved in five relations that are fundamental in the development of every child: (1) the parents' genetic contribution to the child's genotype; (2) the contribution of the child's genotype to his or her own phenotype; (3) the contribution of the child's environment to his or her phenotype; (4) the influence of the child's phenotype on his or her environment; and (5) the influence of the child's environment on his or her genotype. We will now consider each of these relations in turn.

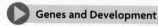

▶ **Genes and Development**

1. Parents' Genotype–Child's Genotype

Relation 1 involves the transmission of genetic material—chromosomes and genes—from parent to offspring. You caught a glimpse of this process in Chapter 2, when we discussed the gametes (one from the mother and one from the father) that conjoin at conception to create a zygote. The nucleus of every cell in the body contains **chromosomes,** long threadlike molecules made up of two twisted strands of **DNA (deoxyribonucleic acid).** DNA carries all the biochemical instructions involved in the formation and functioning of an organism. These instructions are "packaged" in **genes,** the basic unit of heredity in all living things. Genes are sections of chromosomes. More specifically, each gene is a segment of DNA that is the code for the production of particular *proteins.* Some

genotype ■ the genetic material an individual inherits

phenotype ■ the observable expression of the genotype, including both body characteristics and behavior

environment ■ every aspect of an individual and his or her surroundings other than genes

chromosomes ■ molecules of DNA that transmit genetic information; chromosomes are made up of DNA

DNA (deoxyribonucleic acid) ■ molecules that carry all the biochemical instructions involved in the formation and functioning of an organism

genes ■ sections of chromosomes that are the basic unit of heredity in all living things

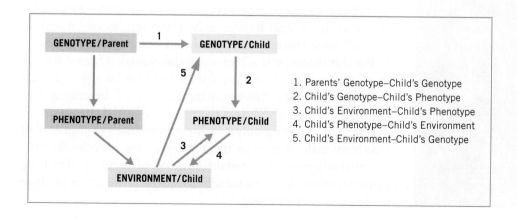

1. Parents' Genotype–Child's Genotype
2. Child's Genotype–Child's Phenotype
3. Child's Environment–Child's Phenotype
4. Child's Phenotype–Child's Environment
5. Child's Environment–Child's Genotype

FIGURE 3.1 Development Development is a combined function of genetic and environmental factors. The five numbered relations are discussed in detail in the text.

sex chromosomes ■ the chromosomes (X and Y) that determine an individual's gender

proteins are the building blocks of the body's cells; others regulate the cells' functioning. Genes affect development and behavior only through the manufacture of proteins.

But here is the blockbuster surprise we mentioned earlier: researchers have discovered that genes—at least "genes" as they have been traditionally defined—make up only about 2% of the human genome (Mouse Genome Sequencing Consortium, 2002). Much of the rest of our genome—once thought to be "junk" DNA—turns out to play a supporting role in influencing genetic transmission by regulating the activity of protein-coding genes. Understanding just how much of this noncoding DNA is vital to functioning, and precisely how it works, is the object of ongoing research efforts (Kellis et al., 2014).

Human heredity Humans normally have a total of 46 chromosomes, divided into 23 pairs, in the nucleus of each cell (see Figure 3.2). The only exception is the sex cells; recall from Chapter 2 that, as a result of the type of cell division that produces gametes, eggs and sperm each contain only 23 chromosomes.

With the exception of the sex chromosomes, the two members of each chromosome pair are of the same general size and shape (roughly the shape of the letter X). Furthermore, each chromosome pair carries, usually at corresponding locations, genes of the same type—that is, sequences of DNA that are relevant to the same traits. One member of each chromosome pair was inherited from each parent. Thus, every individual has two copies of each gene, one on the chromosome inherited from the father and one on the chromosome from the mother. Your biological children will each receive half of your genes, and your biological grandchildren will have one-quarter (just as you have half your genes in common with each of your biological parents and one-fourth with each biological grandparent).

Sex determination As noted, the **sex chromosomes,** which determine an individual's sex, are an exception to the general pattern of chromosome pairs described above. Females have two identical, largish sex chromosomes called X chromosomes, but males have one X chromosome and one much smaller Y chromosome (so called because it is Y-shaped). Because a female has only X chromosomes, the division of her gametes (germ cells) results in all her eggs having an X. However, because a male is XY, half his sperm contain an X chromosome and half contain a Y. For this reason, it is *always* the father who determines the sex of offspring: if an X-bearing sperm fertilizes an egg, a female (XX) zygote results; if an egg is fertilized by a Y-bearing sperm, the zygote is male (XY). It is the *presence* of a Y chromosome—not the fact of having only one X chromosome—that makes an individual male. A gene on the Y chromosome encodes the protein that triggers the prenatal formation of testes by activating genes on other chromosomes. Subsequently, the testes produce the hormone testosterone.

FIGURE 3.2 Karyotype This color-enhanced micrograph, called a karyotype, shows the 23 pairs of chromosomes in a healthy human male. As you can see, in nearly all cases, the chromosomes of each homologous pair are roughly the same size. The notable exception is the sex chromosomes (middle of bottom row): the Y chromosome that determines maleness is much smaller than the X chromosome. A woman's karyotype would contain two X chromosomes.

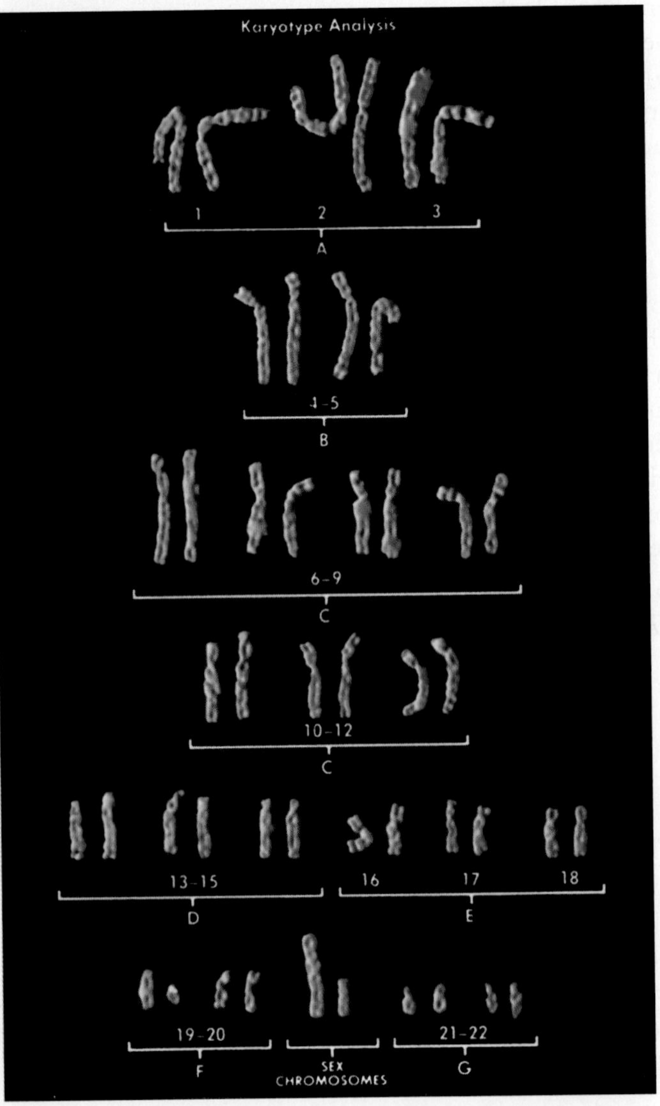

Karyotype Analysis

1 2 3
A
4–5
B
6–9
C
C
10–12
C
13–15   16   17   18
D   E
19–20   SEX   21–22
F   CHROMOSOMES   G

BIOPHOTO ASSOCIATES / SCIENCE SOURCE

Diversity and individuality As we have noted, genes guarantee that humans will be similar to one another in certain ways, both at the species level (e.g., humans are all bipedal and have opposable thumbs) and at the individual level (i.e., family resemblances). Genes also guarantee differences at both levels. Several mechanisms contribute to genetic diversity among people.

One such mechanism is **mutation,** a change that occurs in a section of DNA. Some mutations are random, spontaneous errors; others are caused by environmental factors. Most are harmful. Those that occur in germ cells can be passed on to offspring; many inherited diseases and disorders originate from a mutated gene. (Box 3.1 discusses the genetic transmission of diseases and disorders.)

Occasionally, however, a mutation makes individuals more viable, that is, more likely to survive—perhaps by increasing their resistance to some disease or by increasing their ability to adapt to some crucial aspect of their environment. Such mutations provide the basis for evolution: a person with the favorable mutated gene is more likely to survive long enough to produce offspring, who, in turn, are likely to possess the mutated gene, thus heightening their own chance of surviving and reproducing. Across generations, these favorable genes proliferate in the gene pool of the species.

A second mechanism that promotes variability among individuals is the *random assortment* of chromosomes in the formation of egg and sperm. During gamete division, the 23 pairs of chromosomes are shuffled randomly, with chance determining which member of each pair goes into each new egg or sperm. This means that for each gamete, there are 223, or 8.4 million, possible combinations of chromosomes. Thus, when a sperm and an egg unite, the odds are essentially zero that any two individuals—even members of the same family—would have the same genotype (except, of course, identical twins). Further variation is introduced by a process called **crossing over:** when gametes divide, the two members of a pair of chromosomes sometimes swap sections of DNA. As a result, some of the chromosomes that parents pass on to their offspring are constituted differently from their own.

mutation ■ a change in a section of DNA

crossing over ■ the process by which sections of DNA switch from one chromosome to the other; crossing over promotes variability among individuals

Children inherit half of their genes from their mother and half from their father. But biological mechanisms like random assortment and crossing over, as well as forces influencing the child's phenotype, shape the degree to which a child will resemble one parent, and the degree to which they will vary. In the case pictured here, Prince George (right) bears a strong resemblance to his father, Prince William (left) at age 2.

BOX 3.1 | applications

GENETIC TRANSMISSION OF DISORDERS

Thousands of human disorders—many of them extremely rare—are presently known to have genetic origins. Although our discussion here will focus on the behaviors and psychological symptoms associated with such disorders, most of them also involve a variety of physical symptoms, often including atypical physical appearance (e.g., distorted facial features), organ defects (e.g., heart problems), and atypical brain development. These and other genetically based conditions can be inherited in several different ways.

Dominant–Recessive Patterns

Many genetic disorders involve the dominant–recessive pattern of inheritance, occurring only when an individual has two recessive alleles for the condition. There are thousands of such recessive-gene disorders, including phenylketonuria (PKU) (discussed on page 103) and sickle-cell anemia (discussed below), as well as Tay-Sachs disease, cystic fibrosis, and many others. Disorders that are caused by a dominant gene include Huntington disease (a progressive and always fatal degenerative condition of the brain) and neurofibromatosis (a disorder in which nerve fibers develop tumors). A combination of severe speech, language, and motor difficulties that was first discovered in a particular family in England has been traced to a mutation of a single gene (referred to as FOXP2) that acts in a dominant fashion (Graham & Fisher, 2015).

In some cases, a single gene can have both harmful and beneficial effects. One such case is sickle-cell disease, in which red blood cells are sickle-shaped rather than round, diminishing their capacity to transport oxygen. This disease, which can be debilitating and sometimes fatal, affects about 1 of every 500 African Americans. It is a recessive-gene disorder, so individuals who are homozygous for this trait (inheriting two sickle-cell genes, one from each parent) will suffer from the disease. Individuals who are heterozygous for this trait (carrying one normal and one sickle-cell gene) have some abnormality in their blood cells but usually experience no negative effects. In fact, if they live in regions of the world—like West Africa—where malaria is common, they benefit, because the sickle cells in their blood confer resistance against this deadly disease. In nineteenth-century Africa, malaria came to be known as the "White man's disease" because so many European explorers, lacking the sickle-cell gene, died of it.

Note that even when the root cause of a disorder is a single gene, it does not mean that that one gene is responsible for all manifestations of the disorder. The single gene simply starts a cascade of events, turning on and turning off multiple genes with effects on many different aspects of the individual's subsequent development.

Polygenic Inheritance

Many common human disorders are believed to result from interactions among multiple inherited genes, often in conjunction with environmental factors. Among the many diseases in this category are some forms of cancer and heart disease, type 1 and type 2 diabetes, and asthma. Psychiatric disorders, such as schizophrenia, and behavior disorders, such as attention-deficit hyperactivity disorder, also involve numerous genes. As described in the text, genome-wide association studies (GWAS) suggest that each gene has just a small effect on its own. It is the combination of many genes that leads to heritable traits, including human disorders.

Sex-Linked Inheritance

As mentioned in the text, some single-gene conditions are carried on the X chromosome and are much more common in males. (Females can inherit such conditions, but only if they inherit the culprit recessive alleles on both of their X chromosomes.) Sex-linked disorders range from relatively minor problems, like male-pattern baldness and red–green color blindness, to very serious problems, including hemophilia and Duchenne muscular dystrophy. Another sex-linked disorder is fragile-X syndrome, which involves mutations in the X chromosome and is the most common inherited form of intellectual disability.

Chromosomal Anomalies

Some genetic disorders originate with errors in germ-cell division that result in a zygote

 Genetic Disorders

that has either more or fewer than the normal complement of chromosomes. Most such zygotes cannot survive, but some do. Down syndrome most commonly originates when the mother's egg cells do not divide properly, and an egg that is fertilized contains an extra copy of chromosome 21. The probability of such errors in cell division increases with age, thus the incidence of giving birth to a child with Down syndrome is markedly higher for women older than 35. (Increased paternal age has also been linked to the incidence of Down syndrome, though to a lesser extent [De Souza, Alberman, & Morris, 2009; Hurles, 2012]). The boy pictured on the next page shows some of the facial features common to individuals with Down syndrome, which is also marked by intellectual disability (ranging from mild to severe), a number of physical problems, and a sweet temperament.

Other genetic disorders arise from extra or missing *sex* chromosomes. For example, Klinefelter syndrome, which affects between 1 in 500 to 1000 males in the United States, involves an extra X chromosome (XXY). The physical signs of this syndrome, which can include small testes and elongated limbs, often go unnoticed, but infertility is common. Turner syndrome, which affects 1 in 2500 U.S. women, involves a missing X chromosome (XO) and is usually characterized by short stature, stunted sexual development at puberty, and infertility.

Gene Anomalies

Just as genetic disorders can originate from extra or missing chromosomes, so too can they result from extra, missing, or abnormal genes. One intriguing instance is Williams syndrome. This rare genetic disorder involves a variety of cognitive impairments, most noticeably in spatial and visual skills, but relatively less impairment in language ability (e.g., Musolino & Landau, 2012; Skwerer & Tager-Flusberg, 2011). Individuals with Williams syndrome are also typically characterized by outgoing personalities and friendliness paired with anxiety and phobias.

LAUREN SHEAR / SCIENCE SOURCE

One of the most common identifiable causes of intellectual disability is Down syndrome, which occurs in about 1 of every 1000 births in the United States. The risk increases dramatically with the age of the parents, especially the mother; by the age of 45, a woman has 1 chance in 32 of having a baby with Down syndrome. The degree of disability varies greatly and depends in part on the kind of care and early intervention children receive.

This condition has been traced to the deletion of a small section of approximately 25 genes on chromosome 7. Some individuals, however, have a smaller deletion; in those cases, the degree of impairment is decreased, suggesting a clear relationship between the number of genes deleted and the resulting phenotype (Karmiloff-Smith et al., 2012). Interestingly, some individuals show a duplication of the same section of genes that is deleted in Williams syndrome. In this disorder, known as 7q11.23 duplication syndrome, the pattern of abilities and disabilities is flipped, with individuals exhibiting relatively weak speech and language abilities paired with relatively strong visuo-spatial skills (Mervis & Velleman, 2011; Osborne & Mervis, 2007).

Regulator-Gene Defects

Many disorders are thought to originate from defects in regulator genes, which, as discussed on page 100, control the expression of other genes. For example, a defect in the regulator gene that initiates the development of a male can interrupt the normal chain of events, occasionally resulting in a newborn who has female genitalia but is genetically male. Such cases often come to light when a young woman fails to begin menstruating or when a fertility clinic discovers that the reason a couple has failed to conceive is that the person trying to get pregnant is genetically male.

Unidentified Genetic Basis

In addition to the known gene-disorder links, there are many syndromes whose genetic origins are clear from their inheritance patterns but whose specific genetic cause has yet to be identified. For example, dyslexia is a highly heritable reading disability that probably stems from a variety of gene-based conditions. Another example is Tourette syndrome. Individuals with this disorder generally display a variety of tics, ranging from involuntary twitching and jerking to compulsively blurting out obscenities. Research suggests that Tourette syndrome probably involves a complex pattern of inheritance, making precise determination of the cause very difficult (O'Rourke et al., 2009).

The same is true for *autism spectrum disorder* (*ASD*), which includes both autism and Asperger syndrome and involves a wide range of deficits in social skills and communication. In 2012, in various U.S. districts monitored by the Centers for Disease Control, it was estimated that the ASD prevalence rate among 8-year-olds was 1 in 68 children (age 8 is thought to be the age of peak prevalence); furthermore, boys are 4.5 times more likely than girls to be identified as having the disorder (Christensen et al., 2016). The diagnosis of ASD is based on major impairments in social interaction and communication skills and a limited set of interests or repetitive behaviors. Individuals with Asperger syndrome tend to have a milder array of symptoms and usually do not experience difficulties in language development.

ASD includes individuals with not only a range of disabilities but also, in some cases, remarkable talents in a narrowly focused area, such as mathematics or drawing. ASD is known to be highly heritable: twin studies have revealed that identical twins (who share 100% of their genes) are more than twice as likely as fraternal twins (who share 50% of their genes) to share an autism diagnosis (Ronald & Hoekstra, 2011). The difficulty in identifying the specific genetic basis for autism spectrum disorder is highlighted by the fact that there are between 500 and 1000 candidate genes associated with ASD (Huguet, Benabou, & Bourgeron, 2016). An additional complicating feature of the genetics of ASD is that *de novo* mutations—non-inherited mutations that are not shared between parents and children—are also associated with risk for autism (Neale et al., 2012). Yet progress is being made in identifying the genetic contributions to ASD: researchers recently identified which genetic mutations have the greatest likelihood of leading to autism and which mutations do not (Uddin et al., 2014).

The number of children diagnosed with ASD has increased dramatically in recent years. In the districts tracked by the Centers for Disease Control, the ASD prevalence estimates for 8-year-olds in 2008 represented a 78% increase over those for 2002 (Baio, 2012), with a smaller but still sizable increase between 2008 and 2012 (Christiansen et al., 2016). Part of the increase is believed to be due to greater public awareness of the syndrome, leading to a higher level of detection by parents, teachers, and doctors. In addition, current diagnostic criteria are broader than those of the past. It is thus unclear to what degree the increased level of diagnoses accurately reflects a change in the actual incidence of ASD (e.g., Gernsbacher, Dawson, & Goldsmith, 2005).

One factor that was highly publicized as a possible cause of the so-called autism epidemic—the MMR vaccine that is routinely given to young children to prevent measles, mumps, and rubella—has been *definitively* ruled out (A. W. McMahon et al., 2008; Price et al., 2010). The original study reporting a link between the MMR vaccine and ASD (Wakefield et al., 1998) has been shown to be fraudulent and has been retracted (Godlee, Smith, & Marcovitch, 2011). Unfortunately, however, some parents continue to deny their children this important vaccine, needlessly putting themselves and other members of their communities at risk for the illnesses that the vaccine prevents.

endophenotypes ▪ intermediate phenotypes, including the brain and nervous systems, that do not involve overt behavior

regulator genes ▪ genes that control the activity of other genes

2. Child's Genotype–Child's Phenotype

We now turn to Relation 2 in Figure 3.1, the relation between one's genotype and one's phenotype. Keep in mind that phenotypes include both physical characteristics, such as height and eye color, and behavioral characteristics, such as temperament and intelligence. Genes also influence unobservable aspects of the phenotype that influence behavior, most notably, our brain and nervous systems. These intermediate phenotypes, known as **endophenotypes,** mediate the pathways between genes and behavior.

Our examination of the genetic contribution to the phenotype begins with a key fact: although every cell in your body contains copies of all the genes you received from your parents, only some of those genes are expressed. At any given time in any cell in the body, some genes are active (turned on), while others are not. Some genes that are hard at work in neurons, for example, are totally at rest in toenail cells. As you will see, there are several reasons for this.

Gene expression: Developmental changes Genes influence development and behavior only when they are turned on, and human development proceeds normally, from conception to death, only if genes get switched on and off in the right place, at the right time, and for the right length of time. Some genes are turned on in only a few cells and for only a few hours and then are switched off permanently. This pattern is typical during embryological development when, for example, the genes that are turned on in certain cells lead them to specialize for arm, hand, and fingerprint formation. Other genes are involved in the basic functioning of almost all cells almost all the time.

The switching on and off of genes is controlled primarily by **regulator genes.** The activation or inactivation of one gene is always part of a chain of genetic events. When one gene is switched on, it causes another gene to turn on or off, which has an impact on the status of yet other genes. Thus, genes never function in isolation. Instead, they belong to extensive networks in which the expression of one gene is a precondition for the expression of another, and so on. The continuous switching on and off of genes underlies development throughout life, from the initial prenatal differentiation of cells to the gene-induced events of puberty to many of the changes related to aging.

External factors can affect the switching on and off of genes. A dramatic example is the effect of thalidomide on limb development (described in Chapter 2), in which the sedative interferes with the functioning of genes underpinning normal growth factors (Ito et al., 2010). Another example comes from the fact that early visual experience is necessary for the normal development of the visual system because it causes the switching on of certain genes, which, in turn, switch on other genes in the visual cortex (Maya-Vetencourt & Origlia, 2012). The ramifications of decreased visual experience are observed in cases of children with cataracts that are not removed early in life, as discussed later in this chapter.

The fact that regulator genes can repeatedly switch other genes on and off in different patterns means that a given gene can function multiple times in multiple places during development. All that is required is that the gene's expression be controlled by different regulator genes at different times. This on-again, off-again functioning of individual genes results in enormous diversity in genetic expression. By analogy, consider the fact that this book is written with only 26 letters and probably only a few thousand different words made up of combinations of those letters. The meaning comes from the order in which the letters occur, the order in which they have been "switched on and off" by the authors.

Gene expression: Dominance patterns Many of an individual's genes are never expressed; some others are only partially expressed. One reason is the fact that about one-third of human genes have two or more different forms, known as **alleles.** The alleles of a given gene influence the same trait or characteristic (e.g., eye color), but they contribute to different developmental outcomes (e.g., brown, blue, hazel, gray eyes).

Let's consider the simplest pattern of gene expression—the one discovered by Mendel and referred to as the *dominant–recessive pattern.* The explanation for this pattern (unknown to Mendel) is that some genes have only two alleles, one of which is **dominant** and the other **recessive.** In this pattern, there are two possibilities: (1) a person can inherit two of the same allele—two dominant or two recessive—and thus be **homozygous** for the trait in question; or (2) the person can inherit two different alleles—one dominant and the other recessive—and thus be **heterozygous** for the trait. When an individual is homozygous, with either two dominant or two recessive alleles, the corresponding trait will be expressed. When an individual is heterozygous for a trait, the instructions of the dominant allele will be expressed (see Figure 3.3).

The sex chromosomes present an interesting wrinkle in the story of dominance patterns. The X chromosome carries roughly 1500 genes, whereas the much smaller Y chromosome carries only about 200. Thus, when a female inherits a recessive allele on the X chromosome from her mother, she is likely to have a dominant allele on the chromosome from her father to suppress it, so she will not express the trait in question. In contrast, when a male inherits the same recessive allele on the X chromosome from his mother, he likely will not have a dominant allele from his father to override it, so he will express the trait. Males are thus more likely than females to suffer a variety of sex-linked inherited disorders caused by recessive alleles on their X chromosome (see Box 3.1).

Despite the traditional emphasis given to it, the dominant–recessive pattern of inheritance, in which a single gene affects a particular trait, pertains to relatively few human traits—such as hair color, blood type, abundance of body hair, and the like—as well as to a large number of genetic disorders. Much more commonly, a single gene can affect multiple traits; both alleles can be fully expressed or blended in heterozygous individuals; and some genes are expressed differently, depending on whether they are inherited from the mother or from the father.

Inheritance patterns are vastly more complicated for most of the traits and behaviors that are of primary interest to behavioral scientists. These traits, such as shyness, aggression, thrill-seeking, and language learning, involve **polygenic inheritance,** in which many different genes contribute to any given phenotypic outcome. For this reason, you should be skeptical whenever you encounter news headlines announcing the discovery of "a gene for" a complex human trait or predisposition.

alleles ■ two or more different forms of a gene

dominant allele ■ the allele that, if present, gets expressed

recessive allele ■ the allele that is not expressed if a dominant allele is present

homozygous ■ having two of the same allele for a trait

heterozygous ■ having two different alleles for a trait

polygenic inheritance ■ inheritance in which traits are governed by more than one gene

FIGURE 3.3 Mendelian inheritance patterns Pictured here are the Mendelian inheritance patterns for the offspring of two brown-haired parents who are both heterozygous for hair color. The allele for brown hair (B) is dominant, and that for blond hair (b) is recessive. Note that these parents have three chances out of four of producing children with brown hair. They have two chances in four of producing brown-haired children who carry the gene for blond hair.

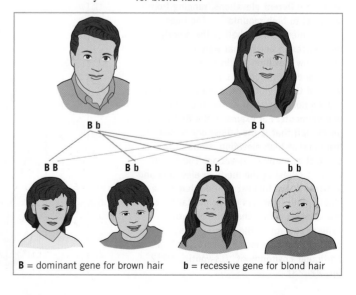

B = dominant gene for brown hair   **b** = recessive gene for blond hair

norm of reaction ▪ all the phenotypes that can theoretically result from a given genotype in relation to all the environments in which it can survive and develop

3. Child's Environment–Child's Phenotype

We now come to Relation 3 in our model—the impact of the environment on the child's phenotype. (Remember, the environment includes everything not in the genetic material itself, including the array of prenatal experiences discussed in Chapter 2.) Because of the continuous interaction of genotype and environment, a given genotype will develop differently in different environments. This idea is expressed by the concept of the **norm of reaction** (Dobzhansky, 1955), which refers to all the phenotypes that could theoretically result from a given genotype in relation to all the environments in which it could survive and develop. According to this concept, for any given genotype developing in varying environments, a range of outcomes would be possible. As will be seen in the discussion of emotional development in Chapter 10, children who are predisposed to be impulsive will exhibit more negative outcomes if raised in a hostile, abusive environment as opposed to a loving, supportive one. A similar relationship between genotype and environment influences aspects of the child's social development and gender development, among other areas of development. (Figure 3.4 offers a classic illustration of the norm of reaction in a genotype–environment interaction.)

Examples of genotype–environment interaction Genotype–environment interactions can be studied directly by randomly assigning nonhuman animals with known genotypes to be raised in a wide variety of environmental conditions.

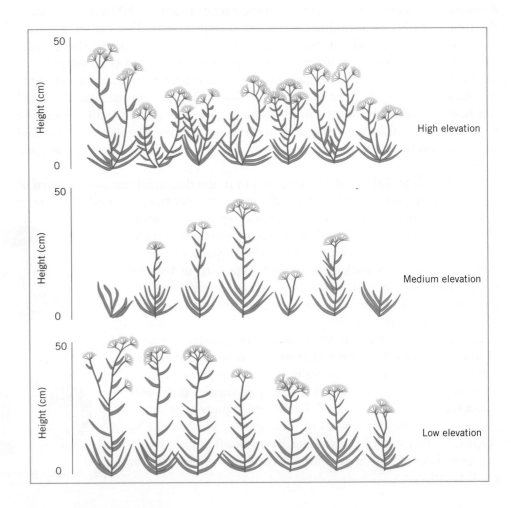

FIGURE 3.4 The norm of reaction concept This classic figure illustrates how a given genotype can develop differently in different environments. Three cuttings were made from each of seven individual plants; thus, the cuttings in each set of three had identical genes. The three cuttings from each plant were then planted at three different elevations, ranging from sea level to high mountains. The question of interest was whether the orderly differences in height that were observed at the low elevation would persist at the two higher elevations. As you can see, the order of the heights of the plants is neither orderly nor consistent across the different environments. For example, the first plant on the left that is the tallest one at sea level and at high elevation is one of the shortest at medium elevation. The fourth plant is tallest at the medium elevation and shortest at the highest. Notice that not a single plant is always either the tallest or the shortest across the three elevations. "The phenotype is the unique consequence of a particular genotype developing in a particular environment" (Lewontin, 1982, pp. 22–23).

If genetically identical animals develop differently in different environments, researchers can infer that environmental factors must be responsible for the different developmental outcomes. Scientists cannot, of course, randomly assign humans to different rearing conditions, but there are powerful naturally occurring examples of genotype–environment interactions for humans.

One such example is **phenylketonuria (PKU),** a disorder related to a defective recessive gene on chromosome 12. Individuals who inherit this gene from both parents cannot metabolize phenylalanine, an amino acid present in many foods (especially red meats) and in artificial sweeteners. If they eat a normal diet, phenylalanine accumulates in the bloodstream, causing impaired brain development that results in severe intellectual impairment. However, if infants with the PKU gene are identified shortly after birth and placed on a stringent diet free of phenylalanine, intellectual impairment can be avoided, as long as the diet is carefully maintained. Thus, a given genotype results in quite different phenotypes—cognitive disability or relatively normal intelligence—depending on environmental circumstances. Because early detection of this genetic disorder has such a positive effect on children's developmental outcomes, all newborn infants in the United States are routinely screened for PKU, as well as for a number of other severe and easily detected genetic disorders. In Box 3.2, we describe the role of genetic testing as it currently relates to children's development, including screening prior to pregnancy, fetal genetic testing, and newborn screening.

A second example of a genotype–environment interaction comes from an important study showing that the effects of abusive parenting vary in severity as a function of the child's genotype (Caspi et al., 2002). The researchers wanted to determine why some children who experience severe maltreatment become violent and antisocial as adults, whereas others who are exposed to the same abuse do not. The results, shown in Figure 3.5, revealed the importance of a *combination* of environmental *and* genetic factors leading to antisocial outcomes—suffering abusive treatment as a child *and* possessing a particular variant of MAOA, an X-linked gene known to inhibit brain chemicals associated with aggression. Young men who had a relatively inactive version of the MAOA gene, and who had experienced severe maltreatment, grew up to be more antisocial than other men. More concretely, 85% of the maltreated group with the relatively inactive gene developed some form of antisocial behavior, and they were almost 10 times more likely to be convicted of a violent crime.

The important point here is that neither factor by itself (possessing the inactive MAOA gene or being abused) predisposed boys to become highly aggressive; the higher incidence of antisocial behavior was observed only for the group with *both* factors. As the authors of that study note, knowledge about specific genetic risk factors that make people more susceptible to particular environmental effects could strengthen multiple-risk models, such as those discussed in the preceding two chapters. (We will revisit Caspi and colleagues' research on environment and genetics in the discussion of temperament in Chapter 10.)

Parental contributions to the child's environment Obviously, a highly salient and important part of a child's environment is the parents' relationship with the child—the manner in which they interact

phenylketonuria (PKU) ■ a disorder related to a defective recessive gene on chromosome 12 that prevents metabolism of the amino acid phenylalanine

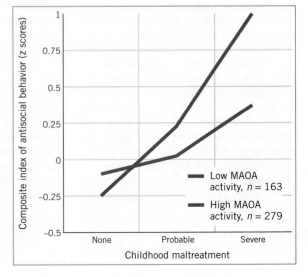

FIGURE 3.5 Genotype and environment This graph shows the level of antisocial behavior observed in young men as a function of the degree to which they had been maltreated in childhood. As this figure shows, those young men who had experienced severe maltreatment were in general more likely to engage in antisocial behavior than were those who had experienced none. However, the effect was much stronger for those individuals who had a relatively inactive MAOA gene. (Data from Caspi et al., 2002, p. 852)

BOX 3.2 | applications

GENETIC TESTING

As our depth of scientific knowledge about human genetics continues to increase, opportunities to use that knowledge to improve human health have become far more widespread. *Genetic testing* is one such application. Genetic testing can be done at any point in an individual's life span in order to diagnose a disease or find genetic clues that predict the likelihood of developing a disease. It is also increasingly used for *pharmacogenomics testing*: using information about an individual's genetic makeup to determine which course of treatment is most likely to be effective.

Genetic testing is frequently used prior to pregnancy to determine whether prospective parents are carriers of a specific disorder. The parents' racial and ethnic background can provide useful information about the likelihood that they carry certain deleterious mutations. For example, **carrier genetic testing** is typically offered to people of Eastern European Jewish descent (Ashkenazi Jews) because they have an increased likelihood of carrying the recessive gene for Tay Sachs disease, a severe birth defect that culminates in death by age 5. Similarly, this testing is typically offered to people of African descent because they have an increased likelihood of carrying the recessive gene for sickle-cell disease, in which red blood cells have an atypical sickle shape causing chronic anemia and pain. If both biological parents are carriers, there is a 25% chance that the child will inherit the atypical gene from both parents and develop the disease, and there is a 50% chance that the child will become a carrier of the disease. This information may influence the decision to become pregnant. Some parents opt for *in vitro fertilization* (IVF) with *preimplantation genetic diagnosis*, where the fertilized eggs are tested for the gene, and eggs that do not carry the gene are chosen for implantation into the mother's uterus.

Prenatal testing involves genetic testing during pregnancy. These tests are offered to all women in the United States and are especially encouraged for fetuses with risk factors that increase the likelihood of a genetic disorder (e.g., fetuses with older parents, as discussed in Chapter 2). Prenatal *screening tests* analyze maternal blood for information about degree of risk for genetic anomalies. Prenatal *diagnostic tests* detect genetic anomalies using fetal cells, either from the placenta (*chorionic villus sampling*, or CVS, usually done between 10 and 13 weeks of pregnancy) or from amniotic fluid (*amniocentesis*, usually done between 15 and 20 weeks of pregnancy). Screening tests are less invasive (and thus less risky) than diagnostic tests, but because they do not provide an actual diagnosis, they can lead to distressing *false positives* (incorrect indications of a disorder that is not actually present). For this reason, if the results of a screening test indicate elevated risk, parents may choose to proceed with diagnostic testing in order to get a definitive diagnosis.

Prenatal testing is used to assess risk for a range of genetic disorders, including *aneuploidy* (missing or extra chromosomes). The severity of the condition depends on the location of the chromosomal abnormality. Trisomy 21, the condition commonly known as Down syndrome, leads to the characteristic phenotype described in Box 3.1. Other trisomies, such as trisomy 18 (Edwards syndrome) and trisomy 13 (Patau syndrome), lead to extremely high rates of fetal and infant mortality. In order to help parents interpret the risks associated with positive genetic tests, they are encouraged to consult with genetic counselors. These health-care professionals, who receive extensive training in both genetics and counseling, can provide families with advice about how to interpret the findings of genetic tests and can offer resources to help them with the difficult decisions that often accompany the diagnosis of a genetic disorder.

Newborn screening is the largest genetic screening program in the United States (Rose & Dolan, 2012). Under this state-based program, all newborn infants are screened for a variety of disorders, both genetic and some that may or may not be of genetic origin (e.g., metabolic and endocrine disorders, hearing loss, and congenital heart disease). Newborns receive a tiny pinprick to their heel to get a blood sample, which is then tested for 30 to 50 different disease biomarkers. The National Institutes of Health's National Human Genome Research Institute is investigating the use of genome sequencing for potential use in newborn screening. Because gene sequencing has become so inexpensive, it may be possible to provide parents with more extensive information about their newborn infant's predisposition for particular diseases. This type of information could be useful in guiding a lifetime of medical care. However, this screening also raises important ethical concerns. Would insurance companies be justified for raising rates if newborn screening reveals an untreatable disease or detects a disorder that won't exhibit symptoms for decades? And could extensive genetic information lead to discrimination?

In 2008, the U.S. government passed the Genetic Information Nondiscrimination Act, intended to prohibit the use of genetic information in decisions about insurance or employment. However, as genetic information becomes ever more easily accessible to individuals through companies such as 23andme, the intersection between genetic testing and discrimination protections remains murky. It is also unclear how people without any training in human genetics will interpret the results of mail-order genetic tests. Whenever possible, parents should seek out trained professionals such as genetic counselors before making important decisions about their children's care.

with him or her; the general home environment they provide; the experiences they arrange for the child; the encouragement they offer for particular behaviors, attitudes, and activities; and so on. Less obvious is the idea that the environment parents provide for their children is due in part to the parents' own genetic makeup. These types of *gene–environment correlations* are observed frequently in the study of child development. Parents' behavior toward their children (e.g., how warm or reserved they are, how patient or short-fused) is genetically influenced, as are the kinds of preferences, activities, and resources to which they expose their children. For example, the child of a highly musical parent is likely to hear more music while growing up than are children whose parents are less musically inclined. Parents who are skilled readers and enjoy and value reading are likely to have lots of books around the house, read frequently to their children, and to take them to the library. In contrast, parents for whom reading is challenging and not a source of pleasure are less likely to provide a highly literate environment for their children. Thus, parents' genes influence not only their children's genes, but also their children's environments (e.g., Knafo & Jaffee, 2013). For these reasons, when researchers observe correlations between parents and children on some trait, such as reading ability (e.g., Swagerman et al., 2016), it is important to find ways to tease apart genetic contributions and environmental contributions, a topic we will address later in this chapter when we discuss behavior genetics designs.

This parent enjoys reading novels for pleasure and reads extensively for her work. She is providing a rich literary environment for her young child. The child may become an avid reader both because his mother's genetic makeup contributed to his enjoyment of reading and because of the physical environment (lots of books) and the social environment (encouragement of an interest in books) that the mother has provided.

4. Child's Phenotype–Child's Environment

Relation 4 in our model restates the *active child* theme—the child as a source of his or her own development. As noted in Chapter 1, children are not just the passive recipients of a preexisting environment. They are active creators of the environment in which they live in two important ways. First, by virtue of their nature and behavior, they actively evoke certain kinds of responses from others. The older child of one of the authors was a very outgoing baby. Because of his engaging personality, he created an environment filled with people—family and strangers alike—smiling and talking to him. The younger child, by contrast, was a very shy infant who actively avoided contact with strangers; her temperament limited the types of interactions she had with unfamiliar adults. Thus, these two children, despite living in the same home with the same parents, experienced very different early environments by virtue of their own behavior.

The second way in which children create their own environment is by actively selecting surroundings and experiences that match their interests, talents, and personality characteristics. As soon as infants become capable of self-locomotion, for example, they start selecting certain objects in the environment for exploration, rather than solely relying on their parents' choices of play objects. Beginning in the preschool years, children's friendship opportunities increasingly depend on their own characteristics, as they choose playmates and pals with whom they feel compatible—the "birds of a feather flock together" phenomenon. And, as noted in Chapter 1, with age, children play an ever more active role in selecting their own environment. As they gain more autonomy, they increasingly select aspects of the environment that fit their temperament and abilities. Returning to the reading example, children who enjoy reading will read more books than will children who find reading tedious. The more they read, the more skillful readers they become, leading them to choose increasingly more challenging books; this, in turn, leads

carrier genetic testing ■ genetic testing used to determine whether prospective parents are carriers of specific disorders

prenatal testing ■ genetic testing used to assess the fetus's risk for genetic disorders

newborn screening ■ tests used to screen newborn infants for a range of genetic and non-genetic disorders

them to acquire advanced vocabulary, improve their language comprehension, and enhance their general knowledge base, resulting in greater success in school. Children's ability to choose their own environment and activities has profound effects on intellectual development, as we will see in Chapter 8.

5. Child's Environment–Child's Genotype

The fifth relationship in our model is perhaps the most surprising. Until fairly recently, geneticists thought of the genotype as being "fixed" at birth. But as discussed in Chapter 1 (page 12), the field of *epigenetics* has turned this conventional wisdom on its head. That is, it is now known that although the structure of DNA remains "fixed" (mutations aside), certain epigenetic mechanisms, mediated by the environment, can alter the functioning of genes and create stable changes in their expression—and some of these changes can be passed on to the next generation.

Epigenetic factors can help explain why identical twins do not have identical pathways through life: different environments can alter gene expression in subtle ways across developmental time. These stable changes in gene expression that are mediated by the environment involve processes including *methylation*, which silences gene expression. Differences in experience over the course of development are reflected in differences in methylation levels. Consider identical twin pairs at age 3 and at age 50. Three-year-old co-twins have had highly overlapping life experiences, whereas many 50-year-old co-twins are likely to have had a far more divergent range of experiences. In a study that measured differences in DNA methylation levels in 3- and 50-year-old identical co-twins, researchers found that, whereas there were virtually no differences in the 3-year-olds' levels, roughly one-third of the 50-year-olds showed "remarkable" differences—and the greater the differences in the twins' lifestyle and experiences, the greater the differences in their methylation levels (Fraga et al., 2005).

How might the environment exert its effects through epigenetic mechanisms? To date, the bulk of the behavioral research on this topic has focused on non-human animal models, with clear evidence that low-quality maternal care has epigenetic effects, permanently changing the animal's pattern of gene expression (e.g., van IJzendoorn, Bakermans-Kranenburg, & Ebstein, 2011). In particular, poor maternal care affects the methylation of genes involved in glucocorticoid receptors, which influence how the animal copes with stress (e.g., T.-Y. Zhang & Meaney, 2010). As you saw in Chapter 1, emerging evidence suggests similar effects of early stress on methylation in humans (e.g., Essex et al., 2013). And indeed, a recent study suggests that children who experienced severe early life stress in the form of child maltreatment show similar patterns of methylation in the glucocorticoid receptor gene as do rodents who received poor parental care (Romens et al., 2015).

Our discussion of the relationships between genotypes, phenotypes, and environments has emphasized the myriad challenges in understanding how genes function in the development of individuals. Nevertheless, the conceptualization we have presented is greatly simplified. This is particularly true for the fifth relationship—epigenetics—which, when considered in full, suggests that the line between genes and environment is blurry at best. In the next section, we will explore the research designs and tools that researchers in the field of behavior genetics have used to make headway in teasing apart nature and nurture in the study of human development.

Review

The five relations shown in Figure 3.1 depict the complex interplay of genetic and environmental forces in development: (1) The course of children's development is influenced by the genetic heritage they receive from their mother and father, with their sex determined solely by their father's chromosomal contribution. (2) The relation between children's genotype and phenotype depends in part on dominance patterns in the expression of some genes, but most traits of primary interest to behavioral scientists are influenced by multiple genes (polygenic inheritance). (3) As the concept of norm of reaction specifies, any given genotype will develop differently in different environments. A particularly salient part of children's environment is their parents, including their parents' own genetic makeup, which influences how parents behave toward their children. (4) Children's own genetic makeup influences how they select and shape their own environment and the experiences they have in it. (5) Conversely, children's experiences can change their genetic expression through epigenetic mechanisms.

Behavior Genetics

The field of **behavior genetics** is concerned with how variation in behavior and development results from the interaction of genetic and environmental factors. Behavior geneticists ask the same sort of question Galton asked about eminence: "Why are people different from one another?" Why, in any group of human beings, do we vary in terms of how smart, sociable, depressed, aggressive, and religious we are? The answer given by behavior geneticists is that all behavioral traits are **heritable;** that is, they are all influenced to some degree by hereditary factors (Bouchard, 2004; Turkheimer, 2000). As noted, the kind of traits that have been of particular interest to behavior geneticists—intelligence, sociability, mood, aggression, and the like—are polygenic, that is, affected by the combination of many genes. They are also **multifactorial,** that is, affected by a host of environmental factors as well as genetic ones. Thus, the potential sources of variation are vast.

To fully answer Galton's question, behavior geneticists try to tease apart genetic and environmental contributions by taking advantage of the differences observed among a population of people or other animals. Two premises underlie this endeavor:

1. To the extent that genetic factors are important for a given trait or behavior, individuals who are genotypically similar should be phenotypically similar. In other words, behavior patterns should "run in families": children should be more similar to their parents and siblings than to second- or third-degree relatives or unrelated individuals.

2. To the extent that shared environmental factors are important, individuals who were reared together should be more similar than people who were reared apart.

Behavior Genetics Research Designs

As it was for Galton, the mainstay of modern behavior genetics research is the *family study.* In order to examine genetic and environmental contributions to a given trait or characteristic, behavior geneticists first measure that trait in people who vary in terms of genetic relatedness—parents and their children, identical and fraternal twins, non-twin siblings, and so on. Next, they assess how highly correlated

behavior genetics ■ the science concerned with how variation in behavior and development results from the combination of genetic and environmental factors

heritable ■ refers to any characteristics or traits that are influenced by heredity

multifactorial ■ refers to traits that are affected by a host of environmental factors as well as genetic ones

"The title of my science project is 'My Little Brother: Nature or Nurture.'"

the measures of the trait are among individuals who vary in the degree to which they are genetically related. (As you may recall from Chapter 1, the strength and direction of a correlation express the extent to which two variables are related; the higher the correlation, the more precisely scores on one variable can be predicted from scores on the other.) Finally, behavior geneticists compare the resulting correlations to see if they are (1) higher for more closely related individuals than for less closely related people, and (2) higher for individuals who share the same environment than for individuals who do not.

There are several specialized family-study designs that are particularly helpful in assessing genetic and environmental influences. One is the *twin-study* design, which compares the correlations for identical (monozygotic, or MZ) twins with those for same-sex fraternal (dizygotic, or DZ) twins. As you will recall, identical twins have 100% of their genes in common (though the expression of these genes is affected by epigenetic factors over the course of development, as discussed in the preceding section), whereas fraternal twins are only 50% genetically similar (just like non-twin siblings). For twins who grow up together, the degree of similarity of the environment is generally assumed to be equal. Known as the *equal environments assumption,* the claim is that both types of twins shared the same womb, were born at the same time, have lived in the same family and community, and are always the same age when tested. Thus, with different levels of genetic similarity and essentially equal environmental similarity, the difference between the correlations for the two types of twins is treated as an index of the importance of genetic factors. If the correlation between identical twins on a given trait or behavior is substantially higher than that between fraternal twins, it is assumed that genetic factors are substantially responsible for the difference.

Another family-study design used for assessing genetic and environmental influences is the *adoption* study. In this approach, researchers examine whether adopted children's scores on a given measure are correlated more highly with those of their biological parents and siblings or with those of their adoptive parents and siblings. Genetic influences are inferred to the extent that children resemble their biological relatives more than they do their adoptive ones.

The ideal behavior genetics design—the *adoptive twin* study—compares identical twins who grew up together versus identical twins who were separated shortly after birth and raised apart, like Oskar Stohr and Jack Yufa whom we discussed at the beginning of this chapter. If the correlations for twins reared apart are similar to those for twins reared together, it suggests that environmental factors have little effect. Conversely, to the extent that the correlations between identical twins who grew up in different environments are lower than those for identical twins who grew up together, environmental influence is inferred.

Family Studies of Intelligence

One of the most common focuses of behavior genetics family studies has been intelligence. Table 3.1 summarizes the results of more than 100 family studies of IQ through adolescence. The pattern of results

TABLE 3.1

Summary of Family Studies of Intelligence

Relationship	Average R Reared-together Biological Relatives	Number of Pairs
Average Familial IQ Correlations (R)		
MZ twins	0.86	4672
DZ twins	0.60	5533
Siblings	0.47	26,473
Parent–offspring	0.42	8433
Half siblings	0.35	200
Cousins	0.15	1176
Reared-apart Biological Relatives		
MZ twins	0.72	65
Siblings	0.24	203
Parent–offspring	0.24	720
Reared-together Nonbiological Relatives		
Siblings	0.32	714
Parent–offspring	0.24	720

Note: MZ = monozygotic; DZ = dizygotic
Source: McGue et al. (1993).

reveals both genetic and environmental influences. Genetic influence is shown by generally higher correlations for higher degrees of genetic similarity. Most notable is the finding that identical (MZ) twins resemble each other in IQ more than do same-sex fraternal (DZ) twins. At the same time, environmental influences are reflected in the fact that identical twins are not identical in terms of IQ. Further evidence for an environmental role is that MZ twins who are reared together are more similar than those reared apart.

Does the relative influence that genes and environment have on intelligence change over the course of development? One might expect that as children get older and have ever more (and more varied) experiences in the world, genetic influences on IQ would decrease. Surprisingly, the actual pattern is exactly the opposite: as twins get older, the degree of variance in IQ accounted for by their genetic similarity increases. In a study of 11,000 twin pairs across four countries, researchers found that the correlations in IQ between co-twins increased with age for MZ twins and decreased with age for DZ twins. These divergent patterns were observed first from childhood to adolescence, and again from adolescence to young adulthood (Haworth et al., 2010). The same pattern of results was revealed in a large longitudinal study that compared MZ and DZ twin pairs in early childhood (2- to 4-year-olds) and middle childhood (7- to 10-year-olds): for the younger children, shared environment accounted for more variance than did shared genes, with the opposite pattern observed for the older children (Davis, Haworth, & Plomin, 2009).

This surprising pattern of results—namely, that genetic influences on intelligence increase with age—is consistent with the idea that people actively construct their own environment: the phenotype–environment correlation (Relation 4) discussed earlier. As children get older, they increasingly control their own experiences, and their parents have less influence over their activities. The effects of education may be particularly relevant to this pattern of results, given that educational experiences and achievements influence children's performance on measurements of intelligence. Younger children have little or no choice about their educational setting and opportunities, whereas older children, teens, and young adults have increasingly greater choices with regard to their educational experiences (choosing more or less challenging courses of study, more or less academically oriented peer groups, and so on). These observations are consistent with evidence suggesting that grade school–aged twins are more similar in their educational achievement (literacy and mathematical skills) than in measures of intelligence (Kovas et al., 2013). As children have more opportunities to shape their own environments based on their genetic propensities, the genetic effects of intelligence become more prominent. By the end of high school, educational achievement is still genetically mediated, but the primary predictor is intelligence, followed by other genetically influenced traits such as personality and psychopathology (Krapohl et al., 2014).

Heritability

In their approach to the nature–nurture question, many behavior geneticists attempt to quantify the degree to which genes contribute to various traits. To estimate how much of the variability in measures of a given trait is attributable to genetic and environmental factors, they derive heritability estimates from correlations of the type shown in Table 3.1. **Heritability** is a statistical estimate of how

heritability ■ a statistical estimate of the proportion of the measured variance on a trait among individuals in a given population that is attributable to genetic differences among those individuals much of the measured variance on a trait among individuals in a given population is attributable to genetic differences among those individuals.

A crucial point to understand about heritability estimates is that they tell us nothing about the relative contributions of genetic and environmental factors to the development of an *individual.* Instead, they estimate how much of the variation among *a given population of people* is due to differences in their genes. The heritability estimate for intelligence, for example, is generally considered to be approximately 50% (Bouchard, 2004; Plomin, 1990). This means that, *for the population studied,* roughly 50% of the variation in IQ scores is due to genetic differences among the members of the population. (It does *not* mean that 50% of your IQ score is due to your genetic makeup and 50% is due to your experience.) Note that this heritability estimate indicates that the environmental contribution to the variation in IQ is also approximately 50%.

Behavior genetics analyses have been applied to many diverse aspects of human behavior, several of which you will encounter in other chapters of this book. Researchers believe that essentially all human traits that have been studied using behavior genetics designs are at least slightly heritable. One large meta-analysis of over 17,000 traits—with over 14 million twin pairs—found that heritability was greater than zero for every trait investigated in the analysis (Polderman et al., 2015). These traits include psychological traits like temperament, which we will discuss further in Chapter 10, as well as many other aspects of personality, cognition, and psychopathology (Plomin et al., 2016; Vukasović & Bratko, 2015). Physical traits such as "sidedness" (right, left, or mixed preferences for hands, feet, eyes, ears) are also heritable (Tran & Voracek, 2015), as are fairly specific psychological traits, including political beliefs and religiosity (Plomin et al., 2013).

The implausibility of "liberal" or "evangelical" genes brings us back to a point we made earlier: despite the common use of the phrase, there are no genes "for" particular behavior patterns. As we have stressed, genes do nothing more than code for proteins, so they affect behavior only insofar as those proteins affect the sensory, neural, and other physiological processes involved in behavior. In addition, *genome-wide association studies (GWAS)*, which are used in attempts to link specific DNA segments with particular traits, have revealed that genetic effects are cumulative. On their own, individual regions of chromosomes do not correlate with traits; it takes a combination of many genes, each with a small effect, to render a heritable trait (Plomin & Deary, 2015).

As compelling as they seem, heritability estimates have also been widely criticized. Part of the criticism stems from ways that the term "heritability" is often misinterpreted or misused by the public. One very common misuse involves the application of the concept of heritability to individuals, despite the fact that, as we have emphasized, *heritability applies only to populations.*

In addition, *a heritability estimate applies only to a particular population living in a particular environment.* Consider the case of height. Research conducted almost exclusively with North Americans and Europeans—most of them White and adequately nourished—puts the heritability of height at around 90%. But what if some segment of this population had experienced a severe famine during childhood, while the rest remained well fed? Would the heritability estimate for height still be 90%? No—because the variability due to environmental factors (poor nutrition) would *increase* dramatically; therefore, the variability that could be attributed to genetic factors would *decrease* to the same degree. The principle of variable heritability also appeared in the discussion of

IQ correlations earlier in this chapter, with the heritability estimates derived from them differing for the same individuals at different points in development (Davis et al., 2009).

Furthermore, it is known that heritability estimates can differ markedly for groups of people who grow up in very different economic circumstances. In the United States, for instance, heritability estimates differ considerably as a function of socioeconomic status (SES), as shown by a large twin study that included families across the SES spectrum (Turkheimer et al., 2003). In this study, almost 60% of the variance in IQ among a sample of 7-year-olds living in poverty was accounted for by shared environment, with almost none of it attributable to genetic similarity. Affluent families follow the opposite pattern, with genetic factors contributing more than environmental ones. In a related study focused on the test scores of adolescent twins, the same pattern was observed: environmental factors trumped genetic factors for poorer teens, while genetic factors trumped environmental factors for wealthier teens (Harden, Turkheimer, & Loehlin, 2007). Although it is not fully clear what causes these differing levels of heritability, both studies suggest that qualitatively different developmental forces may be operating in poor versus affluent environments.

A related, frequently misunderstood point is that *high heritability does not imply immutability*. The fact that a trait is highly heritable does not mean that there is little point in trying to improve the course of development related to that trait. Thus, for example, the fact that the heritability estimate for IQ is relatively high does not mean that the intellectual performance of young children living in poverty cannot be improved by appropriate intervention efforts (see Chapter 8).

Finally, recall the *equal environments assumption:* the claim, underlying many behavior genetics designs, that MZ twins share environments that are equally similar as those shared by DZ twins. If this assumption is not correct—that is, if MZ twins are both genetically more similar and have more similar environments than DZ twins—the confounding of similarity of genes and environments would bias heritability estimates. Traits would appear to be more heritable than they actually are. Clever research designs, including studies of adopted children, and research with twin pairs who were misclassified earlier in life (such that they were treated as more or less similar than they actually are) generally support the equal environments assumption, though criticisms remain (e.g., Conley et al., 2013; Felson, 2014; Matteson, McGue, & Iacono, 2013).

Innovations in molecular genetic techniques are providing new approaches to the study of heritability that may address some of the shortcomings of classic behavior genetics studies. Heritability estimates have traditionally been limited to comparisons based on within-family relationships, but DNA-based methods permit the analysis of genetic influences in large samples of unrelated individuals. One such method, *genome-wide complex trait analysis (GCTA)* takes advantage of actual genetic resemblance across large groups of individuals, rather than estimates of genetic resemblance based on family relationships (Rietveld et al., 2013). By measuring actual genetic similarity, it is possible to tease apart aspects of genes and environment that are confounded within families (e.g., Plomin, 2014). For example, SES is difficult to integrate into traditional measures of heritability because it is shared by twins within families. One recent study used GCTA to determine whether the effects of family SES on school achievement are genetically mediated—a question that could not be answered using traditional twin-based behavior genetics methods (Krapohl & Plomin, 2016). Using a large representative sample of unrelated British schoolchildren, the researchers found that genetic factors explained a substantial portion of the variance in school achievement. More surprisingly, genetic factors accounted for fully half of the correlation between school achievement scores and family SES. Children's educational attainments and social advantage appear to share some of the same genetic roots.

GCTA has also allowed researchers to determine whether the same genes are implicated in measures of a particular trait across development. For example, recall from our earlier discussion of intelligence that heritability tends to increase over age. Since this discovery was first made, researchers have wondered whether this change is due to gene–environment correlations, as discussed above—namely, that with increasing age and independence, children can select their own environments—or whether, instead, different genes affect intelligence at different times in development. By analyzing the DNA of a large sample of children from 7 to 12 years of age, researchers were able to uncover evidence of genetic stability: the same genes are implicated in heritable aspects of intelligence across this age span, with increasing effects of heritability across age (Trzaskowski et al., 2014). Thus, molecular genetic approaches hold promise in providing new ways to answer existing questions about our genetic endowment, while raising many new questions. For example, to the extent that genetic effects on intelligence are mediated by individual differences in brain structure and function, GCTA focused on endophenotypes may help us better understand the relationship between the brain and complex behaviors like intelligence or academic achievement.

Environmental Effects

Every examination of genetic contributions to behavior and development is also necessarily a study of environmental influences: estimating heritability automatically estimates the proportion of variance not attributable to genes. Because heritability estimates rarely exceed 50%, a large contribution from environmental factors is usually indicated.

Behavior geneticists try to assess the extent to which aspects of an environment shared by biologically related people make them more alike and to what extent non-shared experiences make them different. The most obvious source of shared environment is growing up in the same family. Shared-environment effects can also be inferred when twins or other relatives are more similar on some trait than would be expected on the basis of their genetic relatedness. For example, substantial shared-environmental influence has been inferred for positive emotion in toddlers and young children because fraternal and identical twins who were reared together were equally similar in the degree to which they showed pleasure (Goldsmith, Buss, & Lemery, 1997). Shared-environment effects are also being discovered for disorders that have a clear genetic component. For instance, as discussed in Box 3.1, twin studies of autism spectrum disorder (ASD) have consistently provided evidence for genetic effects (with heritability of the disorder being greater for MZ twins than for DZ twins). However, in a recent large-scale study of twin pairs in which at least one co-twin had an ASD diagnosis, researchers found a substantial shared-environment effect on the likelihood that the second twin also had an ASD diagnosis (Hallmayer et al., 2011).

Behavior geneticists' investigations of the effects of non-shared environments arise from the recognition that even children who grow up in the same family do not have all their experiences in common—either inside or outside the family. Indeed, most effects of environment in behavior genetics designs are not shared by children within the same family (Plomin et al., 2016). This may be due to aspects of the family structure. For example, birth order may result in quite different experiences for siblings. The oldest child in a large family may have been reared by young, energetic, but inexperienced, parents, whereas that child's much younger sibling will be parented by older and more sedentary, but more knowledgeable, individuals who are likely to have more resources available than they did as first-time parents. In addition, as discussed in Chapter 1, siblings may experience their parents' behavior toward them differently (the "Mom always loved you best" syndrome).

Outside the family, siblings can also have highly divergent experiences, partly as a result of belonging to different peer groups. Highly active siblings who both like physical challenges and thrills will have very different experiences if one takes up rock climbing while the other hangs out with delinquent peers. Idiosyncratic life events—suffering a serious accident, having an inspiring teacher, being bullied on the playground—can contribute further to the development of individual differences among siblings. Much like the action of genetic factors, in which many genes of small effect work together to influence development, the effects of the environment are likely due to many experiences of small effect working together.

Review

The field of behavior genetics is concerned with how development results from the interaction of genetic and environmental factors. Using the family-study methodology, behavior geneticists compare the correlations among individuals who vary in the degree of genetic relatedness and in similarity of their rearing environments. Contemporary methods like GCTA have allowed researchers to move beyond twin or adoption designs to consider actual genetic overlap among unrelated people. Heritability estimates indicate the proportion of the variance among individuals in a given population on a given trait that is attributable to genetic differences among them. Most behavioral traits that have been measured show substantial heritability; at the same time, heritability estimates reveal the close partnership of heredity and environment in development and the fallacy of considering the influences of nature and nurture as independent of each other.

Brain Development

As you will see, the collaboration between nature and nurture takes center stage in the development of the brain and nervous system. The brain is the font of all thought, memory, emotion, imagination, personality—in short, the behavior, capacities, and characteristics that make us who we are.

Structures of the Brain

In our examination of the structures of the brain, we focus our discussion on two that are central to behavior—the neuron and the cortex, as well as some of their substructures.

neurons ■ cells that are specialized for sending and receiving messages between the brain and all parts of the body, as well as within the brain itself

cell body ■ a component of the neuron that contains the basic biological material that keeps the neuron functioning

dendrites ■ neural fibers that receive input from other cells and conduct it toward the cell body in the form of electrical impulses

axons ■ neural fibers that conduct electrical signals away from the cell body to connections with other neurons

Neurons

The business of the brain is information. The basic units of the brain's remarkably powerful informational system are its more than 100 billion **neurons** (Figure 3.6), which constitute the gray matter of the brain. These cells are specialized for sending and receiving messages between the brain and all parts of the body, as well as within the brain itself. *Sensory neurons* transmit information from sensory receptors that detect stimuli in the external environment or within the body itself. *Motor neurons* transmit information from the brain to muscles and glands; and *interneurons* act as intermediaries between sensory and motor neurons.

Although they vary substantially in size, shape, and function, all neurons are made up of three main components: (1) a **cell body,** which contains the basic biological material that keeps the neuron functioning; (2) **dendrites,** fibers that receive input from other cells and conduct it toward the cell body in the form of electrical impulses; and (3) an **axon,** a fiber (anywhere from a few micrometers to more than a meter in length) that conducts electrical signals away from the cell body to connections with other neurons.

FIGURE 3.6 The neuron The cell body manufactures proteins and enzymes, which support cell functioning, as well as the chemical substances called neurotransmitters, which facilitate communication among neurons. The axon is the long shaft that conducts electrical impulses away from the cell body. Many axons are covered with a myelin sheath, which enhances the speed and efficiency with which signals travel along the axon. Branches at the end of the axon have terminals that release neurotransmitters into the synapses—the small spaces between the axon terminals of one neuron and the dendrites or cell body of another. The dendrites conduct impulses toward the cell body. An axon can have synapses with thousands of other neurons. (Information from Banich, 1997)

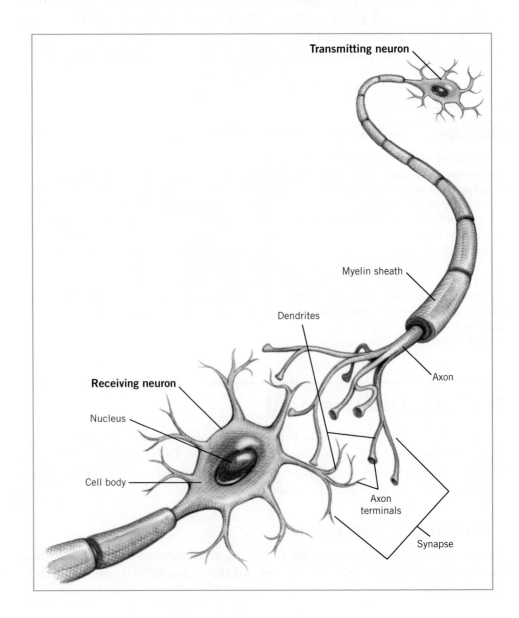

Transmitting neuron

Myelin sheath

Dendrites

Axon

Receiving neuron

Nucleus

Cell body

Axon terminals

Synapse

Neurons communicate with one another at **synapses,** which are microscopic junctions between the axon terminal of one neuron and the dendritic branches of another. In this communication process, electrical and chemical messages cross the synapses and cause the receiving neurons either to fire, sending a signal on to other neurons, or to be inhibited from firing. The total number of synapses in the human brain is staggering—hundreds of trillions—with some neurons having as many as 15,000 synaptic connections with other neurons.

Glial Cells

Glial cells are another essential component of the brain. Until recently, it was believed that glial cells outnumbered neurons 10 to 1. However, with the advent of new methods of cell counting, recent studies suggest that the glial cells and neurons actually appear in equal numbers (von Bartheld, Bahney, & Herculano-Houzel, 2016). Glial cells perform a variety of critical functions, including the formation of a **myelin sheath** around axons, which insulates them and increases the speed and efficiency of information transmission. The importance of myelin is highlighted by the severe consequences that can arise from disorders that affect it. For example, multiple sclerosis is a disease in which the immune system attacks myelin, interfering with neuronal signaling and producing varying degrees of physical and cognitive impairment. Myelin is also implicated in mental illness: individuals with schizophrenia show disruptions in white matter that have been linked to multiple genes that regulate myelination (e.g., Chavarria-Siles et al., 2016).

Glial cells also play a key supportive role in promoting brain health. They function as neural stem and progenitor cells during brain development, and some subsets of these cells continue to do so into adulthood. When the brain is injured, certain types of glial cells react by rapidly increasing in numbers, protecting the brain and potentially aiding in regeneration (e.g., Dimou & Götz, 2014).

The Cortex

Over the course of human evolution, the brain has expanded greatly in size. Almost all of this increase occurred in the **cerebral cortex,** which constitutes 80% of the human brain, a much greater proportion than in other species. The folds and fissures that are apparent in Figure 3.7 form during development as the brain grows within the confined space of the skull; these convolutions make it possible to pack more cortex into the limited space.

The cortex plays a primary role in a wide variety of mental functions, from seeing and hearing to reading, writing, and doing arithmetic to feeling compassion and communicating with others. As Figure 3.7 shows, the major areas of the cortex—the **lobes**—can be characterized in terms of the general behavioral categories with which they are associated. The **occipital lobe** is primarily involved in processing visual information. The **temporal lobe** is associated with memory, visual recognition, speech and language, and the processing of emotion and auditory information. The **parietal lobe** is important for spatial processing. It is also involved in the integration of information from different sensory modalities, and it plays a role in integrating sensory input with information stored in memory and with information about internal states. The **frontal lobe,** the brain's "executive," is involved in cognitive control, including working memory, planning, decision making, and inhibitory control. Information from multiple sensory systems is processed and integrated in the **association areas** that lie in between the major

synapses ■ microscopic junctions between the axon terminal of one neuron and the dendritic branches or cell body of another

glial cells ■ cells in the brain that provide a variety of critical supportive functions

myelin sheath ■ a fatty sheath that forms around certain axons in the body and increases the speed and efficiency of information transmission

cerebral cortex ■ the "gray matter" of the brain that plays a primary role in what is thought to be particularly humanlike functioning, from seeing and hearing to writing to feeling emotion

lobes ■ major areas of the cortex associated with general categories of behavior

occipital lobe ■ the lobe of the cortex that is primarily involved in processing visual information

temporal lobe ■ the lobe of the cortex that is associated with memory, visual recognition, and the processing of emotion and auditory information

parietal lobe ■ governs spatial processing as well as integrating sensory input with information stored in memory

frontal lobe ■ associated with organizing behavior; the one that is thought responsible for the human ability to plan ahead

association areas ■ parts of the brain that lie between the major sensory and motor areas and that process and integrate input from those areas

FIGURE 3.7 The human cerebral cortex This view of the left hemisphere of an adult brain shows the four major cortical regions—known as the lobes—which are divided from one another by deep fissures. Each of the primary sensory areas receives information from a particular sensory system, and the primary motor cortex controls the body's muscles. Information from multiple sensory areas is processed in association areas.

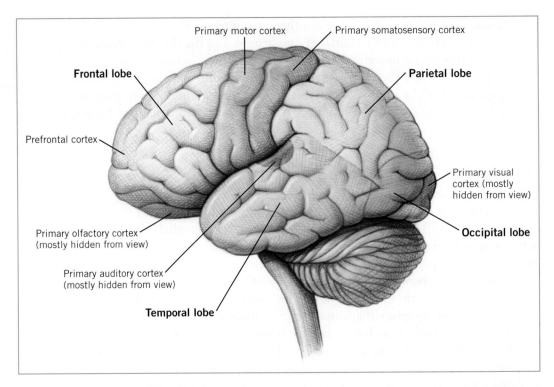

Primary motor cortex

Primary somatosensory cortex

Frontal lobe

Parietal lobe

Prefrontal cortex

Primary visual cortex (mostly hidden from view)

Primary olfactory cortex (mostly hidden from view)

Occipital lobe

Primary auditory cortex (mostly hidden from view)

Temporal lobe

sensory and motor areas. The parts of the human brain that have evolved to be most enlarged compared with other species are also those that grow the most as children develop: prefrontal, parietal, and temporal cortices (e.g., Kaas, 2013). Other brain regions, including sensory and motor areas, expanded less during the evolution of the human brain.

Although it is convenient to think of different cortical areas as if they were functionally specific, they are not. It has become increasingly clear that complex mental functions are mediated by multiple areas of the brain, with an extraordinary degree of interactivity both within and across brain regions. A given area may be critical for some ability, but this does not mean that control of that ability is located in that one area. (Box 3.3 examines some of the techniques that researchers use to learn about brain functioning.)

Cerebral lateralization The cortex is divided into two separate halves, or **cerebral hemispheres.** For the most part, sensory input from one side of the body goes to the opposite side of the brain, and the motor areas of the cortex control movements of the opposite side of the body. Thus, if you pick up a hot pot with your right hand, it is the left side of the brain that receives the sensory response, registers the pain, and initiates the motor response to let go immediately.

The left and right hemispheres of the brain communicate with each other primarily by way of the **corpus callosum,** a dense tract of nerve fibers that connects them. The two hemispheres are specialized for different modes of processing, a phenomenon referred to as **cerebral lateralization.** There are notable similarities across species in hemispheric specialization. For example, most aspects of speech and language are lateralized to the left hemisphere in humans, with a similar asymmetry observed for communicative signals in nonhuman species from mice to primates (Corballis, 1999). However, contrary to popular belief, the data do not support the idea that people are left brain–dominant or right brain–dominant; individuals do not tend to have a general preference to use one hemisphere over the other (e.g., Nielsen et al., 2013).

cerebral hemispheres ■ the two halves of the cortex; for the most part, sensory input from one side of the body goes to the opposite hemisphere of the brain

corpus callosum ■ a dense tract of nerve fibers that enable the two hemispheres of the brain to communicate

cerebral lateralization ■ the specialization of the hemispheres of the brain for different modes of processing

Developmental Processes

How does the incredibly complex structure of the human brain come into being? You will not be surprised to hear that, once again, a partnership of nature and nurture is involved. Some aspects of the construction of the brain are set in motion and tightly controlled by the genes, relatively independent of experience. But, as you will see, other aspects are profoundly influenced by experience.

Neurogenesis and Neuron Development

Neurogenesis, the proliferation of neurons through cell division, begins 42 days after conception (in humans) and is virtually complete by the midway point of gestation (Stiles & Jernigan, 2010). Thus, most of the roughly 100 billion neurons you currently possess have been with you since before you were born. Notably, however, we do continue to generate new neurons throughout life. During bouts of learning, for example, neurogenesis occurs in the hippocampus, a brain region important for memory processes (Gould et al., 1999). Neurogenesis does not always occur, however: it can be inhibited by stress (Mirescu & Gould, 2006). This pattern of results suggests that neurogenesis later in life is not fixed and predetermined but is instead adaptive, increasing under rewarding conditions and decreasing in threatening environments (e.g., Glasper, Schoenfeld, & Gould, 2012).

After their "birth," neurons begin the second developmental process, which involves migration to their ultimate destinations—typically outwards from the center of the brain toward the developing neocortex. Some neurons are pushed along passively by the newer cells formed after them, whereas others actively propel themselves toward their ultimate location. Early in gestation, the brain is very small so the distances traveled are quite short. But as the brain grows, neurons require guides, in the form of a special kind of glial cell (radial glial cells) that provides scaffolding for neurons, to correctly find their destinations.

Once neurons reach their destination, cell growth and differentiation occur. Neurons first grow an axon and then a "bush" of dendrites (refer back to Figure 3.6). Thereafter, they take on the specific structural and functional characteristics of the different structures of the brain. Axons elongate as they grow toward specific targets, which, depending on the neuron in question, might be anything from another neuron in the brain to a bone in the big toe. The main change in dendrites is "arborization"—an enormous increase in the size and complexity of the dendritic "tree" that results from growth, branching, and the formation of **spines** on the branches. Arborization enormously increases the dendrites' capacity to form connections with other neurons. In the cortex, the period of most intense growth and differentiation comes after birth.

The process of **myelination,** the formation of the insulating myelin sheath around some axons, begins in the brain before birth and continues into early adulthood. The myelinated portions of axons are white, leading to the term *white matter,* and lie below the *gray matter* (cell bodies) at the surface of the cortex. As noted earlier, a crucial function of myelin is to increase the speed of neural conduction. Myelination begins deep in the brain and moves upward and outward into the cortex. This process occurs rapidly for the first few months after birth, slows somewhat during toddlerhood, and continues slowly into young adulthood (e.g., Dubois et al., 2014). The various cortical areas thus become myelinated at very different rates, possibly contributing to the different rates of development for various behaviors.

neurogenesis ■ the proliferation of neurons through cell division

spines ■ formations on the dendrites of neurons that increase the dendrites' capacity to form connections with other neurons

myelination ■ the formation of myelin (a fatty sheath) around the axons of neurons that speeds and increases information-processing abilities

 Brain Development: Prenatal, Infants, and Toddlers

 Brain Development: Myelination

BOX 3.3 | a closer look

MAPPING THE MIND

Developmental scientists employ a variety of techniques to determine what areas of the brain are associated with particular behaviors, thoughts, and feelings, as well as how brain functions change with age. The existence of increasingly powerful techniques for investigating brain function has sparked a revolution in the understanding of the brain and its development. Here, we provide examples of some of the techniques most often used to map the mind and its workings in children.

Electrophysiological Recording

One of the techniques most often used by developmental researchers to study brain function is based on *electroencephalographic* (*EEG*) recordings of electrical activity generated by neurons. EEG is completely noninvasive (the recordings are obtained through an electrode cap that simply rests on the scalp and can contain hundreds of electrodes), so this method can be used successfully even with infants (see photo). EEG recordings provide detailed information about the time course of neural events and have provided valuable information about a variety of brain-behavior relations.

An electrophysiological technique that is very useful for studying the relation between brain activity and specific kinds of stimulation is the recording of **event-related potentials (ERPs)**,

that is, changes in the brain's electrical activity that occur in response to the presentation of a particular stimulus. One contribution these measures have made is that they reveal continuity over time. For instance, studies of infants' ERPs in response to native-speech sounds have shown that infants' ability to discriminate among these sounds predicts their language growth over the next few years (Kuhl et al., 2008). A related method, called *magneto-encephalography* (*MEG*), detects magnetic fields generated by electrical currents in the brain. MEG has the added benefit of being the only noninvasive imaging method that can be used to study the fetal brain. Researchers have used MEG to detect fetal

neural responses to auditory stimuli and flashes of light displayed on the mother's abdomen, as well as habituation responses to repeated stimuli (Sheridan et al., 2010). MEG has also allowed researchers to answer more complex questions, such as whether fetuses are sensitive to the number of sounds in a sequence. Just like adults and newborns, fetuses' brains detect when a repeated auditory sequence changes in number, suggesting that during the last trimester, fetuses are encoding information about repetitions of sounds (Schleger et al., 2014).

 Event-Related Potential Research

Functional Magnetic Resonance Imaging

Functional magnetic resonance imaging (*fMRI*) uses a powerful electromagnet to detect fluctuations in cerebral blood flow in different areas of the brain. (fMRI is distinct from structural MRI, which essentially takes a snapshot of the brain.) In fMRI, increased blood flow indicates increased activity, so this technology allows researchers to determine which areas of the brain are activated by different tasks and stimuli. Because a person must be able to tolerate the noise and close confinement of an MRI machine and must also be able to remain very

OLI SCARFF / GETTY IMAGES

This EEG cap holds electrodes snugly against the baby's scalp, enabling researchers to record electrical activity generated from all over the baby's brain.

event-related potentials (ERPs) ■ changes in the brain's electrical activity that occur in response to the presentation of a particular stimulus

This pattern diverges in interesting ways from the pattern found in one of our closest primate relatives, the chimpanzee. Initially, white matter develops more slowly in the prefrontal lobes of infant and juvenile chimpanzees than it does in young humans, suggesting one possible mechanism whereby evolutionary pressure has improved human brain function relative to that of other primates (Sakai et al., 2011). Interestingly, however, the chimpanzee shows a mature pattern of myelination at the point of sexual maturity, far earlier than that observed in humans (Miller et al., 2012). The reasons for the extended period of human myelination remain unknown and might be both positive (facilitating

still, most developmental fMRI studies have been done with children aged 6 years or older, often using practice sessions in a mock scanner to help children acclimate to the MRI environment. However, recent studies have used fMRI methods to investigate neural processes in sleeping infants as young as 2 days old. One such study demonstrated that the areas of the brain that are activated by spoken language from later infancy onward are also activated by speech in neonates (Perani et al., 2011).

Two applications of fMRI that have become increasingly prominent in studies of child development are diffusion tensor imaging (DTI) and resting-state functional magnetic resonance imaging (rs-fMRI). These methods allow researchers to study how brain networks develop. DTI is a variant of conventional MRI that uses the rate of water diffusion as a way to model 3-D spatial location. This technique permits estimates of the white-matter tracts described in the text, and it has been used to model white-matter development and myelination over the course of early postnatal development (Dubois et al., 2014). Resting-state fMRI measures brain activity in the absence of any external stimuli. The results of rs-fMRI studies reveal early-emerging brain networks in infancy, with connections between hemispheres similar to those observed in older children and adults (Cusack et al., 2016).

Other Techniques

Positron emission tomography (*PET*) measures brain activity by detecting the brain's metabolic processes and has provided important information about brain

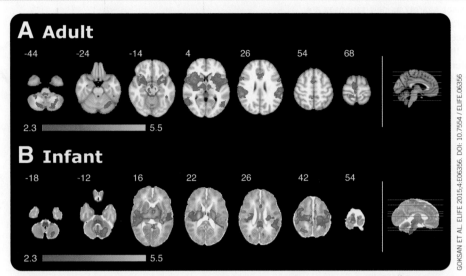

fMRI images This figure shows the areas of the adult and newborn brain that are revealed by fMRI as responsive to mild pain (pinprick sensations). While there are some differences in activation, the patterns are broadly similar across these disparate age groups (Goksan et al., 2015).

GOKSAN ET AL. ELIFE 2015;4:E06356. DOI: 10.7554 / ELIFE.06356

development. However, because PET scans involve injecting radioactive material into the brain, this technique is used primarily for diagnostic purposes.

One of the newest methods to be used in developmental studies is *near-infrared spectroscopy* (*NIRS*), an optical imaging technique that measures neural activity by detecting metabolic changes that lead to differential absorption of infrared light in brain tissue. The infrared light is transmitted to the brain, and its absorption is detected by means of an optical-fiber skullcap or headband. Because NIRS is silent, noninvasive, and does not require rigid stabilization of the head, it is particularly promising for research with infants and

young children. One particularly interesting application of NIRS involved a study of deaf children who had just received a cochlear implant, a surgically implanted electronic hearing device that we will discuss in Chapter 6. Because of concerns about the effects of its magnetic field, fMRI cannot be used to study brain processes in individuals with implants. NIRS was thus used to determine whether the auditory cortices of these children could respond to auditory stimulation. The NIRS showed that, rather remarkably, the auditory cortex of deaf children responded to sound within hours after the implant was activated, even though the cortex had never before been exposed to sound (Sevy et al., 2010).

improvements in executive functions after sexual maturity) and negative (making the human brain more vulnerable to disorders related to myelination, discussed on page 115).

Synaptogenesis

One result of the extraordinary growth of axonal and dendritic fibers is a wildly exuberant generation of neuronal connections. In a process called **synaptogenesis,** each neuron forms synapses with thousands of others, resulting in the formation of the trillions

synaptogenesis ■ the process by which neurons form synapses with other neurons, resulting in trillions of connections

FIGURE 3.8 Synapse production and elimination Mean synaptic density (the number of synapses in a given space) first increases sharply as new synapses are overproduced and later declines gradually as excess synapses are eliminated. Note that the time scale is compressed at later stages. (Information from P. R. Huttenlocher & Dabholkar, 1997)

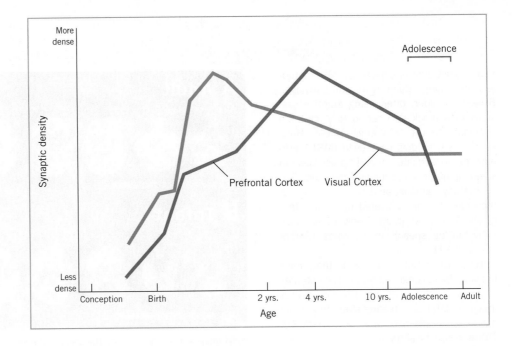

Brain Growth: Infancy Through Age 18

synaptic pruning ■ the normal developmental process through which synapses that are rarely activated are eliminated

of connections referred to earlier. Figure 3.8 shows the time course of synaptogenesis in the cortex. As you can see, it begins prenatally and proceeds very rapidly both before birth and for some time afterward. Note that both the timing and rate of synapse production vary for different cortical areas; synapse generation is complete much earlier in the visual cortex, for example, than in the frontal area. As with myelination, the differential timing of synapse generation across areas of the brain likely contributes to the developmental timing of the onset of various abilities and behaviors.

Synapse Elimination

The explosive generation of neurons and synapses during synaptogenesis results in a huge surplus—many more neural connections than any one brain can use. This overabundance of synapses includes an excess of connections between different parts of the brain: for instance, many neurons in what will become the auditory cortex are linked with those in the visual area, and both of these areas are overly connected to neurons involved in taste and smell. As a consequence of this hyperconnectivity, infants may experience *synesthesia*—the blending of different types of sensory input—because the functional connections between sensory areas have yet to be pruned (e.g., Spector & Maurer, 2009). In the case of the extra connections between auditory and visual cortex, for example, auditory stimulation may produce both auditory and visual sensations.

We now come to what is one of the most remarkable facts about the development of the human brain. Approximately 40% of this great synaptic superfluity is eliminated in a developmental process known as **synaptic pruning.** As you learned in the preceding chapter, cell death is a normal part of development, and nowhere is that more evident than in the systematic pruning of excess synapses that continues for years after birth. This pruning occurs at different times in different areas of the brain. You can see from Figure 3.8 that synapse elimination in the visual cortex begins near the end of the 1st year of life and continues until roughly 10 years of age, whereas synapse elimination in the prefrontal area shows a slower time course.

The brain undergoes substantial changes during adolescence, including a wave of overproduction and pruning akin to that in the first years of life (Giedd et al., 1999; Gogtay et al., 2004). Although the amount of white matter in the cortex shows a steady increase from childhood well into adulthood, the amount of gray matter increases dramatically starting around 11 or 12 years of age. The increase in gray matter proceeds rapidly, peaks around puberty, and then begins to decline as some of it is replaced by white matter (see Figure 3.9). The last area of the cortex to mature is the dorsolateral prefrontal cortex, which is vital for regulating attention, controlling impulses, foreseeing consequences, setting priorities, and other executive functions. It does not reach adult dimensions until after the age of 20, and synaptic pruning continues until individuals are in their 30s (Petanjek et al., 2011). Some subcortical areas, such as the thalamus, show similarly protracted developmental trajectories (Raznahan et al., 2014). Studies like these demonstrate clearly that our brains change substantially over the first few decades of life. As described in the next section, our experiences play a large role in this process, sculpting what will eventually become the mature brain.

The Importance of Experience

What factors determine which of the brain's excess synapses will be pruned and which maintained? Experience plays a central role in what is essentially a case of "use it or lose it." In a competitive process that has been dubbed "neural Darwinism" (Edelman, 1987), those synapses that are frequently activated are selectively preserved. The more often a synapse is activated, the stronger the connection becomes between the neurons involved: in short, neurons that fire together wire together (Hebb, 1949). Conversely, when a synapse is rarely active, it is likely to disappear: the axon of one neuron withdraws and the dendritic spine of the other is "pruned away."

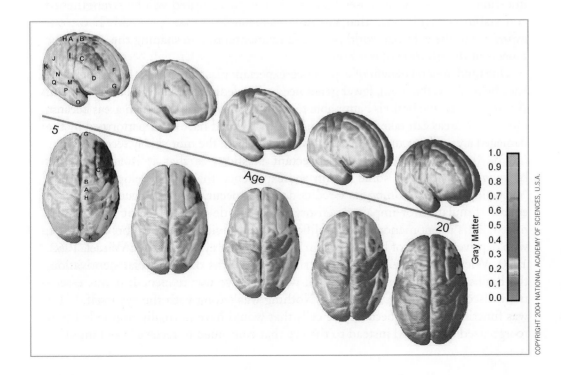

FIGURE 3.9 Brain maturation These views of the right side and top of the brain of 5- to 20-year-olds illustrate maturation over the surface of the cortex. The averaged MRI images come from participants whose brains were scanned repeatedly at 2-year intervals. The bluer the image, the more mature that part of the cortex is (i.e., the more gray matter has been replaced with white matter). Notice that the parts of the cortex associated with more basic functions (i.e., the sensory and motor areas toward the back) mature earlier than the areas involved in higher functions (i.e., attention, executive functioning). Notice particularly that the frontal areas, involved in executive functioning, approach maturity only in early adulthood. (Information from Gogtay et al., 2004)

plasticity ■ the capacity of the brain to be affected by experience

experience-expectant plasticity ■ the process through which the normal wiring of the brain occurs in part as a result of experiences that every human who inhabits any reasonably normal environment will have

The obvious question now is: Why does the human brain—the product of millions of years of evolution—take such a devious developmental path, producing a huge excess of synapses, only to get rid of a substantial proportion of them? The answer appears to be evolutionary economy. The capacity of the brain to be molded or changed by experience, referred to as **plasticity,** means that less information needs to be encoded in the genes. This economizing may, in fact, be a necessity: the number of genes involved in the formation and functioning of the nervous system is enough to specify only a very small fraction of the normal complement of neurons and neural connections. In addition, if brain structures were entirely hard-wired, organisms would be unable to adapt to their postnatal environment. To complete the final wiring of the brain, *nurture* joins forces with *nature.*

The collaboration between nature and nurture in building the brain occurs differently for two kinds of plasticity. One kind involves the general experiences that almost all infants have just by virtue of being human. This form of plasticity is referred to as *experience-expectant.* The second kind, referred to as *experience-dependent,* involves specific, idiosyncratic experiences that children have as a result of their particular life circumstances—such as growing up in the United States or in the Amazon rain forest, experiencing frequent cuddling or abuse, being an only child or one of many siblings, and so on.

Experience-Expectant Processes

The role of general human experience in shaping brain development is known as **experience-expectant plasticity** (Greenough, Black, & Wallace, 1987). According to this view, the normal wiring of the brain is in part a result of the kinds of general experiences that have been present throughout human evolution, experiences that every human with an intact sensory-motor system who inhabits a reasonably normal environment will have: patterned visual stimulation, voices and other sounds, movement and manipulation, and so forth (Greenough & Black, 1992). Consequently, the brain can "expect" input from these reliable sources to fine-tune its circuitry; synapses that are frequently activated will be strengthened and stabilized, and those that are rarely activated will be "pruned." Thus, our *experience* of the external world plays a fundamental role in shaping the most basic aspects of the *structure* of our brain.

One fundamental benefit of experience-expectant plasticity is that, because experience helps shape the brain, fewer genes need to be dedicated to normal development. Another is that the brain is better able to recover from injury to certain areas because other brain areas can take over the function that would have been performed by the damaged area. The younger the brain when damaged, the more likely recovery is.

The downside of experience-expectant plasticity is that it is accompanied by *vulnerability.* If for some reason the experience that the developing brain is "expecting" for fine-tuning its circuits does not occur, whether because of inadequate stimulation or impaired sensory receptors, development may be compromised. This phenomenon is exemplified by the classic work of Hubel & Wiesel, who deprived kittens of light exposure in one of their eyes (Hubel & Wiesel, 1962, 1970; Wiesel & Hubel, 1963). After several months of monocular deprivation, the brains of the kittens reorganized: when the eye was reopened, it was essentially disconnected from the cortex. Nothing was wrong with the eye itself, but it was functionally blind because the cells that would have normally responded to it reorganized to respond instead to the eye that continued to receive visual input.

A human analogy to Hubel & Wiesel's kittens experiment comes from children who are born with cataracts that obscure their vision. The longer a cataract remains in place after birth, the more impaired the child's visual acuity will be once it is removed. Dramatic improvement typically follows early removal, although some aspects of visual processing (especially of faces) remain affected even into adulthood (de Heering & Maurer, 2014). Rather remarkably, these impairments appear to be due to recruitment of areas of visual cortex for use by the auditory system (Collignon et al., 2015). Deprived of visual input, the visual cortices of young infants with cataracts reorganize to process auditory information instead. This reorganization remains detectible in adults, suggesting that early sensory experience (or lack thereof) can have permanent effects on brain organization.

This finding—brain reorganization in the face of absent early sensory experience—is consistent with a wealth of data from nonhuman animals: brain areas can become at least partially reorganized to serve some other function. Evidence of such plasticity and reorganization in humans is also observed in studies of congenitally deaf adults who, as children, had learned American Sign Language, a full-fledged, visually based language. Deaf individuals rely heavily on peripheral vision for language processing; they typically look into the eyes of a person who is signing to them, while using their peripheral vision to monitor the hand and arm motions of the signer. Measures of brain activity show that deaf individuals' responses to peripheral visual stimuli are several times stronger than those of hearing people, and their responses are distributed differently across the brain. Regions of the brain that are typically linked to auditory processing appear to have been co-opted by visual processing in deaf individuals (e.g., Shiell, Champoux, & Zatorre, 2016; Shiell & Zatorre, 2016). *Cross-modal reorganization* thus operates in both directions: individuals with early cataracts (or who are born blind) show auditory takeover of brain areas that are typically part of the visual system, whereas individuals who are deaf show visual takeover of brain areas that are typically part of the auditory system.

Sensitive periods As suggested by the foregoing examples, a key element in experience-expectant plasticity is timing. There are a few sensitive periods when the human brain is especially sensitive to particular kinds of external stimuli. It is as though a time window were temporarily opened, inviting environmental input to help organize the brain. Gradually, the window closes. The neural organization that occurs (or does not occur) during sensitive periods is typically irreversible.

Hubel and Wiesel's work on monocular deprivation in kittens also provides an example of sensitive periods. When mature cats are similarly deprived of visual input in one eye, there are no long-term effects on the brain, unlike the effects on kittens. There appear to be sensitive periods for the organization of sensory systems, like vision, but sensitive periods are not limited to perceptual development. As discussed in Box 1.1, the extreme deprivation that the Romanian orphans suffered early in life, when children normally experience a wealth of social and other environmental stimulation, is considered by some to be an example of a sensitive-period effect. Some investigators speculate that adolescence, during which rapid changes are occurring in the brain, may be another sensitive period for various aspects of development. Yet another sensitive period, one for language learning, will be discussed in Chapter 6.

experience-dependent plasticity ■ the process through which neural connections are created and reorganized throughout life as a function of an individual's experiences

Experience-Dependent Processes

The brain is also sculpted by idiosyncratic experience through what Greenough calls **experience-dependent plasticity.** Neural connections are created and reorganized constantly, throughout life, as a function of an individual's experiences. (If you remember anything of what you have been reading in this chapter, it's because you have formed new neural connections.)

Much of the research on experience-dependent plasticity has been focused on nonhuman animals, whose environments can be readily manipulated. One such method has involved comparisons between animals reared in complex environments full of objects to explore versus animals reared in bare laboratory cages. The brains of rats (and cats and monkeys) that grow up in a complex environment have more dendritic spines on their cortical neurons, more synapses per neuron, and more synapses overall, as well as a generally thicker cortex and more of the supportive tissues (e.g., blood vessels and glial cells) that maximize neuronal and synaptic function. All this extra hardware seems to have a payoff: rats (and other animals) reared in a complex environment (which is more akin to their natural environment) perform better in a variety of learning tasks than do their counterparts raised in bare cages (e.g., Sale, Berardi, & Maffei, 2009).

Highly specific effects of experience on brain structure also occur. For example, rats that are trained to use just one forelimb to get a food reward have increased dendritic material in the particular area of the motor cortex that controls the movement of the trained limb (Greenough, Larson, & Withers, 1985). In humans, research on musicians provides a "natural experiment" in which particular body parts are trained more intensely than others. The results from musician studies mirror the results of nonhuman animal studies. For example, adults who play wind instruments (such as trumpets and French horns) have thicker lip-related cortical areas than adults who do not play wind instruments (Choi et al., 2015). After years of practice, more cortical cells were devoted to controlling the lips of these skilled instrumentalists.

As a result of growing up in a complex environment full of stimulating objects to explore and challenges to master, the brains of the rats in the top photo will contain more synapses than if they had been reared in unstimulating laboratory cages (bottom photo).

SHAWNA LAUFER, THE RAT WHISPERER (WWW.RATWHISPERER.NET)

ENVIRONMENT IMAGES / UIG / GETTY IMAGES

Brain Damage and Recovery

As noted previously, because of its plasticity (especially early in life), the brain can become rewired—at least to some degree—after suffering damage. Children who suffer from brain damage thus have a better chance of recovering lost function than do adults who suffer similar damage. The strongest evidence for this comes from young children who suffer damage to the language area of the cortex and who generally recover most, if not all, of their language functions. This is because after the damage has occurred, other areas of the immature brain can take over language functions. As a result, language is largely spared, though specific linguistic impairments may remain (e.g., Zevin, Datta, & Skipper, 2012). By contrast, adults who sustain the same type of brain damage undergo no such reorganization of language functions and may have a permanent loss in the ability to comprehend or produce speech.

It is not always true, however, that the chance of recovery from early brain injury is greater than it is for later injury. Likelihood of recovery depends on how extensive the damage is and

How would the cortical representations of their fingers be likely to differ for these two professional musicians?

what aspect of brain development is occurring at the time of the damage. Consider, for example, the offspring of Japanese women who, while pregnant, were exposed to massive levels of radiation from the atomic bombs dropped on Hiroshima and Nagasaki in 1945. The rate of intellectual impairment was much higher for surviving children whose exposure had occurred very early in prenatal development, during the time of rapid neurogenesis and migration of neurons (Otake & Schull, 1984). This finding harkens back to our discussion of sensitive periods for prenatal teratogens in Chapter 2. As shown in Figure 2.16, the fetus is more susceptible to damage early in gestation than later in gestation. Similarly, brain injury during early childhood generally results in more severe cognitive impairment in IQ than does later comparable injury (V. Anderson et al., 2012).

Furthermore, even when children appear to have made a full recovery from an early brain injury, deficits may emerge later. This was demonstrated in a cross-sectional study that compared cognitive performance in a group of children who had been born with cerebral damage and a control group of children with no brain damage (Banich et al., 1990). As Figure 3.10 shows, the children with brain damage did not differ from the control group in their performance on two subscales of an IQ test at 6 years of age. However, as the normal children's performance improved with age, the brain-damaged children's performance fell progressively behind. The same pattern of results—decline in IQ over age for children with

FIGURE 3.10 Emergent effects of early brain damage At 6 years of age, children with congenital brain damage scored the same as normal children on two subscales of an intelligence test. However, the children with brain damage failed to improve and fell progressively farther behind the normal children, so that by adolescence there were large differences between the two groups. (Data from Banich et al., 1990; information from Kolb, 1995)

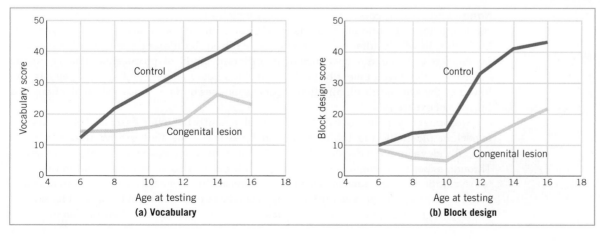

(a) Vocabulary

(b) Block design

brain damage—was also demonstrated in a longitudinal study, in which children who had sustained early damage were tested before and after age 7 (S. C. Levine et al., 2005). These results illustrate the difficulty of predicting the development of children with cerebral injuries: behavior that appears normal early in development may deteriorate.

On the basis of these various aspects of plasticity, we can generalize that the worst time to suffer brain damage is very early, during prenatal development and the 1st year after birth, when neurogenesis is occurring and basic brain structures are being formed. Damage at this point may have cascading effects on subsequent aspects of brain development, with potentially wide-ranging negative effects. In contrast, when brain damage is sustained in early childhood—that is, when synapse generation and pruning are occurring and plasticity is highest—the chances for the brain's rewiring itself and recovering lost function are best.

Atypical patterns of brain wiring are also observed in developmental disorders, in which areas of the brain show unusual patterns of connections in the absence of brain damage. Neuroimaging studies of individuals with autism spectrum disorder (ASD) suggest that rather than atypical brain structures or functions, it is the connections between brain areas that diverge from the typical developmental path. The autistic brain appears to be characterized by both an overabundance and an underabundance of connections relative to the neurotypical brain (Di Martino et al., 2014). Subcortical regions are over-connected, while cortical regions are under-connected. These patterns of connectivity suggest roots for autism early in development. And, given that ASD is amongst the most heritable of developmental disorders (see Box 3.1), it seems likely that the atypical wiring of the autistic brain is at least partially under genetic control.

Wiring abnormalities also occur in another heritable brain disorder, schizophrenia. Data from mouse studies suggest that a gene implicated in schizophrenia produces excessive synaptic pruning (Sekar et al., 2016). As discussed above, there is a burst of synaptic pruning around adolescence, especially around the prefrontal cortex. It is possible that the timing of the onset of schizophrenic symptoms in adolescence and young adulthood is linked to aberrant pruning around puberty.

The brain is thus sculpted by both experience and by genes. While plasticity affords opportunities to compensate for some sorts of neural insults, plasticity gone awry can also have devastating consequences.

Review

Nature and nurture cooperate in the construction of the human brain. Some important brain structures include the neurons, which communicate with one another at synapses; the cortex, in which different functions are localized in different areas; and the cerebral hemispheres, which are specialized for different kinds of processing. The processes involved in the development of the brain include neurogenesis and synaptogenesis, followed by the systematic elimination of some synapses and the preservation of others as a function of experience.

Two forms of plasticity contribute to the development of behavior. As a result of experience-expectant plasticity, the brain is shaped by experiences that are available to every typically developing individual in interaction with every species-typical environment. Through experience-dependent plasticity, the brain is also structured by an individual's idiosyncratic life experiences. Because of the importance of experience in brain development, sensitive periods exist during which specific experience must be present for normal development. Timing is also a crucial factor in the ultimate impact of brain damage.

The Body: Physical Growth and Development

In Chapter 1, we emphasized the multiple contexts in which development occurs. Here we focus on the most immediate context for development—the body itself. Everything we think, feel, say, and do involves our physical selves, and changes in the body lead to changes in behavior. In this section, we present a brief overview of some aspects of physical growth, including some of the factors that can disrupt normal development. Nutritional behavior, a vital aspect of physical development, is featured as we consider the regulation of eating. We concentrate particularly on one of the consequences of poor regulation—obesity. Finally, we focus on the opposite problem—undernutrition.

 Physical Development in Infancy and Toddlerhood

Growth and Maturation

Compared with most other species, humans undergo a prolonged period of physical growth. The body grows and develops for 20% of the human life span, whereas mice, for example, grow during only 2% of their life span. Figure 3.11 shows the most obvious aspects of physical growth: we become 15 to 20 times heavier and 3 times taller between birth and age 20. The figure shows averages, of course, and there are obviously huge individual differences in weight and height, as well as in the timing of physical development.

Growth is uneven over time, as you can tell from the differences in the slopes in Figure 3.11. The slopes are steepest when the most rapid growth is

FIGURE 3.11 Growth curves These growth curves for weight and height from ages 2 to 20 years are based on large national samples of children from across the United States. Each curve indicates the percent of the reference population that falls below the indicated weight and height. (Data from the Centers for Disease Control and Prevention, 2002)

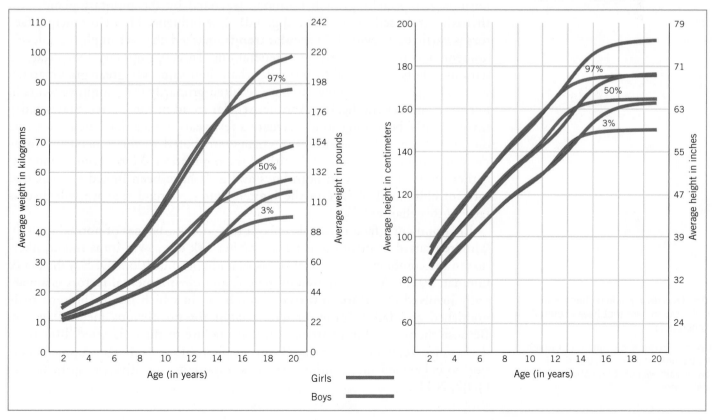

occurring—in the first 2 years and in early adolescence. Early on, boys and girls grow at roughly the same rate, and they are essentially equal in height and weight until around 10 to 12 years of age. Then girls experience their adolescent growth spurt, at the end of which they are somewhat taller and heavier than boys. (Remember those awkward middle-school years when the girls towered over the boys, much to the discomfort of both?) Adolescent boys experience their growth spurt about 2 years after the girls, permanently passing them in both height and weight. Full height is achieved, on average, by around the age of 15½ for girls and 17½ for boys.

Growth is also uneven across the different parts of the body. Following the principle of cephalocaudal development described in Chapter 2, the head region is initially relatively large—fully 50% of body length at 2 months of age. By adulthood, the head is only about 10% of body length. The gawkiness of young adolescents stems in part from the fact that their growth spurt begins with dramatic increases in the size of the hands and feet; it's easy to trip over your own feet when they are disproportionately larger than the rest of you.

Body composition also changes with age. The proportion of body fat is highest in infancy, gradually declining thereafter until around 6 to 8 years of age. In adolescence, it decreases in boys but increases in girls, and that increase helps trigger the onset of menstruation. The proportion of muscle grows slowly until adolescence, when it increases dramatically, especially in boys.

Variability

There is great variability across individuals and groups in all aspects of physical development, due to both genetic and environmental factors. Genes affect growth and sexual maturation in large part by influencing the production of hormones, especially growth hormone (secreted by the pituitary gland) and thyroxine (released by the thyroid gland). The influence of environmental factors is particularly evident in **secular trends,** marked changes in physical development that have occurred over generations. In contemporary industrialized nations, adults are several inches taller than their same-sex great-grandparents were. This change is assumed to have resulted primarily from improvements in nutrition and general health. Another secular trend in the United States today involves girls' beginning to menstruate a few years earlier than their ancestors did over the past few centuries, a change attributed to the general improvement in nutrition and general health of the population. More recent trends for earlier onset of puberty in both boys and girls have been linked to increased rates of childhood obesity in the United States, a trend that we will discuss later in this chapter.

Environmental factors can also play a role in disturbances of normal growth. Children raised in institutions have a higher risk of growth impairment, likely due to the combination of social stressors and poor nutrition (D. E. Johnson & Gunnar, 2011). A combination of genetic and environmental factors is apparently involved in **failure to thrive,** a condition in which infants become malnourished and fail to grow or gain weight for no obvious medical reason. Because the reason for a particular infant's failure to thrive is often difficult to determine, treatment may range from hospitalization to dietary supplementation to behavioral interventions, such as rewards for positive eating behaviors (Jaffe, 2011).

secular trends ■ marked changes in physical development that have occurred over generations

failure to thrive ■ a condition in which infants become malnourished and fail to grow or gain weight for no obvious medical reason

Nutritional Behavior

As suggested by the examples cited above, the health of our bodies depends on what we put into them, including the amount and kind of food we eat. Thus, the development of eating or nutritional behavior is a crucial aspect of child development from infancy onward.

Infant Feeding

Like all mammals, human newborns obtain life-sustaining nourishment through suckling, although they require more assistance in this endeavor than do most other mammals. Throughout nearly the entire history of the human species, the only or primary source of nourishment for infants was breast milk. Mother's milk has many virtues. It is naturally free of bacteria, strengthens the infant's immune system, and contains the mother's antibodies against infectious agents the baby is likely to encounter after birth. Breast-feeding is also good for mothers' health. Among other benefits, women who breast-feed their babies have a lower risk of breast cancer and type 2 diabetes (e.g., Gunderson et al., 2015; Islami et al., 2015).

There have also been suggestions in the literature that the fatty acids in breast milk have a positive effect on cognitive development. A number of studies indicate higher IQ scores for children and adults who were breast-fed as infants, even after controlling for parental IQ (for review, see Kanazawa, 2015; Nisbett et al., 2012). Other studies suggest minimal long-term cognitive benefits of breast-feeding (e.g., von Stumm & Plomin, 2015). Research findings in this area can be difficult to interpret because the choice to breast-feed is correlated with social class in the United States (due to factors ranging from maternal education to working conditions that make it difficult to nurse or pump breast milk on the job), and SES is also correlated with IQ. However, several studies that controlled for social class still found cognitive benefits associated with breast-feeding.

In one of those studies, mother–infant dyads were randomly assigned either to an intervention encouraging breast-feeding or to a control condition without intervention. The results indicated that prolonged and exclusive breast-feeding in infancy led to increased IQ scores at 6½ years of age (Kramer et al., 2008). Another study that examined genetic factors found that children who carry one of two specific alleles that regulate fatty acids showed a substantial cognitive benefit from breast-feeding, while individuals with a different allele showed a smaller benefit (Caspi et al., 2007). These results reflect the kind of genotype–environment interaction discussed earlier in this chapter, with the benefits of a particular environment (in this case, breast milk) delimited by the child's genotype. The relevant endophenotype (intermediate phenotype)—the point at which genes and environment interact—may be brain gray-matter volume, which is larger in children who were breast-fed than those who were not (Luby et al., 2016).

In spite of the well-established nutritional superiority of breast milk, as well as the fact that it is free, many infants in the United States and around the world are exclusively or predominantly formula-fed. Public health efforts have begun to shift this longtime feeding trend by educating parents about the benefits of breast milk and encouraging employers to provide private space for working mothers to

By breast-feeding her infant, this mother is providing her baby with many benefits that are not available in formula.

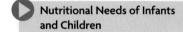
Nutritional Needs of Infants and Children

pump breast milk. Since these efforts were initiated, the number of newborns fed breast milk in the United States has increased annually and, by 2013, had risen to 77% of neonates (Centers for Disease Control and Prevention, 2013). However, this good nutritional start was difficult for parents to maintain; by 6 months of age, only 49% of infants in the United States were still being breast-fed, and by 12 months of age, only 27% were. These rates are high relative to some other wealthy countries like Great Britain, where less than 1% of infants are still breast-fed by 12 months of age. But they are low in comparison to poorer countries in sub-Saharan Africa, South America, and Southeast Asia, where the majority of infants are breast-fed until at least 1 year of age (Victora et al., 2016). High rates of breast-feeding in low-income countries are particularly positive and noteworthy. In the absence of breast-feeding, infant formula is often mixed with polluted water in unsanitary containers. Breast-feeding is thus especially important in promoting positive health outcomes in countries with unsafe drinking water and fewer public health resources.

Development of Food Preferences

Food preferences are a primary determinant of what we eat throughout life, and some of these preferences are clearly innate. Infants display some of the same reflexive facial expressions that older children and adults display in response to basic tastes: sweet, umami (savory), bitter, sour, and salty (e.g., Ventura & Worobey, 2013). The first two flavors produce positive responses: a hint of a smile, lip smacking, sucking. Bitter flavors elicit negative responses, including frowning and nose wrinkling. Sour flavors elicit varied responses: some infants respond negatively while others respond positively. Salty flavors do not elicit much of a reaction until after 4 months of age, when a preference for salt emerges.

Newborns' strong preference for sweetness is reflected both in their positive response to sweet flavors and in the fact that they will drink larger quantities of sweetened water than plain water. These innate preferences may have an evolutionary origin, because poisonous substances are often bitter or sour but almost never sweet. At the same time, recall from Chapter 2 that taste preferences can also be influenced by the prenatal environment, suggesting an important role for experience even in the earliest flavor preferences. Breast milk also takes on some of the flavors of the foods that mothers eat. While the predominant flavor of breast milk is sweetness, it also provides a continually varying array of tastes, unlike the constant flavor set provided by a specific brand of formula. Indeed, formula-fed infants show long-term preferences for the predominant flavor found in their formula (e.g., Ventura & Worobey, 2013).

The transition out of a primarily liquid diet to—in just a few short years—adult table foods brings a variety of opportunities and challenges. Most young children demonstrate *food neophobia*: an unwillingness to eat unfamiliar foods. Avoidance of unknown foods likely evolved as an adaptive response during a period of vulnerability in early childhood, helping to keep children safe (especially important given infants' and toddlers' propensity to put everything they find in their mouths). However, neophobia is often a painful phenomenon for children and parents alike. Research suggests that the best way to overcome children's conservative eating tendencies is to repeatedly introduce new foods, ideally between 6 and 15 times (Ventura & Worobey, 2013). This exposure should also include tasting, as just seeing the novel food is insufficient to override children's paranoia about eating new foods. Pressuring children to try new foods, or bribing them ("If you have two bites of broccoli, you can have dessert"), is likely to backfire. By pairing foods in this fashion, parents unintentionally send the message that broccoli is punishment while dessert is the reward. Parents also inadvertently increase the value of foods by restricting them. When access to certain foods is limited, children will tend to overindulge when they have the opportunity to do so (e.g., Ventura & Worobey, 2013). More generally, parental use of food as a way to control children's behaviors and emotions is a predictor of larger body mass indices (BMI) and other risk factors for obesity (e.g., Larsen et al., 2015).

Eating is an inherently social act, and much of what children learn about food comes from observing others (in Chapter 9, we will discuss the role of observational learning in social development more generally). Toddlers are more likely to accept novel foods from a caregiver than a stranger. They prefer foods modeled by individuals with positive expressions over those with negative expressions, foods modeled by peers over adults, foods modeled by same-gender peers over those modeled by opposite-gender peers, and foods modeled by people who speak their native language (Frazier et al., 2012; Shutts et al., 2009). In general, young children are more likely to choose foods endorsed by others who are similar to them along key social dimensions (Shutts, Kinzler, & DeJesus, 2013). Indeed, infants expect individuals from the same social group to share food preferences—but not preferences for non-food items such as novel objects, suggesting that even infants understand that food choices reflect social conventions (Liberman et al., 2016).

Associative learning, which we will discuss in Chapter 5 in the form of conditioning, also influences children's food choices. Foods marketed to young children are often branded with popular cartoon characters (e.g., Dora the Explorer) and mascots (e.g., the Trix bunny). This branding strategy makes a difference: children are more likely to select, and rate more highly, foods that are branded with familiar characters (e.g., Kraak & Story, 2015). Children's positive associations with these images lead them, in turn, to associate positive feelings with the foods that the characters label. While branding currently predominates as a marketing tool for less healthy foods, nowhere is this strategy more evident than in the toys that fast-food restaurants offer to their youngest customers, leading to nearly a billion child-targeted meals served annually (Longacre et al., 2016). Child-targeted marketing of unhealthy foods, including the pairing of unhealthy foods with enticing toys, is one contributor to the obesity epidemic.

Associative learning via branding can also encourage healthy dining choices. One recent study used branding to market the salad bars in elementary school cafeterias in a large urban school district (Hanks, Just, & Brumberg, 2016). Simply by fastening a banner showing cartoon vegetable characters to the salad bar, the number of students choosing vegetables doubled. When the banner was paired with television advertisements featuring the vegetable characters, the number of students choosing vegetables tripled. Thus, advocates of healthy eating should consider taking advantage of the marketing tools that have so long predominated in the advertising of rather less healthy options.

Obesity

So many people have difficulty regulating their eating appropriately that the most common dietary problems in the United States are related to overeating and its many consequences. The proportion of American children and adolescents who are obese and extremely obese has risen for certain age groups over the past three decades (see Figure 3.12), with the increase being greatest for Latinos and African Americans. While the rates of obesity have leveled off in the past few years, and even declined for children ages 2 to 5, they continue to increase for adolescents (Ogden et al., 2016). Across age groups, 17% of children and teens were obese in 2014.

Childhood obesity is a global problem, with 42 million overweight and obese children worldwide (World Health Organization, 2014). The majority of these children live in developing countries, which have shown a particularly steep rate of increase in obesity. For example, the number of children under the age of 5 in Africa who are overweight or obese has nearly doubled since 1990, from 5.4 million to 10.3 million (World Health Organization, 2016). This situation exists largely because societies all over the world are increasingly adopting a "Western diet" of foods high in fat and sugar and low in fiber. Fast-food restaurants have proliferated around the globe; indeed, after Santa Claus, Ronald McDonald is the second most recognized figure worldwide (K. Brownell, 2004).

Two important questions need to be addressed: Why do some people but not others become overweight, and why is there an epidemic of obesity? Both genetic and environmental factors play roles. Genetic factors are reflected in the findings that (1) the weight of adopted children is more strongly correlated with that of their biological parents than with that of their adoptive parents, and (2) identical twins, including those reared apart, are more similar in weight than fraternal twins are (Plomin et al., 2013). Even the *speed* of eating, which is related both to how much is eaten in a given meal and to the weight of the eater, shows substantial heritability (Llewellyn et al., 2008). Research on dogs has revealed a specific genetic deletion (POMC), occurring in breeds with high rates of obesity, associated with weight and appetite that causes these dogs to be hungrier than others (Raffan et al., 2016). The POMC gene is present in humans, and in rare cases, deficiencies lead to human obesity. However, GWAS studies suggest that like most other complex traits, human obesity risk is polygenic (Tung et al., 2014). While there is no single gene for obesity, genes affect individuals' susceptibility to gaining weight and how much food they eat in the first place, making it relatively difficult or easy for them to avoid becoming part of the obesity epidemic.

Genetic factors have also been shown to influence an individual's temperament, which relates to self-regulation and impulse control. Impulsivity is linked to executive function and cognitive control, as well as to the ability to forgo immediate gratification. Childhood impulsivity is linked to overweight and obesity, and in fact, young children with difficult temperaments tend to gain weight faster, have higher BMIs, and choose obesogenic diets—foods that tend to lead to obesity (Thamotharan et al., 2013; Larsen et al., 2015). Temperament paired with factors in cognitive development may

FIGURE 3.12 Overweight—a growing problem The proportion of children in the United States who are obese and extremely obese has risen over the past three decades, though there are indications that it is plateauing or declining among some age groups. (Data from National Health Examination Surveys II [Ages 6–11] and III [Ages 12–17], 1999–2004; Ogden et al., 2016)

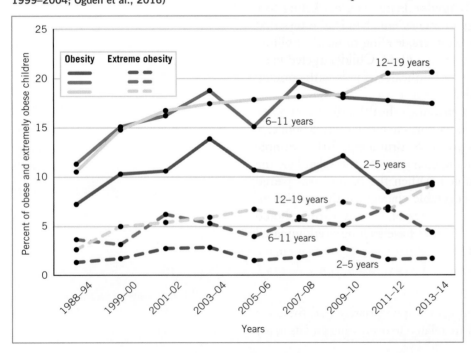

interact in children's differential ability to engage in self-control when confronted with large portions and sweet treats, both staples of the contemporary diet. (The Marshmallow Test described in Chapter 10, which also includes a detailed discussion of temperament, presents a striking demonstration of childhood impulsivity.)

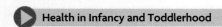

Environmental influences also play a major role in this epidemic, as is obvious from the fact that a much higher proportion of the U.S. population is overweight now than in previous times. Indeed, some have argued that becoming obese in the United States could be considered a normal response to the contemporary American taste for obesogenic high-fat, high-sugar foods in ever larger portion sizes.

A host of other factors fuel the ever-expanding waistlines of today's children. At school, they frequently have no physical education programs or recess activities and often purchase cafeteria lunches consisting of high-fat foods (e.g., pizza, hamburgers) and high-calorie soft drinks. They also spend less time playing outside than their counterparts did in previous generations: fully half of today's preschool-age children spend less than an hour a day engaged in outdoor play (Tandon, Zhou, & Christakis, 2012). Children today also get less exercise because they rarely walk or bike to school. At the same time, children spend increasingly more hours per day in front of screens (a trend that we will discuss in Chapter 9), and screen time is more highly predictive of obesity than amount of physical activity (Maher et al., 2012).

Sleep duration is also associated with weight gain: children who get less sleep are more prone to obesity, as are children with televisions in their rooms (which may also detract from sleep duration) (Appelhans et al., 2014; Wethington, Pan, & Sherry, 2013). Eating meals as a family appears to be a protective factor, with lower rates of obesity among children and teens whose families dine together regularly in non-fast-food contexts (Martin-Biggers et al., 2014). Finally, unhealthy foods are often less expensive and more readily available than healthier foods, especially in inner-city areas that lack full-service supermarkets. In such areas, known as "food deserts," poorer residents often must rely on convenience stores that stock primarily high-calorie prepackaged foods, making it difficult even for motivated parents to provide healthy foods to their children.

Obesity puts children and adolescents at risk for a wide variety of serious health problems, including heart disease and diabetes. In addition, many obese youth suffer the consequences of negative stereotypes and discrimination in a variety of areas. As early as 1st grade, children who are obese are more likely to be withdrawn and depressed (Harrist et al., 2016). According to child, peer, and teacher reports, these children are also more likely to struggle with friendships and are generally poorly treated by their peers, with teasing and rejection especially common for severely obese children (those with a BMI above the 99th percentile). Severely obese children as young as 6 years of age were largely ostracized by their peers. Indeed, body size stigmatization appears to begin in preschool. Three- to 5-year-old girls were tested using a doll paradigm, in which a Barbie-like doll was manipulated to be thin, average, or fat (Worobey & Worobey, 2014). The girls' responses followed the stereotypical pattern, with more positive traits attributed to the thin and average dolls ("smart," "pretty") and more negative traits attributed to the fat doll ("sad," "tired"). While the roots of these negative attributions remain unclear, it is clear that children who are obese have a very challenging road ahead both physically and psychologically.

There is, unfortunately, no easy cure for obesity in children, or clear means of prevention. Some of the techniques often thought to prevent obesity, such as breast-feeding in lieu of formula feeding or delaying the introduction of solid

By exercising together, this father and son may be taking one of the most effective steps they can toward weight control.

foods, do not have strong evidence-based support (Lumeng et al., 2015). However, some hope for the general obesity problem comes from the fact that public awareness is now focused on the severity of the problem and the variety of factors that contribute to it. Many schools have begun serving more nutritious, less caloric foods, including those available in vending machines, and fast-food chains have begun to include low-calorie options and calorie counts on their menus. Prominent national figures, such as First Lady Michelle Obama, have targeted childhood obesity as a key public-health issue, raising hope that campaigns focused on healthy eating and exercise will help families make positive lifestyle choices.

Finally, promising intervention programs are currently underway, including interventions delivered during pediatrician visits and via home visits (Cloutier et al., 2015; Gorin et al., 2014). One such program, HomeStyles, was developed by nutrition scientists as an 18-month intervention focused on educating parents about many of the topics presented in this section, including family meals, sleep duration, physical activity, screen time, and dealing with picky eaters (Martin-Biggers et al., 2015). An innovative strategy of HomeStyles is to nudge parents every few days (via SMS, email, or voicemail) to motivate them to work with their child toward positive health behaviors: "Move to the music and get active"; "Unplug the TV and talk to each other about your day." While data collection is still ongoing, the intervention has great potential to enact change by encouraging parents to alter the home environment in ways that promote positive health outcomes for themselves and their children.

Undernutrition

At the same time that many people are overeating their way to poor health, the health of people in developing nations is compromised by their not getting enough to eat. According to UNICEF, undernutrition contributes to nearly half of all deaths of children under the age of 5 worldwide, especially in Asia and Africa (UNICEF, 2016). Undernutrition impairs children's health by increasing their risk of succumbing to infections. For example, a child who is severely underweight is almost 10 times more likely to die of diarrhea than a child who is not (UNICEF, 2013). These childhood illnesses, in turn, may decrease children's ability to take in nutrients, leading to a vicious cycle between infection and undernutrition.

Undernutrition and malnutrition are virtually always associated with poverty and myriad related factors, ranging from limited access to health care (the primary cause in the United States) to warfare, famine, and natural disasters. As we discuss in Box 3.4, the interaction of malnutrition with poverty and other forms of deprivation adversely affects all aspects of development, from brain development and physical growth (including stunting, or height more than 2 standard deviations below the mean), to downstream effects on cognition, social development, educational attainment, and eventual economic productivity and quality of life. Strategies to counter undernutrition worldwide include improvements in maternal health, breast-feeding supports, access to supplementation of key nutrients (e.g., iodized salt, iron, vitamin A), improved water sanitation, and community-based interventions.

One noteworthy intervention is currently being used in Nepal, where most people live without access to health care. To begin to address the lack of routine

BOX 3.4 | a closer look

POVERTY AND HEALTH DISPARITIES

Throughout this book, we highlight myriad ways in which children growing up in poverty are disadvantaged. Poverty-related health disparities emerge early in life. In the United States, infants living in families with low socioeconomic status (SES) are more likely to die than other infants, potentially due to increased rates of SIDS and fatal accidents (Chen, Oster, & Williams, 2016). Indeed, infants' risk of death actually increases over the 1st year of life in the United States, especially for infants in socioeconomically disadvantaged families, as reflected in the United States' disturbingly high infant mortality rate discussed in Chapter 2.

The effects of poverty are also evident in brain development. As shown in the figure below, brain growth is slowed in infants and toddlers growing up in poverty (e.g., Hanson et al., 2013). Importantly, infants' brains do not start out differently sized as a function of parental SES, as one might expect if differences in brain development were due to prenatal nutrition, preterm birth, or genetic differences that covary with SES (e.g., if the genes that affect brain size also influence parents' educational and occupational attainment). Instead, as shown in the figure below, gray matter is roughly the same in very young infants across socioeconomic groups. But by 12 months of age, gray-matter volume has already begun

to diverge as a function of SES, and by 24 months, there are substantial differences in gray matter in toddlers growing up in families from different socioeconomic groups, a finding consistent with studies of older children and adults (e.g., Mackey et al., 2015; Noble et al., 2015). As yet, it is unclear why these differences in brain size as a function of SES emerge. Possible reasons could be the level of stress in the home, the richness of the environment (recall the earlier discussion on experience-dependent plasticity), toxins in the environment, or any number of other factors correlated with SES.

Children living in poverty are also at heightened risk for a number of health problems. They are more likely than their peers to be overweight or obese, potentially due to their bodies' response to chronic stress (e.g., Miller et al., 2013, 2015). Poverty-related chronic stress also contributes to increased rates of diseases including cardiovascular disease, immune system disorders, and psychiatric illnesses. Heightened rates of illness may be due, in part, to lack of access to good health care. But even when studies control for access to health care, effects of poverty remain. One recent study examined rates of relapse for children with leukemia who were all treated at the same medical center in New York City (Bona et al., 2016). Despite having access to the same treatments at the same

hospital, children with leukemia living in high-poverty neighborhoods were more likely to relapse after treatment than were children living in low-poverty neighborhoods. Thus, family SES influences cancer outcomes even when children receive the same treatment protocols. This may be due to the presence of other underlying health problems, differences in adherence to therapies, or differences in family belief systems related to positive child development outcomes.

Health-care professionals are increasingly taking note of the toll taken on child poverty. In 2016, the American Academy of Pediatrics issued its first ever policy statement about poverty and child health (Gitterman et al., 2016). The policy statement is a call to action for pediatricians to engage in advocacy, research, and community interventions as part of their medical practices, and it concludes with the following statement: "The American Academy of Pediatrics considers child poverty in the United States unacceptable and detrimental to the health and well-being of children and is committed to its elimination." As health-care professionals join developmental scientists, economists, and public-policy experts in focusing increasingly on poverty, their attention to these issues will hopefully lead to renewed efforts to ameliorate the deleterious effects of poverty on children's health and well-being.

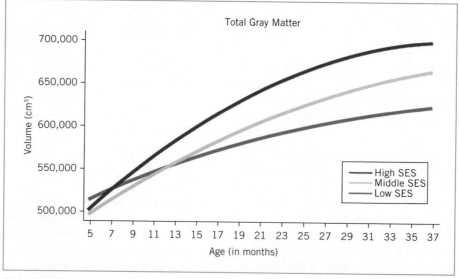

(Data from Hanson et al., 2013)

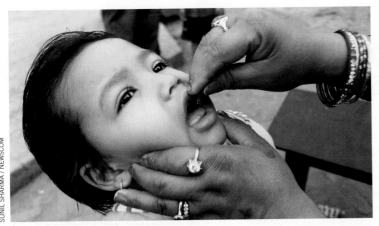

Though most lack extensive health-care training, female community health-care workers in Nepal have played an important role in bringing treatment and medicine to a population that otherwise would not have access to basic health services. Their work may provide a model for improving the outcomes of women and children in impoverished communities.

care, Nepal developed a system of interventions delivered by female community health volunteers (UNICEF, 2013). Nearly 50,000 women travel the country to deliver basic health care, treating common childhood infections such as diarrhea and pneumonia. With their help, Nepal has become the first country to deliver vitamin A supplements every 6 months to children nationwide. And because the volunteers are spread out throughout the country, they are able to intervene rapidly. When women give birth in rural Nepal, volunteers arrive within the hour, prepared to detect and help manage low-birth-weight neonates (Amano et al., 2014). While this program faces challenges—many of the volunteers are illiterate, requiring them to depend on memory about treatments and family histories, and the long walks between villages can hamper opportunities for training—it represents an important step toward improving children's nutritional and physical health in impoverished countries.

Review

Sound nutritional behavior is vital to general health. Preferences for certain foods are evident from birth on, and, as children develop, what they choose to eat is influenced by many factors, including the preferences of their friends and their parents' attempts to influence their eating behavior. Obesity among both adults and children has increased dramatically in the United States and much of the rest of the world in recent decades, as exposure to rich foods in large portions has increased and physical activity has decreased. However, throughout the world, the most common nutritional problem is undernutrition, which is very closely associated with poverty. The combination of malnutrition and poverty is particularly devastating to development.

CHAPTER SUMMARY

Nature and Nurture

■ The complex interplay of nature and nurture was the constant theme of this chapter. In the drama of development, genotype, phenotype, and environment all play starring roles, and the plot moves forward as they interact in many obvious and many not-so-obvious ways.

■ The starting point for development is the genotype—the genes inherited at conception from one's parents. Only some of those genes are expressed in the phenotype, one's observable characteristics. Whether some genes are expressed at all is a function of dominance patterns. Most traits studied by developmental scientists are influenced by multiple genes. The switching on and off of genes over time underlies many aspects of development. This process is affected by experience via methylation.

■ The eventual outcome of a given genotype is always contingent on the environment in which it develops. Parents

and their behavior toward their children are a salient part of the children's environment. Parents' behavior toward their children is influenced by their own genotypes. Similarly, the child's development is influenced by the aspects of the environment he or she seeks out and the different responses the child's characteristics and behavior evoke from other people.

Behavior Genetics

■ The field of behavior genetics is concerned with the joint influence of genetic and environmental factors on behavior. Through the use of a variety of family-study designs, behavior geneticists have discovered a wide range of behavior patterns that "run in families." Many behavior geneticists use heritability estimates to statistically evaluate the relative contributions of heredity and environment to behavior.

Brain Development

- A burgeoning area of developmental research focuses on the development of the brain—the most complex structure in the known universe. Neurons are the basic units of the brain's informational system. These cells transmit information via electrical signals. Impulses are transmitted from one neuron to another at synapses.

- The most human part of the human brain is the cortex, because it is involved in a wide variety of higher mental functions. Different areas of the cortex are specialized for general behavioral categories. The cortex is divided into two cerebral hemispheres, each of which is specialized for certain modes of processing, a phenomenon known as cerebral lateralization.

- Brain development involves several processes, beginning with neurogenesis and differentiation of neurons. In synaptogenesis, an enormous profusion of connections among neurons is generated, starting prenatally and continuing for the first few years after birth. Through synaptic pruning, excess connections among neurons are eliminated.

- Experience plays a crucial role in the strengthening or elimination of synapses and hence in the normal wiring of the brain. The fine-tuning of the brain involves experience-expectant processes, in which existing synapses are preserved as a function of stimulation that virtually every human encounters, and experience-dependent processes, in which new connections are formed as a function of experience and learning.

- Plasticity refers to the fact that nurture is the partner of nature in the normal development of the brain. This fact makes it possible in certain circumstances for the brain to rewire itself in response to damage. It also makes the developing brain vulnerable to the absence of stimulation at sensitive periods in development.

- The ability of the brain to recover from injury depends on the age of the child. Very early damage, during the time when neurogenesis and synaptogenesis are occurring, can have especially devastating effects.

The Body: Physical Growth and Development

- Humans undergo a particularly prolonged period of physical growth, during which growth is uneven, proceeding more rapidly early in life and in adolescence. Secular trends have been observed in increases in average weight and height.

- Food preferences begin with innate responses by newborns to basic tastes, but additional preferences develop as a result of experience. Problems with the regulation of eating are evident in the United States, where an epidemic of obesity is clearly related to both environmental and genetic factors.

- In much of the rest of the world, the dominant problem is getting enough food. Inadequate nutrition is closely associated with poverty, and it leads to a variety of behavioral and physical problems in virtually every aspect of the child's life. Prevention of undernutrition is needed to allow millions of children to develop normal brains and bodies.

Test Yourself

1. The genetic material an individual inherits is called the
   a. chromosome.
   b. genome.
   c. phenotype.
   d. genotype.

2. Marcus has red hair, green eyes, and freckles. He is very active but shy. These characteristics are a reflection of Marcus's
   a. dominant genes.
   b. recessive genes.
   c. genotype.
   d. phenotype.

3. An individual's sex is determined by
   a. whether the mother has a Y chromosome.
   b. the random interaction of the sex chromosomes of the mother and father.
   c. the sex chromosomes contributed by the mother.
   d. the sex chromosomes contributed by the father.

4. The continual switching on or off of specific genes at specific times throughout development is the result of a chain of genetic events primarily controlled by _____ .
   a. alleles
   b. regulator genes

   c. glial cells
   d. synaptogenisis

5. Trevor and Malcolm are identical twins who are being raised in separate homes. According to the concept of norm of reaction, the different environmental factors that these two children experience will
   a. produce a different phenotype in each child, despite the fact that their genotypes are identical.
   b. have no effect on their phenotypes because environmental factors have no influence on an individual's genome.
   c. result in both children displaying the same phenotype, because they share the same genotype.
   d. have no effect on their phenotypes because the genetic input for their parents is unaffected by environmental factors.

6. Traits such as aggression and shyness are the result of the contributions of a complex combination of genes. These traits are examples of which process?
   a. polygenetic inheritance
   b. the norm of reaction
   c. multifactorial inheritance
   d. experience-dependent plasticity

7. A twin-study design project reveals that the correlation between identical (MZ) twins on a given trait is substantially higher than that between fraternal (DZ) twins. Which of the following statements offers the most plausible explanation for the difference in how this trait is correlated in MZ twins compared with DZ twins?
   a. Environmental factors are substantially responsible for the difference in correlation.
   b. Genetic factors are substantially responsible for the difference in correlation.
   c. Environmental and genetic factors are equally responsible for the difference in correlation.
   d. No assumption can be made as to the contributions of environmental or genetic factors for the difference.

8. Which of the following responses would be consistent with the statement "High heritability does not imply immutability"?
   a. The concept of inheritance plays a very small role in dictating an individual's phenotype.
   b. Highly heritable traits affect all individuals in the same way.
   c. Intervention efforts can successfully influence the course of development related to an inherited trait.
   d. There is little point in trying to improve the course of development related to an inherited trait.

9. The points at which neurons communicate with one another are called _____ .
   a. synapses
   b. glial cells
   c. dendrites
   d. myelin sheaths

10. The process of synaptogenesis
    a. involves the formation of connections between neurons.
    b. causes the elimination of excess neurons.
    c. is basically complete before birth.
    d. is the proliferation of neurons through cell division.

11. Before Sidney begins a drawing of her family, she first plans out the family members that she will include in the picture and the colors she will use to draw each one. Which lobe of the cerebral cortex is she using to plan ahead?
    a. frontal lobe
    b. temporal lobe
    c. parietal lobe
    d. occipital lobe

12. The capacity of the brain to be molded or changed by experience is referred to as _____ .
    a. synaptogenesis
    b. associative learning
    c. plasticity
    d. neurogenesis

13. Rats that are raised in cages with toys have more dendritic spines and more synapses per neuron than rats raised in cages without this stimulation. The different responses in the brains of these two groups of rats provide an example of which biological process?
    a. sensitive periods
    b. experience-expectant plasticity
    c. experience-dependent plasticity
    d. neurogenesis

14. Average at-birth length has increased in some industrialized nations over the course of the past few generations, possibly due to improvements in health and nutrition for pregnant women. This development is an example of _____ .
    a. experience-expectant plasticity
    b. secular trends
    c. obesity
    d. genotype–environment interactions

15. Belle is 3 years old. She loves bananas and other yellow foods, but when her father places a piece of broccoli, which she has never eaten, on her plate, she closes her mouth and refuses to open it. Belle is demonstrating
    a. a failure to thrive.
    b. associative learning.
    c. experience-expectant plasticity.
    d. food neophobia.

LaunchPad
macmillan learning

Don't stop now! Research shows that testing yourself is a powerful learning tool. Visit LaunchPad to access the LearningCurve adaptive quizzing system, which gives you a personalized study plan to help build your mastery of the chapter material through videos, activities, and more. **Go to launchpadworks.com.**

Critical Thinking Questions

1. A major focus of this chapter was the interaction of nature and nurture. Consider yourself and your family (regardless of whether you were raised by your biological parents). Identify some aspect of who you are that illustrates each of the five relations depicted in Figure 3.1 and answer these questions: (a) How and when was your sex determined? (b) What are some alleles you are certain or relatively confident you share with other members of your family? (c) What might be an example of a gene–environment interaction in your parents' behavior toward you? (d) What would be an example of your active selection of your own environment that might have influenced your subsequent development? (e) What aspects

of your own environment might have had epigenetic effects on your gene expression?

2. "Fifty percent of a person's IQ is due to heredity and fifty percent to environment." Discuss what is wrong with this statement, describing both what heritability estimates mean and what they do not mean.

3. Relate the developmental processes of synaptogenesis and synapse elimination to the concepts of experience-expectant and experience-dependent plasticity.

4. What aspects of brain development do researchers think may be related to the traits and behaviors of adolescents?

5. Think back over your activities and observations of the past day or so. What aspects of your environment may relate to the epidemic of obesity described in this chapter?

6. Many aspects of children's health are shaped by the world they live in, ranging from broad national differences (e.g., economic stability) to family factors (e.g., socioeconomic status, parental behavior). What are some of the ways that a child's health can be influenced by the environment? If you were a parent, what reasonable, long-lasting steps could you take to improve your child's health outcomes and eating habits?

Key Terms

alleles, p. 101

association areas, p. 115

axons, p. 114

behavior genetics, p. 107

carrier genetic testing, p. 104

cell body, p. 114

cerebral cortex, p. 115

cerebral hemispheres, p. 116

cerebral lateralization, p. 116

chromosomes, p. 95

corpus callosum, p. 116

crossing over, p. 97

dendrites, p. 114

DNA (deoxyribonucleic acid), p. 95

dominant allele, p. 101

endophenotypes, p. 100

environment, p. 95

event-related potentials (ERPs), p. 118

experience-dependent plasticity, p. 124

experience-expectant plasticity, p. 122

failure to thrive (nonorganic), p. 128

frontal lobe, p. 115

genes, p. 95

genome, p. 94

genotype, p. 95

glial cells, p. 115

heritability, p. 109

heritable, p. 107

heterozygous, p. 101

homozygous, p. 101

lobes, p. 115

multifactorial, p. 107

mutation, p. 97

myelin sheath, p. 115

myelination, p. 117

neurogenesis, p. 117

neurons, p. 114

newborn screening, p. 104

norm of reaction, p. 102

occipital lobe, p. 115

parietal lobe, p. 115

phenotype, p. 95

phenylketonuria (PKU), p. 103

plasticity, p. 122

polygenic inheritance, p. 101

prenatal testing, p. 104

recessive allele, p. 101

regulator genes, p. 100

secular trends, p. 128

sex chromosomes, p. 96

spines, p. 117

synapses, p. 115

synaptic pruning, p. 120

synaptogenesis, p. 119

temporal lobe, p. 115

▶ Student Video Activities

Nature vs. Nurture: Growing Up Apart

Separated at Birth

Genes and Development

Genetic Disorders

Brain Development: Prenatal, Infants, and Toddlers

Brain Development: Myelination

Event-Related Potential Research

Brain Growth: Infancy Through Age 18

Physical Development in Infancy and Toddlerhood

Nutritional Needs of Infants and Children

Health in Infancy and Toddlerhood

Answers to Test Yourself

1. d, 2. d, 3. d, 4. b, 5. a, 6. a, 7. b, 8. c, 9. a, 10. a, 11. a, 12. c, 13. c, 14. b, 15. d

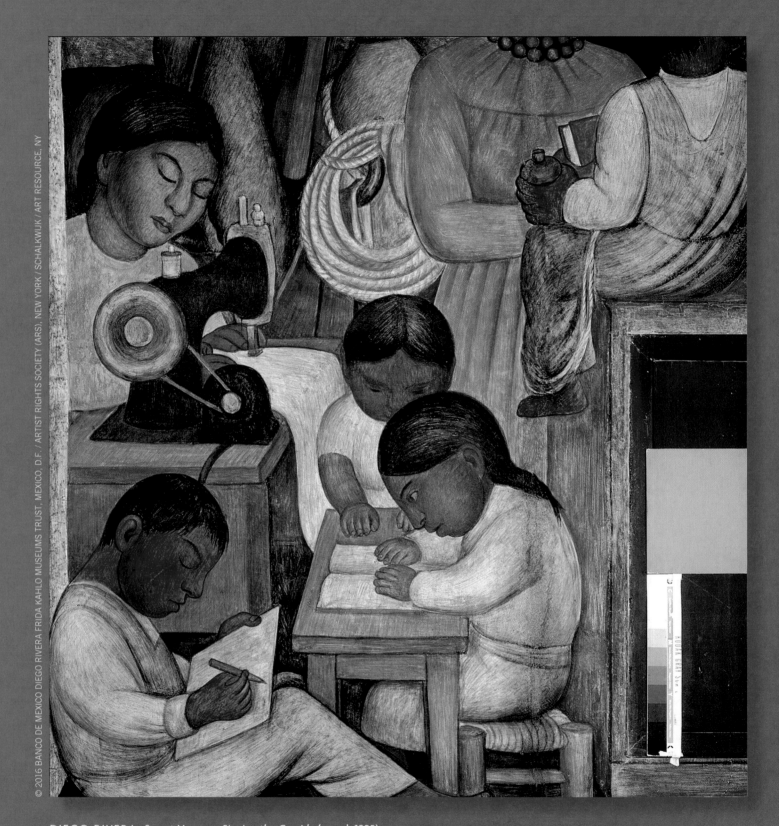

DIEGO RIVERA, *Sweet Home — Singing the Corrido* (mural, 1925)

Theories of Cognitive Development

Themes

- ■ Nature and Nurture
- ■ The Active Child
- ■ Continuity/Discontinuity
- ■ Mechanisms of Change
- ■ The Sociocultural Context
- ■ Individual Differences
- ■ Research and Children's Welfare

The author whose son loved to grab his glasses is not the only one who has encountered this problem. Had the mom in this picture been lucky enough to read this textbook, she may have solved the problem in the same way.

ELIZABETH CREWS

A 7-month-old boy, sitting on his father's lap, becomes intrigued with the father's glasses, grabs one side of the frame, and yanks it. The father says, "Ow!" and his son lets go, but then reaches up and yanks the frame again. The father readjusts the glasses, but his son again grasps them and yanks. How, the father wonders, can he prevent the boy from continuing this annoying routine without causing him to start screaming?

Fortunately, the father, a developmental psychologist, soon realizes that Jean Piaget's theory of cognitive development suggests a simple solution: put the glasses behind his back. According to Piaget's theory, removing an object from a young infant's sight should lead the infant to act as if the object never existed. The strategy works perfectly; after the father puts the glasses behind his back, his son shows no further interest in them and turns his attention elsewhere. The father looks skyward and thinks, "Thank you, Piaget."

This experience, which one of the authors of this textbook actually had, illustrates in a small way how understanding theories of child development can yield practical benefits. It also illustrates three broader advantages of knowing about such theories:

1. Developmental theories provide a framework for understanding important phenomena. Theories help to reveal the significance of what we observe about children, both in research studies and in everyday life. Someone who witnessed the glasses incident but who did not know about Piaget's theory might have found the experience amusing but insignificant. Seen in terms of Piaget's theory, however, this passing event exemplifies a general and profoundly important developmental phenomenon: infants younger than 8 months react to the disappearance of an object as though the object has ceased to exist. In this way, theories of child development place particular experiences and observations in a larger context and deepen our understanding of their meaning.

2. Developmental theories raise crucial questions about human nature. Piaget's theory about young infants' reactions to disappearing objects was based on his informal experiments with infants younger than 8 months. Piaget would cover one of their favorite objects with a cloth or otherwise put it out of sight and then wait to see whether the infants tried to retrieve the object. They rarely did, leading Piaget to conclude that before the age of 8 months, infants do not realize that hidden objects still exist. Other researchers have challenged this explanation. They argue that infants younger than 8 months do in fact understand that hidden objects continue to exist but lack the memory or problem-solving skills necessary for using that understanding to retrieve hidden objects (Baillargeon, 1993). Despite these disagreements about how best to interpret young infants' failure to retrieve hidden objects, researchers agree that Piaget's theory raises a crucial question about human nature: Do infants realize from the first days of life that objects continue to exist when out of sight, or is this something that they only learn later? Do they fear that Mom no longer exists when she disappears from sight?

3. Developmental theories lead to a better understanding of children. Theories also stimulate new research that may support the theories' claims, fail to support them, or require refinements of them, thereby improving our understanding of children. For example, Piaget's ideas led Yuko Munakata and her colleagues (1997) to test whether 7-month-olds' failure to reach for hidden objects was due to their lacking the motivation or the reaching skill to retrieve them. To find out, the researchers created a situation similar to Piaget's object-permanence experiment, except that they placed the object, an attractive toy, under a transparent cover rather than under an opaque one. In this situation, infants quickly removed the cover and regained the toy. This finding seemed to support Piaget's original interpretation by showing that neither lack of motivation nor lack of ability to reach for the toy explained the infants' usual failure to retrieve it.

In contrast, an experiment conducted by Adele Diamond (1985) indicated a need to revise Piaget's theory. Using an opaque covering, as Piaget did, Diamond varied the amount of time between when the toy was hidden and when the infant was allowed to reach for it. She found that even 6-month-olds could locate the toy if allowed to reach immediately, that 7-month-olds could wait as long as 2 seconds and still succeed, that 8-month-olds could wait as long as 4 seconds and still succeed, and so on. Diamond's findings indicated that memory for the location of hidden objects, as well as the understanding that they continue to exist, is crucial to success on the task. In sum, theories of child development are useful because they provide frameworks for understanding important phenomena, raise fundamental questions about human nature, and motivate new research that increases understanding of children.

Because child development is such a complex and varied subject, no single theory accounts for all of it. The most informative current theories focus primarily on either cognitive development or social development. Providing a good theoretical account of development in even one of these areas is an immense challenge, because each of them spans a huge range of topics. Cognitive development includes the growth of such diverse capabilities as perception, attention, language, problem solving, reasoning, memory, conceptual understanding, and intelligence. Social development includes the growth of equally diverse areas: emotions, personality, relationships with peers and family members, self-understanding, aggression, and moral behavior. Given this immense range of developmental domains, it is easy to understand why no one theory has captured the entirety of child development.

Therefore, we present cognitive and social theories in separate chapters. We consider theories of cognitive development in this chapter, just before the chapters on specific areas of cognitive development, and consider theories of social development in Chapter 9, just before the chapters on specific areas of social development. The goal is to help you understand the theories that address fundamental questions about cognitive and social development. These theories provide much of the motivation behind the studies, presented here and in later chapters, that address those fundamental questions in specific contexts (such as language development or the acquisition of academic skills).

This chapter examines five theories of cognitive development that are particularly influential: Piagetian, information-processing, core-knowledge, sociocultural, and dynamic-systems. We consider each theory's fundamental assumptions about children's nature, the central developmental issues on which the theory focuses, and practical examples of the theory's usefulness for educating children.

These five theories are influential in large part because they provide important insights into the basic developmental themes described in Chapter 1. Each one addresses all the themes to some extent, but each emphasizes different ones. For example, Piaget's theory focuses on *nature and nurture, continuity/discontinuity,* and the *active child,* whereas information-processing theories focus on *nature and nurture* and *mechanisms of change* (Table 4.1). Together, the five theories allow a broader appreciation of cognitive development than any one of them alone.

TABLE 4.1

Enduring Themes Addressed by Theories of Cognitive Development

Theory	Main Questions Addressed
Piagetian	Nature and nurture, continuity/discontinuity, the active child
Information-processing	Nature and nurture, how change occurs
Core-knowledge	Nature and nurture, continuity/discontinuity
Sociocultural	Nature and nurture, influence of the sociocultural context, how change occurs
Dynamic-systems	Nature and nurture, the active child, how change occurs

Piaget's theory ■ the theory of Swiss psychologist Jean Piaget, which posits that cognitive development involves a sequence of four stages—the sensorimotor, preoperational, concrete operational, and formal operational stages—that are constructed through the processes of assimilation, accommodation, and equilibration

Piaget's Theory

Jean Piaget's studies of cognitive development are a testament to how much one person can contribute to a scientific field. Before his work began to appear in the early 1920s, there was no recognizable field of cognitive development. Nearly a century later, **Piaget's theory** remains the best-known cognitive developmental theory. What accounts for its longevity?

One reason is that Piaget's observations and descriptions vividly convey the texture of children's thinking at different ages. They remind parents, teachers, nurses, and day-care employees of their own experiences with children of different ages. Another reason is the exceptional breadth of the theory. It extends from infancy through adolescence and examines topics as diverse as conceptualization of time, space, distance, and number; language use; memory; understanding of other people's perspectives; problem solving; and scientific reasoning. A third source of its longevity is that it offers an intuitively plausible depiction of the interaction of nature and nurture in cognitive development, as well as of the continuities and discontinuities that characterize intellectual growth.

View of Children's Nature

Piaget's fundamental assumption about children was that they are mentally active from the moment of birth and that their mental and physical activity both contribute greatly to their development. His approach to understanding cognitive development is often labeled *constructivist,* because it depicts children as constructing knowledge for themselves in response to their experiences. Three of the most important of children's constructive processes, according to Piaget, are generating hypotheses, performing experiments, and drawing conclusions from their observations. If this description reminds you of scientific problem solving, you are not alone: the "child as scientist" is the dominant metaphor in Piaget's theory. Consider this description of his infant son:

> Laurent is lying on his back. . . . He grasps in succession a celluloid swan, a box, etc., stretches out his arm and lets them fall. He distinctly varies the position of the fall. When the object falls in a new position (for example, on his pillow), he lets it fall two or three more times on the same place, as though to study the spatial relation.
>
> (Piaget, 1952b, pp. 268–269)

In simple activities such as Laurent's game of "drop the toy from different places and see what happens," Piaget perceived the beginning of scientific experimentation.

This example also illustrates a second basic Piagetian assumption: children learn many important lessons on their own, rather than depending on instruction from others. To further illuminate this point, Piaget cited a friend's recollection from childhood:

> [H]e put [the pebbles] in a row and he counted them one, two, three up to 10. Then he . . . started to count them in the other direction. . . . and once again he found that he had 10. He found this marvelous. . . .
>
> (Piaget, 1964, p. 12)

Jean Piaget, whose work has had a profound influence on developmental psychology, is seen here interviewing a child to learn about his thinking.

PHOTO RESEARCHERS / GETTY IMAGES

This incident also highlights a third basic assumption of Piaget's: children are intrinsically motivated to learn and do not need rewards from other people to do so. When they acquire a new capability, they apply it as often as possible. They also reflect on the lessons of their experience, because they want to understand themselves and everything around them.

Central Developmental Issues

In addition to his view that children actively shape their own development, Piaget offered important insights regarding the roles of *nature and nurture* and of *continuity/discontinuity* in development.

Nature and Nurture

Piaget believed that nature and nurture interact to produce cognitive development. In his view, nurture includes not just the nurturing provided by parents and other caregivers but every experience children encounter. Nature includes children's maturing brain and body; their ability to perceive, act, and learn from experience; and their tendency to integrate particular observations into coherent knowledge. As this description suggests, a vital part of children's nature is how they respond to nurture.

Sources of Continuity

Piaget depicted development as involving both continuities and discontinuities. The main sources of continuity are three processes—*assimilation, accommodation,* and *equilibration*—that work together from birth to propel development forward.

Assimilation is the process by which people incorporate incoming information into concepts they already understand. To illustrate, when one of our children was 2 years old, he saw a man who was bald on top of his head and had long frizzy hair on the sides. To his father's great embarrassment, the toddler gleefully shouted, "Clown! Clown!" (Actually, it sounded more like "Kown! Kown!") The man apparently looked enough like a "kown" that the boy could assimilate him to his clown concept.

Accommodation is the process by which people improve their current understanding in response to new experiences. In the "kown" incident, the boy's father explained to his son that the man was not a clown and that even though his hair looked like a clown's, he was not wearing a funny costume and was not doing silly things to make people laugh. With this new information, the boy was able to accommodate his clown concept to the standard one, allowing other men with bald pates and long side hair to proceed in peace.

Equilibration is the process by which people balance assimilation and accommodation to create stable understanding. Equilibration includes three phases. First, people are satisfied with their understanding of a particular phenomenon; Piaget labeled this a state of *equilibrium,* because people do not see any discrepancies between their observations and their understanding of the phenomenon. Then, new information leads them to perceive that their understanding is inadequate. Piaget said that this realization puts people in a state of *disequilibrium;* they recognize shortcomings in their understanding of the phenomenon, but they cannot generate a superior alternative. Put more simply, they are confused. Finally, they develop a more sophisticated understanding that eliminates the shortcomings of the old one, creating a more advanced equilibrium within which a broader range of observations can be understood.

assimilation ■ the process by which people translate incoming information into a form that fits concepts they already understand

accommodation ■ the process by which people adapt current knowledge structures in response to new experiences

equilibration ■ the process by which children (or other people) balance assimilation and accommodation to create stable understanding

Perhaps hearing toddlers yelling "Kown, kown!" set Larry, a member of The Three Stooges, on his career path.

EVERETT COLLECTION, INC.

One example of how equilibration works involves the belief—held by most 4- to 7-year-olds in a wide range of cultures (Inagaki & Hatano, 2008)—that animals are the only living things. This belief seems to stem from the assumption that only animals can move in ways that help them survive. Sooner or later, children realize that plants also move in ways that promote their survival (e.g., they bend toward sunlight). This new information is difficult for them to assimilate to their prior thinking. The resulting disparity between their previous understanding of living things and their new knowledge about plants creates a state of disequilibrium, in which they are confused about what it means to be alive. Later, their thinking accommodates the new information about plants: they realize that both animals and plants move in adaptive ways and that, because adaptive movement is a key characteristic of living things, plants as well as animals must be alive (Opfer & Gelman, 2001; Opfer & Siegler, 2004). This realization constitutes a more stable equilibrium because subsequent information about plants and animals will not contradict it. Through innumerable such equilibrations, children acquire knowledge of the world around them.

Sources of Discontinuity

Although Piaget placed some emphasis on continuous aspects of cognitive development, the most famous part of his theory concerns discontinuous aspects, which he depicted as distinct *stages* of cognitive development. Piaget viewed these stages as products of the basic human tendency to organize knowledge into coherent structures. Each stage represents a unified way of understanding one's experience, and each transition between stages represents a discontinuous intellectual leap from one coherent way of understanding the world to the next, higher one. The following are the central properties of Piaget's stage theory:

1. Qualitative change. Piaget believed that children of different ages think in qualitatively different ways. For example, he proposed that children in the early stages of cognitive development conceive of morality in terms of the *consequences* of a person's behavior, whereas children in later stages conceive of it in terms of the person's *intent.* Thus, a 5-year-old would judge someone who accidentally broke a whole jar of cookies as having been naughtier than someone who deliberately stole a single cookie; an 8-year-old would reach the opposite conclusion. This difference represents a *qualitative change,* because the two children are basing their moral judgments on entirely different criteria.

2. Broad applicability. The type of thinking characteristic of each stage influences children's thinking across diverse topics and contexts.

3. Brief transitions. Before entering a new stage, children pass through a brief transitional period in which they fluctuate between the type of thinking characteristic of the new, more advanced stage and the type of thinking characteristic of the old, less advanced one.

4. Invariant sequence. Everyone progresses through the stages in the same order without skipping any of them.

Piaget hypothesized four stages of cognitive development: the *sensorimotor* stage, the *preoperational* stage, the *concrete operational* stage, and the *formal operational* stage. In each stage, children exhibit new abilities that enable them to understand the world in qualitatively different ways than they had previously.

1. In the **sensorimotor stage** (birth to age 2 years), infants' intelligence is expressed through their sensory and motor abilities, which they use to perceive and explore the world around them. These abilities allow them to learn about objects and people and to construct rudimentary forms of fundamental concepts such as time, space, and causality. Throughout the sensorimotor period, infants live largely in the here and now: their intelligence is bound to their immediate perceptions and actions.

2. In the **preoperational stage** (ages 2 to 7 years), toddlers and preschoolers become able to represent their experiences in language and mental imagery. This allows them to remember the experiences for longer periods and to form more sophisticated concepts. However, as suggested by the term *preoperational,* Piaget's theory emphasizes young children's inability to perform certain *mental operations,* such as considering multiple dimensions simultaneously. This leads to children's being unable to form certain ideas, such as the idea that pouring all the water from a short, wide glass into a taller, narrower glass does not change the total amount of water, even though the column of water is higher in the second glass. In other words, they do not recognize that the increased height of the liquid column in the second glass is compensated for by its being narrower.

3. In the **concrete operational stage** (ages 7 to 12 years), children can reason logically about concrete objects and events; for example, they understand that pouring water from one glass to a taller, narrower one leaves the amount of water unchanged. However, concrete operational reasoners cannot think in purely abstract terms or generate systematic scientific experiments to test their beliefs.

4. In the final stage of cognitive development, the **formal operational stage** (age 12 years and beyond), adolescents and adults can think deeply not only about concrete events but also about abstractions and purely hypothetical situations. They can also perform systematic scientific experiments and draw appropriate conclusions from them, even when the conclusions differ from their prior beliefs.

With this overview of Piaget's theory, we can consider in greater depth major changes that take place within each stage and from one stage to another.

The Sensorimotor Stage (Birth to Age 2 Years)

One of Piaget's most profound insights was his realization that the roots of adult intelligence are present in infants' earliest behaviors, such as their seemingly aimless sucking, flailing, and grasping. He recognized that these behaviors are not random but instead reflect an early type of intelligence involving sensory (perceptual) and motor activity. Indeed, many of the clearest examples of the *active child* theme come from Piaget's descriptions of the development of what he called "sensorimotor intelligence."

sensorimotor stage ■ the period (birth to 2 years) within Piaget's theory in which intelligence is expressed through sensory and motor abilities

preoperational stage ■ the period (2 to 7 years) within Piaget's theory in which children become able to represent their experiences in language, mental imagery, and symbolic thought

concrete operational stage ■ the period (7 to 12 years) within Piaget's theory in which children become able to reason logically about concrete objects and events

formal operational stage ■ the period (12 years and beyond) within Piaget's theory in which people become able to think about abstractions and hypothetical situations

 Sensorimotor Intelligence in Infancy and Toddlerhood

Piaget proposed that when infants suck on objects, they gain not only pleasure but also knowledge about the world beyond their bodies.

Over the course of the first 2 years, infants' sensorimotor intelligence develops tremendously. The sheer amount of change may at first seem astonishing. However, when we consider the innumerable new experiences that infants encounter during this period, and the tripling of brain weight between birth and age 3 (with weight being an index of brain development during this period), the huge increase in infants' cognitive abilities is understandable. The profound developments that Piaget described as occurring during infancy call attention to a general principle: *the earlier in development, the more rapidly changes occur.*

Infants are born with many reflexes. When objects move in front of their eyes, they visually track them; when objects are placed in their mouths, they suck them; when objects come into contact with their hands, they grasp them; when they hear noises, they turn toward them; and so on.

Even during their first month, infants begin to modify their reflexes to make them more adaptive. At birth, for example, they suck in a similar way regardless of what they are sucking. Within a few weeks, however, they adjust their sucking according to the object in their mouth. Thus, they suck on a milk-yielding nipple in a way that enhances the efficiency of their feeding and that is different from the way they suck on a finger or pacifier. As this example illustrates, from the first days out of the womb, infants accommodate their actions to the parts of the environment with which they interact.

Over the first few months, infants begin to organize separate reflexes into larger behaviors, most of them centered on their own bodies. For example, instead of being limited to exercising their grasping and sucking reflexes separately, they can integrate them: when an object touches their palm, they can grasp it, bring it to their mouth, and suck on it. Thus, their reflexes serve as components of more complex behaviors.

In the middle of their first year, infants become increasingly interested in the world around them—people, animals, toys, and other objects and events beyond their own bodies. A hallmark of this shift is repetition of actions that produce pleasurable or interesting results, such as repeatedly banging a rattle or squeezing a rubber duck again and again to make it squeak.

Piaget (1954) advanced a striking and controversial claim about a deficiency in infants' thinking during this period—the one referred to in the chapter-opening anecdote about the father hiding his glasses. The claim was that through the age of 8 months, infants lack **object permanence,** the knowledge that objects continue to exist even when they are out of view. This hypothesis, like many of Piaget's claims about development during infancy, was based largely on his observations of his own children, Laurent, Lucienne, and Jacqueline. The following account of an informal experiment with Laurent reflects the type of observation that inspired Piaget's belief about object permanence:

> At age 7 months, 28 days, I offer him a little bell behind a cushion. So long as he sees the little bell, however small it may be, he tries to grasp it. But if the little bell disappears completely he stops all searching. I then resume the experiment using my hand as a screen. Laurent's arm is outstretched and about to grasp the little bell at the moment I make it disappear behind my hand which is open and at a distance of about 15 cm from him. He immediately withdraws his arm, as though the little bell no longer existed.
>
> (Piaget, 1954, p. 39)

Thus, in Piaget's view, for infants younger than 8 months, the adage "out of sight, out of mind" is literally true. They are able to mentally represent (think about) only the objects that they can perceive at the moment.

object permanence ■ the knowledge that objects continue to exist even when they are out of view

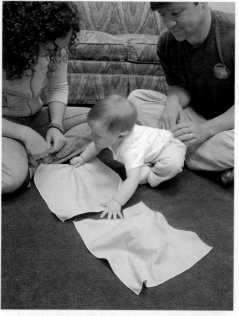

BEN CLORE

FIGURE 4.1 Piaget's A-not-B task A child looks for and finds a toy under the cloth where it was hidden (left frame). After several such experiences, the toy is hidden in a different location (right frame). The child continues to look where he found the toy previously, rather than where it is hidden now. The child's ignoring the visible protrusion of the toy under the cloth in the right frame illustrates the strength of the inclination to look in the previous hiding place.

▶ **Problem Solving and the A-not-B Error**

A-not-B error ■ the tendency to reach for a hidden object where it was last found rather than in the new location where it was last hidden

deferred imitation ■ the repetition of other people's behavior a substantial time after it originally occurred

By the end of the first year, infants search for hidden objects, thus indicating that they mentally represent the objects' continuing existence even when they no longer see them. These initial representations of objects are fragile, however, as reflected in the **A-not-B error.** In this error, once 8- to 12-month-olds have reached for and found a hidden object several times in one place (location A), they tend to reach there again when they see the object hidden at a different place (location B) and are prevented from immediately reaching for it (see Figure 4.1). Not until around their 1st birthday do infants consistently search first at the object's current location.

At around 1 year of age, infants begin to actively and avidly explore the potential ways in which objects can be used. The "child as scientist" example presented earlier, in which Piaget's son Laurent varied the positions from which he dropped different objects to see what would happen, provides one instance of this emerging competency. Similar examples occur in every family with an infant. Few parents forget their 1-year-old sitting in a high chair, banging various objects against the chair's tray—first a spoon, then a plate, then a cup—seemingly fascinated by the different sounds. Nor do they forget their infant dropping bathroom articles into the toilet or pouring a bag of flour on the kitchen floor, just to see what happens.

In the last half-year of the sensorimotor stage (ages 18 to 24 months), according to Piaget, infants become able to form enduring mental representations. The first sign of this new capability is **deferred imitation,** that is, the repetition of other people's behavior minutes, hours, or even days after it occurred. Consider Piaget's observation of 1-year-old Jacqueline:

> Jacqueline had a visit from a little boy . . . who, in the course of the afternoon, got into a terrible temper. He screamed as he tried to get out of a playpen and pushed it backward, stamping his feet. . . . The next day, she herself screamed in her playpen and tried to move it, stamping her foot lightly several times in succession.
>
> (Piaget, 1951, p. 63)

Piaget indicated that Jacqueline had never before thrown such a tantrum. Presumably, she had watched and remembered her playmate's behavior, maintained

COURTESY OF JUDY DELOACHE

This toddler's techniques for applying eye makeup may not exactly mirror those he has seen his mother use, but they are close enough to provide a compelling illustration of deferred imitation, a skill that children gain during their second year.

symbolic representation ■ the use of one object to stand for another

egocentrism ■ the tendency to perceive the world solely from one's own point of view

ILLUSTRATION BY VIVIAN HOXSEY

FIGURE 4.2 A 4-year-old's drawing of a summer day Note the use of simple artistic conventions, such as the V-shaped leaves on the flowers.

FIGURE 4.3 Piaget's three-mountains task When asked to choose the picture that shows what the doll sitting in the seat across the table would see, most children younger than 6 years choose the picture showing how the scene looks to them, illustrating their difficulty in separating their own perspective from that of others.

a representation of it overnight, and imitated it the next day. When we consider Piaget's account of cognitive development during infancy, several notable trends are evident.

■ At first, infants' activities center on their own bodies; later, their activities include the world around them.

■ Early goals are concrete (shaking a rattle and listening to the sound it makes); later goals often are more abstract (varying the heights from which objects are dropped and observing how the effects vary).

■ Infants become increasingly able to form mental representations, moving from "out of sight, out of mind" to remembering a playmate's actions from a full day earlier. Such enduring mental representations make possible the next stage, which Piaget called preoperational thinking.

The Preoperational Stage (Ages 2 to 7)

Piaget viewed the preoperational period as including striking cognitive acquisitions and equally striking limitations. Perhaps the foremost acquisition is *symbolic representations;* among the most notable weaknesses are *egocentrism* and *centration.*

Development of symbolic representations Have you ever seen preschoolers use two sticks to represent a gun or use a playing card to represent an iPhone? Forming such personal symbols is common among 3- to 5-year-olds. It is one of the ways in which they exercise their emerging capacity for **symbolic representation**—the use of one object, word, or thought to stand for another. Typically, objects that toddlers and preschoolers use as personal symbols physically resemble the objects they represent. The shapes of the sticks and playing card resemble those of a gun and an iPhone.

As children develop, they rely less on self-generated symbols and more on conventional ones. For example, when 5-year-olds play games involving pirates, they might wear a patch over one eye and a bandanna over their head because that is how pirates are commonly depicted. Heightened symbolic capabilities during the preoperational period are also evident in the growth of drawing. Children's drawings between ages 3 and 5 make increasing use of symbolic conventions, such as representing the leaves of flowers as Vs (Figure 4.2).

Egocentrism Although Piaget noted important growth in children's thinking during the preoperational stage, he found its limitations to be equally intriguing. One important limitation of their thinking is **egocentrism,** perceiving the world solely from one's own point of view. An example of this limitation involves preschoolers' difficulty in taking other people's spatial perspectives. Piaget and Inhelder (1956/1977) demonstrated this difficulty by having 4-year-olds sit at a table in front of a model of three mountains of different sizes (Figure 4.3). The children were asked to identify which of several photographs depicted what a doll would see if it were sitting on chairs at various locations around the table. Solving this problem required children to recognize that their own perspective was not the only one possible and to imagine what the view would be from another location. Most 4-year-olds, according to Piaget, cannot do this.

The same difficulty in taking other people's perspectives is seen in quite different contexts—for example, in communication. As illustrated in Figure 4.4, preschoolers often talk right past each other, focused only on what they themselves are saying and seemingly oblivious to other people's comments. Preschoolers' egocentric communication also is evident when they make statements that require knowledge they themselves possess but that their listeners couldn't be expected to have. For example, 2- and 3-year-olds frequently tell day-care providers and parents things like "He took it from me," in situations where the person or object to which the child is referring is totally unclear. Egocentric thinking is also evident in preschoolers' explanations of events and behavior. Consider the following interviews with preschoolers that occurred in the original version of the TV show *Kids Say the Darndest Things:*

> *Interviewer:* Any brothers or sisters?
> *Child:* I have a brother a week old.
> *I:* What can he do?
> *C:* He can say "Mamma" and "Daddy."
> *I:* Can he walk?
> *C:* No, he's too lazy.

> *Interviewer:* Any brothers or sisters?
> *Child:* A 2-months-old brother.
> *I:* How does he behave?
> *C:* He cries all night.
> *I:* Why is that, do you think?
> *C:* He probably thinks he's missing something on television.
>
> (Linkletter, 1957, p. 6)

Over the course of the preoperational period, egocentric speech becomes less common. An early sign of progress is children's verbal quarrels, which become increasingly frequent during this period. The fact that a child's statements elicit a playmate's objection indicates that the playmate is at least paying attention to the differing perspective that the other child's comment implies. Children also become better able to envision spatial perspectives other than their own during the preoperational period. We all remain somewhat egocentric throughout our lives—our own perspectives almost always seem more compelling than those of other people—but most of us do become less egocentric with age and experience.

Centration   A related limitation of preschoolers' thinking is **centration,** that is, focusing on a single, perceptually striking feature of an object or event to the exclusion of other relevant but less striking features. Children's approaches to balance-scale problems provide a good example of centration. If presented with a balance scale like that in Figure 4.5 and asked which side will go down, 5- and 6-year-olds center on the amount of weight on each side, ignore the distance of the weights from the fulcrum, and say that whichever side has more weight will go down (Inhelder & Piaget, 1958).

Another good example of centration comes from Piaget's research on children's understanding of conservation. The idea of the **conservation concept** is that merely changing the appearance or arrangement of objects does not necessarily change other key properties, such as the quantity of material. Three variants of the concept that are commonly studied in 5- to 8-year-olds are *conservation of liquid quantity, conservation of solid quantity,* and *conservation of number* (Piaget, 1952a). In all three cases, the tasks used to measure children's understanding employ a three-phase procedure (Figure 4.6). First, as in the figure, children are shown two

FIGURE 4.4 Egocentrism An example of young children's egocentric conversations.

centration ■ the tendency to focus on a single, perceptually striking feature of an object or event

conservation concept ■ the idea that merely changing the appearance of objects does not necessarily change the objects' other key properties

▶ **The Balance-Scale Problem**

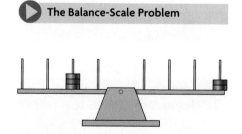

FIGURE 4.5 The balance scale When asked to predict which side of a balance scale, like the one shown above, would go down if the arm were allowed to move, 5- and 6-year-olds almost always center their attention on the amount of weight and ignore the distances of the weights from the fulcrum. Thus, they would predict that the left side would go down, even though it is the right side that would actually drop.

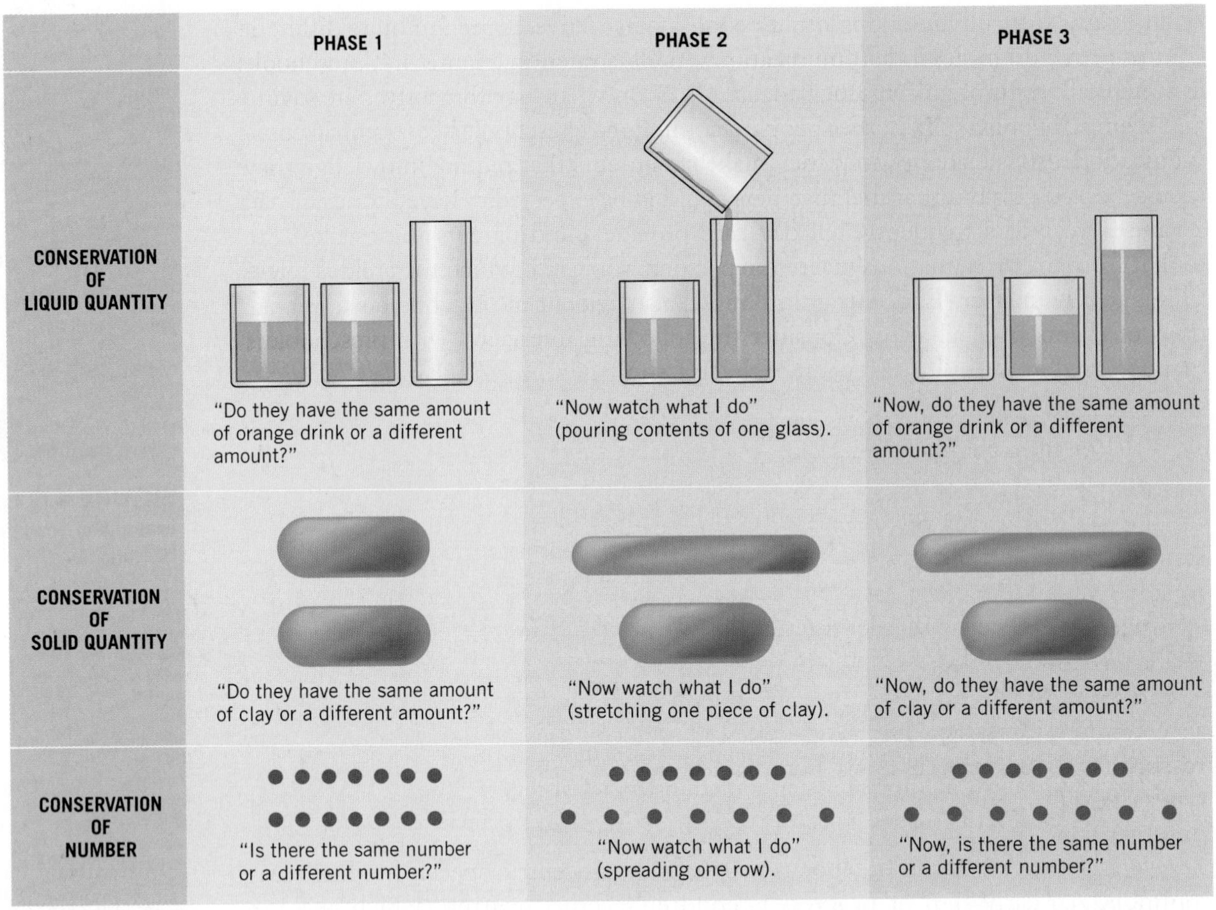

	PHASE 1	PHASE 2	PHASE 3
CONSERVATION OF LIQUID QUANTITY	"Do they have the same amount of orange drink or a different amount?"	"Now watch what I do" (pouring contents of one glass).	"Now, do they have the same amount of orange drink or a different amount?"
CONSERVATION OF SOLID QUANTITY	"Do they have the same amount of clay or a different amount?"	"Now watch what I do" (stretching one piece of clay).	"Now, do they have the same amount of clay or a different amount?"
CONSERVATION OF NUMBER	"Is there the same number or a different number?"	"Now watch what I do" (spreading one row).	"Now, is there the same number or a different number?"

FIGURE 4.6 Procedures used to test conservation of liquid quantity, solid quantity, and number Most 4- and 5-year-olds say that the taller liquid column has more liquid, the longer sausage has more clay, and the longer row has more objects.

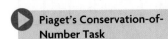

▶ **Piaget's Conservation-of-Liquid Task**

▶ **Piaget's Conservation-of-Number Task**

objects (e.g., two glasses of orange drink, two clay sausages) that are identical in quantity, or two sets of objects (e.g., two rows of pennies) that are identical in number. Once children agree that the dimension of interest (e.g., the amount of orange drink or the number of pennies) is equal in the two objects or sets, they observe a second phase in which the experimenter transforms one object or set in a way that makes it look different but does not change the dimension of interest. Orange drink might be poured into a taller, narrower glass; a short, thick clay sausage might be molded into a long, thin sausage; or a row of pennies might be spread out. Finally, in the third phase, children are asked whether the dimension of interest, which they earlier had said was equal for the two objects or sets of objects, remains equal.

The large majority of 4- and 5-year-olds answer "no." On conservation-of-liquid-quantity problems, they claim that the taller, narrower glass has more orange drink; on conservation-of-solid-quantity problems, they claim that the long, thin sausage has more clay than the short, thick one; and so on. Children of this age make similar errors in everyday contexts; for example, they often think that if a child has one fewer cookie than another child, a fair solution is to break one of the short-changed child's cookies into two pieces, so that he or she will have as many cookies as the other child (Miller, 1984).

A variety of weaknesses that Piaget perceived in preoperational thinking contribute to these difficulties with conservation problems. Preoperational thinkers center their attention on the single, perceptually salient dimension of height or length, ignoring other relevant dimensions. In addition, their egocentrism leads to their failing to understand that their own perspective can be misleading—that just because the tall, narrow glass of orange drink or the long, thin clay sausage looks like it has more orange drink or clay does not mean that it really does. Children's tendency to focus on static states of objects (the appearance of the objects after the transformation) and to ignore the transformation that was performed (pouring the orange drink or reshaping the clay) also contributes to their difficulty in solving conservation problems.

In the next period of cognitive development, the concrete operational stage, children largely overcome these and related limitations.

The Concrete Operational Stage (Ages 7 to 12)

At around age 7, according to Piaget, children begin to reason logically about concrete features of the world. Development of the conservation concept exemplifies this progress. Although few 5-year-olds solve any of the three conservation tasks described in the previous section, most 8-year-olds solve all of them. The same progress in thinking also allows children in the concrete operational stage to solve many other problems that require attention to multiple dimensions. For example, on the balance-scale problem, they consider distance from the fulcrum as well as weight of objects.

However, this relatively advanced reasoning is, according to Piaget, limited to concrete situations. Thinking systematically remains very difficult, as does reasoning about hypothetical situations. These limitations are evident in the types of experiments that concrete operational children perform to solve the pendulum problem (Inhelder & Piaget, 1958) (Figure 4.7). In this problem, children are presented a pendulum frame, a set of strings of varying lengths with a loop at each end, and a set of metal weights of varying weights, any of which can be attached to any string. When the loop at one end of the string is attached to a weight, and the loop at the other end is attached to the frame of the pendulum, the string can be swung. The task is to perform experiments that indicate which factor or factors influence the amount of time it takes the pendulum to swing through a complete arc. Is it the length of the string, the heaviness of the weight, the height from which the weight is dropped, or some combination of these factors? Think for a minute: How would you go about solving this problem?

Most concrete operational children, like most adolescents and adults, begin their experiments believing that the relative heaviness of the weights being dropped is the most important factor, perhaps the only important one. What distinguishes the children's reasoning from that of older individuals is how they test their beliefs. Concrete operational children design biased experiments from which no valid conclusion can be drawn. For example, they might compare the travel time of a heavy weight on a short string dropped from a high position to the travel time of a light weight on a long string dropped from a lower position. When the first string goes faster, they conclude that, just as they thought, heavy weights go faster. This premature conclusion, however, reflects their limited ability to think systematically or to imagine all possible combinations of variables. They fail to imagine that the faster motion might be related to the length of the string or the height from which the string was dropped, rather than the weight of the object.

The Formal Operational Stage (Age 12 and Beyond)

Formal operational thinking, which includes the ability to think abstractly and to reason hypothetically, is the pinnacle of Piaget's stage progression. The

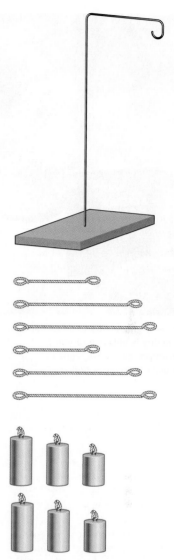

FIGURE 4.7 Inhelder and Piaget's pendulum problem The task is to determine the influence of weight, string length, and dropping point on the time it takes for the pendulum to swing back and forth. Unbiased experiments require varying one and only one variable at a time—for example, comparing a heavier weight to a lighter weight when both are attached to strings of the same length and dropped from the same point. Children younger than 12 usually perform unsystematic experiments and draw incorrect conclusions.

MARK RICHARDS / PHOTOEDIT

Teenagers' emerging ability to understand that their reality is only one of many possible realities may cause teens to develop a taste for science fiction.

difference between reasoning in this stage and in the previous one is clearly illustrated by formal operational reasoners' approach to the pendulum problem. Framing the problem more abstractly than do children in the concrete operational stage, formal operational reasoners see that any of the variables—weight, string length, and dropping point—might influence the time it takes for the pendulum to swing through an arc, and that it is therefore necessary to test the effect of each variable systematically. For example, to test the effect of weight, they compare times to complete an arc for a heavier weight and a lighter weight, attached to strings of equal length dropped from the same position. To test the effect of string length, they compare the travel times of a long and a short string, with equal weight dropped from the same position. Such systematic experiments allow the formal operational thinker to determine that the only factor that influences the pendulum's travel time is the length of the string.

Piaget believed that unlike the previous three stages, the formal operational stage is not universal: not all adolescents (or adults) reach it. For those adolescents who do reach it, however, formal operational thinking greatly expands and enriches their intellectual universe. Such thinking makes it possible for them to see the particular reality in which they live as only one of an infinite number of possible realities. This insight leads them to think about alternative ways that the world could be and to ponder deep questions concerning truth, justice, and morality. It no doubt also helps account for the fact that many people first acquire a taste for science fiction during adolescence. The alternative worlds depicted in science-fiction stories appeal to adolescents' emerging capacity to think about the world they know as just one of many possibilities and to wonder whether a better world is possible.

The attainment of formal operational thinking does not mean that adolescents will always reason in advanced ways, but it does, according to Piaget, mark the point at which adolescents attain the reasoning powers of intelligent adults. (Some ways in which Piaget's theory has been applied to improving education are discussed in Box 4.1.)

Piaget's Legacy

Although Piaget's theory was formulated many years ago, it remains a very influential approach to understanding cognitive development. Some of its strengths were mentioned earlier. It provides a good overview of children's thinking at different points in development (Table 4.2). It includes countless fascinating observations. It offers a plausible and an appealing perspective on children's nature. It surveys a remarkably broad spectrum of developments and covers the entire age span from infancy through adolescence.

However, subsequent analyses (e.g., Miller, 2011) have identified some crucial weaknesses in Piaget's theory. The following four are particularly important:

1. Piaget's theory is vague about the mechanisms that give rise to children's thinking and that produce cognitive growth. Piaget's theory provides any number of excellent descriptions of children's thinking. It is less revealing, however, about the processes that lead children to think in a particular way and that produce changes in their thinking. Assimilation, accommodation, and equilibration have an air of plausibility, but how they operate is unclear.

BOX 4.1 | applications

EDUCATIONAL APPLICATIONS OF PIAGET'S THEORY

Piaget's view of children's cognitive development holds a number of general implications for how children should be educated (Case, 1998; Piaget, 1972). Most generally, it suggests that children's distinctive ways of thinking at different ages need to be considered in deciding how to teach them. For example, children in the concrete operational stage would not be expected to be ready to learn purely abstract concepts such as inertia and equilibrium state, whereas adolescents in the formal operational stage would be.

A second implication of Piaget's approach is that children learn best by interacting with the environment, both mentally and physically. One research demonstration of this principle involved promoting children's understanding of the concept of speed (Levin, Siegler, & Druyan, 1990). The investigation focused on problems of a type beloved by physics teachers: "When a race horse travels around a circular track, do its right and left sides move at the same speed?" It appears obvious that they do, but, in fact, they do not. The side toward the outside of the track is covering a slightly greater distance in the

The child and adult are holding onto a bar as they walk around a circle four times. On the first two trips around, the child holds the bar near the pivot; on the second two trips, the child holds it at its end. The much faster pace needed to keep up with the bar when holding onto its end leads the child to realize that the end was moving faster than the inner portion (Levin et al., 1990).

same amount of time as the side toward the inside and therefore is moving slightly faster.

Levin and her colleagues devised a procedure that allowed children to actively experience how different parts of a single object can move at different speeds. They attached one end of a 7-foot-long metal bar to a pivot that was mounted on the floor. One by one, 6th-graders and an experimenter took four walks around the

pivot while holding onto the bar. On two of the walks, the child held the bar near the pivot and the experimenter held it at the far end; on the other two walks, they switched positions (see figure). After each walk, children were asked whether the inner or outer part of the bar had moved faster.

The difference between the speeds required for walking while holding the inner and the outer parts of the metal bar was so dramatic that the children generalized their new understanding to other problems involving circular motion, such as cars moving around circular tracks on a computer screen. In other words, physically experiencing the concept accomplished what years of formal science instruction usually fail to do. As one boy said to the experimenter, "Before, I hadn't experienced it. I didn't think about it. Now that I have had that experience, I know that when I was on the outer circle, I had to walk faster to be at the same place as you" (Levin et al., 1990). Clearly, relevant physical activities, accompanied by questions that call attention to the lessons of the activities, can foster children's learning.

TABLE 4.2

Piaget's Stages of Cognitive Development

Stage	Approximate Age	New Ways of Knowing
Sensorimotor	Birth to 2 years	Infants know the world through their senses and through their actions. For example, they learn what dogs look like and what petting them feels like.
Preoperational	2–7 years	Toddlers and young children acquire the ability to internally represent the world through language and mental imagery. They also begin to see the world from other people's perspectives, not just from their own.
Concrete operational	7–12 years	Children become able to think logically, not just intuitively. They now can understand that events are often influenced by multiple factors, not just one.
Formal operational	12 years and beyond	Adolescents can think systematically and reason about what might be, as well as what is. This allows them to understand politics, ethics, and science fiction, as well as to engage in scientific reasoning.

2. Infants and young children are more cognitively competent than Piaget recognized. Piaget employed fairly difficult tests to assess most of the concepts he studied. This led him to miss infants' and young children's earliest knowledge of these concepts. For example, Piaget's test of object permanence required children to reach for the hidden object after a delay; Piaget claimed that children do not do this until about 8 months of age. However, alternative tests of object permanence, which analyze where infants *look* immediately after the object has disappeared from view, indicate that by 3 months of age, infants at least suspect that objects continue to exist (Baillargeon, 1987a, b; 1993).

3. Piaget's theory understates the contribution of the social world to cognitive development. Piaget's theory focuses on how children come to understand the world through their own efforts. From the day that children emerge from the womb, however, they live in an environment of adults, older children, and cultural institutions and values that shape their cognitive development in countless ways. A child's cognitive development reflects the contributions of other people, and of the broader culture, to a far greater degree than Piaget's theory acknowledges.

4. The stage model depicts children's thinking as being more consistent than it is. According to Piaget, once children enter a given stage, their thinking consistently shows the characteristics of that stage across diverse concepts. Subsequent research, however, has shown that children's thinking is far more variable than this depiction suggests. For example, most children succeed on conservation-of-number problems by age 6, whereas most do not succeed on conservation of solid quantity until about age 8 (Field, 1987).

These weaknesses of Piaget's theory do not negate the magnitude of his achievement: it remains one of the major intellectual accomplishments of the past century. However, appreciating the weaknesses as well as the strengths of his theory is necessary for understanding why alternative theories of cognitive development have become increasingly prominent.

In the remainder of this chapter, we consider the four most prominent alternative theories of cognitive development: information-processing, core-knowledge, sociocultural, and dynamic-systems. Each can be seen as an attempt to overcome a major weakness of Piaget's approach. *Information-processing theories* emphasize precise characterizations of the mechanisms that give rise to children's thinking and that produce cognitive growth. *Core-knowledge theories* focus on the surprisingly early knowledge and skills that infants and young children show in areas thought to be of evolutionary importance. *Sociocultural theories* emphasize the ways in which children's interactions with other people and with the products of their culture guide cognitive development. *Dynamic-systems theories* highlight the variability of children's thinking, even from moment to moment.

Review

Piaget's theory of cognitive development emphasizes the interaction of nature and nurture, continuities and discontinuities, and children's active contribution to their own development. The continuities of development are produced by assimilation (interpreting incoming information to fit current understanding), accommodation (adapting one's thinking to match new experience), and equilibration (balancing assimilation and accommodation to create stable understandings).

As depicted by Piaget, the discontinuities of cognitive development involve four discrete stages: (1) the sensorimotor stage (the first 2 years), in which infants begin to know the world through the perceptions of their senses and through their motor activities; (2) the preoperational stage (ages 2 to 7), in which children become capable of mental representations but tend to be egocentric and to focus on a single dimension of an event or a problem; (3) the concrete operational stage (ages 7 to 12), in which children reason logically about concrete aspects of the environment but have difficulty thinking abstractly; and (4) the formal operational stage (age 12 and beyond), in which preadolescents and adolescents become capable of systematic thought and experimentation.

Among the important strengths of Piaget's theory are its broad overview of development, its plausible and attractive perspective on children's nature, its inclusion of varied tasks and age groups, and its endlessly fascinating observations. Among the theory's important weaknesses are its vagueness regarding cognitive mechanisms, its underestimation of infants' and young children's cognitive competence, its lack of attention to the contribution of the social world, and its overstatement of the consistency of children's thinking.

Information-Processing Theories

SCENE: DAUGHTER AND FATHER IN THEIR YARD.
A PLAYMATE RIDES IN ON A BIKE.
> *Child:* Daddy, would you unlock the basement door?
> *Father:* Why?
> *Child:* 'Cause I want to ride my bike.
> *Father:* Your bike is in the garage.
> *Child:* But my socks are in the dryer.

(Klahr, 1978, pp. 181–182)

What reasoning could have produced this 5-year-old's enigmatic comment, "But my socks are in the dryer"? David Klahr, an eminent information-processing theorist (and the father in the conversation) formulated the following model of the thought process that led to it:

> *Top goal:* I want to ride my bike.
> > *Bias:* I need shoes to ride comfortably.
> > *Fact:* I'm barefoot.
> *Subgoal 1:* Get my sneakers.
> > *Fact:* The sneakers are in the yard.
> > *Fact:* They're uncomfortable on bare feet.
> *Subgoal 2:* Get my socks.
> > *Fact:* The sock drawer was empty this morning.
> > *Inference:* The socks probably are in the dryer.
> *Subgoal 3:* Get them from the dryer.
> > *Fact:* The dryer is in the basement.
> *Subgoal 4:* Go to the basement.
> > *Fact:* It's quicker to go through the yard entrance.
> > *Fact:* The yard entrance is always locked.
> *Subgoal 5:* Unlock the door to the basement.
> > *Fact:* Daddies have the keys to everything.
> *Subgoal 6:* Ask Daddy to unlock the door.

Klahr's analysis of his daughter's thinking illustrates two notable characteristics of **information-processing theories.**[1] One is the precise specification of the processes involved in children's thinking. To help specify these processes, Klahr used

information-processing theories ■ a class of theories that focus on the structure of the cognitive system and the mental activities used to deploy attention and memory to solve problems

---

[1] Here and throughout this section, we use the plural term "information-processing *theories*" rather than the singular "information-processing *theory*" because information-processing theories consist of a family of related approaches rather than a single theory. For the same reason, in subsequent sections we refer to "core-knowledge theories," "sociocultural theories," and "dynamic-systems theories."

task analysis ■ the research technique of identifying goals, relevant information in the environment, and potential processing strategies for a problem

computer simulation ■ a type of mathematical model that expresses ideas about mental processes in precise ways

task analysis—that is, identification of goals needed to perform the task, obstacles that prevent their immediate realization, information in the environment and prior knowledge relevant to achieving the goals, and potential strategies for reaching the desired outcome.

Task analysis helps information-processing researchers understand and predict children's behavior and to rigorously test precise hypotheses regarding how development occurs. In some cases, it also allows them to formulate a **computer simulation**, a type of mathematical model that expresses ideas about mental processes in precise ways. For example, Simon and Klahr (1995) created computer simulations of the knowledge and mental processes that led young children to fail on conservation problems and of the somewhat different knowledge and mental processes that allowed older children to succeed on them. Comparing the two simulations allowed the researchers to identify the processes that produced the change from failure to success. Computer simulations have been used to model many other aspects of development as well, including object permanence (Munakata & McClelland, 2003), word learning (McMurray, Horst, & Samuelson, 2012), categorization (Rakison & Lupyan, 2008; Rogers & McClelland, 2004), phonology (Thiessen & Pavlik, 2013), working memory (Buss & Spencer, 2014), reading (Seidenberg, 2005), and problem solving (Siegler & Araya, 2005).

A second distinctive feature of information-processing theories is an emphasis on thinking as a process that occurs over time. Often, a single simple behavior, such as the initial request of Klahr's daughter that he open the basement door, reflects an extended sequence of rapid mental operations. Information-processing analyses identify what those mental operations are, the order in which they are executed, and how increasing speed and accuracy of mental operations lead to cognitive growth.

View of Children's Nature

Information-processing theorists see cognitive development as occurring continuously, in small increments that happen at different ages on different tasks. This depiction differs fundamentally from Piaget's belief that children progress through qualitatively distinct, broadly applicable stages at similar ages.

The Child as a Limited-Capacity Processing System

In trying to understand differences in children's thinking at various ages, some information-processing theorists draw comparisons between the information processing of computers and that of humans. A computer's information processing is limited by its hardware and software. The hardware limitations relate to the computer's memory capacity and its speed in executing basic operations. The software limitations relate to the strategies and knowledge that are available for performing particular tasks. People's thinking is limited by the same factors: memory capacity, speed of thought processes, and availability of useful strategies and knowledge. In the information-processing view, cognitive development arises from children's gradually surmounting their processing limitations through (1) expanding the amounts of information they can process at one time, (2) increasing their processing speeds, and (3) acquiring new strategies and knowledge.

The Child as Problem Solver

Also central to the view of human nature held by information-processing theories is the assumption that children are *active problem solvers*. As suggested by

Klahr's analysis of his daughter's reasoning, **problem solving** involves strategies for overcoming obstacles and attaining goals. A description of a younger child's problem solving reveals the same combination of goal, obstacle, and strategy:

> Georgie (a 2-year-old) wants to throw rocks out the kitchen window. . . . Dad says that Georgie can't throw rocks out the window, because he'll break the lawnmower . . . . Georgie . . . goes outside, brings in some green peaches that he had been playing with, and says: "They won't break the lawnmower."

(Waters, 1989, p. 7)

In addition to illustrating the typical goal–obstacle–strategy sequence, this example highlights another basic tenet of information-processing approaches: children's cognitive flexibility helps them attain their goals. Even young children show great ingenuity in surmounting the obstacles imposed by their parents, the physical environment, and their own lack of knowledge.

Central Developmental Issues

Like all the theories described in this chapter, information-processing theories examine how *nature and nurture* work together to produce development. What makes information-processing theories distinctive is their emphasis on precise descriptions of *how change occurs*. The way in which information-processing theories address the issues of nature and nurture and how change occurs can be seen particularly clearly in their accounts of the development of memory and problem solving.

The Development of Memory

Memory is crucial to everything we do. The skills we use on everyday tasks, the language we employ when writing or speaking, the emotions we feel on a given occasion—all depend on our memories of past experiences and the knowledge acquired through them. Indeed, without memories of our experiences, we lose our very identity, a devastating syndrome that has been observed in patients with certain types of amnesia (Reed & Squire, 1998). Memory plays a role in all cognitive developmental theories, but it is especially central to information-processing theories. Most such theories distinguish among *working memory, long-term memory,* and *executive functions.*

Working memory **Working memory** involves actively attending to, gathering, maintaining, and processing information (Cowan, 2016). For example, if immediately after reading a story about birds, a child were asked a question about it, the child would, through working memory, bring together relevant information from the story, inferences made from that information, and prior knowledge about birds, and then attend to and maintain that information in memory long enough to process it and construct a reasonable answer.

Working memory is limited in both its capacity (the amount of information that it can actively attend to at one time) and in the length of time for which it can maintain information in an active state without updating activities. For example, a child might be able to remember a sequence of five digits but not six, and might be able to remember them for 10 seconds without repeating them but not for a longer time. The exact capacity and duration vary with age, the task, and the type of information being processed (Cowan, 2016; Schneider, 2011).

problem solving ■ the process of attaining a goal by using a strategy to overcome an obstacle

working memory ■ memory system that involves actively attending to, gathering, maintaining, storing, and processing information

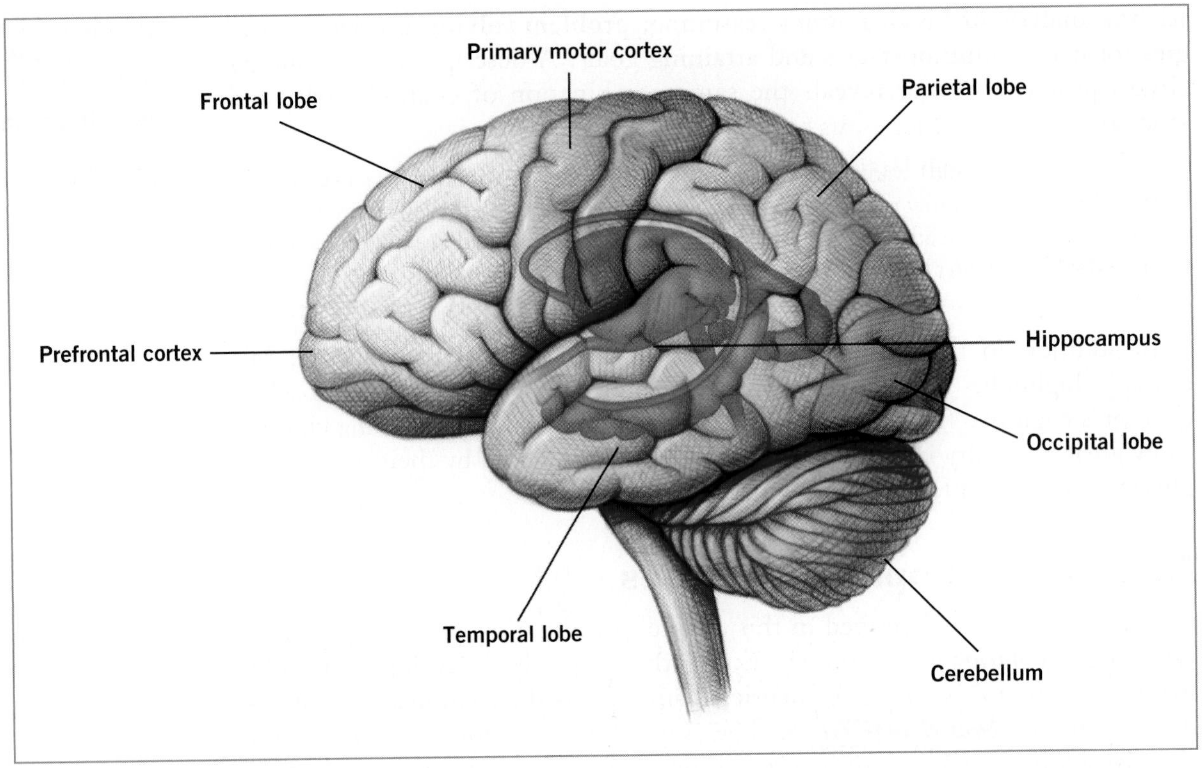

FIGURE 4.8 All the major areas of the cortex shown here continue to mature after birth. Brain maturation continues for a particularly long time, at least into one's 20s, in the prefrontal cortex, an area that is especially involved in planning, inhibiting inappropriate behavior, and adopting new goals in response to changing situations.

The basic organization of working-memory subsystems seems to be constant from early in childhood. However, the capacity and speed of working memory increase greatly during infancy, childhood, and adolescence (Barrouillet & Camos, 2015; Cowan, 2016). These changes are believed to occur in part because of increasing knowledge of the content on which working memory operates and in part because of maturational changes in the brain (Nelson, Thomas, & de Haan, 2006 see Figure 4.8).

In addition to these internal changes, the external environment also influences attention, sometimes in surprising ways. For example, kindergarten classrooms in the United States usually have many colorful posters, photos, artworks, and other decorations. The intent is to make the classroom an appealing environment for learning, but the effect may be that it distracts children's attention away from the lesson being taught. When kindergarteners were taught a series of science lessons either in a brightly decorated room resembling a typical classroom or in a room with no decorations, they learned more of the material being taught when they were in the undecorated room (Fisher, Godwin, & Seltman, 2014). Kindergartners in the highly decorated room spent more time off task (primarily, looking at the decorations), and the more time they spent doing so, the less material from the science lessons they learned.

Long-term memory In contrast to the moment-to-moment nature of working memory, **long-term memory** consists of the knowledge that people accumulate over their lifetime. It includes factual knowledge (e.g., knowing the capitals of different countries or the teams that won the Super Bowl in the past 3 years), conceptual knowledge (e.g., the concepts of justice, mercy, and equality), procedural knowledge (e.g., knowing how to shoot a basketball or play an Xbox game), attitudes (e.g., likes and dislikes regarding political parties or foods), reasoning strategies (e.g., knowing how to take an argument to its logical extreme to question it), and so on. Long-term memory can thus be thought of as the totality of

long-term memory ■ information retained on an enduring basis

one's knowledge, whereas working memory can be regarded as the subset of that knowledge that is being attended to at a given time (Barrouillet & Camos, 2015; Cowan, 2016).

In contrast to the strict limits on the capacity and duration of working memory, long-term memory can retain an unlimited amount of information for unlimited periods of time. To cite one notable example, research shows that people who studied Spanish or algebra in high school often retain a substantial amount of what they learned in the subject 50 years later, despite their not having used the information in the interim (Bahrick & Phelps, 1987).

Executive functioning Executive functions involve the control of cognition. The prefrontal cortex (Figure 4.8) plays a particularly important role in this cognitive control. Three major types of executive functions are *inhibiting* inadvisable actions, such as resisting the temptation to play with one's phone when an important test looms the next day; *enhancing working memory* through use of strategies, such as selectively attending to the most important information; and *being cognitively flexible*, such as imagining someone else's perspective in an argument despite it differing from one's own (Blair, 2016; Diamond, 2013; Rose, Feldman, & Jankowski, 2011).

The ability of executive functions to control thinking and action—enabling the individual to respond appropriately rather than acting impulsively or out of habit—increases greatly during the preschool and early elementary school years. One aspect of this improvement is children's increased cognitive flexibility in shifting goals. For instance, when they are assigned the task of sorting toys by color, then are asked to sort the same toys by shape, then to sort them by color again, and so on, most 3-year-olds have difficulty switching goals, but 5-year-olds easily do so (Baker, Friedman, & Leslie, 2010; Zelazo & Carlson, 2012).

The ability to inhibit habitual responses becomes apparent slightly later and is evident in everyday games such as "Simon Says." Preschoolers have great difficulty inhibiting the impulse to quickly respond to commands that are not preceded by the critical phrase in such games, whereas early elementary school children are much better at inhibiting the impulse to act immediately (Best & Miller, 2010; Dempster, 1995; Sabbagh et al., 2006). As you might anticipate, the need for strong executive functioning continues to pose challenges well beyond early childhood. For example, resisting the temptation to procrastinate, keeping quiet while the teacher is talking, and inhibiting tempting but disrespectful retorts to parents or teachers are difficult even for many adolescents (Bunge & Zelazo, 2006; Munakata, Snyder, & Chatham, 2012).

The quality of executive functioning during early childhood predicts many important later outcomes, including academic achievement in high school, enrollment in college, and income and occupational status during adulthood (Blair & Raver, 2015; Cantin, et al., 2016; Mischel & Ayduk, 2011; Moffitt et al., 2011). Executive functioning is also related to the benefits that children derive from instruction intended to help them gain other skills; for example, preschoolers with strong executive functioning skills learn more than peers from instruction intended to improve their understanding of other people's thinking (Benson et al., 2013). Experiences such as becoming bilingual improve executive functioning (Adesope et al., 2010; Bialystok, 2015), probably in part by providing practice in inhibiting one language while speaking the other.

Several training programs have shown considerable promise for improving young children's executive functioning (Blair & Raver, 2014; Diamond, 2013). In one such training study, kindergartners in 29 schools serving low-income

basic processes ■ the simplest and most frequently used mental activities

encoding ■ the process of representing in memory information that draws attention or is considered important

populations were randomly assigned to either classrooms using a curriculum called *Tools of the Mind,* designed to improve executive functioning, or to a control group (Raver et al., 2011). The curriculum involved instructing teachers in strategies—including stating and implementing clear rules, rewarding positive behaviors, and redirecting negative behaviors in positive directions—that would help children inhibit impulses to disrupt classroom activities and help them sustain attention to the task at hand. When tested immediately after the program ended and one year after that, the behavior and executive functioning of children who were presented *Tools of the Mind* showed substantial improvement. They were superior to peers in the control group in maintaining attention in the face of distractions, keeping information in working memory, and solving novel problems. Especially impressive is that for the next three years, children who had been in the intervention classrooms continued to perform better in math and reading than did children in the control group (Blair & Raver, 2014).

Explanations of memory development Information-processing theorists try to explain both the processes that make memory as good as it is at each age and the limitations that prevent it from being better. These efforts have focused on three types of capabilities: *basic processes, strategies,* and *content knowledge.*

BASIC PROCESSES The simplest and most frequently used mental activities are known as **basic processes.** They include *associating* events with one another, *recognizing* objects as familiar, *recalling* facts and procedures, and *generalizing* from one instance to another. Another basic process, which is key to all the others, is **encoding**—the representation in memory of specific features of objects and events. With development, children execute basic processes more efficiently, enhancing their memory and learning for all kinds of materials.

Most of these basic processes are familiar, and their importance obvious. However, encoding is probably less familiar. Appreciating its significance requires some understanding of the way in which memory works. People often think of memory as something akin to an unedited movie of our experiences, but memory is actually far more selective. People encode information that draws their attention or that they consider relevant, but they fail to encode a great deal of other information. If information is not encoded, it is not remembered later. Failure to encode information is probably evident in your own memory of the American flag; although you have seen it many times, you most likely have not encoded how the stars are arranged or how many red or white bars it contains.

Studies of how children learn to solve balance-scale problems illustrate the importance of encoding for learning, memory, and problem solving. As discussed on page 151, most 5-year-olds predict that the side of the scale with more weight will go down, regardless of the distance of the weights from the fulcrum. Five-year-olds generally have difficulty learning more advanced approaches to solving balance-scale problems that take into account distance as well as weight, because they do not encode information about distance of the weights from the fulcrum. To assess encoding of balance-scale configurations, children are shown a balance scale with varying arrangements of weights on pegs; the scale is then hidden behind an opaque barrier, and the children are asked to reproduce the arrangement on an identical but empty balance scale. Five-year-olds generally reproduce the correct number of weights on each side but rarely put them the correct distance from the

FAMILY CIRCUS © 1997 BIL KEANE, INC. DIST. BY KING FEATURES SYND.

"Mirror, mirror, on the wall, who's the fairest of the mall?"

Misencoding common sayings can lead to memorable confusions.

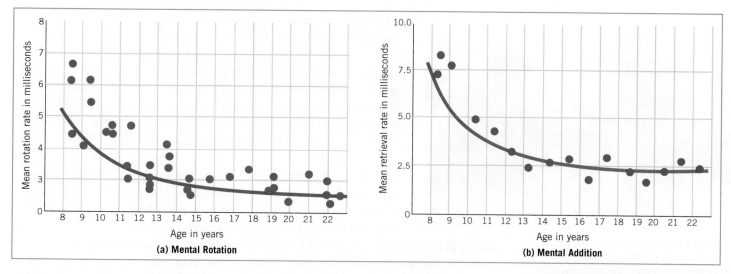

(a) Mental Rotation

(b) Mental Addition

fulcrum (Siegler, 1976). Teaching a randomly chosen group of 5-year-olds to encode distance by telling them that both weight and distance are important enables them to learn more advanced balance-scale rules that peers who were not taught to encode distance failed to learn on their own.

Like improved encoding, improved speed of processing plays a key role in the development of memory, problem solving, and learning. As shown in Figure 4.9, processing speed increases most rapidly at young ages but continues to increase in adolescence (Kail, 1991, 1997).

Two biological processes that contribute to faster speed of processing are myelination and increased connectivity among brain regions (Johnson, 2011; Luna et al., 2004). As discussed in Chapter 3, from the prenatal period through adolescence, increasing numbers of axons become covered with myelin, the insulating substance that promotes faster and more reliable transmission of electrical impulses in the brain (Paus, 2010). Greater connectivity among brain regions also increases processing speed by allowing more direct transmission of information across brain areas.

STRATEGIES Information-processing theories point to the acquisition and growth of strategies as another major source of memory development. Between ages 5 and 8 years, children begin to use a number of broadly useful memory strategies, among them the strategy of **rehearsal,** the repeating of information multiple times in order to remember it. The following excerpt from a newspaper article illustrates the usefulness of rehearsal for remembering information verbatim:

> A 9-year-old boy memorized the license plate number of a getaway car following an armed robbery, a court was told Monday. . . . The boy and his friend . . . looked in the drug store window and saw a man grab a 14-year-old cashier's neck. . . . After the robbery, the boys mentally repeated the license number until they gave it to police.
>
> (*Edmonton Journal,* Jan. 13, 1981, cited in Kail, 1984)

Had the boys witnessed the same event when they were 5-year-olds, they probably would not have rehearsed the numbers and would have forgotten the license number before the police arrived.

Another widely used memory strategy that becomes increasingly prevalent in the preschool and early elementary school years is **selective attention,** the process of intentionally focusing on the information that is most relevant to the current goal (Hanania & Smith, 2010). If 7- and 8-year-olds are shown objects from two

FIGURE 4.9 Increase with age in speed of processing on two tasks Note that the increase is rapid in the early years and more gradual later. (Data from Kail, 1991)

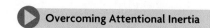
Overcoming Attentional Inertia

rehearsal ■ the process of repeating information multiple times to aid memory of it

selective attention ■ the process of intentionally focusing on the information that is most relevant to the current goal

Through repeated experiences engaging in activities such as chess, children gain content knowledge that improves their memory for and reasoning about subsequent, similar events.

different categories (e.g., several toy animals and several tools) and are told that they later will need to remember the objects in only one category (e.g., "You'll need to remember the animals"), they focus their attention on the objects in the specified category and remember more of them. In contrast, given the same instructions, 4-year-olds pay roughly equal attention to the objects in both categories, which reduces their memory for the objects they need to remember (DeMarie-Dreblow & Miller, 1988).

CONTENT KNOWLEDGE With age and experience, children's knowledge about almost everything increases. This increase in knowledge improves recall of new material by making it easier to integrate the new material with existing understanding (Schneider & Ornstein, 2015). The importance of content knowledge to memory is illustrated by the fact that when children know more than adults about a topic, they often remember more new information about the topic than adults do. For example, when children and adults are provided new information about children's TV programs and books, the children generally remember more of the new information than do the adults (Lindberg, 1980, 1991). Similarly, children who know a lot about soccer learn more from reading new soccer stories than do children who are older and have higher IQs but who know less about soccer (Schneider, Körkel, & Weinert, 1989).

Prior content knowledge improves memory for new information in several different ways. One is through improving encoding. In tests of memory of various arrangements of chess pieces on a board, child chess experts remember far more than do adult novices. The reason is that the child experts' greater knowledge of chess leads to their encoding higher-level chunks of information that include the positions of several pieces relative to one another rather than encoding the location of each piece separately (Chi & Ceci, 1987). Content knowledge also improves memory by providing useful associations. A child who is knowledgeable about birds knows that type of beak and type of diet are associated, so remembering either one increases memory for the other (Johnson & Mervis, 1994). In addition, content knowledge indicates what is and is not possible and therefore guides memory in useful directions. For example, when people familiar with baseball are asked to recall a particular inning of a game that they watched, and they can remember only two outs in that inning, they recognize that there must have been a third out and search their memories for it; people who lack baseball knowledge do not do this (Walker, 1987).

The Development of Problem Solving

Information-processing theories depict children as active problem solvers whose use of strategies often allows them to overcome limitations of knowledge and processing capacity. In this section, we present one prominent information-processing perspective on the development of problem solving—overlapping waves theory.

Piaget's theory depicted children of a given age as using a particular strategy to solve a particular class of problems. For example, he described 5-year-olds as solving conservation-of-number problems (see Figure 4.6) by choosing the longer row of objects, and 7-year-olds as solving the same problems by reasoning that if nothing was added or subtracted, the number of objects must remain the same. According to **overlapping waves theory**, however, individual children usually use a variety of approaches to solve such problems (Siegler, 1996; 2006). For instance, examining 5-year-olds' reasoning on repeated trials of the conservation-of-number problem

overlapping waves theory ■ an information-processing approach that emphasizes the variability of children's thinking

reveals that most children use at least three different strategies (Siegler, 1995). The same child who on one trial incorrectly reasons that the longer row must have more objects will on other trials correctly reason that just spreading a row does not change the number of objects; on yet other trials, the child will count the number of objects in the two rows to see which has more.

Figure 4.10 presents the typical pattern of development envisioned by the overlapping waves approach, with strategy 1 representing the simplest strategy, and strategy 5, the most advanced. At the youngest age depicted, children usually use strategy 1, but they sometimes use strategy 2 or 4. With age and experience, the strategies that produce more successful performances become more prevalent; new strategies also are generated and, if they are more effective than previous approaches, are used increasingly. Thus, by the middle of the age range in Figure 4.10, children have added strategies 3 and 5 to the original group and have almost stopped using strategy 1.

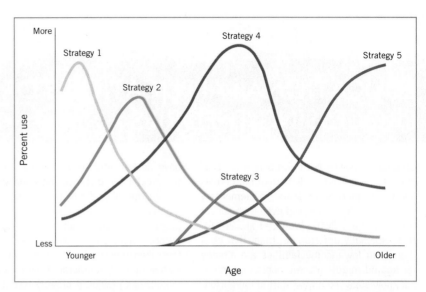

FIGURE 4.10 The overlapping waves model The overlapping waves model proposes that, at any one age, children use multiple strategies; that with age and experience, they rely increasingly on more advanced strategies (the ones with the higher numbers); and that development involves changes in the frequency of use of existing strategies as well as discovery of new approaches.

Overlapping waves theory has been shown to accurately characterize children's problem solving in a wide range of contexts, including arithmetic, time-telling, reading, spelling, scientific experimentation, biological understanding, tool use, and recall from memory (Chen & Siegler, 2000; Fazio, DeWolf, & Siegler, 2016; Lee & Karmiloff-Smith, 2002; Miller & Coyle, 1999; Siegler, 2006; Van der Ven et al., 2012). The theory also specifies several ways in which problem solving improves over the course of development. Children discover new strategies that are more effective than their previous ones, they learn to execute both new and old strategies more efficiently, and they choose strategies that are more appropriate to the particular problem and situation (Miller & Coyle, 1999; Siegler, 2006).

All these sources of cognitive growth are evident in learning single-digit addition. During kindergarten and the first few years of elementary school, children's knowledge of these problems improves greatly. One reason is that children discover new strategies, such as counting-on (e.g., solving 2 + 9 by thinking "9, 10, 11"). Another source of improvement is faster and more accurate execution of all the strategies that children know (e.g., retrieval of answers from memory, counting from one, and counting-on). A third source of improvement is that children choose among strategies increasingly adaptively (e.g., using counting-on most often on problems with a large difference between the addends, such as 2 + 9, but retrieving the answer on easy problems such as 2 + 2; Geary, 2006). (Box 4.2 provides an example of how information-processing analyses can improve education.)

Planning Problem solving is often more successful if people plan before acting. Children benefit from planning the fastest route to friends' houses, how to get their way with parents, and how to break bad news to others in ways that are least likely to trigger angry reactions (Hudson, Sosa, & Shapiro, 1997). Despite the advantages of planning, however, children often fail to plan in situations in which it would help their problem solving (Berg et al., 1997). The question is why.

Information-processing analyses suggest that one reason planning is difficult for children is that it requires inhibiting the desire to solve the problem immediately in favor of first trying to choose the best strategy. Starting to work on an assigned paper without planning what will be written in the paper is one familiar example.

BOX 4.2 | applications

EDUCATIONAL APPLICATIONS OF INFORMATION-PROCESSING THEORIES

Children's knowledge of numbers when they begin kindergarten predicts their mathematics achievement years later—in elementary school, middle school, and even high school (Duncan et al., 2007; Watts, et al., 2015). It is especially unfortunate, then, that children from low-income families are already far behind middle-income peers in numerical knowledge when they start kindergarten.

What might account for these early differences in numerical knowledge of children from different economic backgrounds? An information-processing analysis suggested that experience playing numerical board games such as Chutes and Ladders (known as Snakes and Ladders in some countries) might be one important factor. In Chutes and Ladders, players must move a token across 100 consecutively numbered squares, advancing on each of their turns by the number of spaces determined by a spinner or dice. A task analysis of the game indicated that the higher the number of the square on which a child's token rests at any given point in the game, the greater the number of number names the child will

have spoken and heard during the game, the greater the distance the child will have moved the token from the first square, the greater the time the child will have been playing the game, and the greater the number of discrete hand movements with the token the child will have made. These verbal, spatial, temporal (time-based), and motor cues provide a broadly based, multisensory foundation for knowledge of numerical magnitudes (the quantities indicated by number words), a type of knowledge that is closely related to overall mathematics achievement (Siegler, 2016).

Ramani and Siegler (2008) applied this information-processing analysis to improving the numerical understanding of low-income preschoolers. The researchers randomly assigned 4- and 5-year-olds from low-income families to either an experimental number-board condition or a control color-board condition. The number-board condition was virtually identical to the first row of the Chutes and Ladders board; it included 10 squares numbered consecutively from left to right. On each turn, the

child spun a spinner that yielded a 1 or a 2 and moved his or her token the corresponding number of squares on the board, stating the number on each square in the process. Children in the color-board condition played the same game, except that their board had no numbers and the players would say the name of the color of each square as they advanced their token. Players in both conditions played the game for four sessions, were helped by the experimenter if they did not know the numbers or colors in the squares, were given a pretest that examined their knowledge of numbers before playing the game, and were given a posttest that examined their knowledge of numbers just after the final game-playing session and again 9 weeks later.

On the posttest, children who played the number board game showed improved knowledge of the numbers 1 through 10 on all four tasks that were presented—counting, reading numbers, comparing magnitudes (e.g., "Which is bigger, 8 or 3?"), and estimating the locations of numbers on a number line. Significantly, all the gains were maintained on the follow-up test, 9 weeks later. In contrast, children who played the color board game showed no improvement in any aspect of number knowledge.

Subsequent studies demonstrated that playing the 1–10 board game also improves preschoolers' ability to learn the answers to arithmetic problems, such as 2 + 4 = 6 (Siegler & Ramani, 2009), and that a 0–100 version of the board game improves kindergartners' knowledge of those larger numbers (Laski & Siegler, 2014). Thus, playing numerical board games can represent a quick, effective, and inexpensive means of improving the numerical knowledge of low-income preschoolers and kindergartners.

ROBERT SIEGLER

Playing this number board game improves preschoolers' numerical knowledge.

A second reason why planning is difficult for young children is that they tend to be overly optimistic about their abilities and believe they can solve problems without planning (Bjorklund, 1997; Schneider, 1998). Such overoptimism sometimes leads young children to act rashly. For instance, 6-year-olds who overestimate their physical abilities have more accidents than do peers who evaluate their abilities more realistically, presumably because their confidence leads to them not planning how to avoid potential dangers (Plumert, 1995).

Over time, maturation of the prefrontal cortex, a part of the brain that is especially important for planning, along with experiences that reduce overoptimism or demonstrate the value of planning, lead to increases in the frequency and quality of planning, which improves problem solving (Chalmers & Lawrence, 1993). The improvements in the planning process take a long time, however; in dangerous situations, preadolescents and adolescents are more likely than adults not to plan or to ignore prior plans and take risks (Plumert, Kearney, & Cremer, 2004; Steinberg, 2008).

Review

Information-processing theories envision children as active learners and problem solvers who continuously devise means for overcoming their processing limits and reaching their goals. The capacity and processing speed of working memory and long-term memory influence all information processing. Executive functioning uses information in working memory and long-term memory to flexibly shift goals and inhibit impulses to behave in ways that are inappropriate in the situation; it also updates the contents of working memory so that new goals can be pursued effectively. Overlapping waves theory indicates that individual children use multiple strategies to solve the same type of problem, that children choose adaptively among these strategies, and that problem solving improves through the discovery of more effective strategies, more efficient execution of the strategies, and better choices of when to use each strategy. Improved planning also improves problem solving.

Core-Knowledge Theories

I didn't break the lamp, and I won't do it again.

—*3-year-old, speaking to her mother (cited in Vasek, 1986)*

Although transparent from an adult's perspective, this 3-year-old girl's cover-up reflects rather sophisticated reasoning. She realizes that her mother does not know all that she herself knows about how the lamp was broken, so she attempts to deny responsibility. At the same time, she knows that her mother may not believe her, so she hedges her bets by promising not to do it again. The effort to deceive actually reflects a kind of progress in the child's reasoning; when placed in a situation where they are likely to transgress, the percentage of children who lie about the transgression steadily increases from age 2 to age 7, presumably due to increasing ability to imagine potential negative consequences and to generate ways of avoiding them (see Figure 4.11) (K. Lee, 2013).

Such studies of deception illustrate two characteristic features of research inspired by **core-knowledge theories.** First, research on these theories focuses on areas of knowledge that have been important throughout human evolutionary history, such as understanding and manipulating other people's thinking. Other areas of core knowledge include recognizing the difference between living and nonliving things,

Young children's overoptimism sometimes leads them to engage in dangerous activities. This particular plan worked out fine, but not all do.

core-knowledge theories ■ approaches that view children as having some innate knowledge in domains of special evolutionary importance and domain-specific learning mechanisms for rapidly and effortlessly acquiring additional information in those domains

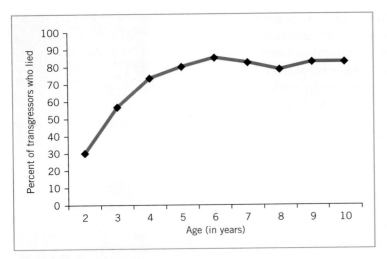

FIGURE 4.11 Children who lie about transgressions by age The percentage of children who lie to cover up transgressions increases substantially with age, perhaps because older children are more imaginative in generating plausible cover-ups. (Data from Lee, 2013)

identifying human faces, finding one's way through space, understanding causes and effects, and learning language.

Deception research reflects a second feature of core-knowledge theories: the assumption that in certain areas of probable importance in human evolution, infants and young children think in ways that are considerably more advanced than Piaget suggested were possible. If preschoolers were completely egocentric, they would assume that other people's knowledge is the same as their own, in which case there would be no point in lying because the other person would know the lies are false. However, preschoolers' attempts to deceive indicate that they have non-egocentric understandings of other people's minds. The question is how children come to have such sophisticated knowledge so early in life.

View of Children's Nature

Core-knowledge theories depict children as active learners. For example, research from the core-knowledge perspective shows that 3-year-olds understand deception much better when they are actively involved in perpetrating the deceit than when they merely witness the same deception being perpetrated by others (Carlson, Moses, & Hix, 1998; Sullivan & Winner, 1993). In this respect, the core-knowledge perspective on children's nature resembles that of Piagetian and information-processing theories.

However, core-knowledge theories differ dramatically from Piagetian and information-processing theories in their view of children's innate capabilities. Piagetian and information-processing theorists propose that children enter the world equipped with only general learning abilities that allow them to gradually increase their understanding of all types of content. By contrast, core-knowledge theorists view children as entering the world equipped not only with general learning abilities but also with specialized learning mechanisms, or mental structures,

Some transgressions are difficult to cover up; sometimes confessing, apologizing, and seeking the judge's mercy works better.

that allow them to quickly and effortlessly acquire information of evolutionary importance. Where the central metaphors within Piagetian and information-processing theories are, respectively, the child as scientist and the child as general purpose computational system, the central metaphor in the core-knowledge approach is the child as well-adapted product of evolution. This metaphor is strikingly apparent in the following statement:

> The brain is no less a product of natural selection than the rest of the body's structures and functions. . . . Hearts evolved to support the process of blood circulation, livers evolved to carry out the process of toxin extraction, and mental structures evolved to enable the learning of certain types of information necessary for adaptive behavior.
> (R. Gelman & Williams, 1998, p. 600)

The basic understandings proposed by core-knowledge theorists are assumed to be **domain specific,** that is, limited to a particular area. Domain-specific understandings in these areas allow children to distinguish between living and nonliving things; to anticipate that inanimate objects they encounter for the first time will remain stationary unless an external force is applied to them; to anticipate that animals they encounter for the first time might well move on their own; and to learn especially quickly in these and other areas of evolutionary importance. Different mechanisms are believed to produce development in each domain; for example, a kind of mechanism that has been labeled a *theory of mind module* (TOMM) is believed to produce learning about one's own and other people's minds, but different specialized mechanisms are believed to produce learning about faces, language, movement, and other important domains (Leslie, Friedman, & German, 2004; Mahy, Moses, & Pfeifer, 2014).

Central Developmental Issue: Nativism Versus Constructivism

Although core-knowledge theorists are united in believing that development reflects the operation of domain-specific as well as general learning mechanisms, they disagree regarding how much knowledge is inborn. Researchers who emphasize innate knowledge are often labeled *nativists*; those who emphasize the generation of increasingly sophisticated domain-specific theories on top of the innate foundation are often labeled *constructivists*.

Nativism

The position that infants are born with substantial knowledge of evolutionarily important domains, as well as the ability to quickly and easily acquire more knowledge in these domains, is called **nativism.** Elizabeth Spelke proposed the most prominent nativist theory, which she labeled "Core-Knowledge Theory" (e.g., Spelke, 2004; Spelke & Kinzler, 2007). She hypothesized that infants begin life with four core-knowledge systems, each of which includes understanding of a particularly important domain. One system represents inanimate objects and their mechanical interactions; a second system represents the minds of people and other animals capable of goal-directed actions; a third system represents numbers, such as numbers of objects and events; and a fourth system represents spatial layouts and geometric relations. Each system has its own principles. For example, infants' understanding of physics includes the knowledge that all objects occupy space, move in continuous ways through it, and cannot simultaneously occupy the same space

domain specific ■ information about a particular content area

nativism ■ the theory that infants have substantial innate knowledge of evolutionary important domains

constructivism ■ the theory that infants build increasingly advanced understanding by combining rudimentary innate knowledge with subsequent experiences

as another object. Consistent with this hypothesis, numerous studies have documented that infants indeed possess these basic understandings (e.g., Baillargeon, 2004; Hespos & vanMarle, 2012).

Language is another domain in which core-knowledge theorists have proposed that children have innate knowledge and a specialized learning mechanism, sometimes labeled the *language acquisition device* (e.g., Chomsky, 1988). Theorists hypothesize that this specialized learning mechanism enables young children to rapidly master the complicated systems of grammatical rules that are present in all human languages. One type of evidence for such specialized mechanisms is the universality of language acquisition. Virtually all children in all societies master the basic grammar of their native language quickly and effortlessly, even though adults almost never directly instruct them about the grammar. In contrast, understanding other complex rule systems—such as those in algebra, formal logic, and kinship relations (e.g., second cousin, twice removed)—is not universal, and learning them requires direct instruction from adults and considerable effort from children. Universality of acquisitions early in life, without apparent effort and without instruction from other people, is characteristic of the domains that are viewed as particularly important by core-knowledge theorists.

Constructivism

As the term is used by core-knowledge theorists, **constructivism** blends elements of nativism, Piagetian theory, and information-processing theories. Like nativists, but unlike Piagetian theorists who use the same term, core-knowledge constructivists theorize that infants possess specialized learning abilities that allow them to quickly and effortlessly begin to understand domains of special evolutionary importance. However, constructivists emphasize that infants' initial knowledge in these domains is rudimentary, and, like Piagetian and information-processing theorists, they believe that construction of more advanced knowledge reflects the interaction of experience with learning mechanisms. (The reason that the term *constructivist* is applied to both these core-knowledge theorists and to Piagetians is their shared assumption that cognitive development occurs in large part through children constructing new understandings by integrating new experience with prior understanding.)

Several core-knowledge constructivists have proposed that young children actively organize their understanding of the most important domains into informal theories (Carey, 2009; S. Gelman & Noles, 2011; Gopnik & Wellman, 2012). In particular, they hypothesize that children form naive theories of physics (knowledge of objects), psychology (knowledge of people), and biology (knowledge of plants and animals). As rudimentary and informal as these theories may be, they share three important characteristics with formal scientific theories:

1. They identify fundamental units for dividing relevant objects and events into a few basic categories.

2. They explain many phenomena in terms of a few fundamental principles.

3. They explain events in terms of unobservable causes.

Each of these characteristics is evident in understanding of biology (Carey, 2009; Inagaki & Hatano, 2008; Legare & S. Gelman, 2014). Consistent with the first characteristic, infants and young children divide all objects into three categories: people, other animals, and nonliving things. Consistent with the second characteristic, preschoolers understand broadly applicable biological principles, such as that a desire for food and water underlies many behaviors of animals. Consistent with the third characteristic, preschoolers know that vital activities of animals, such as reproduction and movement, are caused by something inside the animals themselves, as opposed to the external forces that determine the behavior of objects.

At the same time, core-knowledge constructivists emphasize that initial simple theories grow considerably more complex with age and experience. For example, the prominent core-knowledge constructivists Henry Wellman and Susan Gelman (1998) suggested that the first theory of psychology emerges at about 18 months of age, and the first theory of biology at about 3 years. The first theory of psychology is organized around the understanding that other people's actions, not just one's own, reflect their goals and desires. For example, 2-year-olds realize that another person will want to eat if he or she is hungry, regardless of whether the children themselves are hungry at that moment. The first theory of biology is organized around the realization that people and other animals are living things, different from nonliving things. For example, 3- and 4-year-olds realize that people and animals, but not manufactured objects, can heal themselves (Gelman, 2003).

More advanced theories follow these initial ones. For instance, not until age 7 years do children believe that the category of living things includes plants as well as animals (Inagaki & Hatano, 2008). Similarly, not until age 3 or 4 years

BOX 4.3 | applications

EDUCATIONAL APPLICATIONS OF CORE-KNOWLEDGE THEORIES

Although core-knowledge theorists emphasize what infants and young children understand about certain fundamental concepts, they also recognize that many other fundamental concepts are not mastered until much later, if ever. One such late-developing concept is natural selection, a key part of biological evolution—but one that even many high school and college students struggle to understand (Gregory, 2009). Core-knowledge theorists, such as Gelman (2003), have hypothesized that one reason for the difficulty is that young children are *essentialists*. They believe that members of a species have a fixed inner essence that makes them what they are—that is, dogs have a "dogness," cats a "catness," and so on.

Essentialist thinking has important advantages for drawing valid inferences. For example, it enables preschoolers to reason that if they learn that one dog has a spleen, other dogs also do, and that even if a sheep is raised among goats, it remains a sheep. However, essentialism interferes with learning about natural selection because having

a fixed essence would seem to preclude new species evolving from existing ones. Indeed, even extended instruction often leads to only modest improvement in understanding natural selection (Ferrari & Chi, 1998).

Deborah Kelemen and her colleagues (Kelemen et al., 2014) applied core-knowledge ideas, in particular the emphasis on causal explanations and on young children's ability to understand relatively advanced biological concepts, to help 5- to 8-year-olds learn about natural selection. To do so, they created storybooks about fictitious animals called "pilosas." In the story, the pilosas were suddenly dying off due to extreme climate change, which caused the insects they ate to burrow further underground. The effects of these changes depended on the pilosas' trunks, which they used to get the insects. Some of the pilosas had thin trunks that allowed them to reach into the narrow burrows where the insects had retreated, but other pilosas had trunks too wide to fit into the burrows. These circumstances led to the pilosas with thick trunks starving before they could produce offspring

and to the pilosas with thin trunks surviving to have babies, most of whom had thin trunks like those of their parents. Over generations, the pilosas with thin trunks became the main type of pilosa.

Hearing and seeing the storybook led to children not only learning what they had been told, but also generalizing the logic of natural selection to questions about a different hypothetical species faced with a different environmental challenge. Consistent with core-knowledge theories, storybooks with more information about the causal mechanisms that produced the population-level change led to greater learning than did books with less information about causes. The children's increased understanding of natural selection remained evident 3 months later. These impressive results challenged prior views that children younger than high school age could not understand evolutionary concepts such as natural selection and demonstrated the usefulness of applying core-knowledge theories to educationally important concepts.

do children recognize the role of beliefs as well as desires in influencing their own and other people's actions (Wellman, Cross, & Watson, 2001). Research generated by advocates of the core-knowledge approach is examined in greater depth in Chapter 7. We close this section's overview of core-knowledge theories by examining an intriguing educational application of the approach (Box 4.3).

Review

Core-knowledge theorists envision children as well-equipped products of evolution and focus on the development of understanding in domains of likely evolutionary importance, such as space, time, language, and biology. Some core-knowledge theorists, known as nativists, hypothesize that infants are born with domain-specific understanding and specialized learning mechanisms for acquiring information of evolutionary importance. Other core-knowledge theorists, known as constructivists, hypothesize both some innate understanding and the formation of increasingly advanced theories in response to experience in these vital areas. Both view children as active learners with impressive early understanding of vital concepts and domain-specific learning mechanisms.

Sociocultural Theories

A mother and her 4-year-old daughter, Sadie, assemble a toy, using a diagram to guide them:

> *Mother:* Now you need another one like this on the other side. Mmmmm . . . there you go, just like that.
>
> *Sadie:* Then I need this one to go like this? Hold on, hold on. Let it go. There. Get that out. Oops.
>
> *M:* I'll hold it while you turn it. *(Watches Sadie work on toy)* Now you make the end.
>
> *S:* This one?
>
> *M:* No, look at the picture. Right here *(points to diagram)*. That piece.
>
> *S:* Like this?
>
> *M:* Yeah.
>
> (Gauvain, 2001, p. 32)

This interaction probably strikes you as completely unexceptional—and it is. From the perspective of **sociocultural theories,** however, it and thousands of other everyday interactions like it are of the utmost importance, because they make development happen.

One noteworthy characteristic of the event, from the sociocultural perspective, is that Sadie is learning to assemble the toy in an interpersonal context. Sociocultural theorists emphasize that much of cognitive development takes place through direct interactions between children and other people—parents, siblings, teachers, playmates, and so on—who want to help children acquire the skills, knowledge, beliefs, and attitudes valued by their culture. Thus, whereas Piagetian, information-processing, and core-knowledge theories emphasize children's own efforts to understand the world, sociocultural theories emphasize the developmental importance of children's interactions with other people.

The interaction between Sadie and her mother is also noteworthy because it exemplifies **guided participation,** a process in which older, more knowledgeable individuals organize activities in ways that allow younger, less knowledgeable

sociocultural theories ■ approaches that emphasize that other people and the surrounding culture contribute greatly to children's development

guided participation ■ a process in which more knowledgeable individuals organize activities in ways that allow less knowledgeable people to learn

cultural tools ■ the innumerable products of human ingenuity that enhance thinking

people to engage in them at a higher level than they could manage on their own (Rogoff, 2003). Sadie's mother, for example, holds one part of the toy so that Sadie can screw in another part. On her own, Sadie would be unable to screw the two parts together and therefore could not improve her assembly skills. Similarly, Sadie's mother points to the relevant part of the diagram, enabling Sadie to decide what to do next and also to learn how diagrams convey information. As this episode illustrates, guided participation often occurs in situations in which the explicit purpose is to achieve a practical goal, such as assembling a particular toy, but in which learning more general skills, in this case assembling objects, occurs as a by-product of the activity.

A third noteworthy characteristic of the interaction between Sadie and her mother is that it occurs in a broader cultural context. This context includes not only other people but also the innumerable products of human ingenuity that sociocultural theorists refer to as **cultural tools**—symbol systems, artifacts, skills, values, and the many other ways in which culture influences our thinking. Without the symbol systems of printed diagrams and spoken language, Sadie and her mother would find the task of assembling the toy's pieces difficult if not impossible; without techniques for manufacturing artifacts such as toys, there would be no pieces to fasten; without skills such as Sadie's mother holding one part of the toy so that Sadie could screw in the other, Sadie could not have assembled the toy; without cultural values that encourage girls to learn mechanical skills, this interaction between Sadie and her mother would not have occurred; and so on. Thus, sociocultural theories help us appreciate the many aspects of culture embodied in even the most commonplace interactions.

Through guided participation, parents can help children not only accomplish immediate goals but also learn skills, such as how to use written instructions and diagrams to assemble objects.

View of Children's Nature

The giant of the sociocultural approach to cognitive development, and in many ways its founder, was the Russian psychologist Lev Semyonovich Vygotsky. Although Vygotsky and Piaget were contemporaries, much of Vygotsky's most important work was largely unknown outside Russia until the 1970s. Its appearance created considerable excitement, in part because Vygotsky's view of children's nature was so different from Piaget's.

The Russian psychologist Lev Vygotsky, founder of the sociocultural approach to child development.

Vygotsky's Theory

Vygotsky's theory can be understood by contrasting it with that of Piaget. Whereas Piaget's theory emphasizes children's efforts to understand the world on their own, Vygotsky and subsequent sociocultural theorists portray children as social learners, intertwined with other people who eagerly help them gain skills and understanding. Whereas Piaget viewed children as intent on mastering physical, mathematical, and logical concepts that are the same in all times and places, Vygotsky viewed them as intent on participating in activities that are prevalent in the specific time and place in which they live. Whereas Piaget emphasized abrupt qualitative changes in children's thinking, Vygotsky emphasized gradual continuous changes. These Vygotskian views gave rise to the central metaphor of sociocultural theories: children as social learners, shaped by other people and by their cultural context and gradually becoming immersed in it.

private speech ■ the second phase of Vygotsky's internalization-of-thought process, in which children develop self-regulation and problem-solving abilities by telling themselves aloud what to do, much as their parents did in the first stage

Vygotsky's emphasis on children as social learners is evident in his perspective on the relation between language and thought. Whereas Piaget viewed the two as largely independent, Vygotsky (1934/1962) viewed them as integrally related. In particular, he believed that thought is internalized speech and that thought originates in large part in statements that parents and other adults make to children.

To illustrate the process of internalizing speech, Vygotsky described three phases of its role in the development of children's ability to regulate their own behavior. At first, children's behavior is controlled by other people's statements (as in the example of Sadie's mother telling her how to assemble the toy). Then, children's behavior is controlled by their own **private speech,** in which they tell themselves aloud what to do, much as their parents might have done earlier. Finally, their behavior is controlled by internalized private speech (thought), in which they silently tell themselves what to do. The transition between the second and third phases often involves whispers or silent lip movements; in Vygotsky's terms, the speech "goes underground" and becomes thought. Private speech is most prevalent between ages 4 and 6 years, although older children and adults also use it on challenging tasks, such as assembling furniture or operating unfamiliar devices (Diaz & Berk, 2014; Winsler et al., 2003).

Children as Teachers and Learners

Contemporary sociocultural theorists, such as Michael Tomasello (2009; 2014), have extended Vygotsky's insights. Tomasello proposed that the human species has two unique characteristics that are crucial to our ability to create complex, rapidly changing cultures. One of these is the inclination to teach others of the species; the other is the inclination to attend to and learn from such teaching. In every human society, adults communicate facts, skills, values, and traditions to their young. This is what makes culture possible; it enables the new generation to stand on the shoulders of the old and thus to see farther. The inclination to teach emerges very early: even 1-year-olds spontaneously point to and name objects to call other people's attention to what they themselves find interesting. Only humans engage in such rudimentary teaching behaviors that are not directly tied to survival.

The inclination to teach and the ability to learn from teaching are among the most distinctly human characteristics.

DANITA DELIMONT / GETTY IMAGES

Children as Products of Their Culture

Sociocultural theorists believe that many of the *processes* that produce development, such as guided participation, are the same in all societies. However, the *content* that children learn—the particular symbol systems, artifacts, skills, and values—vary greatly from culture to culture and shape thinking accordingly.

One example of the impact that culturally specific content has on thinking comes from a study of analogical problem solving, a process in which experience with previously encountered problems is applied to new ones. In the study (Chen, Mo, & Honomichl, 2004), students attending universities in the United States and China were asked to solve two problems. One problem required a solution analogous to the strategy of leaving a trail of white pebbles to follow home in

"Hansel and Gretel," a tale well known to the U.S. students but unknown to those in China. The American college students were far more successful in solving that problem, and many of them alluded to the fairy tale, even though they had not heard it in many years. The other problem required a solution analogous to that in a fairy tale well known to the students in China but not those in the United States. College students in China were vastly superior in solving that problem, and many alluded to the relevant fairy tale.

Children's memories of their own experiences also reflect their culture. When 4- to 8-year-olds from China and the United States were asked to describe their earliest memories, their descriptions differed in ways that reflected their culture's attitudes and values (Wang, 2013). Chinese culture prizes and promotes interdependence among people, especially among those in one's inner circle. European American culture, by contrast, prizes and promotes the independence of individuals. Consistent with these cultural emphases, reports of Chinese children's earliest memories included more references to other people than did those of U.S. children, and similar reports by U.S. children included more references to the child's own feelings and reactions. Thus, the attitudes and values of a culture, as well as its artifacts and technologies, shape the thoughts and memories of people in that culture.

Central Developmental Issues

Vygotsky and contemporary sociocultural theorists have proposed a number of specific ideas about *how change occurs* through social interaction. One of these ideas—guided participation—has already been discussed. In this section, we examine two related concepts that play prominent roles in sociocultural analyses of change: *intersubjectivity* and *social scaffolding*, both of which exemplify the themes of *the active child* and the importance of the *sociocultural context*.

Intersubjectivity

Sociocultural theorists believe that the foundation of human cognitive development is our ability to establish **intersubjectivity,** the mutual understanding that people share during communication (Rochat, 2009). The idea behind this imposing term is both simple and profound: effective communication requires participants to focus on the same topic, as well as on each other's reaction to whatever is being communicated. Such a "meeting of the minds" is indispensable for effective teaching and learning.

The roots of intersubjectivity are evident early in infancy. By age 6 months, infants can learn novel behaviors by observing another person's behavior, which requires attending to the actions of the other person (Collie & Hayne, 1999).

This and related developments in early infancy set the stage for the emergence of a process that is at the heart of intersubjectivity— **joint attention.** In this process, infants and their social partners intentionally focus on a common referent in the external environment. The emergence of joint attention is evident in numerous ways. Around their first birthday, infants increasingly look toward objects that are the targets of their social partners' gaze, even if the partner is not acting on the objects. Around the same age, infants begin to actively direct a partner's attention toward objects that they

As illustrated by this photo of an East Asian mother teaching her child to use an abacus, the tools available in a culture shape the learning of children within that culture.

intersubjectivity ■ the mutual understanding that people share during communication

joint attention ■ a process in which social partners intentionally focus on a common referent in the external environment

Joint attention, the process through which social partners focus on the same external object, underlies the human capacity to teach and to learn from teaching.

social scaffolding ■ a process in which more competent people provide a temporary framework that supports children's thinking at a higher level than children could manage on their own

themselves find interesting (Adamson, Bakeman, & Deckner, 2004; Akhtar & Gernsbacher, 2008; Moore, 2008).

Joint attention greatly increases children's ability to learn from other people. One important example involves language learning. When an adult tells a child the name of an object, the adult usually looks or points at it; children who are looking at the same object are in a better position to learn what the word means than ones who are not (Baldwin, 1991). Indeed, the degree to which infants follow other people's gaze when the other person is teaching them a new word predicts their later vocabulary development (Brooks & Meltzoff, 2008) and their subsequent language development in general (Carpenter, Nagell, & Tomasello, 1998).

Joint attention also enables infants to evaluate the competence of other people and to use those evaluations to decide whom to imitate. Infants between 8 and 18 months of age more often attend to, imitate, and learn new labels for objects from adults whom they see pursuing goals competently than from adults they see acting incompetently (Brooker & Poulin-Dubois, 2013; Poulin-Dubois & Brosseau-Liard, 2016; Stenberg, 2013; Tummeltshammer et al., 2014).

Intersubjectivity continues to develop well beyond infancy, as children become increasingly able to take the perspectives of other people. For example, older preschoolers and elementary school-age children are more likely than younger ones to reach agreement with peers on the rules of a game they are about to play and the roles that each child will assume in it (Baines & Blatchford, 2011; Pelligrini, 2009). The continuing development of such perspective-taking abilities also leads to school-age children's increasing ability to teach and learn from one another (Gauvain, 2001).

Social Scaffolding

When putting up tall buildings, construction workers use metal frameworks called *scaffolds* that allow them to work high above the ground. Once a building's main structure is in place, that structure can support further work, thus allowing the scaffolding to be removed. In an analogous fashion, children's learning is aided by **social scaffolding,** in which more competent people provide a temporary framework that supports children's thinking at a higher level than children could manage on their own (Wood, Bruner, & Ross, 1976). Ideally, supplying this framework includes explaining the goal of the task, demonstrating how the task can be done, and helping children with the most difficult parts. This, in fact, is the way parents and teachers tend to instruct children (Bibok, Carpendale, & Müller, 2009; Simons & Klein, 2007).

Through the process of social scaffolding, children are able to work at a higher level than without such help. At first, this higher-level functioning requires extensive support, then it requires less and less support, and eventually it becomes possible without any support. The higher the quality of the scaffolding—that is, the more that instructional efforts are directed at the upper end of the child's capabilities—the greater the learning (Conner, Knight, & Cross, 1997; Gauvain, 2001). The goal of social scaffolding—to allow children to learn by doing—is the same as that of guided participation, but scaffolding tends to involve more explicit instruction and explanation, whereas guided participation tends to involve adults' organizing tasks so that children can take increasingly active and responsible roles in them.

By providing their children with social scaffolding, parents enable them to play with toys and other objects in more advanced ways than would otherwise be possible, which helps the children learn.

SIMON MARCUS / GETTY IMAGES

BOX 4.4 | applications

EDUCATIONAL APPLICATIONS OF SOCIOCULTURAL THEORIES

For some time, the educational system of the United States has been criticized for promoting rote memorization of facts rather than deep understanding, for promoting competition rather than cooperation among students, and for generally failing to create enthusiasm for learning (National Association for the Education of Young Children, 2011; Pellegrino, Chudowsky, & Glaser, 2001). The emphasis of sociocultural theories on the role of culture in cognitive development implies that one way to improve schooling is to change the culture of schools. The culture should be one in which instruction is aimed at helping children gain deep understanding, in which learning is a cooperative activity, and in which learning a little creates a desire to learn more.

One impressive attempt to meet these goals is Ann Brown's (1997) *community-of-learners* program, which has focused on 6- to 12-year-olds, most of them African American children attending inner-city schools in Boston, Massachusetts, and Oakland, California. The main curriculum consists of projects that require research on some large topic, such as interdependence between animals and their habitats. The class divides into small groups, each of which focuses on a particular aspect of the topic. With the topic of the interdependence between animals and habitats, for example, one group might study predator–prey relations; another, reproductive strategies; another, protection from the elements; and so on.

At the end of roughly 10 weeks, new groups are formed, each including one child from each original group. Children in the new groups are asked to solve a problem whose solution incorporates parts of all the topics previously studied. For instance, children might be tasked with designing an "animal of the future" that would be particularly well adapted to its habitat. Because each child's participation in the previous group has resulted in the child's gaining expertise on the aspect of the problem studied by that group, and because no other child in the new group has that expertise, all the children's contributions are essential for the new group to succeed. This technique is sometimes called the *jigsaw approach* because, as in a jigsaw puzzle, all pieces are necessary for the solution.

Participating in communities of learners yielded both cognitive and motivational benefits (Brown, 1997). It helped children become increasingly adept at constructing high-quality solutions to the problems they tried to solve. It also helped them learn such general skills as identifying key questions and comparing alternative solutions to a problem. Finally, because success depended on everyone's contributions, the community-of-learners approach encouraged mutual respect and responsibility. In short, the approach created a culture of learning.

One particularly important way in which parents use social scaffolding is in helping children form **autobiographical memories,** that is, explicit memories of events that took place at specific times and places in the person's past (Nelson & Fivush, 2004). Autobiographical memories include information about one's goals, intentions, emotions, and reactions to these events. Over time, these memories become organized into a more or less coherent narrative about one's life.

When discussing past experiences with their young children, some mothers encourage them to provide many details about past events and often expand on the children's statements. Such a mother might reply to her toddler's statement "Bird fly away" by saying, "Yes, the bird flew away because you got close to it and scared it." Such statements help children remember their experiences by improving their encoding of key information (in this case, their distance from the bird when it flew away) and appreciation of the causal relations among events (Boland, Haden, & Ornstein, 2003; McGuigan & Salmon, 2004). Other mothers ask fewer questions and rarely elaborate on what their children say. Children whose mothers use the more elaborative style remember more about events than do children whose mothers rarely elaborate (Haden, Haine, & Fivush, 1997; Harley & Reese, 1999; Leichtman et al., 2000). As discussed in Box 4.4, concepts from sociocultural theories also have proved useful for improving education in classrooms.

autobiographical memories ■ memories of one's own experiences, including one's thoughts and emotions

dynamic-systems theories ■ a class of theories that focus on how change occurs over time in complex systems

Review

Sociocultural approaches view children as social learners, shaped by, and shaping, their cultural contexts. These approaches emphasize that children develop in a cultural context of other people and human inventions, such as symbol systems, artifacts, skills, and values. Through guided participation, more knowledgeable people help children gain skills in using these cultural tools; children's use of the tools, in turn, further transforms their thinking. Culture is made possible by the human propensity to teach and learn and to establish intersubjectivity and joint attention with other people. Through processes such as social scaffolding and the creation of communities of learners, older and more skilled individuals help children acquire the skills, knowledge, and values of their culture.

Dynamic-Systems Theories

Like all biological processes, thinking serves an adaptive purpose: it helps people and other animals attain goals. However, attaining goals also requires action; without the ability to take effective action, thinking would be pointless (see Figure 4.12). Despite this inherent connection between thinking and acting, most theories of cognitive development have ignored the development of the skilled actions that allow children to realize the fruits of their mental labor.

One exception to this generalization is **dynamic-systems theories,** which focus on how changes in actions occur over time in complex physical and biological systems. Consistent with the dynamic-systems perspective, detailed analyses of the development of infants' basic actions—such as crawling, walking, reaching, and grasping—have yielded impressive insights into how cognitive development occurs. For example, dynamic-systems research has shown that improved reaching allows infants to categorize objects in more advanced ways (Spencer et al., 2006; Thelen & Corbetta, 1994). Dynamic-systems research also has shown that the onset of crawling changes infants' relationships with family members, who may be thrilled to see their baby attain this milestone but less thrilled about the need for increased vigilance and rearrangement of living spaces to avoid harm to one's child and one's possessions (Campos, Kermoian, & Zumbahlen, 1992).

Another contribution of dynamic-systems research has been to demonstrate that the development of seemingly simple actions is far more complex and interesting than it initially seems. For instance, such research has overturned the traditional belief that physical maturation leads infants to attain motor milestones

FIGURE 4.12 Problem solving often requires motor skills A major insight of dynamic-systems theories is that thinking would be pointless without motor capabilities. In these photos, a 12-month-old is shown knocking a barrier out of the way (left frame) and then grasping the edge of a cloth in order to pull the cloth, string, and toy toward him (right frame). If the infant lacked the motor dexterity to grasp the cloth or the strength to pull in the toy, his problem-solving processes would have been fruitless.

COURTESY OF PETER WILLATTS, UNIVERSITY OF DUNDEE, SCOTLAND

in stages, at roughly the same age, in the same way, and in a consistently forward progression. Instead, dynamic-systems research has shown that individual children acquire skills at different ages and in different ways, and that their development entails regressions as well as progress (Adolph, Cole, & Vereijken, 2015).

One example of this type of research is a longitudinal study of the development of infants' reaching conducted by Esther Thelen, who, along with her colleague Linda Smith, founded the dynamic-systems approach to cognitive development. In this particular study, Thelen and colleagues (1993) repeatedly observed the reaching efforts of four infants during their 1st year. Using high-speed motion-capture video systems and computer analysis of the infants' muscle movements, they found that because of individual differences in the infants' physiology, activity level, arousal, motivation, and experience, each child faced different challenges in his or her attempts to master reaching. The following observations illustrate some of the complexities these researchers discovered, including variability in the ages at which infants reach developmental milestones, their patterns of change, and the differing challenges they must overcome. The age at which different infants reach this transition varied greatly. In the following case, Nathan reached the transition at 12 weeks, but Hannah and Justin did not reach it until they were 20 weeks old. Moreover,

> the infants showed periods of rapid change, plateaus, and even regressions in performance. . . . There was in Nathan, Justin, and Hannah a rather discontinuous shift to better, less variable performance. . . . Gabriel's transition to stability was more gradual.
> (Thelen & Smith, 1998, pp. 605, 607)

Individuals also vary in their reaching speeds and typical motions. Returning to the infants in Thelen's study, Gabriel

> had to damp down his very vigorous movements in order to successfully reach, and he did. In contrast, Hannah, who moved slowly and spent considerable time with her hands flexed near her face, had to activate her arms more to extend them out in front of her.
> (Thelen, 2001, pp. 172, 182)

These descriptions help to convey what is meant by the label "dynamic-systems." As suggested by the term *dynamic*, dynamic-systems theories depict development as a process in which change is the only constant. Whereas some approaches to cognitive development hypothesize that development entails long periods of relatively stable stages or theories separated by relatively brief transition periods, dynamic-systems theories propose that at all points in development, thought and action change from moment to moment in response to the current situation, the child's immediate past history, and the child's longer-term history in similar situations.

As suggested by the second term in the label, dynamic-systems theories depict each child as a well-integrated system, in which many subsystems—perception, action, attention, memory, language, social interaction, and so on—work together to determine behavior. For example, success on tasks viewed as measures of conceptual understanding, such as object permanence, is influenced by perception, attention, motor skills, and a host of other factors (Smith et al., 1999). The assumptions that development is dynamic and that it functions as an organized system are central to the theory's perspective on children's nature.

▶ Infant Problem Solving

View of Children's Nature

Dynamic-systems theories are the newest of the five types of theories discussed in this chapter, and their view of children's nature incorporates influences from each of the others. Like Piaget's theory, dynamic-systems theories emphasize children's innate motivation to explore the environment; like information-processing theories, they emphasize precise analyses of problem-solving activity; like core-knowledge theories, they focus on infants' and toddlers' surprising early competence; and like sociocultural theories, they emphasize the formative influence of other people. These similarities to other theories, as well as the differences from them, are evident in dynamic-systems theories' emphasis on motivation and the role of action.

Motivators of Development

To a greater extent than any of the other theories except Piaget's, dynamic-systems theories emphasize that from infancy onward, children are strongly internally motivated to learn about the world around them and to explore and expand their own capabilities (von Hofsten, 2007). This motivation to explore and learn is clearly apparent in the fact that children persist in practicing new skills even when they possess well-practiced skills that are more efficient. Thus, 1-year-olds try to walk down ramps, despite the fact that crawling would get them down more quickly and without the risk of falling (Adolph & Berger, 2015).

Like sociocultural approaches, but unlike Piagetian theory, dynamic-systems theories also emphasize infants' interest in the social world as a crucial motivator of development. As noted in our discussion of the *active child* in Chapter 1, even newborns prefer attending to the sounds, movements, and features of the human face over almost any alternative. By 10 to 12 months of age, infants' interest in the social world is readily apparent in the emergence of intersubjectivity (page 175), as infants look to where the people interacting with them are looking and direct the attention of others to objects and events they themselves find interesting (Deák, 2015; von Hofsten, Dahlström, & Fredriksson, 2005). Dynamic-systems theorists have emphasized that observing other people, imitating their actions, and attracting their attention are all potent motivators of development (Fischer & Bidell, 2006; von Hofsten, 2007).

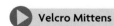

▶ **Velcro Mittens**

Reaching with Velcro-covered mittens for Velcro-covered objects improved infants' later ability to grab and explore ordinary objects without the mittens (Libertus & Needham, 2010).

The Centrality of Action

Dynamic-systems theories are unique in their pervasive emphasis on how children's specific actions shape their development. Piaget's theory asserts the role of actions during infancy, but dynamic-systems theories emphasize that actions contribute to development throughout life. This focus on the developmental role of action has led to a number of interesting discoveries. For example, infants' own reaching for objects helps them infer the goals of other people's reaches; infants who can skillfully reach are more likely to look at the probable target of another person's reaching just after the other person's reach begins (von Hofsten, 2007). Another example of infants' learning from actions comes from research in which infants were outfitted with Velcro mittens that enabled them to "grab" and explore Velcro-covered objects that they otherwise could not have picked up. After 2 weeks of successfully grabbing the Velcro-covered objects with the Velcro-covered mittens, infants showed greater ability to grab and explore ordinary objects without the mittens than did other infants of the same ages (Needham, 2016).

The ways in which actions shape development extend well beyond reaching and grasping in infancy. Actions influence categorization: in one study, encouraging children to move an object up and down led to their categorizing it as one of a group of objects that were easiest to move in that way, whereas encouraging children to move the same object from side to side led them to categorize it as one of a group of objects that were easiest to move in that way (Smith, 2005). Actions also affect vocabulary acquisition and generalization (Gershkoff-Stowe, Connell, & Smith, 2006; Samuelson & Horst, 2008): for example, experimental manipulations that lead children to state an incorrect name for an object impair the child's future attempts to learn the object's correct name. In addition, actions shape memory, as demonstrated by research in which children's past attempts to locate and dig up objects they had seen being hidden in a sandbox altered their recall of the objects' new location after they saw them being re-hidden (Schutte, Spencer, & Schöner, 2003; Zelazo, Reznick, & Spinazzola, 1998). Thus, just as thinking shapes actions, actions shape thinking.

Central Developmental Issues

Two developmental issues that are especially prominent in dynamic-systems theories are how the cognitive system organizes itself and how it changes. These issues exemplify our themes of the *active child* and *mechanisms of change*.

Self-Organization

Dynamic-systems theories view development as a process of self-organization that involves integrating attention, memory, emotions, and actions as needed to adapt to a continuously changing environment. The organizational process is sometimes called *soft assembly*, because the components and their organization change from moment to moment and situation to situation, rather than being governed by rigid stages or rules that are consistently applied across time and situations.

The types of research to which this perspective leads are well illustrated by certain studies of the A-not-B error that 8- to 12-month-olds typically make in Piaget's classic object-permanence task. As noted earlier, this error involves infants' searching for a toy where they previously found it (location A), rather than where they last saw it hidden (location B). Piaget (1954) explained the A-not-B error by hypothesizing that before their 1st birthday, infants lack a clear concept of the permanent existence of objects.

In contrast, viewing the A-not-B error from a dynamic-systems perspective suggested that many factors other than conceptual understanding influence performance on the object-permanence task. In particular, Smith and colleagues (1999) argued that babies' previous reaching toward location A produces a habit of reaching there, which influences their behavior when the object is subsequently hidden at location B. On the basis of this premise, the researchers made several predictions that were later borne out. One was that the more often babies had found an object by reaching to one location, the more likely they would be to reach there again when the object was hidden at a different location.

Also supported was the prediction that increasing the memory demands of the task by not allowing infants to search for the object for 3 seconds after it was hidden at the B location would increase the likelihood of infants' reaching to location A (Clearfield et al., 2009). The reasoning here was that the strength of the new memory, which was based on viewing a single action, would fade rapidly relative to the fading of the habit of reaching to the previous hiding place, which was based on several actions.

The dynamic-systems perspective also suggested that infants' attention would influence their object-permanence performance. Consistent with this view, manipulating infants' attention by tapping one of the locations just as the infants were about to reach usually resulted in their reaching to the tapped location, regardless of where the object was actually hidden. Thus, rather than providing a pure measure of conceptual understanding, infants' performance on the object-permanence task appears to reflect the combined influence of the strength of the habit of reaching to location A, the memory demands of the current task, and the infant's current focus of attention.

Mechanism of Change

Dynamic-systems theories posit that changes occur through mechanisms of variation and selection that are analogous to those that produce biological evolution (Fischer & Bidell, 2006; Steenbeek & van Geert, 2008). In this context, *variation* refers to the use of different behaviors to pursue the same goal. For example, to descend a ramp, a 1-year-old will sometimes walk; sometimes crawl; sometimes do a belly slide; sometimes do a sitting, feet-first slide; and so on (Adolph & Berger, 2015). *Selection* involves increasingly frequent choice of behaviors that are effective in meeting goals and decreasing use of less effective behaviors. For instance, when children first learn to walk, they often are too optimistic about being able to walk down ramps and frequently fall; but after a few months of walking experience, they more accurately judge the steepness of ramps and whether they can walk down them, leading the infants to use another descent strategy if the ramp is too steep.

Children's selection among alternative approaches reflects several influences. Most important is the *relative success* of each approach in meeting a particular goal: as children gain experience, they increasingly rely on approaches that produce desired outcomes. Another important consideration is *efficiency*: children increasingly choose approaches that meet goals more quickly or with less effort than do other approaches. A third consideration is *novelty*, the lure of trying something new. Children sometimes choose new approaches that are no more efficient, or even less efficient, than an established alternative but that have the potential to become more efficient. For example, when they first learn the memory strategy of rehearsal, it does not improve their memory, but they use it anyway, and eventually it does improve their recall of rehearsed information (Miller & Seier, 1994). Such a novelty preference tends to be adaptive because, with practice, a strategy that is initially less efficient than existing approaches often becomes more efficient (Wittmann et al., 2008). As discussed in Box 4.5, the insights of dynamic-systems theories have led to useful applications as well as theoretical progress.

Review

Dynamic-systems theories view children as ever-changing, well-integrated organisms that combine perception, attention, memory, language, and social influences to produce actions that satisfy goals. From this perspective, children's actions are shaped by their remote and recent history, their current physical capabilities, where their attention is focused, and the immediate physical and social environment. The actions, in turn, are viewed as shaping the development of categorization, conceptual understanding, memory, language, and other capabilities. Dynamic-systems theories are unique in their emphasis on how children's actions shape their development, as well as in the range of developmental influences they consider with regard to particular capabilities.

BOX 4.5 | applications

EDUCATIONAL APPLICATIONS OF DYNAMIC-SYSTEMS THEORIES

As noted in Chapter 2, children born prematurely with low birth weight are more likely than other children to encounter developmental difficulties, among them slower emergence of reaching (Fallang et al., 2003). These delays in reaching reduce the rate of development of brain areas involved in reaching, limiting infants' ability to explore and learn about objects (Lobo, Galloway, & Savelsbergh, 2004).

A recent intervention (Heathcock, Lobo, & Galloway, 2008), was quite successful in helping preterm infants improve their reaching. This intervention was inspired by two findings from dynamic-systems research: (1) that some infants' slowness to initiate arm activity impedes their development of reaching (Thelen, et al., 1993), and (2) that providing young infants with experience reaching for and grabbing Velcro-patched objects while

wearing Velcro-covered mittens improves the infants' later ability to reach for and grab ordinary objects barehanded (Needham et al., 2002).

Heathcock, Lobo, and Galloway began their intervention by requesting that caregivers of preterm infants in an experimental group provide the infants with special movement experiences. Specifically, they asked the caregivers to encourage infants' arm movements by (1) tying a bell to the infants' wrists so that arm movements would make it ring, presumably motivating further arm movements, and (2) placing Velcro mittens on the infants' hands to allow them to reach for and grab Velcro-patched toys held in front of them. The caregivers were asked to do this at home as well. Caregivers of preterm infants in a control group were asked to provide their infants with special social experiences that included singing to and

talking with the infants on the same schedule as that of children in the experimental group. Periodically, infants in both groups were brought to the lab to allow project personnel to observe their reaching and exploration under controlled circumstances and during free play.

As might be expected, the reaching of preterm infants in both groups improved over the 8 weeks of the study. However, the infants in the experimental group improved more. They more often touched toys that were held in front of them, and more often did so with the inside rather than the outside part of their hand, as is needed to grasp objects. Such interventions may also help preterm infants avoid other types of cognitive and motor impairments related to delayed development of reaching and may facilitate brain development as well.

CHAPTER SUMMARY

Theories of development are important because they provide a framework for understanding important phenomena, raise major issues regarding human nature, and motivate new research. Five major theories of cognitive development are Piagetian, information-processing, core-knowledge, sociocultural, and dynamic-systems.

Piaget's Theory

- Among the reasons for the longevity of Piaget's theory are that it vividly conveys the flavor of children's thinking at different ages, extends across a broad range of ages and content areas, and provides many fascinating and surprising observations of children's thinking.

- Piaget's theory is often labeled constructivist because it depicts children as actively constructing knowledge for themselves in response to their experience. The theory posits that children learn through two processes that are present from birth—assimilation

and accommodation—and that the contribution of these processes is balanced through a third process, equilibration. These processes produce continuities across development.

- Piaget's theory divides cognitive development into four broad stages: the sensorimotor stage (birth to age 2), the preoperational stage (ages 2 to 7), the concrete operational stage (ages 7 to 12), and the formal operational stage (age 12 and beyond). These stages reflect discontinuities in development.

- In the sensorimotor stage, infants' intelligence is expressed primarily through motor interactions with the environment. During this period, infants gain understanding of concepts such as object permanence and become capable of deferred imitation.

- In the preoperational stage, children become able to represent their experiences in language, mental imagery, and thought; but because of cognitive limitations such as egocentrism and centration, they have difficulty solving many problems, including Piaget's various tests of conservation and egocentrism.

- In the concrete operational stage, children become able to reason logically about concrete objects and events but have difficulty reasoning in purely abstract terms and in succeeding on tasks requiring hypothetical thinking, such as the pendulum problem.

- In the formal operational stage, children become able to think systematically, test hypotheses in valid ways, and reason about hypothetical situations.

- Four weaknesses of Piaget's theory are (1) it only vaguely describes the mechanisms that give rise to thinking and cognitive growth; (2) it underestimates infants' and young children's cognitive competence; (3) it understates the contribution of the social world to cognitive development; and (4) it depicts children's thinking as being more consistent than it is. Each shortcoming has motivated a theory intended in large part to address it.

Information-Processing Theories

- Information-processing theories focus on the specific mental processes that underlie children's thinking. Even in infancy, children are seen as actively pursuing goals; encountering physical, social, and processing limits; and devising strategies that allow them to surmount those limits and attain their goals.

- The memory system includes working memory, long-term memory, and executive functioning.

- Working memory is a system for actively attending to, gathering, maintaining, briefly storing, and processing information.

- Long-term memory is the enduring knowledge accumulated over a lifetime.

- Executive functioning is crucial for inhibiting inadvisable actions, enhancing working memory, and flexibly adapting to changing situations. It develops greatly during the preschool and early elementary school years and is related to later academic achievement and occupational success.

- The development of memory, problem solving, and learning reflects improvements in basic processes, strategies, and content knowledge.

- Basic cognitive processes allow infants to learn and remember from birth onward. Among the most important basic processes are association, recognition, recall, generalization, and encoding.

- Acquisition of strategies and content knowledge enhances learning, memory, and problem solving beyond the level that basic processes alone could provide.

- Important contributors to the growth of problem solving include the development of planning and encoding.

- Overlapping waves theory characterizes development of problem solving as involving acquisition of new strategies, increasingly efficient execution of existing strategies, and increasingly frequent choice of strategies that fit particular situations.

Core-Knowledge Theories

- Core-knowledge theories are based on the view that children begin life with a wide range of specific cognitive competencies.

- Core-knowledge approaches also hypothesize that children are especially adept at acquiring evolutionarily important information, such as language, spatial and numerical information, understanding of other people's thinking, and face recognition.

- These approaches further posit that from early ages, children organize information about the most important areas into domain-specific knowledge structures.

- Nativism is a type of core-knowledge approach that posits that infants are born with substantial knowledge of evolutionarily important domains.

- Core-knowledge constructivism proposes that children generate increasingly advanced theories of areas such as physics, psychology, and biology by combining basic innate knowledge with subsequent learning produced by both domain-general and domain-specific mechanisms.

Sociocultural Theories

- Starting with Vygotsky, sociocultural theorists have focused on how the social world molds development. These theories emphasize that development is shaped not only by interactions with other people and the skills learned from them, but also by the artifacts with which children interact and the beliefs, values, and traditions of the larger society.

- Sociocultural theories view humans as differing from other animals in their propensity to teach and their ability to learn from teaching.

- Establishing intersubjectivity between people through joint attention is essential to learning.

- Sociocultural theories describe people as learning through guided participation and social scaffolding, in which others who are more knowledgeable support the learner's efforts.

Dynamic-Systems Theories

- Dynamic-systems theories view change as the one constant in development. Rather than depicting development as being organized into long periods of stability and brief periods of dramatic change, these theories propose that there is no period in which substantial change is not occurring.

- These theories view each person as a unified system that, in order to meet goals, integrates perception, action, categorization, motivation, memory, language, and knowledge of the physical and social worlds.

■ Dynamic-systems theories view development as a self-organizing process that brings together components as needed to adapt to a continuously changing environment, a process known as soft assembly.

■ Attaining goals requires action as well as thought. Thought shapes action, but action also shapes thought.

■ Just as variation and selection produce biological evolution, they also produce cognitive development.

Test Yourself

1. According to Piaget, development is both continuous and discontinuous. Which of the following aspects of Piagetian theory would be considered a source of discontinuity?
   a. assimilation
   b. accommodation
   c. equilibration
   d. invariant stages

2. Piaget's theory of cognitive development is comprised of four invariant stages from birth to adolescence. Which of the following is the correct chronology of these stages?
   a. Formal operational, preoperational, sensorimotor, and concrete operational
   b. Sensorimotor, preoperational, concrete operational, and formal operational
   c. Sensorimotor, concrete operational, formal operational, and preoperational
   d. Preoperational, concrete operational, formal operational, and sensorimotor

3. A noted accomplishment during Piaget's sensorimotor stage is _____.
   a. symbolic representation
   b. object permanence
   c. conservation
   d. egocentrism

4. Thinking that does not factor in the viewpoints of others is known as _____.
   a. symbolic representation
   b. centration
   c. egocentrism
   d. intersubjectivity

5. According to information-processing theories, the ability to encode, store, and retrieve information is referred to as

   _____.
   a. memory
   b. rehearsal
   c. metacognition
   d. retrieval

6. Information-processing theories note several limits on children's thinking. Which of the following is *not* one of these limits?
   a. memory capacity
   b. implementation of task analysis

   c. speed of processing information
   d. ability to utilize problem-solving strategies

7. Overlapping waves theory explains children's ability to
   a. selectively attend to the most relevant aspect of a problem.
   b. identify the obstacles in achieving a goal.
   c. effectively process mental operations.
   d. discover new strategies that lead to more efficient problem solving.

8. Core-knowledge theories argue that _____ play(s) a role in cognitive development.
   a. evolution
   b. memory strategies
   c. cultural tools
   d. biomechanical actions

9. According to core-knowledge theorists, children possess naïve theories in what three major domains?
   a. mathematics, psychology, and the arts
   b. biology, linguistics, and psychology
   c. biology, physics, and psychology
   d. linguistics, physics, and psychology

10. Sociocultural theories emphasize the child's
    a. individual action in his or her environment.
    b. ability to self-regulate his or her learning.
    c. direct interactions with others.
    d. automatization of basic skills to promote new learning.

11. Five-year-old Marcus is learning gymnastics. He's having trouble on the balance beam, so his teacher assists by holding his hand as he walks across. This interaction can be described as _____.
    a. guided participation
    b. discovery learning
    c. intersubjectivity
    d. the jigsaw approach

12. Jamal is walking with his mother. He taps her on the arm, points to an animal, and says, "Doggie!" This is an example of _____.
    a. social scaffolding
    b. joint attention
    c. cultural tools
    d. directed learning

13. According to Vygotsky's sociocultural theory, young children will often talk aloud to themselves as a means of controlling their behavior. This is referred to as _____.
    a. external speech
    b. egocentric speech
    c. directional speech
    d. private speech

14. Although Piaget argues that infants younger than 8 months fail the A-not-B error test due to a lack of object permanence, proponents of dynamic-systems theories argue their failure is
    a. due to a combination of habit, memory demands, and focus of attention.

b. influenced by the infant's motor abilities.
c. caused by an infant's fragile attachment to the hidden object.
d. influenced by infant fatigue.

15. Although 15-month-old Lena has been walking unassisted for several months, on recent trips to the park her father has noticed Lena walking on some areas of the playground but crawling on others. Lena's regression from walking to crawling in this example is best explained by which theory?
    a. constructivist theory
    b. overlapping waves theory
    c. sociocultural theories
    d. information-processing theories

Don't stop now! Research shows that testing yourself is a powerful learning tool. Visit LaunchPad to access the LearningCurve adaptive quizzing system, which gives you a personalized study plan to help build your mastery of the chapter material through videos, activities, and more. **Go to launchpadworks.com.**

Critical Thinking Questions

1. Piaget's theory has been prominent for almost 100 years. Do you think it will continue to be prominent in the coming years as well? Why or why not?

2. Do you think that the term *egocentric* is a good description of preschoolers' overall way of seeing the world? On the basis of what you learned in this chapter and your own experience, explain your answer and indicate in what ways preschoolers are egocentric and in what ways they are not.

3. Information-processing analyses tend to be more specific about cognitive processes than are analyses generated by other theories. Do you see this specificity as an advantage or a disadvantage? Why?

4. Of the two types of core-knowledge theories, nativist and constructivist, which do you prefer? Why?

5. Imagine that you are trying to help a 6-year-old learn a skill that you possess. Using the sociocultural ideas of guided participation and social scaffolding, describe how you might go about this task.

6. Dynamic-systems theories reflect influences of each of the other theories reviewed in this chapter. Which theoretical influence do you think is strongest: Piagetian, core-knowledge, information-processing, or sociocultural? Explain your reasoning.

Key Terms

A-not-B error, p. 149

accommodation, p. 145

assimilation, p. 145

autobiographical memories, p. 177

basic processes, p. 162

centration, p. 151

computer simulation, p. 158

concrete operational stage, p. 147

conservation concept, p. 151

constructivism, p. 170

core-knowledge theories, p. 167

cultural tools, p. 173

deferred imitation, p. 149

domain specific, p. 169

dynamic-systems theories, p. 178

egocentrism, p. 150

encoding, p. 162

equilibration, p. 145

formal operational stage, p. 147

guided participation, p. 172

information-processing theories, p. 157

intersubjectivity, p. 175

joint attention, p. 175

long-term memory, p. 160

nativism, p. 169

object permanence, p. 148

overlapping waves theory, p. 164

Piaget's theory, p. 144
preoperational stage, p. 147
private speech, p. 174
problem solving, p. 159
rehearsal, p. 163
selective attention, p. 163
sensorimotor stage, p. 147
social scaffolding, p. 176
sociocultural theories, p. 172
symbolic representation, p. 150
task analysis, p. 158
working memory, p. 159

Student Video Activities

Sensorimotor Intelligence in Infancy and Toddlerhood
Problem Solving and the A-not-B Error
The Balance-Scale Problem
Piaget's Conservation-of-Liquid Task
Piaget's Conservation-of-Number Task
Overcoming Attentional Inertia
Infant Problem Solving
Velcro Mittens

Answers to Test Yourself

1. d, **2.** b, **3.** b, **4.** c, **5.** a, **6.** b, **7.** d, **8.** a, **9.** c, **10.** c, **11.** a, **12.** b, **13.** d, **14.** a, **15.** b

MARY STEVENSON CASSATT (1844–1926), *Mother and Child* (oil on canvas, 1900)

Seeing, Thinking, and Doing in Infancy

Themes

- ▪ Nature and Nurture
- ▪ The Active Child
- ▪ Continuity/Discontinuity
- ▪ Mechanisms of Change
- ▪ The Sociocultural Context
- ▪ Individual Differences

Four-month-old Benjamin, perched on the kitchen counter in his infant seat, is watching his parents wash the dinner dishes. What he observes are two people who move on their own, as well as a variety of glass, ceramic, and metal objects of differing sizes and shapes that move only when picked up and manipulated by the people. Other elements of the scene never move. As the people go about their task, distinctive sounds emanate from their moving lips, while different sounds occur as they deposit cutlery, skillets, glasses, and sponges on the kitchen counter. At one point, Benjamin sees a cup completely disappear from view when his father places it on the counter behind a cooking pot; it reappears a moment later when the pot is moved. He also sees objects disappear as they pass through the suds and into the water, but he never sees one object pass through another. The objects that are placed on the counter stay put, until Benjamin's father puts a crystal goblet on the counter with more than half of its base hanging over the counter's edge. The crashing sound that follows startles all three people in the room, and Benjamin is further startled when the two adults begin emitting sharp, loud sounds toward one another, quite unlike the soft, pleasant sounds they had been producing before. When Benjamin begins crying in response, the adults rush to him, patting him and making soft, especially pleasant sounds.

This example, to which we will return throughout the chapter, illustrates the enormous amount of information that is available for an infant to observe and learn from in even the most everyday situations. In learning about the world, Benjamin, like most infants, avidly explores everything and everyone around him, using every tool he has: he gathers information by looking and listening, as well as by tasting, smelling, and touching. His explorations will gradually expand as he becomes capable first of reaching for objects and then of manipulating them, making it possible for him to discover more about them. When he starts to move around under his own power, even more of the world will become available to him, including things

Like Benjamin, this infant will take in a great deal of perceptual information just observing his father washing dishes.

MONALYN GRACIA / CORBIS / VCG / GETTY IMAGES

his parents would prefer that he not investigate—such as electrical outlets and kitty litter. Never will Benjamin explore so voraciously or learn so rapidly as in the first few years of his young life.

In this chapter, we discuss development in four closely related areas: perception, action, learning, and cognition. Our discussion focuses primarily on infancy. One reason for concentrating on this period is that extremely rapid change occurs in all four areas during the first two years of a child's life. A second reason is the fact that infant development in these four domains is particularly intertwined: the minirevolutions that transform infants' behavior and experience in one domain lead to minirevolutions in others. For example, the dramatic improvements in visual abilities that occur in their first few months enable infants to see more of the people and objects around them, thereby greatly increasing the opportunities they have to learn new information.

A third reason for concentrating on infancy in this chapter is the fact that the majority of recent research on perceptual and motor development has been done with infants and young children. There is also a large body of fascinating research on learning and cognition in the first few years. We will review some of this research here and cover subsequent development in these areas in later chapters. A final reason for focusing on infants in this chapter is that the methods used to investigate infants' development in these four domains are, of necessity, quite different from those that researchers are able to use to study older children.

Our examination of key developments in infancy will feature several enduring themes. The *active child* theme is vividly embodied by infants' eager exploration of their environment. *Continuity/discontinuity* arises repeatedly in research that addresses the relation between behavior in infancy and subsequent development. In some sections, the *mechanisms of change* theme is also prominent, as we explore the role that variability and selection play in infants' development. In our discussion of early motor development, we will examine contributions made by the *sociocultural context*.

Underlying much of this chapter, of course, is the theme of *nature and nurture*. For at least 2000 years, an often contentious debate has existed between those philosophers and scientists who have emphasized innate knowledge in accounting for human development and those who have emphasized learning. The desire to shed light on this age-old debate is one reason that an enormous amount of research has been conducted with infants over the past few decades. As you will see, these discoveries have revealed that infant development is even more complicated and remarkable than previously suspected.

Perception

Parents of new babies cannot help wondering what their children experience—how much they can see, how well they can hear, whether they connect sight and sound (as in our opening vignette), and so on. William James, one of the first psychologists, believed that the world of the newborn is a "big blooming, buzzing confusion." Because of remarkable advances in the study of early sensation and perception, modern researchers do not share his view. They have demonstrated that infants come into the world with all their sensory systems functioning to some degree and that subsequent development occurs at a very rapid pace. **Sensation** refers to the processing of basic information from the external world by the sensory receptors in the sense organs (eyes, ears, skin, and so forth) and the brain. **Perception** is the process of organizing and interpreting sensory information about the objects, events, and spatial layout of the world around us. In our opening example, sensation involved light and sound waves activating receptors in Benjamin's eyes, ears, and brain; one instance of perception involved his experiencing the visual and auditory stimulation provided by the crashing goblet as a single coherent event.

In this section, we devote the most attention to vision, both because of its fundamental importance to humans and because so much more research has been conducted on vision than on the other senses. We will also discuss hearing and, to a lesser degree, taste, smell, and touch, as well as the coordination between these multiple sensory modalities. Although these abilities often seem commonplace to us as adults, they are actually some of the most remarkable achievements attained during the 1st year of life.

Vision

Humans rely more heavily on vision than most species do, but as recently as a few decades ago, it was generally assumed that newborns' vision was so poor as to be barely functional. However, once researchers started carefully studying the looking behavior of newborns and young infants, they discovered that this assumption was incorrect. In fact, as soon as newborns enter the world, they begin using their eyes

sensation ■ the processing of basic information from the external world by the sensory receptors in the sense organs (eyes, ears, skin, etc.) and brain

perception ■ the process of organizing and interpreting sensory information

This infant and caregiver are each wearing a head-mounted eye tracker. The intersection of the purple lines shows where the viewer is looking. The top panel indicates that the caregiver's gaze is focused on the infant's face. The lower panel indicates that the infant's gaze is focused on the green object.

preferential-looking technique ■ a method for studying visual attention in infants that involves showing infants two patterns or two objects at a time to see if the infants have a preference for one over the other

visual acuity ■ the sharpness of visual discrimination

to explore. They scan the environment, and when their gaze encounters a person or object, they pause to look at it. Although newborns do not see as clearly as adults do, their vision improves extremely rapidly in their first months. And as you will learn, recent studies have revealed that despite their immature visual systems, even the youngest infants have some surprisingly sophisticated visual abilities.

The evidence that enables us to say this so confidently was made possible by the invention of a variety of ingenious research methods. Because young infants cannot understand or respond to instructions, investigations of infant abilities required researchers to devise methods that are quite different from those used with older children and adults. The first breakthrough was achieved with the **preferential-looking technique,** a method for studying visual attention in infants. In this technique, pioneered by Robert Fantz (1961), two different visual stimuli are typically displayed on side-by-side screens. If an infant looks longer at one of the two stimuli, the researcher can infer that the baby can discriminate between them, and that the infant has a preference for one over the other. Fantz established that newborns, just like everyone else, would rather look at something than at nothing. When a pattern of any sort—black and white stripes, newsprint, a bull's-eye, a schematic face—was paired with a plain surface, the infants preferred (i.e., looked longer at) the pattern.

Modern versions of preferential looking often involve the use of automatic eye trackers. By using a specially designed camera that measures infants' eye movements via infrared light reflection, researchers can automatically detect where infants are looking on a screen. Researchers also use head-mounted infant eye trackers that show where infants are looking as they move their eyes freely around the room.

Another method that is frequently used to study sensory and perceptual development in infants is *habituation,* which you encountered in Chapter 2 as a research tool used in studying fetal development. This procedure involves repeatedly presenting an infant with a particular stimulus until the infant's response to it habituates, that is, declines. Then a novel stimulus is presented. If the infant dishabituates (the response increases) in response to the novel stimulus, the researcher infers that the baby can discriminate between the old and new stimuli. Despite their simplicity, habituation and preferential-looking procedures have turned out to be enormously powerful for studying infants' perception and understanding of the world.

Visual Acuity and Color Perception

The preferential-looking method enables researchers (and eye-care professionals) to assess infants' **visual acuity,** that is, to determine how clearly they can see. This method builds on research showing that infants who can see the difference between a simple pattern and a solid gray field consistently prefer to look at the pattern (Figure 5.1). By varying the patterns and assessing infants' preferences, researchers have learned a great

FIGURE 5.1 Testing infants' visual acuity Paddles like the ones depicted here can be used to assess young infants' visual acuity. Two paddles are shown to the infant simultaneously, one with stripes and one in plain gray. If the infant can detect the contrast difference between the black and white stripes, the infant's gaze should, because of infants' preference for a patterned visual field over a plain one, become oriented toward the striped paddle. The ophthalmologist or researcher presents the infant a succession of paddles with increasingly narrow stripes, with increasingly narrow gaps between them, until the infant can no longer distinguish between the striped paddle and the plain gray one. The thickness of the stripes on the last paddle discriminated provides an indication of the infant's visual acuity.

deal about not only infants' early visual abilities but also about their looking preferences. For example, young infants generally prefer to look at patterns of high visual contrast—such as a black-and-white checkerboard (Banks & Dannemiller, 1987). This is because young infants have poor **contrast sensitivity:** they can detect a pattern only when it is composed of highly contrasting elements.

One reason for this poor contrast sensitivity is the immaturity of the **cone** cells in infants' retinas, the light-sensitive neurons that are highly concentrated in the *fovea* (the central region of the retina) and are involved in seeing fine detail and color. Newborns' cones are spaced 4 times farther apart than adults' cones, with the consequence that cones in newborns catch only about 2% of the light striking the fovea, compared with 65% for adults (for review, see Arterberry & Kellman, 2016). This is partly why in their 1st month, babies have only about 20/120 vision (a level of acuity that would only enable an adult to read the large E at the top of a standard eye chart). Subsequently, visual acuity develops so rapidly that by 8 months of age, infants' acuity approaches that of adults.

Another restriction on young infants' visual experience is that, for the 1st month or so, they do not appear to perceive differences between white and color. However, by 2 months of age, infants' color vision is similar to that of adults. Infants appear to prefer colors that are unique hues, like blue, over colors that are combinations of hues, like blue-green (Arterberry & Kellman, 2016). Thus, it appears that the tendency to paint infants' rooms in pastel colors does not reflect infants' color preferences, but instead reflects their parents' color preferences.

Research on color perception in young infants has been used to address a longstanding debate concerning the origin of color categories. While humans can discriminate between thousands of different colors, languages use only a small number of terms to distinguish broad color categories, and these categories can differ across languages. To what extent is color perception affected by language? This question was recently tested in a study of color perception in infants who do not yet have words for colors (Yang et al., 2016). The researchers used NIRS, one of the brain-measurement methods we discuss in Box 3.3, to determine whether 5-month-old infants categorize colors the same way adults do. The results revealed that like adults, infants' brains respond to a change from a color in one category to a new color in a different category, but not to a new color in the same category. These findings suggest that infants' brains represent at least some color categories prior to the acquisition of language.

Visual Scanning

As noted, newborns start visually scanning the environment right away. From the beginning, they are attracted to moving stimuli. However, they have trouble tracking these stimuli because their eye movements are jerky and often do not stay with whatever they are trying to visually follow. Not until 4 months of age are infants able to track moving objects smoothly, and then they are able to do so only if an object is moving slowly (Rosander, 2007). This developmental achievement

The blurred image on the right is roughly what a 1-month-old infant would perceive. The infant's relatively low level of visual acuity leads some features of the image to pop out—those with higher contrast (e.g., the woman's eyes and hairline).

GOODSHOOT RF / GETTY IMAGES

contrast sensitivity ■ the ability to detect differences in light and dark areas in a visual pattern

cones ■ the light-sensitive neurons that are highly concentrated in the fovea (the central region of the retina)

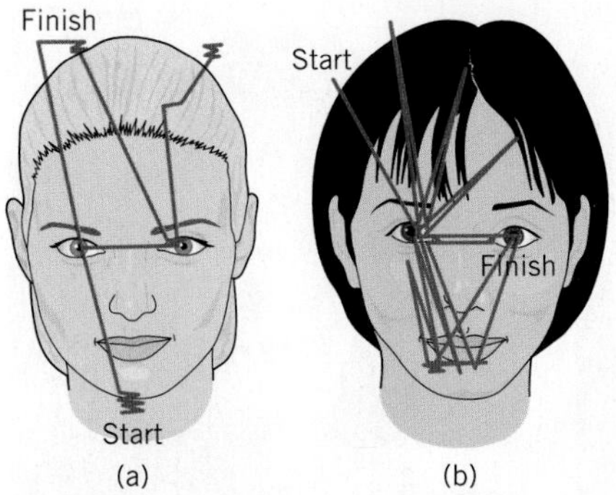

FIGURE 5.2 Visual scanning The lines superimposed on these face pictures show age differences in where two babies fixated on the images. (a) A 1-month-old looked primarily at the outer contour of the face and head, with a few fixations of the eyes. (b) A 2-month-old fixated primarily on the internal features of the face, especially the eyes and mouth. (Information from Maurer & Salapatek, 1976)

appears to be less a function of visual experience than of maturation. Preterm infants, whose neural and perceptual systems are immature, develop smooth visual tracking later than full-term infants do (Strand-Brodd et al., 2011). Additional evidence from preterm infants supports the view that visual tracking reflects neurodevelopment: very preterm infants (born before 32 weeks gestation) who have difficulty tracking moving objects at 4 months of gestational age (i.e., corrected for preterm birth) show poorer cognitive outcomes at 3 years of age than similarly preterm infants (Kaul et al., 2016). Thus, this very early-developing aspect of perceptual development may be an important predictor of later cognitive development.

One reason why visual scanning is so important is that it is one of the few ways that infants have active control over what they observe and learn. Young infants' visual experience of the world (and therefore what they can learn) is highly restricted. With a simple figure like a triangle, infants younger than 2 months old look almost exclusively at one corner. With more complex shapes, like faces, they tend to scan only the outer edges (Haith, Bergman, & Moore, 1977; Milewski, 1976). Thus, as Figure 5.2 shows, when 1-month-olds look at a line drawing of a face, they tend to fixate on the perimeter—on the hairline or chin, where there is relatively high contrast with the background. By 2 months of age, infants scan much more broadly, enabling them to pay attention to both overall shape and inner details. Indeed, as discussed in Box 5.1, faces are among the most preferred and prominent aspects of infants' visual environments.

Talking faces are a particularly important source of information for infant learners. By observing talking faces, infants have the opportunity to begin to draw connections between the motor actions and sounds that will be the basis for their eventual native language. Research on visual scanning with talking faces reveals an interesting pattern of behavior that is consistent with the increasingly important role of talking faces as a learning source (Lewkowicz & Hansen-Tift, 2012). At 4 months of age, before the onset of productive speech, infants watching talking faces primarily fixate on the eyes of the speaker. However, after infants begin babbling, they primarily fixate on the mouth of the speaker, supporting the view that attention to a talking mouth may be related to infants' development of spoken language. Interestingly, bilingual infants show this shift in visual scanning—preferring the mouth of a talking face over the eyes—earlier than do monolingual infants, suggesting that infants acquiring multiple languages take advantage of the information provided in the mouth earlier than infants acquiring just a single language (Pons, Bosch, & Lewkowicz, 2015). We will learn more about how infants accomplish the impressive feat of learning multiple languages in Chapter 6.

Object Perception

One of the most remarkable things about visual perception is how stable the world appears to be. When a person approaches or moves away from us, or slowly turns in a circle, our retinal image of the person changes in size and shape, but we do not have the impression that the person changes in size and shape. Instead, we perceive a constant shape and size, a phenomenon known as **perceptual constancy.** The origin of perceptual constancy was a traditional component in the debates between *empiricists* and *nativists*. As you read in Chapter 4, empiricists maintain that all knowledge arises from experience, whereas nativists—especially coreknowledge theorists—argue that key aspects of knowledge are, in fact, innate, or hard-wired. Thus, empiricists argue that our perception of the constant size and shape of objects develops as a function of spatially experiencing our environment,

perceptual constancy ■ the perception of objects as being of constant size, shape, color, etc., in spite of physical differences in the retinal image of the object whereas nativists argue that this perceptual regularity stems from inherent properties of the nervous system.

The nativist view is supported by evidence of perceptual constancy in newborns and very young infants. In a study of size constancy (Slater, Mattock, & Brown, 1990), newborns were repeatedly shown either a large or a small cube at varying distances. While the cube's actual size remained the same, the size of the retinal image projected by the cube changed from one trial to the next (see Figure 5.3). The question was whether the newborns would perceive these events as multiple presentations of the same object or as presentations of similar objects of different sizes.

To answer this question, the researchers subsequently presented the newborns with the original cube and a second one that was identical except that it was twice as large. The crucial factor was that the second cube was located twice as far away as the original one, so it produced the same-size retinal image as the original. The infants looked longer at the second cube, indicating that they saw it as different in size from the original one. This, in turn, revealed that they had perceived the multiple presentations of the original cube as a single object of a constant size, even though its retinal size varied. Thus, visual experience is not necessary for size constancy.

Another crucial perceptual ability is **object segregation,** the perception of the boundaries between objects. To appreciate the importance of this ability, look at the room around you. How can you tell where one object ends and another begins? If the objects are separated by a visible gap, the boundaries between the objects are obvious. But what if there are no gaps? Suppose, for example, that as baby Benjamin watches his parents washing dishes, he sees a cup sitting on a saucer. An adult would perceive this arrangement as two distinct objects, but will Benjamin? Lacking experience with china, Benjamin may be unsure: the difference in shape suggests two objects, but the common texture suggests only one. Now suppose that Ben's mother picks up the cup to dip it in the suds, leaving the saucer on the table. Will he still be uncertain? No, because even infants treat the independent motion of cup and saucer (or any objects) as a signal that they are separate entities. Is this knowledge innate, or do infants acquire it from observing everyday events in their environment?

The importance of motion as a cue indicating the boundaries between objects was initially demonstrated in a classic experiment by Kellman and Spelke (1983). First, 4-month-olds were presented with the display shown in Figure 5.4a. This display could be perceived either as two pieces of a rod moving on each end of a block of wood or as a single rod moving back and forth behind the block. Importantly, adults perceive displays of this type the latter way. After habituating to the display, the infants were shown the two test displays in Figure 5.4b: a whole rod and a rod broken into two pieces. The investigators reasoned that if the infants, like adults, assumed that there was a single intact rod moving behind the block during habituation, they would look longer at the broken rod because that display would be relatively novel. And that is exactly what the babies did.

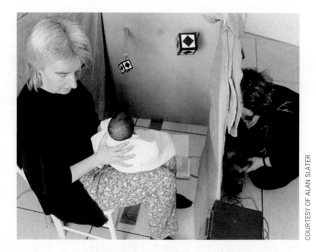

FIGURE 5.3 If this infant looks longer at the larger but farther-away cube, researchers will conclude that the child has size constancy.

object segregation ■
the identification of separate objects in a visual array

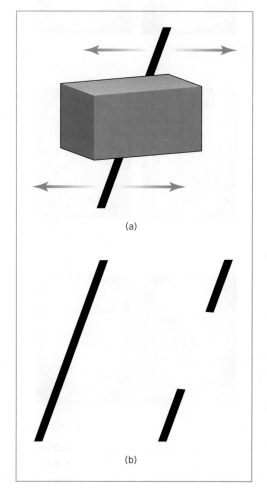

(a)

(b)

FIGURE 5.4 Object segregation Infants who see the combination of elements in (a) perceive two separate objects, a rod moving behind a block. After habituating to the display, they look longer at two rod segments than at a single rod (b), indicating that they find the single rod familiar but the two segments novel. If they first see a display with no movement, they look equally long at the two test displays. This result reveals the importance of movement for object segregation. (Information from Kellman & Spelke, 1983)

BOX 5.1 | a closer look

INFANTS' FACE PERCEPTION

A particularly fascinating aspect of infant perception has to do with the reaction of human infants to that most social of all stimuli—the human face. As we have noted, infants are drawn to faces from birth, leading researchers to ask what initially attracts their attention. The answer, it seems, is a very general bias toward configurations with more elements in the upper half than in the lower half—something that characterizes all human faces (Macchi Cassia, Turati, & Simion, 2004) (see the images in the first column). Evidence in support of a general bias to attend to facelike stimuli comes from studies showing that newborn humans are equally interested in human faces and monkey faces—as long as they are presented right-side up (Di Giorgio et al., 2012).

From paying lots of attention to faces, infants very quickly come to recognize and prefer their own mother's face. After exposure to Mom over the first few days after birth, infants look longer at her face than at the face of another woman, even when controlling for olfactory cues (a necessary step because, as discussed in Chapter 2, newborns are highly attuned to their mother's scent) (Bushnell, Sai, & Mullin, 2011). Over the ensuing months, infants develop a preference for faces depicting the gender of the caregiver they see most often, whether female or male (Quinn et al., 2002).

Faces are incredibly prevalent in infants' environments. Recent studies using infant head cameras have documented the ubiquity of faces. During the first few months of postnatal life, infants are viewing faces for 15 minutes of every hour they are awake (Jayaraman, Fausey, & Smith, 2015; Sugden, Mohamed-Ali, & Moulson, 2014). At this age, infants are primarily exposed to female faces (70%) from individuals of their own race (96%) (Sugden et al., 2014). This heavy focus on faces decreases with age, dropping to about 5 minutes of every hour by the end of the 1st year. By that point, infants are more focused on hands (and the objects they manipulate) than on faces (Fausey, Jayaraman, & Smith, 2016).

Over the course of the 1st year, infants' perception of faces is shaped by their experiences through a process known as *perceptual narrowing*: infants become face specialists, better at discriminating amongst the kinds of faces that are frequently experienced in their environments. Evidence to support perceptual narrowing comes from an intriguing study of infants' and adults' ability to discriminate between individual human faces and individual monkey faces. Adults, 9-month-olds, and 6-month-olds can all readily discriminate between two human faces. However, adults and 9-month-olds have a great deal of difficulty telling the difference between one monkey face and another (Pascalis, de Haan, & Nelson, 2002). Surprisingly, 6-month-olds are just as good at discriminating between monkey faces as they are at discriminating between human faces. These data suggest that while 6-month-olds are still generalists, 9-month-olds have become specialists, better at perceiving the dimensions that matter for discriminating between human faces, but worse at perceiving the dimensions that matter for discriminating between monkey faces.

Another source of evidence suggesting that perceptual narrowing shapes face perception comes from research on the perception of faces from different races. The *other-race effect (ORE)* is a well-established finding, initially observed in adults, in which individuals find it easier to distinguish between faces of individuals from their own racial group than between faces from other racial groups. It was later determined that the ORE emerges in infancy.

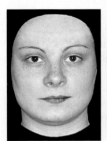
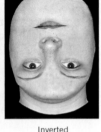

Upright face | Inverted face

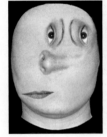
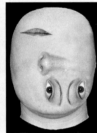

Scrambled Top-heavy | Scrambled Bottom-heavy

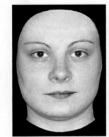
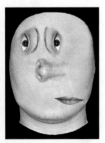

Upright face | Scrambled Top-heavy

When presented with each of these three pairs of stimuli, newborns look longer at the image in the left-hand column, revealing a general preference for top-heavy stimuli that contributes to their preference for human faces (Macchi Cassia et al., 2004; Simion et al., 2002). Notice that this simple preference is all that is needed to result in newborns spending more time looking at their mother's face than at anything else. By 3 months of age, however, infants no longer discriminate between the faces in the middle pair of pictures, suggesting that their visual attention is no longer guided by a general top-heavy bias (Macchi Cassia et al., 2006).

COURTESY OF OLIVER PASCALIS

Do the photographs of the men show the same person or different people? How about the two monkey photos? As an adult human, you no doubt can tell the two men apart quite easily, but you may still not be sure whether the two monkey photos are of different individuals. (They are.)

Whereas newborns show no preference for own-race faces over other-race faces, 3-month-old White, African, and Chinese infants prefer own-race faces (Kelly, Liu et al., 2007; Kelly et al., 2005). Over the second half of the 1st year, infants' face processing continues to become more specialized, as shown by the emergence of the ORE; by 9 months of age, infants have more difficulty discriminating between other-race faces than between own-race faces (Kelly, Quinn et al., 2007; Kelly et al., 2009).

What drives these effects is not the infant's own race per se but, rather, the features of individuals in the infant's immediate environment. For example, 3-month-old African emigrants to Israel who were exposed to both African and White caregivers showed equal interest in African and White faces (Bar-Haim et al., 2006). Further evidence of effects of visual experience on face perception comes from a study suggesting that the

facial-scanning abilities of biracial infants—who are exposed to the facial features characteristic of two races in the home—are more mature than those of monoracial infants (Gaither, Pauker, & Johnson, 2012).

One of the most intriguing aspects of infants' facial preferences is the fact that, along with all the rest of us, babies like a pretty face. From birth, infants look longer at faces that are judged by adults to be highly attractive than at faces judged to be less appealing (Langlois et al., 1991; Langlois et al., 1987; Rubenstein, Kalakanis, & Langlois, 1999; Slater et al., 1998, 2000). Older infants' preference for prettiness, like that of adults, also affects their behavior toward real people. This was demonstrated in a study in which 12-month-olds interacted with a woman whose face was either very attractive or very unattractive (Langlois, Roggman, & Rieser-Danner, 1990). The first key feature of this study was that the attractive

woman and the unattractive woman were one and the same! This duality of appearance was achieved through the use of extremely natural-looking professional masks that were applied before the woman interacted with the infants. On a given day, the young woman who would test the babies emerged from her makeup session looking either fabulous or not so fabulous, depending on which mask she was wearing. The masks conformed to what adults judge to be a very attractive face and a relatively unattractive one.

When interacting with the woman, infant participants behaved differently as a function of which mask she was wearing. They were more positive, became more involved in play, and were less likely to withdraw when she was wearing the attractive mask than when she had on the unattractive one. This study was particularly well designed because the young woman never knew on any given day which mask she had on. Thus, the children's behavior could not have been cued by her behavior; it could only have been due to her pretty or homely appearance.

Finally, face perception may provide important hints about atypical development. Children and adults with autism spectrum disorders (ASD) frequently have difficulty with face perception, often preferring not to look at faces—especially the eyes—and showing impaired memory for faces (e.g., Jones, Carr, & Klin, 2008; Weigelt, Koldewyn, & Kanwisher, 2013). Researchers have proposed that infant preferences for non-faces—in particular, geometric shapes—may provide an early indication that the infant will eventually be diagnosed with ASD. One recent eye-tracking study found that toddlers with ASD disproportionately preferred a display of geometric shapes over a display of dynamic human images, while typically developing toddlers showed the opposite pattern of preference (Pierce et al., 2016). Interestingly, those toddlers with ASD who most strongly preferred the geometric images had poorer language, cognitive, and social abilities than other toddlers with ASD. Infants with less interest in faces may have fewer opportunities to learn about the many types of information carried by faces, from speech sounds to social cues.

What caused the infants to perceive the two rod segments presented during habituation as parts of a unitary object? The answer is *common movement*, that is, the fact that the two segments always moved together in the same direction and at the same speed. Four-month-olds who saw a display that was the same as the one in Figure 5.4a, except that the rod was stationary, looked equally long at the two test displays. In other words, in the absence of common movement, the display was ambiguous.

Common movement is such a powerful cue that it leads infants to perceive disparate elements moving together as parts of a unitary object. It does not matter if the two parts of the object moving behind the block differ in color, texture, and shape, nor does it make much difference how they move (side to side, up and down, and so forth). For infants, common motion may have this effect, in part, because it draws their attention to the relevant aspects of the scene—the moving pieces rather than the block (S. P. Johnson et al., 2008). Strikingly, however, even this seemingly very basic feature of visual perception must be learned. Newborn infants, tested using displays similar to those described above and shown in Figure 5.4, do not appear to make use of common motion as a cue to object identity (Slater et al., 1990, 1996). Only at 2 months of age do infants show any evidence that they use common motion to interpret the occluded rod as a single object, and then only when the task is simplified (S. P. Johnson & Aslin, 1995). Thus, as powerful a cue as common motion may be, infants must develop the ability to exploit it.

As they become older, infants use additional sources of information for object segregation, including their general knowledge about the world (Needham, 1997; Needham & Baillargeon, 1997). Look at the displays shown in Figure 5.5. The differences in color, shape, and texture between the box and the tube in Figure 5.5a suggest that there are two separate objects, although you cannot really be sure. However, your knowledge that objects cannot float in midair tells you that Figure 5.5b has to be a single object; that is, the tube must be attached to the box.

Like you, 8-month-olds interpret these two displays differently. When they see a hand reach in and pull on the tube in Figure 5.5a, they look longer (presumably they are more surprised) if the box and tube move together than if the tube comes apart from the box, indicating that they perceive the display as two separate objects. However, the opposite pattern occurs in Figure 5.5b: now the infants look longer if the tube alone moves, indicating that they perceive a single object. Follow-up studies using the displays in Figure 5.5 with younger infants suggest that younger infants (4½-month-olds) exhibit the adultlike interpretation of these displays, but only when they have been familiarized previously with the box or the tube (Needham & Baillargeon, 1998). Thus, it appears that experience with specific objects helps infants to understand their physical properties. We will return to this idea later in the chapter when we discuss the implications of motor development for infants' knowledge about objects (particularly with respect to reaching, on page 213).

The culture within which an infant develops—which constitutes another form of experience—may also influence his or her attention to the visual world. Decades of research in cultural psychology have documented different patterns of visual attention in different cultures. For example, when processing emotions

FIGURE 5.5 Knowledge and object segregation (a) It is impossible to know for sure whether what you see here is one object or two. (b) Because of your knowledge about gravity and support, you can be sure that this figure is a single (albeit very odd) object. (Information from Needham, 1997)

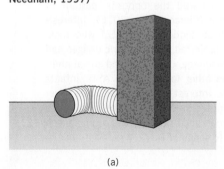
(a)

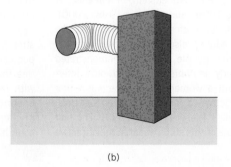
(b)

in faces, Western Caucasian adults are more likely to make use of information in the mouth, while East Asian adults are more likely to make use of information in the eyes (Jack et al., 2012). These cultural differences in visual attention must be learned. And indeed, this pattern of face perception emerges by 7 months of age: Caucasian infants growing up in the United Kingdom were more likely to focus on the mouths of faces shown during an eye-tracking task, while East Asian infants growing up in Japan were more likely to focus on the eyes (Geangu et al., 2016).

Cultural differences are also found in scene perception. Western Caucasian adults tend to fixate on the focal objects in a scene, whereas East Asian adults tend to fixate on the actions and background contexts of the scene (e.g., Nisbett & Miyamoto, 2005). And indeed, by 24 months of age, Caucasian American and Chinese infants display subtly different patterns of visual attention when viewing dynamic scenes: Caucasian American infants pay more attention to objects, whereas Chinese infants pay more attention to actions (Waxman et al., 2016). This emerging difference may be due to cultural differences in what parents are paying attention to—which influences what their infants are paying attention to. Also, as we will see in Chapter 6, mothers in East Asian countries are more likely than mothers in the United States to label actions, which may heighten their salience for infants.

Depth Perception

To navigate through our environment, we need to know where we are with respect to the objects and landmarks around us. We use many sorts of depth and distance cues to tell us whether we can reach the coffee cup on our desk or whether the approaching car is far enough away that we can safely cross in front of it. From the beginning, infants are sensitive to some of these cues, and they rapidly become sensitive to the rest.

One cue that infants are sensitive to very early on is **optical expansion,** in which the visual image of an object increases in size as the object comes toward us, occluding more and more of the background. When the image of an approaching object expands symmetrically, we know that the object is headed right for us, and a sensible response is to duck. Babies cannot duck, but they can blink. Timing this blinking response is critical; if infants blink too soon or too late, they risk having the oncoming object hit their open eye. If you think about it, though, it's not at all obvious how infants would know how to correctly time a blink. Doing so requires infants to rapidly exploit information present in the visual image looming before them, including how rapidly the image is expanding and how much of the visual field is taken up by the image. Rather remarkably, infants as young as 1 month blink defensively at an expanding image that appears to be an object heading toward them (Nález, 1988). Preterm infants show a delayed developmental pattern of blinks to looming objects, suggesting that brain maturation, and not solely postnatal visual experience, is crucial for this developmental achievement (e.g., Agyei, van der Weel, & van der Meer, 2016).

The simple fact that we have two eyes also aids in the early development of depth perception. Because of the distance between our eyes, the retinal image of an object at any instant is never quite the same in both eyes. Consequently, the eyes never send quite the same signal to the brain—a phenomenon known as **binocular disparity.** The closer the object we are looking at, the greater the disparity between the two images; the farther away the object, the less the disparity. In a process known as **stereopsis,**

optical expansion ■ a depth cue in which an object occludes increasingly more of the background, indicating that the object is approaching

binocular disparity ■ the difference between the retinal image of an object in each eye that results in two slightly different signals being sent to the brain

stereopsis ■ the process by which the visual cortex combines the differing neural signals caused by binocular disparity, resulting in the perception of depth

As objects approach, they appear to grow in size. Optical expansion is a basic cue for depth perception.

CHICCODODIFC / GETTY IMAGES

monocular depth (or pictorial) cues ■ the perceptual cues of depth (such as relative size and interposition) that can be perceived by one eye alone

the visual cortex computes the degree of disparity between the eyes' differing neural signals and produces the perception of depth. This form of depth perception emerges quite suddenly at around 4 months of age and is generally complete within a few weeks (Held, Birch, & Gwiazda, 1980).

The development of stereopsis is a classic example of the experience-expectant plasticity discussed in Chapter 3. Given the type of visual experience that infants normally receive, the development of binocular vision—both eyes working together to compute depth cues and other aspects of the visual scene—is a natural outcome of brain maturation. However, if infants are deprived of normal visual input during early postnatal life, they may fail to develop normal binocular vision and will have difficulty making use of stereopsis and other binocular depth cues. There is a sensitive period for this aspect of visual development, which was first discovered in the research with cats discussed in Chapter 3: kittens deprived of vision in one eye before about 3 months of age fail to develop normal binocular vision when vision is restored (Hubel & Wiesel, 1962). The human analogue is a form of visual disruption known as *strabismus,* a disorder in which the two eyes do not line up in the same direction. Children whose strabismus is not treated (usually by corrective surgery) before the age of 3 are at risk for pervasive life-long challenges in binocular vision (Banks, Aslin, & Letson, 1975).

At about 6 or 7 months of age, infants begin to become sensitive to a variety of **monocular depth cues** (so called because they denote depth even if only one eye is open) (Yonas, Elieff, & Arterberry, 2002). These cues are also known as **pictorial cues** because they can be used to portray depth in pictures. Three of them, including relative size, are presented in Figure 5.6.

In one of the earliest studies of infants' sensitivity to monocular depth cues, Yonas, Cleaves, and Pettersen (1978) capitalized on the fact that infants will reach toward whichever of two objects is nearer. The investigators put a patch over one eye of 5- and 7-month-olds (so binocular depth information would not be

FIGURE 5.6 Pictorial cues This Renaissance painting contains multiple examples of pictorial cues. One is interposition—nearer objects occlude ones farther away. The convergence of lines in the distance is another. To appreciate the effectiveness of a third cue—relative size—compare the actual size of the man on the steps in the foreground to the actual size of the woman in the blue dress.

available) and presented them with a trapezoidal window with one side considerably longer than the other (Figure 5.7). (When viewed by an adult with one eye closed, the window appears to be a standard rectangular window sitting at an angle with one side closer to the viewer.) The 7-month-olds (but not the younger babies) reached toward the longer side, indicating that they, as you would, perceived it as being nearer, providing evidence that they used relative size as a cue to depth. (Box 5.2 reviews research on infants' perception of pictures.)

Auditory Perception

Another rich source of infants' information about the world is sound. As discussed in Chapter 2, fetuses can hear sufficiently well to learn basic features of their auditory environment (their mother's heartbeat, the rhythmic patterns of her native language, and so forth). At birth, the human auditory system is well developed relative to the visual system. That said, there are vast improvements in sound conduction from the outer and middle ear to the inner ear over the course of infancy. Similarly, over the 1st year, auditory pathways in the brain mature significantly. Taken together, these developments in the ear and in the brain greatly improve the infant's ability to respond to, and learn from, sound.

Other factors add to infants' improvement in auditory perception. One example involves **auditory localization,** the perception of the spatial location of a sound source. When they hear a sound, newborns tend to turn toward it. However, newborns and young infants are far worse at determining the spatial location of a sound than are older infants and toddlers. To localize a sound, listeners rely on differences in the sounds that arrive at both of their ears: a sound played to their right will arrive at their right ear before reaching their left ear, and will be louder at their right ear than at their left ear, thereby signaling the direction the sound is coming from. Young infants may have more difficulty using this information because their heads are small, thus the differences in timing and loudness in information arriving at each ear are smaller for infants than for toddlers and children with larger heads. Another reason why this information may be difficult for infants to exploit is that the development of an auditory spatial map (i.e., a mental representation of how sounds are organized in physical space—right versus left, up versus down) requires multimodal experiences, through which infants become able to integrate information from what they hear with information from what they see and touch.

Infants are adept at perceiving patterns in the streams of sound they hear. They are remarkably proficient, for example, at detecting subtle differences in the sounds of human speech—an ability we will review in detail in our discussion of language development in Chapter 6. Here, we focus on another realm in which infants display an impressive degree of auditory sensitivity: music.

Music Perception

Caregivers around the world sing while caring for their infants. When adults sing to their infants, they do so in a characteristic fashion which, like the infant-directed speech register we will discuss in Chapter 6, tends to be slower and

FIGURE 5.7 Monocular depth cues This 7-month-old infant is using the monocular depth cue of relative size. Wearing an eye patch to take away binocular depth information, he is reaching to the longer side of a trapezoidal window. This behavior indicates that the baby sees it as the nearer, and hence more readily reachable, side of a regular rectangular window (Yonas et al., 1978).

DR. ALBERT YONAS

auditory localization ■ perception of the location in space of a sound source

BOX 5.2 | a closer look

PICTURE PERCEPTION

A special case of perceptual development concerns pictures. Paintings, drawings, and photographs are ubiquitous in modern societies, and we acquire an enormous amount of information through them. When can infants perceive and understand these important cultural artifacts?

Even young infants perceive pictures in much the same way that you do. In a classic study, Hochberg and Brooks (1962) raised their own infant son with no exposure to pictures at all: no art or family photos; no picture books; no patterns on sheets, clothing, or toys. They even removed the labels from canned foods. Nevertheless, when tested at 18 months, the child readily identified people and objects in photographs and line drawings. Later research established that infants as young as 5 months old can recognize people and objects in photographs and drawings of them (e.g., DeLoache, Strauss, & Maynard, 1979; Dirks & Gibson, 1977), and even newborns can recognize two-dimensional versions of three-dimensional objects (Slater, Morison, & Rose, 1984).

Despite their precocious perception of pictures, infants do not fully understand their nature. The four babies shown here—two from the United States and two from a rural village in West Africa—are all manually exploring depicted objects. Although these 9-month-old babies can perceive the difference between pictures and objects, they do not yet understand what two-dimensionality means; hence, they attempt to treat pictured objects as if they were real objects—with an inevitable lack of success.

One source of evidence suggesting that infants do not fully understand the nature of 2-D images is that they sometimes attempt to pick up pictured objects, suggesting that they think the objects are real. Of particular note is that infants are more likely to attempt to pick up images that look real than images that do not. For instance, 9-month-olds are more likely to attempt to grasp objects depicted in realistic photographs than objects depicted in colored line drawings, and they are more likely to reach for pictured objects than for high-contrast images of non-objects (Pierroutsakos & DeLoache, 2003; Ziemer, Plumert, & Pick, 2012). They do, however, show more grasps for actual objects than for pictured objects, suggesting that they have at least some rudimentary understanding of the distinction between 2-D and 3-D images. They also appear to understand the correspondence between 2-D and 3-D versions of the same object. Nine-month-olds habituated to a 3-D object do not dishabituate when shown a 2-D image of the same object (Jowkar-Baniani & Schmuckler, 2011). This finding may reflect confusion on the part of infants, who are treating the 2-D and 3-D objects as the same thing. Alternatively, it may reflect infants' recognition of the correspondence between 2-D and 3-D representations of objects.

By 19 months of age and after substantial experience with pictures, American infants no longer manually investigate pictures, apparently having learned that pictures are to look at and talk about, but not to feel, pick up, or eat (DeLoache et al., 1998; Pierroutsakos & DeLoache, 2003). In short, they have come to understand the symbolic nature of pictures and appreciate that a depicted object stands for a real object (Uttal & Yuan, 2014). We will discuss the development of symbols further in Chapter 6.

Whereas most Western infants live in environments filled with pictured objects, infants in other cultures often lack experience with such images. Fascinating cross-cultural research suggests that, in fact, infants who grow up in homes and communities without pictured objects do not show the same trajectory of understanding that

---

higher-pitched, and to suggest more positive affect, than does singing directed toward adult listeners. Perhaps because of these characteristics, infants prefer infant-directed singing over adult-directed singing (Masataka, 1999; Trainor, 1996). Indeed, infants appear to enjoy listening to infant-directed singing even more than to infant-directed speech, possibly because mothers smile more while singing than speaking (Trehub, Plantinga, & Russo, 2015). Indeed, infants will listen twice as long to singing as to speaking before becoming distressed (Corbeil, Trehub, & Peretz, 2015).

In many ways, infant music perception is adultlike. One well-studied example is the preference for consonant intervals (e.g., octaves, or perfect fifths like the opening notes of the ABCs song) over dissonant intervals (e.g., augmented fourths like the opening of the theme song from the TV show *The Simpsons*, or minor seconds like the theme from the film *Jaws*). From Pythagoras to Galileo to the present day, many scientists and scholars have argued that consonant tones are inherently pleasing to human ears, whereas dissonant tones are unpleasant

pictures are representations of real objects. In one study, Canadian toddlers and pre-schoolers outstripped their peers from rural India and Peru in their ability to match line drawings of objects to toy objects (Callaghan et al., 2011). Similarly, toddlers from rural Tanzania, who had no prior exposure to pictures, had greater difficulty than did North American toddlers in generalizing the names of objects in color photographs to the objects themselves (Walker, Walker, & Ganea, 2013). These studies suggest that understanding the relationship between 2-D images and 3-D objects requires experience with pictorial media.

Many infants today have increased access to another form of 2-D images—moving images presented via screens, especially on handheld media devices. How do infants come to understand that Grandma on Skype is the same as "real" Grandma? By age 2 years, toddlers are as good at learning labels for objects via video chat as they are from in-person interactions, probably because both of these sources of information provide contingent interactions (Roseberry, Hirsh Pasek, & Golinkoff, 2014). When toddlers are given the same information via non-contingent interactions—as they would if they were watching a television show—they do not learn as well. Thus, it may be the case that 2-D images that interact contingently with infants are more readily understood as representing real objects.

ALL COURTESY JUDY DELOACHE, PIERROUSTAKOS, UTTAL, ROSENGREN, AND GOTTLIEB

These 9-month-old infants—two from the United States and two from West Africa—are responding to pictures of objects as if they were real objects. They do not yet know the true nature of pictures.

(Schellenberg & Trehub, 1996; Trehub & Schellenberg, 1995). To see if infants agree, researchers employ a simple but reliable procedure. They draw infants' attention toward an audio speaker by using a visually interesting stimulus (e.g., a flashing light) and then play music through the speaker. The length of time infants look at the speaker (actually, at the visual stimulus located in the same position as the speaker) is taken as a measure of their interest in, or preference for, the music emanating from the speaker.

Studies have shown that infants pay more attention to a consonant version of a piece of music, whether a folk song or a minuet, than to a dissonant one (Trainor & Heinmiller, 1998; Zentner & Kagan, 1996, 1998). A study by Masataka revealed that even 2-day-old infants show this pattern of preference (Masataka, 2006). This study is particularly notable in that it was conducted with hearing infants whose mothers were deaf, making it unlikely that the infants would have had prenatal exposure to singing. These results suggest that preferences for consonant music as opposed to dissonant music are not due to musical experience. Indeed, other

perceptual narrowing ■ developmental changes in which experience fine-tunes the perceptual system

species (including chicks, macaque monkeys, and chimps) also show preferences for consonant music, supporting the view that preferences for consonance over dissonance are unrelated to musical experience (e.g., Chiandetti & Vallortigara, 2011; Sugimoto et al., 2010).

In certain other aspects of music perception, infants diverge markedly from adult listeners. One of the most interesting differences is in the area of melodic perception, in which infants can make perceptual discriminations that adults cannot. In one set of studies, 8-month-old infants and adults listened to a brief repeating melody that was consistent with the harmonic conventions of Western music. Then, in a series of test trials, they heard the melody again—but with one note changed. On some trials, the changed note was in the same key as the melody; on others, it fell outside the key. Both infants and adults noticed changes that violated the key of the melody, but only the infants noticed the changes that stayed within the key of the melody (Trainor & Trehub, 1992). Does this mean that infants are more musically attuned than adults? Probably not. What appeared to be a heightened musical sensitivity in the infant participants was more likely a reflection of their relative lack of implicit knowledge about Western music. Because it takes years to acquire culture-specific familiarity with musical key structures, the within-key and out-of-key changes were equally salient to the infant listeners (Trainor & Trehub, 1994). For adults, years of hearing music makes it very difficult to detect note changes that stay within a key.

In a similar way, infants are also more "sensitive" to aspects of musical rhythm than are adults. Musical systems vary in the complexity of their rhythmic patterning; the rhythms of most Western music, for example, are relatively simple compared with those of some cultures in Africa, India, and parts of Europe. Hannon and Trehub (2005a, 2005b) tested adults and 6-month-olds on their ability to detect meter-disrupting changes in simple rhythms versus complex rhythms. Notably, some of the adults in this study lived in the Balkans, where the local music contains complex rhythmic patterns; others lived in North America, where popular music is characterized by simpler rhythmic patterns. The results revealed that all groups detected changes in the simple rhythms, but only the North American infants and the Balkan adults detected changes in the complex rhythms. Thus, North American 6-month-olds outperformed North American adults on this task. A follow-up study asked whether North American 12-month-olds and adults could be trained to detect such changes in the complex rhythms. After 2 weeks of exposure to the Balkan rhythms, the 12-month-olds were able to detect changes in complex rhythms, but the adults still failed to do so.

These examples from the musical domain suggest that, with experience, there is a process of **perceptual narrowing.** Infants, who are relatively inexperienced with music, can detect differences between musical stimuli that adults cannot. Developmental changes in which experience fine-tunes the perceptual system are observed across numerous domains. Indeed, you saw this process of perceptual narrowing in our discussion of face perception in Box 5.1, and you will see the same pattern of development when we examine intermodal aspects of speech perception (pages 206–207) and, quite prominently, when we take up language acquisition in Chapter 6. Across all these examples and in other domains, experience leads the young learner to begin to "lose" the ability to make distinctions that he or she could make at earlier points in development. In each case, this perceptual narrowing permits the developing child to become especially attuned to patterns in biological and social stimuli that are important in their environment.

As discussed in Chapter 3, adult musicians' brains are shaped by the instruments that they play, demonstrating substantial plasticity. More generally, musicians are better than nonmusicians at processing aspects of pitch and rhythm—in both speech and music (e.g., Kraus & Chandrasekaran, 2010; Wong et al., 2007). This finding raises a chicken and egg problem: Which comes first, enhanced auditory processing or musical training? That is, perhaps those individuals who persist in musical training are those who started out with unusually good auditory skills. Alternatively, infants are generally similar in their auditory abilities, but musical training leads to enhanced auditory perception in those who receive it. To address this question, a recent study assigned 9-month-old infants to one of two conditions, a musical intervention (12 sessions of musical exposure/play activities in the lab, akin to an infant music class) or a control condition consisting of nonmusical social play in the lab (Zhao & Kuhl, 2016). The researchers then used MEG (one of the brain measures described in Box 3.3) to determine how well the infants' brains detected violations of musical and speech structure. The results suggest that the musical intervention affected how well infants processed these materials: those infants who received additional musical experience were better able to process and detect violations in both music and speech. Thus, these data support the view that experience plays a key role in supporting the development of musical abilities.

These infants are engaging in musical activities as part of an infant music class, which is both enjoyable and provides potential benefits for perceptual development.

Taste and Smell

As you learned in Chapter 2, sensitivity to taste and smell develops before birth, and newborns prefer sweet flavors. Preferences for smells are also present very early in life. Newborns prefer the smell of the natural food source for human infants—breast milk (Marlier & Schaal, 2005). Smell plays a powerful role in how a variety of infant mammals learn to recognize their mothers. It probably does the same for humans, as shown by studies in which infants chose between the scent of their own mother and that of another woman. In one such study, a pad that an infant's mother had worn next to her armpit was placed on one side of the infant's head and a pad worn by a different woman was placed on the other side. Two-day-old infants spent almost twice as long oriented to the pad infused with their mother's unique scent (Marin, Rapisardi, & Tani, 2015).

 The Senses in Infancy and Toddlerhood

Touch

Another important way that infants learn about the environment is through active touch, initially through their mouth and tongue, and later with their hands and fingers. Oral exploration dominates for the first few months, as infants mouth and suck on their own fingers and toes, as well as virtually any object they come into contact with. (This is why it is so important to keep small, swallowable objects away from babies.) Through their ardent oral exploration, babies presumably learn about their own bodies (or at least the parts they can get their mouths on), as well as about the texture, taste, and other properties of the objects they encounter.

From around the age of 4 months, as infants gain greater control over their hand and arm movements, manual exploration increases and gradually takes

Initially, every object that a baby can pick up gets directed to his or her mouth for oral exploration—whether or not it will fit. Later, infants are more inclined to explore objects visually and manually, thereby showing an interest in the object itself.

intermodal perception ■
the combining of information from two or more sensory systems

precedence over oral exploration. Infants actively rub, finger, probe, and bang objects, and their actions become increasingly specific to the properties of the objects. For example, they tend to rub textured objects and bang rigid ones. They also begin to develop mental maps of their own bodies, relating the sensation of being touched to the locations on their bodies that are being touched (Ali, Spence, & Bremner, 2015). Important developments occur as infants become more adept at reaching, as we will discuss later in this chapter.

Intermodal Perception

Most events that both adults and infants experience involve simultaneous stimulation through multiple sensory modalities. In the scenario described at the opening of this chapter, the shattering glass provided both visual and auditory stimulation. Through the phenomenon of **intermodal perception,** the combining of information from two or more sensory systems, Benjamin's parents perceived the auditory and visual stimulation as a unitary, coherent event. It is likely that 4-month-old Benjamin did, too.

According to Piaget (1954), information from different sensory modalities is initially perceived as separate, and only after some months do infants become capable of forming associations between how things look and how they sound, taste, feel, and so on. However, research suggests that from very early on, infants integrate information from different senses. For example, very young infants link their oral and visual experiences. In studies with newborns (Kaye & Bower, 1994) and 1-month-olds (Meltzoff & Borton, 1979), infants sucked on a pacifier that they were prevented from seeing. They were then shown a picture of the pacifier that had been in their mouth and a picture of a novel pacifier of a different shape or texture. The infants looked longer at the pacifier they had sucked on. Thus, these infants could visually recognize an object they had experienced only through oral exploration.

Researchers have also discovered that infants possess various forms of auditory–visual intermodal perception. In studies of this mode of perception, infants simultaneously view two different videos side by side, while listening to a soundtrack that is synchronized with one of the videos but not the other. If an infant responds more to the video that goes with the soundtrack, it is taken as evidence that the infant detects the common structure in the auditory and visual information. Another way to think about these phenomena is that infants prefer to attend to multisensory events that can be perceived as emanating from a single object (Murray et al., 2016).

In a classic study of cross-modal matching using this procedure, Spelke (1976) showed 4-month-olds two videos: one presented a person playing peekaboo, and the other presented a hand beating a drumstick against a block. The infants responded more to the film that matched the sounds they were hearing. When they heard a voice saying "Peekaboo," they looked more at the person, but when they heard a beating sound, they looked longer at the hand. In subsequent studies, infants showed finer discriminations. For instance, 4-month-olds responded more to a film of a "hopping" toy animal in which the sounds of impact coincided with the animal's landing on a surface than they did to a film in which the impact sounds occurred while the animal was in midair (Spelke, 1979).

At this age, infants can also draw more abstract connections between sights and sounds. For example, 3- to 4-month-olds look longer at visual displays in which dimensions in each modality are congruent, such as a ball rising and falling at the same rate as a whistle rising and falling in pitch (Walker et al., 2010; though see Lewkowicz & Minar, 2014, for conflicting results). These findings have been interpreted as an early-emerging form of *synesthesia*, a phenomenon by which a stimulus in one modality leads to a percept in another modality. As discussed in Chapter 2, infants may be especially likely to experience this type of sensory blending because the neural connections between sensory areas have yet to be pruned.

One of the most dramatic demonstrations of auditory–visual blending is an illusion known as *the McGurk effect* (McGurk & MacDonald, 1976). To elicit this illusion, the auditory syllable *ba* is dubbed onto a video of a person speaking the syllable *ga*. Someone watching this display will hear the syllable *da*, which is intermediate between *ba* and *ga* (as you can tell if you speak the three syllables aloud, in succession, and pay attention to the location in your mouth where you create the consonant). In order to experience this illusion, the perceiver must be able to integrate auditory and visual information together. And indeed, 4½-month-olds are able to experience this illusion: they treat the *da* sound as familiar after familiarization with the McGurk stimulus, even though they did not actually ever hear *da* (Burnham & Dodd, 2004; Kushnerenko et al., 2008).

The processes of perceptual narrowing that we have noted elsewhere also occur in intermodal perception. Young infants can detect correspondences between speech sounds and facial movements for nonnative speech sounds (those not present in their native language), but older infants cannot (Pons et al., 2009). Similarly, young infants can detect the correspondence between monkey facial movements and monkey vocalizations, but older infants are unable to do so (Lewkowicz & Ghazanfar, 2006). Experience thus fine-tunes the types of intermodal correspondences that infants detect.

How does intermodal perception develop when one sense is absent early in life? This intriguing question has been the target of investigation in India, a nation with an unusually large population of blind children. For a large number of these children, their blindness is reversible because it is due to cataracts, which can be easily removed surgically. Project Prakash is a scientific and philanthropic organization dedicated to screening children and adults in India in order to remediate preventable blindness. Their research mission is to discover what happens when vision is restored after years or even decades of blindness. One of their research efforts focused on intermodal perception (Held et al., 2011). In particular, they asked: Would newly sighted adults be able to match an object that they felt via touch with an object that they saw? The results showed that immediately after regaining sight, formerly blind adults could not match a visual shape with a tactile shape. However, after just 5 days of visual experience, the adults successfully performed this visual–tactile intermodal matching task. These results suggest that experience is indeed necessary in order to help previously blind learners discover the links between modalities. While it might not require the months that Piaget believed, intermodal processes do appear to be facilitated by sensory experience.

The McGurk Effect

This child is a participant in Project Prakash, an organization dedicated to restoring vision to blind children in India and studying their subsequent perceptual development.

PAWAN SINHA / PROJECT PRAKASH

Review

Using a variety of special techniques, developmental psychologists have discovered an enormous amount about perceptual development in infancy. They have documented rapid development of basic visual abilities from birth over the next few months, discovering that by approximately 8 months of age infants' visual acuity, scanning patterns, and color perception are similar to those of adults. Some forms of depth perception are present at birth, whereas others require visual experience. Infants use many sources of information, including movement and their knowledge of their surroundings, for object segregation. Faces are of particular interest to infant perceivers.

Research on auditory perception has shown that right from birth, babies turn toward sounds they hear. They are quite sensitive to music and display some of the same musical preferences adults do, such as a preference for consonance over dissonance. Infants also show perceptual abilities for music that exceed those of adults, whose auditory processing has been shaped by years of musical listening. Smell and touch both play an important role in infants' interaction with the world around them. The crucial ability to link what they perceive in separate modalities to experience unitary, coherent events is present in a simple form at birth, but more complex associations develop gradually.

There is much in recent research to encourage anyone of a nativist persuasion: neonates show remarkable perceptual abilities that cannot be due to experience, even prenatal experience. At the same time, most perceptual skills also show development over time, much of which clearly involves learning. Infants gradually become more adult-like in their perceptual abilities through perceptual narrowing: as expertise increases (via learning) within and across modalities, infants lose the ability to distinguish between less familiar sights and sounds, becoming increasingly attuned to their native environment.

Motor Development

As you learned in Chapter 2, human movement starts well before birth, as the fetus floats weightlessly in amniotic fluid. After birth, the newborn's movements are jerky and relatively uncoordinated, in part because of physical and neurological immaturity and in part because the baby is experiencing the full effects of gravity for the first time. As you will see in this section, the story of how the uncoordinated newborn, a prisoner of gravity, becomes a competent toddler confidently exploring the environment is remarkably complicated.

Reflexes

Newborns start off with some tightly organized patterns of action known as neonatal **reflexes.** Some reflexes, such as withdrawal from a painful stimulus, have clear adaptive value; others have no known adaptive significance. In the *grasping* reflex, newborns close their fingers around anything that presses against the palm of their hand (see Figure 5.8a). When stroked on the cheek near their mouth, infants exhibit the *rooting* reflex, turning their head in the direction of the touch and opening their mouth (see Figure 5.8b). Thus, when their cheek comes into contact with their mother's breast, they turn toward the breast, opening their mouth as they do. Oral contact with the nipple then sets off a *sucking* reflex, followed by the *swallowing* reflex, both of which increase the baby's chance of getting nourishment and ultimately of surviving (see Figure 5.8c). These reflexes are not *fully* automatic; for example, a rooting reflex is more likely to occur when an infant is hungry.

No benefit is known to be associated with certain other reflexes, such as the *tonic neck* reflex: when an infant's head turns or is turned to one side, the arm on that side of the body extends, while the arm and knee on the other side flex

reflexes ■ innate, fixed patterns of action that occur in response to particular stimulation

FIGURE 5.8 Common neonatal reflexes

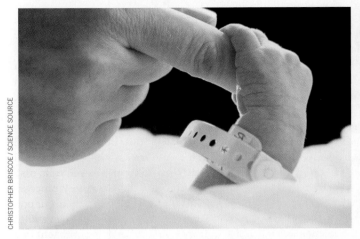

(a) Grasping

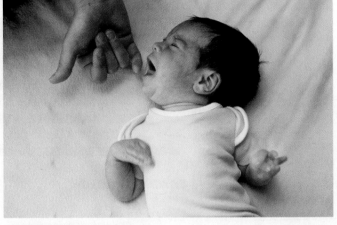

(b) Rooting

(c) Sucking

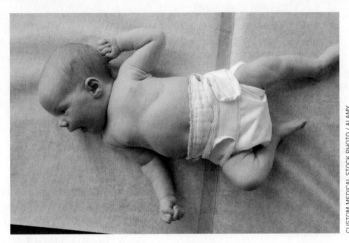

(d) Tonic neck reflex

(see Figure 5.8d). It is thought that the tonic neck reflex involves an effort by babies to get and keep their hand in view (von Hofsten, 2004).

The presence of strong reflexes at birth is a sign that the newborn's central nervous system is in good shape. Reflexes that are either unusually weak or unusually vigorous may signal brain damage. Most of the neonatal reflexes disappear on a regular schedule, although some—including coughing, sneezing, blinking, and withdrawing from pain—remain throughout life. Persistence of a neonatal reflex beyond the point at which it is expected to disappear can indicate a neurological problem.

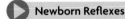 **Newborn Reflexes**

Motor Milestones

Infants progress quickly in acquiring the basic movement patterns of our species, shown in Figure 5.9. As you will see, the achievement of each of the major "motor milestones" of infancy, especially walking, constitutes a major advance. Consistent with the dynamic systems approach described in Chapter 4, infants' acquisition of new ways to interact with the world provides them with new things to learn and new ways to think about the world.

The average ages that Figure 5.9 indicates for the development of each of these important motor skills are based on research with Western, primarily

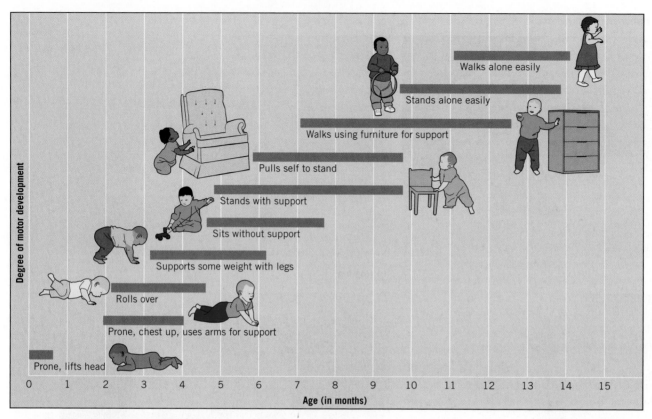

FIGURE 5.9 **The major milestones of motor development in infancy** The average age and range of ages for achievement of each milestone are shown. Note that these age norms are based on research with healthy, well-nourished North American infants.

North American, infants. There are, of course, tremendous individual differences in the ages at which these milestones are achieved. For example, the range for sitting shown in Figure 5.9 is roughly 5 to 7 months of age. However, a cross-cultural study by the World Health Organization found a range of sitting onsets from 3.8 months to 9.2 months (Martorell et al., 2006). These individual differences appear to be at least partially mediated by cultural differences. In a study of the development of sitting in seven different countries, the percentage of 5-month-olds who could sit independently ranged from 0% (in Italy) to 92% (in Cameroon), with the United States falling below average at 17% (Karasik et al., 2015).

These differences in the course of motor development reflect the contexts in which infants are developing. In countries where infants tend to sit independently earlier, they also tend to be placed in locations that offer less postural support, such as on the ground (in Kenya) and on adult furniture (in Cameroon). Infants in the countries where sitting tends to emerge later, such as Italy and the United States, spend more time in child furniture (infant carriers, swings, etc.) or being held. Because their posture is supported for more of the time, these infants have less opportunity to learn how to cope with gravity in order to keep from toppling over.

The degree to which motor skills are encouraged varies from one culture to another. Caregivers in some cultures actively *discourage* early locomotion. In modern urban China, for example, infants are often restricted from crawling due to hygienic concerns (He, Walle, & Campos, 2015). These restrictions make it difficult for infants to develop the muscle strength required to support their upper trunk, which is necessary for crawling. Among the Aché, a nomadic people who live in the rain forest of Paraguay, infants spend almost all of their first 3 years of life being carried by their mothers or kept very close to her because of safety concerns. These infants thus get relatively little opportunity early on to exercise their locomotor skills (Kaplan & Dove, 1987).

In direct contrast, caregivers in other cultures actively encourage their infants' motor development. Motor exercises—including massage, limb manipulation, and other forms of motor stimulation—are a widespread parenting practice in many cultures in sub-Saharan Africa, including the Kipsigis, Kung San, Gusii, Wolof, and Bambora communities. These motor stimulation activities, shown in Figure 5.10, are often accompanied by singing, rhythmic bouncing, and high positive affect from the caregiver, and are chosen intentionally to promote their infants' motor development. As described by one mother, "stretching the legs, the hands, and everything of the body makes the baby physically strong" (Carra, Lavelli, & Keller, 2014).

These widely varying cultural practices can affect infants' development. The infants who undergo these massage and exercise regimes are more advanced in their motor-skill development than North American infants. Infants whose movements are particularly restricted may be less advanced. In one striking example, some families in Northern China use sandbags instead of diapers due to water scarcity; their infants spend more than 16 hours per day lying inside a bag filled with fine sand, with only their arms unrestricted. These infants show significant delays in sitting and walking relative to their peers (Adolph, Karasik, & Tamis-LeMonda, 2010).

Even aspects of infant life that we take for granted in our own culture have an effect on motor development. In a recent study, researchers asked whether diapers—a relatively recent cultural invention—have an impact on walking behavior (Cole, Lingeman, & Adolph, 2012; see Figure 5.11). The researchers found that the same infants exhibited more mature walking behavior when tested naked than when tested diapered, despite the fact that these infants—all residents of New York City—were accustomed to wearing diapers and had rarely walked naked. These data beautifully demonstrate that cultural practices that are undertaken in one domain (toileting) can have unforeseen consequences in another domain (walking behavior).

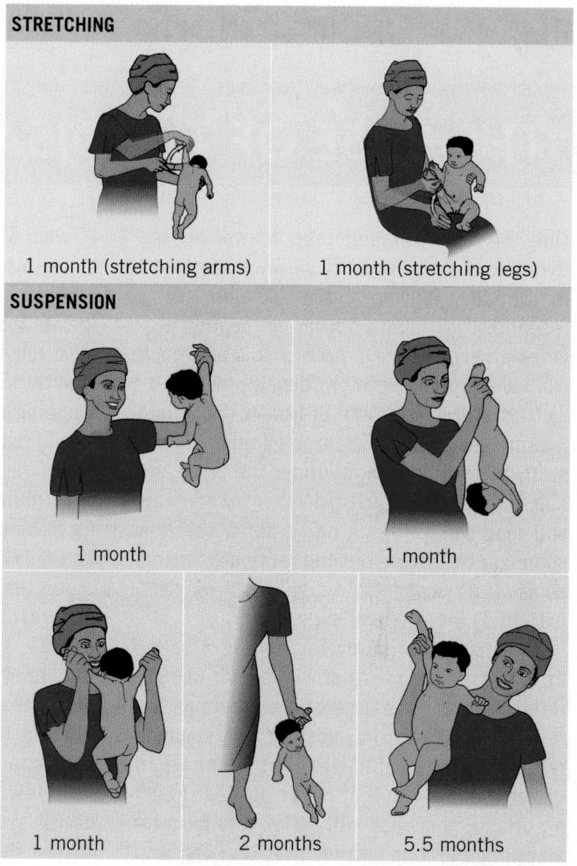

Modern Views of Motor Development

Impressed by the orderly acquisition of skills reflected in Figure 5.9, two early pioneers in the study of motor development, Arnold Gesell and Myrtle McGraw, concluded that infants' motor development is governed by brain maturation (Gesell & Thompson, 1938; McGraw, 1943). In contrast, current theorists emphasize that early motor development results from a confluence of numerous factors that include developing neural mechanisms, increases in infants' strength, posture control, balance, and perceptual skills, as well as changes in body proportions and motivation. (Box 5.3 offers a detailed account of a research program exemplifying this approach.)

FIGURE 5.10 Promoting motor development in West Africa Caregivers in Mali believe it is important to exercise their infants to promote their physical and motor development. The maneuvers shown here hasten their early motor skills. (Information from Bril & Sabatier, 1986)

▶ **West African Exercise Routine**

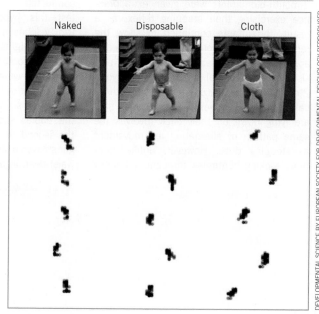

FIGURE 5.11 These images depict the footprint paths for a single infant participant who was tested walking naked, wearing lightweight disposable diapers, and wearing bulkier cloth diapers. The most mature walking behavior was seen in the left-most path, in the absence of diapers (Cole et al., 2012).

BOX 5.3 | a closer look

"THE CASE OF THE DISAPPEARING REFLEX"

One of the primary proponents of the dynamic-systems point of view we discussed in Chapter 4 was Esther Thelen. Early research by Thelen and her colleagues provides an excellent example of this approach to investigating motor development, as well as a good example of how to formulate hypotheses and test them in general. In one study, they held infants under the arms and submerged them waist-deep in water. As you read the following paragraphs, see how soon you can figure out the rationale for this somewhat strange-sounding but, in fact, extremely informative, experiment.

This particular study was one in a series of investigations that Thelen (1995) referred to as "the case of the disappearing reflex." The reflex in question, the **stepping reflex,** can be elicited by holding a newborn under the arms so that his or her feet touch a surface; the baby will reflexively perform stepping motions, lifting first one leg and then the other in a coordinated pattern as in walking. The reflex typically disappears at about 2 months of age. It was long assumed that the stepping reflex disappears from the infant's motor repertoire as a result of cortical maturation.

However, the results of a classic study by Zelazo, Zelazo, and Kolb (1972) were inconsistent with this view. In that research, 2-month-old infants were given extra practice exercising their stepping reflex; as a result, the infants continued to show the reflex long after it would otherwise have disappeared. Other research also showed persistence of the stepping pattern long beyond 2 months of age. For one thing, the rhythmical kicking that babies engage in when they are lying down on their back involves the same pattern of alternating leg movement as stepping does. However, unlike stepping, kicking continues throughout infancy

(Thelen & Fisher, 1982). Furthermore, when 7-month-olds (who neither walk nor typically show the stepping reflex) are supported on a moving treadmill, they step smartly (Thelen, 1986). If the stepping reflex can be prolonged or elicited long after it is supposedly scheduled to disappear, cortical maturation cannot account for it vanishing. Why then does it normally disappear?

A clue was provided by the observation that chubbier babies generally begin walking (and crawling) somewhat later than do slimmer ones. Thelen reasoned that infants' very rapid weight gain in the first few weeks after birth may cause their legs to get heavier faster than they get stronger. More strength is needed to step while upright than to kick while lying down, and more is needed to lift a chubby leg than a thin one. Thus, Thelen hypothesized that the solution to the mystery might have more to do with brawn than with brains.

Thelen and her colleagues conducted two elegant experiments to test this hypothesis (Thelen, Fisher, & Ridley-Johnson, 1984). In one, the researchers put weights on the ankles of very young infants who still had a stepping reflex. The amount of weight was roughly equivalent to the amount of fat typically gained in the first few months. When the weight was added, the babies suddenly stopped stepping. In the second study, older infants who no longer showed a stepping reflex were suspended waist-deep in a tank of water. As predicted,

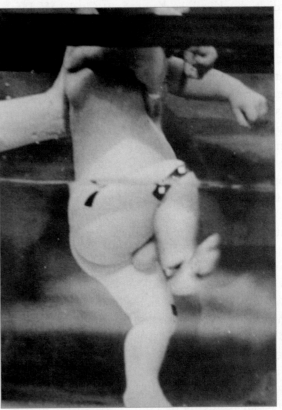

COURTESY OF ESTHER THELEN

This infant, who no longer shows a stepping reflex on dry land, does show it when suspended in water.

the babies resumed stepping when the buoyancy of the water supported their weight. Thus, the scientific detective work of these investigators established that the normal disappearance of the stepping reflex is not caused by cortical maturation, as previously assumed. Rather, the movement pattern (and its neural basis) remains but is masked by the changing ratio of leg weight to strength. Only by considering multiple variables simultaneously was it possible to solve the mystery of the disappearing reflex.

Think for a moment about how each of these factors plays a part in infants' gradual transition from newborns unable even to lift their head to toddlers who walk independently, holding their upper body erect while coordinating the movement of legs that have grown strong enough to support their weight. Every milestone in this transition is fueled by what infants can perceive of the external world and their motivation to experience more of it. The vital role of motivation is especially clear in infants' determined efforts to attempt to walk when they can get around much more efficiently by crawling. Most parents—and many researchers—have the impression that infants derive pleasure from pushing the envelope of their motor skills. And motor development pays off, as we will see in the next section; infants' increasing ability to explore and manipulate the world around them facilitates learning about the world. Indeed, individual differences in motor maturity at 5 months of age—as indexed by motor control and exploratory behavior—predict children's academic achievement at 14 years of age (Bornstein, Hahn, & Suwalsky, 2013). This research suggests that infants who are better able to interact with their environment—by reaching for and manipulating objects, changing their body position, and so on—may have an advantage in perceptual and cognitive development by being better able to seek out new opportunities for stimulation.

The Expanding World of the Infant

Infants' mastery of each of the milestones shown in Figure 5.9 greatly expands their world: there is more to see when they can sit up, more to explore when they can reach for things themselves, and even more to discover when they can move about on their own. In this section, we consider some of the ways that motor development affects infants' experience of the world.

Reaching

The development of reaching sets off a minirevolution in the infant's life: "once infants can reach for and grasp objects, they no longer have to wait for the world to come to them" (Bertenthal & Clifton, 1998). However, reaching takes time to develop. That is because, as discussed in Chapter 4, this seemingly simple behavior actually involves a complex interaction of multiple, independent components, including muscle development, postural control, development of various perceptual and motor skills, and so on.

Initially, infants are limited to **pre-reaching movements**—clumsy swiping toward the general vicinity of objects they see. At about 3 to 4 months of age, they begin successfully reaching for objects, although their movements are initially somewhat jerky and poorly controlled, and their grabs fail more often than not.

Earlier, we noted that infants' achievements in motor development pave the way for new experiences and opportunities to learn. A particularly compelling example comes from studies (described in Chapter 4) in which pre-reaching infants were given Velcro-patched mittens and Velcro-patched toys that allowed them to pick up objects (Needham, Barrett, & Peterman, 2002). The manual exploration of objects made possible by these "sticky mittens" led to the infants' increased interest in objects and the earlier emergence of their ability to reach independently for them. Months later, these infants showed more sophisticated patterns of object exploration than infants who had not experienced the sticky mittens intervention (Libertus, Joh, & Needham, 2015; Wiesen, Watkins, & Needham, 2016).

stepping reflex ■ a neonatal reflex in which an infant lifts first one leg and then the other in a coordinated pattern like walking

pre-reaching movements ■ clumsy swiping movements by young infants toward the general vicinity of objects they see

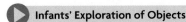 Infants' Exploration of Objects

COURTESY OF RACHEL KEEN

FIGURE 5.12 This right-handed 14-month-old—a participant in research by Rachel Keen and colleagues—is having a hard time getting the applesauce he has been offered into his mouth. As the photo on the left shows, he has been presented the spoon with its handle to his left, but he has grabbed it with his dominant right hand, which makes it extremely difficult to keep the spoon upright on its way to his mouth. A spill ensued.

At about 7 months, as infants gain the ability to sit independently, their reaching becomes quite stable, and the trajectory of their reaches is consistently smooth and straight to the target. The achievement of stable sitting and reaching enables infants to enlarge their sphere of action, because they can now lean forward to capture objects previously out of reach. These increased opportunities for object exploration have ramifications for visual perception. For example, consider the difficulty of perceiving 3-D objects as whole objects. By their very nature, the front portions of 3-D objects block perception of their back portions. Nevertheless, even without X-ray vision, adults readily fill in the nonvisible portions of 3-D objects and perceive them as solid volumes. It turns out that having more experience manipulating objects helps infants to become better at this process of 3-D object completion. Infants with better sitting and manual skills are better at perceiving complete 3-D objects from a limited view than are infants with weaker sitting and manual skills (Soska, Adolph, & Johnson, 2010).

These sources of evidence suggest a great deal of interaction between visual development and motor development. At the same time, infants can perform quite well on some motor tasks in the absence of vision by using auditory or vestibular cues instead. For example, vision is not necessary for accurate reaching: infants in a completely dark room can successfully nab an invisible object that is making a sound (Clifton et al., 1991). In addition, when reaching for objects they can see, infants rarely reach for ones that are too distant, suggesting that they have some sense of how long their arms are (Bertenthal & Clifton, 1998).

With age and practice, infants' reaching shows increasingly clear signs of anticipation; for example, when reaching toward a large object, infants open their fingers widely and adjust their hand to the orientation of the desired object (Lockman, Ashmead, & Bushnell, 1984; Newell et al., 1989). Furthermore, like an outfielder catching a fly ball, infants can make contact with a moving object by anticipating its trajectory and aiming their reach slightly ahead of it (Robin, Berthier, & Clifton, 1996; von Hofsten et al., 1998). Most impressive, 10-month-olds' approach to an object is affected by what they intend to do after they get their hands on it. Like adults, they reach faster for an object that they plan to throw than for one they plan to use in a more precise fashion (Claxton, Keen, & McCarty, 2003). However, as Figure 5.12 illustrates, infants' anticipation skills remain quite limited for some time.

Reaching behavior interacts in interesting ways with other aspects of infants' growing understanding of the world around them. One source of evidence is that by 8 months of age, infants are more likely to reach toward a distant object when an adult is present than when they are alone (Ramenzoni & Liszkowski, 2016). These data suggest that infants' reaching behavior has a social component; infants perceive adults as able to help them accomplish goals when they can't manage on their own. In this study, it did not matter whether the adult was a parent or an unfamiliar experimenter. In either case, infants were more likely to work to get an out-of-reach object when someone was there to help them.

Self-Locomotion

At about 8 months of age, infants become capable for the first time in their lives of **self-locomotion,** that is, of moving around in the environment on their own. No longer limited to being only where someone else carries or puts them, their world must seem vastly larger to them.

Infants' first success at moving forward under their own power typically takes the form of crawling. Many (perhaps most) infants begin by belly crawling or using other idiosyncratic patterns of self-propulsion, one of which researchers refer to as the "inchworm belly-flop" style (Adolph, Vereijken, & Denny, 1998). Most belly crawlers then shift to hands-and-knees crawling, which is less effortful and faster. Other styles of crawling also have colorful names: bear crawls, crab crawls, spider crawls, commando crawls, and bum shuffles (Adolph & Robinson, 2013). The broader point is that infants are remarkably good at finding ways to get around prior to their being able to walk.

When infants first begin walking independently, at about 11 to 12 months, they keep their feet relatively wide apart, which increases their base of support; they flex slightly at the hip and knee, thereby lowering their center of gravity; they keep their hands in the air to facilitate balance; and they have both feet on the ground 60% of the time (as opposed to only 20% for adults) (Bertenthal & Clifton, 1998). As they grow stronger and gain experience, their steps become longer, straighter, and more consistent. Just as with other motor activities, like learning to play a sport or a musical instrument, practice is vital to infants' gradual mastery over their initially weak muscles and precarious balance. And practice they do: Adolph and colleagues (2012) found that their sample of 12- to 19-month-olds in New York City averaged 2368 steps (and 17 falls) per hour! This practice pays off: infants' proficiency at motor tasks is predicted by the number of days since they first began to engage in that behavior (Adolph & Robinson, 2015).

self-locomotion ■ the ability to move oneself around in the environment

© THE METROPOLITAN MUSEUM OF ART. IMAGE SOURCE: ART RESOURCE, NY

Van Gogh's painting *First Steps* may have been inspired by the joy that most parents feel at seeing their baby walk alone for the first time and the joy the baby feels taking those first steps.

The everyday life of the newly mobile crawler or walker is replete with challenges to locomotion—slippery floors, spongy carpets, paths cluttered with objects and obstacles, stairs, sloping lawns, and so on. Infants must constantly evaluate whether their developing skills are adequate to enable them to travel from one point to another. Eleanor Gibson and her colleagues found that infants adjust their mode of locomotion according to their perception of the properties of the

BOX 5.4 | a closer look

"GANGWAY—I'M COMING DOWN"

The interdependence of different developmental domains is beautifully illustrated by a rich and fascinating series of experiments conducted over five decades. This work started with a landmark study by Eleanor Gibson and Richard Walk (1960) that addressed the question of whether infants can perceive depth. It has culminated in research linking depth perception, locomotion, cognitive abilities, emotion, and the social context of development.

To answer the depth-perception question, Gibson and Walk used an apparatus known as the "visual cliff." As the photo shows, the visual cliff consists of a thick sheet of plexiglass that can support the weight of an infant or toddler. A platform across the middle divides the apparatus into two sides. A checked pattern right under the glass on one side makes it look like a solid, safe surface. On the other side, the same pattern is far beneath the glass, and the contrast in the apparent size of the checks makes it look as though there is a dangerous drop-off—a "cliff"—between the two sides.

Gibson and Walk reported that 6- to 14-month-old infants would readily cross the shallow side of the visual cliff. They would not, however, cross the deep side, even when a parent was beckoning to them to come across it. The infants were apparently unwilling to venture over what looked like a precipice—strong evidence that they perceived and understood the significance of the depth cue of relative size.

Karen Adolph, who had been a student of Gibson, has conducted extensive research on the relation between perception and action in infancy. Adolph and her colleagues have discovered surprising discontinuities in infants' learning what

they can and cannot accomplish with their developing locomotor and postural skills (Adolph, 1997, 2000; Adolph, Eppler, & Gibson, 1993; Adolph, Vereijken, & Shrout, 2003; Eppler, Adolph, & Weiner, 1996). This research exemplifies our theme of *mechanisms of change,* in which variation and selection produce developmental change.

As a way of studying the relation between early motor abilities and judgment, the investigators asked parents to try to entice their infants to lean over or crawl across gaps of varying widths in an elevated surface or to crawl or walk down sloping walkways that varied in how steep they were.

Some of these tasks were possible for a given infant; the baby would have no trouble, for example, negotiating a slope of a particular steepness. Others, however, were impossible for that infant. Would the babies identify which tasks were which? (An experimenter always hovered nearby to catch any infant who misjudged his or her prowess.)

The accompanying photos show how infants behaved on slopes when beckoned by an adult (usually their mother). In their first weeks of crawling, infants (averaging about 8½ months in age) unhesitatingly and competently went down shallow slopes. Confronted with slopes that were too steep to crawl down, the babies typically

COURTESY OF PROFESSOR JOSEPH J. CAMPOS, UNIVERSITY OF CALIFORNIA, BERKELEY

This infant is refusing to cross the deep side of the visual cliff, even though his mother is calling and beckoning to him from the other side.

surface they want to traverse (Gibson et al., 1987; Gibson & Schmuckler, 1989). For example, an infant who had promptly walked across a rigid plywood walkway would prudently revert to crawling in order to get across a waterbed. Box 5.4 summarizes a program of research on the development of locomotion and other forms of motor behavior in infancy, focusing specifically on the integration of perception and locomotion.

Integrating perceptual information with new motor skills Researcher Karen Adolph will need to rescue the newly crawling young infant on the left, who does not realize that this slope is too steep for her current level of crawling expertise. In contrast, the experienced walker on the right is judiciously deciding that the slope is too steep for him to walk down.

paused for a moment, but then launched themselves headfirst anyway (requiring the experimenter to catch hold of them). With more weeks of crawling practice, the babies got better at judging when a slope was simply too steep and should be avoided. They also improved at devising strategies to get down somewhat steep slopes, such as turning around and cautiously inching backward down the slope.

However, when the infants started walking, they again misjudged which slopes they could get down using their new mode of locomotion and tried to walk down slopes that were too steep for them. In other words, they failed to transfer what they had learned about crawling down slopes to walking down them. Thus, infants apparently have to learn through experience how to integrate perceptual information with each new motor behavior they develop. With experience comes increased flexibility, allowing access to multiple strategies

for solving previously intractable problems, including laboratory-created challenges such as descending impossibly steep slopes or crossing narrow bridges with wobbly handrails (Adolph & Robinson, 2013).

Infants' decisions in such situations also depend on social information. Infants who are close to being able to make it down a relatively steep walkway can be rather easily discouraged from trying to do so by their mother telling them, "No! Stop!" Conversely, enthusiastic encouragement from a parent can lead an inexperienced crawler or walker to attempt a currently too-steep slope. Thus, the child uses both perceptual and social information in deciding what to do. In this case, the information is obtained through *social referencing,* the child's use of another person's emotional response to an uncertain situation to decide how to behave (see Chapter 10).

A key finding of Adolph's research is that infants have to learn from experience what

they can and cannot do with respect to each new motor skill they master. Just like the new crawlers and walkers who literally plunge ahead when put atop a sloping walkway, an infant who has just developed the ability to sit will lean too far out over a gap in a platform in an attempt to snag an out-of-reach toy and would fall over the edge if not for the ever-present researcher–catcher. And, like the experienced crawlers and walkers who pause to make a prudent judgment about whether or not to try a descent, an infant who has been capable of sitting unsupported for some time can judge whether the gap is too wide to lean across and will stay put if it appears to be so. These highly consistent findings across a variety of motor skills have made a very important contribution to our understanding of how infants learn to interact successfully with their environment.

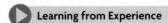 **Learning from Experience**

FIGURE 5.13 Scale errors These three children are making scale errors, treating a miniature object as if it were a much larger one. The girl on the left has just fallen off the toy slide she was trying to go down; the boy in the middle is persistently trying to get into a very small car; and the boy on the right is attempting to sit in a miniature chair. (From DeLoache et al., 2004)

 Scale Errors

The challenge that young children experience in integrating perceptual information in the planning and execution of actions sometimes results in quite surprising behaviors, especially when children fail to meet the challenge. A particularly dramatic example of failure in the integration of perception and action is provided by **scale errors** (Brownell, Zerwas, & Ramani, 2007; DeLoache, Uttal, & Rosengren, 2004; Ware et al., 2006). In this kind of error, very young children try to do something with a miniature replica object that is far too small for the action to be at all possible. For instance, toddlers will attempt, in all seriousness, to sit in a tiny, dollhouse-sized chair or to get into a small toy car (see Figure 5.13). In committing a scale error, the child momentarily, and sometimes repeatedly, fails to take into account the relation between his or her own body and the size of the target object. These errors are hypothesized to result from a failure to integrate visual information represented in two different areas of the brain in the service of action.

Review

Typically developing infants display a similar sequence of milestones in the development of motor behavior, starting with a common set of neonatal reflexes. Although the timing of these milestones varies widely across infants and is affected by cultural differences, their order rarely varies. Researchers emphasize the pervasive interconnectedness between infants' motor behavior, perception, and motivation, as well as the many ways that infants' experience of the world changes as motor skills improve. In the development of self-locomotion (crawling, walking), infants adopt a variety of different movement patterns and strategies to get around and to cope with different environmental challenges. With experience, infants begin to develop the crucial ability to make accurate judgments about what actions they are and are not capable of performing.

Learning

Who do you think learned more today—you or a 10-month-old infant? We'd bet on the baby, just because there is so much that is new to an infant. Think back to baby Benjamin in the kitchen with his parents. A wealth of learning opportunities are embedded in that everyday scene. Benjamin was, for example, gaining experience with some of the differences between animate and inanimate entities, with the particular sights and sounds that occur together in events, with the consequences of objects' losing support (including the effect of this event on his parents' emotional state), and so on. He also experienced consequences of his own behavior, such as his parents' response to his crying.

scale error ■ the attempt by a young child to perform an action on a miniature object that is impossible due to the large discrepancy in the relative sizes of the child and the object

In this section, we review eight different types of learning by which infants profit from their experience and acquire knowledge of the world. Some of the questions that developmental psychologists have addressed with respect to infants' learning include at what age the different forms of learning appear and in what ways learning in infancy is related to later cognitive abilities. Another important question concerns the extent to which infants find some things easier or more difficult to learn. The learning abilities described below are implicated in developmental achievements across every domain of human functioning, from vision to language to emotion to social skills. It is thus impossible to think about development without considering the nature of the learning mechanisms that support developmental change.

Habituation

The simplest form of learning is recognizing something that has been experienced before. As discussed in Chapter 2 and again earlier in this chapter, babies—like everybody else—tend to respond relatively less to stimuli they have previously experienced and relatively more to novel stimuli (see Figure 5.14). The occurrence of habituation in response to repeated stimulation reveals that learning has taken place; the infant has formed a memory representation of the repeated, and now familiar, stimulus. Habituation is highly adaptive: diminished attention to what is familiar enables infants to pay attention to, and learn about, what is new.

The speed with which an infant habituates is believed to reflect the general efficiency of the infant's processing of information. Related measures of attention, including duration of looking and degree of novelty preference, also indicate speed and efficiency of processing. Though the specific factors that predict these individual differences in time to habituation in infancy are not known at this time, these differences appear to be related to aspects of general cognitive ability. For example, infants who are being raised in bilingual households tend to show more efficient (faster) habituation than infants being raised in monolingual households (Singh et al., 2015). This finding is consistent with an array of results, discussed in Box 6.1, suggesting general cognitive benefits of bilingualism. More generally, a substantial and surprising degree of continuity has been found between measures of habituation in infancy and general cognitive ability later in life. Infants who habituate relatively rapidly, who take relatively short looks at visual stimuli,

FIGURE 5.14 Habituation This 3-month-old provides a vivid demonstration of habituation. She is seated in front of a screen on which photographs are displayed. At the first appearance of a photo of a face, her eyes widen and she stares intently at it. With three more presentations of the same picture, her interest wanes and a yawn appears. By its fifth appearance, other things are attracting the baby's attention, and by the sixth even her dress is more interesting. When a new face finally appears, her interest in something novel is evident.
(From Maurer & Maurer, 1988)

CHARLES E. MAURER

The objects surrounding this baby offer a variety of affordances. Some can be picked up, but others are too big for the infant's small hands or too heavy for his limited strength. The stuffed toys can be enjoyably cuddled, but not the plastic cups, which make noise when banged together. Through interacting with the world around them, infants discover these and many other types of affordances.

▶ Cognitive Development in Infancy: Manual Exploration

and/or who show a greater preference for novelty tend to have higher IQs when tested as many as 18 years later (Bornstein, Hahn, & Wolke, 2013; Colombo et al., 2004; Rose & Feldman, 1997).

Perceptual Learning

From their first moments of life, infants actively search for order and regularity in the world around them, and they learn a great deal from simply paying close attention to the objects and events they perceive. According to Eleanor Gibson (1988), the key process in perceptual learning is **differentiation**—extracting the relationships that remain constant from the ever-changing environment. For instance, infants learn the association between tone of voice and facial expression because, in their experience, a pleasant, happy, or eagerly excited tone of voice occurs with a smiling face—not a frowning one—and a harsh, angry tone of voice occurs with a frowning face—not a smiling one. This type of learning is clearly involved in the development of intermodal perception discussed earlier in this chapter.

A particularly important part of perceptual learning is the infant's discovery of **affordances**—that is, the possibilities for action offered, or afforded, by objects and situations (Gibson, 1988). They discover, for example, that small objects—but not large ones—afford the possibility of being picked up, that liquid affords the possibility of being poured and spilled, that chairs of a certain size afford the possibility of being sat on, and so forth. Infants discover affordances by figuring out the relations between their own bodies and abilities and the things around them. As discussed earlier, for instance, infants learn that solid, flat surfaces afford stable walking, whereas squishy, slick, or steeply sloping ones do not.

Perceptual learning also underlies the processes of perceptual narrowing that we have discussed throughout this chapter. Via perceptual learning, infants' attention is honed to focus on dimensions that are relevant to important stimuli in their own environment—native speech sounds, faces, and musical patterns—such that attention is no longer drawn to dimensions that are not relevant in their environment. The perceptual narrowing process is essentially the development of expertise; infants become skilled at processing exactly those stimuli that matter most in their world.

Statistical Learning

A related type of learning also involves simply picking up information from the environment, specifically, detecting statistically predictable patterns (Aslin, Saffran, & Newport, 1998; Kirkham, Slemmer, & Johnson, 2002; Saffran, Aslin, & Newport, 1996). Our natural environment contains a high degree of regularity and redundancy; certain events occur in a predictable order, certain objects appear at the same time and place, and so on. A common example for a baby is the regularity with which the sound of Mom's voice is followed by the appearance of her face.

From quite early on, infants are highly sensitive to the regularity with which one event follows another. In one study, 2- to 8-month-olds were habituated to six simple visual shapes that were presented one after another with specified levels of probability (Kirkham et al., 2002). For example, three pairs of colored shapes always occurred together in the same order (e.g., a square was always followed by a cross),

differentiation ■ extracting from the constantly changing stimulation and events in the environment the relation of those elements that are constant—invariant, or stable

affordances ■ the possibilities for action offered, or afforded, by objects and situations

but the next stimulus could be any of three different shapes (e.g., a cross was followed by a circle, triangle, or square equally often). Thus, the probability that the cross would follow the square was 100%, but the probability that the circle (or triangle or square) would follow the cross was 33%. In a test, the order of appearance of one or more of the shapes was changed. The infants looked longer when the structure inherent in the initial set was violated (e.g., square followed by circle).

Statistical learning abilities have been measured across numerous domains, including music, action, and speech (Roseberry et al., 2011; Saffran & Griepentrog, 2001; Saffran et al., 1996). Even newborn infants track statistical regularities in these domains, suggesting that statistical learning mechanisms are available at birth if not before (Bulf, Johnson, & Valenza, 2011; Kudo et al., 2011; Teinonen et al., 2009). Finally, statistical learning has been proposed to be of vital importance in language learning, as we will discuss in Chapter 6.

Several recent studies suggest that infants prefer to attend to certain types of statistical patterns over others. In particular, they appear to prefer patterns that have some variability over patterns that are very simple (perfectly predictable) or very complex (random) (Gerken, Balcomb, & Minton, 2011; Kidd, Piantadosi, & Aslin, 2012; Kidd, Piantadosi, & Aslin, 2014). This "Goldilocks effect"—avoiding patterns that are either too easy or too hard, while continuing to focus on those that are just right, given the infant's learning abilities—suggests that infants allocate attention differently to different learning problems, preferentially attending to the patterns that are most informative.

Classical Conditioning

Another type of learning, **classical conditioning,** was first discovered by Ivan Pavlov in his famous research with dogs (who learned an association between the sound of a bell and the arrival of food and gradually came to salivate at the sound of the bell alone). Classical conditioning plays a role in infants' everyday learning about the relations between environmental events that have relevance for them. Consider young babies' mealtimes, which occur frequently and have a predictable structure. A breast or bottle contacts the infant's mouth, eliciting the sucking reflex. The sucking causes milk to flow into the infant's mouth, and the infant experiences the pleasurable sensations of a delicious taste and the satisfaction of nourishment, alleviating hunger. Learning is revealed when an infant's sucking motions begin to occur at the mere sight of the bottle or breast.

In terms of classical conditioning, the nipple in the infant's mouth is an **unconditioned stimulus (UCS)** that reliably elicits a reflexive, unlearned response—in this case, the sucking reflex—called the **unconditioned response (UCR).** Learning, or conditioning, occurs when an initially neutral stimulus—the breast or bottle, which is the **conditioned stimulus (CS)**—repeatedly occurs just before the unconditioned stimulus (the baby sees the breast or bottle before receiving the nipple). Gradually, the originally reflexive response becomes a learned behavior, or **conditioned response (CR),** triggered by exposure to the CS (anticipatory sucking movements now begin as soon as the baby sees the breast or bottle). In other words, the sight of the bottle or breast has become a signal of what will follow. Gradually, the infant may also come to associate caregivers with the entire sequence, including the pleasurable feelings that result from feeding. If so, these feelings could eventually be evoked simply by the presence of a caregiver. It is thought that many emotional responses are initially learned through classical conditioning.

classical conditioning ■ a form of learning that consists of associating an initially neutral stimulus with a stimulus that always evokes a particular reflexive response

unconditioned stimulus (UCS) ■ in classical conditioning, a stimulus that evokes a reflexive response

unconditioned response (UCR) ■ in classical conditioning, a reflexive response that is elicited by the unconditioned stimulus

conditioned stimulus (CS) ■ in classical conditioning, the neutral stimulus that is repeatedly paired with the unconditioned stimulus

conditioned response (CR) ■ in classical conditioning, the originally reflexive response that comes to be elicited by the conditioned stimulus

instrumental (or operant) conditioning ■ learning the relation between one's own behavior and the consequences that result from it

positive reinforcement ■ a reward that reliably follows a behavior and increases the likelihood that the behavior will be repeated

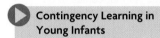
Contingency Learning in Young Infants

FIGURE 5.15 Contingency This young infant learned within minutes that kicking her leg would cause the mobile to move in an interesting way; she learned the contingency between her own behavior and an external event.

CAROLYN ROVEE-COLLIER

Like statistical learning, classical conditioning is displayed by newborn infants. One classical-conditioning task used with newborns is the eye-blink conditioning, in which a tone (CS) is paired with a puff of air (UCS) to the eye, eliciting an eye-blink (UCR). After exposure to the paired tone and air puff, infants will begin to blink in response to the tone alone (CR). Even sleeping newborns learn this response, supporting the view that classical conditioning is a potent form of learning early in postnatal life (Fifer et al., 2010).

Instrumental Conditioning

A key form of learning for infants (and everyone else) is learning the consequences of one's own behavior. In everyday life, infants learn that shaking a rattle produces an interesting sound, that cooing at Dad gets him to coo back, and that exploring the dirt in a potted plant leads to a parental reprimand. This kind of learning, referred to as **instrumental conditioning** (or *operant conditioning*), involves learning the relationship between one's own behavior and the consequences it results in. Most research on instrumental conditioning in infants involves **positive reinforcement,** that is, a reward that reliably follows a behavior and increases the likelihood that the behavior will be repeated. Such research features a *contingency* relation between the infant's behavior and the reward: if the infant performs the target behavior, *then* he or she receives the reinforcement.

Carolyn Rovee-Collier (1997) developed a particularly clever instrumental-conditioning procedure for studying learning and memory in young infants. In this method, experimenters tie a ribbon around a baby's ankle and connect it to a mobile hanging above the infant's crib (Figure 5.15). In the course of naturally kicking their legs, infants as young as 2 months of age quickly learn the relation between their leg movements and the enjoyable sight of the jiggling mobile. They then quite deliberately and often joyfully increase their rate of foot kicking. The interesting mobile movement thus serves as reinforcement for the kicking. This task has been used extensively to investigate age-related changes in how long, and under what circumstances, infants continue to remember that kicking will activate the mobile (e.g., Rovee-Collier, 1999). Among the findings: (1) 3-month-olds remember the kicking response for about 1 week, whereas 6-month-olds remember it for 2 weeks; (2) infants younger than about 6 months of age remember the kicking response only when the test mobile is identical to the training mobile, whereas older infants remember it with novel mobiles.

Infants' intense motivation to explore and master their environment, which we have emphasized in our *active child* theme, shows up in instrumental-learning situations: infants work hard at learning to predict and control their experience, and they display positive emotions during peaks in performance (Angulo-Barroso et al., 2016). Infants may also learn that there are situations over which they have no control. For example, infants of depressed mothers tend to smile less and show lower levels of positive affect than do infants whose mothers are not depressed. In part, this may be because the smiles of infants of depressed mothers are not consistently rewarded by their preoccupied parent; mothers struggling with postpartum depression are more likely to be negative and/or disengaged from their infant than nondepressed mothers (for review, see Brummelte & Galea,

2016). More generally, through contingency situations, whether in a lab or an everyday setting, infants learn more than just the particular contingency relations to which they are exposed. They also learn about the relation between themselves and their environment and the extent to which they can have an impact on it.

Observational Learning/Imitation

A particularly potent source of infants' learning is their observation of other people's behaviors. Parents, who are often amused and sometimes embarrassed by their toddler's reproduction of their own behavior, are well aware that their offspring learn a great deal through simple observation.

The ability to imitate the behavior of other people appears to be present very early in life, albeit in an extremely limited form. Meltzoff and Moore (1977, 1983) found that after newborns watch an adult model slowly and repeatedly stick out his or her tongue, they often stick out their own tongue. However, subsequent studies have found mixed results for neonatal imitation (for review, see Simpson et al., 2014). Of particular note is a recent large-scale study that failed to replicate Meltzoff and Moore's influential finding, calling the existence of newborn imitation into question (Oostenbroek et al., 2016).

By the second half of the 1st year, infant imitation becomes more robust. Infants not only imitate facial gestures, but they also begin to imitate novel, and sometimes quite strange, actions they have seen performed on objects. In one such study, infants observed an experimenter performing unusual behaviors with objects, such as leaning over from the waist to touch his or her forehead to a box, causing the box to light up. The infants were later presented with the same objects the experimenter had acted on. Infants as young as 6 to 9 months imitated some of the novel actions they witnessed, even after a delay of 24 hours (Barr, Dowden, & Hayne, 1996; Bauer, 2002; Hayne, Barr, & Herbert, 2003; Meltzoff, 1988b). Fourteen-month-olds imitated such actions a full week after first seeing them (Meltzoff, 1988a).

In choosing to imitate a model, infants seem to analyze the reason for the person's behavior. If infants see a model lean over and touch a box with her forehead, they later do the same. If, however, the model remarks that she's cold and tightly clutches a shawl around her body as she leans over and touches a box with her forehead, infants reach out and touch the box with their hand instead of their head (Gergely, Bekkering, & Kiraly, 2002). They apparently reason that the model wanted to touch the box and would have done so in a standard way if her hands had been free. Their imitation is thus based on their analysis of the person's intentions. In general, infants are flexible in learning through imitation: as in the case of touching the box, they can copy either the specific behavior through which a model achieves a goal, or they can employ different behaviors to achieve the same goal the model achieved (Buttelmann et al., 2008).

Further evidence of infants' attention to intention comes from research in which 18-month-olds observed an adult attempting, but failing, to pull apart a small dumbbell toy (Meltzoff, 1995a). The adult pulled on the two ends, but his hand "slipped off," and the dumbbell remained in one piece (Figure 5.16a). When the infants were subsequently given the toy, they pulled the two ends apart, imitating what the adult had *intended* to do, not what he had actually done. This research also established that infants' imitative actions are limited to human acts. A different group of 18-month-olds watched a mechanical device with pincers grasp the two ends of the dumbbell. The pincers either pulled apart the dumbbell or slipped off the ends (Figure 5.16b). Regardless of what the infants had seen

FIGURE 5.16 Imitating intentions
(a) When 18-month-olds see a person apparently try, but fail, to pull the ends off a dumbbell, they imitate pulling the ends off—the action the person intended to do, not what the person actually did. (b) They do not imitate a mechanical device at all. (Information from Meltzoff, 1995a)

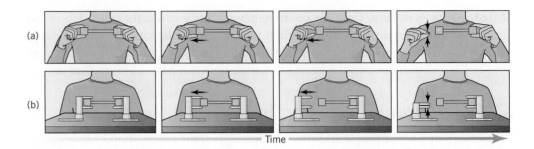

the mechanical device do, they rarely attempted to pull apart the dumbbell themselves. Thus, infants attempt to reproduce the behavior and intentions of other people, but not of inanimate objects.

Imitation is a key component of social learning. Young children use imitation to acquire both *instrumental skills* (object-related knowledge) and *social conventions,* such as rituals and other behaviors specific to a social group (see Legare & Nielsen, 2015). Children in cultures as different as the United States and Vanuatu, a South Pacific chain of islands, show more specific imitation behaviors when learning new social conventions than new instrumental tasks involving objects (Clegg & Legare, 2016). These findings suggest that even young children understand that social conventions should be matched exactly, while actions on objects can be copied more flexibly.

The neural underpinnings of imitative learning have received a great deal of attention. One brain area that is a potential locus for imitation involves the so-called *mirror neuron system,* which was first identified in the ventral premotor cortex in nonhuman primates (e.g., Gallese et al., 1996; Rizzolatti & Craighero, 2004). In research with macaque monkeys, this system becomes activated when the monkey engages in an action; it also is activated when the macaque merely observes another monkey (or a human) engage in an action, as though the macaque itself were engaging in the same action—hence, the name "mirror" neuron system. Mirror neurons were discovered when neuroscientists who were monitoring the brain activity of a monkey noticed that when the monkey happened to see a lab assistant raising an ice cream cone to his mouth, neurons in the monkey's premotor cortex began firing as though the monkey itself were about to eat the ice cream cone. EEG studies in which newborn macaque monkeys observe adult monkeys making facial gestures reveal a pattern of brain activation, known as the *mu rhythm,* that is characteristic of the mirror neuron system (Ferrari et al., 2012).

The degree to which the same system is present in infants, as well as what behavioral domains it might affect, if any at all, is an area of hot debate. Researchers have begun to discover patterns of infant brain activity that are consistent with the hypothesis that mirror neurons are present—namely, patterns of neural firing (the aforementioned mu rhythm) when infants are observing an action that is similar to those they display when they are performing the same action (Marshall & Meltzoff, 2014). These brain patterns have consequences: 7-month-olds whose brains showed greater mu rhythm while observing an experimenter produce a goal-directed action were later more likely to reproduce the action (Filippi et al., 2016). To date, however, it remains unknown how early these brain patterns emerge in development and whether they are present at birth in human infants. Future studies using neuroscientific techniques should be informative about the roots of imitation, identifying what infants are actually encoding as they observe the actions of others, and how that perceptual information is transformed into self-action.

Rational Learning

As adults, we have many beliefs about the world, and we are usually surprised when the world violates our expectations based on those beliefs. We can then adjust our expectations based on the new information we have just received. For example, you can infer from prior meals at your favorite Chinese restaurant that it will be serving Chinese food the next time you go there, and your expectations would be violated if the restaurant turned out to be serving Mexican food on your next visit. You would then, however, update your expectations about the nature of the cuisine at this establishment. Indeed, scientific reasoning is based on precisely this sort of inference from prior data—for instance, using data drawn from a sample of a particular population to make predictions about that population. Infants, too, can use prior experience to generate expectations about what will happen next. This is called **rational learning** because it involves integrating the learner's prior beliefs and biases with what actually occurs in the environment (Xu & Kushnir, 2013).

In an elegant study, Xu & Garcia (2008) demonstrated that 8-month-old infants could make predictions about simple events. Infants were shown a box containing 75 Ping-Pong balls; 70 were red and 5 were white (see Figure 5.17). The infants then observed an experimenter close her eyes (to suggest a random selection) and draw 5 balls from the box—either 4 red and 1 white or 4 white and 1 red—and put them on display. (The experimenter was actually drawing preselected "random samples" from a hidden compartment in the box.) The infants looked longer at the display with the 4 white balls, indicating that they were surprised the experimenter drew mostly white balls from a box that was mostly filled with red balls. (Later in this chapter, we will further discuss the use of so-called *violation-of-expectation* paradigms, which use infants' "surprise" at unexpected outcomes to draw inferences about their expectations.) It is important to note that the infants showed no such surprise when it was clear that the displayed balls did not come from the box (as when the experimenter took them from her pocket) or when they could see that the red balls were stuck to the box and could not be removed (Denison & Xu, 2010; Teglas et al., 2007; Teglas et al., 2011; Xu & Denison, 2009). Infants as young as 6 months of age appear to be sensitive to the distribution of elements (here, colors) as a source of information upon which to base future expectations (Denison, Reed, & Xu, 2013).

Similar findings are emerging across a number of domains, all suggesting that infants generate inferences about the future based on prior data, in tasks ranging from word learning to social interactions, and that infants can use new experiences to adjust these inferences (e.g., Schulz, 2012; Xu & Kushnir, 2013). For example, 16-month-olds confronted with a toy that doesn't work use prior experience to interpret their failure (Gweon & Schulz, 2011). If the infants had previously seen other people fail to operate the toy, they interpreted the toy's malfunction as a property of the toy (and chose a new toy to play with). However, if the

rational learning ■ the ability to use prior experiences to predict what will occur in the future

FIGURE 5.17 The unexpected event After viewing a container dominated by red Ping-Pong balls, 8-month-olds are surprised when they observe the experimenter extract mostly white Ping-Pong balls (the unexpected outcome) (Xu & Garcia, 2008).

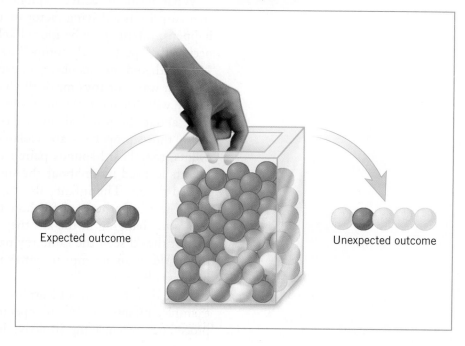

Expected outcome   Unexpected outcome

active learning ■ learning by acting on the world, rather than passively observing objects and events

infants had previously seen other people successfully operate the toy, the infants interpreted the malfunction to be caused by themselves (and passed the toy to their caregivers to operate). In this study, infants behaved rationally. When the problem appeared to be with the toy, infants explored new toys instead. But when the problem appeared to lie in the infants' ability to operate the toy, infants sought help. This study suggests sophisticated reasoning in the context of a simple toy-based interaction.

Active Learning

We often think of learning as a passive process: information-to-be-learned is presented to us by a teacher or some other expert. However, theorists going as far back as Piaget have believed that an important way that infants learn is by acting on the world. As infants develop increasingly sophisticated motor abilities, they can engage with the world in ways that allow them to test hypotheses about how things work. Indeed, *the active child* is one of the themes of this book, and **active learning** is an important aspect of two of the major theories of cognitive development discussed in Chapter 4: Piaget's theory and dynamic-systems theory.

This perspective—that we learn by doing—has been supported by a number of recent experiments with infants. In one such study, 16-month-olds were shown pairs of objects and asked to choose one of them by pointing (Begus Gliga, & Southgate, 2014). The experimenter then showed the infants the function of one of the objects in the pair: either the chosen object or the function of the object that the infant did not choose. The researchers found that infants learned more about the object when they had chosen it themselves during the pointing task. These data support the view that infants learn more when they choose what to learn about. Similarly, toddlers given a computerized learning task learn more about object locations when they are required to actively engage with a touchscreen than when they passively observe the screen (Choi & Kirkorian, 2016). Studies like these suggest that active engagement facilitates learning.

What prompts active exploration of the environment? One hypothesis is that surprise is a driving factor in active learning. When something unexpected happens, infants may be more likely to seek out explanations for what has just occurred. A particularly compelling example comes from a recent study in which 11-month-old infants observed events that violated physical laws: balls passing through walls, or toys magically hanging in the air (Stahl & Feigenson, 2015). As we will discuss in the next section, infants of this age have extensive knowledge about the physical properties of objects, and they tend to watch longer when those properties are violated. As the infants watched these surprising events, they heard sounds paired with the objects. The researchers found that infants learned more about the sound–object pairs when the objects did unexpected things. The infants also explored those objects in specific ways, appearing to test hypotheses about how they worked. For instance, if the infants had seen a toy hanging in the air, they were more likely to explore it by dropping it than if they'd seen the same toy passing through a wall. These infants acted on the world in an attempt to better understand the strange occurrences that they had just observed.

Note that the forms of learning that we have discussed can work together. For example, infants kicking to operate a mobile in an instrumental-conditioning procedure are engaging in active learning, trying to figure out how the mobile works. Rational learning depends on infants' ability to track statistics about their environment, such as the distribution of colors in a box of Ping-Pong balls. Presumably, one reason why infants are such exceptional learners is their ability to integrate multiple types of learning toward the common goal of figuring out how their world works.

Review

Infants begin learning about the world immediately. They habituate to repeatedly encountered stimuli, form expectancies for repeated event sequences, and learn conditioned associations. Infants are highly sensitive to a wide range of contingency relations between their own behavior and what follows it. A particularly powerful form of learning for older infants is observational learning: infants learn many new behaviors simply by watching what other people do. Although an enormous amount of learning goes on during the infancy period, some associations or relations are easier for babies to learn than others. In observational learning, for example, intentionality is a key factor. Finally, infants are able to use their accumulated experience to make rational predictions about the future and engage in active learning in an attempt to discern the underlying structure of their environment.

Cognition

Clearly, infants are capable of learning in a variety of ways. But do they actually *think?* This is a question that has intrigued parents and developmental psychologists alike. Baby Benjamin's parents have no doubt looked with wonderment at their child, asking themselves, "What is he thinking? *Is* he thinking?" Developmental scientists have been working diligently to explore the contents of infants' minds. The resulting explosion of fascinating research has established that infants' cognitive abilities are much more impressive than previously believed, although the nature and origin of these impressive skills is a matter of considerable debate. Theorists of cognitive development vary with respect to the relative roles they attribute to nature and nurture, especially in terms of whether development is guided by innate knowledge structures and special-purpose learning mechanisms or by general learning mechanisms relevant to experiences in all domains.

So once again, the primary debate is between nativists and empiricists. Some nativists argue that infants possess innate knowledge in a few domains of particular importance (e.g., Spelke & Kinzler, 2007). According to this view, infants are born with some knowledge about the physical world, such as the fact that two objects cannot occupy the same space, and that physical objects move only if something sets them in motion. They also propose that infants possess rudimentary understandings in the domains of biology and psychology. As described in Chapter 4, constructivists emphasize *specialized* learning mechanisms that enable infants to acquire this kind of knowledge rapidly and efficiently (e.g., Baillargeon et al., 2012). According to empiricists, infants' mental representations of the physical world are gradually acquired and strengthened through the *general* learning mechanisms that function across multiple domains (e.g., Munakata et al., 1997). The details of this debate are examined in Chapter 7 with respect to conceptual development. In the following sections, we examine findings regarding infants' cognitive abilities and limitations, explanations for which both nativists and empiricists are working to pin down.

violation-of-expectancy ■ a procedure used to study infant cognition in which infants are shown an event that should evoke surprise or interest if it violates something the infant knows or assumes to be true

 Development of Object Permanence in Infancy and Toddlerhood

 Object Permanence: Reaching in the Dark

FIGURE 5.18 Possible versus impossible events In a classic series of tests of object permanence, Renée Baillargeon first habituated young infants to the sight of a screen rotating through 180 degrees. Then a box was placed in the path of the screen. In the possible event, the screen rotated up, occluding the box, and stopped when it reached the top of the box. In the impossible event, the screen rotated up, occluding the box, but then continued on through 180 degrees, appearing to pass through the space where the box was. Infants looked longer at the impossible event, showing that they mentally represented the presence of the invisible box. (Information from Baillargeon, 1987a)

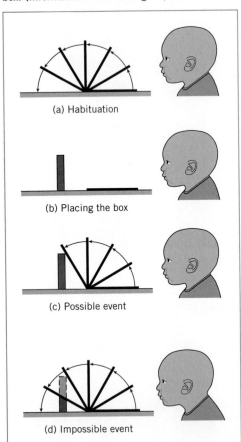

(a) Habituation

(b) Placing the box

(c) Possible event

(d) Impossible event

Object Knowledge

A large part of what we know about infant cognition has come from research on the development of knowledge about objects—research originally inspired by Piaget's theory of sensorimotor intelligence. As you learned in Chapter 4, Piaget believed that young infants' understanding of the world is severely limited by an inability to mentally represent and think about anything that they cannot currently see, hear, touch, and so on. His tests of *object permanence* led him to infer that when an infant fails to search for an object—even a favorite toy—that has disappeared from sight, it is because the object has also disappeared from the infant's mind.

A substantial body of research has provided strong support for Piaget's original observation that young infants do not manually search for hidden objects. However, as noted in Chapter 4, skepticism gradually arose about his explanation of this fascinating phenomenon, and an overwhelming body of evidence has established that young infants are in fact able to mentally represent and think about the existence of objects and events that are currently out of sight.

The simplest evidence for young infants' ability to represent an object that has vanished from sight is the fact that they will reach for objects in the dark, that is, they reach for objects they cannot see. When young infants are shown an attractive object and the room is then plunged into darkness, causing the object (and everything else) to disappear from view, most babies reach to where they last saw the object, indicating that they expect it to still be there (Perris & Clifton, 1988; Stack et al., 1989).

Young infants even seem to be able to think about some characteristics of invisible objects, such as their size (Clifton et al., 1991). When 6-month-olds sitting in the dark heard the sound of a familiar large object, they reached toward it with both hands (just as they had in the light); but they reached with only one hand when the sound they heard was that of a familiar small object.

The majority of the evidence that young infants can represent and think about invisible objects comes from research using the **violation-of-expectancy** procedure. The logic of this procedure is similar to that of the visual-preference method discussed earlier in this chapter. The basic assumption is that if infants observe an event that violates something they know about the world, they will be surprised or at least interested. Thus, an event that is impossible or inconsistent with respect to the infant's knowledge should evoke a greater response (such as longer looking or a change in heart rate) than does a possible or consistent event.

The violation-of-expectancy technique was first used in a classic series of studies designed by Renée Baillargeon and her colleagues (Baillargeon, Spelke, & Wasserman, 1985) to see if infants too young to search for an invisible object might nevertheless have a mental representation of its existence. In some of these studies, infants were first habituated to the sight of a solid screen rotating back and forth through a 180-degree arc (Figure 5.18). Then a box was placed in the screen's path, and the infants saw two test events. In the *possible event*, the screen rotated upward, occluding the box as it did so, and stopped when it contacted the box. In the *impossible event*, the screen continued to rotate a full 180 degrees, appearing to pass through the space occupied by the box (which the experimenter had surreptitiously removed).

Infants as young as 3½ months of age looked longer at the impossible event than at the possible one. The researchers reasoned that the full rotation of the screen (to which the infants had previously been habituated) would be more interesting or surprising than the partial rotation *only* if the infants expected the screen to stop when it reached the box. And the only reason for them to have had that expectation was if they thought the box was still present—that is, if they mentally represented an object they could no longer see. The results also indicate that the infants expected the box to remain in place and did not expect the screen to be able to pass through it.

Other studies have shown that young infants' behavior in this situation is influenced by some of the characteristics of the occluded objects, including height (Baillargeon, 1987a; Baillargeon, 1987b). They expect the screen to stop sooner for a taller object than for a shorter one. This knowledge is refined by learning. For example, exposure to hiding events involving objects of different heights helps infants gain understanding of the relationship between the size of an object and the size of the cover needed to hide it (Wang & Baillargeon, 2008).

Thus, research using two very different assessments—reaching in the dark and visual attention—provides converging evidence that infants who do not yet search for hidden objects nevertheless can represent their continued existence and some of their properties. Note that this is a very different view of infant cognition than that offered by Piaget and discussed in Chapter 4. In Piaget's sensorimotor period, objects did not exist for infants when they were not visible; out of sight is out of mind. Studies by Baillargeon and her colleagues paint a very different picture. While young infants still have much to learn about the properties of objects, they do expect objects to persist when they are out of sight.

Physical Knowledge

Infants' knowledge about the physical world is not limited to what they know and are learning about objects. Other research has examined what they know about physical phenomena, such as gravity. Even in the 1st year of life, infants seem to appreciate that objects do not float in midair, that an inadequately supported object will fall, that a non-round object placed on a stable surface will stay put, and so forth. For example, in a series of studies in which infants observed a ball being released on a slope, 7-month-olds (but not 5-month-olds) looked longer when the ball moved up the slope than when it moved down, indicating that they had expected the ball to go down (Kim & Spelke, 1992). Similarly, they looked longer at an object that traveled more slowly as it rolled down a slope than at one that picked up speed. Infants also seem to understand key physical differences between solids and liquids; 5-month-olds are surprised when a liquid behaves like a solid when it is poured and vice versa (Hespos et al., 2016).

Infants also gradually come to understand under what conditions one object can support another, suggesting an important role for learning. Figure 5.19 summarizes infants' reactions to simple support problems involving boxes and a platform (Baillargeon, Needham, & DeVos, 1992; Needham & Baillargeon, 1993). At 3 months of age, infants are surprised (i.e., they look longer) if a box that is released in midair remains suspended (as in Figure 5.19a), rather than falling. However, as long as there is any contact at

FIGURE 5.19 Infants' developing understanding of support relations Young infants appreciate that an object cannot float in midair, but only gradually do they come to understand under what conditions one object can be supported by another. (Information from Baillargeon, 1998)

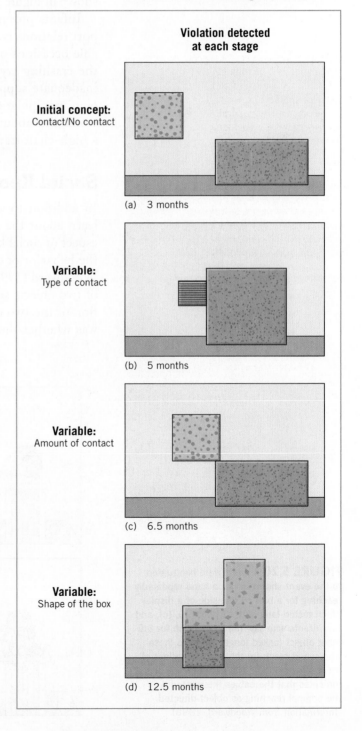

Violation detected at each stage

Initial concept: Contact/No contact

(a) 3 months

Variable: Type of contact

(b) 5 months

Variable: Amount of contact

(c) 6.5 months

Variable: Shape of the box

(d) 12.5 months

all between the box and the platform (as in Figure 5.19b and 5.19c), these young infants do not react when the box remains stationary. By approximately 5 months of age, they appreciate the relevance of the type of contact involved in support. They now know that the box will be stable only if it is released on top of the platform, so they would be surprised by the display in Figure 5.19b. Roughly a month later, they recognize the importance of the amount of contact, and hence they look longer when the box in Figure 5.19c stays put with only a small portion of its bottom surface on the platform. Shortly after their 1st birthday, infants also take into account the shape of the object and hence are surprised if an asymmetrical object like that shown in Figure 5.19d remains stable.

Infants presumably develop this progressively refined understanding of support relations between objects as a result of experience. They observe innumerable occasions of adults placing objects on surfaces, and once in a while, as in the crashing crystal observed by baby Benjamin, they see the consequences of inadequate support. And, of course, they collect additional data through their own manipulation of objects, including lots more evidence than their parents would like about what happens when a milk cup is deposited on the very edge of a high-chair tray.

Social Knowledge

In addition to acquiring knowledge about the physical world, infants need to learn about the social world—about people and their behaviors. An important aspect of social knowledge that emerges relatively early is the understanding that the behavior of others has purpose and is goal-directed. In research by Amanda Woodward (1998), 6-month-old infants saw a hand repeatedly reach toward one of two objects sitting side by side in a display (see Figure 5.20). Then the position of the two objects was reversed, and the hand reached again. The question was whether the infants interpreted the reaching behavior as directed toward a

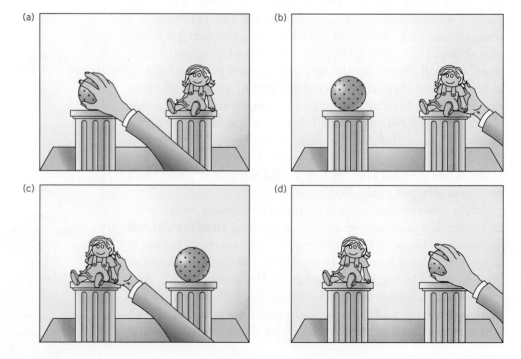

FIGURE 5.20 Infants were habituated to the event shown in (a), a hand repeatedly reaching for a ball on one side of a display. When tested later with displays (b), (c), and (d), infants who saw the hand reach for the other object looked longer than did those who saw it reach for the ball (regardless of the ball's position). The pattern of results indicates that the babies interpreted the original reaching as object-directed. (Information from Woodward, 1998)

particular object. They did, as shown by their looking longer when the hand went to the new object (in the old place) than when it reached for the old object it had reached toward before. Thus, the infants apparently interpreted the reaching behavior as directed toward a particular object; infants even move their eyes to the goal object before the hand gets there (Cannon & Woodward, 2012; Kim & Song, 2015). However, this was true only for a human hand; another group of infants did not react the same way when a mechanical claw did the reaching. (This study may remind you of the one by Meltzoff [1995a] in which older infants imitated the actions of a human but not of a mechanical device.) Older infants even disregard the effort required to select the goal object, expecting the actor to choose their preferred object even when it is more difficult to reach (Scott & Baillargeon, 2013).

Learning is clearly implicated in the development of social knowledge. Infants' understanding of the goal-directed nature of another's actions is related to their own experience achieving a goal. In one study, 3-month-olds, who were not yet able to pick up objects on their own, were fitted with Velcro "sticky mittens" (like those described earlier in this chapter and in Chapter 4) that enabled them to capture Velcro-patched toys (Sommerville, Woodward, & Needham, 2005). Their brief experience successfully "picking up" objects enabled them to interpret the goal-directed reaching of others in the procedure in Figure 5.20 a few months earlier than they would otherwise have been able to do (Skerry, Carey, & Spelke, 2013). Other evidence supporting the role of learning comes from cross-cultural studies manipulating tools used in goal-directed actions. Infants growing up in China are more likely to predict goal-directed actions when an actor uses chopsticks rather than a Western-style spoon (expecting the food to go into the mouth), while infants growing up in Sweden make the opposite prediction, expecting food to be delivered to the mouth by the spoon but not by chopsticks (Green et al., 2016).

How do infants come to understand the intentions of others? One key step is for infants to figure out what kinds of objects can have intentions—that is, what kinds of objects can be agents, behaving like humans. When objects respond contingently, infants are more likely to treat them as agents. In one study, 12-month-olds were introduced to a faceless, eyeless blob that "vocalized" and moved in response to what the experimenter did, simulating a normal human interaction (e.g., Johnson, Shimizu, & Ok, 2007) (see Figure 5.21). Subsequently, when the blob turned toward one of two target objects, the infants treated the blob's behavior as goal-directed. Thus, they seemed to be following the blob's "gaze," just as they would do with a human partner, assuming that the person had turned to look at something. They did not behave this way when the blob's initial behavior was not contingently related to the experimenter's behavior. Indeed, infants are even sensitive to whether the experimenter appears to "play" with the blob, treating it as more like an agent than when the experimenter treats it more neutrally (Beier & Carey, 2014).

FIGURE 5.21 When this amorphous blobby object "responds" contingently to infants, they tend to attribute intention to it. (Information from S. C. Johnson et al., 2008)

PHOTO COURTESY OF SUSAN JOHNSON

Even when observing other humans, infants use cues such as eye gaze and infant-directed speech to determine whether or not to follow the actor's gaze (Senju & Csibra, 2008). If the actor fails to use these cues, infants are less likely to treat them as agents worthy of their attention, or to learn from them (for review, see Csibra & Gergely, 2009).

Infants even interpret quite abstract displays in terms of intention and goal-directed action (Csibra et al., 1999, 2003; Gergely et al., 2002). For instance, 12-month-olds saw a computer animation of a ball repeatedly "jumping" over a barrier toward a ball on the other side. Adults interpret this display as the jumping ball's "wanting" to get to the other ball. So, apparently, did the infants. When the barrier was removed, the infants looked longer when they saw the ball continue to jump, just as it had done before, than when they saw it move straight to the second ball.

Even younger infants seem to attribute intention with respect to simple displays involving small objects. In a study that used a ball, a cube, and a pyramid, all with "googly" eyes attached, 10-month-olds watched as the ball—the "climber"—repeatedly "attempted" to climb up a hill, each time falling back to the bottom (Hamlin, Wynn, & Bloom, 2007; see Figure 5.22). Then the climber was alternately bumped up the hill by the pyramid or pushed back down by the cube. On the subsequent test event, the infants observed the climber alternately approach the "helper" triangle or the "hinderer" cube. The infants looked longer when the climber approached the "hinderer," indicating by their surprise not only their understanding of the "intentions" of all three objects but also their understanding of what the "climber's" response to the "helper" and "hinderer" might be expected to be. Note, however, that several other studies have failed to replicate these effects, suggesting that there may be methodological details that affect infants' preferences in this task (Hamlin, 2015; Salvadori et al., 2015; Scarf et al., 2012).

Infants go beyond attributing intentions to others based on their actions: they exhibit preferences for particular individuals and objects based on the individuals' and objects' actions. Earlier in this chapter, we described research focused on infants' visual preferences (Box 5.1). Infants also exhibit social preferences, as evidenced by their desire to engage with some individuals over others. In one of the first studies to demonstrate early social preferences (Kinzler, Dupoux, & Spelke, 2007), U.S. and French 10-month-olds saw alternating life-sized video projections of two individuals speaking to them, one in English and one in French. They then saw another life-sized video of the same two individuals standing side by side behind a table, both holding an identical plush toy. Silently and simultaneously,

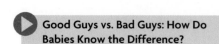
Good Guys vs. Bad Guys: How Do Babies Know the Difference?

FIGURE 5.22 Viewers of the "climber" event described in the text—infants and adults alike—readily interpret it in terms of intentional action. First, they see the ball as "trying" to move up a hill, but then rolling back down, thereby "failing" to achieve its goal of reaching the top. On some trials, after the ball starts to roll back down, a triangle appears below the ball and seems to "push" it upward, "helping" it get to the top. On other trials, a cube appears in front of the ball and "hinders" it by seeming to "push" it down the hill.

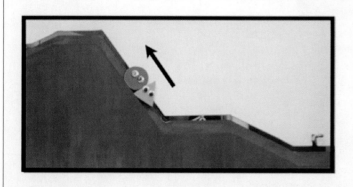

they smiled at the infant, then at the toy, then at the infant again, and then leaned forward, holding the toys out as though giving them to the infant. The moment the toys disappeared from view on the screen, they appeared (through researchers' magic) on a table in front of the infant, creating the impression that they had come directly from the individuals in the video. The infants' responses suggested a social preference for the individual who had spoken their native language: English-learning infants chose the toy offered by the English speaker, whereas French-learning infants chose the toy offered by the French speaker. Crucially, because the toy was offered in silence, these social preferences were attributable to a preference for the individual who shared the infant's language, not for the language itself.

Similar findings emerged in a food-choice paradigm, in which infants were more likely to choose a food offered by a speaker of their language than by a speaker of another language (Shutts et al., 2009). Indeed, even objects similar to those depicted in Figure 5.22 evoke social preferences (Hamlin et al., 2007). In a variation of the "climber" procedure described above, when infants as young as 6 months were presented with the objects they had just observed bumping the "climber" object up the hill or pushing it down the hill, they tended to choose the "helper" object. The social preferences exhibited in studies like these can be quite nuanced. In a study using puppets rather than objects, 5-month-olds uniformly preferred characters who were positive toward "helpers," whereas 8-month-olds preferred characters who were positive toward "helpers" and negative toward "hinderers" (Hamlin et al., 2011).

These and related studies indicate that well before their 1st birthday, infants have already learned a great deal about how humans behave and how their behavior is related to their intentions and goals. Infants and young children can also draw inferences about other people's knowledge states. For example, 15-month-olds can make inferences about what a person will do based on their knowledge of what the person knows (Onishi & Baillargeon, 2005). To succeed in this task, infants need to keep track of what information an adult has about the location of an object. If the object is moved to a new location while an infant—but not the adult—witnesses the move, the infant expects the adult to subsequently search for the object in its *original* location. That is, the infant expects the adult to search where he or she *should believe* the toy to be, rather than in the location where the infant knows it *actually* is. This interpretation is based on the fact that the infants looked longer when the adult searched the object's current location than they did when the adult searched its original location. Thus, this study indicates that 15-month-olds assume that a person's behavior will be based on what the person *believes* to be true, even if the infant knows that the belief is false.

Similar findings with even younger infants have been found using EEG to measure 6-month-olds' sensorimotor cortex activation while watching these types of events (Southgate & Vernetti, 2014). This result suggests that there may be very early precursors of a theory of mind—understanding beliefs and desires (we return to this topic in Chapter 7).

Looking Ahead

The intense activity focused on cognition in infancy has produced a wealth of fascinating findings. This new information has not, however, resolved the basic issues about how cognition develops in infancy. The evidence we have reviewed reveals a remarkable constellation of abilities and deficits. Infants can be both surprisingly smart and surprisingly clueless. They can infer the existence of an unseen object but cannot retrieve it. They appreciate that objects cannot float in midair but think that any kind and amount of contact at all provides sufficient support. The challenge for theorists is to account for both competence and incompetence in infants' thinking.

Review

Building on the insights and observations of Piaget, and using an array of extremely clever methods, modern researchers have made a host of fascinating discoveries about the cognitive processes of infants. They have demonstrated that infants mentally represent not only the continued existence of hidden objects but also characteristics of the objects. Infants' understanding of the physical world grows steadily, as shown by their appreciation of support relations and their increasing ability to solve everyday problems. At the same time, their understanding of the social world also increases, as shown by their interpretation of and preferences concerning the behavior of actors, both human and animated.

CHAPTER SUMMARY

Perception

■ The human visual system is relatively immature at birth; young infants have poor acuity, low contrast sensitivity, and minimal color vision. Modern research has demonstrated, however, that newborns begin visually scanning the world minutes after birth and that very young infants show preferences for strongly contrasted patterns, for the same colors that adults prefer, and, especially, for human faces.

■ Some visual abilities, including perception of constant size and shape, are present at birth; others develop rapidly over the first year. Binocular vision emerges quite suddenly at about 4 months of age, and the ability to identify object boundaries—object segregation—is also present at that age. By 7 months, infants are sensitive to a variety of monocular, or pictorial, depth cues.

■ The auditory system is comparatively well developed at birth, and newborns will turn their heads to localize a sound. Young infants' remarkable proficiency at perceiving pattern in auditory stimulation underlies their sensitivity to musical structure.

■ Infants are sensitive to smell from birth. They learn to identify their mother in part by her unique scent.

■ Through active touching, using both mouth and hands, infants explore and learn about themselves and their environment.

■ Research on intermodal perception has revealed that from very early on, infants integrate information from different senses, linking their visual with their auditory, olfactory, and tactile experiences.

Motor Development

■ Motor development proceeds rapidly in infancy through a series of "motor milestones," starting with the reflexes displayed by newborn babies. The regular pattern of development results from the confluence of many factors, including the development of strength, posture control, balance, and perceptual skills. Some aspects of motor development vary across cultures as a result of different cultural practices.

■ Each new motor achievement, from reaching to self-locomotion, expands the infant's experience of the world but also presents new challenges. Infants adopt a variety of strategies to move around in the world successfully and safely. In the process, they make a variety of surprising mistakes.

Learning

- Various kinds of learning are present in infancy. Infants habituate to repeated stimuli and form expectancies about recurrent regularities in events. Through active exploration, they engage in perceptual learning. They also learn through classical conditioning, which involves forming associations between natural and neutral stimuli as well as through instrumental conditioning, which involves learning about the contingency between one's own behavior and some outcome. They can track statistical patterns in their environment and make use of prior experiences to generate expectations about the future. By acting on the world, infants have the opportunity to make their own choices about what to learn.

- From the second half of the 1st year on, observational learning—watching and imitating the behavior of other people—is an increasingly important source of information. Infants' assessment of the intention of a model affects what they imitate.

Cognition

- Research techniques that enable developmental scientists to assess infants' beliefs—most notably the violation-of-expectancy procedure—have established that infants display impressive cognitive abilities. Much of this work on mental representation and thinking was originally inspired by Piaget's concept of object permanence. But it has been revealed that, contrary to Piaget's belief, young infants can mentally represent invisible objects and even reason about observed events.

- Other research, focused on infants' developing knowledge of the physical world, has demonstrated their understanding of some of the effects of gravity. It takes babies several months to work out the conditions under which one object can provide stable support for another.

- Infants pay particular attention to the intentions of other people and to objects that behave like humans.

Test Yourself

1. A researcher presents an infant with two objects. To determine whether the infant is able to discriminate between the objects and favors one over the other, the researcher measures the amount of time the infant spends looking at each object. Which experimental technique is this researcher using?
   a. contrast sensitivity technique
   b. visual acuity method
   c. preferential-looking technique
   d. active learning method

2. The understanding that two objects are separate, even when they are touching, is referred to as _____ .
   a. object segregation
   b. object permanence
   c. perceptual narrowing
   d. perceptual constancy

3. One-month-old Bella is shown a small cube that is close to her. Next she is shown a larger cube that is farther away from her. Because the two cubes are at different distances from Bella, they appear to be the same size. Bella's actions indicate that she recognizes that the second cube is larger, signifying that she has _____ .
   a. perceptual constancy
   b. intermodal perception
   c. perceptual narrowing
   d. optical expansion

4. Which of the following is a possible explanation for why young infants tend to have more trouble with auditory localization than older infants and children do?
   a. Young infants are not adept at perceiving patterns, particularly sound patterns.
   b. Young infants do not yet understand that sound can come from a variety of sources.

   c. Children's ears do not fully develop until they are close to 1 year old.
   d. Young infants have smaller heads, which makes it more difficult for them to perceive whether a sound is closer to one ear or the other.

5. A 6-month-old and a 9-month-old are shown photographs of two different ostriches, a bird which neither infant has seen before. The 6-month-old more easily distinguishes between the two different birds than does the 9-month-old. The poorer performance of the 9-month-old is a result of what phenomenon?
   a. perceptual narrowing
   b. the McGurk effect
   c. unconditioned response
   d. dishabituation

6. The tendency of an infant to look longer at a smiling face that is paired with a happy voice is an indication of that infant's _____ .
   a. dishabituation
   b. operant conditioning
   c. intermodal perception
   d. optical expansion

7. Five-week-old Johnny is touched on the cheek and promptly turns his head to the side that was touched. Johnny is displaying _____ .
   a. intermodal perception
   b. contrast sensitivity
   c. the rooting reflex
   d. the tonic neck reflex

8. Jane is a 2-month-old infant. She wants to get her hands on the rattle that is lying next to her; however, all she can do is make very clumsy swiping movements in the general vicinity of the toy. Jane's movements are known as _____ .
   a. self-locomotion
   b. rooting reflex
   c. optical expansion
   d. pre-reaching motions

9. Seven-month-old Trevor has learned that small round objects can be rolled across a flat surface. Trevor's discovery is an example of which developmental learning process?
   a. affordances
   b. continuity
   c. differentiation
   d. unconditioned stimulus

10. Five-month-old Kenji is lying in his crib. His mother hides out of view, then pops out above him and yells, "Boo!" Kenji squeals with delight, but after his mother repeats her actions a few times, his excitement dissipates and his attention wanders to the mobile hanging overhead. Kenji's response is an example of _____ .
    a. instrumental conditioning
    b. differentiation
    c. habituation
    d. observational learning

11. The violation-of-expectancy procedure provides evidence of what basic assumption about infants' understanding of their world?
    a. Infants will repeat actions if they receive positive reinforcement from those actions.
    b. Infants' imitative actions are limited to the actions of other humans.
    c. Infants will look longer at an impossible event than at a possible event.
    d. Infants' attention will diminish after repeated exposure to the same stimuli.

12. Understanding that the behavior of others is purposive and goal-directed is an aspect of _____ .
    a. social knowledge
    b. classical conditioning

    c. object permanence
    d. physical knowledge

13. Researchers design an experiment in which 8- to 10-month-old infants are placed in a highchair with a string attached to one of their arms. When they lift their arms, the string tips a small cup that spills cereal onto the table in front of them. A few weeks later, these same infants are placed in a different chair, but outfitted with a similar string and cup mechanism. The fact that these infants will remember that lifting their arms will result in cereal being dispensed is an example of

    _____ .
    a. instrumental conditioning
    b. social referencing
    c. object permanence
    d. intermodal perception

14. How does the element of surprise aid in the process of active learning in infants and children, according to some child psychologists?
    a. Surprise instills fear, which prompts the child to seek out less risky behaviors and situations.
    b. Infants and children are more likely to search for explanations to unexpected events.
    c. Parents can explain unexpected events to their children, thus helping them learn.
    d. Infants are more likely to avoid unexpected events and seek out situations and objects that conform to their understanding.

15. Experiments in which children observe inanimate objects (e.g., a blob on a table or small cubes or balls) perform tasks (e.g., helping or hindering another object) provide evidence for the infants' understanding of which concept?
    a. prosocial behaviors
    b. object permanence
    c. goal-directed behavior
    d. violation-of-expectancy

Don't stop now! Research shows that testing yourself is a powerful learning tool. Visit LaunchPad to access the LearningCurve adaptive quizzing system, which gives you a personalized study plan to help build your mastery of the chapter material through videos, activities, and more. **Go to launchpadworks.com.**

Critical Thinking Questions

1. The major theme throughout this chapter is nature and nurture. Consider the following research findings discussed herein: infants' preference for consonance (versus dissonance) in music, their preference for faces that adults consider attractive, and their ability to represent the existence and even the height of an occluded object. To what extent do you think these preferences and abilities rest on innate factors, and to what extent might they be the result of experience?

2. As you have seen from this chapter, researchers have learned a substantial amount about infants in the recent past. Were you surprised at some of what has been learned? Describe to a friend something from each of the main sections of the chapter that you would never have suspected an infant could do or would know. Similarly, tell your friend a few things that you were surprised to learn infants do not know or that they fail to do.

3. Studying infants' perceptual and cognitive abilities is especially tricky given their limited abilities to respond in a study—they can't respond verbally or even with a reliable reach or point. Consider some of the methods described in this chapter (preferential looking/eye-tracking, conditioning, habituation, violation of expectation, imitation, EEG/ERP, and so on). What kinds of questions are best suited to each method?

4. What is perceptual narrowing? Describe some of the evidence suggesting that perceptual narrowing plays an important role in perceptual development. Of the types of learning discussed in this chapter, which of them might underlie perceptual narrowing and why?

Key Terms

active learning, p. 226

affordances, p. 220

auditory localization, p. 201

binocular disparity, p. 199

classical conditioning, p. 221

conditioned response (CR), p. 221

conditioned stimulus (CS), p. 221

cones, p. 193

contrast sensitivity, p. 193

differentiation, p. 220

instrumental (or operant) conditioning, p. 222

intermodal perception, p. 206

monocular depth (or pictorial) cues, p. 200

object segregation, p. 195

optical expansion, p. 199

perception, p. 191

perceptual constancy, p. 194

perceptual narrowing, p. 204

positive reinforcement, p. 222

preferential-looking technique, p. 192

pre-reaching movements, p. 213

rational learning, p. 225

reflexes, p. 208

scale error, p. 218

self-locomotion, p. 215

sensation, p. 191

stepping reflex, p. 212

stereopsis, p. 199

unconditioned response (UCR), p. 221

unconditioned stimulus (UCS), p. 221

violation-of-expectancy, p. 228

visual acuity, p. 192

▶ Student Video Activities

The Senses in Infancy and Toddlerhood

The McGurk Effect

Newborn Reflexes

West African Exercise Routine

Infants' Exploration of Objects

Learning from Experience

Scale Errors

Cognitive Development in Infancy: Manual Exploration

Contingency Learning in Young Infants

Development of Object Permanence in Infancy and Toddlerhood

Object Permanence: Reaching in the Dark

Good Guys vs. Bad Guys: How Do Babies Know the Difference?

Answers to Test Yourself

1. c, 2. a, 3. a, 4. d, 5. a, 6. c, 7. c, 8. d, 9. a, 10. c, 11. c, 12. a, 13. a, 14. b, 15. c

NICOLA BEALING, *Lucas Talking to a Dog* (oil on board, 2006)

Development of Language and Symbol Use

Themes

- Nature and Nurture
- The Active Child
- The Sociocultural Context
- Individual Differences

symbols ■ systems for representing our thoughts, feelings, and knowledge and for communicating them to other people

These children are intent on mastering one of the many important symbol systems in the modern world.

"Woof." (used at age 11 months to refer to neighbor's dog)

"Hot." (used at age 14 months to refer to stove, matches, candles, light reflecting off shiny surfaces, and so forth)

"Read me." (used at age 21 months to ask mother to read a story)

"Why I don't have a dog?" (27 months of age)

"If you give me some candy, I'll be your best friend. I'll be your two best friends." (48 months of age)

"Granna, we went to Cagoshin [Chicago]." (65 months of age)

"It was, like, ya know, totally awesome, dude." (192 months of age)

These utterances were produced by one boy during the process of his becoming a native English speaker (Clore, 1981). Each one reflects the capacity that most sets humans apart from other species: the creative and flexible use of **symbols,** which include language and many kinds of nonlinguistic symbols (print, numbers, pictures, models, maps, and so forth). We use symbols (1) to represent our thoughts, feelings, and knowledge, and (2) to communicate our thoughts, feelings, and knowledge to other people. Our ability to use symbols vastly expands our cognitive and communicative power. It frees us from the present, enabling us to learn from the generations of people who preceded us and to contemplate the future.

In this chapter, we will focus primarily on the acquisition of the preeminent symbol system: language. We will then discuss children's understanding and creation of nonlinguistic symbols, such as pictures and models. The dominant theme in this chapter will once again be the relative contributions of *nature and nurture.* A related issue concerns the extent to which language acquisition is made possible by abilities that are specialized for language learning versus general-purpose mechanisms that support all sorts of learning.

The *sociocultural context* is another prominent theme and this chapter features research that examines differences in language acquisition across cultures and communities. This comparative work often provides evidence that is crucial to various theories of language development. A third recurring theme is *individual differences.* For any given language milestone, some children will achieve it much earlier, and some much later, than others. The *active child* theme also puts in repeated appearances. Infants and young children pay close attention to language and a wide variety of other symbols, and they work hard at figuring out how to use them to communicate.

Language Development

What is the average kindergartner almost as good at as you are? Not much, with one important exception: using language. By 5 years of age, most children have mastered the basic structure of their native language or languages (the possibility of bilingualism is to be assumed whenever we refer to "native language"), whether spoken or manually signed. Although their vocabulary and powers of expression are less sophisticated than yours, their sentences are as grammatically correct as the ones that you produce. This is a remarkable achievement.

Language use requires **comprehension,** which refers to understanding what others say (or sign or write), and **production,** which refers to actually speaking (or signing or writing). As we have observed for other areas of development, infants' and young children's ability to understand precedes their ability to produce. Children understand words and linguistic structures that other people use months or even years before they include them in their own utterances. This is, of course, not unique to young children; you no doubt understand many words that you never actually use. In our discussion, we will be concerned with the developmental processes involved in both comprehension and production, as well as the relation between them.

The Components of Language

How do languages work? Despite the fact that there are thousands of human languages, they share overarching similarities. All human languages are similarly complex, with different pieces combined at different levels to form a hierarchy: sounds are combined to form words, words are combined to form sentences, and sentences are combined to form stories, conversations, and other kinds of narratives. Children must acquire all of these facets of their native language. The enormous benefit that emerges from this combinatorial process is **generativity;** by using the finite set of words in our vocabulary, we can generate an infinite number of sentences, expressing an infinite number of ideas.

However, the generative power of language carries a cost for young language learners: they must deal with its complexity. To appreciate the challenge presented to children learning their first language, imagine yourself as a stranger in a strange land. Someone walks up to you and says, *"Jusczyk daxly blickets Nthlakapmx."* You would have absolutely no idea what this person had just said. Why?

First, you would probably have difficulty perceiving some of the phonemes that make up what the speaker is uttering. **Phonemes** are the units of sound in speech; a change in phoneme changes the meaning of a word. For example, "rake" and "lake" differ by only one phoneme (/r/ versus /l/), but the two words have quite different meanings to English speakers. Different languages employ different sets of phonemes; English uses just 45 of the roughly 200 sounds found across the world's languages. The phonemes that distinguish meaning in any one language overlap with, but also differ from, those in other languages. For example, the sounds /r/ and /l/ are a single phoneme in Japanese, and do not carry different meanings. Furthermore, combinations of sounds that are common in one language may never occur in others. When you read the stranger's utterance in the preceding paragraph, you probably had no idea how to pronounce the word *Nthlakapmx,* because some of its sound combinations do not occur in English (though they do occur in other languages). Thus, the first step in children's language learning is **phonological development:** the mastery of the sound system of their language.

Another reason you would not know what the stranger had said to you, even if you could have perceived the sounds being uttered, is that you would have had no idea what the sounds mean. The smallest units of meaning are called **morphemes.** Morphemes, alone or in combination, constitute words. The word *dog,* for example, contains one morpheme. The word *dogs* contains two morphemes, one designating a familiar furry entity (*dog*) and the second indicating the plural (*-s*). **Semantic development** involves learning the system for expressing meaning in a language, including words and morphemes.

However, even if you were told the meaning of each individual word the stranger had used, you would still not understand the utterance unless you knew

comprehension ■ with regard to language, understanding what others say (or sign or write)

production ■ with regard to language, speaking (or writing or signing) to others

generativity ■ refers to the idea that through the use of the finite set of words and morphemes in humans' vocabulary, we can put together an infinite number of sentences and express an infinite number of ideas

phonemes ■ the elementary units of meaningful sound used to produce languages

phonological development ■ the acquisition of knowledge about the sound system of a language

morphemes ■ the smallest units of meaning in a language, composed of one or more phonemes

semantic development ■ the learning of the system for expressing meaning in a language, including word learning

ESTA / SUPERSTOCK

By the age of 5, children are capable of generating totally novel sentences that are correct in terms of the phonology, semantics, and syntax of their native language. They are also able to make appropriate pragmatic inferences regarding the content of their partner's utterances.

how words are put together in the stranger's language. To express an idea of any complexity, we combine words into sentences, but only certain combinations are allowed in any given language. **Syntax** refers to the permissible combinations of words from different categories (nouns, verbs, adjectives, etc.). In English, for example, the *order* in which words can appear in a sentence is crucial: "Lila ate the lobster" does not mean the same thing as "The lobster ate Lila." Other languages indicate which noun did the eating and which noun was eaten by adding morphemes, such as suffixes, to the nouns. For example, a Russian noun ending in "a" is likely to refer to the entity doing the eating, while the same noun ending in "u" is likely to refer to the thing that was eaten. **Syntactic development** entails learning how words and morphemes are combined.

Finally, a full understanding of the interaction with the stranger would necessitate having some knowledge of the cultural rules and contextual variations for using language. In some societies, for example, it would be quite bizarre to be addressed by a stranger in the first place, whereas in others it would be commonplace. You would also need to know how to go beyond the speaker's specific words to understand what the speaker was really trying to communicate—to use factors such as the context and the speaker's emotional tone to read between the lines, and to learn how to hold a conversation. Acquiring an understanding of how language is typically used is referred to as **pragmatic development.**

Thus, learning language involves phonological, semantic, syntactic, and pragmatic development. The same factors are involved in learning a sign language, in which the basic linguistic elements are gestures rather than sounds. There are more than 200 languages, including American Sign Language (ASL), that are based on gestures, both manual and facial. They are true languages and are as different from one another as spoken languages are. The course of acquisition of a sign language is remarkably similar to that of a spoken language.

What Is Required for Language?

What does it take to be able to learn a language in the first place? Full-fledged language acquisition is achieved only by humans, so, obviously, one requirement is the human brain. But a single human, isolated from all sources of linguistic experience, could never learn a language; hearing (or seeing) language is a crucial ingredient for successful language development.

syntax ■ rules in a language that specify how words from different categories (nouns, verbs, adjectives, and so on) can be combined

syntactic development ■ the learning of the syntax of a language

pragmatic development ■ the acquisition of knowledge about how language is used

A Human Brain

The key to full-fledged language development lies in the human brain. Language is a *species-specific* behavior: only humans acquire language in the normal course of development. Furthermore, it is *species-universal*: language learning is achieved by typically developing infants across the globe.

In contrast, no other animals naturally develop anything approaching the complexity or generativity of human language, even though they can communicate

with one another. In one of the complex examples of nonhuman animal communication, vervet monkeys reveal the presence and identity of predators through specific calls, telling their listeners whether they should look down to avoid a snake or look up to avoid an eagle (Seyfarth & Cheney, 1993). As sophisticated as this system is compared with other nonhuman communication systems, it is very limited in scope.

Researchers have had limited success in training nonhuman primates to use complex communicative systems. One early effort was an ambitious project in which a dedicated couple raised a chimpanzee (Vicki) with their own children (Hayes & Hayes, 1951). Although Vicki learned to comprehend some words and phrases, she produced virtually no recognizable words. Subsequent researchers attempted to teach nonhuman primates sign language. Washoe, a chimpanzee, and Koko, a gorilla, became famous for their ability to communicate with their human trainers and caretakers using manual signs (Gardner & Gardner, 1969; Patterson & Linden, 1981). Washoe could label a variety of objects and could make requests ("more fruit," "please tickle"). But the general consensus is that, however impressive Washoe's and Koko's "utterances" were, they do not qualify as language because they contained little evidence of syntactic structure (Terrace et al., 1979; Wallman, 1992).

The most successful sign-learning nonhuman is Kanzi, a great ape of the bonobo species. Kanzi's sign-learning began when he observed researchers trying to teach his mother to communicate with them by using a lexigram board, a panel composed of a few graphic symbols representing specific objects and actions ("give," "eat," "banana," "hug," and so forth) (Savage-Rumbaugh et al., 1993). Kanzi's mother never caught on, but Kanzi did, and over the years his lexigram vocabulary increased from 6 words to more than 350. He is now very adept at using his lexigram board to answer questions, to make requests, and even to offer comments. He often combines symbols, but whether they can be considered syntactically structured sentences is not clear.

There are also several well-documented cases of nonprimate animals that have learned to respond to spoken language. Kaminski, Call, and Fischer (2004) found that Rico, a border collie, knew more than 200 words and could learn and remember new words using some of the same kinds of processes that toddlers use (though with important limitations; see also Tempelmann, Kaminski, & Tomasello, 2014; van der Zee, Zulch, & Mills; 2012). Alex, an African-gray parrot, learned to produce and understand basic English utterances, although his skills remained at a toddler level (Pepperberg, 1999).

Whatever the ultimate decision regarding the extent to which trained nonhuman animals should be credited with language, several things are clear. Even their most basic linguistic achievements come only after a great deal of concentrated human effort, whereas human children master the rudiments of their language with little explicit teaching. Furthermore, while the most advanced nonhuman communicators do combine symbols, their utterances show limited evidence of syntactic structure, which is a defining feature of language (Tomasello, 1994). In short, only the human brain acquires a communicative system with the complexity, structure, and generativity of language. Correspondingly, we humans

Kanzi, a bonobo ape, and his caretakers communicate with one another by using a specially designed set of symbols that stand for a wide variety of objects, people, and actions.

This photo shows Rico demonstrating his language comprehension by fetching specific toys on request.

are notoriously poor at learning the communicative systems of other species (Harry Potter's ability to speak Parseltongue with snakes aside). As we will see next, the brains of animals of different species are excellently suited to their respective communicative systems.

Brain–language relations A vast amount of research has examined the relationship between language and brain function. It is clear that language processing involves a substantial degree of functional localization. At the broadest level, there are hemispheric differences in language functioning that we discussed to some extent in Chapter 3. For the 90% of people who are right-handed, language is primarily represented and controlled by the left hemisphere.

Left-hemisphere specialization appears to emerge very early in life. Studies using neuroimaging techniques have demonstrated that newborns and 3-month-olds show greater activity in the left hemisphere when exposed to normal speech than when exposed to reversed speech or silence (Bortfeld, Fava, & Boas, 2009; Dehaene-Lambertz, Dehaene, & Hertz-Pannier, 2002; Pena et al., 2003). An exception to this pattern of lateralization occurs in the detection of pitch in speech, which in infants, as in adults, tends to involve the right hemisphere (Homae et al., 2006).

Although it is evident that the left hemisphere predominantly processes speech from birth, the reasons for this are not yet known. One possibility is that the left hemisphere is innately predisposed to process language but not other auditory stimuli. Another possibility is that speech is localized to the left hemisphere because of its acoustic properties. In this view, the auditory cortex in the left hemisphere is tuned to detect small differences in timing, whereas the auditory cortex in the right hemisphere is tuned to detect small differences in pitch (e.g., Zatorre et al., 1992; Zatorre & Belin, 2001; Zatorre, Belin, & Penhune, 2002). Because speech turns on small differences in timing (as you will see when we discuss voice onset time, page 249), it may be a more natural fit for the left hemisphere.

Critical period for language development If you were to survey your classmates who have studied another language, we predict you would discover that those who learned a foreign language in adolescence found the task to be much more challenging than did those who learned the foreign language in early childhood. A considerable body of evidence suggests that, in fact, the early years constitute a **critical period for language** during which languages are learned relatively easily (though, as discussed in Box 6.5, children with developmental language disorders may struggle with aspects of language development). After this period (which ends sometime between age 5 and puberty), language acquisition is much more difficult and ultimately less successful.

Relevant to this hypothesis, there are several reports of children who barely developed language at all after being deprived of early linguistic experience. The most famous case in modern times is Genie, who was discovered in appalling conditions in Los Angeles in 1970. From the age of approximately 18 months until she was rescued at age 13 years, Genie's parents kept her tied up and locked alone in a room. During her imprisonment, no one spoke to her; when her father brought her food, he growled at her like an animal. At the time of her rescue, Genie's development was stunted—physically, motorically, and emotionally—and she could barely speak. With intensive training, she made some progress, but her language ability never developed much beyond the level of a toddler's: "Father take piece wood. Hit. Cry" (Curtiss, 1977, 1989; Rymer, 1993).

critical period for language ■ the time during which language develops readily and after which (sometime between age 5 and puberty) language acquisition is much more difficult and ultimately less successful

Does this extraordinary case support the critical-period hypothesis? Possibly, but it is difficult to know for sure. Genie's failure to develop full, rich, language after her discovery might have resulted as much from the bizarre and inhumane treatment she suffered as from linguistic deprivation.

Other areas of research provide much stronger evidence for the critical-period hypothesis. As noted in Chapter 3, adults, who are well beyond the critical period, are more likely to suffer permanent language impairment from brain damage than are children, presumably because other areas of the young brain (but not the older brain) are able to take over language functions. Moreover, adults who learned a second language after puberty use different neural mechanisms to process that language than do adults who learned their second language from infancy (e.g., Kim et al., 1997; Pakulak & Neville, 2011). These results strongly suggest that the neural circuitry supporting language learning operates differently (and better) during the early years.

In an important behavioral study, Johnson and Newport (1989) tested the English proficiency of Chinese and Korean immigrants to the United States who had begun learning English either as children or as adults. The results, shown in Figure 6.1, reveal that knowledge of key aspects of English grammar was related to the age at which these individuals began learning English, but not to the length of their exposure to the language. The most proficient were those who had begun learning English before the age of 7.

A similar pattern has been described for first-language acquisition in the Deaf community: individuals who acquired ASL as a first language when they were children become more proficient signers than do individuals who acquired ASL as a first language as teens or adults (Newport, 1990). Johnson and Newport also observed a great deal of variability among "late learners"—those who were acquiring a second language, or a sign language as their first formal language, at puberty or beyond. As in the findings we predicted for your survey of classmates, some individuals achieved nativelike skills, whereas the language outcomes for others were quite poor. For reasons that are still unknown, some individuals continue to be talented language learners even after puberty, while most do not.

Newport (1990) proposed an intriguing hypothesis to explain these results and, more generally, to explain why children are usually better language learners than adults. According to her "less is more" hypothesis, perceptual and memory limitations cause young children to extract and store smaller chunks of the language than adults do. Because the crucial building blocks of language (the meaning-carrying morphemes) tend to be quite small, young learners' limited cognitive abilities may actually facilitate the task of analyzing and learning language.

The evidence for a critical period in language acquisition has some very clear practical implications. For one thing, deaf children should be exposed to sign language as early as possible. For another, foreign-language exposure at school, discussed in Box 6.1, should begin in the early grades in order to maximize children's opportunity to achieve native-level skills in a second language.

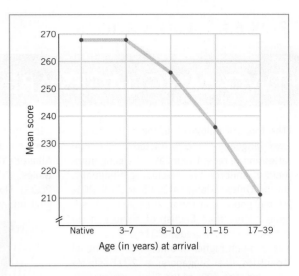

FIGURE 6.1 Test of critical-period hypothesis Performance on a test of English grammar by adults originally from Korea and China was directly related to the age at which they came to the United States and were first exposed to English. The scores of adults who emigrated before the age of 7 were indistinguishable from those of native speakers of English. (Data from J. S. Johnson & Newport, 1989)

A Human Environment

Possession of a human brain is not enough for language to develop. Children must also be exposed to other people using language—any language, signed or spoken.

BOX 6.1 | applications

TWO LANGUAGES ARE BETTER THAN ONE

The topic of **bilingualism,** the ability to use two languages, has attracted substantial attention in recent years as increasing numbers of children are developing bilingually. In the United States in 2013, roughly 20% of the population reported speaking a language other than English at home (United States Census Bureau, 2015). This number is much higher in officially multilingual countries like Singapore; a 2015 survey revealed that 73% of the Singapore population was literate in at least two languages (Department of Statistics Singapore, 2016). Remarkably, despite the fact that bilingual children have twice as much to learn as monolingual children, they show little confusion and language delay. In fact, there is evidence to suggest that being bilingual improves aspects of cognitive functioning in childhood and beyond.

Bilingual learning can begin in the womb. Newborns prenatally exposed to just their native language prefer it over other languages, whereas newborns whose mothers spoke two languages during pregnancy prefer both languages equally (Byers-Heinlein, Burns, & Werker, 2010). Bilingual infants are able to discriminate the speech sounds of their two languages at roughly the same

pace that monolingual infants distinguish the sounds of their one language (e.g., Albareda-Castellot, Pons, & Sebastián-Gallés, 2011; Sundara, Polka, & Molnar, 2008). How might this be, given that bilingual infants have twice as much to learn?

One possibility is that a bilingual infant's attention to speech cues is heightened relative to that of a monolingual infant. For example, bilingual infants are better than monolingual infants at using purely visual information (a silent talking face) to

PAUL CONKLIN / PHOTOEDIT

The issue of bilingualism in the classroom has been a topic of intense debate in the United States and other parts of the world. However, research reveals no costs and various potential benefits of proficiency in multiple languages.

Adequate experience hearing others talk is readily available in the environment of almost all children around the world. Much of the speech directed to infants occurs in the context of daily routines—during thousands of mealtimes, diaper changes, baths, and bedtimes, as well as in countless games like peekaboo and nursery rhymes like the "Itsy Bitsy Spider."

Infants identify speech as something important very early. When given the choice, newborns prefer listening to speech rather than to artificial sounds (Vouloumanos et al., 2010). Intriguingly, newborns also prefer nonhuman primate (rhesus macaque) vocalizations to nonspeech sounds, and show no preference for speech over macaque vocalizations until 3 months of age (Vouloumanos et al., 2010). These results suggest that infants' auditory preferences are fine-tuned through experience with human language during their earliest months.

Infant-directed speech Imagine yourself on a bus listening to a stranger who is seated behind you and speaking to someone. Could you guess whether

bilingualism ■ the ability to use two languages

discriminate between unfamiliar languages (Sebastián-Gallés et al., 2012).

For the most part, children who are acquiring two languages do not seem to confuse them; indeed, they appear to build two separate linguistic systems. Language mixing, also known as code mixing or code switching, is a phenomenon in which bilingual speakers conversing in one language insert words or phrases from their other language. This practice is a normal aspect of bilingual development and does not reflect confusion. When language mixing occurs, it often reflects a gap of knowledge in one language that the child is trying to fill in with the other. It can also reflect the idiomatic language that children hear in their language community (e.g., Byers-Heinlein & Lew-Williams, 2013). Indeed, bilingual parents frequently code switch when addressing their children (Bail, Morini, & Newman, 2015). One study of bilingual families in Montreal, Canada, found that more than 90% of parents mixed their languages in speech to their infants (Byers-Heinlein, 2013). It is thus not at all surprising that most bilingual children engage in language mixing as well.

Children developing bilingually may appear to lag slightly behind monolingual children in each of their languages because their vocabulary is distributed across two languages (Oller & Pearson, 2002). That is, a bilingual child may know how to express some concepts in one language but not the other. However, both the course and the rate of language development are generally very similar for bilingual and monolingual children. For example, bilingual toddlers are just as fast as their monolingual peers at recognizing familiar words (DeAnda et al., 2016). And as we have noted, there are cognitive benefits to bilingualism: children who are competent in two languages perform better on a variety of measures of executive function and cognitive control than do monolingual children (Bialystok & Craik, 2010; Costa, Hernández, & Sebastián-Gallés, 2008; Poulin-Dubois et al., 2011). Even bilingual infants appear to show greater cognitive flexibility in learning tasks (Kovács & Mehler, 2009a, b). The link between bilingualism and improved cognitive flexibility likely lies in the fact that bilingual individuals have had to learn to rapidly switch between languages, both in comprehension and production.

More difficult issues arise with respect to second-language learning in the school setting. Some countries with large but distinct language communities, like Canada, have embraced bilingual education. In Europe, most countries require students to begin foreign language education before age 9 (Eurydice Network, 2012). And in Sri Lanka, the president declared 2012 to be the Year of Trilingualism, kicking off a 10-year plan to ensure that children learn all three of the country's official languages (Sinhala, Tamil, and English). However, the United States has not embraced multilingual schooling. The debate over bilingual education in the United States is tied up with a host of political, ethnic, and racial issues. One side in this debate advocates for total immersion, in which children are communicated with and taught exclusively in English, the goal being to help them become proficient in English as quickly as possible. The other side recommends an approach that initially provides children with instruction in basic subjects in their native language and gradually increases the amount of instruction provided in English (Castro et al., 2011).

In support of the latter view, there is evidence that bilingual children are more successful in learning both of their languages when the school environment provides support for both languages (e.g., McCabe et al., 2013). This research has led the Society for Research in Child Development and the American Academy of Pediatrics to endorse policies aimed at broadening children's access to bilingual educational opportunities.

the stranger was addressing an infant or an adult? We have no doubt that you could, even if the stranger was speaking an unfamiliar language. The reason is that in virtually all cultures, adults adopt a distinctive mode of speech when talking to babies and very young children. This special way of speaking was originally dubbed "motherese" (Newport, Gleitman, & Gleitman, 1977). The current term, **infant-directed speech (IDS),** recognizes the fact that this style of speech is used by both males and females, including parents and nonparents alike. Indeed, even young children adopt it when talking to babies (for review, see Soderstrom, 2007).

CHARACTERISTICS OF INFANT-DIRECTED SPEECH The most obvious quality of IDS is its emotional tone. It is speech suffused with affection—"the sweet music of the species," as Darwin (1877) put it. Another obvious characteristic of IDS is exaggeration. When people speak to babies, their speech is slower and their voice is often higher pitched than when they speak to adults; they also swoop abruptly from high pitches to low pitches and back again. Even their vowels are clearer (Kuhl et al., 1997). All this exaggerated speech is accompanied by exaggerated

infant-directed speech (IDS) ■ the distinctive mode of speech that adults adopt when talking to babies and very young children

The infant-directed talk used by this father grabs and holds his baby's attention.

Around the world, parents in some cultures talk directly to their babies, whereas parents in other cultures, such as this Kwara'ae mother, do not. Almost everywhere, adults and older children use some form of "baby talk" to address infants.

facial expressions. Many of these characteristics have been noted in adults speaking such languages as Arabic, French, Italian, Japanese, Mandarin Chinese, and Spanish (see de Boysson-Bardies, 1996/1999), as well as in deaf mothers signing to their infants (Masataka, 1992).

Beyond expressing emotional tone, caregivers can use various pitch patterns of IDS to communicate important information to infants even when infants don't know the meaning of the words uttered. For example, a word uttered with sharply falling intonation tells the baby that their caregiver disapproves of something, whereas a cooed warm sound indicates approval. These pitch patterns serve the same function in language communities ranging from English and Italian to Japanese (Fernald et al., 1989). Interestingly, infants exhibit appropriate facial emotion when listening to these pitch patterns, even when the language is unfamiliar (Fernald, 1993).

IDS also seems to aid infants' language development. To begin with, it draws infants' attention to speech itself. Indeed, infants prefer IDS to adult-directed speech (ADS) (Cooper & Aslin, 1994; Pegg, Werker, & McLeod, 1992), even when it is in a language other than their own. For example, both Chinese and American infants listened longer to a recording of a Cantonese-speaking woman talking to a baby in IDS than to the same woman speaking normally to an adult friend (Werker, Pegg, & McLeod, 1994). Some studies suggest that infants' preference for IDS may emerge because it is "happy speech"; when speakers' affect is held constant, the preference disappears (Singh, Morgan, & Best, 2002). Perhaps because they pay greater attention to IDS, infants learn and recognize words better when the words are presented in IDS than when they are presented in ADS (Ma et al., 2011; Singh et al., 2009; Thiessen, Hill, & Saffran, 2005). These behavioral effects are mirrored by the reactions of infant brains, which show greater activation when hearing IDS than ADS (e.g., Naoi et al., 2012).

Although IDS is very common throughout the world, it is not universal. In some cultures, such as the Kwara'ae of the Solomon Islands, the Ifaluk of Micronesia, and the Kaluli of Papua New Guinea, it is believed that because infants cannot understand what is said to them, there is no reason for caregivers to speak to them (Le, 2000; Schieffelin & Ochs, 1987; Watson-Gegeo, & Gegeo, 1986). For example, young Kaluli infants are carried facing outward so that they can engage with other members of the group (but not with their caregiver), and if they are spoken to by older siblings, the mother will speak for them (Schieffelin & Ochs, 1987). Thus, even if they are not addressed directly by their caregivers, these infants are still immersed in language.

That infants begin life equipped with the two basic necessities for acquiring language—a human brain and a human environment—is, of course, only the beginning of the story. Of all the things we learn as humans, languages are arguably the most complex; so complex, in fact, that scientists have yet to be able to program computer systems to acquire a human language. The overwhelming complexity of language is further reflected in the difficulty most people have in learning a new language after puberty. How, then, do infants and young children manage to acquire their native language with such astounding success? We turn now to the many steps through which that remarkable accomplishment proceeds.

Review

The process of comprehending and producing language, whether spoken or signed, involves the development of many different kinds of knowledge and skills. The first prerequisite for its full-fledged development is a human brain. Researchers have succeeded in teaching nonhuman animals remarkable symbolic skills but not full-fledged language. A second prerequisite for language development is exposure to language. Much of the language babies hear takes the form of infant-directed speech (IDS), which is characterized by a higher-than-normal pitch; extreme shifts in intonation; a warm, affectionate tone; and exaggerated facial expressions.

The Process of Language Acquisition

Acquiring a language involves listening and speaking (or watching and signing) and requires both comprehending what other people communicate and producing intelligible speech (or signs). Infants start out paying attention to what people say or sign, and they know a great deal about language long before their first linguistic productions.

Speech Perception

The first step in language learning is figuring out the sounds of one's native language. As you saw in Chapter 2, the task usually begins in the womb, as fetuses develop a preference for their mother's voice and the language they hear her speak. The basis for this very early learning is **prosody,** the characteristic rhythmic and intonation patterns with which a language is spoken. Differences in prosody are in large part responsible for why languages—from Japanese to French to Swahili—sound so different from one another.

Speech perception also involves distinguishing among the speech sounds that make a difference in a given language. To learn English, for example, one must distinguish between *bat* and *pat, dill* and *kill, Ben* and *bed*. As you will see next, young infants do not have to learn to hear these differences: they perceive many speech sounds in very much the same way that adults do.

Categorical Perception of Speech Sounds

Both adults and infants perceive speech sounds as belonging to discrete categories. This phenomenon, referred to as **categorical perception,** has been established by studying people's response to speech sounds. In this research, a speech synthesizer is used to gradually and continuously change one speech sound, such as /b/, into a related one, such as /p/. These two phonemes are on an acoustic continuum; they are produced in exactly the same way, except for one crucial difference—the length of time between when air passes through the lips and when the vocal cords start vibrating. This lag, referred to as **voice onset time (VOT),** is shorter for /b/ (less than 25 milliseconds [ms]) than for /p/ (greater than 25 ms). (Try saying "ba"

prosody ■ the characteristic rhythm, tempo, cadence, melody, intonational patterns, and so forth with which a language is spoken

categorical perception ■ the perception of speech sounds as belonging to discrete categories

voice onset time (VOT) ■ the length of time between when air passes through the lips and when the vocal cords start vibrating

and "pa" alternately several times, with your hand on your throat, and you will likely experience this difference in VOT.)

To study the perception of VOT, researchers create recordings of speech sounds that vary along this VOT continuum, so that each successive sound is slightly different from the one before, with /b/ gradually changing into /p/. What is surprising is that adult listeners do not perceive this continuously changing series of sounds. Instead, they hear /b/ repeated several times and then hear an abrupt switch to /p/. All the sounds in this continuum that have a VOT of less than 25 ms are perceived as /b/, and all those that have a VOT greater than 25 ms are perceived as /p/. Thus, adults automatically divide the continuous signal into two discontinuous categories—/b/ and /p/. This perception of a continuum as two categories is a very useful perceptual ability because it allows one to pay attention to sound differences that are meaningful in one's native language, such as, in English, the difference between /b/ and /p/, while allowing meaningless differences, such as the difference between a /b/ with a 10 ms VOT versus a /b/ with a 20 ms VOT, to be ignored.

Young infants draw the same sharp distinctions between speech sounds. This remarkable fact was established using the habituation technique familiar to you from previous chapters. In the original, classic study (one of the 100 most frequently cited studies in psychology), 1- and 4-month-olds sucked on a pacifier hooked up to a computer (Eimas et al., 1971). The harder they sucked, the more often they'd hear repetitions of a single speech sound. After hearing the same sound repeatedly, the babies gradually sucked less enthusiastically (*habituation*). Then a new sound was played. If the infants' sucking rate increased in response to the new sound, the researchers inferred that the infants discriminated the new sound from the old one (*dishabituation*).

The crucial factor in this study was the relation between the new and old sounds—specifically, whether they were from the same or different phonemic categories. For one group of infants, the new sound was from a different category; thus, after habituation to a series of sounds that adults perceive as /b/, sucking now produced a sound that adults identify as /p/. For the second group, the new sound was within the same category as the old one (i.e., adults perceive them both as /b/). A critical feature of the study is that for both groups, the new and old sounds differed *equally* in terms of VOT.

As Figure 6.2 shows, after habituating to /b/, the infants increased their rate of sucking when the new sound came from a different phonemic category (/p/ instead of /b/). Habituation continued, however, when the new sound was within the same category as the original one. Since this classic study, researchers have established that infants show categorical perception of numerous speech sounds from languages around the world.

A fascinating outcome of this research is the discovery that young infants actually make *more* distinctions than adults do. This rather surprising phenomenon occurs because any given language uses only a subset of the large variety of phonemic categories that exist. As noted earlier, the sounds /r/ and /l/ make a difference in English, but not in Japanese. Similarly, speakers of Arabic, but not of English, perceive a difference between the /k/ sounds in "keep" and "cool." Adults simply do not perceive differences in speech sounds that are not important in their

FIGURE 6.2 Categorical perception of speech sounds by infants Infants ages 1 to 4 months were habituated to a tape of artificial speech sounds. (a) One group repeatedly heard a /ba/ sound with a VOT of 20 ms, and they gradually habituated to it. (b) When the sound changed to /pa/, with a VOT of 40 ms, they dishabituated, indicating that they perceived the difference between the two sounds, just as adults do. (c) A different group was habituated to a /pa/ sound with a VOT of 60 ms. (d) When the sound changed to another /pa/ with a VOT of 80 ms, the infants remained habituated, suggesting that, like adults, they did not discriminate between these two sounds. (Data from Eimas et al., 1971)

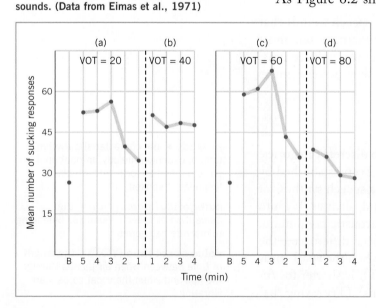

native language, which partly accounts for why it is so difficult for adults to become fluent in a second language.

In contrast, infants can distinguish between phonemic contrasts made in all the languages of the world—about 600 consonants and 200 vowels. For example, Kikuyu infants in Africa are just as good as American babies at discriminating English contrasts not found in Kikuyu (Streeter, 1976). Studies done with infants from English-speaking homes have shown that they can discriminate non-English distinctions made in languages ranging from German and Spanish to Thai, Hindi, and Zulu.

This research reveals an ability that is innate, in the sense that it is present at birth, and experience-independent because infants can discriminate between speech sounds they have never heard before. Being born able to distinguish speech sounds of any language is enormously helpful to infants, priming them to start learning whichever of the world's languages they hear around them. Indeed, the crucial role of early speech perception is reflected in a positive correlation between infants' speech-perception skills and their later language skills. Babies who were better at detecting differences between speech sounds at 6 months scored higher on measures of vocabulary and grammar at 13 to 24 months of age (Tsao, Liu, & Kuhl, 2004).

Developmental Changes in Speech Perception

During the last months of their 1st year, infants increasingly home in on the speech sounds of their native language, and by 12 months of age, they have "lost" the ability to perceive the speech sounds that are not part of it. In other words, their speech perception has become adultlike. This shift was first demonstrated by Janet Werker and her colleagues (Werker, 1989; Werker & Lalonde, 1988; Werker & Tees, 1984), who studied infants ranging in age from 6 to 12 months. The infants, all from English-speaking homes, were tested on their ability to discriminate speech contrasts that are not used in English but that are important in two other languages—Hindi and Nthlakapmx (a language spoken by indigenous First Nations people in the Canadian Pacific Northwest). The researchers used a simple conditioning procedure, shown in Figure 6.3. The infants learned that if they turned their head toward the sound source when they heard a change in the

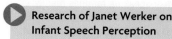
Research of Janet Werker on Infant Speech Perception

FIGURE 6.3 Speech perception This infant is participating in a study of speech perception in the laboratory of Janet Werker. The baby has learned to turn his head to the sound source whenever he hears a change from one sound to another. A correct head turn is rewarded by an exciting visual display, as well as by the applause and praise of the experimenter. To make sure that neither the mother nor the experimenter can influence the child's behavior, they are both wearing headphones that prevent them from hearing what the baby hears. (From Werker, 1989)

PHOTOS COURTESY OF PETER MCLEOD, ACADIA UNIVERSITY

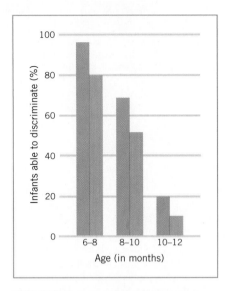

FIGURE 6.4 Percent of infants able to discriminate foreign-language speech sounds Infants' ability to discriminate between speech sounds that are not in their native language declines between 6 and 12 months of age. Most 6-month-olds from English-speaking families readily discriminate between syllables in Hindi (blue bars) and Nthlakapmx (green bars), but most 10- to 12-month-olds do not. (Data from Werker, 1989)

sounds they were listening to, they would be rewarded by an interesting visual display. If the infants turned their heads in the correct direction immediately following a sound change, the researchers inferred that they had detected the change.

Figure 6.4 shows that at 6 to 8 months of age, English-learning infants readily discriminated between the sounds they heard; they could tell one Hindi syllable from another, and they could also distinguish between two sounds in Nthlakapmx. At 10 to 12 months of age, however, the infants no longer perceived the differences they had detected a few months before. Two Hindi syllables that had previously sounded different to them now sounded the same. Other research indicates that a similar change occurs slightly earlier for the discrimination of vowels (Kuhl et al., 1992; Polka & Werker, 1994). Interestingly, this perceptual narrowing does not appear to be an entirely passive process. Kuhl, Tsao, and Liu (2003) found that infants learned more about the phonetic structure of Mandarin from a live interaction with a Mandarin speaker than from watching a videotape of one. This is an example of the benefits of active learning, as discussed in Chapter 5.

Is this process of linguistic perceptual narrowing limited to speech? To answer this question, researchers asked whether this narrowing process also occurs in ASL (Palmer et al., 2012). They began by determining whether infants who had never been exposed to ASL were able to discriminate between highly similar ASL signs that are differentiated only by the shape of the hand. They found that 4-month-olds could, in fact, discriminate between the signs. However, by 14 months of age, only those infants who were learning ASL were able to detect the difference between the hand shapes; infants who were not learning ASL had lost their ability to make this perceptual discrimination. Perceptual narrowing is thus not limited to speech. Indeed, this narrowing process may be quite broad; recall the discussion of perceptual narrowing in the domains of face perception (page 196) and musical rhythm (page 204) discussed in Chapter 5.

Thus, after the age of 8 months or so, infants begin to specialize in their discrimination of speech sounds, retaining their sensitivity to sounds in the native language they hear every day, while becoming increasingly less sensitive to nonnative speech sounds. Indeed, becoming a native listener is one of the greatest accomplishments of the infant's 1st year of postnatal life. This development is also one of the reasons why it is difficult for many people to learn foreign languages later in their lives, a topic we will discuss later in this chapter.

Word Segmentation

As infants begin to tune into the speech sounds of their language, they also begin to discover another crucial feature of the speech surrounding them: words. This is no easy feat. Unlike the words typed on this page, there are no spaces between words in speech, even in IDS. What this means is that most utterances infants hear are strings of words without pauses between them, like "*Lookattheprettybaby! Haveyoueverseensuchaprettybabybefore?*" They then have to figure out where the words start and end. Remarkably, they begin the process of **word segmentation** during the second half of the 1st year.

In the first demonstration of infant word segmentation, Jusczyk & Aslin (1995) used a head-turn procedure designed to assess infants' auditory preferences. In this study, 7-month-olds first listened to passages of speech in which a particular word was repeated from sentence to sentence—for example, "The *cup* was bright and shiny. A clown drank from the red *cup*. His *cup* was filled with milk." After

word segmentation ■ the process of discovering where words begin and end in fluent speech

listening to these sentences several times, infants were tested using the head-turn preference procedure to see whether they recognized the words repeated in the sentences. In this method, flashing lights mounted near two loudspeakers located on either side of an infant are used to draw the infant's attention to one side or the other. As soon as the infant turns to look at the light, an auditory stimulus is played through the speaker, and it continues as long as the infant is looking in that direction. The length of time the infant spends looking at the light—and hence listening to the sound—provides a measure of the degree to which the infant is attracted to that sound.

Infants in this study were tested on repetitions of words that had been presented in the sentences (such as *cup*) or words that had not (such as *bike*). The researchers found that infants listened longer to words that they had heard in the passages of fluent speech, as compared with words that never occurred in the passages. This result indicates that the infants were able to pull the words out of the stream of speech—a task so difficult that even sophisticated speech-recognition computer software often fails at it.

How do infants find words in pause-free speech? They appear to be remarkably good at picking up regularities in their native language that help them to find word boundaries. One example is stress patterning, an element of prosody. In English, the first syllable in two-syllable words is much more likely to be stressed than the second syllable (as in "English," "often," and "second"). By 8 months of age, English-learning infants expect stressed syllables to begin words and can use this information to pull words out of fluent speech (Curtin, Mintz, & Christiansen, 2005; Johnson & Jusczyk, 2001; Thiessen & Saffran, 2003).

Another regularity to which infants are surprisingly sensitive concerns the **distributional properties** of the speech they hear. As discussed in Chapter 5, statistical learning is particularly useful for word segmentation. In every language, certain sounds are more likely to appear together than are others. Sensitivity to such regularities in the speech stream was demonstrated in a series of statistical-learning experiments in which babies learned new words based purely on regularities in how often a given sound followed another (Aslin, Saffran, & Newport, 1998; Saffran, Aslin, & Newport, 1996). The infants listened to a 2-minute recording of four different three-syllable "words" (e.g., *tupiro, golabu, bidaku, padoti*) repeated in random order with no pauses between the "words." Then, on a series of test trials, the babies were presented with the "words" they had heard (e.g., *bidaku, padoti*) and with sequences that were not words (such as syllable sequences that spanned a word boundary—for example, *kupado*, made up from the end of *bidaku* and the beginning of *padoti*). Using the same kind of preferential-listening test described for the Juscyzk & Aslin (1995) study, the researchers found that infants discriminated between the words and the sequences that were not words. To do so, the babies must have registered that certain syllables often occurred together in the sample of speech they heard. For example, "bi" was always followed by "da" and "da" was always followed by "ku," whereas "ku" could be followed by "tu," "go," or "pa." Thus, the infants used predictable sound patterns to fish words out of the passing stream of speech.

The ability to learn from distributional properties extends to real languages as well; English-learning infants, for example, can track similar statistical patterns when listening to Italian IDS (Pelucchi, Hay, & Saffran, 2009). Identifying these regularities in speech sounds supports the learning of words. After repeatedly hearing novel "words" such as *timay* and *dobu* embedded in a long stream of speech sounds, 17-month-olds readily learned those sounds as labels for objects

How quickly could you pick out a word from a stream of speech like the one shown here? It takes 8-month-old infants only 2 minutes of listening.

distributional properties ■ the phenomenon that in any language, certain sounds are more likely to appear together than are others

babbling ■ repetitive consonant–vowel sequences ("bababa . . .") or hand movements (for learners of sign languages) produced during the early phases of language development

(Graf Estes et al., 2007). Similarly, after hearing Italian words like *mela* and *bici* embedded in fluent Italian speech, 17-month-olds who had no prior exposure to Italian readily mapped those labels to objects (J. F. Hay et al., 2011). Having already learned the sound sequences that made up the words apparently made it easier for the infants to associate the words with their referents.

Probably the most salient regularity for infants is their own name. Infants as young as 4½ months will listen longer to repetitions of their own name than to repetitions of a different but similar name (Mandel, Jusczyk, & Pisoni, 1995). Just a few weeks later, they can pick their own name out of background conversations (Newman, 2005). This ability helps them to find new words in the speech stream. After hearing "It's Jerry's cup!" a number of times, 6-month-old Jerry is more likely to learn the word *cup* than if he had not heard it right after his name (Bortfeld et al., 2005). Over time, infants recognize more and more familiar words, making it easier to pluck new ones out of the speech that they hear.

Infants are exceptional in their ability to identify patterns in the speech surrounding them. They start out with the ability to make crucial distinctions among speech sounds but then narrow their focus to the sounds and sound patterns that make a difference in their native language. This process lays the groundwork for their becoming not just native listeners but also native speakers.

Preparation for Production

In their first months, babies are getting ready to talk. Their initial repertoire of sounds is extremely limited. They cry, sneeze, sigh, burp, and smack their lips, but their vocal tract is not sufficiently developed to allow them to produce anything like real speech sounds. Then, at about 6 to 8 weeks of age, infants begin to coo—producing long, drawn-out vowel sounds, such as "ooohh" or "aaahh." Young infants engage in vocal gymnastics, switching from low grunts to high-pitched cries, from soft murmurs to loud shouts. They click, smack, blow raspberries, squeal—all with apparent fascination and delight. Through this practice, infants gain motor control over their vocalizations. While their sound repertoire is expanding, infants become increasingly aware that their vocalizations elicit responses from others, and they begin to engage in dialogues of reciprocal ooohing and aaahing, cooing and gooing with their caregivers. Indeed, infants with more responsive caregivers are more likely to use more mature vocalization patterns (Miller, 2014). The development of language production, like other aspects of language development, is influenced by the degree to which caregivers respond to their infants' bids for communication (Tamis-LeMonda, Kuchirko, & Song, 2014).

Babbling

Sometime between 6 and 10 months of age, but on average at around 7 months, a major milestone occurs: babies begin to babble. Standard **babbling** involves producing syllables made up of a consonant followed by a vowel ("pa," "ba," "ma") that are repeated in strings ("papapa"). Contrary to the long-held belief that infants babble a wide range of sounds from their own and other languages (Jakobson, 1941/1968), research has revealed that babies actually babble a fairly limited set of sounds, some of which are not part of their native language (de Boysson-Bardies, 1996/1999).

Native language exposure is a key component in the development of babbling. Although congenitally deaf infants produce vocalizations similar to those of hearing babies until about 5 or 6 months of age, their vocal babbling occurs very late and is quite limited (Oller & Eilers, 1988). However, congenitally deaf babies who are regularly exposed to sign language do "babble" right on schedule—these infants exposed to ASL babble *manually*. They produce repetitive hand movements that are components of full ASL signs, just as vocally babbled sounds are repeated components of spoken words (Petitto & Marentette, 1991). Thus, like infants learning a spoken language, infants learning sign languages seem to experiment with the elements that are combined to make meaningful words in their native language (Figure 6.5).

As their babbling becomes more varied, it gradually takes on the sounds, rhythm, and intonational patterns of the language infants hear daily. However, it is still very difficult to tell what language an infant is speaking by listening to his or her babbling alone. In one study of English-learning and Chinese-learning 12-month-olds, adult listeners were unable to tell which language the infants were babbling in, unless the infants produced actual words (Lee et al., 2016).

Early interactions

Before we turn to the next big step in language production—uttering recognizable words—it is important to consider the social context that promotes language development in most societies. Even before infants start speaking, they display the beginnings of communicative competence: the ability to communicate intentionally with another person.

The first indication of communicative competence is turn-taking. In a conversation, mature participants alternate between speaking and listening. Jerome Bruner and his colleagues (Bruner, 1977; Ratner & Bruner, 1978) have proposed that learning to take turns in social interactions is facilitated by parent–infant games, such as peekaboo and "give and take," in which caregiver and baby take turns giving and receiving objects. In these "dialogues," the infant has the opportunity to alternate between an active and a passive role, as in a conversation in which one alternates between speaking and listening. These early interactions give infants practice in bidirectional communication, providing infants with a scaffold to learn how to use language to converse with others. Indeed, caregivers' responses to infant babbling may serve a similar function. When an adult labels an object for an infant just after the infant babbles, the infant's learning of the label is more greatly enhanced than when the labeling occurs in the absence of babbling (Goldstein et al., 2010). The results of this study suggest that babbling may serve as a signal to the caregiver that the infant is attentive and ready to learn. This early back-and-forth may also provide infants with practice in conversational turn-taking.

As discussed in Chapter 4, successful communication also requires *intersubjectivity*, in which two interacting partners share a mutual understanding. The foundation of intersubjectivity is *joint attention*, which, early on, is established by the parent's following the baby's lead, looking at and commenting on whatever the infant is looking at. By 12 months of age, infants have begun to understand the communicative nature of pointing, with many also being capable of meaningful pointing themselves (Behne et al., 2012).

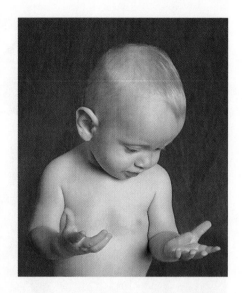

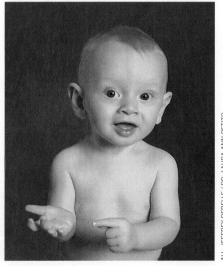

FIGURE 6.5 Manual babbling Babies who are exposed to the sign language of their deaf parents babble with their hands. A subset of their hand movements differs from those of infants exposed to spoken language and corresponds to the rhythmic patterning of adult signs. (Information from Petitto et al., 2001)

This toddler is pointing to get her father to share her attention—to achieve intersubjectivity. Once the father identifies the focus of his daughter's attention, he may even decide to add it to the shopping basket.

reference ■ in language and speech, the associating of words and meaning

A classic problem posed by philosopher Willard Quine was how someone who does not know the word *bunny* could figure out exactly what those sounds refer to. These parents are helping their daughter learn a new word by labeling the referent while it is the focus of their daughter's attention.

We have thus seen that infants spend a good deal of time getting ready to talk. Through babbling, they gain some initial level of control over the production of sounds that are necessary to produce recognizable words. Through early interactions with their parents, they develop conversation-like routines similar to those required in the use of language for communication. We will now turn our attention to the processes that lead to infants' first real linguistic productions: words.

First Words

When babies first begin to segment words from fluent speech, they are simply recognizing familiar patterns of sounds without attaching any meaning to them. But to actually learn and use words, they must recognize that words have meanings. The first step for infants in acquiring the meanings of words is to address the problem of **reference,** that is, to start associating words and meaning. Figuring out which of the multitude of possible referents is the right one for a particular word is, as the philosopher Willard Quine (1960) pointed out, a very complex problem. If a child hears someone say "bunny" in the presence of a rabbit, how does the child know whether this new word refers to the rabbit itself, to its fuzzy tail, to the whiskers on the right side of its nose, or to the twitching of its nose?

Early Word Recognition

Infants begin associating highly familiar words with their highly familiar referents surprisingly early on. When 6-month-olds hear either "Mommy" or "Daddy," they look toward the appropriate person (Tincoff & Jusczyk, 1999). Infants gradually come to understand the meaning of less frequently heard words, with the pace of their vocabulary-building varying greatly from one child to another. Remarkably, parents are often unaware of just how many words their infants recognize. Using an eye-tracking paradigm, Bergelson and Swingley (2012) showed infants pairs of pictures of common foods and body parts and tracked the infants' eye gaze when one of the pictures was named. They found that even 6-month-olds looked to the correct picture significantly more often than would be expected by chance, demonstrating that they recognized the names of these items. Strikingly, most of their parents reported that the infants did not know the meanings of these words. So not only do infants understand far more words than they can produce; they also understand far more words than even their caregivers realize. The same phenomenon occurs for toddlers with autism spectrum disorder, who tend to have delayed language abilities (as we will discuss in Box 6.5): parents think that their autistic toddlers understand fewer words than they actually do, as measured by sensitive eye-tracking tasks (Venker et al., 2016).

One of the remarkable features of infants' early word recognition is how rapidly they understand what they are hearing. To illuminate the age-related dynamics of this understanding, Fernald and her colleagues presented infants with images depicting pairs of familiar objects, such as a dog and a baby, and observed how quickly the infants moved their eyes to the correct object after hearing its label used (e.g., "Where's the *baby*?"). The researchers found that whereas 15-month-olds waited until they had heard the whole word to look at the target object, 24-month-olds looked at the correct object after hearing only the first part of its label, just as adults do (e.g., Fernald, Perfors, & Marchman, 2006). Older infants can also use context to help them recognize words. For example, toddlers who are learning a language that has a grammatical gender system (like Spanish or French) can use the gender of the article preceding the noun (*la* versus *el* in Spanish; *la* versus *le* in French) to speed their recognition of the noun itself (Lew-Williams & Fernald, 2007; Van Heugten & Shi, 2009). Other research using eye gaze measures has shown that older infants can even recognize familiar words when they are mispronounced (e.g., "vaby" for "baby," "gall" for "ball," "tog" for "dog," etc.), though their recognition is slower than when they hear the words pronounced correctly (Swingley & Aslin, 2000).

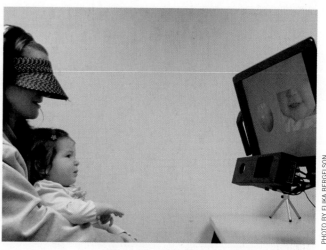

PHOTO BY ELIKA BERGELSON

When this infant hears the word *mouth,* will she look at the picture of the mouth or at the picture of the apple? The speed and accuracy of her looks in response to words provide a useful measure of her vocabulary knowledge.

Early Word Production

Gradually, infants begin to say some of the words they understand, with most producing their first words between 10 and 15 months of age. The words a child is able to say are referred to as the child's *productive vocabulary*.

What counts as an infant's first word? It can be any specific utterance consistently used to refer to something or to express something. Even with this loose criterion, identification of an infant's earliest few words can be problematic. For one thing, doting parents often misconstrue their child's babbling as words. For another, early words may differ from their corresponding adult forms. For example, *Woof* was one of the first words spoken by the boy whose linguistic progress was illustrated at the beginning of this chapter. It was used to refer to the dog next door—both to excitedly name the animal when it appeared in the neighbors' yard and to wistfully request the dog's presence when it was absent.

Infants' early word productions are limited by their ability to pronounce words clearly enough that an adult can recognize them. To make life easier for themselves, infants adopt a variety of simplification strategies (Gerken, 1994).

Baby Blues

BABY BLUES / CARTOONIST GROUP

TABLE 6.1

Rank-Ordered List of Earliest Words in Three Languages*

English	Putonghua (Mandarin)	Cantonese
Daddy	**Daddy**	**Mommy**
Mommy	Aah	**Daddy**
BaaBaa	**Mommy**	*Grandma (paternal)*
Bye	*YumYum*	*Grandpa (paternal)*
Hi	*Sister (older)*	**Hello?/Wei?**
UhOh	**UhOh** (Aiyou)	*Hit*
Grr	*Hit*	Uncle (paternal)
Bottle	**Hello/Wei**	Grab/grasp
YumYum	Milk	*Auntie (maternal)*
Dog	Naughty	**Bye**
No	*Brother (older)*	**UhOh** (Aiyou)
WoofWoof	*Grandma (maternal)*	*Ya/Wow*

*Words in boldface were common across all three languages; those in italics were common for two of the languages.
Information from Tardif et al. (2008).

holophrastic period ■ the period when children begin using the words in their small productive vocabulary one word at a time

overextension ■ the use of a given word in a broader context than is appropriate

FIGURE 6.6 **Language achievement** On average, American children say their first word at about 13 months, experience a vocabulary spurt at about 19 months, and begin to produce simple sentences at about 24 months. However, the bars above and below these means show a substantial amount of variability in when different children achieve each of these milestones. (Data from Bloom, 1998)

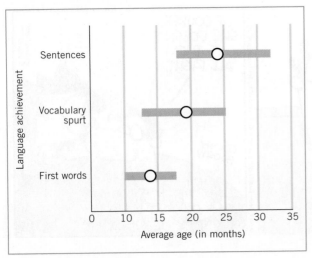

For example, they leave out the difficult bits of words, turning *banana* into "nana," or they substitute easier sounds for hard-to-say ones—"bubba" for *brother*, "wabbit" for *rabbit*. Sometimes they reorder parts of words to put an easier sound at the beginning of the word, as in the common "pisketti" (for *spaghetti*) or the more idiosyncratic "Cagoshin" (the way the child quoted at the beginning of the chapter continued for several years to say *Chicago*).

Once children start talking, what do they talk about? Children name their parents, siblings, pets, and themselves, as well as other personally important objects such as cookies, juice, and balls. Frequent events and routines are also labeled—"up," "bye-bye," "night-night." Important modifiers are also used—"mine," "hot," "all gone." Table 6.1 reveals substantial cross-linguistic similarities in the content of the first 10 words of children in the United States, Beijing, and Hong Kong. As the table shows, many of infants' first words in the three societies referred to specific people or were sound effects (Tardif et al., 2008). Indeed, over the first two years, children's vocabularies across a range of countries are surprisingly similar in their contents (Mayor & Plunkett, 2014).

Initially, infants say the words in their small productive vocabulary only one word at a time. This phase is referred to as the **holophrastic period,** because the child typically expresses a "whole phrase"—a whole idea—with a single word. For example, a child might say "Drink!" to express the desire for a glass of juice. Children who produce only one-word utterances are not limited to single ideas; they manage to express themselves by stringing together successive one-word utterances. An example is a little girl with an eye infection who pointed to her eye, saying "Ow," and then after a pause, "Eye" (Hoff, 2001).

What young children want to talk about quickly outstrips the number of words in their limited vocabularies, so they make the words they do know perform double duty. One way they do this is through **overextension**—using a word in a broader context than is appropriate, as when children use *dog* for any four-legged animal, *daddy* for any man, *moon* for a dishwasher dial, or *hot* for any reflective metal. Most overextensions represent an effort to communicate rather than a lack of knowledge, as demonstrated by research in which children who overextended some words were given comprehension tests (Naigles & Gelman, 1995). In one study, children were shown pairs of pictures of entities for which they generally used the same label—for instance, a dog and a sheep, both of which they normally referred to as "dog." However, when asked to point to the sheep, they chose the correct animal. Thus, these children understood the meaning of the word *sheep*, but because it was not in their productive vocabulary, they used a related word that they knew how to say in order to talk about the animal.

Word Learning

After the appearance of their first words, children typically plod ahead slowly, reaching a productive vocabulary of 50 or so words by about 18 months of age. At this point, the rate of learning appears to accelerate, leading to what appears to be a "vocabulary spurt" (e.g., L. Bloom, 1973; McMurray, 2007). Although scholars disagree about whether learning actually speeds up for all or even most children (Bloom, 2000), it is clear that children's communicative abilities are growing rapidly (Figure 6.6).

What accounts for the skill with which young children learn words? When we look closely, we see that there are multiple sources of support for learning new words, some coming from the people around them, and some generated by the children themselves.

Adult influences on word learning The most important way that caregivers influence word learning is by talking to their children. As we discuss in Box 6.2, the amount and quality of talking that children hear predicts how many words they learn. In addition to using IDS, which makes word learning easier for infants, adults facilitate word learning by highlighting new words. For example, they stress new words (by saying them more loudly and slowly), repeat new words, or place them at the ends of sentences. Another stimulus to word learning that adults provide involves naming games, in which they ask the child to point to a series of named items—"Where's your nose?" "Where's your ear?" "Where's your tummy?" Adults can also enhance word learning by choosing particularly effective moments to provide new words to their children. For example, toddlers show better word learning when the object being labeled is centered in the toddler's visual field, rather than in the periphery (see Figure 6.7; Pereira, Smith, & Yu, 2014).

This young Inuit child is playing a naming game; her mother has just asked her to point to her nose.

COURTESY OF JEAN L. BRIGGS

FIGURE 6.7 Visual information in word learning These images are taken from the infant's perspective; the infant is wearing a head-mounted eye tracker. The infant is more likely to learn the name for the green object when it is centered in the visual field (left panel) than when it is less prominent (right panel) at the moment it is labeled (Pereira, Smith, & Yu, 2014).

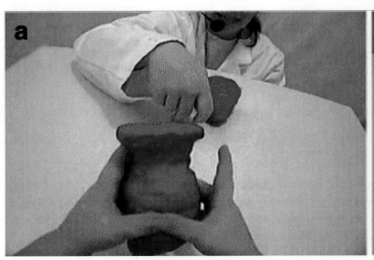
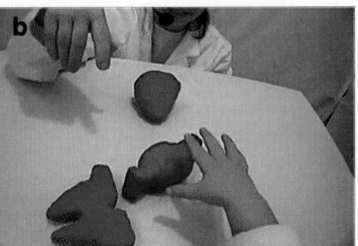

REPUBLISHED WITH PERMISSION OF SPRINGER SCIENCE AND BUS MEDIA B V, FROM PEREIRA, A. F., ET AL. (2013) A BOTTOM UP VIEW OF TODDLER WORD LEARNING. 21:178, 178–185.

BOX 6.2 | individual differences

LANGUAGE DEVELOPMENT AND SOCIOECONOMIC STATUS

Within a family, parents often notice significant linguistic differences among their children. Within a given community, such differences can be greatly magnified. In a single kindergarten classroom, for example, there may be a tenfold difference in the number of words used by different children. What accounts for these differences?

The number of words children know is intimately related to the number of words they hear, which, in turn, is linked to their caregivers' vocabularies. One of the key determinants of the language children hear is the socioeconomic status of their parents. In a seminal study, Hart and Risley (1995) recorded the speech that 42 parents used with their children over the course of 2½ years, from before the infants were talking until they were 3 years of age. Some of the parents were upper-middle class, others were working class, and others were on welfare. The results were astonishing: the average child whose parents were on welfare received half as much linguistic experience (616 words per hour) as did the average working-class parents' child (1251 words per hour) and less than one-third that of the average child in a professional family (2153 words per hour). The researchers did the math and suggested that after 4 years, an average child with upper-middle-class parents would have accumulated experience with almost 45 million words, compared with 26 million for an average child in a working-class family and 13 million for an average child with parents on welfare. This research has brought a great deal of attention to income disparities in language input, resulting in numerous policy initiatives designed to heighten parents' awareness of the amount they talk to their infants, including Bloomburg Philanthropies' Providence

Talks (Rhode Island) and the Thirty Million Words Initiative (Chicago).

Why are researchers and policy makers so worried about the amount of language input that children receive? One reason is that the number of words that children hear predicts the number of words they learn. On average, children from higher-SES groups have larger vocabularies than children from lower-SES groups. Indeed, a study of high-SES and mid-SES mothers and their 2-year-old children found that SES differences in maternal speech (e.g., number and length of utterances, richness of vocabulary, and sentence complexity) predicted some of the differences in children's spoken vocabularies (Hoff, 2003). Such differences in maternal speech even affect how quickly toddlers recognize familiar words: children whose mothers provided more maternal speech at 18 months were faster at recognizing words at 24 months than were children whose mothers provided less input (Hurtado, Marchman, & Fernald, 2008).

Even within groups of parents of similar SES, there is a great deal of variability in the amount of input parents provide, and these differences have ramifications. One study of low-income Spanish-speaking families in California found that 19-month-old infants whose families used more child-directed speech with them had larger vocabularies and were faster at processing words 6 months later (Weisleder & Fernald, 2013). Thus, early differences in language input appear to have cascading effects on language development, potentially contributing to achievement gaps between wealthier and poorer children (e.g., Duncan & Murnane, 2011).

The amount of speech that children hear is not the only determinant of language

learning outcomes. There are also many aspects of input quality that are relevant to language learning. In one study of low-income toddlers, researchers found that the richness of the communicative context, as assessed by such variables as joint engagement, routines and rituals, and fluency, predicted children's language attainment a year later (Hirsh-Pasek, Adamson et al., 2015). Indeed, these indicators of quality of parent–child interaction were a better predictor of language development than the amount of speech the children heard. Another study of quality—indexed by how clearly word meanings could be guessed from the visual context in which they were used—found that again, quality was a better predictor of language outcomes (measured 3 years later) than quantity of speech (Cartmill et al., 2013).

The physical environments in which children learn language also influence the quality of language input. For example, toddlers have more difficulty learning new words in noisy environments (Dombroski & Newman, 2014; McMillan & Saffran, 2016). Children living in poverty are more likely to experience crowded and noisy home environments and to be exposed to street noise and other sources of noise pollution that may make it more difficult for them to process language input.

Similar issues—of both quantity and quality in language input—emerge in the school context. For example, when preschool children with low language skills are placed in classrooms with peers who also have low language skills, they show less language growth than do their counterparts who are placed with classmates who have high language skills (Justice et al., 2011). These peer effects have important implications for

Early word learning and production are also influenced by the contexts in which words are used. New words that are used in very distinct contexts (like kitchens or bathrooms) are produced earlier than words that are used across a range of contexts (Roy et al., 2015). These contexts can be quite specific. For example, while toddlers are generally better at learning the names for solid substances than

Questions for your kids

Where does milk come from?

Which is your favorite vegetable?

These signs were placed around grocery stores in low-income neighborhoods to encourage caregivers to engage in more conversational interactions with their young children—and they worked!

programs like Head Start (discussed fully in Chapter 8), which are designed to enhance language development and early literacy for children living in poverty. Unfortunately, congregating children from lower-SES families together in the same preschool classrooms may limit their ability to "catch up." However, there is the possibility that negative peer effects may be offset by positive teacher effects. For example, one study found that children whose preschool teachers used a rich vocabulary showed better reading comprehension in 4th grade than did children whose preschool teachers used a more limited vocabulary (Dickinson & Porche, 2011).

These results suggest that for a variety of reasons, parents' SES affects the way they talk to their children; in turn, those individual differences have a substantial influence on the way their children talk. These differences can be intensified by the linguistic abilities of children's peers and teachers. For children in low-SES environments, the potential negative effects of these

influences may be offset by interventions including increased access to children's books, which provide enriched linguistic environments by presenting words that their parents may not typically use in conversation with their infants (Montag, Jones, & Smith, 2015). Reach out and Read is an intervention program that provides picture books to parents during pediatrician visits, building on studies that suggest that primary care physicians can influence language outcomes by modeling and promoting reading to young children (High et al., 2014).

Other interventions focus on increasing the amount of time that lower-SES parents spend speaking to their children. In one such intervention, signs were placed in supermarkets in low- and middle-SES neighborhoods, encouraging parents to converse with their children about foods they saw in the market (Ridge et al., 2015). When the signs were present, parents in the low-SES neighborhood increased both the

quality and quantity of talk to their children while shopping (a similar effect was not found in the middle-SES neighborhood). Larger scale interventions like those mentioned earlier—Providence Talks and the Thirty Million Words Initiative—aim to do something similar by providing parents with recording devices that track how much they speak to their baby so that they can monitor and increase their amount of speech. These interventions are motivated by research suggesting that educating parents about their own role in their child's language development has a positive effect on language development outcomes (M. Rowe, 2008; Suskind et al., 2015). Finally, enhancing teacher training and support in low-income school settings is another promising route for intervention (Dickinson, 2011; Hindman, Wasik, & Snell, 2016). Regardless of the source, what goes in is what comes out: we can only learn words and grammatical structures that we hear (or see or read) in the language surrounding us.

non-solid substances, toddlers do better at learning the names for non-solids when seated in a high-chair—a context where they frequently encounter non-solid food items (Perry, Samuelson, & Burdinie, 2014).

There is also some evidence that parents may facilitate their children's word learning by maintaining spatial consistency with the objects they are labeling. For

BOX 6.3 | applications

iBABIES: TECHNOLOGY AND LANGUAGE LEARNING

When adults enter a new language culture, they often have access to many technological aids—from pocket dictionaries to smartphone apps for translations—to help them get around and ask for what they need. They can also harness technology to learn a new language, from online applications like Duolingo to commercial training programs like Rosetta Stone.

What about infants? They, too, are often immersed in technology. Indeed, recent years have seen a "brainy-baby" craze in which businesses earned hundreds of millions of dollars marketing all manner of electronic games, toys, and videos that claimed to enhance babies' intellectual growth. Some of these claims were laughable. For example, one of your authors purchased a teething ring for her baby and was astonished to read on the packaging that the ring supposedly improves an infant's language development by enhancing early oral-motor skills. Other claims seemed more plausible but were subsequently called into serious question by developmental research—so much so that the companies producing these products (e.g., "Baby Einstein") were forced to stop promoting their "educational" value.

However, there is still concern over technology marketed for children younger than 2 years because it reduces the time infants and toddlers spend actively engaged with caregivers and objects, their best source for learning. In one of the most rigorous

studies to date, DeLoache and colleagues (2010) used random assignment and an objective test of vocabulary to determine whether a best-selling "educational" DVD had an impact on language development. The DVD in question was marketed for infants at least 12 months old.

The researchers randomly assigned 12- to 18-month-olds into four groups. Infants in the *video-with-interaction* group watched the video with a parent 5 times a week over 4 weeks; the parent was asked to interact naturally with the infant while watching. Infants in the *video-without-interaction* group received the same amount of exposure, but without a parent watching along with them. This mimics a common situation at home, where parents might be in the same room but are engaged in another activity. Infants in the *parent-teaching group* did not watch the video at all. Instead, their parents were given a list of 25 words featured on the video and asked to teach the infants those words in whatever way felt most natural to them. Finally,

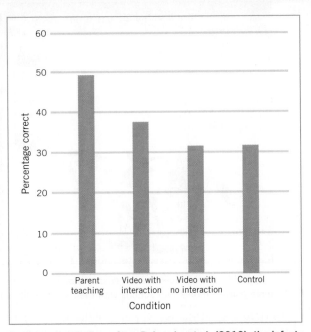

As shown in this figure from DeLoache et al. (2010), the infants who learned from parents (shown in the first column) performed best on the study's measure of word learning. Infants in the two video-learning conditions (middle two columns) did not perform significantly better than the control group (last column).

infants in the *control* group received no intervention, serving as a baseline for typical vocabulary development.

At the beginning and end of the study, the infants were tested on a subset of the words featured on the DVD. Infants in the DVD-viewing conditions were not significantly

---

instance, infants learn the names of objects more readily when the objects are in the same location each time they are labeled (Benitez & Smith, 2012; Samuelson et al., 2011). Presumably, consistency in the visual environment helps children map words onto objects and events in that environment. In Box 6.3, we discuss recent research focused on a currently popular means by which some parents try to "outsource" word learning: technology.

Children's contributions to word learning When confronted with words they haven't heard before, children actively exploit the context in which the new word was used in order to infer its meaning. A classic study by Carey and Bartlett (1978) demonstrated **fast mapping**—the process of rapidly learning a

fast mapping ■ the process of rapidly learning a new word simply from hearing the contrastive use of a familiar and the unfamiliar word

more advanced in vocabulary than infants in the control group. The infants who showed the greatest vocabulary development were the infants in the parent-teaching group. Interestingly, the performance of infants in the DVD-viewing conditions was unrelated to how much parents thought their infant had learned from the DVD. However, there was a correlation between how much the parents liked the DVD themselves and how much they thought their infant had learned: the more parents liked the DVD, the more likely they were to overestimate its positive effects.

While passive viewing does not appear to support learning, infants do seem able to learn when they can actively engage with another human, even if that human is present only on a screen. Several studies have found that when infants are given the opportunity to learn from live video interactions (Skype or FaceTime), they do better than when learning from prerecorded versions of the same interactions (e.g., Myers et al., 2016; O'Doherty et al., 2011; Roseberry, Hirsh-Pasek, & Golinkoff, 2014). The key difference appears to be that live video maintains social contingencies between the infant and the teacher in a way that recorded video does not. And indeed, the 2016 recommendations about screen time from the American Academy of Pediatrics note that live video chat is an acceptable use of technology for infants younger than 2 years of age (AAP Council on Communications and Media, 2016).

Questions about electronic media for infants are only going to increase, given the delight with which young children, and even infants, have embraced the apps on their parents'

smartphones, iPads, and tablets—indeed, Toddler/ Preschool is the most popular category of paid apps in the Apple App store. Although the number of educational apps intended for young children continues to grow, their effect on children's development remains largely unknown (Hirsh-Pasek, Zosh et al., 2015). As with any type of activity, a little here and there probably doesn't hurt. But it is important to approach any claims of "educational value" with a great deal of skepticism. Unfortunately, many companies that market their media as educational do not show appropriate levels of caution in their claims. To take one example, researchers recently tested a media product, "Your Baby Can Read," that purported to teach infants how to read using a kit, which included DVDs, flashcards, and word books (Neuman et al., 2014). Infants were randomly assigned to either the reading condition or a "business as usual" control group, with no intervention. After 7 months of daily training, the infants were tested on precursors to reading. No differences were found between the two groups, though some parents of the participants continued to believe that the program was effective.

Parents should also be aware that their activity choices may affect the amount they talk to their babies. One recent study

Whether they are educationally beneficial or not, it is clear that electronic media are of compelling fascination to infants.

FERNANDO VAZQUEZ MIRAS / GETTY IMAGES

compared the amount of IDS that parents engage in when using different types of toys: electronic toys, traditional toys, and books (Sosa, 2016). The results revealed that when parents played with electronic toys, they talked less and were also less responsive to their infants. Parents' own use of media devices while with their children may also impact language learning and other aspects of child development. As parents become more absorbed in their devices, they may miss opportunities to engage positively with their children; one study found that higher rates of parental absorption were related to more negative parent–child interactions (Radesky et al., 2014). In such cases, technology aimed at adults may actually hinder children's opportunities to learn from their caregivers.

new word simply from hearing the contrastive use of a familiar word and the unfamiliar word. In the course of everyday activities in a preschool classroom, an experimenter drew a child's attention to two trays—one red, the other an uncommon color the child would not know by name—and asked the child to get "the *chromium* tray, not the red one." The child was thus provided with a contrast between a familiar term (*red*) and an unfamiliar one (*chromium*). From this simple contrast, the participants inferred which tray they were supposed to get and that the name of the color of that tray was "chromium." After this single exposure to a novel word, about half the children showed some knowledge of it 1 week later by correctly picking out "chromium" from an array of paint chips.

Some theorists have proposed that the many inferences children make in the process of learning words are guided by a number of assumptions (sometimes referred to as principles, constraints, or biases) that limit the possible meanings children entertain for a new word. For example, children expect that a given entity will have only one name, an expectancy referred to as the *mutual exclusivity* assumption by Woodward and Markman (1998). Early evidence for this assumption came from a study in which 3-year-olds saw pairs of objects—a familiar object for which the children had a name and an unfamiliar one for which they had no name. When the experimenter said, "Show me the blicket," the children mapped the novel label to the novel object, the one for which they had no name (Markman & Wachtel, 1988). Even 16-month-old infants do the same (Graham, Poulin-Dubois, & Baker, 1998). (See Figure 6.8a.) Interestingly, bilingual and trilingual infants, who are accustomed to hearing more than one name for a given object, are less likely to follow the mutual exclusivity principle (Byers-Heinlein & Werker, 2009).

Markman and Woodward (Markman, 1989; Woodward & Markman, 1998) also proposed the *whole-object* assumption, according to which children expect a novel word to refer to a whole object rather than to a part, property, action, or other aspect of the object. Thus, in the case of Quine's rabbit problem (see page 256), the whole-object assumption leads children to map the label "bunny" to the whole animal, not just to its tail or the twitching of its nose.

When confronted with novel words, children also exploit a variety of **pragmatic cues** to their meaning by paying attention to the *social contexts* in which the words are used. For example, children use an adult's focus of attention as a cue to word meaning. In a study by Baldwin (1993), an experimenter showed 18-month-olds two novel objects and then concealed them in separate containers. Next, the experimenter peeked into one of the containers and commented, "There's a modi in here." The adult then removed and gave both objects to the child. When asked for the "modi," the children picked the object that the experimenter had been looking at when saying the label. Thus, the infants used the relation between eye gaze and labeling to learn a novel name for an object before they had ever seen it (see Figure 6.8b).

Another pragmatic cue that children use to draw inferences about a word's meaning is *intentionality* (Tomasello, 2008). For instance, in one study, 2-year-olds heard an experimenter announce, "Let's dax Mickey Mouse." The experimenter then performed two actions on a Mickey Mouse doll, one carried out in a coordinated and apparently intentional way, followed by a pleased comment ("There!"), and the other carried out in a clumsy and apparently accidental way, followed by an exclamation of surprise ("Oops!"). The children interpreted the novel verb *dax* as referring to the action the adult apparently intended to perform (Tomasello & Barton, 1994). Infants can even use an adult's emotional response to infer the name of a novel object that they cannot see (Tomasello, Strosberg, & Akhtar, 1996). In a study establishing this fact, an adult announced her intention to "find the gazzer." She then picked up one of two objects and showed obvious disappointment with it. When she gleefully seized the second object, the infants inferred that it was a "gazzer." (Figure 6.8c depicts another instance in which a child infers the name of an unseen object from an adult's emotional expression.)

The degree to which preschool children take a speaker's intention into account is shown by the fact that if an adult's labeling of an object conflicts with their

pragmatic cues ■ aspects of the social context used for word learning

FIGURE 6.8 Cues for word learning (a) Mutual exclusivity: Because this child already knows the name of the familiar object on the table, she will pick up the novel object when the adult asks her to "show me the blicket."

(b) Pragmatic cues: This child will assume that the novel word she hears the experimenter saying applies to the novel object the experimenter is looking at, even though the child cannot see the object and is looking at a different novel object when she actually hears the word.

(c–d) Pragmatic cues: This child will learn "gazzer" as the name of the novel object that the adult smiles at triumphantly after she had previously announced that she wanted to find "the gazzer."

knowledge of that object, they will nevertheless accept the label if the adult clearly used it intentionally (Jaswal, 2004). When an experimenter simply used the label "dog" in referring to a picture of a catlike animal, preschool children were reluctant to extend the label to other catlike stimuli. However, they were much more willing to do so when the experimenter made it clear that he really intended his use of the unexpected label by saying, "You're not going to believe this, but this is actually a dog." Similarly, if a child has heard an adult

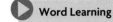

Word Learning

FIGURE 6.9 Linguistic context When Roger Brown, a pioneer in the study of language development, described a drawing like this as "sibbing," "a sib," or "some sib," preschool children made different assumptions about the meaning of "sib."

refer to a cat as "dog," the child will be reluctant to subsequently learn a new word used by that "untrustworthy" adult (e.g., Koenig & Harris, 2005; Koenig & Woodward, 2010; Sabbagh & Shafman, 2009).

Another way young children can infer the meaning of novel words is by taking cues from the *linguistic context* in which the words are used. In one of the first experiments on language acquisition, Roger Brown (1957) established that the grammatical form of a novel word influences children's interpretation of it. He showed preschool children a picture of a pair of hands kneading a mass of material in a container (Figure 6.9). The picture was described to one group of children as "sibbing," to another as "a sib," and to a third as "some sib." The children subsequently interpreted *sib* as referring to the action, the container, or the material, depending on which grammatical form (verb, count noun, or mass noun) of the word they had heard.

Two- and 3-year-old children also use the *grammatical category* of novel words to help interpret their meaning (e.g., Hall, 1994; Hall, Waxman, & Hurwitz, 1993; Markman & Hutchinson, 1984; Waxman, 1990). Hearing "This is a dax," they assume that *dax* refers to an object, as well as to other objects from the same category. In contrast, "This is a dax one" suggests that *dax* refers to a property of the object (e.g., its color or texture), while "This is dax" suggests that *dax* is a proper noun (a name). Even infants and toddlers can draw on some of these links to interpret the meaning of novel words (e.g., Booth & Waxman, 2009; Waxman & Hall, 1993; Waxman & Markow, 1995, 1998).

Children's interpretation of novel words applied to objects is particularly guided by the objects' shape, possibly because shape is a good cue to category membership. Children readily extend a novel noun to novel objects of the same shape, even when those objects differ dramatically in size, color, and texture (Graham & Poulin-Dubois, 1999; Landau, Smith, & Jones, 1988; L. B. Smith, Jones, & Landau, 1992). Thus, a child who hears a U-shaped wooden block called "a dax" will assume that *dax* also refers to a U-shaped object covered in blue fur or to

FIGURE 6.10 Shape bias In one of many studies of the shape bias, children were shown the exemplar at the top of this figure and told that it was a "dax" (or some other nonsense word). Then they were asked which of the objects below the exemplar was also a "dax." The numbers under the objects indicate the proportion of children who thought each object was a "dax." As you can see, they most often thought that the word referred to the object that was of the same shape as the exemplar, even if the surface texture or size was different. (Information from Landau, Smith, & Jones, 1988)

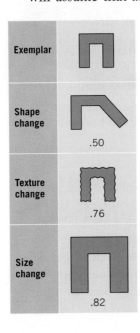

a U-shaped piece of red wire—but not to a wooden block of a different shape (Figure 6.10). A shape bias is also evident in young children's spontaneous extension of familiar words to novel objects that are vaguely similar to familiar entities (e.g., a cone might be referred to as a "mountain") (Samuelson & Smith, 2005). This attention to the shared shape of objects is evident in categorization tasks even before infants have acquired many productive words (Graham & Diesendruck, 2010).

Another potentially useful cue to word meaning is the repeated correspondence between words the child hears and objects the child observes in the world. Any single scene is ambiguous. For example, if the child sees four different novel objects together and hears the label "dax," the child has no way of knowing which object is the dax (this ambiguity is similar to that in Quine's "bunny" example described earlier). But across experiences, the child might observe that whenever "dax" is said, one of those four objects is always present, and thus that object is probably the dax. Through this process of *cross-situational word learning,* even infants can narrow down the possible meanings of new words (e.g., L. Smith & Yu, 2008; Vouloumanos & Werker, 2009).

Children also use the grammatical structure of whole sentences to figure out meaning—a strategy referred to as **syntactic bootstrapping** (Fisher, 1999; Fisher, Gleitman, & Gleitman, 1991; Gertner, Fisher, & Eisengart, 2006; Yuan & Fisher, 2009). An early demonstration of this phenomenon involved showing 2-year-olds a videotape of a duck using its left hand to push a rabbit down into a squatting position while both animals waved their right arms in circles (Figure 6.11) (Naigles, 1990). As they watched, some children were told "The duck is kradding the rabbit"; others were told "The rabbit and the duck are kradding." All the children then saw two videos side by side, one showing the duck pushing on the rabbit and the other showing both animals waving their arms in the air. Instructed to "Find kradding," the two groups looked at the event that matched the syntax they had heard while watching the initial video. Those who had heard the first sentence took "kradding" to mean what the duck had been doing to the rabbit, whereas those who had heard the second sentence thought it meant what both animals had been doing. Thus, the children had arrived at different interpretations for a novel verb based on the *structure* of the sentence in which it was embedded.

As you can see, infants and young children have a remarkable ability to learn new words as object names. Under some circumstances, they are also able to learn nonlinguistic "labels" for objects. Infants between 13 and 18 months of age map an experimenter's gestures or nonverbal sounds (e.g., squeaks and whistles) onto novel objects just as readily as they map words (Namy, 2001; Namy & Waxman, 1998; Woodward & Hoyne, 1999). By 20 to 26 months of age, however, they accept only words as names. And when novel labels are presented via computer rather than through interaction with an adult, even 12-month-olds accept only words as labels, not other nonverbal sounds (MacKenzie, Graham, & Curtin, 2011). Thus, infants learn quite early on that strings of phonemes are more likely to carry meaning than other types of sounds.

Infants also come to understand that some sounds are more relevant than others for identifying words in their language. For example, English-learning 14-month-olds are willing to believe that changing the pitch of a word alters its meaning (something that occurs in languages like Mandarin and Hmong, which use pitch differences in this way). But by 19 months of age, English-learning infants no longer treat pitch changes as cues to meaning changes—they come to understand that English doesn't use pitch as a cue to meaning (Hay et al., 2015). This development suggests a perceptual narrowing process similar to the one described earlier in this chapter for phoneme perception, and provides yet more evidence that children learn a remarkable amount about how their native language works over the course of their first two years.

Putting Words Together

A major landmark in early language development is achieved when children start combining words into sentences, an advance that enables them to express increasingly complex ideas. The degree to which children develop syntax, and the speed with which they do it, is what most distinguishes their language abilities from those of nonhuman primates.

FIGURE 6.11 **Syntactic bootstrapping** When children in Naigles's (1990) study heard an adult describe this filmed scene as "The duck is kradding the rabbit," they used the syntactic structure of the sentence to infer that kradding is what the duck is doing to the rabbit.

syntactic bootstrapping ■ the strategy of using the grammatical structure of whole sentences to figure out meaning

telegraphic speech ■ the term describing children's first sentences that are generally two-word utterances

First Sentences

Most children begin to combine words into simple sentences by the end of their 2nd year. However, in another example of comprehension preceding production, young children know something about word combinations well before they produce any. In one of the first demonstrations of infants' sensitivity to word order, Hirsh-Pasek and Golinkoff (1996) used a preferential-looking paradigm to investigate sentence comprehension. Seventeen-month-old infants viewed a pair of videotaped scenes presented simultaneously on two monitors—one showing Cookie Monster tickling Big Bird, and the other showing Big Bird tickling Cookie Monster. When they heard a sentence like "Where is Cookie Monster tickling Big Bird?" they looked preferentially at the appropriate scene, showing that they understood the meaning of the sentence even though they were months away from producing sentences themselves.

Children's first sentences are two-word combinations; their separate utterances of "More," "Juice," and "Drink" become "More juice" and "Drink juice." These two-word utterances have been described as **telegraphic speech** because, just as in telegrams (where senders paid by the word), nonessential elements are missing (Brown & Fraser, 1963). Consider the following examples of standard two-word utterances: "Read me," "Mommy tea," "Ride Daddy," "Hurt knee," "All wet," "More boy," "Key door," "Andrew sleep" (Braine, 1976). These primitive sentences lack a number of elements that would appear in adult utterances, including function words (such as *a, the, in*), auxiliary verbs (*is, was, will, be*), and word endings (indicating plurals, possessives, or verb tenses). Children's early sentences possess this telegraphic quality in languages as diverse as English, Finnish, Dholuo (Kenya), and Kaluli (Papua New Guinea) (de Boysson-Bardies, 1996/1999). For young children learning languages like English, in which word order is crucial for meaning, their early sentences follow a consistent word order: a child might say "Eat cookie" but would be unlikely ever to say "Cookie eat."

Many children continue to produce one- and two-word utterances for some time, whereas others quickly move on to sentences consisting of three or more words. Figure 6.12 shows the rapid increase in the mean length of utterances of three children in Roger Brown's (1973) classic study of language development. As you can see from the figure, Eve started her explosive increase in sentence length much earlier than the other two children did. The length of children's utterances increases in part because they begin to systematically incorporate some of the elements that were missing from their telegraphic speech.

FIGURE 6.12 Length of utterance This graph shows the relation between age and the mean length of utterance for the three children—Adam, Eve, and Sarah—studied by Roger Brown. (Data from Brown, 1973)

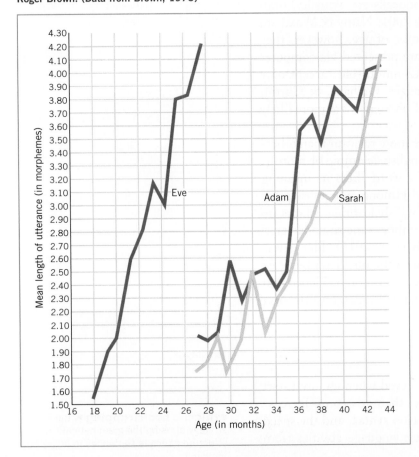

Grammar: A Tool for Building New Words and Sentences

As noted at the beginning of this chapter, human languages are *generative:* through the use of the finite set of words and morphemes in their native vocabulary, individuals can create an infinite number of sentences and express an infinite number of ideas. Each language has a particular set of rules (and exceptions) that governs how linguistic elements can be combined. The power of language derives from the mastery of these regularities, which allows individuals to produce and understand language beyond the specific words and sentences to which they have been exposed. How does this mastery come about, especially in the early years of life?

Much of the research on this topic has focused on morphemes that are added to nouns and verbs. In English, nouns are made plural by adding -*s*, and verbs are put into the past tense by adding -*ed*, with some notable exceptions (e.g., *men, went*). Young children recognize these formations and are able to generalize them to novel words. In a classic experiment by Jean Berko (1958), for example, preschoolers were shown a picture of a nonsense animal, which the experimenter referred to as "a wug." Then a picture of two of the creatures was produced, and the experimenter said, "Here are two of them; what are they?" (See Figure 6.13.) Children as young as 4 readily answered correctly: "Wugs." Since the children had never heard the word *wug* before, their ability to produce the correct plural form for this totally novel word demonstrated that they could generalize beyond the other plurals they had previously heard. The results of this study are taken as evidence that the participants understood how English pluralization works.

Evidence for generalization also comes from the way children treat irregular cases. Consider the plural of *man* and the past tense of *go*. Children initially use the correct irregular forms of these words, saying "men" for the plural of *man* and "went" for the past tense of *go*. However, they then start making occasional **overregularization** errors, in which they treat irregular forms as if they were regular. For instance, a child who previously said "men" and "went" may begin producing novel forms such as "mans" and "goed," as well as "foots," "feets," "breaked," "broked," and even "branged" and "walkeded" (Berko, 1958; Kuczaj, 1977; Xu & Pinker, 1995). Before eventually mastering irregular forms, children sometimes alternate between these overregularization errors and correct irregular forms (Marcus, 1996; 2004). The following dialogue between a 2½-year-old and his father illustrates this kind of error, as well as the difficulty of correcting it:

> *Child:* I used to wear diapers. When I growed up (*pause*)
> *Father:* When you grew up?
> *Child:* When I grewed up, I wore underpants.

(Clark, 1993)

Parents play a role in their children's grammatical development, although a more limited one than you might expect. Clearly, they provide a model of grammatically correct speech. In addition, they frequently fill in missing parts of their children's incomplete utterances, as when a parent responds to "No bed" by saying, "You really don't want to go to bed right now, do you?"

One might think that parents also contribute to their children's language development by correcting their grammatical errors. In fact, parents generally ignore even wildly ungrammatical mistakes, accepting sentences such as "I magicked it," "Me no want go," or "I want dessert in front of dinner" (Brown & Hanlon, 1970;

This is a Wug.

Now there is another one. There are two of them. There are two _____.

JEAN BERKO GLEASON

FIGURE 6.13 Evidence of learning morphology If a child responds to the final query with "Wugs," this is evidence that she understands how to create the English plural (by adding –*s* to the end of the word). The child must be generalizing from prior experience, since she has never heard "wugs" before. (Information from Berko, 1958)

overregularization ■ speech errors in which children treat irregular forms of words as if they were regular

Bryant & Polkosky, 2001). It would be hard to do otherwise, since so much of children's speech is like this. And, as the parent who tried to correct his son's use of "growed" discovered, such efforts are largely futile anyway. In general, parents are more likely to correct factual errors than grammatical errors.

Given this lack of correction, how do infants figure out the ways in which the syntax of their native language works? One approach to answering this question in the lab involves creating miniature languages—known as artificial grammars—and determining which types of linguistic patterns infants are able to learn. After just brief exposure, infants as young as 8 months can learn fairly complex patterns, generalizing beyond the specific items they have heard (e.g., Gerken, Wilson, & Lewis, 2005; Gómez, 2002; Lany & Saffran, 2010; Marcus et al., 1999; Saffran et al., 2008). For example, 8-month-old infants who have heard a list of three-word sequences in which the second word is repeated, such as "le di di, wi je je, de li li . . ." recognize the pattern when it is presented in new syllables, such as "ko ga ga" (Marcus et al., 1999).

Learning how to combine words to create interpretable sentences is the crowning achievement in language acquisition. Possibly no linguistic development is more stunning than the progress children make in a few years from simple two-word utterances to grammatically correct complex sentences. Even their errors reveal an increasingly sophisticated understanding of the structure of their native language. This accomplishment is made all the more impressive given the relative lack of parental feedback they receive.

Conversational Skills

Although young children are eager to participate in conversations with others, their conversational skills lag well behind their burgeoning language skills. For one thing, much of very young children's speech is directed to themselves, rather than to another person. And this is true not just in solitary play: as much as half of young children's speech in the company of other children or adults is addressed to themselves (Schober-Peterson & Johnson, 1991). Vygotsky (1934/1962) believed that this *private speech* of young children serves an important regulatory function: children talk to themselves as a strategy to organize their actions. Gradually, private speech is internalized as thought, and children become capable of mentally organizing their behavior, so they no longer need to talk out loud to themselves.

As noted in Chapter 4, when young children converse with other children, their conversations tend to be egocentric. Piaget (1923/1926) labeled young children's talk with their peers as **collective monologues.** Even when they take turns speaking, their conversations tend to be a series of non sequiturs, with the content of each child's turn having little or nothing to do with what the other child has just said. The following conversation between two preschoolers is a good example of what Piaget observed:

> *Jenny:* My bunny slippers . . . are brown and red and sort of yellow and white. And they have eyes and ears and these noses that wiggle sideways when they kiss.
> *Chris:* I have a piece of sugar in a red piece of paper. I'm gonna eat it but maybe it's for a horse.
> *Jenny:* We bought them. My mommy did. We couldn't find the old ones. These are like the old ones. They were not in the trunk.
> *Chris:* Can't eat the piece of sugar, not unless you take the paper off.

(Stone & Church, 1957, pp. 146–147)

collective monologue ■ conversation between children that involves a series of non sequiturs, the content of each child's turn having little or nothing to do with what the other child has just said

Gradually, children's capacity for sustained conversation increases. In a longitudinal study of parent–child conversations of four children, Bloom, Rocissano, and Hood (1976) found that the proportion of children's utterances that were on the same topic and added new information to what an adult had just said more than doubled (from around 20% to more than 40%) between the ages of 21 months and 36 months. In contrast, the proportion of utterances on unrelated topics fell dramatically (from around 20% to almost 0%) in the same time period.

A particular aspect of young children's conversations that changes dramatically in the preschool period is the extent to which they talk about the past. At most, 3-year-olds' conversations include occasional brief references to past events. In contrast, 5-year-olds produce **narratives**—descriptions of past events that have the form of a story (Miller & Sperry, 1988; K. Nelson, 1993). One thing that makes longer, more coherent narratives possible is better understanding of the basic structure of stories (Peterson & McCabe, 1988; Shapiro & Hudson, 1991; Stein, 1988).

Parents actively assist their children in developing the ability to produce coherent accounts of past events by providing what has been referred to as *scaffolding* (discussed in Chapter 4) for their children's narratives. An effective way to structure children's conversations about the past is to ask them elaborative questions, that is, questions that enable them to say something—anything—that advances the story. Consider this exchange between 27-month-old Harriet and her mother, wherein the mother is helping Harriet explain how she became sick at school by interpreting the child's words and drawing out details:

> *Harriet:* I got [*unintelligible*] my pants fall, fall down.
> *Mother:* You got wee-wees in your pants and you fell down. Is that what you
>   said? . . . Did Helen look after you when you were sick?
> *Harriet:* Yeah.
> *Mother:* . . . Did you fall asleep?
> *Harriet:* I can't close my eyes.

(McCabe & Peterson, 1991, p. 238)

The child in this conversation does not actually say much, but the parent's questions help the child think about the event, and the parent also provides a conversational model. Those toddlers whose parents scaffold their early conversations by asking useful, elaborative questions produce better narratives on their own a few years later (Fivush, 1991; McCabe & Peterson, 1991; Reese & Fivush, 1993).

A crucial aspect of becoming a good conversational partner is the *pragmatic development* that allows children to understand how language is used to communicate. Such understanding is essential with utterances that require listeners to go beyond the words they are hearing to grasp their actual meaning—as in instances of rhetorical questioning, sarcasm, irony, and the use of hyperbole or understatement to make a point. Children's pragmatic abilities develop over the course of the preschool years, facilitating communication with adults and peers. In particular, they learn to take the perspective of their conversational partner,

narratives ■ descriptions of past events that have the basic structure of a story

Parents typically help young children talk about past events. Such conversations contribute to early language development.

something that is clearly lacking in the example of the "conversation" between preschoolers Jenny and Chris, quoted earlier. Kindergarten-age listeners are able to make use of a conversational partner's perspective (e.g., by considering what information relevant to the conversation the partner does or doesn't have) to figure out what the partner means, and to provide a pertinent response (Nadig & Sedivy, 2002; Nilsen & Graham, 2009). They also learn to use information other than words to interpret meaning. For example, older preschoolers can exploit the vocal affect of an ambiguous statement to figure out a speaker's intention (Berman, Chambers, & Graham, 2010). When presented with two dolls—one intact, the other broken—and directed to "Look at the doll," 4-year-olds (but not 3-year-olds) looked at the intact doll when the instruction was given with positive affect, and at the broken doll when the instruction was given with negative affect.

The development of conversational perspective-taking ability is related to children's level of executive function; as children become more able to control their tendency to assume their own perspective, it becomes easier for them to take the perspective of a conversational partner. Several recent studies suggest that children's own experiences with language also influence their ability to take other people's perspective in communication settings. In tasks that require participants to take the experimenter's perspective, infants and young children who are monolingual perform worse than those who are bilingual—and also worse than those who, while not bilingual themselves, live in multilingual environments (Fan et al., 2015; Liberman et al., 2016). Living in a diverse linguistic environment may attune children to the challenges of communication—and the need to take others' perspective in order to effectively communicate—in a way that monolingual environments do not.

We thus see that young children put their burgeoning linguistic skills to good use, becoming more effective communicative partners. Initially, they need substantial support from a more competent partner, but their conversational skills increase quite regularly as other cognitive and social skills develop. Children's growing understanding of narrative structure and their emerging ability to take other people's perspectives are crucial components in the development of their conversational skills.

Later Development

Children continue to develop their language skills beyond the ages of 5 or 6 years, but because the foundational elements of language are typically in place by that point, this later development is less dramatic than in the early years of life. For example, the ability to sustain a conversation, which grew so dramatically in the preschool years, continues to improve into adulthood. School-age children become increasingly capable of reflecting upon and analyzing language, and they master more complex grammatical structures, such as the use of passive constructions.

One consequence of schoolchildren's more reflective language skills is their increasing appreciation of the multiple meanings of words, which is responsible for the emergence of the endless series of puns, riddles, and jokes with which they delight themselves and torture their parents (Ely & McCabe, 1994). They also are able to learn the meaning of new words simply from hearing them defined (Pressley, Levin, & McDaniel, 1987), a factor that helps their comprehension vocabulary expand—from the 10,000 words that the average 6-year-old knows to the 40,000 words estimated for 5th-graders (Anglin, 1993) to the average college-student vocabulary that has been estimated to be as high as 150,000 words (Miller & Gildea, 1987).

Review

Infants have remarkable speech-perception abilities and can exhibit categorical perception of speech sounds, perceiving physically similar sounds as belonging to discrete categories. Infants begin to babble at about 7 months of age, either repeating syllables ("bababa") or, if exposed to sign language, using repetitive hand movements. Gradually, vocal babbling begins to sound more like the baby's native language. By 6 months of age, infants begin to recognize highly familiar words, and during the second half of the 1st year, they are learning how to interact and communicate with other people. Children produce words at about 1 year of age, and in the space of a few years, they take giant steps in mastering the phonology, semantics, syntax, and pragmatics of their native language.

Theoretical Issues in Language Development

As you have seen throughout this chapter, there is ample evidence for both nature and nurture in the process of language development. The two key prerequisites for language acquisition are (1) a human brain and (2) experience with a human language. The former clearly falls on the side of nature, and the latter, on the side of nurture. Despite the obvious interaction between the two, the nature–nurture debate continues to rage fiercely in the area of language development. Why?

Chomsky and the Nativist View

The study of language development emerged from a theoretical debate about the processes through which language is acquired. In the 1950s, B. F. Skinner (1957) wrote a book entitled *Verbal Behavior,* in which he presented a behaviorist theory of language development. As you saw in Chapter 1, behaviorists believed that development is a function of learning through reinforcement and punishment of overt behavior. Skinner argued that parents teach children to speak by means of the same kinds of reinforcement techniques that are used to train animals to perform novel behaviors.

In what was probably the most influential science book review ever published, Noam Chomsky (1959) countered Skinner by pointing out some of the reasons why language cannot be learned through the processes of reinforcement and punishment. One key reason was noted earlier in this chapter: we can understand and produce sentences that we have never heard before (generativity). If language-learning proceeds by means of reinforcement and punishment, how could we know that a sentence like "Colorless green ideas sleep furiously" is a grammatical English sentence, whereas "Green sleep colorless furiously ideas" is not (Chomsky, 1957)? Similarly, how could children produce words they have never heard before, like *wented* or *mouses*? The explanation of such instances must be that we know details about the structure of our native language that we have

According to language theorist Noam Chomsky, all these children rely on the same innate linguistic structures in acquiring their various languages.

not been taught—facts that are unobservable and thus impossible to reinforce—contrary to Skinner's proposal.

In his own explanation of language development, Chomsky proposed that humans are born with a **Universal Grammar,** a hard-wired set of principles and rules that govern grammar in all languages. Chomsky's account, which has been central to the development of the modern discipline of linguistics, is consistent with the fact that, despite many surface differences, the underlying structures of the world's languages are fundamentally similar. His strongly nativist account also provides an explanation for why most children learn language with exceptional rapidity, while nonhumans (who presumably lack a Universal Grammar) do not. (The Universal Grammar hypothesis has been highly relevant to investigations of emerging languages like the Nicaraguan Sign Language discussed in Box 6.4, a language in which children are creating new grammatical structures.)

Universal Grammar ■ a proposed set of highly abstract, unconscious rules that are common to all languages

Ongoing Debates in Language Development

Current theories all acknowledge some of Chomsky's crucial observations. For example, any account of language development must be able to explain why all human languages share so many characteristics. Theories must also explain how it is that language users, from infants to adults, are able to generalize beyond the specific words and sentences they have been exposed to. But the ways in which various accounts handle these facts differ along two key dimensions. The first dimension is the degree to which these explanations lie within the child (*nature*) versus within the environment (*nurture*). The second dimension pertains to the child's contributions: Did the cognitive and neural mechanisms underlying language learning evolve solely to support language learning (*domain specific*), or are they used for learning many different kinds of things (*domain general*)?

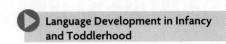

Language Development in Infancy and Toddlerhood

With respect to the first dimension, theorists have countered Chomsky's argument about the universality of language structure by pointing out that there are also universals in children's environments. Parents all over the world need to communicate about certain things with their children, and these things are likely to be reflected in the language that children learn. For example, recall Table 6.1, which shows the remarkable overlap in the earliest words acquired across three diverse cultures (Tardif et al., 2008). These similarities reflect what parents want to talk about with their infants, and what infants want to communicate about.

Indeed, accounts focused on social interaction maintain that virtually everything about language development is influenced by its communicative function. Children are motivated to interact with others, to communicate their own thoughts and feelings, and to understand what other people are trying to communicate to them (Bloom, 1991; Bloom & Tinker, 2001; Snow, 1999). According to this position, children gradually discover the underlying regularities in language and its use by paying close attention to the multitude of clues available in the language they hear, the social context in which language is used, and the intentions of the speaker (e.g., Tomasello, 2008). Some of these conventions may be learned by the same kinds of reinforcement methods originally proposed by Skinner. For example, Goldstein and colleagues have found that both the sounds infants make when babbling and the rate at which they produce them can be influenced by parental reinforcement, such as smiling and touching in response to the babbling (Goldstein, King, & West, 2003; Goldstein & Schwade, 2008). Whether these types of social behaviors can influence less overt aspects of language development, such as the acquisition of syntax, remains unclear.

What of the second dimension—the domain specificity of the processes underlying language acquisition? According to the strongly nativist view espoused by Chomsky, the cognitive abilities that support language development are highly specific to language. As Steven Pinker (1994) describes it, language is "a distinct piece of the biological makeup of our brains . . . distinct from more general abilities to process information or behave intelligently" (p. 18). This claim is taken one step further by the **modularity hypothesis,** which proposes that the human brain contains an innate, self-contained language module that is separate from other aspects of cognitive functioning (Fodor, 1983). The idea of specialized mental modules is not limited to language. As you will see in Chapter 7, innate, special-purpose modules have been proposed to underlie a variety of functions, including perception, spatial skills, and social understanding.

An alternative view suggests that the learning mechanisms underlying language development are actually quite general. Although these learning abilities might

modularity hypothesis ■ the idea that the human brain contains an innate, self-contained language module that is separate from other aspects of cognitive functioning

BOX 6.4 | a closer look

"I JUST CAN'T TALK WITHOUT MY HANDS": WHAT GESTURES TELL US ABOUT LANGUAGE

People around the world spontaneously accompany their speech with gestures. The naturalness of gesturing is revealed by the fact that blind people gesture as they speak just as much as sighted individuals do, even when they know their listener is also blind (Iverson & Goldin-Meadow, 1998).

Gesturing starts early: infants often produce recognizable, meaningful gestures before they speak recognizable words. According to Acredolo and Goodwyn (1990), many "baby signs" are invented by children themselves. One child in their research signed "alligator" by putting her hands together and opening and closing them to imitate snapping jaws; another indicated "dog" by sticking her tongue out as if panting; another signaled "flower" by sniffing. Infants gain earlier motor control of their hands than of their vocal apparatus, facilitating the use of signs during the 1st year.

Interestingly, there is a relationship between early gesturing and later vocabulary (M. L. Rowe, Ozcaliskan, & Goldin-Meadow, 2008). The more children gestured at 14 months, the larger their spoken vocabulary was at 42 months. Moreover, differences

> ▶ **Research on Infant Gestures from Linda Acredolo and Susan Goodwyn**

in the amount of gesturing by high- and low-SES families are one factor that influences the SES effects discussed in Box 6.2 (M. L. Rowe & Goldin-Meadow, 2009).

Especially dramatic evidence of intimate connections between gesture and language comes from remarkable research on children who have *created* their own gesture-based languages. Goldin-Meadow and colleagues studied congenitally deaf American and Chinese children whose hearing parents had little or no proficiency in any formal sign language (Feldman, Goldin-Meadow, & Gleitman, 1978; Goldin-Meadow, 2003; Goldin-Meadow & Mylander, 1998). These children and their parents created "home signs" in order to communicate with one another, and the children's gesture vocabulary quickly outstripped that of their parents.

More important, the children (but not the parents) *spontaneously* imposed a structure—a rudimentary grammar—on their gestures. Both groups of children used a grammatical structure that occurs in some languages but not those of their parents. As a result, the sign systems of the children were more similar to one another than

to those of their own parents. The children's signs were also more complex than those of their parents. A similar phenomenon occurs when deaf children are learning to sign from parents who themselves learned a conventional sign language, like ASL, but whose

SUSAN GOODWYN

This young participant in the research of Acredolo and Goodwyn is producing her idiosyncratic "baby sign" for pig.

be innate, their evolutionary development was not restricted to language learning. For example, researchers have demonstrated that the distributional learning mechanisms discussed earlier in this chapter also help infants track sequences of musical notes, visual shapes, and human actions (e.g., Fiser & Aslin, 2001; Kirkham, Slemmer, & Johnson, 2002; Roseberry et al., 2011; Saffran et al., 1999). Similarly, the fast-mapping mechanisms that support rapid word learning are also used by toddlers to learn facts about objects (Markson & Bloom, 1997). Also relevant is the fact that the "less is more" hypothesis for the critical period for language development, discussed earlier in this chapter, is not tied specifically to language (Newport, 1990). The ability to extract small chunks of information is likely useful in other domains as well, such as music, which also consists of small pieces (notes, chords) organized into higher-level structures (melody, harmony).

signing is ungrammatical (usually because they learned to sign later in life). In such cases, deaf children have been reported to *spontaneously* impose structure that is more consistent than the signs that their parents produce (Singleton & Newport, 2004).

The most extensive and extraordinary example of language creation by children comes from the invention of Nicaraguan Sign Language (NSL), a completely new language that has been evolving over the past 35 years. In 1979, a large-scale education program for the deaf began in Nicaragua (Senghas & Coppola, 2001). The program brought hundreds of deaf children together in two schools in the city of Managua. For most of the children, it was their first exposure to other deaf people.

The teachers in the schools knew no formal sign language, nor did the children, who had only the simple home signs they had used to communicate with their families. The children quickly began to build on one another's existing informal signs, constructing a "pidgin" sign language—a relatively crude, limited communication system. The language was used by the students, both in and outside school, and was learned by each new group of children who entered the community.

What happened next was astonishing. As younger students entered the schools, they rapidly mastered the rudimentary system used by the older students and then gradually transformed it into a complex, fully consistent language (NSL) with its own grammar. The most fluent signers in the NSL community are currently the youngest children, both because NSL has evolved

Nicaraguan deaf children signing together in the language that has emerged in their school community.

into a real language and because they acquired it at an earlier age.

Another emerging sign language was discovered in the Negev desert of Israel (Sandler et al., 2005). The Al-Sayyid Bedouin Sign Language (ABSL) is in its third generation and is about 75 years old. Unlike NSL, ABSL is acquired from birth, because deaf children in this community typically have at least one deaf adult in their extended family. The grammatical structure of ABSL does not resemble those of the local spoken languages (Arabic and Hebrew).

These reports of language invention by deaf children are not just fascinating stories: they provide evidence for the child's contribution to language learning. Over several generations, children have been taking improvised signing that is simple and inconsistent and transforming it into structures much closer to those observed in established languages. Whether this process reflects the operation of a Chomsky-style Universal Grammar or the operation of more general learning mechanisms remains unknown. Regardless, the discovery that children go beyond the linguistic input they receive, spontaneously refining and systematizing these emerging languages, is one of the most fascinating findings in the field of language development.

Finally, recent theories concerning developmental language disorders (discussed in Box 6.5) invoke aspects of general cognitive function, not just language.

As in other areas of child development, computational modeling has played an important role in the development of modern theoretical perspectives. By using computational models, researchers can specify both the innate structure and the environmental input to a computerized learner and attempt to determine what is crucial when simulating children's language acquisition. One influential perspective oriented around computational modeling is **connectionism,** a type of information-processing theory that emphasizes the simultaneous activity of numerous interconnected processing units. Connectionist researchers have developed computer simulations of various aspects of cognitive development, including language acquisition (e.g., Elman et al., 1996). The software learns from

connectionism ■ a type of information-processing approach that emphasizes the simultaneous activity of numerous interconnected processing units

BOX 6.5 | individual differences

DEVELOPMENTAL LANGUAGE DISORDERS

Throughout this chapter, we have emphasized both what is similar and what diverges across children and across cultures over the course of language development. The most significant individual differences fall under the category of developmental language disorders. These range from delays that often disappear by school age to lifelong challenges.

Language disorders are common relative to some of the other disorders described throughout this book. In 2012, roughly 10% of children in the United States between 3 and 8 years of age had received services for speech or language problems in the prior year (Hoffman et al., 2014). However, this number likely underestimates the prevalence of language disorders, because they are often not diagnosed until a child enters school. Of this group, many of the children are considered *late talkers.* This label is applied to toddlers who are developing typically in other domains but whose vocabulary development is lagging at or below the 10th percentile.

Some of these children are so-called late bloomers who will go on to have normal or near-normal language skills. Late-talking toddlers with better word recognition skills, as indexed by the eye-movement tasks described earlier in this chapter, are the most likely to catch up (Fernald & Marchman, 2012). Children who fail to catch up—roughly 7% of school-age children in the United States—are diagnosed with *specific language impairment* (SLI). These children exhibit challenges in many language-related tasks, including speech perception, word segmentation, and grammatical comprehension (e.g., Evans, Saffran, & Robe-Torres, 2009; Fonteneau & van der Lely, 2008; Rice, 2004; Ziegler et al., 2005). They may also exhibit more general challenges in working memory, sequence learning, and processing speed (e.g., Leonard et al., 2007; Tomblin, Mainela-Arnold, & Zhang, 2007).

Children diagnosed with genetically-transmitted developmental disorders, including Down syndrome, fragile-X syndrome, or autism spectrum disorders (ASD), tend to be significantly delayed across all aspects of language development, including both language production and comprehension. Indeed, challenges in communication are one of the diagnostic criteria for ASD. For children with ASD, early language abilities are predictive of later outcomes, including response to treatment (e.g., Stone & Yoder, 2001; Szatmari et al., 2003). Interestingly, younger siblings of children with ASD, who themselves are at greater risk for ASD, have a higher rate of language delay than do their peers (Gamliel et al., 2009). In one large longitudinal study of 12-month-old infants, some of whom were at heightened risk for ASD, infants with lower vocabulary scores (both receptive and expressive) were more likely to later be diagnosed with ASD (Lazenby et al., 2016). Note, however, that not all genetically transmitted developmental disorders have language problems as their hallmark. Children with Williams syndrome, discussed in Box 3.1, show markedly less impairment in language than in other aspects of cognition. They also tend to be very interested in music and other auditory stimuli, and as infants they are able to track the statistical properties of speech in the same manner as typically developing infants (Cashon et al., 2016).

Another group of children who may develop language disorders are deaf children. As noted earlier, if these children have early exposure to a natural sign language like ASL, they will follow a typical language development trajectory. However, 90% of deaf children are born to hearing parents, and many of these children do not have access to sign language. In the absence of hearing, it is very difficult to learn a spoken language. An increasingly popular intervention for profoundly deaf infants, children, and adults is the use of cochlear implants (CIs), surgically implanted devices that translate auditory input into electrical stimulation of the auditory nerve. The signal that CIs provide is quite degraded relative to typical acoustic hearing. Nevertheless, many deaf infants and children are able to learn spoken language with the help of CIs, though the level of success varies widely across individuals. Consistent with other critical-period findings, implantation at a young age is better than at later ages (e.g., Houston & Miyamoto, 2010; Leigh et al., 2013). Even at the outset of learning, though, deaf infants and toddlers who perceive speech through CIs are less accurate and slower to recognize words than are their hearing peers (Grieco-Calub, Saffran, & Litovsky, 2009). Providing these learners with bilingual input (natural sign language and spoken language through CIs) may offer the most successful route to language acquisition.

Cochlear implants are a surgically implanted device used by some deaf and hearing-impaired individuals.

AMELIE-BENOIST / BSIP / THE IMAGE WORKS

experience, gradually strengthening certain connections among units in ways that mimic children's developmental progress. Connectionist accounts have achieved impressive success with respect to modeling specific aspects of language development, including children's acquisition of the past tense in English and the development of the shape bias for word learning (e.g., Rumelhart & McClelland, 1986; Samuelson, 2002). However, connectionist models are always open to criticism regarding the features that were built into the models in the first place (e.g., do they have the same "innate" constraints as infants?) and how well the input provided to them matches the input received by real children.

Review

The current theoretical accounts of language development differ with respect to how much emphasis they put on nature and nurture. Nativists like Chomsky emphasize innate linguistic knowledge and language-specific learning mechanisms, whereas other theorists argue that language learning can emerge from general-purpose learning mechanisms. Children's motivation to understand and interact with other people is also central to many theories. The vast literature on language development provides some support for all of these views, but none of them provide the full story of children's acquisition of this vastly complex and arguably most unique of all human abilities.

Nonlinguistic Symbols and Development

Although language is our preeminent symbol system, humans have invented a wealth of other kinds of symbols to communicate with one another. Virtually anything can serve as a symbol so long as someone intends it to stand for something other than itself. The list of symbols you regularly encounter is long and varied, ranging from the printed words, numbers, graphs, photographs, and drawings in your textbooks to thousands of everyday items such as application icons, maps, and clocks. Because symbols are so central to everyday life, mastering the symbol systems important in their culture is a crucial developmental task for all children.

Symbolic proficiency involves both the mastery of the symbolic creations of others and the creation of new symbolic representations. We will first discuss early symbolic functioning, starting with research on very young children's ability to exploit the informational content of symbolic artifacts. Then we will focus on children's creation of symbols through drawing and writing. In Chapter 7, we will consider children's creation of symbolic relations in pretend play, and in Chapter 8, we will examine older children's development of two of the most important of all symbolic activities—reading and mathematics.

Using Symbols as Information

One of the vital functions of many symbols is that they provide useful information. For example, a map—whether a crude pencil sketch on a scrap of paper or a Google map on your smartphone—can be crucial for locating a particular place. To use a symbolic artifact such as a map requires **dual representation;** that is, the artifact must be represented mentally in two ways at the same time, as a real object and as a symbol for something other than itself (DeLoache, 2002, 2004).

Very young children have substantial difficulty with dual representation, limiting their ability to use information from symbolic artifacts. This has been demonstrated by research in which a young child watches as an experimenter hides a miniature

dual representation ■ the idea that a symbolic artifact must be represented mentally in two ways at the same time—both as a real object and as a symbol for something other than itself

ALL: COURTESY OF JUDY DeLOACHE

FIGURE 6.14 Scale-model task In a test of young children's ability to use a symbol as a source of information, a 3-year-old child watches as the experimenter (Judy DeLoache) hides a miniature troll doll under a pillow in a scale model of an adjacent room. The child searches successfully for a larger troll doll hidden in the corresponding place in the actual room, indicating that she appreciates the relation between the model and room. The child also successfully retrieves the small toy she originally observed being hidden in the model.

toy in a scale model of the regular-sized room next door (Figure 6.14) (DeLoache, 1987). The child is then asked to find a larger version of the toy that the child is told "is hiding in the same place in the big room." Typical 3-year-olds readily use their knowledge of the location of the miniature toy in the model to figure out where the large toy is in the adjacent room. In contrast, most 2½-year-old children fail to find the large toy; they seem to have no idea that the model tells them anything about the full-size room. Because the model is so salient and interesting as a three-dimensional object, very young children have trouble managing dual representation and fail to notice the symbolic relation between the model and the room it stands for.

This interpretation received strong support in a study with 2½-year-old children in which reasoning between a model and a larger space was not necessary (DeLoache, Miller, & Rosengren, 1997). An experimenter showed each child a "shrinking machine" (really an oscilloscope with lots of dials and lights) and explained that the machine could "make things get little." The child watched as a troll doll was hidden in a movable tentlike room (approximately 8 feet by 6 feet) and the shrinking machine was "turned on." Then the child and experimenter waited in another room while the shrinking machine did its job. When they returned, a small-scale model of the tentlike room stood in place of the original. (Assistants had, of course, removed the original tent and replaced it with the scale model.) When asked to find the troll, the children succeeded.

Why should the idea of a shrinking machine enable these 2½-year-olds to perform the task? The answer is that if a child believes the experimenter's claims about the shrinking machine, then in the child's mind the model simply *is* the room. Hence, there is no symbolic relation between the two spaces and no need for dual representation.

The difficulty that young children have with dual representation and symbols is evident in other contexts as well. For example, consider the use of manipulatives in mathematics education: concrete objects, like small blocks or beads, used to represent magnitudes. The goal of using manipulatives to teach math is to help children better understand the relationships among quantities and operations, providing a concrete anchor for abstract concepts. However, educators often overlook the fact that manipulatives are themselves symbols and, as such, are vulnerable to the issues of dual representation described above: manipulatives are objects in their own right that are also serving to represent something else (e.g., Uttal et al., 2009). Therefore, the use of concrete objects as symbols for abstract concepts may not always be effective, especially when the manipulatives are very salient (engaging shapes such as animals).

Another example where symbolic representations may lead to challenges comes from forensic psychology. Investigators often use anatomically detailed dolls to interview young children in cases of suspected sexual abuse, assuming that the relation between the doll and themselves would be obvious. However, children younger than 5 years often fail to make any connection between themselves and the doll, so the use of a doll does not improve their memory reports and may even make them less reliable (e.g., DeLoache & Marzolf, 1995). Research suggests that young children have particular difficulty with self-symbols—symbols intended to represent themselves—even when the symbols are made to be as large as the child (Herold & Akhtar, 2014). For this reason, current practice in child forensics discourages the use of interview props with young children and focuses instead on building rapport, asking open-ended questions, and potentially encouraging children to draw as a way to comfort themselves during stressful interviews (e.g., Johnson et al., 2016; Katz, Barnetz, & Hershkowitz, 2014).

Increasing ability to achieve dual representation—to immediately interpret a symbol in terms of what it stands for—enables children to discover the abstract nature of various symbolic artifacts. For example, unlike younger children, school-age children realize that the red line on a road map does not mean that the real road would be red (Liben & Myers, 2007). This developing ability is affected by children's experiences with symbols. Cross-cultural studies reveal that in cultures where pictures are ubiquitous, as in North America, younger children are more likely to understand that pictures can serve a symbolic function than in cultures where children are rarely exposed to pictures, like India and Peru (Callaghan, Rochat, & Corbit, 2012).

Indeed, the advances in picture perception that we discussed in Box 5.2 provide evidence for early forms of symbolic understanding. For instance, North American infants as young as 13 months of age understand that properties of objects presented in pictures can be extended to real objects (Keates, Graham, & Ganea, 2014). These findings suggest that even at this early age, infants are able to detect links between images of objects and actual objects. By age 4, children interpret images of scenes using the same geometric abilities that guide their navigation in the real world (Dillon & Spelke, 2015). Thus, with experience comes the ability to engage in the kinds of abstractions necessary to understand dual representations like maps and mathematical manipulatives.

Drawing and Writing

Creating pictures and letters is a common symbolic activity encouraged by parents in many societies (Goodnow, 1977). When young children first start making marks on paper, their focus is almost exclusively on the activity per se, with no attempt to produce recognizable images. At about 3 or 4 years of age, most children begin trying to draw pictures *of* something; they try to produce representational art (Callaghan, 1999). Exposure to representational symbols affects the age at which children begin to produce them. One cross-cultural study (Callaghan et al., 2011) found that children from homes filled with pictorial images (a Canadian sample) produce such images earlier and more often than children from homes with few such images (Indian and Peruvian samples).

Initially, children's artistic impulses outstrip their motor and planning capabilities (Yamagata, 1997). Figure 6.15 shows what at first appears simply to be a classic scribble. However, the 2½-year-old creator of this picture was narrating his efforts as he drew, making it possible to ascertain his artistic intentions. While he represented the individual elements of his picture reasonably well, he was unable to coordinate them spatially.

The most common drawing subject for young children is the human figure (Goodnow, 1977). Just as infants who are first beginning to speak simplify the words they produce, young children simplify their drawings, as shown in Figure 6.16. Note that to produce these very simple, crude shapes, the child must plan the drawing

FIGURE 6.15 Early drawing Appearances to the contrary, this is not random scribbling, as shown by what the 2½-year-old who produced it said about his work. As he drew a roughly triangular shape, he said it was a "sailboat." A set of wavy lines was labeled "water." Some scribbled lines under the "sailboat" were denoted as the "person driving the boat." Finally, the wild scribbles all over the rest were "a storm." Thus, each element was representational to some degree, even though the picture as a whole did not appear as such.

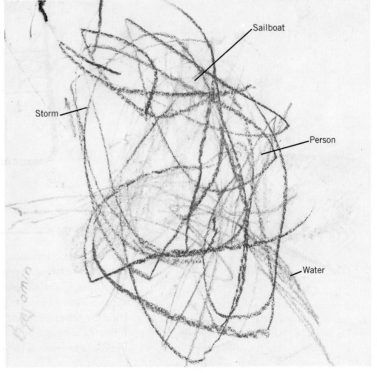

FIGURE 6.16 Tadpole drawings Young children's early drawings of people typically take a "tadpole" form.

and must spatially coordinate the individual elements. Even early "tadpole" people have the legs on the bottom and the arms on the side—although often emerging from the head.

Figure 6.17 reveals some of the strategies children use to produce more complex pictures. The drawing depicts the route from the artist's home to the local grocery store, with several houses along the way. One strategy the child used was to rely on a well-practiced formula for representing houses: a rectangle with a door and a roofline. Another was to coordinate the placement of each house with respect to the road, although at the cost of the overall coordination among the houses. Eventually, some children become highly skilled at representing the relations among the multiple elements in their pictures.

Children's scribbles also reflect their emerging understanding of writing. Even in their earliest scribbles, before age 3, children produce different types of scribbles when writing versus drawing (D. Rowe, 2008). This finding is also true for preschoolers growing up with writing systems with characters that more closely resemble drawings, as in the Chinese system (Treiman & Yin, 2011). By age 4, children understand a key difference between writing and drawing, namely that written words correspond to specific spoken words, whereas a drawing can correspond to many different words (Treiman et al., 2016). As with the development of dual representation described earlier, children initially depend on perceptual similarity between the symbol and what it is intended to represent; for example, longer words may be "written" with longer scribbles (e.g., Uttal & Yuan, 2014).

FIGURE 6.17 More complex drawings This child's drawing relies on some well-practiced strategies, but the child has not yet worked out how to represent complex spatial relationships.

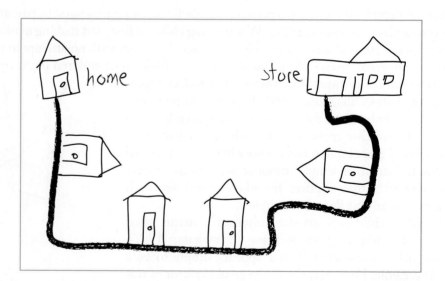

Review

Nonlinguistic symbols play an important role in the lives of young children. As they become increasingly sensitive to the informational potential of symbolic objects created by others, children take an important step toward skillful use of the many symbol systems that are key to modern life. A critical factor in understanding and using the symbols created by others is dual representation—the ability to mentally represent both a symbolic object, such as a map or model, and its relation to what it stands for. The ability to *create* symbols is evident in young children's drawings and early attempts at writing.

CHAPTER SUMMARY

A critical feature of what it means to be human is the creative and flexible use of one or more of a variety of languages and other symbols. The enormous power of language comes from generativity—the fact that a finite set of words can be used to generate an infinite number of sentences.

Language Development

- Acquiring a language involves learning the complex systems of phonology, semantics, syntax, and pragmatics that govern its sounds, meaning, grammar, and use.

- Language ability is species-specific. The first prerequisite for its full-fledged development is a human brain. Researchers have succeeded in teaching nonhuman animals remarkable symbolic skills but not full-fledged language.

- The early years constitute a critical period for language acquisition; many aspects of language are more difficult to acquire thereafter.

- A second prerequisite for language development is exposure to language. Much of the language babies hear takes the form of infant-directed speech (IDS), which is characterized by a higher-than-normal pitch; extreme shifts in intonation; a warm, affectionate tone; and exaggerated facial expressions.

The Process of Language Acquisition

- Infants have remarkable speech-perception abilities. Like adults, they exhibit categorical perception of speech sounds, perceiving physically similar sounds as belonging to discrete categories.

- Young infants are actually better than adults at discriminating between speech sounds not in their native language. As they learn the sounds that are important in their language(s), infants' ability to distinguish between sounds in other languages declines.

- Infants are remarkably sensitive to the distributional properties of language; they notice a variety of subtle regularities in the speech they hear and use these regularities to segment words from fluent speech.

- Infants begin to babble at around 7 months of age, either repeating syllables ("bababa") or, if exposed to sign language, using repetitive hand movements. Gradually, vocal babbling begins to sound more like the baby's native language.

- During the second half of the 1st year, infants are learning how to interact and communicate with other people, including developing the ability to establish joint attention.

- Infants begin to recognize highly familiar words at about 6 months of age.

- Infants begin to produce words at about 1 year of age. They initially say just one word at a time and often make overextension errors, using a particular word in a broader context than is appropriate. Infants make use of a variety of strategies to figure out what new words mean.

- By the end of their 2nd year, most toddlers produce short sentences. The length and complexity of their utterances gradually increase, and toddlers spontaneously practice their emerging linguistic skills.

- In the early preschool years, children exhibit generalization, extending such patterns as "add–s to make plural" to novel nouns, and making overregularization errors.

- Children develop their burgeoning language skills as they go from collective monologues to sustained conversation, improving their abilities to tell coherent narratives about their experiences and to listen and respond to and converse with others.

Theoretical Issues in Language Development

- All current theories of language development agree that there is an interaction between innate factors and experience.

- Nativists, such as the influential linguist Noam Chomsky, posit innate knowledge of Universal Grammar, the set of highly abstract rules common to all languages. They believe that language learning is supported by language-specific skills.

- Theorists focused on social interaction emphasize the communicative context of language development and use. They emphasize the impressive degree to which infants and young children exploit a host of pragmatic cues to figure out what others are saying.

- Other perspectives argue that language can develop in the absence of innate knowledge and that language learning requires powerful general-purpose cognitive mechanisms. Connectionist models have been used to support this view.

Nonlinguistic Symbols and Development

- Symbolic artifacts like maps or models require dual representation. To use them, children must represent mentally both the object itself as well as its symbolic relation to what it stands for. Toddlers become increasingly skillful at achieving dual representation and using symbolic artifacts as a source of information.

- Drawing and writing are popular symbolic activities. Young children's early scribbling quickly gives way to the intention to draw pictures *of* something, with a favorite theme being representations of the human figure. Early attempts at writing, while illegible, contain some characteristics of mature writing systems.

Test Yourself

1. The first step in children's language learning is mastery of the sound system of their native language. This concept is known as _____ development.
   a. pragmatic
   b. phonological
   c. semantic
   d. syntactic

2. The smallest units of meaning in a language, such as the English words *dog* or *mom*, are called _____ .
   a. morphemes
   b. syntactic patterns
   c. phonemes
   d. semantics

3. A deeper understanding of the cultural contexts of language—including shifts in tone and body language, which allow two strangers who speak the same language to successfully communicate—is known as _____ development.
   a. semantic
   b. syntactic
   c. pragmatic
   d. phonological

4. Between 6 and 12 months of age, infants typically experience a linguistic perceptual narrowing. What effect does this change have on their language development?
   a. They become increasingly more sensitive to non-native speech sounds.
   b. They focus more on the words they hear most frequently.
   c. They become increasingly less sensitive to non-native speech sounds.
   d. Their ability to distinguish between speech and other environmental sounds diminishes.

5. Emily is given two pictures: one shows a flower, a word she already knows, and the other shows a unicorn, which is new to her. When asked to point to the "unicorn," Emily points to the unknown image, which is of a unicorn. Which assumption is Emily making in order to learn this new word?
   a. social contexts
   b. intentionality
   c. mutual exclusivity
   d. grammatical categorization

6. Which of the following statements is *not* true of infant-directed speech (IDS)?
   a. The exaggerated tone and pitch of IDS is often accompanied by exaggerated facial expressions.
   b. Infants tend to prefer infant-directed speech to adult-directed speech.
   c. Evidence suggests that IDS is a universal practice across all cultures.
   d. Infant brains show greater activity when exposed to infant-directed speech than when exposed to adult-directed speech.

7. In order to actually learn and use words, infants must first learn to associate words with specific meanings. This concept is referred to as _____ .
   a. reference
   b. prosody
   c. categorical perception
   d. syntactic bootstrapping

8. Thirteen-month-old Christian calls all men "Dad." This is an example of _____ .
   a. pragmatic learning
   b. syntactic bootstrapping
   c. mapping
   d. overextension

9. Stella uses the word "food" to indicate that she wants to eat. Her tendency to use a single word to communicate an entire phrase suggests that Stella is in which phase of language development?
   a. holophrastic period
   b. critical period
   c. babbling phase
   d. semantic phase

10. Two-year-old Ravi goes to the zoo with his mother. Even though he has never heard of a giraffe or seen one before, when his mother points to an animal and calls it a "giraffe," Ravi then calls that animal a giraffe. This exchange demonstrates Ravi's use of _____ .
    a. pragmatic cues
    b. phonemes
    c. language mixing
    d. telegraphic speech

11. Using the structure of a sentence to derive the meaning of a novel word is known as _____ .
    a. telegraphic speech
    b. Universal Grammar
    c. syntactic bootstrapping
    d. semantic development

12. Preschoolers Ahmed and Max are talking together. Ahmed says that his father is old. Max says that he likes cars. Ahmed says that his father is probably more than 10 years old. Max says that he likes blue cars the best. According to Piaget, Ahmed and Max are engaging in _____ .
    a. babbling
    b. private speech
    c. dual representation
    d. collective monologues

13. Chomsky's proposition that humans are born with an understanding of the basic principles and rules that govern all language is known as _____ .
    a. holophrastic theory
    b. the behavior theory of language development
    c. Universal Grammar
    d. the modularity hypothesis

14. *Dual representation* refers to one's ability to
    a. communicate both verbally and nonverbally.
    b. understand a symbolic artifact as both a real object and as a symbol for something else.
    c. understand that a single word may have more than one meaning.
    d. distinguish between the words that someone uses and the intention behind those words.

15. The idea that the human brain contains innate and self-contained modules used for specific cognitive functions, such as language, is known as _____ .
    a. the modularity hypothesis
    b. the behavioral theory of language development
    c. connectionism
    d. symbol theory

LaunchPad
macmillan learning

Don't stop now! Research shows that testing yourself is a powerful learning tool. Visit LaunchPad to access the LearningCurve adaptive quizzing system, which gives you a personalized study plan to help build your mastery of the chapter material through videos, activities, and more. **Go to launchpadworks.com.**

Critical Thinking Questions

1. Drawing on the many references to parental behaviors relevant to language development that were discussed in this chapter, give some examples of how parents are known to influence their children's language development.

2. Language development is a particularly complex aspect of child development, and no single theory successfully accounts for all that is known about how children acquire language. Would you weight the child's contributions (nature) or the environment's contributions (nurture) more strongly?

3. What are overregularization errors, and why do they offer strong evidence for the acquisition of grammatical structures by children?

4. Many parallels were drawn between the process of language acquisition in children learning spoken language and in those learning sign language. What do these similarities tell us about the basis for human language?

Key Terms

babbling, p. 254

bilingualism, p. 246

categorical perception, p. 249

collective monologues, p. 270

comprehension, p. 241

connectionism, p. 277

critical period for language, p. 244

distributional properties, p. 253

dual representation, p. 279

fast mapping, p. 262

generativity, p. 241

holophrastic period, p. 258

infant-directed speech (IDS), p. 247

modularity hypothesis, p. 275

morphemes, p. 241

narratives, p. 271

overextension, p. 258

overregularization, p. 269

phonemes, p. 241

phonological development, p. 241

pragmatic cues, p. 264

pragmatic development, p. 242

production, p. 241

prosody, p. 249

reference, p. 256

semantic development, p. 241

symbols, p. 240

syntactic bootstrapping, p. 267

syntactic development, p. 242

syntax, p. 242

telegraphic speech, p. 268

Universal Grammar, p. 274

voice onset time (VOT), p. 249

word segmentation, p. 252

▶ Student Video Activities

Research of Janet Werker on Infant Speech Perception

Word Learning

Language Development in Early Childhood

Language Development in Infancy and Toddlerhood

Research on Infant Gestures from Linda Acredolo and Susan Goodwyn

Answers to Test Yourself

1. b, **2.** a, **3.** c, **4.** c, **5.** c, **6.** c, **7.** a, **8.** d, **9.** a, **10.** a, **11.** c, **12.** d, **13.** c, **14.** b, **15.** a

JOHN GEORGE BROWN (1813–1913), *The Little Joker* (oil on canvas)

Conceptual Development

Themes

- Nature and Nurture
- The Active Child
- Mechanisms of Change
- The Sociocultural Context

concepts ■ general ideas or understandings that can be used to group together objects, events, qualities, or abstractions that are similar in some way

Shawna, an 8-month-old, crawls into her 7-year-old brother's bedroom. The room contains many objects, among them a bed, a dresser, a dog, a baseball, a baseball mitt, books, magazines, shoes, and dirty socks. To her older brother, the room includes furniture, clothing, reading material, and sports equipment. But what does the room look like to Shawna?

Infants lack concepts of furniture, reading material, and sports equipment. They also lack more specific concepts such as baseball mitts and books. Thus, Shawna does not understand the scene in the same way her older brother does. However, without knowledge of child development research, an observer would not know whether a baby as young as Shawna has formed other concepts relevant to understanding the scene. Has she formed concepts of living and nonliving things that help her understand why the dog runs around but the books never do? Has she formed concepts of heavier and lighter that allow her to understand why she could pick up a sock but not a dresser? Has she formed concepts of before and after that allow her to understand that her brother always puts on his socks before his shoes rather than in the opposite order? Or is it all a jumble?

As this imaginary scene indicates, concepts are crucial for helping people make sense of the world. But what exactly are concepts, and how do they help us understand the world?

Concepts are general ideas that organize objects, events, qualities, or relations on the basis of some similarity. There are infinite possible concepts because there are infinite ways in which objects or events can be similar. For example, objects can have similar shapes (all football fields are rectangular), materials (all diamonds are made of compressed carbon), sizes (all skyscrapers are tall), tastes (all lemons are sour), colors (all colas are brown), functions (all knives are for cutting), and so on.

Concepts help us understand the world and act effectively in it by allowing us to generalize from prior experience. If we like the taste of one carrot, we probably will like the taste of others. Concepts also tell us how to react emotionally to new experiences, as when we fear all dogs after being bitten by one. Life without concepts would be unthinkable: every situation would be new, and we would have no idea what past experience would be relevant in a new situation.

Several themes have been especially prominent in research on conceptual development. One is *nature and nurture:* children's concepts reflect the interaction between their specific experiences and their biological predispositions to process information in particular ways. Another recurring theme is the *active child:* from infancy onward, many of children's concepts reflect their active attempts to make sense of the world. A third major theme is *how change occurs:* researchers who study conceptual development attempt to understand not only what concepts children form but also the processes by which they form them. A fourth is the *sociocultural context:* the concepts we form are influenced by the society in which we live.

Although there is widespread agreement that conceptual development reflects the interaction of nature and nurture, the particulars of this interaction are hotly debated. The controversy parallels the nativist/empiricist controversies described previously in the context of theories of cognitive development (Chapter 4), perceptual development (Chapter 5), and language development (Chapter 6). In the context of conceptual development, nativists, such as Liz Spelke (2011), Alan Leslie (Scholl & Leslie, 2001), and Karen Wynn

What does this infant see when he looks at this room?

CAVAN IMAGES / GETTY IMAGES

(2008), believe that innate understanding of basic concepts plays a central role in development. They argue that infants are born with some sense of fundamental concepts, such as time, space, number, causality, and the human mind, or with specialized learning mechanisms that allow them to acquire rudimentary understanding of these concepts unusually quickly and easily. Within the nativist perspective, nurture plays an important role in helping children move beyond this initial level of conceptual understanding, but not in forming the basic understanding.

By contrast, empiricists, such as Vladimir Sloutsky (2010), Scott Johnson (2010), David Rakison (Rakison & Lupyan, 2008), Lisa Oakes (Baumgartner & Oakes, 2013), and Marianella Casasola (2008), argue that nature endows infants with only general learning mechanisms, such as the ability to perceive, attend, associate, generalize, and remember. Within the empiricist perspective, the rapid and universal formation of fundamental concepts such as time, space, number, causality, and mind arises from infants' massive exposure to experiences that are relevant to these concepts. Empiricists also maintain that the data on which many nativist arguments are based—such as data involving infants' looking times in habituation studies—are not sufficient to support the nativists' conclusions that infants understand the concepts in question (J. J. Campos et al., 2008; Kagan, 2008). The continuing debate between nativists and empiricists reflects a fundamental, unresolved question about human nature: Do children form all concepts through the same learning mechanisms, or do they also possess special mechanisms for forming a few particularly important concepts?

This chapter focuses on the development of fundamental concepts—those that are useful in the greatest number of situations. These concepts fall into two groups. One group of fundamental concepts is used to categorize the kinds of things that exist in the world: human beings, living things in general, and inanimate objects. The other group of fundamental concepts involves dimensions used to represent our experiences: space (where the experience occurred), time (when it occurred), number (how many times it occurred), and causality (why it occurred).

You may have noticed that these fundamental concepts correspond closely to the questions that every news story should answer: Who or what? Where? When? Why? How? The similarity between the concepts that are most fundamental for children and those that are most important in news stories is no accident. Knowing who or what, where, when, how many, and why is essential for understanding any event.

Because early conceptual development is so crucial, this chapter focuses on development in the first 5 years. This does not mean that conceptual growth ends at age 5. Beyond this age, children form vast numbers of more specialized concepts, and their understanding of all types of concepts deepens for many years thereafter. Rather, the focus here on early conceptual development reflects the fact that this is the period in which children acquire a basic understanding of the most crucial concepts—those that are universal, that allow children to understand their own and other people's experiences, and that provide the foundations for subsequent conceptual growth.

Understanding Who or What

How can infants make sense of the innumerable objects they encounter? What they seem to do is adopt a kind of divide-and-conquer strategy, in which they quickly divide the objects into three general categories: inanimate objects, people, and other animals (they are unsure for many years whether plants are more like

category hierarchy ■ a category that is organized by set–subset relations, such as animal/dog/poodle

animals or more like inanimate objects) (S. Gelman & Kalish, 2006). It is no coincidence that these categories are similar to those that are prominent in perceptual development (Chapter 5); children's perceptual systems influence the concepts they form, and the concepts influence how they perceive the world.

Dividing Objects into Categories

Forming these broad divisions is crucial, because different types of concepts apply to different types of objects (Keil, 1979). Some concepts apply to anything—all things, living and nonliving, have height, weight, color, size, texture, and so on. Other concepts apply only to living things—only living things eat, drink, grow, and breathe, for example. Yet other concepts, such as reading, shopping, pondering, and chatting, apply only to people. Forming these general categories of objects allows children to draw accurate inferences about unfamiliar entities. For instance, when told that a platypus is a kind of animal, children know immediately that a platypus can move, eat, grow, reproduce, and so on.

In addition to dividing objects into these very general categories, children form immense numbers of more specific categories: cars, tools, furniture, baseball mitts, and endless others. Children tend to organize these categories of objects into **category hierarchies**—that is, categories organized according to set–subset relations. These category hierarchies help them make finer distinctions among the objects within each level. The furniture/chair/La-Z-Boy hierarchy shown in Table 7.1 is one example. The category "furniture" includes all chairs; the category "chair" includes all La-Z-Boys. Forming such category hierarchies greatly simplifies the world for children by allowing them to draw accurate inferences. Knowing that a La-Z-Boy is a kind of chair allows children to use their general knowledge of chairs to infer that people sit on La-Z-Boys and that La-Z-Boys are neither lazy nor boys.

Of course, infants are not born knowing about La-Z-Boys and chairs, nor are they born knowing the other categories shown in Table 7.1. How do infants and older children form categories that apply to all kinds of objects, living and nonliving?

Categorization of Objects in Infancy

Even in the first months of life, infants form categories of objects. P. C. Quinn and Eimas (1996), for example, found that when 3- and 4-month-olds were shown a series of photographs of very different breeds of cats, they habituated; that is, they looked at new cat photographs for less and less time. However, when

TABLE 7.1

Category Hierarchies

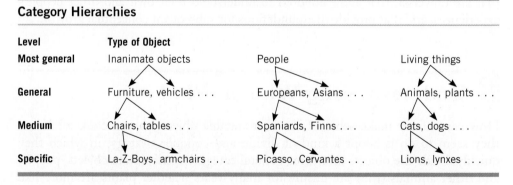

Level	Type of Object		
Most general	Inanimate objects	People	Living things
General	Furniture, vehicles . . .	Europeans, Asians . . .	Animals, plants . . .
Medium	Chairs, tables . . .	Spaniards, Finns . . .	Cats, dogs . . .
Specific	La-Z-Boys, armchairs . . .	Picasso, Cervantes . . .	Lions, lynxes . . .

the infants were subsequently shown a picture of a dog, lion, or other animal, they dishabituated; that is, their looking time increased. Their habituation to the cat photographs suggests that the infants saw all the cats, despite their differences, as members of a single category; their subsequent dishabituation to the photo of the dog or other kind of animal suggests that the infants saw those creatures as members of categories other than cats.

Infants can also form categories more general than "cats." Behl-Chadha (1996) found that 6-month-olds habituated after repeatedly being shown pictures of different types of mammals (dogs, zebras, elephants, and so forth) and then dishabituated when they were shown a picture of a bird or a fish. The infants apparently perceived similarities among the mammals that led to their eventually losing interest in them. The infants also apparently perceived differences between the mammals and the bird or fish that led them to show renewed interest.

As suggested by this example, infants frequently use **perceptual categorization,** the grouping together of objects that have similar appearances (L. B. Cohen & Cashon, 2006; Madole & Oakes, 1999). Prior to participating in the Behl-Chadha (1996) study, few infants would have seen zebras or elephants. Thus, the distinctions the infants made between these mammals and the birds and fish could only have been based on perception of the animals' differing appearances.

Infants categorize objects along many perceptual dimensions, including color, size, and movement. Often their categorization is largely based on specific parts of an object rather than on the object as a whole; for example, infants younger than 18 months rely heavily on the presence of legs to categorize objects as animals, and they rely heavily on the presence of wheels to categorize objects as vehicles (Rakison & Lupyan, 2008; Rakison & Poulin-Dubois, 2001).

During their 2nd year, children increasingly categorize objects on the basis of overall shape. As discussed in Chapter 6, when toddlers are shown an unfamiliar object and told that it is a "dax," they assume that other objects of the same shape are also "daxes," even when the objects differ from each other in size, texture, and color (Landau, Smith, & Jones, 1998). This is a useful assumption, because for many objects, shape indeed is similar for different members of a category. If we see a silhouette of a cat, hammer, or chair, we can tell from the shape what the object is. However, we rarely can do the same if we know only the object's color or size or texture.

Categorization of Objects Beyond Infancy

As children move beyond infancy, they increasingly grasp not only individual categories but also hierarchical and causal relations among categories.

Category hierarchies The category hierarchies that young children form often include three of the levels in Table 7.1: the general one, which is called the **superordinate level;** the very specific one, called the **subordinate level;** and the medium or in-between one, called the **basic level** (Rosch et al., 1976). As its name suggests, the basic level is the one that children usually learn first. Thus, they typically form categories of medium generality, such as "tree," before they form more general categories such as "plant" or more specific ones such as "oak."

It is not surprising that children tend to form basic-level categories first. A basic-level category such as "tree" has a number of consistent characteristics: bark, branches, large size, and so on. In contrast, the more general category "plant" has fewer consistent characteristics: plants come in a wide range of shapes, sizes, and

perceptual categorization ■ the grouping together of objects that have similar appearances

superordinate level ■ the general level within a category hierarchy, such as "animal" in the animal/dog/poodle example

subordinate level ■ the most specific level within a category hierarchy, such as "poodle" in the animal/dog/poodle example

basic level ■ the middle level, and often the first level learned, within a category hierarchy, such as "dog" in the animal/dog/poodle example

colors (consider an oak, a rose, and a house plant). Subordinate-level categories have the same consistent characteristics as the basic-level category, and some additional ones—all oaks, but not all trees, have rough bark and pointed leaves, for example. However, it is relatively difficult to discriminate among different subordinate categories within the same basic-level category (oaks versus maples, for example).

Very young children's basic categories do not always match those of adults. For example, rather than forming separate categories of cars, motorcycles, and buses, young children seem to group these objects together into a category of "objects with wheels" (Mandler & McDonough, 1998). Even in such cases, however, the initial categories are less general than such categories as "moving things" and more general than ones such as "Toyotas."

Having formed basic-level categories, how do children go on to form superordinate and subordinate categories? Part of the answer is that parents and others use the child's basic-level categories as a foundation for explaining the more specific and more general categories (S. Gelman et al., 1998). When parents teach children superordinate categories such as furniture, they typically illustrate properties of the relevant terms with basic-level examples that the child already knows (Callanan, 1990). They might say, "Furniture includes things, like chairs, tables, and sofas that people have inside their houses and that make living there more comfortable."

Parents also refer to basic-level categories to teach children subordinate-level terms (Callanan & Sabbagh, 2004; Waxman & Senghas, 1992). For example, a parent might say, "Belugas are a kind of whale." Preschoolers are sensitive to the nuances of such statements; for example, they generalize more widely from categorical statements such as "Belugas are a kind of whale" than from statements about specific objects, such as "This beluga is a whale" (Cimpian & Scott, 2012). Thus, statements that specify relations among categories of objects allow children to use what they already know about basic-level categories to form superordinate- and subordinate-level categories.

Although parents' explanations clearly enhance children's conceptual understanding, the learning path sometimes involves amusing detours. In one such case, Susan Gelman (2003) gave her 2-year-old son a spoon and a container filled with bite-size pieces of fruit and said, "This is a fruit cup." The boy responded to her description by picking up the "cup" and attempting to drink the fruit in it.

Causal understanding and categorization Toddlers and preschoolers are notorious for their endless questions about causes and reasons. "Why do dogs bark?" "How does the iPhone know where to call?" "Where does rain come from?" Parents are often exasperated by such questions, but respecting and answering children in an informative way can help them learn (Chouinard, 2007).

Understanding causal relations is crucial in forming many categories. How could children form the category of "light switches," for example, if they did not understand that flipping or pushing certain objects causes lights to go on and off? To study how an understanding of causes and effects influences category formation, Krascum and Andrews (1998) told 4- and 5-year-olds about two categories of imaginary animals: wugs and gillies. Some of the preschoolers were provided only physical descriptions of the animals: they were told that wugs usually have claws on their feet, spikes on the end of their tails, horns on their heads, and armor on their backs; gillies were described as usually having wings, big ears, long tails, and long toes. Other children were provided the same physical descriptions, plus a simple causal story that explained why wugs and gillies are the way they are.

These children were told that wugs have claws, spikes, horns, and armor because they like to fight. Gillies, in contrast, do not like to fight; instead, they hide in trees. Their big ears let them hear approaching wugs, their wings let them fly away to treetops, and so on. After the children in both groups were given the information about these animals, they were shown the pictures in Figure 7.1 and asked which animal was a wug and which animal was a gilly.

The children who were told why wugs and gillies have the physical features they do were better at classifying the pictures into the appropriate categories. When tested the next day, those children also remembered the categories better than did the children who were given the physical descriptions without explanations. Thus, understanding cause–effect relations helps children learn and remember.

"Wug"　　　"Gilly"

FIGURE 7.1 Cause–effect relations Hearing that wugs are well prepared to fight and gillies prefer to flee helped preschoolers categorize novel pictures like these as wugs or gillies (Krascum & Andrews, 1998). In general, understanding cause–effect relations helps people of all ages learn and remember.

Knowledge of Other People and Oneself

Although understanding of oneself and others varies greatly from individual to individual, just about everybody has a commonsense level of psychological understanding. This **naïve psychology** is crucial to normal human functioning and is a major part of what makes us people. Adult chimpanzees are the equal of human 2½-year-olds on a wide range of tasks that require physical reasoning, such as how to use tools to obtain food, but they fall far short of the toddlers on tasks requiring social reasoning, such as inferring intentions from behavior (Herrmann et al., 2007; Tomasello, 2008).

At the center of naïve psychology are three concepts that we all use to understand human behavior: desires, beliefs, and actions (Gopnik & Wellman, 2012). We apply these concepts almost every time we think about why someone did something. For example, why did Jimmy go to Billy's house? He *wanted* to play with Billy (a desire), and he *expected* that Billy would be at home (a belief), so he *went* to Billy's house (an action). Why did Jenny turn the TV to Channel 5 at 8:00 A.M. on Saturday? She was *interested in* watching *SpongeBob Squarepants* (a desire) and she *thought* the program was on Channel 5 at 8 in the morning (a belief), so she *selected* that channel at that time (an action).

Three properties of naïve psychological concepts are noteworthy. First, many of them refer to invisible mental states. No one can see a desire or a belief or other psychological concepts such as a perception or a memory. We, of course, can see behaviors related to invisible psychological concepts, such as Jimmy's ringing Billy's doorbell, but we can only infer the underlying mental state, such as Jimmy's desire to see Billy. Second, psychological concepts are linked to one another in cause–effect relations. Jimmy, for instance, might become angry if Billy isn't home because he went to a different friend's house, which could later cause Jimmy to be mean to his younger brother. The third noteworthy property of these naïve psychological concepts is that they develop surprisingly early in life.

Sharp disagreements have arisen between nativists and empiricists regarding the source of this early psychological understanding. Nativists (e.g., Leslie, 2000) argue that the early understanding is possible only because children are born with a basic understanding of human psychology. By contrast, empiricists (e.g., Frye et al., 1996; Ruffman, Slade, & Crowe, 2002) argue that experiences with other

naïve psychology ■ a commonsense level of understanding of other people and oneself

THE FAMILY CIRCUS   By Bil Keane

"Mommy, how much grape juice would be bad for the rug?"

Indirect ways of breaking bad news are a specialty of young children and reflect their understanding that other people's reactions might not be the same as their own.

people and general information-processing capacities are the key sources of the early understanding of other people. There is evidence to support each view.

Naïve Psychology

As we saw in Chapter 5, infants find people interesting, pay careful attention to them, and learn an impressive amount about them in the 1st year. Even very young infants prefer to look at people's faces rather than at other objects. Infants also imitate people's facial movements, such as sticking out their tongue, but they do not imitate the motions of inanimate objects. And it is not just faces that interest infants; they also prefer to watch human bodies moving instead of other displays with equal amounts of movement (Bertenthal, 1993).

This early interest in human faces and bodies helps infants learn about people's behavior. Imitating other people and forming emotional bonds with them encourages the other people to interact more with the infants, creating additional opportunities for the infants to acquire psychological understanding.

As noted earlier, several important aspects of psychological understanding emerge late in the 1st year and early in the 2nd: (1) understanding of intention, the desire to act in a certain way; (2) a sense of self, in which children realize that they are individuals distinct from other people; (3) joint attention, in which two or more people focus intentionally on the same referent; and (4) intersubjectivity, the mutual understanding that people share during communication (Chapter 4).

One-year-olds' understanding of other people also includes some understanding of their emotions. Consider Michael, a 15-month-old who

> is struggling with his friend Paul over a toy. Paul starts to cry. Michael appears concerned and lets go of the toy, so Paul has it. Paul continues crying. . . . Michael pauses again, runs to the next room, gets Paul's security blanket, and gives it to him. Paul stops crying.
>
> (Hoffman, 1976, pp. 129–130)

Although interpreting anecdotes is always tricky, it seems likely that Michael understood that giving Paul something that he liked might make him feel better (or at least stop his crying). Michael's leaving the room, getting Paul's security blanket, and bringing it back to him suggests that Michael had the further insight that Paul's blanket might be useful for soothing his hurt feelings. This interpretation is consistent with a variety of evidence suggesting that 1-year-olds fairly often offer both physical comfort (hugs, kisses, pats) and comforting comments ("You be okay") to unhappy playmates. Presumably, infants' experience of their own emotions and the behaviors that soothe them allows the infants to understand others' emotions and the behaviors that might soothe them (Harris, 2006).

Theory of Mind

▶ Theory of Mind

In the toddler and preschool periods, children build on their early-emerging psychological understanding to develop an increasingly sophisticated comprehension of themselves and other people and to interact with others in increasingly complex ways. One area of especially impressive development is understanding other people's minds.

theory of mind ▪ an organized understanding of how mental processes such as intentions, desires, beliefs, perceptions, and emotions influence behavior

The growth of a theory of mind Infants' and preschoolers' naïve psychology, together with their strong interest in other people, provides the foundation for a **theory of mind,** an organized understanding of how mental processes such as intentions, desires, beliefs, perceptions, and emotions influence behavior. Preschoolers' theory of mind includes, for example, knowledge that beliefs often originate in perceptions, such as seeing an event or hearing someone describe it; that desires can originate either from physiological states, such as hunger or pain, or from psychological states, such as wanting to see a friend; and that desires and beliefs produce actions (S. A. Miller, 2012).

One important component of such a theory of mind—understanding the connection between other people's desires and their actions—emerges by the end of the 1st year. In a study by Phillips, Wellman, and Spelke (2002), 12-month-olds saw an experimenter look at one of two stuffed kittens and say in a joyful voice, "Ooh, look at the kitty!" Then a screen descended, and when it was raised 2 seconds later, the experimenter was holding either the kitty that she had just gushed over or the other one. The 12-month-olds looked longer when the experimenter was holding the other kitty, suggesting that they expected the experimenter to want to hold the kitty that had excited her so much and were surprised that she was holding the other one. In contrast, when presented the same experience, 8-month-olds looked for similar amounts of time regardless of which kitty the experimenter held, suggesting that the understanding that people's desires guide their actions develops toward the end of the 1st year (Phillips et al., 2002). Consistent with this conclusion, 10-month-olds can use information about a person's earlier desires to predict that person's later desires, but only if the earlier and later circumstances are virtually identical (J. Sommerville & Crane, 2009).

The understanding that desires lead to actions is firmly established by age 2 years. Children of this age, for instance, predict that characters in stories will act in accord with their own desires, even when those desires differ from the child's preferences (Gopnik & Slaughter, 1991; Lillard & Flavell, 1992). Thus, if 2-year-olds who would rather play with trucks than with dolls are told that a character in a story would rather play with dolls than with trucks, they predict that, given the choice, the character in the story will choose in accord with the character's own preference, rather than the child's preference.

By age 3 years, children show some understanding of the relation between beliefs and actions. For example, they answer questions such as "Why is Billy looking for his dog?" by referring to beliefs ("He thinks the dog ran away") as well as to desires ("He wants it") (Bartsch & Wellman, 1995). Most 3-year-olds also have some knowledge of how beliefs originate. They know, for example, that seeing an event produces beliefs about it, whereas simply being next to someone who sees the event does not (Pillow, 1988).

At the same time, 3-year-olds' understanding of the relation between people's beliefs and their actions is limited in important ways. These limitations are evident when children are presented with **false-belief problems,** in which another person believes something to be true that the child knows is false. The question is whether the child thinks that the other person will act in accord with his or her own false belief or in accord with the child's correct understanding of the situation. Studying such situations reveals whether children understand that other people's actions are determined by the contents of their own minds rather than by the objective truth of the situation.

In one widely studied false-belief problem, preschoolers are shown a box that has on it a picture of a type of candy called Smarties (Figure 7.2); such boxes ordinarily have Smarties inside them. The experimenter then asks the preschoolers what is inside the box. Logically enough, they say "Smarties." Next, the experimenter opens the box, revealing that it actually contains pencils. Most 5-year-olds

FIGURE 7.2 Testing children's theory of mind The Smarties task is frequently used to study preschoolers' understanding of false beliefs. Most 3-year-olds answer the way the child in this cartoon does, which suggests a lack of understanding that people's actions are based on their own beliefs, even when those beliefs deviate from what the child knows to be true.

false-belief problems ■ tasks that test a child's understanding that other people will act in accord with their own beliefs even when the child knows that those beliefs are incorrect

SUPERSTOCK

Despite leading very different lives, Pygmy children in Africa and same-age peers in industrialized North American and European societies respond to the false-belief task in the same way.

laugh or smile and admit their surprise. When asked what another child would say if shown the closed box and asked to guess its contents, they say the child would answer "Smarties," just as they had. Not 3-year-olds! A large majority of them claim they always knew what was in the box, and they predict that if another child were shown the box, that child would also believe that the box contained pencils (Gopnik & Astington, 1988). The 3-year-olds' responses show they have difficulty understanding that other people act on their own beliefs, even when those beliefs are false, and that other people do not necessarily know what the child knows.

This finding is extremely robust. A review of 178 studies of children's understanding of false beliefs showed that similar results emerged with different forms of the problem, different questions, and different societies (Wellman, Cross, & Watson, 2001). In one noteworthy cross-cultural study, false-belief problems were presented to children attending preschools in Canada, India, Peru, Thailand, and Samoa (Callaghan et al., 2005). Performance improved greatly between ages 3 and 5 years in all five societies; averaged across them, accuracy increased from 14% correct for 3-year-olds to 85% correct for 5-year-olds. Especially striking was the consistency of performance across these very different societies: in no country did 3-year-olds answer more than 25% of problems correctly, and in no country did 5-year-olds answer less than 72% correctly.

Although 3-year-olds generally err on false-belief problems when the problems are presented in the standard way, many children of this age succeed if the task is presented in a manner that facilitates understanding. For example, if an experimenter tells a 3-year-old that the two of them are going to play a trick on another child by hiding pencils in a Smarties box and enlists the child's help in filling the box with pencils, most 3-year-olds correctly predict that the other child will say that the box contains Smarties (K. Sullivan & Winner, 1993). Presumably, assuming the role of deceiver by hiding the pencils in the candy box helps 3-year-olds see the situation from the other child's perspective. Nonetheless, it is striking just how difficult 3-year-olds find standard false-belief problems. To date, no set of conditions has enabled the majority of 3-year-olds to consistently solve standard false-belief questions correctly, though repeated exposure to carefully designed experiences have produced substantial improvements among 3-year-olds who had relatively advanced understanding before the experiences (Rhodes & Wellman, 2013).

Children's theories of mind continue to develop far beyond this early period, with at least some of the development dependent on specific experiences. For example, 14-year-olds who gained experience acting in plays over the course of a school year showed greater understanding of other people's thinking at the end of the year than before their acting experience (T. R. Goldstein & Winner, 2011). In contrast, peers who received other types of arts education (music or visual arts) for the same period did not show comparable improvements in understanding other people's thinking.

Explaining the development of theory of mind People's lives clearly would be very different without a reasonably sophisticated theory of mind. However, the findings on the improvement in a typical child's theory of mind between ages 3 and 5 do not tell us what causes the improvement. This question has generated enormous controversy, and currently there is great disagreement about how to answer it.

Investigators who take a nativist position have proposed the existence of a **theory of mind module (TOMM),** a hypothesized brain mechanism devoted to understanding other human beings (Baron-Cohen, 1995; Leslie, 2000). Advocates of this position argue that among typical children exposed to a typical environment, the TOMM matures over the first 5 years, producing an increasingly sophisticated understanding of people's minds. These investigators cite evidence from brain-imaging studies showing that certain areas of the brain are consistently active in representing beliefs across different tasks, and that the areas are different from those involved in other complex cognitive processes, such as understanding grammar (R. Saxe & Powell, 2006).

Studies of children with autism spectrum disorders (ASD) also are often cited to support the idea of the TOMM. As discussed in Box 7.1, these children have great difficulty with false-belief problems, as well as with understanding people more generally.

theory of mind module (TOMM) ■ a hypothesized brain mechanism devoted to understanding other human beings

BOX 7.1 | individual differences

CHILDREN WITH AUTISM SPECTRUM DISORDERS (ASD)

Although most children readily handle false-belief problems by the age of 5 years, one group continues to find them very difficult even when they are teenagers: children with autism spectrum disorders (ASD). As discussed in Chapter 3, this syndrome, which strikes roughly 1 in 100 children in the United States, most of them male (Centers for Disease Control and Prevention, Autism and Developmental Disabilities Monitoring Network, 2012), involves difficulties in social interaction, communication, and other intellectual and emotional functions.

Children with the most serious forms of ASD (about 1 in 500 children) often engage in solitary, repetitive behaviors, such as continually rocking back and forth or endlessly skipping around a room. They interact minimally with other children and adults, rarely form close relationships, produce little or no language, and tend to be more interested in objects than in people (Willis, 2009). These problems, among others, have led many researchers to speculate that a failure to understand other people underlies these children's limited engagement in the social world.

Recent research supports this hypothesis. Children with ASD tend to have trouble establishing joint attention with other people (Klin et al., 2004). Compared with both typical children and children with abnormally low IQs, children with ASD show less concern when other people appear distressed (Sigman & Ruskin, 1999) or experience circumstances that would lead most people to be distressed (Hobson et al., 2009). These

children also tend to have poor language skills (Tager-Flusberg & Joseph, 2005), which both reflects their lack of attention to other people and limits their opportunities to learn about people's thoughts and feelings through conversation. In line with these patterns, children with ASD are strikingly befuddled by false-belief questions (Baron-Cohen, 1991). For example, fewer than half of 6- to 14-year-olds with ASD solve false-belief problems that are easy for typical 4- and 5-year-olds (Peterson, Wellman, & Liu, 2005). Children with ASD have some understanding of how desire affects behavior, but the ways in which beliefs influence behavior largely elude them (Harris, 2006; Tager-Flusberg, 2007).

Impaired theory-of-mind mechanisms are not the only source of the difficulty that children with ASD encounter in understanding other people. More general deficits in planning, adapting to changing situations, and controlling working memory also contribute (Ozonoff et al., 2004). Nonetheless, impaired theory of mind is a source of particular difficulty, especially in understanding situations in which people's beliefs differ from reality (Baron-Cohen, 1993; Tager-Flusberg, 2007).

Fortunately, many problems caused by ASD can be mitigated by intense and prolonged early treatment. Dawson and colleagues (2010) randomly assigned 1- and 2-year-olds with ASD to receive either Early Start Denver Model (ESDM) treatment or community-based treatment (the control condition). The ESDM treatment included roughly 15 hours per week of sessions with

trained therapists, during which time the therapists and children practiced everyday activities, such as eating and playing, and used operant conditioning techniques to promote desired behaviors. These desired behaviors were chosen by the children's parents, who also were taught how to use the approach and were encouraged to use it with their child during common activities such as playing and bathing. The parents reported using the approach for an average of 16 hours per week, beyond the formal ESDM sessions. The effects of ESDM were compared with those of the community-based treatment, which included comprehensive diagnostic evaluations, the provision of resource manuals and reading materials, and referrals for other types of treatment.

After 2 years, children who received the ESDM treatment showed considerably greater gains in IQ score, language, and daily living skills than did peers who received the community-based treatment. This study and others (e.g., Voos et al., 2013) suggest that early, intensive treatment of ASD can yield large benefits. Applications of the ESDM approach to even younger children (7- to 15-month-olds) have also yielded promising preliminary results (Rogers et al., 2014). These results suggest that the ESDM program may be even more effective during infancy than during the toddler period in helping children with ASD.

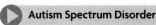 **Autism Spectrum Disorder**

JAN SONNENMAIR / AURORA

The child sitting in his mother's lap shows a distinct lack of interest in her affection. Such lack of interest in other people is common among children with autism spectrum disorders and seems related to their very poor performance on tasks that require an understanding of other people's minds.

Consistent with the idea of a TOMM, one reason for these difficulties in understanding the social world appears to be atypical sizes and activity of certain brain areas that are crucial for understanding people (Amaral, Schumann, & Nordahl, 2008; Dinstein et al., 2012).

Theorists who take an empiricist stance suggest a different explanation for the development of theory of mind, maintaining that psychological understanding arises from interactions with other people (Doherty, 2008; Ruffman, Slade, & Crowe, 2002). They cite evidence that on false-belief tasks, preschoolers who have siblings outperform peers who do not. This finding appears to be strongest when the siblings are older or of the opposite sex, presumably because interacting with people whose interests, desires, and motives are different from their own broadens children's understanding of other people and how they differ from themselves (Jenkins & Astington, 1996; S. A. Miller, 2012). From this perspective, the tendency of children with ASD not to interact much with other people is a major contributor to their difficulty in understanding others.

A third group of investigators also takes an empiricist stance but emphasizes the growth of general information-processing skills as essential to understanding other people's minds. They cite evidence that children's understanding of false-belief problems is substantially correlated with their ability to reason about complex counterfactual statements (German & Nichols, 2003) and with their ability to inhibit their own behavioral propensities when necessary (S. M. Carlson, Mandell, & Williams, 2004; Frye et al., 1996). The ability to reason about counterfactual statements is important because false-belief problems require children to predict what a person would do on the basis of a counterfactual belief (e.g., the belief that the Smarties box contained Smarties). The ability to inhibit behavioral propensities is important because false-belief problems also require children to suppress the assumption that the person would act on the truth of the situation as the child understands it. Investigators in this camp argue that typical children younger than 4 and children with ASD lack the information-processing skills needed to understand others' minds, whereas typical older children can engage in such processing.

All three explanations have merit. Normal development of brain regions relevant to understanding other people, interactions with other people, and improved information-processing capacity all contribute to the growth of psychological understanding during the preschool years. Together, they allow almost all children to achieve a basic, but useful, theory of mind by age 5.

The Growth of Play

One way in which children learn about other people's thinking, and also about many other aspects of the world, is through play. *Play* refers to activities that are pursued for their own sake, with no motivation other than the enjoyment they bring. The earliest play occurs in the 1st year and includes behaviors such as banging spoons on metal high-chair trays and repeatedly throwing food on the floor. These initial play activities tend to be solitary. Over the next few years, children's increasing understanding of other people contributes to their play becoming more social as well as more complex.

One early milestone in the development of play is the emergence, at around 18 months of age, of **pretend play,** make-believe activities in which children

pretend play ■ make-believe activities in which children create new symbolic relations, acting as if they were in a situation different from their actual one

object substitution ■ a form of pretense in which an object is used as something other than itself, for example, using a broom to represent a horse

sociodramatic play ■ activities in which children enact miniature dramas with other children or adults, such as "mother comforting baby"

create new symbolic relations. When engaged in pretend play, children act as if they were in a different situation than their actual one. They often engage in **object substitution,** ignoring many of a play object's characteristics so that they can pretend that it is something else. Typical examples of object substitution are a child's treating a cylindrical wooden block as a bottle and pretending to drink from it or treating a plastic soap dish as a boat and floating it on the water while taking a bath.

About a year later, toddlers begin to engage in **sociodramatic play,** a kind of pretend play in which they enact miniature dramas with other children or adults, such as "mother comforting baby" or "doctor helping sick child" (Lillard et al., 2013). Sociodramatic play is more complex and more social than object substitution. Consider, for example, "tea party" rituals, in which a child and parent "pour tea" for each other from an imaginary teapot, daintily "sip" it, "eat" imaginary cookies, and comment on how delicious the cookies are.

Young children's sociodramatic play is typically more sophisticated when they are playing with a parent or older sibling who can scaffold the play sequence than when they are pretending with a peer (Bornstein, 2007; Lillard, 2007). Such scaffolding during play provides children with opportunities for learning, in particular for improving their storytelling skills (Nicolopoulou, 2007). Consider one mother's comments as her 2-year-old played with two action figures:

> Oh look, Lantern Man is chasing Spider Man. Oh no, he is pushing him down. Spider Man says, "Help, Lantern Man is grabbing me." Look, Spider Man is getting away.
>
> (Kavanaugh & Engel, 1998, p. 88)

Such adult elaboration of implicit storylines in children's play provides a useful model for children to follow in later pretend play with peers or by themselves.

By the elementary school years, play becomes even more complex and social. It begins to include activities such as sports and board games that have conventional rules that participants must follow. The frequent quarrels that arise among young elementary school students regarding who is obeying the rules and playing fair attest to the cognitive and emotional challenges posed by these games (Rubin, Fein, & Vandenberg, 1983).

Pretend play is often thought of as limited to early childhood, but it actually continues far beyond that time. In a survey of college students, the majority reported that they had engaged in pretend play at least weekly when they were 10 or 11 years old, and most reported doing so at least monthly when they were 12 or 13 years old (E. D. Smith & Lillard, 2011). Boys and only children tended to report engaging in pretend play at older ages more than did girls and children with siblings.

In addition to being fun, pretend play may expand children's understanding of the social world. Children who engage in greater amounts of pretend play tend to show greater understanding of other people's thinking (Lillard, 2007) and emotions (Youngblade & Dunn, 1995). The type of pretend play in which children engage also matters: social pretend play is more strongly related to understanding other people's thinking than is nonsocial pretend play (Harris, 2000). Preschoolers also learn from watching others' pretend play (S. L. Sutherland & Friedman,

BETH SIEGLER RETCHLESS

Object substitution enables children to pursue play activities they enjoy, even when they do not have the exact objects for those activities. These twins' costumes were imitations of their father's outfit when he bicycled to work. The fire trucks were their bikes, the hats were their helmets, and the glasses were their goggles. Thanks to their mother (the daughter of one of the authors) for explaining the symbolism.

Children often enjoy having a parent join them in sociodramatic play, which tends to be richer and more informative with a parent's participation because the parent usually provides scaffolding for the play episode. Along with helping to structure the physical situation, the father in this scene might be teaching his son strategies for overcoming adversaries and winning battles.

FANCY COLLECTION / SUPERSTOCK

2012). Such evidence has led some experts in the area (e.g., Hirsh-Pasek et al., 2009; Tomlinson, 2009) to conclude that high levels of pretend play are causally related to increased social understanding. However, a recent comprehensive review of studies of pretend play (Lillard et al., 2013) found limited evidence for such a causal relation. Instead, both frequent pretend play and high levels of social understanding may be caused by parents who promote both. Moreover, some children with high social skills simply enjoy engaging in pretend play and thinking about other people (an example of how children shape their own development through their activities). The jury remains out on whether pretend play is a cause of improved social understanding, but it is clear that such play is not harmful and that it enriches many children's lives.

Children's interest in social play is so strong that many of them do not let the absence of playmates prevent them from engaging in it. For such occasions, and even sometimes when playmates are available, they turn to imaginary companions (Box 7.2).

Knowledge of Living Things

Children are fascinated by living things, especially animals. One sign of their fascination is how often they talk about them. In a study of the first 50 words used by children, the two terms other than "mama" and "dada" that were used by the greatest number of children were "dog" and "cat" (and variants such as "doggie" and "kitty") (K. Nelson, 1973). "Duck," "horse," "bear," "bird," and "cow" also were common early terms. A more recent study of the earliest words spoken by 8- to 16-month-olds in the United States and two regions of China showed similar word choices 35 years later across very different cultures (Tardif et al., 2008).

By the time children are 4 or 5 years old, their fascination with living things translates into impressive knowledge, including knowledge about growth, inheritance, illness, and healing (S. Gelman, 2003). Coexisting with this relatively advanced knowledge, however, are a variety of immature beliefs and types of reasoning. For example, children often fail to understand the difference between artifacts, such as chairs and cars, which are built by people for specific purposes, and living things, such as monkeys, which are not created by people for any purpose. Thus, when Kelemen and DiYanni (2005) asked 6- to 10-year-olds why the first monkey came to exist, the children often referred to how monkeys serve human purposes, such as "The manager of the zoo-place wanted some" and "So then we had somebody to climb trees."

Another weakness in young children's biological knowledge is their incorrect beliefs about which things are living and which are not (as discussed in Chapter 4). For instance, most 5-year-olds believe that plants are not alive, and some believe that the moon and mountains are alive (Hatano et al., 1993; Inagaki & Hatano, 2002). Such erroneous notions have led some investigators to conclude that children have only a shallow and fragmented understanding of living things until they are 7 to 10 years old (Carey, 1999; Slaughter, Jaakkola, & Carey, 1999). In contrast, other investigators believe that by age 5 years, children understand the essential characteristics of living things and what separates them from nonliving things but are just confused on a few points (S. Gelman, 2003). A third view is that young children simultaneously possess both mature and immature biological understanding (Inagaki & Hatano, 2008). With this dispute in mind, we will now consider what young children do and do not know about living things and how they acquire knowledge about them.

BOX 7.2 | individual differences

IMAGINARY COMPANIONS

Many children have an imaginary companion. Hearing one's child talk about an invisible friend sometimes leads parents to worry about the child's sanity, but children's creation of such characters is entirely normal.

Research conducted by Marjorie Taylor (1999) indicates that the majority of children have an imaginary friend at one time or another. She found that 63% of children whom she interviewed at age 3 or 4 years and again at age 7 or 8 years reported having imaginary companions at one or both times. In another study, Taylor and colleagues (2004) found that as many 6- and 7-year-olds as 3- and 4-year-olds said that they had imaginary companions—31% of older children and 28% of younger ones (most children had an imaginary friend at one age but not the other).

Most of the imaginary playmates described by the children in Taylor's studies were ordinary boys and girls who happened to be invisible. Others were more colorful. They included Derek, a 91-year-old man who was said to be only 2 feet tall but able to hit bears; "The Girl," a 4-year-old who always wore pink and was "a beautiful person"; Joshua, a possum who lived in San Francisco; and Nobby, a 160-year-old businessman. Other imaginary companions were modeled after specific people: two examples were MacKenzie, an imaginary playmate who resembled the child's cousin MacKenzie, and "Fake Rachel," who resembled the child's friend Rachel.

As with real friends, children have a variety of complaints about their imaginary companions. In a study of 36 preschoolers with imaginary companions, only one child had no complaints; the other 35 children griped that their imaginary companions argued with them, refused to share, failed to come when invited, and failed to leave when no longer welcome (M. Taylor & Mannering, 2007). In this independence from their creator, the imaginary companions resemble characters invented by novelists, many of whom report that their characters at times seem to act independently, including arguing with and criticizing their creator (M. Taylor & Mannering, 2007).

Contrary to popular speculation, Taylor (1999) found that, in terms of broad characteristics such as personality, intelligence, and creativity, children who invent imaginary playmates are no different from children who do not. This finding is true even for the relatively small number of children who report having imaginary friends in middle school (about 9% of children; Pearson et al., 2001). Although these children tend not to be especially popular among peers during middle school, by the end of high school, they are as well-adjusted as their peers (Taylor, Hulette, & Dishion, 2010).

Taylor and her colleagues identified a few relatively specific differences between children with and without imaginary companions. Children who created imaginary playmates were more likely (1) to be first-born or only children; (2) to watch relatively little television; (3) to be verbally skillful; and (4) to have advanced theories of mind (Carlson et al., 2003; Taylor & Carlson, 1997; Taylor et al., 2004). These relations make sense. Being without siblings may motivate some firstborn and only children to invent friends to keep them company; not watching much television frees time for

Although the sight of their child feeding someone who isn't there might worry some parents, the creation of imaginary friends is entirely normal and the majority of children enjoy the company of such characters at some time in early childhood.

imaginative play; and being verbally skilled and having an advanced theory of mind may enable children to imagine especially interesting companions and especially interesting adventures with them.

Companionship, entertainment, and enjoyment of fantasy are not the only reasons why children invent imaginary companions. Children also use them to deflect blame ("I didn't do it; Blebbi Ussi did"); to vent anger ("I hate you, Blebbi Ussi"); and to convey information that the child is reluctant to state directly ("Blebbi Ussi is scared of falling into the potty"). Many young children also report that when they are sad, their imaginary companions comfort them (Sadeh, Hen-Gal, & Tikotzky, 2008). As Taylor (1999) noted, "Imaginary companions love you when you feel rejected by others, listen when you need to talk to someone, and can be trusted not to repeat what you say" (p. 63). No wonder so many children invent them.

 Imaginary Companions: The Research of Marjorie Taylor

Distinguishing Living from Nonliving Things

As noted previously, infants in their 1st year already are interested in people and distinguish them from nonliving things (Figure 7.3). Other animals also attract infants' interest, though infants act differently toward them than they do toward people. For example, 9-month-olds pay more attention to rabbits than they do to inanimate objects, but they smile less at rabbits than they do at people (Poulin-Dubois, 1999; Ricard & Allard, 1993).

These behavioral reactions indicate that infants in their 1st year distinguish people from other animals and that they distinguish both from inanimate objects. However, the reactions do not indicate when children construct a general category of living things that includes plants as well as animals or when they recognize humans as a type of animal. It is difficult to assess knowledge of these and many other properties of living and nonliving things until the age of 3 or 4 years, when children can comprehend and answer questions about these categories. By this age, they clearly know quite a bit about the similarities among all living creatures and about the differences between living creatures and inanimate objects. This knowledge of living things is not limited to visible properties such as having legs, moving, and making distinctive noises. It also extends to biological processes such as digestion and heredity (S. Gelman, 2003). At least through age 5 or 6, however, many children deny that people are animals (Carey, 1985).

Understanding the life status of plants also presents a challenge to young children. On one hand, most preschoolers know that plants, like animals but unlike inanimate objects, grow (Hickling & Gelman, 1995; Inagaki & Hatano, 1996), heal themselves (Backscheider, Shatz, & Gelman, 1993), and die (Springer, Nguyen, & Samaniego, 1996). On the other hand, most preschoolers believe that plants are not alive; in fact, it is not until age 7 to 9 years that a clear majority of children realize that plants are living things (Hatano et al., 1993). Part of the reason is that children often equate being alive with being able to move in adaptive ways that promote survival; plants do move in this way, but their adaptive movements, such as bending toward sunlight, occur too slowly to observe under ordinary circumstances (Opfer & Gelman, 2001). Consistent with this interpretation, letting 5-year-olds know that plants bend toward sunlight and that their roots grow toward water leads the children to conclude that plants, like animals, are living things (Opfer & Siegler, 2004).

FIGURE 7.3 Distinguishing people from nonliving things These photos show a task used by Poulin-Dubois (1999) to study infants' reactions when they see people and inanimate objects (in this case, a robot) engaging in the same action. Both 9- and 12-month-olds show surprise when they see inanimate objects move on their own, suggesting that they understand that self-produced motion is a distinctive characteristic of people and other animals.

COURTESY OF DIANE POULIN-DUBOIS

(a)   (b)

More generally, culture and direct experience influence the age at which children understand that plants are, in fact, alive. For example, children growing up in rural areas realize that plants are living things at younger ages than do children growing up in cities or suburbs (J. D. Coley, 2000; N. Ross et al., 2003).

Understanding Biological Processes

Preschoolers understand that biological processes, such as growth, digestion, and healing, differ from psychological ones (Wellman & Gelman, 1998). For instance, while 3- and 4-year-olds recognize that desires influence what people do, they also recognize that some biological processes are independent of one's desires. Distinguishing between biological and psychological processes, for example, leads preschoolers to predict that people who overeat but wish to lose weight will not get their wish (Inagaki & Hatano, 1993; Schult & Wellman, 1997).

Children are interested in living things, plants as well as animals—especially when part of the plant tastes good.

Preschoolers also recognize that properties of living things often serve important functions for the organism, whereas properties of inanimate objects do not. Thus, 5-year-olds recognize that the green color of plants is crucial for them to make food, whereas the green color of emeralds has no function for the emerald (Keil, 1992). The extent of preschoolers' understanding of biological processes can be understood more fully by examining their specific ideas about inheritance, growth, and illness.

Inheritance Although 3- and 4-year-olds obviously know nothing about DNA or the mechanisms of heredity, they do know that physical characteristics tend to be passed on from parent to offspring. If told, for example, that Mr. and Mrs. Bull have hearts of an unusual color, they predict that Baby Bull also will have a heart of that color (Springer & Keil, 1991). Similarly, they predict that a baby mouse will eventually have hair of the same color as its parents, even if it is presently hairless.

Older preschoolers also know that certain aspects of development are determined by heredity rather than by environment. For instance, 5-year-olds realize that an animal of one species raised by parents of another species will become an adult of its own species (S. C. Johnson & Solomon, 1997).

Coexisting with this understanding are numerous misguided beliefs about inheritance. Many preschoolers believe that mothers' desires can play a role in their children's inheritance of physical qualities, such as having blue eyes (Weissman & Kalish, 1999). Many preschoolers also believe that adopted children are at least as likely to look like their adoptive parents as like their birth parents (G. E. Solomon et al., 1996). In other situations, preschoolers' belief in heredity is too strong, leading them to deny that the environment has any influence. For example, preschoolers tend to believe that differences between boys and girls in play preferences are due totally to heredity (M. G. Taylor, 1993).

Related to this general belief in the importance of heredity is one of the most basic aspects of children's biological beliefs—**essentialism,** the view that living things have an essence inside them that makes them what they are (S. Gelman, 2003). Thus, most preschoolers (as well as most older children and adults) believe that puppies have a certain "dogness" inside them, kittens have a certain "catness," roses have a certain "roseness," and so on. This essence is what makes all members of the category similar

essentialism ■ the view that living things have an essence inside them that makes them what they are

"I've been getting in touch with the puppy in me."

A fanciful representation of the inner essence that children believe makes a dog a dog, a cat a cat, and so on.

to one another and different from members of other categories; for instance, their inner "dogness" leads to dogs' barking, chasing cats, and liking to be petted. This essence is viewed as being inherited from one's parents and being maintained throughout the organism's life. Thinking in terms of such essences seems to make it difficult, both for children and for many adults, to understand and accept biological evolution (E. M. Evans, 2008; Kelemen et al., 2014). If animals inherit an unchanging essence from their parents, how, they may wonder, would it be possible, say, for mice and whales to have common ancestors? (Recall, though, that carefully designed and informative storybooks can help children understand natural selection (see Chapter 4).

Growth, illness, and healing Preschoolers realize that growth, like inheritance, is a product of internal processes. They recognize, for example, that plants and animals become bigger and more complex over time because of something going on inside them (again, preschoolers are not sure what) (Rosengren et al., 1991). Three- and 4-year-olds also recognize that the growth of living things generally proceeds in only one direction (smaller to larger) at least until old age, whereas inanimate objects such as balloons can become either smaller or larger at any point in time.

Preschoolers also show a basic understanding of illness. Three-year-olds have heard of germs and have a general sense of how they operate. They know that eating food that is contaminated with germs can make a person sick, even if the person is unaware of the germs' presence (Kalish, 1997). Conversely, they realize that psychological processes, such as being aware of germs in one's food, do not cause illness.

Finally, preschoolers know that plants and animals, unlike inanimate objects, have internal processes that often allow them to regain prior states or attributes. For example, 4-year-olds realize that a tomato plant that is scratched can heal itself and that an animal's hair can grow back after being cut but that a scratched chair cannot heal itself and that a doll's hair cannot grow back (Backscheider et al., 1993). Preschoolers also recognize the limits of living things' recuperative processes: they understand that both illness and old age can cause death, from which no recuperation is possible (Nguyen & Gelman, 2002).

How Do Children Acquire Biological Knowledge?

As with other aspects of conceptual development, nativists and empiricists have very different ideas regarding how children acquire biological understanding. Nativists propose that humans are born with a "biology module" much like the theory of mind module described earlier in the chapter. This brain structure or mechanism helps children learn quickly about living things (Atran, 1990, 2002). Nativists use three main arguments to support the idea that people have a biology module.

■ During earlier periods of our evolution, it was crucial for human survival that children learn quickly about animals and plants.

■ Children throughout the world are fascinated by plants and animals and learn about them quickly and easily.

■ Children throughout the world organize information about plants and animals in very similar ways (in terms of growth, reproduction, inheritance, illness, and healing).

Empiricists, by contrast, maintain that children's biological understanding comes from their personal observations and from information they receive from parents, teachers, and the general culture (Callanan, 1990). When mothers read to their 1- and 2-year-olds about animals, for example, many of the mothers' comments suggest that animals have intentions and goals, that different members of the same species have a lot in common, and that animals differ greatly from inanimate objects (S. Gelman et al., 1998). Such teaching is often elicited by children's questions: when 3- to 5-year-olds encounter unfamiliar objects, they ask a higher percentage of questions about the functions of objects that appear to be manmade but ask a higher percentage of questions about the biological properties of objects that look like animals or plants (Margett & Witherington, 2011). Such questions reflect children's biological knowledge and can increase it, too.

The feelings of awe experienced by many children (and adults) upon seeing remains of great animals of the past and present, such as dinosaurs, elephants, and whales, were a major reason for the founding of natural history museums. Despite all the depictions of monsters and superheroes on television, in movies, and in video games, these fossils and models inspire the same sense of wonder in children growing up today.

Empiricists also note that children's biological understanding reflects the views of their culture. For example, 5-year-olds in Japan are more likely than their peers in the United States and Israel to believe that nonliving things and plants are able to feel physical sensations, such as pain and cold (Hatano et al., 1993). This tendency of Japanese children echoes the Buddhist tradition, still influential in Japanese society, which views all objects as having certain psychological properties.

As with the parallel arguments regarding the sources of psychological understanding, both nature and nurture seem certain to play important roles in the acquisition of biological understanding. Young children are innately fascinated by animals and learn about them much more quickly than about aspects of their environment that they find less interesting. At the same time, the particulars of what children learn obviously are influenced by the information, beliefs, and values conveyed to them by their parents and their society. And, as always, nurture responds to nature, as when parents provide informative answers to their children's many questions about living things, which in turn reflect, and sometimes increase, the children's interest in those things.

Review

From early in infancy, children form categories of similar objects. As they gain experience, they form new categories and include new objects within existing categories. They categorize unfamiliar objects on the basis of similarities between the appearance and function of the new object and objects already known to be category members. From infancy onward, they divide objects into three, highly general categories: people, animals, and nonliving things.

From the first days of life, infants are interested in other people and spend a great deal of time looking at them. By age 3 years, they form a simple theory of people's minds that includes some understanding of the causal relations among desires, beliefs, and actions. Not until age 4 or 5 years, however, do most children become able to solve false-belief problems that require them to understand that other people will act in accord with their own beliefs, even if the child knows that those beliefs are wrong. The development of understanding of other people's minds during the preschool period has been attributed to biological maturation of a theory of mind module, to interactions with other people, and to the growth of general information-processing capabilities that allow children to understand increasingly complex social situations.

Understanding of many properties of biological entities—growth, heredity, illness, and death—is evident in the preschool years. Not until children go to school, however, do most of them group plants with animals into a single category of living things. Explanations for children's relatively rapid acquisition of biological knowledge include the extensive expo-sure to biological information provided by families and the broader culture, children's own questions that elicit useful information about plants and animals from other people, and the existence of brain mechanisms that lead children to be interested in living things and to learn about them quickly and easily.

Understanding Why, Where, When, and How Many

Making sense of our experiences requires accurately representing not only who or what was involved in an event but also why, where, when, and how often the event occurred. Development of all these concepts begins in infancy, but major improvements continue throughout childhood and adolescence.

Causality

The famed eighteenth-century Scottish philosopher David Hume described cau-sality as "the cement of the universe." His point was that causal connections unite discrete events into coherent wholes. Consistent with Hume's view, from early in development, children rely heavily on their understanding of causal mechanisms to infer why physical and psychological events occur. When children take apart toys to find out how they work, ask how flipping a switch makes a light go on, or won-der why Mommy is upset, they are trying to understand causal connections. We discussed the development of understanding of psychological causes earlier in this chapter; we will now focus on the development of understanding of physical causes.

Nativists and empiricists fundamentally disagree about the origins of understand-ing of physical causes. The difficulty of making sense of the world without some basic causal understanding and the fact that children show some such understand-ing early in infancy have led nativists to propose that infants possess an innate causal module or core theory that allows them to extract causal relations from the events they observe (e.g., Leslie, 1986; Spelke, 2003). Empiricists, however, have proposed that infants' causal understanding arises from their observations of innumerable events in the environment (e.g., L. B. Cohen & Cashon, 2006; T. T. Rogers & McClelland, 2004) and in their observing the causal effects of their own actions (Rakison & Krogh, 2012; Rakison & Woodward, 2008). One fact both sides agree on is that children show impressive causal reasoning from infancy onward.

Causal Reasoning in Infancy

By 6 months of age, infants perceive causal connections among some physical events (L. B. Cohen & Cashon, 2006; Leslie, 1995). In a typical experiment demonstrating infants' ability to perceive such relations, Oakes and Cohen (1995) presented 6- to 10-month-olds a series of video clips in which a moving object collided with a station-ary object and the stationary object immediately moved in the way one would expect. Different moving and stationary objects were used in each clip, but the basic "plot" remained the same. After seeing a few of these video clips, infants habituated to the collisions. Then the infants were shown a slightly different clip in which the stationary object started moving shortly before it was struck. Infants looked at this event for a longer time than they had looked during the preceding trials, presumably because the new video clip violated their sense that inanimate objects do not move on their own.

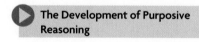

The Development of Purposive Reasoning

Infants' and toddlers' understandings of physical causality influence not only their expectations about inanimate objects but also their ability to remember and imitate sequences of actions. When 9- to 11-month-olds are shown actions that are causally related (e.g., making a rattle by putting a small object inside two cups that can be pushed together to form a single container), they usually can reproduce the actions (Figure 7.4 shows a toddler performing this procedure; Bauer, 1995). In contrast, when similar but causally unrelated actions are shown, babies do not reliably reproduce them until a year later, at age 20 to 22 months (Bauer, 2007).

By the end of their 2nd year, and by some measures even earlier, children can infer the causal impact of one variable based on indirectly relevant information about another. Sobel and Kirkham (2006), for instance, presented 19- and 24-month-olds a box called a "blicket detector" that, the experimenter explained, played music when a type of object called a blicket was placed on it. Then the experimenter placed two objects, A and B, on the blicket detector, and the music played. When the experimenter then placed object A alone on the blicket detector, the music did not play. Finally, the children were asked to turn on the blicket detector. The 24-month-olds consistently chose object B, indicating that seeing the ineffectiveness of object A led them to infer that object B was the blicket. In contrast, the 19-month-olds chose object A as often as they did object B, suggesting that they did not draw this inference.

Another illustration of this growing understanding of causality comes from Z. Chen and Siegler's (2000) study of 1- and 2-year-olds' tool use. The toddlers were presented an attractive toy that was sitting on a table roughly a foot beyond

FIGURE 7.4 Imitating sequences of events Understanding the actions they are imitating helps toddlers perform the actions in the correct order. In this illustration of the procedure used by Bauer (1995) to demonstrate this point, a toddler imitates a previously observed three-step sequence to build a rattle. The child (a) picks up a small block; (b) puts it into the bottom half of the container; (c) pushes the top half of the container onto the bottom, thus completing the rattle; and (d) shakes it.

(a)

(b)

(c)

(d)

ALL: COURTESY OF PATRICIA BAUER

FIGURE 7.5 Toddlers' problem solving
In the task used by Chen and Siegler (2000) to examine toddlers' causal reasoning and problem solving, choosing the right tool for getting the toy turtle required children to understand the importance of both the length of the shaft and the angle of the head relative to the shaft. Compared with younger toddlers, older toddlers had greater understanding of these causal relations, which led them to more often use tools, rather than just reaching for the toy, and to more often choose the right tool for the task.

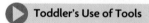

▶ **Toddler's Use of Tools**

Most 5-year-olds find magic tricks thrilling, even though they would have been uninterested in them a year or two earlier.

their reach. Between the child and the toy were six potential tools that varied in length and in the type of head at the end of the shaft (Figure 7.5). To succeed on the task, the toddlers needed to understand the causal relations that would make one tool more effective than the others for pulling in the toy. In particular, they needed to understand that a sufficiently long shaft and a head at right angles to the shaft were essential.

The 2-year-olds succeeded considerably more often than the 1-year-olds did in obtaining the toy, both in their initial efforts to get it on their own and after being shown by the experimenter how they could use the optimal tool to obtain it. One reason for the older toddlers' greater success was that they more often used a tool to try to get the toy, as opposed to reaching for it with their hands or seeking their mother's help. Another reason was that the older toddlers chose the optimal tool in a greater percentage of trials in which they used some tool. A third reason was that the older toddlers more often generalized what they had learned on the first problem to new, superficially different problems involving tools and toys with different shapes, colors, and decorations. All these findings indicate that the older toddlers had a deeper understanding of the causal relations between a tool's features and its usefulness for pulling in the toy.

Causal Reasoning During the Preschool Period

Causal reasoning continues to grow in the preschool period. Preschoolers seem to expect that if a variable causes an effect, it should do so consistently (Schulz & Sommerville, 2006). When 4-year-olds see a potential cause produce an effect inconsistently, they infer that some variable that they cannot see must cause the effect; when the same effect occurs consistently, they do not infer that a hidden variable was important. For example, if 4-year-olds saw some dogs respond to petting by eagerly wagging their tails and other dogs respond to petting by growling, they might infer that some variable other than the petting, such as the dogs' breed, caused the effect. But if all the dogs they had ever seen looked happy when petted, they would not infer that the dogs' breed was relevant.

Preschoolers' emerging understanding that events must have causes also seems to influence their reactions to magic tricks. Most 3- and 4-year-olds fail to see the point of such tricks; they grasp that something strange has happened but do not find the "magic" humorous or actively try to figure out what caused the strange outcome (Rosengren & Hickling, 2000). By age 5, however, children become fascinated with magic tricks precisely because no obvious causal mechanism could produce the effect (Box 7.3). Many want to search the magician's hat or other apparatus to see how such a stunt was possible. This increasing appreciation that even astonishing events must have causes, along with an increasing understanding of the mechanisms that connect causes and their effects, reflect the growth of causal reasoning.

IMAGES-USA / ALAMY

BOX 7.3 | a closer look

MAGICAL THINKING AND FANTASY

Lest you conclude that by age 5, children's causal reasoning is as advanced as that of adults, consider the following conversation between two kindergartners and their teacher:

Lisa: Do plants wish for baby plants?
Deana: I think only people can make wishes. But God could put a wish inside a plant. . . .
Teacher: I always think of people as having ideas.
Deana: It's just the same. God puts a little idea in the plant to tell it what to be.
Lisa: My mother wished for me and I came when it was my birthday.
(Paley, 1981, pp. 79–80)

This is not a conversation that would have occurred among 10-year-olds and their teacher. Rather, as noted by Jacqui Woolley, a psychologist who studies preschoolers' fantasies, it reflects one of the most charming aspects of early childhood: Preschoolers and young elementary school children "live in a world in which fantasy and reality are more intertwined than they are for adults" (Woolley, 1997).

Young children's belief in fantasy and magic, as well as in normal causes, is evident in many ways. Most 4- to 6-year-olds believe that they can influence other people by wishing them into doing something, such as buying a particular present for their birthday (Vikan & Clausen, 1993). They believe that effective wishing takes a great deal of skill, and perhaps magic, but that it can be done. In related fashion, many believe that getting in good with Santa Claus can make their hopes come true. The fantasies can have a dark side as well, such as when children fear that monsters might hurt them (Woolley, 1997).

Research has shown that young children not only believe in magic; they sometimes also act on their belief. In one experiment, preschoolers were told that a certain box was magical and that if they placed a drawing into it and said magical words, the object depicted in the drawing would appear. Then the experimenter left the children alone with the box and a number of drawings. The children put drawings of the most attractive items into the box, said the "magical words," and were visibly disappointed when they opened the box and found only the drawings (Subbotsky, 1993, 1994).

How can we reconcile preschoolers' understanding of physical causes and effects with their belief in magic, wishing, and Santa Claus? The key is to recognize that here, as in many situations, children simultaneously believe a variety of somewhat contradictory ideas (Evans, Legare, & Rosengren, 2011; Harris & Giménez, 2005; Legare & S. Gelman, 2008; Woolley, Cornelius, & Lacy, 2011). They may think that magic or the power of their imagination can cause things to happen, but they may not depend on it when doing so could be embarrassing. In one demonstration of this limited belief in magic and the power of the imagination (Woolley & Phelps, 1994), an experimenter showed preschoolers an empty box, closed it, and then asked them to imagine a pencil inside it. The experimenter next asked the children whether there was now a pencil in the box. Many said "yes." Then an adult came into the room and said that she needed a pencil to do her work. Very few of the preschoolers opened the box or handed it to her. Thus, it appeared that many children said the box contained a pencil when no consequences would follow if they were wrong, but they did not believe in magic strongly enough to act in a way that might look foolish to an adult.

How do children move beyond their belief in magic? One way is learning more about real causes: the more children know about the true causes of events, the less likely they are to explain them in magical terms (Woolley, 1997). Another influence is personal experiences that undermine the child's magical beliefs, such as hearing peers pooh-pooh the idea of Santa Claus or seeing two Santa Clauses on the same street. Sometimes, however, children salvage their hopes by distinguishing between flawed manifestations of the magical being and the magical being itself. They may, for example, fervently distinguish between the real Santa Claus and imposters who dress up to look like him.

3-12
© 2005 Bil Keane, Inc.
Dist. by King Features Synd.
www.familycircus.com

"A real one, or just somebody wearing a funny suit and a painted face?"

Although this world of the imagination is most striking between ages 3 and 6, aspects of it remain evident for years thereafter. In one study that demonstrated the persistence of magical thinking, many 9-year-olds and some adults reverted to magical explanations when confronted with a trick that was difficult to explain in physical terms (Subbotsky, 2005). Moreover, in a recent poll of a representative sample of the American population, 31% of adults said that they believe in ghosts (Rasmussen, 2011). These beliefs in the supernatural cannot be written off as simply reflecting a lack of education. Subbotsky (2005) found that 0 of 17 college-student participants were willing to allow someone who was said to be a witch to cast an evil spell on their lives. Innumerable other adults indulge superstitions such as not walking under ladders, avoiding cracks in sidewalks, and knocking on wood. In explaining certain improbable events, adults actually generate supernatural explanations more often than children (Woolley et al., 2011). Apparently, we never entirely outgrow magical thinking.

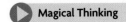 **Magical Thinking**

Space

The nativist/empiricist debate has been vigorous with regard to spatial thinking. Nativists argue that children possess an innate module that is specialized for representing and learning about space and that processes spatial information separately from other types of information (Hermer & Spelke, 1996; Hespos & Spelke, 2004). Empiricists argue that children acquire spatial representations through the same types of learning mechanisms and experiences that produce cognitive growth in general, that children adaptively combine spatial and non-spatial information to reach their goals, and that language and other cultural tools such as jigsaw puzzles shape spatial development (Gentner & Boroditsky, 2001; Jirout & Newcombe, 2015; S. C. Levine et al., 2012; Newcombe, Levine, & Mix, 2015).

Nativists and empiricists agree on some issues. For example, from early in infancy, children show impressive understanding of some spatial concepts, such as *above, below, left of,* and *right of* (Casasola, 2008; P. C. Quinn, 2005). Another common conclusion is that self-produced movement around the environment stimulates processing of spatial information. A third shared belief is that certain parts of the brain are specialized for coding particular types of spatial information; for instance, development of the hippocampus appears to produce improvements in place learning (Sluzenski, Newcombe, & Satlow, 2004; Sutton, Joanisse, & Newcombe, 2010). A fourth common conclusion is that geometric information—information about lengths, angles, and directions—is extremely important in spatial processing. When toddlers and preschoolers are given clues to an object's location, they often weigh such geometric information more strongly than seemingly simpler non-geometric cues, such as the object's being in front of the one blue wall in the room (Hermer & Spelke, 1996; Newcombe & Ratliff, 2007).

Effective spatial thinking requires coding space relative to oneself and relative to the external environment. Next we consider each of these types of spatial coding.

Representing Space Relative to Oneself

From early in infancy, children code the locations of objects in relation to their own bodies. As noted in Chapter 5, when young infants are presented with two objects, they tend to reach for the closer one (van Wermeskerken et al., 2013). This shows that they recognize which object is closer and that they know the direction of that object relative to themselves.

Over the ensuing months, infants' representations of spatial locations become increasingly durable, enabling them to find objects they observed being hidden some seconds earlier. For example, 7-month-olds reach to the correct location for objects that were hidden 2 seconds earlier under one of two identical opaque covers, but not for objects hidden 4 seconds earlier; yet most 12-month-olds accurately reach for objects hidden 10 seconds earlier (A. Diamond, 1985). In part, these increasingly enduring object representations reflect brain maturation, particularly of the dorsolateral prefrontal cortex, an area in the frontal lobe that is involved in the formation and maintenance of plans and in the integration of new and previously learned information (A. Diamond & Goldman-Rakic, 1989; J. K. Nelson, 2005). However, the improved object representations reflect learning as well: infants who are provided a learning experience with a hidden object in one situation show improved location of hidden objects in other situations (S. P. Johnson, Amso, & Slemmer, 2003).

Note that the preceding examples of infants' ability to code space involve infants remaining in a single location and coding locations relative to their bodies. Piaget (1954/1971) proposed that this is the one kind of spatial coding that infants can do. The reason, according to his theory, is that during the sensorimotor period, infants can form only **egocentric spatial representations,** in which the locations of objects are coded relative to the infants' position at the time of the coding. As evidence, Piaget reported experiments showing that if infants repeatedly found a toy located to their right, they would continue to turn right to find it, even if they were repositioned so that the hidden object was now on their left. Subsequent investigators replicated this finding (e.g., L. P. Acredolo, 1978; Bremner, 1978).

Egocentric spatial representation during infancy is not absolute, however. If toys are hidden adjacent to a distinctive landmark, such as a tower, infants usually find the toy despite changes in their own position (Lew, 2011). Still, the question remains: How do young children become able to find objects when their own position has changed and when no landmarks are available to guide their search?

A major factor in helping infants acquire a sense of space independent of their own location appears to be self-locomotion. Infants who crawl or have had experience propelling themselves in walkers more often remember the locations of objects on the object permanence task (Chapter 4) than do infants of the same age without such locomotor experience (Bertenthal, Campos, & Kermoian, 1994; Campos et al., 2000). Similarly, compared with infants who have not yet moved across rooms on their own, those infants who have done so show an earlier understanding of depth and drop-offs on the surfaces they travel; this is evidenced by acceleration in their heart rate as they approach the visual cliff in the procedure described in Chapter 5.

The reasons why self-locomotion enhances infants' representation of space should be familiar to anyone who has both driven a car and been a passenger in one. Just as driving requires continuous updating of information about the surroundings, so does crawling or walking. In contrast, just as being a passenger in a car does not require such continuous updating of one's location, neither does being carried.

As would be expected from this analysis, self-locomotion also enhances older children's spatial coding. Striking evidence for this conclusion emerged from a study in which kindergarteners were tested in the kitchens of their own homes (Rieser, Garing, & Young, 1994). Some kindergartners were asked to stand in place, imagine themselves walking from their seat in the classroom to the teacher's chair, and turning around to face the class. Then they were asked to point from this imagined position in the classroom to the locations of various objects within it—the fishbowl, the alphabet chart, the coatroom door, and so on. Under these conditions, the 5-year-olds' pointing was inaccurate. Other kindergartners went through the same procedure, except that they were instructed to actually walk through their kitchen and turn around as they imagined themselves walking to the teacher's chair and then turning to face the class. Under these conditions, the children's pointing to the imagined objects in their imagined classroom was far more accurate. This result, like those described above with infants, highlights the interconnectedness of the system that produces self-generated motion and the system that produces mental representations of space (Adolph & Robinson, 2015).

Another type of experience that contributes to spatial development beyond infancy is the assembling of puzzles. Children who played with puzzles more often between their 1st and 4th birthdays than their peers did were found to be more successful as 4½-year-olds on the spatial transformation task shown in Figure 7.6

egocentric spatial representations ■ coding of spatial locations relative to one's own body, without regard to the surroundings

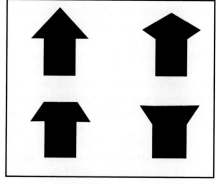

FIGURE 7.6 Measuring early spatial reasoning These are the shapes used by Levine and colleagues (2012) to examine the effects of playing with puzzles on preschoolers' spatial skills. The task was to identify which of the shapes in the top panel could be constructed from the pair of shapes in the bottom panel.

(Levine et al., 2012). The relation between puzzle play and subsequent spatial reasoning occurred irrespective of parents' education, income, and use of spatial terms while interacting with their children. This relation between puzzle play and spatial reasoning makes sense. Assembling puzzles requires identifying appropriate pieces for specific locations and physically rotating them into the proper orientation; mentally rotating pieces to identify plausible candidates for filling empty locations allows more efficient puzzle solving than would otherwise be possible. Such practice in mental rotation seems likely to build spatial-reasoning skills that can be used in future situations.

You might be wondering about blind children, though—do they form representations of space? This question is addressed in Box 7.4.

BOX 7.4 | individual differences

DEVELOPMENT OF SPATIAL CONCEPTS IN BLIND AND VISUALLY IMPAIRED PEOPLE

People often equate spatial thinking with vision, assuming that we can think spatially only about layouts that we have seen. Even in infancy, however, spatial thought can be based on senses other than vision. Thus, when 3-month-olds are brought into a totally dark room in which nothing can be seen, they use sounds emitted by nearby objects to identify the objects' spatial locations and reach for them (Keen & Berthier, 2004).

Although infants can use their auditory sense, as well as other senses, to form spatial representations, visual experience during infancy does play an important role in spatial development. Evidence for this conclusion comes from cases in which surgery restored sight to people who were born either blind (S. Carlson, Hyvärinen, & Raninen, 1986) or with severely impaired vision due to cataracts that prevented patterned stimulation from reaching the retina (Le Grand et al., 2001, 2003). The surgery was performed early—on average at 4 months of age—and those who underwent it subsequently had between 9 and 21 years of postsurgical visual experience before being tested. Despite their extensive visual experience after the corrective surgery, most of these people could not use visual information to represent space as well as other people can. Problems remained even 20 years after the surgery (and thus after 20 years of visual experience). The deficits

extended to aspects of visual processing that might not immediately be viewed as spatial, such as face perception. Young adults with central eye cataracts that prevented any vision until they were removed during their 1st year (on average, at age 4 months) showed reduced brain activity in areas involved in face processing and reduced connectivity among areas involved in face processing and other aspects of spatial processing (Grady et al., 2014). Thus, lack of visual experience in the few months of infancy limited and altered subsequent spatial development.

These findings do not mean that children who are born blind cannot represent space. They actually tend to have a surprisingly good sense of space. On tasks involving the representation of very small spaces, such as being guided in drawing two sides of a triangle on a piece of paper and then being asked to complete the triangle by drawing the third side themselves, children who are born blind perform as well as sighted children who are blindfolded (Thinus-Blanc & Gaunet, 1997). On tasks involving representation of large spaces, such as those formed by exploring unfamiliar rooms, the spatial representations of people born blind also are surprisingly good, about as good as those formed by sighted people who were blindfolded during the exploration period. Thus, although some spatial skills,

Blind adolescents and adults, even those blind from birth, tend to have a quite accurate sense of space, which helps them move around the environment skillfully.

especially face perception, seem to require early visual experience, many blind people develop impressive senses of space without ever seeing the world.

SCOTT T. BAXTER / GETTY IMAGES

Representing Space Relative to the External Environment

As we have noted, infants as young as 6 months can use landmarks to code the location of objects they observe being hidden (Lew, 2011). However, for such young infants to use a landmark successfully, it must be the only obvious landmark in the environment and must be located right next to the hidden object.

With development, infants become increasingly able to choose among alternative potential landmarks. When 12-month-olds are presented a single yellow cushion, a single green cushion, and a large number of blue cushions, they have little trouble finding an object hidden under either the yellow or the green cushion (Bushnell et al., 1995). At 22 months, but not at 16 months, the presence of a landmark improves children's ability to locate an object that is not hidden immediately adjacent to the landmark but fairly close to it (Newcombe et al., 1998). By age 5 years, children can also represent an object's position in relation to multiple landmarks, such as when it is midway between a tree and a street lamp (Newcombe & Huttenlocher, 2006).

Children, like adults, have more difficulty forming a spatial representation when they move around in an environment without distinctive landmarks or when the only landmarks are far from the target location. To understand the challenge of such tasks, imagine walking in a forest without cleared paths and not being able to remember exactly how you arrived at your current location. How easily could you find your way back to your starting point?

Even toddlers show some degree of navigational ability—good enough to lead them in the right general direction (Loomis et al., 1993). In one experiment, 1- and 2-year-olds first saw a small toy hidden in a long, rectangular sandbox and then saw a curtain descend around the sandbox, thus hiding the toy. The toddlers then walked to a different location, after which they were asked to find the toy. Despite no landmarks being present, the toddlers kept track of the hidden toy's location well enough to show better than chance accuracy in their searches (Newcombe et al., 1998).

However, forming relatively precise coding of locations in the absence of straightforward landmarks continues to be difficult for people well beyond 2 years of age (Bremner, Knowles, & Andreasen, 1994). Six- and 7-year-olds are not very good at it (Overman et al., 1996), and adults vary tremendously in their abilities to perform this type of navigation. For example, when adults are asked to walk around the perimeter of an unfamiliar college campus and then to walk straight back to the starting point, some are quite accurate, but many choose routes that take them nowhere near the original location (Cornell et al., 1996).

The degree to which people develop spatial skills is strongly influenced by the importance of such skills in their culture. To demonstrate this point, Kearins (1981) compared the spatial abilities of seminomadic aboriginal children growing up in the Australian desert with those of White peers growing up in Australian cities. Spatial ability is essential within aboriginal culture, because much of life within this culture consists of long treks between distant water holes that vary in which seasons they have water. Needless to say, the aboriginal people cannot rely on road signs or maps; they must rely on their sense of space to get to the water. Consistent with the importance of spatial skills within their everyday lives, aboriginal children are superior to their city-dwelling peers in memory for spatial location, even in board games, a context that is more familiar to the

Spatial skills tend to be especially well developed in cultures in which they are crucial for survival.

urban children (Kearins, 1981). Thus, consistent with the general importance of the sociocultural context, how people make use of spatial thinking in their everyday activities greatly influences their quality of spatial thinking.

Time

What then is time? I know well enough what it is, provided nobody asks me; but if I am asked and try to explain, I am baffled.

—*Saint Augustine, 398 C.E. (2002)*

As this quotation suggests, even the deepest thinkers—from Saint Augustine who wrote in the fourth century to Albert Einstein who wrote in the twentieth—have been mystified by the nature of time. Yet even infants in their 1st half-year have a rudimentary sense of time, including perception of the order and the duration of events (W. J. Friedman, 2008).

Experiencing Time

Probably the most basic sense of time involves knowledge of temporal order, that is, knowing what happened first, what happened next, and so on. Not surprisingly, given how mystifying life would be without such a basic sense of time, infants know the order in which events occur from as early as the capability can be effectively measured. In one study, 3-month-olds were presented a series of interesting photos, first on their left, then on their right, then on their left, and so on. Within 20 seconds, they began to look to the side where each new photo was to appear even before the photo was presented (Adler et al., 2008; Haith, Wentworth, & Canfield, 1993). This looking pattern indicated that the 3-month-olds detected the repetitive order of events over time and used the information to form expectations of where the next photo would appear. The same conclusion has arisen using other experimental methods; for example, 4-month-olds who were habituated to three objects falling in a constant order dishabituated when the order changed (Lewkowicz, 2004).

Infants also have an approximate sense of the duration of events. In one study, 4-month-olds saw periods of light and darkness alternate every 5 seconds for eight cycles, at which point the pattern was broken by the light's failing to appear. Within half a second of the break, infants' heart rates decelerated, a change that is characteristic of increased attention. In this case, the heart-rate deceleration suggested that the infants had a rough sense of the 5-second interval, expected the light to go on at the end of the interval, and increased their attention when it did not appear (Colombo & Richman, 2002).

Infants can also discriminate between longer and shorter durations. The ratio of the durations, rather than differences in their absolute length, is critical for noticing the differences (Brannon, Suanda, & Libertus, 2007). For instance, 6-month-olds discriminate between two durations when their ratio is 2:1 (1 second versus 0.5 second or 3 seconds versus 1.5 seconds), but not when the ratio is 1.5:1 (1.5 seconds versus 1 second or 4.5 seconds versus 3 seconds). Over the course of the 1st year, the precision of these discriminations increases. Thus, 10-month-olds, unlike 6-month-olds, discriminate when the ratio of the durations is 1.5:1.

What about longer periods, such as weeks, months, or years? It is unknown whether infants have a sense of such long periods, but preschoolers do possess some knowledge regarding them. For example, when asked which of two past events occurred more recently, most 4-year-olds knew that a specific event that happened a week before the experiment (Valentine's Day) happened more recently than an event that happened 7 weeks earlier (Christmas) (W. J. Friedman, 1991). However,

preschoolers correctly answer such questions only when the more recent event is quite close in time and much closer than the less recent one. Ability to distinguish more precisely among the timing of past events develops slowly during middle childhood (W. J. Friedman, 2003). For example, when children who had been presented a distinctive classroom experience were asked 3 months later to recall the month in which the experience occurred, correct recall increased from 20% among 5-year-olds to 46% among 7-year-olds to 64% among 9-year-olds (W. J. Friedman & Lyon, 2005).

Understanding of the timing of future events also increases during this age range (W. J. Friedman, 2000, 2003). Preschoolers often confuse past and future. For example, 5-year-olds predict a week after Valentine's Day that the next Valentine's Day will come sooner than the next Halloween or Christmas; they also predict that their next lunch is the same amount of time in the future regardless of whether they are tested just before lunch or just after it. Six-year-olds, by contrast, generally predict correctly in both cases. The improvement in children's sense of future time between the ages of 5 and 6 years is probably influenced by their experience in kindergarten classrooms, where the cycle of seasons, holidays, and daily routines is often emphasized.

Children, like adults, are subject to certain illusions about time, in part because of the role attention plays in time perception. When 8-year-olds' attention is focused on the passage of time (e.g., when they expect a prize at the end of a 2-minute wait), they perceive the duration as longer than the same interval when they are not anticipating a prize. Conversely, when they have little to do, they perceive the duration as longer than when they are very busy (Zakay, 1992, 1993). Thus, the adage "A watched pot never boils" has psychological merit.

Reasoning About Time

During middle childhood, children become increasingly proficient at reasoning about time. In particular, they become able to infer that if two events started at the same time, but one event ended later than the other, then the event that ended later lasted longer.

Children as young as 5 years can sometimes make such logical inferences about time, but only in simple, straightforward situations. For instance, when told that two dolls fell asleep at the same time and that one doll awoke before the other, 5-year-olds reason correctly that the doll that awoke later also slept longer (Levin, 1982). However, when 5-year-olds see two toy trains travel in the same direction on parallel tracks, and one train stops farther down the track, they usually say that the train that stopped farther down the track traveled for a longer time, regardless of when the trains started and stopped moving (C. Acredolo & Schmid, 1981). The problem is that the 5-year-olds' attention is captured by the one train being farther down the track, which leads them to focus on the spatial positions of the trains rather than on their relative starting and stopping times. If this observation reminds you of Piaget's idea of centration (Chapter 4), there is good reason: Piaget's (1969) observations of performance on this task were part of what led him to conclude that children in the preoperational stage often center on a single dimension and ignore other, more relevant ones.

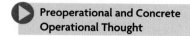

Preoperational and Concrete Operational Thought

Number

Like causality, space, and time, number is a central dimension of human experience. It is hard to imagine how the world would appear if we did not have at least a crude sense of number—we would not know how many fingers, family members, or shoes we have, for example.

numerical equality ■ the realization that all sets of *N* objects have something in common

Unsurprisingly, the nativist/empiricist debate has extended to the concept of number. Nativists argue that children are born with a core concept of number that includes special mechanisms for representing and learning about the relative numbers of objects in sets, counting, and simple addition and subtraction (Feigenson, Dehaene, & Spelke, 2004). As evidence, they note that specific brain areas, particularly the intraparietal sulcus, are heavily involved in representing numerical magnitudes (Ansari, 2008; Nieder & Dehaene, 2009) and that specific neurons respond most strongly when particular numbers of objects (e.g., 5 objects) are displayed (Nieder, 2012). In contrast, empiricists argue that children learn about numbers through the same types of experiences and learning mechanisms that help them acquire other concepts and that infants' numerical competence is not as great as nativists claim (Clearfield, 2006; Lyons & Ansari, 2015). They also note the existence of large differences in numerical understanding among children of different cultures and document the contributions of instruction, language, and cultural values to these differences (Bailey et al., 2015; K. F. Miller et al., 1995). In this section, we review current evidence regarding numerical development as well as nativist and empiricist perspectives on the evidence.

Numerical Equality

Perhaps the most basic understanding of numbers involves **numerical equality,** the idea that all sets of *N* objects have something in common. For example, understanding numerical equality implies recognizing that two dogs, two cups, two balls, and two shoes share the property of "twoness."

Newborns already have some sense of numerical equality in a nonlinguistic (often called "nonsymbolic") sense. One example of this nonsymbolic sense is that after repeatedly hearing sets of four identical syllables, with adjacent sets separated by pauses (e.g., "tu, tu, tu, tu," pause, "tu, tu, tu, tu"), they look more at four objects than at 12; in contrast, after hearing sets of 12 identical syllables, separated by pauses, they look more at the 12 objects (Izard et al., 2009). Although newborns do not know the words "four" or "twelve," they already have a rough concept of these set sizes.

As with discriminations among temporal durations, infants' discriminations between numerical sets depend in large part on the ratio of the number of entities in them. In the study by Izard and colleagues (2009), newborns showed the same tendency to discriminate between 6 and 18 syllables and objects, but not with 4 versus 8, suggesting that they could discriminate the 3:1 ratio but not the 2:1 ratio.

Discrimination among numbers becomes increasingly more precise during the 1st year and beyond. By 6 months of age, infants discriminate between sets with 2:1 ratios (e.g., 16 versus 8 dots or sounds), but they still cannot discriminate between sets with ratios of 3:2 (e.g., 12 versus 8 dots or sounds) (Libertus & Brannon, 2010; Lipton & Spelke, 2003). By 9 months, infants discriminate ratios of 3:2 but not 4:3 ratios (Cordes & Brannon 2008). By adulthood, many people are able to reliably discriminate 8:7 ratios (Halberda & Feigenson 2008).

One exception to the ratio dependence of nonsymbolic number discrimination is that discrimination between very small sets (1 to 4 objects or events) is more accurate, faster, and less variable than would be expected from the ratios alone. For example, infants discriminate two objects from one object and three objects from two objects before they can discriminate larger sets with the same ratio (Piazza, 2011). This phenomenon, which is also apparent in species as varied as guppies, chickens, and monkeys (Agrillo, Piffer, & Bisazza, 2011), indicates that there are

at least two different mechanisms for processing numbers of sights and sounds: one that is used to process very small sets and is based on the specific numbers of objects or events, and one that is based on the ratios of objects or events and is applicable to all numbers of them.

Infants' Arithmetic

In addition to representing nonsymbolic numerical magnitudes, infants can also perform approximate arithmetic on these representations. Four- to 5-month-olds dishabituate when it appears (through trickery) that adding one or two objects to an initial set of one or two objects has produced more or fewer objects than the correct number; infants of the same age also dishabituate when shown unexpected subtractive outcomes with similarly small sets of objects (Wynn, 1992). Older infants dishabituate to surprising addition and subtraction outcomes on larger sets (5 to 10) of objects (McCrink & Wynn, 2004).

Figure 7.7 illustrates the experiment used by Wynn to produce this evidence for infant knowledge of arithmetic. A 5-month-old sees a doll on a stage. A screen comes up, hiding the doll from the infant's sight. Next, the infant sees a hand place a second doll behind the screen and then sees the hand emerge from behind the screen without the doll, thus seeming to have left the second doll with the first one. Finally, the screen drops down, revealing either one doll or two. Most 5-month-olds look longer when there is only one doll, suggesting that they expected that 1 + 1 should equal 2 and that they were surprised when they saw only a single object. Similar results are seen with subtraction: 5-month-olds look longer when the apparent removal of one of two objects results in two objects being present than when the removal results in one object being there (Wynn, 1992).

Counting

Many children begin to count verbally at 2 years of age, but their initial understanding of what they are doing is severely limited. After counting flawlessly from

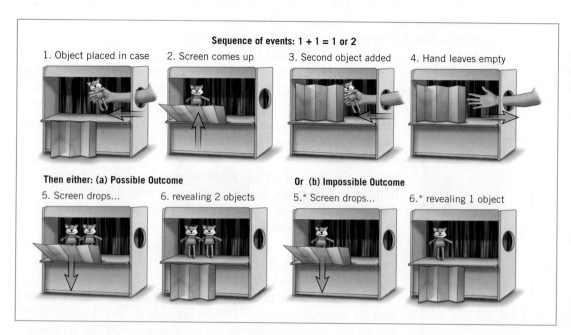

FIGURE 7.7 Infants' understanding of addition On the task used by Wynn (1992) to examine whether infants have a rudimentary grasp of addition, 5-month-olds saw (1) a single doll placed on a stage, (2) a screen raised to hide the doll, (3) a hand with a doll in it move toward and then behind the screen, and (4) the hand return empty after having been behind the screen. Then the screen dropped, revealing either the possible event of two dolls on the stage (5 and 6) or the seemingly impossible event of one doll on the stage (5* and 6*). Infants younger than 6 months looked for a longer time at the seemingly impossible event, suggesting their surprise at seeing one doll rather than two.

1 to 10, many 2-year-olds have no idea whether 3 is bigger than 5 or 5 is bigger than 3 (Le Corre & Carey, 2007). Toddlers' initial counting resembles singing a song in an unfamiliar foreign language.

Learning the meaning of the counting words at first occurs number by number. Toddlers associate the word "1" with one object, a month or two later, they associate "2" with two objects, and a month or two later, they associate "3" with three objects. After this slow early acquisition period, toddlers seem to realize that these counting words indicate differing quantities, and they subsequently learn the link between number words and the quantities they represent much more quickly (Le Corre & Carey, 2007; Le Corre et al., 2006).

In addition to learning counting procedures, preschoolers also acquire understanding of five principles underlying counting (R. Gelman & Gallistel, 1978):

1. *One–one correspondence:* Each object must be labeled by a single number word.

2. *Stable order:* The numbers should always be recited in the same order.

3. *Cardinality:* The number of objects in the set corresponds to the last number stated.

4. *Order irrelevance:* Objects can be counted left to right, right to left, or in any other order.

5. *Abstraction:* Any set of discrete objects or events can be counted.

Much of the evidence that preschoolers understand these principles comes from their judgments when observing two types of counting procedures: incorrect counts and unusual but correct counts. When 4- or 5-year-olds see a puppet counting in a way that violates the one–one correspondence principle—for example, by labeling a single object with two number words (Figure 7.8a)—they consistently say that the counting is incorrect (Frye et al., 1989; R. Gelman, Meck, & Merkin, 1986). In contrast, when they see the puppet count in ways that are unusual but that do not violate any principle—for example, by starting in the middle of a row but counting all the objects (Figure 7.8b)—many (though far from all) 4- and 5-year-olds judge the counting to be correct, even though they say they would not count that way themselves (Briars & Siegler, 1984). The preschoolers' realization that procedures they themselves would not use are nonetheless correct shows that they understand the principles that distinguish correct from incorrect counting.

Although children all over the world learn number words, the rate at which they do so is affected by the specifics of the number system used in their culture. As Kevin Miller and his colleagues (1995) note, for example, most 5-year-olds in China can count to 100 or more, whereas most 5-year-olds in the United States cannot count nearly as high. Part of the reason for this difference in counting proficiency seems to be the greater regularity of the Chinese number system, particularly with respect to numbers in the teens. In both Chinese and English, the words for numbers greater than 20 follow a regular rule: decade name first, digit name second (e.g., twenty-one, twenty-two, and so forth). In Chinese, the words for numbers between 11 and 19 follow the same rule (equivalent to ten-one, ten-two, and so on). In English, however, no simple rule indicates the numbers between 11 and 19; each term has to be learned separately.

Figure 7.9 charts the apparent impact of this cultural difference in number systems. Three-year-olds in the United States and China are comparable in their ability to recite the numbers 1

FIGURE 7.8 Counting procedures Counting procedures similar to those used by Frye and colleagues (1989) and Gelman, Meck, and Merkin (1986): (a) an incorrect counting procedure; (b) an unusual but correct procedure.

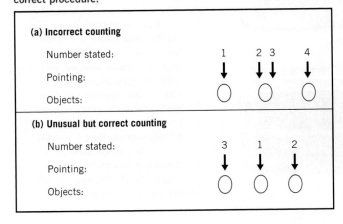

through 10, which do not follow any rule either in the English or the Chinese language. However, Chinese 4-year-olds quickly learn the numbers in the teens and succeeding decades, whereas their U.S. peers experience prolonged difficulty with the teens. The difference in language is not the only reason that the counting skill of U.S. children lags behind that of children in China. Chinese culture places a much greater emphasis on mathematical skill than U.S. culture does, and Chinese preschoolers are consequently more advanced than their U.S. peers in numerical skills generally, including arithmetic and number line estimation (Siegler & Mu, 2008). Still, the greater simplicity of the Chinese system for naming numbers in the teens seems to be one contributor to Chinese children's greater counting proficiency.

Relations Among Understanding of Space, Time, and Number

Piaget (1952) hypothesized that infants possess only a general, undifferentiated concept of magnitude, and lack specific concepts of space, time, and number. That is, he thought that infants have a concept of "bigness" but do not distinguish among larger size, longer time, and greater number. Subsequent research has shown that infants *can* distinguish among size, duration, and number. For example, after habituating to different displays with the same number of objects, infants dishabituate when the number of objects changes, even though the space occupied by the new objects and the time for which they are displayed is the same as previously (F. Xu & Arriaga, 2007; F. Xu & Spelke, 2000).

However, the fact that infants possess specific concepts of space, time, and number does not mean that they lack the type of undifferentiated magnitude concept that Piaget suggested. Indeed, Lourenco and Longo (2010) found that 9-month-olds have a general sense of magnitude that extends to space, number, and time. The infants in their study were initially habituated to the type of display shown at the top of Figure 7.10, in which a particular decoration (e.g., black with white stripes) consistently accompanied the larger of two stimuli on one of the three dimensions (e.g., size). Then the infants were presented displays in which the link between decoration and relative magnitude *on a different dimension* either was maintained or changed. For example, infants who had habituated to a link between black with white stripes and larger size might now see that decoration accompanying either the more numerous set (bottom left in Figure 7.10) or the less numerous one (bottom right in Figure 7.10). Lourenco and Longo found that the infants dishabituated when the decoration that had accompanied the larger stimulus now accompanied the one that was smaller on another dimension, but not when it continued to accompany the larger one. Similar results were obtained regardless of whether the habituated dimension was size, number, or time and regardless of whether the dimension that subsequently varied was size, number, or time.

Other research suggests the same conclusion (de Hevia & Spelke, 2010; Srinivasan & Carey, 2010). For instance, the ratios required for infants of a given age to discriminate between two stimuli are similar regardless of whether the discrimination involves time, space, or number (Brannon, Lutz, & Cordes, 2006; Brannon, Suanda, & Libertus, 2007). Moreover, overlapping brain areas in the intraparietal sulcus are involved in representing all three dimensions (Dehaene & Brannon, 2011). Thus, infants appear to have both the general, undifferentiated concept of magnitude that Piaget hypothesized they have, as well as the more specific concepts of time, space, and number that he hypothesized they lack.

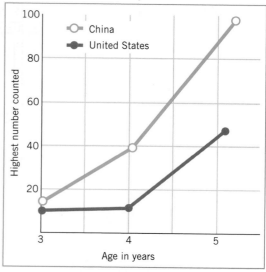

FIGURE 7.9 Counting level Although 3-year-olds in China and the United States can count to about the same point, 4- and 5-year-olds in China can count much higher than their U.S. peers. One reason for the faster development of Chinese children's counting ability appears to be that the Chinese words for numbers in the teens follow a consistent, easily learned pattern, whereas the English words for numbers in the teens must be memorized one by one. (Data from K. F. Miller et al., 1995)

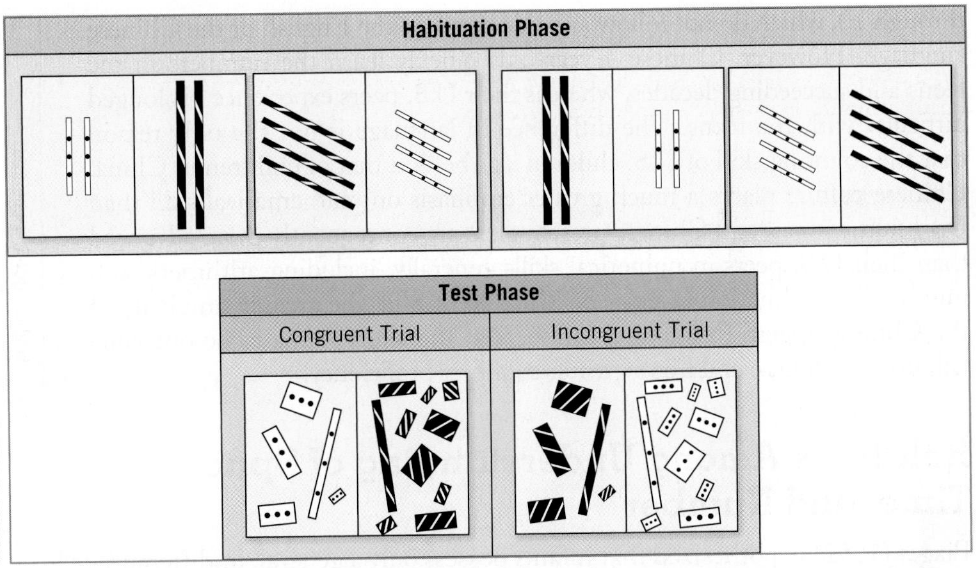

COURTESY OF STELLA LOURENCO

FIGURE 7.10 Infants' general magnitude representations To test whether infants possess a general sense of magnitude, Lourenco and Longo (2010) first presented pairs of figures, such as those in the top panel, in which one decoration (here, black with white stripes) was associated with the larger value of one quantitative dimension (here, larger size). After this habituation phase, the infants were shown either congruent trials (bottom left), in which the same decoration accompanied the choice with the greater quantitative value (here, the greater number of objects), or incongruent trials (bottom right), in which that decoration accompanied the choice with the smaller quantitative value (here, the smaller number of objects). Regardless of the particular pair of quantitative dimensions used during the habituation and test phases, children looked longer during incongruent trials, indicating that they expected that particular decoration to continue to accompany the choice with the larger value on whichever quantitative dimension varied.

Review

A basic understanding of causality emerges extremely early in development. Infants in their 1st year distinguish between physical causes, in which actions are produced by direct contact, and psychological causes, in which actions are produced by desires and beliefs. During the preschool and elementary school periods, children become increasingly adept at inferring causal relations, even when the relations are more complex and require deeper understanding of causes, effects, and the mechanisms that link them. However, belief in magic and the supernatural coexist with this growing understanding of causal mechanisms, especially in the preschool years.

People, like other animals, are biologically prepared to code specific types of spatial information in specific parts of the brain. From the 1st year, children represent spatial locations relative both to their own bodies and to other features of the environment, such as landmarks. Self-produced movement seems crucial in the further development of spatial representations.

A rudimentary sense of time also is present extremely early: by age 3 months, if not earlier, infants possess a sense of the order in which events happened. However, an accurate sense of duration doesn't develop until 3 to 5 years of age, and learning to reason logically about time takes even longer.

A basic recognition of differences between 1 to 4 objects, sounds, or actions is present in the 1st year, as is the ability to discriminate between larger sets whose numbers differ by substantial ratios. With age and experience, children become able to discriminate between increasingly smaller ratios. During the preschool period, children also learn the principles underlying counting, such as that each object must be counted once and only once. Learning of counting is influenced by the regularity of the number system in the child's language as well as by the culture's emphasis on mathematics.

In addition to specific representations of space, time, and number, infants possess a general representation of magnitude that extends across all three dimensions. The overlap in the brain areas in which the three dimensions are represented probably contributes to this general representation of magnitude.

CHAPTER SUMMARY

To understand their experiences, children must learn that the world includes several types of objects: people, other living things, and inanimate objects. Children also need a basic understanding of causality, space, time, and number, so that they will be able to code their experiences in terms of why, where, when, and how often events occurred.

Understanding Who or What

- Early categories of objects are based in large part on perceptual similarity, especially similarity in the shapes of the objects.

- By age 2 or 3 years, children form category hierarchies: animal/dog/poodle, furniture/chair/La-Z-Boy, and so on.

- From infancy onward, children differentiate people from other animals and inanimate objects. For example, infants smile more at people than at either rabbits or robots.

- By age 4 or 5 years, preschoolers develop a rudimentary but well-organized theory of mind for understanding people's behavior. A key assumption of this theory of mind is that desires and beliefs motivate specific actions.

- Understanding that other people will act on their beliefs, even when the beliefs are false, is very difficult for 3-year-olds; many children do not gain this understanding until age 5.

- Animals and plants, especially animals, are of great interest to young children. When animals are present, infants and toddlers pay careful attention to them.

- By age 4 years, children develop an elaborate understanding of living things, including coherent ideas about invisible processes such as growth, inheritance, illness, and healing. Both their natural fascination with living things and the input they receive from the environment contribute to their knowledge about plants and animals.

Understanding Why, Where, When, and How Many

- Debates between nativists and empiricists have increased our understanding of infants' impressive understanding of fundamental concepts regarding cause–effect relations, the human mind, space, time, and number, as well as the experiences and learning mechanisms that contribute to subsequent development of these concepts.

- The development of causal reasoning about physical events begins in infancy. By 6 to 12 months, infants understand the likely consequences of objects colliding. Understanding causal relations among actions helps 1-year-olds remember them.

- By 4 or 5 years, children seem to realize that causes are necessary for events to occur. When no cause is obvious, they search for one. However, many preschoolers believe in magic as well as physical cause–effect relations.

- People, like other animals, are biologically prepared to code space. Early in infancy, they code locations of other objects in relation to their own location and to landmarks. As they gain the ability to move around on their own, children gain a sense of locations relative to the overall environment as well as to their own body's current location.

- Children who are born blind have surprisingly good representations of space, though some aspects of their spatial processing, especially processing of faces, remain poor even if corrective surgery is performed during infancy.

- Just as infants are born with an ability to code some aspects of space, so they are born with an ability to code some aspects of time. Even 3-month-olds code the order in which events occur. Infants of that age can also use consistent sequences of past events to anticipate future events.

- By age 5 years, children can reason about time, in the sense of inferring that if two events started at the same time, and one stopped later than the other, the event that stopped later took longer. However, they can do this only when there are no interfering perceptual cues.

- Infants discriminate differences between the numbers of objects, sounds, or events when the ratio of the numbers is large. During their 1st year, they become able to discriminate smaller ratios of objects and events, a trend that continues to adulthood. From infancy onward, representations of small sets, those with 1 to 4 items, is more precise than those with larger sets.

- By age 3 years, most children learn to count 10 objects. Their counting seems to reflect understanding of certain principles, such as that each object should be labeled by a single number word. Children's subsequent rate of learning about numbers reflects their culture's number system and the degree to which their culture values numerical knowledge.

- From infancy onward, children also possess a general representation of magnitude that extends to space, time, and number.

Test Yourself

1. The belief that infants are born with some sense of fundamental concepts, such as time, space, and number, is a basic component of
   a. naïve psychology.
   b. theory of mind.
   c. nativism.
   d. empiricism.

2. In Krascum and Andrews' experiments, young children were better able to classify wugs and gillies after being told stories explaining each creature's unique appearance. Their findings support the importance of
   a. naïve psychology.
   b. causal relationships.
   c. magical thinking.
   d. false beliefs.

3. Research by Gelman and Kalish (2006) suggests that infants tend to divide objects into three general categories. Which of the following is *not* one of the general categories as identified by their research?
   a. food
   b. inanimate objects
   c. people
   d. other animals

4. Which of the following represents the most typical organization of superordinate, subordinate, and basic category levels that young children tend to form?
   a. animals/dogs/poodles
   b. objects/plants/animals
   c. parents/siblings/grandparents
   d. dogs/animals/poodles

5. Which category level do children tend to form first?
   a. superordinate
   b. subordinate
   c. basic
   d. primary

6. The proposed existence of a theory of mind module, which is the brain mechanism devoted to understanding other human beings, is most closely associated with advocates of which position?
   a. empiricism
   b. existentialism
   c. essentialism
   d. nativism

7. What is the significance of the false-belief problem?
   a. It illustrates that very young children do not understand that other people act on their own beliefs, even when those beliefs are false.
   b. It presents evidence that young children do not fully understand causal relationships.
   c. It proves that there are certain false beliefs that an individual will maintain from early childhood into adolescence.
   d. It supports the view that the age at which a child can understand other people's intentions varies by culture.

8. Which of the following is an example of sociodramatic play?
   a. Ezra is making car noises while pushing a toy car.
   b. Tanya is using her water bottle as a microphone.
   c. Laila is pretending that she is in school and her friend Tosha is the teacher.
   d. LeDonna is flying a kite with her father.

9. Ted believes that the reason his dog barks, wags her tail, and likes to go outside is because the dog has an inner "dogness." Ted's belief is an example of
   a. false belief.
   b. essentialism.
   c. nativism.
   d. perceptual categorization.

10. A mother magically produces a coin from behind her 6-year-old son's ear. Which of the following scenarios describes the response of a typical 6-year-old?
    a. The son searches his mother's hands, up her sleeves, and behind his ear to try to make sense of the event.
    b. The son does not react to this unusual event.
    c. The son does not find the trick funny and storms out of the room.
    d. The son realizes immediately that the mother has hidden the coin in her hand.

11. Nativists and empiricists have intense debates about the development of spatial thinking, but on which of the following points do these two groups tend to agree?
    a. Infants show little to no understanding of spatial concepts.
    b. Self-movement does not appear to aid in the development of spatial learning.
    c. Children are unable to use geometric information in locating objects.
    d. The development of the hippocampus is related to improvements in spatial learning.

12. According to Piaget, children's coding of locations of objects relative to their own bodies is referred to as
    a. landmark representations.
    b. allocentric spatial representations.
    c. egocentric spatial representations.
    d. directional representations.

13. In front of Sue are three balls, three teddy bears, three pencils, and three apples. Sue studies the groups of objects and realizes that they all share the property of "threeness." Sue is demonstrating an understanding of what concept?
    a. stable order
    b. order irrelevance
    c. numerical equality
    d. abstraction

14. Kamar is happily counting all of his holiday candy, reciting a number as he touches each piece: "One, two, three, four, five, six, seven, eight, nine." He holds up the final piece and

states, "I have seven pieces of candy!" Kamar's counting skills suggests he lacks an understanding of _____ .
a. stable order
b. cardinality
c. one–one correspondence
d. abstraction

15. Which of the following statements describes the counting principle of abstraction?
a. Any set of discrete objects or events can be counted.
b. Objects can be counted in any order.
c. Each object must be labeled by a single number word.
d. The numbers should always be recited in the same order.

LaunchPad
macmillan learning

Don't stop now! Research shows that testing yourself is a powerful learning tool. Visit LaunchPad to access the LearningCurve adaptive quizzing system, which gives you a personalized study plan to help build your mastery of the chapter material through videos, activities, and more. **Go to launchpadworks.com.**

Critical Thinking Questions

1. Why is it useful for people to organize categories into hierarchies, such as animal/dog/poodle or vehicle/car/Tesla?

2. Did you have an imaginary companion as a child or know someone who did? What functions did the invisible friend serve, and why do you think you or the other person later stopped imagining the companion?

3. Why do you think 5-year-olds are so much better at false-belief problems than 3-year-olds are?

4. Self-produced movement enhances children's representation of space. What evolutionary purpose might this serve?

5. Describe the thoughts that might go through a 5-year-old's mind when the child sees two Santa Clauses walking past each other.

6. Do infants possess a basic understanding of arithmetic? Why or why not?

7. Why might it be useful for children to have a general representation of quantity, as well as specific representations of space, time, and number?

8. After reading this chapter, do you lean more toward a nativist or an empiricist approach to conceptual development? What reasons led to your conclusion?

Key Terms

basic level, p. 291

category hierarchy, p. 290

concepts, p. 288

egocentric spatial representations, p. 311

essentialism, p. 303

false-belief problems, p. 295

naïve psychology, p. 293

numerical equality, p. 316

object substitution, p. 299

perceptual categorization, p. 291

pretend play, p. 298

sociodramatic play, p. 299

subordinate level, p. 291

superordinate level, p. 291

theory of mind, p. 294

theory of mind module (TOMM), p. 297

▶ Student Video Activities

Theory of Mind

Autism Spectrum Disorder

Imaginary Companions: The Research of Marjorie Taylor

The Development of Purposive Reasoning

Toddler's Use of Tools

Magical Thinking

Preoperational and Concrete Operational Thought

Answers to Test Yourself

1. c, **2.** b, **3.** a, **4.** d, **5.** c, **6.** d, **7.** a, **8.** c, **9.** b, **10.** a, **11.** d, **12.** c, **13.** c, **14.** b, **15.** a

CHARLES HAIGH-WOOD (1856–1927), *Story Time* (oil on canvas, 1893)

Intelligence and Academic Achievement

Themes

- Nature and Nurture
- The Active Child
- Continuity/Discontinuity
- Mechanisms of Change
- The Sociocultural Context
- Individual Differences
- Research and Children's Welfare

In 1904, the minister of education of France faced a problem. France, like other western European and North American countries, had recently introduced universal public education, and it was becoming apparent that some children were not learning well. Therefore, the minister wanted a means of identifying children who would have difficulty succeeding in standard classrooms, so that they could be given special education. His problem was how to identify such children.

One obvious solution was to ask teachers to indicate which of their students were encountering difficulty. However, the minister worried that teachers might be biased in their assessments. In particular, he was concerned that some teachers would be prejudiced against poor children and would claim that those children were unable to learn, even if they actually could. He therefore asked Alfred Binet, a French psychologist who had studied intelligence for many years, to develop an easy-to-administer, objective test of intelligence.

The prevailing view at the time was that intelligence is based on simple skills, such as associating objects with the sounds they make (e.g., ducks with quacking, bells with ringing), responding quickly to stimuli, and recognizing whether two objects are identical. According to this view, children who are more adept than their peers at such simple skills learn more quickly and thus become more intelligent. The theory was plausible—but wrong. It is now clear that differences among children in simple skills are only modestly related to differences among the children in broader, everyday indicators of intelligence, such as school performance.

Binet's theory differed from the prevailing wisdom of his time. He believed that the key components of intelligence were high-level abilities, such as problem solving, reasoning, and judgment, and he maintained that intelligence tests should assess such abilities directly. Therefore, on the test that he and his colleague Théophile Simon devised—the *Binet–Simon Intelligence Test*—children were asked (among other things) to interpret proverbs, solve puzzles, define words, and sequence cartoon panels so that the jokes made sense.

Binet's approach was successful in identifying children who would have difficulty learning from classroom instruction; they were the children who could not interpret the proverbs, solve the puzzles, define the words, and so on. More generally, children's performance on the Binet–Simon Intelligence Test correlated highly not only with their school grades at the time of testing but also with their grades years later. The test was also reasonably successful in meeting a goal of intelligence testing that has been pursued ever since—to provide an objective measure of scholastic aptitude that would allow fairer decisions about children's schooling, including which children should be in honors classes, which are in need of special education, which should be admitted to highly selective colleges, and so on.

In addition to the practical impact of his test, Binet's theoretical approach to intelligence has continued to influence research on the topic to this day. In most areas of cognitive development—perception, language, conceptual understanding, and so forth—the emphasis is on age-related changes: the ways in which younger children differ from older ones. Following Binet's lead, however, research on intelligence has focused on *individual differences*—on how and why children of the same age differ from one another and on the continuity of such individual differences over time.

Questions regarding the development of intelligence excite strong passions, and for good reason. Research in this area raises many of the most basic issues about human nature: the roles of heredity and environment, the influence of ethnic and racial differences, the effects of wealth and poverty, and the possibility of improvement. Almost everyone has opinions, often heartfelt ones, about why some people are more intelligent than others.

Intelligence research has added greatly to understanding all the major themes emphasized in this book: the nature and origins of *individual differences,* the contributions of the *active child* and of the *sociocultural context,* the way in which *nature and nurture* together shape development, the degree of *continuity* in a key human trait, the *mechanisms* that produce changes, and the relation between *research and children's welfare.* Before examining what is known about the development of intelligence, however, we must examine a question that sounds simple but actually lies at the heart of many controversies: What *is* intelligence?

What Is Intelligence?

Intelligence is notoriously difficult to define, but this has not kept people from trying. Part of the difficulty is that intelligence can legitimately be described at three levels of analysis: as one thing, as a few things, or as many things.

Intelligence as a Single Trait

Some researchers view intelligence as a single trait that influences all aspects of cognitive functioning. Supporting this idea is the fact that performance on all intellectual tasks is positively correlated: children who do well on one task tend to do well on others, too (Geary, 2005). These positive correlations occur even among dissimilar intellectual tasks—for example, remembering lists of numbers and folding pieces of paper to reproduce printed designs. Such omnipresent positive correlations have led to the hypothesis that each of us possesses a certain amount of *g,* or **general intelligence,** and that *g* influences our ability to think and learn on all intellectual tasks (J. B. Carroll, 2005; Spearman, 1927).

Numerous sources of evidence attest to the usefulness of viewing intelligence as a single trait. Measures of *g,* such as overall scores on intelligence tests, correlate positively with school grades and achievement test performance (Gottfredson, 2011). At the level of cognitive and brain mechanisms, *g* correlates with information-processing speed (Coyle et al., 2011; Deary, 2000), speed of neural transmission (Vernon et al., 2000), and brain volume (McDaniel, 2005). Measures of *g* also correlate strongly with people's general information about the world (Lubinski & Humphreys, 1997). Such evidence supports the view of intelligence as a single trait that involves the ability to think and learn.

Intelligence as a Few Basic Abilities

There are also good arguments for viewing intelligence as more than a single general trait. The simplest such view holds that there are two types of intelligence: *fluid intelligence* and *crystallized intelligence* (Cattell, 1987):

■ **Fluid intelligence** involves the ability to think on the spot—for example, by drawing inferences and understanding relations between concepts that have not been encountered previously. It is closely related to adaptation to novel tasks, speed of information processing, working-memory functioning, and ability to control attention (C. Blair, 2006; Geary, 2005).

g **(general intelligence)** ■ cognitive processes that influence the ability to think and learn on all intellectual tasks

fluid intelligence ■ ability to think on the spot to solve novel problems

crystallized intelligence ■ factual knowledge about the world

primary mental abilities ■ seven abilities proposed by Thurstone as crucial to intelligence

three-stratum theory of intelligence ■ Carroll's model that places *g* at the top of the intelligence hierarchy, eight moderately general abilities in the middle, and many specific processes at the bottom

■ **Crystallized intelligence** is factual knowledge about the world: knowledge of word meanings, state capitals, answers to arithmetic problems, and so on. It reflects long-term memory for prior experiences and is closely related to verbal ability.

The distinction between fluid and crystallized intelligence is supported by the fact that tests of each type of intelligence correlate more highly with tests of the same type than they do with tests of the other type (J. L. Horn & McArdle, 2007). Thus, children who do well on one test of fluid intelligence tend to do well on other tests of fluid intelligence but not necessarily on tests of crystallized intelligence, and vice versa. In addition, the two types of intelligence have different developmental courses. Crystallized intelligence increases steadily from early in life to old age, whereas fluid intelligence peaks around age 20 and slowly declines thereafter (Salthouse, 2009). The brain areas most active in the two types of intelligence also differ: the prefrontal cortex usually is highly active on measures of fluid intelligence but tends to be much less active in measures of crystallized intelligence (C. Blair, 2006; Jung & Haier, 2007).

A somewhat more differentiated view of intelligence (Thurstone, 1938) proposes that the human intellect is composed of seven **primary mental abilities:** word fluency, verbal meaning, reasoning, spatial visualization, numbering, rote memory, and perceptual speed. The key evidence for the usefulness of dividing intelligence into these seven abilities is similar to that for the distinction between fluid and crystallized intelligence. Scores on various tests of a single ability tend to correlate more strongly with one another than do scores on tests of different abilities. For example, although both spatial visualization and perceptual speed are measures of fluid intelligence, children tend to perform more similarly on two tests of spatial visualization than they do on a test of spatial visualization and a test of perceptual speed. The trade-off between these two views of intelligence is between the simplicity of the crystallized/fluid distinction and the greater precision of the idea of seven primary mental abilities.

Intelligence as Numerous Cognitive Processes

A third view envisions intelligence as comprising numerous, distinct *processes*. Information-processing analyses of how people solve intelligence test items and how they perform everyday intellectual tasks such as reading, writing, and arithmetic reveal that a great many processes are involved (e.g., Geary, 2005). These processes include remembering, perceiving, attending, comprehending, encoding, associating, generalizing, planning, reasoning, forming concepts, solving problems, generating and applying strategies, and so on. Viewing intelligence as "many processes" allows more precise specification of the mechanisms involved in intelligent behavior than do approaches that view it as "a single trait" or as "several abilities."

A Proposed Resolution

How can these competing perspectives on intelligence be reconciled? After studying intelligence for more than half a century, John B. Carroll (1993, 2005) proposed a grand integration: the **three-stratum theory of intelligence** (Figure 8.1). At the top of the hierarchy is *g;* in the middle are several moderately general abilities (which include both fluid and crystallized intelligence and other competencies similar to Thurstone's seven primary mental abilities); at the bottom are many specific

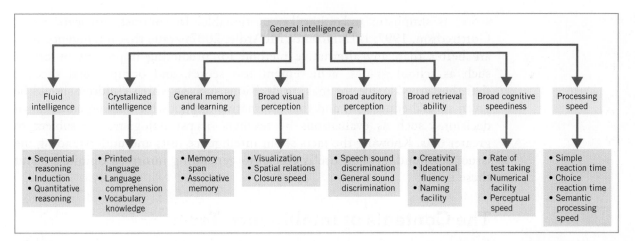

FIGURE 8.1 Carroll's three-stratum theory of intelligence In Carroll's hierarchy, general intelligence (*g*) influences several intermediate-level abilities, and each intermediate-level ability influences a variety of specific processes. As this model suggests, intelligence can be usefully viewed as a single entity, as a small set of abilities, or as a very large number of particular processes.

processes. General intelligence influences all moderately general abilities, and both general intelligence and the moderately general abilities influence the specific processes. For instance, knowing someone's general intelligence allows for a fairly reliable prediction of the person's general memory skills; knowing both of them allows quite reliable prediction of the person's memory span; and knowing all three allows very accurate prediction of the person's memory span for a particular type of material, such as words, letters, or numbers.

Carroll's comprehensive analysis of the research literature indicated that all three levels of analysis that we have discussed in this section are necessary to account for the totality of facts about intelligence. Thus, for the question "Is intelligence a single trait, a few abilities, or many processes?" the correct answer seems to be "All of the above."

Review

Intelligence can be viewed as a single general ability to think and learn; as several moderately general abilities, such as crystallized and fluid intelligence; or as a collection of numerous specific skills, processes, and content knowledge. All three levels are useful for understanding intelligence.

Measuring Intelligence

Although intelligence is usually viewed as an invisible *capacity* to think and learn, any measure of it must be based on *observable behavior*. Thus, when we say that a person is intelligent, we mean that the person acts in intelligent ways. One of Binet's profound insights was that the best way to measure intelligence is by observing people's actions on tasks that require a variety of types of intelligence: problem solving, memory, language comprehension, spatial reasoning, and so on. Modern intelligence tests continue to sample these and other aspects of intelligence.

Intelligence testing is highly controversial. Critics such as Ceci (1996) and Sternberg (2008) argue that measuring a quality as complex and multifaceted as intelligence requires assessing a much broader range of abilities than are assessed by current intelligence tests; that current intelligence tests are culturally biased; and that reducing a person's intelligence to a number (the IQ score) is simplistic and ethically questionable. In contrast, advocates (e.g., Gottfredson, 1997; J. L. Horn & McArdle, 2007) argue that intelligence tests are better than any alternative method for predicting important outcomes such as school grades, achievement test scores, and occupational success; that they are valuable for making decisions such as which children should be given special education; and that alternative methods for making educational decisions, such as evaluations by teachers or psychologists, are subject to greater bias. Knowing the facts about intelligence tests and understanding the issues surrounding their use is crucial to generating informed opinions about these issues.

The Contents of Intelligence Tests

Intelligence is reflected in different abilities at different ages. For example, language ability is not a part of intelligence at 4 months of age because infants this young neither produce nor understand words, but it is obviously a vital part of intelligence at 4 years of age. The items on tests developed to measure intelligence at different ages reflect these changing aspects. For instance, on the Stanford–Binet intelligence test (a descendant of the original Binet–Simon test), 2-year-olds are asked to identify the objects depicted in line drawings (a test of object recognition), to find an object that they earlier saw someone hide (a test of learning and memory), and to place each of three objects in a hole of the proper shape (a test of perceptual skill and motor coordination). The version of the Stanford–Binet presented to 10-year-olds asks them to define words (a test of verbal ability), to explain why certain social institutions exist (a test of general information and verbal reasoning), and to count the blocks in a picture in which the existence of some blocks must be inferred (a test of problem solving and spatial reasoning).

Intelligence tests have had their greatest success and widest application with children who are at least 5 or 6 years old. The exact abilities examined, and the items used to examine them, vary somewhat from test to test, but there is considerable similarity among the leading tests.

The most widely used intelligence testing instrument for children 6 years and older is the **Wechsler Intelligence Scale for Children (WISC).** The current edition, the WISC-V, was revised in 2014 to reflect modern theoretical conceptions of intelligence and the current population of children in the United States, which is more diverse, both linguistically and culturally, than it was when earlier versions of the WISC were published (Kaufman, Raiford, & Coalson, 2016).

The conception of intelligence underlying the WISC-V is consistent with Carroll's three-stratum framework, proposing that intelligence includes general ability (g), several moderately general abilities, and a large number of specific processes. The test yields not only an overall score but also separate scores on five moderately general abilities—verbal comprehension, visual-spatial processing, working memory, fluid reasoning, and processing speed. The WISC-V measures these abilities because they reflect skills that are important within information-processing theories, correlate positively with other aspects of intelligence, and are related to important outcomes, notably school grades and later occupational success. Figure 8.2 provides examples of types of items that appear on the WISC-V (the actual items are protected by copyrights and thus cannot be reprinted).

Wechsler Intelligence Scale for Children (WISC) ■ widely used test designed to measure the intelligence of children 6 years and older

Typical Verbal Comprehension Items

Vocabulary "What is a helicopter?"

Similarities "How are a mountain and a river alike?"

Typical Visual-Spatial Processing Items

Block design "Make these nine blocks look exactlly like the picture."

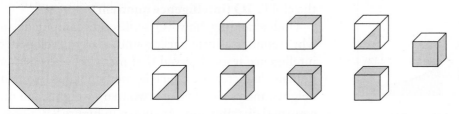

Typical Fluid Reasoning Items

Picture concepts "Pick an object from each pair to make a group of objects that go together"

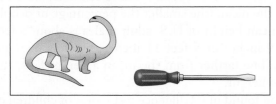

Typical Working Memory Items

Digit span "Repeat the following numbers in order when I'm finished: 5, 3, 7, 4, 9." "Now say these numbers from last to first: 2, 9, 5, 7, 3."

Letter-number sequencing "Repeat the numbers from smallest to biggest, then repeat the letters from earliest to latest in the alphabet: 4, D, 2, G, 7."

Typical Processing Speed Items

Coding "Under each square, put a plus; under each circle, put a minus; under each triangle, put an X."

Symbol search "Does the figure to the left of the vertical line also appear to the right of the line?"

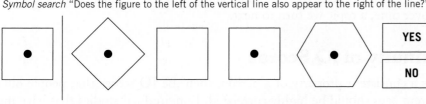

FIGURE 8.2 Four abilities tested by WISC-V This figure shows examples of the types of items used on the WISC-V to measure four aspects of children's intelligence. On most subtests, the measure of performance is simply whether answers are correct, but on some subtests, such as "perceptual speed," the measure of performance is the number of correct answers that are generated in a limited time. These are not actual items from the test but rather are of the same type; copyright laws prevent the reproduction of the actual items.

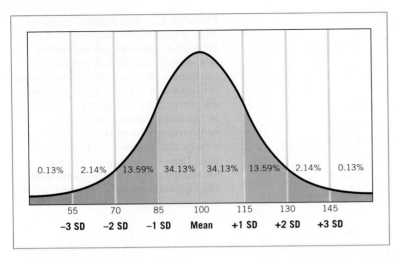

0.13% 2.14% 13.59% 34.13% 34.13% 13.59% 2.14% 0.13%

| 55 | 70 | 85 | 100 | 115 | 130 | 145 |
| -3 SD | -2 SD | -1 SD | Mean | +1 SD | +2 SD | +3 SD |

FIGURE 8.3 A normal distribution of IQ scores Like other measurable human characteristics, IQ scores fall into a normal distribution. Here, the numbers along the base of the graph correspond to IQ scores. The number just below each IQ score indicates how many standard deviation units that score is below or above the mean. Thus, an IQ score of 55 is 3 standard deviations below the mean. The percentages in each interval indicate the percentage of children whose scores fall within that interval; for example, less than 1% of children have IQ scores below 55 and slightly more than 2% score between 55 and 70.

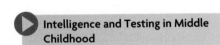

Intelligence and Testing in Middle Childhood

IQ (intelligence quotient) ■ quantitative measure, typically with a mean of 100 and a standard deviation of 15, used to indicate a child's intelligence relative to that of other children of the same age

normal distribution ■ pattern of data in which scores fall symmetrically around a mean value, with most scores falling close to the mean and fewer and fewer scores farther from it

standard deviation (SD) ■ measure of the variability of scores in a distribution; in a normal distribution, 68% of scores fall within 1 SD of the mean, and 95% of scores fall within 2 SDs of the mean

The Intelligence Quotient (IQ)

Intelligence tests such as the WISC and the Stanford–Binet provide an overall quantitative measure of a child's intelligence relative to that of other children of the same age. This summary measure is referred to as the child's **IQ (intelligence quotient).**

Understanding how IQ scores are computed, and why, requires a little background. Early developers of intelligence tests observed that many easy-to-measure human characteristics, such as men's heights, women's heights, men's weights, and women's weights, fall into a **normal distribution.** As shown in Figure 8.3, normal distributions are symmetrical around a mean (average) value, with most scores falling relatively near the mean. The farther a score is from the mean, the smaller the percentage of people who obtain it. For example, the mean height of U.S. adult males is about 5 feet 10 inches. Many men are 5 feet 9 inches or 5 feet 11 inches, but few men are 5 feet 2 inches or 6 feet 6 inches. The farther from the mean a height falls, the smaller the number of men of that height.

Similarly, the normal distribution found in intelligence test scores of children of a given age means that most IQ scores are fairly close to the mean, with relatively few children obtaining very high or very low scores. Early designers of IQ tests made an arbitrary decision that has been maintained ever since: a score of 100 is given to children who score exactly at the mean for their age at the time the test is developed. (The mean score can rise or fall in the years after a particular test is developed, and indeed, as discussed later in this chapter, IQ scores on specific tests have risen throughout the industrialized world over the past century.)

IQ scores reflect not only the mean for the test but also its **standard deviation (SD),** a measure of the variability of scores within a distribution. By definition, in a normal distribution, 68% of scores fall between 1 SD below the mean and 1 SD above it, and 95% of scores fall between 2 SDs below the mean and 2 SDs above it.

On most IQ tests, the standard deviation is about 15 points. Thus, as shown in Figure 8.3, a child scoring 1 standard deviation above the mean for his or her age (a score higher than 84% of children) receives a score of 115 (the mean of 100 plus the 15-point SD). Similarly, a child scoring 1 standard deviation below the mean (a score higher than only 16% of children) receives a score of 85 (the mean of 100 minus the SD of 15). Figure 8.3 also reflects the fact that about 95% of children obtain IQ scores that fall within 2 standard deviations of the mean (between 70 and 130).

An advantage of this scoring system is that IQ scores at different ages are easy to compare, despite the great increases in knowledge that accompany development in all children. A score of 130 at age 5 means that a child's performance exceeded that of 98% of age peers; a score of 130 at age 10 or 20 means exactly the same thing. This property has facilitated analysis of the stability of individuals' IQ scores over time, a topic we turn to next.

Continuity of IQ Scores

If IQ is a consistent property of a person, then the IQ scores that people obtain at different ages should be highly correlated. Longitudinal studies that have measured the same children's IQ scores at different ages have, in fact, shown impressive continuity from age 5 onward. For example, one study indicated that the same children's IQ scores at ages 5 and 15 correlated 0.67 (Humphreys, 1989). This is a remarkable degree of continuity over a 10-year period. (Recall from Chapter 1 that a correlation of 1.00 indicates that two variables are perfectly correlated; a correlation of 0.67 is considered strong.) Indeed, the IQ score may be the most stable of all psychological traits (N. Brody, 1992).

Several variables influence the degree of stability of IQ scores over time. As might be expected, the closer in time that IQ tests are given, the more stability is found. Thus, the same study that found that IQ scores at ages 5 and 15 correlated 0.67 also found that scores at ages 5 and 9 correlated 0.79 and at ages 5 and 6 correlated 0.87. In addition, for any given length of time between tests, scores are more stable at older ages. For instance, in one study, IQ scores of 4- and 5-year-olds correlated 0.80, those of 6- and 7-year-olds correlated 0.87, and those of 8- and 9-year-olds correlated 0.90 (N. Brody, 1992).

Although a person's IQ scores at different ages tend to be similar, the scores are rarely identical. Children who take an IQ test at age 4 and again at age 17 show an average change, up or down, of 13 points; those who take the test at ages 8 and 17 show an average change of 9 points; and those who take it at ages 12 and 17 show an average change of 7 points (N. Brody, 1992). These changes in the same child's score from one age to another are due at least in part to random variation in factors such as the child's alertness and mood on the test days. Changes in the child's environment, such as those associated with parental divorce or remarriage or moving to a better or worse neighborhood, also can produce changes in IQ score; the greater similarity of children's environments over shorter periods of time probably contributes to the greater similarity of scores over shorter periods (Sameroff et al., 1993).

A question of interest to parents and scientists alike is whether it is possible to identify at young ages children who are superior in intelligence or in specific intellectual or artistic abilities. Research on such children, who are often described as "gifted," is presented in Box 8.1.

The IQ scores of children whose parents take an interest in their academic success tend to increase over time.

Review

Intelligence tests examine a range of abilities and types of knowledge, including vocabulary, verbal comprehension, arithmetic, memory, and spatial reasoning. The tests are used to obtain a general measure of intelligence: the IQ score. IQ tests are designed to produce average scores of 100, with higher scores indicating above-average intelligence and lower scores below-average intelligence. After age 5 or 6, IQ scores of individual children tend to be quite stable over long periods, but they vary somewhat from one testing to the next.

IQ Scores as Predictors of Important Outcomes

IQ scores are a strong predictor of academic, economic, and occupational success (Sackett, Borneman, & Connelly, 2008; F. L. Schmidt & Hunter, 2004). They correlate positively and quite strongly with school grades and achievement test

BOX 8.1 | individual differences

GIFTED CHILDREN

At age 18 months, Kyle was already fascinated by numbers. His favorite toys were plastic numbers and blocks with numbers on them. As he played with these toys, he said the number names over and over. When he was 2 years old, he saw a license plate with two 8s on it and said "8 + 8 = 16." Neither he nor his parents could explain how he knew this. By age 3 years, Kyle was playing math games on a computer every day. During one such game, he discovered the idea of prime numbers and thereafter was able to identify new prime numbers. Again, neither he nor his parents knew how he did this.

Before he entered kindergarten, Kyle could add, subtract, multiply, divide, estimate, and solve complex word problems. When asked if he ever got tired of numbers, he said, "No, never" and said that he was a "number boy" (Winner, 1996, pp. 38–39). He went on to represent his state in the national MATHCOUNTS competition when he was a 7th-grader, pursued a master's degree in computer science at an Ivy League university, and did a summer internship at a highly rated medical school, helping to teach machines how to diagnose burns on human skin. He plans to devote his career to improving the efficiency of everyday life activities through the development of superior algorithms (personal communication with Kyle's mother, August 23, 2016).

As noted by Ellen Winner, a psychologist who studies intellectually and artistically gifted children, most, like Kyle, show astonishing early facility in a single area: numbers, music, drawing, reading, or some other realm. A smaller number of children are exceptional over a wide range of intellectual areas. These globally gifted children usually display several signs of giftedness from very early in development (N. M. Robinson & Robinson, 1992):

- Unusual alertness and long attention span in infancy
- Rapid language development
- Curiosity—asking deep questions and being dissatisfied with superficial answers
- High energy levels, often bordering on hyperactivity
- Intense reactions to frustration
- Precocious reading and interest in numbers
- Exceptional logical and abstract reasoning
- Unusually good memory
- Enjoyment of solitary play

Exceptional early ability often foreshadows outstanding later achievement. Consider a long-term study of 320 children who took the SAT by age 13 as part of a national talent search and who scored in the top 1 in 10,000 in verbal or math ability. Among their accomplishments by age 23 were adapting Pink Floyd's *The Wall* into a multimedia rock opera, developing one of the most popular video games in the United States, and inventing a navigation system that was used to land a rocket on Mars (Lubinski et al., 2001). As a group, they had published 11 articles in scientific and medical journals and won numerous major awards in areas ranging from physics to creative writing.

By age 38, more than half of the original sample had received a PhD, MD, or JD (Kell, Lubinski, & Benbow, 2013). Their rate of PhDs was more than 50 times higher than that for the general population, and their rate of patents was 11 times that in the general population. Even within this elite sample, higher initial SAT mathematics scores predicted higher achievement. For example, the higher the score on the SAT math test at age 13, the greater the number of patents and publications in scholarly journals—especially those in science, engineering, and mathematics—at age 38. Those students whose verbal test scores exceeded their math scores tended to make their largest contribution in the arts, humanities, and social sciences, whereas those whose math scores were higher tended to make their main contributions in mathematics, statistics, and computer science (Makel et al., 2016).

Exceptional early ability in an area is no guarantee of outstanding adult achievement in it, however. Factors such as creativity, devotion to the area, ability to work long hours, and perseverance in the face of difficulty are also essential for making exceptional contributions (Makel et al., 2016; Wai et al., 2010). Nonetheless, it is remarkable how scores on a single test, given at age 13 years, predict exceptional achievement 25 years later.

 Interview with Ellen Winner

Exceptionally early readers, such as this 3½-year-old, often continue to be excellent readers throughout life.

PETER BECK / GETTY IMAGES

performance, both at the time of the test and years later (Geary, 2005); for example, IQ and achievement test performance typically correlate between 0.50 and 0.60 (Deary et al., 2007). Substantial relations between IQ score and performance in intellectually demanding occupations are present not only when the person is hired but for at least 10 years after entry into the occupation (Sackett et al., 2008).

In part, the positive relation between IQ score and occupational and economic success stems from the fact that standardized test scores serve as gatekeepers, determining which students gain access to the training and credentials required for entry into lucrative professions. Even among people who initially have the same job, however, those with higher IQ scores tend to perform better, earn more money, and receive better promotions (F. L. Schmidt & Hunter, 2004; Wilk, Desmarais, & Sackett, 1995).

A child's IQ score is more closely related to the child's later occupational success than is the socioeconomic status of the child's family, the school the child attends, or any other variable that has been studied (Ganzach et al., 2013; Kulkofsky & Ceci, 2006). These relations hold even at the top of the test score distribution. Although popular books such as *Outliers* (Gladwell, 2008) claim that people with fairly high test scores achieve grades and occupational success equivalent to those of people with very high scores, empirical research indicates that even at the top of the distribution, the higher the test score, the higher that subsequent achievement is likely to be (Arneson, Sackett, & Beatty, 2011; Lubinsky, Benbow, & Kell, 2014).

Other Predictors of Success

As strong a predictor of academic, economic, and occupational success as IQ score is, it is far from the only influence. A child's other characteristics, such as motivation to succeed, conscientiousness, intellectual curiosity, creativity, physical and mental health, and social skills, also exert important influences (Roberts et al., 2007; Sternberg, 2004; von Stumm, Hell, & Chamorro-Premuzic, 2011). For instance, **self-discipline**—the ability to inhibit actions, follow rules, and avoid impulsive reactions—is more predictive of changes in report card grades between 5th and 9th grades than is IQ score, though IQ score is more predictive of changes in achievement test scores over the same period (Duckworth, Quinn, & Tsukayama, 2012). Similarly, "practical intelligence"—skills useful in everyday life but not measured by traditional intelligence tests, such as accurately reading other people's intentions and motivating others to work effectively as a team—predicts occupational success beyond the influence of IQ score (Cianciolo et al., 2006; Sternberg, 2003). Characteristics of the environment are similarly influential: parents' encouragement and modeling of productive careers predict their children's occupational success (Kalil, Levine, & Ziol-Guest, 2005). Moreover, IQ tests appear to measure motivation to succeed on the test as well as intellect; offering participants material incentives, such as money or candy, to do well on IQ tests increases IQ scores (Duckworth et al., 2011), which would not be expected if all students were maximally motivated to do well on the tests.

Figure 8.4 illustrates how the same set of data can simultaneously provide evidence for the importance of IQ score and other factors. Consistent with the importance of IQ, the figure shows that, among people with the same level of education, those with higher IQ scores earn more money. Consistent with the importance of other factors, the figure shows that, among

self-discipline ■ ability to inhibit actions, follow rules, and avoid impulsive reactions

FIGURE 8.4 Effects of intelligence and education on income Intelligence influences income, but so do other factors, such as education. These data indicate the average income of people who received different levels of education and who scored in different quintiles (fifths) of the IQ distribution. Within any given educational level, people with higher IQ scores earned more. Thus, among people with only a high school education, those who scored in the bottom 20% on an IQ test (the blue bar) averaged only a little more than $250/week, but those who scored in the top 20% (the purple bar) averaged almost $450/week. People in the top 20% in IQ score earned considerably more, but here too education mattered: those with high IQ scores who had only a high school education earned an average of roughly $450/week, whereas those with comparable IQ scores and a four-year college education earned almost $650/week. (Data from Ceci, 1996)

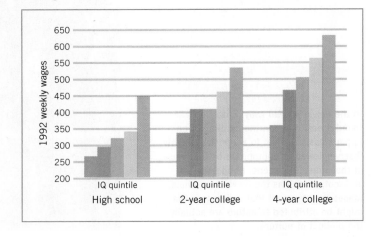

people with comparable IQ scores, those who complete more years of education earn more money. Thus, while IQ is a key contributor to educational, occupational, and economic success, numerous social and motivational factors are also crucial.

Review

IQ scores are positively related to grades in school and achievement test performance, both at the time of the test and in the future. They are also positively related to occupational success in adulthood. However, they are not the only influence on these outcomes. Intellectual curiosity, creativity, self-discipline, social skills, practical intelligence, and a variety of other factors also contribute.

Genes, Environment, and the Development of Intelligence

No issue in psychology has produced more acrimonious debate than the issue of how heredity and environment influence intelligence. Even people who recognize that intelligence, like all human qualities, is constructed through the continuous interaction of genes and environment often forget this fact and take extreme positions that are based more on emotions and ideology than on logic and evidence.

A useful starting point for thinking about genetic and environmental influences on intelligence is Bronfenbrenner's (1993) bioecological model of development (detailed in Chapter 9). This model envisions children's lives as embedded within a series of increasingly encompassing environments. The child, with a unique set of qualities including his or her genetic endowment and personal experiences, is at the center. Surrounding the child is the immediate environment, especially the people and institutions with which the child interacts directly: family, school,

In the movie *My Fair Lady*, Eliza Doolittle found it easier to don the clothing of an upper-class lady than to adopt the haughty reserve viewed as appropriate by that class at that time. This scene, of opening day at Ascot, as well as the movie as a whole, makes the argument that differences that might be attributed to nature are actually the product of nurture.

WARNER BROS / REX / SHUTTERSTOCK

classmates, teachers, neighbors, and so on. Surrounding the immediate environment are more distant, and less tangible, forces that also influence development: cultural attitudes, the social and economic system, mass media, the government, and so on. We now examine how qualities of the child, the immediate environment, and the broader society contribute to the development of intelligence.

Qualities of the Child

Children contribute greatly to their own intellectual development through their genetic endowment, the reactions they elicit from other people, and their choice of environments.

Genetic Contributions to Intelligence

As noted in Chapter 3, the genome substantially influences intelligence. This genetic influence varies greatly with age (Figure 8.5): it is moderate in early childhood and becomes large by adolescence and adulthood (Bouchard, 2004; Krapohl et al., 2014). Reflecting the same trend, IQ scores of adopted children and their biological parents become increasingly correlated as the children develop, even without contact between them, but the scores of adopted children and their adoptive parents become less correlated over the course of development (Plomin et al., 1997).

One reason for this increasing genetic influence is that some genetic processes do not exert their effects until late childhood or adolescence. For example, some types of synchronization of activities of distant brain areas are not evident until adolescence or early adulthood, and the extent of such synchronization reflects genetic influences (Uhlhaas et al., 2010). Another reason is that children's increasing independence with age allows them greater freedom to choose environments that are compatible with their own genetically based preferences but not necessarily with those of the parents who are raising them (McAdams & Olson, 2010).

Advances in genetics have inspired research aimed at identifying genes that explain individual differences in intelligence. These efforts have led to identification of a large number of genes that are associated with mental retardation (Inlow & Restifo, 2004) and a large number of other genes that are consistently related to normal variation in intelligence (Trzaskowski et al., 2014). However, the correlations between individual alleles of genes and IQ are almost all very small. These findings suggest that genetic influences on intelligence reflect small contributions from each of a very large number of genes, as well as complex interactions among them, rather than one or a small number of master genes (Chabris et al., 2015; Mukherjee, 2016; Nisbett et al., 2012).

Genotype–Environment Interactions

As noted in Chapter 3, the environments children encounter are influenced by the children's genotype. Sandra Scarr (1992) proposed that gene–environment relations involve three types of processes: passive, evocative, and active.

■ *Passive effects* of the genotype arise when children are raised by their biological parents. These effects occur not because of anything the children do but

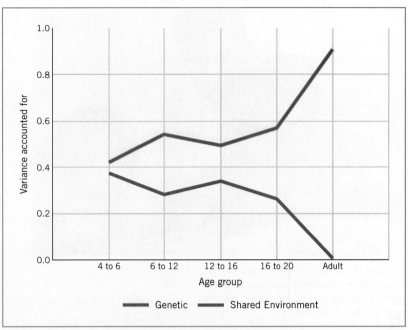

FIGURE 8.5 Changes with age in factors influencing intelligence As children grow into adults, the influence of genetics on individual differences in intelligence increases, whereas the influence of shared aspects of family environment decreases. (Data from McGue et al., 1993)

Children influence their own development: these children's positive reactions to their father's reading ensure that he will want to read to them in the future.

because of the overlap between their parents' genes and their own. Thus, children whose genotypes predispose them to enjoy reading are likely to be raised in homes with plentiful access to reading matter because their parents also like to read. The passive effects of the genotype help explain why some correlations between biological parents' and their children's IQ scores are higher when the children live with their biological parents than when they live with adoptive parents.

■ *Evocative effects* of the genotype emerge through children's eliciting or influencing other people's behavior. For example, even if a child's parents are not avid readers, they will read more bedtime stories to a child who is interested in the stories than to one who is uninterested.

■ *Active effects* of the genotype involve children's choosing environments that they enjoy. A high school student who loves reading will read a great deal, regardless of whether he or she was read to when young.

The evocative and active effects of the genotype help explain how children's IQ scores become more closely related over time to those of their biological parents, even if the children are adopted and never see their biological parents.

Influence of the Immediate Environment

The influence of nurture on the development of intelligence begins with a child's immediate environment of families and schools.

Family Influences

If asked to identify the most important environmental influence on their intelligence, most people probably would say, "My family." Testing the influence of the family environment on children's intelligence, however, requires some means of assessing that environment. How can something as complex and multifaceted as a family environment be measured, especially when it can differ for different children in the same family?

Bradley and Caldwell (1979) tackled this problem by devising a measure known as the HOME (Home Observation for Measurement of the Environment). The HOME samples various aspects of children's home life, including organization and safety of living space; intellectual stimulation offered by parents; whether children have books of their own; amount of parent–child interaction; parents' emotional support of the child; and so on. Table 8.1 shows the items and subscales used in the original HOME, which was designed to assess the family environments of children from birth to age 3 years. Subsequent versions of the HOME have been developed for application with preschoolers, school-age children, and adolescents (Totsika & Sylva, 2004).

Throughout childhood, children's IQ scores, as well as their math and reading achievement scores, are positively correlated with scores on the HOME (Bradley et al., 2001). HOME scores of families of 6-month-olds correlate positively with the IQ scores of the same children at age 4 years; similarly, HOME scores of 2-year-olds correlate positively with IQ scores and school achievement of the

TABLE 8.1

Sample Items and Subscales on the HOME (Infant Version)

I. Emotional and Verbal Responsivity of Mother

    1. Mother spontaneously vocalizes to child at least twice during visit (excluding scolding).

    2. Mother responds to child's vocalizations with a verbal response.

    3. Mother tells child the name of some object during visit or says name of person or object in a "teaching" style.

II. Avoidance of Restriction and Punishment

    4. Mother does not shout at child during visit.

    5. Mother does not express overt annoyance with or hostility toward child.

    6. Mother does not interfere with child's actions or restrict child's movements more than three times during visit.

III. Organization of Physical and Temporal Environment

    7. When mother is away, care is provided by one of three regular substitutes.

    8. Child is taken regularly to doctor's office or clinic.

    9. Child has a special place in which to keep his or her toys and "treasures."

IV. Provision of Appropriate Play Materials

    10. Child has push or pull toy.

    11. Child has stroller or walker, kiddie car, scooter, or tricycle.

    12. Provides learning equipment appropriate to age—cuddly toy or role-playing toys.

V. Maternal Involvement with Child

    13. Mother tends to keep child within visual range and to look at him or her often.

    14. Mother "talks" to child while doing her work.

    15. Mother structures child's play periods.

VI. Opportunities for Variety of Daily Stimulation

    16. Mother reads stories at least three times weekly.

    17. Child eats at least one meal per day with mother and father.

    18. Child has three or more books of his or her own.

Information from Bradley & Caldwell (1984).

same children at age 11 years (Olson, Bates, & Kaskie, 1992). When HOME scores are relatively stable over time, IQ scores also tend to be stable; when HOME scores change, IQ scores also tend to change in the same direction (Totsika & Sylva, 2004). Thus, assessing varied aspects of a child's family environment allows prediction of the child's IQ score.

Given this evidence, it is tempting to conclude that better-quality home environments cause children to have higher IQ scores. Whether that is actually the case, however, is not yet known. The uncertainty reflects two factors. First, the type of intellectual environment that parents establish in the home is almost certainly influenced by their genetic makeup. Second, almost all studies using the HOME have focused on families in which children live with their biological parents.

Stimulating home environments, especially those in which adults and children undertake challenging tasks together, are associated with high IQ scores and high achievement in school.

GHISLAIN AND MARIE DAVID DE LOSSY / GETTY IMAGES

These two considerations may mean that parents' genes influence both the intellectual quality of the home environment and children's IQ scores; thus, the home intellectual environment as such may not cause children to have higher or lower IQ. Consistent with this possibility, in the few studies in which the HOME has been used to study adoptive families, the correlations between it and children's IQ scores are lower than in studies of children living with their biological parents (Plomin et al., 1997). Thus, although scores on the HOME clearly correlate with children's IQ scores, whether causal relations exist between the two remains uncertain.

Shared and non-shared family environments The phrase "family intellectual environment" is often taken to mean characteristics that are the same for all children within the family: the parents' emphasis on education, the number of books in the house, the frequency of intellectual discussions around the dinner table, and so on. As discussed in Chapter 3, however, each child within a given family also encounters unique, non-shared environments. In any family, only one child can be the firstborn and receive the intense, undivided parental attention early in life that this status tends to bring. Similarly, a child whose interests or personality characteristics mirror those of one or both parents may receive more positive attention than other children in the family. If homes that are extremely lacking in intellectual stimulation are excluded from consideration, such within-family variations in children's environment may have a greater impact on the development of intelligence than do between-family variations (Petrill et al., 2004). In addition, the influence of the non-shared environment increases with age, and the influence of the shared environment decreases with age, as children become increasingly able to choose their own friends and activities (Plomin & Daniels, 2011; Segal et al., 2007).

The relative influence of shared environments and genetics varies with family income. Among children and adolescents from low-income families in the United States, the shared environment accounts for more of the variance in IQ scores and academic achievement than genetics does. In contrast, among children and adolescents from middle- and high-income families in the United States, the relative influence of shared environment and genetics is reversed (Harden, Turkheimer, & Loehlin, 2007; D. C. Rowe, Jacobson, & Van den Oord, 1999; Turkheimer et al., 2003). These differing patterns are found as early as age 2 years (Tucker-Drob et al., 2011). Interestingly, the differing relations between shared environments and genetics among richer and poorer families were not found in Great Britain, Germany, Sweden, the Netherlands, or Australia (Tucker-Drob & Bates, 2016). This may be because social policies in those countries ensure access to quality education regardless of family income, thus making the children's intellectual development less dependent on the family in which they grow up.

With age, children increasingly shape their own environments in ways that reflect their personalities and tastes.

DARREN MODRICKER / AGE FOTOSTOCK

Influences of Schooling

Attending school makes children smarter. One type of evidence for this conclusion came from a study that examined IQ scores of older and younger Israeli children within the 4th, 5th, and 6th grades (Cahan & Cohen, 1989). As indicated by the gradual upward trends in the graphs in Figure 8.6, older children within each grade did somewhat better than younger children within that grade on each part of the test. However, the jumps in the graphs between grades indicate that children who were only slightly older, but who had a year more schooling, did much better than the slightly younger children in the grade below them. For example, on the verbal-oddities sub-test (which involves indicating which word in a series does not belong with the others), the results show a small gap between 123- and 124-month-old 4th-graders but a large gap between both of them and 125-month-old 5th-graders. The positive effects of education on IQ scores do not seem to come about through education increasing *g*, but rather through education increasing a number of specific cognitive skills measured on IQ tests, such as inferential reasoning and logical memory (Ritchie, Bates, & Deary, 2015).

Another type of evidence indicating that going to school makes children smarter is that average IQ and achievement test scores rise during the school year but not during summer vacation (Ceci, 1991; J. Huttenlocher, Levine, & Vevea, 1998). The details of the pattern are especially telling. Children from families of low socioeconomic status and those from families of high socioeconomic status make comparable gains in school achievement during the school year. However, over the summer, the achievement test scores of low-SES children tend to stay constant or drop, whereas the scores of high-SES children tend to rise (K. L. Alexander, Entwisle, & Olson, 2007; Burkam et al., 2004). The likely explanation is that during the academic year, schools provide children of all backgrounds with relatively stimulating intellectual environments, but when school is not in session, fewer children from low-SES families have the kinds of experiences that allow them to increase their academic achievement.

Influence of Society

Intellectual development is influenced not only by characteristics of children, their families, and their schools but also by broader characteristics of the societies within which children develop. One reflection of societal influences is that in many countries throughout the world, average IQ scores have consistently risen over the past 80 years, a phenomenon that has been labeled the **Flynn effect** in honor of James Flynn, the researcher from New Zealand who discovered this widespread trend (Flynn, 1987; 2009). In some countries, including the Netherlands and Israel, average IQ scores have risen as much as 20 points; in the United States, the gains have been roughly 10 points (Dickens & Flynn, 2001; Flynn & Weiss, 2007). Given that the gene pool has not changed appreciably over this period, the increase in IQ scores must be due to changes in society.

The specific source of the Flynn effect remains controversial. Some researchers argue that the key factors are improvements in the lives of low-income families, such as improved nutrition (Lynn, 2009), health (Eppig, Fincher, & Thornhill, 2010), and formal education (C. Blair et al., 2005). These researchers point to evidence that the increase in IQ scores has been greatest among those in the lower part of the IQ score

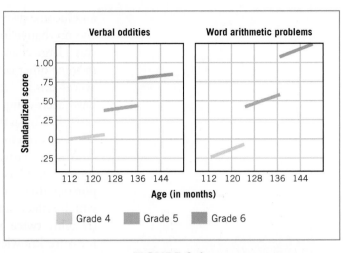

FIGURE 8.6 Relations of age and grade to performance on two parts of an IQ test The jumps between grade levels indicate that schooling exerts an effect on intelligence test performance beyond that of the child's age. (Data from Cahan & Cohen, 1989)

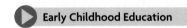
▶ **Early Childhood Education**

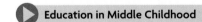
▶ **Education in Middle Childhood**

Flynn effect ■ consistent rise in average IQ scores that has occurred over the past 80 years in many countries

and income distributions. For example, among Danes born from 1942 to 1980, there was no change in the scores of people in the top 10% of the IQ distribution, but there was a large change among those in the bottom 10% (Geary, 2005). IQ score changes in some other countries, including Spain and Norway, show a similar pattern. However, gains in yet other countries, including the United States, France, and Britain, have been comparable throughout the IQ score and income distributions (Nisbett et al., 2012). In the United States, gains in intellectual performance over decades have occurred even in the top 5% of the population (Wai, Putallaz, & Makel, 2012).

An alternative plausible explanation for the increases in IQ scores is increased societal emphasis on abstract problem solving and reasoning (Flynn, 2009). Supporting this interpretation is the fact that scores on tests of fluid intelligence, which reflects abstract problem solving and reasoning, have increased much more (roughly twice as much) than scores on tests of crystallized intelligence, which measure knowledge of facts and procedures, such as vocabulary and arithmetic (Nisbett et al., 2012; Pietschnig & Voracek, 2015). One source of these recent increases in fluid intelligence might be experience with new technologies, such as video games. Several studies have found that playing video games increases performance on a number of measures of fluid intelligence, such as selective attention (e.g., Glass, Maddox, & Love, 2013; Green & Bavelier, 2003). Moreover, Haier and colleagues (2009) found that 3 months of playing a video game led to increased brain thickness in areas of adolescent girls' brains that are specifically activated by playing the game and that are active in the types of spatial tasks that are often used to measure fluid intelligence. Other studies, however, have found weak or no relation between playing video games and fluid intelligence (Hambrick et al., 2010; Powers et al., 2013; Unsworth et al., 2015), so the contribution of video games to fluid intelligence remains controversial.

One conclusion that sparks no controversy is that poverty hinders intellectual development. In the following sections, we consider how poverty affects children's development in different societies, and how it contributes to differences in IQ scores and school achievement among different racial and ethnic groups within the United States. We will also consider risk factors associated with poverty that adversely affect intelligence, as well as programs that enhance poor children's intellectual development.

Effects of Poverty

The negative effects of poverty on children's IQ scores are indisputable. Even after taking into account the mother's education, whether both parents live with the child, and the child's race, the adequacy of family income for meeting family needs is related to children's IQ scores (Duncan & Murnane, 2014). Further, the more years children spend in poverty, the lower their scores tend to be (Korenman, Miller, & Sjaastad, 1995).

Poverty exerts negative effects on intellectual development in numerous ways. Chronic inadequate diet early in life can disrupt brain development; missing meals on a given day (e.g., achievement test day) can impair intellectual functioning on that day; reduced access to health services can result in more absences from school; conflicts between adults in the household can produce emotional turmoil that interferes with learning; insufficient intellectual stimulation can lead to a lack of background knowledge needed to understand new material; and so on.

One source of evidence for the relation between poverty and IQ is the fact that in all countries that have been studied, children from wealthier homes score higher on IQ and achievement tests, on average, than do children from poorer homes (Ganzach et al., 2013). Large differences between children from less and more

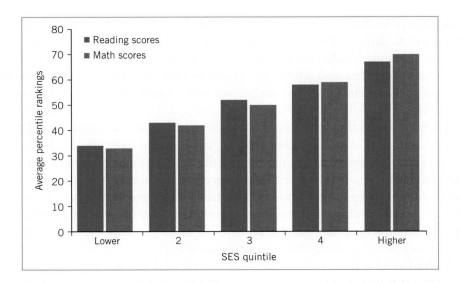

FIGURE 8.7 Reading and math scores
upon entering kindergarten, by SES
Even at the beginning of kindergarten,
children from families with lower incomes
and education lag far behind peers from
more affluent and educated backgrounds.

affluent backgrounds are already present in measures of reading and math knowledge when children enter kindergarten (see Figure 8.7; Larson et al., 2015).

More telling, in those developed countries where the income gap between rich and poor is widest, such as the United States, the difference between the intellectual achievement of children from rich and poor homes is much larger than in countries in which the gap is smaller, such as the Scandinavian countries and, to a lesser degree, Germany, Canada, and Great Britain. As shown in Figure 8.8, children from affluent U.S. families score, on average, about the same on mathematics achievement tests as children from affluent families in some comparison countries with greater income equality. In contrast, children from poor U.S. families have average achievement test scores far below children from poor families in those same comparison countries. The key difference is that poor U.S. families are much poorer, relative to others in their society, than their counterparts in many other developed countries. Thus, in 2014, 21% of U.S. children lived in families with incomes below the federal poverty threshold (Jiang, Ekono, & Skinner, 2016). By contrast, in a set of 35 other developed countries, only 11% of children were from families with this low a percentage of the median income in their country (UNICEF, 2012).

As noted in Chapter 1, within the United States, the percentage of children living in poor families is much higher among Hispanic Americans and African Americans than among European Americans and Asian Americans, and it is much higher in families headed by a single female than in families headed by a married couple. These economic differences help explain the group differences in IQ scores that we examine in the next section.

FIGURE 8.8 Relation in three
countries between fathers' occupational
status and children's math achievement
U.S. children whose fathers hold low-status
jobs perform, on average, far more poorly
on math-achievement tests than do children
whose fathers hold comparable jobs in
Canada or Japan. In contrast, U.S. children
whose fathers have high-status jobs
perform, on average, as well as children
whose fathers have comparable jobs in
Canada and almost as well as children from
similar backgrounds in Japan. (Data from
Case et al., 1999)

Race, Ethnicity, and Intelligence

Few claims stir stronger passions than those surrounding assertions that racial and ethnic groups differ in intelligence. It is therefore especially important to know both the facts about this issue and what can and cannot be concluded from them.

One fact is that the *average* IQ scores of children from different racial and ethnic groups *do* differ. For example, the average IQ score of European American children is about 10 points higher than that of African American children (Dickens & Flynn, 2006). The average scores of Hispanic American and Native American children are a few points higher than those of African American children, and those of

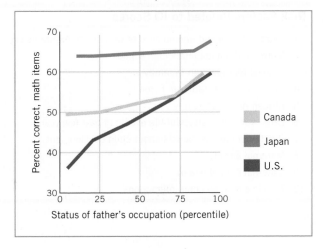

Asian American children are a few points higher than those of European Americans (Nisbett et al., 2012). These differences are explained in part by differences in social-class backgrounds. Within each social class, however, differences in mean IQ scores of African American and European American children also are present, though they are smaller than those that are present when social class is not held constant (L. A. Suzuki & Valencia, 1997).

A second fact is that scientific statements about group differences in IQ scores refer to statistical averages rather than to any individual's score. Understanding this second fact is essential for interpreting the first. Millions of African American children have IQ scores higher than the average European American child, and millions of European American children have IQ scores lower than the average African American child. Far more variability exists *within* each racial group than *between* them. Thus, data on the average IQ score of members of an ethnic or racial group tell us nothing about any individual.

A third crucial fact is that differences in IQ and achievement test scores of children from different racial and ethnic groups describe children's performance only in the environments in which the children live. The findings do not indicate their intellectual potential, nor do they indicate what their scores would be if the children lived in different environments. Indeed, with decreases in discrimination and inequality in the past 50 years, achievement test differences between European American and African American children have decreased considerably. A rigorous analysis of changes over time in intelligence test scores showed that African American schoolchildren reduced the gap with European American schoolchildren by 4 to 7 points between 1972 and 2002 (Dickens & Flynn, 2006); achievement test scores have shown the same trend (N. Brody, 1992).

Risk Factors and Intellectual Development

In the popular media, reports on how to help all children reach their intellectual potential often focus on a single factor—the need to eliminate poverty, or the need to eliminate racism, or the need to preserve two-parent families, or the need for high-quality day care, or the need for universal preschool education, and so on. However, no single factor, nor even any small group of factors, is *the* key. Instead, many factors in combination contribute to the problem of poor intellectual development.

To capture the impact of these multiple influences, Arnold Sameroff and his colleagues developed an *environmental risk scale* (Sameroff et al., 1993) based on 10 features of the environment that put children at risk for low IQ scores (Table 8.2). Each child's risk score is a simple count of the number of major risks facing the child. Thus, a child growing up with a mother who is unemployed, unmarried, highly anxious, and mentally ill, but who has none of the other risk factors in Sameroff's list, would have an environmental risk score of 4.

Sameroff and his colleagues measured the IQ scores and environmental risks of more than 100 children when they were 4-year-olds and again when they were 13-year-olds. They found that the more risks in a child's environment, the lower the child's IQ score tended to be. As shown in Figure 8.9, the effect was large. The average IQ score of children whose environments did not include any of the risk factors was around 115; the average score of children

TABLE 8.2

Risk Factors Related to IQ Scores

1. Head of household unemployed or working in low-status occupation
2. Mother did not complete high school
3. At least four children in family
4. No father or stepfather in home
5. African American family
6. Large number of stressful life events in past few years
7. Rigidity of parents' beliefs about child development
8. Maternal anxiety
9. Maternal mental health
10. Negative mother–child interactions

Information from Sameroff et al. (1993).

whose environments included six or more risks was around 85. The sheer number of risks in the child's environment was a better predictor of the child's IQ score than was the presence of any particular risk. Subsequent studies demonstrated similarly strong relations between the number of risk factors and school grades (Gassman-Pines & Yoshikawa, 2006; Gutman, Sameroff, & Cole, 2003).

The Sameroff (1993) study also provided an interesting perspective on why children's IQ scores are highly stable. It is not just that children's genes remain constant; over time, their environment tends to remain fairly constant as well. The study revealed that there was just as much stability in the number of risk factors in children's environments at ages 4 and 13 years as there was in their IQ scores over that period.

The number of risk factors in a 4-year-old's environment not only correlates highly with the child's IQ score at age 4 but also predicts likely changes in the child's score between ages 4 and 13. That is, if two children have the same IQ score at age 4 but one child lives in an environment with more risk factors, the child facing more risks will, at age 13, probably have an IQ score lower than that of the other child. Thus, environmental risks seem to have both immediate and long-term effects on children's intellectual development. Genetic contributions cannot be ruled out—anxiety, poor mental health, and other risk factors may be biologically transmitted from parent to child—but a greater number of risk factors is definitely associated with lower IQ scores.

Although Sameroff and his colleagues described their measure as a "risk index," it is as much a measure of the quality of a child's environment as of its potential for harm. High IQ scores are associated with favorable environments as much as low scores are associated with adverse ones. This is true for children from low-income families as well as for children in general. Low-income parents who, relative to others with similar incomes, are responsive to their children and provide them with safe play areas and varied learning materials have children with higher IQ scores (Bradley et al., 1994). Thus, high-quality parenting can help offset the risks imposed by poverty.

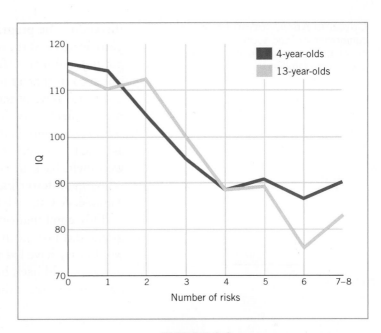

FIGURE 8.9 Risk factors and IQ score For both younger and older children, the more risk factors in the environment, the lower the average IQ score. (Data from Sameroff et al., 1993)

Programs for Helping Poor Children

During the early 1960s, a political consensus developed in the United States—that helping children from poor families was an urgent national priority. Child development research contributed to this consensus by demonstrating that children's environments had significant effects on their cognitive growth (W. Dennis & Najarian, 1957; J. M. Hunt, 1961). As a consequence, over the next decade, many intervention programs were initiated to enhance the intellectual development of preschoolers from impoverished families.

In a comprehensive analysis of 11 of the most prominent early-intervention programs—all of which focused on 2- to 5-year-old African American children from low-income families—Irving Lazar and his colleagues found a consistent pattern (Lazar et al., 1982). Participation in the programs, most of which lasted a year or two, initially increased children's IQ scores substantially—by 10 to 15 points. However, over the next 2 or 3 years, the gains decreased, and by the 4th year after

Carolina Abecedarian Project ■ comprehensive and successful enrichment program for children from low-income families

the end of the programs, no differences were apparent between the IQ scores of participants and those of nonparticipants from the same neighborhoods and backgrounds. Similar effects have been found for math and reading achievement—initial gains that all too quickly fade (Bailey et al., 2016).

Fortunately, other effects of these experimental programs aimed at helping preschoolers from low-income backgrounds are more enduring. In one long-term study, only half as many program participants as nonparticipants were later assigned to special-education classes—14% versus 29%—and fewer participants were held back in school, more participants subsequently graduated from high school, and fewer had been arrested by age 18 (Reynolds et al., 2001; Reynolds, Temple, & Ou, 2010).

This combination of findings may seem puzzling. If the intervention programs did not result in lasting increases in IQ or achievement test scores, why would they have led to fewer children being assigned to special-education classes or being held back in school? A likely reason is that the interventions had long-term effects on children's motivation and conduct. These effects would help

BOX 8.2 | applications

A HIGHLY SUCCESSFUL EARLY INTERVENTION: THE CAROLINA ABECEDARIAN PROJECT

The difficulty of producing enduring gains in poor children's IQ and achievement test scores led some evaluators to conclude that intelligence is unalterable (A. R. Jensen, 1973; Westinghouse Learning Corporation, 1969). However, the same findings motivated other researchers to find out if interventions that started in infancy, continued for a number of years, and attempted to improve many aspects of children's lives might produce enduring increases in IQ, even though briefer, less intensive, later-starting efforts had not. One intervention that yielded a positive answer to these questions is the **Carolina Abecedarian Project,** a program that clearly illustrates the theme of how research can improve children's welfare (F. A. Campbell & Ramey, 2007; Ramey & Ramey, 2004).

Children were selected to participate in the Abecedarian (pronounced "a-bee-ce-darian") program on the basis of low family income, the absence of a father in the home, low maternal IQ score and education, and other factors that put the children at risk for developmental problems. More than 95% of the children who participated were

African American. The program was based on seven principles (Ramey & Ramey, 2004):

1. Encourage exploration.
2. Mentor basic skills.
3. Celebrate developmental advances.
4. Rehearse and generalize new skills.
5. Protect children from inappropriate disapproval, teasing, and punishment.
6. Communicate richly and responsively.
7. Guide and limit behavior.

Children in the program began attending a special day-care center by the time they were 6-month-olds and continued to do so through the age of 5 years. They were at the center for the entire working day (7:45 A.M. to 5:30 P.M.), 5 days per week, 50 weeks per year, for 5 years. The teacher–child ratio was optimal: 1:3 for children aged 3 years and younger and 1:6 for 4- and 5-year-olds. Children aged 3 years and younger received a program that emphasized general social, cognitive, and motor development; for 4- and 5-year-olds, the program also provided systematic instruction in math, science, reading, and

music. At all ages, the program emphasized language development and ensured extensive verbal communication between teachers and children. Program personnel also worked with the children's mothers outside the day-care center to improve their understanding of child development. Families of children in the experimental program were provided with nutritional supplements and access to high-quality health care. Families of children in a control group received similar nutritional and health benefits, but the children did not attend the day-care center.

This well-planned, multifaceted program proved to have lasting positive effects on the IQ scores and achievement levels of children in the experimental group. At the age of 21 years, 15 years after the program had ended, these children had mean IQ scores 5 points higher than the children in the control group: 90 versus 85 (F. A. Campbell et al., 2001). Participants' achievement test scores in math and reading were also higher. As with less encompassing intervention programs, fewer participants were ever held back in school or placed in special-education classes. At age 30, a higher percentage of

children do well enough in the classroom to be promoted with their classmates, which in turn might make them less likely to drop out of high school and less likely to turn to criminal activity, even if improvements in their cognitive abilities fade over time.

Participation also led to benefits after children finished school. As adults, former participants in some intervention programs used the welfare system less, were more likely to enroll in college, and earned larger salaries than did nonparticipants (Garces, Duncan, & Currie, 2002; Reynolds et al., 2010). As discussed in Box 8.2, at least one specialized, intensive program has shown the possibility of producing enduring gains in IQ score and school achievement as well.

Project Head Start In response to the same political consensus of the 1960s that led to small-scale early-intervention programs, the U.S. government initiated a large-scale intervention program: Project Head Start. In the past 50 years, this program has provided a wide range of services to more than 32 million children (Office of Head Start, 2015).

children in the experimental group than in the control group had graduated from college: 23% versus 6% (F. A. Campbell et al., 2012). A replication of the program demonstrated that the lower the mother's educational level, the greater the difference the program made (Ramey & Ramey, 2004).

What general lessons can be drawn from the Abecedarian Project? One important lesson is the benefit of starting interventions early and continuing them for substantial periods. A version of the Abecedarian program that ended at age 3 did not produce long-term effects on intelligence, nor did a version that provided educational support from kindergarten through 2nd grade (Burchinal et al., 1997; Ramey et al., 2000). A second crucial lesson is the need for caregivers to interact with infants in positive, responsive ways. High adult-to-infant ratios in day-care centers make such interactions more likely, as does educating staff members in the need for such interactions. A third lesson is that the gains produced by this and other successful early-intervention programs are likely due more to improvements in children's self-control and perseverance than to changes in their IQ scores (Heckman, 2011; Knudsen et al., 2006). Probably the most important lesson is the most basic: it is possible to design interventions that have substantial, lasting, positive effects on poor children's intellectual development.

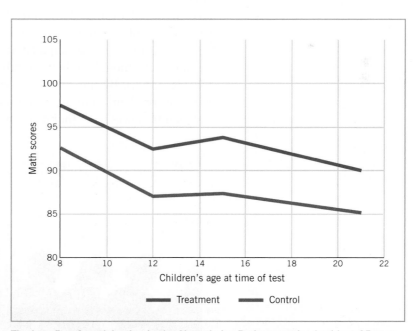

The benefits of participating in the Abecedarian Project remained evident 15 years after the end of the program, as illustrated in this graph of the mathematics achievement of children who participated either in the program or in the control condition. Relative to the average level of mathematics achievement of children in the United States, performance of both groups of children declined somewhat between ages 8 and 21, but at all ages, children who participated in the program performed better than did children from comparably disadvantaged backgrounds who had been in the control condition.

Children who participate in Head Start programs, like the youngsters pictured here, are in later years less likely to be held back in the same grade and more likely to graduate from high school than are children from similar backgrounds who do not participate in these programs.

At present, Head Start serves more than 900,000 preschoolers per year, most of them 4-year-olds. The population served is racially and ethnically diverse: in 2010, 39% were African Americans, 31% European Americans, and 34% Hispanic Americans (the sum is more than 100% because some children were counted in multiple categories) (Schmit, 2011). Almost all children in Head Start are from families with incomes below the poverty line, mostly single-parent families. In the program, children are provided with medical and dental care, nutritious meals, and a safe environment. Many parents of participating children work as caregivers at the Head Start centers, serve on policy councils that help plan each center's directions, and receive help with their own vocational and emotional needs.

Consistent with the findings of the smaller experimental intervention programs that have been aimed at 3- and 4-year-olds, participation in Head Start produces higher IQ and achievement test scores at the end of the program and briefly thereafter. The strongest evidence for this conclusion comes from the Head Start Impact Study (U.S. DHHS, 2010), an especially well-done experiment that included 5000 3- and 4-year-olds from low-income families who were on waiting lists to participate in a Head Start program. Half the children were randomly assigned to participate in Head Start; the other half followed another path of their parents' choosing. The children comprised a nationally representative sample of the low-income population, and the Head Start centers in which the children enrolled were representative in terms of their quality.

The children who participated in Head Start showed better pre-reading and pre-writing skills (though no better math skills) at the end of a year in the program (U.S. DHHS, 2006). By the end of 1st grade, however, children's intellectual outcomes were almost identical to those of nonparticipants (U.S. DHHS, 2010), and no intellectual differences were found at the end of 3rd grade, either (Puma et al., 2012).

Among the benefits of Head Start is the provision of nutritious meals for children who otherwise might be at risk for malnutrition.

On the other hand, participation in Head Start produces a number of other positive effects that do endure, ones that resemble those produced by the experimental preschool programs: improved social skills and health, lower frequency of being held back in school, greater likelihood of graduating from high school and enrolling in college, and lower rates of drug use and delinquency (Love, Chazan-Cohen, & Raikes, 2007; Zigler & Styfco, 2004). These important gains have contributed to the enduring popularity of Head Start.

Review

The development of intelligence is influenced by qualities of the child, the immediate environment, and the broader society. The child's genetic inheritance exerts a large influence, especially for children from middle- and upper-income families; this influence steadily increases over the course of development. The intellectual environment provided by the child's family and the schooling the child encounters are also influential, as are the family's economic status and educational level and whether one or two parents are present. For U.S. children from low-income backgrounds, these shared aspects of the environment seem to exert a stronger influence than do children's genes on differences in their intellectual development. The impact of changes in society is evident in the Flynn effect, which reflects the consistent rise in IQ scores over decades in all economically advanced countries.

Programs such as Project Head Start are often beneficial in a variety of ways, though their effect on IQ and achievement test scores usually fades over time. However, at least one early-intervention program, the Abecedarian Project, reports enduring positive effects on IQ scores and achievement.

Alternative Perspectives on Intelligence

The discussions of intellectual development in this chapter have relied on IQ tests as their main measure. Research using these tests has revealed a great deal about the development of intelligence. However, a number of contemporary theorists have noted that many important aspects of intelligence are not measured by IQ tests. These tests assess verbal, mathematical, and spatial capabilities, but they do not directly examine other abilities that seem to be important parts of intelligence: creativity, social understanding, knowledge of one's own strengths and weaknesses, and so on. This perspective has led Howard Gardner and Robert Sternberg to formulate theories of intelligence that encompass a wider range of human abilities than do traditional theories.

Gardner's Theory

Howard Gardner (1993; 1999) labeled his approach **multiple intelligences theory.** Its basic claim is that people possess at least eight kinds of intelligence: the linguistic, logical-mathematical, and spatial abilities emphasized in previous theories and measured on IQ tests, and also musical, naturalistic, bodily-kinesthetic, intrapersonal, and interpersonal abilities (see Table 8.3). He has also speculated that a ninth ability might be present—existential intelligence, which is concerned with ultimate questions about life and the human condition, such as "why are we here?" (Gardner & Davis, 2013).

Gardner used several types of evidence to arrive at this set of intelligences. One involved deficits shown by people with brain damage. For example, some brain-damaged patients function well in most respects but have no understanding of other

multiple intelligences theory ■ Gardner's theory of intellect, based on the view that people possess at least eight types of intelligence

TABLE 8.3

Gardner's Theory of Multiple Intelligences

Type of Intelligence	Description	Examples
Linguistic intelligence	Sensitivity to the meanings and sounds of words; mastery of syntax; appreciation of the ways language can be used	Poet, political speaker, teacher
Logical-mathematical intelligence	Understanding of objects and symbols, of the actions that can be performed on them, and of the relations between these actions; ability for abstraction; ability to identify problems and seek explanations	Mathematician, scientist
Spatial intelligence	Capacity to perceive the visual world accurately, to perform transformations upon perceptions, and to re-create aspects of visual experience in the absence of physical stimuli; sensitivity to tension, balance, and composition; ability to detect similar patterns	Artist, engineer, chess master
Musical intelligence	Sensitivity to individual tones and phrases of music; an understanding of ways to combine tones and phrases into larger musical rhythms and structures; awareness of emotional aspects of music	Musician, composer
Naturalistic intelligence	Sensitivity to, and understanding of, plants, animals, and other aspects of nature	Biologist, farmer, conservationist
Bodily-kinesthetic intelligence	Use of one's body in highly skilled ways for expressive or goal-directed purposes; capacity to handle objects skillfully	Dancer, athlete, actor
Intrapersonal intelligence	Access to one's own feeling life; ability to draw on one's emotions to guide and understand one's behavior	Novelist, therapist, parent
Interpersonal intelligence	Ability to notice and make distinctions among the moods, temperaments, motivations, and intentions of other people and potentially to act on this knowledge	Political leader, religious leader, parent, teacher, therapist

Information from H. Gardner (1993).

theory of successful intelligence ■ Sternberg's theory of intellect, based on the view that intelligence is the ability to achieve success in life

FINE ART / GETTY IMAGES

Mozart's musical genius was evident from early in childhood, leading some of the greatest musicians of his day to play music with him when he was still a child, as illustrated in this portrait by Louis Carrogis Carmontelle, painted when Mozart was 7 years old.

people (Damasio, 1999). This phenomenon suggested to Gardner that interpersonal intelligence was distinct from other types of intelligence. A second type of evidence that Gardner used to identify this set of intelligences was the existence of prodigies, people who from early in life show exceptional ability in one area but not in others. One such example is Wolfgang Amadeus Mozart, who displayed musical genius while still a child but was unexceptional in many other ways. The existence of highly specialized musical talents such as Mozart's provides evidence for viewing musical ability as a separate intelligence. Although Gardner's theory of multiple intelligences is backed by much less supporting evidence than traditional theories of intelligence, its optimistic message—that children have a variety of strengths on which parents and teachers can build—has led to its having a large influence on education.

Sternberg's Theory

Robert Sternberg (1999; 2007) also argued that the emphasis of IQ tests on the type of intelligence needed to succeed in school is too narrow. However, the alternative view of intelligence that he proposed differs from that proposed by Gardner. Sternberg's **theory of successful intelligence** envisions intelligence as "the ability to achieve success in life, given one's personal standards, within one's sociocultural context" (p. 4). In his view, success in life reflects people's ability to build on their strengths, to compensate for their weaknesses, and to select environments in which they can succeed. When people choose a job, for instance, their understanding of the conditions that will motivate them may be crucial to their success.

Sternberg proposed that success in life depends on three types of abilities: analytic, practical, and creative. *Analytic abilities* involve the linguistic, mathematical, and spatial skills that are measured by traditional intelligence tests. *Practical abilities* involve reasoning about everyday problems, such as how to resolve conflicts with other people. *Creative abilities* involve intellectual flexibility and innovation that allow adaptation to novel circumstances.

The theories proposed by Gardner and Sternberg have inspired rethinking of long-held assumptions about intelligence. Intelligence and success in life clearly involve a broader range of capabilities than traditional IQ tests measure, and assessing a broader range of capabilities may allow more encompassing theories of intelligence. There is not now, nor will there ever be, a single correct theory of intelligence, nor a single best measure of it. What is possible is a variety of theories, and tests based on them, that together reveal the varied ways in which people can be intelligent.

Review

Howard Gardner and Robert Sternberg have formulated novel theories of intelligence. Gardner's multiple intelligences theory proposes that there are at least eight intelligences: linguistic, logical-mathematical, spatial, musical, naturalistic, bodily-kinesthetic, intrapersonal, and interpersonal, and perhaps a ninth that he labeled "existential intelligence." Sternberg's theory of successful intelligence proposes that success in life depends on three types of abilities: analytic, practical, and creative. Both theories conceive of intelligence as a broader set of abilities than those included in traditional theories.

Acquisition of Academic Skills: Reading, Writing, and Mathematics

One important goal to which children apply their intelligence is learning the skills and concepts taught at school. Because these skills and concepts are necessary to academic achievement, because they are central to success in adulthood, and because they can be difficult to master, children spend more than 2000 days in school from 1st through 12th grade. Much of this time is devoted to acquiring proficiency in reading, writing, and mathematics. In this section, we focus on how children learn academic skills, why some children have such difficulty mastering them, and how children's proficiency can be improved.

Reading

Many children learn to read effortlessly, but others do not. You can no doubt remember the painful times classmates—and perhaps you, yourself—seemed to take forever to read aloud simple sentences, even in 2nd and 3rd grade. Why is it that some children learn to read so easily, whereas others experience great difficulty and frustration? To answer this question, we must examine the typical path of reading development as well as how and why children deviate from it.

Chall (1979) described five stages of reading development. These stages provide a good overview of the typical path to mastery:

1. *Stage 0* (birth until the beginning of 1st grade): During this time, many children acquire key prerequisites for reading. These include knowing the letters of the alphabet and gaining **phonemic awareness,** that is, knowledge of the individual sounds within words.

2. *Stage 1* (1st and 2nd grades): Children acquire **phonological recoding skills,** the ability to translate letters into sounds and to blend the sounds into words (informally referred to as "sounding out").

3. *Stage 2* (2nd and 3rd grades): Children gain fluency in reading simple material.

phonemic awareness ■ ability to identify component sounds within words

phonological recoding skills ■ ability to translate letters into sounds and to blend sounds into words; informally called *sounding out*

4. *Stage 3* (4th through 8th grades): Children become able to acquire reasonably complex, new information from written text. To quote Chall, "In the primary grades, children learn to read; in the higher grades, they read to learn" (1983, p. 24).

5. *Stage 4* (8th through 12th grades): Adolescents acquire skill not only in understanding information presented from a single perspective but also in coordinating multiple perspectives. This ability enables them to appreciate the subtleties in sophisticated novels and plays, which almost always include multiple viewpoints.

This description of developmental stages provides a general sense of the reading acquisition process and a framework for understanding how particular developments fit into the broader picture.

Pre-reading Skills

Preschoolers acquire certain basic information about reading just from looking at books and having their parents read to them. They learn that (in English and other European languages) text is read from left to right; that after they reach the right end of a line, the text continues at the extreme left of the line below; and that words are separated by small spaces.

Children with well-educated parents also tend to learn the names of most or all the letters of the alphabet before they enter school. This tends not to be true of children whose parents are poorly educated (Lonigan, 2015). In one study of beginning kindergartners, 86% of children whose mothers graduated from college were proficient in letter recognition, but only 38% of children whose mothers did not complete high school were (J. West, Denton, & Germino-Hausken, 2000).

Kindergartners' mastery of letter names is positively correlated with their later reading achievement through at least 7th grade (Vellutino & Scanlon, 1987). However, no causal relation exists between the two: teaching the names of the letters to randomly chosen preschoolers does not increase their subsequent reading achievement (Piasta & Wagner, 2010). Instead, it appears that other variables, such as children's interest in books and parents' interest in their children's reading, stimulate both early knowledge of the alphabet and later high reading achievement.

Phonemic awareness, on the other hand, is correlated with later reading achievement and is also a cause of it. To measure awareness of the component sounds within words, researchers ask children to decide whether two words start with the same sound, to identify component sounds within a word, and to indicate what would remain if a given sound were removed from a word. Kindergartners' performance on these measures of phonemic awareness is the strongest known predictor of their ability to sound out and spell words in the early grades—stronger even than IQ score or social-class background (Nation, 2008; Rayner et al., 2001). Phonemic awareness continues to be related to reading achievement as many as 11 years later, above and beyond the influence of the child's social-class background (MacDonald & Cornwall, 1995).

Even more impressive, a review of 52 well-controlled experimental studies indicated that teaching phonemic-awareness skills to 4- and 5-year-olds causes them to become better readers and spellers, with the effects enduring for years after the training (Lonigan, 2015; National Reading Panel, 2000). Instructing young children to break words into their component sounds and then writing the letter that best matches each successive sound causes especially large gains in spelling (Levin & Aram, 2013).

Although explicit training can help foster phonemic awareness, most children do not receive such training. Where, then, does phonemic awareness come from in the natural environment? One relevant experience is hearing nursery rhymes. Many nursery rhymes highlight the contribution of individual sounds to differences among words (e.g., "I do not like green eggs and *ham;* I do not like them, *Sam* I *am.*") Consistent with this hypothesis, 3-year-olds' knowledge of nursery rhymes correlates positively with their later phonemic awareness, above and beyond their IQ scores and their mother's educational level (Maclean, Bryant, & Bradley, 1987). Other factors that contribute to the development of phonemic awareness include growth of working memory, increasingly efficient processing of language, and, especially, reading itself (Foorman et al., 2016; McBride-Chang, 2004). Children with greater phonemic awareness read more and read better, which, in turn, leads to further increases in their phonemic awareness and in the quantity and quality of their reading.

The appeal of nursery rhymes to young children has always been obvious, but only recently have the benefits of such rhymes for phonemic awareness and reading acquisition become known.

Word Identification

Rapid, effortless word identification is crucial not only to reading comprehension but also to reading enjoyment. One remarkable finding makes the point: 40% of 4th-graders with poor word identification skills said they would rather clean their rooms than read (Juel, 1988). One child went as far as to volunteer, "I'd rather clean the mold around the bathtub than read." Not only does poor word identification make reading slow and laborious, it also leads children to read no more than is absolutely necessary, which, in turn, limits improvement in reading skills.

Words can be identified in two main ways: *phonological recoding* and *visually based retrieval.* As previously indicated, phonological recoding involves converting the visual form of a word into a verbal, speechlike form and using the speechlike form to determine the word's meaning. **Visually based retrieval** involves processing a word's meaning directly from its visual form.

Most young children use both approaches (Share, 2004), choosing adaptively between them from 1st grade onward. They employ a **strategy–choice process,** in which they choose the fastest approach that is likely to allow correct word identification. In the context of reading, this means that on easy words, children rely heavily on the fast but not always accurate approach of visually based retrieval; on hard words, they resort to the slower but surer strategy of phonological recoding. As shown in Figure 8.10, 1st-graders are very skillful in adjusting their strategies to the difficulty of a particular word.

The mechanisms underlying this adaptive strategy choice involve a form of associative learning in which children's past behavior shapes their future behavior (Siegler, 1996; 2006). Beginning readers rely heavily on phonological recoding, because the associations between words' visual forms and their sounds are too weak to allow much use of retrieval. Correct use of phonological recoding increases the associations between words' visual forms and their sounds, which in turn allows greater use of visually based retrieval. Consistent with this view, the shift to retrieval occurs earliest for words on which children most often execute phonological recoding correctly—words that are short, that have regular letter–sound relations, and that children encounter frequently. Also consistent with this view, children who are better at phonological recoding stop using that approach earlier because their past success with it enables them to shift more rapidly to visually based retrieval. A third correct implication is that reading instruction that

visually based retrieval ■ proceeding directly from the visual form of a word to its meaning

strategy–choice process ■ procedure for selecting among alternative ways to solve a problem

FIGURE 8.10 Young children's strategy choices in reading A strong positive correlation exists between the difficulty of a word, as defined by the percentage of errors children make when reading it, and the frequency of young children's use of an overt strategy, such as audible phonological recoding, to read it. Thus, on words that 1st-graders find easy, such as *in*, they generally retrieve the word's pronunciation, but on words they find difficult, such as *parade*, they often fall back on overt strategies such as sounding out (Siegler, 1986).

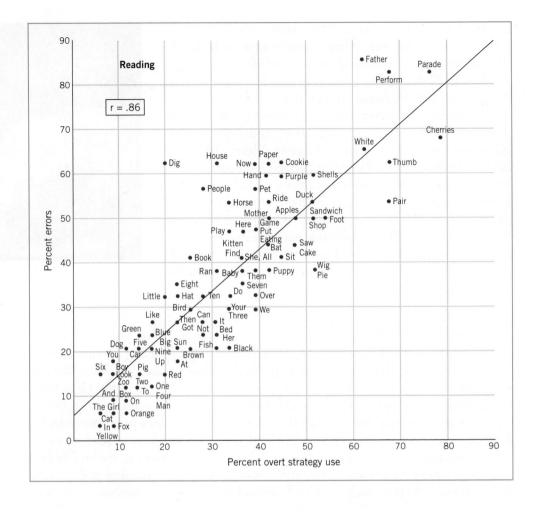

emphasizes phonics, and the strategy of phonological recoding, should help to produce fast and accurate word identification (M. J. Adams, Treiman, & Pressley, 1998; Foorman et al., 2016).

With age and experience, vocabulary knowledge becomes an increasingly important influence on word identification, particularly on words with irregular sound–symbol correspondences (Nation, 2008). This is seen in the positive effect of interventions that teach relevant vocabulary on children's subsequent comprehension of passages that include those terms (Apthorp et al., 2012; Goodson et al., 2010). However, phonological recoding skill also continues to be important, even for adults when they encounter unfamiliar words. Box 8.3 on page 356 discusses the relation between poor phonological recoding skills and the reading disability known as *dyslexia*.

Comprehension

Quickly and accurately identifying individual words is necessary but not sufficient for comprehending the text in which the words appear (Olson et al., 2014). Consistent with this view, word-identification skill and text comprehension are closely related in the early grades, but after 4th grade, the correlation weakens, and reading comprehension is more closely related to listening comprehension than to word identification (Johnston, Barnes, & Desrochers, 2008). In other words, language processing, regardless of whether the language is in printed or oral form, becomes the key determinant of reading comprehension.

Reading comprehension involves forming a **mental model** to represent the situation or idea being depicted in the text and continuously updating it as new

mental model ■ cognitive processes used to represent a situation or sequence of events

information appears (Oakhill & Cain, 2012). All the types of mental operations that influence cognitive development in general—basic processes, strategies, metacognition (knowledge about people's thinking), and content knowledge—also influence the development of reading comprehension.

Basic processes such as encoding (identification of key features of an object or event) and automatization (executing a process with minimal demands on cognitive resources) are crucial to reading comprehension. The reason is simple: children who identify the key features of stories will understand the story better, and children who automatically identify the key features of words will have more cognitive resources left to devote to comprehension. Fast, accurate word identification correlates positively with reading comprehension at all points from 1st grade through adulthood (Cunningham & Stanovich, 1997; Foorman et al., 2016).

Development of reading comprehension is also aided by acquisition of reading strategies. For example, good readers proceed slowly when they need to master written material in depth and speed up when they need only a rough sense of it (Pressley & Hilden, 2006). Proficiency in making such adjustments develops surprisingly late. Even when 10-year-olds are told that some material in a passage is crucial and other material is not, they tend to read all the material at the same speed. In contrast, 14-year-olds skim the nonessential parts and spend more time on the important ones (Kobasigawa, Ransom, & Holland, 1980).

Increasing metacognitive knowledge also enhances reading comprehension. With age and experience, readers increasingly monitor their ongoing understanding and reread passages they do not understand (Nicholson, 1999). Such **comprehension monitoring** differentiates good readers from poor ones at all ages from 1st grade through adulthood. Instructional approaches that focus on comprehension monitoring and other metacognitive skills, such as anticipating questions that a teacher might ask about the material, have been shown to improve reading comprehension (Palincsar & Magnusson, 2001; Rosenshine & Meister, 1994).

Perhaps the most powerful influence on the development of reading comprehension is increasing content knowledge. This content knowledge includes both understanding vocabulary terms and possessing general information about the subject (Perfetti & Stafura, 2014). Relevant content knowledge frees cognitive resources to focus on what is new or complex in the text and allows readers to draw reasonable inferences about information left unstated. Thus, when reading the headline "Blue Jays Maul Giants," readers knowledgeable about baseball realize that the headline concerns a baseball game; it is unclear how readers who lack baseball knowledge would interpret such a headline.

The path to strong or weak reading comprehension begins even before children start school. Hearing stories told or read by their parents helps preschoolers learn how stories tend to go, facilitating their understanding of new stories once they read themselves. It also enhances their general level of language development (Foorman et al., 2016; Whitehurst & Lonigan, 1998). The amount that parents read to their children during the preschool years also partially accounts for the differences between the reading comprehension skills of children from middle- and low-income families. For example, a study conducted in Israel showed that in an affluent school district with high reading-achievement scores, 96% of parents of preschoolers read to them daily. The same was true of only 15% of parents of preschoolers in a poor district with low scores (Feitelson & Goldstein, 1986).

The straightforward implication of these findings is that if preschoolers from poor families were read to daily, they too would become better readers. The evidence is consistent with this inference. Encouraging low-income parents to also actively engage their children in the reading process, such as by asking

comprehension monitoring ■
process of keeping track of one's understanding of a verbal description or text

 Reading and Reading Disorders

BOX 8.3 | individual differences

DYSLEXIA

Some children of normal intelligence whose parents encourage reading nonetheless read very poorly. Such poor reading despite normal intelligence is referred to as **dyslexia,** a condition that affects 5% to 10% of children in the United States (Compton et al., 2014). The causes of dyslexia are not well understood, but genetics are clearly part of the story. If one of a pair of monozygotic twins is diagnosed as dyslexic, the probability of the other twin receiving a similar diagnosis is 84%, whereas if the twins are dizygotic, the corresponding probability is 48% (Kovas & Plomin, 2007; Oliver, Dale, & Plomin, 2004). The extent of genetic influences varies with parental educational level: as with IQ score, genetic influences on dyslexia are larger with children of highly educated parents than with children of less educated parents (Friend, DeFries, & Olson, 2008; Olson et al., 2014).

At a cognitive level of analysis, dyslexia stems primarily from weak ability to discriminate between phonemes, from poor short-term memory for verbal material, from limited vocabulary, and from slow recall of the names of objects (Perfetti & Stafura, 2014). Determining the sounds that go with vowels is especially difficult for children with dyslexia, at least in English, where a single vowel can be pronounced in many ways (consider the sounds that accompany the letter "a" in *ha, hat, hall,* and *hate*). Because of these weaknesses, dyslexic children have great difficulty mastering the letter–sound correspondences used in phonological recoding, especially in languages, such as English, with irregular sound–symbol correspondences (Sprenger-Charolles, 2004).

For instance, as shown in the figure, when asked to read pseudo words such as *parding,* dyslexic 13- and 14-year-olds perform at the same level as typical 7- and 8-year-olds (Siegel, 1993). As would be expected from the strategy–choice model described on page 353, this difficulty with phonological processing causes most dyslexic children to be poor at visually based retrieval, as well as at sounding out words (Compton et al., 2014).

The problem can be a lasting one: most individuals who have poor phonological processing skills in early elementary school remain poor readers as adults (Compton et al., 2014; Ehri, 2014; Olson et al., 2014). This is especially often true for children who are from disadvantaged backgrounds and who attend inferior schools: children with dyslexia who come from more advantaged family backgrounds and who attend better schools are more likely to show substantial improvements (S. E. Shaywitz, Mody, & Shaywitz, 2006).

Studies of brain functioning support the view that poor phonological processing is at the heart of dyslexia. When dyslexic children read, two areas of their brains are less active than the corresponding areas in typical children reading the same words (Schlaggar & Church, 2009; Tanaka et al., 2011). One such area is directly involved in discriminating phonemes; the other area is involved in integrating visual and auditory data (in this

 Dyslexia: Expert and Children

 Adolescent Discusses Impact of Dyslexia

them to relate what is being read to their own experiences or to explain the characters' goals and motivations, helps even more (Zevenbergen & Whitehurst, 2003). Persuading low-income parents to enroll in such programs and read to their children on a continuing basis is not easy because of time demands and, in many cases, the pressures of being a single parent (Whitehurst et al., 1999), but when parents do so, their children's reading comprehension benefits.

Once children enter school, the amount of material they read varies greatly and has a large effect on their reading comprehension. For instance, U.S. 5th-graders whose reading-achievement test scores are in the 90th percentile for their grade report roughly 200 times as much discretionary reading as peers who score in the 10th percentile (Anderson, Wilson, & Fielding, 1988). High reading ability leads children to read more; children who read more, in turn, show greater gains over time in reading comprehension than do children of equal ability who read less (Guthrie et al., 1999).

Individual Differences

Individual differences in reading ability tend to be stable over time. Children who have relatively advanced reading skills when they enter kindergarten tend to be better readers through elementary, middle, and high school (Duncan et al., 2007; Harlaar, Dale, & Plomin, 2007). Studies of adoptive and non-adoptive siblings

dyslexia ■ inability to read and spell well despite having normal intelligence

case, integrating letters on the page with accompanying sounds).

How can dyslexic children be helped? One tempting idea is that because these children have difficulty learning phonics, they would learn better through an approach that de-emphasizes letter–sound relations and instead emphasizes either visually based retrieval or reliance on context. These alternative methods work poorly, however (Compton et al., 2014); there is simply no substitute for being able to sound out unfamiliar words. Instead, teaching children with dyslexia to use strategies that enhance their phonological recoding appears to be at least somewhat helpful. Effective strategies include drawing analogies to known words with similar spellings; generating alternative pronunciations of vowels when the first attempt at sounding out does not yield a plausible word; and, with long words, "peeling off" prefixes and suffixes and then trying to identify the rest of the word. Using such strategies helps many children with dyslexia to improve their reading-achievement scores (Compton et al., 2014).

After reviewing interventions that used such strategic approaches, however, Compton and colleagues concluded that

"unfortunately, our best attempts at developing potent interventions . . . can best be described as producing limited successes" (2014, p. 56). The improvements in word

identification produced by teaching word-identification strategies have not yielded large gains in reading comprehension (Solis et al., 2012). These researchers and others (e.g., Miller & Keenan, 2009; Perfetti & Stafura, 2014) argue that the only way to substantially improve the reading comprehension of dyslexic children is to greatly increase their vocabulary and general information about the world. Pursuing this path poses daunting challenges because of the vast amount of vocabulary and general information to be learned, but substantially improving reading comprehension of dyslexic children may require it.

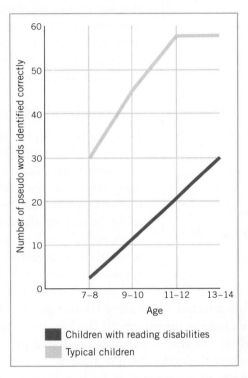

This chart shows the number of pseudo words identified correctly by 7- to 14-year-olds with and without reading disabilities. Note that 13- and 14-year-olds with reading disabilities correctly identified no more items than did typical 7- and 8-year-olds. The poor phonological recoding skills of children with reading disabilities lead them to have special difficulty with pseudo words that, because they are totally unfamiliar, can be pronounced only by using phonological recoding. (Data from Siegel, 1993)

and of monozygotic and dizygotic twins indicate that these continuities of individual differences reflect both shared genes and shared environments (Petrill et al., 2007; Wadsworth et al., 2006). As we have noted, genetic and environmental influences are mutually reinforcing: parents who are good and frequent readers are likely to provide both genes and environments that make it likely that their children will be relatively good readers when they are young, which makes it more likely that the children will seek out reading opportunities as they get older, which will further improve their reading, and so on (Petrill et al., 2005).

Writing

Much less is known about the development of children's writing than about the development of their reading, but what is known shows interesting parallels between the two.

Pre-writing Skills

The development of writing, like the development of reading, begins before children receive formal schooling. Figure 8.11 displays writing efforts typical of a 3½-year-old. The marks are not conventional letters of the alphabet, but they look vaguely

FIGURE 8.11 A 3½-year-old's effort at writing The child's symbols, although unconventional, indicate an understanding that words require separate symbols.

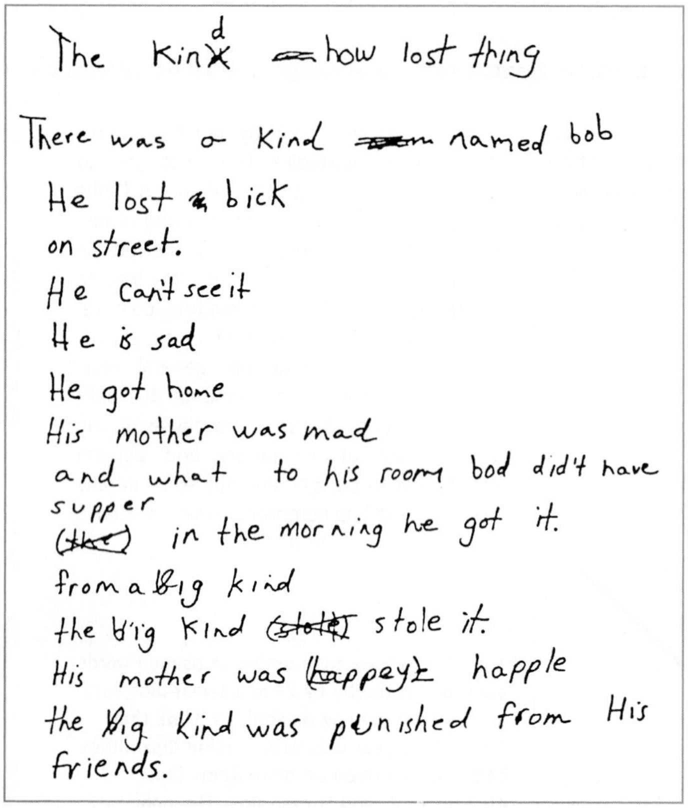

> The Kind ⟶ how lost thing
>
> There was a kind ⟶ named bob
>
> He lost a bick
> on street.
> He can't see it
> He is sad
> He got home
> His mother was mad
> and what to his room bod did't have
> supper
> (the) in the morning he got it.
> from a big kind
> the big kind (stole) stole it.
> His mother was (happey) happle
> the big kind was punished from His
> friends.

FIGURE 8.12 A 4th-grader's story The intended title of this story was *The Kid Who Lost Things*. See if you can figure out the rest.

script ■ typical sequence of actions used to organize and interpret repeated events, such as eating at restaurants, going to doctors' appointments, and writing reports

like them and are arranged along a roughly horizontal line. By age 4, children's "writing" is sufficiently advanced that adults have no trouble distinguishing it from the figures 4-year-olds produce when asked to draw a flower or a house (Tolchnisky, 2003).

Preschoolers' "writing" indicates that they expect meaning to be reflected in print. They use more marks to represent words that signify many objects, such as "forest," than to represent words that signify a single object, such as "tree" (Levin & Korat, 1993). Similarly, when asked to guess which of several words is the name for a particular object, they generally choose longer words for larger objects (Bialystok, 2000). Although written language does not work this way, the children's guess seems reasonable.

Generating Written Text

Learning to write, in the sense of composing an essay or story, is a good deal more difficult than learning to read. This is not surprising, because writing requires focusing simultaneously on numerous goals, both low level and high level. The low-level goals include forming letters, spelling words, and using correct capitalization and punctuation. The high-level goals include making arguments comprehensible without the intonations and gestures that help us communicate when we speak, organizing individual points in a coherent framework, and providing the background information that readers need to understand the writing (Berninger & Richards, 2002b). The difficulties children have in meeting both the low-level and high-level goals result in their often writing the type of flat story illustrated in Figure 8.12.

As with development of reading comprehension, growth of writing proficiency reflects improvements in basic processes, strategies, metacognition, and content knowledge. Automatizing low-level skills, such as spelling and punctuation, aids writing not only because correct spelling and punctuation make writing easier to understand but also because automatizing the low-level skills frees cognitive resources for pursuing the higher-level communicative goals of writing. Consistent with this conclusion, children's proficiency at low-level skills such as spelling correlates positively with the quality of the children's essays (Juel, 1994).

Acquisition of strategies also contributes to improvements in writing. One common strategy is to sequence high-level goals in a standard organization, or **script,** a set of actions or events that occur repeatedly. Harriet Waters, a psychologist whose proud mother saved all her daughter's "class news" assignments from 2nd grade, was one child who employed such an approach (Waters, 1980). As shown in Table 8.4, in each class news essay, Waters first noted the date, then described the weather, and then discussed events of the school day—a strategy that greatly simplified her writing task. For older children, formulating outlines serves a similar purpose of dividing the task of writing into manageable parts: first figure out what you want to say, then figure out the best order for making your main points, then figure out how to make each point.

Metacognitive understanding plays several crucial roles in writing. Perhaps the most basic type of metacognitive understanding is recognizing that readers may not have the same knowledge as the writer and that the writing therefore needs to include all the information that readers will need to allow them to grasp what is being said. Good writers consistently exhibit such understanding by high school;

TABLE 8.4

Stories Written at Beginning, Middle, and End of Year for Class News Assignment

SEPTEMBER 24, 1956

Today is Monday, September, 24, 1956. It is a rainy day. We hope the sun will shine. We got new spelling books. We had our pictures taken. We sang Happy Birthday to Barbara.

JANUARY 22, 1957

Today is Tuesday, January 22, 1957. It is a foggy day. We must be careful crossing the road. This morning, we had music. We learned a new song. Linda is absent. We hope she comes back soon. We had arithmetic. We made believe that we were buying candy. We had fun. We work in our English books. We learned when to use is and are.

MAY 27, 1957

Today is Monday, May 27, 1957. It is a warm, cloudy day. We hope the sun comes out. This afternoon, we had music. We enjoyed it. We went out to play. Carole is absent. We hope she comes back soon. We had a spelling lesson, we learned about a dozen. Tomorrow we shall have show and tell. Some of us have spelling sentences to do for homework. Danny brought in a cocoon. It will turn into a butterfly.

Information from H. S. Waters (1980).

poor writers often do not (Berninger & Richards, 2002b). A second crucial type of metacognitive knowledge involves understanding the need to plan one's writing rather than just jumping in and starting to write. Good writers spend much more time than do poor writers planning what they will say before they begin writing—making notes, constructing outlines, and so on (Graham et al., 2012). Understanding the need for revision is a third key type of metacognitive knowledge. Good writers spend more time revising their already relatively good first drafts than poor writers spend revising their poorer ones (Fitzgerald, 1992).

Fortunately, as with reading, instruction aimed at inculcating metacognitive understanding can enhance writing skills (S. Graham & Harris, 1996; Graham et al., 2012). In particular, the writing of both typical and learning-disabled children improves when they are taught to revise other children's work and to ask themselves several basic questions: Who is the main character in this story? What does the main character do? How do the other characters respond? How does the main character respond to the other characters' responses? What happens in the end? Asking children to reflect on the relative quality of essays written by other children and on why some essays are better than others also can improve writing (Braaksma et al., 2004).

Finally, as in reading, content knowledge plays a crucial role in writing. Children generally write better when they are familiar with the topic than when they are not (Bereiter & Scardamalia, 1982; Graham et al., 2012). Children can gain content knowledge through reading, which is one reason why children who are skillful readers and read more than most peers also tend to be good writers (Graham et al., 2012).

Mathematics

In Chapter 7, we examined infants' early-developing nonverbal number sense and the emergence of counting between ages 2 and 4 years. Here we examine subsequent mathematical development, including development of arithmetic.

Arithmetic

People often think of arithmetic learning as a process of rote memorization, but it is actually far more complex and interesting. How well children learn arithmetic

BARBARA SMALLER THE NEW YORKER COLLECTION / THE CARTOON BANK

"Maybe it's not a wrong answer—maybe it's just a different answer."

Learning arithmetic is harder than it looks.

depends on the strategies they use, the precision of their representations of numerical magnitudes, and their understanding of basic mathematical concepts and principles.

Strategies From age 4 or 5 years, when most children begin to learn arithmetic, they use a variety of problem-solving strategies. The most common initial strategies are counting from 1 (e.g., solving 2 + 2 by putting up two fingers on each hand and counting "1, 2, 3, 4") and retrieval (recalling answers from memory). At first, children can use these strategies to answer only a few simple problems, such as 1 + 2 and 2 + 2, but they gradually expand use of the strategies to a wider range of single-digit problems (Geary, 2006; Siegler, 1996).

When children begin to do arithmetic on a daily basis, in kindergarten or 1st grade, they add several new strategies. One is *counting from the larger addend* (e.g., solving 3 + 9 by counting, "9, 10, 11, 12"). Another strategy is *decomposition*, which involves dividing a problem into two easier ones (e.g., solving 3 + 9 by thinking "3 + 10 = 13; 13 − 1 = 12"). Children continue to use the earlier developing strategies as well; most 1st-graders use three or more strategies to add single-digit numbers (Siegler, 1987).

Children use similarly varied strategies on all four arithmetic operations. For example, to solve a multiplication problem such as 3 × 4, children sometimes

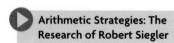

Arithmetic Strategies: The Research of Robert Siegler

write three 4s and add them, sometimes make three bundles of four hatch marks and count them, and sometimes retrieve 12 from memory (Mabbott & Bisanz, 2003). Use of these arithmetic strategies is surprisingly enduring: even college students use strategies other than retrieval on 15% to 30% of single-digit problems (LeFevre et al., 1996; Lemaire, 2010).

Just as children's choices among word-identification strategies are highly adaptive, so are their choices among arithmetic strategies (Siegler, 1996). Even 4-year-olds choose in sensible ways, usually solving easy problems such as 2 + 2 quickly and accurately by using retrieval and usually solving harder problems such as 5 + 2 less quickly but still accurately by counting from 1. As children gain experience with the answers to single-digit arithmetic problems, their strategy choices shift increasingly toward using retrieval of those answers. The learning process seems to be the same as with the corresponding shift toward visually based retrieval in reading. The more often children generate the correct answer to a problem, regardless of the strategy they use to generate it, the more often they will be able to retrieve that answer, thereby avoiding the need to use slower counting strategies.

Understanding numerical magnitudes **Numerical magnitude representations** are mental models of the way quantities are ordered along a less-to-more dimension. Regardless of whether "7" refers to a distance (7 inches), a weight (7 pounds), a duration (7 hours), or a set size (7 people), the magnitude represented by "7" is larger than that indicated by "6"—and smaller than that indicated by "8"—of the same unit.

numerical magnitude representations ■ mental models of the sizes of numbers, ordered along a less-to-more dimension

The idea that symbolically expressed numbers represent magnitudes might seem obvious, but accurately linking such numbers and the magnitudes they represent actually constitutes a major challenge for children over a prolonged period of development. Here are some examples: many preschoolers who can count flawlessly from 1 to 10 do not know whether 4 or 8 indicates the greater number of objects (Le Corre & Carey, 2007); many elementary school children estimate the location of 150 as being near the midpoint of a number line with 0 and 1000 at the two ends (Laski & Yu, 2014; Thompson & Opfer, 2010); and many adolescents and adults have no idea whether 3/5 is larger or smaller than 5/11 (Fazio, DeWolf, & Siegler, 2016; Meert, Grégoire, & Noël, 2010). What is lacking in all these cases is accurate representations of numerical magnitudes.

Although the learning process takes a prolonged period, the range of numbers whose magnitudes children represent reasonably precisely, as indicated by the accuracy of their magnitude comparisons and number-line estimates, increases greatly with age and experience (Figure 8.13). Accuracy of magnitude representations of the numbers 1–10 increases greatly between ages 3 and 6 (Bertelletti et al., 2010); that of numbers 1–100, between ages 6 and 8 (Geary et al., 2007); that of numbers 1–1000, between ages 8 and 12 (Siegler & Opfer, 2003); and so on. These ages reflect when children are first gaining substantial experience with each numerical range: most children learn to count from 1–10 in the preschool period; they learn to count, add, and subtract numbers from 1–100 in early elementary school and so on.

Children of any given age differ considerably in their knowledge of numerical magnitudes. These differences are related to the children's overall mathematical knowledge. During elementary school, children who more accurately estimate whole-number magnitudes on number lines have higher math achievement. During middle school, the same is true for children who accurately estimate fraction

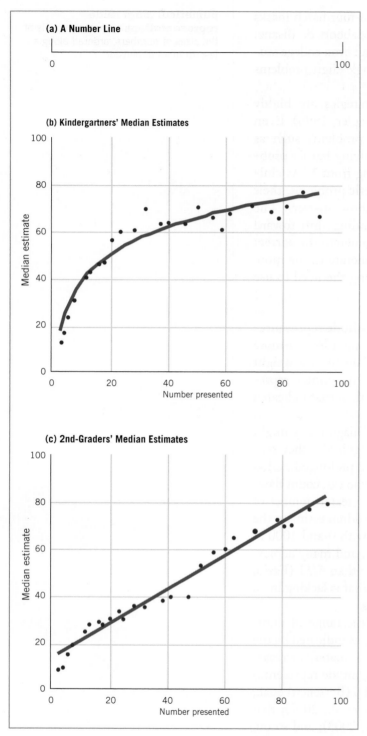

FIGURE 8.13 The number-line task and typical developmental changes on it (a) On each trial with a 0–100 number line, children need to estimate a different number's location on the line. (b) Kindergartners' median estimates for each number on the 0–100 number-line task increased with the number being estimated, but in a way that involved overestimates of relatively small numbers and underestimates of large ones. (c) 2nd-graders' median estimates for each number on the same task increased linearly with the size of the number being estimated, and were quite accurate. (Data from Siegler & Booth, 2004)

magnitudes (Jordan et al., 2013; Siegler & Pyke, 2013; Siegler, Thompson, & Schneider, 2011).

Part of the reason for this relation is that more accurate magnitude representations help children learn arithmetic. The more precisely a child understands numerical magnitudes, as measured by his or her accuracy in estimating the position of numbers on a number line, the greater the child's arithmetic proficiency (J. L. Booth & Siegler, 2006; 2008; Geary et al., 2007). Moreover, instruction that improves the accuracy of children's symbolic numerical magnitude representations also improves their subsequent learning of arithmetic (J. L. Booth & Siegler, 2008; L. S. Fuchs et al., 2013; Siegler & Ramani, 2009). Accurate magnitude representations may enhance arithmetic learning by suggesting plausible answers and eliminating implausible ones from consideration. Accurate magnitude representations, in turn, are related to some of the same cognitive processes that contribute to reading, writing, and mathematics more generally, especially basic processes, such as working memory, and strategy use (Jordan et al., 2013; Vukovic et al., 2014)

Conceptual understanding of arithmetic Understanding why some arithmetic procedures are appropriate and others inappropriate poses a major challenge for many children, even those who have memorized the correct procedure. Such conceptual understanding of arithmetic begins developing during the preschool period; for example, many 4-year-olds understand the *commutative law of addition*, the principle that adding a + b is the same as adding b + a (Canobi, Reeve, & Pattison, 2002). Not until years later, however, do they master more advanced arithmetic concepts, such as **mathematical equality**—the idea that the values on the two sides of the equal sign must balance. On almost all problems in which young children encounter the equal sign, numbers appear only to the left of it (e.g., 3 + 4 = __; 3 + 4 + 5 = __). For purposes of solving such problems, children can interpret the equal sign merely as a signal to start adding.

Eventually, however, children encounter arithmetic problems with numbers on both sides of the equal sign, such as 3 + 4 + 5 = __ + 5. As late as 4th grade, most children in the United States answer such problems incorrectly (Goldin-Meadow, Cook, & Mitchell, 2009). The most common incorrect approach is to

mathematical equality ■ concept that the values on each side of the equal sign must be equivalent

add all the numbers to the left of the equal sign, which in the above problem sum to 12, and to assume that this sum is the answer to the problem. Such errors reflect interference from the vast amount of practice children have had solving typical addition problems, which have no number following the equal sign (McNeil et al., 2011), as well as a lack of understanding that the equal sign means that the values on both sides of it must be equivalent.

In many cases, children's hand gestures reveal that they have somewhat better understanding of mathematical equality than is revealed by their answers or explanations. For example, on the problem $3 + 4 + 5 = \_\_ + 5$, children often answer "12" and explain that they solved the problem by adding $3 + 4 + 5$, but during their explanation, they point to all four numbers rather than just to the three preceding the equal sign. This pointing suggests an implicit recognition that the fourth number might be important, even though the child did not include it in the calculation (Goldin-Meadow & Alibali, 2002). Children who initially show such **gesture–speech mismatches,** in which their gesturing conveys more information than their verbal statements, learn more from instruction on mathematical equality problems than do peers whose gesturing and speech before the instruction were consistent (i.e., those who said "12" and pointed only to the three numbers that they added).

The gestures play a causal role in learning as well: children who are encouraged to gesture appropriately while explaining answers to mathematical equality problems learn more than children asked not to gesture (Goldin-Meadow et al., 2009). The positive relation between gesture–speech mismatches and subsequent learning has emerged on number conservation and physics problems as well as on mathematical equality problems. These findings illustrate a widespread phenomenon: variability of thought and action (e.g., generating gestures that differ from one's speech or advancing multiple explanations of a phenomenon rather than just one) often indicates heightened readiness to learn (Church, 1999; Siegler, 2006; Thelen & Smith, 2006).

Cultural influences Knowledge of arithmetic varies greatly among countries. Children in China, Japan, South Korea, and other East Asian countries acquire far greater proficiency than those in even high-achieving European and North American countries (e.g., Finland, the Netherlands, and Canada), who in turn tend to know more than peers in other European and North American countries, including the United States, Spain, and Italy (Bailey et al., 2015; Geary, Berch, & Mann Koepke, 2015; Torbeyns et al., 2015). The differences start even before the child enters formal schooling (Siegler & Mu, 2008) and appear to be related to cultural emphasis (or lack of emphasis) on math, quality of math teachers and textbooks, and time spent on math in classrooms and homes (Bailey et al., 2015; Geary, 2006; Leung et al., 2015).

One cultural influence on math learning is language. As noted in Chapter 7, the Chinese, Japanese, and Korean languages express whole-number names in more straightforward ways than English (e.g., ten-one, ten-two, etc.), and the differences appear to contribute to the superior mathematics learning of East Asian children. Linguistic differences also make fractions easier to learn for East Asian children. For example, the Korean term for 1/3, *sam bun, ui, il,* which translates roughly to "of three parts one," helps Korean 1st- and 2nd-graders more accurately match fractions to pictorial representations of the fraction (in the case of 1/3, one of three equal parts of an object is shaded) (Miura et al., 1999). Teaching U.S. children English translations of the Korean way of

gesture–speech mismatches ■ phenomenon in which hand movements and verbal statements convey different ideas

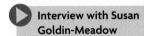 **Interview with Susan Goldin-Meadow**

expressing fractions led to substantial gains in their ability to match the numerical symbol to the pictorial representation (Paik & Mix, 2003). Language is only one of many factors that contribute to the superior math learning of East Asian children, and other factors, in particular the cultural value that learning math is extremely important for all children, probably play an even larger role (Hatano, 1990). There can be no doubt that environmental variables greatly influence children's math learning.

Mathematics Anxiety

Many children experience *mathematics anxiety*, a negative emotional state that leads to fear and avoidance of math (Ashcraft & Ridley, 2005). Such anxiety can be evident as early as 1st grade (Ramirez et al., 2012) and for many people presents a lifelong problem. Mathematics evokes more anxiety than other school subjects, probably because of the unambiguous right/wrong status of answers to many mathematics problems, the widespread belief that mathematics is closely linked to intelligence, and the frustrating periods with no apparent progress that mathematics learning often entails.

Although, as will be discussed in Chapter 15, mean math achievement of boys and girls is almost identical (Halpern et al., 2007), mathematics anxiety is considerably more prevalent in girls than in boys (Devine et al., 2012). Not surprising, it is more common among people who do poorly in math, though some people experience it despite having high mathematics achievement and not suffering from high anxiety in general (Maloney & Beilock, 2012; Moore & Ashcraft, 2013). The dread that math can inspire contributes to the negative outcomes that are feared; a likely reason is that the anxiety reduces the working memory resources needed to solve mathematics problems (Beilock & Willingham, 2014). Consistent with this interpretation, when presented with mathematics tasks, people with math anxiety show both unusually great activity on the right side of the amygdala, a part of the brain involved in processing negative emotions, and depressed activity in brain areas crucial to working memory (C. B. Young, Wu, & Menon, 2012).

How do some children become anxious about math? The mechanisms are not well understood, but one contributor appears to be the views of adults who are important in the children's lives. Parents and teachers who are themselves anxious about mathematics tend to convey their beliefs and feelings to their children. The problem seems to be especially great for girls whose parents and teachers are pessimistic about girls' mathematical abilities (Beilock et al., 2010; Meece, Wigfield, & Eccles, 1990).

The negative impact of anxiety on mathematics learning has prompted efforts to find ways of reducing the anxiety. One promising intervention is surprisingly simple: have students write a brief description of their emotions just before taking a test. Such expressive writing reduces anxiety and boosts performance in a variety of areas in which negative emotions interfere with learning and performance, including mathematics (Ramirez & Beilock, 2011). Putting the negative thoughts on paper might help students think about the situation more objectively and thus allow them to concentrate on the math problems.

Even among children with mathematics anxiety, most learn the basics reasonably well. However, as noted in Box 8.4, the learning process goes seriously awry with certain children who suffer from the general difficulty in thinking about numbers that is known as *mathematics disability*.

BOX 8.4 | applications

MATHEMATICS DISABILITIES

Between 5% and 8% of children perform so poorly in math that they are classified as having a mathematics disability (Shalev, 2007). These children have IQ scores in the normal range (85 or higher) but perform extremely poorly in mathematics. In the first few grades, they tend to be slow to learn to count, to learn the relative magnitudes of numbers, and to accurately solve single-digit arithmetic problems (Geary et al., 2008; Jordan, 2007). Their performance improves with experience, but even in later grades and adulthood, most continue to be slow at single-digit arithmetic and to have difficulty with the many mathematical skills that build on it, such as multi-digit arithmetic, fractions, and algebra (Geary et al., 2012; Hecht & Vagi, 2010).

Although people often think of mathematics as a type of knowledge necessary for school but not afterward, the experience of adults with mathematics disabilities illustrates the lifelong debilitating effects of this problem:

> I worked for Nabisco. As a mixer, you had to know the correct scale and formulas. I kept messing up. I lost my job.
> (Curry, Schmitt, & Waldron, 1996, p. 63)

> Dairy Queen wouldn't hire me because I couldn't make change in my head.
> (Curry, Schmitt, & Waldron, 1996, p. 63)

> For as long as I can remember, numbers have not been my friend.
> (Blackburn, cited in M. McCloskey, 2007, p. 415)

Several specific problems contribute to mathematics disabilities (Geary et al., 2012). In severe cases, damage to one or more brain areas that are central to numerical processing, such as the intraparietal sulcus, is often the cause (Butterworth, 2010; T. J. Simon & Rivera, 2007). In less severe cases, minimal exposure to numbers prior to beginning school often contributes. Children who start school lacking knowledge of the key mathematical concepts and skills that their peers possess tend to lag far behind throughout school (Duncan et al., 2007). Other variables that are associated with, and might cause, mathematics disabilities are poor working memory for numbers, poor executive functioning, slow processing of numerical information, and mathematics anxiety (C. Blair & Razza, 2007; Lyons &

Beilock, 2012; Mazzocco & Kover, 2007; Raghubar, Barnes, & Hecht, 2010).

A variety of programs have been designed to improve the mathematics knowledge of children with mathematics disabilities. One particularly successful program (L. S. Fuchs et al., 2013) emphasized learning of fraction magnitudes through instruction in magnitude comparison (e.g., "Which is larger: 1/2 or 1/5?") and number-line estimation (e.g., "Where would 1/5 go on this number line?"). The instruction, which was implemented with 9- and 10-year-olds, not only improved the children's learning of these capabilities but also improved their learning of fraction arithmetic, relative to that of children who received a greater amount of fraction arithmetic instruction in the classroom but less instruction in understanding fraction magnitudes. Such findings indicate that effective instruction can reduce the problems associated with mathematics disabilities.

Review

Learning to read begins in preschool, when many children come to recognize the letters of the alphabet and gain phonemic awareness. Early in elementary school, children learn to identify words through two main processes—phonological recoding and visually based retrieval—and they choose adaptively between these strategies. Reading comprehension improves through automatization of word identification, development of strategies, and acquisition of metacognition and content knowledge. How much parents read to their children and, later, how much the children themselves read also influence reading development.

Learning to write well is difficult. It requires focusing simultaneously on low-level goals (proper spelling, punctuation, and capitalization) and high-level goals (making arguments clear and persuasive). Many Western children enter school knowing that writing proceeds in a horizontal sequence from left to right, that the text on one line continues on the next, and that words are separated by small spaces. Improvements in writing with age and experience reflect automatization of low-level goals, new organizational strategies, growing metacognitive understanding of what readers need to be told, and increasing content knowledge.

Mathematical development follows a similar general pattern. Most children enter school with some useful knowledge, such as knowing how to count from 1 to solve addition problems. Once in school, children learn a wide range of strategies for solving arithmetic and other mathematical problems, and they generally choose among these strategies in sensible ways. They also learn about an increasing range of numerical magnitudes, which improves their arithmetic learning. Understanding underlying concepts and principles also is an essential part of learning mathematics. On the other hand, mathematics anxiety can interfere with performance and learning, because the heightened emotions reduce working-memory resources. Knowledge of arithmetic varies greatly among countries, and there can be no doubt that environmental variables, such as the particular language children speak and the value of math learning in their culture, greatly influence children's math learning.

CHAPTER SUMMARY

■ Alfred Binet and his colleague Théophile Simon developed the first widely used intelligence test. Its purpose was to identify children who were unlikely to benefit from standard instruction in the classroom. Modern intelligence tests are descendants of the Binet–Simon test.

■ One of Binet's key insights was that intelligence includes diverse high-level capabilities that need to be assessed in order to measure intelligence accurately.

What Is Intelligence?

■ Intelligence can be viewed as a single trait, such as *g;* as a few separate abilities, such as Thurstone's primary mental abilities; or as a very large number of specific processes, such as those described in information-processing analyses.

■ Intelligence is often measured through use of IQ tests, such as the Stanford–Binet and the WISC. These tests examine general information, vocabulary, arithmetic, language comprehension, spatial reasoning, and a variety of other intellectual abilities.

Measuring Intelligence

■ A person's overall score on an intelligence test, the IQ score, is a measure of general intelligence. It reflects the individual's intellectual ability relative to age peers.

■ Most children's IQ scores are quite stable over periods of years, though scores do vary somewhat over time.

IQ Scores as Predictors of Important Outcomes

■ IQ scores correlate positively with long-term educational and occupational success.

■ Other factors, such as social understanding, creativity, and motivation also influence success in life.

Genes, Environment, and the Development of Intelligence

■ Development of intelligence is influenced by the child's own qualities, by the immediate environment, and by the broader societal context.

■ Genetic inheritance is one important influence on IQ score. This influence tends to increase with age, in part due to some genes not expressing themselves until late childhood or adolescence, and in part due to genes influencing children's choices of environments.

■ A child's family environment, as measured by the HOME, is related to the child's IQ score. The relation reflects within-family influences, such as parents' intellectual and emotional support for the particular child, as well as between-family influences, such as differences in parental wealth and education.

■ Schooling positively influences IQ score and school achievement.

■ Broader societal factors, such as poverty and discrimination against racial and ethnic minorities, also influence children's IQ scores.

■ To alleviate the harmful effects of poverty, the United States has undertaken both small-scale preschool intervention programs and the much larger Project Head Start. Both have initial positive effects on intelligence and school achievement, though the effects fade over time. On the other hand, the programs have enduring positive effects on the likelihood of not being held back in a grade and the likelihood of completing high school.

- Intensive intervention programs, such as the Carolina Abecedarian Project, that begin in the child's 1st year and provide optimal childcare circumstances and structured academic curricula have produced increases in intelligence that continue into adolescence and adulthood.

Alternative Perspectives on Intelligence

- Novel approaches to intelligence, such as Gardner's multiple intelligences theory and Sternberg's theory of successful intelligence, attempt to broaden traditional conceptions of intelligence.

Acquisition of Academic Skills: Reading, Writing, and Mathematics

- Many children learn letter names and gain phonemic awareness before they start school. Both skills correlate with later reading achievement, and phonemic awareness also is causally related to it.
- Word identification is achieved by two main strategies: phonological recoding and visually based retrieval.
- Reading comprehension benefits from automatization of word identification, because it frees cognitive resources for understanding the text. Use of strategies, metacognitive understanding, and content knowledge also influence

reading comprehension, as does the amount that parents read to their children and the amount that children themselves read.

- Although many children begin to write during the preschool period, writing well remains difficult for many years. Much of the difficulty comes from the fact that writing well requires children to attend simultaneously to low-level processes, such as punctuation and spelling, and to high-level processes, such as anticipating what readers will and will not know.
- As with reading, automatization of basic processes, use of strategies, metacognitive understanding, and content knowledge influence development of writing.
- Most children use several strategies to learn arithmetic, such as adding by counting from 1, counting from the larger addend, and retrieving answers from memory. Children typically choose in adaptive ways, using more time-consuming and effortful strategies only on the more difficult problems where such approaches are needed to generate correct answers.
- Precise representations of numerical magnitudes are crucial for learning arithmetic and other mathematical skills.
- As children encounter more advanced math, conceptual understanding becomes increasingly important. Understanding mathematical equality, for example, is essential for grasping advanced arithmetic and algebra problems.
- Mathematics anxiety can interfere with performance and learning because the heightened emotions reduce working-memory resources.

Test Yourself

1. Who developed the first objective intelligence test that directly assessed specific high-level abilities identified as key components of intelligence?
   a. Spearman
   b. Wechsler
   c. Gardner
   d. Binet

2. Chris is an elementary school student who is good at putting together puzzles, identifying which object doesn't belong to a given set, and thinking on the spot. Chris's proficiency in these various intellectual tasks is an indication of his level of _____ intelligence.
   a. crystallized
   b. fluid
   c. emotional
   d. processing

3. Which of the following best describes Carroll's three-stratum theory of intelligence?
   a. Intelligence is best measured by reading, writing, and mathematics concepts.

   b. Each individual can be categorized into one of three levels intelligence.
   c. Successful intelligence involves analytic, practical, and creative abilities.
   d. General intelligence influences intermediate abilities, which influence specific processes.

4. The summary measure that is the result of an intelligence test is referred to as a person's _____ .
   a. normal distribution
   b. intelligence quotient
   c. general intelligence
   d. individual quantitative measure

5. As an individual moves from early childhood into adolescence and adulthood, the influence of genetic factors on intelligence _____ .
   a. increases
   b. fluctuates
   c. remains stable
   d. decreases

6. Six-year-old Aliya loves to read. Her parents aren't particularly engaged in reading themselves, but because of Aliya's evident interest, they surround her with books and read to her. According to Sandra Scarr, the relationship between Aliya's interests and her parents' actions is an example of
   _____ .
   a. passive effects
   b. active effects
   c. evocative effects
   d. mental modeling

7. HOME was developed to measure the complex influences of family environment on a child's intelligence. Though this measure can be used to predict a child's IQ score, why are researchers not able to conclude that better home environment leads to higher scores?
   a. Children's IQ scores tend to fluctuate widely with age.
   b. This measure does not account for the influence of parents' genes on the home environment and the child's intelligence.
   c. Children's IQ scores are not normally distributed and therefore cannot be used to draw causal relationships.
   d. Subsequent measures have shown that home environment has little influence on intelligence.

8. Which of the following statements is true regarding the relationship between environmental risk and intelligence, according to the environmental risk scale?
   a. Parental education level is the key factor in predicting a child's intellectual development.
   b. The impact of additional risks diminishes greatly after the presence of three risk factors.
   c. The total number of risks is a better predictor of IQ than the presence of any single risk.
   d. Though IQ score remains stable over time, the number of risk factors in a child's environment is highly variable.

9. The fact that certain types of brain damage can lead to deficiencies in specific areas (e.g., interpersonal skills) and that prodigies show remarkable ability in specific areas (e.g., musical intelligence) but not in others led to the development of which theory?
   a. Sternberg's theory of successful intelligence
   b. the Flynn effect
   c. Gardner's theory of multiple intelligences
   d. Thurston's theory of primary mental abilities

10. What are the three components of Sternberg's theory of successful intelligence?
    a. analytic abilities, practical abilities, and creative abilities
    b. linguistic intelligence, logical-mathematical intelligence, and spatial intelligence
    c. passive effects, evocative effects, and active effects
    d. general intelligence, intermediate-level abilities, and specific processes

11. Performance on measures of _____ is the strongest predictor of a kindergartner's later ability to sound out and spell words.
    a. phonemic awareness
    b. letter name mastery
    c. IQ
    d. phonological recoding skills

12. Comprehension monitoring describes an individual's ability to
    a. process a word's meaning from its visual form.
    b. translate letters into sounds and blend those sounds into words.
    c. keep track of one's ongoing understanding of a text.
    d. recognize that readers may not have the same knowledge as the writer.

13. Which high-level writing strategy involves the repetition of a certain sequence of actions, such as determining a thesis, outlining the main points, and figuring out how to support those points?
    a. following a script
    b. comprehension monitoring
    c. planning
    d. strategy–choice processing

14. The idea that the number 5 represents a unit that falls between the numbers 4 and 6, regardless of whether one is referring to distance, weight, set size, or some other measurement, is known as _____ .
    a. mathematical equality
    b. decomposition
    c. numerical magnitude representations
    d. mental modeling

15. When asked to solve the problem $2 + 3 + 4 = \_\_ + 4$, 10-year-old Nevin gives the incorrect answer 9, but explains his answer by pointing to all four numbers, rather than just the three that come before the equal sign. Nevin's behavior illustrates _____ .
    a. mathematical inequality
    b. gesture–speech mismatch
    c. decomposition
    d. visual retrieval error

LaunchPad
macmillan learning

Don't stop now! Research shows that testing yourself is a powerful learning tool. Visit LaunchPad to access the LearningCurve adaptive quizzing system, which gives you a personalized study plan to help build your mastery of the chapter material through videos, activities, and more. **Go to launchpadworks.com.**

Critical Thinking Questions

1. Intelligence can be viewed as a single ability, several abilities, or many processes. List the characteristics that you think are the most important components of intelligence and explain their relevance.

2. Individual differences in intelligence are more stable than individual differences in other areas of psychological functioning such as emotional regulation or aggression. Why do you think this is so?

3. Among children from middle- and upper-income families, genetics are more influential than the shared environment on individual differences in intelligence, but among children from low-income families, the opposite is the case. Why do you think that is?

4. Participation in Head Start does not lead to higher IQ or achievement test scores by the end of high school, but it does lead to lower rates of dropping out or being placed in special-education classes. Why do you think this is the case?

5. Explain Chall's (1979) statement: "In the primary grades, children learn to read; in the higher grades, they read to learn."

6. The development of reading, writing, and mathematics shows a number of similarities. What are these similarities, and why do you think development occurs in similar ways in the three areas?

Key Terms

Carolina Abecedarian Project, p. 346

comprehension monitoring, p. 355

crystallized intelligence, p. 328

dyslexia, p. 356

fluid intelligence, p. 327

Flynn effect, p. 341

g (general intelligence), p. 327

gesture–speech mismatches, p. 363

IQ (intelligence quotient), p. 332

mathematical equality, p. 362

mental model, p. 354

multiple intelligences theory, p. 349

normal distribution, p. 332

numerical magnitude representations, p. 361

phonemic awareness, p. 351

phonological recoding skills, p. 351

primary mental abilities, p. 328

script, p. 358

self-discipline, p. 335

standard deviation (SD), p. 332

strategy–choice process, p. 353

theory of successful intelligence, p. 350

three-stratum theory of intelligence, p. 328

visually based retrieval, p. 353

Wechsler Intelligence Scale for Children (WISC), p. 330

▶ Student Video Activities

Intelligence and Testing in Middle Childhood

Interview with Ellen Winner

Early Childhood Education

Education in Middle Childhood

Dyslexia: Expert and Children

Adolescent Discusses Impact of Dyslexia

Reading and Reading Disorders

Arithmetic Strategies: The Research of Robert Siegler

Interview with Susan Goldin-Meadow

Answers to Test Yourself

1. d, 2. b, 3. d, 4. b, 5. a, 6. c, 7. b, 8. c, 9. c, 10. a, 11. a, 12. c, 13. a, 14. c, 15. b

ANDREW MACARA, *Cricket, Sri Lanka* (oil on canvas, 1998)

Theories of Social Development

Themes

- ■ Nature and Nurture
- ■ The Active Child
- ■ Continuity/Discontinuity
- ■ Mechanisms of Change
- ■ The Sociocultural Context
- ■ Individual Differences
- ■ Research and Children's Welfare

Imagine yourself interacting face-to-face with an infant. What is it like? You naturally smile and speak in an affectionate tone of voice, and the infant probably smiles and makes happy sounds back at you. If for some reason you speak in a loud, harsh voice, the baby becomes quiet and wary. If you look away, the infant follows your gaze, as though assuming there is something interesting to see in that direction. Of course, the baby does not just respond to what you do; the baby also engages in independent behaviors, examining various objects or events in the room or fussing for no obvious reason. Your interaction with the baby evokes emotions in you—joy, affection, frustration, and so on. Over time, through repeated interactions, you and the infant learn about each other and smile and vocalize more readily to each other than to someone else.

Now imagine that you are asked to interact with Kismet, the robot pictured below, just as you would with a human infant. Although the request might seem strange, Kismet's facelike features make you willing to give it a try. So you smile and speak in an affectionate tone—"Hi, Kismet, how are you?" Kismet smiles back at you and gurgles happily. You speak harshly, "Kismet, stop that right now." The robot looks surprised—even a bit frightened—and makes a whimpering sound. You find yourself spontaneously attempting to console Kismet: "I'm sorry; I didn't mean it." After just a few moments, you have lost your feeling of self-consciousness and find the interaction with your new metallic friend remarkably natural. You may even start to feel fond of Kismet.

Kismet was one of the world's first "social robots." Unlike robots that are programmed to behave in specific ways (like a vacuuming Roomba), social robots are programmed to learn from their interactions with humans, just as infants do. Accordingly, Kismet was designed as a sociable, "cute" robot that could elicit "nurturing" from humans. Kismet's behavior is readily interpretable in human terms, and the robot even seems to have internal mental and emotional states and a personality. Kismet learns from its interactions with people—from their instructions and from their reactions to its behavior. Through these interactions, Kismet

Like that between a mother and her infant, a face-to-face interaction between Kismet and its designer involves talking, cooing back and forth, and responding to each other's facial expressions.

PETER MENZEL / SCIENCE SOURCE

figures out how to interpret facial expressions, how to communicate, what behaviors are acceptable, and so on (Breazeal, 1998). Thus, Kismet develops over time as a function of the interaction between the "innate" structure built into it and its subsequent socially mediated experience. Just like a baby!

The challenge for Kismet's designers was in many ways like the task of developmental scientists who attempt to understand how children's development is shaped through their interactions with other people. Any successful account of social development must include the many ways we influence one another, starting with the simple fact that no human infant can survive without intensive, long-term care by other people. We learn how to behave on the basis of how others respond to our behavior; we learn how to interpret ourselves according to how others treat us; and we interpret other people by analogy to ourselves—all in the context of social interaction and human society. Pioneers in robotics have continued to use machines as a way to better understand the role of social dynamics from infancy onward. In one recent application of robotics to social development, researchers modeled the development of infant smiling by having undergraduate students interact with a baby-faced robot named Diego-San, programmed to both perceive and produce smiling behavior (Ruvolo, Messinger, & Movellan, 2015). The researchers found that by carefully timing Diego-San's smiles, it can elicit the maximum amount of adult smiling. Thus, by using robots, researchers can carefully control aspects of "infant" behavior that would otherwise be extremely difficult to manipulate, allowing them to test specific hypotheses about the development of social behavior.

In this chapter, we review some of the most important and influential general theories of social development, theories that attempt to account for how children's development is affected by the people and social institutions around them. In our survey of cognitive theories in Chapter 4, we discussed some of the reasons why theories are important; those reasons apply equally well to theories of social development.

Theories of social development attempt to account for many important aspects of development, including emotion, personality, attachment, self, peer

Advances in artificial intelligence and robotics have allowed researchers to test theories of social and behavioral development in unique ways. Diego-San, pictured here, is being used to study the motivation and timing of mother and infant smiles.

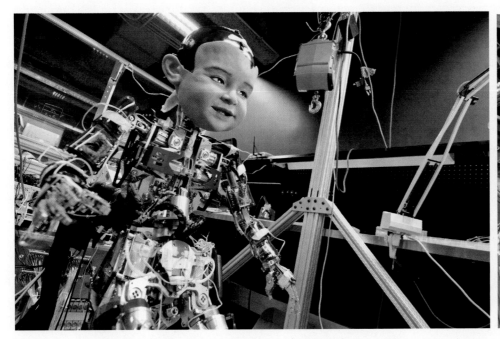

relationships, morality, and gender. In this chapter, we will describe four types of theories that address these topics, reflecting, in turn, the psychoanalytic, learning, social cognitive, and ecological perspectives. We will discuss the basic tenets of each theory and examine some of the relevant evidence.

Every one of our seven themes appears in this chapter, with three of them being particularly prominent. The theme that pervades this chapter most extensively is *individual differences,* as we examine how the social world affects children's development. The theme of *nature and nurture* helps us distinguish between the theories, because they vary in the degree to which they emphasize biological and environmental factors. The *active child* theme is also a major focus: some of the theories emphasize children's active participation in, and effect on, their own socialization, whereas others view children's development as shaped primarily by external forces.

Psychoanalytic Theories

No psychological theory has had a greater impact on Western culture and on thinking about personality and social development than the psychoanalytic theory of Sigmund Freud (1856–1939). The life-span developmental theory of Erik Erikson (1902–1994), a successor to Freud's theory, has also been quite influential.

View of Children's Development

In both Freud's and Erikson's theories, development is largely driven by biological maturation. For Freud, behavior is motivated by the need to satisfy basic drives. These drives, and the motives that arise from them, are mostly unconscious, and individuals often have only the dimmest understanding of why they do what they do. In Erikson's theory, development is driven by a series of developmental crises related to age and biological maturation. To achieve healthy development, the individual must successfully resolve these crises.

Central Developmental Issues

Three of our seven themes—*continuity/discontinuity, individual differences,* and *nature and nurture*—play prominent roles in psychoanalytic theory. Like Piaget's theory of cognitive development, the developmental accounts of Freud and Erikson are stage theories. However, within the framework of discontinuous development, psychoanalytic theories stress the continuity of individual differences, emphasizing that children's early experiences have a major impact on their subsequent development. The interaction of nature and nurture arises in terms of Freud's and Erikson's emphasis on the biological underpinnings of developmental stages and how they interact with the child's experience.

Freud's Theory of Psychosexual Development

Freud began his career as a neurologist and soon became interested in the origins and treatment of mental illness. He was particularly intrigued by the fact that sometimes his patients' symptoms—such as loss of feeling in a hand or blindness—had no apparent physical cause. After listening to his patients talk about their problems, he came to the conclusion that these unexplained symptoms could be attributed to completely unconscious but powerful feelings of guilt, anxiety, or fear—such as the fear of touching or seeing something forbidden. Freud's interest in development grew as he became increasingly convinced that the majority of his patients' emotional problems originated in their early childhood relationships, particularly those with their parents. Freud made fundamental, lasting contributions to developmental psychology; however, as we will discuss later in this chapter, his current influence is limited to broad psychological concepts, not the specifics of his theory.

Freud's theory is referred to as a theory of *psychosexual* development because he thought that even very young children have a sexual nature that motivates their behavior and influences their relationships. He proposed that children pass through a series of universal developmental stages. In each successive stage, **psychic energy**—the biologically based, instinctual drives that fuel behavior, thoughts, and feelings—becomes focused in different **erogenous zones,** that is, areas of the body that are erotically sensitive (e.g., mouth, anus, and genitals). Freud believed that in each stage, children encounter conflicts related to a particular erogenous zone, and he maintained that their success or failure in resolving these conflicts affects their development throughout life.

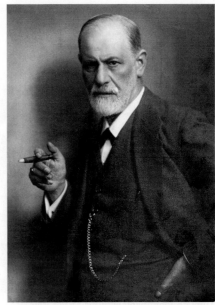

Sigmund Freud, the father of psychoanalysis, has had a lasting influence on developmental psychology through his emphasis on the lifelong impact of early relationships.

The Developmental Process

In Freud's view, development starts with a helpless infant beset by instinctual drives, foremost among them hunger. The distress associated with hunger is expressed through crying, prompting the mother to breast-feed the baby. (In Freud's day, virtually all babies were breast-fed.) The resulting satisfaction of the infant's hunger, as well as the experience of nursing, is a source of intense pleasure for the infant. The instinctual drives with which the infant is born constitute the **id**—the earliest and most primitive of three personality structures posited by Freud. The id, which is totally unconscious, is the source of psychic energy. The id is ruled by the *pleasure principle*—the goal of achieving maximal gratification as quickly as possible. Whether the gratification involves eating, drinking, eliminating, or physical comfort, the id wants it *now.* The id remains the source of psychic energy throughout life, with its operation most apparent in selfish or impulsive behavior in which immediate gratification is sought with little regard for consequences.

During the 1st year of life, the infant is in Freud's first stage of psychosexual development, the **oral stage,** so called because the primary source of gratification and pleasure is oral activity, such as sucking and eating. For Freud, the baby's feelings for his or her mother are "unique, without parallel," and through them the mother is "established unalterably for a whole lifetime as the first and strongest love-object and as the prototype for all later love-relations" (Freud, 1940/1964). However, maternal security does not come without costs. As always with Freud, there is a dark side: infants "pay for this security by a fear of loss of love" (1940/1964). For Freud, common fearful reactions to being alone or in the dark are based on "missing someone who is loved and longed for" (Freud, 1926/1959).

Later in the 1st year, the second personality structure, the **ego,** arises out of the need to resolve conflicts between the id's unbridled demands for immediate gratification and the restraints imposed by the external world. Whereas "the id stands for the untamed passions," the ego "stands for reason and good sense" (Freud, 1933/1964). Over time, as it continually seeks resolution between the demands of the id and those of the real world, the ego begins to develop into the individual's sense of self. Nevertheless, the ego is never fully in control.

psychic energy ■ Freud's term for the collection of biologically based instinctual drives that he believed fuel behavior, thoughts, and feelings

erogenous zones ■ in Freud's theory, areas of the body that become erotically sensitive in successive stages of development

id ■ in psychoanalytic theory, the earliest and most primitive personality structure. It is unconscious and operates with the goal of seeking pleasure.

oral stage ■ the first stage in Freud's theory, occurring in the 1st year, in which the primary source of satisfaction and pleasure is oral activity

ego ■ in psychoanalytic theory, the second personality structure to develop. It is the rational, logical, problem-solving component of personality.

MEDIACOLORS / ALAMY

Through identifying with his father, this young boy should, according to Freud's theory, develop a strong superego.

anal stage ■ the second stage in Freud's theory, lasting from the 2nd year through the 3rd year, in which the primary source of pleasure comes from defecation

phallic stage ■ the third stage in Freud's theory, lasting from age 3 to age 6, in which sexual pleasure is focused on the genitalia

superego ■ in psychoanalytic theory, the third personality structure, consisting of internalized moral standards

internalization ■ the process of adopting as one's own the attributes, beliefs, and standards of another person

Oedipus complex ■ Freud's term for the conflict experienced by boys in the phallic period because of their sexual desire for their mother and their fear of retaliation by their father

Electra complex ■ Freud's term for the conflict experienced by girls in the phallic stage when they develop unacceptable romantic feelings for their father and see their mother as a rival

latency period ■ the fourth stage in Freud's theory, lasting from age 6 to age 12, in which sexual energy gets channeled into socially acceptable activities

genital stage ■ the final stage in Freud's theory, beginning in adolescence, in which sexual maturation is complete and sexual intercourse is a major goal

During the infant's 2nd year, maturation facilitates the development of control over some bodily processes, including urination and defecation. At this point, the infant enters Freud's second stage, the **anal stage,** which lasts until roughly age 3. In this stage, the child's erotic interests focus on the pleasurable relief of tension derived from defecation. Conflict ensues when, for the first time, the parents begin to make specific demands on the infant, most notably their insistence on toilet training.

Freud's third stage, the **phallic stage,** spans the ages of 3 to 6. In this stage, the focus of sexual pleasure again migrates, as children become interested in their own genitalia and curious about those of parents and playmates. Freud believed that during the phallic stage, children identify with their same-sex parent, giving rise to gender differences in attitudes and behavior. Freud also believed that young children experience intense sexual desires during the phallic stage, and he proposed that their efforts to cope with them leads to the emergence of the third personality structure, the **superego.** The superego is essentially what we think of as conscience and is based on the child's **internalization,** or adoption, of the parents' standards for acceptable behavior. The superego guides the child to avoid actions that would result in guilt, which the child experiences when violating these internalized standards.

For boys, the path to superego development is through the resolution of the **Oedipus complex,** a psychosexual conflict in which a boy experiences a form of sexual desire for his mother and wants an exclusive relationship with her. Freud thought that girls experience a similar but less intense conflict—the **Electra complex,** involving erotic feelings toward the father. Although these ideas may seem outlandish, many family stories are consistent with them. For example, when one of our sons was a 5-year-old, he told his mother that he wanted to marry her someday. She said that she was sorry, but she was already married to Daddy, so he would have to marry someone else. The boy replied, "I have a good idea. I'll put Daddy in a big box and mail him away somewhere. Then we can get married!"

The fourth developmental stage, the **latency period,** lasts from about age 6 to age 12. It is, as its name implies, a time of relative calm. Sexual desires are safely hidden away in the unconscious, and psychic energy gets channeled into constructive, socially acceptable activities, including both intellectual and social pursuits.

The fifth and final stage, the **genital stage,** begins with the advent of sexual maturation. The sexual energy that had been kept in check for several years reasserts itself with full force, directed toward peers. Ideally, the individual has developed a strong ego that facilitates coping with reality and a superego that is neither too weak nor too strong.

According to Freud, if fundamental needs are not met during any of the stages of psychosexual development, children may become *fixated* on those needs, continually attempting to satisfy them and to resolve associated conflicts. In Freud's view, these unsatisfied needs, and the person's ongoing attempts to fulfill them, are unconscious and are expressed in indirect or symbolic ways. For example, if an infant's needs for oral gratification are not adequately satisfied during the oral stage, later in life the individual may repeatedly engage in substitute oral activities, such as excessive eating, nail-biting, smoking, and so on. Similarly, if toddlers are subjected to very harsh toilet training during the anal stage, they may remain preoccupied with issues related to cleanliness, becoming either compulsively tidy and psychologically rigid or extremely sloppy and lax. Thus, in Freud's view, the child's passage through the stages of psychosexual development shapes the individual's personality for life. (With regard to oral and anal fixations, it is interesting that Freud smoked 20 cigars a day for more than 50 years—in fact, he found it impossible to work without them—and over the same period followed the same rigid, ritualized schedule nearly every day.)

Erikson's Theory of Psychosocial Development

Of the many followers of Freud, none has had greater influence in developmental psychology than Erik Erikson. Erikson accepted the basic elements of Freud's theory but incorporated social factors into it, including cultural influences and contemporary issues, such as juvenile delinquency, changing sexual roles, and the generation gap. Consequently, his theory is regarded as a theory of *psychosocial* development.

The Developmental Process

Erikson proposed eight age-related stages of development that span infancy to old age. Each stage is characterized by a specific *crisis,* or set of developmental issues, that the individual must resolve. If the dominant issue of a given stage is not successfully resolved before the onset of the next stage, the person will continue to struggle with it. In the following summary of Erikson's stages, we discuss only the first five stages, which focus on development in infancy, childhood, and adolescence.

1. *Basic Trust Versus Mistrust (the 1st year).* The crucial issue for the infant is developing a sense of trust. If the mother is warm, consistent, and reliable in her caregiving, the infant learns that she can be trusted. More generally, the baby comes to feel good and reassured by being close to other people. If the ability to trust others when it is appropriate to do so does not develop, the person will have difficulty forming intimate relationships later in life.

2. *Autonomy Versus Shame and Doubt (ages 1 to 3½).* The challenge for the child is to achieve a strong sense of autonomy while adjusting to increasing social demands. Going well beyond Freud's focus on toilet training, Erikson pointed out that during this period, the dramatic increases that occur in every realm of children's real-world competence—including motor skills, cognitive abilities, and language—foster children's desires to make their own choices. Infants' newfound ability to explore the environment on their own (as discussed in Chapter 5) changes the family dynamics, initiating a long-running battle of wills with caregivers. If parents provide a supportive atmosphere that allows children to achieve self-control without the loss of self-esteem, children gain a sense of autonomy. In contrast, if children are subjected to severe punishment or ridicule, they may come to doubt their abilities.

3. *Initiative Versus Guilt (ages 4 to 6).* Like Freud, Erikson saw this period as the time during which children come to identify with, and learn from, their parents: "[The child] hitches his wagon to nothing less than a star: he wants to be like his parents, who to him appear very powerful and very beautiful" (Erikson, 1959/1994). The child is constantly setting goals, in play and in school, and working to achieve them. Like Freud, Erikson believed that a crucial attainment is the development of conscience. The challenge for the child is to achieve a balance between initiative and guilt.

Erik Erikson, who was born in Germany, took a long time to settle into a career. Instead of attending college, he wandered around Europe pursuing his interest in art for several years. Eventually, he was hired as an art instructor in a school run by Anna Freud, Sigmund Freud's daughter, and became an analyst. He moved to the United States in the early 1930s, when fascism was on the rise in Germany.

 Theories of Emotional Development in Infancy and Toddlerhood

Many parents witness scenes like the one depicted here. Should this toddler be made to feel shame for his natural exploratory behavior?

4. *Industry Versus Inferiority (age 6 to puberty).* This stage is crucial for ego development. Children master cognitive and social skills that are important in their culture, and they learn to work industriously and to cooperate with peers. Successful experiences give the child a sense of competence, but failure can lead to excessive feelings of inadequacy or inferiority.

5. *Identity Versus Role Confusion (adolescence to early adulthood).* Erikson accorded great importance to adolescence, seeing it as a critical stage for the achievement of a core sense of *identity*. The dramatic physical changes of puberty and the emergence of strong sexual urges are accompanied by new social pressures, including a need to make educational and occupational decisions. Caught between their past identity as a child and the many options and uncertainties of their future, adolescents must resolve the question of who they really are or live in confusion about what roles they should play as adults. As you will see in Chapter 11, developmental scientists have devoted a good deal of attention to the stage of identity versus role confusion in modern multicultural societies.

Current Perspectives

Freud's most significant contributions to developmental psychology are his emphasis on the importance of early emotional relationships and his recognition of the role of subjective experience and unconscious mental activity. Erikson's emphasis on the quest for identity in adolescence has had a lasting impact, providing the foundation for a wealth of research on this aspect of adolescence. The signal weakness of both theories is that their major theoretical claims are too vague to be testable, and many of their specific elements, particularly in Freud's theory, are generally regarded as highly questionable. Nevertheless, there is no doubt that both of these theories have been enormously influential.

Freud's emphasis on the importance of early experience and close relationships was especially influential in setting the foundation for modern-day attachment theory and research (which you will read about in Chapter 11). The research in this area strongly suggests that the nature of infants' relationships with their parents not only affects behavior in infancy but also has important long-term effects on close relationships throughout life. In addition, Freud's remarkable insight that much of our mental life occurs outside the realm of consciousness is fundamental to modern cognitive psychology and brain science.

Our behavior is also influenced by implicit attitudes of which we are unaware, attitudes that are often antithetical to what we consciously believe. For example, many individuals who believe that they lack racial prejudice nevertheless unconsciously associate members of some racial groups with a variety of negative characteristics (Greenwald & Banaji, 1995; Nosek & Banaji, 2009). Even children as young as 7 years of age exhibit implicit racial biases: White children show an in-group bias for other Whites, while Black children showed no bias in either direction (Newheiser & Olson, 2012). To experience this phenomenon firsthand, visit http://implicit.harvard.edu/ and take any number of the different Implicit Attitudes Tests; the results may surprise you (although they would probably not have surprised Freud).

The vast abundance of cartoons about Freud and psychoanalysis testify to his enormous impact on society.

"To this day, I can hear my mother's voice—harsh, accusing. 'Lost your mittens? You naughty kittens! Then you shall have no pie!'"

How might psychoanalytic theories be useful to Kismet's designers? They have already adopted the goal of making Kismet as sociable as possible. Probably the most important further step they can take, based on Freud's and Erikson's theories, is to program Kismet to form a few very close relationships with others. Certain people should become much more important to Kismet than other people with whom it interacts. Ideally, Kismet should derive some sense of security and well-being from those relationships. Furthermore, those relationships should have a lasting effect on Kismet's internal organization so that they continue to influence the robot throughout its "life." Consistent with Freud's and Erikson's theories, Kismet clearly has an unconscious life (given that consciousness presumably eludes robots). But could a robot ever develop unconscious biases and prejudices as humans do?

Review

The psychoanalytic theories of Freud and Erikson propose that social and emotional development proceeds in a series of stages, with each stage characterized by a particular task or crisis that must be resolved for subsequent healthy development. Maturational factors play a key role in both theories, especially with respect to the physical body. Psychic energy and sexual impulses are emphasized by Freud as major forces in development, whereas Erikson places greater emphasis on social factors. Both theories maintain that early experiences in the context of the family have a lasting effect on the individual's relationships with other people. While the specifics of these theories have been called into question, the approach taken by Freud and Erikson has had enormous, continuing impact on thought and culture.

Learning Theories

I imagine the minds of children as easily turned this or that way, as water itself.

—John Locke, from his essay "Some Thoughts Concerning Education"

As you may recall from Chapter 1, the empiricist philosopher John Locke believed that experience shapes the nature of the human mind. The intellectual descendants of Locke are psychologists who consider learning to be the primary factor in social and personality development.

View of Children's Development

In contrast to Freud's emphasis on the role of internal forces and subjective experience, learning theorists emphasize the role of external factors in shaping social behavior. They have often made very bold claims about the extent to which development can be guided by how people reinforce some behaviors and punish or ignore others.

Central Developmental Issues

The primary developmental question on which learning theories take a unanimous stand is that of *continuity/discontinuity:* they all emphasize continuity. Because the same principles control learning and behavior throughout life, there are no qualitatively different stages in development. Like information-processing theorists, learning theorists focus on the role of specific *mechanisms of change*—which, in

systematic desensitization ■ a form of therapy based on classical conditioning, in which positive responses are gradually conditioned to stimuli that initially elicited a highly negative response. This approach is especially useful in the treatment of fears and phobias.

their view, involve learning principles, such as reinforcement and observational learning. They believe that children become different from one another primarily because they have different histories of reinforcement and learning opportunities. The theme of *research and children's welfare* is also relevant here in that therapeutic approaches based on learning principles have been widely used to treat children with a variety of problems. Contemporary learning theorists emphasize the theme of the *active child*: the role that children play in their own development.

Watson's Behaviorism

John B. Watson (1878–1958), the founder of behaviorism, believed that development is determined by the child's social environment, via learning through conditioning (see Chapter 5). He believed that psychologists should study visible behavior, not the "mind."

The extent of Watson's (1924) faith in the power of conditioning is clear in his famous boast:

> Give me a dozen healthy infants, well-formed, and my own specified world to bring them up in, and I'll guarantee to take any one at random and train him to become any type of specialist I might select—doctor, lawyer, artist, merchant-chief, and yes, even beggar man and thief, regardless of his talents, penchants, tendencies, abilities, vocations, and race of his ancestors.
>
> (p. 104)

On a much less ambitious scale, Watson demonstrated the power of classical conditioning in a famous—and by present standards, unethical—experiment with a 9-month-old infant referred to as "Little Albert" (Watson & Rayner, 1920). Watson first exposed Little Albert to a perfectly nice white rat in the laboratory. Initially, Albert reacted positively to the rat. On subsequent exposures, however, the researchers repeatedly paired the presentation of the rat with a loud noise that clearly frightened Albert. After a number of such pairings, Albert became afraid of the rat itself.

Our everyday lives are filled with examples of conditioned responses. Young children, for example, often show fear at the sight of a doctor or nurse in a white lab coat, based on their previous association between people wearing white coats and painful injections. (To counteract this problem, modern medical personnel wear lab coats with cheerful designs, hoping to elicit a positive response in their young patients.)

Watson's work on classical conditioning laid the foundation for treatment procedures that are based on the opposite process— the *deconditioning*, or elimination, of fear. A student of Watson's (M. C. Jones, 1924) treated 2-year-old Peter, who was deathly afraid of white rabbits (as well as white rats, white fur coats, white feathers, and a variety of other white things). To decondition Peter's fear, the experimenter first gave him a favorite snack. Then, as Peter ate, a white rabbit in a cage was very slowly brought closer and closer to him—but never close enough to make him afraid. After repeatedly being exposed to the feared object in a context that was free of distress and paired with the positive experience of a snack, Peter got over his fear. Eventually, he was even able to pet the rabbit. This approach, now known as **systematic desensitization,** is still widely used to rid people of fears and phobias of everything from dogs to dentists.

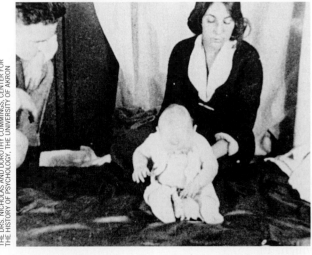

To demonstrate the power of conditioning, John B. Watson and his assistant Rosemary Raynor conditioned "Little Albert" to fear a white rat. Albert had not been afraid of the rat until its presentation was paired several times with a loud, frightening sound.

Believing that he had established the power of learning in development, Watson placed the responsibility for guiding children's development squarely on the shoulders of their parents. In his child-rearing manual, *Psychological Care of Infant and Child* (1928), he offered parents stern advice for fulfilling this responsibility. One particular piece of Watson's advice that was widely adopted in the United States was to put infants on a strict feeding schedule. The idea was that the baby would become conditioned to expect a feeding at regular intervals and therefore would not cry for attention in between. To help implement this strict regimen, Watson advised parents to achieve distance and objectivity in their relations with their children (just as he exhorted psychologists to be objective in their research):

> Treat them as though they were young adults. Dress them, bathe them with care and circumspection. Let your behavior always be objective and kindly firm. Never hug and kiss them, never let them sit on your lap. If you must, kiss them once on the forehead when they say good night. Shake hands with them in the morning. Give them a pat on the head if they have made an extraordinarily good job on a difficult task. Try it out. In a week's time you will find how easy it is to be perfectly objective with your child and at the same time kindly. You will be utterly ashamed of the mawkish, sentimental way you have been handling it.
>
> (pp. 81–82)

Watson's overly strict child-rearing advice gradually fell from favor with the publication and widespread success of Dr. Benjamin Spock's *The Common Sense Guide to Baby and Child Care*, first published in 1946 (Spock's thinking about early development and child rearing was very strongly influenced by Freud). However, Watson's emphasis on the environment as the key factor in determining behavior persisted in the work of B. F. Skinner.

Skinner's Operant Conditioning

B. F. Skinner (1904–1990) was just as forceful as Watson in proposing that behavior is under environmental control, once claiming that "a person does not act upon the world, the world acts upon him" (Skinner, 1971, p. 211). As described in Chapter 5, a major tenet of Skinner's theory of operant conditioning is that we tend to repeat behaviors that lead to favorable outcomes—that is, reinforcement—and suppress those that result in unfavorable outcomes—that is, punishment. Skinner believed that everything we do in life—every act—is an operant response influenced by the outcomes of past behavior.

Skinner's research on the nature and function of reinforcement led to many discoveries, including two that are of particular interest to parents and teachers. One is the fact that *attention* can by itself serve as a powerful reinforcer: children often do things "just to get attention" (Skinner, 1953, p. 78). Thus, the best strategy for discouraging a child who throws temper tantrums from continuing to do so is to ignore that behavior whenever it occurs. The popular behavior-management strategy of *time-out*, or temporary isolation, involves systematically withdrawing attention and thereby removing the reinforcement for inappropriate behavior, with the goal of extinguishing it.

When the toddler son of one of the authors first graduated to a "big-boy bed," he repeatedly got up after having been put to bed, using one pretext after another to join his parents. This undesirable behavior was extinguished in just a few nights by his father, who sat in a chair outside the bedroom door. Every time the child appeared, his father gently, but firmly and silently, put him back in his bed. The key

B. F. Skinner, who once appeared in 40th place in a popular magazine's list of the 100 most important people who ever lived (P. H. Miller, 2002), believed that children's development is primarily a matter of their reinforcement history.

intermittent reinforcement ■ inconsistent response to the behavior of another person—for example, sometimes punishing an unacceptable behavior and sometimes ignoring it

behavior modification ■ a form of therapy based on principles of operant conditioning in which reinforcement contingencies are changed to encourage more adaptive behavior

to this successful intervention was the fact that there was no reinforcement for getting out of bed—no talking, no yelling, no drink of water, no interaction of any sort—in short, none of the potent reinforcers that parental attention provides.

A second important discovery was the difficulty of extinguishing behavior that has been *intermittently reinforced*, that is, that has sometimes been followed by reward and sometimes not. As Skinner discovered in his research with animals, **intermittent reinforcement** makes behaviors resistant to extinction. If a behavior is only occasionally rewarded, an animal is likely to maintain the expectation that the next performance of the behavior may produce the reward, leading to persistence of the behavior even in the absence of reward. Inadvertently, parents often encourage unwanted behavior in their children by applying intermittent reinforcement. We try not to reward children's whiny or aggressive demands, but—being human—we sometimes give in. Such intermittent reinforcement is very powerful: if a parent who had occasionally given in to whining never did so again, the child would nevertheless continue to resort to whining for a long time, assuming that because it worked in the past, it might work again in the future.

Skinner's work on reinforcement led to a form of therapy known as **behavior modification,** which can be quite useful for changing undesirable behaviors. A simple example of this approach involved a preschool child who spent too much of his time in solitary activities. Observers noticed that the boy's teachers were unintentionally reinforcing his withdrawn behavior: they talked to him and comforted him when he was alone but tended to ignore him when he played with other children. The boy's withdrawal was modified by reversing the reinforcement contingencies: the teachers began paying attention to the boy whenever he joined a group but ignored him whenever he withdrew. Soon the child was spending most of his time playing with his classmates (F. R. Harris, Wolf, & Baer, 1967).

Social-Learning Theory

Although scolding has the goal of causing a child to stop doing something that the parent disapproves of, the fact that it is also a form of paying attention to a child may actually reinforce undesirable behaviors and cause them to persist.

STOCKBYTE / GETTY IMAGES

Social-learning theory, like other learning-oriented theories, attempts to account for personality and other aspects of social development in terms of learning mechanisms. However, unlike Skinner's focus on reinforcement, social-learning theory emphasizes observation and imitation. Albert Bandura (1977, 1986), for example, has argued that most human learning is inherently *social* in nature and is based on observation of the behavior of other people. Children learn rapidly and efficiently simply from watching what other people do and then imitating them. Although direct reinforcement can increase the likelihood of imitation, it is not necessary for learning. Children can learn from indirect models, that is, from reading books and from watching TV or movies, in the absence of any direct reinforcement for their behavior (see Box 9.1).

Over time, Bandura increasingly emphasized the cognitive aspects of observational learning, eventually renaming his view "social cognitive theory." Observational learning clearly depends on basic cognitive processes of *attention* to others' behavior, *encoding* what is observed, *storing* the information in memory, and *retrieving* it at some later time in order to reproduce the behavior observed earlier. Thanks to observational learning, many young children know quite a bit about adult activities—such as driving a car (you insert and turn the ignition key, press on the accelerator, turn the steering wheel)—long before being allowed to engage in them themselves.

Unlike earlier learning theorists like Watson and Skinner, Bandura emphasized the active role of children in their own development, describing development as a **reciprocal determinism** between children and their social environment. The basic idea of this concept is that every child has characteristics that lead him or her to seek particular kinds of interactions with the external world. The child is affected by these interactions in ways that influence the kinds of interactions he or she seeks in the future. For example, a child who enjoys playing violent video games (a topic we will address later in this chapter) may encourage peers to begin playing violent games together. The child may then seek out these peers above others; as their skill level in the games mounts, the members of the group may become desensitized to violence in games, encourage each other to behave more aggressively, and be rejected by other peers, thereby becoming even more committed to their social group (e.g., Anderson & Bushman, 2001).

reciprocal determinism ■ Bandura's concept that child–environment influences operate in both directions; children are affected by aspects of their environment, but they also influence the environment

Current Perspectives

In contrast to psychoanalytic theories, learning theories are based on principles derived from experiments. As a result, they allow explicit predictions that can be empirically tested. Partly for this reason, they have inspired an enormous amount of research concerning parental socialization practices and how children learn social behaviors. They have also led to important practical applications, including clinical procedures of systematic desensitization and behavior modification. The primary weakness of the learning approach is that because it is focused on behavior, not brains or minds, it lacks attention to biological influences and, except for Bandura's theory, to the role of cognition in influencing behavior.

Kismet's designers took learning theories of development to heart from the very beginning by giving the robot the crucial capacity for learning that is mediated by humans. The emotional and verbal reactions of people to its behaviors instruct Kismet regarding the appropriateness of what it has done. Kismet also has the capacity to acquire new behaviors by modeling what it "sees" and "hears" humans do. Kismet's ability to learn from people is a crucial aspect of what makes it seem truly sociable. But to what extent can Kismet learn via reciprocal determinism, shaping its own environment? Contemporary social robots, like the baby-faced smiling robot discussed earlier in the chapter (Ruvolo et al., 2015), do have the capacity to shape their environment and to learn how to control the behavior of those around it. This innovation may be one of the most important "social" developments in artificial intelligence.

Review

Learning theorists believe that social development is primarily attributable to what children learn through their interactions with other people. Early behaviorists such as Watson and Skinner emphasized the reinforcement history of the individual: social behavior is shaped by the pattern of rewards and punishments they receive from others. Social-learning theorists, most prominently Bandura, emphasize the role of cognition in social learning, noting that children learn a great deal simply from observing the behavior of other people, including the ramifications of observed behavior (such as the rewards and punishments observed in the Bobo doll experiments described in Box 9.1). Learning approaches have inspired a variety of treatment methods useful for a wide range of behavioral problems in children.

BOX 9.1 │ a closer look

BANDURA AND BOBO

A series of classic studies by Albert Bandura and his colleagues (Bandura, 1965; Bandura, Ross, & Ross, 1963) will give you a good sense of the kind of questions and methods that typify social-learning-theory research. The investigators began by having preschool children individually watch a short film in which an adult model performed highly unusual aggressive actions on a Bobo doll (an inflatable toy, with a weight in the bottom so it pops back up as soon as it is knocked down). The model punched the doll, hit it with a mallet while shouting "Sockeroo," threw balls at it while shouting "Bang bang," and so on.

In one study, three groups of children observed the adult model receive different consequences for these aggressive behaviors. One group saw the model receive rewards (an adult gave the model candy and soda and praised the "championship performance"). Another group saw the model punished (scolded). The third group saw the model experience no consequences. The question was whether **vicarious reinforcement**—observing someone else receive a reward or a punishment—would affect the children's subsequent reproduction of the behavior. After viewing the film, each child was left alone in a playroom with a Bobo doll, and hidden observers recorded whether the child imitated what he or she had seen the model do. Later, whether or

not they had imitated the model, the children were offered juice and prizes to reproduce all the model's actions that they could remember.

The results are shown in the figure. The children who had seen the model punished imitated the behavior less than did those in the other two groups. However, the children in all conditions had *learned* from observing the model's behavior and remembered what they had seen; when offered rewards to reproduce the aggressive actions, they did so, even if they had not spontaneously performed them in the initial test.

One particularly interesting feature of this research is the gender differences that emerged: boys were more physically aggressive toward the Bobo doll than girls were. However, the girls had learned as much about the modeled behaviors as the boys had, as shown by their increased level of imitation when offered a reward. Presumably, boys and girls generally learn a great deal about the behaviors considered appropriate to both genders but inhibit those they believe to be inappropriate for their own gender.

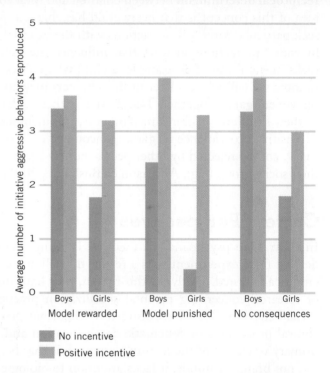

This graph shows the average number of aggressive behaviors children imitated after seeing a model rewarded, punished, or receiving no consequences for aggressive behavior. In the no-incentive test, the children were simply left alone in the room with the Bobo doll and were given no instructions. In the positive-incentive test, they were offered a reward to do what they had seen the model do. The results clearly show that the children had learned from what they observed and that they had learned more than they initially showed. (Data from Bandura, 1965)

vicarious reinforcement ▪ observing someone else receive a reward or punishment

Theories of Social Cognition

How do children come to understand their own and other people's thoughts, feelings, motives, and behaviors? Like adults, children are active processors of social information. They pay attention to what other people do and say, and they are constantly drawing inferences, forming interpretations, constructing explanations, or making attributions regarding what they observe. They process information about their own behavior and experiences in the same way.

The complexity of children's thinking and reasoning about the social world is related to, and limited by, the complexity of their thought processes in general.

This classic research thus demonstrates that children can quickly acquire new behaviors simply as a result of observing others, that their tendency to reproduce what they have learned depends on whether the person whose actions they observed was rewarded or punished, and that what children learn from watching others is not necessarily evident in their behavior.

These photographs show an adult performing a series of aggressive actions on a Bobo doll. The boy who had observed the adult's behavior subsequently imitated it when left alone in the room with the Bobo doll. The girl, who did not initially reproduce the model's aggressive actions, did imitate the model's behavior when offered a reward to do so.

 Observation Learning of Aggression: Bandura's Bobo Doll Study

After all, the same mind that solves arithmetic and conservation problems also solves problems having to do with making friends and resolving moral dilemmas. With advances in cognitive development, the way that children think about themselves and other people deepens and becomes more abstract.

View of Children's Development

Social cognitive theories provide a sharp contrast to the emphasis that psychoanalytic and learning theories place on external forces as the primary source of development. Instead, social cognitive theories emphasize the process of **self-socialization**—children's active shaping of their own development. According

self-socialization ■ the idea that children play a very active role in their own socialization through their activity preferences, friendship choices, and so on

role taking ■ being aware of the perspective of another person, thereby better understanding that person's behavior, thoughts, and feelings

to this view, children's knowledge and beliefs about themselves and other people lead them to adopt particular goals and standards to guide their own behavior.

Central Developmental Issues

The central theme of most relevance to social cognitive theories is the *active child*. Another prominent theme is *individual differences*, particularly in the comparisons that are often drawn between the thinking and behavior of males and females, aggressive and nonaggressive children, and so on. The theme of *continuity/discontinuity* is important in some prominent stage theories that emphasize age-related qualitative changes in how children think about the social world. Information-processing theories, on the other hand, stress continuity in the processes involved in social reasoning. In the following discussions, we will consider these two types of social cognitive theories. The first type is represented by Selman's stage theory of role taking; the second type is represented by Dodge's information-processing theory of social problem solving and by Dweck's attributional account of academic achievement.

Selman's Stage Theory of Role Taking

In formulating his theory of social cognition, Robert Selman (1980; Yeates & Selman, 1989) focused on the development of **role taking**—the ability to think about something from another's point of view. He proposed that adopting the perspective of another person is essential to understanding others' thoughts, feelings, and motives.

According to Selman, young children's social cognition is limited by their inability to engage in role-taking behavior. Indeed, Selman, like Piaget, suggested that before the age of 6 years, children are virtually unaware that there is any perspective other than their own. Perhaps failure to recognize the discrepant view of someone else underlies those endless sibling arguments of the familiar form "Did so," "Did not," "Did so," "Did not."

Selman proposed that children go through four increasingly complex and abstract stages in their thinking about other people. In stage 1 (roughly ages 6 to 8), children come to appreciate that someone else can have a perspective different from their own, but they assume that the different perspective is merely due to that person's not possessing the same information they do. In stage 2 (ages 8 to 10), children not only realize that someone else can have a different view, but they also are able to think about the other person's point of view. However, it is not until stage 3 (ages 10 to 12) that children can systematically compare their own point of view with another person's. In this stage, they can also take the perspective of a third party and assess the points of view of two other people. In stage 4 (age 12 and older), adolescents attempt to understand another's perspective by comparing it with that of a "generalized other," assessing whether the person's view is the same as that of most people in their social group.

Notice that in Selman's stages of role taking, as children become less egocentric in their reasoning, they become increasingly capable of considering multiple perspectives simultaneously (e.g., their own, another person's, and "most people's"). This growth in social cognition mirrors the cognitive changes identified by Piaget (and discussed in Chapter 4). Not surprisingly,

Many of young children's arguments with others stem from their difficulty appreciating that another person can have a point of view different from their own.

JOHN BIRDSALL / AGE FOTOSTOCK

children's progress through Selman's stages of role taking is strongly related to their progress through Piaget's stages of cognitive development (Keating & Clark, 1980).

Dodge's Information-Processing Theory of Social Problem Solving

The information-processing approach emphasizes the crucial role of cognitive processes in social behavior. This approach to social cognition is exemplified by Dodge's analysis of children's use of aggression as a problem-solving strategy (Dodge, 1986; Dodge, Dishion, & Lansford, 2006). In the research that originally motivated Dodge's theory, elementary-school-age children were presented with stories that involved a child who suffers because of another child's actions, the intentions of which are ambiguous. For example, in one story, as a child is working hard to assemble a puzzle, a peer bumps into the table, scattering the puzzle pieces, and merely says "Oops." The children were then asked to imagine themselves as the victim in this scenario and to describe how they would respond and why. Some children interpreted the other child's knocking into the table as an accident and said that they would simply ignore the event. Others concluded that the peer bumped the table on purpose, and they reported that they would find a way to get even (many thought that punching the offender would be a good way to achieve that goal).

Dodge and his colleagues have found that some children have a **hostile attributional bias:** a general expectation that others are antagonistic to them (Crick & Dodge, 1994; S. Graham & Hudley, 1994). This bias leads such children to search for evidence of hostile intent on the part of the peer in the above scenario and to attribute to the peer a desire to harm them. They are likely to conclude that retaliation is the appropriate response to the peer's behavior. Hostile attributional biases become self-fulfilling prophecies: a child's aggressive retaliation to the presumed hostile act of a peer elicits counterattacks and rejection by his or her peers, further fueling the child's belief in the hostility of others. The development of hostile attributional biases does not appear to be specific to a particular cultural group or gender. A recent large-scale study including boys and girls from a wide range of locations (including cities and towns in China, Colombia, Jordan, Kenya, and Sweden) observed the same pattern: children with hostile attributional biases asserted that they would react aggressively to a provocation (Dodge et al., 2015).

Why might children begin to attribute hostile intent to those around them? Early harsh parenting predicts social information-processing biases that persist into early adulthood (Pettit et al., 2010). Children who have been physically abused are particularly likely to attribute anger to others, even in neutral situations (Pollak et al., 2000). It may be that the experience of physical abuse leads children to be especially sensitive to anger cues. For example, physically abused children are better at recognizing angry facial expressions than are children who have not experienced abuse, and the speed with which they do so is related to the degree of anger and hostility to which they have been subjected (as reported by their parent) (Pollak et al., 2009).

Physically abused children also have difficulty reasoning about negative emotions. In one study, abused children had difficulty determining which situations might trigger anger in parents, endorsing both positive and negative events as potential causes of parental anger (Perlman, Kalish, & Pollak, 2008). For instance, when presented hypothetical stories about child–parent situations, the abused children saw anger as a plausible response to positive events, such as a child's winning a prize at school or helping around the house. A tendency to assume anger in others (even when it is not present), paired with difficulty understanding what

hostile attributional bias ■ in Dodge's theory, the tendency to assume that other people's ambiguous actions stem from a hostile intent

might provoke anger in others, is likely to result in a hostile attributional bias. (We will examine child maltreatment in more detail later in this chapter.)

School systems have particular problems in dealing with children who have a hostile attributional bias. One strategy is to remove them from regular classrooms because of their disruptive behavior and put them into special classrooms in which they can be more closely supervised (Dodge, Lansford, & Dishion, 2006). However, by grouping children with hostile attributional biases together, there can be other negative consequences. First, social grouping provides children with evidence supporting their existing expectation of hostility from others, raising the possibility that they will reinforce one another's aggressive tendencies. At the same time, children at risk are segregated from well-adjusted peers from whom they might learn more effective social strategies.

An alternative intervention strategy targets social cognitive processes themselves. The Fast Track project is a multi-year preventive intervention program focused on aggression, targeting high-risk kindergartners with small-group activities, parent training, peer coaching, and other programming (e.g., Conduct Problems Prevention Research Group, 2002a, b, c). The Fast Track intervention and prevention trial has shown long-term benefits of decreased aggression through improved social cognitive processing. Children in the program were more likely to assume benign intent on the part of others, responded more competently to social challenges, and viewed aggression as detrimental (Dodge, Godwin, & Conduct Problems Prevention Research Group, 2013). Thus, by directly targeting children's thinking about social behavior—both their own and others—it may be possible to decrease the likelihood of later antisocial behavior.

Dweck's Theory of Self-Attributions and Achievement Motivation

Imagine two grade-school children, Mia and Ava, both hard at work trying to solve math problems and both initially failing. Coming to the realization that the problems are quite difficult, Mia feels excited about meeting the challenge and works persistently to get the answers. Ava, in contrast, feels anxious and makes only a half-hearted effort to solve the problems. What explains this difference in the children's reaction to failure?

According to Carol Dweck's social cognition perspective (2006), the difference in their reaction is attributable to a difference in their **achievement motivation**—that is, in whether they are motivated by *learning goals,* seeking to improve their competence and master new material, or by *performance goals,* seeking to receive positive assessments of their competence or to avoid negative assessments. From this perspective, Mia has an *incremental* view of intelligence, the belief that intelligence can be developed through effort. She focuses on mastery—on meeting challenges and overcoming failures, and she generally expects her efforts to be successful. Indeed, her increased effort and persistence following failure will in all likelihood improve her subsequent performance.

Ava, on the other hand, has an *entity* view of intelligence, the belief that her intelligence is fixed. Her goal is to be successful, and as long as she is succeeding, all is well. However, when she fails at something, she feels "helpless." Not succeeding leads her to feel bad and doubt her abilities and self-worth.

Underlying these two patterns of achievement motivation are differences in the attributions children make about themselves, particularly with regard to their sense of their self-worth. Children with an **entity/helpless orientation** tend to base their sense of self-worth on the approval they receive (or do not receive) from

achievement motivation ■ refers to whether children are motivated by *learning goals,* seeking to improve their competence and master new material, or by *performance goals,* seeking to receive positive assessments of their competence or to avoid negative assessments

entity/helpless orientation ■ a general tendency to attribute success and failure to enduring aspects of the self and to give up in the face of failure

other people about their intelligence, talents, and personal qualities. To feel good about themselves, they seek out situations in which they can be assured of success and receive praise, and they avoid situations in which they might be criticized. In contrast, the self-esteem of children with an **incremental/mastery orientation** is based more on their own effort and learning and not on how others evaluate them. Because they do not equate failure on a task with a personal flaw, they can enjoy the challenge of a hard problem and persist in the attempt to solve it.

These different motivation patterns are evident as early as preschool (Smiley & Dweck, 1994). Given a choice of working on a puzzle they have already solved or on one they had previously failed to solve, some 4- and 5-year-old children strongly prefer the one they already know how to do, whereas others want to continue working on the one they had failed to solve.

Older children's cognitions about themselves involve more complex concepts and reasoning than those of younger children. Some have what Dweck and her colleagues (Cain & Dweck, 1995; Dweck, 1999; Dweck & Leggett, 1988) refer to as an **entity theory** of intelligence. This way of thinking about oneself, like Ava's view of her own intelligence, is rooted in the idea that intelligence is fixed and unchangeable. Over time, it comes to include the belief that success or failure in academic situations depends on how smart one is. When evaluating their own performance, children with an entity theory of intelligence focus on outcomes—success or failure—not on effort or learning from mistakes. Thus, when they experience failure (as everyone does some of the time), they think they are not very smart and that there is nothing they can do about it. They feel helpless.

Other children subscribe to an **incremental theory** of intelligence. This theory, like Mia's view of her own intelligence, is rooted in the idea that intelligence can grow as a function of experience. Children who hold an incremental theory of intelligence believe that academic success is achievable through effort and persistence. When evaluating their performance, they focus on what they have learned, even when they have failed, and they believe they can do better in the future by trying harder. They feel hopeful.

Given what you have just read, what kind of praise and criticism do you think would reinforce these two patterns? The answer depends on the focus of the feedback. An incremental/mastery pattern is reinforced by focusing on children's effort, praising them for a good effort ("You really worked hard on that," "I like the way you kept at it") and criticizing them for an inadequate one ("Next time you need to put in some more work," "I think you can do better if you try harder"). In contrast, an entity/helpless pattern is reinforced by both praise and criticism focused on children's enduring traits or on the child as a whole ("You're very smart at these problems," "You just can't do math").

Do these two different types of internal theories have real-world ramifications? As you read in Chapter 1, Dweck and her colleagues have demonstrated that the answer is yes. In an important study conducted in New York City public schools, Dweck and her colleagues found that 7th-graders with an incremental theory of intelligence showed an upward trajectory in math scores over the next 2 years, while the scores of 7th-graders with an entity theory of intelligence remained flat (Blackwell, Trzesniewski, & Dweck, 2007). The investigators then provided an 8-session intervention to a new group of

incremental/mastery orientation ■ a general tendency to attribute success and failure to the amount of effort expended and to persist in the face of failure

entity theory ■ a theory that a person's level of intelligence is fixed and unchangeable

incremental theory ■ a theory that a person's intelligence can grow as a function of experience

The comments this teacher is offering his student on her work could be either beneficial or detrimental, depending on whether he focuses on how smart she is or on the effort she has made.

BLUE JEAN IMAGES / ALAMY

7th-graders who had an entity theory of intelligence. Students in this group were taught an incremental theory of intelligence based on some of the same concepts from basic neuroscience that you read about in Chapter 3: the brain is plastic and always changing; learning forges new connections among synapses; and so on. A control group received training in basic study skills. Remarkably, the children who received the intervention showed a positive change in motivation as well as improvements in grades, while the children in the control group showed a decline in grades.

Do these two types of internal views—entity theories and incremental theories—have implications for children's development in domains beyond academic achievement? Again, the answer appears to be yes. For example, recall the hostile attributional bias discussed in the previous section. Adolescents who maintain an entity theory about personality traits are more likely to demonstrate a hostile attributional bias than are adolescents who endorse an incremental theory (Yeager et al., 2013). In other words, if they hold the view that people's behaviors are due to fixed personality traits (some people are good, others are bad), rather than due to situations or circumstances, they are more likely to interpret other people's harmful behavior as hostile rather than as accidental or situational. If this is the case, then learning to take a more incremental view should diminish their tendency to make hostile attributions. And indeed, when adolescents received an intervention about neuroscience concepts (as described in the previous paragraph) designed to shift their perspectives away from the fixed-entity view and closer to the incremental view, there was a reduction in participants' hostile attributions. Thus, internal theories about traits of self and others have important implications for diverse aspects of development.

Where do these individual differences in internal theories come from? One obvious source is parents, who often try very hard to enhance their child's self-esteem. Unfortunately, doing something that might seem purely positive—praising a child for being good at something—can actually undermine the child's motivation for improvement. When parents instead praise their toddlers' effort, the children are more likely to have an incremental perspective in elementary school (Gunderson et al., 2013). Another obvious source is teachers. The way teachers comfort poor-performing students when the teacher has an entity perspective (as seen in teacher comments like "It's okay; not everyone can be good at math") can seriously undermine their students' motivation and self-expectations (Rattan, Good, & Dweck, 2012). Parents and teachers alike should be aware that some kinds of praise and comfort are beneficial, whereas others are not.

Current Perspectives

Social cognitive theorists have made many important contributions to the study of social development. One is their strong emphasis on children as active seekers of information about the social world. Another contribution is the insight that the effect of children's social experience depends on their interpretation of those experiences. Thus, children who make different attributions about a given social event (such as someone's causing them harm) or an academic event (such as doing poorly on a test) will respond differently to that event. In addition, a large amount of research has supported the social cognitive position. Although these theories have provided a very healthy antidote to social theories that left children's cognition out of the picture, they too provide an incomplete account. Most notably, social cognitive theories, like learning theories, have very little to say about biological factors in social development. However, this is beginning to change. As discussed in Box 9.2, current

BOX 9.2 | a closer look

DEVELOPMENTAL SOCIAL NEUROSCIENCE

How does the social environment affect the developing brain? And what are the neural mechanisms underlying the development of social behavior? These are the types of questions being asked in the emerging field of developmental social neuroscience.

While many of the theories of social development we discussed in this chapter invoke biological mechanisms, from instincts to imprinting to genetic adaptation, they largely avoid invoking brain systems. A number of contemporary accounts, however, take their inspiration from neuroscience. One such approach emerged from the literature on caregiving in nonhuman animals. Hormonal systems appear to be disrupted by adverse experience early in the lives of nonhuman animals. In particular, the development of the hypothalamic–pituitary–adrenal (HPA) axis, which regulates hormones that are critically involved in the body's response to stress, is impacted by exposure to adverse rearing conditions in rodents and nonhuman primates (e.g., Meaney, 2001; Parker & Maestripieri, 2011).

Taking their lead from lab studies of nonhuman animals, developmental social neuroscientists have studied "experiments in nature" in which human children have been exposed to adverse rearing conditions. One such group of children are international adoptees who experienced institutional neglect. These children were raised in orphanages abroad, in settings that lacked consistent emotional and physical contact from caregivers, prior to being adopted into households in the United States. Like the nonhuman animals that received aberrant early care, these children show aberrant hormonal responses in social situations (Wismer Fries et al., 2005; Wismer Fries, Shirtcliff, & Pollak, 2008). By examining the neural consequences of early social stress, it is possible to begin to understand why some children, such as those reared in institutions, show pervasive social challenges, including difficulties with attachment to their adoptive families.

Developmental social neuroscience methods have also been used to investigate interventions that may be effective in improving the outcomes of children growing

up in adverse conditions. One such intervention was used in Bucharest, Romania, to ameliorate the negative impacts of orphanage-rearing discussed in Chapter 1. The Bucharest Early Intervention Project randomly selected a group of institutionalized children to move into foster homes, while their peers remained behind in orphanage settings (Nelson et al., 2007). The results of a structural MRI study several years after assignment to foster care showed that the children who had left the orphanage had more white matter in their brains than did the children still living in the orphanage (Sheridan et al., 2012), suggesting improvements in neural information transmission. Remarkably, the brains of the children who had transitioned to foster care were indistinguishable from other Romanian children who had grown up at home with their families. The use of neuroimaging methods thus provides clear evidence that our brains are resilient; moving out of the stark orphanage setting into foster care had a palliative effect on these children's brains.

Research in adult social and affective neuroscience also inspires new approaches to studying development. One current example lies in the potentially beneficial effects of mindfulness meditation on the brain. Over the past decade, the emerging field of contemplative neuroscience has provided evidence that at least for adults, there are numerous benefits of meditation, ranging from effects on the immune system to those parts of the brain associated with attention. Neuroimaging studies suggest that the brain bases of these effects reside largely in the prefrontal cortex, in areas that are responsible for such behaviors as emotion regulation, selective attention, and empathy (e.g., Davidson et al., 2012). These findings have led to a great deal of interest in the potential use of meditation and other contemplative practices with children and teens, especially given the fact that developing brains are more plastic than adult brains (e.g., Sanger & Dorjee, 2015). In one recent study, researchers used a mediation-based (mindfulness) Kindness Curriculum

DAVID TAYLOR / ALAMY

in a preschool setting. After 12 weeks, they observed improvements in the children's social competence and measures of executive function relative to a wait-list control group (Flook et al., 2015).

To date, however, no developmental studies have gone beyond behavioral measures to demonstrate neural changes as a function of meditation. And, despite a great deal of interest in developing meditation-based interventions for a range of developmental disorders, including ADHD and autism, it is important to be cautious about the cause of any observed positive effects. For example, one study focused on rumination behavior— a tendency to focus on one's negative emotions, which, as you'll see in Chapter 10, is a risk factor for adolescent depression. The results suggested that distraction— that is, purposely directing one's attention to happier thoughts or activities—was just as effective as meditation in reducing rumination (Hilt & Pollak, 2012). Thus, while mindfulness is a promising route to healthier minds, brains, and bodies, it may not be the only, or even the best, route to positive outcomes.

research efforts are taking advantage of cognitive neuroscience methods to begin to uncover the underlying neural processes that lead to optimal—or suboptimal—social development.

Kismet is designed to shape its own development through its understanding of the behavior of humans toward it—a form of self-socialization emphasized by social cognition theorists. What would it take, however, for Kismet to go further and draw inferences about others' cognitions, feelings, and motivations? For example, will it ever be possible for Kismet to make different attributions about a given behavior, based on subtle aspects of the social context of its history with a person? Even more challenging, will Kismet come to know that people can hold points of view different from one another and from its own? Finally, can Kismet develop some sense of self-worth that will affect its attributions about itself? These questions about Kismet's potential to mimic social cognition highlight the vast complexity of human social development and the challenge faced by theorists trying to understand it.

Review

Theories of social cognition stress the role of cognitive processes—attention, knowledge, reasoning, attribution, explanation—in children's social development. A key aspect of these theories is an emphasis on the process of self-socialization, through which children actively shape their own development. Selman's theory of role taking proposes that children go through stages in terms of their ability to appreciate that different people can have different points of view. The information-processing approach taken by Dodge to the study of aggression emphasizes the role of children's interpretation of other people's behavior. Aggressive children often have a hostile attributional bias, a general expectation that other people will be hostile to them. According to Dweck's theory of achievement motivation, children's response to their success or failure depends on whether they attribute the outcome to their effort or their ability.

Ecological Theories of Development

We now turn to a set of theories united by the fact that they take a very broad view of the context of social development. Virtually all psychological theories, and certainly those that we have reviewed in the chapter thus far, emphasize the role of the environment in the development of individual children. However, the "environment" in many of these theories is narrowly construed as immediate contexts—family, peers, schools. The first two approaches discussed here—ethological and evolutionary psychology views—relate children's development to the grand context of the evolutionary history of our species. The third approach—the bioecological model—considers how multiple levels of environmental influence simultaneously affect development.

View of Children's Development

Ethological and evolutionary theories view children as inheritors of genetically based abilities and predispositions. The focus of these theories is largely on aspects of behavior that serve, or once served, an adaptive function.

The bioecological model stresses the effects of context on development, but it also emphasizes the child's active role in selecting and influencing those contexts.

Children's personal characteristics—temperament, intellectual ability, athletic skill, and so on—lead them to choose certain environments over others and also influence the people around them. This last point is reminiscent of Bandura's concept of *reciprocal determinism,* discussed earlier in the chapter.

Central Developmental Issues

The developmental issue that is front and center in ecological theories is the interaction of *nature and nurture.* The importance of the *sociocultural context* and the *continuity* of development are implicitly emphasized in all these theories. Another central focus is the *active role* children play in their own development.

Ethological and Evolutionary Theories

Ethological and evolutionary theories are concerned with understanding development and behavior in terms of a given animal's evolutionary heritage. Of particular interest are species-specific behaviors—behaviors that are common to members of a particular species (such as humans) but not typically observed in other species.

Ethology

Ethology, the study of behavior within an evolutionary context, attempts to understand behavior in terms of its adaptive or survival value. According to ethologists, a variety of innate behavior patterns in animals were shaped by evolution just as surely as their physical characteristics were.

Ethological approaches have frequently been applied to developmental issues. The prototypical, and best-known, example is the study of imprinting made famous by Konrad Lorenz (1903–1989), who is often referred to as the father of modern ethology (Lorenz, 1935, 1952). **Imprinting** is a process by which newborn birds and mammals of some species become attached to their mother at first sight and follow her everywhere, a behavior that ensures that the baby will stay near a source of protection and food. For imprinting to occur, the infant has to encounter its mother during a specific *critical period* very early in life.

The basis for imprinting is not actually the baby's mother per se; rather, the infants of some species are genetically predisposed to follow around the first moving object with particular characteristics that they see after emerging into the world. In chickens, for example, imprinting is elicited specifically by the sight of a bird's head and neck regions (M. H. Johnson, 1992). Which particular object the individual will dutifully trail after is thus a matter of experience-expectant processes (discussed in Chapter 3). Usually, the first moving object any chick sees *is* its mother, so everything works out just fine.

Although human newborns do not "imprint," they do have strong tendencies that draw them to members of their own species. Examples noted in Chapter 5 include an early-emerging visual preference for faces, which seems to result from an attraction to a face shape with more "stuff" in the top half. Even though this attraction is not based on a specific human face template, it gets the infant to pay attention to other humans in the environment. Also, like other mammals, human newborns orient to sounds, tastes, and smells familiar from their experience in the womb—a predisposition that inclines them toward their own mother

ethology ■ the study of the evolutionary bases of behavior

imprinting ■ a form of learning in which the newborns of some species of birds and mammals become attached to and follow adult members of the species (usually their mother)

This famous photograph shows Konrad Lorenz (1952) and a gaggle of greylag goslings that were imprinted on him and followed him all over his farm. Lorenz discovered that mallard ducklings are more discriminating: they would imprint on him only if he squatted low and dragged himself around, quacking all the while, for hours on end. He was a very dedicated scientist.

THOMAS D. MCAVOY / GETTY IMAGES

(see Chapter 2). One of the most influential applications of ethology to human development, which we discuss in Chapter 11, is Bowlby's (1969) extension of the concept of imprinting to the process by which infants form emotional attachments to their mother. According to Bowlby, attachment is essentially an emotional version of imprinting, an adaptive relationship that increases the helpless infant's chances of survival by creating reciprocal emotional ties between caregiver and infant. When the attachment relationship is positive, the infant has a secure base from which to begin exploring the world.

Another example of human behavior to which an ethological perspective has been applied is the existence of differences in the play preferences of males and females (which you will read more about in Chapter 15). For example, many (but not all) boys prefer to play with vehicle toys, which afford action play, whereas many (but not all) girls prefer dolls, which are conducive to nurturant play. The standard accounts for these differences, which come from social-learning and social cognitive theories, maintain that children (especially boys) are encouraged by their parents to play with "gender-appropriate" toys, and they do so because they want to be like others of their own sex. However, some researchers argue that these accounts are not the whole story and that evolved predispositions fuel these preferences. In one study, for instance, newborn girls looked longer at social stimuli—human faces—than at nonsocial stimuli such as mobiles, whereas the reverse was true for boys (Connellan et al., 2000). Similarly, 1-year-old boys watched a video of moving cars for longer than they watched a video of an active human face, whereas girls did the opposite (Lutchmaya & Baron-Cohen, 2002). These findings may point to genetic preferences as a function of the child's sex, rather than socially learned gender norms.

Evolutionary Psychology

Closely related to ethology, evolutionary psychology applies the Darwinian concepts of natural selection and adaptation to human behavior (Bjorklund, 2007; Geary, 2009). The basic idea is that in the evolutionary history of our species, certain genes predisposed individuals to behave in ways that solved the adaptive challenges they faced (obtaining food, avoiding predators, establishing social bonds). These individuals were more likely to survive, mate, and reproduce, passing along their genes to their offspring. These adaptive genes became increasingly common

According to evolutionary psychology, gender differences in play probably have their origin in the evolutionary history of the human species, with males being predisposed to dominance, and females, to nurturing.

and were passed down to modern humans; thus, many of the ways we behave today are a legacy of the demands on our prehistoric ancestors (Geary, 2009).

One of the most important adaptive features of the human species—one that clearly distinguishes us from other species—is the large size of our brains (relative to body size). The trade-off for this is that human children experience a prolonged period of immaturity and dependence. We are "a slow-developing, big-brained species" (Bjorklund & Pellegrini, 2002), as illustrated in Figure 9.1. In Chapter 2, we discussed how the size of the human brain at birth is limited by the size of the female pelvis. As modern humans evolved, enlargement of our brains was made possible by birth occurring at a more "premature" stage of development than is characteristic of other mammals. These evolutionary changes were made possible by increased social complexity, which is necessary for successful caregiving of extremely helpless offspring. A related consequence of our large brains and slow development is our species-typical high level of neural plasticity that supports our unrivaled capacity for learning from experience. As Bjorklund (1997) points out, in addition to its adaptive benefits, this extended immaturity is a necessity for humans who

> must survive by their wits; human communities are more complex and diverse than those of any other species, and this requires that they have not only a flexible intelligence to learn the conventions of their societies but also *a long time to learn them*.
>
> (p. 153, emphasis added)

Many evolutionary psychology theorists have suggested that *play*, which is one of the most salient forms of behavior during the period of immaturity of most mammals, is an evolved platform for learning (Bjorklund & Pellegrini, 2002). Children develop motor skills by racing and wrestling with one another, throwing toy spears, or kicking a ball into a goal. They try out and practice a variety of social roles (as mentioned in Chapter 7), enacting what they know about being, say, a parent or a police officer. One of the main virtues of play is that children can experiment in a situation with minimal consequences; no one gets hurt if a baby doll is accidentally dropped on its head or a Nerf gun is fired at a "bad guy."

To benefit from their protracted immature status, children must, of course, survive it, and their survival and development require that parents spend an enormous amount of time, energy, and resources in raising them (Bjorklund, 2007). Why are parents willing to sacrifice so much for the benefit of their offspring? According to **parental-investment theory** (Trivers, 1972), a primary source of motivation for parents to make such sacrifice is the drive to perpetuate their genes in the human gene pool, which can happen only if their offspring survive long enough to pass those genes on to the next generation.

Parental-investment theory also points to a potential dark side of the evolutionary picture—the so-called Cinderella effect—which refers to the fact that rates of child maltreatment are considerably higher for stepparents than for biological parents. As Figure 9.2 shows, estimates of the rate of murder committed by stepfathers against children residing with them is hundreds of times higher than the rate for fathers and their biological children. Furthermore, in families in which both natural and stepchildren reside, abusive parents typically target their abuse toward their stepchildren (Daly & Wilson, 1996). Notably, this pattern is not just

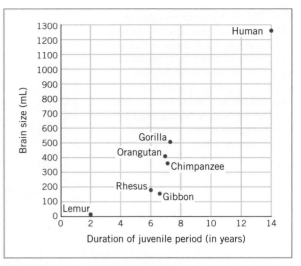

FIGURE 9.1 Brain sizes of various primates and humans Humans are "a slow-developing, big-brained species" compared with other primates. The larger the brain size of various primates, the longer their developmental period. (Data from Bonner, 1988)

parental-investment theory ■ a theory that stresses the evolutionary basis of many aspects of parental behavior, including the extensive investment parents make in their offspring

FIGURE 9.2 Estimated rates of child homicide committed by genetic fathers versus stepfathers in Canada from 1974 to 1990 As is shockingly clear, stepchildren, especially very young ones, are much more likely to be murdered by a stepfather than other children are likely to be murdered by their biological fathers. (Data from Daly & Wilson, 1996)

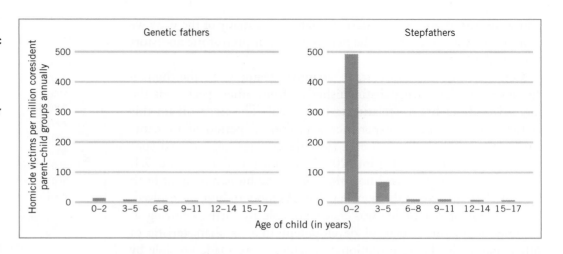

present in Canada, where the original Daly and Wilson study was conducted, but in countries ranging from Australia to South Korea to Colombia (Archer, 2013). Similar findings suggest that unintended child fatalities (e.g., drowning) are also more likely to occur in homes with a resident stepparent than in homes with no stepparent, suggesting that there is less commitment to protecting children in stepparent homes (Tooley et al., 2006).

These findings are consistent with parent-investment theory; that is, because parenting is so costly, it is not, from an evolutionary point of view, worth investing in children who cannot contribute to the perpetuation of one's own genes. However, it is also possible that there are contextual differences that contribute to these effects. For example, a large longitudinal study in Australia found that while there were indeed more injuries to children living in stepfamilies, this pattern can be explained by other risk factors correlated with family structure, including maternal alcohol use and child behavior problems (Malvaso et al., 2015). The next section focuses on approaches to social development that are squarely focused on the effects of the contexts in which children develop.

The Bioecological Model

The most encompassing model of the general context of development is Urie Bronfenbrenner's bioecological model (Bronfenbrenner, 1979; Bronfenbrenner & Morris, 1998). This perspective treats the child's environment as "a set of nested structures, each inside the next, like a set of Russian dolls" (1979, p. 22). Each structure represents a different level of influence on development (Figure 9.3). The child is at the center, with his or her particular constellation of characteristics (genes, gender, age, temperament, health, intelligence, physical attractiveness, and so on).

Over the course of development, the child's characteristics interact with the environmental forces present at each level. The different levels vary in how immediate their effects are, but Bronfenbrenner emphasizes that *every* level, from the intimate context of a child's home to the general culture in which the family lives, has an impact on that child's development. Note that each of the levels depicted in Figure 9.3 is labeled as a "system," emphasizing the complexity and interconnectedness of what goes on in each level. This theory is ecological in the sense that, just as in the study of the ecology of other living things, it considers how multiple levels of context influence outcomes. It just

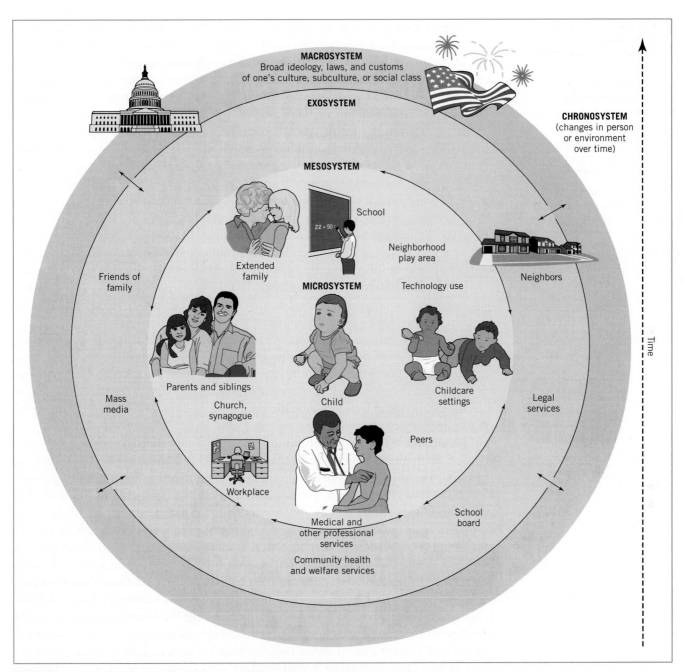

FIGURE 9.3 The bioecological model Urie Bronfenbrenner considers the child's environment as composed of a series of nested structures, including the microsystem (the immediate environment with which the child directly interacts), the mesosystem (the interconnections that exist among microsystems), the exosystem (social settings that the child is not a part of but that nevertheless affect the child's development), and the macrosystem (the general cultural context in which all the other systems are embedded). These systems all exist within the chronosystem, which describes the changes to beliefs, values, customs, technologies, and circumstances that occur over time. This figure illustrates the environment of a child living in the United States. (Information from Bronfenbrenner, 1979)

happens that instead of the soil and rainfall that might be the relevant ecological contexts for plants, the ecological systems influencing children range from families to neighborhoods to governments. The ecological levels in which children develop range from quite narrow (microsystem) to extremely broad (macrosystem).

microsystem ■ in the bioecological model, the immediate environment that an individual child personally experiences and participates in

mesosystem ■ in the bioecological model, the interconnections among immediate, or microsystem, settings

exosystem ■ in the bioecological model, environmental settings that a child does not directly experience but that can affect the child indirectly

macrosystem ■ in the bioecological model, the larger cultural and social context within which the other systems are embedded

chronosystem ■ in the bioecological model, historical changes that influence the other systems

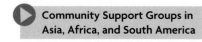

Community Support Groups in Asia, Africa, and South America

The first level in which the child is embedded is the **microsystem**—the activities and relationships in which the child *directly* participates. The child's family is a crucial component of the microsystem, and its influence is predominant in infancy and early childhood. The microsystem becomes richer and more complex as the child grows older and interacts increasingly often with peers, teachers, and others in settings such as school, neighborhood, organized sports, arts, clubs, religious activities, and so on. The child has some influence on their microsystem through their choices of peers, activities, and technology (for example, the use of certain media outlets and social technologies). Other aspects are heavily influenced by family expectations and resources. Bronfenbrenner stresses the *bidirectional* nature of all relationships within the microsystem. For example, the parents' marital relationship may affect how they treat their child, and their child's behavior may, in turn, have an impact on the marital relationship.

The next two levels in Bronfenbrenner's model move outward from the child's home into the child's community. His second level, the **mesosystem,** encompasses the *interconnections* among various microsystems, such as family, peers, and schools. Supportive relations among these contexts can benefit the child. For instance, a child's academic success is facilitated when his parents and peers value scholastic endeavors. When interconnections in the mesosystem are non-supportive, negative outcomes are more likely. The third level of social context, the **exosystem,** comprises settings that the child may not directly be a part of but that can still influence his development. The parents' workplaces, for example, can affect the child in many ways, including policies about parental leave, flexible work hours, and on-site childcare.

The outer level of Bronfenbrenner's model is the **macrosystem,** which consists of the general beliefs, values, customs, and laws of the larger society in which all the other levels are embedded. It includes the general cultural, sub-cultural, or social-class groups to which the child belongs. Cultural and class differences permeate almost every aspect of a child's life, including differences in beliefs about what qualities should be fostered in children and how best to foster them. National laws can also have a major impact on child development. For example, consider paid parental-leave policies around the world. According to the United Nations, the United States is one of just three countries (out of 185 surveyed) that currently does not mandate paid maternity leave (Addati, Cassirer, & Gilchrist, 2014). There are also huge national differences in the duration of parental leave (up to a year in many countries, but only 12 weeks in the United States) and in other policies that influence child-rearing practices, such as federally mandated breast-feeding breaks in the workplace. National policies and priorities can render stark differences in the options available to parents.

Finally, Bronfenbrenner's model has a temporal dimension, the **chronosystem.** In any given society, beliefs, values, customs, social circumstances, and technologies (such as devices and systems) change over time, with consequences for the child's development. For instance, as we discuss later in this chapter, children today have access to a vast realm of digital information and entertainment unimaginable to previous generations. This access influences children's relationships with their parents, peers, community, and the broader culture. In addition, the impact of environmental events depends on the timing of those events: the effects of a divorce on children in the household are likely to be much more pronounced initially than they will be several years later. Another important aspect of the temporal dimension, which we have noted on several occasions, is the fact

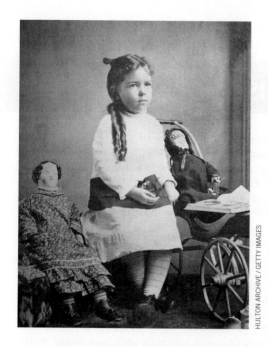

What different experiences were available to these girls born in different historical times? How did their educational and employment opportunities differ?

that as children become older, they take an increasingly active role in their own development, making their own decisions about their friends, activities, and environments. As Box 9.3 on attention-deficit hyperactivity disorder suggests, the chronosystem can even be a factor in developmental disorders.

To provide a better sense of how these contextual levels influence children's development, we will now discuss examples from a large 2015 survey conducted by the Pew Research Center entitled *Parenting in America* (December 17, 2015). This survey contrasts parents from different economic brackets with respect to the experiences of their children and their attitudes about parenting. It gives an intriguing glimpse into the very different contexts in which children living in the same country are growing up.

Beginning with the microsystem, the Pew survey gives us a sense of how parental education and income influence some of the ways that children spend their time. For example, 71% of parents with a bachelor's degree report reading to their young children every day; this number drops to 33% for parents with a high school diploma or less. Similarly, 84% of higher-income parents (earning over $75K/year) report that their child participated in sports in the past year; this number drops to 59% for lower-income parents (earning under $30K/year). The Pew survey also reveals mesosystem-level influences that are mediated by parental income. While 78% of higher-income families rated their neighborhood as an excellent/very good place to raise their children, only 42% of lower-income families endorsed a positive view of their neighborhood.

An aspect of the exosystem that has a major influence on child development is mass media, especially electronic media. According to the Pew survey, 80% of kids younger than 6, and 90% of kids older than 6, have daily screen time; these statistics suggest ample opportunities for children to be influenced by media, including social media for older children. Later in this chapter, we will discuss some of the ways in which electronic media impact child development.

Finally, the Pew survey reveals broad cultural differences in parents' aspirations for their children, showing the influence of the macrosystem. For example, African American and Hispanic parents in the United States

BOX 9.3 | individual differences

ATTENTION-DEFICIT HYPERACTIVITY DISORDER

Many developmental disorders can be profitably examined with the different levels of the bioecological model in mind. Influences and interventions from different levels can make it easier or harder for children to manage the challenges they face. A good case in point is **attention-deficit hyperactivity disorder (ADHD).**

Children with ADHD tend to be of normal intelligence and do not typically show serious emotional disturbances. However, they have difficulty sticking to plans, following rules and regulations, and persevering on tasks that require sustained attention (especially ones they find uninteresting). Many are hyperactive, constantly fidgeting, drumming on their desks, and moving around. Children with ADHD typically have difficulty acquiring academic skills, such as reading and writing, since these skills require focusing attention for prolonged periods. Many also have problems suppressing aggressive reactions when they are frustrated. All these symptoms seem to reflect an underlying difficulty in inhibiting impulses to act. The difficulty is greatest when interesting distractors are present.

An analysis of data collected by the Centers for Disease Control and Prevention for 2011–2012 suggests that 6.4 million children aged 4 to 17 received a diagnosis of ADHD at some time in their life. In other words, roughly 11% of school-age children in the United States have been given a diagnosis of ADHD. This represents a 16% increase in ADHD diagnoses for this age group since 2007 and a whopping 41% increase over the prior decade. Even more remarkably, 20% of high school boys in

the 2011–2012 data were given a diagnosis of ADHD at some point in their lives, compared with 10% of high school girls. According to a more recent study, while the prevalence of ADHD is still higher amongst boys than girls, the rate of diagnosis for girls is increasing more sharply than the rate of diagnosis for boys (Collins & Cleary, 2016). As with autism spectrum disorder (discussed in Chapter 3), it is currently unclear whether the steep increase in rates of diagnosis of ADHD reflects an actual increase in prevalence, increased awareness of the disorder, changing standards for ADHD diagnoses, or all of the above.

The causes of ADHD are quite varied. Genetic factors clearly play a role. Heritability estimates from twin studies fall in the 70% to 90% range (Chang et al., 2013; Larsson et al., 2014). Indeed, heritability for ADHD is greater than any other developmental disorder, with the possible exception of autism spectrum disorder. ADHD appears to share gene variations with several other psychiatric illnesses, including schizophrenia, autism, major depression, and bipolar disorder—though with hundreds of genes involved, it's difficult to parse the genetic overlap between disorders (Cross-Disorder Group of the Psychiatrics Genomics Consortium, 2013). Also complicating the picture is the likelihood of vicious cycles between genes and environment. For example, a child's behavioral challenges may frustrate his parent, who reacts harshly rather than providing him with the extra support he needs (Hinshaw & Arnold, 2015). In such a case, the child's genes (predisposing him to

develop ADHD) may elicit an environment (hostile parenting) that is particularly conducive to the development of the disorder.

Environmental factors in the microsystem also influence the development of ADHD. As discussed in Chapter 2, prenatal exposure to alcohol and tobacco smoke affects brain development, and both have been linked to the development of ADHD (Han et al., 2015). Prenatal exposure to numerous other teratogens, including lead and household pesticides, has also been linked to greater risk for ADHD (Nigg, 2012). Synthetic food additives, including artificial colors, have also been implicated as a potential cause, and restriction diets that avoid these elements may benefit some children with ADHD (Nigg et al., 2012). Social factors that have been associated with the development of ADHD include low SES, high levels of parent–child conflict, and severe early deprivation (Thapar et al., 2013).

Note, however, that while all of these factors have been associated with ADHD, it is very difficult to establish causality. For example, mothers who smoke while pregnant may also pass genetic risk for ADHD to their offspring. Indeed, recent studies examining the effects of paternal smoking during pregnancy have also shown enhanced risk of ADHD, suggesting that at least some of the risk factors associated with tobacco may lie in other genetic or household factors, rather than solely exposure in the uterus via the mother (Langley et al., 2012; Zhu et al., 2014).

Current treatment for ADHD involves agents in the microsystem (the family

attention-deficit hyperactivity disorder (ADHD) ■ a syndrome that involves difficulty in sustaining attention

are almost twice as likely as Caucasian parents to say it is extremely important to them that their children earn a college degree. Parental concerns are also influenced by cultural differences. Twice as many Caucasian parents than African American parents report fears that their child may eventually have problems with drugs or alcohol, whereas twice as many African American parents than Caucasian parents report fears that their child may get shot. This last finding is likely a result of recent and widespread fatal police shootings

doctor), the exosystem (the drug/pharmaceutical industry), and the macrosystem (the government). The most common approach taken by physicians is to prescribe stimulant medications, such as Ritalin. Although it seems paradoxical that stimulants could help children who are already overly active, they improve symptoms in 70% to 90% of children for whom they are prescribed. The reason is that the brain systems in these children are actually underaroused; the children's restless and sometimes disruptive behavior is actually an attempt to wake the brain up. Appropriate medication, which stimulates neurotransmitter systems, allows children with ADHD to focus their attention better and to be less distractible. This leads to improved academic achievement, better relationships with classmates, and reduced activity levels (Barbaresi et al., 2007a, 2007b).

As with many medications, there are numerous potential side effects associated with medication used to treat ADHD, some of which can be quite serious, including loss of appetite, disrupted sleep patterns, and high blood pressure. Because of these and other concerns, many parents who choose stimulants for their children limit use to school days. As it's become possible to follow children over decades of treatment, important concerns about prolonged use of medication have been alleviated. For example, stimulant treatment over many years had no negative effects on height, despite long-standing worries about stunted growth (Harstad et al., 2014).

It is important to realize, however, that the benefits of Ritalin continue only as long as children take the medication. Longer-lasting gains require not only

BEN GARVIN / THE NEW YORK TIMES / REDUX

Standing desks, such as the one used by this elementary school student, might help children who have trouble sitting quietly for long periods of time.

medication but also behavioral treatments. Behavioral interventions can target youth directly, or they target parents and teachers, providing tools to help promote the child's self-regulation. Combination treatments, integrating both medication and

psychosocial interventions, have been the focus of large-scale longitudinal studies. The data suggest that combination treatments are particularly effective, especially when parents are also able to reduce their negative or ineffective disciplinary practices (Hinshaw & Arnold, 2015). Developmental social neuroscience may offer new ways to think about treatment, such as the mindfulness meditation approach discussed in Box 9.2.

The availability of medications helpful to those with ADHD is a function of the exosystem; in order to research and develop medications, the pharmaceutical companies must perceive that they can profit from a drug targeted for this problem. It also depends on the medication's receiving a favorable evaluation from the FDA, based on research to determine the drug's efficacy and potential side effects. Thus, the fate of a child in need of medication could be quite different, depending on factors far outside the influence of his or her family.

But would any intervention be necessary in the first place if it were not the case that every school-age child is expected to spend a substantial amount of time on most days sitting quietly at a desk, concentrating on tasks that he or she may have little interest in? Pointing to the highest level of the bioecological model—the chronosystem—many experts have suggested that ADHD may have emerged as a serious problem only in recent times—specifically, only since the advent of compulsory schooling. Before then, an individual who had attentional difficulties that would have posed problems in a classroom might very well have been able to function successfully in an environment where such difficulties were inconsequential, even unnoticed.

that raise significant concerns about racial profiling, suggesting an effect of the chronosystem.

To further illustrate the richness of the bioecological model for thinking about and investigating child development, we will consider three examples in which the interactions among multiple levels of the model are particularly clear and relevant: child maltreatment, children and electronic media, and SES and development.

Child Maltreatment

One of the most serious threats to children's development in the United States is **child maltreatment,** defined as intentional abuse or neglect that endangers the well-being of anyone younger than 18. In 2014, roughly 702,000 children were confirmed victims of child maltreatment (U.S. Department of Health and Human Services Administration for Children and Families, 2016). The majority of cases involved maltreatment by parents, and the victims included nearly equal numbers of girls and boys. The highest rate of victimization was for infants younger than 1 year: 24.4 out of every 1,000 U.S. infants in this age group were maltreated in 2014. More tragic still, more than 1,580 children—most of them younger than 4—died from abuse or neglect, and 4/5 of those children were killed by one or both of their parents. Consistent with the bio-ecological model, a variety of factors, including characteristics of the child, the parents, and the community, are implicated in the causes and consequences of child abuse.

Causes of maltreatment At the level of the microsystem, certain characteristics of parents increase the risk for maltreatment. Among these are low self-esteem, strong negative reactions to stress, and poor impulse control. Parental alcohol and drug dependence also increase the probability of maltreatment. So does an abusive spousal relationship: mothers who are abused by their partner are more likely to abuse their children. In addition, certain characteristics of children—including low birth weight, physical or cognitive challenges, and difficult temperament—are associated with increased risk for parental abuse (e.g., Bugental & Happaney, 2004).

Child maltreatment tends to be associated with additional factors in the meso-system and exosystem that increase stress on parents. Many of these factors are related to low family income. They include high levels of unemployment, inadequate housing, and community violence.

Often a particularly important exosystem contributor to child maltreatment is a family's social isolation and lack of social support (more common in lower-income families). Such isolation may have multiple causes—mistrust of other people, a lack of the social skills needed to maintain positive relationships, frequent moves from place to place because of economic factors, or living in a community characterized by violence and transience. The importance of social support is highlighted by the fact that impoverished parents are less likely to maltreat their children if they live in a neighborhood in which there is a prevailing sense of community, with neighbors who care about and help one another (Belsky, 1993; Coulton et al., 1995; Garbarino & Kostelny, 1992).

Consequences of maltreatment The consequences of child maltreatment are manifested primarily in the microsystem (although they can extend to, and be moderated by, factors in the mesosystem and exosystem such as child-protection policies and agencies). The effects emerge early: 3-month-old infants who have been physically abused show increased rates of fearfulness, anger, and sadness while interacting with their mother (Cicchetti & Ng, 2014). In later infancy, maltreated infants are at risk for developing an unusual attachment pattern to their caregivers, known as the disorganized/disoriented attachment pattern, which will be discussed in Chapter 11 (Cyr et al., 2010). As they continue to develop, children who are victims of maltreatment are vulnerable to a host of mental and physical health challenges (Jaffee & Christian, 2014). Not only are they more likely

child maltreatment ■ intentional abuse or neglect that endangers the well-being of anyone under the age of 18

than their peers to be diagnosed with a psychiatric disorder in adolescence or adulthood, but their disorders are likely to develop earlier, be more severe, and be less amenable to treatment (McCrory & Viding, 2015).

Not surprisingly, peer relations are also affected. Maltreated children tend to either withdraw from peer interactions or to show heightened aggression. There is also a subgroup of children who are both aggressive and withdrawn; these children appear to be the most socially challenged (Cicchetti & Toth, 2015). Maltreatment also impacts cognition: maltreated children's autobiographical memories are more general than those of their peers, lacking details about specific events (Valentino, Toth, & Cicchetti, 2009).

The more chronic the abuse, the worse the outcome is likely to be, in childhood and beyond. As shown in Figure 9.4, the number of maltreatment reports a child received is correlated with the number of adverse outcomes for that child later in life, including substance abuse, violent delinquency, and suicide attempts (Johnson-Reid, Kohl, & Drake, 2012). There are also significant health consequences of child maltreatment, ranging from negative effects on the immune system in childhood to increased rates of coronary heart disease and other biological risk factors in adulthood (Friedman et al., 2015; Miller, Chen, & Parker, 2011; Shirtcliff, Coe, & Pollak, 2009). Of particular concern is the fact that the association between physical abuse in childhood and negative health outcomes in adulthood persists decades after the abuse has occurred and is not accounted for by the victim's adult SES or health behaviors.

We can examine the effects of maltreatment at an even more micro level. In our earlier discussion of the hostile attributional bias, we noted that children who are the victims of physical abuse show a heightened response to anger cues. This heightening is observed in increased aggressive behavior; in brain responses including both event-related potentials and fMRI; in physiological responses including heart rate and skin conductance; and in negative emotion, as measured via facial musculature (McCrory et al., 2013; Pollak et al., 2005; Shackman & Pollak, 2014). Although such responses might be maladaptive in many social situations, leading children to misinterpret or overreact to emotional cues, an ecological perspective suggests that overattention to negative emotions might be highly adaptive for children growing up in a home marked by threat and danger. By considering children's responses to their environments as adaptive in some contexts but maladaptive in others, an ecological perspective may help explain why maltreatment has the particular constellation of effects that it does, as well as which interventions might be most effective (Cicchetti, 2016; Frankenhuis & de Weerth, 2013).

Taking a different kind of micro perspective, recall the discussion of the MAOA gene in Chapter 3 (Figure 3.5). Individuals who were maltreated as children, and who possess a particular variant of the MAOA gene, are more resilient to the negative effects of child abuse (Caspi et al., 2002). Genetic differences may also impact the effects of interventions, such that some maltreated individuals may be especially susceptible to the positive effects of intervention (Belsky & van IJzendoorn, 2015). Of course, the ideal situation would be to prevent child maltreatment altogether. (For one promising approach to preventing child abuse, see Box 9.4).

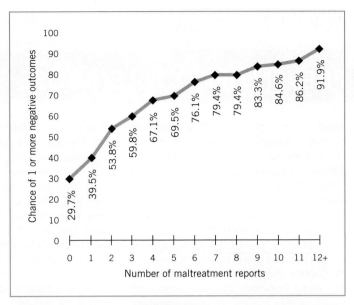

FIGURE 9.4 Long-term outcomes of maltreatment Children who are maltreated more often are at greater risk for negative outcomes during adolescence and adulthood. (Data from Johnson-Reid et al., 2012)

BOX 9.4 | applications

PREVENTING CHILD ABUSE

Given the multiple factors that contribute to child maltreatment, preventing or ameliorating the problem of abuse is extremely difficult. However, one very promising intervention program was developed from research financed by federal funding agencies at the macrosystem level and is carried out at the microsystem level.

The program, reflecting a social cognitive perspective, was designed and implemented by Daphne Bugental and her colleagues, who found that many abusive parents have inappropriate models of their relationship with their children. They tend to see themselves and their children as locked in a power struggle—a conflict in which they view *themselves* as the victims (Bugental, Blue, & Cruzcosa, 1989; Bugental & Happaney, 2004). Thus, they might interpret their baby's prolonged crying as evidence that the baby is mad at them, and they might think that a child who continues to beg for a withheld toy or treat is intentionally trying to subvert their authority.

The goal of this program was to help parents at risk for abusing their children achieve more realistic interpretations of their difficulties in caring for their children (Bugental et al., 2002). The researchers targeted high-risk parents of newborn infants. Parental risk factors included parents' own histories (of being maltreated themselves, of substance abuse, and of criminality), as well as belief systems that put their child at risk (belief in harsh punishment, parental perception of the child as difficult, unrealistic child expectations, and ambivalence about the child).

The intervention involved frequent home visits from trained professionals over the course of the infants' 1st year of life. Parents were asked to give examples of recent problems they had had with their children and to indicate what they thought had been the cause of the problem. They were then led to identify a cause that did not focus blame on the children (i.e., something other than deliberate misbehavior by their children), as well as to come up with potential strategies for solving the problem.

A particularly important factor in assessing this program is that at-risk families were *randomly assigned* to the intervention condition or to two comparison conditions. Thus, any difference in outcomes could not be due to initial differences among the groups.

The program was remarkably successful: the prevalence of physical abuse in the intervention group was only 4%, compared with about 25% in the two comparison groups. This intervention program, targeted at the microsystem level, suggests that home-visiting programs that focus on altering parents' cognitive interpretations have a high potential for preventing physical abuse. Subsequent to this initial study, the intervention was applied successfully to a different high-risk group: parents of newborns with health complications (Bugental & Schwartz, 2009). As discussed in Chapter 2, preterm infants and others who are medically at risk can be especially challenging to parent. Consistent with the

BOB KALMAN / THE IMAGE WORKS

parent-investment theory discussed earlier in the context of evolutionary psychology, the program led parents to begin to invest more caregiving in their at-risk (preterm) infants (Bugental, Beaulieu, & Silbert-Geiger, 2010). As parents developed a greater understanding of the needs—and the potential—of their infants, they subsequently increased their investment in their offspring, who later showed substantial health benefits.

Children and the Media: The Good, the Bad, and the Awful

Another good illustration of the multiple levels in which children's development is embedded is the impact of various media—television, movies, video games, You-Tube, social media, and popular music. In terms of the bioecological model, media are situated in the exosystem, but they are subject to influences from the chronosystem, as indicated earlier; from the macrosystem (including cultural values and government policies); from other elements in the exosystem (such as economic pressures); and from the microsystem (such as parental monitoring). All these factors are at play every time children log on or power up.

A recent economic study demonstrates how the introduction of educational television, in the form of *Sesame Street*, had positive long-term effects on those children who had access to it (Kearney & Levine, 2015). When *Sesame Street* was introduced in 1969, its content was designed to enhance school readiness, and roughly 1/3 of American children between the ages of 2 and 5 watched it regularly. But because the show was aired on broadcast television, there were disparities in the quality of the signal that families' TV antennae received. Kearney & Levine (2015) used differences in the chronosystem (cohorts of children before and after *Sesame Street* began airing) and the macrosystem (whether or not households were located in counties with good television reception) to investigate the long-term effects of *Sesame Street* viewing using census data. The researchers found that quality of television reception did not affect educational outcomes (as measured by age at grade level) before *Sesame Street* started broadcasting. However, after *Sesame Street* began airing, children living in counties with better television reception were 14% more likely not to fall behind appropriate grade level. This effect was most pronounced for boys, African Americans, and children living in impoverished areas. The authors of the study describe *Sesame Street* as the first MOOC (Massive Open Online Course), and their results are consistent with numerous smaller-scale findings of social and cognitive benefits from *Sesame Street* viewing around the world (Mares & Pan, 2013).

Researchers found that broadcast quality for programing like *Sesame Street* had an impact on educational outcomes. Would researchers find similar results for access and speed of Internet service?

As screens have become ever more pervasive, moving from living rooms to bedrooms to children's pockets, and as streaming video and social media have become commonplace, concerns about screen time have mounted. In a 2016 policy statement, the American Academy of Pediatrics recommended no screen time other than video chatting (such as Skype) for infants under 18 months of age, and no more than 1 hour daily for children 2 to 5 years of age (AAP Council on Communications and Media, 2016a). Parents of older children are advised to develop and follow a family media use plan designed to place appropriate limits on media use (AAP Council on Communications and Media, 2016b). But consider the following statistics, all from 2015: 8- to 12-year-olds averaged 6 hours of entertainment media daily, while 13- to 18-year-olds averaged about 9 hours—excluding time spent at school or on homework (Rideout, 2015). According to the Pew Research Center, 92% of teens reported that they are online daily, and 24% said they are online "almost constantly" (Lenhart, 2015).

Very young children are increasingly active participants in this media immersion. In a 2015 study of children under age 4 in a low-income area of Philadelphia, almost all of the participants had used mobile devices for media content delivery (97%), and fully three-fourths of the 4-year-olds had their own mobile device (Kabali et al., 2015). In a national study, parents of 2- to 10-year-olds reported that they participate in their children's media usage about one-third of the time (watching videos together or playing games together), and that nearly 50% of their children's time is spent on shows and apps that they consider to be educational (though parents may have quite divergent views about what is educational for their child; over 10% of parents rated Angry Birds and SpongeBob to be at least somewhat educational; Rideout, 2014). Three-quarters of the parents surveyed by Kabali et al. (2015) reported that they used the mobile device to keep

Some researchers have concluded that viewing media violence increases the incidence of aggression and violent behavior, though the degree and nature of this relationship remains a topic of debate.

their child calm in public or to distract their child so they could complete chores, and one-quarter of the parents used the device to help their child fall asleep. Thus, parents appear to have many motivations for engaging their children in digital media, from educational aspirations to behavior management.

Concerns about children's exposure to media The nature and amount of children's media exposure have aroused a variety of concerns, ranging from the possible effects of media violence and pornography to those of isolation and inactivity.

MEDIA VIOLENCE Foremost among the concerns that have been raised is fear that a steady diet of watching violent television shows, playing violent video games, and listening to music with violent lyrics will cause children to behave violently. The concern originally arose from the fact that television was awash in violence, as indexed by a comprehensive study reporting that 61% of programs on television between 1994 and 1997 contained episodes of violence (B. J. Wilson et al., 1997). Somewhat more recent estimates suggest that 90% of movies include depictions of violence, as do 68% of video games, 60% of TV shows, and 15% of music videos (Wilson, 2008). Aggression in television, games, and movies is particularly concerning because it tends to be glamorized and trivialized—particularly the violence perpetrated by heroes/heroines, who are rarely punished or condemned for their actions.

Extensive reviews of the vast amount of research on this issue have led many researchers to conclude that media violence increases aggression and violence and is therefore a risk factor for positive youth development. However, as discussed in Chapter 1, a recent meta-analysis by Ferguson (2015) suggests that video games in particular may have only minimal effect on children's and adolescents' aggression. This paper was published alongside a number of rebuttals by other scientists, who argue that the Ferguson (2015) analysis suffers from methodological weaknesses and underestimates the negative effects of video games (e.g., Boxer, Groves, & Docherty, 2015; Gentile, 2015; Rothstein & Bushman, 2015; Valkenberg, 2015). The presence of such heated debate in the pages of a major scientific journal clearly demonstrates the high stakes on both sides of the issue, as well as the societal importance of better understanding the effects of media violence on children.

Exposure to media violence can have an impact in four different ways (C. A. Anderson et al., 2003). First, seeing actors engage in aggression teaches aggressive behaviors and inspires imitation of them, as you saw earlier in this chapter in the discussion of Bandura's studies with the Bobo doll. Second, viewing aggression activates the viewer's own aggressive thoughts, feelings, and tendencies. This heightened aggressive mindset makes it more likely that the individual will interpret new interactions and events as involving aggression and will respond aggressively. Furthermore, when aggression-related thoughts are frequently activated, they may become part of the individual's normal internal state. These factors may lead to a hostile attributional bias, as described by Dodge and discussed earlier in this chapter.

Third, media violence is exciting and arousing for most youth, and their heightened physiological arousal makes them more likely to react violently to provocations right after watching violent films. Finally, frequent long-term exposure to media violence gradually leads to emotional desensitization—a reduction in the level of unpleasant physiological arousal most people experience when observing violence. Because this arousal normally helps inhibit violent behavior, emotional desensitization can render violent thoughts and behaviors more likely. These factors, taken together, can help to explain disturbing findings like those from a recent longitudinal study in New Zealand: individuals who watched more television during childhood were more likely to engage in antisocial behaviors later in their lives, including criminal convictions, and receive diagnoses of antisocial personality disorders (Robertson, McAnally, & Hancox, 2013).

SOCIAL MEDIA Technology now plays a major role in adolescent social relationships. In 2015, 73% of American teens had access to a smartphone and 55% texted their friends at least once daily (Lenhart, 2015). The majority of teens reported that they had made at least one new friend online, and one-third reported online flirting with a potential partner (Lenhart, 2015; Lenhart, Smith, & Anderson, 2015). Unfortunately, this behavior is not always welcome; one-quarter of all teens reported that they had unfriended or blocked someone on social media whose flirting made them uncomfortable. And after relationships end, 13% of teen daters report that partners spread rumors about them on social media. Furthermore, while social media may depict less in the way of physical violence than other forms of media, hate speech is prevalent on social media; one in four teen social-media users say that they "often" encounter racist, sexist, or homophobic comments online (Rideout, 2012). As one teen wrote: "Once you read it, it can be deleted from the computer but not from your head" (Smahel & Wright, 2014).

PHYSICAL INACTIVITY Another concern has to do with the fact that a child who is glued to a screen is not outside playing or otherwise engaging in robust physical activity. In addition, the thousands of commercials that bombard children every year (at an advertiser cost of billions of dollars per year) consist largely of advertisements for sugary cereals, candy, and fast-food restaurants. The sedentary nature of screen time, combined with the onslaught of commercials encouraging the consumption of sweet, fatty foods, have been linked to the recent increase in childhood obesity discussed in Chapter 3. More generally, there is a negative relationship between screen time and physical activity in the tween and teen years, such that heavy users of screen media are less likely to be physically active on a daily basis (Rideout, 2015). And when a child both exceeds screen time recommendations and has a TV in their bedroom—as do more than half of 8- to 18-year-olds (Rideout, 2015)—the child is at heightened risk of becoming obese (Wethington, Pan, & Sherry, 2013).

The common practice of spending a great deal of time watching TV while consuming high-fat snacks and meals increases the likelihood of childhood obesity.

EFFECTS ON ACADEMIC ACHIEVEMENT According to a study by the Kaiser Family Foundation, there is a strong relationship between media use and school grades (Rideout, Foehr, & Roberts, 2010). For example, children who are heavy users of screen media (more than 16 hours per day) are far more likely to report fair/poor grades (Cs or below) than are those who are moderate users (3 to 16 hours per day) or light users (fewer than 3 hours per day). Specific aspects of electronic media usage may be particularly problematic; for instance, teen girls who feel a compulsive need to text have worse grades and perceived academic competence than their peers (Lister-Landman, Domoff, & Dubow, 2015). Of course, there are many other confounding factors that might account for links between media usage and grades, such as generally poor parental supervision, or a family culture (parents included) that deemphasizes reading and other academic pursuits in favor of screen time.

However, one cleverly designed study was able to draw causal conclusions about the relation between video games and school achievement (Weis & Cerankosky, 2010). Boys in the 1st through 3rd grades who did not already own a video game console were randomly assigned to an experimental group, whose members were given a console at the beginning of the study, or to a comparison group, whose members were, in the name of fairness, given a console after the study was completed. The boys who received the game console at the beginning of the study subsequently spent less time on after-school academic pursuits than did the boys in the comparison group. Four months into the study, they performed more poorly on measures of literacy and had a higher rate of teacher-reported academic problems than did the comparison group. Boys who spent the most time with the games showed the poorest academic outcomes.

PORNOGRAPHY A serious concern for many parents is children's exposure to pornography on television and the Internet, whether inadvertent or intentional. And their children are worried, too; in a large 2014 sample of European children and teens, pornography was the most frequent concern that participants voiced about their own online activities (Smahel & Wright, 2014). Research suggests that exposure to pornography can make children and teens more tolerant of aggression toward women, as well as more accepting of premarital and extramarital sex (Greenfield, 2004).

Of special concern is pornography featuring children. Child pornography is a multibillion-dollar industry that has increased dramatically since the advent of the Internet and other digital technologies (U.S. Department of Justice, 2015). Today, pedophiles commonly use the Web, including chat rooms, to share illegal photographs of children and to lure children into sexual relationships.

The most effective weapons against the various negative effects of media on children operate at the microsystem level, with parents exercising control over their children's access to undesirable media. As children get older, parents become less vigilant; a recent study found that while 68% of parents of 13- to 14-year-olds check their child's Web-browsing history, this number drops to 56% for 15- to 17-year-olds (Pew Research Center, 2016). The burden of online safety clearly shifts from parent to child over the course of development, suggesting effects of the chronosystem. There are also impacts at the macrosystem level, with legal controls and government programs designed to minimize the negative features of the media with which children interact. Effective control is complicated, however, by concerns about freedom of speech and, in the case of Internet pornography, the global nature of the problem.

SES and Development

As we have frequently noted, the family's SES has profound effects on children's development. These effects originate at every level of the bioecological model. In the microsystem, children are affected by the nature of their family's housing and their neighborhood, and in the mesosystem, by the condition of their school and the quality of their teachers. Exosystem influences include the nature of the parents' employment or lack of employment. Macrosystem factors include the government policies that affect employment opportunities and establish programs like Project Head Start, geared to low-income families.

Chronosystem factors also come into play with respect to changes over time in the kind and number of jobs that are available. For example, in the United States, the number of well-paying manufacturing jobs has been shrinking for many years, ravaging whole communities with skyrocketing unemployment. The shrinking tax base in those communities, and in others affected by the economic downturn of the past several years, has resulted in fewer resources to support schools, health care, and other community resources important for developing children.

The pervasive effects of poverty In many of our discussions throughout this book, we focus on a number of factors that affect the development of children living in poverty. However, the factors we discuss are only the tip of the iceberg. Table 9.1

TABLE 9.1

The Environment of Childhood Poverty

Some ways that the physical and social environments of children growing up in poverty differ from the environments of more well-off children:

PHYSICAL ENVIRONMENT

Home

- Inadequate housing
- Structural deficiencies
- Inadequate heat
- Unsafe drinking water
- Poor air quality in house (including parental smoking)
- Rodent infestation
- Few safety features (e.g., smoke alarms)
- Crowding (number of people in home)
- Small yards (if any)

Neighborhood

- Exposure to toxins
  - o Air pollution (e.g., near highways, factories)
  - o Water, soil pollution (factories, toxic waste dumps)
  - o Exposure to contaminants (lead, pesticides)
- Few parks or open spaces
- Few places for informal gatherings
- Inadequate municipal services (garbage, police, fire)
- Few stores, services, including supermarkets
- Less bus, taxi service
- More bars, taverns
- More physical hazards (traffic volume, street crossings, playground safety)

SOCIAL ENVIRONMENT

Home

- Low parental education
- Low parental income
- Employment instability
- Frequent change of residence
- Social isolation (small social networks)
- Less social support
- Lower marital quality (conflict)
- More domestic violence (spousal, child abuse)
- Higher divorce rate
- More single-parent households
- Harsher, punitive parenting
- Low monitoring of children
- Less emotional support
- More corporal punishment
- Less speech from parents
- Less frequent literacy activities
- Fewer computers/older computers
- Less access to Internet
- More TV watching

School

- Poor-quality day care
- Aggressive, violent peers
- Unstable peer relations
- Poorer quality teachers
- High teacher turnover
- High student absenteeism
- Less parent involvement in school
- Less sense of belonging to school
- Inadequate buildings (plumbing, heating, lighting, etc.)
- Overcrowding

Neighborhood

- High crime rates
- High level of violence
- Widespread unemployment
- Fewer positive adult role models
- Few social resources

Source: G. W. Evans (2004).

How might the conditions of a child's school affect development? What environmental risk factors might students in a poorer school face (see top photo), compared with students in a wealthier school (bottom photo)?

lists a wide variety of ways in which the environment of poor children in the United States differs from that of more affluent children (summarized from G. W. Evans, 2004). Many of the items in the table will be familiar to you, but you may never have considered some of the others. As you look over the table, think about how these various aspects of impoverished environments interact and what their cumulative impact might be. Also, consider how the many detrimental factors listed in the table relate to the different levels of the bioecological model, from government priorities and policies to the physical health of the individual child growing up in poverty.

As you look over the table, you should also keep in mind two points from our discussion of the multiple-risk model in Chapter 2. First, it is the *accumulated* exposure to multiple environmental risk factors that is crucial (Evans & Whipple, 2013). A child whose parents are neglectful might cope reasonably well, but doing so would be more difficult if the child also goes to a poor-quality school in a dangerous neighborhood. Second, as discussed in Chapters 10 and 11, individual children differ with respect to how susceptible they are to environmental influences, both positive and negative (Hartman & Belsky, 2015).

Because many specific effects of poverty on development are discussed throughout the book, we will not feature them here; instead, we will examine a developmental effect of SES that often goes unnoticed: the costs of affluence.

The costs of affluence Contrary to popular assumption, growing up in highly affluent families can have negative effects on development. The stereotype of the "poor little rich kid" seems to have some basis in fact, leading to a recently coined term: *affluenza*. Affluent teens report markedly higher levels of substance use than their peers, especially alcohol use. In one study of affluent high school students, over half of the girls and two-thirds of the boys reported being drunk in the prior month, compared with about one-third in less affluent samples of high school students (Luthar & Barkin, 2012). Peer envy is also especially common among more affluent teens, particularly among girls (Lyman & Luthar, 2014). We also see effects at the mesosystem level, with evidence that merely living in an affluent neighborhood confers psychological challenges; middle-income boys living in affluent neighborhoods reported higher levels of delinquency, and middle-income girls living in affluent neighborhoods reported higher levels of anxiety and depression, than their peers growing up in middle-income neighborhoods (Lund & Dearing, 2013).

In attempting to account for these findings, Luthar and Becker (2002) note that affluent parents tend to pressure their children to excel both academically and in extracurricular activities. At the same time, these parents often provide their children with less emotional support. Increased substance use among affluent teens, for example, is more common in families where parents are unaware of their children's whereabouts after school, and for teens who believed that their parents would be lax in imposing consequences (Luthar & Barkin, 2012). Given the relative safety of their neighborhoods, affluent parents may not feel the need to be as vigilant—but there may be costs to lax monitoring. The same appears to be true of online behavior: higher-income parents talk much less frequently with their teens about their online behavior and content viewing than do low-income parents (Pew Research Center, 2016).

In recent years, the popular press has drawn attention to the perils of stressed-out teens who face tremendous pressure to achieve and résumé-build in preparation for college admissions. Despite heavily publicized examples of "tiger moms" and negative parental pressure, the number of hours that affluent teens spend on extracurricular activities was not related to levels of maladjustment (Luthar & Barkin, 2012). This finding is consistent with data from the 2015 Pew survey on Parenting in America, with which we began this section: while 20% of wealthier parents think that their children's schedules are too busy, this number is not all that different from middle-income (13%) and lower-income (8%) families. Concerns about overscheduling outside of school may be over-blown, at least to some extent. It may be more important for the parents of affluent teens to focus on staying engaged and attuned to their child's friends and activities.

Current Perspectives

The three theoretical positions discussed in this section have all made valuable contributions to developmental science by placing individual development in a much broader context than is typically done in mainstream psychology. All of them challenge researchers to look beyond the lab—far beyond it.

The primary contribution of ethology and evolutionary psychology comes from the emphasis on children's biological nature, including genetic tendencies grounded in evolution. Evolutionary psychology has provided fascinating insights into human development, but it has also come in for serious criticism. One frequent complaint is that, like psychoanalytic theories, many of the claims of evolutionary psychologists are impossible to test. Often, a behavioral pattern that is consistent with an evolutionary account is at least equally consistent with social learning or some other perspective. Finally, evolutionary psychology theories tend to overlook one of the most remarkable features of human beings, a feature strongly emphasized by Bronfenbrenner—our capacity to transform our environments and ourselves.

Bronfenbrenner's bioecological model has made an important contribution to our thinking about development. His emphasis on the broad context of development and the many different interactions among factors at various levels has highlighted how complex the development of every child is. The main criticism of this model is its lack of emphasis on biological factors.

What is the relevance of ecological theories to Kismet's design? Evolution is basically irrelevant to it. Evolutionary change does not apply to individual development, and, without the possibility for reproduction, it simply cannot occur.

With respect to the bioecological model, Kismet developed in an extremely limited microsystem—a lab at the Massachusetts Institute of Technology—populated with a relatively small number of people. It has no mesosystem at present, although that could change in the future. This fact makes Kismet's experience quite different from that of most human children. The development of social robots could be affected by the macrosystem at any time, if changes in research priorities of the federal government cut off funding for the project. In terms of the chronosystem, such a remarkable robot was unimaginable until recently, and even more remarkable ones are currently being developed to follow in Kismet's footsteps.

It is interesting that the most difficult parallels to draw between Kismet's development and that of children and theories of social development concern the larger context of human development. Part of what is unique about the human species is the fact that every individual is embedded in multiple layers of human interactions, institutions, traditions, and history.

Review

The theories we have grouped under the label "ecological theories" examine development in a much broader context than those found in other theoretical approaches. Theories of development based on ethology and evolutionary psychology emphasize the influence of the evolutionary history of the human species on the development of individual children. Parental-investment theory proposes that the perpetuation of one's genes underlies the enormous effort that parents invest in raising their children.

Other evolutionary theories emphasize the adaptive function of prolonged immaturity in the development of human children. Urie Bronfenbrenner's highly influential bioecological model conceptualizes the environment in which children develop as a set of nested systems, or contexts. The systems range from aspects of the environment that the individual child directly experiences on a daily basis to the broader society and historical time in which the child lives.

CHAPTER SUMMARY

Four major types of social development theories present contrasting views of the social world of children.

Psychoanalytic Theories

- The psychoanalytic theory of Sigmund Freud has had an enormous impact on developmental psychology and psychology as a whole, primarily through Freud's emphasis on the importance of early experience for personality and social development, his depiction of unconscious motivation and processes, and his emphasis on the importance of close relationships.

- Freud posited five biologically determined stages of psychosexual development (oral, anal, phallic, latency, genital) in which psychic energy becomes focused in different areas of the body. Children face specific conflicts at each stage, and these conflicts must be resolved for healthy development to proceed. Freud also posited three structures of personality—id (unconscious urges), ego (rational thought), and superego (conscience).

- Erik Erikson extended Freud's theory by identifying eight stages of psychosocial development extending across the entire life span. Each stage is characterized by a developmental crisis that, if not successfully resolved, will continue to trouble the individual.

Learning Theories

- John Watson believed strongly in the power of environmental factors, especially reinforcement, to influence children's development.

- B. F. Skinner held that all behavior can be explained in terms of operant conditioning. He discovered the importance of intermittent reinforcement and the powerful reinforcing value of attention.

- Albert Bandura's social-learning theory and his empirical research established that children can learn simply by observing other people. Bandura has increasingly stressed the importance of cognition in social learning.

Theories of Social Cognition

- Social cognitive theories assume that children's knowledge and beliefs are vitally important in social development.

■ Robert Selman's theory proposes that children go through four stages in the development of the ability to take the role or perspective of another person. They progress from the simple appreciation that someone can have a view different from their own to being able to think about the view of a "generalized other."

■ The social information-processing approach to social cognition emphasizes the importance of children's attributions regarding their own and others' behavior. The role of such attribution is clearly reflected in the hostile attributional bias, described by Dodge, which leads children to assume hostile intent on the part of others and to respond aggressively in situations in which the intention of others is ambiguous.

■ Dweck's theory of self-attribution focuses on how children's achievement motivation is influenced by their attributions about the reasons for their successes and failures. Children with an incremental/mastery orientation enjoy working on challenging problems and tend to be persistent in trying to solve them, whereas children with an entity/helpless orientation prefer situations in which they expect to succeed and tend to withdraw when they experience failure.

Ecological Theories of Development

■ Ethological theories examine behavior within the evolutionary context, trying to understand its adaptive or survival value. The research of Konrad Lorenz on imprinting has been particularly relevant to certain theories of social development in children. Sex differences have been documented in children's toy and play preferences.

■ Evolutionary psychologists apply Darwinian concepts of natural selection to human behavior. Characteristic of their approach are parental-investment theory and the idea that the long period of immaturity and dependence in human infancy enables young children to learn and practice many of the skills needed later in life.

■ Bronfenbrenner's bioecological model conceptualizes the environment as a set of nested contexts, with the child at the center. These contexts range from the microsystem, which includes the activities, roles, and relationships—the environment—in which a child directly participates on a regular basis, to the chronosystem, the historical context that affects all the other systems.

Test Yourself

1. The first signs of superego development appear during which stage of Freud's psychoanalytic theory?
   a. the oral stage
   b. the anal stage
   c. the phallic stage
   d. the genital stage

2. Each of Erikson's stages is characterized by
   a. the intervention of a caregiver or mentor.
   b. a crisis that the individual must resolve.
   c. individual goal-setting.
   d. mastery of social skills, however rudimentary.

3. Which of the following best describes a parenting style influenced by Watson's theories?
   a. rigid and strict
   b. overprotective
   c. permissive
   d. child-centered

4. According to Skinner, everything we do in life is an operant response influenced by
   a. the immediate sociocultural context.
   b. the outcomes of past behavior.
   c. the behavior of peers.
   d. behavior modification.

5. Social learning theory emphasizes _____ as the primary mechanisms of development.
   a. observation and imitation
   b. genetic encoding
   c. reinforcement
   d. social influences

6. Bandura's Bobo doll experiment demonstrated
   a. the pleasure principle.
   b. vicarious reinforcement.
   c. operant conditioning.
   d. basic trust versus mistrust.

7. Dodge's approach to social cognition centers on the use of _____ as a problem-solving strategy.
   a. negotiation
   b. role-taking
   c. aggression
   d. the "generalized other"

8. According to Dweck, whether a child meets a new challenge with a sense of excitement or with a sense of anxiety depends on that child's _____ .
   a. skill level
   b. achievement motivation
   c. parental engagement
   d. level of internalization

9. A person with an entity view of intelligence believes that his or her intelligence level:
   a. is based on family circumstances.
   b. can change with effort.
   c. rises and falls on a continuum.
   d. is fixed and unchangeable.

10. What is the term used to describe the study of behavior within an evolutionary context?
    a. ethology
    b. biology
    c. sociology
    d. mesosystem

11. Parental-investment theory stresses the _____ basis of many aspects of parental behavior.
    a. evolutionary
    b. empirical
    c. behaviorist
    d. bioecological

12. Lisa's peers are picking on her at recess because she wears glasses. Which level of Bronfenbrenner's bioecological model is affecting Lisa?
    a. the macrosystem
    b. the exosystem
    c. the microsystem
    d. the mesosystem

13. Which level of Bronfenbrenner's model would account for how changes in a society's customs over time affect the development of a child?
    a. the macrosystem
    b. the exosystem
    c. the chronosystem
    d. the mesosystem

14. At which level of Bronfenbrenner's model do the consequences of child maltreatment primarily manifest themselves?
    a. the microsystem
    b. the exosystem
    c. the macrosystem
    d. the mesosystem

15. According to Caspi and colleagues, children who possess a particular variant of the MAOA gene are _____ to the negative effects of child abuse.
    a. completely immune
    b. especially susceptible
    c. more resilient
    d. slightly more prone

 **LaunchPad**
macmillan learning

Don't stop now! Research shows that testing yourself is a powerful learning tool. Visit LaunchPad to access the LearningCurve adaptive quizzing system, which gives you a personalized study plan to help build your mastery of the chapter material through videos, activities, and more. **Go to launchpadworks.com.**

Critical Thinking Questions

1. What influences of Freud's theory of development can you identify in modern society?

2. The concept of self-socialization plays a prominent role in social cognitive theories. Explain what is meant by this term. To what extent and in what ways do the other major theories reviewed in the chapter allow for the possibility of self-socialization?

3. Consider your behavior when preparing for and taking tests and when receiving feedback on your academic performance. Do you see yourself as having primarily an incremental/mastery orientation or an entity/helpless orientation to academic achievement?

4. Imagine yourself raising a child. Identify one or two things from each of the four types of theories discussed in this chapter that you think might be helpful to you as a parent.

5. Consider Box 9.3 on attention-deficit hyperactivity disorder and analyze what is discussed there in terms of Bronfenbrenner's bioecological model.

Key Terms

hostile attributional bias, p. 387

id, p. 375

imprinting, p. 393

incremental theory, p. 389

incremental/mastery orientation, p. 389

intermittent reinforcement, p. 382

internalization, p. 376

latency period, p. 376

macrosystem, p. 398

mesosystem, p. 398

microsystem, p. 398

Oedipus complex, p. 376

oral stage, p. 375

parental-investment theory, p. 395

phallic stage, p. 376

psychic energy, p. 375

reciprocal determinism, p. 383

role taking, p. 386

self-socialization, p. 385

superego, p. 376

systematic desensitization, p. 380

vicarious reinforcement, p. 384

▶ Student Video Activities

Theories of Emotional Development in Infancy and Toddlerhood

Theories of Middle Childhood Development

Observation Learning of Aggression: Bandura's Bobo Doll Study

Community Support Groups in Asia, Africa, and South America

Answers to Test Yourself

1. c, **2.** b, **3.** a, **4.** b, **5.** a, **6.** b, **7.** c, **8.** b, **9.** d, **10.** a, **11.** a, **12.** c, **13.** c, **14.** a, **15.** c

FREDERICK MORGAN (1856–1927), *Never Mind!* (oil on canvas, 1884)

Emotional Development

Themes

- Nature and Nurture
- The Active Child
- Continuity/Discontinuity
- The Sociocultural Context
- Individual Differences

I magine the following situation: a young girl is taken to a room in her preschool where an experimenter shows her some tasty treats, such as M&M's, marshmallows, or pretzels. The experimenter tells the girl that he is going to leave the room "for a while" and that she has two choices: if she waits until he returns to the room, she can have two of the treats; or if she wishes, she can ring a bell and the experimen ter will return immediately—but she will get only one treat. The child is then left alone for a considerable period, say 15 to 20 minutes, or until she rings the bell.

You may have heard of this famous experiment, commonly known as "the marshmallow test" (Mischel, 2015). Walter Mischel and his colleagues first used this procedure with a group of preschoolers in the 1960s to study their ability to delay immediate gratification in order to obtain larger rewards. The researchers were interested in whether or not the children would wait for the second treat, but they also wanted to observe the children's strategies for coping with the long wait. Videos showed them using a variety of strategies: some distracted themselves by talking, singing, trying to sleep, or making up games to play; others stared at the treats or at the bell; and some, of course, just rang the bell and ate the single treat right away, preferring one immediate but guaranteed treat to the possibility of more treats later.

Mischel believed that a child's ability to delay eating one marshmallow for the reward of eating two marshmallows later was an indicator of that child's self-control or willpower in the face of immediate pleasure or happiness (however fleeting). The ability to exhibit self-control early in life, he reasoned, predicted success later in life. After all, much of success in adulthood depends on working toward long-term goals, whether in matters related to higher education, professional career, or exercise and physical health. Success also entails resisting temptation and exercising self-restraint.

To test his theory, Mischel interviewed the children who participated in his original marshmallow test at regular intervals over the subsequent four decades. At every 10-year interval, those children who were able to wait the longest were found to be more intelligent, attentive, strategic, and self-reliant than those who displayed less patience (Mischel, 2015; Mischel, Shoda, & Peake, 1988; Peake, Hebl, & Mischel, 2002). Once they got to high school, they obtained higher SAT scores and scored higher on a behavioral measure requiring control of one's attention and behavioral responses on a computer task (Eigsti et al., 2006; Shoda, Mischel, & Peake, 1990); and at about age 30, they had achieved a higher educational level, had higher self-esteem, and were reported to be better able to cope with stress (Ayduk et al., 2000; Mischel & Ayduk, 2004; Peake & Mischel, 2000).

The marshmallow test was designed to determine how well children can delay gratification—in other words, how well they manage the frustration of waiting to eat one treat in order to get two treats in the future.

Furthermore, in computer-task assessments 40 years after the original experiment, those who scored low in delay of gratification in Mischel's study continued to exhibit greater difficulty in delaying responses to rewarding stimuli than did those who scored high in delay (Casey et al., 2011).

Given the importance of this ability to delay gratification, researchers have turned to studying whether self-control is innate (*nature*) or learned (*nurture*), and if any part of it is learned, how it can be taught. Some of the children in Mischel's original study underwent brain scans in their 40s, which revealed differences in the prefrontal cortex between adults who had been high-delay and low-delay preschoolers, suggesting at least some biological basis (Casey et al., 2011)—although whether that difference comes from genes or from influences in the early environment is yet to be determined. Schools around the country now promote self-control, along with self-regulation and the ability to get along with others (collectively called social-emotional skills), through social emotional learning (SEL), or character-building, programs. A review of 200 SEL programs found that they did improve social and emotional skills and had the added benefit of improving academic achievement as well (Durlak et al., 2011).

Emotions are a basic part of human experience, but how children learn to regulate them and their behavior can have lifelong consequences. In this chapter, we examine the development of children's emotions, as well as the development of their ability to regulate their emotions and the behavior associated with them. In addition, we consider links between children's temperaments and their behavior, as well as links between emotional stress and mental health. In the course of our discussion, we will give particular emphasis to several of our themes. Key among them will be the theme of *individual differences,* as we examine differences among children in various aspects of their emotional functioning. We also discuss the origins of these differences, including heredity, parental socialization practices, cultural beliefs related to emotion, and how the child's behavior in a given context affects his or her physiological reactions. Thus, the themes of *nature and nurture* and the *sociocultural context* will also be prominent. The theme of the *active child* is also touched upon with respect to children's attempts to regulate their own emotions and behavior. Finally, the theme of *continuity versus discontinuity* is discussed briefly in regard to the emergence of self-conscious emotions.

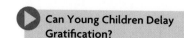
Can Young Children Delay Gratification?

The Development of Emotions

Most people equate emotions with "feelings." However, emotions are more complicated than simply sensations or reactions. Developmentalists working in this area attempt to explain why we experience emotions and why we express them outwardly on our faces or in our voices. They view **emotions** as a combination of physiological and cognitive responses to thoughts or experiences. Emotions have several components (Izard, 2010; Saarni et al., 2006):

1. Neural responses

2. Physiological factors, including heart rate, breathing rate, and hormone levels

3. Subjective feelings

4. Emotional expressions

5. The desire to take action, including the desire to escape, approach, or change people or things in the environment

emotions ■ neural and physiological responses to the environment, subjective feelings, cognitions related to those feelings, and the desire to take action

The following example illustrates how each of these components contributes to the experience of emotion. Imagine you are walking in your neighborhood and come across a growling dog without a leash or an owner nearby. You stop suddenly, realize you may be trapped, and begin to feel a sense of dread that you label as fear (subjective feeling). You recognize that your heart is racing and your eyes are widening (physiological factors) and that your eyebrows are raised and your mouth is pulled back (emotional expression), all as you try to figure out how to get away from the dog and toward someplace safe (desire to take action). Although not observable by you, your brain is rapidly processing information about the dog and the environment around you, as well as about the likely odds of success of any action you might take, and signaling the production of hormones that will help you mobilize your muscles to flee from the terrorizing dog (neural responses). All of these responses happen in a split second—so fast, in fact, that it is hard to say which comes first.

The nearly simultaneous nature of these components has led researchers to consider whether emotion is mostly innate (*nature*) or mostly learned (*nurture*) (Izard, 2010; Lindquist et al., 2013; Moors et al., 2013). Do we experience the physiological reaction first and then learn to call it "fear"? Or do we cognitively assess a situation as one that is fear-inducing and then experience the corresponding physiological reactions and facial expressions? In other words, what role does cognition play in our experience of emotion? Research on these questions is ongoing. This chapter will explore some of the possible explanations currently under investigation, as well as some of the aspects of emotion and emotional development about which some consensus has emerged.

Theories on the Nature and Emergence of Emotion

Determining whether emotions are innate or learned relies in large part on knowing whether humans are born with the ability to experience key emotions. Consequently, research on emotional development tends to focus on infants. One view, known as **discrete emotions theory,** argues that neurological and biological systems have evolved to allow humans, from infancy, to experience and then express a set of basic emotions through adaptation to our surroundings (Ekman & Cordaro, 2011; Izard, Woodburn, & Finlon, 2010). Given its emphasis on evolution and adaptation, it is not surprising that this theory was first put forward by Charles Darwin in his 1872 book *The Expression of the Emotions in Man and Animals.* Based on careful observation of facial, verbal, and gestural expressions, Darwin argued that the expressions for certain basic emotional states are innate to the species and therefore are similar across all peoples, including young babies. According to discrete emotions theory, emotional responses are largely automatic and not based on cognition.

Adherents to discrete emotions theory point to several aspects of emotional development to support the proposition that emotions are innate and evolved over the course of human evolution. Infants express a set of recognizable, discrete emotions, well before they can be actively taught about them (Izard et al., 2010). Also, similar emotional facial expressions have been observed around the world, including in remote tribes, although cultures do vary in how they label these expressions (Ekman & Cordaro, 2011). Vocalizations of basic emotions such as anger, joy, and sadness are recognizable across very different cultural groups, from individuals living in England to members of the seminomadic Himba tribe in Namibia (Sauter et al., 2010).

discrete emotions theory ■ a theory about emotions, held by Tomkins, Izard, and others, in which emotions are viewed as innate and discrete from one another from very early in life, and each emotion is believed to be packaged with a specific and distinctive set of bodily and facial reactions

TABLE 10.1

The Goals, Meanings, and Actions Associated with Particular Emotions

Emotion type	Goal connected with the emotion	Meaning regarding the self	Action tendency
Disgust	Avoiding contamination or illness	This stimulus may contaminate me or make me ill	Rejection of the thing causing disgust
Fear	Maintaining one's own physical and psychological integrity	This stimulus is threatening to me	Flight or withdrawal
Anger	Attaining the end state that the individual currently is invested in	There is an obstacle to my obtaining my goal	Forward movement, especially to eliminate obstacles to one's goal
Sadness	Attaining the end state that the individual currently is invested in	My goal is unattainable	Disengagement and withdrawal
Shame	Maintaining others' respect and affection; preserving self-esteem	I am bad (my self-esteem is damaged) and others notice how bad I am	Withdrawal; avoiding others, hiding oneself
Guilt	Meeting one's own internalized values	I have done something contrary to my values, and perhaps hurt someone else	Movement to make reparation, to inform others, or to punish self

In contrast, the **functionalist perspective** argues that individuals experience emotions in order to manage the relationship between themselves and the environment (J. J. Campos et al., 1994; Saarni et al., 2006). According to this perspective, emotions are partly a response to how an individual appraises the environment and whether factors in the environment are promoting or hindering his or her well-being (Moors et al., 2013). Emotions and emotional expressions are thus goal-driven; if a child wants something to stop, he cries, whereas if he wants something to continue, he smiles and laughs. Table 10.1 provides some examples of the goals, goal meanings, and the actions they may precipitate. These appraisal processes most often occur at the subconscious level in both children and adults. The exceptions occur when children realize that people can fake emotions, and that faking emotions can be another way to reach their goals. For example, a 4-year-old may fake crying after a fight with her big sister to evoke sympathy from an unsuspecting mother. We will return to this idea of fake emotions later in the chapter.

Although these two perspectives differ regarding whether distinct emotions emerge early in life, each with its own set of physiological components, they both agree that cognition and experience shape emotional development.

The Emergence of Emotions

Researchers agree that there are several basic emotions—happiness, fear, anger, sadness, surprise, and disgust—that are universal in all human cultures. Each of these basic emotions serves important survival and communication functions (Sullivan & Lewis, 2003). These basic emotions appear very early in life, lending support to the discrete emotions theory that emotions have at least a core innate component (Box 10.1 describes the coding schemes researchers have developed for recognizing these emotions in infants).

Happiness

The first clear sign of happiness that infants express is a smile. During the 1st month, they exhibit fleeting smiles primarily during the REM phase of sleep; after the 1st month, they sometimes smile when they are stroked gently. These early smiles may be reflexive and seem to be evoked by some biological state rather than by social interaction (Sullivan & Lewis, 2003), although there is some evidence

functionalist perspective ■ a theory of emotion, proposed by Campos and others, arguing that the basic function of emotions is to promote action toward achieving a goal. In this view, emotions are not discrete from one another and vary somewhat based on the social environment.

BOX 10.1 | a closer look

BASIC EMOTIONAL EXPRESSIONS IN INFANTS

Emotions are internal states, of course, but they typically are expressed through facial expressions and body movements. As part of the effort to determine whether emotions are innate (*nature*) or learned (*nurture*), researchers have studied whether infants express recognizable emotions in response to external stimuli. Early expressions of emotion would seem to support a biological and evolutionary basis. To make their own interpretations of infants' emotions more objective, researchers have devised highly elaborate systems for identifying the emotional meaning of infants' facial expressions. These systems involve coding dozens of facial cues—whether an infant's eyebrows are raised or knitted together; whether the eyes are wide open, tightly closed, or narrowed; whether the

lips are pursed, softly rounded, or retracted straight back; and so on—and then analyzing the combinations in which these cues are present.

AFFEX is a prominent system for coding emotions in infants that links particular facial expressions and facial muscle movements with particular emotions (Izard & Dougherty, 1980). Many of the training videos for AFFEX use footage from children getting their vaccinations, an experience that elicits a range of negative emotional expressions. Once researchers have been trained in the AFFEX systems, they can then watch videotapes of infants' and older children's faces and make note of which facial and muscle movements they see. The videotapes are played in slow motion to adequately capture

expressions that sometimes last a second or less.

The following table provides brief descriptions and photographs of the combinations of muscle and facial movements that result in the recognition of six basic emotions.

The AFFEX system has been used to demonstrate links between children's emotional expressions and their emotion regulation skills and social behaviors. In one recent study conducted with 3- to 5-year-old children attending a Head Start center, the more the 3- to 5-year-old children expressed anger and sadness in a laboratory task, the more they displayed mental health and behavior problems in their classrooms six months later (Morgan, Izard, & Hyde, 2014).

Happiness: smiling, either with a closed mouth or with an open upturned mouth; raised cheeks, which in turn make the eyes squint a bit

ROSS WHITAKER / GETTY IMAGES

Sadness: down-turned corners of the mouth, lips pushed together and possibly trembling, slightly furrowed brow

LEUNGCHOPAN / GETTY IMAGES

Anger: strongly furrowed brow that comes down in the center, almost making an X of the brow muscles; open square-shaped mouth, sometimes baring teeth; flared nostrils

HEATHER PERRY / GETTY IMAGES

Fear: eyes wide open; brows raised in the middle, making a triangle shape; corners of mouth pulled back into a grimace, with mouth either open or closed

BELYNDA WEBB / SUPERSTOCK

Surprise: eyes wide open; eyebrows raised into arches; mouth open in round O shape

MILLA1974 / GETTY IMAGES

Disgust: nose crinkled and nostrils flared; mouth open wide with lips pulled back and possibly with tongue sticking out

ANATOLS / GETTY IMAGES

that even newborns less than a day old smile when they are being touched (see Cecchini et al., 2011).

Between the 3rd and 8th week of life, infants begin to smile in reaction to external stimuli, including touching, high-pitched voices, or other stimuli that engage their attention (Sullivan & Lewis, 2003). After about 3 or 4 months of age, infants laugh as well as smile during a variety of activities that give them pleasure. For example, they are likely to laugh when a parent tickles them or blows on their tummy, bounces them on a knee or swings them around in the air, or shares a favorite activity such as bathing with them. Around the same time, babies also begin to exhibit **social smiles,** that is, smiles directed toward people (B. L. White, 1985); they also smile more at people, even strangers, than at puppet-like foam balls that resemble people, are animated, and "talk" to the infant (Ellsworth, Muir, & Hains, 1993). Social smiles frequently occur during interactions with a parent or other familiar people and tend to elicit the adult's delight, interest, and affection (Camras, Malatesta, & Izard, 1991; Huebner & Izard, 1988). In turn, this response usually inspires more social smiling from the infant. Thus, the infant's early social smiles likely promote care from parents and other adults and strengthen the infant's relationships with other people.

Infants also show happiness when they realize they can control a particular event. In one study that demonstrated this, researchers attached a string to an arm of each infant in the study. For half of the infants, music played when they pulled the string; for the other half, music played randomly, regardless of their actions. The infants who caused the music to play by pulling on the string showed more interest and smiling when the music came on than did the infants whose string-pulling had no connection to the music's being played (M. Lewis, Alessandri, & Sullivan, 1990).

At about 7 months of age, infants start to smile primarily at *familiar* people, rather than at people in general. (In fact, as you will see, unfamiliar people often elicit distress at this age.) These selective smiles tend to delight parents and motivate them to continue interacting with the infant. In turn, infants of this age often respond to parents' playfulness and smiles with excitement and joy, which also prolongs their positive social interactions (Weinberg & Tronick, 1994). Such exchanges of positive affect, especially when they occur with parents but not with strangers, make parents feel special to the infant and strengthen the bond between them.

Children's expression of happiness increases across the 1st year of life (Rothbart & Bates, 2006), perhaps because they are able to understand and respond to more interesting and positive events and stimuli. By late in the 1st year of life, children's cognitive development allows them to take pleasure from unexpected or discrepant events such as a family member making a funny noise or wearing a silly hat (Kagan, Kearsley, & Zelazo, 1978). As their language skills develop along with their understanding of people and events, children in the preschool years begin to find humor and enjoyment in words, including jokes (Dunn, 1988).

Fear

Although there is little firm evidence of distinct fear reactions in infants during the first months of life (Witherington et al., 2010), by 4 months of age, infants do seem wary of unfamiliar objects and events (Sroufe, 1995). At around the age of 6 or 7 months, initial signs of fear begin to appear (Camras et al., 1991), most notably the fear of strangers in many circumstances. In part, this shift likely reflects infants' recognition that unfamiliar people do not provide the comfort and pleasure that familiar people do. In general, the fear of strangers intensifies and lasts until about age 2. However, it should be noted that the

social smiles ■ smiles that are directed at people; they first emerge as early as 6 to 7 weeks of age

Social smiles directed toward people typically first appear during the infant's 3rd month.

Young children who were not afraid of strangers at 6 months of age often suddenly show fear of them at 7 or 8 months of age.

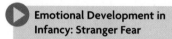

▶ **Emotional Development in Infancy: Stranger Fear**

separation anxiety ■ feelings of distress that children, especially infants and toddlers, experience when they are separated, or expect to be separated, from individuals to whom they are emotionally attached

FIGURE 10.1 Development of fear and anger across the first 16 months of life Fear has a steep early increase that then levels off, whereas anger shows a more steady increase across the entire period. (Data from Braungart-Rieker et al., 2010)

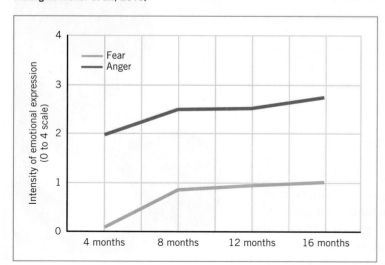

fear of strangers is quite variable (Sroufe, 1995), depending on both the infant's temperament (which we will discuss later in this chapter) and the specific context, such as whether a parent is present and the manner in which the stranger approaches (e.g., abruptly and excitedly or slowly and calmly).

To determine when fear develops in infants, one team of researchers repeated the same procedure with infants every four months from age 4 months to age 16 months (Braungart-Rieker, Hill-Soderlund, & Karrass, 2010). An experimenter, a stranger to the infant, slowly approached the infant while the mother sat close by; the stranger talked to the infant and picked him or her up. Observers rated the infants' facial expressions of fear using the AFFEX code described in Box 10.1 on a scale from 0 (no evidence of fear) to 4 (strong evidence of fear); they also rated the amount of distress in the infants' vocalizations. The results are displayed in Figure 10.1. Infants were found to display no fear of the approaching stranger at 4 months but experienced a steep increase in expressions of fear up to 8 months, suggesting the fear of strangers was clearly in place by 8 months. There was little change in how much fear was expressed between 8 and 16 months, suggesting that after 8 months infants have more experience with novel situations and thus maintain some wariness but do not become increasingly distressed in fear-inducing situations (Braungart-Rieker et al., 2010).

The emergence of fear of strangers and novel situations is clearly adaptive. Because babies often do not have the ability to escape from potentially dangerous situations on their own, they must rely on their parents to protect them, and expressions of fear and distress are powerful tools for bringing help and support when they are needed. Individual differences in the decline in these kinds of fears seem to be related to the quality of children's relationships with their mothers and how effectively their mothers deal with their children's expressions of fear (K. A. Buss & Kiel, 2011; Kochanska, 2001).

An especially salient and important type of fear or distress that emerges at about 8 months of age is **separation anxiety**—distress due to separation from the parent who is the child's primary caregiver. When infants experience separation anxiety, they typically whine, cry, or otherwise express fear and upset. However, the degree to which children exhibit such distress varies with the context. For example, infants show much less distress when they crawl or walk away from a parent than when the parent does the departing (Rheingold & Eckerman, 1970). Separation anxiety tends to increase from 8 to 13 or 15 months of age, and then begins to decline (Kagan, 1976). This pattern of separation anxiety occurs across many cultures, displayed by infants reared in environments as disparate as the U.S. middle class, Israeli kibbutzim (communal farming communities), and !Kung San hunting-and-gathering groups in the Kalahari Desert in Africa (Kagan, 1976). Some amount of separation anxiety is both normal and adaptive, as it encourages infants to stay in close proximity to adults who can protect them and provide for their needs. However, at extreme levels, fear and anxiety can develop into a mental health disorder, which will be discussed later in this chapter.

In the preschool years, as their cognitive ability to represent imaginary phenomena develops, children are prone to magical thinking and often fear imaginary creatures such as ghosts or monsters (see Chapter 7 for a more detailed discussion). As they approach school age (i.e., age 5 or 6), children learn to differentiate between real and imaginary fears (Zisenwine et al., 2013). Their anxieties and fears tend to be related to real-life issues, such as challenges at school (tests and grades, being called on in class, and pleasing teachers), health (their parents' and their own), and personal harm (being robbed, mugged, or shot) (Silverman, La Greca, & Wasserstein, 1995).

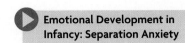

Emotional Development in Infancy: Separation Anxiety

Anger

Anger is a child's response to a frustrating or threatening situation and is largely an interpersonal experience. According to the functionalist perspective on emotions, a child (or an adult) is more likely to be angry with another person than an object, and is more likely to be angry in certain contexts more than others (Sears et al., 2014). Anger is rarely expressed by infants as a single emotion; rather, it is often blended with sadness, which suggests that infants are expressing a general state of distress and that they have yet to differentiate whether a stimulus is making them sad or angry (Sullivan & Lewis, 2003). By their 1st birthday, however, infants clearly and frequently express anger (Radke-Yarrow & Kochanska, 1990). In the same experiment described above in which fear was induced by the actions of a stranger, anger was elicited by having the mother gently hold the infant's arms while an attractive toy was put on the table in front of them (Braungart-Rieker et al., 2010)—clearly a frustrating experience for infants who at 4 months have just developed the ability to reach for objects (see Chapter 5). Infants' expressions were again coded using the AFFEX system (see Box 10.1). As the red line in Figure 10.1 shows, infants displayed moderate anger at 4 months, which steadily increased in intensity over the subsequent year (Braungart-Rieker et al., 2010).

Children's tendency to react to a situation with anger appears to peak around 18 to 24 months of age (P. M. Cole et al., 2011); and from age 3 to 6 years, children show less negative emotion on structured laboratory tasks designed to elicit it (Durbin, 2010). The general decline in children's expressions of anger is likely due to children's increasing ability to express themselves with language (Kopp, 1992) and to regulate their emotions, which will be discussed later in this chapter.

The causes of anger also change as children develop a better understanding of others' intentions and motives. For example, in the early preschool years, a child is likely to feel anger when harmed by a peer, whether or not the harm was intentional. In contrast, young school-age children are less likely to be angered if they believe that harm done to them was unintentional or that the motive for some harmful action was benign rather than malicious (Coie & Dodge, 1998; Dodge, Murphy, & Buchsbaum, 1984). As they become older, children tend to express more anger at home with their families, although their anger is typically low in intensity (Sears et al., 2014), perhaps in conjunction with their developing identities as individuals separate from their parents (see Chapter 11).

Sadness

Infants often exhibit sadness in the same types of situations in which they show anger, such as after a painful event and when they cannot control outcomes in their environment, although displays of sadness appear to be somewhat less frequent at this age than displays of anger or distress (Izard, Hembree, & Huebner, 1987; Izard et al., 1995; M. Lewis et al., 1990; Shiller, Izard, & Hembree, 1986). Older infants or young children also exhibit intense and prolonged displays of sadness when they are separated from their parents for extended periods and are not given sensitive care during this period (Bowlby, 1973; J. Robertson & Robertson, 1971). Like fear, sadness is clearly adaptive because it can draw in the attention and support from a caregiver who can help the child regulate her emotion with a calming touch and soft words.

Surprise

Surprise is an emotional reaction to a sudden, unexpected event. It is more than just the physical reaction to being startled by something like a loud noise, which, as we saw in Chapter 5, infants display from birth, but rather involves a cognitive understanding that something is not as it usually is. Most infants begin to express surprise by the age of 6 months (Sullivan & Lewis, 2003). Expressions of surprise tend to be brief, and they usually transform into another emotional expression, such as happiness (Sullivan & Lewis, 2003). The extent to which infants express surprise to novel events is influenced by the emotional environment provided by their parents. In one study conducted in Scotland, infants whose mothers had symptoms of depression expressed less surprise in reaction to a jack-in-the-box than did infants of mothers without depressive symptoms (Reissland & Shepherd, 2006). This same study also found that mothers with depressive symptoms themselves expressed lower intensity of surprise in reaction to the jack-in-the-box, which suggests that how infants express emotions is influenced by how strongly their caregivers express emotions (Reissland & Shepherd, 2006).

Disgust

The emotional experience of disgust is thought to have an evolutionary basis, as it helps humans avoid potential poisons or disease-causing bacteria (Curtis, De Barra, & Aunger, 2011). However, individuals learn what is considered disgusting; for example, eating insects is a normal practice in some countries, such as Thailand, but it is considered unacceptable and disgusting by most cultures in the United States, Canada, and Europe. Children learn, at least in part, from the behaviors of adults what they should react to with disgust, such as how their caregivers react to particular foods (Widen & Russell, 2013). Of course, most children younger than 3 or 4 years of age do not know the words "disgust" or "disgusting," or their equivalent in other languages; however, even at this young age, children are able to express feelings of disgust using other words to convey that something is *yucky* or *gross* (Widen & Russell, 2013).

The Self-Conscious Emotions

self-conscious emotions ■ emotions such as guilt, shame, embarrassment, and pride that relate to our sense of self and our consciousness of others' reactions to us

The emotions above are thought to be innate and to occur well before children are able to communicate with others. There is another set of emotions that are considered **self-conscious emotions** because they require that children have a sense of themselves as separate from other people (M. Lewis, 1998)—an ability which is not fully developed until children are 2 or 3 years old, as will be discussed in greater detail in Chapter 11. The expression of these emotions is an example of *discontinuous growth:* there is an abrupt, qualitative change in children's abilities to experience self-conscious emotions that is linked to the emergence of a sense of self (M. Lewis, 1998; Mascolo, Fischer, & Li, 2003). The emergence of self-conscious emotions is also fostered by children's growing sense of what adults and society expect of them and their acceptance of these external standards (Lagattuta & Thompson, 2007; M. Lewis, Alessandri, & Sullivan, 1992; Mascolo et al., 2003). The set of self-conscious emotions includes guilt, shame, jealousy, empathy, pride, and embarrassment. For brevity, the discussion that follows is limited to the development of guilt and shame; however, all of the self-conscious emotions develop in a similar fashion.

Guilt and shame are sometimes mistakenly thought of as equivalent, but they are actually quite distinct. Guilt is associated with empathy for others and involves feelings of remorse and regret about one's behavior, as well as the desire to undo the consequences of that behavior (M. L. Hoffman, 2000). In contrast, shame does not seem to be related to concern about others. When children feel shame, their focus is on themselves: they feel that they are exposed, and they often feel like hiding (N. Eisenberg, 2000; Tangney, Stuewig, & Mashek, 2007).

Shame and guilt can be distinguished fairly early, as documented by a study in which researchers arranged for 2-year-olds to play with a doll that had been rigged so that one leg would fall off during play while the experimenter was out of the room. When the "accident" occurred, some toddlers displayed a pattern of behavior that seemed to reflect shame—they avoided the adult when she returned to the room and delayed telling her about the mishap. Other children showed a pattern of behavior that seemed to reflect guilt—they repaired the doll quickly, told the adult about the mishap shortly after she returned to the room, and showed relatively little avoidance of her (Barrett, Zahn-Waxler, & Cole, 1993). In general, the degree of association of guilt feelings with bad or hurtful behavior increases in the 2nd to 3rd year (Aksan & Kochanska, 2005), and the individual differences in children's guilt observed at 22 months of age remain relatively stable across the early preschool years (Kochanska, Gross et al., 2002).

In everyday life as well, the same situation often elicits shame in some individuals and guilt in others. Which emotion children experience partly depends on parental practices. Studies of North American children have found that they are more likely to experience guilt than shame if, when they have done something wrong, their parents emphasize the "badness" of the behavior ("You did a bad thing") rather than of the child ("You're a bad boy"). In addition, children are more likely to feel guilt rather than shame if their parents help them understand the consequences their actions have for others, teach them the need to repair the harm they have done, avoid publicly humiliating them, and communicate respect and love for their children even when disciplining them (M. L. Hoffman, 2000; Tangney & Dearing, 2002).

The situations likely to induce self-conscious emotions in children vary across cultures, as does the frequency with which specific self-conscious emotions are likely to be experienced (P. M. Cole, Tamang, & Shrestha, 2006). For instance, the Japanese culture frowns upon bestowing praise on the individual because to do so would encourage a focus on the self rather than on the needs of the larger social group

Children in the preschool years often exhibit shame or guilt when they do something wrong.

(M. Lewis, 1992). Japanese children are thus less likely to report experiencing pride as a consequence of personal success than are American children (Furukawa, Tangney, & Higashibara, 2012).

In many Asian or Southeast Asian cultures that emphasize the welfare of the group rather than the individual, not living up to social or familial obligations is likely to evoke shame or guilt (Mascolo et al., 2003), and children in these cultures report experiencing guilt and shame more than do children in the United States (Furukawa et al., 2012). In such cultures, parents' efforts to elicit shame from their young children are often direct and disparaging (e.g., "You made your mother lose face," "I've never seen any 3-year-old who behaves like you") (Fung & Chen, 2001). This kind of explicit belittling appears to have a more positive effect on children in these Asian cultures than it does on children in Western cultures.

Review

Emotions are fundamental to much of human functioning and undergo change in the early months and years of life. As with many areas of development, both *nature* and *nurture* play a role: there is evidence to support the argument that emotions are innate (the discrete emotions theory) and to support the argument that emotions are dependent on interactions with the environment (the functionalist perspective).

Researchers point to six basic emotions that are recognized across cultures: happiness, fear, anger, sadness, surprise, and disgust. Happiness begins with reflexive smiles but quickly becomes linked with social smiles by 3 or 4 months of age. Fear does not emerge until 6 months or so, when anxiety over strangers and novel situations develops. In the 2nd year, many children develop separation anxiety in response to the absence of their caregivers. The capacity to express anger develops over the course of the 1st year and peaks around 18 to 24 months of age, while sadness, surprise, and disgust all emerge in the 1st year.

The self-conscious emotions—guilt, shame, jealousy, empathy, pride, and embarrassment—likely emerge in the 2nd year of life, somewhat later than the basic emotions. Their emergence is tied in part to the development of a rudimentary sense of self and to an appreciation of others' reactions to the self. Situations that evoke these emotions vary across cultures.

▌Understanding Emotions

In addition to the development of children's capacity to *feel* emotions, another key influence on children's emotional reactions and regulation is their *understanding* of emotion—that is, their understanding of how to identify emotions, as well as their understanding of what emotions mean, their social functions, and what factors affect emotional experience. Because an understanding of emotion affects social behavior, it is critical to the development of social competence. Children's understanding of emotions is primitive in infancy but develops rapidly over the course of childhood.

Identifying the Emotions of Others

The first step in developing an understanding of emotion is the recognition of different emotions in others. By 3 months of age, infants can distinguish facial expressions of happiness, surprise, and anger (Grossmann, 2010). This ability is determined through the use of the habituation paradigm, which was first discussed in the infant learning section of Chapter 5. Three- or 4-month-olds who were first habituated to pictures of happy faces before being presented with a picture of a face depicting surprise showed renewed interest by looking longer at the new picture. By 7 months of age, infants appear to discriminate a number of additional expressions such as fear, sadness, and interest (Grossmann, 2010). For example, 7-month-olds exhibit different patterns of brain waves when they observe fearful and angry facial expressions, a finding that suggests some ability to discriminate these emotions (Kobiella et al., 2008).

Infants have also been shown to perceive others' emotional expressions as meaningful. For instance, if infants are shown a video in which a person's facial expression and voice are consistent in their emotional expression (e.g., a smiling face and a bubbly voice) and a video in which a person's facial expression and voice are emotionally discrepant (e.g., a sad face and a bubbly voice), they will attend more to the presentation that is emotionally consistent (Walker-Andrews & Dickson, 1997). Infants younger than 7 months generally do not seem to notice the difference between the two presentations.

An experiment compared a group of children aged 12 to 14 months with a second group aged 16 to 18 months, to determine when children develop the ability to relate facial expressions of emotion and emotional tones of voice to events in the environment (Martin et al., 2014). Individually, the children were shown an object and a video of a facial expression at the same time; specific toys were associated with each of six different emotional expressions—anger, fear, sadness, surprise, happiness, and a neutral expression. The children were then presented with both an emotion-paired toy and a neutral toy that had not been paired with an emotion; experimenters observed which toy the children reached for. As seen in Figure 10.2, an age difference clearly emerged. The 12- to 14-month-old children did not differentiate between objects that had been associated with each emotion—they reached for all of them at about the same rates. However, children just a few months older at 16 to 18 months of age strongly preferred the toys associated with surprise and happy faces, whereas they strongly avoided toys that had been associated with anger or fear (Martin et al., 2014).

Such skills are evident in children's **social referencing**—that is, their use of a parent's or other adult's facial expression or vocal cues to decide how to deal with novel, ambiguous, or possibly threatening situations. In laboratory studies of this phenomenon, infants are typically exposed to novel people or toys while their mother, at the experimenter's direction, shows a happy, fearful, or neutral facial expression. In studies of this type, 12-month-olds tend to stay near their mother when she shows fear, to move toward the novel person or object if she expresses positive emotion, and to move partway toward the person or object if she shows no emotion (L. J. Carver & Vaccaro, 2007; Moses et al., 2001; Saarni et al., 2006). Similar results have been found in research on 12-month-olds' ability to read their mother's tone of voice. When prevented from seeing their mother's face as they were being presented with novel toys, infants were

social referencing ■ the use of a parent's or other adult's facial expression or vocal cues to decide how to deal with novel, ambiguous, or possibly threatening situations

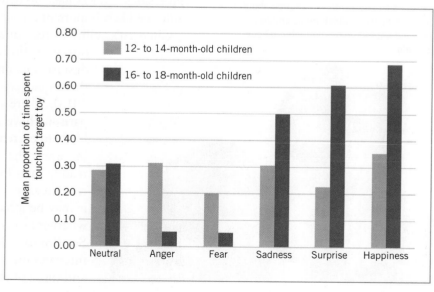

FIGURE 10.2 Developmental change in ability to associate emotions with objects Differences by age group in proportion of time spent touching a toy that had been associated with each facial emotion. (Data from Martin et al., 2014)

more cautious and exhibited more fear when the mother's voice was fearful than when it was neutral (Mumme, Fernald, & Herrera, 1996). By 14 months of age, the emotion-related information obtained through social referencing has an effect on children's touching of the object even an hour later (Hertenstein & Campos, 2004). Children seem to be better at social referencing if they receive both vocal and facial cues of emotion from the adult, and the use of vocal cues seems to be more effective than just visual cues alone (Vaillant-Molina & Bahrick, 2012; Vaish & Striano, 2004).

By the age of 3, children in laboratory studies demonstrate a rudimentary ability to label a fairly narrow range of emotional expressions displayed in pictures or on puppets' faces (Bullock & Russell, 1985; Denham, 1986; J. A. Russell & Bullock, 1986). Young children—even 2-year-olds—are skilled at labeling happiness (usually by pointing to pictures of faces that reflect happiness; Michalson & Lewis, 1985). The ability to label anger, fear, and sadness emerges and increases in the next year or two, with the ability to label surprise and disgust gradually appearing in the late preschool and early school years (N. Eisenberg, Murphy, & Shepard, 1997; J. A. Russell & Widen, 2002; Widen & Russell, 2003, 2010a). Most children cannot label the self-conscious emotions of pride, shame, and guilt until early to mid-elementary school (Saarni et al., 2006), but the scope and accuracy of their emotion labeling improve thereafter into adolescence (Montirosso et al., 2010).

The ability to discriminate and label different emotions helps children respond appropriately to their own and others' emotions. If a child understands that he or she is experiencing guilt, for example, the child may understand the need to make amends to diminish the guilt. Similarly, a child who can see that a peer is angry can devise ways to avoid or appease that peer. In fact, children who are more skilled than their peers at labeling and interpreting others' emotions are also rated higher in social competence (Denham et al., 2003; R. S. Feldman, Philippot, & Custrini, 1991; Izard et al., 2008) and lower in behavior problems or social withdrawal (Alonso-Alberca et al., 2012; Fine et al., 2003; Schultz et al., 2001).

Children's facility for reading others' emotions can also be determined by their environments. Children who grow up in environments with violence or without adults they can trust may develop heightened awareness to emotional cues of conflict. A study of homeless, orphaned children in Sierra Leone found that they were much more likely than children living in homes with their families to detect anger in facial expressions and less likely to detect sadness (Ardizzi et al., 2015). These tendencies, sadly, are likely important aspects of self-preservation for living on the streets.

Children's ability to recognize the facial expression of disgust in others develops over time; very few children of preschool age recognize disgust, but one-third of 12- to 14-year-olds recognize it, and three-quarters of 15- to 17-year-olds do (Widen & Russell, 2013). There are cultural differences as well: cross-cultural comparisons have found that school-age French children are more likely to correctly match a disgust face to a story about a disgusting event than are American children, who in turn do so more readily than Palestinian children (Widen & Russell, 2013). The exact reason for such cultural differences is not clear, although it may be affected by the languages spoken in each culture and whether terms like "disgust" have literal translations across them. See Box 10.2 for a discussion of emotional intelligence and some interventions to help children better understand their emotions and those of others.

The ability to read peers' facial expressions provides children with information about a peer's motives, which helps children respond appropriately in a potential conflict situation.

ISTOCK / GETTY IMAGES

BOX 10.2 | a closer look

EMOTIONAL INTELLIGENCE

Cognitive intelligence, as discussed in Chapter 8, refers to the ability to reason about, learn from, and remember verbal or visual information. **Emotional intelligence** refers to an individual's ability to cognitively process information about emotions and to use that information to guide both their thoughts and behaviors (Mayer, Roberts, & Barsade, 2008). Importantly, emotional intelligence involves the ability to understand one's own emotions as well as the emotions of others, as perceived through their facial expressions, body movements, and verbal tone.

To measure emotional intelligence in children and adolescents, researchers typically ask participants to respond to direct statements about themselves and their abilities. For example, one commonly used measure known as the Trait Emotional Intelligence Questionnaire asks adolescents to rate the truth of statements such as "I can control my anger when I want to" and "I'm good at getting along with my classmates" (Petrides et al., 2006).

Emotional intelligence has been linked to a range of positive outcomes in both childhood and adolescence. Children high in emotional intelligence are better able to manage their own emotions and are less likely to engage in aggressive behavior than are children with lower emotional intelligence (Lomas et al., 2012). A review of studies conducted in a diverse set of countries (Australia, China, Spain, Trinidad, the United Kingdom, and the United States) found that children high in emotional intelligence in adolescence have fewer mental health problems, lower risk behaviors, and better strategies for coping with stress than do children low in emotional intelligence (Resurrección, Salguero, & Ruiz-Aranda, 2014). Emotional intelligence also appears to predict these positive outcomes over and above other related factors such as self-esteem, personality, and cognitive intelligence (Resurrección et al., 2014).

Such findings have led researchers to develop interventions to promote emotional intelligence as a way of reducing aggressive and antisocial behavior. One intervention for elementary school students, called RULER, focuses on building their emotion *recognition,* emotion *understanding,* emotion *labeling,* and emotion *expression* and *regulation* (Rivers et al., 2012). An experimental study in New York City found that students in classrooms randomly assigned to participate in the RULER program were observed to be more emotionally supportive and respectful of others' perspectives than were those in the control classrooms (Rivers et al., 2012).

Another intervention for middle and high school students in Spain focuses on enhancing aspects of emotional intelligence, such as perceiving emotions in others and being aware of how emotions influence thought processes. For example, one activity uses emotionally laden music, poems, and short stories as a springboard for a discussion of the role and usefulness of emotion in daily life (Castillo et al., 2013). In an experimental evaluation, students who participated in the intervention engaged in less verbal and physical aggression and reported fewer mental health problems than did students not in the program (Castillo et al., 2013; Salguero, Palomera, & Fernández-Berrocal, 2012).

As this research shows, emotional intelligence is a helpful concept for understanding how emotion-related skills affect children's interactions with others and provides a useful target for interventions aimed at improving children's social-emotional skills and mental health.

Understanding the Causes and Dynamics of Emotion

Knowing the causes of emotions is also important for understanding one's own and others' behavior and motives (Saarni et al., 2006). It likewise is key for regulating one's own behavior and, hence, for social competence (Denham et al., 2003; Izard et al., 2008; Schultz et al., 2001). Consider, for example, a child who is being rebuffed or insulted by a friend whom the child has just bested in a game or on an exam. If the child understands that, in this situation, the friend may be lashing out not because the friend is nasty but because the friend feels threatened and inadequate, the child may be much better able to control his or her own response.

Various studies have shown rapid development over the preschool and school years in children's understanding of the kinds of emotions that certain situations tend to evoke in others. In a typical study of this understanding, children are told short stories about characters in situations such as having a birthday party or losing a pet. Children are then asked how the character in the story feels. By age 3, children are quite good at identifying situations that make people feel happy.

emotional intelligence ■ the ability to cognitively process information about emotions and to use that information to guide both thought and behavior

At age 4, they are fairly accurate at identifying situations that make people sad (Borke, 1971; Denham & Couchoud, 1990), and by age 5, they can identify situations likely to elicit anger, fear, or surprise (N. Eisenberg et al., 1997; Widen & Russell, 2010b).

Children's ability to understand the circumstances that evoke self-conscious social emotions such as pride, guilt, shame, embarrassment, and jealousy often emerges after age 7. Researchers have found these abilities to be similar across school-age children (ages 5 to 14) from industrialized countries (England and the Netherlands) and from a remote Himalayan village (P. L. Harris et al., 1987). From age 4 until at least age 10, children are generally better at identifying emotions from stories depicting the cause of an emotion than from pictures of facial expressions such as fear, disgust, embarrassment, and shame (an exception is for surprise) (Widen & Russell, 2010a). This is probably because facial expressions of emotions such as anger, fear, sadness, and disgust are often interpreted as indicating more than one emotion (Widen & Naab, 2012).

Another way to assess children's understanding of the causes of emotions is to record what they say about emotions in their everyday conversations and to ask them to discuss and explain others' emotions. In this kind of research, even 28-month-olds mention emotions such as happiness, sadness, anger, and fear in appropriate ways during their conversations (e.g., "You sad, Daddy?" or "Don't be mad"), and sometimes they even mention the causes of those emotions (e.g., "Santa will be happy if I pee in the potty" or "Grandma mad. I wrote on wall") (Bretherton & Beeghly, 1982).

By age 4 to 6, children can give accurate explanations for why their peers expressed negative emotions in their preschool (e.g., because they were teased or lost the use of a toy) (Fabes et al., 1988). Children get more skilled at explaining the causes of emotion across the preschool and school years (Fabes et al., 1991; Sayfan & Lagattuta, 2009; Strayer, 1986). For example, 3rd- and 6th-graders are more likely than kindergartners to believe that someone caught being dishonest will be scared (Barden et al., 1980).

With age, children also come to understand that people can feel particular emotions brought on by reminders of past events. For instance, in one study, 3- to 5-year-olds were told stories about children who experienced a negative event and later saw reminders of that event. One story was about a girl named Mary who has a pet rabbit that lives in a typical rabbit cage. One day Mary's rabbit is chased away by a dog and is never seen again. In different versions of the story, Mary later sees one of three reminders of her loss—the culprit dog, her rabbit's cage, or a photograph of her rabbit. At this point, the children were told that Mary started to feel sad and were asked, "Why did Mary start to feel sad right now?" On stories such as these, 39% of 3-year-olds, 83% of 4-year-olds, and 100% of 5-year-olds understood that the story characters were sad because a memory cue had made them think about a previous unhappy event (Lagattuta, Wellman, & Flavell, 1997). Similarly, from ages 3 to 5, children increasingly can explain that when people are in a situation that reminds them of a past negative event, they may worry and change their behavior to avoid future negative events (Lagattuta, 2007). Understanding that memory cues can trigger emotions associated with past events helps children explain their own and others' emotional reactions in situations that in themselves seem emotionally neutral.

In the elementary school years, children become increasingly sophisticated in their understanding about how, when, and why emotions occur. For example, they become more aware of cognitive processes related to regulating emotion and of the fact that emotional intensity wanes over time. They also come to recognize that people can experience more than one emotion at the same time (P. L. Harris, 2006; Harter & Buddin, 1987; F. Pons & Harris, 2005). In addition, they increasingly understand how the mind can be used to both increase and reduce fears and that thinking positively can improve one's emotion while thinking negatively can worsen it (Bamford & Lagattuta, 2012; Sayfan & Lagattuta, 2009). At around age 10, children begin to understand emotional ambivalence and realize that people can have mixed feelings about events, others, and themselves (Donaldson & Westerman, 1986; Reissland, 1985). Taken together, these developments allow children to better understand the complexities of emotional experience in context.

Understanding Real and False Emotions

An important component in the development of emotional understanding is the realization that the emotions people express do not necessarily reflect their true feelings. The beginnings of this realization are seen in 3-year-olds' occasional (and usually transparent) attempts to mask their negative emotions when they receive a disappointing gift or prize (P. M. Cole, 1986). By age 5, children's understanding of false emotion has improved considerably; in one study, a group of 3- to 5-year-olds were presented with stories that involved children feeling emotions, such as the following:

> Michelle is sleeping over at her cousin Johnny's house today. Michelle forgot her favorite teddy bear at home. Michelle is really sad.... But, she doesn't want Johnny to see how sad she is because Johnny will call her a baby. So, Michelle tries to hide how she feels.
>
> (M. Banerjee, 1997)

After the children were questioned to ensure that they understood each story, they were presented with illustrations of various emotional expressions and given instructions such as, "Show me the picture for how Michelle really feels" and "Show me the picture for how Michelle will try to look on her face." Although only half of 3- and 4-year-olds chose the appropriate pictures for four or more of the stories, more than 80% of 5-year-olds chose correctly (M. Banerjee, 1997). These findings suggest that the younger children did not appreciate that someone could express one emotion while feeling another, whereas the older children did. Studies with both Japanese and Western children also confirm that between 4 and 6 years of age, children increasingly understand that people can be misled by others' facial expressions (D. Gardner et al., 1988; D. Gross & Harris, 1988).

Part of the improvement in understanding false emotion involves a growing understanding of **display rules,** which are a social or cultural group's informal norms about when, where, and how much one should show emotions, as well as when and where displays of emotion should be suppressed or masked by displays of other emotions (Saarni, 1979). Display rules sometimes require that children express an emotion that is not matched with their felt emotion. The two main strategies for engaging in display rules are simulating an emotion (such as pretending to love an aunt's cooking) and masking an emotion (such as pretending not to be afraid of an approaching bully). Displaying context-appropriate emotion and avoiding uncontrolled emotions are key to successful social interactions (Saarni et al., 2006).

Children as young as 1½ years of age can recognize exaggerated and fake emotional displays (Walle & Campos, 2014). Over the preschool and elementary school years, children develop a more refined understanding of when and why

display rules ■ a social group's informal norms about when, where, and how much one should show emotions and when and where displays of emotion should be suppressed or masked by displays of other emotions

display rules are used (M. Banerjee, 1997; Rotenberg & Eisenberg, 1997; Saarni, 1979). With age, children also better understand that people tend to break eye contact and avert their gaze when lying, and they are increasingly able to use this knowledge to conceal their own deception (McCarthy & Lee, 2009).

In order to determine how display rules develop, researchers conducting a study of 4-, 6-, and 8-year-olds in Germany devised a scenario to encourage children to fake emotions in order to win a prize (Kromm, Färber, & Holodynski, 2015). The children were shown three boxes with lids. One box had an attractive gift (e.g., a glitter tattoo), one had an unattractive gift (e.g., a broken pencil), and the third had no gift at all. The children were instructed to look in each box and then try to trick the experimenter into thinking one of the boxes *without* the attractive toy was in fact the box *with* the attractive toy; if they succeeded in tricking the experimenter, they could keep the attractive toy. In fact, the experimenter always "guessed" incorrectly, and so all children got to take home the preferred toy, but the experimenters videotaped the children's facial expressions during the task. They found that the 4-year-olds were not successful in following display rules; they were unable to mask their disappointment, and they were unable to simulate joy to trick the experimenter. Yet as Figure 10.3 shows, children became increasingly better at these two aspects of emotion display rules with age, such that nearly 60% of 8-year-olds could simulate joy to trick the experimenter and only 28% failed to mask their disappointment with the unattractive toy (Kromm et al., 2015). This study provides clear evidence that children experience a steep increase in their understanding and implementation of display rules in middle childhood.

These age-related advances in children's understanding of real versus false emotion and display rules are linked to increases in children's cognitive capacities (Flavell, 1986; P. L. Harris, 2000). However, social factors also seem to affect children's understanding of display rules. For example, 10-year-olds in Iran are more likely to report using display rules around happiness, fear, and sadness than are 10-year-olds in the Netherlands (Novin et al., 2009). In many cultures, display rules are somewhat different for males and females and reflect societal beliefs about how males and females should feel and behave (Ruble, Martin, & Berenbaum, 2006; Van Beek, Van Dolderen, & Demon Dubas, 2006). Elementary school girls in the United States, for instance, are more likely than boys to feel that openly expressing emotions such as pain is acceptable (Zeman & Garber, 1996). In some cultures, girls are also somewhat more attuned than boys to the need to inhibit emotional displays that might hurt others' feelings (P. M. Cole, 1986; Saarni, 1984). This is especially true for girls from cultures such as India, in which females are expected to be deferential and to express only socially appropriate emotions (M. S. Joshi & MacLean, 1994). These findings obviously are consistent with the gender stereotypes that girls are more likely both to try to protect others' feelings and to be more emotional than boys.

Parents' beliefs and behaviors—which often reflect cultural beliefs—likely contribute to children's understanding and use of display rules (Friedlmeier, Corapci, & Cole, 2011). As discussed later in this chapter, the emphasis placed on controlling emotional displays in Nepal varies by subculture. Correspondingly, the degree to which Nepali children report masking certain emotions varies with the degree to which mothers in different Nepali subcultures report teaching their children how to manage emotions (P. M. Cole & Tamang, 1998). Thus, children seem to be attuned to display rules that are valued in their culture or that serve an important function in the family.

FIGURE 10.3 Development of display rules Percent of children simulating joy to deceive an experimenter about an unattractive gift (successful use of display rule) and percent of children expressing their actual disappointment in the unattractive gift (a failure to mask their emotion), by age of the child. (Data from Kromm et al., 2015)

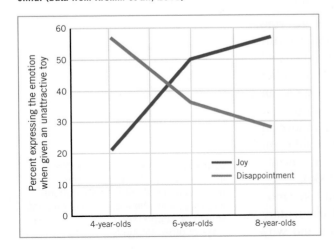

Review

Children's understanding of emotions plays an important role in their emotional functioning. Although infants can detect differences in various emotional expressions such as happiness and surprise by 3 to 4 months of age, it is not until they are about 6 months of age that they start to treat others' emotional expressions as meaningful. Around the same time, children begin to connect facial expressions of emotion or an emotional tone of voice with other events in the situation, as evidenced by their use of social referencing. By the 2nd year of life, children engage in social referencing by using their caregivers' emotions and tone of voice as a guide to understanding novel situations. By age 3, children demonstrate a rudimentary ability to label facial expressions and understand simple situations that are likely to cause happiness.

As children move through the preschool and elementary school years, their understanding of others' emotions and the situations that elicit them grows in range and complexity. In addition, they increasingly appreciate that the emotions people show may not reflect their true feelings and that display rules govern which emotions should be expressed in certain situations.

Emotion Regulation

Throughout life, being able to regulate one's emotions is crucial to successful development across domains, including cognitive and behavioral. **Emotion regulation** is a set of both conscious and unconscious processes used to both monitor and modulate emotional experiences and expressions. Emotion regulation develops gradually over the course of childhood and paves the way for success both in social interactions as well as in academic settings.

The Development of Emotion Regulation

Imagine you are an infant lying in a crib. One of your toes is caught on the inside of your pajamas and is causing pain. You are powerless to stop it—you don't know how to roll over yet and you can't talk, so you're unable to tell anyone what is happening. Your only option is to cry out in pain and frustration. Your father rushes in and picks you up and tries to figure out what's wrong. He holds you close, pats you on the back, and talks soothingly to you. You slowly calm down. There is no more pain in your toe.

When young infants are distressed, frustrated, or frightened, like the one in this scenario, there is little they can do to fix the situation. Their parents typically try to help them regulate their emotional arousal by attempting to soothe or distract them (Gianino & Tronick, 1988). For example, mothers tend to use caressing and other affectionate behavior to calm a crying 2-month-old. Over the next few months, they increasingly include vocalizations (e.g., talking, singing, "shushing") in their calming efforts, as well as in their attempts to divert the infant's attention. Holding or rocking upset young infants while talking soothingly to them seems to be the most reliable approach, and feeding them if they are not highly upset is also effective (Jahromi, Putnam, & Stifter, 2004). Thus, the emotional states of young infants are externally controlled by a process known as **co-regulation,** in which a caregiver provides the needed comfort or distraction to help the child reduce his or her distress.

emotion regulation ■ a set of both conscious and unconscious processes used to both monitor and modulate emotional experiences and expressions

co-regulation ■ the process by which a caregiver provides the needed comfort or distraction to help a child reduce his or her distress

Parents often help young children regulate themselves by physically calming them or distracting them with an object.

When distressed, many young children engage in self-soothing behaviors, such as rubbing their body, sucking a thumb, or clinging to well-loved objects such as a favorite blanket.

▶ Developing Self Control in Early Childhood

self-comforting behaviors ■ repetitive actions that regulate arousal by providing a mildly positive physical sensation

self-distraction ■ looking away from an upsetting stimulus in order to regulate one's level of arousal

As children develop in their abilities to control their own bodies and to understand their environments, they are gradually able to take control of regulating their own emotions. By 5 months of age, infants show signs of rudimentary emotion regulation in aversively arousing or uncertain situations. One strategy used by infants is known as **self-comforting behaviors,** which are repetitive actions that regulate arousal by providing a mildly positive physical sensation; examples include sucking fingers or rubbing hands together (Planalp & Braungart-Rieker, 2015). Another strategy infants use is **self-distraction,** which involves looking away from the upsetting stimulus in order to regulate their level of arousal (Ekas, Lickenbrock, & Braungart-Rieker, 2013); for instance, an infant may turn his head away from an older sibling jangling a set of keys in front of his face. Over the course of the 1st year of life, infants decrease their use of self-comforting behaviors in stressful situations and increase their use of self-distraction (Planalp & Braungart-Rieker, 2015).

These changes in children's self-regulation are at least partly due to the increasing maturation of the neurological systems—including the portion of the frontal lobes that are central to managing attention and inhibiting thought and behaviors (A. Berger, 2011; Smith et al., 2016). They are also partly due to changes in what adults expect of children. As children age, adults increasingly expect them to manage their own emotional arousal and behavior. Once children are capable of crawling, for example, they are viewed as more responsible for their behavior and for complying with parental expectations (J. J. Campos, Kermoian, & Zumbahlen, 1992). At about 9 to 12 months of age, children start to show awareness of adults' demands and begin to regulate themselves accordingly (Kopp, 1989). Their compliance grows rapidly in the 2nd year of life (Kaler & Kopp, 1990), making them increasingly likely to heed simple instructions, such as to not touch dangerous objects.

In the 2nd year of life, children also show increased ability to inhibit their motor behavior when asked to do so—such as slowing down their walking or not touching certain attractive objects (N. P. Friedman et al., 2011; Kochanska, Murray, & Harlan, 2000). Although these abilities are quite limited in the toddler years, they improve considerably by age 3 to 5 (Moilanen et al., 2009; Putnam, Gartstein, & Rothbart, 2006) and further improve in the school years and beyond (Bedard et al., 2002; B. C. Murphy et al., 1999; Sinopoli, Schachar, & Dennis, 2011).

Over the course of the early years, children develop and improve their ability to distract themselves by playing on their own when distressed. They also become less likely to seek comfort from their parents when they are upset (Bridges & Grolnick, 1995). And because of their growing ability to use language, when they are upset by parental demands, they are more likely to discuss and negotiate the situation with the parent than to engage in an emotional outburst (Campos, Frankel, & Camras, 2004; Klimes-Dougan & Kopp, 1999; Kopp, 1992). For example, if a preschooler is unhappy when told by a parent to stop playing and instead clean up his or her room, the child may verbally protest and lobby for extra playtime or work out a timetable for cleaning up rather than throwing a fit.

Children's ability to regulate their attention improves across the early years (Rueda, Posner, & Rothbart, 2011). As a result, children are increasingly able to conform to adults' expectations, such as not hurting others when angry and staying seated at school when they would much prefer to get up and talk or play with classmates. In adolescence, the neurological changes that occur in the cortex (see Chapter 3 for details) further contribute to self-regulation and other cognitive functioning. They also likely contribute to the decline in risk taking and the improvement in judgment that often occur in the transition from adolescence to young adulthood (Steinberg, 2010).

Whereas younger children regulate their emotional distress primarily by using behavioral strategies (e.g., distracting themselves with play), older children are also able to use cognitive strategies and problem solving to adjust to emotionally difficult situations (Zimmer-Gembeck & Skinner, 2011). Finding themselves caught in unpleasant or threatening circumstances, they may rethink their goals or the meaning of events so that they can adapt gracefully to the situation. This ability helps children avoid acting in ways that might be counterproductive. When older children are teased by peers, for instance, they may be able to defuse the situation by downplaying the importance of the teasing rather than reacting to it in a way that would provoke more teasing.

The Selection of Appropriate Regulatory Strategies

In dealing with emotion, children, over time, improve in their ability to select cognitive or behavioral strategies that are appropriate for the particular situation and stressor (Brenner & Salovey, 1997). One reason is that, with age, children are more aware that the appropriateness of a particular coping behavior depends on their specific needs and goals, as well as on the nature of the problem. For example, children are increasingly likely to realize that it is better to try to find alternative ways to obtain a goal rather than simply give up in frustration when their initial efforts fail (C. A. Berg, 1989). Another reason is that planning and problem-solving skills, which likely contribute to the selection and use of appropriate strategies, improve across childhood and across adolescence (Albert & Steinberg, 2011; Zimmer-Gembeck & Skinner, 2011).

Children's improving ability to use appropriate strategies for dealing with negative situations is also aided by their growing ability to distinguish between stressors that can be controlled (such as homework) and those that cannot be controlled (such as painful but necessary medical procedures). Older children, for example, are more aware than younger children that in situations they cannot control, it is easier to manage their emotion by simply adapting to the situation rather than trying to change it (e.g., Altshuler et al., 1995; Hoffner, 1993; Rudolph, Dennig, & Weisz, 1995). Faced with having to undergo major surgery, for instance, older children may adapt by trying to think about the benefits of having the surgery, such as being in better health afterward, or by distracting themselves with enjoyable activities. Younger children, in contrast, are more likely to insist that they do not need the operation.

The Relation of Emotion Regulation to Social Competence and Adjustment

As we noted earlier, the development of emotion regulation has important consequences for children, especially with regard to their social competence. **Social competence** is a set of skills that helps individuals achieve their personal goals in social interactions while maintaining positive relationships with others (Rubin, Bukowski, & Parker, 1998). A variety of studies indicate that children who have the ability to inhibit inappropriate behaviors, delay gratification, and use cognitive

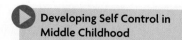
Developing Self Control in Middle Childhood

This little girl is using signs to communicate that she wants to take a nap. Children who can indicate their wants and needs with language or signs are less likely to get frustrated and to exhibit unregulated behavior.

social competence ■ the ability to achieve personal goals in social interactions while simultaneously maintaining positive relationships with others

Children who exhibit positive affect and laughter tend to be well liked by peers.

FRANCISCO VILLAFLOR / ALAMY

methods of controlling their emotion and behavior tend to be well-adjusted and liked by their peers and by adults (Diener & Kim, 2004; Doan, Fuller-Rowell, & Evans, 2012; Olson et al., 2011; see N. Eisenberg, Spinrad, & Eggum, 2010).

Moreover, children and adolescents who are able to deal constructively with stressful situations—negotiating with others to settle conflicts, planning strategies to resolve upsetting situations, seeking social support, and so on—generally are better adjusted than are children who lack these skills, including those who avoid dealing with stressful situations altogether (K. A. Blair et al., 2004; Compas et al., 2001; Jaser et al., 2007). Children who are unable to successfully regulate their emotions are at higher risk of becoming victims of bullying compared with their peers who are better at emotion regulation (Morelen, Southam-Gerow, & Zeman, 2016). Well-regulated children also do better in school than their less regulated peers do, likely because they are better able to pay attention, are better behaved and better liked by teachers and peers, and, consequently, like school better (Denham et al., 2012; Duckworth, Quinn, & Tsukayama, 2012; Ponitz et al., 2009; Rimm-Kaufman et al., 2009).

Review

Children's efforts to regulate their emotions and emotionally driven behaviors change with age. Whereas young infants must rely on adults to manage their emotions, older infants and young children increasingly regulate their own emotions and behavior through the use of self-comforting behaviors and self-distraction. Their ability to inhibit their actions also improves with age. Improvements in children's regulatory capacities likely are based on increases in brain maturation that allow them to better control their attention and their own bodies, as well as on changes in adults' expectations of them.

In contrast to young children, who often try to cope with their emotions by taking direct action, older children also are able to use cognitive modes of coping, such as focusing on positive aspects of a negative situation or trying to think about something else altogether. In addition, they are increasingly able to select and use ways of regulating themselves and coping with stress that are appropriate to the requirements of specific situations.

The abilities to regulate one's emotions and related behavior, and to deal constructively with stressful situations, are associated with high social competence and low levels of problem behavior.

Temperament

Although the overall development of emotions and emotion-regulation capabilities is roughly similar for most children, there are also very large individual differences in children's emotional functioning. Some infants and children are relatively mellow: they do not become upset easily and they usually do not have difficulty calming down when they are upset. Other children are quite emotional; they get upset quickly and intensely, and their negative emotion persists for a long time. Moreover, children differ in their timidity, in their expression of emotions, and in the ways they deal with their emotions. Compare these two 3-year-old children, Maria and Bruce, as they react to Teri, an adult female stranger:

> When Teri walks over to Maria and starts to talk with her, Maria smiles and is eager to show Teri what she is doing. When Teri asks Maria if she would like to go down the hall to the play room (where experiments are conducted), Maria jumps up and takes Teri's hand.

> In contrast, when Teri walks over to Bruce, Bruce turns away. He doesn't talk to her and averts his eyes. When Teri asks him if he wants to play a game, Bruce moves away, looks timid, and softly says "no."

> (N. Eisenberg, laboratory observations)

Children also vary in the speed with which they express their emotions, as illustrated by the differences in these two preschool boys:

> When someone crosses Taylor, his wrath is immediate. There is no question how he is feeling, no time to correct the situation before he erupts. Douglas, though, seems almost to consider the ongoing emotional situation. One can almost see annoyance building until he finally sputters, "Stop that!"

> (Denham, 1998, p. 21)

Such differences in how individual children react to similar situations led researchers to develop the concept of temperament. **Temperament** refers to individual differences in emotion, activity level, and attention that are exhibited across contexts and that are present from infancy; thus, they are thought to be genetically based (Bornstein et al., 2015). As we will see below, the temperament of any given child is influenced both by his or her genes and by the environment in which he or she lives; therefore, the construct of temperament is highly relevant to our themes of *individual differences* and the role of *nature and nurture* in development.

Alexander Thomas and Stella Chess are the pioneers of temperament research (Thomas & Chess, 1977; Thomas, Chess, & Birch, 1968). They began by interviewing a sample of parents, repeatedly and in depth, about their infants' specific behaviors. To reduce the possibility of bias in the parents' reports, the researchers asked that instead of interpretive characterizations, such as "he's often cranky" or "she's interested in everything," the parents provide detailed descriptions of their infant's specific behaviors. On the basis of those interviews, nine characteristics of children were identified, including their mood, adaptability, activity level, attention span, and persistence. Further analyzing the interview results in terms of these characteristics, the researchers classified the infants into three groups:

1. *Easy babies* adjusted readily to new situations, quickly established daily routines such as sleeping and eating, and generally were cheerful in mood and easy to calm.

2. *Difficult babies* were slow to adjust to new experiences, tended to react negatively and intensely to novel stimuli and events, and were irregular in their daily routines and bodily functions.

3. *Slow-to-warm-up babies* were somewhat difficult at first but became easier over time as they had repeated contact with new objects, people, and situations.

temperament ■ individual differences in emotion, activity level, and attention that are exhibited across contexts and that are present from infancy and thus thought to be genetically based

 Temperament in Infancy and Toddlerhood

Due partly to variations in temperament, children often show very different reactions to the same situation.

ALFRED EISENSTAEDT / TIME LIFE PICTURES / GETTY IMAGES

Who could resist this toddler? Children whose temperaments are happy and agreeable are likely to elicit more positive reactions from adults than children who are highly irritable.

In the initial study, 40% of the infants were classified as easy, 10% as difficult, and 15% as slow-to-warm-up. The rest did not fit into one of these categories. Of particular importance, some dimensions of temperament showed relative stability within children over time, with temperament in infancy predicting how children were doing years later. For example, "difficult" infants tended to have problems with adjustment at home and at school, whereas few of the "easy" children had such problems.

Measuring Temperament

Since the groundbreaking efforts of Thomas and Chess, researchers studying temperament no longer group children into categories such as easy, difficult, or slow-to-warm up, which reflects what is known as a *between-person* approach to understanding development. Rather, researchers now characterize every child along the same set of dimensions of temperament—a *within-person* approach to understanding development. According to this new approach, every child has some level of each dimension of temperament. Not all researchers agree on exactly how many dimensions of temperament there are; however, one of the leading experts in this area, Mary Rothbart, has identified five key dimensions of temperament: fear, distress/anger/frustration, attention span, activity level, and smiling and laughter (Gartstein & Rothbart, 2003; Rothbart et al., 2001). She has created measures of temperament in both infancy (the Infant Behavior Questionnaire) and early childhood (the Child Behavior Questionnaire) that ask parents, teachers, or observers to rate each child along several dimensions of temperament (Gartstein & Rothbart, 2003; Rothbart et al., 2001). These measures ask parents, teachers, or observers to indicate how well a range of statements describes the target child. The participants are then asked to respond to several items about each dimension of temperament; then their responses are averaged together so that each child gets a score reflecting how high or low he or she rates on that dimension. Table 10.2 presents examples

TABLE 10.2

Measuring Infant and Child Temperament: The Infant Behavior Questionnaire and the Child Behavior Questionnaire

Temperament dimension	Description	Infant Behavior Questionnaire (for ages 0 to 12 months) Sample items in measure for infants (aged 0 to 12 months), rated from 1 (never) to 7 (always)	Child Behavior Questionnaire (for ages 3 to 7) Sample items in measure for children (aged 3 to 7), rated from 1 (extremely untrue of your child) to 7 (extremely true of your child)
Fear	Tendency to experience unease, worry, or nervousness to novel or potentially threatening situations	"How often during the last week did the baby startle to a sudden or loud noise?"	"My child is not afraid of large dogs and/or other animals" (reversed for scoring).
Distress at limitations (infant) or anger/frustration (in childhood)	Negative emotional response related to having ongoing task interrupted or blocked	"When placed on his/her back, how often did the baby fuss or protest?"	"My child has temper tantrums when s/he doesn't get what s/he wants."
Attention span	Attention to an object or task for an extended period of time	"How often during the last week did the baby stare at a mobile, crib bumper, or picture for 5 minutes or longer?"	"When picking up toys or other jobs, my child usually keeps at the task until it's done."
Activity level	Rate and extent of gross motor body movements	"When put into the bath water, how often did the baby splash or kick?"	"My child seems always in a big hurry to get from one place to another."
Smiling and laughter	Positive emotional response to a change in the intensity, complexity, or incongruity of a stimulus	"How often during the last week did the baby smile or laugh when given a toy?"	"My child laughs a lot at jokes and silly happenings."

Information from the Revised Infant Behavior Questionnaire (Gartstein & Rothbart, 2003) and the Child Behavior Questionnaire (Rothbart et al., 2001).

of these items for each of these two measures of temperament. Ratings of temperament tend to be fairly stable over time and to predict later development in such areas as behavioral problems, anxiety disorders, and social competence (A. Berger, 2011; Rothbart, 2011; Rothbart & Bates, 2006).

In addition to measuring temperament through the use of rating scales, researchers also use physiological measures of emotional reactions to laboratory situations to assess temperament. For example, researchers have found that children with different temperaments exhibit differences in the variability of their heart rate (Kagan, 1998; Kagan & Fox, 2006). Heart-rate variability—how much an individual's heart rate normally fluctuates—is believed to reflect, in part, the way the central nervous system responds to novel situations and the individual's ability to regulate emotion (Porges, 2007; Porges, Doussard-Roosevelt, & Maiti, 1994). Another commonly used physiological measure of temperament is electroencephalographic recordings (see Chapter 3) of frontal-lobe activity. Activation of the left frontal lobe of the cortex as measured with an electroencephalogram (EEG) has been associated with approach behavior, positive affect, exploration, and sociability.

In contrast, activation of the right frontal lobe has been linked to withdrawal, a state of uncertainty, fear, and anxiety (Kagan & Fox, 2006). When confronted with novel stimuli, situations, or challenges, infants and children who show greater right frontal activation on the EEG are more likely to react with anxiety and avoidance (Calkins, Fox, & Marshall, 1996; Kagan & Fox, 2006), whereas individuals who show left frontal activation are more likely to exhibit a relaxed, often happy mood and an eagerness to engage in new experiences or challenges (Kagan & Fox, 2006; L. K. White et al., 2012).

The key advantage of parents' reports of temperament is that parents have extensive knowledge of their children's behavior in many different situations. One important disadvantage of this method is that parents may not always be objective in their observations, as suggested by the fact that their reports sometimes do not correspond with what is found with laboratory measures (Rothbart & Bates, 2006). Another disadvantage is that many parents do not have wide knowledge of other children's behavior to use as a basis for comparison when reporting on their own children (what is irritability to some parents, for example, may be near-placidness to others). In contrast, the key advantage of laboratory observational data is that such data are less likely to be biased than is an adult's personal view of the child. A key disadvantage is that children's behavior usually is observed in only a limited set of circumstances. Consequently, laboratory observational measures may reflect a child's mood or behavior at a given moment, in a particular context, rather than reflecting the child's general temperament. No measure of temperament is perfect, and it is prudent to assess temperament with a variety of different methods (Rothbart & Bates, 2006).

Temperament is considered to be relatively consistent across time and across situations. Using parents' ratings on the Infant Behavior Questionnaire, one study found that an infant's level on each dimension of temperament is considerably stable across the 1st year of life, but that there is some evidence of change over time as well (Bornstein et al., 2015). Across early childhood, children who are prone to more anger and distress than their peers at age 3 tend to be more angry and distressed than their peers at ages 6 and 8 (Guerin & Gottfried, 1994; Rothbart, Derryberry, & Hershey, 2000); those prone to display happiness remain relatively happy across the same age range (Durbin et al., 2007; Sallquist et al., 2009). But that is not to say that temperament is entirely immutable—it can and does change over time. Children aged 3 to 6 have much more stable temperaments than do children 0 to 3 (Roberts & DelVecchio, 2000). There is now evidence that some aspects of temperament may not emerge until childhood or adolescence and may change considerably at different ages (Saudino & Wang, 2012; Shiner et al., 2012). Changes in when and how much temperament is expressed at different ages likely occur because genes switch on and off throughout development, so there are changes in the degree to which behaviors are affected by genes (Saudino & Wang, 2012).

Determinants of Temperament

Temperament is believed to have a strong basis in biology and genetics (Saudino & Wang, 2012). Evidence for a genetic component to temperament comes from dozens of studies. For example, identical twins are more similar to each other in these aspects of their emotion and regulation than are fraternal twins (Rasbash et al., 2011; Saudino & Wang, 2012). Recent studies have shown connections between an individual's genes and aspects of temperament such as self-regulatory capacity (Depue & Fu, 2012; Goldsmith, Pollak, & Davidson, 2008; Saudino & Wang, 2012). For example, genes related to the functioning of dopamine and other neurotransmitters that affect voluntary attentional processes (executive attention) appear to be especially relevant for self-regulation (Posner, Rothbart, & Sheese, 2007).

Although genes are clearly important for temperament, the environment does play a role as well, even from before birth. In Chapter 2, we learned about teratogens, which are external agents that can cause birth defects in a fetus. Teratogens such as nutritional deficiencies, exposure to cocaine, or maternal stress and anxiety during pregnancy have each been found to predict infants' and young children's temperament-based abilities to regulate their attention and behavior (Huizink, 2008, 2012; T. Dennis et al., 2006). As children age, the behaviors of their parents become a strong influence on temperament. Children who grow up in home environments that are harsh or unstable tend to have problems with self-regulation and the expression of emotion (E. E. Lewis et al., 2007). Warm and responsive parenting can have the opposite effect; in a twin study, the twin who received more warm and responsive parenting had fewer emotional problems and exhibited more positive affect and more prosocial behaviors than their twin sibling (Deater-Deckard et al., 2001).

Yet, as suggested by the *active child* theme, children's temperamental characteristics can affect their environments and particularly their parents' behaviors (Belsky, Bakermans-Kranenburg, & van IJzendoorn,, 2007; N. Eisenberg et al., 1999; K. J. Kim et al., 2001; E. H. Lee et al., 2013). For example, parents of angry, unregulated children may eventually become less patient and more punitive with their children; in turn, this intensification of discipline may cause their children to become even more angry and unregulated. Alternatively, children who are high in regulation and in sociability may elicit more warmth from parents, which in turn predicts continued regulation and sociability in children. Thus, temperament plays a role in the development of children's social and psychological adjustment, but that role is complex and varies as a function of the child's social environment and the degree to which a child represents a challenge to the parent (Ganiban et al., 2011).

To determine whether genes or the environment have more influence over temperament, a group of researchers (Lemery-Chalfant et al., 2013) used a twin study, which is a research design we learned about in Chapter 3. In this study, parents of 807 pairs of twins (301 monozygotic [identical], 263 same-sex dizygotic [fraternal], and 243 opposite-sex dizygotic) reported on both of their children's temperaments, and then statistical analyses were used to determine how similar the twins were. If monozygotic twins in the same home environment were more similar than dizygotic twins who shared the same home environment, then they would conclude that temperament is more determined by genes than the environment.

Indeed, that is what they found—a large portion of the variance in three aspects of temperament (effortful control, negative affectivity, and extraversion) was explained by heritability (Lemery-Chalfant et al., 2013). They also found that key aspects of the home environments, namely how chaotic and unsafe they were, had a heritable component as well—parents' temperaments affected children both directly through genetic transmission and indirectly through the home environment they created (Lemery-Chalfant et al., 2013). This latter contribution of genes to children's temperament is referred to as a passive gene–environment correlation, a concept discussed in Chapter 8 with regard to the heritability of intelligence. Undoubtedly, a combination of genetic and environmental factors jointly contributes to individual differences in children's emotions and related behaviors (C. S. Barr, 2012; Rasbash et al., 2011; Saudino & Wang, 2012).

The Role of Temperament in Social Skills and Maladjustment

One of the reasons for researchers' interest in temperament is that it plays an important role in determining children's social adjustment. Consider a boy who is prone to anger and has difficulty controlling this emotion. Compared with other boys, he is likely to sulk, yell at others, and be defiant with adults and aggressive with peers. Such behaviors often lead to long-term adjustment problems. Consequently, it is not surprising that where children fall on such dimensions of temperament as anger/irritability, positive emotion, and the ability to inhibit behavior is closely linked with their social competence and maladjustment (Coplan & Bullock, 2012; Eiden et al., 2009; N. Eisenberg et al., 2010; Kagan, 2012; Kochanska et al., 2008). For example, children who are too inhibited are more likely than other children to have problems such as anxiety, depression, and social withdrawal at older ages (Biederman et al., 1990; Fox & Pine, 2012; Hirshfeld-Becker et al., 2007; Moffitt et al., 2007). Different problems with adjustment seem to be associated with different temperaments.

The links between early temperament and later behavior are highlighted by a large longitudinal study conducted in New Zealand by Caspi and colleagues. These researchers found that participants who were angrier and more unregulated as young children tended as adolescents or young adults to have more problems with adjustment, such as not getting along with others, than did peers with different temperaments. They were also more likely to engage in illegal behaviors and to get in trouble with the law (Caspi et al., 1995; Caspi & Silva, 1995; B. Henry et al., 1996). At age 21, they reported getting along less well with whomever they

Children high in the anger or irritability dimensions of temperament are more likely to be defiant with adults.

goodness of fit ■ the degree to which an individual's temperament is compatible with the demands and expectations of his or her social environment

differential susceptibility ■ a circumstance in which the same temperament characteristic that puts some children at high risk for negative outcomes when exposed to a harsh home environment also causes them to blossom when their home environment is positive

were sharing living quarters (e.g., roommates) and reported being unemployed more often. They also tended to have few people from whom they could draw social support (Caspi, 2000) and were prone to emotions like anxiety (Caspi et al., 2003). At age 32, they had poorer physical health and personal resources, greater substance dependence, more criminal offenses, and more problems with gambling (Moffitt et al., 2011; Slutske et al., 2012). Children with moderate levels on each dimension of temperament and who were thus considered well-adjusted in early childhood were most likely to continue to be doing well in adulthood, with no increased risk for problem behavior or mental health disorder (Caspi, 2000; Slutske et al., 2012).

The effect of temperament on behavior is clearly illustrated in the reactions that different children can have to the same situation. For example, imagine two 4-year-old boys arrive at a loud and chaotic birthday party. The child who has a high activity level will immediately join in, whereas the child high in fearfulness will observe from the perimeter before finding a way to play with the other children. The high activity child is in his element; the high fearfulness child is decidedly not. How well a child's temperament matches the demands of a particular context is called **goodness of fit**.

The family provides arguably the most important context for issues related to goodness of fit. Research indicates that children who are impulsive or low in emotion regulation seem to have more problems and are less sympathetic to others if exposed to hostile, intrusive, and/or negative parenting rather than to supportive parenting (Hastings & De, 2008; Kiff, Lengua, & Zalewski, 2011; Lengua et al., 2008; Valiente et al., 2004; see also Rothbart & Bates, 2006). Similarly, children prone to emotions such as anger are more likely to have behavioral problems such as aggression if exposed to hostile parenting or low levels of positive parenting (Calkins, 2002; Lengua, 2008; Mesman et al., 2009; Morris et al., 2002; see also Bates, Schermerhorn, & Petersen, 2012, for a review). A study in Canada found that children whose parents rated them as high in shyness had fewer problems with peers and fewer emotional problems if their mothers were high in warmth (Coplan, Arbeau, & Armer, 2008).

It is important to note, however, that some children's temperaments make them highly reactive to both positive and negative family environments. These children exhibit a characteristic known as **differential susceptibility,** which means that the same temperament characteristic that puts some children at high risk for negative outcomes when exposed to a harsh home environment also causes them to blossom when their home environments are positive (Belsky & Pluess, 2009). For example, children with impulsive temperaments have been found to exhibit high levels of behavior problems in adolescence if they are raised in harsh family environments; but if raised in positive family environments, they exhibit low levels of behavior problems (Rioux et al., 2016b).

Children with such susceptible, or highly responsive, temperaments have been described as "orchids" who thrive when conditions are good but wither when they are bad. In contrast, children who are less sensitive to their environments and do well in all but the most high-risk environments are thought of as "dandelions" (Boyce & Ellis, 2005). Although evidence for differential susceptibility has been found in several longitudinal studies (Rioux et al., 2016a), it is also the case that all children benefit from positive parenting environments regardless of whether their genetic and temperamental characteristics make them likely to be reactive to their environments (Belsky et al., 2015).

Review

Temperament refers to individual differences in various aspects of children's emotional reactivity, regulation, and other characteristics such as behavioral inhibition and activity level. Although many dimensions of temperament have been identified, researchers have not agreed on exactly how many dimensions there are. Some of the commonly accepted dimensions are fearfulness, attention, anger/frustration, and activity level. Temperament is believed to have a genetic basis, but it is also affected by experiences in the environment, particularly the type of parenting children receive. Temperament tends to be stable over time and across situations, although the degree of its stability varies depending on the quality of the environment.

Temperament plays an important role in adjustment and maladjustment. Children high on problematic dimensions of temperament, such as anger and inattention, are more likely to exhibit problem behaviors, whereas children low on these dimensions will not. Similarly, children high in fearfulness will have difficulty in new situations while children low in fearfulness will not. The goodness of fit between a child's temperament and his or her environment is an important determinant of future behavior. Children whose temperaments put them at risk for poor adjustment often do well if they receive sensitive and appropriate parenting and if there is a good fit between their temperament and their social environment.

The Role of Family in Emotional Development

As children's primary environment during the early stages of emotional development, families in general and parents in particular have an important influence on how children interpret and respond to emotions in others, as well as on how they interpret and regulate their own emotions. Some of the ways that parents affect emotional development are implicit, such as through the quality of their relationships with their children and their own expressions of emotion to their children; others are more explicit, such as parents' reactions to their children's emotions and their explicit teaching of emotion display rules.

Quality of Parent–Child Relationships

The parent–child relationship influences children's sense of security and how they feel about themselves and other people (R. A. Thompson, 2015; see Chapter 11 for more detail on this relationship). In turn, these feelings affect children's tendencies to express certain emotions. For instance, children who are *securely attached*—who have high-quality, trusting relationships with their parents—tend to show more happiness and less social anxiety and anger than do children who are *insecurely attached*—that is, whose relationships with their parents are low in trust and support (e.g., Bohlin, Hagekull, & Rydell, 2000; Borelli et al., 2010; Kochanska, 2001). Securely attached children also tend to be more open and honest in their expression of emotion (Becker-Stoll, Delius, & Scheitenberger, 2001; Zimmermann et al., 2001), as well as more advanced in their understanding of emotion (Steele, Steele, & Croft, 2008)—perhaps because their parents are more likely to discuss feelings and other mental states with them (McElwain, Booth-LaForce, & Wu, 2011; McQuaid et al., 2007; Raikes & Thompson, 2006). This enhanced understanding of emotion is likely to help these children recognize when and how to regulate their emotion. A longitudinal study in Israel further demonstrated the links between parent–child relationships and children's emotional development. The more children have mutually responsive relationships with their parents, the better those children are at emotion regulation—and vice versa (Feldman, 2015).

Parents' Expression of Emotion

Parents' expressions of emotion have been shown to influence children's views about themselves and others in their social world (Dunsmore & Halberstadt, 1997). For example, children exposed to high levels of anger and hostility from their parents may come to view themselves as individuals who anger people and may eventually believe that most people are hostile. In addition, parents' expression of emotion provides children with a model of when and how to express emotion (Denham, Zoller, & Couchoud, 1994; Dunn & Brown, 1994). This modeling also may affect children's understanding of what types of emotional expressions are appropriate and effective in interpersonal relations (Halberstadt et al., 1995; Morris et al., 2007). In families in which parents tend not to express emotions, children may get the message that emotions are basically bad and should be avoided or inhibited (Gottman, Katz, & Hooven, 1997). Finally, the parental emotions to which children are exposed may affect their general level of distress and arousal in social interactions, in turn affecting their ability to process important information about the interactions (e.g., others' verbal and nonverbal cues) that would help them moderate their behavior (N. Eisenberg, Cumberland, & Spinrad, 1998; M. L. Hoffman, 2000).

Whatever the underlying reason, it is clear that the consistent and open expression of emotions in the home is associated with children's emotional expressions as well as their behavior. In a review of studies, Halberstadt and colleagues found that when positive emotions like happiness are prevalent in the home, children tend to express happiness themselves. These children in turn are socially skilled, well-adjusted, low in aggression, able to understand others' emotions, and typically high in self-esteem (Halberstadt & Eaton, 2003; see also Barry & Kochanska, 2010; Brophy-Herb et al., 2011; McCoy & Raver, 2011).

In contrast, when negative emotions such as anger are prevalent in the home, especially when they are intense, children tend to exhibit low levels of social competence and to experience and express negative emotion themselves, including depression and anxiety (Crockenberg & Langrock, 2001; N. Eisenberg et al., 2001; Raval & Martini, 2011; Stocker et al., 2007). Even when the conflict and anger in the home is not directed at the children, there is an increased likelihood that they will develop anger, behavior problems, and deficits in social competence and self-regulation (Grych & Fincham, 1997; Kouros, Cummings, & Davies, 2010; Rhoades, 2008; Rhoades et al., 2011). These outcomes are also more likely when children are exposed to high levels of parental depression (Blandon et al., 2008; Cicchetti & Toth, 2006; Downey & Coyne, 1990), perhaps in part because children of depressed parents are especially attentive to expressions of sadness in others (Lopez-Duran et al., 2013).

Parents' failure to express emotion, particularly in situations where children expect some kind of emotional reaction, can also influence

Children who are exposed to relatively high levels of positive emotion in the family tend to express more positive emotion and are more socially skilled and better adjusted than children who are exposed to high levels of negative emotion.

JACK HOLLINGSWORTH / GETTY IMAGES

children's emotional development. In the 1970s, Edward Tronick and his colleagues developed an experimental procedure known as the Still-Face Paradigm (Tronick et al., 1978). For this procedure, mothers and their infants, usually around 4 months of age, are brought into the laboratory; the infants are strapped in a highchair and the mothers are seated a foot and a half away, where they can easily interact with their infants. Mothers in the control group are instructed by the experimenters to play with their child for 10 minutes. Mothers in the experimental group first are instructed to play normally for 2 minutes with their baby; then, they are told to sit back in their chair, maintain a neutral expression, and not talk to, touch, or otherwise react to their baby—in other words, to keep a "still face." After 2 minutes, they again alternate another play episode with a still-face episode, before concluding with a final play episode.

What is remarkable about the findings from this research is how quickly the infants become distressed when their mothers do not express emotion or react to the infants' emotional expressions. The accompanying photos show the change in the infant's emotions and behavior from a play episode to a still-face episode; remember that each episode is only two minutes long! Using data from a recent study (DiCorcia et al., 2016), Figure 10.4 compares the amount of time in each episode the infants looked at their mothers or expressed distress; infants show a steep decrease in the time spent looking at their mothers during the still-face episodes, which is a clear example of infants using the self-distraction method. The infants' emotional distress increases during the still-face episodes, with a more intense distress reaction occurring in the second still-face episode. These results illustrate that even at a few months of age, infants are attuned to their mothers' emotional expressions and behaviors and experience distress when their mothers do not react as they have come to expect.

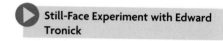

Still-Face Experiment with Edward Tronick

Parents' Socialization of Children's Emotional Responses

In addition to being affected by the overall parent–child relationship, children's emotional development is influenced by parents'

LOVETT STORIES + STRATEGIES

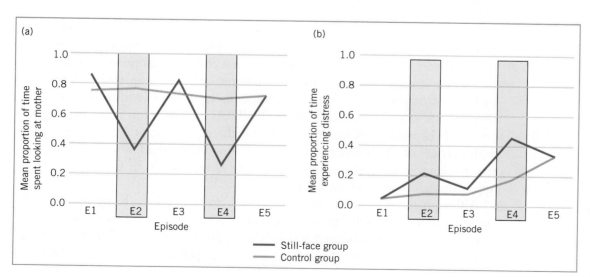

FIGURE 10.4 Children's reactions to mothers' still faces An infant happily interacting with her mother (top panel of photo series) quickly becomes distressed when the mother keeps a still face and does not interact with the infant (bottom panel). The two graphs highlight the episodes when mothers kept a still face in the experimental condition; mothers in the control condition continued to play with their babies normally across all episodes. Infants significantly reduce the time they spend looking at their mothers during still-face episodes and increase their expressions of negative affect. (Data from DiCorcia et al., 2015)

emotion socialization ■ the process through which children acquire the values, standards, skills, knowledge, and behaviors that are regarded as appropriate for their present and future role in their particular culture

emotion socialization of their children—that is, the direct and indirect influence that parents have on their children's standards, values, and ways of thinking and feeling. Parents socialize their children's emotional development through their reactions to their children's expression of emotion and through the discussions they have with their children about emotion and emotional regulation. These avenues of socialization, which are often interrelated, can affect not only children's emotional development but also their social competence (J. K. Baker, Fenning, & Crnic, 2011; Thompson, 2015).

Parents' Reactions to Children's Emotions

Parents' reactions to their children's emotions influence the children's own tendencies to express emotions, as well as their social competence and adjustment. Consider, for example, the different parental messages conveyed in the following two instances:

> Jeremy . . . watched the movie *Jaws,* against his mother's better judgment. He fearfully, animatedly asked many questions about the movie afterwards, and anxiously discussed it in great detail (e.g., "What was that red stuff?"). His mother and father answered all the questions and supported him as he resolved these things in his mind. Jeremy's emotions were accepted, and he was able to regulate them, as well as to learn about what makes things "scary."
>
> (Denham, 1998, p. 106)

> Scott's parents, who are punitive socializers, show disregard and even contempt when his best friend moves away. These parents tease Scott for his tender feelings, so that in the end he is let down not only by the disappearance of his friend, but by their reactions as well. . . . [H]e is very lonely and still feels very bad.
>
> (Denham, 1998, p. 120)

Parents who, like Scott's, dismiss or criticize their children's expressions of sadness and anxiety communicate to their children that their feelings are not valid. Parents send similar messages when they react to their children's anger with threats, belligerence, or dismissive comments. In turn, their children are likely to be less emotionally and socially competent than are children whose parents are emotionally supportive. They tend, for example, to be lower in sympathy for others, less skilled at coping with stress, and more prone to express anger and to engage in problem behaviors such as aggression (N. Eisenberg, Fabes, & Murphy, 1996; Engle & McElwain, 2011; Luebbe, Kiel, & Buss, 2011; Lunkenheimer, Shields, & Cortina, 2007; J. Snyder, Stoolmiller et al., 2003).

In contrast, parents who are supportive when their children are upset help their children regulate their emotional arousal and find ways to express their emotions constructively. This process can start early in a child's development. In the !Kung San hunter-gatherer community of Botswana, mothers keep their infants close by for the first years of their lives and respond very quickly (within 10 seconds) to their infants' cries (Kruger & Konner, 2010). As a result, even at the peak age for crying (1–12 weeks), !Kung infants cry for the equivalent of 1 minute per hour, with only 6% of all observed crying bouts lasting longer than 30 seconds; compare this tendency with Western newborns who, as we learned in Chapter 2, cry for approximately 8 minutes per hour.

Although not all parents can be as quick to respond as !Kung mothers, the more mothers acknowledge and respond contingently to their children's emotions, the more their children feel validated. In turn, these children tend to be better adjusted and more competent with their peers and to perform better in school (Klimes-Dougan et al., 2007; Raval & Martini, 2011). Supportive parental reactions may be especially helpful in reducing problem behaviors for those children who have difficulty regulating their physiological responses to challenges (Hastings & De, 2008).

Another striking example of cultural influences in emotional socialization is provided by the Tamang in rural Nepal. The Tamang are Buddhists who place great value on keeping one's *sem* (mind–heart) calm and clear of emotion, and they believe that people should not express anger because it has disruptive effects on interpersonal relationships. Consequently, although Tamang parents are responsive to the distress of infants, they often ignore or scold children older than age 2 when those children express anger, and they seldom offer explanations or support to reduce children's anger. Such parental reactions are not typical of all Nepali groups, however; for instance, parents of Brahman Nepali children respond to children's anger with reasoning and yielding.

Of particular interest is the fact that although nonsupportive parental behavior comparable to that of the Tamang has been associated with low social competence in U.S. children, it does not seem to have a negative effect on the social competence of Tamang children. Because of the value placed on controlling the expression of emotion in Tamang culture, parental behaviors that would seem dismissive and punitive to American parents likely take on a different meaning for Tamang parents and children and probably have different consequences (P. M. Cole & Dennis, 1998; P. M. Cole et al., 2006).

Interviews with children in remote villages in Nepal allowed Pamela Cole and her colleagues to examine how Buddhist and Hindu values contribute to children's understanding of emotion.

Parents' Discussion of Emotion

Family conversations about emotion are therefore an important aspect of children's emotional socialization. By discussing emotions with their children, parents teach them about the meanings of emotions, the circumstances in which they should and should not be expressed, and the consequences of expressing or not expressing them (N. Eisenberg et al., 1998; LaBounty et al., 2008; R. A. Thompson, 2006). An additional help in emotional socialization is *emotion coaching,* in which parents not only discuss emotions with their children but also help them learn ways to cope with their emotions and express them appropriately (Gottman et al., 1997; Power, 2004). Children who receive this type of guidance tend to display better emotional understanding than children who do not.

A longitudinal study by Judy Dunn and her colleagues found, for example, that the degree to which children are exposed to, and participate in, discussions of emotions with family members at ages 2 and 3 predicts their understanding of others' emotions until at least age 6 (J. R. Brown & Dunn, 1996; Dunn, Brown, & Beardsall, 1991; Dunn, Brown et al., 1991). In two similar studies, mothers' references to their children's desires at 15 months of age predicted their children's understanding of emotions and use of emotion language at 24 months. In fact, mothers' verbal references to others' thoughts and knowledge when describing a series of pictures to their children at 24 months of age predicted children's use of emotion language and understanding of emotion at 33 months of age (Taumoepeau & Ruffman, 2006, 2008). Indeed, in these same two studies, as well as in another (Ensor & Hughes, 2008), mothers' references to others' mental states predicted children's emotion understanding better than did mothers' references to emotions themselves, perhaps because references to mental states help children understand the thoughts that accompany and motivate emotional states.

Parents actively teach children about emotions through emotion coaching.

Researchers have also found that children whose parents use emotion coaching are more socially competent with peers, more empathic, and less likely to exhibit problem behaviors or depression than are children who do not receive such guidance (Brophy-Herb et al., 2011; Katz, Maliken, & Stettler, 2012; Stocker et al., 2007). Of course, children's own characteristics—such as their ability to sustain attention and their initial understanding of emotions—may affect the degree to which adults talk about emotion with them. For instance, in one study, parents engaged in more conversations about emotional past events with their 5- and 6-year-olds if the children were relatively well regulated and if their expression of negative emotions such as anger, sadness, or fear was consistent with what their parents expected from a child of their age (Bird, Reese, & Tripp, 2006).

Parents' ideas about the usefulness of specific emotions also vary depending on the context in which the family lives; in some contexts, emotions that typically hamper social interactions, such as anger or fear, can be adaptive. For example, in a study of African American mothers living in dangerous neighborhoods, mothers valued and promoted their daughters' readiness to express anger and aggressiveness in situations related to self-protection because they wanted their daughters to act quickly and decisively to defend themselves when necessary. One way they did this was to play-act the role of an adversary, teasing, insulting, or challenging their daughters in the midst of everyday interactions. An example of this is provided by Beth's mother, who initiated a teasing event by challenging Beth (27 months old) to fight:

> "Hahahaha, Hahaha. Hahahaha. [Provocative tone:] You wanna fight about it?" Beth laughed. Mother laughed. Mother twice reiterated her challenge and then called Beth an insulting name, "Come on, then, chicken." Beth retorted by calling her mother a chicken. The two proceeded to trade insults through the next 13 turns, in the course of which Beth marked three of her utterances with teasing singsong intonation and aimed a shaming gesture (rubbing one index finger across the other) at her mother. The climax occurred after further mock provocation from the mother, when Beth finally raised her fists (to which both responded with laughter) and rushed toward her mother for an exchange of ritual blows.
>
> (P. Miller & Sperry, 1987, pp. 20–21)

It is unlikely that mothers in a less difficult and dangerous neighborhood would encourage their children, especially their daughters, to express anger and to act aggressively. Thus, consistent with Bronfenbrenner's bioecological model (Chapter 9), the norms, values, and socioeconomic circumstances of the context in which a family lives contribute substantially to differences among families in their expression and discussion of emotion.

Cultural differences also influence which emotional expressions are encouraged or discouraged. When asked about norms for emotional expression, adults from 48 countries (3 from North America, 4 from South America, 17 from Europe, 7 from Africa, 16 from Asia, and Australia) varied widely in the extent to which they believed children should display happiness, fearfulness, or anger (Diener & Lucas, 2004). These cultural differences are often reflected in parents' socialization of emotion because parents are typically the ones responsible for guiding children in social norms.

Chinese cultures strongly emphasize the need to be aware of oneself as embedded in a larger group and to maintain a positive image within that group. Thus, shame would be expected to be a powerful emotion—important for self-reflection and self-perfection (Fung, 1999; Fung & Chen, 2001) and particularly useful for inducing compliance in children. In fact, Chinese (Taiwanese) parents frequently try to induce shame in their preschool children when they transgress, typically pointing out that the child's behavior is judged negatively by people outside the family and that the child's shame is shared by other family members (Fung & Chen, 2001). Because of this cultural emphasis, it is likely that children in this society experience shame more frequently than do children in many Western cultures.

Moreover, when children in Western cultures do experience shame or sadness, their mothers seem to be most concerned with helping them feel better about themselves. In contrast, Chinese mothers more often than Western mothers use the situation as an opportunity to teach proper conduct and help their child understand how to conform to social expectations and norms—for example, asking "Isn't it wrong for you to get mad at Papa?" (Cheah & Rubin, 2004; Friedlmeier et al., 2011; Q. Wang & Fivush, 2005). When teaching about emotion, Chinese immigrant parents are more likely to focus on behaviors that can cause, or resolve, emotional states, whereas European American parents are more likely to talk about internal emotional states (Doan & Wang, 2010).

Culture also plays a role in whether, and to what extent, children display anger. In one study, Japanese and American preschoolers were asked to say what they would do in hypothetical situations of conflict and distress, such as being hit or seeing a peer knock down a tower of blocks they had just built. American preschoolers expressed more anger and aggression in response to these vignettes than did Japanese children. This difference may have to do with the fact that American mothers appear to be more likely than Japanese mothers to encourage their children to express their emotions in situations such as these (Zahn-Waxler et al., 1996). These tendencies are in keeping with the high value the European American culture places on independence, self-assertion, and the expression of emotions (Zahn-Waxler et al., 1996). In contrast, Japanese culture emphasizes interdependence, the subordination of oneself to one's group, and, correspondingly, the importance of maintaining harmonious interpersonal relationships. A similar contrast is found in other East Asian cultures, such as in China, where mothers often discourage their children from expressing anger (Markus & Kitayama, 1991; Matsumoto, 1996; Mesquita & Frijda, 1992). As a consequence, children in such societies learn not to express their anger or frustration (Raval & Martini, 2009).

Review

Children's emotional development is influenced by their relationship with their parents. Children who have positive and secure relationships with their parents tend to show more happiness and greater emotional understanding than do children who have insecure relationships with their parents. Parents also affect children's emotional development through their own emotional expressions; hostility and anger have a particularly negative impact on developing children. Parents who fail to express any affect can also be upsetting to children, as seen in the still-face paradigm.

Parents' positive reactions to specific emotions will make those emotions more likely to recur, whereas their negative reactions will have the opposite effect. Parents can also influence emotional development by engaging in emotion coaching, although exactly which emotions are encouraged can be contextually and culturally determined.

mental health ■ children's sense of well-being both internally, such as in their emotions and stress levels, as well as externally, such as in their relationships with family members and peers

stress ■ a physiological reaction to some change or threat in the environment

toxic stress ■ the experience of overwhelming levels of stress without support from adults to help mitigate the effects of that stress

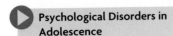
Psychological Disorders in Adolescence

Mental Health, Stress, and Internalizing Mental Disorders

Mental health is an important component of emotional development. It reflects children's sense of well-being both internally, such as in their emotions and stress levels, as well as externally, such as in their relationships with family members and peers. Developmentalists are concerned with mental health at every stage of development, from infancy through adolescence. Mental health is a continuum and children (or adults, of course) can be at the high end one day but at the low end another. An individual's mental health becomes a source of concern if one spends many days on the low end of the continuum. Mental health is promoted when children have safe and healthy environments as well as supportive and nurturing caregivers. The absence of one or both of these factors increases the risk of the development of stress and related mental health disorders, as do certain genetic predispositions, as discussed below.

Stress

When children are in situations or environments that they perceive to be frightening, threatening, or overwhelming, they can experience **stress**—a physiological reaction to some change or threat in the environment. The stress response involves increased heart rate, secretion of stress hormones, increased flow of blood to the brain, and a heightened feeling of vigilance and fear (Shonkoff, Boyce, & McEwen, 2009). Each of these physiological reactions underlies the body's "fight or flight" response to a threat in the environment. In reaction to a challenging situation, the adrenal cortex secretes steroid hormones such as cortisol, which helps to activate energy reserves (Danese & McEwen, 2012). Sometimes individual differences in children's cortisol baseline—that is, their typical cortisol level—have been related to levels of internalizing problems such as inhibition, anxiety, and social withdrawal (Granger, Stansbury, & Henker, 1994; Smider et al., 2002), to emotion regulation (Gunnar et al., 2003), and to behavior problems (Gunnar & Vazquez, 2006; Shirtcliff et al., 2005; Shoal, Giancola, & Kirillova, 2003).

Stress can be a common experience in childhood and adolescence, when the pressures of school, extracurricular activities, family obligations, and peer relationships may be overwhelming at times. In most cases, periodic stress serves the beneficial and adaptive function of mobilizing the child to take actions to reduce or manage exposure to the stimulus in the environment that is provoking the anxiety. For example, a stress response can prompt a child to flee a dangerous situation, or to focus and work hard for an important test. If the stress is not constant or if a child has an adult who can provide support and help him or her manage the stress, then the child can learn how to cope with the periodic stress.

Stress becomes problematic when it is chronic (see Box 10.3 for a more in-depth discussion of toxic stress). Exposure to repeated stressors such as conflict between parents in the home, or a single mother's entrance into a new romantic relationship or cohabitation arrangement, increases children's experience of emotions such as fear and anxiety (Bachman, Coley, & Carrano, 2011; Davies, Cicchetti, & Martin, 2012; Rhoades, 2008).

Although some stress can be adaptive, too much stress can interfere with children's daily activities and relationships.

LEAH-ANNE THOMPSON / SHUTTERSTOCK

BOX 10.3 | applications

TOXIC STRESS AND ADVERSE CHILDHOOD EXPERIENCES

Children who experience chronic high levels of stress, and who lack supportive adults to help mitigate the effects are said to experience **toxic stress** (Shonkoff et al., 2009; Shonkoff, Garner et al., 2012). When a child's stress response system is overworked by toxic stress, regions of the brain that regulate fear (e.g., amygdala, hippocampus) become overloaded and suffer atrophying of neuron dendrites and shrinkage (Danese & McEwen, 2012). Some changes are permanent and may lead to long-term changes both in responses to stress and in stress-related chronic disease in adulthood (Shonkoff et al., 2012).

Children are threatened by several sources of toxic stress. Maltreatment, such as physical abuse or neglect, has been linked with changes in brain structure and functioning (Jaffee & Christian, 2014; Teicher, Anderson, & Polcari, 2012). Poverty and material deprivation have been linked with low academic achievement, high rates of behavior and mental problems, and poor physical health (Yoshikawa, Aber, & Beardslee, 2012). Exposure to war is also linked to stress-related and mental health problems (Slone & Mann, 2016).

Although poverty, maltreatment, and war have long been recognized as threats to children's development, a landmark study known as the Adverse Childhood Experiences Study has linked such potential sources of toxic stress in childhood to later mental and physical health in adulthood. In this study, over 17,000 adult participants indicated their exposure to various adverse childhood experiences (or ACEs), which were summed to give each participant an ACE score. Nearly 64% of the participants had at least one ACE and 12.5% had an ACE score of 4 or higher (Anda et al., 2006). Physical abuse was the most common ACE (28%), followed by having a household member with a substance abuse problem (27%), and having parents who separated or divorced (23%; see the table).

The more ACEs the participants had experienced, the greater their risk of having high levels of stress, depression, anxiety, severe obesity, smoking, and alcoholism. As shown in the figure, the relationship between ACEs and problems in adulthood followed a clear and consistent pattern: as the number of ACEs increased, the likelihood of experiencing a mental or physical health problem

increased. This pattern is consistent regardless of the participant's gender, race, or level of education. The fact that ACEs are linked with increased high stress in adulthood suggests that experiences of toxic stress in childhood may prime children to experience high levels of stress in adulthood as well.

There is some evidence that exposure to non-stressful environments and treatment can reverse some of the harmful effects of toxic stress. For example, children who had been maltreated by their families but were removed to foster-care homes that provided consistent discipline and positive reinforcement showed normalization of levels of the stress hormone cortisol and reduction in behavior problems (Fisher et al., 2000). Trauma-focused mental health interventions such as cognitive behavioral therapy, play therapy, multisystemic therapy, and parent–child interaction therapy are also effective in helping victims of maltreatment (Saunders, Berliner, & Hanson, 2004).

Of course, public health research is also focused on preventing the events or circumstances that trigger toxic stress in the first place. The American Academy of Pediatrics (AAP) has called for public policies and community-based programs aimed at reducing toxic stress exposure in children's lives (Shonkoff et al., 2012). Maltreatment ACEs in particular could be prevented through individual and community-wide parenting education and alternatives to harsh parenting (Prinz

et al., 2009). The AAP's Early Brain and Child Development initiative seeks to focus the attention of pediatricians and other public health workers on understanding, recognizing, and preventing toxic stress (American Academy of Pediatrics, 2016). Research on toxic stress is still in its infancy, and as more interventions are tested, experts will know more about how to treat and prevent toxic stress.

Adverse Childhood Experience (ACE) Categories, Definitions, and Prevalence in a Sample of 17,337 Adults

Category	Prevalence
Emotional abuse	11%
Physical abuse	28%
Sexual abuse	21%
Someone in household engaged in substance abuse	27%
Someone in household had mental illness	19%
Mother was treated violently	13%
Someone in household was incarcerated	5%
Parents were separated or divorced	23%

Source: Data from Table 1 of Anda et al. (2006).

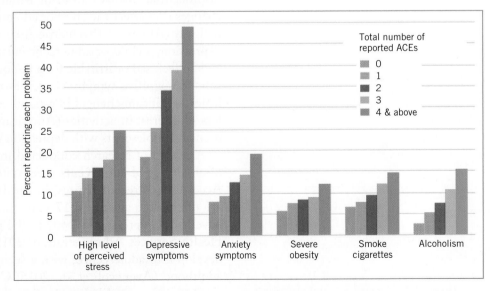

ACEs and adult health The more ACEs adults recall from their childhoods, the more mental, physical, and behavioral health problems they report. (Data from Anda et al., 2006)

mental disorder ■ a state of having problems with emotional reactions to the environment and with social relationships in ways that affect daily life

equifinality ■ the concept that various causes can lead to the same mental disorder

multifinality ■ the concept that certain risk factors do not always lead to a mental disorder

depression ■ a mental disorder that involves a sad or irritable mood along with physical and cognitive changes that interfere with daily life

rumination ■ the act of focusing on one's own negative emotions and negative self-appraisals and on their causes and consequences, without engaging in efforts to improve one's situation

co-rumination ■ extensively discussing and self-disclosing emotional problems with another person

Sometimes a single major negative event can trigger a form of stress known as *traumatic stress.* Children and adolescents who are directly exposed to sudden, catastrophic events, such as natural disasters or terrorist attacks, tend to experience unusually high levels of emotions such as fear and anxiety and to experience mood disorders such as depression and post-traumatic stress disorder (N. Eisenberg & Silver, 2011; Gershoff et al., 2010; Slone & Mann, 2016; Weems et al., 2010).

Internalizing Mental Disorders

Exposure in childhood to repeated or traumatic stress can lead to the development of **mental disorders,** which are chronic conditions that may persist throughout childhood and into adulthood (Perou et al., 2013). Psychologists have identified several categories of mental disorders, including psychotic disorders, eating disorders, personality disorders, and behavior disorders. In this section, we will focus on internalizing mental disorders. Because they involve internal emotional states, internalizing mental health disorders are often difficult to identify and diagnose, compared with behavior disorders (also called externalizing disorders), which manifest in disruptive or aggressive actions. (Behavior disorders will be discussed in Chapter 14.)

As we will see, there is no single pathway to a disorder; rather, the prediction of disorders follows a concept known as **equifinality,** which means that various factors (such as genetic predisposition, chaotic home environment, or a traumatic event) can each lead to the same mental disorder. Yet disorders can also exhibit a quality known as **multifinality,** which refers to the fact that certain risk factors do not always lead to a disorder (Hinshaw, 2015; Masten & Cicchetti, 2010). For example, though children who have been maltreated are twice as likely to develop depression or anxiety in adolescence or young adulthood than non-maltreated children (Scott, Smith, & Ellis, 2010), not every maltreated child develops a disorder.

Depression

According to the *Diagnostic and Statistical Manual of Mental Disorders* (DSM-5), the definitive clinical guide for diagnosing mental disorders, **depression** is a mental disorder that involves a sad or irritable mood along with physical and cognitive changes that affect the child or adolescent's ability to behave and interact in a normal way (American Psychiatric Association, 2013). In order to be diagnosed with depression, a child or adolescent must report feeling, or be observed by their parents to feel, sad or irritable for a period of two weeks, and they must exhibit physical and cognitive symptoms such as difficulties sleeping (either too much or too little), significant changes in weight (either loss or gain), inability to concentrate, or loss of interest in activities (American Psychiatric Association, 2013). Some children and adolescents with depression will also think about or even attempt suicide.

A review of research conducted in 27 different countries determined that 3% of children and adolescents meet criteria for depression (Polanczyk et al., 2015). According to recent figures, in the United States specifically, at any given time 2% of children aged 3 to 17 years have depression (Perou et al., 2013), and 11% have had a depressive episode in the previous year (Substance Abuse and Mental Health Services Administration, 2015). Risk of depression increases as children develop into adolescence, with a second uptick in risk when they age into young adulthood (Avenevoli et al., 2015; Costello, Copeland, & Angold, 2011). Girls are 2 to 3 times as likely as boys to develop depression (Avenevoli et al., 2015), a fact that is discussed more in depth in Box 10.4.

BOX 10.4 | individual differences

GENDER DIFFERENCES IN ADOLESCENT DEPRESSION

One of the most striking features of adolescent depression is the gender-related differences in its occurrence (D. M. Costello et al., 2008; Twenge & Nolen-Hoeksema, 2002). As children develop, they have an increased likelihood of experiencing depression, but girls face a steeper increase in this risk over time—so much so that by age 17, girls are 2 to 3 times more likely than boys to experience both severe and non-severe depression (Avenevoli et al., 2015). Although the chance of depression at some point in their lifetime increases across adolescence for both boys and girls, the increase is twice as fast for girls (Hankin et al., 2015; see the figure). Similar gender differences in the patterns of adolescent depression have been found in Canada, Great Britain, and New Zealand (Galambos, Leadbeater, & Barker, 2004; Hankin et al., 1998; Wade, Cairney, & Pevalin, 2002).

Why are adolescent girls more likely than boys to experience depression? One reason is that in early and middle childhood, a period just before the steep increase in depression, girls tend to express more internalizing emotions, such as sadness and anxiety, than do boys (Chaplin & Aldao, 2013). Another reason is that the biological changes brought on by puberty tend to be more difficult for girls and may contribute to girls' vulnerability (Hilt & Nolen-Hoeksema, 2009). Girls are also more affected by chronic stress from social interactions with peers (e.g., lack of friendships or conflict with friends), which in turn predicts depressive symptoms (Hankin et al., 2015). Important stressors may include concerns about one's body and appearance (Hankin, Mermelstein, & Roesch, 2007).

As discussed in Chapter 15, adolescent girls in the United States report greater dissatisfaction with their bodies than boys report with theirs. This dissatisfaction, fueled by a cultural obsession with an "ideal" body type attainable only by a few, seems to contribute substantially to low self-esteem and depression in adolescent girls (Compian, Gowen, & Hayward, 2004; Hankin & Abramson, 1999; Harter, 2006; Wichstrom, 1999).

Another stressor for girls can be the social consequences of early puberty, which represent a clear risk for depression (Negriff & Susman, 2011). Early maturity, for example, may lead young adolescent girls to become involved with older adolescent boys, who may pressure them to engage in sexual activity, drinking, or delinquency. Many younger girls often are not cognitively and socially mature enough to cope with these pressures (Ge, Conger, & Elder, 1996; Ge et al., 2003). In contrast, for boys, early puberty has been less consistently related to internalizing problems such as depression. However, recent evidence suggests that boys who enter puberty early and move through it quickly are, in fact, at risk for depression (Ge et al., 2003; Mendle et al., 2010), in part because of a decline in the quality of their relationships with peers (Mendle et al., 2012). For both sexes, early puberty is especially likely to be associated with depressive symptoms if it is accompanied by low popularity (Teunissen et al., 2011). For boys, starting puberty later than one's peers is a predictor of depression as well (Negriff & Susman, 2011).

Also appearing to contribute to the higher rates of depression for adolescent girls is the fact that they, more than their male peers, are prone to repeatedly focus on causes, consequences, and symptoms of their sadness or frustration ("I'm so fat" or "I'm so tired") and on the meaning of their distress ("What's wrong with my life?") without engaging in efforts to remedy their situation (Hankin, Stone, & Wright, 2010; Nolen-Hoeksema, Larson, & Grayson, 1999). The more adolescents engage in such thinking about stress events, called **rumination,** the more likely they are to be depressed, with girls more likely to engage in rumination in response to stress than boys (Abela et al., 2012; Nolen-Hoeksema, 2012).

One study found that the gender difference in rumination was not present in a sample of 11-year-olds, but it was present in a sample of 15-year-olds (Cox, Mezulis, & Hyde, 2010), suggesting that girls begin ruminating more after the transition to adolescence. Tendencies to ruminate are particularly strong among girls who have a more feminine gender role identity and whose mothers encourage their daughters' emotion expression; thus, gender differences in rumination are likely an example of girls conforming to gender-linked behaviors (Cox et al., 2010). Moreover, **co-rumination**—that is, extensively and almost exclusively discussing and self-disclosing emotional problems with another person, usually a peer (A. J. Rose, 2002)—is more common for girls and accounts for the gender difference in depression (Hankin et al., 2010; Schwartz-Mette & Rose, 2012; L. B. Stone et al., 2011).

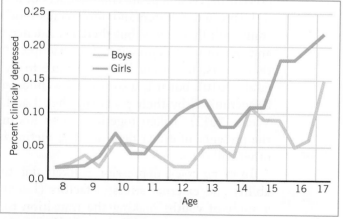

Gender differences in adolescent depression Beginning around age 11, boys and girls diverge dramatically in their risk for becoming clinically depressed. (Data from Hankin et al., 2015)

Both *nature* and *nurture* influence whether a child experiences depression. On the side of nature, children and adolescents with depression tend to have elevated levels of the stress hormone cortisol, and to exhibit differences in brain structure and function, compared with their peers who are not depressed (Klein et al., 2013). Depression also has a genetic component; it often runs in families. The heritability of depression is 40%; that is, an individual's genetic makeup explains 40% of the likelihood that he or she will experience depression (American Psychiatric Association, 2013; see Chapter 3 for a more detailed discussion of heritability). Children whose mothers or fathers have a history of depression exhibit a pattern of activation in the prefrontal cortex and amygdala that is associated with greater sadness, withdrawal, and reactivity to the environment—factors that increase the likelihood that the children will themselves experience depression (Chai et al., 2015; Cicchetti & Toth, 2006; Joormann et al., 2012).

On the nurture side, a variety of family factors likely also contribute to depression in youth. In particular, low levels of parental sensitivity, support, or acceptance and high levels of parental negativity have each been linked with higher levels of depressive symptoms in children (Auerbach et al., 2011; Kiff, Lengua, & Bush, 2011; O. S. Schwartz et al., 2012). Depressed parents are more likely than nondepressed parents to be insensitive and disengaged, yielding an environmental pathway through which parent depression increases the likelihood of child depression (Belsky, Schlomer, & Ellis, 2012; S. B. Campbell et al., 2007; Garber & Cole, 2010; Lovejoy et al., 2000). Adverse childhood experiences, such as those discussed in Box 10.3, are also risk factors for depression, as are stressful life events (American Psychiatric Association, 2013; Brennan et al., 2002; Karevold et al., 2009; H. K. Kim, Capaldi, & Stoolmiller, 2003).

Depression also has a cognitive component. Depressed children and adolescents tend to have unrealistic expectations about social relationships and see themselves, rather than external or chance events, as the cause of negative events (Klein et al., 2013). Depressed individuals also tend to ruminate extensively about negative events in their lives (Abela et al., 2012; Nolen-Hoeksema, 2012; see Box 10.4). Research to date has not yet been able to determine whether these cognitive factors precede depression or are consequences of it.

Depressed children and adolescents tend to have problems in their relationships with their peers, but there is evidence that such problems are both a cause and outcome of depression. For example, the more children are victimized by their peers, the more likely they are to develop depression (Witvliet, Olthof et al., 2010), but it is also true that children with depression are more likely to be victimized by their peers (Kochel, Ladd, & Rudolph, 2012; Tran, Cole, & Weiss, 2012). Taken together, these findings suggest a vicious cycle whereby the presence of either depression or victimization increases the chances that the other will occur.

In many cases, depression is likely due to a combination of personal vulnerability and external stressful factors (Lewinsohn, Joiner, & Rohde, 2001). In a study of youths making the transition to middle school, for instance, those who felt that they had little control over their success in school and who demonstrated little investment in school were especially likely to show an increase in depressive symptoms if they also experienced the transition as stressful (Rudolph et al., 2001). Other research found that girls who were low in the regulation of sadness were prone to depressive symptoms in preadolescence if their parents were not especially caring and supportive (Feng et al., 2009). In addition, the combination of family difficulties (e.g., separation from parents) in early childhood and high levels of interpersonal stress later on may increase youths' vulnerability to depression (Rudolph & Flynn, 2007), perhaps because early stress can affect the child's ability to adapt physiologically years later (Gunnar & Vazquez, 2006).

Anxiety Disorders

Anxiety disorders involve the inability to regulate the emotions of fear and worry (Weems & Silverman, 2013) such that the individual experiences excessive and uncontrollable fear of real or perceived threats and worries about future threats (American Psychiatric Association, 2013). Unlike the temporary fear or anxiety that an individual may feel in response to a threat in their environment, anxiety disorders manifest as intense fear or anxiety that lasts days or even months and impairs the individual's ability to interact with others or to concentrate on tasks (Weems & Silverman, 2013). Anxiety disorders are believed to involve over-activation of areas of the brain associated with reaction to threat, including the amygdala and hippocampus brain structures, as well as the sympathetic nervous system (Weems & Silverman, 2013).

In young children, the most common anxiety disorder is separation anxiety disorder, which involves persistent fear about being separated from a caregiver or about a caregiver being in danger (American Psychiatric Association, 2013). As noted earlier in this chapter, some separation anxiety is normative in young children and, as will be discussed in Chapter 11, is often seen in the positive development of secure attachment with caregivers. However, if the separation anxiety becomes severe and persistent and interferes with behavior, then it is considered a disorder. Children with anxiety disorder may be described by adults as intrusive and demanding of constant attention (American Psychiatric Association, 2013). Children and adolescents with an anxiety disorder may also suffer from panic attacks, which are sudden and intense surges of fear and discomfort, or from phobias about certain animals or about certain social situations (American Psychiatric Association, 2013).

Around the world, 7% of children and adolescents meet criteria for an anxiety disorder (Polanczyk et al., 2015). In the United States, the prevalence is slightly lower at 3% of children aged 3 to 17 years (Perou et al., 2013), with girls twice as likely to be diagnosed with anxiety as boys (American Psychiatric Association, 2013). Over the course of development from childhood to adolescence and into young adulthood, there is an increase in several types of anxiety disorder, namely panic disorder and agoraphobia (the fear of open or public spaces), but a decrease in separation anxiety disorder and in other phobias (Costello et al., 2011). Anxiety disorder typically develops in childhood and can persist into adulthood if not treated (American Psychiatric Association, 2013).

Like depression, both genetic (*nature*) and environmental (*nurture*) factors contribute to the onset of anxiety disorder. About one-third of the variance in anxiety is thought to be heritable, with some of that heritability coming from temperament: children who have fearful or inhibited temperaments are more likely to experience problems with anxiety (Weems & Silverman, 2013). Yet the environment also plays an important role. Children can come to associate

anxiety disorders ■ a set of mental disorders that involve the inability to regulate fear and worry certain people or events with fear and anxiety, even when fear and anxiety are not warranted. This association may come about either through conditioning (e.g., a child is bitten by a dog and develops a strong fear of dogs), through observation (e.g., a child's mother is afraid of dogs and the child adopts that same fear), or through instruction (e.g., hearing about a rabid dog terrorizing a neighborhood) (Weems & Silverman, 2013).

Parenting behavior has also been implicated as a precursor of children's anxiety disorders. Mothers' overprotective, overinvolved, and controlling behaviors have been linked to anxiety in children. To a lesser extent, fathers' encouragement for their children to engage in risky behavior outside their comfort zone has also been associated with anxiety in children (Möller et al., 2016).

Treatment of Internalizing Mental Disorders

Drug therapy is a common treatment for depression in children and adolescents; however, the drugs typically used to treat children and adolescents (serotonin reuptake inhibitors, or SRIs) are different from the class of drugs used to treat depression in adults (tricyclic antidepressants) (Maughan, Collishaw, & Stringaris, 2013). Significant concerns have been raised about the possibility that antidepressants may increase the risk of suicidal thinking and suicidal behavior among some adolescents (Calati et al., 2011).

An alternative, psychotherapeutic approach known as cognitive behavioral therapy (CBT) has been found to be very effective in treating both depression and anxiety in children. In CBT, children learn to recognize when they are having maladaptive thoughts and learn ways to actively modify those thoughts and their reactions to them (Hofmann et al., 2012). CBT has been found to be more effective at reducing anxiety symptoms than other forms of treatment, including traditional child-centered therapy (Hofmann et al., 2012; Silk et al., 2016). CBT is as effective at treating depression as drug therapy, and the combination of CBT and drug therapy can be particularly effective in reducing depressive symptoms (Hofmann et al., 2012).

Although effective therapies exist for both depression and anxiety, unfortunately many children and adolescents with these disorders do not receive treatment. In the United States, only 44% of children aged 6 to 17 with severe impairment from mental health disorders receive any mental health treatment. In addition, among those with severe disorders, non-White children are less likely to receive treatment than are White children (Olfson, Druss, & Marcus, 2015; Substance Abuse and Mental Health Services Administration, 2015). Children living in disadvantaged families are also less likely to receive services or treatment, despite having a higher rate of diagnosed mental disorders than their advantaged peers (Bringewatt & Gershoff, 2010). There is generally a shortage of children's mental health care providers in the United States, but professionals working in this area anticipate that the trend will change in the future as a result of the passage of the Mental Health Parity and Addiction Equity Act (2008) and the Patient Protection and Affordable Care Act (2010), which require that health insurers cover mental health to the same extent as physical health.

Children with internalizing mental disorders have been shown to benefit from psychotherapy. (Photo is being used for illustrative purposes only; person depicted in photo is a model.)

KATARZYNABIALASIEWICZ / GETTY IMAGES

Review

Mental health is an important aspect of emotional development. Exposure to stressful events, especially when chronic or at toxic levels, can be extremely harmful to children's emotional and physical health. Although stress in small amounts does serve an important function in mobilizing children's responses to a threatening event or circumstance, in large or repeated amounts it can be debilitating.

Mental disorders arise when children or youth experience problems in their cognitions and emotions that affect their daily lives. Depression and anxiety are two common mental health problems that affect substantial numbers of children and adolescents. Effective therapies exist for helping children and adolescents with depression and anxiety, but unfortunately large proportions of children diagnosed with these disorders do not receive treatment.

CHAPTER SUMMARY

The Development of Emotions

- Discrete-emotions theorists believe that a set of biological and neurological reactions to the environment have evolved so that humans experience a core set of basic emotions that are universal across all human cultures. In contrast, proponents of the functionalist perspective believe that emotions reflect what individuals are trying to do in specific situations—that is, their concerns and goals at the moment—and that there is not a set of innate, discrete emotions but many emotions based on people's many different interactions with the social world. As with many aspects of development, there is evidence to support both the *nature* (discrete emotions) and *nurture* (functionalist) interpretations of emotion.

- Researchers have identified six basic emotions: happiness, fear, anger, sadness, surprise, and disgust. Each of these emotions can be reliably identified in infants and each is thought to play an important role in both survival and social communication.

- Emotions undergo change in the early months and years of life. Smiles become social around the 2nd to 3rd month of life, and what makes children smile and laugh changes with cognitive development.

- Fear appears by 6 to 7 months of age, such as when infants become distressed in the presence of strangers. At around 8 months of age, infants begin to exhibit separation anxiety when separated from their parents.

- Infants begin expressing anger and frustration by 4 months of age and peak in their likelihood of responding with anger by 24 months of age. As they age, children increasingly match their anger to the situation, getting angrier if an act was intentional than if it was unintentional.

- Sadness, surprise, and disgust each appear in the 1st year as well. How often and to what stimuli children express each of these emotions is closely tied to their home and cultural environment.

- The self-conscious emotions—guilt, shame, jealousy, empathy, pride, and embarrassment—emerge in the 2nd year of life. Their emergence is tied in part to the development of a rudimentary sense of self and to an appreciation of others' reactions to the self.

Understanding Emotions

- An important aspect of emotional development is children's understanding of different types of emotion, what they mean, and what events cause them. These skills are important for interacting successfully with others in their environments. Between 5½ and 12 months of age, infants start to perceive that others' emotional expressions are meaningful and start to exhibit social referencing.

- By age 3, children demonstrate a rudimentary ability to use words to label facial expressions.

- Children's understanding of the situations that cause emotions, display rules, and the complexities of emotional experience increases in the preschool and elementary school years.

Emotion Regulation

▪ Emotion regulation involves a set of both conscious and unconscious processes used to both monitor and modulate emotional experiences and expressions. Emotion regulation develops gradually over the course of childhood and paves the way for success both in social interactions as well as in academic settings.

▪ Newborns are not able to regulate their own emotions and must rely on adults to manage their emotions. However, beginning after the 5th month, infants can engage in self-comforting and self-distraction behaviors when they are in stressful situations. Improvements in children's regulatory capacities are based on increases in both their cognitive development and their ability to control their own bodies, as well as on changes in others' expectations of them.

▪ Emotion regulation is generally associated with high social competence and low problem behavior.

Temperament

▪ Temperament—individual differences in emotion, activity level, and attention exhibited across contexts—is relatively stable but can undergo some change over time.

▪ Temperament can be measured through laboratory assessments or through parent reports; both strategies have strengths and weaknesses.

▪ Temperament is thought to be determined both by genetic and environmental factors.

▪ Children do best when there is a goodness of fit between their temperament and their environments.

▪ Children may experience differential susceptibility, such that they do very poorly in harsh conditions but very well in enriched conditions.

The Role of Family in Emotional Development

▪ Children's emotional development is affected indirectly by the quality of their early social relationships and by their parents' own expressions of emotion.

▪ Infants have a strong negative reaction when their mothers do not react emotionally to them, as is demonstrated in still-face experiments.

▪ Parents engage in active emotion socialization to teach children about the appropriateness of emotion expression and about circumstances that require emotion regulation.

▪ Cultural factors have been shown to influence what emotions parents encourage their children to express, with certain emotions more encouraged or discouraged in some cultures than others.

Mental Health, Stress, and Internalizing Mental Disorders

▪ Mental health involves children's sense of well-being both internally, such as in their emotions and stress levels, as well as externally, such as in their relationships with family members and peers.

▪ Stress, although adaptive and beneficial in short doses as a means of organizing a response to a threatening event, can be problematic when experienced repeatedly over long periods or at toxic levels.

▪ Children who have difficulties with their emotional reactions to their environments are said to have a mental disorder. The same mental disorder can be caused by different risks across different people (equifinality); however, the presence of a risk factor does not always lead to a disorder (multifinality).

▪ Three percent of all children and adolescents around the world experience depression, which involves a combination of sad or irritable mood with physiological and cognitive changes affecting one's ability to conduct normal interactions. Depression appears to have both biological and environmental causes.

▪ Seven percent of all children have an anxiety disorder, which involves excessive and uncontrollable fear of or worry about real or perceived threats. Anxiety is typically manifested as separation anxiety disorder in early childhood and as panic disorder and agoraphobia in later childhood and adolescence.

▪ Both depression and anxiety disorders can be successfully treated through psychotherapy, drug treatment, or a combination of both.

Test Yourself

1. Which of the following statements best summarizes the findings by Mischel and his colleagues from their famous marshmallow test?
   a. The ability to exhibit self-control early in life can predict success later in life.
   b. The ability to experience and express emotion is a result of human evolution.
   c. Individuals experience emotions in order to manage their relationship to their environment.
   d. Infants across all cultures are born with the ability to express the six basic human emotions.

2. Tom is walking down the street and suddenly encounters a dog that is crouched and growling. Tom begins to perspire, his breathing quickens, and his heart rate increases. This reaction is an example of which component of emotion?
   a. neural responses
   b. physiological factors
   c. subjective feelings
   d. the desire to take action

3. The notion that humans have evolved to experience a basic set of emotions through adaptation to their surroundings is central to which theory?
   a. discrete emotions theory
   b. functionalist perspective theory
   c. the AFFEX approach
   d. display rules theory

4. How do self-conscious emotions differ from the set of basic emotions discussed in this chapter?
   a. Self-conscious emotions are thought to be innate.
   b. Self-conscious emotions tend to occur very early in infancy.
   c. Self-conscious emotions develop after the child has acquired a sense of himself as separate from others.
   d. Self-conscious emotions have a consistently negative effect on development.

5. Based on your understanding of the chapter, how would a 12-month-old respond to a novel stimulus in a given situation if his or her parent expressed positive emotion?
   a. The infant is likely to stay near his or her parent.
   b. The infant is likely to move closer to the novel stimulus.
   c. The infant will stay in between the parent and novel stimulus.
   d. The infant will show a fear response and avoid the novel stimulus.

6. _____ refer(s) to an individual's ability to understand his or her own emotions, as well as the emotions of others.
   a. Emotion regulation
   b. Temperament traits
   c. Display rules
   d. Emotional intelligence

7. _____ refer(s) to the social and cultural norms related to emotion expression.
   a. Emotion regulation
   b. Temperamental traits
   c. Display rules
   d. Emotional intelligence

8. An infant is startled by a loud noise and begins to cry. Her mother calms her by playing with her and speaking soothingly to her. This interaction is an example of _____.
   a. co-regulation
   b. self-comforting
   c. emotion socialization
   d. co-rumination

9. A decreased reliance on self-comforting behaviors, an increased ability to inhibit motor behavior, and an improved ability to distract oneself when distressed are all the result of developments in _____.
   a. emotional intelligence
   b. emotion regulation
   c. temperament
   d. social competence

10. Which of the following is *not* one of the five key dimensions of temperament, according to research by Mary Rothbart?
    a. disgust
    b. smiling
    c. attention span
    d. fear

11. Twin studies conducted by Lemery-Chalfant and colleagues have led to which important conclusion regarding temperament?
    a. Temperament is most strongly affected by environmental factors.
    b. Temperament is completely determined by genetic factors.
    c. Temperament is determined more by genes than environment.
    d. Genes and environment play an equal role in determining temperament.

12. Researchers conducting Tronick's famous Still-Face Paradigm found that during the distressing still-face episodes, infants spent very little time looking at their mothers. This response is an example of which of the following behaviors?
    a. anxiety disorder
    b. self-distraction
    c. self-comforting
    d. co-rumination

13. What are the two components of mental health?
    a. genetics and environment
    b. physical health and emotional stability
    c. internal well-being and external relationships
    d. parents and peers

14. Two 6-year-old boys, Cal and Sam, accompany their class to the library. Sam grabs a book from the shelf and sits quietly to read. Cal is unable to sit still or quietly and ends up disrupting other children. The different reactions that these two boys have to this situation are the result of _____.
    a. emotion socialization
    b. goodness of fit
    c. toxic stress
    d. differential susceptibility

15. The fact that a variety of factors can each lead to a given mental disorder is known as _____.
    a. multifinality
    b. equifinality
    c. differential susceptibility
    d. rumination

LaunchPad
macmillan learning

Don't stop now! Research shows that testing yourself is a powerful learning tool. Visit LaunchPad to access the LearningCurve adaptive quizzing system, which gives you a personalized study plan to help build your mastery of the chapter material through videos, activities, and more. **Go to launchpadworks.com.**

Critical Thinking Questions

1. How might differences in children's intelligence contribute to (a) the emotions they display and (b) their understanding of emotions? What other factors might contribute to children's understanding of their own and others' emotions?

2. List at least five aspects of children's temperament. What aspects of adults' personality might each predict?

3. Suppose that you wanted to assess changes with age in children's regulation of emotion. Think of five different tasks you could use to assess age-related changes. Which would be best to use in early childhood and which would better reflect changes at older ages?

4. Recall from Chapter 7 the development of children's theory of mind. How might advances in children's understanding of theory of mind relate to their understanding of emotion? What aspects of understanding emotion might be mostly associated with an understanding of theory of mind?

5. Imagine that you are devising an intervention that will enhance children's emotional development in the preschool years. On what skills would you focus? On whom would you focus your efforts—the children, their parents, their teachers, or their peers?

Key Terms

anxiety disorders, p. 457

co-regulation, p. 435

co-rumination, p. 455

depression, p. 454

differential susceptibility, p. 444

discrete emotions theory, p. 420

display rules, p. 433

emotions, p. 419

emotional intelligence, p. 431

emotion regulation, p. 435

emotion socialization, p. 448

equifinality, p. 454

functionalist perspective, p. 421

goodness of fit, p. 444

mental disorder, p. 454

mental health, p. 452

multifinality, p. 454

rumination, p. 455

self-comforting behaviors, p. 436

self-conscious emotions, p. 426

self-distraction, p. 436

separation anxiety, p. 424

social competence, p. 437

social referencing, p. 429

social smiles, p. 423

stress, p. 452

temperament, p. 439

toxic stress, p. 453

▶ Student Video Activities

Can Young Children Delay Gratification?

Emotional Development in Infancy: Stranger Fear

Emotional Development in Infancy: Separation Anxiety

Developing Self Control in Early Childhood

Developing Self Control in Middle Childhood

Temperament in Infancy and Toddlerhood

Still-Face Experiment with Edward Tronick

Psychological Disorders in Adolescence

Answers to Test Yourself

1. a, **2.** b, **3.** a, **4.** c, **5.** b, **6.** d, **7.** c, **8.** a, **9.** b, **10.** a, **11.** c, **12.** b, **13.** c, **14.** b, **15.** b

HECTOR MCDONNELL (B. 1947), *Refugee Mother and Baby, Goma* (oil on canvas, 1997)

Attachment to Others and Development of the Self

Themes

- Nature and Nurture
- The Active Child
- The Sociocultural Context
- Individual Differences
- Research and Children's Welfare

Between 1937 and 1943, numerous childcare professionals in both North America and Europe reported instances of a disturbing phenomenon: children who seemed to have no concern or feeling for anyone but themselves. Some of the children were withdrawn and isolated; others were overactive and abusive toward their peers. By the time they were adolescents, these children often had histories of persistent stealing, violence, and sexual misdemeanors. Many of these children had been reared in institutions in which they received adequate physical care but experienced little social interaction; others had been shifted from foster home to foster home in infancy and early childhood (Bowlby, 1953).

Around the same time, similar disturbances were being observed among children who had been orphaned or separated from their parents during World War II and were in refugee camps or other institutional settings. John Bowlby, an English psychoanalyst who worked with many of these children, reported that they were listless, depressed or otherwise emotionally disturbed, and mentally stunted. Older refugee children often seemed to have lost all interest in life and were possessed by feelings of emptiness (Bowlby, 1953). These children, like the Romanian orphans discussed in Box 1.1, tended not to develop normal emotional attachments with other people.

On the basis of such observations, René Spitz, a French psychoanalyst who had worked with Freud, conducted a series of classic studies of how the lack of adequate caregiving affects development (Spitz, 1945, 1946, 1949). Spitz filmed infants (a methodological innovation) residing in orphanages, most of whom had been born to unmarried mothers and had been given up for adoption. The films were extremely poignant and painful to watch. They documented the fact that, despite receiving good institutional care, the infants were generally sickly and developmentally impaired. In many cases, the infants seemed unmotivated to live: their death rate was about 37% over 2 years' time, compared with no deaths in an institution where children had daily contact with their mothers. The films' most important contribution, however, was their evidence of intense and prolonged grief and depression in infants who had been separated from their mothers after developing a loving relationship with them. Psychologists of the time did not believe that infants could experience such emotions (Emde, 1994).

Taken together, these early observations also challenged the more central belief then held by many childcare professionals, that if children in institutions such as orphanages received good physical care, including proper nourishment and health care, they would develop normally. These professionals placed little emphasis on the emotional dimensions of caregiving. As a result of the studies of children who lost their parents in the 1940s, it became generally recognized that, no matter how hygienic and competently managed, institutions like orphanages put babies at high risk because they did not provide the kind of caregiving that enables infants to form close socioemotional bonds. Foster care and adoption—the earlier, the better—came to be viewed as far better options.

Although we no longer put children into orphanages in the United States, there are other circumstances in which separation from parents can have significant implications for a child's development. These circumstances range from short-term separation, such as placement in a childcare center or with a non-parent caregiver while parents are at work, to long-term separations, as when a parent is deployed overseas or an abused or neglected child is removed from the home. How children adapt to these separations has become an important focus of developmental science. Indeed, one important outcome of Bowlby's work and that of others who studied institutionalized children was the beginning of systematic research on how the quality of parent–child interactions affects children's development in families, especially their development of emotional attachments to other people. This research, which continues today, has led to a much deeper understanding of the ways in which the early parent–child emotional bond likely influences children's interactions with others from infancy into adulthood. It has also provided new insight into the development of children's sense of self, as well as of their emotions, including their feelings of self-worth.

In this chapter, we will first explore how children develop **attachments**—close and enduring emotional bonds to parents or other primary caregivers. Then we will examine the ways in which the nature of these attachments to others seems to set the stage for the child's near- and long-term development. As you will see, the attachment process appears to be biologically based, yet it unfolds in different ways, depending on the familial and cultural context. Thus, the themes of *nature and nurture* and the *sociocultural context* will be important in our discussion of this topic. You will also see that although most children in normal social circumstances develop attachments to their parents, the quality of these attachments differs in important ways and has implications for each child's social and emotional development. The theme of *individual differences* will therefore figure prominently in our discussion as well. The theme of *research and children's welfare* is also relevant to our examination of experimental interventions designed to enhance the quality of mother–child attachment.

Next we will examine a related issue—the development of children's sense of self, that is, their self-understanding, self-identity, and self-esteem. Although many factors influence these areas of development, the quality of children's early attachments lays the foundation for how children feel about themselves, including their sense of security and well-being. Over time, children's self-understanding, self-esteem, and self-identity are also shaped by how others perceive and treat them, by biologically based characteristics of the child, and by children's developing abilities to think about and interpret their social worlds. Thus, the themes of *nature and nurture, individual differences,* the *sociocultural context,* and the *active child* will be evident in our discussion of the development of self.

attachment ■ an emotional bond with a specific person that is enduring across space and time. Usually, attachments are discussed in regard to the relation between infants and specific caregivers, although they can also occur in adulthood.

The Caregiver–Child Attachment Relationship

Following the very disturbing observations made in the 1930s and 1940s regarding children separated from their parents early in life, researchers began to conduct systematic studies of this phenomenon. Much of the early research, such as that conducted by Spitz, focused on how the development of young children who had been orphaned or otherwise separated from their parents was affected by the quality of the caregiving they subsequently received. The research on children adopted from institutions in Romania (discussed in Chapter 1) is probably the best known of recent studies on this topic, all of which support the idea that institutional deprivation in the first years of life hinders optimal social, emotional, and cognitive development (Bick et al., 2015; McCall et al., 2011; Rutter et al., 2010), presumably because it deprives the child of meaningful relationships with any caregivers. Although there was agreement among researchers that children and their parents share a special

Time infant rhesus monkeys spent on the cloth and wire mothers in Harlow's famous experiment.

bond, exactly why they do was initially a matter of debate. Proponents of *behaviorism* (see Chapter 9) argued that food, such as breast milk, is the basis for the bond. Infants link food to mothers through the process of classical conditioning, in which food is the *unconditioned stimulus* that causes the infant to experience pleasure and mothers are the *conditioned stimulus* linked with the food. Mothers evoke pleasure in the infant only because of this association (Dollard & Miller, 1950).

Psychologist Harry Harlow proposed another idea, based on his work with rhesus monkeys. Harlow had seen firsthand that infant monkeys reared in a laboratory setting away from their mothers were physically healthy but developed emotional and behavioral problems unless they were given some form of affection and something soft to cling to. Harlow decided to test whether the pleasure of food or the pleasure of comfort was most important to infant monkeys.

Harlow constructed two "surrogate mothers" made of wire and wood: one was covered in terrycloth over sponge rubber (the "cloth mother") and the other was left uncovered. Harlow then took infant monkeys from their mothers and put them in cages with these two surrogate mothers. He varied which of the two surrogates provided milk to the infant and watched how much time the infant monkeys spent on each one. Both groups of infants spent more time on the cloth mothers, though initially the group fed by the cloth mother spent more time with it than did the monkeys fed by the wire mother (see Figure 11.1). Interestingly, the monkeys fed by the wire mothers increased the amount of time spent on the cloth mothers as they got older, such that eventually they spent as much time on the cloth mother as did the monkeys who were fed by the cloth mother (Harlow, 1958). These results provided Harlow with evidence that infant monkeys strongly preferred, and thus likely needed, the comfort provided by the cloth mother.

Harlow also found that when infant monkeys were put in an unfamiliar situation without a surrogate mother, they would cower and engage in self-comforting behaviors, such as rocking and thumb-sucking. Yet when the cloth surrogate mother was introduced, they would initially cling to it but then eventually explore the room, periodically returning to the cloth mother. Harlow concluded that the cloth mother functioned as "a source of security, a base of operations" and that it "provides its young with a sense of security . . . when mother and child are in a strange situation" (Harlow, 1958, pp. 678–679).

Harlow's experiments taught developmentalists about the importance of physical comfort for infant monkeys, but it did so at a severe cost. Many of the monkeys

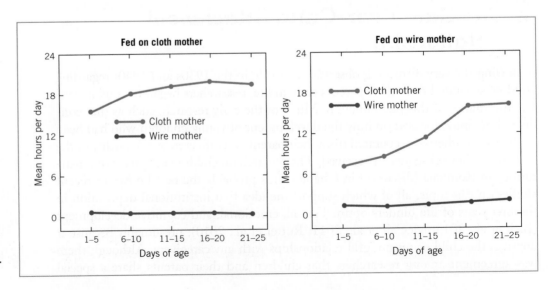

FIGURE 11.1 Time infant rhesus monkeys spent on the cloth and wire mothers in Harlow's famous experiment. (Data from Harlow, 1958)

in Harlow's experiments were extremely disturbed and had difficulties in their later lives. His research has been criticized as unnecessarily cruel and unethical, but he established without a doubt that infants need more than their physical needs met to thrive in the world.

Attachment Theory

The findings from observations of children and monkeys separated from their parents were so dramatic that psychiatrists and psychologists were compelled to rethink their ideas about early development. Foremost in this effort were John Bowlby, who proposed **attachment theory,** and his colleague, Mary Ainsworth, who extended and tested Bowlby's ideas.

Bowlby's theory of attachment (1953) was initially influenced by several key tenets of Freud's theories, especially the idea that infants' earliest relationships with their mothers shape their later development. However, Bowlby replaced the psychoanalytic notion of a "needy, dependent infant" with the idea of a "competence-motivated infant" who uses his or her primary caregiver as a **secure base** (E. Waters & Cummings, 2000). As with Harlow's use of the term with infant monkeys, the general idea of the secure base for infant humans is that the presence of a trusted caregiver provides them with a sense of security that allows them to explore the environment and hence to become generally knowledgeable and competent. In addition, the primary caregiver serves as a haven of safety when the infant feels threatened or insecure, and the child derives comfort and pleasure from being near the caregiver. Infants thus develop an attachment to their caregiver.

Attachment serves several important purposes. First, it enhances the infant's chance of survival by keeping the caregiver (who is also the source for food and protection) in close proximity. Second, attachment helps the child feel emotionally secure, which allows him or her to explore the world without fear. Third, it serves as a form of *co-regulation* (see Chapter 10) that helps children manage their levels of arousal and their emotions. Bowlby was directly influenced by Harlow's work as well as by ethological theories, particularly the concept of *imprinting* identified by Konrad Lorenz (see Chapter 9). Bowlby proposed that the attachment process between infant and caregiver is rooted in evolution and increases the infant's chance of survival. Just like imprinting, this attachment process develops from the interaction between species-specific learning biases (such as infants' strong tendency to look at faces) and the infant's experience with his or her caregiver. Thus, the attachment process is viewed as having an innate basis, but the development and quality of infants' attachments are highly dependent on the nature of their experiences with caregivers.

According to Bowlby (1969), the initial development of attachment takes place in four phases:

1. *Preattachment* (birth to age 6 weeks). In this phase, the infant produces innate signals, most notably crying, that summon caregivers, and the infant is comforted by the ensuing interaction.

2. *Attachment-in-the-making* (age 6 weeks to 6 to 8 months). During this phase, infants begin to respond preferentially to familiar people. Typically they smile, laugh, or babble more frequently in the presence of their primary caregiver and are more easily soothed by that person. Like Freud and Erikson, Bowlby saw this phase as a time when infants form expectations about how their caregivers will respond to their needs and, accordingly, do or do not develop a sense of trust in them.

attachment theory ■ theory based on John Bowlby's work that posits that children are biologically predisposed to develop attachments to caregivers as a means of increasing the chances of their own survival

secure base ■ refers to the idea that the presence of a trusted caregiver provides an infant or toddler with a sense of security that makes it possible for the child to explore the environment

John Bowlby, who laid the foundations of attachment theory, was influenced by psychoanalytic work and research on animals' social behavior.

COURTESY OF SIR JOHN BOWLBY

internal working model of attachment ■ the child's mental representation of the self, of attachment figure(s), and of relationships in general that is constructed as a result of experiences with caregivers. The working model guides children's interactions with caregivers and other people in infancy and at older ages.

3. *Clear-cut attachment* (between 6 to 8 months and 1½ years). In this phase, infants actively seek contact with their regular caregivers. They happily greet their mother when she appears and, correspondingly, may exhibit *separation anxiety or distress* when she departs (see Chapter 10). For the majority of children, the mother now serves as a secure base, facilitating the infant's exploration and mastery of the environment.

4. *Reciprocal relationships* (from 1½ or 2 years on). During this final phase, toddlers' rapidly increasing cognitive and language abilities enable them to understand their parents' feelings, goals, and motives and to use this understanding to organize their efforts to be near their parents. As a result, a more mutually regulated relationship gradually emerges as the child takes an increasingly active role in developing a working partnership with his or her parents. Correspondingly, separation distress declines.

The usual outcome of these phases is an enduring emotional tie uniting the child and caregiver. In addition, the child develops an **internal working model of attachment,** a mental representation of the self, of attachment figures, and of relationships in general. This internal working model is based on the young child's perception of the extent to which his or her caregiver can be depended on to satisfy the child's needs and provide a sense of security. Bowlby believed that this internal working model guides the individual's expectations about relationships throughout life. If caregivers are accessible and responsive, young children come to expect interpersonal relationships to be gratifying and they feel worthy of receiving care and love. As adults, they look for, and expect to find, satisfying and security-enhancing relationships similar to the ones they had with their attachment figures in childhood. If children's attachment figures are unavailable or unresponsive, children develop negative perceptions of relationships with other people and of themselves (Bowlby, 1973, 1980; Bretherton & Munholland, 1999). Thus, children's internal working models of attachment are believed to influence their overall adjustment, social behavior, perceptions of others, and the development of their self-esteem and sense of self (R. A. Thompson, 2006).

Measurement of Attachment Security

Attachment encompasses how a child thinks and feels about a caregiver. It is usually measured by observing children's behaviors with their caregivers or by interviewing parents and children about each other's behaviors and the quality of their relationship.

Ainsworth's Strange Situation Procedure

Mary Ainsworth, who began working with John Bowlby in 1950, provided empirical support for Bowlby's theory, extending it in important ways and further emphasizing the concept of the primary caregiver as a secure base. In research conducted in both Uganda (Ainsworth, 1967) and the United States (Ainsworth et al., 1978), Ainsworth studied mother–infant interactions during infants' explorations and separations from their mother. On the basis of her observations, she came to the conclusion that two key factors provide insight into the quality of the infant's attachment to the caregiver: (1) the extent to which an infant is able to use his or her primary caregiver as a secure base, and (2) how the infant reacts to brief separations from, and reunions with, the caregiver (Ainsworth, 1973; Ainsworth et al., 1978).

With these factors in mind, Ainsworth designed a laboratory test for assessing the security of an infant's attachment to his or her parent. This test is called the **Strange Situation** because it is conducted in a context that is unfamiliar to the child and likely to heighten the child's need for his or her parent (similar to Harlow's strange situation for the rhesus monkey infants). In this test, the child, accompanied by the parent, is placed in a laboratory playroom equipped with interesting toys. After the experimenter introduces the parent and child to the room, the child is exposed to seven episodes, including two separations from, and reunions with, the parent, as well as two interactions with a stranger—one when the parent is out of the room and one when the parent is present (see Table 11.1). Each episode lasts approximately 3 minutes unless the child becomes overly upset. Throughout these episodes, observers rate the child's behaviors, including attempts to seek closeness and contact with the parent, resistance to or avoidance of the parent, interactions with the stranger, and interactions with the parent from a distance using language or gestures. Particularly important to determining a child's attachment is his or her reaction to the parent when that parent returns after the separation (Steps 5 and 8 in Table 11.1).

Through her use of the Strange Situation, Ainsworth and her colleagues (1978) discerned three distinct patterns of infants' behavior that seemed to indicate the quality or security of their attachment bonds and that are associated with distinct patterns of parenting behavior. These patterns have been replicated many times in research with mothers and fathers. On the basis of these patterns, Ainsworth identified three attachment categories.

The first attachment category—the one into which the majority of infants fall—is **secure attachment.** Babies in this category use their mother as a secure

Strange Situation ■ a procedure developed by Mary Ainsworth to assess infants' attachment to their primary caregiver

secure attachment ■ a pattern of attachment in which infants or young children have a positive and trusting relationship with their attachment figure. In the Strange Situation, a securely attached infant, for example, may be upset when the caregiver leaves but may be happy to see the caregiver return, recovering quickly from any distress. When children are securely attached, they can use caregivers as a secure base for exploration.

TABLE 11.1

Episodes in Ainsworth's Strange Situation Procedure

Episode	Events	Aspect of Attachment Behavior Assessed
1	Experimenter introduces caregiver and infant to the unfamiliar room; shows toys to baby; then leaves.	None
2	Caregiver and child are alone; caregiver is told not to initiate interaction but to respond to baby as appropriate.	Exploration and use of parent as a secure base
3	Stranger enters and is seated quietly for 1 minute; then talks to caregiver for 1 minute; then tries to interact with the baby for 1 minute.	Reaction to the stranger
4	Mother leaves child alone with the stranger, who lets baby play but offers comfort if needed. Segment is shortened if the baby becomes too distressed.	Separation distress and reaction to stranger's comforting
5	Caregiver calls to baby from outside door, enters the room, and pauses by the door. Stranger leaves. Caregiver lets infant play or may comfort infant if distressed.	Reaction to reunion with parent
6	Parent leaves infant alone in the room. Segment is ended if infant is too distressed.	Separation distress
7	Stranger enters room, greets infant, and pauses. She sits or comforts infant if the infant is upset. Segment is ended if the infant is very upset.	Ability to be soothed by stranger
8	Caregiver calls from outside the door, enters and greets infant and pauses. Caregiver sits if infant is not upset but may provide comfort if infant is distressed. Caregiver allows infant to return to play if interested.	Reaction to reunion

Source: Information from Ainsworth et al. (1978).

insecure attachment ■ a pattern of attachment in which infants or young children have a less positive attachment to their caregiver than do securely attached children. Insecurely attached children can be classified as insecure/resistant (ambivalent), insecure/avoidant, or disorganized/disoriented.

insecure/resistant (or ambivalent) attachment ■ a type of insecure attachment in which infants or young children are clingy and stay close to their caregiver rather than exploring their environment. In the Strange Situation, insecure/resistant infants tend to become very upset when the caregiver leaves them alone in the room. When their caregiver returns, they are not easily comforted and both seek comfort and resist efforts by the caregiver to comfort them.

insecure/avoidant attachment ■ a type of insecure attachment in which infants or young children seem somewhat indifferent toward their caregiver and may even avoid the caregiver. In the Strange Situation, they seem indifferent toward their caregiver before the caregiver leaves the room and indifferent or avoidant when the caregiver returns. If the infant gets upset when left alone, he or she is as easily comforted by a stranger as by a parent.

disorganized/disoriented attachment ■ a type of insecure attachment in which infants or young children have no consistent way of coping with the stress of the Strange Situation. Their behavior is often confused or even contradictory, and they often appear dazed or disoriented.

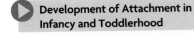

Development of Attachment in Infancy and Toddlerhood

base during the initial part of the session, leaving her side to explore the many toys available in the room. As they play with the toys, these infants occasionally look back to check on their mother or bring a toy over to show her. They are usually, but by no means always, distressed to some degree when their mother leaves the room, especially when they are left totally alone. However, when their mother returns, they make it clear that they are glad to see her, either by simply greeting her with a happy smile or, if they have been upset during her absence, by going to her to be picked up and comforted. If they have been upset, their mother's presence comforts and calms them, often enabling them to explore the room again. Between 50 and 60% of children in the United States whose mothers are not clinically disturbed fall into this category (R. A. Thompson, 1998; van IJzendoorn, Schuengel, & Bakermans-Kranenburg, 1999).

The other two attachment categories that Ainsworth originally identified involve children who are rated as **insecurely attached,** that is, who have less positive attachment to their caregivers than do securely attached children. One type of insecurely attached infant is classified as **insecure/resistant,** or **ambivalent.** Infants in this category are often clingy from the beginning of the Strange Situation, staying close to the mother instead of exploring the toys. When their mother leaves the room, they tend to get very upset, often crying intensely. In the reunion, the insecure/resistant infant typically reestablishes contact with the mother, only to then rebuff her efforts at offering comfort. For example, the infant may rush to the mother bawling, with outstretched arms, signaling the wish to be picked up—but then, as soon as he or she is picked up, arch away from the mother or begin squirming to get free from her embrace. About 9% of children in the United States fall into the insecure/resistant category (van IJzendoorn et al., 1999).

The other type of insecurely attached infant is classified as **insecure/avoidant.** Children in this category tend to avoid their mother in the Strange Situation. For example, they often fail to greet her during the reunions and ignore her or turn away while she is in the room. Approximately 15% children fall into the insecure/avoidant category (van IJzendoorn et al., 1999).

Subsequent to Ainsworth's original research, attachment investigators found that the reactions of a small percentage of children in the Strange Situation did not fit well into any of Ainsworth's three categories. These children seem to have no consistent way of coping with the stress of the Strange Situation. Their behavior is often confused or even contradictory. For example, they may exhibit fearful smiles and look away while approaching their mother, or they may seem quite calm and contented and then suddenly display angry distress. They also frequently appear dazed or disoriented and may freeze in their behavior and remain still for a substantial period of time. These infants, labeled **disorganized/disoriented,** seem to have an unsolvable problem: they want to approach their mother, but they also seem to regard her as a source of fear from which they want to withdraw (Main & Solomon, 1990). About 15% of middle-class American infants fall into this category. However, this percentage may be considerably higher among maltreated infants (van IJzendoorn et al., 1999), among infants whose parents are having serious difficulties with their own working models of attachment (van IJzendoorn, 1995), and among preschoolers from lower socioeconomic backgrounds (Moss, Cyr, & Dubois-Comtois, 2004; van IJzendoorn et al., 1999).

A key question, of course, is whether there is some similarity between infants' behavior in the Strange Situation and their behavior at home. The answer is yes (J. Solomon & George, 1999). For example, compared with infants who are insecurely attached, 12-month-olds who are securely attached exhibit more enjoyment of physical contact, are less fussy or difficult, and are better able to use their

mothers as a secure base for exploration at home (Pederson & Moran, 1996). Thus, they are more likely to learn about their environments and to enjoy doing so. In addition, children's behavior in the Strange Situation correlates with attachment scores derived from observing children's interactions with their mother over several hours (van IJzendoorn et al., 2004).

The Strange Situation remains the standard means of measuring infants' attachment security, but it has been criticized on several fronts. First, the Strange Situation requires substantial resources; it must be conducted in a laboratory with video-recording equipment and an extensively trained staff (Tryphonopoulos, Letourneau, & Ditommaso, 2014). Second, some psychologists argue that, rather than falling into categories, the attachment security of parent–child relationships should be measured along multiple continuous dimensions. This possibility was demonstrated in a sample of several thousand children: security dimensions provided a better explanation of children's observed attachment behaviors than did categories (Fraley & Spieker, 2003). Despite these findings, researchers continue to overwhelmingly prefer attachment categories.

A third critique of the Strange Situation is that it is no longer so "strange" in a world where 61% of children under the age of five are cared for by someone other than their mothers on a daily basis (Laughlin, 2013). However, a study of children's behavior toward their parents at drop-off and pickup from childcare found that 67% were classified as secure, 9% were insecure/avoidant, 14% were insecure/resistant, and 10% were disorganized/disoriented (Bick, Dozier, & Perkins, 2012)—numbers similar to those found by the Strange Situation measure. This study also found that children's behavior in these childcare settings matched their behavior during the laboratory-based Strange Situation (Bick et al., 2012). See Box 11.1 for more information about the connection between childcare and attachment security.

Other Measures of Attachment Security

Over the past few decades, several other tools have been developed to measure attachment. One widely used alternative is the Attachment Q-Sort (Waters & Deane, 1985). To complete a Q-sort, parents, teachers, or observers take a large number of cards (75 or more) with descriptions of child behaviors and sort them into nine equal piles according to how well they describe the target child. In this way, the child is characterized on a continuum from secure to insecure. The Attachment Q-Sort has been found to have good *reliability* and *validity* (see Chapter 1) in the United States and across a variety of countries (e.g., China, Japan, Norway, Portugal, South Africa, and Thailand; Tryphonopoulos et al., 2014).

Attachment is not a fixed quality. Although there is moderate stability in attachment security, children's level of attachment to their parents can change throughout childhood (Pinquart, Feussner, & Ahnert, 2013). However, because the Strange Situation is not relevant after infancy, researchers have developed measures to determine attachment security in older children. Children in middle childhood and adolescence can be asked directly about their relationships with their parents in interviews, such as the Adult Attachment Interview (Main & Goldwyn, 1998), or through questionnaires, such as the Inventory of Parent and Peer Attachment (Armsden & Greenberg, 1987), which, as its name suggests, also taps into adolescents' growing reliance on peers for emotional support. Attachment security takes different forms in older childhood and adolescence; only in early childhood do we expect children to react with distress to their parent leaving the room. However, researchers have found that securely attached adolescents

BOX 11.1 | a closer look

DOES CHILDCARE INTERFERE WITH ATTACHMENT?

Attachment develops in the 1st year of life, but many parents have to work out of the home during their children's 1st year. This predicament has led researchers and parents to wonder if time away from primary caregivers, particularly mothers, and in the care of nonparental caregivers might interfere with children's ability to form secure attachments with their parents.

Growing interest in the effects of childcare on infants and toddlers prompted the National Institute of Child Health and Human Development (NICHD) to fund a large, longitudinal study of children and families from 10 cities around the United States. Started in 1991, the Study of Early Child Care and Youth Development (SECCYD) studied the development of 1364 children from birth to adolescence and kept careful track of their various childcare arrangements in their early years. The study measured (1) characteristics of children's families and their childcare settings, (2) children's attachment to their mothers using the Strange Situation procedure, (3) the quality of their mothers' interactions with them, and (4) their social behavior, cognitive development, and health status. The SECCYD has provided the strongest examination into potential links between childcare and attachment to date.

The first important finding was that 15-month-olds in childcare were just as likely to be securely attached to their mothers as were children not in childcare (NICHD Early Child Care Research Network, 1997a). The same thing was found with children at 36 months of age: differences in the number of hours in childcare, the type of childcare, the number of childcare arrangements, the age the child entered childcare, and the quality of childcare did not predict children's security of attachment (NICHD Early Child Care Research Network, 2001).

Second, the SECCYD found that for children age 15 months and 36 months, maternal sensitivity was a very strong predictor of children's attachment security, even when aspects of the children's childcare arrangements and other aspects of the family (income, mother education, mother depressive symptoms) were accounted for (NICHD Early Child Care Research Network, 1997a, 2001). Aspects of childcare were related to attachment security when children experienced risks in both the childcare and home contexts, namely poor-quality care in the childcare setting *and* insensitive or unresponsive parenting in the home setting (NICHD Early Child Care Research Network, 1997a).

Additionally, the study found evidence that high-quality childcare can serve a compensatory function. Specifically, children who had insensitive and unresponsive mothers were more likely to be securely attached to those mothers if they experienced high-quality childcare than if they experienced low-quality childcare (NICHD Early Child Care Research Network, 1997a). This finding demonstrates that, in addition to not undermining parent–child attachment security, under some circumstances childcare can actually promote attachment security in the parent–child relationship.

Other studies have replicated these findings. A meta-analysis of studies comparing links between maternal and nonmaternal care and children's development found no evidence that children in childcare are less securely attached than other children or that they display less positive behavior in interactions with their mothers (Erel, Oberman, & Yirmiya, 2000). As with the SECCYD findings, the only time that childcare appears to interfere with attachment is when the care is of low quality (e.g., frequent turnover in caregivers or a high ratio of infants per caregiver) (M. E. Lamb, 1998; Sagi et al., 2002).

continue to use their parents as secure bases as they begin to establish their own autonomy (Allen et al., 2003).

Cultural Variations in Attachment Styles

Because human infants are believed to be biologically predisposed to form attachments with their caregivers, one might expect attachment behaviors to be similar in different cultures. In fact, in large measure, infants' behaviors in the Strange Situation are similar across numerous cultures, including those of China, Western Europe, and various parts of Africa. In all these cultures, there are securely attached, insecure/resistant, and insecure/avoidant infants, with the average percentages approximating those established in the United States (van IJzendoorn & Sagi, 1999; van IJzendoorn et al., 1999). Relatively few studies in non-Western cultures include the category "disorganized/disoriented," but in those that do, the percentage of babies who fall into this category is roughly the same as that in Western countries (Behrens, Hesse, & Main, 2007; van IJzendoorn et al., 1999).

Despite these general consistencies in attachment ratings, some important differences in children's behavior in the Strange Situation have been noted in certain other cultures (van IJzendoorn & Sagi-Schwartz, 2008; Zevalkink, Riksen-Walraven, & Van Lieshout, 1999). For example, while Japanese infants in one study showed roughly the same percentage of secure attachment in the Strange Situation as middle-class U.S. infants do (about 62% to 68%), in some research, there was a notable difference in the types of insecure attachment they displayed. All the insecurely attached Japanese infants were classified as insecure/resistant, which is to say that none exhibited insecure/avoidant behavior (Takahashi, 1986). Similarly, in a sample of Korean families, insecure/avoidant children were very rare (Jin et al., 2012).

One possible explanation is that Japanese culture exalts the idea of oneness between mother and child; correspondingly, its child-rearing practices, compared with those in the United States, foster greater mother–infant closeness and physical intimacy, as well as infants' greater dependency on their mother (Rothbaum et al., 2000). Thus, in the Strange Situation, Japanese children may desire more bodily contact and reassurance than do U.S. children and therefore may be more likely to exhibit anger and resistance to their mother after being deprived of contact with her (Mizuta et al., 1996).

Another explanation is that the Strange Situation might not always have been a valid measure because it is possible that some Japanese parents were self-conscious and inhibited in the Strange Situation setting, which, in turn, could have affected their children's behavior. It is also possible that how young children react in the Strange Situation is affected by their prior experience with unfamiliar situations and people. Thus, part of the difference in the rates of insecure/resistant attachment shown by Japanese and U.S. infants may be due to the fact that, at the time that many of the studies in question were conducted (the 1980s), very few infants in Japan were enrolled in day care and thus did not experience frequent separations from their mother. Consistent with this argument, a more recent study, which looked at the reunion behaviors of 6-year-old Japanese children who had all attended preschool, did not find a high number of insecure/resistant attachments (Behrens et al., 2007). It is therefore possible that differences in children's experiences with separation within or across cultures contribute substantially to the variability in children's behavior in the Strange Situation.

One study of mothers and their young children in nine countries (Canada, Colombia, France, Italy, Japan, Peru, Portugal, Taiwan, and the United States) found that across all countries children used their mothers as a secure base when exploring new surroundings (Posada et al., 2013). This finding supports the notion that attachment security is a universal phenomenon. However, this study also revealed some behavioral differences: Children in Colombia and Peru were least likely to remain in close physical proximity to their mothers, while children in Italy and Portugal were much more likely than children in other countries to maintain physical contact with their mothers (Posada et al., 2013).

The degree to which children are encouraged to be independent varies across cultures and can affect whether children are categorized as insecure/resistant.

 Assessment of Attachment in the Efe Culture: Interview with Gilda Morelli

Sources of Individual Differences in Attachment Styles

If children are biologically disposed to form attachments to their caregivers, why are some children securely attached and some insecurely attached? Two main sources for these individual differences are parental sensitivity and genetic predispositions.

The mothers of securely attached infants generally respond warmly to their offspring and are sensitive to their needs.

CULTURA CREATIVE (RF) / ALAMY

Parenting and Attachment Styles

Given that attachment security is a marker of the quality of the relationship between a parent and child, it makes sense that parental behavior should be a strong predictor of children's attachment styles. Indeed, after developing the Strange Situation procedure, Ainsworth and her colleagues (1978) checked the validity of their measure by observing whether mothers' behavior in the home was linked with their children's attachment classifications. They found that it was, and several subsequent studies have found similar relationships across the three original classifications as well as the disorganized/disoriented classification (see Table 11.2 for a summary of behaviors associated with each classification).

One key aspect of parenting that has been consistently linked with attachment styles is **parental sensitivity,** which is caregiving behavior that involves the expression of warmth as well as contingent and consistent responsiveness to children's needs. The mothers of securely attached 1-year-olds tend to read their babies' signals accurately, responding quickly to the needs of a crying baby and smiling back at a beaming one. Positive exchanges between mother and child, such as mutual smiling and laughing, making sounds at each other, or engaging in coordinated play, are a characteristic of sensitive parenting that may be particularly important in promoting secure attachment (De Wolff & van IJzendoorn, 1997; Nievar & Becker, 2008).

TABLE 11.2

Patterns of Child and Parent Behavior Characteristic of the Four Styles of Attachment

Style of Attachment	Child's Behaviors During Strange Situation Procedure	Parent's Behaviors Toward Child at Home
Secure	Uses parent as secure base; is upset at separation; seeks parent at reunion and is easily soothed by the parent	Is responsive and sensitive to the child's signals; is affectionate and expressive; initiates frequent close contact with the child
Insecure/Avoidant	Readily separates to explore; avoids or ignores the parent; does not prefer the parent to the stranger	Is insensitive to the child's signals; avoids close contact and rejects child's bids for contact; may be angry, irritable, or impatient
Insecure/Resistant	Does not separate to explore; is wary of the stranger even when the parent is present; is extremely upset at separation; is not soothed by the parent and resists the parent's attempts to soothe	Is inconsistent or awkward in reacting to child's distress; seems overwhelmed with tasks of caregiving
Disorganized/Disoriented	Goes to parent reluctantly, perhaps looking away from parent; may express fear when with parent; may seem to "freeze" their behavior and expressions for short periods	Is intrusive; is emotionally unavailable; may dissociate or be in a trance-like state; confuses or frightens the child; may be harsh or abusive

Information from Ainsworth et al. (1978); Hesse & Main (2006); Isabella (1993); Leerkes, Parade, & Gudmundson (2011); Main & Solomon (1990).

parental sensitivity ■ caregiving behavior that involves the expression of warmth and contingent responsiveness to children, such as when they require assistance or are in distress

In contrast, the mothers of insecure/resistant infants tend to be inconsistent in their early caregiving: they sometimes respond promptly to their infants' distress, but sometimes they do not. These mothers often seem highly anxious and overwhelmed by the demands of caregiving. Mothers of insecure/avoidant infants tend to be indifferent and emotionally unavailable, sometimes rejecting their baby's attempts at physical closeness (Isabella, 1993; Leerkes, Parade, & Gudmundson, 2011).

Mothers of disorganized/disoriented infants sometimes exhibit abusive, frightening, or disoriented behavior and may be dealing with unresolved loss or trauma (L. M. Forbes et al., 2007; Madigan, Moran, & Pederson, 2006; van IJzendoorn et al., 1999). In response, their infants often appear to be confused or frightened (E. A. Carlson, 1998; Hesse & Main, 2006). By age 3 to 6, perhaps in an attempt to manage their emotions, these children often try to control their mother's activities and conversation, either in an excessively helpful and emotionally positive way, basically trying to cheer her up, or in a hostile or aggressive way (Moss et al., 2004; J. Solomon, George, & De Jong, 1995).

The association between maternal sensitivity and the quality of infants' and children's attachment has been demonstrated in studies involving a variety of cultural groups (Beijersbergen et al., 2012; Mesman, van IJzendoorn, & Bakermans-Kranenburg, 2012; Posada et al., 2016; Valenzuela, 1997; van IJzendoorn et al., 2004). Particularly striking is the finding that infants whose mothers are insensitive show only a 38% rate of secure attachment, which is almost half the typical rate (van IJzendoorn & Sagi, 1999). An association between fathers' sensitivity and the security of their children's attachment has also been found, though it is somewhat weaker than that for mothers (G. L. Brown, Mangelsdorf, & Neff, 2012; Lucassen et al., 2011; van IJzendoorn & De Wolff, 1997).

Given that all the research discussed above involves correlations between parental sensitivity and children's attachment status, it is impossible to determine whether parents' sensitivity was actually responsible for their children's security of attachment or was merely associated with it. It could be that some other factor, such as the presence or absence of marital conflict, affected both the parents' sensitivity and the child's security of attachment. However, evidence that parental sensitivity does in fact have a causal effect on infants' attachment has been provided by short-term experimental interventions designed to enhance the sensitivity of mothers' caregiving. These interventions, discussed in Box 11.2, have been found to increase not only mothers' sensitivity with their infants but also the security of their infants' attachment (Bakermans-Kranenburg, van IJzendoorn, & Juffer, 2003; van IJzendoorn, Juffer, & Duyvesteyn, 1995). Moreover, in twin studies of infants' attachment, nearly all the variation in attachments was due to environmental factors (Bokhorst et al., 2003; Roisman & Fraley, 2006).

Although secure attachments are more likely when parents display sensitivity, children can still develop secure attachments to their parents even when they are not consistently sensitive. In a study of preschoolers, half of whom were involved in the child protective system because their mothers had maltreated them, the maltreated preschoolers were indeed more likely to be insecure or disorganized than the non-maltreated children. However, 23% of the maltreated children had secure attachments to the mothers who had maltreated them (Stronach et al., 2011). Though surprising, this finding likely derives from the fact that abusive parents can also be loving and sensitive at times, factors that promote children's attachment. The findings also demonstrate that the biological drive to be securely attached to a caregiver is powerful enough to overcome frightening and painful parental behavior.

BOX 11.2 | applications

INTERVENTIONS TO IMPROVE ATTACHMENT

Clinicians who work with families have developed programs to intervene in parent–child relationships in order to promote attachment security. A meta-analysis of 10 attachment interventions for families at risk for insecure attachments found that infants were nearly 3 times as likely to have a secure attachment classification if they and their parents participated in an attachment intervention, compared with infants and parents who did not (Letourneau et al., 2015). The interventions were most effective if they occurred early (when children were between 3 and 9 months of age) and if the family had a history of maltreatment. Some of these efforts are directed entirely at parenting behavior but others are directed at both parents and children.

One commonly used intervention targeted at parenting behavior is called the Circle of Security (Powell et al., 2014). Parents are encouraged to reflect on their own mental representations of how parents and children should interact and then are guided by trained therapists to change any maladaptive representations, such as assuming the child should automatically know what the parent wants or that the role of the child is to comfort the parent rather than vice versa. A study in Australia evaluated the effectiveness of the Circle of Security intervention with a sample of young children with documented behavior problems and their caregivers. After 20 weeks, the caregivers developed more positive representations and the number of children with a disorganized/disoriented attachment style decreased (Huber, McMahon, & Sweller, 2015).

Another intervention known as the Attachment and Biobehavioral Catch-Up (ABC) was developed specifically for mothers identified as at risk for maltreating their children (Bernard et al., 2012). ABC focuses on changing parents' behaviors, rather than changing mental representations. Trainers teach parents to achieve three goals: provide nurturance to the child, follow the child's lead, and avoid frightening behaviors. Trainers observe parent–child interactions and give the parents immediate positive feedback and concrete suggestions to implement in the moment. ABC also includes structured parent–child activities (such as preparing a simple snack) to help parents practice their new skills.

The ABC intervention has been found to be very effective at changing both parents' behaviors and children's security. Maltreated children who participated in the ABC intervention with their parents were more likely to have secure attachments, compared with maltreated children who were not in the intervention (52% versus 33%), and they were less likely to have disorganized attachments (43% versus 57%; Bernard et al., 2012). The ABC intervention shows promise for changing such insensitive behavior; maltreating mothers who participated in ABC showed improvement in their attention to and processing of infant emotional expressions (Bernard, Simons, & Dozier, 2015). As we saw in Chapter 10, contingent and appropriate responses to children's emotions are key to promoting children's own positive emotional and social development.

These interventions together demonstrate that even very problematic parent–child relationships can be improved, with clear benefits for children's attachment security.

Genetic Influences

An important source of individual differences in attachment lies within children themselves—namely, in their genes (S. C. Johnson & Chen, 2011). One recent study focused on the possible influence that allelic variants of the serotonin transporter gene, SLC6A4 (formerly named 5HTT), might have on behavior in the Strange Situation. The participants were Ukrainian preschoolers, some of whom had been raised in institutions and some of whom had been raised in their biological family. The researchers found that children with an SLC6A4 variant that is frequently associated with vulnerability in the face of stress exhibited less attachment security and more attachment disorganization if they grew up in an institution than did preschoolers with the same variant who lived with their family. In contrast, preschoolers who were raised in an institution but had a different SLC6A4 genotype, one that is frequently associated with less reactivity and less vulnerability, did not exhibit adverse attachment behavior (Bakermans-Kranenburg, Dobrova-Krol, & van IJzendoorn, 2012).

There is also some research indicating that a gene, called DRD4, involved in the dopamine system is associated with disorganized/disoriented attachment when an infant is in a stressful environment (as when the mother is suffering from trauma or loss) but is associated with greater attachment security in a less stressful context (Bakermans-Kranenburg & van IJzendoorn, 2007). This research, along with the study discussed above and other recent work, highlights the concept of *differential susceptibility* described in Chapter 10. That is, it suggests that certain genes result in children being differentially susceptible to the quality of their rearing environment, such that those with the "reactive" genes benefit more from having a secure attachment (e.g., are better adjusted and more prosocial than their peers) but do more poorly if they have an insecure attachment (Bakermans-Kranenburg & van IJzendoorn, 2007, 2011; Kochanska, Philibert, & Barry, 2009).

The links between attachment security and genetic makeup have been found to last into adulthood. One longitudinal study followed children from infancy, when attachment was assessed with the Strange Situation, all the way to age 26, when attachment was assessed with the Adult Attachment Interview. Researchers found that the continuity in individuals' attachment security depended on which variant of an oxytocin receptor gene OXTR they had, although not on variations in DRD4 (Raby et al., 2013). Taken together, these studies indicate that individuals' genetic makeup affects both the way in which environmental forces influence their attachment security in childhood and the continuity of attachment security into adulthood.

Attachment and Social-Emotional Development

Children's attachment status, both in infancy and later in childhood, has been found to predict their later social-emotional development, with securely attached infants experiencing better adjustment and more social skills than insecurely attached children. One explanation for this may be that children with a secure attachment are more likely to develop positive and constructive internal working models of attachment. (Recall that children's working models of attachment are believed to shape their adjustment and social behavior, their self-perceptions and sense of self, and their expectations about other people; there is also some direct evidence for this belief [e.g., S. C. Johnson & Chen, 2011; S. C. Johnson, Dweck, & Chen, 2007].) In addition, children who experience the sensitive, supportive parenting that is associated with secure attachment are likely to learn that it is acceptable to express emotions in an appropriate way and that emotional communication with others is important (Cassidy, 1994; Kerns et al., 2007; Riva Crugnola et al., 2011). In contrast, insecure/avoidant children, whose parents tend to be nonresponsive to their signals of need and distress, are likely to learn to inhibit emotional expressiveness and to not seek comfort from other people (Bridges & Grolnick, 1995).

Consistent with these patterns, children who were securely attached in infancy or later in childhood seem to have closer, more harmonious relationships with peers than do children who were insecurely attached (McElwain, Booth-LaForce, & Wu, 2011; Pallini et al., 2014). For example, securely attached children are higher in self-regulation, sociability, and social competence with peers than are insecurely attached children (Drake, Belsky, & Fearon, 2014; Lucas-Thompson & Clarke-Stewart, 2007; Panfile & Laible, 2012; Vondra et al., 2001). Correspondingly, they are less anxious, depressed, or socially withdrawn (Brumariu & Kerns, 2010; Madigan et al., 2016)—especially compared with children who had insecure/resistant attachments (Groh et al., 2012)—as well as less aggressive and delinquent (Fearon et al., 2010; Groh et al., 2012; Hoeve et al., 2012; Madigan et al., 2016; NICHD Early Child Care Research Network, 2006). They are also better able to understand others' emotions (Steele, Steele, & Croft, 2008; R. A. Thompson, 2008)

Toddlers who were securely attached as infants are more likely to engage in prosocial behavior, such as trying to comfort someone who is sad, than are those who were insecurely attached as infants.

and display more helping, sharing, and concern for peers (N. Eisenberg, Fabes, & Spinrad, 2006; Kestenbaum, Farber, & Sroufe, 1989; Panfile & Laible, 2012).

Securely attached children are also more likely to report positive emotion and to exhibit normal rather than abnormal patterns of reactivity to stress (Bernard & Dozier, 2010; Borelli et al., 2010; Luijk et al., 2010). Secure attachment in infancy predicts positive peer and romantic relationships and emotional health in adolescence (E. A. Carlson, Sroufe, & Egeland, 2004; Collins et al., 1997) and early adulthood (Englund et al., 2011), as well as physical health in adulthood (Puig et al., 2013).

Although there are only a few studies in which infants' attachments to both parents were assessed, it appears that children may be most at risk if they have insecure attachments to both their mother and their father. In a study in which attachment was assessed at 15 months of age, children with insecure attachments to both parents were especially prone to problem behaviors such as aggression and defiance in elementary school. Having secure attachment(s) with one or both parents was associated with low levels of problem behaviors (Kochanska & Kim, 2013). However, it is not clear yet if having one secure attachment buffers against other types of negative outcomes, such as internalizing problems (e.g., anxiety, depression) or problems in interpersonal relations.

Yet, as noted above, children's attachment to their parents can change over time, such as when aspects of their environments change—for example, with the onset or termination of stress and conflict in the home (Frosch, Mangelsdorf, & McHale, 2000; M. Lewis, Feiring, & Rosenthal, 2000; Moss et al., 2004) or a pronounced shift in the mother's typical behavior with the child (L. M. Forbes et al., 2007) or in her sensitivity (Beijersbergen et al., 2012). In such cases, current parent–child interactions or parenting behaviors predict the child's social and emotional competence at that age better than measures of attachment taken at younger ages (R. A. Thompson, 1998; Youngblade & Belsky, 1992). Quality of attachment in adolescence has been found to predict changes in behavior and mental health, with securely attached adolescents experiencing fewer behavioral and mental health problems than insecurely attached adolescents (Allen et al., 2007).

Review

Influenced by research with human and monkey infants demonstrating the importance of consistent, caring relationships with adults, John Bowlby proposed that a secure attachment provides infants and children with a secure base for exploration and contributes to a positive internal working model of relationships in general. According to attachment research, pioneered by Mary Ainsworth and based on results from her Strange Situation test, children's attachment relationships with caregivers can be classified as secure, insecure/avoidant, insecure/resistant, and disorganized/disoriented. Children in these categories display behavioral similarities across cultures, although the percentage of children in different attachment groups sometimes varies across cultures or subcultures.

Factors that appear to influence the security of attachment include parents' sensitivity and responsiveness to their children's needs, as well as some aspects of children's genes. Children's security of attachment to their caregivers has been found to predict their later behaviors and mental health, with secure children displaying better behavior, higher self-regulation, and fewer mental health problems than insecure children.

The Self

Who are you? The answer could involve a description of physical characteristics; personality traits; personal preferences; social and familial relationships; or details of ethnicity, culture, or national origin. The self is in fact all of these things and, over the course of development, children assimilate each of them into a sense of who they are. This section will focus on three main aspects of the self and how each develops across childhood: self-concept, self-esteem, and identity. Self-concept is how individuals view themselves, whereas self-esteem refers to how they evaluate and feel about themselves. Self-concept and self-esteem are thus internal to the individual (Baumeister, 2005).

In contrast, identity involves descriptions or categories that are often externally imposed, such as through membership or participation in a family, religion, race/ethnic group, or school (Baumeister, 2005). To understand the difference between self-concept and identity, think of a newborn baby; he does not have a conscious self-concept, but he does have an identity because he has a name and is part of a family, which in turn is part of a larger community (Baumeister, 2005). As we will see below, children and adolescents can—and do—have multiple identities based on various facets of their lives, including ethnic identity and sexual identity.

Self-Concept

Self-concept refers to a system made up of one's thoughts and attitudes about oneself. This conceptual system can include thoughts about one's own physical being (e.g., body, possessions), social characteristics (e.g., relationships, personality, social roles), and internal characteristics (e.g., thoughts, psychological functioning). It is also an understanding of how the self changes or remains the same over time, of beliefs about one's own role in shaping these processes, and even of reflections on one's own consciousness of selfhood (Damon & Hart, 1988). The development of the self is important because individuals' self-conceptions, including the ways they view and feel about themselves, influence their overall feelings of well-being and self-confidence when faced with external criticism (Harter, 2012a). As we will see, children's self-concept develops primarily through interactions with people in their environments.

Self-Concept in Infancy

Self-concept starts as an appreciation of one's physical self. Infants must first differentiate themselves from the environment, which they do by developing the sense that they are physical beings (Oyserman, Elmore, & Smith, 2012). Infants do this in part by realizing that some things are always present, such as their hands, while other things come and go, such as their parents or toys. Eventually, infants understand that the things that are always present are part of their own bodies (Baumeister, 2005).

In their theories of cognitive development, both Piaget and Vygotsky argue that children learn by interacting with their environments (see Chapter 4). One important lesson infants learn through experience is that they can affect their environments. For example, over the first few months of life an infant learns that if she cries, a parent will come and provide comfort and that if she grabs a toy, she can bring it closer to play with or suck on. Through such interactions, infants gradually appreciate that they are separate from the people and objects in their environments and that they can influence these people and objects to meet their own needs.

self-concept ■ a conceptual system made up of one's thoughts and attitudes about oneself

There is compelling evidence that infants have a rudimentary self-concept in the first months of life. As noted in Chapters 5 and 10, by 2 to 4 months of age, infants have a sense of their ability to control objects outside themselves, as is clear both from their enthusiasm when they can make a mobile move by pulling a string attached to their arm and from their anger when their efforts no longer have an effect. They also seem to have some understanding of their own bodily movements.

Self-concept becomes much more distinct at about 8 months of age. According to attachment theory, this is the age when infants react with separation distress if kept apart from a parent, suggesting that they recognize that they and their mother are separate entities. Thus, the development of self-concept is the first necessary step in the development of attachment to a caregiver.

As discussed in Chapter 4, around their 1st birthday, infants begin to show joint attention with respect to objects in the environment. For example, they will visually follow a caregiver's pointing finger to find the object that the caregiver is calling attention to, and then turn back to the caregiver to confirm that they are indeed looking at the intended object (Stern, 1985). They sometimes will also give objects to an adult in an apparent effort to engage the adult in their activities (M. J. West & Rheingold, 1978). By around 15 months of age, most children are able to distinguish themselves and others by both gender and age (Damon & Hart, 1988).

An emerging recognition of the self becomes more directly apparent by 18 to 20 months of age, when many children can look into a mirror and recognize themselves (Asendorpf, Warkentin, & Baudonnière, 1996; M. Lewis & Brooks-Gunn, 1979; Nielsen, Suddendorf, & Slaughter, 2006), which requires that they have memories of their appearance that they can match to the image in the mirror (Oyserman et al., 2012). A commonly used test of this ability is the mirror self-recognition test or "rouge test," in which an experimenter surreptitiously puts a dot of rouge on a child's face, places the child in front of a mirror, and observes the child's reaction. Children younger than 18 months old typically respond by either trying to touch the image in the mirror or doing nothing, suggesting that they do not recognize the image as themselves. Most children between 18 and 24 months old will touch the rouge on their own face, indicating that they recognize themselves in the mirror (Courage, Edison, & Howe, 2004), although children with autism spectrum disorder (ASD) have significant difficulties in this regard (see Box 11.3). Interestingly, 2-year-old chimpanzees have also been found to show self-recognition through the mirror self-recognition test (Bard et al., 2006).

The rouge test was developed in the United States, and when it has been tried in developing countries, even children much older than 2 years of age often fail to recognize themselves in the mirror (Broesch et al., 2010). Researchers wondered whether these children really had less self-recognition or whether differences in autonomy due to cultural factors accounted for the different test results. For instance, children in interdependent cultures may ignore the mark because they assume the experimenter put it there on purpose, while children in independent cultures are more disposed to explore the mark on their own (Ross et al., 2016).

To examine this idea, researchers administered the mirror self-recognition test to infants in Scotland, Turkey, and Zambia, along with a second test known as the "body-as-obstacle" task.

▶ **Self-Awareness and the Rouge Test**

This girl recognizes that the child in the mirror with a spot on her cheek is herself.

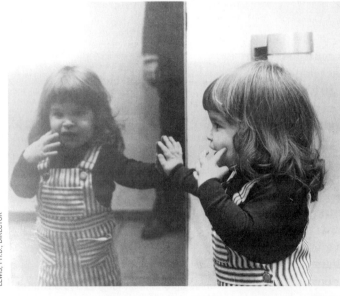

THE SELF ■ 483

BOX 11.3 | individual differences

DEVELOPMENT OF SELF-AWARENESS AMONG CHILDREN WITH AUTISM

Children with autism spectrum disorder (ASD) have a variety of cognitive and emotional difficulties, including impairments in the development of a theory of mind and in their ability to identify with others (American Psychiatric Association, 2013; also see Boxes 3.1 and 7.1). Researchers have wondered whether the difficulties children with ASD have in interacting with other people, as well as in behaviors such as maintaining personal hygiene, derive in part from the fact that they have an impaired sense of self-awareness (Duff & Flattery, 2014).

Researchers have found that children with ASD typically refer to themselves in the third person (Duff & Flattery, 2014). In addition, children with ASD have difficulties differentiating themselves from other people—difficulties that they may be aware of. Take for example this quote from a high-functioning young adult with ASD:

> I really didn't know there were people until I was seven years old. I then suddenly realized there were people. But not

like you do. I still have to remind myself that there are people . . . I never could have a friend. I really don't know what to do with other people.

> (Cohen, 1980, p. 388)

Therapists and teachers have designed interventions to improve these children's self-awareness, with the hope that they will develop the skills to function independently. One such intervention promotes self-awareness among adolescents with ASD through joint attention activities, which involve attracting the attention of another person in order to share interest in an object or event (e.g., "Look at that pretty butterfly!"). Participants are first taught about reflected mirror images using joint attention. This ability is then generalized over time such that eventually the participants can recognize themselves in the mirror. Participation in these activities did in fact lead to greater self-awareness in the participants who did not already have it (Duff & Flattery, 2014), indicating

that children with ASD can be guided into having greater self-awareness.

Another intervention goes a step further by focusing on this disorder as an identity. PsychoEducational Groups for Autism Spectrum Understanding and Support (known as PEGASUS) teaches high-functioning children with ASD about their diagnosis in order to foster ASD-related self-awareness (Gordon et al., 2015). Participants have experienced significant gains in ASD self-awareness and, importantly, did not experience an accompanying decrease in self-esteem (Gordon et al., 2015). Although PEGASUS can only be helpful to high-functioning children with ASD, such as those who can speak and understand a language, it does illustrate that self-awareness can be fostered through direct instruction. This intervention thus points to a potentially valuable strategy for working with the two-thirds of children with ASD who do not also have intellectual disability (Centers for Disease Control and Prevention, 2014).

In this task, children are made to stand on a mat that is attached to a toy cart and are then encouraged to push the cart to their mothers. Children who realize they must step off the mat in order to push the cart are considered to have a sense of self-concept. In this three-country study, children from Scotland did best on the mirror self-recognition test, whereas children from Zambia did best on the body-as-obstacle task (see Figure 11.2). Cultural differences in infants' self-awareness behaviors have also been linked to differences in parenting behavior; children whose mothers emphasize verbal communication were more likely to pass the mirror test, whereas the children whose mothers were more physically and verbally directive were not (Ross et al., 2016). These findings make clear that cultural contexts can influence how children think about themselves and their environments.

By age 2, many children can recognize themselves in photographs. In one study, 63% of a group of 20- to 25-month-olds picked themselves out when presented with pictures of themselves and two same-sex, same-age children. By approximately age 30 months, 97% of the children immediately picked their own photograph (Bullock & Lütkenhaus, 1990). During their 3rd year, children's self-awareness becomes quite clear in other ways as well. Similar to how memory

FIGURE 11.2 Percent of children in three countries who show self-awareness in two different tasks Children in the more interdependent country (Zambia) did best on the task that required meeting a social goal, namely pushing a toy to their mothers. (Data from Ross et al., 2016)

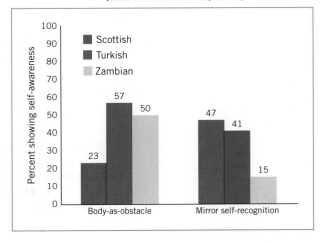

aids in self-recognition, young children use language to store memories of their own experiences and behaviors, which they then use to construct narratives of their own "life story" and develop more enduring self-concepts (Harter, 2012a; R. A. Thompson, 2006). As we saw in Chapter 10, 2-year-olds exhibit embarrassment and shame—emotions that obviously require a self-concept (M. Lewis, 1998). The strength of 2-year-olds' awareness of self is even more evident in their notorious self-assertion, which has led to the period between ages 2 and 3 being called the "terrible twos." During this time, children often try to determine their activities and goals independent of, and often in direct opposition to, what their parents (and other adults) want them to do (Bullock & Lütkenhaus, 1990).

Parents contribute to the child's expanding self-concept by providing descriptive information about the child ("You're such a big boy"), evaluative descriptions of the child ("You're so smart"), and information about the degree to which the child has met rules and standards ("Good girls don't hit their baby sisters"). As noted in Chapter 4, parents also collaborate in children's construction of autobiographical memory by reminding them of their past experiences (Snow, 1990).

Self-Concept in Childhood

As children progress through childhood, their self-concept becomes increasingly complex. Susan Harter, a leading researcher on children's emerging sense of self, argues that sense of self is largely a social construction based on the observations and evaluations of others, particularly of caregivers (Harter, 2012a). These evaluations can be both direct and indirect. For instance, if a teacher tells a child that she is doing very well on her math tests, the child will internalize that she is a person who is good at math; the teacher has directly influenced the child's sense of self. Indirect influences come from how children are treated by others. As seen in the discussion of attachment, a child who is nurtured, loved, and supported develops an internal working model of herself as a lovable, worthy person. In contrast, a child who is treated in a punitive and rejecting manner can develop an internal working model that she is incompetent and unworthy of love (Harter, 2012a). The evaluations of others also can lead to self-conscious emotions (see Chapter 10): for example, praise from others leads to feelings of pride, whereas criticism and blame lead to shame and guilt (Harter, 2012a).

Combining statements made by a wide array of children in a number of empirical studies, Harter has constructed composite examples of children's typical self-descriptive statements at different ages. The following is a composite example of how 3- to 4-year-olds describe themselves:

> I'm 3 years old, I'm a boy, and my name is Jason. I live with my mommy and daddy who really love me. My mommy makes me yummy spaghetti! I am going to get my own baby sister for Christmas! I have blue eyes and a kitty that is orange and a television in my own room, it's all mine! I know all of my ABC's, listen: A, B, C, D, E, F, G, H, J, L, K, O, P, Q, R, X, Y, Z. I can run real fast, faster than when I was 2. And I can kick a soccer ball real far, all the way from one end of the field to the other. I'm a lot bigger now. When I look in the mirror at me, I can tell I grew. My daddy puts marks on the mirror to show how much taller I get. I have a nice teacher at preschool, she thinks I'm great at everything! I can count up to 100, want to hear me? I can climb to the top of the jungle gym, I'm not scared! I'm never scared! I'm always happy. I'm really strong. I can lift this chair, watch me! My mommy and I like to make up stories about me, she helps me remember things I did or said.
>
> (Harter, 2012a, p. 28)

As this composite self-description demonstrates, at age 3 to 4, children understand themselves in terms of concrete, observable characteristics related to physical attributes ("I have blue eyes"), physical activities and abilities ("I can run real fast"), and psychological traits ("I'm not scared! I'm never scared!"). For example, even when the child made a general statement about himself/herself ("I'm really strong"), this statement was closely tied to actual behavior (lifting a chair). Young children also describe themselves in terms of their preferences ("yummy spaghetti") and possessions ("I have . . . a kitty . . . and a television").

The composite example reflects another characteristic typical of children's self-concept during the preschool years: their self-appraisals are unrealistically confident (Trzesniewski, Kinal, & Donnellan, 2010). These overly positive views of themselves are not attempts to lie or brag but rather are a result of cognitive limitations (Harter, 2012a). Young children seem to think that they are really like what they want to be (Harter & Pike, 1984; Stipek, Roberts, & Sanborn, 1984). For example, the child in the composite self-description claimed mastery of the ABCs but clearly lacked it. Maintaining positive illusions about themselves is relatively easy for young children because they usually do not consider their own prior successes and failures when assessing their abilities. Even if they have failed badly at a task several times, they are likely to believe that they will succeed on the next try (Ruble et al., 1992).

Children begin to refine their conceptions of self in elementary school, in part because they increasingly engage in **social comparison,** comparing themselves with others in terms of their characteristics, behaviors, and possessions ("He is bigger than me"). At the same time, they increasingly pay attention to discrepancies between their own and others' performance on tasks ("She got an A on the test and I only got a C") (Chayer & Bouffard, 2010).

By middle to late elementary school, children's conceptions of self have begun to become integrated and more broadly encompassing, as is illustrated by the following composite self-description that would be typical of a child between the ages of 8 and 11:

> I'm in fourth grade this year. It's a little tougher than when I was younger, in the "baby" grades. I'm pretty popular, at least with the girls who I spend time with, but not with the super-popular girls who think they are cooler than everybody else. With my friends, I know what it takes to be liked, so I'm nice to people and helpful and can keep secrets. . . . At school, I'm feeling pretty smart in certain subjects like language arts and social studies, someday I will probably get a job that depends on having good English skills. . . . But I'm feeling pretty dumb in math and science, especially when I see how well a lot of the other kids are doing . . . I also like myself because I know my parents like me and so do the other kids in my classes. . . . But you also have to look and dress a certain way, if you want other kids to like you. . . . At school, I try not to act like I'm better than other people. But some kids are show-offs and they make fun of others in class who aren't doing as well as they are. . . . If you ask me, they are just acting like they're totally awesome but I think they really aren't that sure of themselves.
>
> (Harter, 2012a, p. 59)

The developmental changes in older children's self-concept reflect cognitive advances in their ability to use higher-order concepts that integrate more specific behavioral features of the self. For example, the child in the preceding self-description was able to relate being "popular" to several behaviors, such as being "nice to others" and being able to "keep secrets." In addition, older children can coordinate opposing self-representations ("smart" and "dumb") that, at a younger

In describing themselves, young children often make reference to their preferences and possessions such as a family pet.

social comparison ■ the process of comparing aspects of one's own psychological, behavioral, or physical functioning to that of others in order to evaluate oneself

PAUL RADENFELD/GETTY IMAGES

In middle childhood, children start to refine their sense of self by comparing their own attributes and behavior with those of their peers. This process of social comparison involves a variety of areas, ranging from physical abilities and academic achievement to material well-being.

age, they would have considered mutually exclusive (Harter, 2012a; Marsh, Craven, & Debus, 1998). This new cognitive capacity to form higher-order conceptions of the self allows older children to construct more global views of themselves and to evaluate themselves as a person overall. These abilities result in a more balanced and realistic assessment of the self, although they also can result in feelings of inferiority and helplessness (see the discussion of achievement motivation in Chapter 9).

The preceding self-description also reflects the fact that schoolchildren's self-concepts are increasingly based on others' evaluations of them, especially those of their peers. Consequently, their self-descriptions often contain a pronounced social element and focus on characteristics that may influence their place in their social networks, as reflected in the following interview:

WHAT ARE YOU LIKE? I am friendly.
WHY IS THAT IMPORTANT? Other kids won't like you if you aren't.
(Damon & Hart, 1988, p. 60)

Because older school-age children's conceptions of self are strongly influenced by the opinions of others, children at this age are vulnerable to low self-esteem if others view them negatively or as less competent than their peers (Harter, 2006).

Self-Concept in Adolescence

Children's self-concept changes in fundamental ways across adolescence, due in part to the emergence of abstract thinking during this stage of life (see Chapter 4). The ability to use this kind of thinking allows adolescents to conceive of themselves in terms of abstract characteristics that encompass a variety of concrete traits and behaviors. Adolescents typically develop multiple selves (Harter, 2012a)—the self they are with their parents is different from the self they are with their friends, and both of these are different from the self they are in school or at a job. Initially, adolescents may lack the ability to integrate these different selves into a coherent whole, resulting in feelings of uncertainty and internal conflict. However, as they develop, adolescents are able to appreciate that they can act differently in different situations and still be the same person, thereby resolving this sense of confusion (Harter, 2012a). See Figure 11.3.

Consider the following composite self-description of a young adolescent, 11 to 13 years old:

I'm an extrovert with my friends: I'm talkative, cheerful, and funny. My friends really like me. So I like myself a lot when I'm around my friends but not so much when I'm with my mom and dad. . . . I spend a lot of time worrying about what other people think of me. . . . In school, it seems like I'm pretty intelligent, because I feel smart and sometimes creative. . . . Socially, I can be a real introvert around people I don't know well. . . . How much I like myself really depends on what other kids think about me, I have to admit it. . . . I try to tell myself that what I think is the most important, that I should just be my true self. I shouldn't be phony and act like I'm somebody else. But sometimes you have to because it's very important to seem as if you really like yourself, it's a big deal to show that you have high self-esteem.
(Harter, 2012a, pp. 74–75)

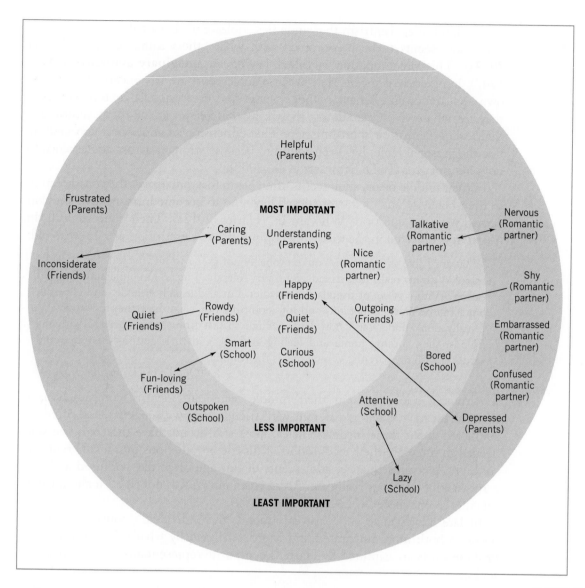

FIGURE 11.3 The multiple selves of a prototypical 15-year-old girl The girl represented by this diagram views herself as being different in different contexts or with different people. For example, she is happy with her friends but depressed with her parents, and she is both attentive and lazy at school. (Information from Harter, 2012a)

As is evident in this composite example, young people's concern over their social competence and their social acceptance, especially by peers, intensifies in early adolescence (Damon & Hart, 1988). The example also illustrates young adolescents' ability to arrive at higher-level, abstract self-descriptions such as "extrovert" based on personal traits such as "talkative," "cheerful," and "funny." Particularly notable is the fact that adolescents can conceive of themselves in terms of a variety of selves, depending on the context. The adolescent in the composite, for instance, describes himself/herself as a somewhat different person with friends and with parents, as well as with familiar and unfamiliar people.

Thinking about the self in early adolescence is characterized by a form of egocentrism called the **personal fable,** in which adolescents overly differentiate their feelings from those of others and come to regard themselves, and especially their feelings, as unique and special (Elkind, 1967). They may believe that only they can experience whatever misery or rapture or confusion they are currently feeling. This belief is typified in the adolescent assertions "But you don't know how it feels!" and "My parents don't understand me, what do *they* know about what it's like to be a teenager?" (Harter, 2012a, p. 95). The tendency to exhibit this type of egocentrism is often still evident in late adolescence (P. D. Schwartz, Maynard, & Uzelac, 2008).

personal fable ■ a form of adolescent egocentrism that involves beliefs in the uniqueness of one's own feelings and thoughts

imaginary audience ■ the belief, stemming from adolescent egocentrism, that everyone else is focused on the adolescent's appearance and behavior

The kind of egocentrism that underlies adolescents' personal fables also causes many adolescents to be preoccupied with what others think of them (Harter, 2012a). This preoccupation is called having an **imaginary audience** (Elkind, 1967); in practice, it means that because adolescents are so concerned with their own appearance and behavior, they assume that everyone else is, too. Wherever they are, whatever they are doing, they think that all eyes are on them, scrutinizing their every blemish or social misstep. This dimension of adolescent egocentrism, like the personal fable, has been found to become stronger across adolescence for boys but not girls (P. D. Schwartz et al., 2008).

In their middle teens, adolescents often begin to agonize over the contradictions in their behavior and characteristics. They tend to become introspective and concerned with the question "Who am I?" (Harter, 2012a). Their concern with this question is reflected in the following composite self-description of a 15-year-old:

> What am I like as a person? You're probably not going to understand. I'm complicated! With my really *close* friends, I am very tolerant, I mean I'm understanding and caring. With a *group* of friends I'm rowdier. I'm also usually friendly and cheerful, but I can be pretty obnoxious and intolerant if I don't like how they're acting. . . . I really don't understand how I can switch so fast from being cheerful with my friends, then coming home and feeling anxious, and then getting frustrated and sarcastic with my parents. Which one is the *real* me?
>
> (Quoted in Harter, 2012a, p. 94)

Although adolescents in their middle teens can identify contradictions in themselves, such as being different with friends than with parents, and often feel conflicted about these inconsistencies, most still do not have the cognitive skills needed to integrate their recognition of these contradictions into a coherent self-concept. As a consequence, adolescents of this age often feel confused and concerned about who they really are. As one teen put it, "It's not right, it should all fit together in one piece!" (Harter, 2012a, p.100).

In late adolescence and early adulthood, the individual's conception of self becomes both more integrated and less determined by what others think. Both of these shifts are captured by Harter's composite representation of a high school senior:

> I'd like to be an ethical person who treats other people fairly; that's why I want to be a lawyer. Sometimes I do something that doesn't feel that ethical. When that happens I get a little depressed because I don't like myself as a person. But I tell myself that it's natural to make mistakes, so I don't really question the fact that deep down inside, the real me is a moral person. Basically, I like who I am. . . . Being athletic isn't that high on my own list of what is important, even though it is for a lot of the kids in our school. But I don't really care what they think anymore, at least I try to convince myself that I don't. I try to believe that what *I* think is what counts. After all, I have to live with myself as a person and to respect that person, which I do now, more than a few years ago.
>
> (Quoted in Harter, 2012a, p. 118)

As in the case of this prototypical senior, older adolescents' conceptions of self frequently reflect internalized personal values, beliefs, and standards. Many of these were instilled by others in the child's life but are now accepted and generated by adolescents as their own. Thus, older adolescents place less emphasis on what other people think than they did at younger ages and are more concerned with meeting their own standards and with their future self—what they are becoming or who they are going to be (Harter, 2012a; Higgins, 1991).

Older adolescents are also more likely to have the cognitive capacity to integrate opposites or contradictions in the self that occur in different contexts or at different times (Higgins, 1991). They may explain contradictory characteristics in terms of the need to be flexible, and they may view variations in their behavior with different people as "adaptive" because one cannot act the same with everyone. Similarly, they may integrate changes in emotion under the characteristic "moody." Moreover, they are likely to view their contradictions and inconsistencies as a normal part of being human, which likely reduces feelings of conflict and upset.

Whether older adolescents are able to successfully integrate contradictions in themselves likely depends not only on their own cognitive capacities but also on the help they receive from parents, teachers, and others in understanding the complexity of personalities. The support and tutelage of others in this regard allow adolescents to internalize values, beliefs, and standards that they feel committed to and to feel comfortable with who they are (D. Hart & Fegley, 1995; Harter, 1999, 2012a).

Self-Esteem

Self-esteem ■ an individual's overall subjective evaluation of his or her worth and the feelings he or she has about that evaluation

Self-esteem incorporates a child's overall subjective evaluation of his or her worth and the feelings he or she has about that evaluation (Orth & Robins, 2014). Self-esteem does not emerge until children reach age 8 or so (Harter, 2012a). To measure children's self-esteem, researchers ask children, verbally or by questionnaire, about their perceptions of themselves. As reflected in Table 11.3, the questions assess children's sense of their own physical attractiveness, athletic competence,

TABLE 11.3

Sample Items from Susan Harter's Self-Perception Profile for Children, a Commonly Used Measure of Self-Esteem and Self-Perceptions

Really True for Me	Sort of True for Me				Sort of True for Me	Really True for Me
		Scholastic Competence				
☐	☐	Some kids feel that they are very good at their school work.	BUT	Other kids worry about whether they can do the school work assigned to them.	☐	☐
		Social Competence				
☐	☐	Some kids find it hard to make friends.	BUT	Other kids find it's pretty easy to make friends.	☐	☐
		Athletic Competence				
☐	☐	Some kids do very well at all kinds of sports.	BUT	Other kids don't feel that they are very good when it comes to sports.	☐	☐
		Physical Appearance				
☐	☐	Some kids are happy with the way they look.	BUT	Others kids are *not* happy with the way they look.	☐	☐
		Behavioral Conduct				
☐	☐	Some kids often do not like the way they behave.	BUT	Other kids usually like the way they behave.	☐	☐
		Global Self-Worth				
☐	☐	Some kids are often unhappy with themselves.	BUT	Other kids are pretty pleased with themselves.	☐	☐

Source: Information from Harter (2012b).

social acceptance, scholastic ability, and the appropriateness of their behavior. In addition, the researchers ask children about their global self-worth—how they feel about themselves in general.

Individuals with high self-esteem tend to feel good about themselves and hopeful in general, whereas individuals with low self-esteem tend to feel worthless and hopeless (Harter, 2012a). In particular, low self-esteem in childhood and adolescence is associated with problems such as aggression, depression, substance abuse, social withdrawal, suicidal ideation (Boden, Fergusson, & Horwood, 2008; Donnellan et al., 2005; Rubin, Coplan, & Bowker, 2009; Sowislo & Orth, 2013), and cyberbullying (both as perpetrator and victim) (Modecki, Barber, & Vernon, 2013; S. J. Yang et al., 2013).

Low self-esteem in childhood has also been linked with certain problems in adulthood, including mental health problems, substance abuse and dependence, criminal behavior, weak economic prospects, and low levels of satisfaction with life and with relationships—but these associations are relatively weak (Boden et al., 2008; Orth, Robins, & Roberts 2008; Trzesniewski et al., 2006).

It should also be noted that high self-esteem, especially if not based on positive self-attributes, may have costs for children and adolescents (K. Lee & Lee, 2012). For example, high self-esteem in aggressive children is associated with their increasingly valuing the rewards that they derive from their aggression and their belittlement of victims (Menon et al., 2007). The combination of high self-esteem and narcissism—grandiose views of the self, inflated feelings of superiority and entitlement, and exploitative interpersonal attitudes—has been associated with especially high levels of aggression in young adolescents (Thomaes et al., 2008).

Sources of Self-Esteem

There are several sources of individual differences in self-esteem. One is age: an individual's self-esteem is not constant and varies by developmental stage. Self-esteem tends to be high in childhood before declining in adolescence and then rebounding in adulthood (Orth & Robins, 2014). Physical attributes, such as attractiveness, also are linked with self-esteem. In childhood and adolescence, attractive individuals are much more likely to report high self-esteem than are those who are less attractive (Erkut et al., 1999; Harter, 2012a), possibly because attractive people are viewed more positively by others and receive better treatment than people who are considered less attractive.

Gender is another source of individual differences in self-esteem. Numerous studies in Western countries have established that boys tend to have higher overall self-esteem than girls, and that this tendency persists across the life span (Orth & Robins, 2014). Although this gender difference has been found for overall self-esteem, it may be that females have higher self-esteem than males in certain domains. A meta-analysis of studies examining domain-specific self-esteem found that males have higher self-esteem than females in the domains of athletics, personal appearance, and self-satisfaction, whereas females were higher in the domains of behavioral conduct (perceiving themselves as well-behaved) and moral-ethical self-esteem (see Figure 11.4; Gentile et al., 2009). No gender differences were found in self-esteem related to academic performance, which suggests that although girls may have lower self-esteem in some domains, this does not prevent them from seeing themselves as able to do well in school (Gentile et al., 2009).

Perhaps the most important influence on children's self-esteem is the approval and support they receive from others, particularly their parents. Early theories

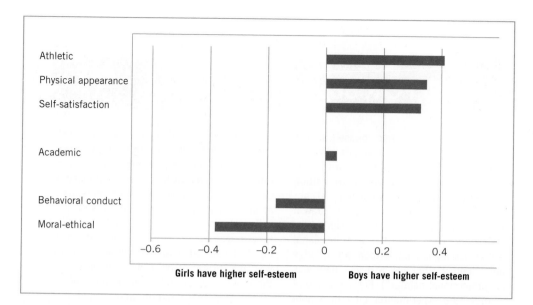

FIGURE 11.4 Gender differences in self-esteem by domain Boys are higher in self-esteem in terms of athletics, personal appearance, and self-satisfaction. Girls have higher self-esteem when it comes to behavioral conduct and moral-ethical behavior. There is no gender difference in academic self-esteem. (Data from Gentile et al., 2009)

viewed self-esteem as the internalization of the views of ourselves held by important people in our lives. In this view, self-esteem is a reflection of what others think of us, or our "looking glass self" (Cooley, 1902). Similar ideas were proposed by Erikson (1950) and Bowlby (1969), who argued that children's self-esteem is grounded in the quality of their relationships with their parents. If children feel loved when young, they come to believe that they are lovable and worthy of others' love; if they feel unloved when young, they come to believe the opposite. Indeed, securely attached children with sensitive and responsive parents tend to have higher self-esteem (Boden et al., 2008; Cassidy et al., 2003; Verschueren, Marcoen, & Schoefs, 1996).

Parents' behavior with and discipline of their children affect the children's self-esteem. Parents who are accepting of and involved with their children and who use supportive yet firm child-rearing practices tend to have children and adolescents with high self-esteem (Awong, Grusec, & Sorenson, 2008; Behnke et al., 2011; S. M. Cooper & McLoyd, 2011; Lamborn et al., 1991). In contrast, parents who regularly react to their children's unacceptable behavior with belittlement or rejection—in effect, condemning the child rather than the behavior—are likely to instill in their children a sense of worthlessness and of being loved only to the extent that they meet parental standards (Harter, 1999, 2006; Heaven & Ciarrochi, 2008). Parents can also undermine children's self-esteem by constantly relying on social comparison as a means of motivating children (e.g., "Why can't you be helpful like your sister?"). They can also give children unrealistically high self-esteem by praising too often (see Box 11.4).

Over the course of childhood, children's self-esteem is increasingly affected by peer acceptance (Harter, 1999). Indeed, in late childhood, children's feelings of competence about their appearance, athletic ability, and likability may be affected more by their peers' evaluations than by their parents'. This tendency to evaluate the self on the basis of peers' perceptions has been associated with a preoccupation with approval, fluctuations in self-esteem, lower levels of peer approval, and lower self-esteem (Harter, 2012a).

Although far from being the only factors in shaping a child's self-esteem, the quality and nature of interactions with parents and other caregivers are among the more important influences.

GOLDEN PIXELS LLC / ALAMY

BOX 11.4 | a closer look

IS TOO MUCH PRAISE BAD FOR SELF-ESTEEM?

The vast majority (87%) of adults in Western society believe that children need to be praised in order to have a positive view of themselves (Brummelman, Crocker, & Bushman, 2016). Such beliefs have led to the recent trend of rewarding participation rather than achievement (the "everybody gets a trophy" phenomenon). This trend finds the most support among young adults aged 18 to 24 (51%), compared with adults 45 to 55 (41%), 55 to 53 (38%), and 65 and older (29%) (Ekins, 2014).

Researchers have become concerned with one particular kind of praise known as *inflated praise,* which involves exaggerated language ("Wow! Your drawing is amazing!" or "You are the best at building sandcastles!"). Adults have been observed using inflated praise twice as often with children who have low self-esteem than with children who have high self-esteem (Brummelman et al., 2014), suggesting that adults think such language will be especially effective with children who are not feeling good about themselves.

To test how inflated praise affects children's behavior, researchers in the Netherlands did an experiment with 240 children ages 8 to 12 who were visiting a science museum (Brummelman et al., 2014). Children were first asked to draw a copy of a famous painting (Van Gogh's *Wild Roses*) and were told that a professional painter working in another room would judge their painting (this was a ruse—there was no "professional painter"). For one group of children, the experimenter brought a note back from the "painter" that said, "You made an *incredibly* beautiful drawing!"—this was the inflated praise condition. For a second group of children, the message said, "You made a beautiful drawing!"—this constituted the non-inflated praise condition. The last group was the no-praise condition; these children did not receive any communication from the painter.

In the second half of the experiment, each child was given the option of two pictures to copy: one easy and one difficult. The data revealed that inflated praise in the first part of the experiment decreased children's challenge-seeking behavior in the second part, but only among children who rated themselves as having low self-esteem before the experiment started (Brummelman et al., 2014). Yet when children with low self-esteem were given non-inflated praise, they sought out the more challenging drawing task. In other words, inflated praise was backfiring—it was most harmful to the children whom adults think most need it. Instead, only children who started the experiment with high self-esteem were more likely to accept the challenge of the difficult drawings if they were given inflated praise for their initial drawing.

Why does inflated praise undermine the effort of children with low self-esteem? The researchers surmised that inflated praise sets high standards (e.g., you must be "perfect" or "the best" at something to get praise) which in turn leads these children to avoid activities where they might fail, as a form of self-protection (Brummelman et al., 2014). Interestingly, children did not rate the inflated praise as less sincere than the non-inflated praise, which suggests that they are taking the praise at face value. This finding emphasizes the importance such word choices have for children's behavior.

So what is a well-meaning parent or teacher to do? Praising children for their *effort* rather than for their ability or for the products of their effort is one way to encourage children to persist in the face of challenges. Another important take-away is that, contrary to their instincts, adults should avoid using inflated praise with children who have low self-esteem. Instead, they should target such praise at children with high self-esteem. Of course, if you don't know the level of a child's self-esteem, then it may be best to avoid inflated praise in the first place. And you may want to rethink giving everyone trophies.

Although many adults think giving everyone a medal for participation is good for self-esteem, research suggests otherwise.

SUSAN CHIANG / GETTY IMAGES

At the same time, children's self-esteem likely affects how peers respond to them. Youth who see themselves as competent in their peer relationships tend to be well liked (M. S. Caldwell et al., 2004), perhaps because their behavior is confident and socially engaging.

Adolescents' self-esteem is also affected by the standards and values of important people and cultural groups in their lives (Harter, 2012a). These standards and values can refer to physical appearance, activities, and relationships. Experts agree that adolescents who continue to base their self-evaluations on others' standards and approval are at risk for psychological problems, at least in Western industrialized cultures where an autonomous, relatively stable sense of self is valued (Harter, 2012a; Higgins, 1991).

Children's and adolescents' self-esteem can also be affected by their school and neighborhood environments. The effect of the school environment is most apparent in the decline in self-esteem that is associated with the transition from elementary school to junior high (Eccles et al., 1989). The junior high environment often is not a good developmental match for 11- and 12-year-olds because many children of that age are distressed by the switch from having one teacher whom they know well and who is well acquainted with their skills and weaknesses to having many teachers who know little about them. In addition, the transition to junior high forces students to enter a new group of peers and to go from the top of one school's pecking order to the bottom of another's. Especially in poor, overcrowded, urban schools, young adolescents often do not receive the attention, support, and friendship they need to do well and to feel good about themselves (Seidman et al., 1994; Wigfield et al., 2006). At the same time, schools become more competitive environments in which students are subjected to repeated social comparison (Harter, 2012a). But there is a bright spot—support from teachers does promote higher self-esteem in adolescents (Sterrett et al., 2011).

Aspects of the neighborhoods in which adolescents live have also been linked with self-esteem. Living in impoverished and violent neighborhoods is associated with lower self-esteem among adolescents in the United States (Behnke et al., 2011; Ewart & Suchday, 2002; Paschall & Hubbard, 1998; Turley, 2003). This may be due to high levels of stress that undermine the quality of parenting, prejudice from more affluent peers and adults, and inadequate material and psychological resources (Behnke et al., 2011; K. Walker et al., 1995).

Children who do poorly in school tend to have lower self-esteem than do their more successful peers. However, children's perceptions of their academic competence tend to be less important to their overall self-esteem than are their perceptions of their appearance.

Culture and Self-Esteem

In various cultures, the sources, form, and function of self-esteem may be different, and the criteria that children use to evaluate themselves may vary accordingly. Between Asian and Western cultures, for example, there are fundamental differences that appear to affect the very meaning of self-esteem. In Western cultures, self-esteem is related to individual accomplishments and self-promotion. By contrast, in Asian societies such as Japan and China, which traditionally have had a collectivist (or group) orientation, self-esteem is believed to be more related to contributing to the welfare of the larger group and affirming the norms of social interdependence. In this cultural context, self-criticism and efforts at self-improvement may be viewed as evidence of commitment to the group (Heine et al., 1999). But in terms of standard measures of self-esteem (i.e., those used by U.S. researchers), this motivation toward self-criticism is reflected as lower self-evaluation (Harter, 2012a).

Cultures differ in the skills they value. Children learn what abilities are valued in their group through participation in the family and larger community and evaluate their own competence accordingly.

RICHARD CUMMINS/GETTY IMAGES

It is not surprising, then, that scores on standard measures of self-esteem vary considerably across cultures. Self-esteem scores tend to be lower in China, Japan, and Korea than in the United States, Canada, Australia, and some parts of Europe (Harter, 2012a). These differences seem to be partly due to the greater emphasis that the Asian cultures place on modesty and self-effacement—which results in less positive self-descriptions (Cai et al., 2007; Suzuki, Davis, & Greenfield, 2008; Q. Wang, 2004). Indeed, European American and African American adolescents tend to be more comfortable with being praised and with events that make them look good and cause them to stand out than are Asian American and Latino adolescents (Suzuki et al., 2008); this could affect the degree to which they report high self-esteem, and hence could account for the pattern of ethnic differences in self-esteem (Harter, 2012a).

In addition, in some Asian societies, people tend to be more comfortable acknowledging discrepancies in themselves—for example, the existence of both good and bad personal characteristics—than are people in Western cultures; this tendency results in reports of lower self-esteem in late adolescence and early adulthood (Hamamura, Heine, & Paulhus, 2008; Spencer-Rodgers et al., 2004). The same types of cultural influences may affect measures of self-esteem in U.S. subcultures that have maintained traditional non-Western ideas about the self and its relation to other people.

Surprisingly, studies have shown that culture does not appear to be a factor in gender differences related to self-esteem. A large study of 1 million adolescents and adults in 48 countries (including Argentina, Canada, China, Egypt, India, Japan, Malaysia, South Africa, Thailand, and the United States) confirmed that males have higher self-esteem on average than females, and that while self-esteem increases from age 16 on for both genders, females' self-esteem on average never reaches that of males (Bleidorn et al., 2015). Why is there such a stark gender difference in self-esteem across countries and cultures? The reasons are not entirely clear, though they may derive from gender roles and stereotypes. However, this same study found that the gender differences in self-esteem were largest in countries that were wealthy, individualistic, and egalitarian, where women officially have the same freedoms as men, rather than in highly patriarchal countries where gender roles are traditionally more restrictive (Bleidorn et al., 2015).

Identity

An **identity** is a definition of the self. Importantly, each of us has multiple identities that are more salient than others at certain times or in certain situations. If you are on a college campus, you might say you are a student. If you are at a family reunion, you could say you are a son, daughter, or grandchild. You can be a friend, a coworker, a teammate, a member of a religious group.

Adolescence is the period at which children appreciate their multiple identities and begin to forge new identities that may be distinct from those of their family and childhood friends. The earliest theory of identity formation was proposed by Erik Erikson, as briefly described in Chapter 9. Erikson argued that all adolescents experience an identity crisis, in part as a means of separating from their parents, in the psychosocial stage of development he called **identity versus role confusion** (Erikson, 1968). In his view, the challenge is as follows: "From among all possible and imaginable relations, [the person] must make a series of ever-narrowing selections of personal, occupational, sexual, and ideological commitments" (1968, p. 245). Successful resolution of this crisis results in **identity achievement**—that is, an integration of various aspects of the self into a coherent whole that is stable over time and across events.

In the decades after Erikson published his theory, researchers rejected the idea that all individuals must go through an identity crisis (Baumeister, 2005). A psychologist named James Marcia (1980) developed an alternate way of describing adolescents' identity development by considering where an individual falls on the dimensions of identity crisis and identity commitment. On the basis of an adolescent's responses in a structured interview, he or she is classified into one of four categories of identity status (see Table 11.4).

More recently, researchers have delineated some additional distinctions in identity status. During a status of **moratorium,** individuals explore possible commitments in two different ways. Some may explore them in *breadth,* trying out a variety of candidate identities before choosing one (Luyckx, Goossens, & Soenens, 2006; Luyckx, Goossens, Soenens, & Beyers, 2006). For example, a person might consider being a musician, artist, or historian. Others may make an initial commitment and explore it in *depth,* through continuous monitoring of current commitments in order to make them more conscious (Meeus et al., 2010). Thus, they may try out various types of art (painting, sculpture) before committing to being an artist.

identity ■ a description of the self that is often externally imposed, such as through membership in a group

identity versus role confusion ■ the psychosocial stage of development, described by Erikson, that occurs during adolescence. During this stage, the adolescent or young adult either develops an identity or experiences an incomplete and sometimes incoherent sense of self.

identity achievement ■ an integration of various aspects of the self into a coherent whole that is stable over time and across events

moratorium ■ period in which the individual is exploring various occupational and ideological choices and has not yet made a clear commitment to them

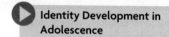 **Identity Development in Adolescence**

TABLE 11.4

The Four Groups of Identity Status Developed by Marcia (1980)

	Crisis	No Crisis
Commitment	**Identity achievement** The individual has achieved a coherent and consolidated identity based on personal decisions regarding occupation, ideology, and the like. The individual believes that these decisions were made autonomously and is committed to them.	**Identity foreclosure** The individual has not engaged in any identity experimentation and has established a vocational or ideological identity based on the choices or values of others.
No commitment	**Moratorium** The individual is exploring various occupational and ideological choices and has not yet made a clear commitment to them.	**Identity diffusion** The individual does not have firm commitments regarding the issues in question and is not making progress toward developing them.

JOHN WARBURTON-LEE PHOTOGRAPHY / ALAMY

In some traditional cultures, adolescents have few role options and, consequently, know from a young age what their adult identity will be.

identity diffusion ■ period in which the individual does not have firm commitments regarding the issues in question and is not making progress toward developing them

identity foreclosure ■ period in which the individual has not engaged in any identity experimentation and has established a vocational or ideological identity based on the choices or values of others

DEVON STEPHENS / GETTY IMAGES

Trying out various "looks" can be an aspect of the self-discovery that occurs among many adolescents in some cultures.

Researchers using interview methods similar to Marcia's have found that most young adolescents seem to be in **identity diffusion** or **identity foreclosure** and that the percentage of youth in moratorium status is highest at ages 17 to 19 (Nurmi, 2004; Waterman, 1999). In the course of adolescence and early adulthood, individuals generally progress slowly toward identity achievement (Kroger, Martinussen, & Marcia, 2010; Meeus, 2011). The most typical sequences of change appear to be from diffusion → early foreclosure → achievement, or from diffusion → moratorium → closure → achievement (Meeus, 2011). There is little evidence that many adolescents have the kind of sustained identity confusion that Erikson maintained could lead to severe psychological disturbance (Meeus, 2011).

Researchers generally have found that, at least in modern Western societies, the identity status of adolescents and young adults is related to their adjustment, social behavior, and personality. Those who have made a commitment, whether through foreclosure or identity achievement, tend to be low in depression and anxiety, and high in personality characteristics of extroversion and agreeableness (Crocetti et al., 2008; Luyckx et al., 2005; Luyckx, Goossens, Soenens, & Beyers, 2006; Meeus, 1996). Young adults who explore possible commitments more in depth than in breadth tend to be extroverted, agreeable, and conscientious (reliable, regulated), whereas those who explore more in breadth tend to be prone to negative emotionality but open to experience (Dunkel & Anthis, 2001; Luyckx, Soenens, & Goossens, 2006). Individuals who have made commitments through foreclosure tend to be low on substance use (Luyckx et al., 2005) and aggression (Crocetti et al., 2008; Luyckx et al., 2008). In contrast, adolescents who are in moratorium, especially when they are experimenting in breadth, seem to be relatively likely to take drugs or to have unprotected sex (J. T. Hernandez & Diclemente, 1992; R. M. Jones, 1992; Luyckx, Goossens, Soenens, & Beyers, 2006).

A number of factors influence adolescents' identity formation. One key factor is the approach parents take with their offspring. Adolescents who experience warmth and support from parents tend to have a more mature identity and less identity confusion (Meeus, 2011; S. J. Schwartz et al., 2009). In addition, parents tend to react with support when young college students explore in depth and make identity commitments (Beyers & Goossens, 2008), and this support may reinforce their children's choices. Youths who are subject to parental psychological control tend to explore in breadth and are lower in making commitment to an identity (Luyckx et al., 2007). Adolescents are also more likely to explore identity options rather than go into foreclosure if they have at least one parent who encourages in them both a sense of connection with the parent and a striving for autonomy and individuality (Grotevant, 1998).

Identity formation is also influenced by both the larger social context and the historical context (Bosma & Kunnen, 2001). The historical context plays a role in identity formation as well, because of the changes it brings about in identity options over time. Until a few decades ago, for instance, most adolescent girls focused their search for identity on the goal of marriage and family. Even in developed societies, few career opportunities were available to women. Today, women in many cultures are more likely to base their identity on both family and career. Thus, familial, individual, socioeconomic, historical, and cultural factors all contribute to identity development.

Ethnic and Racial Identity

Ethnic and racial identity is especially salient in adolescence. An **ethnic and racial identity** encompasses the beliefs and attitudes an individual has about the ethnic or racial groups to which they belong (Umaña-Taylor et al., 2014). Ethnicity refers to the relationships and experiences a child has that are linked with their cultural or ethnic ancestry, whereas race refers to experiences children have that are the result of their membership, which may be assigned by others, in historical racial groups such as "Black," "White," "Asian," or "Hispanic or Latino" (Umaña-Taylor et al., 2014).

Children have different understandings of their ethnic and racial identity at different points of their development. Preschool children do not really understand the significance of being a member of an ethnic group, although they may be able to label themselves as belonging to an ethnic group or race. Even if they engage in behaviors that characterize their ethnic or racial group and have some simple knowledge about the group, they do not understand that ethnicity and race are lasting features of the self.

By the early school years, ethnic-minority children know the common characteristics of their ethnic or racial group, start to have feelings about being members of the group, and may have begun to form ethnically based preferences regarding foods, traditional holiday activities, language use, and so forth (Ocampo, Bernal, & Knight, 1993). Children tend to identify themselves according to their ethnic or racial group between the ages of 5 and 8; shortly thereafter, they begin to understand that their ethnicity or race is an unchanging feature of themselves (Bernal et al., 1990; Ocampo, Knight, & Bernal, 1997). By late elementary school, minority children in the United States often have a very positive view of their ethnic or racial group (D. Hughes, Way, & Rivas-Drake, 2011).

The family and the larger social environment play a major role in the development of children's ethnic and racial identity. Parents and other family members and adults can be instrumental in teaching their children about the strengths and unique features of their ethnic culture or race and instilling them with pride (A. B. Evans et al., 2012; Hughes et al., 2006; Vera & Quintana, 2004). Such instruction can be especially important for the development of a positive ethnic identity when the child's racial or ethnic group is the object of prejudice and discrimination in the larger society (Gaylord-Harden, Burrow, & Cunningham, 2012; M. B. Spencer & Markstrom-Adams, 1990).

The issue of ethnic or racial identity often becomes more central in adolescence, as young people try to forge their overall identity (S. E. French et al., 2006). Minority-group members in particular may be faced with difficult and painful decisions as they try to decide the degree to which they will adopt the values of their ethnic group or those of the dominant culture (Phinney, 1993; M. B. Spencer & Markstrom-Adams, 1990).

One difficulty for ethnic- or racial-minority adolescents is that they are more likely than they were at younger ages to be aware of discrimination against their group and consequently may feel ambivalent about the group and their own ethnic status (M. L. Greene, Way, & Pahl, 2006; Seaton et al., 2008; Szalacha et al.,

ethnic and racial identity ■ the beliefs and attitudes an individual has about the ethnic or racial groups to which they belong

Much of young children's learning about their ethnic group takes place in the family. Parents teach their children the specific practices associated with their group and can instill in them pride in their ethnic heritage.

2003). Ethnic-minority children may also be faced with basic conflicts between the values of their ethnic group and those of the dominant culture (Parke & Buriel, 2006; Qin, 2009). For example, many ethnic groups place a premium on family obligation, including values and behaviors related to children's assisting, supporting, and respecting members of the nuclear and extended family. Thus, adolescents in traditional Mexican American families, for instance, may be expected to spend after-school time helping take care of elderly or young family members or earning money for the family. At the same time, the majority culture may be urging them to participate in school-related activities—such as sports, clubs, or study groups—that can lead to expanded opportunities.

Research suggests that higher levels of ethnic and racial identity are generally associated with high self-esteem, well-being, and low levels of emotional and behavioral problems (Berkel et al., 2009; M. D. Jones & Galliher, 2007; Kiang et al., 2006; Neblett, Rivas-Drake, & Umaña-Taylor, 2012). Adolescents with a positive ethnic and racial identity appear to be buffered from the negative effects of discrimination (Gaylord-Harden et al., 2012; Tynes et al., 2012). The benefits of high ethnic and racial identification appear to hold more consistently for African American and Latino youth than for Asian American youth (Umaña-Taylor, 2011).

Establishing a clear ethnic identification may be more difficult and less consistent for some adolescents, such as multi-ethnic or multi-racial youth, who could develop identifications with more than one ethnic or racial group (Marks, Patton, & Garcia Coll, 2011; Nishina et al., 2010). However, when ethnic- or racial-minority parents actively socialize their children by teaching about their culture and instilling pride, children tend to have a more positive ethnic and racial identity (Neblett et al., 2012; Umaña-Taylor, Bhanot, & Shin, 2006; Umaña-Taylor & Guimond, 2010) and are less susceptible to the negative effects of discrimination (Harris-Britt et al., 2007; Neblett et al., 2008; M.-T. Wang & Huguley, 2012).

In some cases, ethnic- and racial-minority youth develop a *bicultural identity* that includes a comfortable identification with both the majority culture and their own ethnic culture. Although trying to straddle two cultures can be stressful, it is not always so, and for some minority youths it can provide certain benefits, such as positive perceptions of opportunities in the majority society (Fuligni, Yip, & Tseng, 2002; Kiang & Harter, 2008; Kiang, Yip, & Fuligni, 2008; LaFromboise, Coleman, & Gerton, 1993). However, for adolescents in some traditional cultures (e.g., Canadian First Nations), a bicultural identity can be associated with lower levels of some strengths that are part of successful identity development, such as certain traditional values, as well as fidelity (loyalty and commitment) and wisdom (Gfellner & Armstrong, 2012).

Ethnic and racial identities are also linked with adolescents' self-esteem. Despite the fact that African American children and adolescents experience discrimination and stereotyping, they have higher self-esteem on average than their European American peers (Gray-Little & Hafdahl, 2000). This may be the case because ethnic and racial identity is an important aspect of self-concept for many African Americans, and the emphasis by parents and other adults in the community on the positive features of being African American may enhance African American children's and adolescents' self-esteem (Gray-Little & Hafdahl, 2000; Herman, 2004).

Engaging in activities that promote the welfare of others in their ethnic or racial group may contribute to adolescents' having a positive sense of ethnic identity. The adolescents shown here are members of a youth-development group that carries out community projects ranging from cleaning parks and painting neighborhood murals to tending community gardens and working in a food pantry for the needy.

FRESH YOUTH INITIATIVES

Less is known about the self-esteem of Latino and other minority children. Because of the poverty and prejudice that many Latino Americans experience, one might expect their self-esteem to be consistently much lower than that of European Americans at all ages, and it is, at least through elementary school. Beginning in adolescence, however, the difference becomes much smaller (Twenge & Crocker, 2002). In part, this change may be due to the fact that Latino (e.g., Mexican American) parents encourage their children's identification with the family and with the larger ethnic group (Parke & Buriel, 2006), which can provide a buffer against some of the negative effects that poverty and prejudice often have on self-esteem. Increases in Latino adolescents' self-esteem are also associated with growth in their exploration of their ethnic identity (Umaña-Taylor, Gonzales-Backen, & Guimond, 2009). Especially in communities where Latinos are in the majority, Latino youth who identify with their ethnic group, in comparison with those who do not, tend to have higher self-esteem (Umaña-Taylor, Diversi, & Fine, 2002).

Other minority groups in the United States show different patterns of self-esteem. Asian American children, for instance, report higher self-esteem in elementary school than do European Americans and African Americans; but by high school, their reported self-esteem is lower than that of European Americans (Herman, 2004; Twenge & Crocker, 2002). In fact, in one recent study, Asian Americans had lower self-esteem by 6th grade (Witherspoon et al., 2009). As discussed earlier in this chapter, cultural factors may contribute to the lower levels of self-esteem reported in some ethnic-minority groups.

Although discrimination can have a negative effect on adolescents' self-esteem, how ethnic minority children and adolescents think about themselves is influenced much more strongly by acceptance from their family, neighbors, and friends than by reactions from strangers and the society at large (Galliher, Jones, & Dahl, 2011; Seaton, Yip, & Sellers, 2009). Thus, minority-group parents can help their children develop high self-esteem and a sense of well-being by instilling them with pride in their culture and by being generally supportive (Bámaca et al.,

sexual identity ■ one's sense of oneself as a sexual being

sexual orientation ■ a person's preference in regard to males or females as objects of erotic feelings

sexual-minority youth ■ young people who experience same-sex attractions

2005; Berkel et al., 2009; S. M. Cooper & McLoyd, 2011). For example, African American adolescents whose mothers support them and help them cope with problems hold more positive attitudes toward their race and express greater pride in being African American than do adolescents with less supportive mothers. In turn, this greater pride predicts lower levels of perceived stress and, consequently, better adjustment (C. H. Caldwell et al., 2002).

Having positive peer and adult role models from their own ethnic group also contributes to ethnic minority children's positive feelings about themselves and their ethnicity (A. R. Fischer & Shaw, 1999; K. Walker et al., 1995). One study found that Black girls had higher self-esteem on average than White girls, and that this difference was partly explained by the fact that Black mothers are more likely to encourage independence in and to have higher academic aspirations for their daughters (Ridolfo, Chepp, & Milkie, 2013).

Sexual Identity

In childhood and especially adolescence, an individual's identity includes his or her **sexual identity,** which refers to one's sense of oneself as a sexual being. Sexual identity includes **sexual orientation**—an individual's romantic or erotic attractions to people of the opposite gender, same gender, both, or neither. Sexual identity is thus separate from gender identity, which is an individual's awareness of himself or herself as a male, as a female, or as transgendered and will be discussed in Chapter 15.

Puberty, during which there are large rises in gonadal hormones, is the most likely time for youth to begin experiencing feelings of sexual attraction to others (Diamond, Bonner, & Dickenson, 2015). Most current theorists believe that whether those feelings are directed toward members of the opposite sex or one's own is based primarily on biological factors (Savin-Williams & Cohen, 2004). Studies using a variety of methodologies, including twin and adoption studies, as well as epigenetic studies, indicate that a person's sexual orientation is at least partly hereditary: identical twins, for example, are more likely to exhibit similar sexual orientations than are fraternal twins (Ngun & Vilain, 2014).

Sexual-Minority Identity

The majority of adolescents, like the majority of adults, are heterosexual—they are attracted to members of the opposite biological sex. In surveys compiled by the Centers for Disease Control and Prevention from across the United States, 88.8% of high school students reported a heterosexual identity, 6.0% reported a bisexual identity, 2.0% reported a gay or lesbian identity, and 3.2% were not sure (Kann et al., 2016). A heterosexual identity is normative, meaning that it is what most people experience, and so the research literature has largely been unconcerned with the sexual identities of heterosexual adolescents.

There is, however, concern—as well as significant research—about the sexual identities of **sexual-minority youth,** namely those adolescents who are attracted to people from their same biological sex or from both sexes. Sexual-minority youth and adults continue to be discriminated against, both in law and in practice, and are frequent targets for harassment and violence; the massacre at a gay nightclub in Orlando, Florida, in June 2016 was a tragic recent example of such violence. Even with the growing acceptance of lesbian, gay, and bisexual (LGB) people in Western society, and with the legality of same-sex marriage in Canada, the United States, and several other countries, hate crimes against LGB individuals are still prevalent, making up one-fifth of all hate crimes in the United States (Federal Bureau of Investigation, 2014).

Throughout childhood and adolescence, sexual-minority youth often feel "different" (Savin-Williams & Cohen, 2007), and some even display cross-gender behaviors from a relatively early age—for example, in their preferences for toys, clothes, or leisure activities (Drummond et al., 2008). However, these youth may take a long time to recognize that they are lesbian, gay, or bisexual. This process begins with the *first recognition*—an initial realization that one is somewhat different from others, accompanied by feelings of alienation from oneself and others. At this point, the individual is generally aware that same-sex attractions may be the relevant issue but does not reveal this to others.

Figure 11.5 displays data from a study of sexual-minority adults. Across genders, sexual identities, and age, most participants reported experiencing their first same-sex attraction between ages 10 and 15, but did not identify themselves as LGB until after age 15 (Martos, Nezhad, & Meyer, 2015). On average, disclosure of their sexual identity did not occur until after age 20, though there was considerable variation by age cohort: young adults (18 to 29) reported disclosing their sexual identity before age 20, whereas adults aged 45 to 59 did not disclose until age 25 (Martos et al., 2015). This finding likely reflects the growing acceptance of homosexual and bisexual identities in U.S. society; identifying as homosexual had more negative consequences for the older generation than for the younger generation.

Sometimes self-identification as gay, lesbian, or bisexual does not occur until after the individual has engaged in same-sex sexual activities. During this period, referred to as *test and exploration,* the individual may feel ambivalent about his or her same-sex attractions; but eventually, after limited sexual contact with gays or lesbians, he or she starts to feel alienated from heterosexuality (Savin-Williams, 1998a). This contact may lead to *identity acceptance,* which is marked by a preference for social and sexual interaction with other sexual-minority individuals,

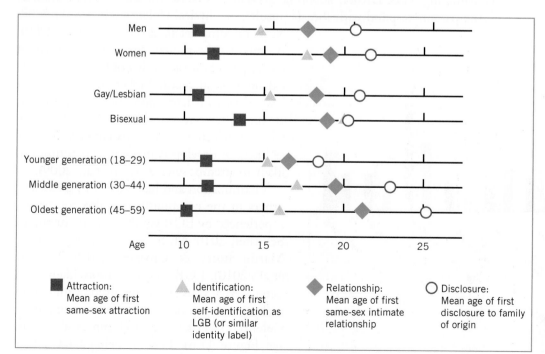

FIGURE 11.5 Milestones of sexual identity and behavior recalled by LGB adults The younger generation (18–29) experienced milestones earlier and with smaller gaps than did the oldest generation (45–59) in the study, reflecting the differences in the social standing of LGB individuals across generations. (Data from Martos, Nezhad, & Meyer, 2015)

the development of positive feelings about sexual identity, and the disclosure of sexual identity to family or friends. (Note that this latter stage, which involves self-identification, sometimes precedes sexual exploration.)

One factor that complicates the study of sexual identity is the fact that, especially for females, there is considerable instability in adolescents' and young adults' reports of same-sex attraction or sexual behavior (Savin-Williams & Ream, 2007). By college age, for example, a notable number of young women identify themselves as "mostly straight"—that is, mostly heterosexual but somewhat attracted to females (Diamond et al., 2015). One longitudinal study that followed 79 lesbian, bisexual, and unlabeled (those with some same-sex involvement who were unwilling to attach a label to their sexuality) women ages 18 to 25 found that, over a 10-year period, two-thirds changed the identity labels they had claimed at the beginning of the study and one-third changed labels two or more times (L. M. Diamond, 2008). Overall, females are more likely to describe themselves as bisexual or "mostly heterosexual" than are males (Saewyc, 2011). Male youth who have engaged in same-sex sexual experiences show an increasing preference for males from adolescence to early adulthood (Smiler, Frankel, & Savin-Williams, 2011).

Consequences of Coming Out

When they do "come out," or publicly self-identify as LGB, sexual-minority youths usually disclose to a best friend (typically a sexual-minority friend), to a peer to whom they are attracted, or to a sibling, and they do not tell their parents until a year or more later, if at all (Savin-Williams, 1998b). If they do reveal their sexual identity to their parents, they usually tell their mothers before telling their fathers, often because the mother asked or because they wanted to share that aspect of their lives with their mother (Savin-Williams & Ream, 2003).

Although many parents react in a supportive or only slightly negative manner to their children's coming out, it is not unusual for parents to initially respond to such a disclosure with anger, disappointment, and especially denial (Heatherington & Lavner, 2008; Savin-Williams & Ream, 2003). Unfortunately, some parents respond with threats, insults, or physical violence (Bos et al., 2008; M. S. Friedman et al., 2011; Ryan et al., 2009). As might be expected, sexual-minority youth whose parents are accepting of their child's sexual orientation report higher self-esteem and lower levels of depression and anxiety (Floyd et al., 1999; Savin-Williams, 1989a). Those who are rejected by their parents are 6 times as likely to develop depression and 8 times as likely to attempt suicide (Ryan et al., 2009).

Victimization and harassment by peers and others in the community are also commonly experienced by LGB youth (Coker, Austin, & Schuster, 2010; M. S. Friedman et al., 2011; Martin-Storey & Crosnoe, 2012; Toomey et al., 2010). LGB youth are more likely than heterosexual youth to be involved or injured in a physical fight and to be the victim of dating violence or sexual assault (Kann et al., 2016; see Figure 11.6). Fear of being harassed or

FIGURE 11.6 Exposure to violence and internalizing mental health problems by sexual orientation LGB youth report more of all forms of violence than heterosexual youth, and report higher sadness and likelihood to attempt suicide. (Data from Kann et al., 2016)

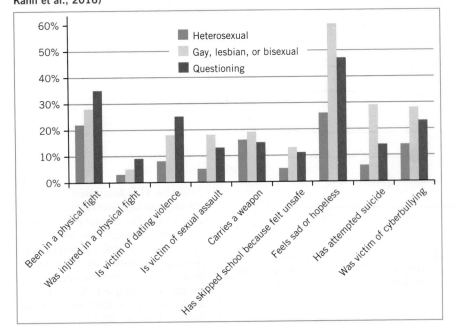

rejected outside the home is one reason many sexual-minority youth hide their sexual identity from heterosexual peers. In fact, many heterosexual adolescents are unaccepting of same-sex preferences in their peers (Bos et al., 2008; L. M. Diamond & Lucas, 2004). These high rates of victimization may also explain why LGB youth are more likely to engage in truancy (Kann et al., 2016).

In a recent survey, the top three most important life problems listed by LGB youth were non-accepting families, bullying at school, and fear of being open about their sexual identity; in contrast, the top three problems listed by non-LGB youth were grades, college, and financial pressures (Human Rights Campaign, 2012). Clearly, the lives of LGB youth are strongly affected by their sexual identities, and related concerns may prevent them from focusing on the day-to-day issues that concern most adolescents. The daily struggles of sexual-minority youth lead them to be twice as likely as non-LGB youth to say they will need to move to another town to feel that they are accepted (Human Rights Campaign, 2012).

Given these levels of harassment and violence, it is not surprising that sexual-minority youth are vulnerable to a number of social and psychological problems. They are prone to experience negative affect, depression, low self-esteem, and low feelings of control in their romantic relationships (Bos et al., 2008; Coker et al., 2010; Human Rights Campaign, 2012). They also report higher levels of school-related problems and substance abuse than do other youth (Bos et al., 2008; Marshal et al., 2008). They are also more likely to be homeless or involved in street life, frequently because they have run away from, or have been kicked out of, their home (Coker et al., 2010). Finally, sexual-minority youth have higher reported rates of attempted suicide than do their heterosexual peers (M. S. Friedman et al., 2011; Human Rights Campaign, 2012).

High rates of suicide among LGB youth led to the creation of the It Gets Better Project (www.itgetsbetter.org) in 2010. Over 50,000 videos have been uploaded and viewed more than 50 million times across six continents (It Gets Better Project, n.d.). Such efforts seem to be having an impact; a survey of LGB youth in 2012 found that 77% said that they knew their lives would get better (Human Rights Campaign, 2012). Connecting with other LGB individuals through social media may help sexual-minority adolescents cope with the stress of their lives; 73% of sexual-minority youth say they are more honest about themselves online, compared with only 43% of non-LGB youth (Human Rights Campaign, 2012).

LGB youth who are also of minority race or ethnic status are a special source of concern, given that they may experience discrimination on two fronts. However, a study of over 1000 sexual-minority young women found that LGB women found no difference in the ranges of mental health problems (depression, anxiety) and health-related behaviors (alcohol consumption, smoking) across African American, Latino American, Asian American, and White American groups (Balsam et al., 2015).

Despite the heightened risks, it is important to emphasize that in most ways sexual-minority children and adolescents are developmentally indistinguishable from their heterosexual peers: they deal with many of the same family and identity issues in adolescence and generally function just as well. Three-quarters of youth now say that they hear positive messages about sexual-minority identities online and in the media, at school, or by elected leaders (Human Rights Campaign,

Sexual-minority youth deal with many of the same family and identity issues as do other adolescents, and they are generally equally as adjusted as other teens. However, they face special challenges if their peers and family do not accept their sexual identity. In what may be a sign of changing attitudes, these two Minnesota high school seniors, who were among the students elected to their school's ceremonial "royal court," filed a civil suit to gain the right to walk together as a couple in the royal court's opening procession. Their legal victory and their appearance together in the procession brought cheers from many of their schoolmates.

AP PHOTO/JIM MONE

2012). The increasing positive portrayals of sexual-minority people in the media, as well as increasing social equality and cultural acceptance of sexual minorities, may also contribute to this positive trend (Diamond et al., 2015; Saewyc, 2011).

Review

The self is made up of three key components, namely self-concept (how one views oneself), self-esteem (how one feels about oneself), and identify (how others see one). Self-concept changes with age, shifting from being based on physical characteristics and overt behavior to being based on internal qualities and relationships with others. Young children tend to view themselves in positive ways and to overestimate their abilities. Older children tend to be more realistic about their strengths and weaknesses. In late childhood, children's self-concepts become more complex and integrated, and increasingly incorporate the perceptions of others. Adolescents' self-conceptions are more abstract than younger children's and accommodate different selves in different contexts. Adolescents develop a form of egocentrism that expresses itself as the "personal fable" and the critical "imaginary audience." In late adolescence and early adulthood, self-concepts become much more integrated and are more likely to reflect internalized values, beliefs, and standards.

Self-esteem emerges in middle childhood and is affected by the approval of parents and peers, physical attractiveness, academic competence, and social factors. Cultural differences affect how self-esteem is expressed, and there are consistent gender differences in levels of self-esteem.

Every individual has multiple identities, which are determined in part by one's membership in families, groups, communities, and cultures. Most adolescents move toward identity achievement by making a series of ever-narrowing selections of personal, occupational, sexual, and ideological commitments. Exploration of one's identity is affected by cultural surroundings.

The development of an ethnic and racial identity begins in childhood and reflects the beliefs and attitudes a child has about the ethnic or racial groups to which he or she belongs. Parents and community members may provide information about and foster pride in a child's ethnic and racial groups. Minority children and adolescents become aware that their group is discriminated against and conflicts with the dominant culture. Yet ethnic and racial identities are also sources of pride and are linked with children's self-esteem.

With the onset of puberty, adolescents begin to develop a sexual identity, which includes their sexual orientation. Most adolescents who identify as lesbian, gay, or bisexual recognize their same-sex attractions in late childhood and identify themselves as LGB, but they do not publicly reveal this identity until young adulthood. LGB individuals face significant discrimination and harassment, including from their own families. Though the majority of LGB youth experience outcomes similar to heterosexual youth, there is a heightened risk for mental health disorder and suicide among this population.

CHAPTER SUMMARY

The Caregiver–Child Attachment Relationship

- Harlow demonstrated through studies with monkeys that infants need and prefer a "cloth mother" over a wire one that provides food, and they use the cloth mothers as a secure base for exploration.

- According to Bowlby's theory, attachment is a biologically based process, rooted in evolution, that increases the helpless infant's chance of survival. A secure attachment provides children with a secure base for exploration. Children's early relationships with their parents and other caregivers provide children with internal working models of relationships.

- Ainsworth's Strange Situation can be used to categorize the quality of a child's attachment to his or her primary caregiver as securely attached, insecurely attached (insecure/resistant, insecure/avoidant), or disorganized/disoriented. Children are more likely to be securely attached if their caregivers are sensitive and responsive to their needs.

- There are similarities in children's attachments across many cultures, although the percentages of children in different attachment categories sometimes vary across cultures or subcultures.

- Intervention programs demonstrate that parents can be trained to be more sensitive, attentive, and stimulating in their parenting. These changes are associated with increases in infants' sociability, exploration, ability to soothe themselves, and security of attachment.

The Self

- Young children's conceptions of themselves are concrete—based on physical characteristics and overt behavior—and usually positive. As children age, their self-concepts are increasingly based on internal qualities and the quality of relationships with others; they also become more realistic, integrated, abstract, and complex.

- According to Elkind, because young adolescents focus on what others think of them, they think about an "imaginary audience" and develop "personal fables."

- Children's self-esteem is affected by many factors, including genetic predispositions, the quality of parent–child and peer relationships, physical attractiveness, academic competence, and various social factors.

- Concepts of how a person should think and behave differ across cultures, and therefore self-evaluations and self-esteem scores also differ.

- According to Erikson, adolescence is marked by the crisis of identity versus role confusion.

- The development of an ethnic and racial identity involves identifying oneself as a member of an ethnic or racial group, developing an understanding of group constancy, engaging in ethnic-role behaviors, acquiring knowledge about one's group, and developing a sense of belonging to the group. Family and community influence these aspects of development.

- Minority adolescents often start to explore the meaning of their ethnicity or race and its role in their identity. Many youth initially tend to be diffused or foreclosed in regard to their identities, and then become increasingly interested in exploring their ethnicity or race (search/moratorium). Some come to embrace their ethnicity or race; others gravitate toward the majority culture; still others become bicultural.

- Sexual-minority (lesbian, gay, or bisexual) youth are similar to others in their development of identity and self, although they face special difficulties. Many have some awareness of their same-sex attractions by late childhood. The process of self-identification and disclosure among LGB youth may involve several phases: first recognition, test and exploration, identity acceptance, and identity integration. However, not all LGB individuals go through all these stages, or go through them in the same order, and some have difficulty accepting and revealing their sexual-minority identity.

Test Yourself

1. Critical to an infant's growth is the development of a positive emotional connection to a primary caregiver, such as a parent. This enduring emotional bond is known as
   _____ .
   a. co-regulation
   b. attachment
   c. co-dependency
   d. imprinting

2. In both Harlow's work with rhesus monkeys and Ainsworth's Strange Situation paradigm, researchers observed the baby monkey or child continually return to the mother after exploring an unfamiliar space or situation. This behavior is an example of
   a. disoriented behavior.
   b. ambivalent attachment.
   c. secure attachment.
   d. parental sensitivity.

3. According to attachment theory as proposed by John Bowlby, which of the following is an example of a child in the *attachment-in-the-making* phase?
   a. Juan favors his father more than others and tends to laugh and smile more in his presence.
   b. Ava is easily soothed by anyone who picks her up when she cries.
   c. Devon actively seeks the company of his grandmother and is emboldened to explore the environment in her presence.
   d. Serena shows a clear preference for her mother and demonstrates visible distress upon separation.

4. Three attachment types were initially identified in research by Mary Ainsworth. Which attachment type was later added to categorize those that did not fit well into Ainsworth's initial three categories?
   a. securely attached
   b. disorganized/disoriented

    c. insecure/resistant

    d. insecure/avoidant

5. Which measure of attachment security pays careful attention to children's reactions to their caregivers after a separation?

    a. attachment Q-Sort

    b. inventory of parent and peer attachment

    c. Strange Situation

    d. internal working model

6. A father who responds quickly to the needs of his child and shows emotional warmth by smiling, laughing, and communicating positively to his child is demonstrating

    a. caregiver responsibility.

    b. reciprocal attachment.

    c. parental security.

    d. parental sensitivity.

7. Studies have shown that the link between attachment security and genetic make-up

    a. disappears by adulthood.

    b. can be differentially impacted by the quality of the child's environment.

    c. can be changed by altering the levels of oxytocin in the brain.

    d. is proof that genetic markers cause specific attachment security types.

8. _____ involves a person's overall subjective evaluation of oneself and the feelings associated with that evaluation.

    a. Self-esteem

    b. Self concept

    c. Self-reflection

    d. Self-measure

9. Two-year-old Lani walks by a mirror and notices chocolate around her mouth. She uses the bottom of her shirt to carefully wipe it off. Lani is displaying _____ .

    a. self-recognition

    b. self-consciousness

    c. self-determination

    d. self-esteem

10. Susan Harter argues that a child's sense of self-concept

    a. is a social construct influenced in large part by the evaluations of others.

    b. is an innate sense that is based entirely on evolutionary mechanisms.

    c. does not begin to emerge until middle childhood, around the ages of 6–9 years.

    d. is fully developed by the time the child enters elementary school, at about age 6.

11. As children's cognitive abilities increase, their self-concepts shift from focusing on _____ characteristics to _____ qualities.

    a. physical; concrete

    b. abstract; personal

    c. personal; psychological

    d. concrete; abstract

12. Self-concept in adolescence is characterized by a reemergence of a form of egocentrism, exemplified by the individual overly differentiating his or her feelings from those of others. This type of egocentrism is called the

    a. looking-glass self.

    b. personal fable.

    c. imaginary audience.

    d. introspective mirror.

13. According to James Marcia's theory of identity development, which stage is noted by the exploration of identity status?

    a. identify diffusion

    b. identity foreclosure

    c. confusion

    d. moratorium

14. Which of the following statements is *not* true about racial and ethnic identity during adolescence?

    a. The more an adolescent identifies with his or her ethnic and racial identity, the lower his or her self-esteem.

    b. Minority-group members can face challenges in adopting the values of their ethnic group or those of the dominant culture.

    c. Because they may have had early experiences with discrimination, ethnic- and racial-minority adolescents may feel ambivalent about their own ethnic status.

    d. Development of a bicultural identity can lead to positive benefits for some minority youth and can lead to challenges for others.

15. For sexual-minority youth, the process of *first recognition* is noted by

    a. feelings of alienation resulting from the realization that they are different from others.

    b. a preference for social interaction with other sexual-minority individuals.

    c. an individual's first experience with same-sex sexual activities.

    d. an individual's initial disclosure about his/her sexual identity.

LaunchPad
macmillan learning

Don't stop now! Research shows that testing yourself is a powerful learning tool. Visit LaunchPad to access the LearningCurve adaptive quizzing system, which gives you a personalized study plan to help build your mastery of the chapter material through videos, activities, and more. **Go to launchpadworks.com.**

Critical Thinking Questions

1. Some theorists believe that early attachment relationships have enduring long-term effects. Others think that such effects depend on the quality of the ongoing parent–child relationship, which tends to be correlated with the security of children's early attachment to parents. How do you think researchers might go about examining this issue?

2. Based on what you have read about attachment and the development of the self, what negative effects might children experience as a result of being placed in a series of different foster-care homes? How might these effects vary with the age of the child?

3. Recall Erikson's psychosocial stages of development (Chapter 9). How might a person's self-esteem be affected by the events and outcomes associated with each of the stages?

4. What are some of the practical and conceptual difficulties of determining when children first recognize that they are physically attracted to same-sex or other-sex individuals?

Key Terms

attachment, p. 467

attachment theory, p. 469

disorganized/disoriented attachment, p. 472

ethnic and racial identity, p. 497

identity, p. 495

identity achievement, p. 495

identity diffusion, p. 496

identity foreclosure, p. 496

identity versus role confusion, p. 495

imaginary audience, p. 488

insecure attachment, p. 472

insecure/avoidant attachment, p. 472

insecure/resistant (or ambivalent) attachment, p. 472

internal working model of attachment, p. 470

moratorium, p. 495

parental sensitivity, p. 476

personal fable, p. 487

secure attachment, p. 471

secure base, p. 469

self-concept, p. 481

self-esteem, p. 489

sexual identity, p. 500

sexual orientation, p. 500

sexual-minority youth, p. 500

social comparison, p. 485

Strange Situation, p. 471

▶ Student Video Activities

Development of Attachment in Infancy and Toddlerhood

Assessment of Attachment in the Efe Culture: Interview with Gilda Morelli

Self-Awareness and the Rouge Test

Identity Development in Adolescence

Answers to Test Yourself

1. b, **2.** c, **3.** a, **4.** b, **5.** c, **6.** d, **7.** b, **8.** a, **9.** a, **10.** a, **11.** d, **12.** b, **13.** d, **14.** a, **15.** a

ANNA BELLE LEE WASHINGTON (1924–2000), *The Fair* (oil on canvas)

The Family

Themes

- Nature and Nurture
- The Active Child
- The Sociocultural Context
- Individual Differences
- Research and Children's Welfare

As noted in Chapter 2, in 1980, the People's Republic of China instituted a sweeping new policy that would affect Chinese families dramatically. Out of fear of national overpopulation, the government ordered a limit of one child per family. In the decade before the one-child policy was implemented, China's population was doubling every five years (United Nations, 2015). Backed up by a system of economic rewards for those who complied and sometimes severe sanctions, including forced abortions, imposed against those who did not, this policy was quite effective at controlling China's dramatic population growth.

One unintended and distressing consequence of the one-child policy, however, was an epidemic of female abortion and infanticide related to the strong preference for male offspring in Chinese culture. As a result, China saw an imbalance between males and females, with the 2015 ratio of males to females (106 males per every 100 females) higher than the worldwide average (102:100) and significantly higher than that of the U.S. and Canada (98.3:100 and 98.4:100, respectively; United Nations, 2015). In addition, between 2010 and 2015, China's population actually shrank by 50% (United Nations, 2015), leading to concerns over an imbalance between the young and the old (Buckley, 2015). The "success" of the one-child policy at controlling population coupled with these concerns led China to adopt a "two-child policy" in 2015 (Buckley, 2015).

China's attempt to use policy to control its population has provided developmental psychologists with a "natural experiment" in which to study how a national change in family size might affect children's development. Think about the differences in upbringing that might occur when parents have one child as opposed to two or more. To begin with, an only child is likely to receive more individual attention from parents and more of the family's resources. In addition, an only child does not have to cooperate and share with siblings—although, of course, he or she will miss out on the warmth and closeness many siblings feel for one another. Because of differences such as these, many people predicted that the new generation of single children raised in China would be overindulged and have little experience in compromising and cooperating with others and would become spoiled "little emperors" (Falbo & Poston, 1993).

After years of studying these only children, however, researchers have found no consistent support for these concerns. There is some evidence that Chinese only children, especially in urban areas, perform better on tests of academic performance and intelligence than do children from families with more than one child (Falbo & Poston, 1993; Falbo et al., 1989; Jiao, Ji, & Jing, 1996). And although some initial studies found that only children in China were viewed by peers as more self-interested and less cooperative than children with siblings (e.g., Jiao, Ji, & Jing, 1986), later studies found little evidence that only children have more behavioral problems (Hesketh et al., 2011; D. Wang et al., 2000; S. Zhang, 1997).

Moreover, large survey studies have indicated that only children are no more prone to depression and anxiety than are children with siblings

China's one-child policy provided an opportunity to assess the effects of being an only child and to consider the impact of its unintended consequences, such as the birth and survival of a disproportionately high number of male children.

EPA / ADRIAN BRADSHAW / NEWSCOM

(G. D. Edwards et al., 2005; Hesketh & Ding, 2005), despite the potential for heightened family pressures on them to fulfill parental goals and needs. In fact, there appears to be virtually no difference between only children and sibling children in regard to personality or social behavior, including positive behaviors needed for getting along with others, negative behaviors such as aggression and lying, and respect and support for other family members (Deutsch, 2006; Falbo & Poston, 1993; Fuligni & Zhang, 2004; Poston & Falbo, 1990). The difference between the early and later findings may be due to a change in parents' behaviors toward only children as one-child families have become more common and expected—the consequence being that only children are no more likely to be spoiled than are children with siblings.

The one-child policy in China is a good example of how the size and composition of families can change and of how, consistent with Bronfenbrenner's model discussed in Chapter 9, the larger society affects what goes on within families. Culture, as well as social and economic events, can have a tremendous effect on the structure of families and interactions among family members. In industrialized Western societies as well, a variety of social changes in the past several decades have had marked effects on the structure of the family. For example, families are smaller today than in the past, many more mothers work outside the home, more people are choosing to have children outside of marriage, and same-sex parenting is increasingly common and accepted. Such changes in the family can affect the resources available to the child, as well as the parents' child-rearing practices and behavior.

In this chapter, we examine many developmental aspects of family interaction. We begin by considering how family functioning and children's development may have been affected by certain social changes that have occurred in the United States over the past seven decades—from the increased age of first-time parenthood to increased rates of divorce, remarriage, and maternal employment. We then discuss the ways in which parents' approach to parenting can influence their children's development, the ways in which children can influence their parents' parenting, and the ways in which siblings may influence one another. Finally, we explore the impact that factors such as poverty and culture may have on developmental outcomes.

As you will see, the theme of *nature and nurture* is central to the study of the role of the family because a child's heredity and rearing influence each other and jointly affect the child's development. In addition, the theme of the *active child* is evident in our discussion of how children influence the way their parents socialize them. The theme of *sociocultural context* is also key, in that parenting practices are strongly influenced by cultural beliefs, biases, and goals and are related to different outcomes for children in different cultures. Furthermore, the issue of *individual differences* is a major theme in this chapter because different styles of parenting, child-rearing practices, and family structures are associated with differences in children's social and emotional functioning. Finally, because parenting influences the quality of children's day-to-day experience, as well as children's beliefs and behaviors, understanding patterns of family functioning has relevance for our theme of *research and children's welfare*.

Some family forms, such as families headed by same-sex parents, are more common and accepted now than in the past.

SARAHWOLFEPHOTOGRAPHY / GETTY IMAGES

family structure ■ the number of and relationships among the people living in a household

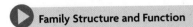

Family Structure and Function

Family Structure

What is a family? When you first think of your family, you likely think of your parents and siblings, if you have any. You may then think about your extended family, which includes your grandparents, aunts, uncles, and cousins; you may be close with some members of your extended family and have little interaction with others. The adult family members that will have the biggest effects on children's development are those they live with, both because they will have regular contact with the children and because they financially support and raise the children.

Family structure refers to the number of and relationships among the people living in a household. Alterations in the family structure due to births, deaths, divorce, remarriage, or other factors can also influence interactions among family members and may affect family routines and norms, as well as children's emotional well-being (Bachman, Coley, & Carrano, 2012; Dush, Kotila, & Schoppe-Sullivan, 2011; Lam, McHale, & Crouter, 2012). In many cases, the effects of such shifts in family dynamics tend to be gradual and continuous. However, a single event such as a traumatic divorce or the death of a parent may cause a fairly dramatic change in a child's behavior and emotional adjustment. In this section, we will first consider recent changes in family structure before reviewing in depth what is known about three family structures about which there has been some concern and much debate: same-sex parents, divorced parents, and stepparents.

Changes in Family Structure in the United States

If asked to describe the typical family structure, most Americans would list a mother, a father, and one or more children biologically related to both of them. In 1960, that characterization was correct: 73% of children lived in family structures fitting this description (Pew Research Center, 2015). However, according to data collected by the U.S. Census (Laughlin, 2014; Pew Research Center, 2015), that is no longer the case. The following changes in family structure over the past 50 or more years are the most important ones for the understanding of child development and family life.

More Children Live with Single or Unmarried Parents

In 2014, only 7% of children in the United States lived with parents who were in their first marriage, compared with the 73% in 1960 noted above. As displayed in Figure 12.1, this drop was accompanied by a large increase, from 9% in 1960 to 26% in 2014, in the number of children living with a single parent. In addition, 7% of

FIGURE 12.1 The family structures in which children live have changed dramatically over the past 50 years Children were much more likely in 2014 to be living with single parents or with unmarried cohabitating parents than in 1960. (*Note:* Data for cohabitating parents was unavailable for 1960.) (Data from Pew Research Center, 2015)

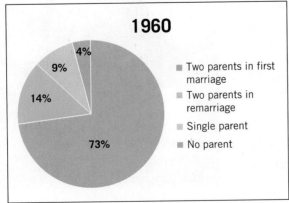

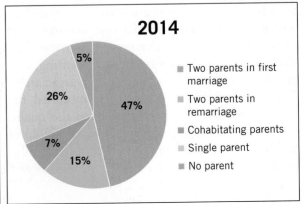

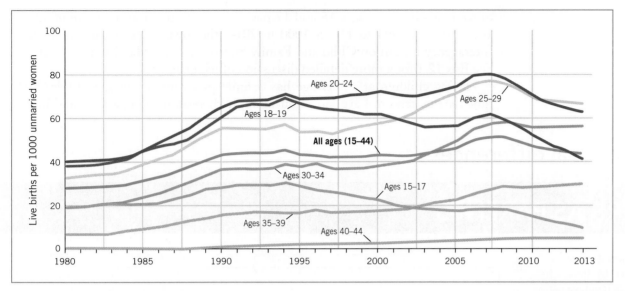

FIGURE 12.2 Birth rates for unmarried women by age of the mother The proportion of births for unmarried women in general rose sharply from 1980 to 2005, although rates have recently declined. The rate of births for unmarried teen girls aged 15 to 17 has dropped substantially between 1994 and 2013, from 32 per 1000 to 12 per 1000 teens. (Data from Federal Interagency Forum on Child and Family Statistics, 2015)

children live with cohabiting (non-married) parents, which was not tracked by the Census in 1960. The number of births to unmarried women began to increase in the 1980s. As seen in Figure 12.2, in 2013, there were 44 births for every 1000 unmarried women aged 15 to 44 (Federal Interagency Forum on Child and Family Statistics, 2015). Rates for 15- to 17-year-olds and for 18- to 19-year-olds dropped steeply, while the rates for all other groups increased—at least until 2010 or so. It is important to note that about half the unmarried women who give birth are cohabitating with the fathers of their children (Kennedy & Bumpass, 2008).

As Figure 12.1 makes clear, family structures have changed dramatically in the last 50 years (Pew Research Center, 2015). However, these averages obscure some important qualifications—for example, the likelihood that a child in the United States will live with a single parent is greater for some racial and ethnic groups, and for some socioeconomic groups, than for others. More than half (54%) of Black children and 29% of Latino children live with a single parent, compared with 19% of White children and 13% of Asian children (Pew Research Center, 2015). In addition, children of parents with college degrees are much less likely to live with a single parent (12%), compared with children whose parents only went to high school (41%; Pew Research Center, 2015).

Family structure has big implications for family income. Forty-one percent of children living with single parents live below the federal poverty line, compared with 14% of children living with two married parents (Laughlin, 2014). Another major implication of living with a single parent is that the parent has less time to spend with each child because she or he must do all the household tasks alone and often must have more than one job in order to support the family. As a result, single parents are much less likely to read to their children than married parents, although they are not less likely to eat breakfast with their children (Laughlin, 2014).

First-Time Parents Are Older than in the Past

The average age at which women have their first child has increased over the last several decades, from 21 years in 1970, to 26 years in 2014 (Pew Research Center, 2015). This average has increased both because women are delaying when they have children and because the teen birth rate has been decreasing. Births to teen girls between ages 15 and 17 have steeply declined, from a rate of 32 per 1000 teens in 1994 to 11 per 1000 in 2014, the lowest rate on record (Federal Interagency Forum on Child and Family Statistics, 2015; Hamilton et al., 2015). See Box 12.1 for a more detailed discussion of teen parenting.

Having children at a later age has definite parenting advantages. Older first-time parents tend to have more education, higher-status occupations, and higher

BOX 12.1 | individual differences

TEENAGERS AS PARENTS

Although most adolescents live with and are cared for by their parents, a significant percentage of adolescents are parents themselves. When teen pregnancies were at their peak in the 1990s, more than 10% of teenage girls in some racial and ethnic groups had given birth to children. The good news is that this rate has dropped dramatically over the last couple of decades. In 2014, there were 11 babies born per every 1000 adolescents aged 15 to 17 years in the United States (Hamilton et al., 2015). This rate represents a decline of 72% from 1991 (which was the peak year for teen births) and was the lowest rate in the seven decades for which national data are available.

Declines in teen births occurred across all racial and ethnic groups (see figure); from 1991 to 2014, there was a 60% decline in births to non-Hispanic White teens, a 70% drop in births to non-Hispanic Black teens, a 68% decline in births to American Indian or Alaska Native teens, a 72% decline in births to Asian or Pacific Islander teens, and a 64% decline in births to Hispanic teens (Hamilton et al., 2015). This decline is likely due in large part to better sex education and to greater availability of birth control and abortion services. Nevertheless, the current rate is still much higher than public health officials would like and is higher than that in other industrialized countries (National Campaign to Prevent Teen and Unplanned Pregnancy, 2014).

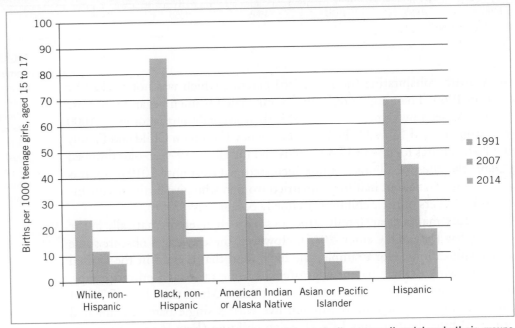

The birth rate for teenage girls aged 15 to 17 has dropped dramatically across all racial and ethnic groups in the United States. (Data from Hamilton et al., 2015)

A number of factors affect U.S. girls' risk for childbearing during adolescence. Two factors that reduce the risk are living with both biological parents and being involved in school activities and religious organizations (B. J. Ellis et al., 2003; K. A. Moore et al., 1998). Factors that substantially increase the risk include being raised in poverty by a single or adolescent mother (R. L. Coley & Chase-Lansdale, 1998; J. B. Hardy et al., 1998), having low school achievement and dropping out of school (Freitas et al., 2008), having significant family problems (e.g., death of a parent, drug or alcohol abuse in the family; Freitas et al., 2008), having an older adolescent sibling who is sexually active or is already a parent (East & Jacobson, 2001; B. C. Miller, Benson, & Galbraith, 2001), and having friends who are sexually active (East, Felice, & Morgan, 1993; Scaramella et al., 1998).

Having a child in adolescence is associated with many negative consequences for both the adolescent mother and the child (Jaffee, 2002). Motherhood curtails the mother's opportunities for education, career development, and normal relationships with peers. Even if teenage mothers marry, they are very likely to get divorced and to spend many years as single mothers (R. L. Coley & Chase-Lansdale,

incomes than younger parents do. Older parents are also more likely to have planned the birth of their children and to have fewer children overall. Thus, they have more financial resources for raising a family. They are also less likely to get divorced within 10 years if they are married (Bramlett & Mosher, 2002). In addition, older parents tend to be more positive in their parenting of infants than younger parents are. For example, one study found that, compared with people who became parents between the ages of 18 and 25, older mothers and fathers had

Teenage mothers face a number of challenges that make it difficult for them to stay in school.

SYRACUSE NEWSPAPERS / JOHN BERRY / THE IMAGE WORKS

1998; M. R. Moore & Brooks-Gunn, 2002). In addition, adolescent mothers often have poor parenting skills and are more likely than older mothers to provide low levels of verbal stimulation to their infants, to expect their children to behave in ways that are beyond their years, and to neglect and abuse them (Ekéus, Christensson, & Hjern, 2004).

Given these deficits in parenting, it is not surprising that children of teenage mothers are more likely than children of older mothers to exhibit disorganized/disoriented attachment status, low impulse control, problem behaviors, and delays in cognitive development in the preschool years and thereafter. As adolescents themselves, children born to teenagers have higher rates of academic failure, delinquency, incarceration, and early sexual activity than do adolescents born to older mothers (M. R. Moore & Brooks-Gunn, 2002;

Wakschlag et al., 2000). Not surprisingly, they also tend to have less education, income, and life satisfaction as young adults (Lipman, Georgiades, & Boyle, 2011).

This does not mean that all children born to adolescent mothers are destined to poor developmental outcomes. Those whose mothers have more knowledge about child development and parenting and who exhibit more authoritative parenting than most teen mothers do tend to display fewer problem behaviors and better intellectual development (L. Bates, Luster, & Vandenbelt, 2003). In addition, those who experience a positive mother–child relationship, including consistent and sensitive parenting, appear more likely to stay in school and obtain employment in early adulthood (Jaffee et al., 2001). Supportive parents and other relatives are also likely to provide childcare so that young mothers have the opportunity to continue their schooling.

A number of factors likewise affect adolescent males' risk for becoming fathers. Chief among these are being poor, being prone to substance abuse and behavioral problems, being involved with deviant peers, and having a police record (Miller-Johnson et al., 2004; D. R. Moore & Florsheim, 2001).

Many young unmarried or absent fathers see their children regularly, at least during the first few years, but rates of contact decrease over time (Marsiglio et al., 2000). Contact is less likely to be maintained when the unmarried non-cohabitating father is an adolescent (M. Wilson & Brooks-Gunn, 2001). Young unmarried fathers remain more involved with their children if they have a warm, supportive relationship with the mother in the weeks after delivery and if the mother does not experience many stressful life events (particularly financial problems) during and soon after the pregnancy (Cutrona et al., 1998). They are also more likely to be involved with their infants if they have social support from their own parents for the parenting role and if their level of stress related to fatherhood or other factors is low (Fagan, Bernd, & Whiteman, 2007).

The presence and support of the father can be beneficial to both the child and the mother. Adolescent mothers feel more competent as a parent and less likely to be depressed when they are satisfied with the level of the father's involvement (Fagan & Lee, 2010). The children of adolescent mothers fare better in their own adolescence if they have a good relationship with their biological father (or a stepfather), especially if he lives with the child. However, exposure to a fathering figure may have little beneficial effect on children of adolescent mothers if the father–child relationship is not positive or the father figure has a criminal history (Jaffee et al., 2001).

On average, older fathers engage in more verbal interactions with their preschool-age children than do younger fathers.

LYN WALKERDEN PHOTOGRAPHY / GETTY IMAGES

lower rates of observed harsh parenting with their 2-year-olds, which, in turn, predicted fewer problem behaviors a year later (Scaramella et al., 2008). Furthermore, men who delay parenting until approximately age 30 or later are likewise more positive about the parenting role and tend to be more responsive, affectionate, and cognitively and verbally stimulating with their infants than are younger fathers (Cooney et al., 1993; NICHD Early Child Care Research Network, 2000a).

More Children Live with Grandparents

 Grandparents as Parents

Almost 10% of all children in the United States live with a grandparent, either with or without their own parents; these rates vary with the child's race or ethnicity: 14% of Black children, 14% of Asian children, 12% of Latino children, and 7% of White non-Hispanic children live with their grandparents (Ellis & Simmons, 2014). Since 1970, the percentage of children who have grandparents as their primary caregivers (i.e., the grandparents are functioning in the parent role) has doubled, from 3% to 6%, such that 2.7 million grandparents nationwide are the primary caregivers for their grandchildren (Ellis & Simmons, 2014).

Grandparent-headed families tend to be poorer than households not headed by grandparents, as grandparents have the added cost of caring for children on what may be fixed retirement incomes (Ganong, Coleman, & Russell, 2015). Parenting as a grandparent is particularly difficult because most grandparents have experienced a long gap since the last time they parented. It is also difficult for grandparents raising grandchildren to maintain a social support network, as friends their age are often not struggling with raising a new generation of children and they are not of the same generation as the parents of their grandchildren's friends (Ganong et al., 2015). Unfortunately, children raised by grandparents experience a range of emotional and behavioral problems (Fergusson, Maughan, & Golding, 2008), although it is impossible to know if the difficulties are a result of grandparenting, of poor parenting from their biological parents, or of the trauma of separation from their biological parents (Strong, Bean, & Feinauer, 2010).

Families Are Smaller

Families are smaller now than in the past, which can be attributed to women delaying pregnancies because they have careers, as well as to increased access to birth control. The percentage of women who had four or more children dropped from 40% in 1976 to 14% in 2014, while the percent of women who had one child rose (11% to 22%), as did the percent of women who had two children (24% to 41%), over that same period (Pew Research Center, 2015). This change, of course, means that fewer children have multiple, if any, siblings.

Family Structures Are More Fluid

A commonly repeated statistic is that 50% of marriages end in divorce. This is still the case, if you look over the course of 20 years. Specifically, a couple in a first marriage has a 69% chance of staying together for 10 years and a 54% chance of staying together for 20 years—rates that have remained relatively unchanged since the 1970s (Copen et al., 2012). This high rate of divorce means that a substantial proportion of children experience some, and sometimes repeated, changes in family structure through the entrance or exit of a parent or parent's cohabitating partner. Nearly one-fifth of all children experience a change in family structure as a result of separation, divorce, remarriage, cohabitation, or parental death over a three-year period (Laughlin, 2014). The more family structure transitions a child experiences, the more behavior problems they can develop (Cavanagh & Huston, 2006; Osborne & McLanahan, 2007).

Next, we look at several specific family structures and how they influence child development: same-sex parents, divorced parents, and stepparents.

Same-Sex Parents

The number of gay and lesbian parents has risen dramatically in recent years, as legislation and public attitudes have changed. According to the 2010 U. S. Census, 115,000 same-sex couples reported that they were raising children (Lofquist, 2011). Most children of lesbian or gay parents were born when one of their parents was in a heterosexual marriage or relationship, meaning that 59% of children in same-sex parent households are biologically related to one of their parents (Goldberg, Gartrell, & Gates, 2014). In many such cases, the biological parents divorced when one parent came out as lesbian or gay.

In addition to legal barriers, same-sex couples face obvious practical barriers to becoming parents. Some lesbian women turn to artificial insemination, and some gay men seek out surrogate mothers who will donate their eggs or carry the gay couple's baby. Most states allow the nonbiological parent to adopt their same-sex spouse's biological child in a process known as second-parent adoption. Other same-sex parents choose to become foster or adoptive parents, although several states still have legal barriers to such adoptions, despite the fact that the U.S. Supreme Court ruled in *Oberfegell v. Hodges* in 2015 that same-sex marriages are constitutional.

Although the practice of same-sex couples raising children has likely existed for hundreds of years, the lack of

A growing body of research suggests that the development of children of gay and lesbian parents does not differ from that of children of heterosexual parents.

JAMIE CHOMAS / GETTY IMAGES

social acceptance of same-sex relationships meant that these instances were largely hidden. With the increasing acceptance of same-sex couples and same-sex parenting, more and more same-sex couples have become parents. At the same time, many members of the public have voiced concerns about the capability of same-sex couples to be "good" parents. Many researchers have set out to test whether same-sex parents are any different from different-sex parents, and whether the children of same-sex parents experience different outcomes from the children of different-sex parents. This growing body of research has consistently shown that children with same-sex parents are not different from children of heterosexual parents in terms of adjustment, personality, relationships with peers, and academic achievement (Bos et al., 2016; Farr, Forssell, & Paterson, 2010; Gartrell & Bos, 2010; Potter, 2012; Wainright & Patterson, 2006, 2008).

In addition, these children are also similar in their sexual orientation and in the degree to which their behavior is gender-typed (J. M. Bailey et al., 1995; Fulcher, Sutfin, & Patterson, 2008; Golombok et al., 2003), as well as in their romantic involvements and sexual behavior as adolescents (Wainright, Russell, & Patterson, 2004). Perhaps surprisingly, children of lesbian and gay parents generally report low levels of stigmatization and teasing (Tasker & Golombok, 1995), although they sometimes feel excluded, or gossiped about, by peers (Bos & van Balen, 2008).

As in families with heterosexual parents, the adjustment of children with lesbian and gay parents seems to depend on family dynamics, including the closeness of the parent–child relationship (Wainright & Patterson, 2008), how well the parents get along, parental supportiveness, regulated discipline, and the degree of stress parents experience in their parenting (Farr et al., 2010; Farr & Patterson, 2013). In addition, children of lesbian parents are better adjusted when their parents are not highly stressed (R. W. Chan, Raboy, & Patterson, 1998), when they report sharing childcare duties evenly (C. J. Patterson, 1995), and when they are satisfied with the division of labor in the home (R. W. Chan et al., 1998). When gay adoptive fathers have low levels of social support and a less positive gay identity, they experience more stress regarding parenting and are more likely to have poor relationships with their children (Tornello, Farr, & Patterson, 2011)— responses that are likely to affect their children's adjustment. In families with a gay father and his partner, a son's happiness with his family life is related to the inclusion of the partner in family activities and the son's having a good relationship with the partner as well as with his biological father (Crosbie-Burnett & Helmbrecht, 1993).

The consistency in these findings has led professional organizations such as the American Academy of Pediatrics to reaffirm that there is no evidence of a causal link between parents' sexual orientation and children's development across a range of domains (Siegel et al., 2013).

Divorced Parents

In 2015, 4.8 million U.S. children lived with only their divorced mother, while 1.3 million children lived with only their divorced father (U.S. Census Bureau, 2015). Moreover, about 40% of remarriages involving children end in divorce within 10 years (Bramlett & Mosher, 2002). Given the number of children in these situations, the effects of divorce and remarriage on children have been the subjects of extensive research (Amato, 2010).

Mechanisms by Which Divorce Can Affect Children

Before we discuss *whether* divorce affects children, let us first consider *why* it might do so, combining the themes of the *mechanisms of development* and the *contexts of development*. Divorce precipitates a number of changes in a child's life (Amato, 2010). The parents separate and live in different residences, with the child typically staying with the mother. The parent whom the child lives with now has to function as a single parent, which is both more time intensive and more financially costly, even with child support from the noncustodial parent. As a result of the stress associated with these changes, the parenting of newly divorced mothers, compared with that of mothers in two-parent families, often tends to be characterized by more irritability and coercion and by less warmth, emotional availability, consistency, and supervision of children (Hetherington, Bridges, & Insabella, 1998; K. E. Sutherland, Altenhofen, & Biringen, 2012). This is unfortunate because children tend to be most adjusted during and after the divorce if their custodial parent is supportive and emotionally available (Altenhofen, Sutherland, & Biringen, 2010; DeGarmo, 2010).

Sometimes as a result of the financial hardship that accompanies being a single parent, and sometimes for other practical reasons, the custodial parent (or both parents, if they have joint custody) may move the children to a new neighborhood and a new school; children then must go through an often wrenching transition to a new home, neighborhood, school, and peer group at the same time that they are adjusting to a new family structure (Braver, Ellman, & Fabricius, 2003; Fabricius & Braver, 2006). Divorce can thus disrupt children's routines and social networks. All of these potentially stressful life changes during and after divorce can affect children's mental health directly (Sun & Li, 2011) but can also affect children indirectly by undermining positive parenting and enjoyable family interactions (Ge, Natsuaki, & Conger, 2006).

Divorce may also result in positive outcomes, particularly if the parents were engaged in high levels of conflict while married. Parental conflict has been linked to increased emotional problems as well as increased behavioral problems in children and adolescents (Buehler, Lange, & Franck, 2007; Davies, Cummings, & Winter, 2004; Grych, Harold, & Miles, 2003). Indeed, Amato and colleagues (1995) found that among children raised in high-conflict families, those whose parents divorced were better adjusted than those whose parents stayed together, whereas the reverse was true for low-conflict families. Thus, for children from high-conflict families, divorce is a positive change if it can disrupt that conflict.

Of course, divorce can also lead to an exacerbation of conflict between parents about finances or parenting decisions. This ongoing conflict is especially likely to have negative effects on children if they feel caught in the middle—for example, if they are forced to act as intermediaries between their parents or to inform one parent of the other's activities. Similar pressures may arise if children feel the need to hide from one parent information about, or their loyalty to, the other parent—or if the parents inappropriately disclose to them sensitive information about the divorce and each other. Adolescents who feel that they are caught up in their divorced parents' conflict are at increased risk for being depressed or anxious and for

Because ongoing marital conflict poses a variety of risks for children, research suggests that staying together "for the sake of the children" may be more harmful than divorce in highly conflictual marriages.

engaging in problematic behavior such as drinking, stealing, cheating at school, fighting, or using drugs (Afifi et al., 2007, 2008; Afifi, Afifi, & Coho, 2009; Afifi & McManus 2010; Buchanan, Maccoby, & Dornbusch, 1991; Kenyon & Koerner, 2008).

Children's Adjustment to Divorce

Most experts agree that children of divorce are at greater risk for a variety of short-term and long-term problems than are most children who are living with both their biological parents. Compared with the majority of their peers in intact families, for instance, they are more likely to experience depression and sadness, to have lower self-esteem, and to be less socially responsible and competent (Amato, 2001; Ge et al., 2006; Hetherington et al., 1998). In addition, children of divorce, especially boys, may be prone to higher levels of externalizing problem behaviors such as aggression and antisocial behavior, both soon after the divorce and years later (Burt et al., 2008; Hartman, Magalhães, & Mandich, 2011; Malone et al., 2004). Problems such as these may contribute to the drop in academic achievement that children of divorce often exhibit (Potter, 2010). Adolescents whose parents divorce exhibit a greater tendency to drop out of school, engage in delinquent activities and substance abuse, and have children out of wedlock (Hetherington et al., 1998; Song, Benin, & Glick, 2012).

As adults, children from divorced and remarried families are at greater risk for divorce than are their peers from intact families (Bumpass, Martin, & Sweet, 1991; Mustonen et al., 2011; Rodgers, Power, & Hope, 1997). Within this group, women, but not men, appear to also be at risk for poorer-quality intimate relationships; lower self-esteem; and lower satisfaction with social support from friends, family members, and other people (Mustonen et al., 2011). Being less likely to have completed high school or college, children of divorce often earn lower incomes in early adulthood than do their peers from intact families (Hetherington, 1999; Song et al., 2012). As adults, they are also at slightly greater risk for serious emotional disorders such as depression, anxiety, and phobias (Chase-Lansdale, Cherlin, & Kiernan, 1995).

Despite all these greater risks, however, most children whose parents divorce do not suffer significant, enduring problems as a consequence (Amato, 2010). In fact, although divorce usually is a very painful experience for children, the differences between children from divorced families and children from intact families in terms of their psychological and social functioning are small overall (e.g., Burt et al., 2008). In addition, these differences often reflect an extension of the differences in the children's and/or their parents' psychological functioning that existed for years prior to the divorce (Clarke-Stewart et al., 2000; Emery & Forehand, 1996).

Although older children and adolescents are better able to understand a divorce than are younger children, they are nonetheless particularly at risk for problems with adjustment, including poor academic achievement and negative relationships with their parents. Adolescents who live in neighborhoods characterized by a high crime rate, poor schools, and an abundance of antisocial peers are at especially high risk (Hetherington et al., 1998), most likely because the opportunities to get into trouble are amplified when there is only one parent—who most likely is at work during the day—to monitor the child's activity. College students are less reactive

Divorced parents who are single often have to deal with increased levels of stress, which can affect the quality of their parenting.

BRUCE AYRES / GETTY IMAGES

to their parents' divorce, probably because of their maturity and relative independence from the family (Amato & Keith, 1991). With regard to their parents' remarriage, young adolescents appear to be more negatively affected than younger children. One possible explanation is that young adolescents' struggles with the issues of autonomy and sexuality are heightened by the presence of a new parent who has authority to control them and is a sexual partner of their biological parent (Hetherington, 1993; Hetherington et al., 1992).

A key factor that affects children's adjustment after divorce is the quality of the contact with the noncustodial parent. Children who have contact with competent, supportive, authoritative noncustodial fathers show better adjustment and do better in school than children who have frequent but superficial or disruptive contact with their noncustodial fathers (Amato & Gilbreth, 1999; Hetherington, 1989; Hetherington et al., 1998; Whiteside & Becker, 2000). In contrast, contact with nonresidential fathers who have antisocial traits predicts an increase in children's noncompliance (DeGarmo, 2010). Less is known about noncustodial mothers, but research has found that the more the noncustodial mothers maintain regular and positive involvement with their children, the better adjusted their children are (Gunnoe & Hetherington, 2004; King, 2007).

Stepparents

As seen in Figure 12.1, 15% of children live in households with stepparents (Pew Research Center, 2015). Stepfamilies can have a variety of structures, including *simple* stepfamily households, in which a new stepparent joins another parent and his or her children, or *complex* or *blended* stepfamilies which add both a new stepparent and stepsiblings (Ganong et al., 2015). The majority of stepfamilies are formed through divorce and remarriage, but some are formed after the death of one of a child's biological parents.

The introduction of a stepparent into a child's life can affect him or her in a number of ways. A parent's remarriage often leads to less frequent contact with the noncustodial parent, which can be stressful to the child and can lead to difficulties adjusting to the stepparent (Ganong et al., 2015). A custodial parent's remarriage can have a positive effect on family income, although if a stepparent is supporting his or her own biological children from a previous marriage, that impact will be diminished (Ganong et al., 2015). A child who bonds with the stepparent also gains another trusted adult in his or her life, which can have positive benefits for emotional and behavioral health (Ganong et al., 2011).

Both the benefits and challenges in stepfamilies may differ somewhat for families with stepfathers and those with stepmothers. Although most stepfathers want their new families to thrive, they generally feel less close to their stepchildren than do fathers in intact families (Hetherington, 1993). At first, stepfathers tend to be warm toward their stepchildren and less controlling than are fathers in intact families (Kurdek & Fine, 1993). New stepfathers may be especially helpful in providing a male role model for stepsons (Parke & Buriel, 1998); indeed, an adolescent's likelihood of engaging in delinquent activities is reduced if the adolescent's parent remarries (Burt et al., 2008). Overall, with time, children often become as close to their stepfathers as they are to their nonresidential biological fathers, and sometimes even closer (Falci, 2006), usually without affecting their relationship with the biological father (King, 2009). For adolescents, having a close relationship with both their stepfather and their biological father, and believing that they matter to both, is associated with better adolescent outcomes (Schenck et al., 2009).

BRAUNS / GETTY IMAGES

Children of divorce benefit from interaction with noncustodial fathers only if that interaction is of high quality.

Nevertheless, on average, conflict between stepfathers and stepchildren tends to be greater than that between fathers and their biological offspring (Bray & Berger, 1993; Hakvoort et al., 2011; Hetherington et al., 1992, 1999), perhaps in part because stepfathers are more likely to see the children as burdens than their biological fathers are (A. O'Connor & Boag, 2010). It is thus not surprising that children with stepfathers tend to have higher rates of depression, withdrawal, and disruptive problem behaviors than do children in intact families (Hetherington & Stanley-Hagan, 1995).

Preadolescent girls in particular are likely to have problems with their stepfathers. Often the difficulty arises from the fact that prior to the remarriage, divorced mothers have had a close, confiding relationship with their daughters, and the entry of the stepfather into the family disrupts this relationship. These changes can lead to resentment in the daughter and conflict with both her mother and the stepfather (Hetherington et al., 1992; Hetherington & Stanley-Hagan, 2002). Because there are decidedly fewer stepmothers than stepfathers, much less research has been devoted to their role as stepparents. However, it appears that stepmothers generally have more difficulty with their stepchildren than do stepfathers (Gosselin & David, 2007) and are at risk for depressive symptoms (D. N. Shapiro & Stewart, 2011). Often fathers expect stepmothers to take an active role in parenting, including monitoring and disciplining the child, although children frequently resent the stepmother's being the disciplinarian and may reject her authority or accept it only grudgingly. This may help explain why stepmothers are more likely than biological mothers to feel resentment toward their children and view them as a burden (A. O'Connor & Boag, 2010). Children of both sexes are most adjusted in stepfamilies when the stepparent is warm and involved and supports the custodial parent's decisions rather than trying to exert control over the children independently (Bray & Berger, 1993; Hetherington et al., 1998).

An additional factor in children's adjustment in stepfamilies is the attitude of the noncustodial biological parent toward the stepparent and the level of conflict between the two (Wallerstein & Lewis, 2007). If the noncustodial parent has hostile feelings toward the new stepparent and communicates these feelings to the child, the child is likely to feel caught in the middle, increasing his or her adjustment problems (Buchanan et al., 1991). The noncustodial parent's hostile feelings may also encourage the child to behave in a hostile or distant manner with the stepparent. Not surprisingly, children in stepfamilies fare best when the relations between the noncustodial parent and the stepparent are supportive and the relations between the biological parents are cordial (Golish, 2003). Thus, the success or failure of stepfamilies is affected by the behavior and attitudes of all involved parties.

Review

The American family has changed dramatically in recent decades. More children are living with single mothers or with grandparents, first-time parents are older, families are smaller, and divorce and remarriage are common occurrences. Same-sex parenting is also more prevalent and accepted than in the past, and research shows that the development of children of same-sex parents is no different from the development of children with heterosexual parents.

Parental divorce can be disruptive for children, although it can be a positive event if the parents' marriage was characterized by high levels of conflict. Experiencing divorce puts children at higher risk for behavior problems and achievement problems, but most children adjust well to parental divorce. How well children cope is determined in part by the amount and quality of contact with their parents post-divorce.

Conflict is common in stepfamilies, especially when the children are adolescents. Stepparents tend to be less involved with their stepchildren than are biological parents. Children in stepfamilies tend to do best if all parents involved are supportive.

Family Dynamics

Families fulfill several vital functions, including ensuring the survival of children to maturity, providing the means for children to acquire skills needed to be economically productive, and teaching children the basic values of the culture (R. A. LeVine, 1988). How well a family fulfills these basic child-rearing functions obviously depends on a great many factors. Not the least of these is **family dynamics,** that is, how family members interact through various relationships: mother with each child, father with each child, mother with father, and siblings with one another. In subsequent sections, we discuss the ways in which individual family members contribute to a child's development. However, it is important to frame these discussions with a clear appreciation of the overall impact of family dynamics. Families are complex social units whose members are all interdependent and reciprocally influence one another.

Parenting

Socialization is the process through which children acquire the values, standards, skills, knowledge, and behaviors that are regarded as appropriate for their present and future roles in their particular culture (Maccoby, 2015). When asked about the characteristics they want their children to exemplify as adults, the majority of parents say they want them to be honest and ethical (71%), caring and compassionate (65%), and hardworking (62%) (Pew Research Center, 2015). With these long-term goals in mind, parents engage in a variety of socialization behaviors that they hope will foster these characteristics in their children. We will focus on two key aspects of parenting that are particularly important for children's development: parents' use of discipline and their overall parenting style.

Discipline

Discipline is the set of strategies and behaviors parents use to teach children how to behave appropriately. Parental discipline is effective when the child (1) stops engaging in an undesirable misbehavior (e.g., hitting a sibling to get a toy), and ideally (2) engages in a preferred behavior (e.g., taking turns to share a toy). Discipline is considered to be most effective if it leads to a permanent change in the child's behavior because the child has learned and accepted the desired behavior; this process is called **internalization** (Grusec & Goodnow, 1994).

Reasoning focused on the effects of a behavior on other people, referred to as *other-oriented induction,* is particularly effective at promoting internalization. For example, if a parent emphasizes that being hit hurts the other child's body and hurts their feelings, the child will begin to understand why it is better not to engage in the original misbehavior. The use of other-oriented induction has the added benefit of teaching children empathy for others, which is a foundational skill for

family dynamics ■ the way in which family members interact through various relationships: mother with each child, father with each child, mother with father, and siblings with one another

socialization ■ the process through which children acquire the values, standards, skills, knowledge, and behaviors that are regarded as appropriate for their present and future roles in their particular culture

discipline ■ the set of strategies and behaviors parents use to teach children how to behave appropriately

internalization ■ effective discipline that leads to a permanent change in the child's behavior because the child has learned and accepted the desired behavior

punishment ■ a negative stimulus that follows a behavior to reduce the likelihood that the behavior will occur again

parenting style ■ parenting behaviors and attitudes that set the emotional climate in regard to parent–child interactions, such as parental responsiveness and demandingness

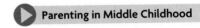

Parenting in Middle Childhood

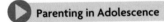

Parenting in Adolescence

acting prosocially toward others. Indeed, reasoning and other-oriented induction have been linked with greater social competence in children (Hastings, Miller, & Troxel, 2015). Thankfully, reasoning is the most common form of discipline, with three-quarters of parents reporting that they use reasoning on a regular basis (Pew Research Center, 2015).

Internalization occurs best when parents apply the right amount of psychological pressure on the child. If they apply too little, the child will discount the parents' message and do what they want. If parents apply too much pressure, the child may comply but only because they feel they are being forced to do so; children then attribute their compliance to this external force (i.e., their parents) rather than internalizing the reason for doing so (Maccoby & Martin, 1983). Children in this situation will likely act in desirable ways only when they know there is the risk that they will get caught by their parents.

Discipline techniques that apply too much psychological or even physical pressure on children are not effective at promoting internalization. Most punishments fall into this category. **Punishment** is a negative stimulus that follows a behavior to reduce the likelihood that the behavior will occur again (Hineline & Rosales-Ruiz, 2012). Punishments, such as time-out or taking away privileges, make clear that the parent disapproves of the misbehavior, but on their own they do not teach the child how to behave in the future. While mild punishments, such as those listed above, can provide the minimally sufficient pressure needed for internalization, it is important to remember that a parent's slightly raised voice or disapproving look are often all the pressure that is needed to get a child to comply.

A large body of research indicates that spanking, a form of physical punishment, is not effective at teaching children how to behave and is linked with a range of unintended negative consequences for children (Gershoff & Grogan-Kaylor, 2016a; see Box 12.2). Other forms of punishment, like yelling, time-out, taking away privileges, and love withdrawal (withholding affection from a child because of their behavior) have also been found to be ineffective and linked with negative outcomes for children (Gershoff et al., 2010), despite the fact that between 20% and 40% of parents report using each of these methods (Pew Research Center, 2015).

Parenting Styles

Although specific parenting behaviors can influence child development, parents' overall style of interacting with their children can also govern the parent–child relationship and children's developmental outcomes (Darling & Steinberg, 1993). **Parenting style** is the constellation of parenting behaviors and attitudes that set the emotional climate of parent–child interactions. Some parents, for example, are strict rule-setters who expect complete and immediate compliance from their children. Others are more likely to allow their children some leeway in following the standards they have set for them. Still others seem oblivious to what their children do. Parents also differ in the overall emotional tone they bring to their parenting, especially with regard to the warmth and support they convey to their children.

In trying to understand the impact that parents can have on children's development, researchers have identified two dimensions of parenting style that are particularly important: (1) the degree of parental warmth and responsiveness, and (2) the degree of parenting control and demandingness (Maccoby & Martin, 1983).

BOX 12.2 | applications

SHOULD PARENTS SPANK THEIR CHILDREN?

Spanking typically involves an open hand, although some parents also use objects, such as a wooden spoon. The percentage of parents who spank their children has dropped significantly over the last several decades in both the United States (Zolotor et al., 2011) and Canada (Clément & Chamberland, 2014). However, the majority of parents still spank their children at some point (Gershoff et al., 2012). Spanking has been the subject of hundreds of research studies and debates among experts, and the following conclusions are now clear:

- **Spanking does not improve children's behavior.** A meta-analysis of the research on spanking determined that spanking does not increase children's immediate compliance (Gershoff & Grogan-Kaylor, 2016a). Spanking also does not improve children's behavior in the long term; the more children are spanked, the less likely they are to behave appropriately in the future, and the more likely they are to behave aggressively or to engage in antisocial behavior (Gershoff & Grogan-Kaylor, 2016a). This finding holds even when the tendency for children's aggression or antisocial behavior to elicit more spanking from parents has been taken into account through longitudinal research designs (Berlin et al., 2009; Gershoff et al., 2012; Lee, Altschul, & Gershoff, 2013).

- **Spanking increases children's risk for a range of negative outcomes.** In addition to not improving children's behavior, spanking has been linked with a range of negative, unintended outcomes that can be thought of as negative "side effects." The more children are spanked, the more mental health problems they have, the more problems they have in their relationships with their parents, the lower their self-esteem, and the lower their cognitive ability (Gershoff, 2013; Gershoff & Grogan-Kaylor, 2016a).

  The most serious outcome linked with spanking is physical abuse. The more parents spank, the greater the likelihood they will use harsh methods that can injure children (Zolotor et al., 2011). Parents who spanked their children at age 1 had a 33% greater likelihood of being suspected of physically abusing their children by the time they were age 5 (Lee, Grogan-Kaylor, & Berger, 2014). A review of child maltreatment cases in Canada revealed that a majority of physical abuse cases start out as physical punishment (Durrant et al., 2006).

- **Spanking is linked with negative outcomes equally across cultural groups.** As discussed in this chapter, culture can determine which parenting practices are seen as both normal and advisable. Cultural groups, particularly those defined by race or ethnicity, do differ in how often they use spanking (Gershoff et al., 2012). However, the extent to which spanking is linked with negative outcomes, such as increased aggression, does not vary across racial and ethnic groups: spanking is linked with more aggression and more externalizing behavior problems across all racial and ethnic groups (Berlin et al., 2009; Gershoff et al., 2012; Gershoff & Grogan-Kaylor, 2016b) and even across countries with differing levels of spanking use (Gershoff et al., 2010).

For these reasons, among others, the United Nations has declared that spanking and physical punishment are forms of violence against children that violate their human rights to protection from violence (United Nations, Committee on the Rights of the Child, 2006). In response to this growing body of evidence linking spanking with harm to children, 49 countries have banned all physical punishment of children, including that by parents (Global Initiative to End All Corporal Punishment of Children, 2016).

Though the United States is not among these countries, the American Academy of Pediatrics (1998), the American Academy of Child and Adolescent Psychiatry (2012), the American Professional Society on the Abuse of Children (2016), and the National Association of Pediatric Nurse Practitioners (2011) all recommend that parents stop spanking their children because of the risks it poses to children. In addition, the Centers for Disease Control and Prevention (Fortson et al., 2016) have identified reducing the use of spanking and other forms of physical punishment as a key step to ending physical abuse.

Parents who exhibit warmth are affectionate with their children and enjoy being with them. Parental responsiveness refers to how quickly and appropriately parents respond to children's needs, requests for assistance, or distress. Parental control, on the other hand, is the extent to which parents monitor and manage their children's behavior through rules and consequences, and demandingness refers to an expectation of conformance to parents' desires and a low tolerance for children's own interests and desires.

A pioneering research study on parenting style was conducted by Diana Baumrind (1973), who differentiated among four styles of parenting related to

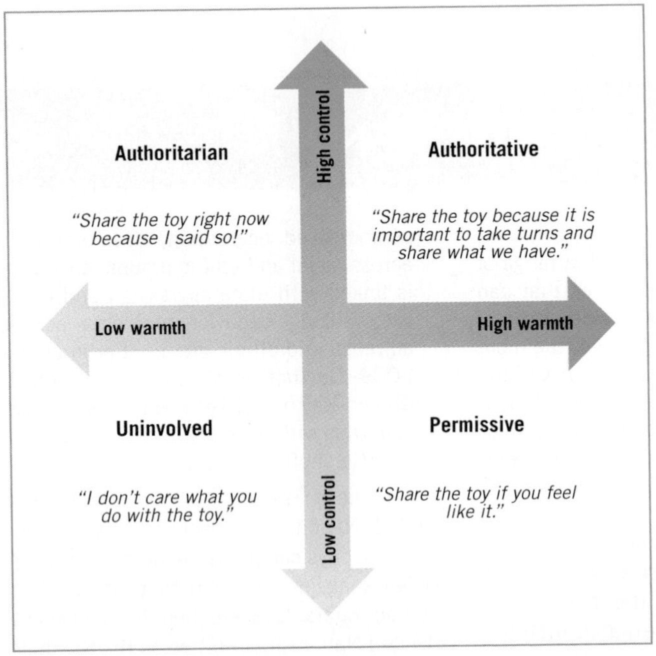

FIGURE 12.3 Parental control and warmth In Baumrind's typology of parenting styles, every parent falls somewhere on the dimensions of warmth and control. Baumrind grouped parents into one of four potential parenting styles. This figure shows the four potential responses of parents reacting to a child who will not share a toy. (Information from Baumrind, 1973)

authoritative parenting ■ a parenting style that is high in demandingness and supportiveness. Authoritative parents set clear standards and limits for their children and are firm about enforcing them; at the same time, they allow their children considerable autonomy within those limits, are attentive and responsive to their children's concerns and needs, and respect and consider their children's perspective.

authoritarian parenting ■ a parenting style that is high in demandingness and low in responsiveness. Authoritarian parents are nonresponsive to their children's needs and tend to enforce their demands through the exercise of parental power and the use of threats and punishment. They are oriented toward obedience and authority and expect their children to comply with their demands without question or explanation.

permissive parenting ■ a parenting style that is high in responsiveness but low in demandingness. Permissive parents are responsive to their children's needs and do not require their children to regulate themselves or act in appropriate or mature ways.

the dimensions of support and control. These styles are referred to as *authoritative, authoritarian, permissive,* and *uninvolved* (Baumrind, 1973, 1991b) (Figure 12.3).

According to Baumrind, **authoritative parenting** is a style that tends to be demanding but also warm and responsive. Authoritative parents set clear standards and limits for their children, monitor their children's behavior, and are firm about enforcing important limits. However, they allow their children considerable autonomy within those limits, are not restrictive or intrusive, and are able to engage in calm conversation and reasoning with their children. They are attentive to their children's concerns and needs and communicate openly with their children about them. They are also measured and consistent, rather than harsh or arbitrary, in disciplining them. Authoritative parents usually want their children to be socially responsible, assertive, and self-controlled.

Baumrind found that children of authoritative parents tend to be competent, self-assured, and popular with peers. They are also able to behave in accordance with adults' expectations and are low in antisocial behavior. Children with authoritative parents seem to accept their parents' socialization efforts; for example, in one study children with authoritative parents were more likely to share and take turns with an unfamiliar peer than were children of authoritarian parents (Hastings et al., 2007). As adolescents, children from authoritative families tend to be relatively high in social and academic competence, self-reliance, and coping skills and relatively low in drug use and problem behavior (Baumrind, 1991a; Driscoll, Russell, & Crockett, 2008; Hoeve et al., 2011; Lamborn et al., 1991).

Authoritarian parenting is a style that tends to be cold and unresponsive to children's needs. Authoritarian parents are high in control and demandingness and expect their children to comply without question. Authoritarian parents tend to enforce their demands through the exercise of parental power, especially the use of threats and punishment and psychological control. Examples include parents' cutting off children when they want to express themselves, threatening to withdraw love and attention if they do not behave as expected, exploiting children's sense of guilt, belittling their worth, and discounting or misinterpreting their feelings.

Such behaviors on behalf of authoritarian parents engender hostility in children and a refusal to accept parents' attempts at socialization (Hastings et al., 2015). Children of authoritarian parents tend to be relatively low in social and academic competence, unhappy and unfriendly, and low in self-confidence, with boys being more negatively affected than girls in early childhood (Baumrind, 1991b). Authoritarian parenting has also been linked with children's inability to cope with everyday stressors (Zhou et al., 2008) and with high levels of depression, aggression, delinquency, and alcohol problems (Bolkan et al., 2010; Driscoll et al., 2008; Kerr, Stattin, & Özdemir, 2012; Rinaldi & Howe, 2012).

Permissive parenting is a style that is responsive to children's needs and wishes, but so much so that parents are overly lenient with them. Permissive parents do not require their children to regulate themselves or act in appropriate ways. The children of permissive parents tend to be impulsive, low in self-regulation, high in externalizing problems, and low in school achievement (Baumrind, 1973, 1991a, 1991b; Rinaldi & Howe, 2012). As adolescents, they engage in more school misconduct and drug or alcohol use than do peers with authoritative parents (Driscoll et al., 2008; Lamborn et al., 1991).

Uninvolved parenting is a style that is low in both demandingness and responsiveness to children; in other words, uninvolved parents are generally disengaged. They do not set limits for children or monitor their behavior and are not supportive of them. Sometimes they are rejecting or neglectful of their children altogether. These parents are focused on their own needs rather than their children's. Children who have uninvolved parents tend to have disturbed attachment relationships when they are infants or toddlers and to have problems with peer relationships as older children (Parke & Buriel, 1998; R. A. Thompson, 1998). In adolescence, they tend to exhibit a wide range of problems, from antisocial behavior and low academic competence to internalizing problems (e.g., depression, social withdrawal), substance abuse, and risky or promiscuous sexual behavior (Baumrind, 1991a, 1991b; Driscoll et al., 2008; Hoeve et al., 2011; Lamborn et al., 1991). The negative effects of this type of parenting appear to continue to accumulate and worsen over the course of adolescence (Steinberg et al., 1994).

In addition to the broad effects that different parenting styles seem to have on children, they also establish an emotional climate that affects the impact of whatever specific parenting practices may be employed (Darling & Steinberg, 1993). For instance, children are more likely to view punishment as being justified and indicating serious misbehavior when it comes from an authoritative parent than when it comes from a parent who generally is punitive and hostile. Moreover, parenting style affects children's receptiveness to parents' practices. Children are more likely to listen to and care about their parents' preferences and demands if the parents are generally supportive and reasonable than if they are distant, neglectful, or expect obedience in all situations (Grusec, Goodnow, & Kuczynski, 2000; M. L. Hoffman, 1983).

Although parenting style appears to have an effect on children's adjustment, it is important to keep in mind that children's behavior sometimes shapes parents' typical parenting style as well. In a recent study, adolescents' reports of relatively high levels of externalizing problems (e.g., delinquency, loitering, and intoxication) and internalizing problems (e.g., low self-esteem, depressive symptoms) predicted a decline in parents' authoritative parenting styles (as reported by the youths) 2 years later, whereas an increase or decline in authoritative parenting over the same 2 years did not predict a change in the adolescents' adjustment (Kerr et al., 2012).

More recent research has moved away from the idea that parents have a single style or that parents can be easily placed into one of Baumrind's four categories (Hastings et al., 2015). Rather, whether parents exhibit, for example, an authoritative or authoritarian style at any given moment depends on contextual factors, such as whether the child's misbehavior is dangerous, whether the parent and child are running late for an appointment, or whether the parent and child are in a good mood (Maccoby, 2015).

Positive social and academic outcomes seem more likely when levels of parental warmth and control are both high.

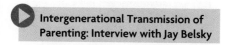

Intergenerational Transmission of Parenting: Interview with Jay Belsky

Differences in Mothers' and Fathers' Interactions with Their Children

Although fathers are engaged in child rearing more now than in the past, differences remain in mothers' and fathers' child-rearing behaviors. For example, there is a major difference in the amount of time mothers and fathers spend caring for

uninvolved parenting ■ a parenting style that is low in both demandingness and responsiveness to their children; in other words, this style describes parents who are generally disengaged their children. Although in most Western cultures today spouses share childcare responsibilities to some degree, in the majority of families, mothers—including those who work outside the home—still spend an average of an hour and a half more with their children each day than fathers do (Biehle & Mickelson, 2012; Yavorsky, Kamp Dush, & Schoppe-Sullivan, 2015).

There is also a difference in what types of child-rearing behaviors mothers and fathers engage in. Mothers are more likely to provide physical care and emotional support than are fathers (M. Moon & Hoffman, 2008); for instance, in a sample of families in the Netherlands, mothers were warmer and more responsive to their children than were fathers (Hallers-Haalboom et al., 2014). In contrast, fathers in modern industrialized cultures spend a greater proportion of their available time playing with their children, both in infancy and childhood, than do mothers, and the type of play they engage in differs from mothers' play as well (Parke & Buriel, 1998). In the United States, mothers are more likely than fathers to say that they are overprotective and that they praise their children too much, whereas fathers are more likely than mothers to have coached their children's sports teams (Pew Research Center, 2015).

Although these general patterns prevail in many cultures, there are also some cultural variations. Fathers in Sweden, Malaysia, and India, for example, do not report much play at all with their children (C. P. Hwang, 1987; Roopnarine, Lu, & Ahmeduzzaman, 1989). Indeed, both mothers and fathers in some cultures simply play less with their children than American parents do (Göncü, Mistry, & Mosier, 2000; Roopnarine & Hossain, 1992). In a study of Gusii infants and parents in Kenya, fathers were seldom seen within 5 feet of their infants, and mothers spent 60% less time playing with infants than American mothers typically do (R. A. LeVine et al., 1996). The degree of maternal and paternal involvement in parenting and the nature of parents' interactions with children vary as a function of cultural practices and such factors as the amount of time parents work away from home and children spend at home.

Fathers tend to engage in more physical play with their children than do mothers.

Economic and educational factors also seem to be related to the degree to which mothers engage in various caregiving activities. In a study of mothers in 28 developing countries who had children younger than 5, those in countries that had higher levels of education and higher gross national product were more likely to engage in caregiving activities that are cognitively stimulating (e.g., reading books, counting, naming objects) and were less likely to leave their children alone or in the care of another child younger than 10. It is likely that cultural differences in the importance placed on literacy and cognitive growth account for these differences in mothers' caregiving activities (Bornstein & Putnick, 2012).

Despite these distinctions in amount and type, however, the effects of mothers' and fathers' parenting on child development are the same. A meta-analysis of studies from 22 countries found that both mothers' and fathers' acceptance of and warmth toward their children were linked with children's positive psychological adjustment (Khaleque & Rohner, 2012); in other words, parenting from mothers and fathers were equally important for children's mental health, and this is true across a range of countries (Bangladesh, Colombia, Egypt, Mexico, Nigeria, Sweden, Turkey, and the United States) (Khaleque & Rohner, 2012). Thus, warm and responsive parenting, whether from mothers or fathers, is beneficial for children.

The Child's Influence on Parenting

Among the strongest influences on both parental discipline and on parenting style is children's own behavior. Thus, *individual differences* in children contribute to the parenting they receive, which, in turn, contributes to differences among children in their behavior and personalities. Consistent with the theme of the *active child*, children also actively shape the parenting process through their behavior and expressions of temperament. Children who are disobedient, angry, or challenging, for example, make it more difficult for parents to use authoritative parenting than do children who are compliant and positive in their behavior (Kerr et al., 2012).

How children behave with their parents—including the degree to which they express anger, low self-regulation, or disobedience—can be due to a number of factors. The most prominent of these are genetic factors related to temperament (Saudino & Wang, 2012). In line with our discussion of *differential susceptibility* in Chapter 10, some children may be more reactive to the quality of parenting they receive than are others. For instance, children with anxious temperaments tend to become fearful and immobilized in response to harsh and demanding parenting; in contrast, these same children are eager to please and comply with warm and responsive parents (Beach et al., 2012; Kiff, Lengua, & Zalewski, 2011; Pluess & Belsky, 2010). At the genetic level, some children have an allele of the serotonin transporter gene SLC6A4 that makes them especially responsive to their rearing environment, whether it be warm and responsive parenting or controlling and demanding parenting (Kochanska et al., 2011).

Children's noncompliance and externalizing problems offer further insight into the complex ways in which children can affect their parents' behavior toward them. In resisting their parents' demands, for example, children may become so whiny or aggressive that their parents back down; the parents' behavior has been affected by the children's behavior, and the children's behavior has been reinforced by the parents' behavior. As these parents become frustrated, they may escalate their negative behaviors (e.g., yelling or spanking), which evoke even more

The quality of parents' relationships with their children is related to how well siblings interact.

FLORIAN FRANKE / ALAMY

bidirectionality of parent–child interactions ■ the idea that parents and their children are mutually affected by one another's characteristics and behaviors

negative behavior from children. Such patterns have been called *coercive cycles* (G. R. Patterson, 1982). By adolescence, such patterns appear to be influenced more by the child than the parent: youths who are noncompliant and antisocial, in part due to their heredity, evoke harsh parenting from their parents to a greater degree than their parents' harshness leads to the youths' externalizing problems (Marceau et al., 2013).

Over time, the mutual influence, or **bidirectionality,** of parent–child interactions reinforces and perpetuates each other's behavior (Combs-Ronto et al., 2009; Morelen & Suveg, 2012). For example, parents' use of spanking at age 1 predicts greater child aggression at age 3, which in turn predicts more parental spanking at age 5 (Altschul, Lee, & Gershoff, 2016)—yet another coercive cycle. Similarly, when parents are hostile and inconsistent in enforcing standards of conduct with their adolescent children, their children, in turn, are hostile, insensitive, disruptive, and inflexible with them (Conger & Ge, 1999; Rueter & Conger, 1998) and exhibit increased levels of problem behaviors (Roche et al., 2011; Scaramella et al., 2008). Bidirectionality is also a key factor in parent–child relationships that exhibit a pattern of cooperation, positive affect, harmonious communication, and coordinated behavior, with the positive behavior of each partner eliciting analogous positive behavior from the other (Aksan, Kochanska, & Ortmann, 2006; Altschul et al., 2016; Denissen, van Aken, & Dubas, 2009).

Sibling Relationships

Siblings influence one another's development and the functioning of the larger family system in many ways, both positive and negative. They serve not only as playmates for one another but also as sources of support, instruction, security, assistance, and caregiving (Gamble, Yu, & Kuehn, 2011; Gass, Jenkins, & Dunn, 2007). The sibling relationship is unique. Siblings are often the same age as peers, but in some cases sibling relationships are like peer relationships in that they are characterized by sharing and reciprocity (Dirks et al., 2015). However, in other cases, sibling relationships are more like parent–child relationships, in which one (the older) sibling has more power and influence over the other (younger) sibling (Dirks et al., 2015). Children in the middle of sibling groups may thus have both types of sibling relationships.

Siblings, of course, also can be rivals and sources of mutual conflict and irritation—they live in close proximity to one another and are often in competition for resources, from toys to parents' time. In some cases, sibling conflict can contribute to the development of undesirable behaviors, such as disobedience, delinquency, and drinking (Bascoe, Davies, & Cummings, 2012; Dirks et al., 2015; Low, Shortt, & Snyder, 2012), as well as depression, anxiety, and social withdrawal (Compton et al., 2003; S. M. McHale et al., 2007; Morgan, Shaw, & Olino, 2012). In addition, high levels of sibling aggression and conflict predict low self-regulation (Padilla-Walker, Harper, & Jensen, 2010) and risky sexual behavior in one or both siblings (S. M. McHale, Bissell, & Kim, 2009). Sibling conflict can also be a crucible for learning important life skills: research with families in Ontario, Canada, has found that when parents are taught how to mediate sibling conflicts, siblings successfully learn constructive means of conflict resolution (Ross & Lazinksi, 2014).

Young children are more likely than older children to respond poorly when they perceive that an infant sibling receives more attention than they themselves do.

Siblings' relationships tend to be less hostile and more supportive when their parents are warm and accepting of them (Grych, Raynor, & Fosco, 2004; Ingoldsby, Shaw, & Garcia, 2001; J.-Y. Kim et al., 2006). Siblings also have closer, more positive relationships with each other if their parents treat them similarly (G. H. Brody et al., 1992; S. M. McHale et al., 1995). If parents favor one child over another, the sibling relationship may suffer, and the less favored child may experience distress, depression, and other problems with adjustment, especially if the child does not have a positive relationship with his or her parents (Feinberg & Hetherington, 2001; Meunier et al., 2013; Shanahan et al., 2008; Solmeyer et al., 2011). Differential treatment by parents is particularly influential in early and middle childhood, with less favored siblings being likelier to experience worry, anxiety, or depression than their more favored siblings (Coldwell, Pike, & Dunn, 2008; Dunn, 1992). When children view differential treatment by parents as justified, they report more positive relationships with their sibling and their parents than when they feel that differential parental treatment is unfair (Kowal & Kramer, 1997; Kowal, Krull, & Kramer, 2004; S. M. McHale et al., 2000).

Cultural values may also play a role in children's evaluations of, and reactions to, differential parental treatment. For example, in a study of Mexican American families, older siblings who embraced the cultural value of *familism*, which emphasizes interdependence, mutual support, and loyalty among family members, were not put at risk of higher levels of depressive symptoms or risky behaviors by their parents' preferential treatment of younger siblings (S. M. McHale et al., 2005). A study that compared a sample of Moroccan siblings to a sample of Dutch siblings found that the children from the collectivist culture of Morocco had less conflict than the siblings from the individualistic culture of the Netherlands. However, for the children from both cultures, when sibling conflict was present, mental health and behavior problems were also found (Buist et al., 2014).

Another factor that can affect the quality of siblings' interactions is the nature of the parents' relationship with each other. Siblings get along better if their parents get along with each other (Erel, Margolin, & John, 1998; McGuire, McHale, & Updegraff, 1996). In contrast, siblings whose parents fight with each other are likely to have more hostile interactions because their parents not only model negative behavior for their children but also may be less sensitive and appropriate in their efforts to manage their children's interactions with one another (N. Howe, Aquan-Assee, & Bukowski, 2001).

Rivalry and conflict between siblings tend to be higher in divorced families and in remarried families than in non-divorced families, even between biological siblings. Although some siblings turn to one another for support when their parents divorce or remarry (Jenkins, 1992), they may also compete for parental affection and attention, which often are scarce in those situations. Relationships between half-siblings can be especially emotionally charged, perhaps because the older sibling may resent the younger sibling who is born to both parents in the new marital relationship (Hetherington, 1999). In general, the more a child in a blended family perceives a parent's preferential treatment of a sibling—whether a full sibling or a half-sibling—the worse the child's relationship is with that sibling (Baham et al., 2008).

Thus, the quality of sibling relationships differs across families depending on the ways that parents interact with each child and with each other and children's perceptions of their treatment by other family members. Such differences highlight the fact that families are complex, dynamic social systems and that all members contribute to one another's functioning.

Review

Parents discipline their children in order to teach them appropriate behavior. Discipline is most effective when it is focused on reasoning, rather than on punishment. Parents' interactions with their children are also governed by general parenting styles, which are thought to have two main components: warmth and control. A style that balances both warmth and reason, sometimes called an authoritative parenting style, is best for promoting children's social competence.

Mothers typically interact with their children much more than fathers do. The nature of mother–child and father–child interactions also tends to differ, with fathers engaging in more physical play with their children. Parent–child interactions differ across cultures; for example, in some cultures, parents play little or not at all with their children. Parents and children mutually affect each other's behavior in a process known as bidirectionality.

Siblings are sources of learning and support, as well as rivalry and conflict. Siblings get along better if they have good relationships with their parents and if they do not feel that their parents treat them differently. Sibling relationships are, on average, more hostile and conflicted in divorced and remarried families than in non-divorced families, and thus like all family relationships, must be viewed in the context of the larger family system.

The Socioeconomic Context

Parent–Adolescent Relationship and Contexts of Family Life: Interview with Anne Petersen

According to Bronfenbrenner's bioecological model (see Chapter 9), children's development is affected by a variety of contexts that are nested into a set of hierarchical systems. The family is the child's most proximal context and thus the one that has the most direct influence on development. Yet the family itself is affected by the contexts in which it is embedded, including cultural contexts, economic contexts, and work contexts.

To see how each of these contexts relate, consider the diverse ways in which family members affect one another in the following scenario. A man loses his job because of company cutbacks, and the ensuing stress causes him to become very irritable with his wife and children. His wife, in turn, has to work extra hours to make ends meet, and her increasing fatigue makes her less patient with the children and more likely to fight with her husband. The mother's increased workload also means that the couple's 8-year-old daughter is expected to do more of the household chores. This makes the daughter angry because her 6-year-old brother is not required to help her out. Soon the daughter becomes hostile to both her parents and her brother. Not surprisingly, the brother starts to fight with his sister, further upsetting the parents. Over time, tension and conflict among all family members increase, adding to the stress created by the family's economic situation.

As is clear from this example, a change from outside the family (e.g., the father's workplace) creates a cascading series of events that alter each of the relationships within the family. In the next sections, we will consider how cultural contexts, economic contexts, and work contexts affect family life, particularly parenting behaviors, and child development.

Cultural Contexts

Parents' beliefs about what constitutes optimal child development as well as their decisions about how to behave with and discipline their children have a strong basis in their culture (Rogoff, 2003). Culture reflects those beliefs and practices that are linked with a family's country, religion, ethnic group, race, or similar group or affiliation. In the United States, much cross-cultural research on families has been focused on cultural similarities and differences between ethnic and racial groups. Internationally, research has focused on similarities and differences across countries. In this section, we briefly review research from each of these categories.

Research in this area has tended to look at two aspects of parenting: the degree to which parents in different cultures engage in specific disciplinary practices, and the degree to which similar parental behaviors affect child outcomes across different cultures. Several studies have investigated whether parents around the world use similar methods of discipline with their children. A study of families in eight countries (Colombia, Italy, Jordan, Kenya, Philippines, Sweden, Thailand, and the United States) found that mothers and children in each of the countries reported high levels of positive discipline, such as inductive reasoning, and of parental warmth (Pastorelli et al., 2016). This finding suggests that both positive discipline and warm parenting were favored by parents across cultures.

A separate study in some of the same countries (China, India, Italy, Kenya, Philippines, and Thailand) found both cross-country similarities and differences in how often mothers reported using a variety of discipline techniques (Gershoff et al., 2010; see Figure 12.4). Mothers in all six countries reported teaching children about good and bad behavior very often, with most averaging between once a week and almost every day. The mothers in this international sample were also similar in the method they used least often, namely love withdrawal, with mothers in Italy and the Philippines saying they rarely used this method of discipline. For the four types of punishment in the middle of Figure 12.4, there was more variation: mothers in Italy were much more likely to yell or scold than were mothers from other countries; mothers from Kenya were much more likely to threaten punishment and to use physical punishment; and mothers from the Philippines were more likely to say they would take away privileges (something the Kenyan mothers said they almost never do).

FIGURE 12.4 Differences in frequency with which mothers reported each of 6 discipline techniques across 6 countries Mothers across all countries report high rates of teaching about good and bad behavior and low rates of love withdrawal. However, some clear country-level differences are seen in how often parents yell or scold, threaten punishment, take away privileges, and use physical punishment. (Data from Gershoff et al., 2010)

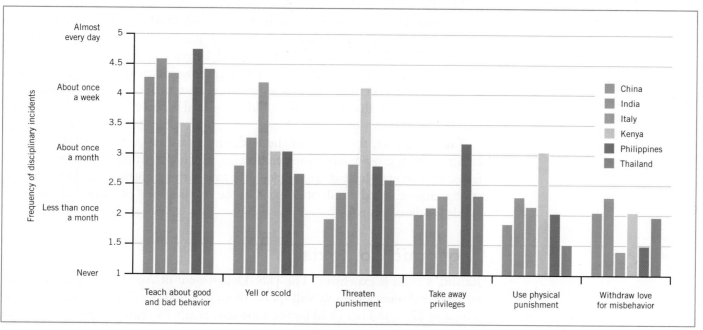

Other studies have looked at differences across racial and ethnic groups within the United States. For example, several studies have found that African American parents spank their children more often than European American, Latino American, or Asian American parents do (Gershoff et al., 2012), and in some surveys African American parents are twice as likely as European American and Latino parents to say they spank their children regularly (Pew Research Center, 2015).

Given these differences in the frequency with which parents use different discipline techniques, the next question is whether they matter—are certain techniques more effective in some cultures than others? Such differences in whether a particular technique is effective could arise from the different parenting beliefs and values held by different cultures. Some researchers have argued that the extent to which a disciplinary technique predicted negative or positive outcomes in children depends on how normative it is in their wider culture (Deater-Deckard & Dodge, 1997). As with cross-cultural comparisons on how often parents use various techniques, there are some similarities and some differences across cultures in how parenting behaviors predict children's development.

For instance, in European American families, authoritative parenting, as noted above, seems to be associated with a close relationship between parent and child and with children's positive psychological adjustment and academic success. Although a somewhat similar relation between authoritative parenting and adjustment has been found in China, it tends to be weaker (Chang et al., 2004; Cheah et al., 2009; C. A. Nelson, Thomas, & de Haan, 2006; Zhou et al., 2004, 2008). In fact, some features of parenting that are considered appropriate in traditional Chinese culture are more characteristic of authoritarian parenting than of authoritative parenting. Compared with American mothers, for example, Chinese American mothers are more likely to believe that children owe unquestioning obedience to their parents and thus use scolding, shame, and guilt to control them (Chao, 1994). Although such a pattern of parental control generally fits the category of authoritarian parenting, it appears to have few negative effects for Chinese American and Chinese children, at least prior to adolescence. Rather, for younger Chinese children, it is primarily physical punishment that is related to negative outcomes (N. Eisenberg, Chang et al., 2009; Zhou et al., 2004, 2008).

The Pastorelli study (2016) described above also found similarity across all eight countries in the extent to which children high in prosocial behavior did elicit more positive discipline and warmth from their parents over time (Pastorelli et al., 2016). This study focused on children 9 and 10 years of age, and it may be that positive parenting plays its strongest role in promoting prosocial behavior before that age (Newton et al., 2014), such that the parental effect is evident before adolescence, and then the effect of the child's prosocial behavior on positive parenting comes later.

Taken together, the results of the research to date suggest that while there are cultural, often cross-country, differences in which parenting behaviors are preferred by parents, there is strong evidence that for any given parenting behavior, strong cross-cultural similarities exist in the implications of those behaviors for children's development.

Economic Contexts

Raising a child is expensive. The U.S. Department of Agriculture estimates that an average American family will spend about $14,000 per child per year, reaching a total of $245,340 per child by the time they reach 18 years of age (Lino, 2014).

Yet there is considerable variation around that average: parents in the lowest one-third of incomes spend around $10,000 per child per year, while parents in the highest one-third spend $25,000 or more per child per year—2.5 times as much (Lino, 2014). High-income parents can buy more and better quality goods (such as books or electronics) and experiences (such as music lessons and sports team memberships) for their children than can low-income parents (Pew Research Center, 2015). Lower-income parents also have a harder time paying for basic necessities like food, clothing, medicine, and shelter. Low-income children thus experience a range of material hardships that the majority of high-income children will never personally experience.

In addition to differences in what families can buy, income influences the amount and quality of time parents spend with their children. Low-income parents may need to work multiple jobs, or jobs with irregular or night hours; such jobs make it difficult for parents to spend time helping their children with homework or taking them to extracurricular activities—in other words, to "invest" in their children (Yoshikawa, Aber, & Beardslee, 2012). Having difficulty making ends meet and experiencing material hardships also creates stress for low-income parents, and that stress can lead to depression, irritability, harsh parenting, and marital conflict (Benner & Kim, 2010; Gershoff et al., 2007). Adequate family income thus matters to parents and children, both for what it can buy and for the stress it can alleviate.

Sadly, far too many children live in poor and low-income families, both in the United States and around the world. One in five children in the United States lives in poverty, a rate that has been steady for the past 35 years (Proctor, Semega, & Kollar, 2016) and is the second highest of the world's 35 richest nations (UNICEF Innocenti Research Centre, 2012). As seen in Figure 12.5, children in the United States are nearly twice as likely as adults to be living in poverty. Around the world, children make up one-third of the world's population but constitute half of the people living in extreme poverty, defined as living on less than $1.25 per day (Partners United in the Fight Against Poverty, 2015).

Because living in poverty can mean living without food, medical care, adequate shelter, or safe schools and neighborhoods, poor children's development suffers across a range of domains. Poor families are also at risk for becoming homeless, a crisis state, which of course exacerbates all the stressors the parents and children experience (see Box 12.3). It is thus not surprising that children in poverty have lower academic achievement, more mental health problems, more behavioral problems, and more health problems than their higher-income peers (Benner & Kim, 2010; Doan, Fuller-Rowell, & Evans, 2012; Yoshikawa et al., 2012).

Low-income parents are twice as likely as high-income parents to be afraid their child will get shot or will get in trouble with the law (Pew Research Center, 2015). All parents, regardless of income, worry that their child will be bullied and will have alcohol or drug problems, but low-income parents are more likely to also be afraid that their child will be physically assaulted. These fears likely stem from the qualities of the neighborhoods in which they live; low-income parents are 3 times as likely

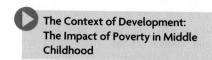

The Context of Development: The Impact of Poverty in Middle Childhood

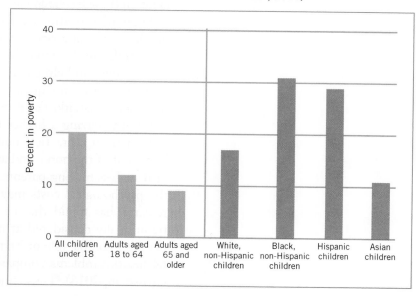

FIGURE 12.5 Poverty rates in the United States Minority children in the United States—especially children with Black race or Hispanic ethnic identity—are more than 3 times more likely to live in poverty than are White children. (Data from Proctor et al., 2016)

BOX 12.3 | a closer look

HOMELESSNESS

One-third of the homeless population in the United States are families with children (National Alliance to End Homelessness, 2016). The United States Department of Education, which tracks child homelessness, reports that more than 1.3 million homeless children and adolescents were enrolled in public schools in the 2013–2014 school year (U.S. Department of Education, 2016). This number represents a doubling of the number of homeless children enrolled in public schools in the 2006–2007 school year (U.S. Department of Education, 2016), most likely a result of the Great Recession that lasted from 2007 to 2009.

Homelessness is considered an adverse childhood experience (see Chapter 10) that puts children at risk in a variety of ways (Masten et al., 2014). At the most basic level, these children lack a regular routine and often lack adequate food and medical care. They may move frequently, which results in chronic absences from school, if they attend school at all (U.S. Department of Education, 2016). They also frequently change schools, which has been shown to undermine academic achievement (National Research Council, 2010). As a result of these risks, homeless children suffer a range of negative outcomes. They score lower on math and reading tests than their peers (Masten et al., 2014). Compared with poor children who are not homeless, homeless children experience

AMY SANCETTA / AP IMAGES

Children in homeless families, including those living in shelters, are at risk for depression, behavioral problems, and academic failure.

as high-income parents to view their neighborhoods as not a good place to raise children (Pew Research Center, 2015).

Supportive relationships with relatives, friends, neighbors, or others who can provide material assistance, childcare, advice, approval, or a sympathetic ear can help moderate the potential impact of economic stress on parenting. Such positive connections can help parents feel more successful and satisfied as parents and can actually improve the quality of their parenting (C.-Y. Lee, Lee, & August, 2011; McConnell, Breitkruez, & Savage, 2011).

Clearly, having a higher income makes parenting and raising children easier, at least from a practical point of view. However, if parents have to spend long hours out of the home and away from their children in order to earn that income, or if high-achieving parents put extra pressure on their children and adolescents, the psychological costs may diminish the material benefits. A growing body of research has found that children living in high-income families, and thus not traditionally considered at risk for behavior problems and delinquency, actually manifest comparable or higher rates of drug use, delinquent behavior, and mental health problems compared with their low-income peers (Luthar, Barkin, & Crossman, 2013). These findings are not intended to equate the experiences and

more internalizing problems, such as depression, social withdrawal, and low self-esteem (Buckner et al., 1999; DiBiase & Waddell, 1995; Rafferty & Shinn, 1991), and suffer more from both health and behavioral problems (Tobin & Murphy, 2013).

Exceptions to this pattern tend to include children who have a close relationship with their parents, especially if their parents are involved in their education (Herbers et al., 2011), children who are temperamentally well regulated (Obradović, 2010), and children with high early (e.g., at 1st grade) reading ability (Herbers et al., 2012) and high executive functioning (see Chapter 4; Masten et al., 2012). However, those who are well regulated also tend to be better adjusted and to get along better with peers (Obradović, 2010).

One particularly at-risk group are homeless youth living on their own, either because they have been kicked out of or have run away from their homes. Each year, approximately 400,000 youth under the age of 18 remain away from home for a week or more and are thus considered homeless (National Alliance to End Homelessness, 2016). Runaway youth report a range of adverse childhood experiences that preceded their being without a home. Among a sample of homeless youth in Los Angeles, 59% had suffered emotional abuse, 51% had been physically abused, and 33% had been sexually abused; 40% had been removed from their homes by child protective services because of such maltreatment. Additionally, 27% had been in juvenile detention, 83% were a racial or ethnic minority, and 42% had a minority sexual orientation. While homeless, 37% had been the victim of a physical assault and 13% of a sexual assault (Wong, Clark, & Marlotte, 2016). Both the adverse experiences before homelessness and the assaults experienced while homeless predicted greater depression, self-injury, and post-traumatic stress disorder (Wong et al., 2016).

Worldwide, there are between 10 million and 15 million homeless children, often referred to as "street children" (Naterer & Lavrič, 2016). In many underdeveloped countries, homeless children often have been orphaned because of AIDS or military conflicts; have been abandoned because their families cannot feed or care for them; or have fled to escape sexual, mental, or physical abuse at home (Aptekar & Ciano-Federoff, 1999). In some cases, children living on the streets do so in order to earn money for their very poor families and reside at least part of the time with a parent or other relative (Aptekar & Stoecklin, 2014). Street children are at risk of being coerced into prostitution or sexual slavery or into organized crime (Aptekar & Stoecklin, 2014). Yet many street children form family-like groups (Naterer & Godina, 2011).

Various intervention strategies have been attempted to help homeless and street children. Given that these children are at immediate physical risk and often already suffer from mental health and drug problems, deciding which problem to tackle first is a serious challenge for those working with the homeless. An organization known as the Canadian Homelessness Research Network (Gaetz et al., 2013) has compiled several examples of successful strategies, including providing mental health care, providing substance abuse treatment, providing job training, and reconnecting them with family. With such a complex population, helping homeless children requires a multipronged approach, whether they are in the United States, Canada, or elsewhere.

difficulties of children from poor and high-income families. Children in high-income families do not experience the stress of survival that low-income children and adolescents do. What these studies do make clear is that there is more than a single pathway to certain maladaptive outcomes, a phenomenon known as *equifinality* (Cicchetti & Rogosch, 1996).

Parents' Work Contexts

In families throughout the world, one or both parents have to work outside the home in order to support their children. The workplace environment can provide parents with a sense of accomplishment and a social network, both of which can enhance their mental health and, in turn, the quality of their parenting. However, work can also cause stress, and many parents, wittingly or not, bring that stress home.

Two studies in Australia provide insight into the effect of work on family life and child development. In the first study, nearly 3000 employed parents of 4- and 5-year-olds were asked about their work and family life (Strazdins et al., 2013). Most parents reported that they found work rewarding, but one-third also admitted that they experienced family difficulties and conflicts as a result of working. The extent to which a family experienced work–family conflict was in turn related to higher levels of emotional and behavioral problems in their children; this finding was true even when family income was accounted for, suggesting that the harm of conflict from a stressful job was not outweighed by the benefits of higher income (Strazdins et al., 2013). The second Australian study hinted at potential mechanisms for these findings. In a separate survey of 2151 mothers of young children, work–family conflict was linked with more parent irritability and less parental warmth, whereas work–family reward was associated with more warmth and more consistency (Cooklin et al., 2015).

The fact that many more mothers work now than in past generations means that many more families may be susceptible to work–family conflict. In 1955, only 18% of mothers with children younger than 6 were employed outside the home (U.S. Department of Health and Human Services, 2006). In 2013, 57% of mothers with infants younger than 1 year, 64% of mothers with children younger than 6, and 75% of mothers with children aged 6 to 17 years old worked outside the home (U.S. Department of Labor, 2016). These changes in the rates of maternal employment reflect a variety of factors, including greater acceptance of mothers who work outside the home, more workplace opportunities for women, and an increase in women who obtain college and graduate degrees, most of whom work (Pew Research Center, 2015).

The dramatic rise in the number of mothers working outside the home raised a variety of concerns. Some experts predicted that maternal employment, especially in an infant's 1st year, would seriously diminish the quality of maternal caregiving and that the mother–child relationship would suffer accordingly. Others worried that "latch-key" children who were left to their own devices after school would get into serious trouble, academically and socially. Over the past two decades, much research has been devoted to addressing such concerns. For the most part, the findings have been reassuring.

Taken as a whole, research does not support the idea that maternal employment has negative effects on children's development. There is little consistent evidence, for example, that the quality of mothers' interactions with their children necessarily diminishes substantially as a result of their employment (Gottfried et al., 2002; Huston & Aronson, 2005; Paulson, 1996). Although working mothers typically spend less time with their children than do nonworking mothers, the difference is largely offset by the fact that, compared with nonworking mothers, working mothers spend a greater portion of their childcare time engaged in social interactions with their infants rather than in straightforward caregiving activities (Huston & Aronson, 2005).

Even in the area of greatest debate—the effects of maternal employment on infants in their 1st year of life—when negative relations between maternal work and children's cognitive or social behavior have been found, the results have not been consistent across studies, ethnic groups, or the type of analyses applied to the data (L. Berger et al., 2008; Brooks-Gunn, Han, & Waldfogel, 2010; Burchinal & Clarke-Stewart, 2007). For example, some research suggests that early maternal employment is associated with better adjustment at age 7 for children in low-income African American families, whereas no such effect was found for those in a study of low-income Hispanic American families (R. L. Coley & Lombardi, 2013).

Studies of maternal employment extending beyond infancy also reveal contextual variation in the effects that maternal employment can have on children's development. For instance, a study of 3- to 5-year-olds found that those whose mother worked a night shift (starting at 9:00 P.M. or later) tended to exhibit more aggressive behavior, anxiety, and depressive symptoms than did the children whose mothers worked a typical daytime schedule (Dunifon et al., 2013). In another study, researchers found that mothers who worked more often at night (starting at 9:00 P.M. or later) spent less time with their adolescents and that their adolescents had a lower-quality home environment (e.g., in terms of the quality of mother–child interactions, the cleanliness and safety of the home, and so on), which in turn predicted higher levels of adolescents' risky behaviors. These effects were especially strong for boys in low-income families. However, similar negative effects were not found in the case of mothers who worked evening shifts that ended by midnight or who had other nonstandard work schedules (e.g., those with varying hours) that allowed them greater knowledge of their children's whereabouts (Han, Miller, & Waldfogel, 2010).

One aspect of work life in the United States that poses a particular challenge to working families is the lack of a paid family-leave policy, which we explore in depth in Box 12.4.

Childcare Contexts

Because so many mothers work outside the home, a large number of infants and young children receive care on a regular basis from someone besides their parents. In the United States in 2011, 35% of children with working mothers were placed

BOX 12.4 | applications

FAMILY-LEAVE POLICIES

Caring for a new baby, whether because of a birth or an adoption, takes both time and energy on the part of parents. As we learned in Chapter 2, infants wake up often and eat often, meaning that one or both parents have to get up repeatedly to take care of them. We also learned in Chapter 11 that the early months of life are an important time for establishing attachment bonds that will form the basis of the parent–child relationship. For much of human history, the bulk of the responsibility of caring for young children fell to mothers. However, with the increase of women in the workforce, more and more women cannot stay home to care for their children. This fact has necessitated family-leave policies that allow one or both parents to take an extended absence from work while not being worried about losing their jobs.

In the United States, family leave is made possible by the Family and Medical Leave Act (known as FMLA) of 1993. FMLA allows parents to take 12 weeks off of work and guarantees that their job will be there for them when they get back. However—and this is a big *however*—FMLA does not require that companies pay their employees when they take family leave, and it exempts small businesses. As a result, many parents can take family leave only if they can afford the loss of income, have saved sick or vacation days they can take, file for disability payments, happen to work at a company that does offer paid family leave (which is true for 13% of all workers, and does not include employees of the federal government), or live in one of the few states that has passed a law guaranteeing paid family leave, which at the time of publication includes California, New Jersey, or Rhode Island.

The United States is the only industrialized country, and indeed one of only three countries in the world, that does not provide paid family leave for new parents. The majority of industrialized countries provide at least one year of paid leave to new mothers, with six countries providing two or more years (OECD Family Database, 2016). Parents around the world thus have the option of staying home to care for their new babies without having to worry about threats to their employment or financial security—unless they live in the United States.

Paid maternity leave allows women to recover from pregnancy and childbirth and to care for their newborns. Children whose mothers were able to stay home for 12 weeks were more likely to be breast-fed, to be taken to regular medical checkups, and to have all recommended immunizations (Berger, Hill, & Waldfogel, 2005). Family leave can also be used when a parent is ill or when he or she has to care for a spouse or their own parent. Paid family leave can prevent a family from falling into poverty because of a medical emergency and has been linked with higher immunization rates (Adema, Clarke, & Frey, 2015).

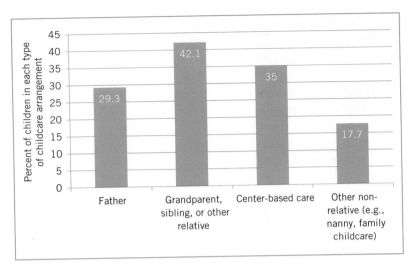

FIGURE 12.6 **Percentage of children with employed mothers, from birth through age 4, in each type of care arrangement** In 2011, 53% of children under the age of 5 (nearly 11 million) had mothers who were working for pay. More than half of these children were in care provided by centers or by nonrelatives in their homes or family childcare settings during the hours their mothers were at work. Note that these categories are not mutually exclusive. (Data from Laughlin, 2013)

in center-based childcare and 18% were cared for by a nonrelative in a home environment (e.g., babysitter, family day-care provider, nanny) (Laughlin, 2013; see Figure 12.6). A majority of children of high-income working parents are cared for in organized childcare centers or preschools (66%), whereas the majority of children in low-income families are cared for by family members other than the parents (Pew Research Center, 2015).

The increase in the number of children in non-parental childcare began in the 1970s. Initially, the greatest concern among researchers studying this trend was that it might undermine the early mother–child relationship (e.g., Belsky, 1986). For example, on the basis of attachment theory (see Chapter 11), it has been argued that young children who are frequently separated from their mothers are more likely to develop insecure attachments to their mothers than are children whose daily care is provided by their mothers. Yet as we saw in Box 11.1, that concern was unfounded. Several other outcomes have been linked with children's experiences in childcare, some to the children's benefit and some not.

Adjustment and Social Behavior

Much research has considered whether children in childcare centers develop more aggression because they compete for resources (e.g., crayons, toy cars, and the time of their teachers). The findings have been mixed and sometimes depend on the specific mode of analysis (e.g., Crosby et al., 2010) and the country in which the research was conducted. A number of investigators have found that children who are in childcare do not differ in problem behavior from those reared at home (Barnes, Beaver, & Miller, 2010; Erel, Oberman, & Yirmiya, 2000; M. E. Lamb, 1998). Indeed, in two recent large studies in Norway, a country in which the quality of childcare is uniformly high, researchers found little consistent relation

In 2011, among children in families in poverty, 27% were in center-based care or preschools as their primary arrangement, compared with 35% of children in families above the poverty line (Laughlin, 2013).

between amount of time in childcare and children's externalizing problems, such as aggression and noncompliance, or social competence (Solheim et al., 2013; Zachrisson et al., 2013).

These findings are in notable contrast to those from the NICHD study in the United States, where the quality of childcare is more variable. The NICHD study indicates that many hours a day in childcare or a number of changes in caregivers in the first 2 years of life predicted lower social competence and more noncompliance with adults at age 2 (NICHD Early Child Care Research Network, 1998a). At 4½ years of age, children in extensive childcare were viewed by care providers (but not by mothers) as exhibiting more problem behaviors, such as aggression, noncompliance, and anxiety/depression (NICHD Early Child Care Research Network, 2006). The relation between more hours in center care and teacher-reported externalizing problems (e.g., aggression, defiance) was also found in the elementary school years but generally was not significant by 6th grade (Belsky, Bakermans-Kranenburg, & van IJzendoorn, 2007). However, more hours of nonrelative care predicted greater risk-taking and impulsivity at age 15 (Vandell et al., 2010).

Significantly, the finding that greater time in childcare is related to increased risk for adjustment problems appears not to apply to children from very low-income, high-risk families (Côté et al., 2008). In fact, longer time in childcare has been found to be positively related to the better adjustment of such children, unless the quality of care is very poor (Votruba-Drzal, Coley, & Chase-Lansdale, 2004). Similarly, in a large study of children from high-risk families in Canada, physical aggression was less common among children who were in group childcare than among those who were looked after by their own families (Borge et al., 2004). High-quality childcare that involves programs designed to promote children's later success at school may be especially beneficial for disadvantaged children. As in the case of Project Head Start, discussed in Chapter 8, children who experience these programs show improvements in their social competence and declines in conduct problems (Keys et al., 2013; M. E. Lamb, 1998; Peisner-Feinberg et al., 2001; Webster-Stratton, 1998; Zhai, Brooks-Gunn, & Waldfogel, 2011).

Thus, it appears that most children in childcare never develop significant behavior problems, but for some, the risk that they will develop such problems increases with an increase in hours spent in childcare, especially center care (R. L. Coley et al., 2013). In the NICHD study, this risk was higher when children spent many hours with a large group of peers and in low-quality childcare (the overall risk was modest and was not due to the characteristics of children who are put in childcare for longer hours) (McCartney et al., 2010). More generally, higher-quality childcare in the NICHD study was related to fewer externalizing problems in the early years (McCartney et al., 2010) and at age 15 (Vandell et al., 2010)—a relation primarily seen in children and adolescents who were prone to negative emotion (Belsky & Pluess, 2012; Pluess & Belsky, 2010) or who had a particular variant of gene DRD4, which, as discussed in Chapter 11, is associated with being susceptible to the effects of the environment (Belsky & Pluess, 2013).

In addition, it must be remembered that the background characteristics (e.g., family income, parental education, parental personality) of children who are in childcare for long hours likely differ in a variety of ways from those of children in childcare for fewer hours. Therefore, cause-and-effect relations cannot be assumed, even when the effects of some of these factors are taken into account (Bolger & Scarr, 1995; NICHD Early Child Care Research Network, 1997). Furthermore, the number of hours spent in childcare is less relevant than the quality of childcare provided: no matter what their SES background, children in high-quality childcare programs tend to be well adjusted and to develop social competencies (Love et al., 2003; NICHD Early Child Care Research Network, 2003; Votruba-Drzal et al., 2004).

As noted earlier, another factor related to the effects of childcare on children's adjustment is the number of changes in the childcare provided. In the NICHD study, increases in the number of nonparental childcare arrangements were associated with increases in children's problem behaviors and lower levels of positive behavior such as compliance and constructive expression of emotion (Morrissey, 2009). Instability of childcare was also related to poorer adjustment in an Australian study (Love et al., 2003).

Cognitive and Language Development

The possible effects of childcare on children's cognitive and language performance are of particular concern to educators as well as to parents. Research suggests that high-quality childcare can have a modest, positive effect on these aspects of children's functioning (Keys et al., 2013), although the effects sometimes weaken over time (Côté et al., 2013). The NICHD study found that, overall, the number of hours in childcare did not correlate with cognitive or language development when demographic variables such as family income were taken into account. However, higher-quality childcare that included specific efforts to stimulate children's language development was linked to better cognitive and language development in the first 3 years of life (NICHD Early Child Care Research Network, 2000b). Children in higher-quality childcare (especially center care) scored higher on tests of pre-academic cognitive skills, language abilities, and attention than did those in lower-quality care (NICHD Early Child Care Research Network, 2002, 2006; NICHD Early Child Care Research Network & Duncan, 2003).

Higher-quality care also predicted mothers' greater involvement in their children's schooling when the children were in kindergarten. This would be expected to foster children's school performance (Crosnoe, Augustine, & Huston, 2012); promote higher vocabulary (but not reading and math) scores in elementary school (Belsky, Vandell et al., 2007); and cultivate higher cognitive and academic achievement at age 15 (Vandell et al., 2010). Moreover, for children in high-quality care, low income was less likely to predict underachievement at 4½ to 11 years of age (Dearing, McCartney, & Taylor, 2009).

Other research also suggests that childcare may have positive effects on cognition and that these effects are larger for higher-quality centers (Peisner-Feinberg et al., 2001). For instance, in Sweden and the United States, a number of researchers have found that children enrolled in out-of-home childcare perform better on cognitive tasks, even in elementary school (Erel et al., 2000; M. E. Lamb, 1998). In addition, children from low-income families who spend long hours in childcare, compared with those who spend fewer hours, tend to show increases in quantitative skills (Votruba-Drzal et al., 2004). It is likely that childcare, unless it is of low quality, provides greater cognitive stimulation than is available in some low-income homes.

Availability and Quality of Childcare

It is not surprising that the quality of care children receive outside the home is related to some aspects of their development. Several organizations, including the American Academy of Pediatrics and the American Public Health Association, have established minimal standards that should ensure a childcare center is both safe for children and promotes their development:

- A child-to-caregiver ratio of 3:1 for children aged 12 months or younger; 4:1 for 13- to 35-month-olds; 7:1 for 3-year-olds; and 8:1 for 4-and 5-year-olds

- Maximum group sizes of 6 for 12-months-olds and younger; 8 for 13- to 35-month-olds; 14 for 3-year-olds; and 16 for 4- and 5-year-olds

- Formal training for caregivers, with lead teachers having (1) a bachelor's degree in early childhood education, school-age care, child development, social work, nursing, or other child-related field, or an associate's degree in early childhood education and currently working toward a bachelor's degree; (2) at least one year of on-the-job training in providing a nurturing environment and meeting children's out-of-home needs (American Academy of Pediatrics, American Public Health Association, & National Resource Center for Health and Safety in Child Care and Early Education, 2011).

In the NICHD study in the United States, children in a form of childcare that met more of these guidelines tended to score higher on tests of language comprehension and readiness for school, and they had fewer behavior problems at age 36 months. The more standards that were met, the better the children performed at 3 years of age (NICHD Early Child Care Research Network, 1998b). Quality was generally highest in nonprofit centers that were not religiously affiliated; intermediate in nonprofit religiously affiliated centers and in for-profit independent centers; and lowest in for-profit chains (Sosinsky, Lord, & Zigler, 2007).

Unfortunately, a majority of working parents with infants and preschool children report that it is difficult to find childcare that is both high in quality and affordable (Pew Research Center, 2015), in part because most childcare centers in the United States do not meet the recommended minimal standards listed above. Another major factor is cost. In some regions of the country, keeping a child in a licensed childcare center requires up to one-third of a family's budget (Gould & Cooke, 2015), making it cost-prohibitive. Indeed, in half of states, childcare for a 4-year-old for one year exceeds the cost of in-state tuition at a public university, sometimes by over 200% (Gould & Cooke, 2015). It is thus not surprising that policymakers, including President Obama (The White House, 2015) and New York City mayor Bill de Blasio (Office of the Mayor of New York City, 2014) have each cited childcare affordability as an issue in need of urgent policy attention.

The positive academic outcomes associated with high-quality preschool childcare have been found to persist into elementary grades.

Review

Consistent with Bronfenbrenner's bioecological model, families are affected by the social and economic contexts in which they are embedded. One important context is culture, which affects parents' choice of behaviors, such as discipline. However, how these behaviors affect children is largely similar across cultures.

One-fifth of children in the United States live in poor families. Low family income restricts the resources that can be dedicated to a child, which can affect his or her cognitive development, and increases parents' stress and use of harsh parenting behaviors, which can affect the child's level of behavior problems.

The bulk of recent research on maternal employment indicates that it often benefits children and mothers and that it has few negative effects on children if they are in childcare of acceptable quality and are supervised and monitored. Recent research on childcare indicates that, on the whole, nonmaternal care has small, if any, effect on the quality of the mother–child relationship. Children who spend long hours in centers tend to exhibit more aggressive behavior at schools, but the effects are modest and likely are nonsignificant for high-quality childcare. High-quality care does appear to have some modest benefits for cognitive development and especially language development.

CHAPTER SUMMARY

Family Structure

- Family structure has changed in the United States over the past few decades: first-time parents are older, more children are being born to single mothers, families are smaller, and divorce and remarriage are common occurrences.

- A disproportionate number of adolescent parents come from impoverished backgrounds. Adolescent mothers tend to be less effective at parenting than older mothers, and their children are at risk for behavioral and academic problems, delinquency, and early sexual activity. Children of adolescent mothers fare better if their mothers have more knowledge about parenting and if the children themselves have a warm, involved relationship with their fathers.

- There is no evidence that children raised by lesbian or gay parents differ from children of heterosexual parents in their sexual orientation or in their cognitive and social adjustment.

- Although most children adjust well after parental divorce, some children do experience enduring negative outcomes. The major factor contributing to negative outcomes for children of divorce is the occurrence of hostile, dysfunctional family interactions, including continuing conflict between ex-spouses.

- Parents' remarriage can have both positive impacts on children, including greater resources and a new trusted adult in their lives, and negative impacts, such as increased conflict in the family. Children do best if all parents are supportive.

Family Dynamics

- Parents socialize their children's development through direct instruction; through their modeling of skills, attitudes, and behavior; and through their managing of children's experiences and social lives.

- The use of discipline that emphasizes reasoning has been linked with better compliance and social competence. Punishments, such as spanking, have been linked with worse behavior in children over time.

- Researchers have identified several types of parenting styles related to the dimensions of warmth and control. A style that balances both warmth and reason, sometimes called an authoritative parenting style, is best for promoting children's social competence.

- The significance and effects of different parenting styles or practices may vary somewhat across cultures.

- Parenting styles and practices are affected by characteristics of the children, including their attractiveness, behavior, and temperament.

- Economic stressors can undermine the quality of marital and parent–child interactions, increasing children's risk for depression, academic failure, disruptive behavior, and drug use.

- Mothers typically interact with their children much more than fathers do. Fathers' play tends to be more physical than mothers' play. However, the nature of parent–child interactions differs across cultures.

- Siblings learn from one another, can be sources of support for one another, and sometimes engage in conflict with one another. Siblings get along better if they have good relationships with their parents and if they feel that their parents treat them equally well.

The Socioeconomic Context

- A family's culture affects the parents' choice of behaviors, such as discipline, but the effect of these behaviors on children is largely similar across cultures.

- Parenting behaviors and, in turn, children's development are affected by the family's economic resources. Fully 20% of children in the United States are from poor families, putting them at risk for a range of cognitive and behavioral problems.

- Children and mothers reap some benefits from maternal employment, and maternal employment has few negative effects on children if they are in childcare of acceptable quality and are supervised and monitored by adults. New parents in the United States have to make difficult choices about staying home or working, given that many parents do not have the option of paid family leave.

- Children in high-quality care do better in their cognitive and language development than children in low-quality care. Whether childcare has positive or negative effects on children's functioning probably depends in part on the characteristics of the child, the child's relationship with his or her mother, and the quality of the childcare.

Test Yourself

1. A recent trend in family structure in the United States is the increasing ages of first-time parents. Which of the following is *not* true of these older parents compared with younger parents?
   a. Older parents tend to be more highly educated.
   b. Older parents tend to earn higher incomes.
   c. Older parents tend to use a harsher parenting style.
   d. Older parents are less likely to get divorced within 10 years of having a child.

2. Recent research has shown which of the following to be true of children of same-sex parents, compared with children of heterosexual parents?
   a. They report higher levels of stigmatization and teasing.
   b. They tend to perform better socially and academically.
   c. They are similar in their sexual orientation and degree of gender-typed behavior.
   d. They report higher levels of parental aggression in adolescence.

3. Which of the following statements is *not* true of divorce?
   a. Young children tend to react more negatively to their parent's remarriage than young adolescents.
   b. For children in high-conflict families, divorce may increase the likelihood of positive outcomes for their adjustment.
   c. Children from divorced and remarried families are at greater risk for becoming divorced themselves as adults.
   d. Most children do not suffer significant, enduring problems as a result of their parents' divorce.

4. The process through which children acquire the values, knowledge, and behaviors that are regarded as appropriate in their culture is known as _____ .
   a. parenting style
   b. socialization
   c. behaviorism
   d. joint attention

5. Which of the following factors has *not* been shown to influence children's adjustment in stepfamilies?
   a. The age of the child at the time of the parent's remarriage
   b. The relationship between the noncustodial parent and stepparent
   c. The genders of the child and stepparent
   d. The age difference between the biological parent and stepparent

6. Which of the following descriptions best fits the definition of other-oriented induction?
   a. After a toddler has taken a toy from his friend, the toddler's mother scolds him and makes him apologize.
   b. A father spanks his toddler after that toddler has taken a toy from her friend.
   c. A mother puts her toddler in a time-out after he has taken a toy from his friend.
   d. A father explains to his toddler that by taking a toy from her friend, she has hurt her friend's feelings.

7. Internalization is best described as
   a. the feelings of guilt that a child may experience after his or her parents divorce.
   b. the process by which parent–child interactions reinforce and perpetuate the parent's and child's behavior.
   c. the process through which a child learns and accepts a desired behavior as a result of appropriate discipline.
   d. the negative impact harsh punishment can have on a child's sense of self-esteem.

8. Which of the following statements is an accurate description of punishment?
   a. Punishment is a more effective form of discipline.
   b. Punishment, though more harsh than other forms of discipline, can teach the child how to behave.
   c. Punishments, such as yelling and revoking privileges, have been found to be successful at encouraging internalization.
   d. Punishments, when mild, provide minimally sufficient pressure for internalization.

9. Jayden wants to go to a party at a friend's house. When she asks her father for permission, he immediately says no. Jayden asks why and her father angrily says, "Because I said so!" Jayden's father is displaying which parenting style?
   a. permissive
   b. authoritarian
   c. authoritative
   d. uninvolved

10. Eric and his friend are playing a game that could become dangerous. Eric's father tells them to stop. Eric pleads with him to let them continue. His father firmly restates his refusal and explains why he thinks their game is dangerous. He then suggests some alternative activities. Eric's father is displaying which parenting style?
    a. permissive
    b. authoritarian
    c. authoritative
    d. friendly

11. Which of the following is *not* an area in which mothers and fathers tend to differ in interactions with their children?
    a. The type of play they tend to engage in with their children
    b. The amount of time they spend with their children
    c. The effect that their parenting style has on their children's mental health
    d. The amount of physical care and emotional support they provide for their children

12. Six-year-old Trevor has a tendency to act aggressively in order to get his way. His parents react to this behavior with harsh discipline, including spanking. Trevor's response, however, is to act out even more, which escalates his parents' reactions. This cycle of parent–child behavior is an example of what concept?
    a. bidirectionality
    b. interdependence
    c. equifinality
    d. child effects only

13. Which of the following statements is *not* true about sibling relationships?
    a. Differential treatment by parents affects children most in late adolescence.
    b. Children are likely to report positive relationships with their parents and sibling if they feel that differential treatment is justified rather than unfair.
    c. Children from collectivist cultures have been shown to report less sibling conflict than children from individualistic cultures.
    d. Siblings get along better in families where the parents get along well together.

14. Which of the following statements is true of the potential effect of socioeconomic context on child development?
    a. Poverty has little impact on children's academic achievement.
    b. Children living in high-income families tend to show lower rates of drug use, delinquency, and mental health problems than their low-income peers.
    c. Parents' relationships with supportive relatives and friends can help moderate the impact of economic stress on their children's development.
    d. Maternal employment tends to significantly diminish the quality of mothers' interactions with their children.

15. Which of the following has *not* been found to influence the positive or negative effects of childcare on a child's development?
    a. number of hours per day the child spends in childcare
    b. type of relationship the child has with his or her mother
    c. quality of the childcare facility
    d. number of siblings the child has

LaunchPad
macmillan learning

Don't stop now! Research shows that testing yourself is a powerful learning tool. Visit LaunchPad to access the LearningCurve adaptive quizzing system, which gives you a personalized study plan to help build your mastery of the chapter material through videos, activities, and more. **Go to launchpadworks.com.**

Critical Thinking Questions

1. It often is assumed that parental socialization of children's behavior is a bidirectional process, with the parent affecting the child's behavior and the child's behavior also evoking some socialization practices or behaviors. Provide examples of bidirectional causality in regard to (a) the relation between spanking and children's aggression, and (b) the relation between parental use of punitive control and children's self-regulation.

2. In some cultures, respect for parental authority is valued more than in many Western industrialized countries. How might this cultural variation affect interactions between parents and children and the relation of parenting styles to children's social and emotional development?

3. Think about the ways your parents interacted with you when you were a child. Based on Baumrind's categories of parenting style, which type of parenting did your mother and/or father display? What specific behaviors did you use to classify their parenting?

4. Make a list of the advantages and disadvantages of joint custody for children of divorce. How would the advantages and disadvantages vary for families in which the parents either (a) argue a lot or get along and (b) live 50 miles apart or 5 miles apart after the divorce?

5. In the past few decades, the number of children being cared for by nonparents or in childcare centers has increased dramatically. What are the potential benefits and costs to parents for putting their children in childcare or preschool? What are the benefits and costs to children? To society?

Key Terms

authoritarian parenting, p. 526

authoritative parenting, p. 526

bidirectionality of parent–child
 interactions, p. 530

discipline, p. 523

family dynamics, p. 523

family structure, p. 512

internalization, p. 523

parenting style, p. 524

permissive parenting, p. 526

punishment, p. 524

socialization, p. 523

uninvolved parenting, p. 527

▶ Student Video Activities

Family Structure and Function

Grandparents as Parents

Parenting in Middle Childhood

Parenting in Adolescence

Intergenerational Transmission of Parenting:
 Interview with Jay Belsky

Parent–Adolescent Relationship and Contexts of
 Family Life: Interview with Anne Petersen

The Context of Development: The Impact of
 Poverty in Middle Childhood

Answers to Test Yourself

1. c, **2.** c, **3.** a, **4.** b, **5.** d, **6.** d, **7.** c, **8.** d, **9.** b, **10.** c, **11.** c, **12.** a, **13.** a, **14.** c, **15.** d

WINSLOW HOMER (1836–1910), *Snap the Whip* (oil on canvas, 1872)

Peer Relationships

Themes

- Nature and Nurture
- The Active Child
- Continuity/Discontinuity
- The Sociocultural Context
- Individual Differences
- Research and Children's Welfare

peers ■ people of approximately the same age and status who are unrelated to one another

The videos Amanda Todd made about her experiences as a victim of cyberbullying have been viewed tens of millions of times.

MLADEN ANTONOV / GETTY IMAGES

"Why did you do all this for me?" he asked. "I don't deserve it. I've never done anything for you."

"You have been my friend," replied Charlotte. "That in itself is a tremendous thing."

– E. B. White, Charlotte's Web

As this quote from E. B. White's classic work of children's literature suggests, friendships motivate many of our behaviors, actions, and beliefs. They influence the formation of our identities and provide powerful indications of who we are and who we might become. Friends—and peers in general—are an important part of our lives, whether they are from our workplace, our school, our community, or even our past. In the digital era, peer relationships can span the globe and develop between individuals who have never met in person, but who communicate in real-time through online video or messaging applications. The Internet has made it much easier to connect with friends and associates, and texts and instant messaging have made keeping in touch quicker and easier than ever. Facebook even made "friend" into a verb—which of course was quickly followed by its antithetical verb, "unfriend."

Unfortunately, social media has also facilitated the darker side of peer interactions by making it easy to harass and bully others. The emergence of *cyberbullying*, which is the use of technology including text, e-mail, websites, videos, embarrassing photos, and fake profiles to harass or upset another person, is a major concern. Though adults sometimes use social media to frighten and shame others, the prevalence of cyberbullying among children is particularly alarming given numerous recent stories of suicides by children and adolescents who were the victims of these online attacks (this issue is discussed in depth in Box 13.2).

The cyberbullying and subsequent suicide of Amanda Todd, an adolescent living in Port Coquitlam, British Columbia, has received worldwide attention. Amanda was blackmailed and bullied by a man she met online, who circulated a revealing photo of her throughout her community and more publicly on Facebook. Spurred on by these acts, a group of her peers bullied and shamed her online, ostracized her at school, and physically assaulted her. In the aftermath, she engaged in a variety of risk behaviors, including drinking, drug use, and sex, and began cutting herself. After a suicide attempt that was prevented by her family, her peers continued to post hurtful comments online, going so far as to say they wished her attempt had been successful. Her original tormentor followed her online when she moved schools, and then digitally distributed the photo to her new classmates, starting the cycle all over again. She posted a video to YouTube describing her ordeal as a cyberbullying victim, though doing so did not give her solace or the support she clearly needed. Sadly, several weeks later she killed herself on October 10, 2012, at the age of 15.

Clearly, the people in children's lives outside their families can have a strong influence on them, both for good and for bad. This becomes increasingly true as children become older and spend more time with their **peers,** who are children of their own age and status to whom they are not related (Rubin, Bukowski, & Bowker, 2015). And though children can have close and warm relationships with their siblings, the peers that a child considers to be friends are uniquely different from siblings because they are chosen by the child.

In this chapter, we consider the special nature of peer interactions and their implications for children's social development. First, we look at friendships, the most intimate form of peer relationships, and consider questions such as: How do children's interactions with friends differ from those with other peers? How do friendships change with age? What do children get out of friendships and how do they think about them?

Next, we consider children's relationships in the larger peer group. These relationships are discussed separately from friendships because they appear to play a somewhat different role in children's development, particularly in regard to the provision of intimacy. We consider questions such as: What are the differences among children who are liked, disliked, or not noticed by their peers? Does children's acceptance or rejection by peers have long-term implications for their behavior and psychological adjustment?

The discussion of children's relationships with their peers will incorporate the theme of *individual differences* and the ways in which differences in peer relationships may cause differences in development. In addition, we will focus on the influence that the *sociocultural context* has on peer relationships, the contributions that both *nature and nurture* make to the quality of children's peer relationships, and the role of the *active child* in choosing friends and activities with peers. We will also consider whether changes in children's thinking about friendships exhibit *continuity or discontinuity*. Finally, we will examine issues of *research and children's welfare* related to interventions to improve children's interactions with other children.

Friendships

Many theorists throughout the years have argued that peer relationships provide special opportunities for children's development. Piaget (1932/1965) suggested that because children are relatively equal in social status, they tend to be more open and spontaneous when expressing their ideas and beliefs with peers than with adults. Similarly, Vygotsky (1978) observed that children learn new skills and develop their cognitive capacities in peer interactions; he emphasized the ways in which children's working together helps to build new skills and abilities, as well as to convey the knowledge and skills valued by the culture.

Most children, at every stage of development and across all cultures, have at least one same-sex peer whom they consider to be a friend (Rubin et al., 2015). Researchers generally agree that friends are people who like to spend time together and feel affection for one another. In addition, their interactions are characterized by *reciprocities;* that is, friends have mutual regard for one another,

Theorists have emphasized both disagreement and cooperation within the context of peer relationships as important contributors to children's cognitive development. Even something as seemingly simple as establishing the ground rules for an informal game of softball can hone children's skills in debate and compromise.

ROBIN SACHS / PHOTOEDIT

friend ■ a person with whom an individual has an intimate, reciprocated, positive relationship

exhibit give-and-take in their behavior (such as cooperation and negotiation), and benefit in comparable ways from their social exchanges (Bukowski, Newcomb, & Hartup, 1996). In brief, a **friend** is a peer with whom an individual has an intimate, reciprocated, and positive relationship.

Children's Choice of Friends

What factors influence a child's friendship decisions? Not surprisingly, children tend to be friends with peers who are sociable and who act prosocially toward others (Rubin et al., 2015). Another key determinant of friendship is similarity of interests and behavior. Children tend to like peers who are similar to themselves in the cognitive maturity of their play (Rubin et al., 1994) and in the levels

---

BOX 13.1 | individual differences

CULTURE AND CHILDREN'S PEER EXPERIENCE

The patterns of peer development described in this chapter reflect trends averaged across groups of children and sometimes across cultures. These averages mask interesting cultural differences in how children approach relationships with their peers. For example, children in China who are unsociable and avoid peer groups tend to have adjustment problems (Liu et al., 2015a), in part because Chinese culture places a strong emphasis on collectivism, which values the good of the group over individual needs or wants (Du, Li, & Lin, 2015). Such cultural norms also affect how Chinese children interact with one another; for example, whereas children in the United States who do well on a test tend to boast to their classmates, high-scoring Chinese children instead emphasize their interest in helping their peers improve (Heyman, Genyue, & Lee, 2008).

Cultural differences also influence the roles of peers and families as sources of support and companionship. Children in some cultures are much more likely to rely on family than on peers for support, and this appears especially true for children from Latino cultures. For instance, in a study comparing children from Canada, Cuba, and Spain, Canadian children with Anglo-European backgrounds rated friends as an important support, while children in Cuba and Spain did not (Vitoroulis et al., 2012).

Although cross-cultural studies often reveal differences, they often identify similarities as

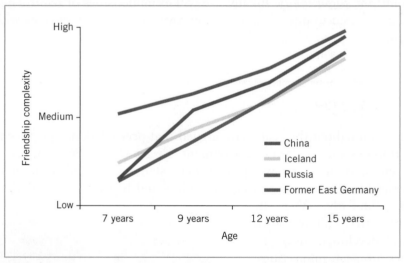

Change in complexity of friendship descriptions across childhood From age 9 on, children in the four different countries listed here increase in the complexity of their friendship descriptions at the same rate, and all are nearly equal in their high ratings of complexity by age 15. (Data from Gummerum & Keller, 2008)

well. One ambitious study followed children from ages 7 to 15 in four different countries: China, Iceland, Russia, and the former East Germany (Gummerum & Keller, 2008). Children were interviewed at four different ages about what makes someone a friend and why friends are important. Researchers coded their responses according to friendship complexity. Despite the differences in these cultures, the children followed a remarkably similar pattern of development in the

complexity of their friendship descriptions across childhood (see the figure). Findings such as these provide evidence that some universal aspects of the development of peer and friend relationships exist across childhood and adolescence.

A classic study of cross-cultural differences in peer relationships was conducted by researchers Beatrice Whiting and Carolyn Edwards (1988). They compared children from six cultures, namely India, Japan,

of their cooperativeness, antisocial behavior, acceptance by peers, and shyness (X. Chen, Cen et al., 2005; Haselager et al., 1998; A. J. Rose, Swenson, & Carlson, 2004). Friends in both childhood and adolescence are also more similar than nonfriends in their academic motivation and self-perceptions of competence (Altermatt & Pomerantz, 2003; Dijkstra, Cillessen, & Borch, 2013; Rubin et al., 2015). Friends also tend to share similar levels of negative emotions such as distress and depression (Haselager et al., 1998; Hogue & Steinberg, 1995) and are similar in their tendencies to attribute hostile intentions to others (Halligan & Philips, 2010; see Chapter 9 for more on hostile attribution bias).

For young children, proximity is an obvious key factor—they tend to become friends with peers who are physically nearby, such as neighbors, playgroup members, or preschool classmates. However, as Box 13.1 points out, young children's

Kenya, Mexico, the Philippines, and the United States. They found that in some communities, such as in Okinawa, Japan, children were free to wander in the streets and public areas of town and had extensive contact with peers. By contrast, Kenyan children were confined primarily to the family yard and therefore had relatively little contact with peers other than their siblings.

Cultures also differ in terms of the total number of hours that children typically spend with peers. In many cultures, especially in unschooled, nonindustrial populations, boys tend to spend more time with peers than girls do, likely because they are less closely monitored and are allowed greater freedom to be away from home (Larson & Verma, 1999). For example, 6- to 12-year-old Indian boys were found to spend 3 times more time with peers outside their families than girls did (Saraswati & Dutta, 1988). The cross-cultural differences in the amount of peer interaction adolescents engage in are likely due, at least in part, to cultural differences in values.

A recent study of adolescents in 11 countries found that the greater the importance of traditional family values—defined as high feelings of family obligations, acceptance of children's duty to be obedient, and an orientation toward the family instead of a focus on autonomy and individualism—the less peer acceptance was related to adolescents' life satisfaction (Schwarz et al., 2012). Thus, in cultures with traditional family values, the peer group appears to be less important, and adolescents' well-being is less related to how well-liked they are by peers.

In some groups in Kenya, children are discouraged from forming relationships with peers who are not related. Thus, children interact primarily with siblings and adult relatives.

Cultural differences have also been found in how children interact with their peers. A major study across nine countries (China, Colombia, Italy, Jordan, Kenya, the Philippines, Sweden, Thailand, and the United States) asked children how often in the previous month they had engaged in physical aggression (e.g., "hitting or slapping other children") or in relational aggression (e.g., "trying to keep others from liking someone by saying mean things about that person") (Lansford et al., 2012). Children in China, Italy, and Thailand reported engaging in more relational than physical aggression, whereas children in Jordan and Kenya were more physically than relationally aggressive; children in the other countries engaged in both kinds of aggression at equal rates. Countries did show similarities in one key aspect of aggression: the role of gender. In each country, boys were more likely than girls to engage in physical aggression, but there were no consistent gender differences for relational aggression across the nine countries (Lansford et al., 2012). These findings suggest that not only are there different cultural norms about what type of aggression is more acceptable, but also that there is a shared norm that it is more acceptable for boys to be physically aggressive than girls.

NIGEL PAVITT / GETTY IMAGES

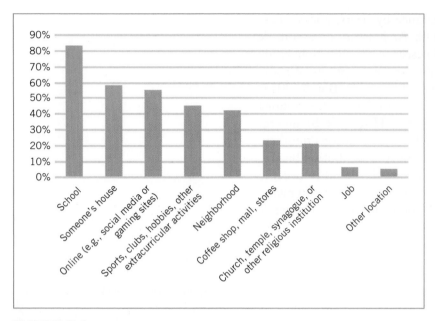

FIGURE 13.1 Main places adolescents say they hang out with close friends Physical proximity still plays a key role in both whom teens are friends with and where they spend time together, although online platforms are used by more than half of teens to spend time with their close friends. (Data from Lenhart, 2015)

access to peers can vary widely by culture. Although proximity becomes less important with age, it continues to play a role in individuals' choices of friends into adolescence (Clarke-McLean, 1996; Dishion, Andrews, & Crosby, 1995), in part because of involvement in similar activities at school (e.g., sports, academic activities, arts), which appear to promote the development of new friendships. One study found that when two adolescents participated in the same activity, they were on average 2.3 times more likely to be friends than were adolescents who did not participate in the same activity (Schaefer et al., 2011).

As seen in Figure 13.1, the vast majority of adolescents (83%) report that school is the most common setting where they spend time with their close friends. Nearly half of the teens surveyed regularly spend time with friends while doing extracurricular activities (45%) or in their neighborhoods (42%), and one-fifth spend time with friends who attended the same religious institution (21%). Of course, physical proximity is no longer necessary for children who have regular access to the Internet; 55% of adolescents regularly spend time with friends online, either through social media or gaming sites (Lenhart, 2015). We will discuss the role of technology in friendships more in depth later on.

In most industrialized countries, similarity in age is also a major factor in friendship, with most children tending to make friends with age-mates (Aboud & Mendelson, 1996; Dishion et al., 1995). In part, this may be due to the fact that in most industrialized societies, children are segregated by age in school: in societies where children do not attend school or otherwise are not segregated by age, they are more likely to develop friendships with children of different ages.

Another powerful factor in friend selection is a child's gender: girls tend to be friends with girls, and boys, with boys (Knecht et al., 2011; C. L. Martin et al., 2013; A. J. Rose & Rudolph, 2006). Cross-gender friendships, though not uncommon, tend to be more fragile (L. Lee, Howes, & Chamberlain, 2007; Maccoby, 2000; see Chapter 15). The preference for same-gender friends emerges in preschool and continues through childhood (Hartup, 1983). The liking of other-gender peers increases over the course of childhood and into early adolescence (Poulin & Pedersen, 2007), with other-gender close friendships increasing in frequency from 8th grade to 11th grade (Arndorfer & Stormshak, 2008).

To a lesser degree, children tend to be friends with peers of their own racial/ethnic group, although this tendency varies across groups and contexts (Knecht et al., 2011). In general, efforts to establish friendships outside one's own racial/ethnic group are less likely to be reciprocated than are efforts within the group (Vaquera & Kao, 2008); and when they are reciprocated, they often are not as long lasting (L. Lee et al., 2007). Youths who maintain cross-racial/ethnic friendships tend to be leaders and relatively inclusive in their social relationships (Kawabata & Crick, 2008), as well as socially competent and high in self-esteem (N. Eisenberg, Valiente et al., 2009; Fletcher,

Rollins, & Nickerson, 2004; Kawabata & Crick, 2011). For majority-group children, having cross-ethnic friendships has been associated with positive attitudes toward people in other groups in the future (Feddes, Noack, & Rutland, 2009). However, cross-race friendships can have costs. For example, middle-school African American and Asian American youths whose best friends are all of a different race from their own tend to be lower in emotional well-being than those with best friends only from the same racial group, perhaps because their friends of different races are not subject to the same forms of racial discrimination and are less able to provide support when they are faced with it (McGill, Way, & Hughes, 2012).

Thus, birds of a feather do tend to flock together. The fact that friends tend to be similar on a number of dimensions underscores the difficulty of knowing whether friends actually affect one another's behavior or whether children simply seek out peers who think, act, and feel as they do.

Early Peer Interactions and Friendships

Children appear to have friends as early as their 2nd year of life. Children as young as 12 to 18 months of age display a preference for some children over others by touching the preferred children, smiling at them, and engaging in positive interactions with them more than they do with other peers (D. F. Hay, Caplan, & Nash, 2009; Shin, 2010). By the time they reach 24 months of age, children have begun to develop skills that allow greater complexity in their social interactions, including imitating peers' social behaviors, engaging in cooperative problem solving, and trading roles during play (C. A. Brownell, Ramani, & Zerwas, 2006; C. Howes, 1996; C. Howes & Matheson, 1992; Seehagen & Herbert, 2011).

By age 3 or 4, children can make and maintain friendships with peers (Dunn, 2004) and most have at least one friendship (M. Quinn & Hennessy, 2010). Even in these early years, children can identify their "best friends" and characterize their relationships with best friends as more positive than their relationships with other friends (Sebanc et al., 2007). Especially with friends, cooperation and coordination in children's interactions continue to increase substantially from the toddler to the preschool years (C. Howes & Phillipsen, 1998).

This is particularly evident in shared pretend play (Dunn, 2004), which, as discussed in Chapter 7, involves symbolic actions that must be mutually understood by the play partners. Pretend play occurs more often among friends than among peers, probably because friends' experiences with one another allow them to trust that their partner will work to interpret and share the meaning of symbolic actions (C. Howes, 1996). The degree to which preschoolers engage in, and are competent at, such pretend play is related to their prosocial behaviors such as kindness, cooperation, sharing, and empathy (Spivak & Howes, 2011)—behaviors considered in depth in Chapter 14.

While the rate of cooperation and positive interactions among young friends is higher than among nonfriends, so is the rate of conflict. Preschool friends quarrel with one another as much as or more than nonfriends do and express more hostility toward one another by means of assaults, threats, and refusing requests

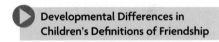

Developmental Differences in Children's Definitions of Friendship

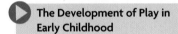

The Development of Play in Early Childhood

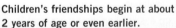

Children's friendships begin at about 2 years of age or even earlier.

ELIZABETH CREWS

TABLE 13.1

Strategies Chosen by Schoolchildren When a Peer Says Something Mean to, or About, Them

	Percent of Children Selecting Each Strategy When the Peer Is:	
	Their Best Friend	A Classmate (Neither a Friend nor Enemy)
Talk to friend/classmate	43%	19%
Think about what to do	24%	14%
Hit, kick, yell	9%	10%
Hold anger in	8%	5%
Quit thinking about it	6%	20%
Get away from what happened	4%	17%
Talk to someone else about it	4%	11%
Do nothing	1%	4%

Source: Information from Whitesell & Harter (1996).

TABLE 13.2

Dimensions on Which Elementary School Children Often Evaluate Their Friendships

Validation and Caring

Makes me feel good about my ideas.

Tells me I am good at things.

Conflict Resolution

Make up easily when we have a fight.

Talk about how to get over being mad at each other.

Conflict and Betrayal

Argue a lot.

Doesn't listen to me.

Help and Guidance

Help each other with school work a lot.

Loan each other things all the time.

Companionship and Recreation

Always sit together at lunch.

Do fun things together a lot.

Intimate Exchange

Always tell each other our problems.

Tell each other secrets.

Source: Information from Parker & Asher (1993).

(Fabes et al., 1996; D. C. French et al., 2005; Hartup et al., 1988). The higher rate of conflict for friends is likely due, in part, to the greater amount of time friends spend together. Children also are more likely to resolve conflicts in direct ways with friends, such as by talking with the person directly or thinking about what to do, whereas they are more likely to avoid nonfriends with whom they are fighting (Whitesell & Harter, 1996; see Table 13.1). Moreover, friends are more likely than nonfriends to resolve conflicts in ways that result in equal outcomes rather than in one child's winning and another's losing. Thus, after a conflict, friends are more likely than nonfriends to resume their interactions and to have positive feelings for one another.

Developmental Changes in Friendship

From about age 5 years on, many of the patterns apparent in the interactions among preschool-age friends and nonfriends persist and become more sharply defined. As mentioned earlier, friends, in comparison with nonfriends, communicate more often and better with one another and cooperate and work together more effectively (Hartup, 1996). They also fight more often—but again, they are more likely to negotiate their way out of the conflict (Laursen, Finkelstein, & Betts, 2001). In addition, they now have the maturity to take responsibility for the conflict and to give reasons for their disagreement, increasing the likelihood of their maintaining the friendship (Fonzi et al., 1997; Hartup et al., 1993; Whitesell & Harter, 1996).

Although children's friendships remain similar in many aspects as the children grow older, they do change in one important dimension: the level and importance of intimacy. This change is reflected both in the nature of friends' interactions with one another and in the way children conceive of friendship. Between ages 6 and 8, for example, children define friendship primarily on the basis of actual activities with their peers and tend to define "best" friends as peers with whom they play all the time and share everything (Gummerum & Keller, 2008). At this age, children also tend to view friends in terms of rewards and costs (Bigelow, 1977). In this respect, friends tend to be in close proximity, have interesting toys, and have similar expectations about play activities. Nonfriends tend to be uninteresting or difficult to get along with. Thus, in the early school years, children's views of friendship are instrumental and concrete (Rubin, Bukowski, & Parker, 2006) (see Table 13.2).

In contrast, between the early school years and adolescence, children in both Asian and Western countries increasingly define their friendships in terms of characteristics such as companionship, similarity in attitudes/interests, acceptance, trust, genuineness, mutual admiration, and loyalty (Furman & Buhrmester, 1992; Gummerum & Keller, 2008; McDougall & Hymel, 2007). At about 9 years of age, children seem to become more sensitive to the needs of others and to the inequalities among people. For children at this age, friends are those peers who take care of one another's physical and material needs, provide general assistance and help with school work, reduce loneliness and the sense of being excluded, and share feelings.

As children age into middle childhood and adolescence, the willingness to lend support and help, including with homework, becomes an important dimension of friendship.

Adolescent friends are more likely to share confidences with one another than are younger friends.

Adolescents use friendship as a context for self-exploration and working out personal problems (Gottman & Mettetal, 1986). Thus, friendships become an increasingly important source of intimacy and disclosure with age, as well as a source of honest feedback. Friendships also become more exclusive in adolescence, as adolescents begin to focus on having just a few close friends (Rubin et al., 2015). These changes may explain why adolescents perceive the quality of their friendships as improving from middle to late adolescence and why they value them so highly (Way & Greene, 2006). However, friendships in adolescence can also be less stable than they were in middle childhood; whereas 75% of friendships at age 10 persist for the entire school year, only half endure in adolescence (Rubin et al., 2015).

What accounts for the various age-related changes that occur in children's friendships, particularly with regard to their concept of friendship? Selman (1980) suggested that changes in children's reasoning about friendships are a consequence of age-related qualitative changes in their ability to take others' perspectives (see Chapter 9). In the view of Selman, as well as of Piaget and others, young children have limited awareness that others may feel or think about things differently than they themselves do. Consequently, their thinking about friendships is limited by the degree to which they consider issues beyond their own needs. As children begin to understand others' thoughts and feelings, they realize that friendships involve consideration of both parties' needs so that the relationship is mutually satisfying. Selman's descriptions of friendship development have been confirmed in research with children in North America and across Europe (Rubin et al., 2015).

The Role of Technology in Friendships

Social technologies, such as online social media, instant messaging, and texting, play an increasingly significant role in peer interactions of children and especially of adolescents. In a large survey of 12- to 17-year-olds, the majority said that texting is one of the three most common ways they contact their closest friends, with phone calls and social networking sites just slightly less popular (Lenhart, 2015). As shown in Figure 13.2, there is a gender difference regarding which modes of communication are most often used; girls prefer texts, phone calls, and social media more than boys, while boys are more than 12 times as likely to use gaming sites to connect with friends.

Researchers have identified several key ways in which electronic communication facilitates the creation and maintenance of friendships among children (Schneider, 2016), including the following:

- *Greater anonymity* leads children and youth to reduce their social inhibitions, which, particularly for temperamentally shy children, could help them interact with others online. It goes without saying, however, that children can get carried away with this disinhibition.

- *Less emphasis on physical appearance* when conversation is done through typing or audio allows children and youth to connect with others based on their shared interests and their personalities rather than on their appearance. This tendency will be less true for video communication, of course.

- *More control over interactions* because they can control when, how, and with whom they connect leads children and youth to feel they are in charge of their social lives.

- *Finding similar peers* is much easier in the Internet age than in the past, which allows youth to connect with others who share their interests, thereby increasing their sense of belongingness and well-being.

- *24/7 access* means that children and youth can connect with friends and peers throughout their day. The downside is that such ubiquitous access can also interfere with school and sleep.

- *It's fun* to connect with friends online and to share thoughts, photos, videos, and game time online.

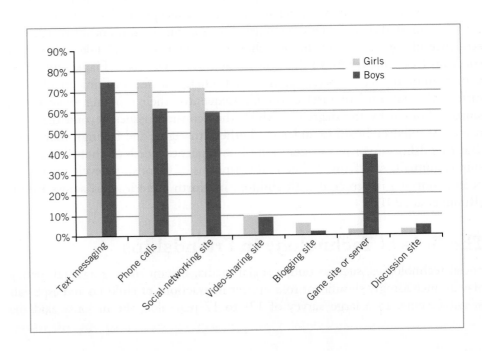

FIGURE 13.2 How adolescents stay in touch with their best friends Texting, phone calls, and social networks are the most common ways adolescents contact their best friends, although girls are more likely than boys to use each of these modes of communication. Boys, on the other hand, are much more likely than girls to use gaming sites to contact friends. (Data from Lenhart, 2015)

The potential for communication through technology to enhance friendships has been confirmed by research. A longitudinal study involving nearly 700 Dutch children ages 10 to 17 years found that the more they used instant messaging, the more comfortable they were introducing themselves to new people and suggesting to new friends that they hang out sometime (Koutamanis et al., 2013).

Given youths' tremendous use of digital technologies for their social interactions, social and behavioral scientists, as well as parents, have expressed concern about the effects that these modes of communication may have on social development—and especially on social relationships. Two major perspectives have guided research on this issue. One view is the *rich-get-richer hypothesis,* which proposes that those youths who already have good social skills benefit from the Internet and related forms of technology when it comes to developing friendships (Peter, Valkenburg, & Schouten, 2005; Schneider, 2016). In contrast, according to the *social-compensation hypothesis,* social media may be especially beneficial for lonely, depressed, and socially anxious adolescents. Specifically, because they can take their time thinking about and revising what they say and reveal in their messages, these youths may be more likely to make personal disclosures online than offline, which eventually fosters the formation of new friendships.

In support of the rich-get-richer hypothesis, researchers have found that adolescents who are not socially anxious or lonely use the Internet for communication more often than do adolescents who are anxious and lonely (Valkenburg & Peter, 2007; Van den Eijnden et al., 2008). Moreover, youths who were better adjusted at ages 13 to 14 were found to use social networking more at ages 20 to 22 and to exhibit a similarity in their online and offline social competence (e.g., in peer relationships, friendship quality, adjustment) (Mikami et al., 2010). By contrast, youth who are shy or withdrawn tend to inappropriately vent anger online, which impairs further interactions with peers (Laghi et al., 2013). Thus, socially competent people may benefit most from the Internet because they are more likely to interact in appropriate and positive ways when engaged in social networking.

However, consistent with the social-compensation hypothesis, lonely and socially anxious youths seem to prefer online communication over face-to-face communication (Peter et al., 2005; Pierce, 2009). Evidence also suggests that youths with high levels of depressive symptoms use online communication to make friends and to express their feelings (J. M. Hwang, Cheong, & Feeley, 2009), and that such use is associated with less depression for youths with low-quality best-friend relationships (Selfhout et al., 2009). Thus, the use of online technology often may provide depressed youths or those with low-quality offline friendships a method of communicating and obtaining emotional intimacy with peers.

Internet-based communication technologies appear to facilitate communication among existing friends, allowing them to maintain and enhance the closeness of their relationships (J. A. Bryant, Sanders-Jackson, & Smallwood, 2006; Peter et al., 2005; Valkenburg & Peter, 2011). In existing friendships, online communication seems to foster self-disclosure, which enhances friendship quality. In fact, many adolescents tend to use social-networking sites to connect with people they know offline and to strengthen these preexisting relationships (Reich, Subrahmanyam, & Espinoza, 2012). Similarly, the use of instant messaging has been associated with an increase in the quality of adolescents' existing friendships over time (Valkenburg & Peter, 2009). In contrast, high levels of Internet use primarily for entertainment (e.g., playing games, surfing) or for communication with strangers can harm the quality of friendships (Blais et al., 2008; Punamäki et al., 2009; Valkenburg & Peter, 2007) and predicts increases in anxiety and depression (Selfhout et al., 2009).

As described at the beginning of the chapter, cyberbullying represents another hazard of online communication. Box 13.2 explores this problem and interventions to reduce it around the world.

Effects of Friendships on Psychological Functioning and Behavior

The most important benefits of friendship, noted by Piaget, Vygotsky, and others, are emotional support and the validation of one's own thoughts, feelings, and worth, as well as opportunities for the development of important social and cognitive skills. However, there are some ways in which friends can have a negative influence on a child's development.

BOX 13.2 | a closer look

CYBERBULLYING

The tragic case of Amanda Todd described at the beginning of this chapter is an example of the extreme psychological harm that can result from cyberbullying. Unfortunately, instances of cyberbullying have been on the rise in recent years. According to a national survey of high school students, 7% of all adolescents aged 12 to 18 (roughly 1.7 million individuals) have reported some form of cyberbullying in the past school year (U.S. Department of Education, 2015). When asked whether they had ever been cyberbullied, 34% of adolescents in 2015 indicated that they had, compared with 19% in 2007 (Hinduja & Patchin, 2015). In a single year, twice as many students report being a victim of cyberbullying as report being a perpetrator. Frequent forms of cyberbullying are displayed below, with spreading rumors being the most common.

Several key groups seem to be in particular danger of cyberbullying. Girls and LGBTQ youth tend to report more cyberbullying than their peers (Rice et al., 2015). A large study of over 16,000 youth in Finland found that cyberbullying is more common in classrooms where students are accepting

of bullying, agreeing with such statements as, "Kids who are weak are just asking for trouble" (Elledge et al., 2013, p. 702).

Cyberbullies and cybervictims tend to be the same youths who are bullies or victims offline (Kowalski et al., 2014; Twyman et al., 2010). Cyberbullies tend to believe aggression is an acceptable way to solve problems and to be high in moral disengagement (Kowalski et al., 2014). Cybervictims, like victims offline, tend to be high in social anxiety, psychological distress, and symptoms of depression, as well as to have aggressive tendencies, poor anger management, and problems at school (Kowalski et al., 2014; Valkenburg & Peter, 2011). However, many cybervictims are also cyberperpetrators, perhaps in retaliation (Kowalski et al., 2014). This fact, and the fact that nearly all the relevant research is correlational, makes it difficult for researchers to tease apart the causes and effects of either cybervictimization or cyberperpetration.

Disturbingly, the perpetrators of cyberbullying may actually benefit socially from their behavior. A longitudinal study of adolescents in Belgium examined their Internet and texting use at age 13 and their peers'

sociometric ratings of them 8 months latter (Wegge et al., 2016). The children on average sent 40 text messages and spent 90 minutes online each day. For the purposes of the study, they reported the names of up to eight fellow students who either physically bullied them or cyberbullied them. About 10% of students reported being victims of cyberbullying, and the victims identified 10% of the students as perpetrators of cyberbullying; cyberbullying behavior was significantly correlated with physical bullying behavior. Adolescents who were perpetrators of cyberbullying at the beginning of the study were rated as being more popular over time by their peers, suggesting that the act of cyberbullying contributed to the increase in their social status—most likely through the sharing of their actions with other peers (Wegge et al., 2016).

In response to concerns among parents, school personnel, and children all around the world, a variety of school-based interventions to reduce cyberbullying have been developed and shown to be effective. The No Trap! intervention in Italy, which uses peer educators to increase awareness

Support and Validation

Friends can provide a source of emotional support and security, even at an early age. Children with best friends and with intimate, supportive friendships experience less loneliness than children who do not have a best friend or whose friends are less caring and intimate (Asher & Paquette, 2003; Erdley et al., 2001; Kingery, Erdley, & Marshall, 2011). Children who experience chronic friendlessness are more likely than children with friends to develop symptoms of depression and social withdrawal (Engle, McElwain, & Lasky, 2011; Ladd & Troop-Gordon, 2003; Palmen et al., 2011; S. Pedersen et al., 2007).

The support of friends can be particularly important during periods of transition. For example, young children have more positive initial attitudes toward school if they begin school with a large number of established friends as classmates (Ladd & Coleman, 1997; Ladd, Kochenderfer, & Coleman, 1996), likely because the presence of established friends in the early weeks of school reduces the strangeness of the new environment. Similarly, as children move into junior high or middle school, they are more likely to increase their levels of sociability and leadership if they have stable, high-quality, intimate friendships (Berndt, Hawkins, & Jiao, 1999).

Friendships may also serve as a buffer against unpleasant experiences, such as being yelled at by the teacher, being excluded or victimized by peers (Bukowski, Laursen, & Hoza, 2010; Ladd et al., 1996; Waldrip, Malcolm, &

among adolescents of the harms of cyberbullying, has succeeded in reducing both cyberbullying and cybervictimization (Palladino, Nocentini, & Menesini, 2016). A successful intervention implemented in Spain focuses on correcting children's beliefs that cyberbullying is normative by showing them that in fact only a small proportion of their peers engage in cyberbullying (Del Rey, Casas, & Ortega, 2016). In Germany, the Media Heroes program successfully reduces cyberbullying by increasing students' empathy for cybervictims (Schultze-Krumbholz et al., 2016). Schools in Australia that implemented the Cyber Friendly Schools program, which emphasizes appropriate and responsible online behavior ("netiquette"), experienced a decrease in cyberbullying and cybervictimization (Cross et al., 2016). Each of these programs is promising and together they illustrate that there are multiple effective strategies for reducing cyberbullying.

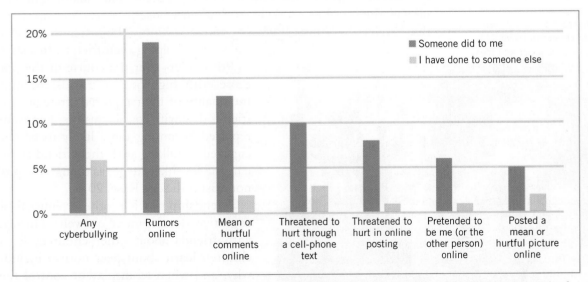

Most common forms of cyberbullying victimization and perpetration in a one-month period, as reported by a sample of 11- to 15-year-olds in the United States. (Data from Hinduja & Patchin, 2015)

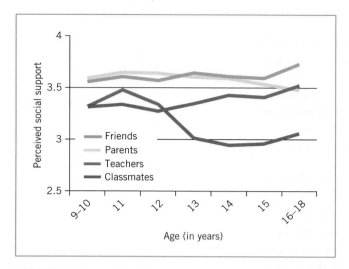

FIGURE 13.3 Age trends in social support from various sources Support from parents and support from friends are relatively stable across childhood and adolescence. Support from teachers drops dramatically once children enter adolescence, while at the same time support from nonfriend classmates increases slightly. (Data from Bokhorst, Sumter, & Westenberg, 2010)

Jensen-Campbell, 2008), or being socially isolated (i.e., having low levels of involvement with peers more generally; Laursen et al., 2007). This is especially true if friends provide intimacy, security, and help when needed (Kawabata, Crick, & Hamaguchi, 2010; M. E. Schmidt & Bagwell, 2007). In one study that demonstrated this effect, 10- and 11-year-olds reported on their negative experiences over a 4-day period, indicating shortly after each bad experience how they felt about themselves and whether or not a best friend had been present during each episode. The researchers also recorded the children's cortisol levels multiple times each day, as a measure of the children's stress reactions. The study showed that when a best friend was not present, the more negative children's everyday experiences were, the greater the increase in their cortisol levels and the greater the decline in their sense of self-worth following each experience (R. E. Adams, Santo, & Bukowski, 2011). In contrast, when a best friend was present, there was less change in cortisol response and in the child's self-worth due to negative experiences.

As noted previously, the degree to which friends provide caring and support generally increases from childhood into adolescence (De Goede, Branje, & Meeus, 2009). Indeed, around age 16, adolescents, especially girls, report that friends are more important confidantes and providers of support than their parents are (Bokhorst, Sumter, & Westenberg, 2010; Furman & Buhrmester, 1992; Helsen, Vollebergh, & Meeus, 2000; Hunter & Youniss, 1982) (Figure 13.3).

The Development of Social and Cognitive Skills

Friendships provide a context for the development of social skills and knowledge that children need to form positive relationships with other people. Throughout childhood, positive behaviors such as cooperation and negotiation are all more common among friends than among nonfriends. In addition, young children who discuss emotions with their friends develop a better understanding of others' mental and emotional states than do children whose peer relationships are less close (C. Hughes & Dunn, 1998; Maguire & Dunn, 1997). Children can use these skills when helping their friends. In a study of 3rd- to 9th-graders over the course of the school year, those with high-quality friendships improved in the quality of their reported strategies for helping friends deal with social stressors. For example, they reported becoming more likely to be emotionally engaged in talking with their friend about a problem and less likely to act as though the problem did not exist (Glick & Rose, 2011).

Friendship provides other avenues to social and cognitive development as well. Through gossip with friends about other children, for example, children learn about peer norms, including how, why, and when to display or control the expression of emotions and other behaviors (McDonald et al., 2007). As Piaget pointed out, friends are more likely than nonfriends to criticize and expand

Interactions with friends provide children with opportunities to get constructive feedback regarding their behavior and ideas.

on one another's ideas and to elaborate and clarify their own ideas (Azmitia & Montgomery, 1993).

This kind of openness promotes cognitive skills and enhances performance on creative tasks (Miell & MacDonald, 2000; Rubin et al., 2015). One demonstration of this was provided by a study in which teams of 10-year-olds, half of them made up of friends and the other half made up of nonfriends, were assigned to write a story about rain forests. The teams consisting of friends engaged in more constructive conversations (e.g., they posed alternative approaches and provided elaborations more frequently) and were more focused on the task than were teams of nonfriends. In addition, the stories written by friends were of higher quality than those written by nonfriends (Hartup, 1996).

Because friendships fill important needs for children, it is not surprising that having friends enhances children's social and emotional health. In fact, having close, reciprocated friendships in elementary school has been linked to a variety of positive psychological and behavioral outcomes for children, not only during the school years but also years later in early adulthood. In a longitudinal study, researchers looked at children when they were 10 years of age and again when they were young adults. They found that children who had best friends were viewed by classmates as more mature and competent, less aggressive, and more socially prominent (e.g., they were liked by everyone or were picked for such positions as class president or team captain). Thirteen years later, individuals who had best friends at age 10 reported greater success in college and in their family and social lives than did individuals who had not had a best friend at age 10. They also reported higher levels of self-esteem, fewer legal problems, and less psychopathology (e.g., depression) (Bagwell, Newcomb, & Bukowski, 1998). Thus, having a best friend in preadolescence relates not only to positive social outcomes in middle childhood but also to self-perceived competence and adjustment in adulthood.

The Possible Costs of Friendships

There can be costs to having friends, if the friends engage in or encourage negative behaviors rather than positive ones (Simpkins, Eccles, & Becnel, 2008). Friends who have behavioral problems may exert a detrimental influence, contributing to the likelihood that a child or adolescent will engage in violence, drug use, or other negative behaviors.

Aggression and disruptiveness In the elementary school years and early adolescence, children who have antisocial and aggressive friends tend to exhibit antisocial, delinquent, and aggressive tendencies themselves (Brendgen, Vitaro, & Bukowski, 2000; J. Snyder et al., 2008). However, the research in this area is correlational, so it is difficult to know if children pick friends who are like them, or if children become more like their friends over time. Aggressive and disruptive children may gravitate toward peers who are similar to themselves in temperament, preferred activities, or attitudes, thereby taking an active role in creating their own peer group (Knecht et al., 2010; Mrug, Hoza, & Bukowski, 2004). At the same time, friends appear to affect one another's behavior (Vitaro, Pedersen, & Brendgen, 2007). Through their talk and behavior, youths who are antisocial may both model and reinforce aggression and deviance in one another by making these behaviors seem acceptable, a process known as *deviancy training* (Dishion & Tipsord, 2011; Piehler & Dishion, 2007). Deviancy training has been found to begin as early as age 5 and to predict antisocial and delinquent behaviors into adolescence (Snyder et al., 2012).

The factors accounting for the association between friends' antisocial behavior may change with age. One longitudinal study found that early adolescents both affected and were affected by their peers, but that from ages 16 to 20, antisocial behavior was reinforced only through socialization by friends. After age 20, an age past which youths become more resistant to peer influence, there was little evidence of either process occurring (Monahan, Steinberg, & Cauffman, 2009).

Alcohol and substance abuse As in the case of aggression, adolescents who abuse alcohol or drugs tend to have friends who do so also (Jaccard, Blanton, & Dodge, 2005; Scholte et al., 2008). And again, as in the case of aggression, it is not clear if friends' substance abuse is a cause or merely a correlate of adolescents' substance abuse, or if the relation between the two is bidirectional.

There is some evidence that adolescents tend to choose friends who are similar to themselves in terms of drinking and the use of drugs (Knecht et al., 2011), and this may be especially true for those youths who are highly susceptible to peer pressure (Schulenberg et al., 1999). Yet there is also evidence that peers also cause adolescents to engage in drug and alcohol use (Branstetter, Low, & Furman, 2011). For example, adolescents who start drinking or smoking tend to have a close friend who has been using alcohol or tobacco (Selfhout, Branje, & Meeus, 2008; Urberg, Değirmencioğlu, & Pilgrim, 1997). Youths who are highly susceptible to the influence of their close friends seem particularly vulnerable to any pressure from them to use drugs and alcohol (Allen, Porter, & McFarland, 2006), and, as in the case of aggression, this is especially the case if those friends have high status in the peer group (Allen et al., 2012). There is also evidence that adolescents' use of alcohol and drugs and their friend's alcohol and substance use mutually reinforce each other, often resulting in an escalation of use (Bray et al., 2003; Popp et al., 2008; Poulin et al., 2011).

Yet another factor in the association between adolescents' abuse of drugs and alcohol and that of their friends is their genetic makeup. Youths with similar genetically based temperamental characteristics such as risk-taking may be drawn both to one another and to alcohol or drugs (Dick et al., 2007; J. Hill et al., 2008). Thus, friends' alcohol and drug abuse may be correlated because of their similarity in genetically based characteristics as well as in their socialization experiences, although the effect of a group of friends on youths' drinking is not due solely to genetics (Cruz, Emery, & Turkheimer, 2012).

The extent to which friends' use of drugs and alcohol may put individuals at risk for use themselves seems to depend, in part, on the nature of the child–parent relationship. Adolescents with substance-using close friends are at risk primarily if those adolescents' parents are uninvolved—low in warmth and low in control and monitoring (Kiesner, Poulin, & Dishion, 2010; Mounts & Steinberg, 1995; Pilgrim et al., 1999). If the adolescents' parents are authoritative in their parenting—high in control but also high in warmth (see Chapter 12)—those adolescents are more likely to be protected against peer pressure to

Peers can encourage youths to use alcohol, but it is also the case that youths who are prone to drinking may seek out peers who are similarly inclined.

OCEAN / CORBIS

use drugs. If the adolescents' parents are more authoritarian—high in control but low in warmth—those adolescents are more susceptible to peers' drug use and thus to using drugs themselves (Mounts, 2002).

Gender Differences in the Functions of Friendships

As children grow older, gender differences emerge in what girls and boys feel they want and get from their friendships. Girls are more likely than boys to desire closeness and dependency in friendships and also to worry about abandonment, loneliness, hurting others, peers' evaluations, and loss of relationships if they express anger (A. J. Rose & Rudolph, 2006). By age 12, girls, compared with boys, feel that their friendships are more intimate and provide more validation, caring, help, and guidance (Bauminger et al., 2008; A. J. Rose & Rudolph, 2006; Zarbatany, McDougall, & Hymel, 2000). For instance, girls are more likely than boys to report that they rely on their friends for advice or help with homework, that they and their friends share confidences and stick up for one another, and that their friends tell them that they are good at things and make them feel special.

Probably as a consequence of this intimacy, girls also report getting more upset than do boys when friends betray them, are unreliable, or do not provide support and help (MacEvoy & Asher, 2012). Girls also report more friendship-related stress, such as when a friend breaks off a friendship or reveals their secrets or problems to other friends, and greater stress from dealing emotionally with stressors that their friends experience (A. J. Rose & Rudolph, 2006). Ironically, the very intimacy of girls' close friendships may make them more fragile, and therefore of shorter duration, than those of boys (Benenson & Christakos, 2003; A. Chan & Poulin, 2007; C. L. Hardy, Bukowski, & Sippola 2002).

As discussed in Chapter 10, girls are also more likely than boys to *co-ruminate* with their close friends, that is, to extensively discuss problems and negative thoughts and feelings (R. L. Smith & Rose, 2011; see Box 10.4). Compared with their male counterparts, girls who are socially anxious or depressed seem more susceptible to the anxiety or depression of their friends (Giletta et al., 2011; M. H. Van Zalk et al., 2010; N. Van Zalk et al., 2011). Unfortunately, while providing support, a co-ruminating anxious or depressed friend may also reinforce the other friend's anxiety or depression, especially in young adolescent girls (A. J. Rose, Carlson, & Waller, 2007; Schwartz-Mette & Rose, 2012).

Girls and boys are less likely to differ in the amount of conflict they experience in their best friendships (A. J. Rose & Rudolph, 2006). Boys' and girls' friendships also do not differ much in terms of the recreational opportunities they provide (e.g., doing things together, going to one another's house) (Parker & Asher, 1993), although they often differ in the time spent together in various activities (e.g., sports versus shopping; A. J. Rose & Rudolph, 2006).

Review ————————————————————————

Children tend to become friends with peers who are similar in age, sex, race and ethnicity, and social behavior. This makes it especially difficult to distinguish between characteristics that children bring to friendships and the effects of friends on one another. Peers, especially friends, provide intimacy, support, and rich opportunities for the development of play and for the exchange of ideas. Children engage in more complex and cooperative play, and in more conflict, with friends than with nonfriends, and they tend to resolve conflicts with friends in more appropriate ways. With age, the dimensions of children's friendships change somewhat. Whereas young children define friendship primarily on the basis of actual activities with their peers and on the rewards and costs involved, older children increasingly rely on their friends to provide a context for self-disclosure, intimacy, self-exploration, and problem solving. Technology plays a strong role in how children initiate and maintain friendships, both for children who are outgoing and children who are more reserved. As was suggested by Piaget and Vygotsky, friends also provide opportunities for the development of important social and cognitive skills. However, friends can have negative effects on children if they engage in problematic behaviors such as aggression or substance abuse.

Peer Interactions

Most children usually have a small number of very close friends and some additional friends with whom they are less close but spend time or share activities. These groups tend to exist within a larger social network of peers that hangs together loosely. Although differential status of children in peer groups has been observed even in young children (Rubin et al., 2015), developmentalists have been especially interested in the emergence and functions of peer groups in adolescence and how status in such groups affects development.

Before examining peer status, however, we need to consider the nature of social groups in middle childhood and early adolescence.

Cliques and Social Networks in Middle Childhood and Early Adolescence

Starting in middle childhood, most children are part of a clique. **Cliques** are peer groups that children voluntarily form or join themselves. In middle childhood, clique members are usually of the same sex and race and typically number between 3 and 10 (X. Chen, Chang, & He, 2003; Kwon, Lease, & Hoffman, 2012; Neal, 2010; Rubin et al., 2006). Boys' groups tend to be larger than those of girls (Benenson, Morganstein, & Roy, 1998), although this difference decreases with age (Neal, 2010). By age 11, many of children's social interactions—from gatherings in the school lunchroom to outings at the mall—occur within the clique (Crockett, Losoff, & Petersen, 1984). Although friends tend to be members of the same clique, many members of a clique do not view one another as close friends (Cairns et al., 1995).

A key feature that underlies cliques and binds their members together is the similarities the members share. Like friends, members of cliques tend to be similar in their degree of academic motivation (Kindermann, 2007; Kiuru et al., 2009); in their aggressiveness and bullying; and in their shyness, attractiveness, popularity, and adherence to conventional values such as politeness and cooperativeness (Espelage, Holt, & Henkel, 2003; Kiesner, Poulin, & Nicotra, 2003; Leung, 1996; Salmivalli & Voeten, 2004; Witvliet, Olthof, et al., 2010). Not only do like individuals tend to group together in cliques, but membership in a clique also seems to increase the likelihood that children will exhibit behaviors similar to those of other group members (Espelage et al., 2003).

Despite the social glue of similarity, the membership of cliques tends to be relatively unstable (Cairns et al., 1995). In a study of 11- to 13-year-olds, only about

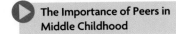
The Importance of Peers in Middle Childhood

cliques ■ friendship groups that children voluntarily form or join themselves

60% of the members of cliques maintained their group ties over the school year (Kindermann, 2007). The degree to which cliques remain stable appears to depend in large part on whether children are assigned to the same classroom from one year to the next (Neckerman, 1996).

Cliques in middle childhood serve a variety of functions: they provide a ready-made pool of peers for socializing; they offer validation of the characteristics that the group members have in common; and, perhaps most important, they provide a sense of belonging. By middle childhood, children are quite concerned about being accepted by peers, and issues of peer status become a common topic of children's conversation and gossip (Gottman, 1986; Kanner et al., 1987; Rubin, Bukowski, & Parker, 1998). Being a welcomed member of a larger peer group and being accepted by others who are similar to oneself in various ways provides a sense of personal affirmation.

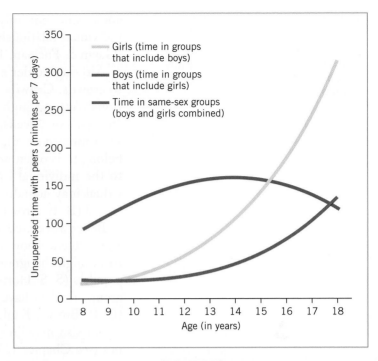

Cliques and Social Networks in Adolescence

From ages 11 to 18, there is a marked drop in the number of adolescents who belong to a single clique and an increase in the number of adolescents who have ties to many cliques or to peers at the margins of cliques (Shrum & Cheek, 1987). In addition, membership in a clique is fairly stable across the school year by 10th grade (Değirmencioğlu et al., 1998).

Although cliques at younger ages contain mostly same-sex members, by 7th grade, about 10% of cliques contain both boys and girls (Cairns et al., 1995). Thereafter, dyadic dating relationships become increasingly common (Richards et al., 1998); thus, by high school, cliques of friends often include adolescents of both genders (La Greca, Prinstein, & Fetter, 2001). As seen in Figure 13.4, time in groups with only same-sex peers peaks around age 13 years, whereas time in groups that include opposite-sex peers increases steadily from age 10 years onward—although this increase is much steeper for girls than for boys (Lam, McHale, & Crouter, 2014).

The dynamics of cliques also vary at different ages in adolescence. During early and middle adolescence, children report placing a high value on being in a popular group and in conforming to the group's norms regarding dress and behavior. Failure to conform—even something as seemingly trivial as wearing the wrong brand or style of jeans or belonging to an afterschool club that is viewed as uncool—can result in being ridiculed or shunned by the group. In comparison with older adolescents, younger adolescents also report more interpersonal conflict with members of their group as well as with members of other groups. In later adolescence, the importance of belonging to a clique and of conforming to its norms appears to decline, which may account for the decline in friction and antagonism within and between groups. With increasing age,

FIGURE 13.4 Change in the amount of unsupervised time children spend with same-sex and opposite-sex peers from age 8 to age 18 After age 13, time exclusively with same-sex peers decreases, while time with opposite-sex peers increases, although more so for girls than for boys. (Data from Lam, McHale, & Crouter, 2014)

 The Importance of Peers in Adolescence

Children and adolescents in cliques tend to spend a lot of time together and often dress similarly.

MARTIN THOMAS PHOTOGRAPHY / ALAMY

crowds ■ groups of adolescents who have similar stereotyped reputations

gang ■ a loosely organized group of adolescents or young adults who identify as a group and often engage in illegal activities

adolescents not only are more autonomous, but they also tend to look more to individual relationships than to group relationships to fulfill their social needs (Gavin & Furman, 1989; Rubin et al., 1998).

Although older adolescents seem less tied to cliques, they still often belong to crowds. **Crowds** are groups of people who have similar stereotyped reputations. Among high school students, typical crowds may include the "jocks," "freaks," or "geeks," (B. B. Brown & Klute, 2003; Delsing et al., 2007; Doornwaard et al., 2012; La Greca et al., 2001). Which crowd adolescents belong to is often not their choice; crowd "membership" is frequently assigned to the individual by the consensus of the peer group, even though the individual may actually spend little time with other members of that designated crowd (B. B. Brown, 1990).

Being associated with a crowd may enhance or hurt adolescents' reputations and influence how they are treated by peers. For example, someone labeled a freak might be ignored or ridiculed by people in groups such as the jocks or the populars (S. S. Horn, 2003). Thus, it is not surprising that youths in high-status groups tend to have higher self-esteem than do youths in less desirable crowds (B. B. Brown, Bank, & Steinberg, 2008). Being labeled as part of a particular crowd also may limit adolescents' options with regard to exploring their identities (see Chapter 11). This is because crowd membership may "channel" adolescents into relationships with other members of the same crowd rather than with a diverse group of peers (B. B. Brown, 2004; Eckert, 1989). Adolescents in one crowd, for instance, might be exposed to their peers' acceptance of violence or drug use, whereas members of another crowd may find that their peers value success in academics or sports (La Greca et al., 2001).

An example of the potential consequences of such channeling comes from a large study in Holland that found that adolescents' persistent self-identification with smaller and potentially nonconventional crowds (e.g., hip-hoppers, nonconformists, and metalheads) was associated with more consistent problem behaviors throughout adolescence, whereas adolescents' consistent identification with conventional groups was generally associated with less problematic behavior (Doornwaard et al., 2012). Thus, experiences in a crowd, like interactions with friends, may help shape youths' behavior.

Negative Influences of Cliques and Social Networks

Like close friends, members of the clique or the larger peer network can sometimes lead the child or adolescent astray. Preadolescents and adolescents are more likely to goof off in school, smoke, drink, use drugs, or engage in violence, for example, if members of their peer group do so (Lacourse et al., 2003; Loukas et al., 2008). Adolescents who are willing to do anything to be liked by peers are particularly at risk for chancy behaviors if engaging in them secures peer acceptance (Fuligni et al., 2001). Adolescents who are low in the ability to regulate their attention and behavior are also at increased risk if their peers are antisocial (T. W. Gardner, Dishion, & Connell, 2008).

Perhaps the greatest potential for negative peer-group influence comes with membership in a **gang,** which is a loosely organized group of adolescents or young adults who identify as a group and often engage in illegal activities. Gang members often say that they join or stay in a gang for protection from other gangs. Gangs provide members with a sense of belonging and a way to spend their time, but they also encourage—and indeed sometimes require—adolescents to engage in more illegal activities such as delinquency and drug abuse when they are in a gang than when they are not (Alleyne & Wood, 2010). The heightened risk for such activities seems to be due to both preexisting characteristics of the adolescents who join gangs and their experience of being in a gang (Barnes, Beaver, & Miller, 2010; DeLisi et al., 2009).

The potential for peer-group influence to promote problem behavior is affected by family and cultural influences. As noted in our discussion of friendship, having authoritative, involved parents helps protect adolescents from peer pressure to use drugs, whereas having authoritarian, detached parents increases adolescents' susceptibility to such pressure. Correspondingly, youths who have poor relationships with their mothers may be especially vulnerable to pressure from the peer group (Farrell & White, 1998).

One consequence of gang membership, and often a prerequisite for it, is the commission of violence, either against rival gang members or against random civilians. Increasingly, gangs are using social media to taunt rival gang members, such as by taking photos or videos in the rivals' neighborhood and posting them for rivals to see (e.g., "We're in your neighborhood . . . Ha, ha"; Patton et al., 2016, p. 3). Gangs also use social media to identify targets for violence; a gang outreach worker in Chicago described such a case:

> A kid got killed for having his face on Facebook and he wasn't even a bad guy. He wasn't a thug. . . . A car went by and they remembered his face on Facebook and that's why they killed him.
>
> (Patton et al., 2016, p. 4)

Gang members who engage in violence are also often victims of violence themselves, such as from fellow gang members or through fights with rival gangs (Pyrooz, Moule, & Decker, 2014). Shared experiences of violence perpetration and victimization often help shape the identity of the gang (Densley, 2012). Although many gang members act tough and do not express sympathy for their victims, they are not immune to the violence they perpetrate. Indeed, youth in gangs tend to exhibit symptoms of posttraumatic stress, especially if they have been forced to engage in violence toward others (Kerig et al., 2016).

Bullying and Victimization

Of course, many negative interactions among peers are initiated not by groups like gangs but by single individuals, often called bullies. Bullying takes four major forms (Huang & Cornell, 2015):

- **Physical bullying:** physically hurting or threatening to hurt someone
- **Verbal bullying:** insulting, teasing, harassing, or intimidating someone
- **Social bullying:** purposely excluding someone from conversations or activities, spreading rumors, or withholding friendship
- **Cyberbullying:** the use of technology including texts, e-mails, websites, videos, embarrassing photos, and fake profiles to harass or upset another person (see Box 13.2 for a more detailed discussion of cyberbullying)

Bullying is unfortunately not a rare experience in the lives of many children and adolescents. A recent study of over 7000 high school students in the United States found that while only 6% had been physically bullied, 11% had experienced cyberbullying, 19% had experienced social bullying, and 31% had experienced verbal

physical bullying ■ physically hurting or threatening to hurt someone

verbal bullying ■ insulting, teasing, harassing, or intimidating someone

social bullying ■ purposely excluding someone from conversations or activities, spreading rumors, or withholding friendship

cyberbullying ■ the use of technology, including texts, e-mails, websites, videos, embarrassing photos, and fake profiles, to harass or upset another person

bullying (Huang & Cornell, 2015). In this same survey, 13% of the adolescents admitted to bullying others in the previous year.

Why do some children bully others? In the moment, children engage in bullying in order to seem powerful to their peers and to gain status (Rodkin, Espelage, & Hanish, 2015). Yet if we consider why some children are bullies and others are not, a complex picture emerges. Consistent with Bronfenbrenner's bioecological model (see Chapter 9), bullying behavior is influenced by a range of individual, home, school, neighborhood, and societal factors (Swearer & Hymel, 2015). Children who are bullies tend to be callous and antisocial, susceptible to peer pressure, and higher in social status (Swearer & Hymel, 2015) and tend to have harsh and insensitive parents (Rodkin et al., 2015).

Victims, on the other hand, are likely to be rejected by peers, feel depressed, and do poorly in school, although some are aggressive as well (Barker et al., 2008; D. Schwartz et al., 1998; J. Snyder, Brooker et al., 2003; Swearer & Hymel, 2015; Tom et al., 2010). In addition, hereditary factors associated with aggression appear to predict peer victimization, suggesting that temperamental or other personal characteristics may increase the likelihood of children becoming both aggressive and victimized (Brendgen et al., 2011). For example, low self-regulation is related to both aggression and peer victimization (N. Eisenberg, Sallquist et al., 2009; Iyer et al., 2010) and may contribute to both. Of course, these same characteristics that elicit bullying may also be the result of bullying, and research suggests that there is a bidirectional relationship between aggression and victimization, with each leading to more of the other over time (Barker et al., 2008; Kawabata et al., 2010; Reijntjes et al., 2011; van Lier et al., 2012).

A small proportion of children (20% or less) are both perpetrators and victims of bullying and thus tend to be more aggressive, like bullies—yet are also more anxious, like victims (Lereya et al, 2015). Researchers speculate that these children may have developed hostile attributional biases as a result of being victims and that such biases make them more likely to act aggressively toward others in the future whom they suspect may harm them (Lereya et al., 2015). In one study in Ontario, Canada, that followed several hundred children from age 10 to age 14 (and thus included the transition into high school), about 6% of children started off as victims but transitioned into bullies themselves; these victims-to-bullies had rates of anxiety and depression that were as high as or higher than children who were just victims (Haltigan & Vaillancourt, 2014).

Although some children cope with bullies by ignoring or avoiding them, other children choose to stand up to bullies on behalf of victims. Research in Finland found that three-quarters of victims report having a classmate who defends them against bullies (Sainio et al., 2011) and that the children who defend others against bullies tend to have empathy for the victims and confidence that they will be successful (Peets et al., 2015). Importantly, when children stand up against bullies, they help protect the intended target in the immediate situation yet also help reduce bullying behavior in the classroom in the long-term (Hawkins, Pepler, & Craig, 2001; Sainio et al., 2011).

Unfortunately, peer victimization is not an uncommon event and can begin quite early. In one study in the United States, approximately one-fifth of kindergartners were repeatedly victimized by peers (Kochenderfer & Ladd, 1996). Over time, victimization by peers likely increases children's aggression, withdrawal, depression, and loneliness (Nylund et al., 2007; D. Schwartz et al., 1998), leading to hanging out with peers who are engaged in deviant behaviors (Rudolph

Understanding Bullying: An Interview with Robert Selman

et al., 2013), as well as problems at school and absenteeism (Juvonen, Nishina, & Graham, 2000; Kochenderfer & Ladd, 1996; Nakamoto & Schwartz, 2010). Although the rate of victimization generally appears to be lower among older children (Olweus, 1994), peer victimization is a serious problem that warrants concern, especially since the same children tend to be victimized again and again (Hanish & Guerra, 2000).

Romantic Relationships with Peers

Romantic relationships with peers tend to develop across early and middle adolescence in a typical sequence, progressing from no such relationship, to one casual relationship, to multiple casual relationships, and then finally to a single more committed relationship (Furman & Rose, 2015). On average, over half of 15-year-olds have dated someone (Price et al., 2016). As we saw in Chapter 11, for sexual-minority youth this relationship milestone used to occur in the late teens, but in younger generations of LGBT youth, relationships are beginning closer to the age 15 average (Martos et al., 2015; see Figure 11.6).

Young adolescents tend to be drawn to, and choose, romantic partners on the basis of characteristics that bring status—such as being stylish and having the approval of peers (Pellegrini & Long, 2007). By middle to late adolescence, traits such as kindness, honesty, intelligence, and interpersonal skills are also important factors in selecting a romantic partner (Ha et al., 2010; Regan & Joshi, 2003). Older adolescents are more likely than younger ones to select partners based on compatibility and characteristics that enhance intimacy, such as caring and compromise (Collins, 2003).

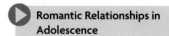

> ▶ Romantic Relationships in Adolescence

For many adolescents, being in a romantic relationship is important for a sense of belonging and status in the peer group (W. Carlson & Rose, 2007; Connolly et al., 1999). By late adolescence, having a high-quality romantic relationship is also associated with feelings of self-worth and a general sense of competence (Collins, Welsh, & Furman, 2009; Connolly & Konarski, 1994), and it can improve functioning in adolescents who are prone to depression, sadness, or aggression (V. A. Simon, Aikins, & Prinstein, 2008).

However, romantic relationships can also have negative effects on development. Early dating and sexual activity, for example, are associated with increased rates of current and later problem behaviors, such as drinking and using drugs, as well as with social and emotional difficulties (e.g., Davies & Windle, 2000; Zimmer-Gembeck, Siebenbruner, & Collins, 2001). This is especially true if the romantic partner is prone to delinquent behavior (Lonardo et al., 2009; S. Miller et al., 2009). When a romantic relationship breaks up, hurt feelings are typical outcomes for both, and adolescents of both genders can experience mental health problems during the dissolution stage of relationships (Price et al., 2016).

The quality of adolescents' romantic relationships appears to mirror the quality of their other relationships. Adolescents who have had poor-quality relationships with parents and peers are likely to have romantic relationships characterized by low levels of intimacy and commitment (Ha et al., 2010; Oriña et al., 2011; Seiffge-Krenke, Overbeek, & Vermulst, 2010) and by aggression (Stocker & Richmond, 2007; Zimmer-Gembeck, Siebenbruner, & Collins, 2004).

It is also believed that adolescents' working models of relationships with their parents tend to be reflected in their romantic relationships. This belief is supported by the finding that children who were securely attached at age 12 months were more socially competent in elementary school, which predicted more secure

The importance of compatibility and caring in romantic relationships increases with age in adolescence.

relationships with friends at age 16. The security of these friendships, in turn, predicted more positive daily emotional experiences in romantic relationships at ages 20 to 23 and less negative affect in conflict resolution and collaborative tasks with romantic partners (J. A. Simpson et al., 2007). Related research suggests that individuals who were securely attached in infancy, in contrast to those with insecure attachments, rebound better from conflicts with their romantic partners in early adulthood (Salvatore et al., 2011). Thus, romantic relationships appear to be affected in multiple ways by youths' history of relationships with parents and peers (Rauer et al., 2013).

Review

Very young children often interact with peers in groups, and dominance hierarchies emerge in these groups by preschool age. By middle childhood, most children belong to cliques of same-gender peers who often are similar in their aggressiveness and orientation toward school.

In adolescence, the importance of cliques tends to diminish, and adolescents typically belong to more than one group. The degree of conformity to the norms of the peer group regarding dress, talk, and behavior decreases over the high school years. Nonetheless, adolescents often are members of crowds—that is, groups of people with similar reputations. Even though adolescents often do not choose what crowd they belong to, belonging to a particular crowd may affect their reputations, their treatment by peers, and their exploration of identities.

Peer groups sometimes contribute to the development of antisocial behavior and the use of alcohol and drugs, although children and adolescents may also select peers with problem behaviors that are similar to their own. Membership in a gang is particularly likely to encourage problem behavior. The degree to which the peer group influences adolescents' antisocial behavior or drug abuse appears to vary according to family and cultural factors.

Involvement in romantic relationships increases with age in adolescence, and youths increasingly select partners based on intimacy, compatibility, and caring rather than on criteria such as social status and stylishness. Involvement in romantic relationships often is related to a sense of belonging, high self-esteem, and reduced depressive feelings, but it can also lead to involvement in risky behaviors, such as drinking and using drugs, and to feelings of rejection if one partner treats the other poorly. The quality of youths' romantic relationships tends to mirror the quality of their relationships with parents and friends.

Status in the Peer Group

Children and adolescents are often extremely concerned with their peer status: being popular is of great importance, and peer rejection can be a devastating experience. Rejection by peers is associated with a range of developmental outcomes for children, such as dropping out of school and problem behaviors, and these relations can hold independent of any effects of having, or not having, close friends (Gest, Graham-Bermann, & Hartup, 2001).

Because of the central role that peer relations play in children's lives, developmental researchers have devoted a good deal of effort to studying the concurrent and long-term effects associated with peer status. In this section, we will examine children's status in the peer group, including how it is measured, its stability, the characteristics that determine it, and the long-term implications of being popular with, or being rejected by, peers.

Measurement of Peer Status

The most common method developmentalists use to assess peer status is to ask children to rate how much they like or dislike each of their classmates. Alternatively, they may ask children to nominate classmates whom they like the most or the least, or whom they do or don't like to play with. The information from these procedures is used to calculate each child's **sociometric status,** or peer acceptance—that is, the degree to which a child is liked or disliked by the peers as a group. The most commonly used sociometric system classifies children into one of five groups: popular, rejected, neglected, average, or controversial (see Table 13.3) (Bukowski, Cillessen, & Velasquez, 2012).

Do popular children always remain at the top of the social heap? Do rejected children sometimes become better liked? In other words, how stable is a child's sociometric status in the peer group? The answer depends in part on the particular time span and sociometric status that are in question.

Over relatively short periods such as weeks or a few months, children who are popular or rejected tend to remain so, whereas children who are neglected or controversial are likely to acquire a different status (Asher & Dodge, 1986; X. Chen, Rubin, & B. Li, 1995; Newcomb & Bukowski, 1984; S. Walker, 2009). Over longer periods, children's sociometric status is more likely to change. In one study in which children were rated by their peers in 5th grade and again 2 years later, only those children who had initially been rated average maintained their status overall, whereas nearly two-thirds of those who had been rated popular, rejected, or controversial received a different rating later on (Newcomb & Bukowski, 1984). Over time, sociometric stability for rejected children is generally higher than for popular, neglected, or controversial children (Harrist et al., 1997; Parke et al., 1997; S. Walker, 2009) and may increase with the age of the child (Coie & Dodge, 1983; Rubin et al., 1998).

Characteristics Associated with Sociometric Status

Why are some children liked better than others? One obvious factor is physical attractiveness. From early childhood through adolescence, children who are rated as objectively attractive by observers are much more likely to be popular, and are less likely to be victimized by peers, than are children who are considered unattractive (Langlois et al., 2000; Rosen, Underwood, & Beron, 2011; Vannatta

sociometric status ■ a measurement that reflects the degree to which children are liked or disliked by their peers as a group

TABLE 13.3

Common Sociometric Categories for Peer Ratings

Popular—Children are designated as popular if they are rated by their peers as being highly liked and accepted and highly impactful.

Rejected—Children are designated as rejected if they are low in acceptance and preference and high in rejection but also high in impact.

Neglected—Children are designated as neglected if they are low in social impact—that is, if they receive few positive or negative ratings. These children are not especially liked or disliked by peers; they simply go unnoticed.

Average—Children are designated as average if they receive moderate ratings on both impact and preference.

Controversial—Children are designated as controversial if they are rated as very high in impact but average in preference. They are noticed by peers and are liked by quite a few children and disliked by quite a few others.

Source: Bukowski et al. (2012).

popular (peer status) ■ a category of sociometric status that refers to children or adolescents who are viewed positively (liked) by many peers and are viewed negatively (disliked) by few peers

et al., 2009). Athleticism is also related to high peer status, albeit more strongly for boys than for girls (Vannatta et al., 2009). Further affecting peer status is the status of one's friends: having popular friends appears to boost one's own popularity (Eder, 1985; Sabongui, Bukowski, & Newcomb, 1998). Beyond these simple determiners, sociometric status also seems to be affected by a variety of other factors, including children's social behavior, personality, cognitions about others, and goals when interacting with peers.

Popular and Likeable Children

Popular children—those who, in sociometric procedures, are rated by peers as being both accepted and impactful and thus have high status in the peer group—are not necessarily the most likeable. Children can be seen as influential in their peer group without necessarily being someone with whom everyone wants to be friends. One key difference between the two appears to be in levels of aggression; children who are likeable tend to be highly prosocial, while children who are popular exhibit both prosocial and aggressive behaviors (Cillessen, 2011).

Popular and prosocial children do tend to have a number of social skills in common. They tend to be skilled at initiating interaction with peers and at maintaining positive relationships with others (Rubin et al., 2015). Popular children are perceived by their peers, teachers, and adult observers as cooperative, friendly, sociable, helpful, and sensitive to others (Lansford et al., 2006; Rubin et al., 2015). They are also able to regulate their own emotions and behaviors (Kam et al., 2011) and tend to have a relatively high number of low-conflict reciprocated friendships (Litwack, Wargo Aikins, & Cillessen, 2012).

Children who are perceived as having high status in the group—those who are often labeled "popular" by other children and often seen as "cool"—tend to be viewed as above average in aggression and to use their aggressiveness to obtain their goals (P. H. Hawley, 2003; Kuryluk, Cohen, & Audley-Piotrowski, 2011; Prinstein & Cillessen, 2003). This association between aggression and perceived popularity has been observed among children as early on as preschool (Vaughn

HILL STREET STUDIOS / AGE FOTOSTOCK

Physically attractive children and teens tend to be more popular than their less attractive peers.

et al., 2003); for example, children rated by peers as being the leaders of their class are also observed to engage in more exclusion of other children, saying things like "There are too many kids here right now; maybe you can play with us later" and "You hate her, right?" (Fanger, Frankel, & Hazen, 2012, p. 235).

Many children engage in social bullying behaviors that are known as **relational aggression,** such as excluding others from the group, withholding friendship to inflict harm, and spreading rumors to ruin a peer's reputation. Unlike physical aggression, which harms the victim physically and perhaps emotionally, relational aggression is aimed at damaging the victim's peer relationships. It is particularly common among high-status children, particularly high-status girls (Cillessen & Mayeux, 2004; K. E. Hoff et al., 2009; Prinstein & Cillessen, 2003). Youth who are perceived as having high status, especially if they are aware of this perception, tend to increasingly use both relational and physical aggression, perhaps because they tend to be arrogant and are allowed by their peers to get away with it (Cillessen & Mayeux, 2004; Mayeux & Cillessen, 2008; A. J. Rose, Swenson, & Waller, 2004). Yet they may also use either physical or relational aggression as a means of both securing and maintaining their status in the peer group (Rubin et al., 2015). One troubling trend in relational aggression is the rise of cyberbullying (see Box 13.2).

Through the process of deviancy training mentioned earlier, high-status adolescents have particular influence over the negative behaviors of lower-status peers in their groups (Laursen et al., 2012; Prinstein, Brechwald, & Cohen, 2011). Highly aggressive children may even have high peer acceptance in some special cases, such as among adolescent males (but not females) who perform poorly in school (Kreager, 2007), in peer groups in which the popular members tend to be relatively aggressive (Dijkstra, Lindenberg, & Veenstra, 2008), or in social situations (e.g., classrooms) that have a strong hierarchy in terms of peer status (Garandeau, Ahn, & Rodkin, 2011).

Rejected Children

Rejected children tend to differ from more popular children in their social motives and in the way they process information related to social situations (Lansford et al., 2010). For example, rejected children are more likely than better-liked peers to be motivated by goals such as "getting even" with others or "showing them up" (Crick & Dodge, 1994). Rejected children also have more trouble than other children do in finding constructive solutions to difficult social situations, such as wanting to take a turn on a swing when someone else is using it. When asked how they would deal with such situations, rejected children suggest fewer strategies than do their more popular peers, and the ones they suggest are more hostile, demanding, and threatening (Dodge et al., 2003; Harrist et al., 1997; Rubin et al., 1998). (Box 13.3 discusses programs designed to help rejected children gain peer acceptance.)

Perhaps one reason rejected children are more likely to select inappropriate strategies is that their *theory of mind* (see Chapter 7) is less developed than that of their better-liked peers; they may therefore have greater difficulty understanding others' feelings and behaviors. In support of this idea, a longitudinal study of 5-year-olds in Italy found that children with lower theory of mind abilities had lower prosocial behavior one year later and then higher rejection by their peers two years later (Caputi et al., 2012).

A majority of rejected children tend to fall into one of two categories: those who are overly aggressive and those who are withdrawn.

relational aggression ■ a kind of aggression that involves excluding others from the social group and attempting to do harm to other people's relationships; it includes spreading rumors about peers, withholding friendship to inflict harm, and ignoring peers when angry or frustrated or trying to get one's own way

rejected (peer status) ■ a category of sociometric status that refers to children or adolescents who are liked by few peers and disliked by many peers

BOX 13.3 | applications

FOSTERING CHILDREN'S PEER ACCEPTANCE

Given the difficult and often painful outcomes commonly associated with a child's being rejected or having few friends, a number of interventions have been developed with the goal of improving children's peer interactions by helping them understand and communicate about their own and others' emotions, as well as regulate their own behavior (Domitrovich, Cortes, & Greenberg, 2007; Izard et al., 2008; P. C. McCabe & Altamura, 2011). As we saw in Chapter 10, emotion recognition and empathy are key skills children acquire as they develop. Thus, these interventions aim to improve children's relationships with their peers by enhancing aspects of their emotional development.

A notable example of this approach is the PATHS (Promoting Alternative Thinking Strategies) curriculum, in which children from 4 to 11 years of age learn to identify emotional expressions (using pictures, for example) and to think about the causes and consequences of different ways to express emotions (Domitrovich et al., 2007; Domitrovich et al., 2010). In addition, the program provides children with opportunities to develop conscious strategies for self-control through verbal mediation (self-talk) and practicing ways to self-regulate. The PATHS approach is illustrated by the Control Signals Poster (CSP), which, like the Turtle Technique discussed in Chapter 1, is designed to remind children how to deal with troubling social situations. As with a traffic light, the CSP uses the colors red, yellow, and green to encourage calming behaviors. When confronted with a stressful social situation, red signals children to stop and calm down, which they can do by breathing deeply and calmly identifying the problem and their feelings about it. Next, yellow signals children to take it slow, consider potential solutions, and decide on a productive course of action. Finally, green signals children to go and try out their chosen solution. A final step in this process encourages reflection and evaluation of the results, and the formulation of new plans if necessary (Riggs et al., 2006).

Programs like this one tend to succeed in fostering knowledge about emotions, self-regulation, prosocial behavior, and social competence—and sometimes in reducing social withdrawal and aggression as well (e.g., Bierman et al., 2010; Domitrovich et al., 2007; Izard et al., 2008; Riggs et al., 2006). Such improvements have been found especially for children with numerous problem behaviors and for children in disadvantaged schools (Bierman et al., 2010). The PATHS curriculum has been shown to be effective in randomized control trials in the United States (e.g., Crean & Johnson, 2013) and has been successfully adapted for use in a number of countries, including China (Kam, Wong, & Fung, 2011) and Pakistan (Inam, Tariq, & Zaman, 2015). The increases in social competence that often result as a consequence of participation in such an intervention would be expected to promote children's social status, although this issue usually has not been specifically tested.

Programs such as PATHS can help young children learn self-regulation and problem-solving skills.

STEVE DEBENPORT / GETTY IMAGES

Aggressive-rejected children According to reports from peers, teachers, and adult observers, 40% to 50% of rejected children tend to be aggressive. These **aggressive-rejected** children are especially prone to hostile and threatening behavior, physical aggression, disruptive behavior, and delinquency (Lansford et al., 2010; Newcomb, Bukowski, & Pattee, 1993; S. Pedersen et al., 2007; Rubin et al., 2006). When they are angry or want their own way, many rejected children also engage in relational aggression (Cillessen & Mayeux, 2004; Crick, Casas, & Mosher, 1997; Tomada & Schneider, 1997).

aggressive-rejected (peer status) ■ a category of sociometric status that refers to children who are especially prone to physical aggression, disruptive behavior, delinquency, and negative behavior such as hostility and threatening others

Even though they start out aggressive, aggressive-rejected children are at risk for increases in their aggression and delinquent behaviors over time, as well as for increases in symptoms of hyperactivity and attention-deficit disorder, conduct disorder, and substance abuse (Criss et al., 2009; Gooren et al., 2011; Lansford et al., 2010; Modin, Östberg, & Almquist, 2011; Sturaro et al., 2011; Vitaro et al., 2007). In one longitudinal study that followed more than 1000 U.S. children from 3rd to 10th grade (Coie et al., 1995), boys and girls who were assessed as rejected in 3rd grade were, according to parent reports, higher than their peers in behavior problems and in depression and loneliness 3 years and 7 years later.

Research in a variety of regions, including North America, China, and Indonesia, further indicates that rejected children, especially those who are aggressive, are more likely than their peers to have academic difficulties (X. Chen, Wang, & Cao, 2011; Chung-Hall & Chen, 2010; D. C. French, Setiono, & Eddy, 1999; Véronneau et al., 2010; Wentzel, 2009). In particular, they have higher rates of school absenteeism (DeRosier, Kupersmidt, & Patterson, 1994) and lower grade-point averages (Wentzel & Caldwell, 1997). Those who are aggressive are especially likely to be uninterested in school and to be viewed by peers and teachers as poor students (Hymel, Bowker, & Woody, 1993; Wentzel & Asher, 1995). Longitudinal research, conducted mostly in the United States, indicates that students' classroom participation is lower during periods in which they are rejected by peers than during periods when they are not, and that the tendency of rejected children to do relatively poorly in school worsens across time (Coie et al., 1992; Ladd, Herald-Brown, & Reiser, 2008; Ollendick et al., 1992). Approximately 25% to 30% of rejected children drop out of school, compared with approximately 8% or less of other children (Parker & Asher, 1987; Rubin et al., 1998). Clearly, children who are rejected by peers are at risk for academic and adjustment problems.

The key question is whether peer rejection actually *causes* problems at school and in adjustment, or whether children's maladaptive behavior (e.g., aggression) leads to both peer rejection and problems in adjustment (Parker et al., 1995; L. J. Woodward & Fergusson, 1999). Although conclusive evidence is not yet available, findings suggest that peer status and the quality of children's social behavior have partially independent effects on subsequent adjustment (Coie et al., 1992; DeRosier et al., 1994). The links are likely cyclical as well, such that children who are aggressive may become rejected by their peers, which then leads them to be both lonely and angry, which they express through more aggression (Leadbeater & Hoglund, 2009). Thus, it is likely that there are complex bidirectional relations among children's adjustment, social competencies, and peer acceptance (Boivin et al., 2010; Fergusson, Woodward, & Horwood, 1999; Lansford et al., 2010; Obradović & Hipwell, 2010).

Withdrawn-rejected children The second group of rejected children includes those who are **withdrawn-rejected.** These children, who make up 10% to 25% of the rejected category, are socially withdrawn and wary and, according to some research, are often timid and socially anxious (Booth-LaForce et al., 2012; Rubin et al., 2006). They frequently are victimized by peers, and many feel isolated, lonely, and depressed (Booth-LaForce & Oxford, 2008; Katz et al., 2011; Rubin, Coplan, & Bowker, 2009; Woodhouse, Dykas, & Cassidy, 2012). Friendlessness, friendship instability, and exclusion in 5th grade predict

withdrawn-rejected (peer status) ■ a category of sociometric status that refers to rejected children who are socially withdrawn, wary, and often timid

Children who are initially withdrawn may be rejected by their peers, leading them to withdraw from interactions even more.

increases in socially withdrawn behavior through 8th grade (Oh et al., 2008). Thus, as with aggression, social withdrawal may be both a cause and consequence of peer exclusion and rejection.

Over the course of childhood, withdrawn behavior seems to become a more reliable predictor of peer rejection. By the middle to late elementary school years, children who are highly withdrawn stand out, tend to be disliked, and appear to become increasingly alienated from the group as time goes on (Rubin et al., 1998). In some cases, however, children who are not initially socially withdrawn have social isolation forced upon them as they progress through school (A. Bowker et al., 1998). That is, children who are disliked and rebuffed by peers may increasingly isolate themselves from the group even if they initially were not withdrawn (Coie, Dodge, & Kupersmidt, 1990; Rubin et al., 1998).

Neglected Children

Research suggests that children who are withdrawn with peers but are relatively socially competent tend to be merely **neglected**—that is, they are not nominated as either liked or disliked by peers (Booth-LaForce & Oxford, 2008). These children tend to be both less sociable and less disruptive than average children (Rubin et al., 1998) and are likely to back away from peer interactions that involve aggression (Coie & Dodge, 1988). Children and adolescents who are simply not social and prefer solitary activities may not be especially prone to peer rejection (J. C. Bowker & Raja, 2011; Coplan & Armer, 2007). Neglected children perceive that they receive less support from peers (S. Walker, 2009; Wentzel, 2003), yet they are not particularly anxious about their social interactions (Hatzichristou & Hopf, 1996; Rubin et al., 1998). In fact, other than being less socially interactive, neglected children display few behaviors that differ greatly from those of many other children (Bukowski et al., 1993; S. Walker, 2009). They appear to be neglected primarily because they are simply not noticed by their peers.

Controversial Children

In some ways, the most intriguing group of children are **controversial** children, who, as indicated, are liked by numerous peers and disliked by numerous others. Controversial children tend to have characteristics of both popular and rejected children (Rubin et al., 1998). For example, they tend to be aggressive, disruptive, and prone to anger, but they also tend to be cooperative, sociable, good at sports, and humorous (Bukowski et al., 1993; Coie & Dodge, 1988). In addition, they are very socially active and tend to be group leaders (Coie et al., 1990). Aggressive children sometimes develop a network of aggressive friends and are accepted in their peer group (Xue & Meisels, 2004), and some elementary school and preadolescent children who start fights and get into trouble are viewed as "cool" and are central in their peer group (K. E. Hoff et al., 2009; Rodkin et al., 2000, 2006). At the same time, controversial children tend to be viewed by peers as arrogant and snobbish (Hatzichristou & Hopf, 1996), which could explain why they are disliked by some peers even if they are perceived as having high status in the peer group (D. L. Robertson et al., 2010).

neglected (peer status) ■ a category of sociometric status that refers to children or adolescents who are infrequently mentioned as either liked or disliked; they simply are not noticed much by peers

controversial (peer status) ■ a category of sociometric status that refers to children or adolescents who are liked by quite a few peers and are disliked by quite a few others

Cross-Cultural Similarities and Differences in Factors Related to Peer Status

Most of the research on behaviors associated with sociometric status has been conducted in the United States, but findings similar to those discussed here have been obtained in a wide array of cross-cultural research. In countries ranging from Canada, Italy, Australia, the Netherlands, and Greece to Indonesia, Hong Kong, Japan, and China, socially rejected children tend to be aggressive and disruptive; and, in most countries, popular (i.e., well-liked) children tend to be described as prosocial and as having leadership skills (Attili, Vermigli, & Schneider, 1997; Chung-Hall & Chen, 2010; D. C. French et al., 1999; Gooren et al., 2011; Hatzichristou & Hopf, 1996; Kawabata et al., 2010; D. Schwartz et al., 2010; Tomada & Schneider, 1997; S. Walker, 2009; Y. Xu et al., 2004).

Similar cross-cultural parallels have been found with regard to withdrawal and rejection. Various studies done in Germany, Italy, and Hong Kong, for example, have shown that, as in the United States, withdrawal becomes linked with peer rejection in preschool or elementary school (Asendorpf, 1990; Attili et al., 1997; Casiglia, Lo Coco, & Zappulla, 1998; D. A. Nelson et al., 2010; D. Schwartz et al., 2010).

Research has also demonstrated that there are certain cultural and historical differences in the characteristics associated with children's sociometric status. One notable example involving both types of differences is the status associated with shyness among Chinese children. In studies conducted in the 1990s, Chinese children who were shy, sensitive, and cautious or inhibited in their behavior were—unlike their inhibited or shy Western counterparts—viewed by teachers as socially competent and as leaders, and they were liked by their peers (X. Chen, Rubin, & B. Li, 1995; X. Chen, Rubin, & Z.-y. Li, 1995; X. Chen et al., 1999; X. Chen, Rubin, & Sun, 1992). A probable explanation for this difference is that Chinese culture traditionally values self-effacing, withdrawn behavior, and Chinese children are encouraged to behave accordingly (Ho, 1986).

In contrast, because Western cultures place great value on independence and self-assertion, withdrawn children in these cultures are likely to be viewed as weak, needy, and socially incompetent. However, Chen found that since the early 1990s, shy, reserved behavior in Chinese elementary school children has become increasingly associated with lower levels of peer acceptance, at least for urban children (X. Chen, Chang et al., 2005). Chen argues that the economic and political changes in China in the past decade have been accompanied by an increased valuing of assertive, less inhibited behavior. For children from rural areas who have had only limited exposure to the dramatic cultural changes in China in recent years, shyness is associated with high levels of both peer liking and disliking, albeit more to liking; thus, for groups somewhat less exposed to cultural changes, shyness is viewed with some ambivalence by peers (X. Chen et al., 2011; X. Chen, Wang, & Wang, 2009). In addition, for the rural children, being unsociable—that is, uninterested

Children who are well liked tend to have similar characteristics in many cultures, as do children who are rejected by their peers.

DESIGN PICS INC / ALAMY

in social interaction—is associated with peer rejection (X. Chen et al., 2009), whereas among North American children it often is not, at least for younger children. Thus, culture and changes in culture appear to affect children's evaluations of what is desirable behavior.

Review

Children's sociometric status is assessed by peers' reports of their liking and disliking of one another. On the basis of such reports, children typically have been classified as popular, rejected, average, neglected, or controversial. Well-liked, popular children tend to be attractive, socially skilled, prosocial, well regulated, and low in aggression that is driven by anger, vengefulness, or satisfaction in hurting others. Some children are rejected for being aggressive, while others are rejected for being withdrawn. Neglected children interact less frequently with peers than other children and display relatively few behaviors that differ greatly from those of many other children. Controversial children display characteristics of both popular and rejected children and tend to be very socially active. Culture plays a role in determining which child behaviors lead children to be rejected by their peers.

BOX 13.4 | a closer look

PARENTS' STRATEGIES FOR SHAPING PEER RELATIONSHIPS

Parents can play a number of active roles in their children's competencies in peer relationships. Two of the more salient ones are in monitoring their children's social life and in coaching their children in social skills.

Monitoring

Parents, especially those of young children, typically spend considerable time orchestrating and monitoring their children's interactions with peers. Parents decide with whom the children interact and how much time they spend with peers doing various activities. However, some parents are more thoughtful and active in this role than are others (Mounts, 2002). Preschoolers whose parents arrange and oversee opportunities for them to interact with peers tend to be more positive and social with peers, have a larger and more stable set of play partners, and more easily initiate social interactions with peers than do other children—so long as their parents are not overly controlling (Ladd & Golter, 1988; Ladd & Hart, 1992). Similarly, elementary school children whose parents allow them to engage in numerous social activities in the neighborhood

ANNA MOLLER / GETTY IMAGES

Parents may contribute to their children's development of social competence by arranging opportunities for their children to interact with peers.

and extracurricular activities at school are more socially competent and liked by peers (McDowell & Parke, 2009).

When children reach adolescence, they spend more time out of the home and with peers, and increasingly in unsupervised

The Role of Parents in Children's Peer Relationships

As we saw in Chapter 12, there is ample evidence that parents affect children's development in a multitude of ways. It is also true that parents affect children's peer relationships, both indirectly (through their interactions with their children) and directly (through monitoring and coaching; see Box 13.4). Attachment theorists (see Chapter 11) as well as social learning theorists (see Chapter 9) have asserted that early parent–child interactions are linked to children's peer interactions at an older age. We will explore some of these links below.

Relations Between Attachment and Competence with Peers

Attachment theory maintains that whether a child's attachment to the parent is secure or insecure affects the child's future social competence and the quality of the child's relationships with others, including peers. Attachment theorists have

---

situations (see Figure 13.5); thus, parental monitoring becomes especially important. Knowing where a child is and with whom at all times is important for his or her safety and well-being, and research has shown that it can reduce adolescents' engagement in risky behaviors in the future. A survey of over 5000 children between 12 and 14 years of age asked them how much their parents knew about their social lives: who their best friends are, who the parents of their best friends are, whom they are with when they are not at home, who their teachers are, and how they are doing in school (Abar, Jackson, & Wood, 2014). Those children who reported high levels of parental knowledge were less likely to get involved in heavy drinking, marijuana use, and delinquency in the ensuing four years. In addition, the more children engaged in these risky behaviors early in adolescence, the more they perceived their parents as monitoring them (Abar et al., 2014). Adolescents are thus both affected by parents' monitoring behavior and actively elicit monitoring through their own behavior.

In adolescence, monitoring may be affected by parents' cultural orientation. For example, in Mexican American families, parents who had a stronger orientation toward Mexican culture and the traditional Mexican value of familism—which emphasizes closeness in the family, family obligations, and consideration of the family in making decisions—placed more restrictions on adolescents' peer relationships than did parents whose orientation was less traditional. Parents who strongly identified with Mexican culture were also more likely to restrict their adolescents'—especially a daughter's—contact with peers if the adolescent reported associating with deviant peers (Updegraff et al., 2010).

Coaching

Preschool children tend to be more socially skilled and more likely to be accepted by peers if their parents effectively coach them on how to interact with unfamiliar peers (Laird et al., 1994; McDowell & Parke, 2009). Mothers of accepted children tend to teach their children group-oriented strategies for gaining entry into a group of peers; for instance, they may make suggestions about what to say when entering the group or they may discourage the child from disrupting the group's current activities. In contrast, mothers of children who are low in sociometric status often try to direct the group's activity themselves or urge their child to initiate activities that are inconsistent with what the group is currently doing (Finnie & Russell, 1988; A. Russell & Finnie, 1990).

Children may also benefit in their peer relations when their parents provide emotion coaching (see Chapter 10)—that is, explanations about the acceptability of emotions and how to appropriately deal with them (L. F. Katz, Maliken, & Stettler, 2012). Children whose parents use high levels of emotion coaching are, for example, more likely to use appropriate conflict-avoidance strategies (e.g., laughter) to deflect teasing, and they are less likely to display socially inappropriate behaviors when dealing with peers' provocations (L. F. Katz, Hunter, & Klowden, 2008). Some evidence suggests that a fairly high level of parental advice giving is sometimes associated with low levels of children's social competence and peer acceptance; but, in part, this may be because parents are more likely to try to help when their children are experiencing a high level of problems (McDowell & Parke, 2009). It is likely that coaching needs to be provided in a sensitive, skilled manner to be effective; that is, it should convey clear, useful information about others' feelings and behavior, along with strategies for dealing with them, and it should be presented in a way that does not overwhelm children or derogate them. For reasons that are not yet clear, mothers' coaching may be especially important for enhancing girls' social skills (Pettit et al., 1998).

suggested that a secure attachment between parent and child promotes competence with peers in at least three ways (Elicker, Englund, & Sroufe, 1992). First, securely attached children develop positive social expectations and are thus inclined to interact readily with other children, expecting these interactions to be positive and rewarding. Second, because of their experience with a sensitive and responsive caregiver, they develop the foundation for understanding reciprocity in relationships. Consequently, they learn to give and take in relationships and to be empathic to others. Finally, securely attached children are likely to be confident, enthusiastic, and friendly—characteristics that are attractive to other children and that facilitate social interaction.

Conversely, attachment theorists argue, an insecure attachment is likely to impair a child's competence with peers. If parents are rejecting and hostile or neglectful, young children are likely to become hostile themselves and to expect negative behavior from other people. They may be predisposed to perceive peers as hostile and, consequently, are likely to be aggressive toward them. These children may also expect rejection from other people and may try to avoid experiencing it by withdrawing from peer interaction instead (Furman et al., 2002; Renken et al., 1989).

There is a good deal of evidence to support these theoretical views. Children who are not securely attached do, in fact, tend to have difficulties with peer relationships. Toddlers and preschoolers who were insecurely attached as infants tend to be aggressive, whiny, socially withdrawn, and low in popularity in elementary school (Bohlin, Hagekull, & Rydell, 2000; Burgess et al., 2003; Erickson, Sroufe, & Egeland, 1985). Throughout childhood, these children, in comparison with securely attached children, express less happiness with peers, as well as less sympathy and prosocial behavior, and they demonstrate poorer skills in resolving conflicts (Elicker et al., 1992; Fox & Calkins, 1993; Kestenbaum, Farber, & Sroufe, 1989; Panfile & Laible, 2012; Raikes & Thompson, 2008).

Securely attached children, on the other hand, tend to be generally happy and to have good social skills; thus, not surprisingly, they tend to have high-quality friendships and to be relatively popular with peers—both as preschoolers (LaFreniere & Sroufe, 1985; McElwain, Booth-LaForce, & Wu, 2011) and in elementary school and adolescence (Granot & Mayseless, 2001; Kerns, Klepac, & Cole, 1996; B. H. Schneider, Atkinson, & Tardif, 2001; see Chapter 11). Even in late childhood and early adolescence, children with more and higher-quality (e.g., more intimate and supportive) friendships tend to be those with a history of a secure attachment (Dwyer et al., 2010; Freitag et al., 1996; B. H. Schneider et al., 2001; J. A. Simpson et al., 2007). Some recent research suggests that the security of attachment with fathers may be especially important for the quality of children's and adolescents' friendships (e.g., Doyle, Lawford, & Markiewicz, 2009; Veríssimo et al., 2011).

Thus, security of the parent–child relationship is linked with quality of peer relationships. This link probably arises from both the early and the continuing effect that parent–child attachment has on the quality of social behavior, as well as children's working models of relationships (Shomaker & Furman, 2009). However, it is also possible that

Children who have secure attachment relationships with their parents tend to develop better social skills than do their peers who are not securely attached.

PEATHEGEE INC / GETTY IMAGES

the individual characteristics of each child, such as sociability, influence both the quality of attachments and the quality of his or her relationships with peers.

Quality of Ongoing Parent–Child Interactions and Peer Relationships

Ongoing parent–child interactions are associated with peer relations in much the same way that attachment patterns are. For example, socially competent, popular children tend to have mothers who are warm in general; discuss feelings with them; and who use warm control, positive verbalizations, reasoning, and explanations in their approach to parenting (C. H. Hart et al., 1992; Kam et al., 2011; McDowell & Parke, 2009; Updegraff et al., 2010). Research that has investigated ongoing father–child interactions has found that they, too, can play a role in children's peer relationships. For example, fathers' warmth and affection toward their children have been linked to the positivity of children's interactions with close friends in the preschool years (Kahen, Katz, & Gottman, 1994; Youngblade & Belsky, 1992) and to children's peer acceptance in elementary school (McDowell & Parke, 2009).

Overall, research in this area suggests that when the family is generally characterized by a warm, involved, and harmonious family style, young children tend to be sociable, socially skilled, liked by peers, and cooperative in childcare (R. Feldman & Masalha, 2010). These associations may occur because such parenting fosters children's self-regulation (Eiden et al., 2009; N. Eisenberg, Zhou et al., 2005; Kam et al., 2011). In contrast, parenting that is characterized by harsh, authoritarian discipline and low levels of child monitoring is often associated with children's being unpopular and victimized (Dishion, 1990; Duong et al., 2009; C. H. Hart, Ladd, & Burleson, 1990; Ladd, 1992).

In considering findings such as these, it is generally assumed that quality of parenting influences the degree to which children behave in socially competent ways, which in turn affects whether children are accepted by peers. But as in the case of attachment, it is difficult to prove that quality of parenting actually has a causal influence on children's social behavior with peers. As noted in Chapter 12, it may be that children who are aggressive and disruptive because of constitutional factors (e.g., heredity, prenatal influences) elicit both negative parenting and negative peer responses (Rubin et al., 1998); or it may be that both harsh parenting and the children's negative behavior with peers are due to heredity. The most likely possibility is that the causal links are bidirectional—that parents' behavior affects their children's social competence and vice versa—and that both environmental and biological factors play a role in the development of children's social competence with peers.

Parents can also serve as a buffer when their children's peer relationships are not going well. A longitudinal study of several hundred 7- to 9-year-olds found that children having difficulty with their peers were less likely to experience increases over time in depressive symptoms if they had positive, close relationships with their parents (see Figure 13.5; Hazel et al., 2014). Similarly, maternal supportiveness has been found to buffer the links between adolescents' romantic stress and their later depressive symptoms (Anderson, Salk, & Hyde,

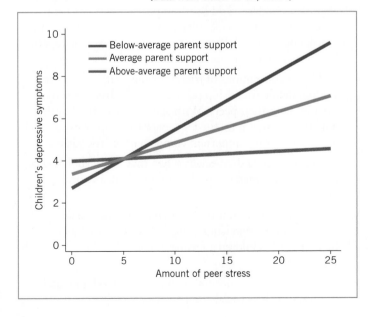

FIGURE 13.5 Associations among peer stress, parent support, and children's depressive symptoms When children have high peer stress and low parent support, they experience high levels of depressive symptoms. In contrast, children have the same level of depressive symptoms regardless of the amount of stress from their peers if they have supportive parents. (Data from Hazel et al., 2014)

2015). As with many aspects of children's lives, a risk factor in one relationship can be counteracted with a protective factor in another relationship. Parents do matter, even when it comes to children's relationships with their peers—and as displayed in Figure 13.5, relationships with parents may have a stronger link to mental health than peer relationships.

Review

Although differences in children's social behavior likely are based in part on constitutional factors that influence temperament and personality, parents appear to influence children's competence with peers. Attachment theorists have suggested that a secure attachment between parent and child promotes peer competence because securely attached children develop positive social expectations, the foundation for understanding reciprocity in relationships, and a sense of self-worth and self-efficacy. In fact, securely attached children tend to be more positive in their behavior and affect, more socially skilled with peers, and better liked than insecurely attached children. Parents can also influence their children's competence with peers through their beliefs and the social behaviors they teach their children. Parents can also buffer their children from some of the mental health problems linked with negative peer interactions.

CHAPTER SUMMARY

Friendships

- Children tend to become friends with peers who are similar in age, sex, and race, and who are similar in behaviors such as aggression, sociability, and cooperativeness—although each of these factors matters less as children age into adolescence.

- Even very young children have friends whom they prefer over other children. Toddlers and preschoolers engage in more complex and cooperative play with friends than with nonfriends, although because they spend more time together, they also engage in more conflict.

- Children's conceptions of friends change with age. Young children define friendship primarily on the basis of actual activities with their peers. With age, issues such as loyalty, mutual understanding, trust, cooperative reciprocity, and self-disclosure become important components of friendship.

- As children age and especially when they reach adolescence, friendships are characterized by more self-disclosure and intimacy.

- Electronic communication facilitates both the creation and maintenance of friendships, largely because it is available all the time, gives children a feeling of control, is fun, and can be anonymous.

- Having friends is associated with positive developmental outcomes, such as social competence and adjustment.

However, having friends who engage in problematic behaviors such as violence or substance abuse increases the risk that a child or adolescent will engage in such behaviors.

- Intervention programs can be helpful in teaching children social skills.

- The degree to which adults encourage children to play with unrelated peers varies greatly in different cultures, as does the degree to which parents expect their children to develop social skills with peers (e.g., negotiating, taking initiative, standing up for their rights). In addition, the hours children spend with unrelated peers varies considerably across cultures.

Peer Interactions

- Cliques are common beginning in middle childhood, with most clique members being of the same sex and having similar levels of aggressiveness and orientation toward school. Membership in these cliques is not very stable over time and clique members may not necessarily consider one another to be friends.

- In adolescence, the importance of cliques tends to diminish, and adolescents tend to belong to more than one group. With increasing age, adolescents are not only more autonomous but also tend to look more to individual relationships rather than to a social group to fulfill their social needs. Nonetheless, adolescents often are members of crowds. In adolescence, girls and boys associate with one another more with increasing age, both as members of social groups and in dyadic relationships.

■ In some circumstances, the peer group may contribute to the development of antisocial behavior, alcohol consumption, and substance use, although youths may also actively seek out peers who engage in similar levels of these behaviors.

■ Bullying is a relatively common experience among children and adolescents. Children who engage in bullying do so to gain power and status. Children who are the victims of bullying tend to suffer both behavioral and mental health problems.

■ Romantic relationships with peers are increasingly common in adolescence and can fulfill adolescents' need for intimacy. The quality of romantic relationships in adolescence mirrors the quality of other relationships, especially those with parents.

Status in the Peer Group

■ On the basis of their sociometric ratings, children typically have been classified as popular, rejected, neglected, average, or controversial, although these statuses can change over time.

■ Children's status in the larger peer group varies as a function of their social behavior and thinking about their social interactions, as well as their physical attractiveness.

■ Popular children, who are well liked by their peers, tend to be high in social skills and in regulation of their emotions and behaviors. In contrast, children who are high status may not be well liked and may use their status to engage in relational aggression.

■ Children who are rejected by their peers tend to be either aggressive or socially withdrawn. Aggressive-rejected children are low in social skills, tend to make hostile attributions about others' intentions, and have trouble coming up with constructive strategies for dealing with difficult social

situations. Withdrawn-rejected children tend to feel isolated, lonely, and depressed over time.

■ Neglected children—those who are not nominated by peers as either liked or disliked—tend to be less sociable, aggressive, and disruptive than average children. They display relatively few behaviors that differ greatly from those of average children and appear not to be noticed by other children.

■ Controversial children tend to have characteristics of both popular and rejected children: they tend to be aggressive, disruptive, and prone to anger, as well as helpful, cooperative, sociable, good at sports, and humorous.

■ Across numerous cultures, children who are popular or rejected share similar characteristics. However, reticent behavior may be more valued in some East Asian cultures and has, at least until recently, been related in China to others' perceptions of a child's social competence.

The Role of Parents in Children's Peer Relationships

■ Consistent with the predictions of attachment theorists, securely attached children tend to be more positive in their behavior and affect, more socially skilled, and better liked than insecurely attached children.

■ Parents of socially competent and popular children are more likely than parents of less competent children to use warm control, positive verbalizations, reasoning, and explanations in interactions with their children. They also hold more positive beliefs about their children's abilities. It is likely that the causal links between quality of parenting and children's social competence are bidirectional and that both environmental and biological factors play a role in the development of children's social competence with peers.

■ Positive relationships with parents can buffer children against the potential negative effects of peer relationships.

Test Yourself

1. Friendships emerge in early childhood as children become more capable of cooperation and coordinated interactions, and as they learn to trust those individuals whom they consider to be friends. Which of the following statements is not true of these early childhood friendships?
   a. Preschool friends are more likely than nonfriends to resume interactions with each other following a conflict.
   b. Preschool friends quarrel less with each other than they do with nonfriends.
   c. Preschool friends tend to resolve conflicts in an equitable manner.
   d. Pretend play occurs more often between friends than nonfriends.

2. Research indicates that friendships change in what significant respect as children grow older?
   a. Average duration of children's friendships lengthens.
   b. Level and importance of the intimacy increases.
   c. Children are more willing to display aggressive behaviors with their friends.
   d. The total number of close friends that an individual reports having increases.

3. Friendships in adolescence tend to be more _____ .
   a. stable
   b. co-dependent
   c. harmful
   d. exclusive

4. Tyler is 15 years old. He thinks of himself as socially awkward. He has a few close friends, but tends to be shy and anxious around most peers and adults. Tyler is more comfortable in online chat rooms and other social media forums, and he tends to express his emotions more openly among his peers in these settings. Tyler's experience supports which perspective on the impact of social media on development?
   a. the rich-get-richer hypothesis
   b. the sociometric status perspective
   c. the social-compensation hypothesis
   d. Selman's perspective

5. What does the term *deviancy training* refer to?
   a. An intervention to discourage aggressive tendencies by encouraging supportive peer interactions
   b. Parental interactions that have the unintended consequence of increasing risky and aggressive behaviors in children
   c. The process through which antisocial youth reinforce aggressive and deviant tendencies in one another
   d. A school-based intervention to provide methods for teachers and other adults to maintain order among at-risk children

6. According to research, which of the following is true of relationships between girls in middle childhood and adolescence compared with those of boys of the same ages?
   a. Girls' friendships tend to last longer than those of boys.
   b. Girls are less likely than boys to discuss their problems and negative thoughts.
   c. Girls are more likely than boys to desire closeness and to worry about abandonment from their friends.
   d. Girls tend to engage in more conflict with their best friends than do boys.

7. In the context of child development, a group of people who have similar stereotyped reputations is called a _____ .
   a. crowd
   b. clique
   c. gang
   d. network

8. Over the course of adolescence, membership in cliques _____ .
   a. becomes increasingly gender-specific
   b. remains stable
   c. increases
   d. diminishes

9. Bullying and victimization are said to have a bidirectional relationship. Which of the following statements best describes that relationship?
   a. Bullying may lead to behavioral changes in victims (e.g., becoming withdrawn) that in turn elicit more bullying from the bullies.
   b. Both bullies and victims often have insecure attachments to their parents.

   c. Aggressors tend to choose as victims individuals who they feel may threaten them in the future.
   d. Both aggressive children and victimized children tend to befriend other children who share their status.

10. The degree to which a child is liked or disliked by peers is a measure of that child's _____ .
    a. sociometric status
    b. relational aggression
    c. social-compensation level
    d. social compensation

11. Alex tends to be cooperative and sociable, but he is also prone to outbursts and can be disruptive in class. He is well liked by some of his classmates, but disliked by others. Which of the following best describes Alex's sociometric status?
    a. confused
    b. aggressive-rejected
    c. controversial
    d. popular-unpopular

12. Beth often ascribes negative motives to others when she doesn't get her way; consequently, she will sometimes lash out at other children as a way to get even for perceived slights. Rather than cooperate or take turns with other children, she is more apt to cut in line or push another child out of the way. Which of the following best describes Beth's sociometric status?
    a. popular
    b. rejected
    c. neglected
    d. controversial

13. Popular and likeable children can both be influential in their peer group, but popular children are more likely than likeable children to be _____ .
    a. socially perceptive
    b. securely attached
    c. aggressive
    d. intelligent

14. Children who are neither liked nor disliked by their peers are considered to be _____ .
    a. controversial
    b. neglected
    c. withdrawn-rejected
    d. aggressive-rejected

15. Which of the following is *not* one of the three ways that secure parent–child attachment promotes peer competence, according to attachment theorists?
    a. Securely attached children develop positive social expectations.
    b. Securely attached children understand reciprocity in relationships.
    c. Securely attached children have exclusive friendships with one or two people.
    d. Securely attached children are more likely to exhibit appealing qualities such as confidence and enthusiasm.

LaunchPad
macmillan learning

Don't stop now! Research shows that testing yourself is a powerful learning tool. Visit LaunchPad to access the LearningCurve adaptive quizzing system, which gives you a personalized study plan to help build your mastery of the chapter material through videos, activities, and more. **Go to launchpadworks.com.**

Critical Thinking Questions

1. What are some of the ways in which same-age peer relationships and relationships with older or younger siblings might differ? On what dimensions are they typically the same?

2. What procedures and methods might someone use to assess which 2-year-old playmates in a group are close friends? How would these methods be the same or different if one were assessing close friendships at ages 6, 11, and 17?

3. What are the similarities and differences between popular and controversial children? Between aggressive-rejected and withdrawn-rejected children?

4. Given what you read about bullies in this chapter, design an intervention that can both reduce bullying behavior and support the victims of bullying.

5. Consider a child who is growing up in an isolated area with few peers nearby and is being schooled at home. In what ways might his or her daily experience differ from that of children attending school? How might this affect his or her development, positively or negatively? What factors might mitigate or increase these effects?

6. Electronic communication can be a great way for children and adolescents to connect with new and old friends, but it exposes them to potential cyberbullying. What are some ways that parents and schools can ensure children enjoy the benefits of electronic communication without its risks?

Key Terms

aggressive-rejected (peer status), p. 576
cliques, p. 566
controversial (peer status), p. 578
crowds, p. 568
cyberbullying, p. 569
friend, p. 552

gang, p. 568
neglected (peer status), p. 578
peers, p. 550
physical bullying, p. 569
popular (peer status), p. 574
rejected (peer status), p. 575

relational aggression, p. 575
social bullying, p. 569
sociometric status, p. 573
verbal bullying, p. 569
withdrawn-rejected (peer status), p. 577

▶ Student Video Activities

Developmental Differences in Children's Definitions of Friendship
The Development of Play in Early Childhood
The Importance of Peers in Middle Childhood

The Importance of Peers in Adolescence
Understanding Bullying: An Interview with Robert Selman
Romantic Relationships in Adolescence

Answers to Test Yourself

1. b, **2.** b, **3.** d, **4.** c, **5.** c, **6.** c, **7.** a, **8.** d, **9.** a, **10.** a, **11.** c, **12.** b, **13.** c, **14.** b, **15.** c

VICTOR GILBERT (1847–1933), *Make Believe*

Moral Development

Themes

- ■ Nature and Nurture
- ■ The Active Child
- ■ Continuity/Discontinuity
- ■ Mechanisms of Change
- ■ The Sociocultural Context
- ■ Individual Differences
- ■ Research and Children's Welfare

On April 15, 2013, two homemade bombs detonated near the finish line of the Boston Marathon. Three people were killed, including an 8-year-old boy, and more than 260 were injured. The bombs were later found to have been made and brought to the site by 26-year-old Tamerlan Tsarnaev and his 19-year-old brother, Dhzokhar Tsarnaev. The brothers also shot and killed a campus police officer at the Massachusetts Institute of Technology. Tamerlan was later killed during a shootout with police, while Dzhokhar was captured by police, put on trial, and convicted of 30 federal charges that included the use of a weapon of mass destruction.

In the sentencing phase of the trial, Dzhokhar's lawyers argued that he was overly influenced by his older brother, Tamerlan, who wanted to punish the United States for its involvement in wars in Muslim countries. The lawyers also cited teachers and friends who said that they had known Dzhokhar to be thoughtful, respectful, kind, and considerate. Despite these claims, the jury found Dzhokhar to be accountable for the crimes committed and, in May of 2015, sentenced him to death for his involvement in the Boston Marathon bombing (Rosen, 2015).

A year prior to that bombing, Malala Yousafzai, a young girl living in the Swat Valley of Pakistan, had been advocating for the education of girls in defiance of local Taliban leaders who banned girls from attending school and even attacked some girls' schools. She gave speeches, wrote a blog for the BBC, and was the subject of a documentary by the *New York Times*. She was awarded the first National Peace Prize of Pakistan in 2011.

Then, in October of 2012, when Malala was 15 years old, a Taliban gunman shot her point blank in the head right after she had boarded a bus to return home after school. She survived the assassination attempt and received extensive medical treatment in England. She was unable to return to Pakistan, because the Taliban made clear that it still planned to kill her. She currently is living in exile with her family.

Despite these considerable obstacles, Malala remains undeterred from her main goal. She has continued to advocate for children's education in general and for girls' education in particular. She has given speeches to the United Nations, wrote a best-selling autobiography, and was the subject of a major 2015 documentary. Two million people signed a right–to-education petition started in her honor. She now heads the Malala Fund (www.malala.org), which works to support the education and empowerment of girls throughout the world.

In recognition of her efforts to promote access to education for all children, Malala was awarded the 2014 Nobel Peace Prize, which she shared with Kailash Satyarthi, an advocate for the rights of children in India. At 17, Malala was the youngest recipient of the prize in history.

Why do some children and adolescents act in moral and prosocial ways, like Malala, while others act in immoral and antisocial ways, like Dzhokhar? The starting point for answering this question lies in understanding the aspects of children's thinking and behavior that contribute to morality. To act in moral ways on a regular basis, children must have an understanding of right and wrong and the reasons why certain actions are moral or immoral. In addition, they must have a conscience—that is, they must be concerned about acting in a moral manner and feel guilty when they do not.

When studying moral development, researchers have focused on a number of different questions related to these requirements. How do children think about

HANDOUT / GETTY IMAGES

Dzhokhar Tsarnaev's lawyers argued that he was overly influenced by his older brother in carrying out the Boston Marathon bombing; a jury rejected that argument and held him accountable for his involvement in the crime.

moral issues, and how does that thinking change as they age? Does children's reasoning about moral issues relate to their behavior? How early do caring and sharing, or their opposites aggression and cruelty, first appear in children? What factors contribute to differences among children in the degree to which they display helpful and caring behaviors or *antisocial behaviors*—namely, disruptive, hostile, or aggressive behaviors? Can steps be taken to help children develop caring and helpful behaviors and reduce the likelihood of their developing immoral or antisocial behaviors?

We start our discussion of moral development by examining children's moral judgment—that is, how children think about situations involving moral decisions. Then we examine findings on the early emergence of conscience and the development of *prosocial* behaviors—behaviors such as helping and sharing that benefit others. Next, we turn to aggression and other antisocial behaviors such as stealing. As you will see, children's moral development is influenced by advances in their social and cognitive capacities, as well as by both genetic factors and environmental factors (see Chapter 3), including family and culture. Therefore, the themes of *individual differences, nature and nurture,* and the *sociocultural context* will be prominent in our discussion of moral development. Theory and research on moral judgment grew out of Piaget's work in this area, which, like his theory of cognitive development (see Chapter 4), involves stages of development and assumes that children actively try to understand the world around them. Consequently, the themes of *continuity/discontinuity, mechanisms of change,* and the *active child* are evident in our consideration of the development of moral judgment as well. Also in play is the theme of *research and children's welfare,* as we survey intervention programs that are designed to promote prosocial thinking and behavior and to prevent antisocial behavior.

At age 15, Malala Yousafzai survived an assassination attempt by the Taliban for her advocacy of education for girls, and at age 17 she became the youngest recipient of the Nobel Peace Prize.

Moral Judgment

The morality of a given action is not always obvious. Consider a girl who steals food to feed her starving sister. Stealing is usually regarded as an immoral behavior, but obviously the morality of this girl's behavior is not so clear. Or consider an adolescent male who offers to help fix a friend's bike but does so because he wants to borrow it later, or perhaps because he wants to find out if the bike is worth stealing. Although this adolescent's behavior may appear altruistic on the surface, it is morally ambiguous, at best, in the first instance and clearly immoral in the second. These examples illustrate that the morality of a behavior is based partly on the thinking—including conscious intentions and goals—that underlies the behavior.

Indeed, some psychologists (as well as philosophers and educators) argue that the reasoning behind a given behavior is critical for determining whether that behavior is moral or immoral, and they maintain that changes in moral reasoning form the basis of moral development (Turiel, 2014). As a consequence, much research on children's moral development has focused on how children think when they try to resolve moral conflicts and how their reasoning about moral issues changes with age. The most important contributors to current understanding of the development of children's moral reasoning are Jean Piaget and Lawrence Kohlberg, both of whom took a cognitive developmental approach to studying the development of morality.

Piaget's Theory of Moral Judgment

The ideas presented in Piaget's book *The Moral Judgment of the Child* (1932/1965) form the foundation of cognitive theories about the origin of morality. Piaget describes how children's moral reasoning changes from a rigid acceptance of the dictates and rules of authorities to an appreciation that moral rules are a product of social interaction and are therefore modifiable. Piaget believed that interactions with peers, more than adult influence, account for advances in children's moral reasoning.

Piaget initially studied children's moral reasoning by observing children playing games, such as marbles, in which they often deal with issues of rules and fairness. In addition, Piaget interviewed children to examine their thinking about questions such as what constitutes a transgression of a rule, what role a person's intentions plays in morality, whether certain punishments are just, and how goods can be distributed among individuals fairly. In these open-ended interviews, he typically presented children with pairs of short vignettes such as the following:

> A little boy who is called John is in his room. He is called to dinner. He goes into the dining room. But behind the door there was a chair, and on the chair there was a tray with fifteen cups on it. John couldn't have known that there was all this behind the door. He goes in, the door knocks against the tray, bang go the fifteen cups, and they all get broken!
>
> Once there was a little boy whose name was Henry. One day when his mother was out he tried to get some jam out of the cupboard. He climbed up onto a chair and stretched out his arm. But the jam was too high up and he couldn't reach it and have any. But while he was trying to get it he knocked over a cup. The cup fell down and broke.
>
> (Piaget, 1932/1965, p. 122)

After children heard these stories, they were asked which boy was naughtier, and why. Children younger than 6 years typically said that the child who broke 15 cups was naughtier. In contrast, older children said that the child who was trying to pilfer jam was naughtier, even though he broke only one cup. Partly on the basis of children's responses to such vignettes, Piaget concluded that there are two stages of development in children's moral reasoning, one in which the outcome is more important than the intention and a second stage in which the intention is seen as paramount, as well as a transitional period between them.

The Stage of Heteronomous Morality

The first of Piaget's stages of moral development, which he referred to as *heteronomous morality,* is most characteristic of children who have not achieved Piaget's stage of concrete operations—that is, children younger than 7 years who are in the preoperational stage (see Chapter 4). Children in this stage regard rules and duties to others as unchangeable "givens." In their view, justice is whatever authorities (adults, rules, or laws) say is right, and authorities' punishments for noncompliance are always justified. Acts that are not consistent with rules and authorities' dictates are "bad"; acts that are consistent with them are "good." It is in this stage that children believe that what determines whether an action is good or bad are the consequences of the action, not the motives or intentions behind it.

Piaget suggested that young children's belief that rules are unchangeable is due to two factors, one social and one cognitive. First, Piaget argued that parental control of children is coercive and unilateral, leading to children's unquestioning respect for rules set by adults. Second, children's cognitive immaturity causes them to believe that rules are "real" things, like chairs or gravity, that exist outside people and are not the product of the human mind.

The Transitional Period

According to Piaget, the period from about age 7 or 8 through age 10 represents a transition from the heteronomous morality of constraint to the next stage. During this transitional period, which occurs as children are reaching the concrete operational stage of cognitive development, children typically have more interactions with peers than they did previously; these interactions are more egalitarian, with more give-and-take, than in their interactions with adults. In games with peers, for instance, children learn that rules can be constructed and changed by the group. Whereas the preoperational stage is characterized by egocentrism and an inability to take perspectives other than their own (see Chapter 4), children in this transitional period leading to the concrete operational stage increasingly learn to take one another's perspective and to cooperate. As a consequence, children start to value fairness and equality and begin to become autonomous in their thinking about moral issues. Piaget viewed children as taking an active role in this transition, using information from their social interactions to figure out how moral decisions are made and how rules are constructed.

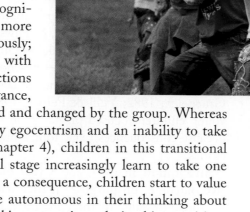

CORBIS

Piaget argued that through games children learn that rules are a creation of human beings—that they are not absolute but rather interpreted and that they can be changed by the consensus of the peer group.

The Stage of Autonomous Morality

By about age 11 or 12, Piaget's second stage of moral reasoning emerges. In this stage, referred to as the stage of *autonomous morality*, children no longer accept blind obedience to authority as the basis of moral decisions. They fully understand that rules are the product of social agreement and can be changed if the majority of a group agrees to do so. In addition, they consider fairness and equality among people as important factors to consider when constructing rules. Children at this stage believe that punishments should "fit the crime" and that adults are not always fair in how they deliver punishment. They also consider individuals' motives and intentions when evaluating their behavior; thus, they view breaking one cup while trying to pilfer jam as worse than accidentally breaking 15 cups.

According to Piaget, children typically progress from the heteronomous morality of constraint to autonomous moral reasoning. Individual differences in the rate of children's progress are due to numerous factors, including differences in cognitive maturity, in opportunities for interactions with peers and for reciprocal role-taking, and in how authoritarian and punitive parents are with them.

Critique of Piaget's Theory

Piaget's general vision of moral development has received some support from empirical research. Studies of children from many countries and various racial or ethnic groups have shown that as they age, boys and girls increasingly take motives and intentions into account when judging the morality of actions (N. E. Berg & Mussen, 1975; Lickona, 1976). In addition, parental punitiveness has been

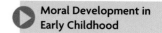

▶ Moral Development in Early Childhood

associated with less mature moral reasoning and moral behavior, as Piaget predicted (Laible, Eye, & Carlo, 2008). Finally, consistent with Piaget's belief that cognitive development plays a role in the development of moral judgment, children's performances on tests of perspective-taking skills, Piagetian logical tasks, and IQ have all been associated with their level of moral judgment (N. E. Berg & Mussen, 1975; Lickona, 1976).

Some aspects of Piaget's theory of moral judgment, however, have been soundly faulted. For example, there is little evidence that peer interaction automatically stimulates moral development (Lickona, 1976). Rather, it seems likely that the quality of peer interactions—such as whether or not they involve cooperative interactions—is more important than the mere quantity of interaction with peers. Piaget also underestimated young children's ability to appreciate the role of intentionality in morality (Nobes, Panagiotaki, & Pawson, 2009). When Piagetian moral vignettes are presented in ways that make the individuals' intentions more obvious—such as by using videotaped dramas—preschoolers and early elementary school children are more likely to recognize individuals with bad intentions (Chandler et al., 1973; Grueneich, 1982; Yuill & Perner, 1988). It is probable that in Piaget's research, young children focused primarily on the consequences of the individuals' actions because consequences (e.g., John's breaking the 15 cups) were very salient in his stories.

In addition, many 4- and 5-year-olds do *not* think that a person caused a negative outcome "on purpose" if they have been explicitly told that the person had no foreknowledge of the consequences of his or her action or believed that the outcome of the action would be positive rather than negative (Pellizzoni, Siegal, & Surian, 2009). Moreover, even younger children seem to use knowledge of intentionality to evaluate others' behavior. In one study, 3-year-olds who saw an adult intend (but fail) to hurt another adult were less likely to help that person than they were if the person's behavior toward the other adult was neutral (intended to neither help nor hurt the other). In contrast, the 3-year-olds helped an adult who accidentally caused harm as much as they helped an adult whose behavior was neutral (Vaish, Carpenter, & Tomasello, 2010).

Equally impressive, 21-month-olds in another study were more likely to help an adult who had tried (but failed) to assist them in retrieving a toy than an adult who had been unwilling to assist them. They were also more likely to help an adult who had tried (but failed) to assist them than an adult whose intentions had been unclear (Dunfield & Kuhlmeier, 2013). Finally, as you will see later in the chapter, it is clear that young children do not believe that some actions, such as hurting others, are right even when adults say they are.

Despite its shortcomings, Piaget's theory provided clear and interesting arguments for subsequent research on the development of moral judgment to support or refute. The most notable example is the more complexly differentiated theory of moral reasoning formulated by Kohlberg.

Kohlberg's Theory of Moral Reasoning

Heavily influenced by the ideas of Piaget, Lawrence Kohlberg (1976; Colby & Kohlberg, 1987) was primarily interested in the sequences through which children's moral reasoning develops over time. On the basis of a longitudinal study in which he first assessed the moral reasoning of three cohorts of boys (beginning at ages 10, 13, and 16, respectively), Kohlberg proposed that the development of moral reasoning proceeds through a specific series of stages that are discontinuous and hierarchical. That is, each new stage reflects a qualitatively different, more advanced way of thinking than the one before it.

Kohlberg's Measure of Moral Reasoning

Kohlberg assessed moral reasoning by presenting children with hypothetical moral dilemmas and then questioning them about the issues involved. The most famous of these is known as the Heinz dilemma:

> In Europe, a woman was near death from a special kind of cancer. There was one drug that the doctors thought might save her. It was a form of radium that a druggist in the same town had recently discovered. The drug was expensive to make, but the druggist was charging 10 times what it cost him to make. He paid $200 for the radium and charged $2,000 for a small dose of the drug. The sick woman's husband, Heinz, went to everyone he knew to borrow the money, but he could only get together about $1000, which is half of what it cost. He told the druggist that his wife was dying, and asked him to sell it cheaper or let him pay later. But the druggist said, "No, I discovered the drug and I'm going to make money from it." So Heinz gets desperate and considers breaking into the man's store to steal the drug for his wife.

(Colby et al., 1983, p. 77)

Kohlberg (pictured here), like Piaget, argued that stages of moral reasoning involve a qualitative change in reasoning and that each stage represents a new way of thinking that replaces the child's thinking at prior, lower levels.

After relating this dilemma to an initial sample of boys aged 10 to 16, Kohlberg asked them questions such as: Should Heinz steal the drug? Would it be wrong or right if he did? Why? Is it a husband's duty to steal the drug for his wife if he can get it no other way? Kohlberg was not interested in whether the children said Heinz should or should not steal the drug; instead, he was interested in the moral reasoning behind their choices. For example, the response that "Heinz should steal the drug because he probably won't get caught and put in jail" was considered less advanced than "Heinz should steal the drug because a human life is more important than property or profits."

Kohlberg's Levels of Moral Reasoning

Based on his interviews with children, Kohlberg proposed that there are three levels of moral reasoning—preconventional, conventional, and postconventional (sometimes called principled). *Preconventional moral reasoning* is self-centered; it focuses on getting rewards and avoiding punishment. *Conventional moral reasoning* is centered on social relationships; it focuses on compliance with social duties and laws. *Postconventional moral reasoning* is centered on ideals; it focuses on moral principles. Each level has two stages within it, as follows:

 Kohlberg Heinz Moral Dilemma and Moral Development in Middle Childhood

Preconventional Level

Stage 1: Punishment and Obedience Orientation. At Stage 1, what is seen as right is obedience to authorities. Children's "conscience" (what makes them decide what is right or wrong) is fear of punishment, and their moral action is motivated by avoidance of punishment. The child does not consider the interests of others or recognize that those interests might differ from his or her own.

Stage 2: Instrumental and Exchange Orientation. At Stage 2, what is right is what is in one's own best interest or involves equal exchange between people (tit-for-tat exchange of benefits).

social-conventional domain than are nonreligious youths. For the religious youths, the crucial factor for nonmoral (conventional) issues is God's word as written in the Bible (i.e., whether or not the Bible says a particular social convention is wrong; Vainio, 2011).

Socioeconomic class can also influence the way children make such designations. Research in the United States and Brazil indicates that children of lower-income families are somewhat less likely than middle-class children to differentiate sharply between moral and social-conventional actions and, prior to adolescence, are less likely to view personal issues as a matter of choice. These differences may be due to the tendency of individuals of low socioeconomic status to place a greater emphasis on submission to authority and to allow children less autonomy (Nucci, 1997). This social-class difference in children's views may evaporate as youths approach adolescence, although Brazilian mothers of lower-income adolescents still claim more control over personal issues than do mothers of middle-income youths (Lins-Dyer & Nucci, 2007).

Review

How children think about moral issues provides one basis for their moral or immoral behavior. Piaget delineated two moral stages—heteronomous morality of constraint and autonomous morality—separated by a transitional stage. In the first stage, children regard rules as fixed and tend to weigh consequences more than intentions in evaluating actions. According to Piaget, a combination of cognitive growth and egalitarian, cooperative interactions with peers brings children to the autonomous stage, in which they recognize that rules can be changed by group consent and in which they judge the morality of actions based on intentions more than consequences. Some aspects of Piaget's theory have not held up well to criticism—for example, children use intentions to evaluate behavior at a younger age than Piaget believed they could—but his theory provided the foundation for Kohlberg's work on stages of moral reasoning.

Kohlberg outlined three levels of moral judgment—preconventional, conventional, and postconventional—each initially containing two stages (Stage 6 was subsequently dropped). He hypothesized that his sequence of stages reflected age-related discontinuous changes in moral reasoning and that children everywhere go through the same stage progression (although they may stop development at different points). Several aspects of Kohlberg's theory are controversial, including whether children's moral reasoning moves through discontinuous stages of development; whether the theory is valid for all cultures; and whether there are gender differences in moral judgment.

Research on other types of moral judgment, such as prosocial-moral judgment, suggests that children's concerns about the needs of others emerge at a younger age than Kohlberg's work indicates. However, with age, prosocial-moral reasoning, like Kohlberg's justice-oriented moral reasoning, becomes more abstract and based on internalized principles.

An individual's conscience reflects the moral standards he or she has internalized; it restrains the child from engaging in immoral behavior and causes the child to feel guilt when he or she misbehaves. Children are more likely to internalize parental standards if they have secure attachments with their parents and if their parents use reasoning in their discipline rather than excessive parental power. Factors that promote the development of conscience differ somewhat among children, depending on their temperament and genetic inheritance.

There are important differences among the moral, social-conventional, and personal domains of behavior and judgment—differences that even children recognize. For example, young children believe that moral transgressions, but not social-conventional or personal violations, are wrong regardless of whether adults say they are unacceptable. There are some cultural differences in whether a given behavior is viewed as having moral implications, but it is likely that people in all cultures differentiate among moral, social-conventional, and personal domains of functioning.

Prosocial Behavior

Malala, whose experiences and activism are described briefly at the beginning of this chapter, has lived a life driven by the desire to act prosocially. While not all children (or even adults) are that selfless, all children are capable of prosocial behaviors. They vary, however, in how often they engage in these behaviors and in their reasons for doing so. Consider the interactions between these three pairs of preschool children:

In their 2nd year, most children are willing to share objects and treats with their parents and with other children.

> Sara is drawing a picture and has a box of crayons. Erin is sitting across from her, and wants to draw. But Erin has only a single crayon and all the rest are in use by other children. She looks around for crayons of other colors. After a short time, Erin looks somewhat distressed. Sara notices that Erin is looking for crayons and is distressed, so she smiles and hands Erin a few of her own crayons, saying, "Here, do you want to use these?"
>
> Marc is sitting at a table drawing with crayons when Manuel comes over and wants to draw. Manuel can't find any crayons and shows signs of upset. Marc looks at Manuel and then returns to his own drawing. Finally, Manuel asks Marc, "Can I have some crayons?" At first Marc ignores Manuel. After Manuel asks for crayons again, Marc hands Manuel three crayons without any comment or display of emotion.
>
> Sakina is drawing when Darren comes to the table, picks up a piece of paper, and looks around for crayons. When Darren can't find any, he exhibits mild distress and then asks Sakina for some crayons. Sakina just ignores him. When Darren tries to take a crayon that Sakina is not using, Sakina angrily pushes him away.
>
> (Eisenberg, unpublished laboratory observations)

Seeing that someone else is sad or in distress, Sara gladly shares without even being asked. Marc shares only if asked repeatedly. Sakina doesn't share at all and does not seem to care if other children are upset. Do these differences in behavior forecast consistent differences in Sara's, Marc's, and Sakina's positive moral behavior as they are growing up?

The answer is yes: there is developmental consistency in children's readiness to engage in prosocial behaviors, such as sharing, helping, and comforting (N. Eisenberg & Fabes, 1998; Knafo et al., 2008). In fact, children who, like Sara, share spontaneously with peers tend to be more concerned with others' needs throughout childhood and adolescence and even in early adulthood. One longitudinal study found that, in comparison with their peers, they were more likely to assist other people even when doing so involved a cost to themselves. As young adults, they reported that they felt responsible for the welfare of others and that they usually tried to suppress aggression toward others when angry. Such children's friends rated them as more sympathetic than peers who engaged in less spontaneous prosocial behavior in preschool (N. Eisenberg et al., 2002; N. Eisenberg, Guthrie et al., 1999). In contrast, children like Marc are unlikely to be concerned with others' needs and feelings when they are older.

Of course, not all prosocial behaviors have the same meaning. Sometimes children help or share to get something in return, to gain social acceptance from peers, or to avoid their anger ("I'll share my doll if you'll be my friend"). However, most

Children's ability to sympathize with others appears to increase with age in early and middle childhood. These boys have just participated in a head-shaving event to show support for children with cancer and to help raise funds for cancer research.

altruistic motives ■ helping others for reasons that initially include empathy or sympathy for others and, at later ages, the desire to act in ways consistent with one's own conscience and moral principles

parents and teachers want children to perform prosocial behaviors for altruistic reasons. **Altruistic motives** initially include empathy or sympathy for others and, at later ages, the desire to act in ways consistent with one's own conscience and moral principles (N. Eisenberg, 1986).

The Development of Prosocial Behavior

The origins of altruistic prosocial behavior are rooted in the capacity to feel empathy and sympathy. As discussed in Chapter 10, *empathy* is an emotional response to another's emotional state or condition (e.g., sadness, poverty) that reflects the other person's state or condition (Eisenberg, Spinrad, & Knafo-Noam, 2015). For example, if a child becomes sad upon observing another person's sadness or pain, the child is experiencing empathy. To experience empathy, children must be able to identify the emotions of others (at least to some degree) and understand that another person is feeling an emotion or is in some kind of need.

Sympathy is a feeling of concern for another in response to the other's emotional state or condition. Although sympathy often is an outcome of empathizing with another's negative emotion or negative situation, what distinguishes sympathy from empathy is the element of concern: people who experience sympathy for another person are not merely feeling the same emotion as the other person.

Young children who view another child's distress sometimes respond with looks of concern or attempts to console or help the distressed peer. Recognizing others' emotions is necessary before children can feel empathy or act prosocially.

In order for children to express empathy or sympathy, they must be able to take the perspective of others. Although early theorists such as Piaget believed that children are unable to do this until age 6 or 7 (Piaget & Inhelder, 1956/1977), it is now clear that children have some ability to understand others' perspectives much earlier (Vaish, Carpenter, & Tomasello, 2009). By 14 months of age, children become emotionally distressed when they see other people who are upset (Knafo et al., 2008; Roth-Hanania et al., 2011) and express verbal and nonverbal concern for an adult who has been hurt (Hastings et al., 2014). These studies suggest that children feel empathy and sympathy by the 2nd year of life.

ELIZABETH CREWS

By 18 to 25 months of age, toddlers in laboratory studies sometimes share a personal object with an adult whom they saw being harmed by another (e.g., by having a piece of personal property taken away or destroyed). They also will sometimes comfort an adult who appears to be injured or distressed, or help an adult retrieve a dropped object or obtain food (Dunfield et al., 2011; Vaish et al., 2009). Such behaviors are especially likely to occur if the adult explicitly and emotionally communicates his or her need (C. A. Brownell, Svetlova, & Nichols, 2009), but they sometimes occur even when the adult does not express an emotional reaction (Vaish et al., 2009).

In displaying empathy, children in the 2nd year of life also are more likely to try to comfort someone who is upset than to become upset themselves, indicating that they know who it is that is suffering. For example, researchers in one study observed an 18-month-old girl who got visibly upset by a crying baby; she responded by bringing offerings of toys and cookies to the baby and by trying to get her own mother to help soothe the child (Radke-Yarrow & Zahn-Waxler, 1984).

ANDY COX / GETTY IMAGES

In the 2nd to 4th years of life, some types of prosocial behaviors increase while others decrease. In one laboratory study, 2-, 3-, and 4-year-olds were equally likely to help an adult get something that was out of reach

(Dunfield & Kuhlmeier, 2013; see Figure 14.3). There were no statistically significant age differences for sharing stickers or food with an adult who did not have any. However, 3- and 4-year-olds were much more likely than 2-year-olds to provide assistance or verbal reassurance to adults who were emotionally distressed because they had broken a toy or hurt themselves. This finding suggests that young children may not be able to act on their feelings of sympathy when others are distressed until they reach age 3, in part because that is the age at which they begin to understand social norms (Tomasello & Vaish, 2013).

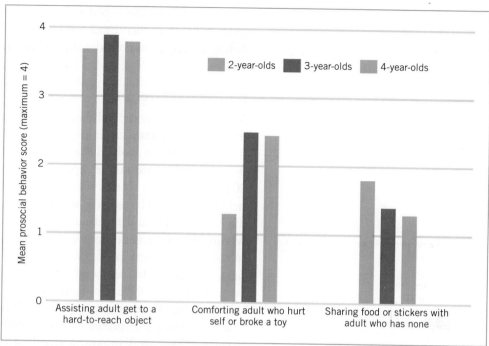

Cooperation is another form of prosocial behavior, one that may be driven by sympathy but may also be driven by a child's sense of fairness. Children as young as 14 months of age are able to cooperate with another child or adult to reach a goal that will benefit them both, namely getting prizes (Warneken & Tomasello, 2007). In a display of a different type of cooperation, children also tend to divide prizes evenly if they are initially given to the children unevenly (Tomasello & Vaish, 2013). In contrast, when this research team repeated the task with chimpanzees, the chimps' interactions were characterized by competition rather than cooperation. This finding lends support to the idea that cooperative prosocial behavior may have evolved especially in humans (Tomasello & Vaish, 2013).

FIGURE 14.3 Observed prosocial behavior by age in response to adults expressing three types of needs An age difference was observed for children's comforting of adults who displayed distress. (Data from Dunfield & Kuhlmeier, 2013, p. 1772)

As children age through middle childhood and into adolescence, their increasingly higher levels of moral reasoning and of their perspective-taking ability lead to accompanying increases in how often they engage in prosocial behaviors such as helping, sharing, and donating (Knafo et al., 2008; Luengo Kanacri et al., 2013; Nantel-Vivier et al., 2009).

However, young children do not always act in prosocial ways (S. Lamb & Zakhireh, 1997). Between the ages of 2 and 3, children often ignore their siblings' distress or need, or they simply watch without intervening. Occasionally, they even make the situation worse with teasing or aggression. One study asked 7-, 11-, and 16-year-olds to describe their reasons behind a specific instance in which they hurt a friend and one in which they helped a friend; each age group focused on their own perspective and on external constraints when explaining hurtful actions (e.g., "He crashed his sled into me") but focused on their friends' perspectives in describing the reasons behind their helpful behaviors (e.g., "He was cold without a jacket"; Recchia et al., 2015).

The Origins of Individual Differences in Prosocial Behavior

Although children's prosocial behaviors change with age, consistent with the theme of *individual differences*, there is great variation among children of the same age in their propensity to help, share with, and comfort others. Recall the behaviors of Sara,

Marc, and Sakina, described earlier in this section. Why do children of the same ages differ so much in their prosocial behavior? To identify the origins of these individual differences, we must consider the themes of *nature and nurture* and *sociocultural context*.

Biological Factors

Many biologists and psychologists have proposed that humans are biologically predisposed to be prosocial (Hastings, Zahn-Waxler, & McShane, 2005). They believe that humans have evolved the capacity for prosocial behavior because collaboration in foraging for food and in repelling enemies ensured survival (Tomasello & Vaish, 2013). According to this view, people who help others are more likely than less helpful people to be assisted when they themselves are in need and, thus, are more likely to survive and reproduce (Trivers, 1983). In addition, assisting those with whom they share genes increases the likelihood that those genes will be passed on to the next generation (E. O. Wilson, 1975). In support of the view that humans have evolved to be prosocial, researchers at the University of British Columbia have shown that 2-year-olds are happier when giving treats to others than when taking treats for themselves (Aknin, Hamlin, & Dunn, 2012). Moreover, this tendency holds true across cultures: both adults and 2-year-olds living in a rural, isolated village in Vanuatu, a small island nation in the Pacific, show the same emotional rewards of giving (Aknin et al., 2015). Evolutionary explanations for prosocial behavior, however, pertain to the human species as a whole and do not explain individual differences in empathy, sympathy, and prosocial behavior.

Genetic factors do contribute to individual differences in these characteristics (e.g., Waldman et al., 2011). In studies with adults, twins' reports of their own empathy and prosocial behavior are considerably more similar for identical than for fraternal twins (Gregory et al., 2009; Knafo & Israel, 2010). In one of the few twin studies of children's prosocial behaviors, researchers observed young twins' reactions to adults' simulations of distress in the home and in the laboratory and had the twins' mothers report on their everyday prosocial behavior. On the basis of *heritability* estimates (see Chapter 3) derived from this study, it appears that the role of genetic factors in the children's prosocial concerns for others and in their prosocial behavior increases with age (Knafo et al., 2008).

Recently, researchers have identified specific genes that might contribute to individual differences in prosocial tendencies (Knafo & Israel, 2010). For example, certain genes are associated with individual differences in oxytocin, a hormone that plays a role in pair bonding and parenting and that has been associated with parental attachment, empathy, and prosocial behavior (N. Eisenberg, Spinrad, & Knafo-Noam, 2015; R. Feldman, 2012; K. MacDonald & MacDonald, 2010; Striepens et al., 2011).

How else might genetic factors affect empathy, sympathy, and prosocial behavior? One likely path is through differences in temperament. For instance, differences in children's ability to regulate emotion are related to their empathy and sympathy. Children who tend to experience emotion without getting overwhelmed by it are especially likely to experience sympathy and to act prosocially (N. Eisenberg, Fabes, & Murphy, 1996; N. Eisenberg et al., 2007; Trommsdorff, Friedlmeier, & Mayer, 2007). Moreover, children who are not responsive to others' emotions or are too inhibited to help others may be relatively unlikely to act prosocially (Liew et al., 2011; S. K. Young, Fox, & Zahn-Waxler, 1999). Regulation is also related to children's theory of mind (see Chapter 7), and theory of mind predicts children's prosocial behavior (Caputi et al., 2012). Thus, the effect of heredity on sympathy and prosocial behavior might be through individual differences in social cognition as well as in temperament.

The Socialization of Prosocial Behavior

A number of environmental factors also contribute to sympathy and prosocial behavior (Knafo & Plomin, 2006a, 2006b; Volbrecht et al., 2007). The primary environmental influence on children's development of prosocial behavior probably is their socialization in the family. Researchers have identified three ways in which parents socialize prosocial behavior in their children: (1) by modeling and teaching prosocial behavior; (2) by arranging opportunities for their children to engage in prosocial behavior; and (3) by disciplining their children and eliciting prosocial behavior from them. Parents also communicate and reinforce cultural beliefs about the value of prosocial behavior (see Box 14.1).

Children are more likely to donate to charity if they see others donate and if adults explain to them how donating helps others.

Modeling and the communication of values Consistent with social-learning theory's emphasis on observation and imitation (see Chapter 9), children tend to imitate other people's helping and sharing behavior, including even that of strangers (N. Eisenberg & Fabes, 1998). Children are especially likely to imitate the prosocial behavior of adults with whom they have a positive relationship (D. Hart & Fegley, 1995; Yarrow, Scott, & Zahn-Waxler, 1973). This may help explain the fact that parents and children tend to be similar in their levels of prosocial behavior and sympathy (Clary & Miller, 1986; N. Eisenberg et al., 1991; Stukas et al., 1999), although heredity may also contribute to the similarity between parent and child in sympathy and helpfulness.

In a particularly interesting study, individuals who had risked their lives to rescue Jews from the Nazis in Europe during World War II were interviewed many years later, along with "bystanders" from the same communities who had not been involved in rescue activities (Oliner & Oliner, 1988). As shown in Table 14.1, when recalling the values they had learned from their parents and other influential adults, 44% of the rescuers mentioned generosity and caring for others, whereas only 21% of bystanders mentioned the same values. Rescuers were 7 times more likely than bystanders to report that their parents taught them that values related to caring should be applied to everyone (28% of rescuers; 4% of bystanders), commenting:

> They taught me to respect all human beings.
>
> He taught me to love my neighbor—to consider him my equal whatever his nationality or religion.
>
> (Oliner & Oliner, 1988, p. 165)

Bystanders also reported that their parents emphasized ethical obligations to family, community, church, and country, but they rarely reported that their parents emphasized their having such obligations to other people. Thus, the values parents convey to their children may influence not only *whether* children are prosocial but also *toward whom* they are prosocial.

One effective way for parents to teach their children prosocial values and behaviors is to have discussions with

TABLE 14.1

Percentage of Rescuers and Bystanders Who Reported Learning a Given Type of Value from Parents

Type of Value	Rescuers (%)	Bystanders (%)
Economic competence	19	34
Independence	6	8
Fairness/equity (including reciprocity)	44	48
Fairness/equity applied universally	14	10
Caring	44	21
Caring applied universally	28	4

Data from Oliner & Oliner (1988).

BOX 14.1 | a closer look

CULTURAL CONTRIBUTIONS TO CHILDREN'S PROSOCIAL AND ANTISOCIAL TENDENCIES

The amount of prosocial and antisocial behavior that children display can be influenced by the particular culture of which they are a part (Graves & Graves, 1983; Wainryb & Recchia, 2014). For example, children from traditional communities and subcultures (e.g., Mexicans and Mexican Americans) are more likely to cooperate on laboratory tasks than are children from urban, Westernized groups (N. Eisenberg & Mussen, 1989; Knight, Cota, & Bernal, 1993). Similar patterns have been found in observations of children interacting at home and in their neighborhoods (Whiting & Edwards, 1988; Whiting & Whiting, 1975): children in traditional societies in Kenya, Mexico, and the Philippines helped, shared, and offered support to others in their families and communities more than did children in the United States, India, and Japan.

In the more prosocial cultures, children often lived in extended families with many relatives. At a young age, they were assigned chores that were very important for the welfare of other family members, such as caring for younger children and tending herds. As a result of taking on these duties, children may have learned that they were responsible for others and that their helping behavior was expected and valued by adults.

However, there may be cultural differences in the people toward whom children's caring behavior is directed. For example, in the research just discussed, Philippine children were more prosocial toward relatives than toward nonrelatives, whereas U.S. children were more prosocial toward nonrelatives than toward relatives (de Guzman, Carlo, & Edwards, 2008). Children in traditional cultures may be socialized to help people with

whom they have close ties but may be relatively disinclined to help people with whom they do not have a close connection.

The multicultural study cited above also revealed cultural differences in children's aggression (Whiting & Whiting, 1975). Children's tendencies to assault, berate, and scold others were related primarily to family structure and interactions among parents. Children

Cross-cultural research has shown that girls who live in societies in which they are expected to take care of younger children are more prosocial than are girls who live in societies that do not have this expectation.

with lower rates of assaulting and reprimanding tended to live in cultures in which fathers were closely involved with their wives and children, helped their wives with the care of infants, and were relatively unlikely to assault their wives. In such family circumstances,

children may have learned nonaggressive modes of social interaction from their fathers and were relatively unlikely to have been exposed to aggressive adult models.

Even in various industrial societies today, there are differences in cultural values regarding prosocial and antisocial behavior. For instance, Mexican American youths are more prosocial if they espouse the traditional Mexican value of familism—a set of norms that promotes emotional and economic interdependence within an extended network of kin—rather than mainstream U.S. norms of individualism (Armenta et al., 2011). Along similar lines, the incidence of children's sharing, helping, and comforting is higher in Taiwan and Japan than it is in the United States (Rao & Stewart, 1999; Stevenson, 1991). Again, in contrast to the U.S. valuing of self and competition, Chinese and Japanese cultures traditionally place great emphasis on teaching children to share and to be responsible for the needs of others in the group (the family, class, or community).

In Japan, there also is an emphasis on creating a "community of learners" in the elementary school classroom—that is, teaching children to respond supportively to one another's thoughts and feelings (M. Lewis, 1995). However, the traditional emphasis on prosocial behavior in many Asian cultures seems to be eroding (L. C. Lee & Zhan, 1991), perhaps due to increasing economic modernization and exposure to Western culture and values. This may explain why Asian children have not been found to be more prosocial than Western children in several relatively recent studies outside the classroom (Kärtner, Keller, & Chaudhary, 2010; Trommsdorff et al., 2007).

CATHERINE URSILLO / SCIENCE SOURCE

them that appeal to their ability to sympathize. In laboratory studies, when elementary school children heard adults explicitly point out the positive consequences of prosocial actions for others (e.g., "Poor children . . . would be so happy and excited if they could buy food and toys"), they were more likely to donate money anonymously to help other people (Eisenberg-Berg & Geisheker, 1979; Perry, Bussey, & Freiberg, 1981). Children were less likely to donate anonymously if adults simply said that helping is "good" or "nice" and did not provide sympathy-arousing rationales for helping or sharing (Bryan & Walbek, 1970; N. Eisenberg & Fabes, 1998).

Opportunities for prosocial activities Providing children with opportunities to engage in helpful activities can increase their willingness to take on prosocial tasks at a later time (N. Eisenberg et al., 1987). In the home, opportunities to help others include household tasks that are performed on a routine basis and benefit others (Richman et al., 1988; Whiting & Whiting, 1975), although performance of household tasks may foster prosocial actions primarily toward family members (Grusec, Goodnow, & Cohen, 1996). For adolescents, voluntary community service such as working in homeless shelters or other community agencies also can be a way of gaining experience in helping others and deepening feelings of prosocial commitment (M. K. Johnson et al., 1998; Lawford et al., 2005; Pratt et al., 2003; Yates & Youniss, 1996). Service learning, which is an educational strategy that integrates community service with instruction to promote learning, is increasingly common in middle and high schools (see Box 14.4 in the last section of this chapter for more on positive youth development and service-learning programs).

Participation in prosocial activities may also give children and adolescents opportunities to take others' perspectives, to increase their confidence that they are competent to assist others, and to experience emotional rewards for helping. Even mandatory school-based service activities have been associated with future prosocial values (D. Hart et al., 2007), as well as with increased voluntary service at a later date for those high school youths who were not initially inclined to engage in such activities (Metz & Youniss, 2003). It should be noted, however, that forcing older adolescents or young adults into service activities can sometimes backfire and undermine their motivation to help (Stukas, Snyder, & Clary, 1999).

Discipline and parenting style High levels of prosocial behavior and sympathy in children tend to be associated with constructive and supportive parenting, including authoritative parenting (Day & Padilla-Walker, 2009; Houltberg et al., 2014; Knafo & Plomin, 2006a; Michalik et al., 2007). When parents are involved with and close to their children, the children are higher in sympathy and regulation, which in turn predicts higher levels of prosocial behavior (Padilla-Walker & Christensen, 2011). Parental support of, and attachment to, the child have been found to be especially predictive of prosocial behavior for youths who are low in fearfulness (Padilla-Walker & Nelson, 2010). It is important to note, however, that not only might supportive, authoritative parenting promote sympathy and prosocial behavior, but prosocial, sympathetic children might also elicit more support from their parents (Miklikowska, Duriez, & Soenens 2011; Padilla-Walker et al., 2012). In contrast, a parenting style that involves physical punishment, threats, and an authoritarian approach (see Chapter 12) tends to be associated with a lack of sympathy and prosocial behavior in children and adolescents (Asbury et al., 2003; Hastings et al., 2000; Houltberg et al., 2014; Krevans & Gibbs, 1996; Laible et al., 2008).

The way in which parents attempt to directly elicit prosocial behavior from their children is

When adults point out the consequences of a child's transgressions against others, children are more likely to respond with sympathy and prosocial behavior in other situations.

SKYNESHER / GETTY IMAGES

also important. If children are regularly punished for failing to engage in prosocial behavior, they may start to believe that the reason for helping others is primarily to avoid punishment (Dix & Grusec, 1983; M. L. Hoffman, 1983). Similarly, if children are given material rewards for prosocial behaviors, they may come to believe that they helped solely for the rewards and, thus, may be less motivated to help when no rewards are offered (Fabes et al., 1989; Warneken & Tomasello, 2008).

What does seem particularly likely to foster children's voluntary prosocial behavior is discipline that involves reasoning (Carlo, Mestre et al., 2010). This is especially true when the reasoning points out the consequences of the child's behavior for others (Krevans & Gibbs, 1996) and encourages perspective taking (B. M. Farrant et al., 2012). Such reasoning also encourages sympathy for others and provides guidelines children can refer to in future situations (C. S. Henry, Sager, & Plunkett, 1996; M. L. Hoffman, 1983). Maternal use of reasoning oriented toward others (e.g., "Can't you see that Tim is hurt?") seems to increase prosocial behavior even for 1- to 2-year-olds, as long as mothers state their reasoning in an emotional tone of voice (Zahn-Waxler, Radke-Yarrow, & King, 1979). Emotion in the mother's voice likely catches her toddler's attention and communicates that she is very serious about what she is saying.

The combination of parental warmth and certain parenting practices—not parental warmth by itself—seems to be especially effective for fostering prosocial tendencies in children and adolescents. Therefore, children tend to be more prosocial when their parents are not only warm and supportive but also when they model prosocial behavior, include reasoning and references to moral values and responsibilities in their discipline, and expose their children to prosocial models and activities (i.e., use authoritative parenting; Hastings et al., 2007; Janssens & Deković, 1997; Yarrow et al., 1973).

The Role of Parenting in Moral Development

Peer influences Relationships with other children are another key way that children learn and practice moral principles, such as fairness, justice, reciprocity (e.g., sharing and taking turns), conflict resolution, and not hurting or taking advantage of others (Killen & Smetana, 2015; Turiel, 2014). This practice in moral reasoning within peer relationships translates into prosocial behavior. A study of adolescents and their best friends found that those pairs that had the highest levels of moral reasoning also were most successful at resolving conflict (McDonald et al., 2014). Children are motivated to do nice things for their friends, both because they care about them and because doing so increases the likelihood that those friends will do nice things for them in return.

Interventions Because most of the research on the socialization of prosocial responding is correlational in design, it does not allow firm conclusions about cause-and-effect relations. However, some school interventions have been effective at promoting prosocial behavior in children, so environmental factors must contribute to its development (see Box 14.2). The research underlying such interventions indicates that experience in helping and cooperating with others, exposure to prosocial values and behaviors, and adults' use of reasoning in discipline contribute to the development of prosocial behavior.

Review

Prosocial behaviors emerge by the 2nd year of life and increase in frequency during the toddler years. At least some types of prosocial behavior continue to increase in frequency and sensitivity in the preschool years and elementary school years. Early individual differences in prosocial behavior predict differences among children in these types of behaviors years later.

Prosocial behavior may increase with age during childhood partly because of children's developing abilities to sympathize and take others' perspectives. Differences among children in their empathy, sympathy, responses to others' distress, and perspective taking also contribute to individual differences in children's prosocial behavior. Furthermore, biological factors, which may contribute to differences among children in temperament, likely affect how empathic and prosocial children become.

The development of prosocial behavior also is related to children's upbringing. In general, a positive relationship between parents and children is linked to prosocial-moral development, especially when supportive parents use effective parenting practices. Authoritative, positive discipline—including explanations of reasoning by parents and teachers and exposure to prosocial models, values, and activities—is associated with the development of sympathy and prosocial behavior. Cultures differ in the degree to which they value and teach prosocial behavior, and these differences are reflected in how much children help, share with, and are concerned about other people and perhaps even whom they assist.

Intervention programs in schools designed to foster prosocial behavior sometimes have been found to increase children's prosocial behavior and prosocial-moral reasoning. Whether a given intervention is effective probably depends on its content, length, and the degree to which it is effectively administered. Such findings convincingly demonstrate that social factors (as well as heredity) contribute to the development of prosocial tendencies.

Antisocial Behavior

Pick up any newspaper or open any news site and you are inevitably reminded of the **antisocial behavior**—defined as disruptive, hostile, or aggressive behaviors that violate social norms or rules and that harm or take advantage of others—from highly publicized cases like Dhzokhar Tsarnaev to everyday incidents of bullying and aggression. In the United States in 2010, juveniles younger than 18 were involved in 8% of murder arrests, 12% of aggravated assault arrests, 23% of burglary arrests, 24% of robbery arrests, 14% of rapes, 14% of all violent crimes, and 22% of all property crimes (Sickmund & Puzzanchera, 2014). However, it is important to note that the number of juveniles arrested decreased 38% between 1980 and 2010, such that juveniles accounted for only 6.6% of arrests in 2010, even though they constitute 24% of the population (Sickmund & Puzzanchera, 2014).

Of course, many children in this juvenile population are too young to be involved in crime. Any juvenile crime is one too many, and thus statistics like those cited above, along with incidents like the Boston Marathon bombing described at the beginning of the chapter, raise questions such as: Why do some children and adolescents exhibit aggression and antisocial behavior? Are youths who commit violent or antisocial acts already aggressive in childhood? How do levels of aggression change with development? What factors contribute to individual differences in children's antisocial behavior? As we address these issues, the themes of *individual differences, nature and nurture,* the *sociocultural context,* and *research and children's welfare* will be particularly salient.

The Development of Aggression and Other Antisocial Behaviors

Aggression is behavior intended to physically or emotionally harm others (Eisner & Malti, 2015), and it emerges quite early. How early? Instances of aggression over possessing objects occur between infants before 12 months of age—especially behaviors such as trying to tug objects away from each other (D. F. Hay, Mundy et al.,

antisocial behavior ■ disruptive, hostile, or aggressive behaviors that violate social norms or rules and that harm or take advantage of others

aggression ■ behavior aimed at harming or injuring others

BOX 14.2 | applications

SCHOOL-BASED INTERVENTIONS FOR PROMOTING PROSOCIAL BEHAVIOR

Knowledge about the socialization of helping and sharing behavior has been used to design school interventions aimed at fostering such behavior. One popular approach used in more than 16,000 schools around the country is Positive Behavioral Interventions and Supports (PBIS; Bradshaw, Waasdorp, & Leaf, 2012). PBIS is a schoolwide intervention program that aims to change the overall school climate and thereby reduce negative behaviors and increase positive behaviors among staff and students (Sugai & Horner, 2006). PBIS is based on principles from learning theories (see Chapter 9), namely, that positive student behavior can be increased by praising it when it does occur (i.e., behaviorism) and by having staff model such behavior so that students will in turn imitate it (i.e., social-learning theory). To achieve these goals, some PBIS schools reward children who are "caught" behaving well; for example, children who are observed spontaneously picking up litter outside school or helping a teacher carry materials are given a voucher for a small prize, such as a treat at lunch. By paying special attention to positive behavior rather than only noting negative behavior, PBIS schools hope to increase the frequency of positive behavior.

Research on prevention programs (that attempt to prevent a problem from occurring) and intervention programs (that aim to help children who already exhibit a

Posters with positive behavioral messages are displayed throughout a school as part of the PBIS approach.

problem) divides the programs into three levels: (1) primary prevention (targeting all children in a setting, e.g., school); (2) secondary prevention (targeting individuals at risk for developing a problem); and (3) tertiary intervention (targeting individuals who already exhibit a problem). The PBIS program uses all three levels of prevention and intervention:

1. **Primary prevention** is universal and thus aimed at all children and staff in a

school. Posters that clearly state behavioral expectations are displayed around the school and are aimed directly at the students; an example of a common PBIS poster message is, "Be Safe; Be Responsible; Be Respectful." School staff, including teachers, are trained to model appropriate behavior and to praise children when they behave appropriately. This level of the intervention is aimed at preventing problem behaviors from occurring in the first place

primary prevention ■ a program targeting all individuals in a particular setting (e.g., a school) in order to prevent the occurrence of a problematic behavior or condition

2011)—but most do not involve bodily contact such as hitting (Coie & Dodge, 1998). Beginning around 18 months of age, physical aggression such as hitting and pushing—particularly over the possession of objects—is normative in development and increases in frequency until about age 2 or 3 (Alink et al., 2006; D. F. Hay, Hurst et al., 2011; D. S. Shaw et al., 2003). Then, with the growth of language skills (see Chapter 6), physical aggression decreases in frequency, and verbal aggression such as insults and taunting increases (Bonica et al., 2003; Dionne et al., 2003; Mesman et al., 2009; Miner & Clarke-Stewart, 2008).

Among the most frequent causes of aggression in the preschool years are conflicts between peers over possessions (Fabes & Eisenberg, 1992; Shantz, 1987) and conflict

and increasing the likelihood that positive behaviors will be repeated (Sugai & Horner, 2006).

2. **Secondary prevention** is targeted toward children who are deemed at risk for problem behavior. These children may exhibit problems with attention, self-regulation, or peer interactions that the staff recognize as leading to potential behavior problems. These children are given extra attention and monitoring from staff, who praise them when they engage in appropriate behavior and provide reminders about expected behavior when they do not. This level of intervention is projected to target about 15% of the student population, with the goal of reducing problem behavior (Sugai & Horner, 2006).

3. **Tertiary intervention** is focused on children who consistently engage in inappropriate, aggressive, or antisocial behavior. The school staff create an individualized plan for each student at this level of intervention; the plan may include interactions with school counselors, special education teachers, and other specialists. The goal at this level of intervention is to reduce the frequency and severity of problem behavior (Sugai & Horner, 2006).

These three levels of prevention and intervention are typically thought of as a pyramid, with the largest number of children receiving primary prevention and the smallest number receiving tertiary intervention. Given that the programs and treatment involved at the level of tertiary intervention tend to be intensive and require specialized training to administer,

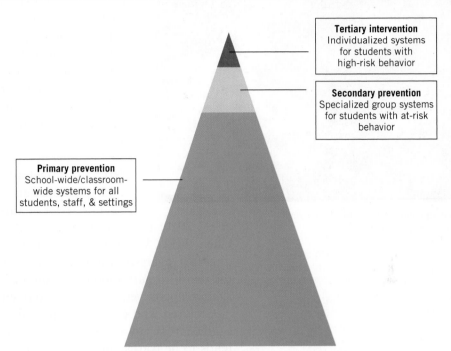

PBIS incorporates three levels of intervention to promote positive behavior in schools. (Information from Sugai & Horner, 2006)

they tend to be more expensive than primary prevention even though they involve fewer children.

The effectiveness of PBIS has been evaluated systematically through research around the country. A study of PBIS in 37 elementary schools, in which schools were randomly assigned to implement PBIS or not, found that children in PBIS schools had significantly fewer attention or behavior problems and improved prosocial behavior up to 4 years later (Bradshaw et al., 2012). Another study of PBIS implemented in all 474 schools in the state of Maryland found that the more comprehensively a school implemented PBIS, the greater reductions they experienced in student truancy and student suspensions (Pas & Bradshaw, 2012). Importantly, PBIS was also associated in this study with significant improvements in children's math and reading achievement (Pas & Bradshaw, 2012), indicating that an intervention focused on improving student behavior can impact student academic outcomes as well.

between siblings over almost anything (Abramovitch, Corter, & Lando, 1979). Conflict over possessions often is an example of **instrumental aggression,** that is, aggression motivated by the desire to obtain a concrete goal, such as gaining possession of a toy or getting a better place in line. Preschool children sometimes also use *relational aggression* (Crick, Casas, & Mosher, 1997), which, as explained in Chapter 13, is intended to harm others by damaging their peer relationships. Among preschoolers, this typically involves excluding peers from a play activity or a social group (M. K. Underwood, 2003). This relational (or indirect) aggression has been linked to theory-of-mind skills, particularly for those children with low levels of prosocial skills (see Chapter 7 for more details on theory of mind). For instance,

secondary prevention ■ a program designed to help individuals at risk for developing a problem or condition, with the goal of preventing the problem or condition

tertiary intervention ■ a program designed to help individuals who already exhibit a problem or condition

instrumental aggression ■ aggression motivated by the desire to obtain a concrete goal

Aggressive conflicts over objects are very common among young children.

a longitudinal study of young children in Canada demonstrated that theory-of-mind skills at age 5 predicted levels of relational aggression one year later, but only for those children who were rated as low to average on prosocial behavior (Renouf et al., 2010).

The drop in physical aggression in the preschool years is likely due not only to children's increasing ability to use verbal and relational aggression but also their developing ability to use language to resolve or pursue conflicts and to control their own emotions and actions (Coie & Dodge, 1998). Overt physical aggression continues to remain low or to decline in frequency for most children during elementary school, although a relatively small number of children—most of them boys (Moffitt & Caspi, 2001; NICHD Early Child Care Research Network, 2004)— develop frequent and serious problems with aggression and anti-social behavior at this age (Cairns et al., 1989; S. B. Campbell et al., 2010; D. S. Shaw et al., 2003) or in early adolescence (Xie, Drabick, & Chen, 2011). Whereas aggression in young children is usually instrumental (goal-directed), aggression in elementary school children often is hostile, arising from the desire to hurt another person, or is motivated by the need to protect oneself against a perceived threat to self-esteem (Dodge, 1980; Hartup, 1974).

Children who engage in physical aggression tend to also engage in relational aggression (Card et al., 2008); the degree to which they use one or the other tends to be consistent across childhood (Ostrov et al., 2008; Vaillancourt et al., 2003). Overall, the frequency of physical aggression decreases for most teenagers (Di Giunta et al., 2010; Loeber, 1982), at least after mid-adolescence (Karriker-Jaffe et al., 2008).

Despite this overall developmental trend toward less physical aggression, serious acts of violence increase markedly in mid-adolescence, as do property offenses and status offenses such as drinking and truancy (Lahey et al., 2000). As illustrated in Figure 14.4, adolescent violent crime peaks at age 17, when 29% of males and 12% of females report committing at least one serious violent offense. As the figure also shows, male adolescents and adults engage in much more violent behavior and crime than do females (Coie & Dodge, 1998; Elliott, 1994)—although in 2012, 29% of the arrests among juveniles were of females

FIGURE 14.4 Prevalence of self-reported violent crime for males and females at different ages At all ages, males report engaging in more violent behavior than do females. (Data from Coie & Dodge, 1998)

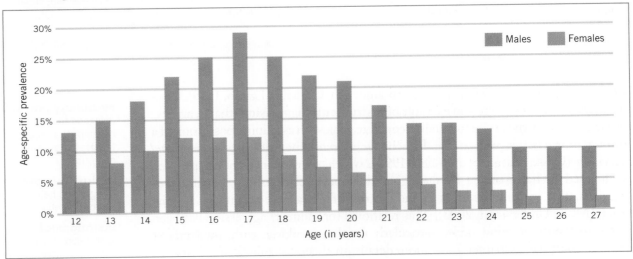

(Puzzanchera, 2014), who made up 19% of the juvenile arrests for violent crime and 35% of the juvenile arrests for property crime.

There is considerable consistency in individual differences in both girls' and boys' aggression across childhood and adolescence. Children who are the most aggressive and prone to conduct problems such as stealing in middle childhood tend to be more aggressive and delinquent in adolescence than children who first develop conduct problems at a later age (Broidy et al., 2003; Burt et al., 2011; Lahey, Goodman et al., 1999; Schaeffer et al., 2003). This holds especially true for boys (Fontaine et al., 2009). In one classic study, children who had been identified as aggressive by their peers when they were 8 years old had more criminal convictions and engaged in more serious criminal behavior at age 30 than did those who had not been identified as aggressive (see Figure 14.5) (Eron et al., 1987). In another study of girls only, relational aggression in childhood was related to subsequent *conduct disorders* (Keenan et al., 2010). (Conduct disorders are discussed in Box 14.3.)

Many children who are aggressive from early in life have neurological deficits (i.e., brain dysfunctions) that underlie such problems as hyperactivity and difficulty in paying attention (Eisner & Malti, 2015; Gatzke-Kopp et al., 2009; Moffitt, 1993a; Speltz et al., 1999; Viding & McCrory, 2012). These deficits, which may become more marked with age (Aguilar et al., 2000), can result in troubled relations with parents, peers, and teachers that further fuel the child's aggressive, antisocial pattern of behavior. Problems with attention are particularly likely to have this effect because they make it difficult for aggressive children to carefully consider all the relevant information in a social situation before deciding how to act; thus, their behavior often is inappropriate for the situation. In addition, callous, unemotional traits, which often accompany aggression and conduct disorder (e.g., Keenan et al., 2010), appear to be associated with a delay in cortical maturation in brain areas involved in decision making, morality, and empathy (De Brito et al., 2009).

Early-onset conduct problems are also associated with a range of family risk factors. These include the mother's being single at birth; the mother's being stressed prenatally and during the child's preschool years; the mother's being psychologically unavailable in the preschool years; parental antisocial tendencies; low maternal education and poverty; and child neglect and physical abuse (S. B. Campbell et al., 2010; D. F. Hay et al., 2011; K. M. McCabe et al., 2001; NICHD Early Child Care Research Network, 2004; M. Robinson et al., 2011).

Adolescents with a long childhood history of troubled behavior represent only a minority of adolescents who engage in the much broader problem of "juvenile delinquency" (Hämäläinen & Pulkkinen, 1996). Indeed, most adolescents who perform delinquent acts have no history of aggression or antisocial behavior before age 11 (Elliott, 1994). For some, delinquency may occur in response to the normal pressures of adolescence, as when teenagers attempt to assert their independence from adults or win acceptance from their peers. However, the onset of antisocial behavior in adolescence is also predicted by economic disadvantage, being a member of an ethnic minority, interacting with deviant peers (see Chapter 13), and having a difficult, irritable temperament from infancy onward (K. M. McCabe et al., 2001; 2004; Roisman et al., 2010).

Youths who develop problem behaviors in adolescence typically stop engaging in antisocial behavior later in adolescence or early adulthood (Moffitt, 1993a).

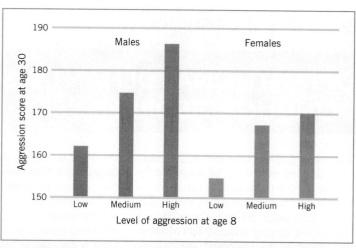

FIGURE 14.5 The relation of peer-nominated aggression at age 8 to self-reported aggression at age 30 Boys and girls who were nominated as high in aggression at age 8 were higher in self-reported aggression at age 30 than were their peers who had been nominated as lower in aggression. (Data from Eron et al., 1987)

BOX 14.3 | a closer look

OPPOSITIONAL DEFIANT DISORDER AND CONDUCT DISORDER

If a child's problem behaviors become serious, the child is likely to be diagnosed by psychologists and physicians as having a clinical disorder. Two such disorders that involve antisocial behavior are *oppositional defiant disorder* and *conduct disorder*, both of which are defined in the *Diagnostic and Statistical Manual of Mental Disorders, 5th edition* (*DSM-V*: American Psychiatric Association, 2013). **Oppositional defiant disorder (ODD)** is characterized by angry, defiant behavior that is age-inappropriate and persistent (lasting at least 6 months). Children with ODD typically lose their temper easily, arguing with adults and actively defying adults' requests or rules. They are also prone to blame others for their own mistakes or misbehavior and are often spiteful or vindictive.

Conduct disorder (CD) includes more severe antisocial and aggressive behaviors that inflict pain on others (e.g., bullying, initiating fights, cruelty to animals) or that involve the destruction of property or the violation of the rights of others (e.g., stealing, robberies). Other diagnostic signs of CD include frequently running away from home, staying out all night before age 13 despite parental prohibitions, or being truant from school beginning prior to age 13. To warrant a diagnosis of ODD or CD, children must exhibit multiple, persistent symptoms that are clearly impairing their social relationships and school performance, distinguishing them from children who display the designated behaviors on an infrequent or inconsistent basis (American Psychiatric Association, 2013; Hinshaw & Lee, 2003).

There is debate in the field regarding how antisocial behavior, including ODD and CD, should be conceptualized. Some experts argue that antisocial behavior should be viewed in terms of a continuum from infrequent to frequent displays of symptoms. Others argue that extreme forms of antisocial behavior are qualitatively different from garden-variety types of problem behaviors. In other words, there is a question regarding whether children with ODD or CD simply have more, or more severe, problem behaviors than do better-adjusted youth, or whether their problems are of an altogether different type. The answer to this question is not clear. However, the fact that exhibiting more ODD or CD symptoms in early childhood predicts serious diagnosed problems in adolescence or adulthood (Biederman et al., 2008; Côté et al., 2001; Hinshaw & Lee, 2003) is viewed by some as evidence that serious antisocial behavior problems differ in their origins from less severe types of such behavior.

Estimates of the prevalence of ODD and CD range widely (Hinshaw & Lee, 2003). The rate of ODD among preschoolers has been found to range from 2% to 17% across different studies, while the rate of CD in preschoolers ranges from 2% to 5% (Egger & Angold, 2006; Rowe et al., 2005). Among both children and adults, 3.3% of the population meets criteria for ODD and 4% meets the criteria for CD (American Psychiatric Association, 2013). The average age of onset for ODD is approximately 6 years; for CD it is 9 years of age (Hinshaw & Lee, 2003). Unfortunately, few children with CD receive treatment (American Psychiatric Association, 2013).

Although there is debate in regard to the relation between ODD and CD, some children develop both CD and ODD, whereas others do not. Children and adolescents with CD often, but not always, develop ODD first (Loeber & Burke, 2011; van Lier et al., 2007). In many instances, youth with ODD or CD also have been diagnosed with other disorders such as anxiety disorder or attention-deficit hyperactivity disorder (about half of youth with ODD or CD also have attention-deficit hyperactivity disorder) (Hinshaw & Lee, 2003). When a child is diagnosed with two distinct mental disorders, the disorders are said to be **comorbid.** The two disorders also seem to differ somewhat in their prediction of later problem behaviors: CD has been found to predict primarily behavioral problems in early adulthood, including antisocial behavior, whereas ODD shows stronger prediction of emotional disorders in early adulthood (Loeber & Burke, 2011; R. Rowe et al., 2010).

The factors related to the development of CD or ODD are similar to those related to the development of aggression. Genetics play a role, although heritability seems to be stronger for early-onset and overt types of antisocial behavior (such as aggression) than for later-onset or covert forms of antisocial behavior (such as stealing) (Hinshaw & Lee, 2003; Lahey, Goodman et al., 2009; Maes et al., 2007; Meier et al., 2011). Environmental risks for these disorders include such factors as living in a disadvantaged, risky neighborhood or in a stressed, lower-SES family; parental abuse; poor parental supervision; and harsh and inconsistent discipline (Goodnight et al., 2012; Hinshaw & Lee, 2003; R. Rowe et al., 2010). Peer rejection and associating with deviant peers are also linked with ODD and CD (Hinshaw & Lee, 2003; Loeber & Stouthamer-Loeber, 1986). It is likely that a variety of these factors jointly contribute to children's developing ODD or CD and that the most important factors vary according to the age of onset, the specific problem behaviors, and individual characteristics of the children, including their temperament and intelligence.

oppositional defiant disorder (ODD) ■ a disorder characterized by age-inappropriate and persistent displays of angry, defiant, and irritable behaviors

conduct disorder (CD) ■ a disorder that involves severe antisocial and aggressive behaviors that inflict pain on others or involve destruction of property or denial of the rights of others

However, some—especially those who have low impulse control, poor regulation of aggression, and a weak orientation toward the future (Monahan et al., 2009)—continue to engage in troublesome behaviors and to have some problems with their mental health and substance dependence until at least their mid-20s (Moffitt et al., 2002).

Characteristics of Aggressive and Antisocial Behavior of Children and Adolescents

Aggressive-antisocial children and adolescents differ, on average, from their nonaggressive peers in a variety of characteristics. These include having a difficult temperament and the tendency to process social information in negative ways.

Temperament and Personality

Children who develop problems with aggression and antisocial behavior tend to exhibit a difficult temperament and a lack of self-regulatory skills from a very early age (Espy et al., 2011; Rothbart, 2012; Yaman et al., 2010). Longitudinal studies have shown, for example, that infants and toddlers who frequently express intense negative emotion and demand unusually large amounts of attention tend to have higher levels of problem behaviors such as aggression from the preschool years through high school (J. E. Bates et al., 1991; Joussemet et al., 2008; Olson et al., 2000). Similarly, preschoolers who exhibit lack of control, impulsivity, high activity level, irritability, and distractibility are prone to fighting, delinquency, and other antisocial behavior at ages 9 through 15. They also are inclined toward aggression and criminal behavior in late adolescence and, in the case of men, to violent crime in adulthood (Caspi et al., 1995; Caspi & Silva, 1995; Tremblay et al., 1994). However, children who use aggression to achieve instrumental goals are less prone to unregulated negative emotion and physiological responding than are those who exhibit angry responses to provocation (Scarpa, Haden, & Tanaka, 2010; Vitaro et al., 2006).

Some aggressive children and adolescents tend to feel neither guilt nor empathy nor sympathy for others (de Wied et al., 2012; Lotze, Ravindran, & Myers, 2010; R. J. McMahon, Witkiewitz, & Kotler, 2010; Pardini & Byrd, 2012; Stuewig et al., 2010). They are often charming, but insincere and callous. The combination of impulsivity, problems with attention, and callousness in childhood is especially likely to predict aggression, antisocial behavior, and run-ins with the police in adolescence (Christian et al., 1997; Frick & Morris, 2004; Hastings et al., 2000) and perhaps in adulthood as well (Lynam, 1996).

Social Cognition

In addition to their differences in temperament, aggressive children differ from nonaggressive children in their social cognition. As discussed in Chapter 9, aggressive children tend to interpret the world through an "aggressive" lens. They are more likely than nonaggressive children to attribute hostile motives to others in contexts in which the other person's motives and intentions are unclear; this process has been called the "hostile attributional bias" (Dodge et al., 2006; Lansford et al., 2010; MacBrayer et al., 2003; D. A. Nelson, Mitchell, & Yang, 2008). Compared with nonaggressive peers, their goals in such social encounters are also more likely to be hostile and inappropriate to the situation, typically involving attempts to intimidate or get back at a peer (Crick & Dodge, 1994; Slaby & Guerra, 1988). For example, aggressive children are more likely to interpret an ambiguous situation—such as a child spilling a drink on them in the cafeteria—as intentional rather than accidental, and to think they need to "get back at" that child (Dodge et al., 2006). Correspondingly, when asked to come up with possible solutions to a negative social situation, aggressive children generate fewer options than do nonaggressive

comorbid ■ being present simultaneously, as in the same individual developing another mental disorder

Proactive aggression (purposeful aggression not evoked by emotion) is used by children to bully others and to get what they want from them.

children, and those options are more likely to involve aggressive or disruptive behavior (Deluty, 1985; Slaby & Guerra, 1988).

In line with these tendencies, aggressive children and adolescents are also inclined to evaluate aggressive responses more favorably, and prosocial responses less favorably, than do their nonaggressive peers (Crick & Dodge, 1994; Dodge et al., 1986; Fontaine et al., 2010). In part, this is because they feel more confident of their ability to perform acts of physical and verbal aggression (Barchia & Bussey, 2011; Quiggle et al., 1992), and they expect their aggressive behavior to result in positive outcomes (e.g., getting their way) as well as to reduce negative treatment by others (Dodge et al., 1986; Perry, Perry, & Rasmussen, 1986). Given all this, it is not surprising that aggressive children are predisposed to aggressive behavioral choices (Calvete & Orue, 2012; Dodge et al., 2006). This aggressive behavior, in turn, appears to increase children's subsequent tendency to positively evaluate aggressive interpersonal behaviors, further increasing the level of future antisocial conduct (Fontaine et al., 2008).

It is important to note, however, that although all these aspects of functioning contribute to the prediction of children's aggression, not all aggressive children exhibit the same biases in social cognition. Children who are prone to emotionally driven, hostile aggression—labeled **reactive aggression**—are particularly likely to perceive others' motives as hostile (Crick & Dodge, 1996), to initially generate aggressive responses to provocation, and to evaluate their responses as morally acceptable (Arsenio, Adams, & Gold, 2009; Dodge et al., 1997). In contrast, children who are prone to **proactive aggression**—which, like instrumental aggression, is aimed at fulfilling a need or desire—tend to anticipate more positive social consequences for aggression (Arsenio, Adams, & Gold, 2009; Crick & Dodge, 1996; Dodge et al., 1997; Sijtsema et al., 2009).

The Origins of Aggression and Antisocial Behavior

What are the causes of aggression and antisocial behavior in children? Key contributors include genetics, socialization by family members, the influence of peers, and cultural factors.

Biological Factors

Biological factors undoubtedly contribute to individual differences in aggression, but their precise role is not very clear (Eisner & Malti, 2015). Twin studies suggest that antisocial behavior runs in families and is partially due to genetics (Arsenault et al., 2003; Rhee & Waldman, 2002; Waldman et al., 2011). In addition, heredity appears to play a stronger role in aggression in early childhood and adulthood than it does in adolescence, when environmental factors are a major contributor to it (Rende & Plomin, 1995; J. Taylor, Iacono, & McGue, 2000). Heredity also contributes to both proactive and reactive aggression; but in terms of stability of individual differences in aggression and the association of aggression with psychopathic traits (e.g., callousness, lack of affect, including lack of remorse, and manipulativeness), the influence of heredity is greater for proactive aggression (Bezdjian et al., 2011; Tuvblad et al., 2009).

We have already noted one genetically influenced contributor to aggression—difficult temperament. Hormonal factors are also assumed to play a role in aggression, although the evidence for this assumption is mixed. For example, testosterone levels seem to be related to activity level and responses to provocation, and high

reactive aggression ■ emotionally driven, antagonistic aggression sparked by one's perception that other people's motives are hostile

proactive aggression ■ unemotional aggression aimed at fulfilling a need or desire

testosterone levels sometimes have been linked to aggressive behavior (Archer, 1991; Hermans, Ramsey, & van Honk, 2008). However, the relation of testosterone to aggression, although statistically significant, is quite small (Book, Starzyk, & Quinsey, 2001).

Another biological contributor to aggression discussed earlier is neurological deficits that affect attention and regulatory capabilities (Moffitt, 1993b): children who are not well regulated are likely to have difficulty controlling their tempers and inhibiting aggressive impulses (N. Eisenberg, Spinrad, & Eggum, 2010; N. Eisenberg, Valiente et al., 2009; Y. Xu, Farver, & Zhang, 2009).

Whatever their specific role, the biological correlates of aggression probably are neither necessary nor sufficient to cause aggressive behavior in most children. Genetic, neurological, or hormonal characteristics may put a child at risk for developing aggressive and antisocial behavior, but whether the child becomes aggressive will depend on numerous factors, including experiences in the social world—in other words, nature and nurture both play a role.

Socialization of Aggression and Antisocial Behavior

Children who experience harsh or low-quality parenting are at greater risk of becoming aggressive or antisocial than are other children (Dodge et al., 2006; Scaramella et al., 2002). For example, children in chaotic homes—characterized by a lack of order and structure, few predictable routines, and noise—tend to be relatively high in disruptive behavior, and this relation appears not to be due to genetics (Jaffee et al., 2012). Although it is unclear to what degree poor parenting and chaotic homes, in and of themselves, may account for children's antisocial behavior, it is clear that they comprise several factors that can promote such behavior.

Parental punitiveness Many children whose parents often use harsh but non-abusive physical punishment are prone to problem behaviors in the early years, aggression in childhood, and criminality in adolescence and adulthood (Burnette et al., 2012; Gershoff, 2002; Gershoff et al., 2010; Gershoff et al., 2012; Olson, Lopez-Duran, et al., 2011). This is especially true when the parents are cold and punitive in general (Deater-Deckard & Dodge, 1997), when the child does not have an early secure attachment (Kochanska et al., 2009; Kochanska & Kim, 2012), and when the child has a difficult temperament and is chronically angry and unregulated (Kochanska & Kim, 2012; Mulvaney & Mebert, 2007; Y. Xu et al., 2009; Yaman et al., 2010).

Although some researchers have argued that the relation between physical punishment and children's antisocial behavior varies across racial, ethnic, and cultural groups (Deater-Deckard & Dodge, 1997), longitudinal studies with large samples have not found this to be true. One study of more than 13,000 American families found that although African American parents did spank their 5-year-olds more than did White, Latino, or Asian American families, spanking predicted increases in children's aggression over time across all four race and ethnic groups (Gershoff et al., 2012). In an international study, both spanking and yelling were associated with higher levels of aggression in children in six countries—China, India, Kenya, Italy, Philippines, and Thailand—although this relation was weaker if children viewed such parenting as normal (Gershoff et al., 2010).

Harsh or abusive punishment is also consistently associated with the development of antisocial tendencies (Deater-Deckard et al., 1995; Luntz & Widom, 1994; Weiss et al., 1992). Very harsh physical discipline appears to lead to the

There is a reciprocal relation between children's behavior and their parents' punitive discipline. That is, children who are high in antisocial behavior or low in self-regulation tend to elicit harsher parenting. The harsher parenting in turn elicits more problematic behavior from the child, leading to a coercive cycle.

ACE STOCK LIMITED / GETTY IMAGES

kinds of social cognition that are associated with aggression, such as assuming that others have hostile intentions, generating aggressive solutions to interpersonal problems, and expecting aggressive behavior to result in positive outcomes (Alink et al., 2012; Dodge et al., 1995).

In addition, parents who use abusive punishment provide salient models of aggressive behavior for their children to imitate (Dogan et al., 2007). Ironically, children who are subjected to such punishment are likely to be anxious or angry and therefore unlikely to attend to their parents' instructions or demands or to be motivated to behave as their parents wish (M. L. Hoffman, 1983).

There is probably a reciprocal relation between children's behavior and their parents' punitive discipline (Arim et al., 2011; N. Eisenberg, Fabes et al., 1999). That is, children who are high in antisocial behavior, who exhibit psychopathic traits (e.g., are callous, unemotional, manipulative, remorseless), or who are low in self-regulation tend to elicit harsh parenting (Lansford et al., 2009; Salihovic et al., 2012); in turn, harsh parenting increases the children's problem behavior (Sheehan & Watson, 2008). However, some recent research suggests that harsh physical punishment has a stronger effect on children's behavior problems than vice versa (Lansford et al., 2011).

Ineffective discipline is often evident in the pattern of troubled family interaction described by G. R. Patterson (1982, 1995; J. Snyder et al., 2005), discussed in Chapter 1. In this pattern, the aggression of children who are out of control may be unintentionally reinforced by parents who, once their efforts to coerce compliance have failed, give in to their children's fits of temper and demands (J. Snyder, Reid, & Patterson, 2003). This is especially probable in the case of out-of-control boys, who are much more likely than other boys to react negatively to their mother's attempts to discipline them (G. R. Patterson, Reid, & Dishion, 1992). Whether maternal coercion elicits the same pattern of response from girls as from boys is not yet known because most of the relevant research has been done with boys, but there is some reason to believe that it does not (McFadyen-Ketchum et al., 1996).

The relation between punitive parenting and children's aggression can, of course, have a genetic component, as was discussed in Chapter 3. Parents whose genes predispose them to aggressive or punitive parenting will pass those genes onto their children; thus, punitive parenting can be linked to antisocial and aggressive behavior in children both directly through genes and indirectly through a punitive home environment (Davies et al., 2012; Dogan et al., 2007; Thornberry et al., 2003). Recall that this indirect effect of a parent's genes on a child's behavior is called a *passive gene–environment correlation* (see Chapter 8 and Chapter 10). Both factors appear to be at play; twin studies indicate that the relation between punitive parenting and children's antisocial behavior is not entirely due to hereditary factors (Boutwell et al., 2011; Jaffee et al., 2004a; Jaffee et al., 2004b), which suggests that something about the environment the parents provide for their children accounts for whether those children display antisocial behavior.

Poor parental monitoring Another factor that can increase children's antisocial behavior is parents' monitoring of where their children are, whom they are with, and what they are doing. One reason parental monitoring may be important is that it reduces the likelihood that older children and adolescents will associate with deviant, antisocial peers (Dodge et al., 2008; G. R. Patterson, Capaldi, & Bank, 1991). It also makes it more likely that parents will know whether their children are engaging in antisocial behavior. This notion is supported by data from the U.S. Department of Justice, which finds that juvenile crimes peak from 3 P.M. to 7 P.M. on weekdays (see Figure 14.6)—the potentially unsupervised hours between the end of school and when parents get home from work. Once adolescents begin engaging in aggressive and antisocial behaviors, they become even harder to monitor; parents of antisocial or aggressive youth find that monitoring can lead to such high conflict with their children that they are forced to back off (Laird et al., 2003).

Parental conflict Children who are frequently exposed to verbal and physical violence between their parents tend to be more antisocial and aggressive than other children (Cummings & Davies, 2002; R. Feldman, Masalha, & Derdikman-Eiron, 2010; Keller et al., 2008; Van Ryzin & Dishion, 2012). This relation holds true even when genetic factors that might have caused it are taken into account (Jaffee et al., 2002). One obvious reason is that embattled parents model aggressive behavior for their children. Another is that children whose mothers are physically abused tend to believe that violence is an acceptable, even natural part of family interactions (Graham-Bermann & Brescoll, 2000). Compared with spouses who get along well with each other, embattled spouses also tend to be less skilled and responsive, and more hostile and controlling, in

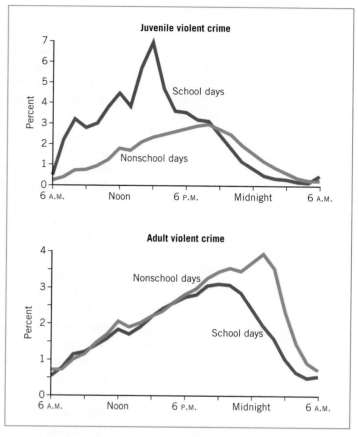

FIGURE 14.6 **Juvenile crimes by time of day and day of week** Nearly 1 in 5 juvenile crimes occurs between the hours of 3 P.M. and 7 P.M. on school days. Adult crimes do not vary dramatically by school and non-school days. (Data from Sickmund & Puzzanchera, 2014)

Children are more likely to develop aggressive and antisocial behavior if they are exposed to marital conflict, especially violence. Parents who are in unhappy marriages tend to be withdrawn from and not supportive of their children, which appears to contribute to their children's problems with adjustment.

their parenting (Buehler et al., 1997; Davies et al., 2012; Emery, 1989; Gonzales et al., 2000), which, in turn, can increase their children's aggressive tendencies (Li, Putallaz, & Su, 2011). This pattern—in which marital hostility predicts hostile parenting, which, in turn, predicts children's aggression—has also been found in families with an adopted child, so these relations cannot be due solely to genes shared by parents and children (Stover et al., 2012).

Socioeconomic status and children's antisocial behavior Children from low-income families tend to be more antisocial and aggressive than children from more prosperous homes (Goodnight et al., 2012; Keiley et al., 2000; NICHD Early Child Care Research Network, 2004; Stouthamer-Loeber et al., 2002). This pattern is highlighted by the finding that when families escaped from poverty, 4- to 7-year-old children tended to become less aggressive and antisocial, whereas families' remaining in poverty or moving into poverty for the long term was associated with an increase in children's antisocial behavior (Macmillan, McMorris, & Kruttschnitt, 2004). There are many reasons that might account for such differences in trajectories.

One major reason is the greater amount of stressors experienced by children in poor families, including stress in the family (illness, domestic violence, divorce, legal problems) and neighborhood violence (Vanfossen et al., 2010). In addition, as discussed in Chapter 12, low SES tends to be associated with living in a single-parent family or being an unplanned child of a teenage parent, and stressors of these sorts are linked to increased aggression and antisocial behavior (Dodge, Pettit, & Bates, 1994; Linares et al., 2001; Tolan, Gorman-Smith, & Henry, 2003; Trentacosta et al., 2008). Also, because of the many stressors they face, impoverished parents are more likely than other parents to be rejecting and low in warmth; to use erratic, threatening, and harsh discipline; and to be lax in supervising their children (Conger et al., 1994; Dodge et al., 1994; Odgers et al., 2012). Children in low-income families tend to live in low-income neighborhoods that tend to have more violence and crime, and to attend low-income schools, which are under-resourced and rate high in violence (Gershoff & Benner, 2014). Such neighborhoods also lack appropriate mentors, job opportunities, and constructive activities (e.g., clubs and sports) that could engage children and youth and divert them from potential antisocial behavior.

Peer Influence

As discussed in Chapter 13, aggressive children tend to socialize with other aggressive children and often become more delinquent over time if they have close friends who are aggressive. Moreover, the expression of a genetic tendency toward aggression is stronger for individuals who have aggressive friends (Brendgen et al., 2008).

The larger peer group with whom older children and adolescents socialize may influence aggression even more than their close friends do (Coie & Dodge, 1998). In one study, boys exposed to peers involved in overt antisocial behaviors, such as violence and the use of a weapon, were more than 3 times as likely as other boys to engage in such acts themselves (Keenan et al., 1995). Associating with delinquent peers tends to increase delinquency because these peers model and reinforce antisocial behavior in the peer group. At the same time, participating in delinquent activities brings adolescents into contact with more delinquent peers (Dishion,

Véronneau, & Myers, 2010; Dishion, Ha, & Véronneau, 2012; Lacourse et al., 2003; Thornberry et al., 1994).

Although research findings vary somewhat, it appears that children's susceptibility to peer pressure to become involved in antisocial behavior increases in the elementary school years, peaks at about 8th or 9th grade, and declines thereafter (Berndt, 1979; B. B. Brown, Clasen, & Eicher, 1986; Steinberg & Silverberg, 1986). Although not all adolescents are susceptible to negative peer influence (Allen, Porter, & McFarland, 2006), even popular youth in early adolescence tend to increase participation in minor levels of drug use and delinquency if these behaviors are approved by peers (Allen et al., 2005).

Peer approval of relational aggression increases in middle school, and students in peer groups supportive of relational aggression become increasingly aggressive (N. E. Werner & Hill, 2010). However, there are exceptions to this overall pattern that appear to be related to cultural factors. For example, Mexican American immigrant youth who are less acculturated, and therefore more tied to traditional values, appear to be less susceptible to peer pressure toward antisocial behavior than are Mexican American children who are more acculturated. Thus, it may be that peers play less of a role in promoting antisocial behavior for adolescents who are embedded in a traditional culture oriented toward adults' expectations (e.g., deference and courtesy toward adults and adherence to adult values) (Wall, Power, & Arbona, 1993).

Biology and Socialization: Their Joint Influence on Children's Antisocial Behavior

As should be clear by now, it is very difficult to separate the specific biological, cultural, peer, and familial factors that affect the development of children's antisocial behavior (Van den Oord, Boomsma, & Verhulst, 2000). Nonetheless, it is clear that parents' treatment of their children affects children's aggression and antisocial behavior. Direct evidence of the role of parental effects can be found in intervention studies. When parents are trained to deal with their children in an effective manner, there are improvements in their children's conduct problems (A. Connell et al., 2008; Dishion et al., 2008; Hanish & Tolan, 2001). Similar effects have been obtained in intervention studies in schools. For example, the Fast Track program, a federally funded intervention for children at high risk for antisocial behavior, trained students in a special curriculum designed to promote understanding and communication of emotions, positive social behavior, self-control, and social problem solving (Conduct Problems Prevention Research Group, 1999a; 1999b; Greenberg et al., 1995). Children with the most serious behavior problems participated in an intensive intervention. The program was quite successful, with classrooms as a whole exhibiting less aggression and disruptive behavior and a more positive atmosphere.

Numerous other programs have been used to combat bullying in schools, and many appear to reduce the incidence of bullying considerably; the more effective programs target adolescents rather than younger children (Cross et al., 2011; Salmivalli, Kärnä, & Poskiparta, 2011; Ttofi & Farrington, 2011). There are also community-based programs that aim to reduce antisocial behavior by increasing positive behavior through an approach called *positive youth development;* see Box 14.4 to learn more about this approach. Effects such as these indicate that socialization in and of itself plays a role in the development of antisocial behavior.

BOX 14.4 | applications

POSITIVE YOUTH DEVELOPMENT AND SERVICE LEARNING

Communities and governments have long sought ways to reduce youth problem behaviors and increase positive behaviors. Beginning in the late 1800s, organizations such as the Young Men's Christian Association (YMCA), Boy Scouts of America, Camp Fire Girls, and Girls Scouts of America were established to promote leadership, citizenship, and life skills among youth. While these organizations continue to serve millions of young people throughout the United States, a new generation of services has developed under the mantle of positive youth development.

Interventions that take a **positive youth development** approach focus attention on youths' strengths and assets, rather than on their weaknesses and deficits, and work to develop and nurture those strengths and assets (Lerner et al., 2005). The positive youth development approach emphasizes what are known as the Five Cs (Eccles & Gootman, 2002; Lerner et al., 2005):

- Competence (skill development in social, academic, cognitive, and vocational domains)
- Confidence (self-efficacy and self-worth)
- Connection (positive bonds with adults and peers in the community)
- Character (integrity and morality)
- Caring and compassion (sympathy and empathy for others)

The positive youth development approach recognizes that youth are developing within social and cultural contexts that both influence and are influenced by the youth themselves, and that when youth contribute to their communities they also benefit (Sanders & Munford, 2014). A panel convened by the National Academy of Sciences concluded that the most successful positive youth development programs are those that ensure the participants' physical and psychological safety, involve a clear structure and adult supervision, endorse positive social norms, mentor participants in skills to develop self-efficacy, and provide opportunities to belong (Eccles & Gootman, 2002).

Service learning is a strategy for promoting positive youth development that integrates school-based instruction with community involvement in order to promote youths' civic responsibility and enhance their learning (Celio, Durlak, & Dymnicki, 2011). Service-learning programs promote positive behaviors by giving students opportunities to design and develop service projects, engage with their communities, and reflect on the benefits of their experiences, both for themselves and for the community (Chung & McBride, 2015). Participation in these activities can increase students' empathy for the needs of others, awareness of larger social issues, ability to participate in a cooperative activity, and capacity for making responsible decisions (Chung & McBride, 2015).

Dozens of research studies have examined whether service learning succeeds in promoting positive youth development. A review of 62 such studies concluded that service-learning programs at the elementary school through college levels had a positive effect on youths' feelings of self-esteem and self-efficacy, attitudes toward school, civic engagement, social skills, and academic achievement (Celio et al., 2011). Students who participate in service learning also have higher grade point averages, fewer behavior problems, and greater civic knowledge than students who do not participate in service learning (Schmidt, Shumow, & Kackar, 2007).

There is some concern that requiring students to engage in service activities could undermine their interest, enjoyment, and intrinsic motivation to participate in volunteer work, thus counteracting any benefit service learning may have to participants. However, when examined by researchers, no differences have been found between voluntary and mandatory service—both have positive benefits for students (Schmidt et al., 2007). Furthermore, proponents of service learning argue that it can initiate habits of civic engagement and public service that will persist throughout life. The results summarized above appear to support this conclusion.

The District of Columbia and the state of Maryland now require that high school students engage in 100 and 75 hours, respectively, of community service in order to graduate (Education Commission of the States, 2016). In addition, 23 states allow students to receive credit toward graduation for community service or for service learning courses (Education Commission of the States, 2016). Perhaps as a result of such requirements, over half of high school students across the U.S. report engaging in service learning (Schmidt et al., 2007).

Youth who engage in service learning projects, like cleaning up a park, experience increases in self-efficacy and other positive outcomes.

PAMELA MOORE / GETTY IMAGES

Nonetheless, recent genetically informed research illustrates that often it is the combination of genetic and environmental factors that predict children's antisocial, aggressive behavior and that some children are more sensitive to the quality of parenting than are others. As noted in our previous discussions of differential susceptibility (see Chapter 10), children with certain gene variants related to serotonin or dopamine, which affect neurotransmission, appear to be more responsive to their environment than are children with different variants. For example, under adverse conditions (e.g., chronic stress, poor parenting, socioeconomic deprivation), children with particular variants of the serotonin transporter gene (SLC6A4), the dopamine receptor gene (DRD4), or the MAOA gene (which controls the enzyme that metabolizes serotonin and dopamine) tend to be more aggressive than children with different variants of these genes (Caspi et al., 2002; C. C. Conway et al., 2012). By comparison, those same children tend to be less aggressive when they are in a supportive, resource-rich environment (Simons et al., 2011; Simons et al., 2012).

In other cases, such gene variants are related to higher risk for aggression in adverse situations like maltreatment and divorce but are not related to aggression in the absence of the adverse conditions (Cicchetti, Rogosch, & Thibodeau, 2012; Nederhof et al., 2012). Regardless of the exact nature of the gene–environment interaction, it seems clear that the degree of aggression is affected by a combination of heredity and the environment (see Chapter 3 for further discussion of gene–environment interactions related to aggression).

positive youth development ▪ an approach to youth intervention that focuses on developing and nurturing strengths and assets rather than on correcting weaknesses and deficits

service learning ▪ a strategy for promoting positive youth development that integrates school-based instruction with community involvement in order to promote civic responsibility and enhance learning

Review

Aggressive behavior emerges by the 2nd year of life and increases in frequency during the toddler years. Physical aggression starts to decline in frequency in the preschool years; in elementary school, children tend to exhibit more nonphysical aggression (e.g., relational aggression) than at younger ages, and some children increasingly engage in antisocial behaviors such as stealing. Early individual differences in aggression and conduct problems predict antisocial behavior in later childhood, adolescence, and adulthood. Children who first engage in aggressive, antisocial acts in early to mid-adolescence are less likely to continue their antisocial behavior after adolescence than are children who are aggressive and antisocial at a younger age.

Biological factors, including those related to temperament and neurological problems, likely affect children's degree of aggression. Social cognition is also associated with aggressiveness in a variety of ways, including the attribution of hostile motives to others, having hostile goals, constructing and enacting aggressive responses in difficult situations, and evaluating aggressive responses favorably.

Children's aggression is affected by a range of environmental factors, as well as by heredity. In general, low parental support, poor monitoring, or the use of disciplinary practices that are abusive or inconsistent are related to high levels of children's antisocial behavior. Parental conflict in the home and many of the stresses associated with family transitions (e.g., divorce) and poverty can increase the likelihood of children's aggression. In addition, involvement with antisocial peers likely contributes to antisocial behavior, although aggressive children also seek out antisocial peers. Cultural values and practices, as communicated in the child's social world, also contribute to differences among children in aggressive behavior. Intervention programs can be used to reduce aggression, which provides evidence of the role of environmental factors in children's aggression.

CHAPTER SUMMARY

Moral Judgment

- Piaget delineated two age-related moral stages and a transitional period. In the first stage, heteronomous morality of constraint, young children tend to believe that rules are unchangeable and tend to weigh consequences more than intentions in evaluating the morality of actions. In the autonomous stage, children realize that rules are social products that can be changed, and they consider motives and intentions when evaluating behavior. Several aspects of Piaget's theory have not held up well to scrutiny, but his theory provided the foundation for subsequent work on moral reasoning.

- Kohlberg outlined three levels of moral judgment—preconventional, conventional, and postconventional—each originally containing two stages (Stage 6 was eventually dropped from Kohlberg's scoring procedure). Kohlberg hypothesized that his sequence of stages reflects age-related, discontinuous (qualitative) changes in moral reasoning that are universal. According to Kohlberg, these changes stem from cognitive advances, particularly in perspective taking. Although there is support for the idea that higher levels of moral reasoning are related to cognitive growth, it is not clear that children's moral reasoning moves through discontinuous stages of development or develops the same way in all cultures and for all kinds of moral issues (e.g., prosocial-moral reasoning).

- The conscience involves internalized moral standards and feelings of guilt for misbehavior: it restrains the individual from engaging in unacceptable behavior. The conscience develops slowly over time, beginning before age 2. Children are more likely to internalize parental standards if they are securely attached and if their parents do not rely on excessive parental power in their discipline, depending on their temperament.

- There are important differences among the moral, social-conventional, and personal domains of behavior and judgment. Young children, like older children, differentiate among domains of social judgment. Which behaviors are considered matters of moral, social-conventional, or personal judgment varies somewhat across cultures.

Prosocial Behavior

- Prosocial behavior is voluntary behavior intended to benefit another, such as helping, sharing, and comforting others. Young children who are prosocial, especially those who spontaneously engage in sharing even at a personal cost, tend to be prosocial when older.

- Prosocial behaviors emerge by the 2nd year of life and increase in frequency with age, probably due to age-related increases in children's abilities to sympathize and take others' perspectives. Differences among children in these abilities contribute to individual differences in children's prosocial behavior.

- Heredity, which contributes to differences among children in temperament, likely affects how empathic and prosocial children are.

- A positive parent–child relationship; authoritative parenting; the use of reasoning by parents and teachers; and exposure to prosocial models, values, and activities are associated with the development of sympathy and prosocial behavior. Cultural values and expectations also appear to affect the degree to which children exhibit prosocial behavior and toward whom.

- School-based intervention programs designed to promote cooperation, perspective taking, helping, and prosocial values are associated with increased prosocial tendencies in children.

Antisocial Behavior

- Aggressive behavior emerges by the 2nd year of life and increases in frequency during the toddler years; physical aggression starts to decline in frequency in the preschool years. In elementary school, children tend to exhibit more nonphysical aggression (e.g., relational aggression) than at younger ages, and some children increasingly engage in antisocial behaviors such as stealing.

- From preschool on, boys are more physically aggressive than girls and are more likely to engage in delinquent behavior.

- Early individual differences in aggression and conduct problems predict antisocial behavior in later childhood, adolescence, and adulthood.

- Biological factors that contribute to differences among children in temperament and neurological functioning likely affect how aggressive children become. Social cognition also affects aggression: aggressive children tend to attribute hostile motives to others and to have hostile goals themselves.

- Children's aggression is promoted by a range of environmental factors, including low parental support; chaotic families; poor monitoring; abusive, coercive, or inconsistent disciplining; and stress or conflict in the home. In addition, involvement with antisocial peers likely contributes to antisocial behavior, although it is also likely that aggressive children seek out antisocial peers. Aggression also varies somewhat across cultures, suggesting that cultural values, norms, and socialization practices may also contribute to individual differences in aggression and antisocial behavior.

■ Children who are diagnosed with an antisocial behavior disorder such as conduct disorder or oppositional defiant disorder display relatively severe forms of problematic behaviors.

■ In high-risk schools, interventions designed to promote understanding and communication of emotions, positive social behavior, self-control, and social problem solving can reduce the likelihood that children will develop behavior problems, including aggression.

Test Yourself

1. According to Piaget, which of the following factors is most influential in the development of children's moral reasoning?
   a. interactions with peers
   b. adult influence
   c. societal norms
   d. heredity

2. Luis does not write on his desk because the rules of the classroom forbid it, and he wants to set a good example for his classmates. According to Kohlberg's hierarchy, Luis is in which stage of moral development?
   a. universal ethical principles
   b. punishment and obedience orientation
   c. instrumental and exchange orientation
   d. social system and conscience orientation

3. Sarah is mad and wants to break her mother's favorite vase. However, she doesn't want to get into trouble for her actions, so she decides to punch a pillow instead. According to Kohlberg's hierarchy, Sarah is in which level of moral development?
   a. preconventional
   b. developmental
   c. conventional
   d. postconventional

4. In discussions of moral development, prosocial behavior is best defined as:
   a. behavior based on personal benefit.
   b. voluntary behavior intended to benefit another.
   c. actions that contribute to society as a whole.
   d. behavior intended to win approval.

5. Children develop a conscience:
   a. through identification with the same-gender parent, at about age 4 to 6.
   b. slowly over time, affected by parental disciplinary practices.
   c. in a discontinuous process.
   d. in a standard sequence, regardless of parental practices.

6. For children with a specific variant of the gene SLC6A4, low maternal responsiveness is associated with high levels of conscience in early childhood. This pattern is an example of
   _____.
   a. Piaget's stages of moral development
   b. Kohlberg's levels of moral reasoning

   c. goodness of fit between temperament and environment
   d. prosocial behavior

7. Which of the following has been shown to influence the development of conscience?
   a. parental discipline style
   b. genetic factors
   c. temperament
   d. all of the above

8. At approximately what age do children begin to believe that it is more important to follow moral rules than social conventions?
   a. 12 months
   b. 6 years
   c. 12 years
   d. 3 years

9. Jaden is playing with a toy car. Sam comes over and takes it from her, which makes Jaden sad. Omar watches this happen and feels sad as well. Omar is displaying what kind of emotional response?
   a. sympathy
   b. prosocial behavior
   c. altruism
   d. empathy

10. Cooperation is a form of prosocial behavior that may be driven by both sympathy and a child's sense of

    _____.
    a. shame
    b. empathy
    c. fairness
    d. justice

11. Which of the following has been shown to influence the development of prosocial tendencies?
    a. parental discipline style
    b. genetic factors
    c. temperament
    d. all of the above

12. Physical aggression is normative in development and increases in frequency beginning at around _____ of age.
    a. 5–6 years
    b. 6 months
    c. 18 months
    d. 3 years

13. Severe antisocial and aggressive behaviors, such as cruelty to animals and patterns of bullying, are examples of _____.
   a. conduct disorder
   b. reactive aggression
   c. oppositional defiant disorder
   d. negative youth development

14. In the school cafeteria, Lynn pushes other children out of the way in order to get ahead in the line. What type of aggression is Lynn using?
   a. reactive
   b. proactive

   c. antisocial
   d. relational

15. During which stage of development is aggression influenced more by environment than by hereditary factors?
   a. adolescence
   b. early childhood
   c. infancy
   d. adulthood

Don't stop now! Research shows that testing yourself is a powerful learning tool. Visit LaunchPad to access the LearningCurve adaptive quizzing system, which gives you a personalized study plan to help build your mastery of the chapter material through videos, activities, and more. **Go to launchpadworks.com.**

Critical Thinking Questions

1. Recall a recent moral dilemma in your own life. What sorts of reasoning did you use when thinking about the dilemma? On what dimensions did it differ from Kohlberg's Heinz dilemma? How might these differences have affected your reasoning about this dilemma?

2. How would you design a study to determine why aggressive children and adolescents have aggressive friends? How would you determine whether aggressive youth simply choose aggressive friends or whether aggressive friends tend to make youth become more aggressive?

3. Suppose you wanted to assess children's helping behavior that was altruistic and not due to factors such as the expectation of personal gain or concern about others' approval. How would you design a study to assess altruistic helping in 5-year-olds? How would you alter the procedure if you wanted to assess altruistic helping in 16-year-olds?

4. Using the tenets of social-learning theory (see Chapter 9), outline ways in which parents might deter the development of aggression in their children.

5. Some advocates within the criminal justice system have pushed in the last two decades to try youth who commit offenses as adults. Given what you have learned about moral development, should youth be considered as culpable as adults for their actions?

6. Schools are increasingly being called upon to teach children how to behave morally. What are the pros and cons of schools as settings for teaching these skills? What are the pros and cons of leaving this job solely to parents?

7. Given the pattern of juvenile violent crime peaking between 3 P.M. and 4 P.M. on school days (see Figure 14.6), what could communities do to reduce juvenile violent crime during these hours?

Key Terms

aggression, p. 613

altruistic motives, p. 606

antisocial behavior, p. 613

comorbid, p. 618

conduct disorder (CD), p. 618

conscience, p. 600

instrumental aggression, p. 615

moral judgments, p. 602

oppositional defiant disorder (ODD), p. 618

personal judgments, p. 602

positive youth development, p. 626

primary prevention, p. 614

proactive aggression, p. 620

prosocial behavior, p. 599

reactive aggression, p. 620

secondary prevention, p. 615

service learning, p. 626

social-conventional judgments, p. 602

tertiary intervention, p. 615

▶ Student Video Activities

Moral Development in Early Childhood

Kohlberg Heinz Moral Dilemma and Moral
Development in Middle Childhood

Good Guys vs. Bad Guys: How Do Babies
Know the Difference?

The Role of Parenting in Moral Development

Answers to Test Yourself

1. a, **2.** d, **3.** a, **4.** b, **5.** b, **6.** c, **7.** d, **8.** d, **9.** d, **10.** c, **11.** d, **12.** c, **13.** a, **14.** b, **15.** a

LAURIE WIGHAM, *Birch Lake Lagoon* (watercolor, 2015)

Gender Development

Themes

- Nature and Nurture
- The Active Child
- The Sociocultural Context
- Individual Differences

If you think about the children that you knew while growing up, you probably recall that there were many individual differences among them. Within any group of children, individual interests, personalities, and abilities will vary. Consider four hypothetical North American 12-year-olds: Casey likes playing on the school soccer team and gets bored when sitting for too long; Taylor likes to watch science fiction programs and belongs to the school computer club; Kim likes dance classes and puts a lot of thought into what to wear each day; Alex is a cheerleader at school and babysits for extra money. You might expect that Casey and Taylor are boys and that Kim and Alex are girls. This thinking would be consistent with commonly held expectations for girls and boys in North America. In some instances, these expectations might reflect general trends among many boys and many girls. However, as we will explore in this chapter, empirical research challenges many widely held expectations about gender. For example, returning to the children that we just described, Casey or Taylor might well be girls—as many girls like sports and physical activity, as well as science fiction and computers. At the same time, Kim or Alex could be boys—as some boys enjoy dancing and dressing up, as well as belong to cheerleading squads and babysit.

Despite the illustration offered in the opening paragraph, the notion that girls and boys are fundamentally different in their dispositions and behavior remains popular. The phrase "the opposite sexes" is commonly used to refer to girls and boys (and women and men). However, scientists find that girls and boys are *not* opposites. As discussed in the chapter, only a few cognitive abilities and social behaviors actually show consistent gender differences, and most of those average differences tend to be fairly small.

Even when researchers find an average gender difference in a behavior, there is considerable overlap between the genders when individuals are considered. For instance, consider the temperamental trait of activity level (see Chapter 10). On average, boys exhibit higher activity levels than girls (see Table 15.1 on page 656). However, many boys are lower in activity level than the average girl, and many girls are higher in activity level than the average boy. Thus, to understand gender development it is important to keep in mind two points: first, girls and boys generally are not opposites; similarities are more common than differences (Hyde, 2005). Second, not all girls are alike, and not all boys are alike. There is considerable variability within each gender in abilities and behavior.

In this chapter, we consider what might account for gender differences or similarities between girls and boys. Why do they have different preferences?

Developmental psychologists generally acknowledge the combined influences of biological, psychological, and cultural processes on gender development (Leaper, 2013, 2015a), but they differ among themselves in how much they stress particular factors in their explanations for observed gender differences. Some researchers argue that certain differences in boys' and girls' behavior reflect underlying biological differences that emerged over the course of human evolution (Bjorklund & Pellegrini, 2002; Geary, 2010). In their view, average gender differences in some behaviors are partly attributable to genetic sex differences in brain structures and hormone effects. By contrast, other psychologists place more emphasis on social and cognitive influences (Bussey & Bandura, 1999; C. L. Martin, Ruble, & Szkrybalo, 2002).

Many girls and boys are similar in their interests and behaviors. For example, approximately 40% of girls and 50% of boys participate in organized sports.

CHRISTOPHER FUTCHER / GETTY IMAGES

They focus on the social influences of family, peers, teachers, and the culture at large, as well as on the impact of cognitive processes such as gender-related beliefs and gender identity. In general, developmental psychologists agree that gender development is a combination of *nature and nurture*, even if they might disagree on the relative influences of each.

We examine two main questions in this chapter: (1) How similar or different are girls and boys in terms of psychological variables? (2) What might account for any differences? We first consider the biological, cognitive-motivational, and cultural influences that may contribute to gender development. Next, we outline the major milestones in children's development of gender stereotypes and gender-typed behavior. Then we compare what actually is known about the similarities and differences between girls and boys in specific areas of development, including physical development, cognitive abilities and achievement, and personality and social behavior.

Throughout our discussion, we use the terms *sex* and *gender* in distinct ways. **Sex** tends to imply biological origins for any differences between males and females, based on one's sex chromosomes (see Chapter 3). **Gender** tends to be a more neutral term that refers to people's categorization of other individuals or one's self-categorization as either female or male (or possibly neither). (As explained later, transgender individuals may identify with a gender category that is different from the one assigned at birth.) We use the term *sex* only when referring explicitly to biological processes, such as those involving sex hormones or genetic sex. In addition, the terms **gender-typed** and **cross-gender-typed** refer, respectively, to behaviors stereotyped for a given person's gender and to behaviors contrary to those stereotyped for a given person's gender. For example, playing with dolls is gender-typed for girls and cross-gender-typed for boys. Finally, the term **gender typing** refers broadly to the process of gender socialization during development.

Four of our seven themes are particularly prominent in this chapter. The theme of *nature and nurture* appears repeatedly, as perspectives vary in emphasizing the roles played by biological and environmental factors in gender development. The theme of the *active child* is apparent in cognitive theories of gender development that emphasize children's roles in discovering what it means to be male or female and in socializing their peers into gender-appropriate roles. The *sociocultural context* is reflected in theories that emphasize the central roles that parents, teachers, peers, and the media play in shaping children's gender development. Finally, the theme of *individual differences* also pervades the chapter as we attempt to account for the ways in which males and females are similar and different.

sex ■ distinction between genetic females (XX) and genetic males (XY)

gender ■ social assignment or self-categorization as female or male (or possibly neither or a different category)

gender-typed ■ behaviors stereotyped or expected for a given person's gender

cross-gender-typed ■ behaviors stereotyped or expected for the gender other than that of a given person

gender typing ■ the process of gender socialization

Theoretical Approaches to Gender Development

Researchers variously point to the influences of biological, cognitive-motivational, and cultural factors on gender development. First, biological differences between females and males—including the influence of sex hormones and brain structure differences—may partly account for average gender differences in some behaviors. Second, cognition and motivation—learning gender-typed roles through observation and practice—can shape children's gender development. As highlighted in cognitive-motivational explanations, boys and girls are systematically provided different role models, opportunities, and incentives for gender-typed behavior by parents, teachers, peers, and the media. Finally, cultural factors, including the relative status of women and men in society, may shape children's gender development.

As you will see in this section, there is empirical evidence for the role of each type of influence in certain behaviors. Indeed, it is likely that most aspects of gender development result from the complex interaction of all three sets of factors.

Biological Influences

Some researchers interested in biological influences on development emphasize possible ways that gender differences in behavior may have emerged during the course of human evolution. Other biologically oriented researchers focus more directly on identifying hormonal factors and differences in brain functioning as possible influences on gender differences in behavioral development.

Evolutionary Approaches

Among the most consistent average gender differences seen across cultures are girls' and boys' preferences for gender-typed play, as well as higher average incidences of physical aggression among boys than girls. However, there is variation within each gender in these trends.

As discussed in Chapter 9, evolutionary theory proposes that certain characteristics that facilitate survival and reproduction (and thereby lead to the transmission of genes to succeeding generations) have been favored over the course of human evolution. Developmental psychologists generally agree that evolution is important for understanding children's development. However, there are different views regarding the proposal that females and males evolved different behavioral dispositions (inherited tendencies to think and act in certain ways). Two examples are *evolutionary psychology theory* and *biosocial theory*.

Evolutionary psychology theory According to evolutionary psychology theory, certain behavioral tendencies occur because they helped humans survive during the course of evolution. Some evolutionary psychology theorists propose that particular gender differences in behavior reflect evolved personality dispositions. These theorists argue that sex-linked dispositions evolved to increase the chances that women and men would successfully mate and protect their offspring (Benenson, 2014; Bjorklund & Pellegrini, 2002; D. M. Buss, 2014; Geary, 2010; Kenrick, Trost, & Sundie, 2004).

As noted in Chapter 9, studies of children's play behavior show average gender differences that have been interpreted as consistent with the evolutionary perspective. For example, more boys than girls tend to engage in physically active, rough-and-tumble, and competitive types of play (Benenson, 2014; Maccoby, 1998). Many boys devote considerable effort to jockeying with their male peers for dominance in groups. Geary (1999) proposed that boys' play-fighting may represent an "evolved tendency to practice the competencies that were associated with male–male competition during human evolution" (p. 31). A propensity to engage in physical aggression is thought to have provided reproductive advantages for males in competition with other males for resources, including access to females (Geary, 2004, 2010).

In contrast, girls are more likely than boys on average to devote effort to establishing and maintaining positive social relations, spend time in smaller groups of close female friends, and tend to avoid open conflict in their interactions (Benenson, 2014; Maccoby, 1998). Girls also engage in much more play-parenting, including play with dolls,

ASIA IMAGES GROUP / GETTY IMAGES

JOHNER / GETTY IMAGES

than boys do. From the evolutionary psychology perspective, these behaviors reflect evolved dispositions because maternal care in the form of breast-feeding was required for infants' survival. In addition, nurturance and other affiliative behaviors may have increased the probability that their offspring would survive long enough to reproduce.

Evolutionary psychology theory is a popular approach, but some of its proposals regarding gender differences are controversial. Critics have raised two notable issues. First, some biologists and psychologists argue that many of evolutionary psychology theory's claims about sex differences in personality traits cannot be tested (S. J. Gould, 1997; Lickliter & Honeycutt, 2003; W. Wood & Eagly, 2002, 2012). These critics argue that some of the theory's explanations are based on circular reasoning: if an average sex difference in behavior occurs—such as women being more likely than men to express nurturance—it is seen as having helped humans survive during the course of evolution; that is, the difference is considered as having been adaptive during evolution because the average gender difference exists today. Such an argument merely asserts its premise as its conclusion—and therefore it is a difficult argument to test! Perhaps the clearest way to establish evidence of evolutionary influences would be to link sex differences in particular behaviors to genetic variations on sex chromosomes. Advances in molecular genetics may someday allow researchers to address these assumptions in evolutionary psychology theory. A second concern is that evolutionary psychology theory can be construed as a rationalization for maintaining the status quo in traditional gender roles; that is, some versions of the theory focus on biological constraints in gender development (see Angier, 1999; S. J. Gould, 1997).

An alternate evolutionary approach, called *biosocial theory*, emphasizes humans' capacity for behavioral adaptation to changing environmental conditions (e.g., Wood & Eagly, 2002, 2012; also see Lickliter & Honeycutt, 2003). We review this theory next.

Biosocial theory Biosocial theory focuses on the evolution of observable *physical* differences between the sexes. By proposing that these differences can have behavioral and social consequences, this theory emphasizes the capacity for behavioral flexibility as an adaptation to environmental variability (Wood & Eagly, 2002, 2012). Proponents of biosocial theory argue that for much of human history, the most important physical differences have been (1) men's greater average size, strength, and foot speed and (2) women's childbearing and nursing capacities. Men's physical abilities gave them an advantage in activities such as hunting and combat and, in turn, tended to confer status and social dominance in the society. In contrast, bearing and nursing children limited women's mobility and involvement in many forms of economic subsistence such as hunting.

However, according to biosocial theory, biology does not necessarily determine destiny. First, in our current technological societies, men's strength and other physical qualities are not relevant for most means of subsistence. For example, strength is irrelevant to succeeding as a manager, lawyer, physician, or engineer. Accordingly, as gender equality has increased, greater numbers of women have entered these high-status occupations (although gender equality is not fully realized in any of them). In addition, reproductive control and day care provide women greater flexibility to maintain their involvement in the labor force. Thus, according to biosocial theory, both physical sex differences and social ecology shape the different gender roles assigned to men and women—as well as the socialization of boys and girls.

As we have seen, some claims associated with evolutionary psychology theory are criticized for emphasizing biological determinants of gender differences. However, evolutionary psychologists take issue with biosocial theory, asserting that the body and the mind evolved together and that biosocial theory addresses only the body's impact on gender development (Archer & Lloyd, 2002; Luxen, 2007). In sum, evolutionary psychology theory and biosocial theory both acknowledge the importance of evolution and the physical differences between women and men. But evolutionary psychology theorists place relatively more emphasis on sex differences in evolved genetic traits leading to differences in behavioral dispositions in women and men.

Neuroscience Approaches

Researchers who take a neuroscience approach focus on testing whether and how genes, hormones, and brain functioning relate to variations in gender development (Hines, 2013). Some neuroscience researchers also frame their work in terms of an evolutionary psychology perspective (Geary, 2004, 2010).

Genes Biological sex is determined by whether a person has XX (genetically female) or XY (genetically male) chromosome pairs. (There are rare conditions when a person may have a missing or an extra sex chromosome; see Box 3.1.) Although no research with humans has provided evidence for direct genetic influences on gender-typed behavior, research with rodents indicates some relevant effects (Hines, 2013). For instance, studies with mice indicate links between genes on the Y chromosome and later levels of some aspects of aggressive and parenting behaviors (Hines, 2013). However, to reiterate, there are no studies documenting direct links between genes and gender-typed behavior in humans. As described next, there is indirect evidence of possible genetic effects mediated by the production of hormones.

Hormones and brain functioning In the study of gender development, much attention has been paid to the possible effects of **androgens,** a class of steroid hormones that includes testosterone. As discussed in Chapter 2, during normal prenatal development, the production of androgens leads to the formation of male genitalia in genetic males; in the absence of high levels of androgens, female genitalia are formed in genetic females.

Androgens can also have *organizing* or *activating* influences on the nervous system. **Organizing influences** occur when certain sex-linked hormones affect brain differentiation and organization during prenatal development or at puberty. For example, sex-related differences in prenatal androgens may influence the organization and functioning of the nervous system; in turn, this may be related to later average gender differences in certain play preferences (see Hines, 2013). Although androgen levels are typically higher in genetic males than genetic females during prenatal development, there are conditions in which genetic females are exposed to high levels of androgens. These girls are more likely to prefer certain masculine-stereotyped activities in childhood (see Box 15.1). **Activating influences** occur when fluctuations in sex-linked hormone levels influence the contemporaneous activation of certain brain and behavioral responses (Hines, 2013). For instance, as described later, the body increases androgen production in response to perceived threats, with possible implications for gender differences in aggression.

Brain structure and functioning Adult male and female brains show some small differences in physical structure (Hines, 2004, 2013). However, these differences do not appear to result in any clear advantage to cognitive performance (D. F. Halpern, 2012). Furthermore, an important limitation of research documenting sex differences in brain structure is that it is mostly based on brain-imaging

androgens ■ class of steroid hormones that normally occur at higher levels in males than in females and that affect physical development and functioning from the prenatal period onward

organizing influences ■ potential result of certain sex-linked hormones affecting brain differentiation and organization during prenatal development or at puberty

activating influences ■ potential result of certain fluctuations in sex-linked hormone levels affecting the contemporaneous activation of the nervous system and corresponding behavioral responses

gender dysphoria ■ psychiatric diagnosis included in the DSM-5 to refer to children who experience distress because they do not identify with the gender assigned to them at birth

transgender ■ individuals who do not identify with the gender assigned at birth (or their biological sex)

cisgender ■ individuals who identify with their gender assigned at birth (or their biological sex)

congenital adrenal hyperplasia (CAH) ■ condition during prenatal development in which the adrenal glands produce high levels of androgens; sometimes associated with masculinization of external genitalia in genetic females and sometimes associated with higher rates of masculine-stereotyped play in genetic females

androgen insensitivity syndrome (AIS) ■ condition during prenatal development in which androgen receptors malfunction in genetic males, impeding the formation of male external genitalia; in these cases, the child may be born with female external genitalia

BOX 15.1 a closer look

GENDER IDENTITY: MORE THAN SOCIALIZATION?

Most children's gender identification is consistent with their observable genitalia and gender socialization. That is, children's view of themselves as "a girl" or "a boy" is consistent with their genetic sex and the gender-role expectations others hold for them. However, in some rare cases, children believe that their gender is not the one that others take it to be. Studies of such cases suggest that, once established, the child's initial gender identification is often impervious to parental attempts to socialize the child as a member of what the child perceives as the "wrong" gender.

The potential power of children's preferences over gender socialization is evident when children identify with the other gender. Some boys indicate a preference to identify as a girl, and some girls express a preference to identify as a boy. These children usually favor cross-gender-typed play activities and clothing and dislike gender-typed activities (Zucker & Bradley, 1995). Such discrepant gender identity usually appears very early in development, occurs mostly in boys, and can be difficult to alter even with parental socialization efforts. These cases suggest that gender identification has a biological component. The biological perspective points to the prenatal impact of sex hormones on the developing fetal brain. Such biological influences seem to contribute to gender identity as well as to behavioral gender differences.

There is currently a debate in psychology over whether children with discrepant gender identities should be classified as having a psychiatric disorder. In the *Diagnostic and Statistical Manual of Mental Disorders, Fifth Edition (DSM-5)*, the latest version of the American Psychiatric Association's (2013) compendium, these children may receive the diagnosis of **gender dysphoria** (replacing the former classification of "gender identity disorder") if they do not identify with the gender assigned to them at birth. Some clinicians contend that children with an alternative gender identity are distressed and require care (Zucker, 2006). Other psychologists argue that assigning a psychiatric label to children with nonconforming gender identities and interests reflects societal expectations for gender-role conformity rather than an inherent disorder (Bartlett, Vasey, & Bukowski, 2000).

Along these lines, some people argue for a broader notion of gender that goes beyond thinking only of the two categories of "female" or "male." This includes acceptance of **transgender** youth and adults, individuals who do not identify with their gender assigned at birth. Transgender individuals may prefer to identify with the other gender, with both genders, or with neither gender. In contrast, the term **cisgender** is used to refer to children who identify with their assigned gender at birth.

The reasons are unclear as to why some children identify as transgender. Psychologists have only recently begun to study the topic (Boskey, 2014; Dragowski, Scharrón-del Río, Sandigorsky, 2011). As noted, many psychiatrists and clinical psychologists have labeled these children as having a "gender identity disorder." However, as gender roles have become more flexible in many cultures, there has been an increasing tolerance and acceptance of transgender children by parents and others (Riley et al., 2013). Despite these cultural changes, many transgender and other gender-nonconforming (e.g., lesbian and gay) youth are rejected and victimized by family members, teachers, and peers, which places them at risk for suicide (Haas et al., 2011; see also Chapter 11).

Another group of individuals who seek to broaden the gender spectrum include those born with intersex conditions (Preves, 2003). *Intersex* conditions are due to recessive genes that cause, in rare instances, a person of one genetic sex to develop genital characteristics typical of the other genetic sex. (Intersex individuals may also consider themselves transgender.) Two such intersex conditions are *congenital adrenal hyperplasia* and *androgen insensitivity syndrome.*

High levels of androgens produced during the prenatal development of genetic females can lead to **congenital adrenal hyperplasia (CAH),** a condition that involves the formation of male (or partly masculinized) genitalia. Researchers have studied girls with CAH to infer the possible influence of androgens on gender development. They have found that, compared with other girls, those with CAH are more likely to choose physically active forms of play, such as rough-and-tumble play, and to avoid sedentary forms of play, such as playing with dolls (Hines, 2013; Nordenström et al., 2002).

By contrast, **androgen insensitivity syndrome (AIS),** a rare syndrome in genetic males, causes androgen receptors to malfunction. In these cases, genetic males may be born with female external genitalia. These individuals commonly self-identify as girls (and later as women), and they generally show preferences for feminine-stereotyped interests (Hines, 2013).

Cases of children with CAH and AIS offer evidence to support the premise that prenatal androgens may partly contribute to boys' and girls' gender identities and to gender-typed play preferences. In addition, this kind of evidence is sometimes used to support evolutionary accounts of gender development (G. M. Alexander, 2003).

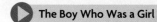 **The Boy Who Was a Girl**

studies performed on adults. Given the continual interaction of genes and experience during brain development, it is unclear to what extent any differences in adult brain structure or functioning are due to genetic or environmental influences. It is also unclear to what extent these small differences in brain structure determine any gender differences in ability and behavior (D. F. Halpern, 2012).

self-socialization ■ active process during development whereby children's cognitions lead them to perceive the world and to act in accord with their expectations and beliefs

gender identity ■ self-identifying as a boy or a girl

gender stability ■ awareness that gender remains the same over time

gender constancy ■ realization that gender is invariant despite superficial changes in a person's appearance or behavior

Cognitive and Motivational Influences

Cognitive theories of gender development emphasize the ways that children learn gender-typed attitudes and behaviors through observation, inference, and practice. According to these explanations, children form expectations about gender that guide their behavior. Cognitive theories stress children's active **self-socialization:** individuals use their beliefs, expectations, and preferences to guide how they perceive the world and the actions they choose. Self-socialization occurs in gender development when children seek to behave in accord with their gender identity as a girl or a boy. However, cognitive theories also emphasize the role of the environment—the different role models, opportunities, and incentives that girls and boys might experience. We next discuss four pertinent cognitive theories of gender development: cognitive developmental theory, gender schema theory, social identity theory, and social cognitive theory. As you will see below, these theories complement one another in many respects (also see Leaper, 2011).

Cognitive Developmental Theory

Lawrence Kohlberg's (1966) cognitive developmental theory of gender-role development reflects a Piagetian framework (reviewed in Chapter 4). Kohlberg proposed that children actively construct knowledge about gender in the same ways that Piaget theorized children construct knowledge about the physical world. There are two distinctive contributions of Kohlberg's theory. First, he posited that children actively seek to understand the meaning of gender through observing and interacting with the world around them. (As described later, this feature is shared by other cognitive theories, including gender schema theory and social cognitive theory.) Second, Kohlberg proposed cognitive developmental changes in children's understanding of gender during early childhood.

Kohlberg maintained that children's understanding of gender involves a three-stage process that occurs between approximately 2 and 6 years of age. First, by around 30 months of age, young children acquire a **gender identity,** categorizing themselves usually as either a girl or a boy (Fagot & Leinbach, 1989). However, they do not yet realize that gender is permanent. For example, young children may believe that a girl could grow up to be a father (Slaby & Frey, 1975). The second stage, which begins at about 3 or 4 years of age, is **gender stability,** wherein children come to realize that gender remains the same over time ("I'm a girl, and I'll always be a girl"). However, they are still not clear that gender is independent of superficial appearance and thus believe that a boy who has put on a dress and now looks like a girl has indeed become a girl.

The basic understanding of gender is completed in the third stage, around 6 years of age, when children achieve **gender constancy,** the understanding that gender is invariant across situations ("I'm a girl, and nothing I do will change that"). Kohlberg noted that this is the same age at which children begin to succeed on Piagetian conservation problems (see Chapter 4), and he argued that both achievements reflect the same underlying thinking processes. Kohlberg maintained that children's understanding that gender remains constant even when superficial changes occur is similar to their understanding that the amount of a substance is conserved even when its appearance is altered. For example, a ball of clay maintains the same volume after it has been mashed flat; in a similar manner, a girl remains the same gender after she gets her hair cut short and starts wearing baseball shirts. According to

As predicted by cognitive theories, children learn a great deal about gender roles by observing other people. Television, movies, and video games provide many examples of gender stereotypes for both sexes.

FELIX VOGEL / MEDIA BAKERY

Kohlberg, once gender constancy is attained, children begin to seek out and attend to same-gender models to learn how to behave ("Since I'm a girl, I should like to do girl things, so I need to find out what those are").

Subsequent research has supported the idea that children's understanding of gender develops in the sequence Kohlberg hypothesized and that the attainment of gender constancy occurs at more or less the same age as success on conservation problems (e.g., D. E. Marcus & Overton, 1978; C. L. Martin et al., 2002; Munroe, Shimmin, & Munroe, 1984). Some studies also indicate that acquiring gender constancy might increase the likelihood of some gender-typed behaviors (C. L. Martin et al., 2002). That is, once most children consolidate their understanding of gender, they tend to use their gender concepts to interpret the world. Gender schema theory, reviewed next, also addresses ways whereby attaining a concept of gender can affect children's gender development.

Gender Schema Theory

Other developmental psychologists proposed gender schema theory as an alternative to Kohlberg's explanation of children's gender development (Liben & Signorella, 1980; Martin & Halverson, 1981). In contrast to Kohlberg's view that gender-typed interests emerge after gender constancy is achieved, gender schema theory holds that the motivation to enact gender-typed behavior begins as soon as children can label other people's and their own gender—in other words, usually by about 3 years of age (see C. L. Martin et al., 2002), which is younger than gender constancy is attained.

Accordingly, children's understanding of gender develops through their construction of **gender schemas,** which are mental representations that incorporate everything the child knows about gender. Gender schemas include memories of one's own experiences with males and females, gender stereotypes transmitted directly by adults and peers ("boys don't cry," "girls play with dolls"), and messages conveyed indirectly through the media. Children use an *ingroup/outgroup* gender schema to classify other people as being either "the same as me" or not. The motivation for cognitive consistency leads them to prefer, pay attention to, and remember more about others of their own gender. As a consequence, an *own-gender schema* is formed, consisting of detailed knowledge about how to do things that are consistent with one's own gender. Simply learning that an unfamiliar object is "for my gender" makes children like it more. Figure 15.1 illustrates how this process leads children to acquire greater knowledge and expertise with gender-consistent entities.

gender schemas ■ organized mental representations (concepts, beliefs, memories) about gender, including gender stereotypes

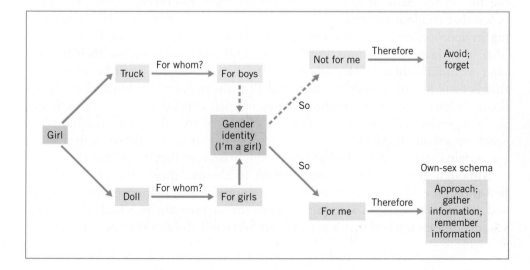

FIGURE 15.1 Gender schema theory According to gender schema theory, children classify new objects and activities as "for boys" or "for girls." They tend to investigate objects and activities that are relevant to their gender and to ignore those that are associated with the other gender.

gender schema filter ■ initial evaluation of information as relevant for one's own gender

interest filter ■ initial evaluation of information as being personally interesting

In one illustrative study that tested the impact of gender schemas on children's information processing (Bradbard et al., 1986), researchers presented 4- to 9-year-olds with three boxes. Each contained unfamiliar, gender-neutral objects, and each was separately labeled as "boys," "girls," or "boys and girls/girls and boys." The children spent more time exploring objects in boxes labeled for their own gender (or for both genders) than objects in the box labeled only for the other gender. One week later, not surprisingly, they remembered more details about the objects they had explored than about the ones with which they had spent less time.

Children regularly look to their peers to infer gender-appropriate behavior. In an observational study conducted in a preschool classroom, boys were influenced by the number and the proportion of same-gender children who were playing with a set of toys: they approached toys that were being played with primarily by boys and shunned those that seemed popular mainly with girls (Shell & Eisenberg, 1990).

Gender schemas are also responsible for *biased* processing and remembering of information about gender. Consistent with the research described above, studies show that children tend to remember more about what they observe from same-gender role models than from cross-gender ones (see Blakemore, Berenbaum, & Liben, 2009; C. L. Martin et al., 2002). They are also more likely to accurately encode and remember information about story characters that behave in gender-consistent ways and to forget or distort information that is gender-inconsistent (Blakemore et al., 2009; Liben & Signorella, 1993; C. L. Martin et al., 2002). For example, in one study children were shown a series of pictures than included a combination of gender-typed images (e.g., a girl baking cookies) and cross-gender-typed images (e.g., a girl sawing wood) (C. L. Martin & Halverson, 1983). When they were later asked to recall the pictures, they showed a greater tendency to mistakenly recall cross-gender-typed images as gender-typed (e.g., remembering a picture of a girl sawing wood as a boy sawing wood) than the reverse (e.g., remembering a picture of a girl baking cookies as a boy baking cookies). This tendency to retain information that is schema-consistent and to ignore or distort schema-inconsistent information helps to perpetuate gender stereotypes that have little or no basis in reality.

Liben and Bigler (2002) proposed that children use two kinds of filters when processing information about the world. One is a **gender schema filter** ("Is this information relevant for my gender?") and the other is an **interest filter** ("Is this information interesting?"). When encountering a new toy, for example, children might decide that it is something for girls or for boys and thus explore or ignore the toy on the basis of their gender schema filter. However, Liben and Bigler noted that children sometimes find a new toy attractive without initially evaluating its appropriateness for their gender. In these instances, they use their interest filter to evaluate information. Furthermore, children sometimes use their interest filter to modify their gender schemas ("If I like this toy, it must be something that is okay for my gender"). Liben and Bigler's modification to gender schema theory helps to account for findings indicating that children are often inconsistent in their gender-typed interests. (For example, they are often more traditional in some areas than others.) It also allows for the fact that some children actively pursue certain cross-gender-typed activities simply because they enjoy them.

Although gender schemas are resistant to change, they often can be modified through explicit instruction. Such an approach was demonstrated by Bigler and Liben, who created a cognitive intervention program in which elementary school children learned that a person's interests and abilities (but not gender) are important for the kind of job that the person could have (Bigler & Liben, 1990; Liben & Bigler, 1987). (The children were encouraged to see, for instance, that if Mary was strong and liked to build things, a good job for her would be to work as a carpenter.) Children who participated in this week-long program showed decreased gender stereotyping and also had better memory for gender-inconsistent stimuli (such as a picture of a girl holding a hammer). However, a limitation of interventions aimed at reducing gender stereotyping is that their impact typically fades once the intervention ends (Bigler, 1999). That is, children gradually revert back to their old gender stereotypes. Given the pervasiveness of gender stereotyping in children's everyday lives, cognitive interventions need to be sustained to have a longer-lasting effect.

Children's stereotyped beliefs about gender can be changed through cognitive intervention programs. Children who learned that a person's interests and abilities were important for the kind of job the person could have showed significant reductions in gender stereotyping.

Social Identity Theory

Henri Tajfel and John Turner's (1979) social identity theory addresses the influence of group membership on people's self-concepts and behavior with others. Developmental psychologists have applied the theory to understand how group processes contribute to children's socialization and to highlight the importance of gender as a social identity in children's development (e.g., Bigler & Liben, 2007; J. R. Harris, 1995; Leaper, 2000; Nesdale, 2007; Powlishta, 1995). Indeed, gender may be the *most* central social identity in most children's lives (Bem, 1993). Children's commitment to gender as a social identity is most readily apparent through their primary affiliation with same-gender peers (Leaper, 1994; Maccoby, 1998).

Two influential processes that occur when a person commits to an ingroup are *ingroup bias* and *ingroup assimilation*. **Ingroup bias** refers to the tendency to evaluate individuals and characteristics associated with the ingroup as superior to those associated with the outgroup. For example, Kimberly Powlishta (1995) observed that children showed same-gender favoritism when rating peers on likeability and favorable traits. Ingroup bias is related to the process of **ingroup assimilation,** whereby individuals are socialized to conform to the group's norms. That is, peers expect ingroup members to demonstrate the characteristics that define the ingroup. Thus, they anticipate ingroup approval for preferring same-gender peers and same-gender-typed activities, as well as for avoiding other-gender peers and cross-gender-typed activities (R. Banerjee & Lintern, 2000; C. L. Martin et al., 1999). As a result, children tend to become more gender-typed in their preferences as they assimilate into their same-gender peer groups (C. L. Martin & Fabes, 2001).

A corollary of social identity theory is that the characteristics associated with a high-status group are typically valued more than are those of a low-status group. In male-dominated societies, masculine-stereotyped attributes such as assertiveness and competition tend to be valued more highly than feminine-stereotyped attributes such as affiliation and nurturance (Hofstede, 2000). Related to this pattern is the tendency of cross-gender-typed behavior to be more common among girls than among boys. Indeed, masculine-stereotyped behavior in a girl can sometimes enhance her status, whereas feminine-stereotyped behavior in a boy typically tarnishes his status (see Leaper, 1994).

ingroup bias ■ tendency to evaluate individuals and characteristics of the ingroup as superior to those of the outgroup

ingroup assimilation ■ process whereby individuals are socialized to conform to the group's norms, demonstrating the characteristics that define the ingroup

intersectionality ■ the interconnection of social identities such as gender, race, ethnicity, sexual orientation, and class, especially in relation to overlapping experiences of discrimination

tuition ■ learning through direct teaching

enactive experience ■ learning to take into account the reactions one's past behavior has evoked in others

observational learning ■ learning through watching other people and the consequences others experience as a result of their actions

Social identity theory helps to explain why gender-typing pressures tend to be more rigid for boys than for girls (Leaper, 2000). Members of high-status groups, for example, are usually more invested in maintaining group boundaries than are members of low-status groups. In most societies, males are accorded greater status and power than are females (Wood & Eagly, 2012). Consistent with social identity theory, boys are more likely than girls to initiate and maintain role and group boundaries (Fagot, 1977; Sroufe et al., 1993). Boys are also more likely to endorse gender stereotypes (Rowley et al., 2007) and to hold sexist attitudes (C. S. Brown & Bigler, 2004).

Of course, gender is not the only social identity that shapes people's lives. As discussed in Chapter 11, many people identify with social groups based on race/ethnicity, religion, sexual orientation, social class, club membership, and so forth. Moreover, developmental psychologists are increasingly trying to understand how the intersection of multiple identities affects a person's experiences. This phenomenon is known as **intersectionality** (Cole, 2009). For instance, the expectations for a girl or a boy in a suburban upper-middle-class family may differ somewhat from the expectations in a poor or working-class family in an inner city. In the latter context, there may be more housework and childcare responsibilities assigned to girls in the home than would be seen in wealthier communities (Bornstein et al., 2016; Hilton & Haldeman, 1991). Also, in the poor inner-city environment, establishing one's physical and emotional toughness may be more fundamental to boys' gender identity than it would be in the suburbs; correspondingly, concerns with toughness may more often undermine boys' academic motivation in these communities than in higher-income suburbs (Anderson, 1999; Farkas & Leaper, 2016). Furthermore, as highlighted by the intersectionality approach, individuals can experience biases from multiple group identities (e.g., gender, ethnicity/race, sexual orientation, class, religion, and so on). When youth experience harassment and discrimination based on multiple group identities, it generally compounds the negative effects on their adjustment (Bucchianeri et al., 2014).

Social Cognitive Theory

Kay Bussey and Albert Bandura (1999, 2004) proposed a theory of gender development based on Bandura's (1986, 1997) social cognitive theory (see pages 384–385). The theory depicts a *triadic model of reciprocal causation* among personal factors, environmental factors, and behavior patterns. Personal factors include cognitive, motivational, and biological processes. Although the theory acknowledges the potential influence of biological factors, it primarily addresses cognition and motivation. Among its key features are sociocognitive modes of influence, observational learning processes, and self-regulatory processes.

According to social cognitive theory, learning occurs through *tuition, enactive experience,* and *observation.* **Tuition,** which refers to direct teaching, occurs during gender socialization—as when a father shows his son how to throw a baseball, or a mother teaches her daughter how to change a baby's diaper. **Enactive experience** occurs when children learn to guide their behavior by taking into account the reactions their past behavior has evoked in others. For instance, girls and boys usually receive positive reactions for behaviors that are gender-stereotypical and negative reactions for behaviors that are counter-stereotypical (Bussey & Bandura, 1999; Harris, 1995; Witt, 2000); they tend to use this feedback to regulate their behavior in relevant situations. Finally, **observational learning**—the most common form of learning—occurs through seeing and encoding the consequences other people experience as a result of children's own actions. Thus, children learn a great deal about gender simply through observing the behavior of their parents, siblings, teachers, and peers. They also learn about gender roles through media such as television, films, the Internet, and video games (see Box 15.2).

Observational learning of gender-role information involves four key processes: attention, memory, production, and motivation. To learn new information, it must, of course, be *attended* to (noticed) and then stored in *memory*. As we have noted, children often notice information that is consistent with their existing gender stereotypes. (This is the main premise of gender schema theory.) Next, children need to practice the behavior (*production*) they have observed (assuming that the behavior is within their capabilities). Finally, children's *motivation* to repeat a gender-typed behavior will depend on the incentives or disincentives they experience relative to the behavior. These sanctions can be experienced either directly (as when a parent praises a daughter for helping to prepare dinner) or indirectly (as when a boy observes another boy getting teased for playing with a doll). Over time, external sanctions are usually internalized as personal standards and become self-sanctions that motivate behavior.

According to social cognitive theory, children monitor their behavior and evaluate how well it matches personal standards. After making this evaluation, children may feel pride or shame, depending on whether they meet their standards. When individuals experience positive self-reactions for their behavior, they gain the sense of personal agency referred to as *self-efficacy*. Self-efficacy can develop gradually through practice (as when a son regularly plays catch with his father), through social modeling (as when a girl observes a female friend do well in math and thinks that maybe she could do well herself), and by social persuasion (as when a coach gives a pep talk to push the boys' performances on the baseball field). Researchers consistently find a strong relation between feelings of self-efficacy and motivation. For example, self-efficacy in math predicts girls' as well as boys' likelihood of taking advanced math courses (Stevens et al., 2007).

Cultural Influences

The theoretical approaches we have discussed so far emphasize biological and cognitive-motivational processes involved in gender development. Complementing these approaches are theories that address the larger cultural and social-structural factors that can shape gender development. One relevant theory that reflects this approach is the bioecological model, which emphasizes how cultural practices mirror and perpetuate the gender divisions that are prevalent in a society.

Bioecological Model

As described in Chapter 9, Urie Bronfenbrenner's bioecological model of human development differentiates among interconnected systems within the child (biological and cognitive processes) and in the child's environment. The environmental systems range from the microsystem (the immediate environment) to the macrosystem (the culture) and chronosystem (changes in the environment over the course of the child's development). These systems interact to influence children's development over time (see Figure 9.3) (Bronfenbrenner, 1979; Bronfenbrenner & Morris, 1998).

BOX 15.2 | applications

WHERE ARE SPONGESALLY SQUAREPANTS AND CURIOUS JANE?

Before reading further, take a moment to list your five favorite television programs. Now count how many of the major characters are female and how many are male. Which characters are most prominent and/or have positions of power on the show? How would you characterize the general nature of your programs—action-packed adventures, romantic comedies, sports shows, reality series? What would be different if you made a list of the programs you liked best as a child?

We would be willing to bet that for most readers your list of major characters includes more males than females, probably by a substantial degree. We also suspect that more male than female readers would list action and sports as favorite programs, whereas more female than male readers would have romantic shows on their lists. Furthermore, the imbalance in female and male characters in your favorite shows today is probably not much different from what you would find in the shows you watched in your youth.

Differences in the gender representation of TV and movie characters have been well documented, are very large, and have changed surprisingly little over the past four decades (Leaper et al., 2002; Scharrer, 2013; Signorielli, 2012). In fact, according to a recent analysis of TV and movie characters, the prevalence of female characters was 28% in family films, 39% in prime-time television programs, and 31% in children's shows (Smith et al., 2013a). A study of children's cartoons, however, did indicate that female and male characters were more equal in number and less gender-stereotyped in their portrayals on public television than on commercial television (Leaper et al., 2002).

Yet the differential treatment of the sexes in the media is not limited to numbers. Portrayals of males and females tend to be highly stereotypical in terms of appearance, personal characteristics, occupations, and the nature of the characters' roles. On average, male characters tend to be older, hold an occupation outside the home, and are depicted in more powerful roles; in contrast,

females tend to be young, attractive, provocatively dressed, and concerned with their appearance (Diekman & Murnen, 2004; Gerding & Signorielli, 2014; Gooden & Gooden, 2001; Leaper et al., 2002; Scharrer, 2013; Signorielli, 2012).

Do the large differences in both the number and type of gender portrayals on TV and in other media matter? Keep in mind that for U.S. children, average media consumption (which now includes TV, digital programming, and online streaming) is more than 6 hours daily for school-age children (Rideout, 2015). In addition, for most young children, television and online programming is a major source of information about the world at large (Gerbner et al., 2002). From a gender-typing perspective, the fact that children have so much exposure to highly stereotyped gender models matters a great deal. For example, children who watch a lot of televised and online programs have more highly stereotypic beliefs about males and females and prefer gender-typed activities to a greater extent than do children who are less avid viewers (Oppliger, 2007). Furthermore, several experimental studies have established a causal relationship between TV viewing and gender stereotyping (Oppliger, 2007). For instance, when children are randomly assigned to watch shows with either gender-stereotyped or neutral content, they are more likely to endorse gender stereotypes themselves after watching the gender-stereotyped programs.

Children are, of course, exposed to media other than television, but similar gender disparities have been documented in those areas as well. For example, children's books still contain far more male than female characters, and characters of both sexes

are often portrayed in gender-stereotypic ways. Males tend to be depicted as active and effective in the world at large, whereas females are frequently passive and prone to problems that require the help of males to solve (DeWitt, Cready, & Seward, 2013; Diekman & Murnen, 2004; Gooden & Gooden, 2001; Hamilton et al., 2006). Thus, although it is now possible to find more counter-stereotypical role models in children's media (e.g., Katniss from *The Hunger Games* series), most female and male characters continue to be gender-stereotyped. Computer and online games are beginning to displace television as the primary source of children's media entertainment. Unfortunately, like television programming, many computer games portray gender in highly stereotyped ways (Downs & Smith, 2010; Scharrer, 2013). Most characters are male, and they commonly engage in highly aggressive acts; and when female characters are present, they are commonly portrayed in highly sexualized ways (e.g., Lara Croft in *Tomb Raider*).

JOHN GREIM / GETTY IMAGES

Computer and online games are beginning to displace television as the primary source of children's media entertainment. Unfortunately, like television programming, many computer games portray the sexes in highly stereotyped ways.

A fundamental feature of the macrosystem is its **opportunity structure,** that is, the economic and social resources it offers and people's understanding of those resources (Leaper, 2000; Ogbu, 1981). Opportunities for members of a cultural community can vary depending on gender, income, and other factors, and they are reflected by the dominant adult roles within that community. According to the bioecological approach, child socialization practices in the family, peer group, classroom, and other facets of the child's microsystem serve to prepare children for these adult roles. Thus, traditional gender-typing practices perpetuate as well as reflect the existing opportunity structures for women and men in a particular community at a particular time in history (Whiting & Edwards, 1988). To the extent that family and occupational roles tend to be divided on the basis of gender, different behaviors (roles) are expected of women and men, as well as of girls and boys. In many countries, women have been traditionally underrepresented in politics, business, science, technology, and various other fields—a trend that continues in many societies today. In turn, girls are not expected to develop interests and skills that lead toward professions in those fields, which simply perpetuates girls' exclusion from them.

To the extent that children's development is largely an adaptation to their existing opportunities, changes in children's macrosystems and microsystems can lead to greater gender equality (see Leaper, 2000). For example, increased academic and professional opportunities for girls in the United States have led to a dramatic narrowing of the gender gap in math and science within the past few decades (D. F. Halpern, 2012; D. F. Halpern et al., 2007). In summary, the bioecological model highlights how institutionalized roles impose both opportunities and constraints on people's behavior and beliefs in the home, schools, the labor force, and political institutions.

opportunity structure ■ the economic and social resources offered by the macrosystem in the bioecological model, and people's understanding of those resources

Review

To varying degrees, biological, cognitive-motivational, and cultural factors relate to different aspects of gender development. In their theories and work, researchers tend to focus on one set of factors—although they usually acknowledge that other influences are also important.

In trying to explain gender differences in behavior, some researchers focus on biological factors. Those who adopt an evolutionary perspective argue that gender differences in behavior emerged over the course of human evolution because they offered reproductive advantages to males and females. Disagreement exists, however, regarding the degree to which evolution led to different behavioral predispositions for females and males. Other biological approaches focus on measureable physiological processes that may be related to variations in development, such as sex-related hormonal influences and sex differences in brain functioning.

Researchers who focus on cognitive-motivational processes emphasize how children's gender-related beliefs, expectations, and preferences guide their behavior. Once children begin to identify with members of their own gender, they are typically motivated to acquire interests, values, and behavior in accord with their social identity as girls or boys. Self-socialization plays a prominent role in cognitive theories because it is primarily children themselves who initiate and enforce many forms of gender-typed behavior.

Cross-cultural comparisons and historical change within the United States and other countries underscore ways that gender roles are tied to culture. Societal values and cultural practices can limit or enhance the role models and opportunities that girls and boys experience during development.

gender segregation ■ children's tendency to associate with same-gender peers and to avoid other-gender peers

Milestones in Gender Development

Developmental psychologists have identified general patterns that tend to occur over the course of children's gender development. As reviewed in this section, gender-related changes are evident in children's physical, cognitive, and social development. Recall that these changes begin during prenatal development, when sexual differentiation occurs.

Infancy and Toddlerhood

During their 1st year, infants' perceptual abilities allow them to figure out that there are two groups of people in the world: females and males. As we saw in Chapter 5, much research indicates that infants can detect complex regularities in perceptual information. Clothing, hairstyle, height, body shape, motion patterns, vocal pitch, and activities all tend to vary with gender, and these differences provide infants with gender cues. For example, habituation studies of infant perception and categorization indicate that by about 6 to 9 months of age, infants can distinguish males from females, usually on the basis of hairstyle (Intons-Peterson, 1988). Infants can also distinguish between male and female voices and make intermodal matches on the basis of gender (Blakemore et al., 2009; C. L. Martin et al., 2002). For instance, they expect a female voice to go with a female face rather than with a male face. Although we cannot conclude that infants understand anything about what it *means* to be female or male, it does appear that older infants recognize the physical difference between females and males by using multiple perceptual cues.

> ▶ **Gender Development in Early Childhood**

Shortly after entering toddlerhood, children begin exhibiting distinct patterns of gender development. By the latter half of their 2nd year, children have begun to form gender-related expectations about the kinds of objects and activities typically associated with males and females. As observed in one study, 18-month-olds looked longer at a doll than at a toy car after viewing a series of female faces, and looked longer at a toy car than at a doll after habituating to male faces (Serbin et al., 2001). Another study with 24-month-olds found that counter-stereotypical matches of gender and action (e.g., a man putting on lipstick) led to longer looking times; it appeared that the children were surprised by the action's gender inconsistency (Poulin-Dubois et al., 2002).

The clearest evidence that children have acquired the concept of gender occurs around 2½ years of age, when they begin to label other people's genders. For example, researchers might assess this ability by asking children to put pictures of children into "boys" and "girls" piles. Toddlers can also make simple gender matches, such as choosing a toy train over a doll when asked to point to the "boy's toy" (A. Campbell, Shirley, & Caygill, 2002). Children typically begin to show understanding of their own *gender identity* within a few months after labeling other people's gender. By age 3, most children use gender terms such as "boy" and "girl" in their speech to refer themselves and other children (Fenson et al., 1994).

Gender self-labeling is usually consistent with children's gender assignment at birth (based on their

In the United States, children's play becomes differentiated by gender during the preschool period; most girls prefer to play with soft toys and to spend time in the "housekeeping" area, and most boys prefer to play with blocks and transportation toys.

MICHELLE D. BRIDWELL / PHOTOEDIT

external genitals). However, in some cases, children do not identify with their assigned gender as they advance into the preschool years and older; instead, these *transgender* children may identify with the other gender category, with both gender categories, or with neither gender category. These children usually have strong cross-gender-typed behavioral preferences (see Box 15.1).

Preschool Years

During the preschool years (approximately ages 3 to 5), children quickly learn gender stereotypes—the activities, traits, and roles associated with each gender. By about 3 years of age, most children begin to attribute certain toys and play activities to each gender. By about 5 years of age, they usually stereotype affiliative characteristics (e.g., nurturance, warmth) to females and assertive characteristics (e.g., directness, aggression) to males (Best & Thomas, 2004; Biernat, 1991; Liben & Bigler, 2002; Serbin, Powlishta, & Gulko, 1993). During this period, children usually lack *gender constancy:* they do not understand that gender remains stable across time and is consistent across situations. For example, a preschooler might think that a girl becomes a boy if she cuts her hair, or that a boy becomes a girl if he wears a dress. Indeed, as explained earlier in this chapter, most young children rigidly endorse gender stereotypes until they develop more cognitive flexibility during middle childhood.

Gender-Typed Behavior

Many children begin to demonstrate preferences for some gender-typed toys by about 2 years of age. These preferences become stronger for most children during the preschool years (Cherney & London, 2006; Pomerleau et al., 1990). Indeed, during childhood, one of the largest average gender differences is in toy and play preferences. Girls are more likely than boys to favor dolls, toy cooking sets, and dress-up materials. Girls are also more likely to invoke domestic themes (such as playing house) in their fantasy play. In contrast, boys are more likely than girls to prefer cars, trucks, building toys, and sports equipment. Boys are also more likely than girls to engage in rough-and-tumble play and to enact action-and-adventure themes (such as playing superheroes) in their fantasy play.

Although studies find large average gender differences in play preferences, there is still some variability. First, variation exists within each gender in how strongly individual children favor gender-typed over cross-gender-typed play. That is, some children are very rigid in their preferences for gender-typed toys and play activities, whereas others are more flexible (Blakemore et al., 2009). Second, some children strongly prefer cross-gender-typed play and dislike gender-typed play. This latter group includes girls with congenital adrenal hyperplasia (CAH), who were exposed to high levels of prenatal androgens (Hines, 2013), and transgender children who may identify with a gender different from the one assigned to them at birth (Boskey, 2014). (Girls with CAH generally do identify with their assigned gender.)

The preschool period is also when **gender segregation** emerges. Most children begin to prefer playing with same-gender peers and to avoid other-gender peers (Leaper, 1994; Maccoby, 1998). Gender segregation increases steadily between about 3 and 6 years of age, then remains stable throughout childhood (Figure 15.2). Preference for same-gender peers is commonly seen across different cultures (Maccoby, 1998; Whiting & Edwards, 1988).

MYRLEEN PEARSON / PHOTOEDIT

During preschool, children begin to avoid peers who violate gender-role norms, and by age 5 to 7 years, they will actively tease peers who cross gender-role boundaries. This is especially true for boys: the one in this photo is likely to experience peer rejection if he continues to play with dolls and other toys strongly stereotyped as appropriate for girls.

FIGURE 15.2 Gender segregation in play This graph reflects the increase in social playtime between preschool and 1st grade that children spent with playmates of their own gender and the decrease in playtime with playmates of the other gender. (Data from Maccoby, 1998)

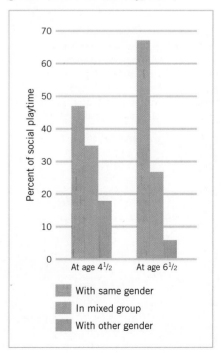

Gender-segregated peer groups are a laboratory for children to learn what it means to be a girl or a boy. Peers are both role models and enforcers of gender-typed behavior. Martin and Fabes (2001) identified what they termed a "social dosage effect" of belonging to same-gender peer groups during early childhood. The amount of time that preschool or kindergarten children spent with same-gender peers predicted subsequent changes in gender-typed behavior over 6 months. For example, boys who spent more time playing with same-gender peers showed increases over time in aggression, rough-and-tumble play, activity level, and gender-typed play. Girls who spent more time playing with same-gender peers showed increases in gender-typed play and decreases in aggression and activity level.

The reasons for children's same-gender peer preferences seem to involve a combination of temperamental, cognitive, and social forces (Leaper, 2015a; Maccoby, 1998). Their relative influences change over time. At first, children appear to prefer same-gender peers because they have more compatible behavioral styles and interests. For instance, girls may avoid boys because boys tend to be rough and unresponsive to girls' attempts to influence them, whereas boys may prefer the company of other boys because they share similar activity levels. Around the time that children begin to exhibit a same-gender peer preference, they are also establishing a gender identity and therefore are further drawn to peers who belong to the same ingroup.

As children become older, peer pressures may additionally motivate them to favor same-gender peers. Thus, behavioral compatibility may become a less important factor with age. For instance, physically active girls might frequently play with boys during early childhood; however, as these girls become older, they tend to affiliate more with girls—even though their activity preferences may be more compatible with those of boys (Pellegrini et al., 2007). Therefore, ingroup identity and conformity pressures may supersede behavioral compatibility as reasons for gender segregation as children become older.

Middle Childhood

By about 6 years of age, children have usually attained *gender constancy,* and their ideas about gender are more consolidated. At this point, children often show a bit more flexibility in their gender stereotypes and attitudes than they did in their younger years (P. A. Katz & Ksansnak, 1994; Liben & Bigler, 2002; Serbin et al., 1993). For example, they may recognize that some boys don't like playing baseball and that some girls don't wear dresses. However, most children continue to be highly gender-stereotyped in their views.

At approximately 9 or 10 years of age, children start to show an even clearer understanding that gender is a social category. They typically recognize that gender roles are social conventions as opposed to biological outcomes (D. B. Carter & Patterson, 1982; Conry-Murray, 2015; Killen, 2007; Stoddart & Turiel, 1985). As children come to appreciate the social basis of gender roles, they may recognize that some girls and boys may not want to do things that are typical for their gender. Some children in this age group may even argue that, in such cases, other girls and boys should be allowed to follow their personal preferences. For instance, Damon (1977) found that children would say that a boy who liked to play with dolls should be allowed to do so. However, children also recognized that the boy would probably be teased and that they themselves would not want to play with him. That is, children understood the notion of individual variations in gender typing, but they were also aware that violating gender role norms would have social costs.

Another development in some children's thinking in the middle childhood years is an awareness of when gender discrimination occurs, as well as the realization that it is unfair (C. S. Brown & Bigler, 2005; Killen, 2007). Killen and Stangor (2001) demonstrated this when they told children stories about a child who was excluded from a group because of the child's gender. Examples included a boy who was kept out of a ballet club and a girl who was kept out of a baseball-cards club. The researchers observed that 8- and 10-year-olds usually judged it unfair for a child to be excluded from a group solely because of gender. Yet despite their capacity to see this as wrong, children commonly exclude other children from activities based on their gender (Killen, 2007; Maccoby, 1998).

Brown and Bigler (2005) identified various factors that affect whether children recognize gender discrimination. First among them are cognitive prerequisites, such as an understanding of cultural stereotypes, the ability to make social comparisons, and a moral understanding of fairness and equity. These abilities are typically reached by middle childhood. People's awareness of sexism can also be influenced by individual factors such as their own self-concepts or beliefs. For instance, girls with gender-egalitarian beliefs were more likely to recognize sexism (C. S. Brown & Bigler, 2004; Leaper & Brown, 2008). Finally, the situation can affect children's likelihood of noticing discrimination. For instance, some children are more likely to notice discrimination directed toward someone else than toward themselves. Also, they are more apt to recognize gender discrimination from someone already known to be prejudiced (C. S. Brown & Bigler, 2005).

Gender-Typed Behavior

As previously noted, most girls and boys spend time primarily in same-gender peer groups throughout childhood. On average, boys' and girls' peer groups establish somewhat different norms for behavior (A. J. Rose & Rudolph, 2006). For this reason, some researchers have suggested that each gender usually constructs its own "culture" during childhood (Maccoby, 1998; Maltz & Borker, 1982; Thorne & Luria, 1986). The gender-role norms seen in the social interactions of many girls and boys tend to reflect differences in the balance of assertion and affiliation. **Assertion** refers to one's attempts to exert influence over the environment (e.g., directive statements), whereas **affiliation** refers to making connections with others (e.g., expressing support). However, the goals of assertion and affiliation are not mutually exclusive: they are often blended together in a style known as **collaboration** (Leaper, 1991; Leaper, Tenenbaum, & Shaffer, 1999). For example, a proposal for joint action ("Let's play a game together") or a statement that builds positively on another's idea are each simultaneously affiliative (connecting to the other) and self-assertive (influencing the situation). Thus, girls are more likely than boys to use collaborative communication that affirms both the self and the other (e.g., proposals for joint activity), whereas boys are more likely than girls to use power-assertive communication that primarily affirms the self (e.g., giving commands).

Average gender differences in girls' and boys' peer cultures reflect the organization of gender in the larger society (Leaper, 2000). The traditional masculine role in most societies stresses self-assertion and downplays interpersonal affiliation. In line with this tendency, boys' peer groups are more likely than girls' peer groups to maintain norms emphasizing dominance, self-reliance, competition, and hiding vulnerability. In contrast, the traditional feminine role stresses affiliation. Accordingly, girls' peer groups are more likely than boys' peer groups to reinforce norms that value interpersonal sensitivity, supportiveness, and affection (Bassen & Lamb, 2006; Best & Williams, 1993; A. J. Rose & Rudolph, 2006). However,

assertion ■ tendency to take action on behalf of the self through competitive, independent, or aggressive behaviors

affiliation ■ tendency to affirm connection with others through being emotionally open, empathetic, or supportive

collaboration ■ coordination of assertion and affiliation in behavior, such as making initiatives for joint activity

During the elementary school years, boys' and girls' groups rarely mix. Children themselves enforce gender segregation; this tendency does not seem to be due to adult influences.

valuing affiliation is not necessarily incompatible with self-assertion. Hence, collaborative styles of social interaction are somewhat more common among girls than among boys (Leaper, 1991; Leaper & Smith, 2004; Leaper et al., 1999). As with most average gender differences, there is also considerable overlap between girls and boys in collaboration and other styles of social behavior.

As we have noted, when children violate gender-role norms, their peers often react negatively (e.g., Fagot, 1977; Harris, 1995; Thorne & Luria, 1986), including mercilessly teasing someone who has crossed gender "borders." The following description of an event in a U.S. elementary school clearly illustrates the degree to which children enforce gender segregation on their own:

> In the lunchroom, when the two second-grade tables were filling, a high-status [popular] boy walked by the inside table, which had a scattering of both boys and girls, and said loudly, "Oooo, too many girls," as he headed for a seat at the far table. The boys at the inside table picked up their trays and moved, and no other boys sat at the inside table, which the pronouncement had effectively made taboo.
>
> (Thorne, 1992, p. 171)

Although most children typically favor same-gender peers, in certain contexts friendly cross-gender contacts regularly occur in many cultures (Sroufe et al., 1993; Strough & Covatto, 2002; Thorne, 1993; Thorne & Luria, 1986). At home and in the neighborhood, the choice of play companions is frequently limited. As a result, girls and boys often play cooperatively with one another. In more public settings, the implicit convention is that girls and boys can be friendly if they can attribute the reason for their cross-gender contact to an external cause. For example, this might occur when a teacher assigns them to work together on a class project or when they are waiting in line together at the cafeteria. However, beyond such exceptions, the risk of peer rejection is high when children violate the convention to avoid cross-gender contact (Sroufe et al., 1993). In some cultural settings, there are strict rules regarding cross-gender contacts, especially as youth enter adolescence. For example, in Orthodox Jewish, Islamic, and Amish societies, girls and boys are separated and any cross-gender contact must be supervised by family.

Gender segregation persists through childhood. Cross-gender teasing is used to maintain gender boundaries.

Overall, gender typing during childhood tends to be more rigid among boys than among girls (Leaper, 1994; Levant, 2005). As noted earlier, boys are more likely to endorse gender stereotypes than are girls, whereas girls are more likely than boys to endorse gender-egalitarian attitudes (C. S. Brown & Bigler, 2004). In addition, girls are less gender-typed in their behavior. For instance, girls are more likely than boys to play with cross-gender-typed toys. Also, girls frequently pursue play activities traditionally associated with boys, such as soccer and basketball. In contrast, it is relatively rare to see boys engage in activities traditionally associated with girls, such as playing house. Furthermore, girls tend to be more flexible in coordinating interpersonal goals. For instance, as explained earlier, girls commonly coordinate both affiliative and assertive goals in their social interactions (Leaper, 1991; Leaper & Smith, 2004).

Adolescence

According to some developmental psychologists, adolescence is a period when gender roles might become more rigid (*gender-role intensification*) or more relaxed (*gender-role flexibility*), depending on individual and contextual factors. As explained in Chapter 11, adolescence is a time when many youth are exploring their personal identities, including their values and beliefs regarding gender roles (e.g., Cooper & Grotevant, 1987). Many girls and boys internalize traditional gender roles in their personal values. As a consequence, concerns with adhering to gender-role expectations may increase (Galambos, Almeida, & Petersen, 1990; J. P. Hill & Lynch, 1983). This **gender-role intensification** commonly occurs in the context of heterosexual dating when adolescents usually adhere to traditional heterosexual scripts. For example, it remains common for both boys and girls to expect that boys will initiate and pay for dates (see Leaper & Robnett, 2016).

Gender-role intensification is also related to increases in gender discrimination during the course of adolescence (American Association of University Women, 2011; Leaper & Brown, 2008). A national survey conducted in the United States found that most adolescent girls and boys experienced sexual harassment, and the rates increased with age—especially for girls (American Association of University Women, 2011). Also, instances of sexual harassment and bullying are more likely directed toward gender-nonconforming children (e.g., boys who are not athletic, girls who are not viewed as pretty or feminine), as well as lesbian, gay, bisexual, and transgender individuals (American Association of University Women, 2011; Mitchell, Ybarra, & Korchmaros, 2014).

Alternatively, some adolescents may reject traditional gender roles as social conventions. This inclination may lead to **gender-role flexibility,** whereby these youths pursue a flexible range of attitudes and interests (D. B. Carter & Patterson, 1982; P. A. Katz & Ksansnak, 1994). As in childhood, greater gender-role flexibility during adolescence is more likely among girls than among boys. For instance, many girls and young women in the United States and other countries participate in sports and pursue careers in business (traditionally male-dominated domains), whereas relatively few boys and young men show similar levels of interest in childcare or homemaking (traditionally female-dominated domains). For girls and boys, gender-role flexibility will partly depend on the breadth of opportunities they perceive in society for their gender ingroup (Wood & Eagly, 2012). Social support (and the absence of rejection) for gender-role flexibility from peers, family, teachers, and others is also important (Witt, 2000).

Gender-Typed Behavior

During early adolescence, peer contacts are primarily members of the same gender. However, in many cultural communities cross-gender interactions and friendships become more common during adolescence (see Figure 15.3) (Poulin & Pedersen, 2007). As described in Chapter 13, these interactions can open

gender-role intensification ■ heightened concerns with adhering to traditional gender roles that may occur during adolescence

gender-role flexibility ■ recognition of gender roles as social conventions and adoption of more flexible attitudes and interests

Parents, peers, and teachers are much more tolerant of girls who engage in masculine-stereotyped activities than they are of boys who engage in feminine-stereotyped activities.

JIM CUMMINS / AGE FOTOSTOCK

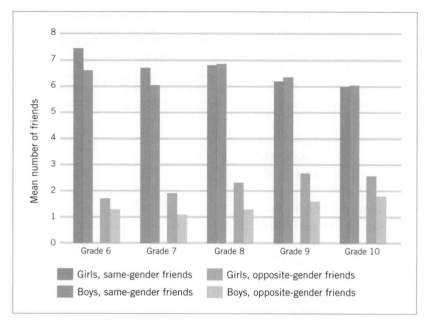

FIGURE 15.3 Friends by gender and grade The data shown in this figure demonstrate that younger children tend to be friends with children who are the same gender as they are. As children move into adolescence, the number of cross-gender friends tends to increase for both boys and girls. (Data from Poulin & Pedersen, 2007)

the way to romantic relationships. Adolescence is also a period of increased intimacy in same-gender friendships. For many girls and boys, increased emotional closeness is often attained through sharing personal feelings and thoughts, although there appears to be more variability among boys in the ways they experience and express closeness in friendships (Camarena, Sarigiani, & Petersen, 1990). While some boys attain intimacy through shared disclosures with same-gender friends, other boys tend to avoid self-disclosure with same-gender friends because they wish to appear strong. Instead, they usually attain a feeling of emotional closeness with friends through shared activities, such as playing sports. At the same time, many boys who avoid expressing feelings with male friends will do so with their female friends or girlfriends (Youniss & Smollar, 1985).

Self-disclosure and supportive listening are generally associated with relationship satisfaction and emotional adjustment (Leaper & Anderson, 1997; Rubin, Bukowski, & Parker, 2006). However, it is possible to have too much of a good thing. This occurs when friends dwell too long on upsetting events by talking to one another about them over and over. As discussed in Chapter 10, this process of *co-rumination* is more common among girls than among boys (A. J. Rose, Carlson, & Waller, 2007). Although it may foster feelings of closeness between friends, co-rumination appears to increase depression and anxiety in girls (but not in boys). To be clear, self-disclosure is generally positive for emotional adjustment, but it can be a problem when friends persistently focus on upset feelings without exploring proactive ways to cope with the distress.

Review

By about 6 to 9 months of age, infants can distinguish between females and males on the basis of perceptual cues. Between ages 2 and 3 years, children identify their own gender, after which they begin acquiring stereotypes regarding culturally prescribed activities and traits associated with each gender. They also start to demonstrate gender-typed play preferences. During the preschool period, children begin a process of self-initiated gender segregation that lasts through childhood and is strongly enforced by peers.

Around 6 years of age, children have acquired gender constancy and consolidate their understanding of gender. During middle childhood, children are capable of recognizing gender discrimination. Adolescence is a period that can involve increased gender-role rigidity or flexibility. It is also a time when girls are more likely to experience gender discrimination (sexism). Throughout childhood and adolescence, gender-role rigidity tends to be more common among boys, and gender-role flexibility tends to be more common among girls. Friendship intimacy also increases during adolescence, although intimacy is more common among girls than among boys.

Comparing Girls and Boys

Given existing gender stereotypes as well as children's early adoption of gender-typed behavior discussed up to this point, you might assume that the actual differences between girls and boys are many and deep. Contrary to this assumption, only a few cognitive abilities, personality traits, and social behaviors actually show consistent gender differences—and most of those gender differences tend to be fairly small.

When evaluating gender group comparisons for different behaviors, it is often the case that one gender differs only *slightly* from the other: the overlap between genders is considerable, meaning that many girls and boys are similar (see Hyde, 2005). In addition, substantial variation appears within each gender: not all members of the same gender are alike. Both these patterns appear in many observed gender differences studied by researchers. Therefore, besides knowing whether a group difference on some attribute is statistically significant—that is, unlikely to be caused by chance—it is important to consider both the *magnitude* of difference between two groups' averages and the *amount* of overlap in their distributions. This statistical index, known as **effect size,** is illustrated in Figure 15.4.

Researchers generally recognize four levels of effect sizes: *negligible* (trivial) if the two distributions overlap more than 85%; *small* but meaningful if the distributions overlap between 67% and 85% (Figure 15.4a); *medium* if the distributions overlap between 53% and 66% (Figure 15.4b); and *large* if the overlap is less than 53% (Figure 15.4c) (J. Cohen, 1988). Thus, sometimes even a small group difference can be statistically significant. That is, a statistically significant ($p < .05$) gender difference can have a trivial effect size!

Across different research studies, contradictory findings are common regarding gender differences or similarities in particular outcomes. Contradictory findings can occur because studies vary in the characteristics of their samples (e.g., participants' ages and backgrounds) and the methods used (e.g., surveys, naturalistic observation, or experiments). To infer overall patterns, scientists use a statistical technique known as **meta-analysis** to summarize the average effect-size and statistical significance across studies (see Chapter 1). When available, in this section we have used meta-analyses to summarize research on gender differences and similarities. Table 15.1 compiles average gender differences and effect sizes for specific behaviors. For some gender comparisons, the effect sizes are large (e.g., physical strength, toy preferences); but for most gender comparisons, the effect sizes are small or medium, and many are trivial or close to zero (e.g., math achievement, talkativeness).

Because statistically significant gender differences in cognitive abilities and social behaviors are often in the small range of effect sizes, Janet Hyde (2005) has advocated "the gender similarities hypothesis." She argued that, when comparing girls and boys, it is important to appreciate that similarities far outweigh differences on most attributes. When reviewing research findings, we acknowledge this importance by noting in Table 15.1 whether the effect size of any average gender

effect size ■ magnitude of difference between two group's averages and the amount of overlap in their distributions

meta-analysis ■ statistical method used to summarize average effect size and statistical significance across several research studies

FIGURE 15.4 Effect sizes in three typical distributions of scores The effect sizes shown in graphs (a), (b), and (c) depict the overlap between males and females on three hypothetical dimensions and are typical of most gender differences. The distribution shown in yellow on each graph represents one gender, and the distribution shown in red represents the other gender. On many attributes, differences in average performance are statistically significant but very small, and the overlap between the scores for girls and boys is considerable. Note also the considerable variation on each graph within each gender, as revealed by the bell-shaped curves.

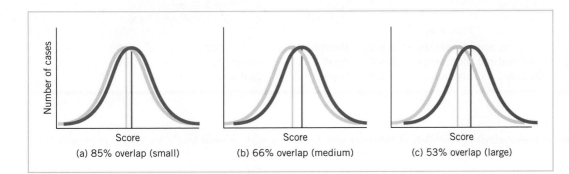

(a) 85% overlap (small) (b) 66% overlap (medium) (c) 53% overlap (large)

TABLE 15.1

Summary of Average Gender Differences and Effect Sizes for Gender-Typed Cognitions and Behaviors

Statistically significant differences between two groups on any measure can range from trivial to very large. Guidelines for interpreting the effect size (magnitude of average difference) between two groups are based on the amount of overlap between the two groups' distributions of scores (see Figure 15.4). When the overlap is greater than 85%, the difference is considered *trivial*. More meaningful differences are considered *small* if the overlap is between 67% and 85%, *medium* between 53% and 66%, and *large* if less than 53% (J. Cohen, 1988). In this table, an overlap less than 30% indicates a *very large* difference.

Measure	Age Range	Average Finding*	Effect Size	Source
Motor Abilities				
Physical strength	Childhood	B > G	Medium	J. R. Thomas & French, 1985
	Adolescence	B > G	Very large	J. R. Thomas & French, 1985
Running speed	Childhood	B > G	Medium	J. R. Thomas & French, 1985
	Adolescence	B > G	Very large	J. R. Thomas & French, 1985
Achievement and Test Performance				
Overall school grades	Childhood and adolescence	G > B	Small	Voyer & Voyer, 2014
Overall verbal ability[†]	Childhood	G ≥ B	Trivial	Hyde & Linn, 1988
Reading achievement[†]	Childhood	G > B	Small	Nowell & Hedges, 1998, Reilly, 2012
Writing achievement[†]	Childhood	G > B	Medium	Nowell & Hedges, 1998
Spatial ability (mental rotation and spatial perception)	Childhood and adolescence	B > G	Small	Voyer, Voyer, & Bryden, 1995
Math achievement[†]	Childhood	B = G	None	Lindberg et al., 2010
	Adolescence	B > G	Small	Lindberg et al., 2010
Life sciences achievement[†]	Adolescence	B = G	None	D. F. Halpern et al., 2007; Lindberg et al., 2010
Physical sciences achievement[†]	Adolescence	B > G	Small	D. F. Halpern et al., 2007; Lindberg et al., 2010
Gender Stereotyping	Childhood	B > G	Small	Signorella, Bigler, & Liben, 1997
Gender-Typed Play				
Preference for feminine-stereotyped toys	Childhood	G > B	Very large[††]	Cherney & London, 2006
Preference for masculine-stereotyped toys	Childhood	B > G	Very large[††]	Cherney & London, 2006
Rough-and-tumble play	Childhood	B > G	Large[††]	DiPietro, 1981
Ability Beliefs				
Athletic self-concept	Childhood and adolescence	B > G	Small	Wilgenbusch & Merrell, 1999
Verbal self-concept	Childhood and adolescence	G > B	Small	Wilgenbusch & Merrell, 1999
Math self-concept	Childhood and adolescence	B > G	Small	Wilgenbusch & Merrell, 1999
Science self-concept	Childhood and adolescence	B > G	Trivial	Weinburgh, 1995
Computing self-concept	Childhood	B = G	None	Whitley, 1997
	Adolescence	B > G	Medium	Whitley, 1997
Personality Traits				
Activity level	Infancy	B > G	Small	Eaton & Enns, 1986
	Childhood	B > G	Medium	Eaton & Enns, 1986
Self-control	Childhood	G > B	Small to large	Else-Quest et al., 2006
Risk taking	Childhood	B > G	Small	Byrnes, Miller, & Schafer, 1999
Interpersonal Goals				
Dominance and control goals	Childhood and adolescence	B > G	Small[††]	A. J. Rose & Rudolph, 2006
Intimacy and support goals	Childhood and adolescence	G > B	Medium[††]	A. J. Rose & Rudolph, 2006
Communication with Peers				
Talkativeness	Childhood and adolescence	G = B	None	Leaper & Smith, 2004
Directive speech	Childhood and adolescence	B > G	Small	Leaper & Smith, 2004
Collaborative speech	Childhood and adolescence	G > B	Small	Leaper & Smith, 2004
Self-disclosure	Childhood	G > B	Small[††]	A. J. Rose & Rudolph, 2006
	Adolescence	G > B	Medium[††]	A. J. Rose & Rudolph, 2006
Aggression				
Direct physical aggression	Childhood and adolescence	B > G	Medium to large	Archer, 2004; Card et al., 2008
Direct verbal aggression	Childhood and adolescence	B > G	Small	Archer, 2004; Card et al., 2008
Indirect aggression	Childhood and adolescence	G ≥ B	Trivial	Card et al., 2008

*B indicates boys; G indicates girls.

[†]Achievement based on performance on standardized tests.

[††]Effect size *not* based on a meta-analysis but refers either to magnitude of difference seen in a single study or trend from a few studies summarized in the source.

difference in behavior or cognition is trivial, small, medium, or large. Keep in mind, however, that even when there is a large average difference on any particular measure, many girls and boys are similar to one another. Also, some members of the group with the lower average exceed some members of the group with the higher average (see Figure 15.4). For example, there is a very large average gender difference in adult height: men are generally taller than women. At the same time, many women and men are the same height, and some women are taller than the average man.

Physical Growth: Prenatal Development Through Adolescence

Sex differences in physical development appear early in prenatal development. The most dramatic of these, of course, is the emergence of male or female genitalia. Thereafter, the differences that occur between males and females are relatively subtle prior to the onset of puberty. In the following sections, we review the role of androgens in initiating prenatal sex differences; the average differences in male and female size, strength, and physical abilities in childhood; and the development of secondary sex characteristics in adolescence.

Prenatal Development, Infancy, and Childhood

As noted in our earlier discussions, a key prenatal factor in sexual development is the presence or absence of androgens. Research suggests that prenatal exposure to androgens may influence the organization of the nervous system, and these effects may be partly related to some average gender differences in behavior seen at later ages. The presence of prenatal androgens, normally triggered by the Y chromosome in genetic males 6 to 8 weeks after conception, stimulates the formation of male external organs and internal reproductive structures; the absence of androgens results in the formation of female genital structures. In unusual circumstances known as intersex conditions (see Box 15.1), an overproduction of androgens may occur during prenatal development (congenital adrenal hyperplasia). In genetic females, this can lead to the formation of masculinized genitals. Conversely, a rare syndrome in genetic males (androgen insensitivity syndrome) causes the androgen receptors to malfunction. In these cases, female external genitalia may form.

At birth, males, on average, weigh only about half a pound more than females do; through infancy, male and female babies look so similar that, if they are dressed in gender-neutral clothing, people cannot guess their gender. As discussed in Chapter 3, during infancy and into childhood, girls and boys grow at roughly the same rate and are essentially equal in height and weight. But during childhood, boys become notably stronger on average compared to girls.

Adolescence

A series of dramatic bodily transformations during adolescence is associated with **puberty,** the developmental period marked by the ability to reproduce—that is, for boys, the ability to inseminate, and for girls, the ability to menstruate, gestate, and lactate (Gaddis & Brooks-Gunn, 1985; Jorgensen, Keiding, & Skakkebaek, 1991). In girls, puberty typically begins with enlargement of the breasts and the general growth spurt in height and weight, followed by the appearance of pubic

 Puberty

puberty ■ developmental period marked by the ability to reproduce and other dramatic bodily changes

JUSTIN PUMFREY / GETTY IMAGES

In early puberty, girls are typically taller than boys because of girls' earlier physical maturation. By the end of adolescence, boys catch up and surpass girls in average height and weight.

menarche ■ onset of menstruation

spermarche ■ onset of capacity for ejaculation

body image ■ an individual's perception of, and feelings about, his or her own body

adrenarche ■ period prior to the emergence of visible signs of puberty during which the adrenal glands mature, providing a major source of sex steroid hormones; correlates with the onset of sexual attraction

hair and then **menarche** (the onset of menstruation). Menarche is triggered in part by the increase in body fat that typically occurs in adolescence. In boys, puberty generally starts with the growth of the testes, followed by the appearance of pubic hair, the general growth spurt, growth of the penis, and **spermarche** (the capacity for ejaculation).

For both sexes, there is considerable variability in physical maturation due to both genetic and environmental factors. Genes affect growth and sexual maturation in large part by influencing the production of hormones, especially growth hormone (secreted by the pituitary gland) and thyroxin (released by the thyroid gland). The influence of environmental factors is particularly evident in the changes in physical development that have occurred over generations (see Chapter 3). In the United States today, girls begin menstruating several years earlier than their ancestors did 200 years ago. This change is thought to reflect improvement in nutrition over the generations.

With the changes in body composition that occur in early adolescence, particularly the substantial increase in muscle mass in boys, the gender gap in physical and motor skills greatly increases. After puberty, average gender differences are very large in strength, speed, and size: few adolescent girls can run as fast or throw a ball as far as most boys can (Malina & Bouchard, 1991; J. R. Thomas & French, 1985). These are among the largest average differences in abilities seen between females and males (see Table 15.1).

The physical changes that boys and girls experience during puberty are accompanied by psychological and behavioral changes. For example, in some cultures, the increase in body fat that adolescent girls undergo may be related to gender differences in **body image**—how an individual perceives and feels about his or her physical appearance. On average, American girls tend to have more negative attitudes toward their bodies than American boys do, and teenage girls typically want to lose several pounds regardless of how much they actually weigh (Tyrka, Graber, & Brooks-Gunn, 2000). A survey of more than 10,000 U.S. adolescents found that roughly half of boys and two-thirds of girls were dissatisfied with their bodies. Girls were mostly concerned about losing weight; boys, with being more muscular (A. E. Field et al., 2005). Dissatisfaction with body image has long been associated with a host of difficulties, ranging from low self-esteem and depression to eating disorders. This survey added another item to the list: the use of unproven and potentially harmful substances to control weight or build muscle—a practice acknowledged by 12% of the boys and 8% of the girls surveyed. These problems do not appear limited to only girls and boys in North America, either. Surveys across different cultures indicate similar patterns of body image and eating disorders (Levine & Smolak, 2010).

Another change that accompanies physical maturation is the onset of sexual attraction, which usually begins before the physical process of puberty is complete. According to the recollections of a sample of adults in the United States, sexual attraction is first experienced at about 10 years of age—regardless of whether the attraction was for individuals of the other sex or the same sex (McClintock & Herdt, 1996). The onset of sexual attraction correlates with the maturation of the adrenal glands, which are the major source of sex steroids other than the testes and ovaries. This stage has been termed **adrenarche,** although the child's body does not yet show any outside signs of maturation. (Sexual identity and romantic relationships are reviewed in Chapters 11 and 13.)

Cognitive Abilities and Academic Achievement

The following sections summarize the evidence comparing boys' and girls' cognitive abilities and academic achievement. When average gender-differences in cognitive ability or performance have been observed, the effect sizes have usually been small (D. F. Halpern, 2012; D. F. Halpern et al., 2007; see Table 15.1). Somewhat greater differences appear when it comes to motivation for particular subjects. After summarizing these comparisons, we consider biological, cognitive-motivational, and cultural influences that might account for these findings. The relationship between gender and academic achievement during childhood and adolescence has important implications for adult gender roles and equality. To the extent that girls and boys develop different cognitive abilities, academic interests, and achievement, gender differences in their future occupations and income may follow.

Adrenarche, the onset of sexual interest, has been linked to the maturation of the adrenal glands, which produce sex steroid hormones in both boys and girls.

General Intelligence

Despite widespread belief to the contrary, boys and girls are equivalent in most aspects of intelligence and cognitive functioning. The average IQ scores of girls and boys are virtually identical (D. F. Halpern, 2012). However, proportionally more boys than girls scored at both the lowest and the highest extremes. That is, somewhat more boys than girls are diagnosed with intellectual disabilities or are classified as intellectually gifted (D. F. Halpern, 2012).

Overall Academic Achievement

Although girls and boys are similar in general intelligence, they tend to differ in academic achievement from elementary school through college. Recent statistics in the United States indicate that girls tend to show higher levels of school adjustment and achievement than do boys (Child Trends Data Bank, 2015; T. D. Snyder & Dillow, 2010; Voyer & Voyer, 2014). In one meta-analysis, there was a small average difference indicating that girls tended to attain higher overall school grades than did boys (Voyer & Voyer, 2014). Also, in 2014, the high school dropout rate was higher for boys (7.1%) than for girls (5.9%); boys accounted for 55% of all high school dropouts. In addition, in that same year, 57% of bachelor's degrees were awarded to women. The magnitude of gender difference in academic achievement varies somewhat across different cultural and ethnic groups and socioeconomic levels.

Verbal Skills

Compared with boys, girls tend to be slightly advanced in early language development, including fluency and clarity of articulation and vocabulary development (Gleason & Ely, 2002). On standardized tests of children's overall verbal ability, there is a negligible average gender difference favoring girls (Hyde & Linn, 1988). Larger average differences are seen when specific verbal skills are examined. Girls tend to achieve higher average performance in reading and writing from elementary school to high school; the effect sizes of the average differences were small for reading and medium for writing (Hedges & Nowell, 1995; Nowell & Hedges, 1998; Reilly, 2012; Voyer & Voyer, 2014; see Table 15.1). Boys are more likely to suffer speech-related problems, such as poor articulation and stuttering, as well as more reading-related problems such as dyslexia (D. F. Halpern, 2012).

Spatial Skills

On average, boys tend to perform somewhat better than girls in some aspects of visual-spatial processing (see Table 15.1). This difference emerges between 3 and 4 years of age and becomes more substantial during adolescence and adulthood (D. F. Halpern, 2012). Gender differences are most pronounced on tasks that involve mental rotation of a complex geometric figure in order to decide whether it matches another figure presented in a different orientation (Figure 15.5a); boys tend to perform better than girls in that area. However, other spatial tasks, such as finding a hidden figure embedded within a larger image, show much smaller gender differences (Figure 15.5b). Thus, the conclusion that more boys than girls have superior spatial ability depends on the particular type of spatial ability.

Mathematical and Related Skills

Until recent decades in the United States, boys tended to perform somewhat better on standardized tests of mathematical ability than did girls. As we have noted, however, the gender gap in mathematics achievement has closed dramatically as a result of efforts made by schools and parents to improve girls' performance. According to the most recent studies, no average gender differences in standardized test performance are seen in the elementary or middle school levels (Lindberg et al., 2010), and only a small average difference (favoring boys) is indicated at the high school level (D. F. Halpern et al., 2007; Lindberg et al., 2010; see Table 15.1). Furthermore, U.S. girls and women are maintaining their interest in math beyond high school at rates higher than seen in earlier decades. The percentage of bachelor's degrees in mathematics awarded to women in the United States increased from 37% in 1970 to 43% in 2012 (National Science Foundation, 2015; T. D. Snyder & Dillow, 2010).

Mathematics is considered a key gateway for careers in science, technology, and engineering (D. F. Halpern et al., 2007; Watt, 2006). Patterns of gender differences in these subject areas are mixed in the United States. In the life sciences (e.g., biology),

FIGURE 15.5 Tests of spatial skills Gender differences vary according to the type of task. Boys tend to perform better than girls do on tasks that involve mental rotation, such as the one in (a), in which children have to determine which response matches the standard. In contrast, gender differences are small or nonexistent on tasks like that in (b), which requires children to find the simple geometric figure on the left embedded in the adjoining complex figure.

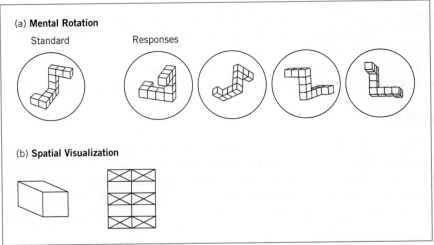

girls and women appear to be doing well. At the high school level, there is no average gender difference in achievement. At the college level, women earned 59% of recent bachelor's degrees in biological sciences (National Science Foundation, 2015).

In contrast, girls and women are not as well represented in the physical sciences (e.g., physics) and technological fields (e.g., engineering). Among recently awarded bachelor's degrees, for example, women accounted for 20% in physics, 18% in computer science, and 19% in engineering (National Science Foundation, 2015). Following the attention paid to the gender gap in math achievement a few decades ago, educators and researchers are increasingly addressing the gender gap in the physical sciences and technology.

Next, we will explore possible reasons for gender differences in academics and achievement, including the influence of culture, in terms of an individual's family, peer group, and society.

Explanations for Gender Differences in Cognitive Abilities and Achievement

Researchers have variously pointed to biological, cognitive-motivational, and cultural factors in relation to gender-related variations in cognitive abilities and achievement. We now examine each possible area of influence.

Biological influences Some researchers have proposed that sex differences in brain structure and function may underlie some differences in how male and female brains process different types of information. However, because the research supporting this interpretation has often been based on adults, it is impossible to determine whether any differences in brain structure and function are due to genetic or environmental influences. Also, a slight biological difference can get exaggerated through differential experience (D. F. Halpern, 2012). For example, boys may initially have a slight average advantage over girls in some types of spatial processing. Yet when boys spend more time playing video games and sports than girls do, they practice their spatial skills more (Moreau et al., 2012; I. Spence & Feng, 2010). As a consequence, the magnitude of the gender difference in spatial ability may widen. However, several studies indicate that spatial skills can be substantially improved in girls as well as boys through training (Uttal et al., 2013).

Stronger evidence for possible biological influences is suggested by research showing that some sex differences in brain structure may be partly due to the influence of sex-related hormones on the developing fetal brain (Hines, 2013). For example, androgens may affect parts of the brain associated with spatial skills (Grön et al., 2000; Hines, 2013). Because males are exposed to higher levels of androgens than are females during typical prenatal development, this difference may lead to greater hemispheric specialization in the male brain and more proficiency in spatial ability later in life. Support for this hypothesis comes from studies that have linked very high levels of prenatal androgens in girls with above-average spatial ability (Grimshaw, Sitarenios, & Finegan, 1995; Hines et al., 2003; Mueller et al., 2008). Conversely, it has been found that males with androgen insensitivity syndrome (see Box 15.1) tend to score lower than average in spatial ability (Imperato-McGinley et al., 1991/2007).

Cognitive and motivational influences The process of self-socialization emphasized in cognitive motivational theories plays a role in children's academic achievement. According to Eccles's *expectancy-value model of achievement*

PHOTODISC / GETTY IMAGES

Some studies find that mothers are more talkative with daughters than with sons. Studies also find that, on average, girls acquire language at a faster rate than do boys. Does mothers' greater talkativeness with girls contribute to girls' faster language acquisition? Or does girls' faster language acquisition influence mothers' talkativeness with them?

(Eccles & Wigfield, 2002), children are most motivated to achieve in areas in which they view themselves as competent (expectations for success) and that they find interesting and important (value). Gender stereotypes can shape the kinds of subjects that girls and boys tend to value (see Table 15.1). For instance, many children internalize gender stereotypes that science, technology, and math are for boys and that reading, writing, and the arts are for girls (Kessels, 2015; Papastergiou, 2008; Plante, Théorêt, & Favreau, 2009). However, these stereotypes seem to be less and less prevalent (Plante et al., 2009)—possibly due to the efforts of many educators, policymakers, and parents over the years.

To the extent that gender stereotyping about academic subjects does persist, perhaps it is not surprising, then, that average gender differences in interest and ability beliefs exist in these academic areas (Eccles & Wigfield, 2002; Else-Quest, Hyde, & Linn, 2010; Simpkins, Fredricks, & Eccles, 2015; Wilgenbusch & Merrell, 1999) and that these self-concepts predict academic achievement and occupational aspirations (Eccles & Wigfield, 2002; D. F. Halpern, 2012; D. F. Halpern et al., 2007). As discussed next, social and cultural factors also influence the development of girls' and boys' academic self-concepts and achievement. That is, children are influenced by the role models, opportunities, and incentives that they recognize in their environments.

Parental influences As noted in Chapter 6, parents' talking to their children is a strong predictor of children's language learning. A meta-analysis of studies conducted with mostly Western, middle-class families found that mothers tended to have average higher rates of verbal interaction with daughters than with sons (Leaper, Anderson, & Sanders, 1998). Thus, one possibility is that young girls learn language at a slightly faster rate than do boys at least partly because mothers spend more time talking with daughters than sons. Conversely, girls' faster language acquisition may lead mothers to talk more to them than to their sons (Leaper & Smith, 2004). Finally, both patterns may tend to occur—a possible bidirectional influence whereby both mothers and daughters tend to be talkative and reinforce this behavior in one another.

Parents' gender stereotyping is also related to children's academic achievement. Many parents accept the prevailing stereotypes about boys' and girls' relative interest in and aptitude for various academic subjects (Eccles, 2015; Eccles et al., 2000; Leaper, 2013, 2015a), and these gender-typed expectations can affect children's achievement motivation (Eccles, 2015; Eccles et al., 2000). Observational research suggests that parents may communicate their own gender-stereotyped expectations to their children through differential encouragement (Bhanot & Jovanovic, 2005; Crowley et al., 2001; Tenenbaum & Leaper, 2003). You might think that parents' beliefs about their children's academic potential would be based primarily on their children's own self-concepts and achievement, but researchers find that parents often hold gender-typed beliefs before any average gender differences in academic interest or performance occur. In fact, longitudinal research indicates that parents' expectations can be a stronger predictor of children's later achievement than the children's earlier performance in particular subject areas (Bleeker & Jacobs, 2004).

Teacher influences Teachers can influence gender differences in children's academic motivation and achievement. Some teachers may hold gender-stereotyped beliefs about girls' and boys' abilities. When this occurs, they may expect higher

Some teachers hold gender-stereotyped expectations about girls' and boys' abilities that may affect their interactions with students.

VSTOCK / ALAMY

school achievement in girls than in boys (S. Jones & Myhill, 2004), or they may stereotype boys as being better at math and science (Riegle-Crumb & Humphries, 2012; Tiedemann, 2000). When teachers hold gender-typed expectations, they may differentially assess, encourage, and pay attention to students according to their gender. In this manner, teachers can lay the groundwork for self-fulfilling prophecies that affect children's later academic achievement (see D. F. Halpern, 2012; D. F. Halpern et al., 2007). However, many educators have become more aware of gender bias over the years, and have made proactive efforts to promote girls' participation in math, science, and technology programs (e.g., Stake & Mares, 2005).

Peer influences Children's interests often are shaped by the activities and values they associate with their classmates and friends. Consequently, peers can shape children's academic achievement. This influence begins with the kinds of play activities children practice with their peers. As we have noted, many activities commonly favored among boys—including construction play, sports, and video games—provide them with opportunities to develop their spatial abilities as well as math- and science-related skills. In contrast, the types of play more common among girls—such as domestic role-play—are talk-oriented and build verbal skills (Leaper, 2015a; Leaper & Bigler, in press).

Girls and boys may be more likely to strive in particular school subjects when they are viewed as compatible with peer norms. For example, one study found that U.S. high school students who viewed their friends as supportive of science and math were more likely to express interest in a future science-related career (Robnett & Leaper, 2013). The association between friends' science support and science career interest held for both girls and boys—but boys were more likely than girls to report having a friendship group supportive of science. It is also notable that friends' support of English (reading and writing) was not related to science career interest; thus, peer norms regarding particular academic subjects may be related to how likely girls or boys are to value those subjects (Leaper, 2015b).

Peer norms can have a strong impact on girls' and boys' achievement motivation. For example, research indicates that girls are more likely to maintain their interest in science and computers when their friends support achievement in these subjects.

▶ **Educating Girls of the World**

Traditional masculinity norms emphasizing dominance and self-reliance may undermine some boys' academic achievement in the United States and other Western industrialized countries (Levant, 2005; Renold, 2001; Steinmayr & Spinath, 2008; Van Houtte, 2004). That is, some boys may not consider it masculine to do well in certain subjects or possibly in school overall. For instance, doing well in school or expressing interest in certain subjects, such as reading, may be devalued as being feminine (Andre et al., 1999; Martinot, Bagès, & Désert, 2012). Indeed, some research suggests that boys' endorsement of traditional masculinity is related to lower average performances in reading and writing and lower rates of high school graduation in North America and Europe (Kessels & Steinmayr, 2013; Levant, 2005; Renold, 2001; Van de Gaer et al., 2006; Van Houtte, 2004). At the same time, some U.S. research suggests that gender-role flexibility is related to stronger interest in nontraditional majors among male undergraduates (Jome & Tokar, 1998; Leaper & Van, 2008).

Cultural influences The bioecological model maintains that socialization practices prepare children for their adult roles in society. If women and men tend to hold different occupations, then different abilities and preferences are apt to be encouraged in girls and boys. Therefore, where there are cultural variations in girls' and boys' academic achievement, there should be corresponding differences in socialization.

A meta-analysis conducted by Else-Quest, Hyde, and Linn (2010) pointed to cultural influences on gender-related variations in mathematics achievement. Gender differences on standardized math tests varied widely across nations: in some, boys scored higher; in others, girls scored higher; and in still others, no gender difference appeared. To assess possible cultural influences, the researchers considered the representation of women in higher education in the country. They found that average gender differences in several math-related outcomes were less likely in nations with higher percentages of women in higher levels of education. This was seen for adolescents' test performance, self-confidence, and intrinsic motivation regarding math. As we noted earlier, the narrowing gender gap in math achievement in the United States over the past few decades has been accompanied by a steady increase in the proportion of women in science and engineering (National Science Foundation, 2015).

Other cultural factors have also been found to predict gender-related variations in academic achievement within Western industrialized societies. Average gender differences in overall academic success and verbal achievement tend to be less common among children from higher-income neighborhoods, among children of highly educated parents, and among children of egalitarian heterosexual parents (Burkam, Lee, & Smerdon, 1997; Croft et al., 2014; Ferry, Fouad, & Smith, 2000; Melby et al., 2008; Updegraff, McHale, & Crouter, 1996). Furthermore, the local community in which children are raised may have an impact. In one study (Riegle-Crumb & Moore, 2014), a comparison of different communities in the United States found the gender gap in physics achievement (usually favoring boys) was smaller in high schools in which more women were employed in science and technology occupations within the community.

Interpersonal Goals and Communication

One of the most popular self-help books about relationships has been John Gray's (1992) *Men Are from Mars, Women Are from Venus.* The author (who is not a scientist) purported that gender differences in interpersonal goals and communication style are so great that it is almost as if the sexes came from different planets. The scientific evidence, however, indicates that average gender differences in adults' communication are not nearly as dramatic as Gray portrayed them. Although average gender differences in women's and men's speech have been documented, the magnitude of the differences has usually been in the small-to-medium range (Leaper & Ayres, 2007). The average gender differences in communication and interpersonal goals during childhood and adolescence have likewise been found to be modest (see Table 15.1).

In terms of interpersonal goals, researchers have found average gender differences that are consistent with traditional gender roles (A. J. Rose & Rudolph, 2006). More boys than girls tend to emphasize dominance and power as goals in their social relationships. In contrast, more girls than boys tend to favor intimacy and support as goals in their relationships. The effect sizes for these differences, however, tend to be small to medium.

Researchers have also observed some average gender differences among children's communication styles with peers. Contrary to the stereotypes of talkative girls and taciturn boys, studies generally do not find average differences in talkativeness after early childhood (Leaper & Smith, 2004). However, with regard to self-disclosure about personal thoughts and feelings, there tends to be a small-to-medium gender difference, with higher average rates among girls than boys (A. J. Rose & Rudolph, 2006). Girls also tend to be somewhat more likely than boys to use collaborative statements, which reflect high affiliation and high assertion. In contrast, boys tend to be more likely than girls to use directive statements, which reflect high assertion and low affiliation (see Box 15.3).

As with most average gender differences, there is considerable overlap between girls and boys in communication style. Although some children act in gender-stereotypical ways, many girls use controlling speech and many boys use high levels of collaborative speech. Indeed, as we have seen throughout this chapter, girls and boys are quite similar to one another in a wide variety of behaviors.

Explanations for Gender Differences in Interpersonal Goals and Communication

As we have seen regarding other types of behaviors, researchers have identified a variety of factors that are related to the likelihood of average gender differences in interpersonal goals and communication. Some of the cognitive-motivational, social-interactional, and cultural influences that have been implicated in research studies are described below.

Cognitive and motivational influences The average gender differences in interpersonal goals and communication style are related. To the extent that some girls and boys differ in their primary goals for social relationships, they are apt to use different language styles to attain those goals (Crosby, Fireman, & Clopton, 2011; P. M. Miller, Danaher, & Forbes, 1986; Strough & Berg, 2000). For example, if a boy is especially interested in establishing dominance, using directive

BOX 15.3 | a closer look

GENDER AND CHILDREN'S COMMUNICATION STYLES

Several studies conducted by Leaper and colleagues have examined gender-related variations in children's and adults' communication patterns (e.g., Leaper, 1991; Leaper et al., 1999; Leaper et al., 1995; Leaper & Gleason, 1996; Leaper & Holliday, 1995). In one study of 5- and 7-year-olds, Leaper (1991) placed children in same- or mixed-gender pairs to play with a set of hand puppets. He recorded the children's conversations and classified each statement the children made in terms of affiliation and assertion. As diagrammed in the figure below, a statement can be high or low on each dimension, which allows for four speech act (statement) categories:

1. *Collaborative statements* are high in both affiliation (engaging the other person) and assertion (guiding the action). Examples include suggestions for joint activity ("Let's play superheroes") or elaborations on what the other speaker previously said.

2. *Controlling statements* are high in assertion but low in affiliation. Examples include directives ("Do this") or negative comments.

3. *Obliging statements* are high in affiliation and low in assertion. Examples include expressions of agreement or going along with the other's proposal ("Sure, that's fine").

4. *Withdrawing acts* reflect low assertion and low affiliation. This includes being nonresponsive to another person's statement.

For girls and boys in both age groups, collaborative conversations were the most common. There were no average gender differences in any of the types of statements among the younger children and there were no average differences in obliging statements or withdrawing acts among the older children. However, significant gender differences were seen among the older children in the percentages of collaborative and controlling statements. Among the 7-year-olds, the average percentage of collaborative statements was significantly higher among girl–girl pairs (mean = 56%) than either boy–boy pairs (mean = 39%) or mixed-gender pairs (mean = 43%).

Following is an example of reciprocal collaboration between one pair of girls. The type of speech act is indicated in brackets next to each statement.

> *Jennifer:* Let's go play on the slide. (Makes sliding noises) [Collaborate]
> *Sally:* Okay. [Oblige] *(Makes sliding noises)* I'll do a choo-choo train with you. [Collaborate]
> *Jennifer:* Okay. [Oblige]
> *Sally:* You can go first. [Collaborate]
> *Jennifer:* Ch . . . *(Gasp)* [Collaborate]
> *Sally:* Ch . . . *(Gasp)* [Collaborate]
>
> (Leaper, 1991, p. 800)

Another average gender difference was the percentage of controlling speech. Rates were significantly lower in girl–girl pairs (mean = 13%) than either boy–boy pairs (mean = 26%) or mixed-gender pairs (mean = 24%).

Within the mixed-gender pairs, no gender differences appeared in collaborative or controlling speech. Thus, it appears that girls tended to decrease their amount of collaborative speech and increase their use of controlling speech when interacting with boys (compared with when they interacted with girls). Conversely, boys tended to use similar amounts of collaborative and controlling speech in same-gender and mixed-gender interactions.

According to Leaper (1991), it is important to acknowledge, first, that collaboration was the most common type of speech for both girls and boys. Despite this similarity, collaboration was even more frequent in the average speech of girls than of boys. Conversely, controlling speech was more common among boys than among girls. Contrary to old stereotypes of girls being unassertive, girls were not more likely than boys to make statements low in assertion (obliging speech or withdrawing). Instead, girls were more likely to coordinate affiliative and assertive goals in their communication. Finally, in mixed-gender interactions, there was more evidence of girl's accommodating to the speech style of boys than the reverse; that is, girls tended to show more of the pattern associated with boys' same-gender interactions (more controlling and less collaborative speech) during mixed-gender interactions, whereas boys tended to show similar average patterns in same- and mixed-gender interactions. Other studies have found similar average gender differences in communication patterns among children from different ethnic and socioeconomic backgrounds (Filardo, 1996; Leaper et al., 1999; Leman, Ahmed, & Ozarow, 2005).

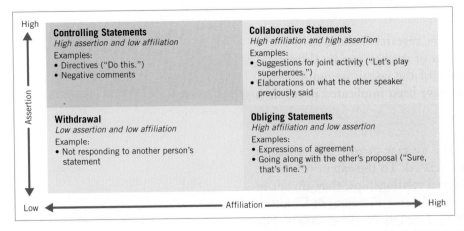

Communication strategies The figure illustrates the two-dimensional model of social interaction and communication. Assertion ranges from high to low along the vertical axis, and affiliation ranges from high to low along the horizontal axis. Collaborative acts are high in both affiliation and assertion. Controlling acts are high in assertion and low in affiliation. Obliging acts are high in affiliation and low in assertion. Withdrawing acts are low in both affiliation and assertion.

statements may help him attain that goal; and if a girl wants to establish intimacy, then talking about personal feelings or elaborating on the other person's thoughts would help realize that goal.

Parental influences Many children observe their parents modeling gender-typed communication patterns. One meta-analysis summarized trends across studies (most of which were conducted with Western middle-class families) comparing mothers' and fathers' speech to their children (Leaper et al., 1998). The results indicated small average effect sizes: first, mothers were more likely than fathers to use affiliative speech; in contrast, fathers were more likely than mothers to use controlling (high in assertion and low in affiliation) speech.

Peer influences The social norms and activities traditionally practiced within children's gender-segregated peer groups foster different interpersonal goals in girls and boys. For example, many girls commonly engage in domestic scenarios ("playing house") that are structured around collaborative and affectionate interchanges. Boys' play is more likely to involve competitive contexts ("playing war" or sports) that are structured around dominance and power. The impact of same-gender peer norms was implicated in Leaper and Smith's (2004) meta-analysis, which found that gender differences in communication were more likely to be detected in studies of same-gender interactions than in mixed-gender interactions.

Cultural influences Cross-cultural comparisons generally find a similar pattern of average gender difference in social behavior. That is, affiliative social behavior tends to be more common among girls and women than among boys and men, whereas directive social behavior tends to more common among boys and men than among girls and women (Best, 2010). However, there are cultural variations in the degree to which these behaviors might be seen. For instance, in many Asian cultures, such as Japan, it is generally considered important for boys as well as girls to show high levels of affiliation in social interaction. Yet, within these cultures, boys and men tend to be more direct in their speech than do girls and women (Smith, 1992). Also, there are cultural variations within diverse nations, such as the United States. For example, some researchers have observed highly direct social interactions among African American girls from working-class and low-income neighborhoods in contrast to European American girls from middle-class communities (Kyratzis, 2004).

Aggressive Behavior

The conventional wisdom is that boys are more aggressive than girls. In support of this expectation, research studies indicate a reliable average gender difference in aggression. But the magnitude of the gender difference is not as great as many people expect. Also, this difference depends partly on the type of aggression being considered.

As noted in Chapter 13, researchers distinguish between direct and indirect forms of aggression (Archer & Coyne, 2005; Björkqvist, Österman, & Kaukiainen, 1992). *Direct aggression* involves overt physical or verbal acts openly intended to cause harm, whereas *indirect aggression* (also known as relational or social aggression) involves attempts to damage a person's social standing or group acceptance through covert means such as negative gossip and social exclusion.

SPENCER GRANT / PHOTOEDIT

Rates of indirect aggression are higher for girls than for boys. Indirect aggression includes behaviors such as criticizing and spreading rumors about a peer or excluding a peer from the friendship group.

Average gender differences in the incidence of physical aggression emerge gradually during the preschool years (D. F. Hay, 2007). In a comprehensive meta-analysis of studies comparing boys' and girls' aggressive behavior, John Archer (2004) found that both physical and verbal forms of direct aggression occurred more often among boys than among girls. The average difference was small during childhood and medium to large during adolescence. Although direct aggression generally declines for both boys and girls with age, the decline is more pronounced for girls than for boys.

There appears to be no average gender difference during childhood in the use of indirect aggression. In a meta-analysis of studies testing for such gender differences, Card and colleagues (2008) found only a negligible effect size during adolescence, with girls slightly more likely than boys to use indirect aggression. The trivial effect size may seem surprising given the popular notion of "mean girls" who use indirect strategies such as negative gossip and social exclusion. However, because direct aggression is less likely among girls than boys, girls tend to use proportionally more indirect than direct aggression than boys, on average. Thus, when most girls do express aggression, it may be indirect rather than direct physical or verbal aggression (Leaper, 2013).

Average gender differences in aggression have been found primarily in research on same-gender interactions. Research conducted with mostly European American children suggests that different rules may apply when some girls and boys have conflicts with one another. Beginning in early childhood, boys are more likely than girls to ignore the other gender's attempts to exert influence (Maccoby, 1998). Thus, when they are more assertive and less affiliative, boys may be more apt to get their way in unsupervised mixed-gender groups.

Studies in the United States comparing children's behavior in same-gender versus cross-gender conflicts revealed another interesting pattern. In same-gender conflicts, boys were more likely to use power-assertive strategies (e.g., threats, demands) and girls were more likely to use conflict-mitigation strategies (e.g., compromise, change the topic). Yet in cross-gender conflicts, girls' use of power-assertive strategies increased, while boys' use of conflict-mitigation strategies did not change (P. M. Miller et al., 1986; Sims, Hutchins, & Taylor, 1998). These studies suggest that girls often may find it necessary to play by the boys' rules to gain influence in mixed-gender settings.

Explanations for Gender Differences in Aggression

Possible explanations for gender differences in aggression range from the effects of biological factors to the socializing influences of family, peers, the media, and the culture at large. Each factor likely has a contributing role.

Biological influences It is well known that, on average, males have higher baseline levels of testosterone than do females. Many people assume that this accounts for gender differences in aggression. Contrary to this popular belief, there does *not* appear to be a direct association between aggression and baseline testosterone levels (Archer, Graham-Kevan, & Davies, 2005). However, there is an indirect one: the body increases its production of testosterone in response to perceived threats and challenges, and this increase can lead to more aggressive behavior (Archer,

2006). Furthermore, people who are impulsive and less inhibited are more likely to perceive the behavior of others as threatening. Thus, because boys, on average, have more difficulty regulating emotional arousal (Else-Quest et al., 2006), they may be more prone to engage in direct aggression (D. F. Hay, 2007). Conversely, greater average emotion regulation among girls (compared to boys) may contribute to higher rates of prosocial behavior.

Cognitive and motivational influences Average gender differences in empathy and prosocial behavior may be related to differences in boys' and girls' rates of aggression (Knight, Fabes, & Higgins, 1996; Lemerise & Arsenio, 2000; Levant, 2005; Mayberry & Espelage, 2007). On average, girls are somewhat more likely than boys to report feelings of empathy and sympathy in response to people's distress (N. Eisenberg & Fabes, 1998), and they also tend to display more concern in their behavioral reactions (e.g., looks of concern and attempts to help). Direct aggression may be more likely among children who are less empathetic and have fewer prosocial skills. In support of this explanation, one study found average gender differences, with boys scoring higher on direct aggression and lower on empathy than girls, but both aggressive girls and aggressive boys scored lower on empathy than did nonaggressive girls and boys (Mayberry & Espelage, 2007).

The gender-typed social norms and goals regarding assertion and affiliation may further contribute to the average gender difference in conflict and aggression (P. M. Miller et al., 1986; A. J. Rose & Rudolph, 2006; see Table 15.1). More boys than girls tend to favor assertive over affiliative goals (e.g., being dominant), whereas more girls than boys tend to endorse affiliative goals or a combination of affiliative and assertive goals (e.g., maintaining intimacy). When some boys focus on dominance goals, they may be more likely to appraise conflicts as competitions that require the use of direct aggression. In addition, some boys may initiate direct aggression as a way to enhance their status.

In contrast, by emphasizing intimacy and nurturance goals, many girls may be more likely to view relationship conflicts as threats to interpersonal harmony that need to be resolved through compromise (P. M. Miller et al., 1986). The normative social pressures among many girls to act "nice" may also lead them to avoid direct confrontation. However, when girls who adhere to these norms are unable to resolve a conflict, they may try to hurt one another through indirect strategies such as criticizing or excluding the offender or sharing secret information about the offender with other girls (Murray-Close, Ostrov, & Crick, 2007; Underwood, 2003). This may be one reason for a paradox noted in Chapter 13: even though girls, on average, have more intimate friendships than do boys, girls' same-gender friendships tend to be less stable over time (Benenson & Christakos, 2003). That is, when conflict occurs in same-gender friendships and indirect aggression occurs, girls may be more likely than boys to take it personally and see it as a reason to end the relationship.

Parental and other adult influences In general, most parents and other adults disapprove of physical aggression in both boys and girls. After the preschool years, however, adults tend to be more tolerant of aggression in boys and often adopt a "boys will be boys" attitude toward it (J. Martin & Ross, 2005). In a classic experiment demonstrating this effect, researchers asked people to watch a short film of two children engaged in rough-and-tumble play in the snow and to rate the level of the play's aggressiveness (Condry & Ross, 1985). The children were dressed in gender-neutral snowsuits and filmed at a distance that made their gender undeterminable. Some viewers were told that both children were boys; others were told that the children were both girls; still others were told that the children were a boy and girl. Viewers who thought that both children were boys rated their play as much less aggressive than did viewers who thought that both children were girls.

Children also appear aware of this "boys will be boys" bias. They believe that physical aggression is more acceptable, and less likely to be punished, when enacted by boys than when enacted by girls (Giles & Heyman, 2005; Perry, Perry, & Weiss, 1989). Thus, girls' reliance on strategies of aggression that are covert—and easily denied if detected—may reflect their recognition that displays of physical aggression on their part will attract adult attention and punishment.

Parenting style may also factor into children's manifestations of aggression. Harsh, inconsistent parenting and poor monitoring increase the likelihood of physical aggression in childhood (Leve, Pears, & Fisher, 2002; Vitaro et al., 2006). Children who experience such parenting may learn to mistrust others and make hostile attributions about other people's intentions (Crick & Dodge, 1996). The association between harsh parenting and later physical aggression is stronger for boys than for girls. Also, as noted in Chapter 14, poor parental monitoring increases children's susceptibility to negative peer influences and is correlated with

BOX 15.4 | applications

SEXUAL HARASSMENT AND DATING VIOLENCE

Sexual harassment commonly affects both boys and girls and can involve direct (physical or verbal) or indirect (relational) aggression. Physical sexual harassment involves inappropriate touching or forced sexual activity. Verbal sexual harassment involves unwanted, demeaning, or homophobic sexual comments, whether spoken directly to the target or indirectly, behind her or his back. Also, verbal harassment commonly spreads via electronic media (Ybarra & Mitchell, 2007).

Surveys in the United States and Canada indicate that the vast majority of both girls and boys have experienced sexual harassment during adolescence (American Association of University Women, 2011; Leaper & Brown, 2008; McMaster et al., 2002; Mitchell et al., 2014). Most teen sexual harassment occurs in school hallways and classrooms, and the perpetrators are more likely to be peers rather than teachers or other adults. In an American Association of University Women (AAUW) national survey (2011), 56% of girls and 40% of boys in middle and high school reported having experienced sexual harassment at least once during the prior year (see the

figure). Two of the most frequent forms of reported sexual harassment in the AAUW survey were unwanted sexual comments or gestures (46% of girls, 22% of boys) and being called gay or lesbian in a negative way (18% of girls, 19% of boys).

A recent online survey of adolescent Internet users (Mitchell et al., 2014) examined rates of reported sexual harassment separately for youth based on their gender and self-identified sexual orientation. Across ages (13 to 18 years), the percent reporting sexual harassment was 43% for heterosexual girls, 72% for lesbian girls, 66% for bisexual girls, 23% for heterosexual boys, 66% for gay boys, and 50% for bisexual boys. (The researchers did not use exactly the same measures of sexual harassment employed in the AAUW survey.) The findings from Mitchell and colleagues' survey are consistent with other reports that rates of sexual harassment may be higher for sexual-minority (lesbian, gay, bisexual, transgender, and intersex) youths (AAUW, 2011; Williams et al., 2005). In a recent nationwide survey of 9th- to 12th-grade students in the United States, 18% of gay, lesbian, and bisexual respondents

reported being forced to have unwanted sexual intercourse, compared with 5% of heterosexual respondents; in addition, 18% of gay, lesbian and bisexual students reported being victims of dating violence in the past year, compared with 8% of heterosexual students (Kann et al., 2016). Although these surveys were conducted in the United States, other studies indicate that sexual harassment is also a problem for teens in many parts of the world (see Leaper & Robnett, 2016).

When the adolescents in the AAUW (2011) survey were asked to indicate whether and how sexual harassment affected them, girls were more likely than boys to report negative effects (also found in Mitchell et al., 2014). The most common responses to sexual harassment in the AAUW survey included not wanting to go to school (37% of girls, 25% of boys) and finding it difficult to study (34% of girls, 24% of boys). Boys were more likely than girls to report that experiences with sexual harassment had no effect on them (17% of boys, 10% of girls).

Girls may tend to have more negative reactions to sexual harassment than do boys—partly because girls are somewhat

higher rates of aggression and delinquency (K. C. Jacobson & Crockett, 2000). Thus, the fact that parents monitor daughters more closely than sons may contribute to gender differences in aggression.

Peer influences Gender differences in aggression are consistent with the gender-typed social norms of girls' and boys' same-gender peer groups. However, it is worth noting that children who are high in aggression *and* low in prosocial behavior are typically rejected in both male and female peer groups (P. H. Hawley, Little, & Card, 2008). These children tend to seek out marginal peer groups of other similarly rejected peers; these contacts strengthen the likelihood of physical aggression over time (N. E. Werner & Crick, 2004).

Another peer influence on aggression may be boys' regular participation in aggressive contact sports, which sanction the use of physical force and may contribute to higher rates of direct aggression among boys (Kidd, 2013; Messner, 2002). Support for this proposal is the finding that participation in aggressive sports, such as football, in high school is correlated with a higher likelihood of sexual aggression in college (G. B. Forbes et al., 2006). As explained in Box 15.4, aggressive behaviors may also involve sexual harassment.

more likely than boys to experience repeated sexual harassment (AAUW, 2011). Also, because of traditional masculine socialization, boys may be more reluctant to admit vulnerability (Farkas & Leaper, 2016). Regardless of the individual's gender, repeated experiences with sexual harassment can have long-term negative consequences on girls' and boys' self-esteem and adjustment (S. E. Goldstein et al., 2007; Gruber & Fineran, 2008).

Sexual harassment and violence also occur in dating relationships. Physical aggression occurs in an estimated one-fourth of adolescent heterosexual dating relationships (Hickman, Jaycox, & Aronoff, 2004; O'Leary et al., 2008), with boys the more likely perpetrators (Swahn et al., 2008; Wolitzky-Taylor et al., 2008). As a consequence, many girls come to regard demeaning behaviors as normal in heterosexual relationships (Witkowska & Gådin, 2005) and therefore may be at risk for dysfunctional and abusive relationships in adulthood. Although there have been fewer studies of dating violence in lesbian and gay teens' relationships, some surveys have indicated the prevalence of dating violence among sexual-minority youths was similar to (Freedner et al., 2002) or greater than (Dank et al., 2014) that among heterosexual youths.

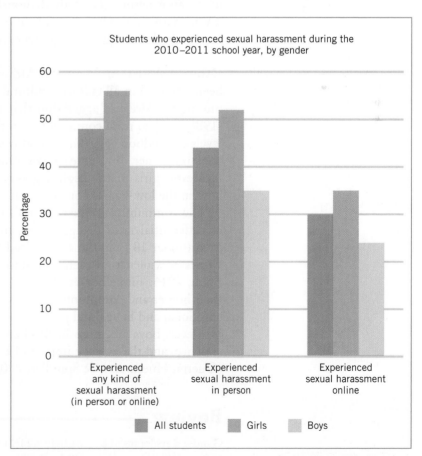

As depicted in the figure, many girls and boys experienced sexual harassment in person or online. However, the rates were higher for girls than for boys. (Data from AAUW, 2011)

Rates of violence are high in many U.S. communities, and boys are more likely to witness violent events. These experiences may contribute to higher rates of aggression for boys compared with girls.

Media influences A common question raised by parents and researchers is whether frequently watching violent TV shows and movies or playing violent video games has a negative impact on children. As you might expect, boys are more likely than girls to devote time to these activities (Cherney & London, 2006). One possible inference is that consuming more violent media may contribute to average gender differences in physical aggression.

Our discussion of media violence in Chapter 9 makes clear that viewing aggression in movies, TV programming, and video games is associated with children's aggressive behavior and that this holds true for girls as well as boys. The degree and nature of this relationship remains a topic of debate. According to a recent meta-analysis of studies testing the link between video game violence and aggressive behavior, the overall association was weak (Ferguson, 2015). However, exposure to violent media may lead to increased arousal and decreased inhibition, which may stimulate aggression in children who are also prone to aggressive behavior for additional reasons (Coyne & Archer, 2005).

Whereas boys are more likely than girls to favor TV shows and movies with violent content, one study found that adolescent girls were more likely than boys to prefer shows depicting indirect aggression (Coyne & Archer, 2005). Furthermore, an experimental study demonstrated that observing indirect aggression on TV increased the subsequent likelihood of indirect aggressive behavior but had no impact on direct aggression (Coyne, Archer, & Eslea, 2004).

Other cultural influences Although gender differences in aggression have been observed in all cultures, cultural norms also play an important role in determining the levels of aggression that are observed in boys and girls. Douglas Fry (1988) studied rural communities in the mountains of Mexico and found that the levels of childhood aggression that were considered normal varied widely from one area to another. Boys in each community showed more aggression than girls did. However, girls in the high-aggression communities were more aggressive than boys in the low-aggression communities.

The community context must also be considered in relation to the emergence of differential rates of aggression among U.S. youth. More than 60% of children (under 18 years) in the United States are estimated to have experienced or witnessed violence in their community within the past year (Child Trends Data Bank, 2016; Finkelhor et al., 2009). When children are exposed to violence in their homes and communities, boys and girls both experience an increased risk of emotional and behavioral problems and show an increase in aggressive behaviors. However, boys are more likely than girls to be exposed to the highest levels of violence, and the average impact of exposure is also greater for boys than for girls (Guerra, Huesmann, & Spindler, 2003).

Review

Gender development begins before birth when the genes program the developing embryo to form female or male genitalia. In the absence of androgen hormones triggered by the Y chromosome, female genitalia form. The higher production of androgens in genetic males (and, in rare cases, in genetic females) may influence brain organization and functioning.

Physical changes during puberty typically lead to increased muscle mass in boys as well as large average advantages in strength, speed, and size. Also, puberty leads to bodily transformations that allow for each sex's reproductive ability.

Although the common impression is that girls and boys are inherently and deeply different in their cognitive and social behaviors, in most respects the similarities between them outweigh the differences. As summarized in Table 15.1, even when differences are consistently reported, they tend to be fairly small. Also, many average differences do not emerge until later in childhood or adolescence. The most substantial differences are found in physical strength and speed, specific spatial abilities (e.g., mental rotation), academic achievement, self-regulation, activity level, and physical aggression. Small average gender differences are seen in verbal ability, risk taking, interpersonal goals, and communication style. A combination of biological, cognitive-motivational, and cultural influences are implicated to varying degrees in most of these differences.

CHAPTER SUMMARY

Theoretical Approaches to Gender Development

- One major approach to gender development is biological, including evolutionary psychology, biosocial theory, and neuroscience approaches.

- According to evolutionary psychology theory, *behavioral* differences between males and females served adaptive functions in our evolutionary past and have been passed down as inherited behavioral dispositions. For example, direct aggression in males is interpreted as an advantage in mating competition, whereas nurturance in females is viewed as facilitating the survival of offspring.

- Biosocial theory focuses on the impact of evolved *physical* differences between females (childbearing and nursing capacities) and males (greater strength, speed, and size) in relation to the social ecology. For example, men's strength and women's childbearing may have made certain roles more appropriate for men and women in hunter-gatherer societies, but physical differences impose fewer constraints on roles in technological societies.

- Other biological researchers take a neuroscience approach to gender development by focusing on sex differences in brain organization and the influences of sex hormones (such as androgens) both before birth and after. A striking example of hormonal influence involves cases of girls with congenital adrenal hyperplasia (CAH), who tend to show a stronger inclination toward play emphasizing physical activity and tend to perform somewhat better on spatial abilities than do girls without CAH.

- A second approach, which addresses cognitive and motivational influences on gender development, includes cognitive developmental theory, gender schema theory, social identity theory, and social cognitive theory. All emphasize children's active participation in learning gender roles and adopting the preferences and behaviors considered appropriate for their gender, thereby highlighting how gender development is largely a process of self-socialization.

- According to cognitive developmental theory, once children realize that their gender is consistent across situations (gender constancy), they pay close attention to same-gender models to learn how to behave.

- Gender schema theory maintains that children construct mental representations of gender based on their own experience and the gender-related ideas they are exposed to. It proposes that children begin to acquire same-gender interests and values as soon as they can identify their own gender. Subsequently, children pay greater attention to, and learn more about, those things that they regard as relevant for their own gender.

- Social identity theory, which also stresses the importance of adopting a gender identity, proposes that children tend to form an ingroup bias favoring attributes associated with their own gender and also to enforce conformity to gender-role norms.

- Social cognitive theory addresses many processes involved in learning gender-typed values and behaviors, including observing others' behavior and determining the consequences of particular behaviors in relation to one's own or other people's gender. Children internalize gender-typed norms, standards that they use to monitor their own behavior.

■ The third theoretical approach focuses on cultural influences and includes the bioecological model. The bioecological model characterizes children's development as embedded in nested systems ranging from the microsystem (immediate environment) to the macrosystem (society). A key feature of the macrosystem is its opportunity structure and the corresponding roles available to women and men that shape the ways in which girls and boys are socialized.

Milestones in Gender Development

■ Between 6 and 8 weeks of prenatal development, sexual differentiation begins. External and internal genitalia are normally completed by the end of the first trimester.

■ During their 1st year, infants learn to distinguish male from female faces. Between ages 2 and 3, children learn to identify their own gender, start to acquire stereotypes about males and females, and begin to prefer gender-typed toys and play activities.

■ During preschool, children begin to gravitate toward same-gender peers, and a strong tendency for children to self-segregate by gender persists until adolescence. Preschool children also stereotype certain traits and activities for each gender. Preferences for gender-typed play become stronger from early to middle childhood.

■ At about 6 years of age, children develop gender constancy. In addition, during middle childhood, they come to understand that gender roles are social conventions. They also may understand that gender discrimination is unfair and notice when it occurs. Average gender differences in social behavior begin to emerge, with boys more likely than girls to stress assertion over affiliation, and girls more apt to emphasize affiliation or a combination of affiliation and assertion.

■ During adolescence, gender roles sometimes become more flexible (due to increased cognitive flexibility) or more rigid (due to concerns with heterosexual roles and adoption of conventional gender attitudes). Intimacy in friendships and romantic relationships also increases for both girls and boys, although friendship intimacy is more common among girls.

■ Throughout childhood and adolescence, gender-role flexibility is more likely among girls than among boys. Peers and parents tend to react more negatively to cross-gender-typed behavior in boys than in girls. This asymmetry may be related to the higher status and power traditionally accorded to males.

Comparing Girls and Boys

■ Actual differences in girls' and boys' psychological functioning are decidedly fewer than commonly portrayed by gender stereotypes. Even on measures in which, on average, one gender scores higher than the other, the effect size often is trivial for many attributes. Moreover, considerable overlap usually occurs in the distribution of scores for males and females even when gender differences in effect size are greater.

■ Boys and girls are quite similar in physical development until puberty, which begins earlier for girls than for boys. Among the largest average gender differences are physical strength, speed, and size after puberty, and a moderate difference exists in physical activity level.

■ Girls and boys score similarly on tests of general intelligence. Slight-to-small average gender differences have been reported in specific cognitive abilities: boys show higher proficiency with certain types of spatial reasoning and mathematic ability, and girls show a small advantage in verbal ability. In academic achievement, girls have tended to do better than boys in reading and writing, whereas boys have tended to do better than girls in the physical sciences. Girls also tend to do better in overall school performance.

■ Biological, cognitive-motivational, and cultural factors may contribute to gender-related variations in academic achievement. Biological processes, such as prenatal hormones, may influence girls' and boys' brain development; however, the degree to which these factors lead to gender differences in cognitive functioning is unclear. The evidence for cognitive-motivational and cultural influences on average gender differences in academic achievement is more clearly established. Researchers find academic achievement in particular domains is related to the expectations of parents, peers, and teachers. The gender gap in U.S. math achievement has dramatically closed in recent decades, and such differences are less likely in societies characterized by greater overall gender equality.

■ Direct (physical and verbal) aggression is associated with an average gender difference of moderate effect size, with higher rates among boys than among girls. No meaningful average gender difference appears in indirect aggression (such as social exclusion or negative gossip). However, indirect aggression constitutes a larger proportion of all aggressive behaviors among girls than among boys. Lower average levels of self-regulation may be partly related to the higher incidence of direct aggression among boys. Cognitive and motivational factors are important as well. For example, boys often practice aggressive themes and behaviors in their play, and aggression is tolerated more in boys than in girls. Some cultural variations in the magnitude of gender difference in direct aggression are related to the degree that behaviors such as sexual harassment are tolerated in a particular culture.

Test Yourself

1. Gender typing refers to
   a. the identification of an individual based on sex chromosomes.
   b. an individual's personal identification as male, female, or neither.
   c. the process of gender socialization that occurs during development.
   d. the genetic forces that determine an individual's sex during prenatal development.

2. The assertion that the tendency for girls to play with dolls is the result of an evolved predisposition toward maternal care is based on the premise of which theory?
   a. evolutionary psychology theory
   b. biosocial theory
   c. social learning theory
   d. gender schema theory

3. Which of the following statements represents a major difference between evolutionary psychology theory and biosocial theory?
   a. Biosocial theory does not account for the influence of evolutionary forces in gender differences.
   b. Evolutionary psychology theory places greater emphasis on the physical differences between the sexes.
   c. Biosocial theory places greater emphasis on the capacity for behavioral flexibility influenced by social and technological factors.
   d. Evolutionary psychology theory asserts that, from an evolutionary perspective, there are no significant differences between the sexes.

4. Exposure to high levels of prenatal androgens in genetic females may influence the development of their nervous system in such a way that results in certain cross-gender-typed behaviors. This example demonstrates the effect of _____.
   a. activating influences
   b. cisgender disposition
   c. organizing influences
   d. self-socialization

5. Kohlberg proposed that there are three stages of children's understanding of gender: gender identity, gender stability, and gender constancy. Which of the following statements is most representative of gender constancy?
   a. "Girls can have babies, boys cannot."
   b. "I am a boy today, but could be a girl tomorrow."
   c. "Even if I cut my hair and dress like a boy, I am a girl."
   d. "I will always be a girl."

6. The complex web of influences—including gender, sexual orientation, race, social class, and other group affiliations—that shape an individual's social identity and experiences is known as _____.
   a. gender schema
   b. in-group assimilation
   c. intersectionality
   d. collaboration

7. Alex is a 6-year-old boy. His father disapproves when Alex plays with his sister's dolls, but happily engages with him when Alex plays with trucks. This scenario is an example of the influence of _____ in shaping Alex's gender identity.
   a. observational learning
   b. collaboration
   c. enactive experience
   d. intersectionality

8. Gender segregation refers to
   a. the tendency of young children to associate with same-gender peers and avoid other-gender peers.
   b. the difference between the sexes in cognitive and behavioral tendencies.
   c. the tendency for an individual to engage in gender-typed behaviors.
   d. the tendency of an individual to retain information that is gender schema-consistent.

9. The tendency of adolescents to integrate elements of traditional gender roles into their personal values, which can lead to increased gender discrimination, is known as _____.
   a. gender-role flexibility
   b. gender-role intensification
   c. assimilation
   d. collaboration

10. The gender similarities hypothesis emphasizes that in areas of cognitive behaviors and social abilities
    a. all measurable differences between the sexes are trivial.
    b. boys and girls develop on parallel but unequal tracks.
    c. similarities between boys and girls far outweigh differences.
    d. differences between boys and girls outweigh similarities.

11. Which of the following statements regarding physical maturation is *not* true?
    a. Genetic and environmental factors significantly affect the variability in physical maturation seen among individuals of both sexes.
    b. The gender gap in physical and motor skills greatly increases as a result of puberty.
    c. Despite the physical changes that occur during puberty, researchers have found no evidence of similar psychological or behavioral changes.
    d. Researchers have found cross-cultural evidence of patterns of body image and eating disorders related to puberty.

12. The combined influence of gender stereotypes and a child's own perceived competence in a given academic subject is described by which of the following theories?
    a. gender intensification model
    b. evolutionary psychology theory
    c. expectancy-value model of achievement
    d. Piaget's theory of gender development

13. Small but consistent gender differences have been found in all of the following domains except _____.
  a. self-concept
  b. general intelligence
  c. communication skills
  d. mental spatial rotation tasks

14. An individual who is high in both assertion and affiliation is likely to display which of the following communication styles?
  a. collaboration
  b. withdrawal
  c. obliging statements
  d. controlling statements

15. Rose is a 9-year old girl. She strongly prefers wearing t-shirts and jeans to dresses and other "girly" clothes. She loves sports and hates playing with dolls. Rose's preferences are an example of _____.
  a. gender-role intensification
  b. cross-gender-typed behavior
  c. cisgender modeling
  d. gender segregation

Don't stop now! Research shows that testing yourself is a powerful learning tool. Visit LaunchPad to access the LearningCurve adaptive quizzing system, which gives you a personalized study plan to help build your mastery of the chapter material through videos, activities, and more. **Go to launchpadworks.com.**

Critical Thinking Questions

1. The four children described at the start of the chapter were portrayed to highlight variations in gender-typed behavior and interests both between gender and within genders. How would the different theories outlined in this chapter attempt to explain these differences and similarities? How would different theories account for other children who have more flexible gender-typed behaviors and interests?

2. Think about how females and males were portrayed in shows, movies, and video games as you were growing up. How might these depictions have affected your gender development?

3. Imagine that you wanted to raise your own children to be as minimally gender-typed as possible. Which of the theoretical perspectives outlined in the chapter would you rely on most?

Do you think you would be more likely to achieve your goal with a daughter or a son?

4. Suppose you are speaking with an evolutionary psychology theorist who tells you that biology makes gender differences in behavior inevitable. What evidence could you use to challenge this view? What evidence could you use to support it?

5. Historically, men have held dominant status in society, but in the last century, women have significantly increased their status and power in the United States and in many other countries. Women now occupy top ranks in many occupations, and men are more involved in childcare and housework. Do you think this trend toward gender equality among adults will affect the kinds of play activities and behaviors in which girls and boys engage in the future?

Key Terms

activating influences, p. 638

adrenarche, p. 658

affiliation, p. 651

androgen insensitivity syndrome (AIS), p. 639

androgens, p. 638

assertion, p. 651

body image, p. 658

cisgender, p. 639

collaboration, p. 651

congenital adrenal hyperplasia (CAH), p. 639

cross-gender-typed, p. 635

effect size, p. 655

enactive experience, p. 644

gender, p. 635

gender constancy, p. 640

gender dysphoria, p. 639

gender identity, p. 640

gender schema filter, p. 642

gender schemas, p. 641

gender segregation, p. 649

gender stability, p. 640

gender typing, p. 635

gender-role flexibility, p. 653

gender-role intensification, p. 653

gender-typed, p. 635

ingroup assimilation, p. 643

ingroup bias, p. 643

interest filter, p. 642

▶ Student Video Activities

The Boy Who Was a Girl
Gender Development in Early Childhood

Puberty
Educating Girls of the World

Answers to Test Yourself

1. c, **2.** a, **3.** c, **4.** c, **5.** c, **6.** c, **7.** c, **8.** a, **9.** b, **10.** c, **11.** c, **12.** c, **13.** b, **14.** a, **15.** b

LINCOLN SELIGMAN, *Kite Flying* (watercolor on paper, 2000)

Conclusions

Themes

- Nature and Nurture
- The Active Child
- Continuity/Discontinuity
- Mechanisms of Change
- The Sociocultural Context
- Individual Differences
- Research and Children's Welfare

In the preceding 15 chapters, you were presented with a great deal of information about how children develop. You learned about the development of perception, attachment, conceptual understanding, language, intelligence, emotional regulation, peer relations, aggression, morality, gender, and a host of other vital human characteristics. Although these are all important parts of child development, the sheer amount of information may seem daunting: getting lost in the trees and losing a sense of the forest is a real danger. We therefore devote this final chapter to providing an overview of the forest by organizing many of the specifics that you have learned into an integrative framework. A likely side benefit of reading this chapter is that you will probably discover that you understand much more about child development than you realized.

The integrative framework that organizes this chapter consists of the seven themes that were introduced in Chapter 1 and highlighted throughout the book. As we have noted, most child-development research is ultimately aimed at understanding fundamental issues related to these themes. This is true regardless of the type of development that the research addresses and regardless of whether the research focuses on fetuses, infants, toddlers, preschoolers, school-age children, or adolescents. Beneath the myriad details, the seven themes emerge again and again.

Theme 1: Nature and Nurture: All Interactions, All the Time

When people think of a child's nature, they typically focus on the biological characteristics with which the child enters the world. When they think of the child's nurture, they focus on the child-rearing experiences provided by parents, caregivers, and other adults. Within this view, nurture is like a sculptor, shaping the raw material provided by the child's nature into closer and closer approximations of its final form.

Although this metaphor is appealing, the reality is much more complex. Unlike the sculptor's passive media of marble and clay, children are active participants in their own development. They seek out experiences based on their inclinations and interests. They also influence other people's behavior toward them: from birth onward, their nature influences the nurture they receive. In addition, rather than nature doing its work before birth and nurture doing its work after, nurture influences development even before birth, and nature is just as influential in adolescence and adulthood as earlier. In this section, we review how nature and nurture interact to produce development.

Nature and Nurture Begin Interacting Before Birth

When prenatal development proceeds normally, it is easy to think of it as a simple unfolding of innate potential, one in which the environment matters little. When things go wrong, however, the interaction of nature and nurture is all too evident. Consider the effects of teratogens. Prenatal exposure to these potentially harmful substances—which include toxins in the general environment, such as mercury, radiation, lead, insects (e.g., mosquitos carrying the Zika virus), and air pollution, as well as toxins that depend on parental behavior (e.g.., cigarettes, alcohol, and illegal drugs)—can cause a wide variety of physical and cognitive impairments. Nevertheless, whether and how much a given baby will actually be affected depends on innumerable interactions among the genetics of the mother, the genetics of the fetus, and a host of environmental factors such as the particular teratogen and the timing and amount of exposure.

The interaction of nature and nurture during the prenatal period is also evident in fetal learning. The experience of hearing their mother's voice while in the womb leads newborns to prefer her voice to that of other women once they enter the world. Fetuses can also learn taste preferences from their mother's diet during pregnancy. Thus, even qualities that are present at birth, which are often thought of as being determined purely by nature, reflect the fetus's experience as well.

Infants' Nature Elicits Nurture

Nature equips babies with a host of qualities that elicit appropriate nurture from parents and other caregivers. One big factor in babies' favor is that they are cute; most people enjoy watching and interacting with them. By looking and smiling at other people, babies motivate others to feel warmly toward them and to care for them. Their emotional expressions—cries, coos, and smiles—guide caregivers' efforts to figure out what to do to make them happy and comfortable. In addition, their attentiveness to sights and sounds that they find interesting encourages others to talk to them and to provide the stimulation necessary for learning. One simple example of this interactive relationship is the fact that parents everywhere sing to their infants; infants throughout the world find singing soothing, bounce in response to rhythm, and respond positively to melodies.

Timing Matters

The effects of an experience on development depend on the state of the organism at the time of the experience. As already noted, timing of exposure to teratogens greatly influences their effects on prenatal development. For example, if a pregnant woman comes down with rubella early in pregnancy, when the developing visual and auditory systems are at a particularly sensitive point, her baby may be born deaf or blind; if she comes down with rubella later in pregnancy, no damage will occur.

Timing also influences many aspects of development in the months and years following birth. The development of perceptual capabilities presents numerous illustrations of the importance of appropriate experience at the appropriate time. The general rule in such cases is "use it or lose it": for normal development to occur, children must encounter the relevant experiences during a certain window of time.

Auditory development provides a good example. Until 8 months of age, infants can discriminate between phonemes regardless of whether they occur in the language the infants hear daily. By age 12 months, however, infants lose the ability to hear the difference between similar sounds that they do not ordinarily encounter or that are not meaningfully different in their native language.

Infants' expressions of contentment and happiness when engaging in certain activities motivate their parents and other adults to engage in the activities with them.

Similar sensitive periods occur in grammatical development. Children from East Asia who move to the United States and begin to learn English as a second language before age 7 acquire grammatical competence in English that eventually matches that of native-born American children. Those who arrive between ages 7 and 11 learn almost as well. However, individuals who immigrate at later ages rarely gain comparable mastery of English grammar, even after many years of hearing and speaking the language of their adopted land. Deaf children's learning of American Sign Language shows a similar pattern: early exposure results in more complete grammatical mastery.

The importance of normal early experience is also evident in social, emotional, and intellectual development. Infants and toddlers who do not have an emotional connection with any caregiver, such as the children who spent their first years in the infamous orphanages of Romania in the 1980s or in concentration camps during World War II, often continue to interact abnormally with other people after being placed in loving homes. Those who spent their first two years or more in the Romanian orphanages also had unusually high rates of low IQ for many years after they were adopted into loving homes in Great Britain. Thus, in many aspects of the development of perception, language, intelligence, emotions, and social behavior, the timing of experience is crucial: normal early experience is vital for successful later development.

Nature Does Not Reveal Itself All at Once

Many genetically influenced properties do not become evident until middle childhood, adolescence, or adulthood. One obvious example is the physical changes that occur at puberty. A less obvious example involves nearsightedness. Many children are born with genes that predispose them to become nearsighted, but most do not become so until late childhood or early adolescence. The more close work, including reading, they do during childhood, the more likely that the genetic predisposition will eventually be realized. A third example involves children who are born with certain types of brain damage. These children's performance on IQ tests is comparable to that of other children through age 6 years but falls considerably behind thereafter.

The development of schizophrenia follows a similar path. Schizophrenia is highly influenced by genes inherited at conception, but most people who become schizophrenic do not do so until late adolescence or early adulthood. As with other aspects of development, the emergence of schizophrenia reflects a complex interplay between nature and nurture. Children with a schizophrenic biological parent who are raised by nonschizophrenic parents are more likely to become schizophrenic themselves than are the biological children of the nonschizophrenic parents. Children who are raised in troubled homes are also more likely than others to become schizophrenic. However, the only children with a substantial likelihood of becoming schizophrenic are those who grew up in a troubled family *and* have a biological parent who is schizophrenic. As in other contexts, the interaction between the children's nature and the nurture they receive is crucial.

Perhaps the most surprising and compelling evidence for the interaction of nature and nurture comes from the emerging field of epigenetics. Although people often think of the genotype as being "fixed"

Differences in running speeds are partially attributable to genetic differences that are present at birth, but nature takes time to reveal itself. Who could have looked at these children when they were newborns and predicted who would be the best runners?

POLKA DOT IMAGES / GETTY IMAGES

at birth, experience can enhance or silence gene expression. Early stressful environments, such as those imposed by poverty, seem to especially influence later gene expression. Thus, adults who grew up in low-income families exhibit different patterns of gene expression decades later than do adults who grew up in high-income homes, regardless of their incomes as adults. Even more remarkably, some of these effects of the early environment on the genome are passed down to the next generation. Thus, not only does nature not reveal itself all at once, but nature itself changes as a result of nurture.

Everything Influences Everything

One common reaction to learning about the complex interactions between nature and nurture is "It sounds like everything influences everything else." This reaction is basically accurate. Consider some of the factors that influence children's and adolescents' self-esteem. Genes matter; the closer the biological relation between two children or adolescents, the more similar their degree of self-esteem is likely to be. A large part of the reason for this genetic influence on self-esteem is that genes influence a wide range of *other* characteristics that themselves influence self-esteem. For example, genes strongly affect attractiveness, athletic talent, and academic success, all of which contribute to self-esteem.

Factors other than genes also play large roles in the development of self-esteem. Support from one's family and peers contribute in a positive way; poverty and unpopularity contribute in a negative way. Unrelated adults also can have positive or negative influences on self-esteem; for example, having a teacher who is supportive can promote a child's self-esteem; conversely, having a teacher who is hostile or demeaning can reduce it. Values of the broader society are also influential. East Asian societies tend to emphasize the importance of self-criticism, and children and adolescents in those societies report lower levels of self-esteem than do peers in Western societies.

Complex interactions are not limited to the development of self-esteem or to social development; they are characteristic of development in all areas. For example, in the development of intelligence, the influence of genetics seems to be greater than that of shared environment for children from middle- and upper-income backgrounds, but the opposite is true for children from impoverished backgrounds. Similarly, parental involvement in school is more closely related to academic achievement in low-income families than in more affluent families. Thus, children's nature—their genes, personal characteristics, and behavioral tendencies—interact with the nurture they receive from parents, teachers, peers, the broader society, and the physical environment in ways that shape their self-esteem, intellect, and other qualities.

Theme 2: Children Play Active Roles in Their Own Development

Children are physically active even before they leave the womb; the fetal kicking that thrills prospective parents is just the most obvious example. Less obvious is that fetuses are also mentally active. While still in the womb, they can learn enough about the sounds in a story their mother repeatedly reads aloud that, as newborns, they react differently to that story than to ones their mother did not

As this infant's eager gaze suggests, children's choices of where to look are among the ways in which they shape their own development.

Children's choices of activities shape their development. This child's interest in print led him to learn to read and write at age 3; the fact that he is one of the authors' children also probably had something to do with his early interest in these skills. (He also is now the father of the baby in the preceding photo.)

read aloud. Moreover, from their first minutes outside the womb, infants selectively focus on objects and events that interest them, rather than passively gazing at whatever appears before their eyes.

Infants' and older children's actions also produce reactions in other people, which further shape the children's development. In this section, we examine four ways in which children contribute to their own development—through physically interacting with the environment, interpreting their experience, regulating their behavior, and eliciting reactions from other people.

Self-Initiated Activity

Even in the womb, normal development depends on the fetus's being active. Fetuses make breathing movements that strengthen their lungs, and they swallow amniotic fluid that prepares their digestive system to function properly after birth. They also "work out" various muscles by tugging on their umbilical cord, sucking their thumb, kicking, and turning somersaults.

From the day they are born, infants display looking preferences that guide their attention to the most informative aspects of the environment that their processing abilities can handle and thus enhance their learning. They like looking at objects rather than at blank fields. They like looking at moving objects rather than at stationary ones and at the edges of objects rather than at their interiors. And they particularly like looking at faces, especially their mother's.

Infants' ability to interact with the environment expands greatly during the 1st year. At about 3 months, most infants become able to follow moving objects fairly smoothly with their eyes, which improves their ability to learn about the actions occurring around them. At 6 or 7 months, most become able to crawl on their bellies, and soon after on their hands and knees; as a result, they no longer have to wait for the world to come to them. By 8 or 9 months, most can hold up their heads, which allows them to reach accurately for objects even when they are not being supported. And by 13 or 14 months, most begin to walk independently, opening new frontiers for exploration.

As development proceeds, children's self-initiated activity extends to additional domains such as language. Toddlers delight in telling their parents the names of objects, for no reason beyond the joy of doing so. They practice talking in their cribs, even when nobody else is present to hear them. They and older children, both deaf and hearing, invent gestures and words to represent objects and events. As their language proficiency develops, children become skilled at initiating conversations that bring them information, allow them to express their feelings and desires, and help them regulate their emotions.

The effects of self-initiated activities are also seen at older ages in other areas, such as self-socialization and antisocial behavior. Throughout the world, boys and girls choose to play predominantly with members of their own gender, especially between the ages of 6 and 10 years. The play patterns reflect the children's own choices: gender segregation is rarely imposed by adults; rather, it arises from differences in the kinds of play that boys and girls tend to prefer. Beginning in the school years, these preferences tend to be reinforced by ridicule from peers when a child crosses the "gender border."

In later childhood and adolescence, children's choices of friends and peer groups become important influences on their own behavior, in that children tend to increasingly act like their friends and others in their social group in both positive and negative ways. Thus, from the prenatal period through adolescence, children's self-initiated activities contribute to their development.

Active Interpretation of Experience

Children also contribute to their development by trying to understand the world around them. Even in the 1st year, infants develop a sense of what is possible in the physical world. Thus, they look longer at an "impossible" event—such as when one solid object appears to move through the space occupied by another object, or when an object seems to be suspended in midair without support—than they do at an event that is similar but physically possible. Toddlers' and preschoolers' continuous "why" questions, and school-age children's searching for the explanations of magic tricks, provide other compelling examples of children's eagerness to understand the world.

This desire to understand also motivates young children to construct informal theories concerning inanimate objects, living things, and people. These theories allow children to go beyond the data provided by their senses to infer underlying causes. For example, preschoolers reason that there must be something inside animals that causes them to grow, breathe, have babies, get sick, and so on, even though they do not know what that something is. They also reason that inanimate objects must have different material inside them than living things do.

Children's and adolescents' interpretations of their experiences extend to inferences about themselves as well as about the external world. When some children fail on a task, for example, they feel sad and question their ability. Other children who fail on the same task take the failure as a challenge and an opportunity to learn. Similarly, in ambiguous situations, aggressive children tend to attribute hostile intentions to others even when the others' motives are unclear; this interpretation sometimes leads the aggressive children to lash out before the other person can hurt them. Thus, subjective interpretations of experiences, as well as objective reality, shape development.

Self-Regulation

Another way in which children contribute to their development is by regulating their behavior. Consider how they regulate their emotions. In the first months after they are born, infants rely almost entirely on parents and other caregivers to help them cope with fright and frustration. By age 6 months, they learn to cope with some upsetting situations by rubbing their bodies to soothe themselves. During the toddler and preschool periods, children become increasingly adept at using physical strategies, such as looking away, when faced with stressors or temptation. During elementary school, they increasingly use cognitive strategies, such as reminding themselves that an unpleasant experience will soon be over, to cope with negative situations. Across a wide range of ages, children who successfully regulate their emotions tend to be more popular and more socially competent than those who are less skilled at emotional regulation.

These early self-regulation skills are related to long-term developmental outcomes. For example, boys who exhibit strong self-regulation abilities in the preschool and early elementary school periods are less likely as adults to use cocaine and other drugs. Children's early self-control also has been found to be a strong predictor of their later grades in school and of occupational and economic success in adulthood.

Over the course of childhood and adolescence, children increasingly regulate their development through their choice of activities. Whether young children go to sports events, movies, libraries, or religious services depends mainly on whether their parents take them there. Whether adolescents engage in the same activities depends mainly on their own preferences. Selecting moral values, choosing a romantic partner, pursuing an occupation, and deciding whether to have children are just a few of the major decisions that adolescents and young adults face. The wisdom of their choices strongly influences their subsequent lives.

Eliciting Reactions from Other People

Because children of all ages differ from one another in behavior and appearance, they evoke different reactions from other people. For example, babies with easy temperaments elicit more positive reactions from their parents than do cranky or fussy babies. Similarly, attractive babies elicit more affectionate and playful mothering than do less attractive ones. And in trying times, attractive children are less likely to suffer parental rejection and punishment than are less attractive ones. Other adults also are influenced by children's actions. For example, when children encounter difficulty learning particular material, teachers act in more encouraging ways if the child has generally been well behaved than if the child has been badly behaved in the past.

The effects that children's initial inclinations have on their parents' behavior toward them multiply over time. Most parents of children who are disobedient, angry, and challenging try to be supportive but firm with them. However, if the bad behavior and defiance continue, many parents become hostile and punitive. Other parents, faced with belligerence and aggression, back down from confrontations and increasingly give in to their children's demands. Once such negative cycles are established, they are difficult to stop. If teenagers act disruptively, and parents respond with hostility, problems generally worsen over the course of adolescence.

It is all too easy for relations between parents and children to spiral downward, with disobedience and anger from children eliciting anger and hostility from parents, which then elicits more disobedience and anger from children, and so on.

MARY KATE DENNY / PHOTOEDIT

Children's characteristics and behavior influence not just their parents' and teachers' reactions but also those of their peers. At all ages, children who are cooperative, friendly, sociable, and sensitive to others tend to be popular with their peers, whereas those who are aggressive or disruptive tend to be disliked and rejected. In some cases, peers' reactions to one another's behavior change with age; for example, kindergartners tend to neither like nor dislike withdrawn peers, but older elementary and middle school students tend to dislike such children. Peer reactions to children's behavior often have long-term consequences; rejected children are more likely than popular children to have difficulty later in school and to engage in criminal activity. In many ways, then, children influence their development, not only by initiating actions, interpreting their experiences, and regulating their emotions, but also by eliciting reactions from other people that then shape their own subsequent behavior.

Theme 3: Development Is Both Continuous and Discontinuous

Long before there was a scientific discipline of child development, philosophers and others interested in human nature argued about whether development is continuous or discontinuous. Current disputes between those who believe that development is continuous, such as social-learning theorists, and those who believe it is discontinuous, such as stage theorists, thus have a long history. There is good reason why both positions have endured so long: each captures important truths about development, yet neither captures the whole truth. Two particularly important issues in this longstanding debate involve continuity/discontinuity of individual differences and continuity/discontinuity of the standard course of development with age.

Continuity/Discontinuity of Individual Differences

One sense of continuity/discontinuity involves stability of individual differences over time. The basic question is whether children who initially are higher or lower than most peers in some quality continue to be higher or lower in that quality years later. It turns out that many individual differences in psychological properties are moderately stable over the course of development, but the stability is always far from 100%.

Consider the development of intelligence. Some stability is present from infancy onward. For instance, the faster that infants habituate to repeated presentation of the same display, the higher their IQ scores tend to be 10 or more years later. Infants' patterns of electrical brain activity also are related to their speed of processing and attention regulation more than 10 years later. The amount of stability increases with age. IQ scores show some stability from age 3 to age 13, considerable stability from age 5 to age 15, and substantial stability from age 8 to age 18.

Even in older children, however, IQ scores vary from occasion to occasion. For example, when the same children take IQ tests at ages 8 and 17, the two scores differ on average by 9 points. Part of this variability reflects random fluctuations in how sharp the person is on the day of testing and in the person's knowledge about the particular questions on each test. Another part of the variability reflects the fact that even if two children start out with equal intelligence, one may show greater intellectual growth over time.

Individual differences in social and personality characteristics also show some continuity over time. Shy toddlers tend to grow into shy children, fearful toddlers into fearful children, aggressive children into aggressive adolescents, generous children into generous adults, and so on. The continuity also carries over into situations quite different from any that the children faced at the earlier time; for example, secure attachments in infancy predict positive romantic relationships in adolescence.

Although there is some continuity of individual differences in social, emotional, and personality development, the degree of continuity is generally lower than in intellectual development. For example, whereas children who are high in reading and math achievement in 5th grade generally remain so in 7th grade, children who are popular in 5th grade may or may not be popular in 7th grade. In addition, aspects of temperament such as fearfulness and shyness often change considerably over the course of early and middle childhood.

Regardless of whether the focus is on intellectual, social, or emotional development, the stability of individual differences is influenced by the stability of the environment. For instance, an infant's attachment to his or her mother correlates positively with the infant's long-term security, but the correlation is higher if the home environment stays consistent than if serious disruptions occur. Similarly, IQ scores are more stable if the home environment remains stable. Thus, continuities in individual differences reflect continuities in children's environments as well as in their genes.

Continuity/Discontinuity of Overall Development: The Question of Stages

Many of the most prominent theories of development divide childhood and adolescence into a small number of discrete stages. Piaget's theory of cognitive development, Freud's theory of psychosexual development, Erikson's theory of psychosocial development, and Kohlberg's theory of moral development all describe development in this way. The enduring popularity of these stage approaches is easy to understand: they simplify the enormously complicated process of development by dividing it into a few distinct periods; they point to important characteristics of behavior during each period; and they impart an overall sense of coherence to the developmental process.

Although stage theories differ in their particulars, they share four key assumptions: (1) development progresses through a series of qualitatively distinct stages; (2) when children are in a given stage, a fairly broad range of their thinking and behavior exhibits the features characteristic of that stage; (3) the stages occur in the same order for all children; and (4) transitions between stages occur quickly.

Development turns out to be considerably less tidy than stage approaches imply, however. For example, children who exhibit preoperational reasoning on some tasks often exhibit concrete operational reasoning on others; children who reason in a preconventional way about some moral dilemmas often reason in a conventional way about others; and so on. Rarely is a sudden change evident across a broad range of tasks.

In addition, developmental processes often show a great deal of continuity. Throughout childhood and adolescence, there are gradual, continuous increases in the ability to regulate emotions, make friends, take other people's perspectives, remember events, solve problems, and engage in many other activities.

This does not mean that there are no sudden jumps. When we consider specific tasks and processes, rather than broad domains, we see many discontinuities. Typically, 3-month-olds move from having almost no binocular depth perception to having adultlike levels within a week or two. Before age 7 months, infants rarely fear strangers, but thereafter, wariness of them develops quickly. Many toddlers move in a single day from being unable to walk without support to walking unsupported for a number of steps. After acquiring about one word per week between ages 12 and 18 months, toddlers undergo a vocabulary explosion, in which the number of words they know and use expands rapidly for years thereafter. Thus, although broad domains, such as intelligence and personality, rarely show discontinuous changes, specific aspects of development fairly often do.

Whether development appears to be continuous or discontinuous often depends on whether the focus is on behavior or on underlying processes. Behaviors that emerge or disappear quite suddenly may reflect continuous underlying processes. Recall the case of infants' stepping reflex. For the first two months after birth, if infants are supported in an upright position with their feet touching the ground, they will first lift one leg and then the other in a pattern similar to walking. At around age 2 months, this reflex suddenly disappears. Underlying the abrupt change in behavior, however, are gradual changes in two dimensions that underlie the behavioral change—weight and leg strength. As babies grow, their gain in weight temporarily outstrips their gain in leg strength, and they become unable to lift their legs without help. Thus, when babies who have stopped exhibiting the stepping reflex are supported in a tank of water, making it easier for them to lift their legs, the stepping reflex reappears.

Whether development appears continuous or discontinuous also depends on the timescale being considered. Recall that when a child's height was measured every 6 months from birth to 18 years, the growth looked continuous (see Figure 1.3, page 16). When height was measured daily, however, development looked discontinuous, with occasional "growth days" sprinkled among numerous days without growth.

One useful framework for thinking about developmental continuities and discontinuities is to envision development as a road trip through the United States, from New York City to San Francisco. In one sense, the drive is a continuous progression westward along Interstate 80. In another sense, the drive starts in the East and then proceeds (in an invariant order, without the possibility of skipping a region) through the Midwest and the Rocky Mountains before reaching its end point in California. The East includes the Atlantic coast and the Appalachians, and it tends to be hilly, cloudy, and green; the Midwest tends to be flatter, dryer, and sunnier; the Mountain states are dryer and sunnier still, with extensive mountainous areas; and most of California is dry and sunny, with both extensive flat and extensive mountainous areas. The differences between the successive regions in climate, color, and topography are large and real, but the boundaries between them are arbitrary. Is Ohio the westernmost eastern state or the easternmost midwestern state? Is eastern Colorado part of the Midwest or part of the Rocky Mountain region?

The continuities and discontinuities in development are a lot like those on the road trip. Consider children's conceptions of the self. At one level of analysis, the development of the self is continuous. Over the course of development, children (and adults) understand more and more about themselves. At another level of analysis, milestones characterize each period of development. During infancy, children come to distinguish between themselves and other people, but they rarely if

A trip along I-80 from New York to San Francisco takes a driver through four time zones in which the main features of the land change dramatically. The changes in topography, like those in development, however, are not discontinuous. Adjacent areas tend to be highly similar, and classification of a border area as being in one zone or another is often quite arbitrary. In all of these ways, the journey resembles psychological development.

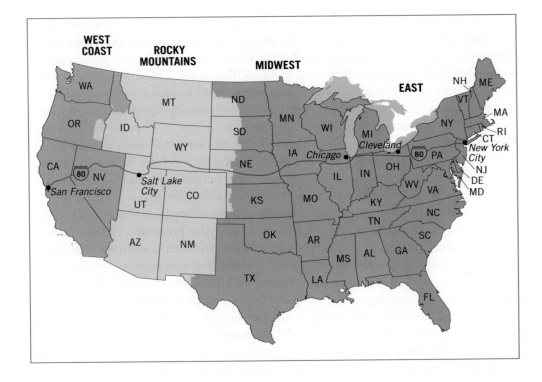

ever see themselves from another person's perspective. During the toddler period, children increasingly view themselves as others might, which allows them to feel such emotions as shame and embarrassment. During the preschool period, children realize that certain of their personal characteristics, such as their gender, are fundamental and permanent, and they use this knowledge to guide their behavior. During the elementary school years, children increasingly think of themselves in terms of their competencies relative to other children's (intelligence, athletic skill, popularity, and so forth). During adolescence, they come to recognize how differently they themselves act in different situations.

Thus, any statement about when a given competency emerges is somewhat arbitrary, much like a statement about where a geographic region begins. Nonetheless, identifying the milestones helps us understand roughly where we are on the map.

Theme 4: Mechanisms of Developmental Change

As with so many issues, contemporary thinking about developmental change owes a large debt to the ideas of Jean Piaget. Within Piaget's theory, change occurs through the interaction of assimilation and accommodation. Through assimilation, children interpret new experiences in terms of their existing mental structures; through accommodation, they revise their existing mental structures in accord with the new experiences. Thus, when we hear a truly unfamiliar type of music (for most of us, Javanese 12-tone music would fit this description), we assimilate the sounds to more familiar musical patterns, to the extent we can. At the same time, our understanding accommodates to the experience, so that when we next encounter the unfamiliar music, it will be a little easier to grasp and will feel a little less strange.

A great deal has been learned about developmental mechanisms since Piaget formulated his theory. Some of the advances have come in understanding change at the biological level, others in understanding it at the behavioral level, and still others in understanding it at the level of cognitive processes.

Biological Change Mechanisms

Biological change mechanisms come into play from the moment a sperm unites with an egg. The sperm and the egg each contain half of the DNA that will constitute the child's genotype throughout life. The genotype contains instructions that specify the rough outline of development, but all particulars are filled in by subsequent interactions between the genotype and the environment.

The way in which the brain forms after conception illustrates the complexity of change at the biological level. The first key process in brain development is *neurogenesis*, which by the 3rd or 4th week after conception is producing roughly 10,000 brain cells *per minute*. About 100 days later, the brain contains just about all of the neurons it ever will have. As neurons form, a process of *cell migration* causes many of them to travel from where they were produced to their long-term location.

Once neurons reach their destination, they undergo a process of *differentiation*, in which dendrites and axons grow out from the original cell body. Later in the prenatal period, the process of *myelination* adds an insulating sheath over certain axons, which speeds up the rate of transmission of electrical signals along them. Myelination continues through childhood and into adolescence.

Yet another process, *synaptogenesis*, involves formation of synapses between the end of axons and the beginning of dendrites that allow neurotransmitters to transmit signals from neuron to neuron. The number of synapses increases rapidly from the prenatal period to early or middle childhood (depending on the particular brain area). By the end of this period of explosive growth, the number of synapses in a given area far exceeds the number in the brains of adults. A process of *pruning* then reduces the number of synapses. The greatest pruning occurs at different times in different brain areas; in some areas, notably the prefrontal cortex, the pruning process occurs throughout adolescence. Those synapses that are frequently used are maintained; those that are not are eliminated ("use it or lose it" at the biological level). The pruning of unused synapses makes information processing more efficient.

The brain includes a number of areas that are specialized for specific functions. This specialization makes possible rapid and universal development of these functions and thus enhances learning of the relevant type of information. Some of the functions are closely linked to sensory and motor systems. The visual cortex is particularly active in processing sights; the auditory cortex is particularly active in processing sounds; the motor cortex is particularly active in making movements; and so on.

Other brain areas are specialized for functions that are not specific to any one sensory or motor system. The limbic system, located in the lower part of the brain, is particularly prominent in producing emotions. The prefrontal cortex is particularly involved in executive functioning. Some areas in the parietal lobe are particularly active in processing space, time, and number. All of these areas are involved in numerous other types of processing, and all types of processing involve

The group average pattern of brain activation for each of three increasingly difficult items (from left to right) on a problem-solving task that requires both executive functioning and spatial processing As shown, the amount of activation in this slice of the brain increases with difficulty in the prefrontal cortex (toward the front of the brain, often involved in executive functioning) and in the superior parietal cortex (toward the back of the brain, often involved in spatial processing).

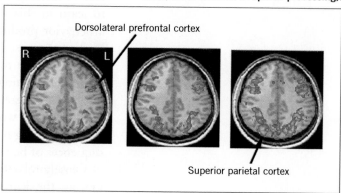

Dorsolateral prefrontal cortex

Superior parietal cortex

numerous brain areas, but each of the areas is especially active in processing the type of information associated with it. Thus, biological mechanisms underlie both very specific and very general changes.

Behavioral Change Mechanisms

Behavioral change mechanisms describe responses to environmental contingencies that contribute to development. These learning mechanisms shape behavior from the prenatal period onward.

Habituation, Conditioning, Statistical Learning, and Rational Learning

The capacity to habituate to familiar stimuli begins before fetuses leave the womb. By 30 weeks after conception (8 to 10 weeks before the typical time of birth), the central nervous system is sufficiently developed for habituation to occur, as reflected in a fetus's heart rate initially slowing down (a sign of interest) when a bell is rung next to the mother's belly and then its returning toward the typical rate as the bell is rung repeatedly. Habituation continues after birth as well, and it is seen in changes in looking patterns as well as in heart-rate patterns. For example, when a picture of a face is shown repeatedly, infants reduce the time they spend looking at it, but they show renewed interest when a different face appears. Habituation motivates babies to seek new stimulation when they have learned from an experience and thus helps them learn more.

From their first days in the outside world, infants also can learn through classical conditioning. If an initially neutral stimulus is repeatedly presented just before an unconditioned stimulus, it comes to elicit a similar response to that elicited by the unconditioned stimulus. Recall Little Albert, who, after repeatedly seeing a harmless white rat and then hearing a frightening loud noise immediately after, came to fear the white rat (and also came to fear doctors and nurses wearing white lab coats).

The fact that an infant would become afraid not only of the white rat but also of people with white coats illustrates another key learning ability that is present from infancy: generalization. Although infants' learning tends to be less general than that of older children, it is never completely literal. Infants generalize the lessons of their past experience to new situations that differ at least in a few details from the original ones.

Like older children, infants also learn through instrumental conditioning; behaviors that are rewarded become more frequent, and behaviors that do not lead to rewards become less frequent. Even young infants appear highly motivated to learn in this way: 2-month-olds express joy and interest while learning that a behavior produces a desired outcome, and they cry and express anger when a learned response no longer produces the expected results.

Yet another mechanism that allows infants to acquire information rapidly is statistical learning. From birth onward, infants quickly learn the likelihood that one sight or sound will follow another. Because many events, including the sounds within words and certain daily activities, occur in predictable orders, statistical learning helps infants anticipate other people's actions and generate similar sequences of behavior themselves.

Closely related to statistical learning is rational learning, which involves integrating the learner's prior beliefs and biases with what actually occurs in the environment. When, for example, infants observe an adult pulling balls of two different colors out of a box, seemingly at random, and the ratio of the colors of those balls deviates greatly from that of the total set of balls in the box, the infants' looking times suggest that they are surprised. Together with habituation, classical conditioning, generalization, and instrumental and statistical learning, such rational learning allows infants to acquire knowledge of the world from the first days following birth.

Social Learning

Children (and adults) learn a great deal from observing and interacting with other people. This social learning pervades our lives to such an extent that it is difficult to think of it as a specific learning capability. However, when we compare humans with other animals, even close relatives such as chimpanzees and other apes, the omnipresence of social learning in people's lives becomes apparent. Humans are far more skillful than any other animal in learning what others are trying to teach us; we also are far more inclined to teach others what we know. Among the crucial contributors to this social learning are imitation, social referencing, language, and guided participation.

The first discernible form of social learning is imitation. At first, the imitation is limited to behaviors that infants sometimes spontaneously produce on their own, such as sticking out their tongue. However, by age 6 months, infants begin to imitate novel behaviors that they never make spontaneously. By 15 months, toddlers not only learn novel behaviors, but they can also remember them and continue to produce them for at least a week. This imitation is not just "monkey see, monkey do." When children of this age see a model try to do something but do so ineffectively, they imitate what the model was trying to do rather than what the model actually did.

Social learning influences socioemotional development as well as acquisition of knowledge. When an unfamiliar person enters the room, 12-month-olds look to their mother for guidance. If the mother's face or voice shows fear, the baby tends to stay close to her; if the mother smiles, the baby is more likely to approach the stranger. Similarly, in the laboratory, a baby of this age will often cross the visual

Imitation starts in infancy.

cliff—in which a transparent plexiglass floor is placed over what looks like a steep drop off—but only if the mother smiles; they rarely will cross if she looks worried.

Social learning also shapes children's standards and values. From the 2nd year of life, toddlers internalize their parents' values and standards and use them to guide and evaluate their own conduct. Later in development, peers, teachers, and other adults also influence children's standards and values through the process of social learning. Peers, in particular, play a steadily increasing role over the course of childhood and adolescence.

Imitation is not the only mechanism of social learning. Another is social scaffolding. In this change mechanism, an older and

Using tools to build and repair things is a common context for social scaffolding, in which the older and more experienced person helps the younger and less experienced person to operate at a higher level than would otherwise be possible.

COMSTOCK / GETTY IMAGES

more knowledgeable person provides the learner with an overview of a given task, demonstrates how to do the most difficult parts, provides help with the difficult parts if necessary, and offers suggestions to the learner on how to proceed. Such scaffolding allows a beginner to do more than he or she could without help. Then, as the learner masters the basics of the task, the more expert person transfers more and more responsibility to the learner until the learner is doing the entire task. Thus, children and other people collaborate to produce social learning.

Cognitive Change Mechanisms

Many of the most compelling analyses of developmental change are at the level of cognitive processes. Both general and specific information-processing mechanisms play important roles.

General Information-Processing Mechanisms

Four categories of information-processing mechanisms are especially general and pervasive: basic processes, strategies, metacognition, and content knowledge.

Basic processes are the simplest, most broadly applicable, and earliest-developing general information-processing mechanisms. They overlap considerably with behavioral learning processes and include associating events with each other, recognizing objects as familiar, recalling facts and procedures, encoding key features of events, and generalizing from one instance to another. Changes with age occur in the speed and efficiency of these basic processes, but all of the basic processes are present from infancy onward. These basic processes provide a foundation that allows infants to learn about the world from their very first days.

Strategies also contribute to many types of development. Toddlers, for example, form strategies for achieving such goals as obtaining a toy that is out of reach or descending a steep surface; preschoolers form strategies for counting and solving arithmetic problems; school-age children form strategies for playing games and getting along with others; and so on. Often, children acquire multiple strategies for solving a single kind of problem—for example, strategies for approaching unfamiliar children on a playground or for solving arithmetic problems. Knowing multiple strategies allows children to adapt to the demands of different problems and situations.

Metacognition is a third type of cognitive process that contributes to development in large ways. For instance, increasing use of memory strategies stems in large part from children's increasing realization that they are unlikely to remember large amounts of material verbatim without using such strategies. Among the most important applications of metacognition is adaptive choice among alternative strategies, such as in deciding whether rereading is necessary to understand text, whether to count or state a retrieved answer to solve an arithmetic problem, and whether to write an outline before beginning an essay. The cognitive control involved in executive functioning—for example, inhibiting tempting but counterproductive actions, being cognitively flexible, and considering other people's perspectives—is another crucial type of metacognition.

Content knowledge is a fourth pervasive contributor to cognitive change. The more children know about any topic—whether it be chess, soccer, dinosaurs, or language—the better able they are to learn and remember new information about it. Knowledge also facilitates learning of unfamiliar content by allowing children to draw analogies between the new content and content that is familiar to them.

Exceptional content knowledge can outweigh all of adults' usual intellectual advantages over children. On the day this photograph was taken, this 8-year-old boy became the youngest person ever to defeat a chess grandmaster (the ranking awarded to the greatest chess players in the world).

Domain-Specific Learning Mechanisms

Infants acquire some complex competencies surprisingly rapidly, including basic perception and understanding of the physical world, language comprehension and production, interpretation of emotions, and attachment to caregivers. What seems to unite the varied capabilities that children acquire especially rapidly is their apparent evolutionary importance. Virtually everyone quickly and easily acquires abilities that are important to survival.

A number of theorists have posited that the nearly universal, rapid learning in these evolutionarily important domains is produced by domain-specific learning mechanisms that operate on everyday experience to produce accurate conclusions about the world. For example, even infants in their 1st year seem to expect bigger moving objects to produce stronger effects than smaller moving objects. Similarly, toddlers' word learning seems to be aided by the whole-object assumption (the idea that words used to label objects refer to the whole object rather than to a part of it) and the mutual exclusivity assumption (the idea that each object has a single name). These assumptions are usually correct for the words that young children hear, thus helping them learn what the words mean.

Children's informal theories about the main types of entities in the world— inanimate objects, people, and other living things—also facilitate their learning about them. The value of learning rapidly about the properties of people, other living things, and inanimate objects is clear; saying "More juice" to another person, for example, is considerably more likely to yield the desired outcome than is saying the same words to the family dog. Crucial in children's informal theories, as in scientists' formal ones, are causal relations that explain a large number of observations in terms of a few basic unobservable processes.

Possessing basic understanding of key concepts—such as inertia and solidity for inanimate objects; goal-directed movement and growth for living things; and intentions, beliefs, and desires for people—helps children act appropriately in new situations. For example, when preschoolers meet an unfamiliar peer, they assume that the other child will have intentions, beliefs, and desires—an assumption that helps them understand that child's actions and react appropriately to them. These assumptions about other people's minds aid the social understanding of children in all societies. Thus, both general and domain-specific cognitive learning mechanisms help children understand the world around them.

Change Mechanisms Work Together

Although it is often easiest to discuss different change mechanisms separately, it is crucial to remember that biological, cognitive, and behavioral mechanisms all reflect interactions between the person and the environment and that all types of mechanisms work together to produce change. For instance, consider effortful attention. The development of this capability reflects a combination of biological and environmental factors. On the biological side, genes influence the production of neurotransmitters that affect children's ability to concentrate and ignore distractions. Effortful attention also relies on the development of connections between two parts of the brain—the anterior cingulate, which is active in attention to goals, and the limbic area, which is active in emotional reactions. On the environmental side, the development of effortful attention can be influenced by the quality of parenting a child receives—though this is true primarily for children with a particular genotype. For children with one form of a relevant gene, quality of parenting influences the development of effortful attention, whereas for children with another form of the gene, quality of parenting has little effect on its development.

Specific experiences can also be influential; for example, playing specially designed computer games increases the activity of the anterior cingulate and thus may aid the ability to sustain attention on both experimental tasks and intelligence tests. In short, varied types of mechanisms work together to produce development of even a single capability.

Theme 5: The Sociocultural Context Shapes Development

Children develop within a personal context of other people: families, friends, neighbors, teachers, and classmates. They also develop within an impersonal context of historical, economic, technological, and political forces, as well as societal beliefs, attitudes, and values. The impersonal context is important in shaping development, just as the personal one is. There is little reason to think that parents in developed societies in the twenty-first century love their children more than parents of the past did. Yet their children die less often, get sick less often, eat a more nutritious diet, and receive more formal education than did children from even the wealthiest families of 100 or 200 years ago. Thus, when and where children grow up profoundly influences their lives.

Growing Up in Societies with Different Practices and Values

Values and practices that people within a society take for granted as "natural" often vary substantially among societies. These variations influence the rate and form of development. Throughout the book, you encountered examples of this in every aspect of development, including in domains that are commonly thought of as governed entirely by maturation. For example, people often assume that the timing of walking and other motor skills in infancy is determined solely by biology, but babies who grow up in African tribes that strongly encourage infants' motor development tend to walk and reach other motor milestones earlier than do infants in the United States. Similarly, infants in societies where babies sleep with their mothers for several years exhibit less fear at bedtime than do children in the United States, where babies rarely sleep in the same bed or even the same room as their mothers past the first 6 months of their lives.

Emotional reactions provide another example of how cultural practices and values influence behavior, even when we might not expect them to do so. Infants in all societies that have been studied show the same attachment patterns, but the frequency of occurrence of each pattern varies with the values of the society. Relative to babies in the United States, for instance, Japanese babies who are placed in the Strange Situation (see Chapter 11) more often become very upset, showing the insecure/resistant attachment pattern. These differences in attachment patterns appear to be due to differing cultural values and practices. Japanese mothers traditionally encourage dependence in children and rarely leave their babies alone, which may lead the babies to become especially upset when they are left alone in the Strange Situation. In contrast, U.S. parents emphasize independence to a greater degree and more often leave babies alone in a room or with other people.

Cultural influences such as these continue well beyond infancy. Japanese culture, for instance, places a higher value on hiding negative emotions, especially anger, than does American culture, and Japanese mothers discourage their children from expressing negative emotions. Quite likely because of these cultural influences, Japanese preschoolers and school-age children less often express anger and other negative emotions than do U.S. peers. Similarly, child rearing in rural Mexican villages emphasizes cooperation and caring about others, and children raised in these villages are more likely to share their possessions than are children from Mexican cities or the United States.

Culture influences not only parents' actions but also children's interpretations of those actions. For example, Chinese American mothers use a great deal of scolding and guilt to control their children. In the broader U.S. population, use of this disciplinary approach is associated with negative outcomes, but that association is not present among Chinese American children. The differing effectiveness of the disciplinary approaches may reflect children's interpretations of their parents' behavior. If children believe that scolding or authoritarian parenting is in their best interest, those behaviors can be effective. However, if children see such disciplinary approaches as reflecting negative parental feelings toward them, the discipline tends to be ineffective or harmful.

Sociocultural differences exert a similar influence on cognitive development.

The Wisdom of Generations: Boys' and Girls' Initiations Among the Cokwe and Related People

The culture of Mexican villages successfully encourages cooperation and helping among children and others.

YURI CORTEZ / GETTY IMAGES

They help determine which skills and knowledge children acquire—for instance, whether children learn to operate abacuses, iPads, or both. They also influence how well children learn skills that everyone acquires to some degree; for example, Australian aboriginal children, whose adult lives will depend on their ability to trek through the desert to distant oases, develop spatial skills superior to those of urban Australian children. Finally, cultural values influence the educational system, which in turn influences what and how deeply children learn. For instance, students in community-of-learners classrooms learn about fewer scientific topics than do children in traditional classrooms, but they learn about them in greater depth.

Growing Up in Different Times and Places

When and where children grow up profoundly influences their development. As noted earlier, in modern societies, children's lives are greatly improved over what they were in the past, in terms of health, nutrition, shelter, and so on. Not all of the changes in modern societies have promoted children's well-being, however. For example, in North America and Europe, far more children grow up with divorced parents than in the past, and these children are at risk for many problems. On average, they are more prone to sadness and depression, have lower self-esteem, do less well in school, and are less socially competent than peers who live in intact families. Although most children from divorced families do not have serious problems, a minority do: engaging in delinquent activities, dropping out of school, and having children out of wedlock all are more common among children whose parents are divorced.

Other historical changes result in children's lives being different, but not necessarily better or worse. The great expansion of childcare outside the home represents one such case. In the United States, about half of infants and three-fourths of 4-year-olds currently receive childcare outside their homes—5 times the rates in 1965. As this change was occurring, many people feared that such care would weaken attachment between babies and mothers. Others expressed hopes that such care would greatly stimulate cognitive development, especially of children from impoverished backgrounds, because of the greater opportunities for interaction with other children and adults. In fact, the data indicate that neither the fears nor the hopes were justified. In almost all respects, children who receive care outside the home tend to develop similarly, both emotionally and cognitively, to those who do not.

More generally, the same cultural or technological change can bring either positive or negative effects, depending on who the child is and how the innovation is used. For instance, the Internet can be used to communicate with friends, which tends to strengthen friendships, but it can also be used for cyberbullying. Playing certain Internet games stimulates development of attention, but very high frequency of playing Internet games can harm the quality of friendships. Thus, in terms of health, comfort, intellectual stimulation, and material well-being, children growing up today in modern societies are, on the whole, better off than those who grew up in the past—but in other ways, the picture is more mixed.

This evocative photograph makes us wonder how the severe poverty faced by this Depression-era family affected the children's subsequent lives.

Growing Up in Different Circumstances Within a Society

Even among children growing up at the same time in the same society, differences in economic circumstances, family relationships, and peer groups lead to large differences in children's lives.

Economic Influences

In every society, the economic circumstances of a child's family considerably influence the child's life. However, the degree of economic inequality within each society influences how large a difference the economic circumstances make. In societies with large income inequalities, such as the United States, poor children's academic achievement is far lower than that of children from wealthier families. In societies with smaller inequalities, such as Japan and Sweden, children from affluent families also do better academically than children from poorer families, but the differences are smaller.

It is not just academic achievement that is influenced by economic circumstances; all aspects of development are. Infants from impoverished families more often are insecurely attached to their mothers. Children and adolescents from impoverished families more often are rejected as friends and more often are lonely. Illegal substance use, crime, and depression also are more common among poor adolescents than among peers from wealthier backgrounds.

These negative outcomes are unsurprising, given the many disadvantages that poor children face. Relative to children who grow up in more affluent environments, poor children more often live in dangerous neighborhoods; grow up in homes with one or no biological parents; attend inferior day-care centers and schools; less often are read to and spoken to by their parents; and have fewer books, magazines, and other intellectually stimulating material in their homes. The cumulative burden of these disadvantages, rather than any one of them, poses the greatest obstacle to successful development.

Influences of Family and Peers

Families and peer groups vary considerably in ways other than income, and many of these differences also have a substantial influence on development. In some families, regardless of income, parents are sensitive to babies' needs and form close attachments with them; in others, this does not occur. In some families, again regardless of income, parents read to their children each night, thus helping the children learn to read; in others, this practice does not occur.

The influence of friends, other peers, teachers, and other adults varies in as many ways as that of families. Friends, for example, can provide companionship and feedback, contribute to self-esteem, and serve as a buffer against stress; during adolescence, they can be particularly important sources of sympathy and support. On the other hand, friends can also have a negative influence, drawing children and adolescents into reckless and aggressive behavior, including crime, drinking, and drug use. Thus, personal relationships, like economic circumstances, culture, and technology, influence development, but the effects of these influences vary with the particulars.

Theme 6: Individual Differences

Children differ on a huge number of dimensions—demographic characteristics (gender, race, ethnicity, socioeconomic status), psychological characteristics (intellect, personality, artistic ability), experiences (where they grow up; whether their parents are divorced; whether they participate in plays, bands, or organized sports), and so on. How can we tell which individual differences are the crucial ones for understanding children and predicting their futures?

As illustrated in Figure 16.1, three characteristics—breadth of related characteristics, stability over time, and predictive value—are crucial in determining the importance of any dimension of individual differences. First, as shown by the red arrows, children's status on the most important dimensions is associated with their status at that time on other important dimensions. Thus, one reason why intelligence is considered a central individual difference is that the higher a child's IQ at a given age, the higher the child's grades, achievement test scores, and general knowledge tend to be at the same time. A second key characteristic is stability over time (the blue arrows in Figure 16.1). A dimension of individual differences is of greater interest if the higher or lower that children score on it early in development, the higher or lower they are likely to score on it later. Thus, another reason for interest in IQ is that children with high (or low) IQs usually grow into adults with high (or low) IQs. A third characteristic of major dimensions of individual differences is that a child's status on the dimension predicts outcomes on other important characteristics in the future (the green arrows in Figure 16.1). Thus, a third reason for interest in IQ scores is that a person's IQ during middle childhood and adolescence predicts that person's later earnings, occupational status, and years of education.

These three characteristics make clear why demographic variables such as gender, race, ethnicity, and SES are studied so often. Consider gender, for example. Gender differences are related to a wide variety of other differences. Boys tend to be larger, stronger, more physically active, and more aggressive; to play in larger groups; to be better at some forms of spatial thinking; and more often to have ADHD and math or reading disabilities. Girls tend to be more verbal, quicker

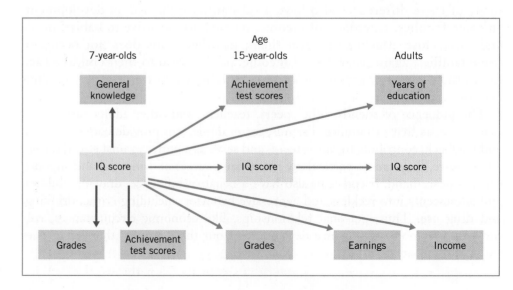

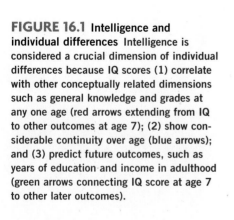

FIGURE 16.1 Intelligence and individual differences Intelligence is considered a crucial dimension of individual differences because IQ scores (1) correlate with other conceptually related dimensions such as general knowledge and grades at any one age (red arrows extending from IQ to other outcomes at age 7); (2) show considerable continuity over age (blue arrows); and (3) predict future outcomes, such as years of education and income in adulthood (green arrows connecting IQ score at age 7 to other later outcomes).

to perceive emotions, better at writing, and more likely to express sympathy and empathy for people in distress. Being male or female obviously is also stable over time. Finally, being male or female predicts future individual differences. If a newborn is female, it is likely that, compared with males, she will be more self-revealing with friends, more vulnerable to depression, more inclined to prosocial behavior, and more disposed to using relational aggression.

We next consider the extent to which several other variables show these three key characteristics of major individual differences.

Breadth of Individual Differences at a Given Time

Individual differences are not randomly distributed. Children who are high on one dimension also tend to be high on other, conceptually related dimensions. Thus, children who do well on one measure of intellect—language, memory, conceptual understanding, problem solving, reading, or mathematics—tend to do well on others. Similarly, children who do well on one measure of social or emotional functioning—relations with parents, relations with peers, relations with teachers, self-esteem, prosocial behavior, and lack of aggression and lying—also tend to do well on others. Sometimes, as with the relation between intelligence and school achievement, the connections are very strong. More often, the relations are moderate. Thus, although children who get along well with their parents also tend to get along well with peers, there are many exceptions.

Beyond intelligence and gender, two other crucial dimensions of individual differences are attachment and self-esteem. Compared with their insecurely attached peers, a toddler who is securely attached to his or her mother tends to be more enthusiastic and positive about solving problems with her, to comply more often with her directives, and to obey her requests even when she isn't present. Such children also tend to get along better with other toddlers and to be more sociable and more socially competent. Similarly, children and adolescents who are high in self-esteem also tend to be strong on many other dimensions of social and emotional functioning. They tend to be generally hopeful and popular, to have many friends, and to have good academic and self-regulation skills. In contrast, those with low self-esteem tend to feel hopeless and to be prone to problems such as depression, aggression, and social withdrawal.

Stability Over Time

Many individual differences show moderate stability over time. For instance, people who have easy temperaments during infancy tend to continue to have easy temperaments in middle and later childhood. Similarly, elementary school children with ADHD, reading disabilities, or mathematics disabilities usually have lifelong difficulties in those areas.

The reasons for such stability of psychological characteristics are to be found in the stability of both genes and environment. A child's genotype remains identical over the course of development (though particular genes switch on and off at different times). Most children's environments remain fairly stable as well. Families that are middle-class when a child is born tend to remain middle-class; families that value education when the child is born usually continue to value education; parents who are sensitive and supportive generally remain that way; and so on. Major changes, such as divorce and unemployment, do occur, and they affect children's happiness, self-esteem, and other characteristics. Nonetheless, the stability of children's environments, like the stability of their genes, contributes to the stability of their psychological functioning over time.

Predicting Future Individual Differences on Other Dimensions

Individual differences on some dimensions are related not only to future status on that dimension but also to future status on other dimensions. For instance, children who are securely attached as infants tend as toddlers and preschoolers to have more social ties to their peers than do children who were insecurely attached as infants. When they reach school age, these securely attached children tend to understand other children's emotions relatively well and to be relatively skilled in resolving conflicts. When they reach adolescence and adulthood, they tend to form close attachments with romantic partners. All of these outcomes are consistent with the view that secure early attachment provides a working model that influences subsequent relationships with other people.

As with stability over time of a single dimension, the relative stability of most children's environments contributes to these long-term continuities of psychological functioning. If children's environments change in important ways, the typical continuities may be disrupted. Thus, stressful events such as divorce reduce the likelihood that children who were securely attached during infancy will continue to show the positive relations with peers usually associated with secure attachment.

Determinants of Individual Differences

Individual differences, like all aspects of development, are ultimately attributable to the interaction of children's genes and the environments they encounter.

Genetics

For a number of important characteristics—including IQ, prosocial behavior, and empathy—about 50% of the differences among individuals in a given population are attributable to differences in genetic inheritance. The degree of genetic influence on individual differences tends to increase over the course of development. For example, correlations between the IQs of adopted children and their biological parents steadily increase over the course of childhood and adolescence, even if the children never meet or have any contact with their biological parents. One reason is that many genes related to intellectual functioning do not exercise their effects until late childhood or adolescence. Another reason is that over the course of development, children become increasingly free to choose environments that are in accord with their genetic predispositions.

Experience

Individual differences reflect children's experiences as well as their genes. Consider just one

Genetic similarities sometimes produce a striking physical resemblance between parent and child. We can only wonder whether this baby, as she develops, will come to resemble her father in other ways as well.

major environmental influence: the parents who raise the children. The more speech that parents address to their toddlers, the more rapidly the toddlers recognize familiar words and learn new ones. The more that parents aim their scaffolding at, but not beyond, the upper end of their children's capabilities, the greater the improvement in their children's problem solving. The more stimulating and responsive the home intellectual environment, the higher children's IQ tends to be.

Parents exert at least as large an influence on their children's social and emotional development as on their intellectual development. For example, the likelihood that children will adopt their parents' standards and values appears to be influenced by the type of discipline their parents use with them. Similarly, parents influence their children's willingness to share, especially if they discuss the reasons for sharing with their children and have good relationships with them.

The effect of different types of parenting, like the effects of children's other experiences, depends on the child. One example of this involves the development of conscience. For fearful children, the key factor determining whether the child internalizes the parents' moral values is gentle discipline. Fearful children may become so anxious in the face of rigorous discipline that they cannot focus on the moral values that the parents are trying to instill. For fearless children, on the other hand, the key factor is a positive relationship with one's parents. Such fearless children often do not respond to gentle discipline; they tend to internalize their parents' values only if they feel close to them. As an old adage states, "It's a wise parent who knows his child."

Theme 7: Child-Development Research Can Improve Children's Lives

One of the few goals shared by virtually everyone is that children be as happy and healthy as possible. Understanding how children develop can contribute to this goal. Theories of development provide general principles for interpreting children's behavior and for analyzing their problems. Empirical studies yield specific lessons regarding how to promote children's physical well-being, positive relationships with other people, and learning. In this section, we review practical implications of child-development research for raising children, educating them, and helping them overcome problems.

Implications for Parenting

Several principles of good parenting are so obvious that noting them might seem unnecessary. However, the number of children who are harmed each year by poor parenting makes it clear that these principles cannot be stated too often.

Pick a Good Partner

The first principle of good parenting comes into play before parenthood even begins: pick a good partner. Given the importance of genetics, pick a partner whose physical, intellectual, and emotional characteristics suggest that he or she will provide your child with good genes. Given the importance of the environment, pick a partner who will be a good mother or father. In terms of your child's development, no decision is more important than picking a good partner.

Ensure a Healthy Pregnancy

An expectant mother should maintain a healthy diet, have regular checkups, and keep stress levels as low as possible to increase the likelihood of a successful pregnancy. Equally important is avoiding teratogens such as tobacco, alcohol, and harmful drugs.

Know Which Decisions Are Likely to Have a Long-Term Impact

In addition to the joy they feel when their baby is born, new parents face a daunting number of decisions. Fortunately, babies are quite resilient. In the context of a loving and supportive home, a wide range of choices work out about equally well. Some decisions that seem minor, however, can have important effects. One such decision involves the baby's sleeping position: having a baby sleep on his or her back, rather than on his or her stomach, reduces the possibility of SIDS.

In other cases, the lesson of child-development research is that early problems are often transitory, so there is no reason to worry about them. Colic, which affects about 10% of babies, is one such problem. A colicky baby's frequent, high-pitched, grating, sick-sounding cries are difficult for parents to bear, but they have no long-term implications for the baby's development. In the short run, the best approach is to soothe the baby to the extent possible and not feel at fault if the effort fails. In the longer run, the best path for parents is to relax, seek social support, and obtain help to allow some time off from caregiving—and to remember that colic usually ends by the time babies are 3 months old.

Form a Secure Attachment

Most parents have no difficulty forming a secure attachment with their baby, but some parents and babies do not form such bonds. One reason is genetics: variant forms of certain genes can influence the likelihood of a child's forming a secure parental attachment, in at least some circumstances. Of course, no one can control the genes that babies inherit, but parents and other caretakers can maximize the likelihood of a baby's becoming securely attached by maintaining a positive approach in their caregiving and by being responsive to the baby's needs. This is easier said than done, of course, and other dimensions of a baby's temperament, as well as the parents' attitude and responsiveness, influence the quality of attachment. However, even when babies are initially irritable and difficult, programs that teach parents how to be responsive and positive with them can lead to more secure attachments.

Provide a Stimulating Environment

The home environment has a great deal to do with children's learning. One good example involves reading acquisition. Reading to young children positively influences their later reading achievement. One reason is that such activities promote phonological awareness (the ability to identify the component sounds within words). Nursery rhymes seem to be particularly effective in this regard; children who repeatedly hear *Green Eggs and Ham,* for instance, generally learn to appreciate the similarities and differences in *Sam, ham, am,* and related words. Phonological awareness helps children learn to sound out words, which, in turn, helps them learn to retrieve the words' identities quickly and effortlessly. Successful early reading leads children to read more, which helps them improve their reading

Family activities, such as looking at photo albums and reminiscing about the people and settings they depict, provide both stimulation and warm, positive feelings for many children.

ASIA IMAGES GROUP PTE LTD / ALAMY

further over the course of schooling. More generally, the more stimulating the intellectual environment, the more eager children will be to learn.

Implications for Education

Theories and research on child development hold a number of further lessons for how to educate children most effectively. Consider the instructional implications of several major theories of cognitive development.

Piaget's theory emphasizes the importance of the child's active involvement, both mental and physical, in the learning process. This active involvement is especially important in helping children master counterintuitive ideas. For example, the physical experience of walking around a pivot while holding a long metal rod at points close to and far from the pivot allowed children to overcome a widely held misconception that previous paper-and-pencil physics lessons had failed to correct—the misconception that all parts of an object must move at the same speed.

Information-processing theories suggest that analyzing the types of information available to children in everyday activities can improve learning. One such analysis indicated that the simple board game Chutes and Ladders provides visual, auditory, kinesthetic, and temporal information that could help children learn the sizes of numbers. Consistent with this analysis, having children from low-income families play a game based on Chutes and Ladders improved the children's understanding of the sizes of numbers, as well as their counting, recognition of numbers, and arithmetic learning.

Sociocultural theories emphasize the need to turn classrooms into communities of learners in which children cooperate with one another in their pursuit of knowledge. Rather than following the traditional model of instruction in which teachers lecture and children take notes, community-of-learners classrooms follow an approach in which teachers provide the minimum guidance needed for children to learn and gradually decrease their directive role as children's competence increases. Such programs also encourage children to make use of the resources of the broader community—children and teachers at other schools, outside experts, reference books, websites, and so on. The approach can be effective not only in building intellectual skills but also in promoting desirable values, such as personal responsibility and mutual respect.

Implications for Helping Children at Risk

Several principles that have emerged from empirical research offer valuable guidance for helping children at risk for serious developmental problems.

The Importance of Timing

Providing interventions at the optimal time is crucial in a variety of developmental contexts. One important example involves efforts to help children at risk for learning difficulties. All theories of cognitive development indicate that such difficulties should be addressed early, before children lose confidence in their ability to learn and before they become resentful toward schools and teachers. This realization, together with research documenting that many children from impoverished backgrounds have difficulty in school, laid the groundwork for Project Head Start and a variety of experimental preschool programs. Evaluations of the programs' effects indicate that both the small experimental programs and Project Head Start increase children's IQs and achievement test scores by the end of the programs and briefly thereafter. Subsequently, the positive effects on IQ and academic achievement usually fade, but other positive effects continue. At-risk children who participate in such programs are less likely to ever be held back in school or assigned to special-education classes than are those who do not participate, and they are more likely to graduate from high school and go to college. These are important gains.

Even greater positive effects of early educational programs are possible, as illustrated by the Abecedarian Project. Designed to show what could be achieved through an optimally staffed, highly funded, and carefully designed program that started during infancy and lasted through age 5, the Abecedarian Project produced large gains in both academic achievement and social skills that continued throughout childhood and adolescence. Its results demonstrate that it is possible

Experiences such as this one in a Project Head Start classroom lead to a variety of lasting benefits.

for intensive programs that start early to have substantial, lasting benefits on poor children's academic achievement.

Early detection of child maltreatment, and rapid intervention to end it, is also crucial. Neglect, physical abuse, and sexual abuse are the three most common forms of child maltreatment. Parents who are stressed economically, have few friends, use alcohol and illegal drugs, or are being abused by their partner are the most likely to mistreat their children.

Knowing the characteristics of abused and neglected children can help teachers and others who come into contact with children recognize potential problems early and alert social service agencies so that they can investigate and remedy the problems. Children who are maltreated tend to have difficult temperaments, to have few friends, to be in poor physical or mental health, to do poorly in school, and to show abnormal aggression or passivity. Adolescents who are maltreated may be depressed or hyperactive, use drugs or alcohol, and have sexual problems such as promiscuity or abnormal fearfulness. Early recognition of such signs of abuse can literally save a child's life.

Biology and Environment Work Together

Another principle with important practical implications is that biology and environment work together to produce all behavior. This principle has proved important in designing treatments for ADHD. Although stimulant drugs such as Ritalin are the best-known treatment for this problem, research has shown that when medications are used alone, their benefits usually end as soon as children stop taking them. Longer-lasting benefits require behavioral therapy as well as medication. One effective behavioral treatment is to teach the children cognitive strategies for screening out distractions. The medications calm children with ADHD sufficiently that they can benefit from the therapy; the therapy helps them learn effective ways for dealing with their problems and for interacting with other people.

Every Problem Has Many Causes

An additional principle that has proved useful for helping children with developmental problems is that trying to identify *the* cause of any particular problem is futile; problems almost always have multiple causes. The greater the number of risks, the more likely children will have low IQs, poor socioemotional skills, and psychiatric disorders. Accordingly, providing effective treatment often requires addressing many particular difficulties. This principle has provided useful guidance for intervening with children who are rejected by other children. Helping these children gain better social skills requires increasing their understanding of other people. It also requires helping them learn new strategies, such as how to enter an ongoing group interaction unobtrusively and how to resolve conflicts without resorting to aggression. It also requires helping them learn from their own experience—for example, by monitoring the success of the different strategies they try and, when necessary, analyzing what went wrong. Together, these approaches can help rejected children make friends and become better accepted.

Improving Social Policy

Even if you do not have children of your own, your actions as a citizen can influence the lives of the children in your community. Votes in elections and referenda, opinions expressed in informal discussions, and participation in advocacy organizations all can make a difference. Knowledge of child-development research can inform your perspectives on many issues relevant to children. The conclusions that you reach will, and should, reflect your values as well as the evidence. For example, reductions in class size in kindergarten through 3rd-grade classrooms have had variable effects on student achievement. A large-scale, well-implemented study in Tennessee indicated positive effects on student achievement (Krueger, 1999), whereas a large-scale, well-implemented study in California did not show any effect on achievement (Stecher, McCaffrey, & Bugliari, 2003). Teachers and parents appeared to be pleased with the class-size reductions in both cases and believed that the smaller classes helped their children.

Are these outcomes worth the many billions of dollars that hiring the number of teachers needed to implement such reform would cost? Research cannot answer this question, because the answer depends on values as well as data. How expensive is too expensive? Nonetheless, as the example illustrates, knowing the scientific evidence can help us, as citizens, make better-informed decisions.

Maternity Leave

Should society require employers to grant paid maternity leave in the months after a baby is born, and if so, for how long? Knowing that long hours of day care before an infant is 9 months old may have negative effects on early social development argues in favor of society's making it easier for parents to take maternity leave for that period of time. However, other considerations, such as economic costs, are also important; as noted above, the scientific evidence alone can never be determinative.

Day Care

Similar debates have arisen about whether the general society should subsidize day-care payments for parents of young children. One argument against such a policy has been the claim that children develop more successfully if they stay at home with one of their parents or other relatives than if they attend day care. This argument has turned out to be flawed, however. Children who attend good-quality day care develop similarly to children who receive care at home from their parents.

Eyewitness Testimony

Understanding child development is also vital for deciding whether children should be allowed to testify in court cases and for obtaining the most accurate testimony possible from them. Each year, more than 100,000 children in the United States testify in court, many of them in trials involving allegations of abuse. Often, the child and the accused are the only ones who witnessed the events. Research indicates that, in general, the accuracy of testimony increases with age; 8-year-olds recall more than do 6-year-olds, and 6-year-olds recall more than do 4-year-olds. However, when children are shielded from misleading and repeated questioning, even 4- and 5-year-olds usually provide accurate testimony about the types of issues that are central in court cases. Given the high stakes in such cases, using the lessons of research to elicit the most accurate possible testimony from children is essential for just verdicts.

Child-development research holds lessons for numerous other social problems as well. Research on the causes of aggression has led to programs such as Fast Track, which are designed to teach aggressive children to manage their anger and avoid

Children are naturally curious about the world; encouraging this curiosity, and channeling it in fruitful directions, is among the most vital goals facing parents and society alike.

BLUE JEAN IMAGES / ALAMY

violence. Research on the roots of morality has led to programs such as the Child Development Project, designed to encourage students to help others who are in need. Research on the effects of poverty has provided the basis for the Abecedarian Project and other early education efforts. There is no end of social problems; understanding child development can help address the ones that affect children's futures.

Test Yourself

1. Which of the following statements accurately describes the interaction of nature and nurture?
   a. Nature does its work before birth, and nurture takes over only after birth.
   b. Nature's influence continues through infancy before giving way to the influence of nurture.
   c. Nature and nurture begin interacting on the fetus in the womb, and both continue to shape the individual's development throughout life.
   d. The role that both nature and nurture play in development is often overstated.

2. Which of the following is an example of the crucial role that timing plays in the potential impact of a teratogen?
   a. The diet of a pregnant mother will influence taste preferences that the fetus will exhibit after birth.
   b. By age 12 months, infants lose the ability to hear the difference between similar sounds that they do not encounter on a regular basis.
   c. A virus will cause damage to the development of a fetus if contracted by the pregnant mother at specific sensitive times during pregnancy.
   d. It is more difficult for children older than 11 or 12 years of age to gain competence in a new language than it is for younger children.

3. The emerging field of epigenetics has helped to explain the ways in which a child's environment can influence gene expression. Which of the following is an example of this interaction?
   a. Children with certain types of brain damage will preform on par with other children on IQ tests up to a certain age, but will fall behind after that point.
   b. It is more difficult for children older than 11 or 12 years of age to gain competence in a new language than it is for younger children.
   c. A child who loses capability in one sense, such as sight, will often compensate with enhanced ability in another sense.
   d. The amount of stress that a mother experiences during her child's infancy can affect that child's ability to regulate reaction to stress later in life.

4. Looking preferences, self-initiated activities, self-socialization, and even the manner in which infants react to their parents are all examples of
   a. the active role children play in their development.
   b. the greater influence that nurture plays compared with nature in child development.
   c. the ways in which development is discontinuous.
   d. the ways in which the sociocultural context shapes development.

5. Which of the following is an example of the theme of the active child?
   a. The stability of IQ scores on average tends to increase with age.
   b. Stressful maternal experiences, such as a periodic shortage of food at certain points during pregnancy, will influence the future physical development of the child.
   c. Children who exhibit preoperational reasoning in some contexts may also exhibit concrete operational reasoning in others.
   d. Children who are better able to regulate their emotions tend to be more socially competent, and therefore elicit more positive reactions from other people, than those who are less skilled at emotion regulation.

6. Piaget's theory of cognitive development, Freud's theory of psychosexual development, and Erikson's theory of psychosocial development are all examples of _____ .
   a. social learning theory
   b. the stage approach to development
   c. theories based on an empiricist perspective of development
   d. theories based on the nativist approach to child development

7. An infant's attachment to his or her mother will more reliably predict that child's long-term security if there are no significant disruptions in the home environment. This example illustrates
   a. the degree to which genetic influence on individual differences tends to decrease over time.
   b. how continuity in individual differences is influenced by continuity in the environment.
   c. the manner in which sociocultural differences exert influence on cognitive development.
   d. the role of domain-specific learning mechanisms in child development.

8. Which of the following statements accurately expresses a key understanding regarding the continuity and discontinuity of development?
   a. Child psychologists today generally believe that, for the vast majority of traits, development occurs in a discontinuous manner.
   b. Very few individual differences in psychological properties show stability over time.
   c. Contrary to the theories by early behavioral psychologists like Piaget and Erikson, developmental processes rarely show a great deal of continuity.
   d. The apparent continuity or discontinuity of a given developmental trait depends on the timescale on which it is considered.

9. Before writing an essay, a child first considers what readers already know about the topic. Which of the four general information-processing mechanisms is illustrated by this example?
   a. strategy formation
   b. basic processes
   c. metacognition
   d. content knowledge

10. Which of the following statements is *not* true of the development of a child's cognitive abilities?
    a. A child's content knowledge in a given area can outweigh an adult's general intellectual ability.
    b. Statistical learning emerges in middle childhood, after the child has begun to understand basic mathematical properties.
    c. Understanding basic causal relationships allows children to infer explanations for a wide variety of observations.
    d. Knowing multiple strategies for achieving goals helps children adapt to different problems and situations they will face.

11. Babies who grow up in African tribes that strongly encourage infants' motor development tend to walk and reach other motor milestones earlier than do infants in the United States. This is an example of the effect of _____ on development.
    a. change mechanisms
    b. historical change
    c. discontinuity
    d. the sociocultural context

12. Which of the following is *not* a reason why demographic variables such as gender, race, ethnicity, and socioeconomic status are particularly useful to child development researchers?
    a. Each of these variables relates directly to a wide variety of other individual differences.
    b. These variables tend to remain stable over time.
    c. These variables have been shown to be a reliable predictor of some future outcomes.
    d. These variables tend to be unaffected by environmental factors.

13. Which of the following is an important contribution that Piaget's theory has made to children's education?
    a. Piaget helped to delineate the interactions between a child's genes and his or her environment.
    b. Piaget's theory emphasizes the importance of the child's active involvement in the learning process.
    c. Piaget brought attention to the role that cultural influences play in a child's learning.
    d. Piaget explained cognitive development in terms of a continuous process, rather than as a series of stages.

14. Habituation is a learning process in which a child becomes familiar with a repeated stimulus. This process can motivate the child to seek out new stimulation. Besides illustrating the role of behavioral mechanisms in a child's development, this example also demonstrates which other theme of child development?
    a. The sociocultural context of an individual's development
    b. The role of the active child
    c. The discontinuity of change over time
    d. The influence of nature over nurture

15. What is meant by the following statement? Individual differences are not randomly distributed.
    a. A child's performance in one area of development will predict the child's achievement in another, related area.
    b. A child's genotype will always exert a stronger influence on the child's outcomes than any environmental factors.
    c. Each individual child is different from all other children.
    d. A child's performance on one measure of intelligence will not predict the child's performance in another.

LaunchPad
macmillan learning

Don't stop now! Research shows that testing yourself is a powerful learning tool. Visit LaunchPad to access the LearningCurve adaptive quizzing system, which gives you a personalized study plan to help build your mastery of the chapter material through videos, activities, and more. **Go to launchpadworks.com.**

Critical Thinking Questions

1. What qualities of children influence the way that other people act toward them, and how do these actions influence their development?

2. Individual differences show some stability over time. How do genes and environment contribute to this stability?

3. How would growing up in one developed society rather than another—for example, the United States rather than Japan—be expected to influence a child's development?

4. How have the changes that have taken place in the United States over the past century influenced children's development? Has the overall effect of the changes on children been predominantly beneficial or predominantly harmful?

5. What findings that you read about in this book surprised you the most? Were there any findings or conclusions that you just don't believe?

6. What practical lessons have you learned from this course that will influence how you might raise your children if you have them?

▶ Student Video Activity

The Wisdom of Generations: Boys' and Girls' Initiations Among the Cokwe and Related People

Answers to Test Yourself

1. c, **2.** c, **3.** d, **4.** a, **5.** d, **6.** b, **7.** b, **8.** d, **9.** c, **10.** b, **11.** d, **12.** d, **13.** b, **14.** b, **15.** a

Glossary

accommodation the process by which people adapt current knowledge structures in response to new experiences (p. 145)

achievement motivation refers to whether children are motivated by *learning goals*, seeking to improve their competence and master new material, or by *performance goals*, seeking to receive positive assessments of their competence or to avoid negative assessments (p. 388)

activating influences potential result of certain fluctuations in sex-linked hormone levels affecting the contemporaneous activation of the nervous system and corresponding behavioral responses (p. 638)

active learning learning by acting on the world, rather than passively observing objects and events (p. 226)

adrenarche period prior to the emergence of visible signs of puberty during which the adrenal glands mature, providing a major source of sex steroid hormones; correlates with the onset of sexual attraction (p. 658)

affiliation tendency to affirm connection with others through being emotionally open, empathetic, or supportive (p. 651)

affordances the possibilities for action offered, or afforded, by objects and situations (p. 220)

aggression behavior aimed at harming or injuring others (p. 613)

aggressive-rejected (peer status) a category of sociometric status that refers to children who are especially prone to physical aggression, disruptive behavior, delinquency, and negative behavior such as hostility and threatening others (p. 576)

alleles two or more different forms of a gene (p. 101)

altruistic motives helping others for reasons that initially include empathy or sympathy for others and, at later ages, the desire to act in ways consistent with one's own conscience and moral principles (p. 606)

amniotic sac a transparent, fluid-filled membrane that surrounds and protects the fetus (p. 50)

amygdala an area of the brain that is involved in emotional reactions (p. 7)

anal stage the second stage in Freud's theory, lasting from the 2nd year through the 3rd year, in which the primary source of pleasure comes from defecation (p. 376)

androgen insensitivity syndrome (AIS) condition during prenatal development in which androgen receptors malfunction in genetic males, impeding the formation of male external genitalia; in these cases, the child may be born with female external genitalia (p. 638)

androgens class of steroid hormones that normally occur at higher levels in males than in females and that affect physical development and functioning from the prenatal period onward (p. 638)

antisocial behavior disruptive, hostile, or aggressive behaviors that violate social norms or rules and that harm or take advantage of others (p. 613)

anxiety disorders a set of mental disorders that involve the inability to regulate fear and worry (p. 457)

apoptosis genetically programmed cell death (p. 49)

assertion tendency to take action on behalf of the self through competitive, independent, or aggressive behaviors (p. 651)

assimilation the process by which people translate incoming information into a form that fits concepts they already understand (p. 145)

association areas parts of the brain that lie between the major sensory and motor areas and that process and integrate input from those areas (p. 115)

attachment an emotional bond with a specific person that is enduring across space and time. Usually, attachments are discussed in regard to the relation between infants and specific caregivers, although they can also occur in adulthood (p. 467)

attachment theory theory based on John Bowlby's work that posits that children are biologically predisposed to develop attachments to caregivers as a means of increasing the chances of their own survival (p. 469)

attention-deficit hyperactivity disorder (ADHD) a syndrome that involves difficulty in sustaining attention (p. 400)

auditory localization perception of the location in space of a sound source (p. 201)

authoritarian parenting a parenting style that is high in demandingness and low in responsiveness. Authoritarian parents are nonresponsive to their children's needs and tend to enforce their demands through the exercise of parental power and the use of threats and punishment. They are oriented toward obedience and authority and expect their children to comply with their demands without question or explanation (p. 526)

authoritative parenting a parenting style that is high in demandingness and supportiveness. Authoritative parents set clear standards and limits for their children and are firm about enforcing them; at the same time, they allow their children considerable autonomy within those limits, are attentive and responsive to their children's concerns and needs, and respect and consider their children's perspective (p. 526)

autobiographical memories memories of one's own experiences, including one's thoughts and emotions (p. 177)

axons neural fibers that conduct electrical signals away from the cell body to connections with other neurons (p. 114)

babbling repetitive consonant–vowel sequences ("bababa . . .") or hand movements (for learners of sign languages) produced during the early phases of language development (p. 254)

basic level the middle level, and often the first level learned, within a category hierarchy, such as "dog" in the animal/dog/poodle example (p. 291)

basic processes the simplest and most frequently used mental activities (p. 162)

behavior genetics the science concerned with how variation in behavior and development results from the combination of genetic and environmental factors (p. 107)

behavior modification a form of therapy based on principles of operant conditioning in which reinforcement contingencies are changed to encourage more adaptive behavior (p. 382)

bidirectionality of parent–child interactions the idea that parents and their children are mutually affected by one another's characteristics and behaviors (p. 530)

bilingualism the ability to use two languages (p. 246)

binocular disparity the difference between the retinal image of an object in each eye that results in two slightly different signals being sent to the brain (p. 199)

body image an individual's perception of, and feelings about, his or her own body (p. 658)

Carolina Abecedarian Project comprehensive and successful enrichment program for children from low-income families (p. 346)

carrier genetic testing genetic testing used to determine whether prospective parents are carriers of specific disorders (p. 105)

categorical perception the perception of speech sounds as belonging to discrete categories (p. 249)

category hierarchy a category that is organized by set–subset relations, such as animal/dog/poodle (p. 290)

cell body a component of the neuron that contains the basic biological material that keeps the neuron functioning (p. 114)

centration the tendency to focus on a single, perceptually striking feature of an object or event (p. 151)

cephalocaudal development the pattern of growth in which areas near the head develop earlier than areas farther from the head (p. 51)

cerebral cortex the "gray matter" of the brain that plays a primary role in what is thought to be particularly humanlike functioning, from seeing and hearing to writing to feeling emotion (p. 115)

cerebral hemispheres the two halves of the cortex; for the most part, sensory input from one side of the body goes to the opposite hemisphere of the brain (p. 116)

cerebral lateralization the specialization of the hemispheres of the brain for different modes of processing (p. 116)

child maltreatment intentional abuse or neglect that endangers the well-being of anyone under the age of 18 (p. 402)

chromosomes molecules of DNA that transmit genetic information; chromosomes are made up of DNA (p. 95)

chronosystem in the bioecological model, historical changes that influence the other systems (p. 398)

cisgender individuals who identify with their gender assigned at birth (or their biological sex) (p. 638)

classical conditioning a form of learning that consists of associating an initially neutral stimulus with a stimulus that always evokes a particular reflexive response (p. 221)

clinical interview a procedure in which questions are adjusted in accord with the answers the interviewee provides (p. 28)

cliques friendship groups that children voluntarily form or join themselves (p. 566)

colic excessive, inconsolable crying by a young infant for no apparent reason (p. 79)

collaboration coordination of assertion and affiliation in behavior, such as making initiatives for joint activity (p. 651)

collective monologue conversation between children that involves a series of non sequiturs, the content of each child's turn having little or nothing to do with what the other child has just said (p. 270)

comorbid being present simultaneously, as in the same individual developing another mental disorder (p. 619)

comprehension monitoring process of keeping track of one's understanding of a verbal description or text (p. 355)

comprehension with regard to language, understanding what others say (or sign or write) (p. 241)

computer simulation a type of mathematical model that expresses ideas about mental processes in precise ways (p. 158)

conception the union of an egg from the mother and a sperm from the father (p. 46)

concepts general ideas or understandings that can be used to group together objects, events, qualities, or abstractions that are similar in some way (p. 288)

concrete operational stage the period (7 to 12 years) within Piaget's theory in which children become able to reason logically about concrete objects and events (p. 147)

conditioned response (CR) in classical conditioning, the originally reflexive response that comes to be elicited by the conditioned stimulus (p. 221)

conditioned stimulus (CS) in classical conditioning, the neutral stimulus that is repeatedly paired with the unconditioned stimulus (p. 221)

conduct disorder (CD) a disorder that involves severe antisocial and aggressive behaviors that inflict pain on others or involve destruction of property or denial of the rights of others (p. 618)

cones the light-sensitive neurons that are highly concentrated in the fovea (the central region of the retina) (p. 193)

congenital adrenal hyperplasia (CAH) condition during prenatal development in which the adrenal glands produce high levels of androgens; sometimes associated with masculinization of external genitalia in genetic females and sometimes associated with higher rates of masculine-stereotyped play in genetic females (p. 638)

connectionism a type of information-processing approach that emphasizes the simultaneous activity of numerous interconnected processing units (p. 277)

conscience an internal regulatory mechanism that increases the individual's ability to conform to standards of conduct accepted in his or her culture (p. 600)

conservation concept the idea that merely changing the appearance of objects does not necessarily change the objects' other key properties (p. 151)

constructivism the theory that infants build increasingly advanced understanding by combining rudimentary innate knowledge with subsequent experiences (p. 170)

continuous development the idea that changes with age occur gradually, in small increments, like that of a pine tree growing taller and taller (p. 14)

contrast sensitivity the ability to detect differences in light and dark areas in a visual pattern (p. 193)

control group the group of participants in an experimental design who are not presented the experience of interest but in other ways are treated similarly (p. 33)

controversial (peer status) a category of sociometric status that refers to children or adolescents who are liked by quite a few peers and are disliked by quite a few others (p. 578)

co-regulation the process by which a caregiver provides the needed comfort or distraction to help a child reduce his or her distress (p. 435)

core-knowledge theories approaches that view children as having some innate knowledge in domains of special evolutionary importance and domain-specific learning mechanisms for rapidly and effortlessly acquiring additional information in those domains (p. 167)

corpus callosum a dense tract of nerve fibers that enable the two hemispheres of the brain to communicate (p. 116)

correlation the association between two variables (p. 30)

correlational designs studies intended to indicate how two variables are related to each other (p. 30)

co-rumination extensively discussing and self-disclosing emotional problems with another person (p. 454)

counting-on strategy counting up from the larger addend the number of times indicated by the smaller addend (p. 36)

critical period for language the time during which language develops readily and after which (sometime between age 5 and puberty) language acquisition is much more difficult and ultimately less successful (p. 244)

cross-gender-typed behaviors stereotyped or expected for the gender other than that of a given person (p. 635)

crossing over the process by which sections of DNA switch from one chromosome to the other; crossing over promotes variability among individuals (p. 97)

cross-sectional design a research method in which participants of different ages are compared on a given behavior or characteristic over a short period (p. 34)

crowds groups of adolescents who have similar stereotyped reputations (p. 568)

crystallized intelligence factual knowledge about the world (p. 328)

cultural tools the innumerable products of human ingenuity that enhance thinking (p. 172)

cyberbullying the use of technology, including texts, e-mails, websites, videos, embarrassing photos, and fake profiles, to harass or upset another person (p. 569)

dendrites neural fibers that receive input from other cells and conduct it toward the cell body in the form of electrical impulses (p. 114)

dependent variable a behavior that is measured to determine whether it is affected by exposure to the independent variable (p. 33)

depression a mental disorder that involves a sad or irritable mood along with physical and cognitive changes that interfere with daily life (p. 454)

developmental resilience successful development in spite of multiple and seemingly overwhelming developmental hazards (p. 85)

differential susceptibility a circumstance in which the same temperament characteristic that puts some children at high risk for negative outcomes when exposed to a harsh home environment also causes them to blossom when their home environment is positive (p. 444)

differentiation extracting from the constantly changing stimulation and events in the environment the relation of those elements that are constant—invariant, or stable (p. 220)

direction-of-causation problem the concept that a correlation between two variables does not indicate which, if either, variable is the cause of the other (p. 31)

discipline the set of strategies and behaviors parents use to teach children how to behave appropriately (p. 523)

discontinuous development the idea that changes with age include occasional large shifts, like the transition from caterpillar to cocoon to butterfly (p. 14)

discrete emotions theory a theory about emotions, held by Tomkins, Izard, and others, in which emotions are viewed as innate and discrete from one another from very early in life, and each emotion is believed to be packaged with a specific and distinctive set of bodily and facial reactions (p. 420)

dishabituation the introduction of a new stimulus rekindles interest following habituation to a repeated stimulus (p. 56)

disorganized/disoriented attachment a type of insecure attachment in which infants or young children have no consistent way of coping with the stress of the Strange Situation. Their behavior is often confused or even contradictory, and they often appear dazed or disoriented (p. 472)

display rules a social group's informal norms about when, where, and how much one should show emotions and when and where displays of emotion should be suppressed or masked by displays of other emotions (p. 433)

distributional properties the phenomenon that in any language, certain sounds are more likely to appear together than are others (p. 253)

DNA (deoxyribonucleic acid) molecules that carry all the biochemical instructions involved in the formation and functioning of an organism (p. 95)

domain specific information about a particular content area (p. 169)

dominant allele the allele that, if present, gets expressed (p. 101)

dose–response relation a relation in which the effect of exposure to an element increases with the extent of exposure (prenatally, the more exposure a fetus has to a potential teratogen, the more severe its effect is likely to be) (p. 61)

dual representation the idea that a symbolic artifact must be represented mentally in two ways at the same time—both as a real object and as a symbol for something other than itself (p. 279)

dynamic-systems theories a class of theories that focus on how change occurs over time in complex systems (p. 178)

dyslexia inability to read and spell well despite having normal intelligence (p. 356)

effect size magnitude of difference between two group's averages and the amount of overlap in their distributions (p. 655)

egocentric spatial representations coding of spatial locations relative to one's own body, without regard to the surroundings (p. 311)

egocentrism the tendency to perceive the world solely from one's own point of view (p. 150)

ego in psychoanalytic theory, the second personality structure to develop. It is the rational, logical, problem-solving component of personality (p. 375)

Electra complex Freud's term for the conflict experienced by girls in the phallic stage when they develop unacceptable romantic feelings for their father and see their mother as a rival (p. 376)

embryo the name given to the developing organism from the 3rd to 8th week of prenatal development (p. 47)

embryonic stem cells embryonic cells, which can develop into any type of body cell (p. 49)

emotion regulation a set of both conscious and unconscious processes used to both monitor and modulate emotional experiences and expressions (p. 435)

emotion socialization the process through which children acquire the values, standards, skills, knowledge, and behaviors that are regarded as appropriate for their present and future role in their particular culture (p. 448)

emotional intelligence the ability to cognitively process information about emotions and to use that information to guide both thought and behavior (p. 431)

emotions neural and physiological responses to the environment, subjective feelings, cognitions related to those feelings, and the desire to take action (p. 419)

enactive experience learning to take into account the reactions one's past behavior has evoked in others (p. 644)

encoding the process of representing in memory information that draws attention or is considered important (p. 162)

endophenotypes intermediate phenotypes, including the brain and nervous systems, that do not involve overt behavior (p. 100)

entity/helpless orientation a general tendency to attribute success and failure to enduring aspects of the self and to give up in the face of failure (p. 388)

entity theory a theory that a person's level of intelligence is fixed and unchangeable (p. 389)

environment every aspect of an individual and his or her surroundings other than genes (p. 95)

epigenesis the emergence of new structures and functions in the course of development (p. 45)

equifinality the concept that various causes can lead to the same mental disorder (p. 454)

equilibration the process by which children (or other people) balance assimilation and accommodation to create stable understanding (p. 145)

erogenous zones in Freud's theory, areas of the body that become erotically sensitive in successive stages of development (p. 375)

essentialism the view that living things have an essence inside them that makes them what they are (p. 303)

ethnic and racial identity the beliefs and attitudes an individual has about the ethnic or racial groups to which they belong (p. 497)

ethology the study of the evolutionary bases of behavior (p. 393)

event-related potentials (ERPs) changes in the brain's electrical activity that occur in response to the presentation of a particular stimulus (p. 118)

exosystem in the bioecological model, environmental settings that a child does not directly experience but that can affect the child indirectly (p. 398)

experience-dependent plasticity the process through which neural connections are created and reorganized throughout life as a function of an individual's experiences (p. 124)

experience-expectant plasticity the process through which the normal wiring of the brain occurs in part as a result of experiences that every human who inhabits any reasonably normal environment will have (p. 122)

experimental control the ability of researchers to determine the specific experiences of participants during the course of an experiment (p. 33)

experimental designs a group of approaches that allow inferences about causes and effects to be drawn (p. 32)

experimental group the group of participants in an experimental design who are presented the experience of interest (p. 33)

external validity the degree to which results can be generalized beyond the particulars of the research (p. 27)

failure to thrive a condition in which infants become malnourished and fail to grow or gain weight for no obvious medical reason (p. 128)

false-belief problems tasks that test a child's understanding that other people will act in accord with their own beliefs even when the child knows that those beliefs are incorrect (p. 295)

family dynamics the way in which family members interact through various relationships: mother with each child, father with each child, mother with father, and siblings with one another (p. 523)

family structure the number of and relationships among the people living in a household (p. 512)

fetal alcohol spectrum disorder (FASD) the harmful effects of maternal alcohol consumption on a developing fetus. Fetal alcohol syndrome (FAS) involves a range of effects, including facial deformities, mental retardation, attention problems, hyperactivity, and other defects. Fetal alcohol effects (FAE) is a term used for individuals who show some, but not all, of the standard effects of FAS (p. 66)

fetus the name given to the developing organism from the 9th week to birth (p. 47)

fluid intelligence ability to think on the spot to solve novel problems (p. 327)

Flynn effect consistent rise in average IQ scores that has occurred over the past 80 years in many countries (p. 341)

formal operational stage the period (12 years and beyond) within Piaget's theory in which people become able to think about abstractions and hypothetical situations (p. 147)

fraternal twins twins that result when two eggs happen to be released into the fallopian tube at the same time and are fertilized by two different sperm; fraternal twins have only half their genes in common (p. 50)

friend a person with whom an individual has an intimate, reciprocated positive relationship (p. 552)

frontal lobe associated with organizing behavior; the one that is thought responsible for the human ability to plan ahead (p. 115)

functionalist perspective a theory of emotion, proposed by Campos and others, arguing that the basic function of emotions is to promote action toward achieving a goal. In this view, emotions are not discrete from one another and vary somewhat based on the social environment (p. 421)

***g* (general intelligence)** cognitive processes that influence the ability to think and learn on all intellectual tasks (p. 327)

gametes (germ cells) reproductive cells—egg and sperm—that contain only half the genetic material of all the other cells in the body (p. 46)

gang a loosely organized group of adolescents or young adults who identify as a group and often engage in illegal activities (p. 568)

gender constancy realization that gender is invariant despite superficial changes in a person's appearance or behavior (p. 640)

gender dysphoria psychiatric diagnosis included in the DSM-5 to refer to children who experience distress because they do not identify with the gender assigned to them at birth (p. 638)

gender identity self-identifying as a boy or a girl (p. 640)

gender-role flexibility recognition of gender roles as social conventions and adoption of more flexible attitudes and interests (p. 653)

gender-role intensification heightened concerns with adhering to traditional gender roles that may occur during adolescence (p. 653)

gender schema filter initial evaluation of information as relevant for one's own gender (p. 642)

gender schemas organized mental representations (concepts, beliefs, memories) about gender, including gender stereotypes (p. 641)

gender segregation children's tendency to associate with same-gender peers and to avoid other-gender peers (p. 648)

gender social assignment or self-categorization as female or male (or possibly neither or a different category) (p. 635)

gender stability awareness that gender remains the same over time (p. 640)

gender-typed behaviors stereotyped or expected for a given person's gender (p. 635)

gender typing the process of gender socialization (p. 635)

generativity refers to the idea that through the use of the finite set of words and morphemes in humans' vocabulary, we can put together an infinite number of sentences and express an infinite number of ideas (p. 241)

genes sections of chromosomes that are the basic unit of heredity in all living things (p. 95)

genital stage the final stage in Freud's theory, beginning in adolescence, in which sexual maturation is complete and sexual intercourse is a major goal (p. 376)

genome each person's complete set of hereditary information (p. 12); the complete set of genes of any organism (p. 94)

genotype the genetic material an individual inherits (p. 95)

gesture–speech mismatches phenomenon in which hand movements and verbal statements convey different ideas (p. 363)

glial cells cells in the brain that provide a variety of critical supportive functions (p. 115)

goodness of fit the degree to which an individual's temperament is compatible with the demands and expectations of his or her social environment (p. 444)

guided participation a process in which more knowledgeable individuals organize activities in ways that allow less knowledgeable people to learn (p. 172)

habituation a simple form of learning that involves a decrease in response to repeated or continued stimulation (p. 56)

heritability a statistical estimate of the proportion of the measured variance on a trait among individuals in a given population that is attributable to genetic differences among those individuals (p. 109)

heritable refers to any characteristics or traits that are influenced by heredity (p. 107)

heterozygous having two different alleles for a trait (p. 101)

holophrastic period the period when children begin using the words in their small productive vocabulary one word at a time (p. 258)

homozygous having two of the same allele for a trait (p. 101)

hostile attributional bias in Dodge's theory, the tendency to assume that other people's ambiguous actions stem from a hostile intent (p. 387)

hypotheses testable predictions of the presence or absence of phenomena or relations (p. 25)

id in psychoanalytic theory, the earliest and most primitive personality structure. It is unconscious and operates with the goal of seeking pleasure (p. 375)

identical twins twins that result from the splitting in half of the zygote, resulting in each of the two resulting zygotes having exactly the same set of genes (p. 50)

identity a description of the self that is often externally imposed, such as through membership in a group (p. 495)

identity achievement an integration of various aspects of the self into a coherent whole that is stable over time and across events (p. 495)

identity diffusion period in which the individual does not have firm commitments regarding the issues in question and is not making progress toward developing them (p. 496)

identity foreclosure period in which the individual has not engaged in any identity experimentation and has established a vocational or ideological identity based on the choices or values of others (p. 496)

identity versus role confusion the psychosocial stage of development, described by Erikson, that occurs during adolescence. During this stage, the adolescent or young adult either develops an identity or experiences an incomplete and sometimes incoherent sense of self (p. 495)

imaginary audience the belief, stemming from adolescent egocentrism, that everyone else is focused on the adolescent's appearance and behavior (p. 488)

imprinting a form of learning in which the newborns of some species of birds and mammals become attached to and follow adult members of the species (usually their mother) (p. 393)

incremental/mastery orientation a general tendency to attribute success and failure to the amount of effort expended and to persist in the face of failure (p. 389)

incremental theory a theory that a person's intelligence can grow as a function of experience (p. 389)

independent variable the experience that participants in the experimental group receive and that those in the control group do not receive (p. 33)

infant-directed speech (IDS) the distinctive mode of speech that adults adopt when talking to babies and very young children (p. 247)

infant mortality death during the 1st year after birth (p. 79)

information-processing theories a class of theories that focus on the structure of the cognitive system and the mental activities used to deploy attention and memory to solve problems (p. 157)

ingroup assimilation process whereby individuals are socialized to conform to the group's norms, demonstrating the characteristics that define the ingroup (p. 643)

ingroup bias tendency to evaluate individuals and characteristics of the ingroup as superior to those of the outgroup (p. 643)

insecure attachment a pattern of attachment in which infants or young children have a less positive attachment to their caregiver than do securely attached children. Insecurely attached children can be classified as insecure/resistant (ambivalent), insecure/avoidant, or disorganized/disoriented (p. 472)

insecure/avoidant attachment a type of insecure attachment in which infants or young children seem somewhat indifferent toward their caregiver and may even avoid the caregiver. In the Strange Situation, they seem indifferent toward their caregiver before the caregiver leaves the room and indifferent or avoidant when the caregiver returns. If the infant gets upset when left alone, he or she is as easily comforted by a stranger as by a parent (p. 472)

insecure/resistant (or ambivalent) attachment a type of insecure attachment in which infants or young children are clingy and stay close to their caregiver rather than exploring their environment. In the Strange Situation, insecure/resistant infants tend to become very upset when the caregiver leaves them alone in the room. When their caregiver returns, they are not easily comforted and both seek comfort and resist efforts by the caregiver to comfort them (p. 472)

instrumental aggression aggression motivated by the desire to obtain a concrete goal (p. 615)

instrumental (or operant) conditioning learning the relation between one's own behavior and the consequences that result from it (p. 222)

interest filter initial evaluation of information as being personally interesting (p. 642)

intermittent reinforcement inconsistent response to the behavior of another person—for example, sometimes punishing an unacceptable behavior and sometimes ignoring it (p. 382)

intermodal perception the combining of information from two or more sensory systems (p. 206)

internalization effective discipline that leads to a permanent change in the child's behavior because the child has learned and accepted the desired behavior (p. 523)

internalization the process of adopting as one's own the attributes, beliefs, and standards of another person (p. 376)

internal validity the degree to which effects observed within experiments can be attributed to the factor that the researcher is testing (p. 26)

internal working model of attachment the child's mental representation of the self, of attachment figure(s), and of relationships in general that is constructed as a result of experiences with caregivers. The working model guides children's interactions with caregivers and other people in infancy and at older ages (p. 470)

interrater reliability the amount of agreement in the observations of different raters who witness the same behavior (p. 26)

intersectionality the interconnection of social identities such as gender, race, ethnicity, sexual orientation, and class, especially in relation to overlapping experiences of discrimination (p. 644)

intersubjectivity the mutual understanding that people share during communication (p. 175)

IQ (intelligence quotient) quantitative measure, typically with a mean of 100 and a standard deviation of 15, used to indicate a child's intelligence relative to that of other children of the same age (p. 332)

joint attention a process in which social partners intentionally focus on a common referent in the external environment (p. 175)

latency period the fourth stage in Freud's theory, lasting from age 6 to age 12, in which sexual energy gets channeled into socially acceptable activities (p. 376)

lobes major areas of the cortex associated with general categories of behavior (p. 115)

longitudinal design a method of study in which the same participants are studied twice or more over a substantial length of time (p. 35)

long-term memory information retained on an enduring basis (p. 160)

low birth weight (LBW) a birth weight of less than 5½ pounds (2500 grams) (p. 80)

macrosystem in the bioecological model, the larger cultural and social context within which the other systems are embedded (p. 398)

mathematical equality concept that the values on each side of the equal sign must be equivalent (p. 362)

meiosis cell division that produces gametes (p. 46)

menarche onset of menstruation (p. 658)

mental disorder a state of having problems with emotional reactions to the environment and with social relationships in ways that affect daily life (p. 454)

mental health children's sense of well-being both internally, such as in their emotions and stress levels, as well as externally, such as in their relationships with family members and peers (p. 452)

mental model cognitive processes used to represent a situation or sequence of events (p. 354)

mesosystem in the bioecological model, the interconnections among immediate, or microsystem, settings (p. 398)

meta-analysis a method for combining the results from independent studies to reach conclusions based on all of them (p. 5)

meta-analysis statistical method used to summarize average effect size and statistical significance across several research studies (p. 655)

methylation A biochemical process that influences behavior by suppressing gene activity and expression (p. 13)

microgenetic design a method of study in which the same participants are studied repeatedly over a short period (p. 35)

microsystem in the bioecological model, the immediate environment that an individual child personally experiences and participates in (p. 398)

mitosis cell division that results in two identical daughter cells (p. 47)

modularity hypothesis the idea that the human brain contains an innate, self-contained language module that is separate from other aspects of cognitive functioning (p. 275)

monocular depth (or pictorial) cues the perceptual cues of depth (such as relative size and interposition) that can be perceived by one eye alone (p. 200)

moral judgments decisions that pertain to issues of right and wrong, fairness, and justice (p. 602)

moratorium period in which the individual is exploring various occupational and ideological choices and has not yet made a clear commitment to them (p. 495)

morphemes the smallest units of meaning in a language, composed of one or more phonemes (p. 241)

multifactorial refers to traits that are affected by a host of environmental factors as well as genetic ones (p. 107)

multifinality the concept that certain risk factors do not always lead to a mental disorder (p. 454)

multiple intelligences theory Gardner's theory of intellect, based on the view that people possess at least eight types of intelligence (p. 349)

mutation a change in a section of DNA (p. 97)

myelination the formation of myelin (a fatty sheath) around the axons of neurons that speeds and increases information-processing abilities (p. 117)

myelin sheath a fatty sheath that forms around certain axons in the body and increases the speed and efficiency of information transmission (p. 115)

naïve psychology a commonsense level of understanding of other people and oneself (p. 293)

narratives descriptions of past events that have the basic structure of a story (p. 271)

nativism the theory that infants have substantial innate knowledge of evolutionary important domains (p. 169)

naturalistic observation examination of ongoing behavior in an environment not controlled by the researcher (p. 28)

nature our biological endowment; the genes we receive from our parents (p. 11)

neglected (peer status) a category of sociometric status that refers to children or adolescents who are infrequently mentioned as either liked or disliked; they simply are not noticed much by peers (p. 578)

neural tube a groove formed in the top layer of differentiated cells in the embryo that eventually becomes the brain and spinal cord (p. 50)

neurogenesis the proliferation of neurons through cell division (p. 117)

neurons cells that are specialized for sending and receiving messages between the brain and all parts of the body, as well as within the brain itself (p. 114)

neurotransmitters chemicals involved in communication among brain cells (p. 17)

newborn screening tests used to screen newborn infants for a range of genetic and non-genetic disorders (p. 105)

non-REM sleep a quiet or deep sleep state characterized by the absence of motor activity or eye movements and more regular, slow brain waves, breathing, and heart rate (p. 74)

normal distribution pattern of data in which scores fall symmetrically around a mean value, with most scores falling close to the mean and fewer and fewer scores farther from it (p. 332)

norm of reaction all the phenotypes that can theoretically result from a given genotype in relation to all the environments in which it can survive and develop (p. 102)

numerical equality the realization that all sets of *N* objects have something in common (p. 316)

numerical magnitude representations mental models of the sizes of numbers, ordered along a less-to-more dimension (p. 361)

nurture the environments, both physical and social, that influence our development (p. 11)

object permanence the knowledge that objects continue to exist even when they are out of view (p. 148)

object segregation the identification of separate objects in a visual array (p. 195)

object substitution a form of pretense in which an object is used as something other than itself, for example, using a broom to represent a horse (p. 298)

observational learning learning through watching other people and the consequences others experience as a result of their actions (p. 644)

occipital lobe the lobe of the cortex that is primarily involved in processing visual information (p. 115)

Oedipus complex Freud's term for the conflict experienced by boys in the phallic period because of their sexual desire for their mother and their fear of retaliation by their father (p. 376)

opportunity structure the economic and social resources offered by the macrosystem in the bioecological model, and people's understanding of those resources (p. 647)

oppositional defiant disorder (ODD) a disorder characterized by age-inappropriate and persistent displays of angry, defiant, and irritable behaviors (p. 618)

optical expansion a depth cue in which an object occludes increasingly more of the background, indicating that the object is approaching (p. 199)

oral stage the first stage in Freud's theory, occurring in the 1st year, in which the primary source of satisfaction and pleasure is oral activity (p. 375)

organizing influences potential result of certain sex-linked hormones affecting brain differentiation and organization during prenatal development or at puberty (p. 638)

overextension the use of a given word in a broader context than is appropriate (p. 258)

overlapping waves theory an information-processing approach that emphasizes the variability of children's thinking (p. 164)

overregularization speech errors in which children treat irregular forms of words as if they were regular (p. 269)

parental-investment theory a theory that stresses the evolutionary basis of many aspects of parental behavior, including the extensive investment parents make in their offspring (p. 395)

parental sensitivity caregiving behavior that involves the expression of warmth and contingent responsiveness to children, such as when they require assistance or are in distress (p. 476)

parenting style parenting behaviors and attitudes that set the emotional climate in regard to parent–child interactions, such as parental responsiveness and demandingness (p. 524)

parietal lobe governs spatial processing as well as integrating sensory input with information stored in memory (p. 115)

peers people of approximately the same age and status who are unrelated to one another (p. 550)

perception the process of organizing and interpreting sensory information (p. 191)

perceptual categorization the grouping together of objects that have similar appearances (p. 291)

perceptual constancy the perception of objects as being of constant size, shape, color, etc., in spite of physical differences in the retinal image of the object (p. 194)

perceptual narrowing developmental changes in which experience fine-tunes the perceptual system (p. 204)

permissive parenting a parenting style that is high in responsiveness but low in demandingness. Permissive parents are responsive to their children's needs and do not require their children to regulate themselves or act in appropriate or mature ways (p. 526)

personal fable a form of adolescent egocentrism that involves beliefs in the uniqueness of one's own feelings and thoughts (p. 487)

personal judgments decisions that refer to actions in which individual preferences are the main consideration (p. 602)

phallic stage the third stage in Freud's theory, lasting from age 3 to age 6, in which sexual pleasure is focused on the genitalia (p. 376)

phenotype the observable expression of the genotype, including both body characteristics and behavior (p. 95)

phenylketonuria (PKU) a disorder related to a defective recessive gene on chromosome 12 that prevents metabolism of the amino acid phenylalanine (p. 103)

phonemes the elementary units of meaningful sound used to produce languages (p. 241)

phonemic awareness ability to identify component sounds within words (p. 351)

phonological development the acquisition of knowledge about the sound system of a language (p. 241)

phonological recoding skills ability to translate letters into sounds and to blend sounds into words; informally called *sounding out* (p. 351)

phylogenetic continuity the idea that because of our common evolutionary history, humans share many characteristics, behaviors, and developmental processes with other animals, especially mammals (p. 57)

physical bullying physically hurting or threatening to hurt someone (p. 569)

Piaget's theory the theory of Swiss psychologist Jean Piaget, which posits that cognitive development involves a sequence of four stages— the sensorimotor, preoperational, concrete operational, and formal operational stages—that are constructed through the processes of assimilation, accommodation, and equilibration (p. 144)

placenta a support organ for the fetus; it keeps the circulatory systems of the fetus and mother separate, but as a semipermeable membrane permits the exchange of some materials between them (oxygen and nutrients from mother to fetus and carbon dioxide and waste products from fetus to mother) (p. 50)

plasticity the capacity of the brain to be affected by experience (p. 122)

polygenic inheritance inheritance in which traits are governed by more than one gene (p. 101)

popular (peer status) a category of sociometric status that refers to children or adolescents who are viewed positively (liked) by many peers and are viewed negatively (disliked) by few peers (p. 574)

positive reinforcement a reward that reliably follows a behavior and increases the likelihood that the behavior will be repeated (p. 222)

positive youth development an approach to youth intervention that focuses on developing and nurturing strengths and assets rather than on correcting weaknesses and deficits (p. 627)

pragmatic cues aspects of the social context used for word learning (p. 264)

pragmatic development the acquisition of knowledge about how language is used (p. 242)

preferential-looking technique a method for studying visual attention in infants that involves showing infants two patterns or two objects at a time to see if the infants have a preference for one over the other (p. 192)

premature any child born at 37 weeks after conception or earlier (as opposed to the normal term of 38 weeks) (p. 80)

prenatal testing genetic testing used to assess the fetus's risk for genetic disorders (p. 105)

preoperational stage the period (2 to 7 years) within Piaget's theory in which children become able to represent their experiences in language, mental imagery, and symbolic thought (p. 147)

pre-reaching movements clumsy swiping movements by young infants toward the general vicinity of objects they see (p. 213)

pretend play make-believe activities in which children create new symbolic relations, acting as if they were in a situation different from their actual one (p. 298)

primary mental abilities seven abilities proposed by Thurstone as crucial to intelligence (p. 328)

primary prevention a program targeting all individuals in a particular setting (e.g., a school) in order to prevent the occurrence of a problematic behavior or condition (p. 614)

private speech the second phase of Vygotsky's internalization-of-thought process, in which children develop self-regulation and problem-solving abilities by telling themselves aloud what to do, much as their parents did in the first stage (p. 174)

proactive aggression unemotional aggression aimed at fulfilling a need or desire (p. 620)

problem solving the process of attaining a goal by using a strategy to overcome an obstacle (p. 159)

production with regard to language, speaking (or writing or signing) to others (p. 241)

prosocial behavior voluntary behavior intended to benefit another, such as helping, sharing with, and comforting others (p. 599)

prosody the characteristic rhythm, tempo, cadence, melody, intonational patterns, and so forth with which a language is spoken (p. 249)

psychic energy Freud's term for the collection of biologically based instinctual drives that he believed fuel behavior, thoughts, and feelings (p. 375)

puberty developmental period marked by the ability to reproduce and other dramatic bodily changes (p. 657)

punishment a negative stimulus that follows a behavior to reduce the likelihood that the behavior will occur again (p. 524)

questionnaire a method, similar to the structured interview, that allows researchers to gather information from a large number of participants simultaneously by presenting them with a uniform set of questions (p. 28)

random assignment a procedure in which each participant has an equal chance of being assigned to each group within an experiment (p. 32)

rapid eye movement (REM) sleep an active sleep state characterized by quick, jerky eye movements under closed lids and associated with dreaming in adults (p. 74)

rational learning the ability to use prior experiences to predict what will occur in the future (p. 225)

reactive aggression emotionally driven, antagonistic aggression sparked by one's perception that other people's motives are hostile (p. 620)

recessive allele the allele that is not expressed if a dominant allele is present (p. 101)

reciprocal determinism Bandura's concept that child–environment influences operate in both directions; children are affected by aspects of their environment, but they also influence the environment (p. 383)

reference in language and speech, the associating of words and meaning (p. 256)

reflexes innate, fixed patterns of action that occur in response to particular stimulation (p. 208)

regulator genes genes that control the activity of other genes (p. 100)

rehearsal the process of repeating information multiple times to aid memory of it (p. 163)

rejected (peer status) a category of sociometric status that refers to children or adolescents who are liked by few peers and disliked by many peers (p. 575)

relational aggression a kind of aggression that involves excluding others from the social group and attempting to do harm to other people's relationships; it includes spreading rumors about peers, withholding friendship to inflict harm, and ignoring peers when angry or frustrated or trying to get one's own way (p. 575)

reliability the degree to which independent measurements of a given behavior are consistent (p. 26)

role taking being aware of the perspective of another person, thereby better understanding that person's behavior, thoughts, and feelings (p. 386)

rumination the act of focusing on one's own negative emotions and negative self-appraisals and on their causes and consequences, without engaging in efforts to improve one's situation (p. 454)

scale error the attempt by a young child to perform an action on a miniature object that is impossible due to the large discrepancy in the relative sizes of the child and the object (p. 218)

scientific method an approach to testing beliefs that involves choosing a question, formulating a hypothesis, testing the hypothesis, and drawing a conclusion (p. 25)

script typical sequence of actions used to organize and interpret repeated events, such as eating at restaurants, going to doctors' appointments, and writing reports (p. 358)

secondary prevention a program designed to help individuals at risk for developing a problem or condition, with the goal of preventing the problem or condition (p. 615)

secular trends marked changes in physical development that have occurred over generations (p. 128)

secure attachment a pattern of attachment in which infants or young children have a positive and trusting relationship with their attachment figure. In the Strange Situation, a securely attached infant, for example, may be upset when the caregiver leaves but may be happy to see the caregiver return, recovering quickly from any distress. When children are securely attached, they can use caregivers as a secure base for exploration (p. 471)

secure base refers to the idea that the presence of a trusted caregiver provides an infant or toddler with a sense of security that makes it possible for the child to explore the environment (p. 469)

selective attention the process of intentionally focusing on the information that is most relevant to the current goal (p. 163)

self-comforting behaviors repetitive actions that regulate arousal by providing a mildly positive physical sensation (p. 436)

self-concept a conceptual system made up of one's thoughts and attitudes about oneself (p. 481)

self-conscious emotions emotions such as guilt, shame, embarrassment, and pride that relate to our sense of self and our consciousness of others' reactions to us (p. 426)

self-discipline ability to inhibit actions, follow rules, and avoid impulsive reactions (p. 335)

self-distraction looking away from an upsetting stimulus in order to regulate one's level of arousal (p. 436)

self-esteem an individual's overall subjective evaluation of his or her worth and the feelings he or she has about that evaluation (p. 489)

self-locomotion the ability to move oneself around in the environment (p. 215)

self-socialization active process during development whereby children's cognitions lead them to perceive the world and to act in accord with their expectations and beliefs (p. 640)

self-socialization the idea that children play a very active role in their own socialization through their activity preferences, friendship choices, and so on (p. 385)

semantic development the learning of the system for expressing meaning in a language, including word learning (p. 241)

sensation the processing of basic information from the external world by the sensory receptors in the sense organs (eyes, ears, skin, etc.) and brain (p. 191)

sensitive period the period of time during which a developing organism is most sensitive to the effects of external factors; prenatally, the sensitive period is when the fetus is maximally sensitive to the harmful effects of teratogens (p. 60)

sensorimotor stage the period (birth to 2 years) within Piaget's theory in which intelligence is expressed through sensory and motor abilities (p. 147)

separation anxiety feelings of distress that children, especially infants and toddlers, experience when they are separated, or expect to be separated, from individuals to whom they are emotionally attached (p. 424)

service learning a strategy for promoting positive youth development that integrates school-based instruction with community involvement in order to promote civic responsibility and enhance learning (p. 627)

sex distinction between genetic females (XX) and genetic males (XY) (p. 635)

sex chromosomes the chromosomes (X and Y) that determine an individual's gender (p. 96)

sexual identity one's sense of oneself as a sexual being (p. 500)

sexual-minority youth young people who experience same-sex attractions (p. 500)

sexual orientation a person's preference in regard to males or females as objects of erotic feelings (p. 500)

small for gestational age babies who weigh substantially less than is normal for whatever their gestational age (p. 80)

social bullying purposely excluding someone from conversations or activities, spreading rumors, or withholding friendship (p. 569)

social comparison the process of comparing aspects of one's own psychological, behavioral, or physical functioning to that of others in order to evaluate oneself (p. 485)

social competence the ability to achieve personal goals in social interactions while simultaneously maintaining positive relationships with others (p. 437)

social-conventional judgments decisions that pertain to customs or regulations intended to secure social coordination and social organization (p. 602)

socialization the process through which children acquire the values, standards, skills, knowledge, and behaviors that are regarded as appropriate for their present and future roles in their particular culture (p. 523)

social referencing the use of a parent's or other adult's facial expression or vocal cues to decide how to deal with novel, ambiguous, or possibly threatening situations (p. 429)

social scaffolding a process in which more competent people provide a temporary framework that supports children's thinking at a higher level than children could manage on their own (p. 176)

social smiles smiles that are directed at people; they first emerge as early as 6 to 7 weeks of age (p. 423)

sociocultural context the physical, social, cultural, economic, and historical circumstances that make up any child's environment (p. 19)

sociocultural theories approaches that emphasize that other people and the surrounding culture contribute greatly to children's development (p. 172)

sociodramatic play activities in which children enact miniature dramas with other children or adults, such as "mother comforting baby" (p. 298)

socioeconomic status (SES) a measure of social class based on income and education (p. 21)

sociometric status a measurement that reflects the degree to which children are liked or disliked by their peers as a group (p. 573)

spermarche onset of capacity for ejaculation (p. 658)

spines formations on the dendrites of neurons that increase the dendrites' capacity to form connections with other neurons (p. 117)

stage theories approaches proposing that development involves a series of large, discontinuous, age-related phases (p. 15)

standard deviation (SD) measure of the variability of scores in a distribution; in a normal distribution, 68% of scores fall within 1 SD of the mean, and 95% of scores fall within 2 SDs of the mean (p. 332)

state level of arousal and engagement in the environment, ranging from deep sleep to intense activity (p. 74)

stepping reflex a neonatal reflex in which an infant lifts first one leg and then the other in a coordinated pattern like walking (p. 213)

stereopsis the process by which the visual cortex combines the differing neural signals caused by binocular disparity, resulting in the perception of depth (p. 199)

Strange Situation a procedure developed by Mary Ainsworth to assess infants' attachment to their primary caregiver (p. 471)

strategy–choice process procedure for selecting among alternative ways to solve a problem (p. 353)

stress a physiological reaction to some change or threat in the environment (p. 452)

structured interview a research procedure in which all participants are asked to answer the same questions (p. 27)

structured observation a method that involves presenting an identical situation to each participant and recording the participant's behavior (p. 29)

subordinate level the most specific level within a category hierarchy, such as "poodle" in the animal/dog/poodle example (p. 291)

sudden infant death syndrome (SIDS) the sudden, unexpected death of an infant less than 1 year of age that has no identifiable cause (p. 65)

superego in psychoanalytic theory, the third personality structure, consisting of internalized moral standards (p. 376)

superordinate level the general level within a category hierarchy, such as "animal" in the animal/dog/poodle example (p. 291)

swaddling a soothing technique, used in many cultures, that involves wrapping a baby tightly in cloths or a blanket (p. 78)

symbolic representation the use of one object to stand for another (p. 150)

symbols systems for representing our thoughts, feelings, and knowledge and for communicating them to other people (p. 240)

synapses microscopic junctions between the axon terminal of one neuron and the dendritic branches or cell body of another (p. 115)

synaptic pruning the normal developmental process through which synapses that are rarely activated are eliminated (p. 120)

synaptogenesis the process by which neurons form synapses with other neurons, resulting in trillions of connections (p. 119)

syntactic bootstrapping the strategy of using the grammatical structure of whole sentences to figure out meaning (p. 267)

syntactic development the learning of the syntax of a language (p. 242)

syntax rules in a language that specify how words from different categories (nouns, verbs, adjectives, and so on) can be combined (p. 242)

systematic desensitization a form of therapy based on classical conditioning, in which positive responses are gradually conditioned to stimuli that initially elicited a highly negative response. This approach is especially useful in the treatment of fears and phobias (p. 380)

task analysis the research technique of identifying goals, relevant information in the environment, and potential processing strategies for a problem (p. 158)

telegraphic speech the term describing children's first sentences that are generally two-word utterances (p. 268)

temperament individual differences in emotion, activity level, and attention that are exhibited across contexts and that are present from infancy and thus thought to be genetically based (p. 439)

temporal lobe the lobe of the cortex that is associated with memory, visual recognition, and the processing of emotion and auditory information (p. 115)

teratogen an external agent that can cause damage or death during prenatal development (p. 60)

tertiary intervention a program designed to help individuals who already exhibit a problem or condition (p. 615)

test–retest reliability the degree of similarity of a participant's performance on two or more occasions (p. 26)

theory of mind an organized understanding of how mental processes such as intentions, desires, beliefs, perceptions, and emotions influence behavior (p. 294)

theory of mind module (TOMM) a hypothesized brain mechanism devoted to understanding other human beings (p. 297)

theory of successful intelligence Sternberg's theory of intellect, based on the view that intelligence is the ability to achieve success in life (p. 350)

third-variable problem the concept that a correlation between two variables may stem from both being influenced by some third variable (p. 31)

three-stratum theory of intelligence Carroll's model that places *g* at the top of the intelligence hierarchy, eight moderately general abilities in the middle, and many specific processes at the bottom (p. 328)

toxic stress the experience of overwhelming levels of stress without support from adults to help mitigate the effects of that stress (p. 452)

transgender individuals who do not identify with the gender assigned at birth (or their biological sex) (p. 638)

tuition learning through direct teaching (p. 644)

umbilical cord a tube containing the blood vessels connecting the fetus and placenta (p. 51)

unconditioned response (UCR) in classical conditioning, a reflexive response that is elicited by the unconditioned stimulus (p. 221)

unconditioned stimulus (UCS) in classical conditioning, a stimulus that evokes a reflexive response (p. 221)

uninvolved parenting a parenting style that is low in both demandingness and responsiveness to their children; in other words, this style describes parents who are generally disengaged (p. 527)

Universal Grammar a proposed set of highly abstract, unconscious rules that are common to all languages (p. 274)

validity the degree to which a test measures what it is intended to measure (p. 26)

variables attributes that vary across individuals and situations, such as age, sex, and popularity (p. 30)

verbal bullying insulting, teasing, harassing, or intimidating someone (p. 569)

vicarious reinforcement observing someone else receive a reward or punishment (p. 384)

violation-of-expectancy a procedure used to study infant cognition in which infants are shown an event that should evoke surprise or interest if it violates something the infant knows or assumes to be true (p. 228)

visual acuity the sharpness of visual discrimination (p. 192)

visually based retrieval proceeding directly from the visual form of a word to its meaning (p. 353)

voice onset time (VOT) the length of time between when air passes through the lips and when the vocal cords start vibrating (p. 249)

Wechsler Intelligence Scale for Children (WISC) widely used test designed to measure the intelligence of children 6 years and older (p. 330)

withdrawn-rejected (peer status) a category of sociometric status that refers to rejected children who are socially withdrawn, wary, and often timid (p. 577)

word segmentation the process of discovering where words begin and end in fluent speech (p. 252)

working memory memory system that involves actively attending to, gathering, maintaining, storing, and processing information (p. 159)

zygote a fertilized egg cell (p. 46)

References

AAP Council on Communications and Media. (2016). Media and young minds. *Pediatrics, 138*(5), e20162591.

AAP Council on Communications and Media. (2016). Media use in school-aged children and adolescents. *Pediatrics,138*(5), e20162592.

AAP Task Force on Sudden Infant Death Syndrome. (2016). SIDS and other sleep-related infant deaths: Updated 2016 recommendations for a safe infant sleeping environment. *Pediatrics, 138*(5), e20162938.

Abela, J. R., Hankin, B. L., Sheshko, D. M., Fishman, M. B., & Stolow, D. (2012). Multi-wave prospective examination of the stress-reactivity extension of response styles theory of depression in high-risk children and early adolescents. *Journal of Abnormal Child Psychology, 40,* 277–287. doi:10.1007/s10802-011-9563-x

Abar, C. C., Jackson, K. M., & Wood, M. (2014). Reciprocal relations between perceived parental knowledge and adolescent substance use and delinquency: The moderating role of parent–teen relationship quality. *Developmental Psychology, 50,* 2176–2187. doi:10.1037/a0037463

Aboud, F. E., & Mendelson, M. J. (1996). Determinants of friendship selection and quality: Developmental perspectives. In W. M. Bukowski, A. F. Newcomb, & W. W. Hartup (Eds.), *The company they keep: Friendship in childhood and adolescence* (pp. 87–112). New York, NY: Cambridge University Press.

Abramovitch, R., Corter, C., & Lando, B. (1979). Sibling interaction in the home. *Child Development, 50,* 997–1003. doi:10.2307/1129325

Acredolo, C., & Schmid, J. (1981). The understanding of relative speeds, distances, and durations of movement. *Developmental Psychology, 17,* 490–493. doi:10.1037/0012-1649.17.4.490

Acredolo, L. P. (1978). Development of spatial orientation in infancy. *Developmental Psychology, 14,* 224–234.

Acredolo, L. P., & Goodwyn, S. W. (1990). Sign language in babies: The significance of symbolic gesturing for understanding language development. In R. Vasta (Ed.), *Annals of child development* (Vol. 7, pp. 1–42). London, England: Jessica Kingsley.

Adams, M. J., Treiman, R., & Pressley, M. (1998). Reading, writing, and literacy. In W. Damon (Series Ed.) & I. E. Sigel &

K. A. Renninger (Vol. Eds.), *Handbook of child psychology: Vol. 4. Child psychology in practice* (5th ed., pp. 275–355). Hoboken, NJ: Wiley.

Adams, R. E., Santo, J. B., & Bukowski, W. M. (2011). The presence of a best friend buffers the effects of negative experiences. *Developmental Psychology, 47,* 1786–1791. doi:10.1037/a0025401

Adamson, L. B., Bakeman, R., & Deckner, D. F. (2004). The development of symbol-infused joint engagement. *Child Development, 75,* 1171–1187. doi:10.1111/j.1467-8624.2004.00732.x

Addati, L., Cassirer, N., & Gilchrist, K. (2014). *Maternity and paternity at work: Law and practice across the world.* International Labour Office, Geneva. Retrieved from http://www.ilo.org/wcmsp5/groups/public/—dgreports/—dcomm/—publ/documents/publication/wcms_242615.pdf

Adema, W., Clarke, C., & Frey, V. (2015). *Paid parental leave: Lessons from OECD countries and selected U.S. states* (OECD Social, Employment and Migration Working Papers, No. 172). Paris, France: OECD Publishing. Retrieved from http://dx.doi.org/10.1787/5jrqgvqqb4vb-en

Adesope, O. O., Lavin T., Thompson, T., & Ungerleider C. (2010). A systematic review and meta-analysis of the cognitive correlates of bilingualism. *Review of Educational Research, 80*(2): 207–245. doi:10.3102/0034654310368803

Adler, S. A., Haith, M. M., Arehart, D. M., & Lanthier, E. C. (2008). Infants' visual expectations and the processing of time. *Journal of Cognition and Development, 9,* 1–25.

Adolph, K. E. (2000). Specificity of learning: Why infants fall over a veritable cliff. *Psychological Science, 11,* 290–295. doi:10.1111/1467-9280.00258

Adolph, K. E., & Berger, S. E. (2015). Physical and motor development. In M. H. Bornstein & M. E. Lamb (Eds.), *Developmental Science: An advanced textbook* (7th ed., pp. 261–333). New York: Psychology Press/Taylor & Francis.

Adolph, K. E., Cole, W. G., Komati, M., Garciaguirre, J. S., Badaly, D., Lingeman, J. M., . . . Sotsky, R. B. (2012). How do you learn to walk? Thousands of steps and dozens of falls per day. *Psychological Science, 23,* 1387–1394. doi:10.1177/0956797612446346

Adolph, K. E., Cole, W. G., & Vareijken, B. (2015). Intra-individual variability in the development of motor skills in childhood.

In M. Diehl, K. Hooker, & M. Sliwinski (Eds.), *Handbook of Intra-Individual Variability Across the Lifespan* (pp. 59–83). New York: Routledge/Taylor & Francis.

Adolph, K. E., Eppler, M. A., & Gibson, E. J. (1993). Crawling versus walking infants' perception of affordances for locomotion over sloping surfaces. *Child Development, 64,* 1158–1174. doi:10.1111/j.1467-8624.1993.tb04193.x

Adolph, K. E., Karasik, L. B., & Tamis-LeMonda, C. S. (2010). Motor skills. In M. H. Bornstein (Ed.), *Handbook of Cultural Developmental Science* (pp. 61–88). New York, NY: Taylor & Francis.

Adolph, K. E., & Robinson, S. R. (2013). The road to walking: What learning to walk tells us about development. In P. D. Zelazo (Ed.), *Oxford handbook of developmental psychology: Vol. 1. Body and mind* (pp. 403–446). New York, NY: Oxford University Press.

Adolph, K. E., & Robinson, S. R. (2015). Motor development. In R. M. Lerner (Series Eds.) & L. Liben & U. Muller (Vol. Eds.), *Handbook of child psychology and developmental science: Vol. 2: Cognitive processes* (7th ed., pp. 114–157). Hoboken, NJ: Wiley. doi:10.1002/9781118963418.childpsy204

Adolph, K. E., Vereijken, B., & Denny, M. A. (1998). Learning to crawl. *Child Development, 69,* 1299–1312.

Adolph, K. E., Vereijken, B., & Shrout, P. E. (2003). What changes in infant walking and why. *Child Development, 74,* 475–497.

Afifi, T. D., Afifi, W. A., & Coho, A. (2009). Adolescents' physiological reactions to their parents' negative disclosures about the other parent in divorced and nondivorced families. *Journal of Divorce and Remarriage, 50,* 517–540. doi:10.1080/10502550902970496

Afifi, T. D., Afifi, W. A., Morse, C. R., & Hamrick, K. (2008). Adolescents' avoidance tendencies and physiological reactions to discussions about their parents' relationship: Implications for postdivorce and nondivorced families. *Communication Monographs, 75,* 290–317. doi:10.1080/03637750802342308

Afifi, T. D., & McManus, T. (2010). Divorce disclosures and adolescents' physical and mental health and parental relationship quality. *Journal of Divorce and Remarriage, 51,* 83–107. doi:10.1080/10502550903455141

Afifi, T. D., McManus, T., Hutchinson, S., & Baker, B. (2007). Inappropriate parental divorce disclosures, the factors that prompt them, and their impact on parents' and adolescents' well-being. *Communication Monographs, 74*, 78–102. doi:10.1080/03637750701196870

Agrillo, C., Piffer, L., & Bisazza, A. (2011). Number versus continuous quantity in numerosity judgments by fish. *Cognition, 119*(2), 281–287. doi:10.1016/j.cognition.2010.10.022

Aguilar, B., Sroufe, L. A., Egeland, B., & Carlson, E. (2000). Distinguishing the early-onset/persistent and adolescence-onset antisocial behavior types: From birth to 16 years. *Development and Psychopathology, 12*, 109–132.

Agyei, S. B., van der Weel, F. R., & van der Meer, A. L. (2016). Development of visual motion perception for prospective control: Brain and behavioral studies in infants. *Frontiers in Psychology, 7*(100). doi:10.3389/fpsyg.2016.00100

Ainsworth, M. D. (1967). *Infancy in Uganda: Infant care and the growth of love.* Baltimore, MD: Johns Hopkins Press.

Ainsworth, M. D. S. (1973). The development of infant-mother attachment. In B. M. Caldwell & H. N. Ricciuti (Eds.), *Review of child development research* (Vol. 3, pp. 1–94). Chicago, IL: University of Chicago Press.

Ainsworth, M. D. S., Blehar, M. C., Waters, E., & Wall, S. (1978). *Patterns of attachment: A psychological study of the strange situation.* Hillsdale, NJ: Erlbaum.

Akhtar, N., & Gernsbacher, M. A. (2008). On privileging the role of gaze in infant social cognition. *Child Development Perspectives, 2*, 59–65. doi:10.1111/j.1750-8606.2008.00044.x

Aksan, N., & Kochanska, G. (2005). Conscience in childhood: Old questions, new answers. *Developmental Psychology, 41*, 506–516. doi:10.1037/0012-1649.41.3.506

Aksan, N., Kochanska, G., & Ortmann, M. R. (2006). Mutually responsive orientation between parents and their young children: Toward methodological advances in the science of relationships. *Developmental Psychology, 42*, 833–848. doi:10.1037/0012-1649.42.5.833

Albareda-Castellot, B., Pons, F., & Sebastián-Gallés, N. (2011). The acquisition of phonetic categories in bilingual infants: New data from an anticipatory eye movement paradigm. *Developmental Science, 14*, 395–401.

Albert, D., & Steinberg, L. (2011). Age differences in strategic planning as indexed by the Tower of London. *Child Development, 82*, 1501–1517.

Alexander, G. M. (2003). An evolutionary perspective of sex-typed toy preferences: Pink, blue, and the brain. *Archives of Sexual Behavior, 32*, 7–14. doi:10.1023/A:1021833110722

Alexander, K. L., Entwisle, D. R., & Olson, L. S. (2007). Lasting consequences of the summer learning gap. *American Sociological Review, 72,* 167–180.

Ali, J. B., Spence, C., & Bremner, A. J. (2015). Human infants' ability to perceive touch in external space develops postnatally. *Current Biology, 25*(20), R978–R979.

Alink, L. R. A., Cicchetti, D., Kim, J., & Rogosch, F. A. (2012). Longitudinal associations among child maltreatment, social functioning, and cortisol regulation. *Developmental Psychology, 48*, 224–236. doi:10.1037/a0024892

Alink, L. R. A., Mesman, J., Van Zeijl, J., Stolk, M. N., Juffer, F., Koot, H. M., . . . van IJzendoorn, M. H. (2006). The early childhood aggression curve: Development of physical aggression in 10- to 50-month-old children. *Child Development, 77*, 954–966. doi:10.1111/j.1467-8624.2006.00912.x

Allen, J. P., Chango, J., Szwedo, D., Schad, M., & Marston, E. (2012). Predictors of susceptibility to peer influence regarding substance use in adolescence. *Child Development, 83*, 337–350. doi:10.1111/j.1467-8624.2011.01682.x

Allen, J. P., McElhaney, K. B., Land, D. J., Kuperminc, G. P., Moore, C. M., O'Beirne-Kelley, H., & Kilmer, S. L.. (2003). A secure base in adolescence: Markers of attachment security in the mother–adolescent relationship. *Child Development, 74*, 292–307.

Allen, J. P., Porter, M. R., & McFarland, F. C. (2006). Leaders and followers in adolescent close friendships: Susceptibility to peer influence as a predictor of risky behavior, friendship instability, and depression. *Development and Psychopathology, 18*, 155–172. doi:10.1017/S0954579406060093

Allen, J. P., Porter, M. R., McFarland, F. C., Marsh, P., & McElhaney, K. B. (2005). The two faces of adolescents' success with peers: Adolescent popularity, social adaptation, and deviant behavior. *Child Development, 76*, 747–760. doi:10.1111/j.1467-8624.2005.00875.x

Allen, J. P., Porter, M., McFarland, F. C., McElhaney, K. B., & Marsh, P. (2007). The relation of attachment security to adolescents' paternal and peer relationships, depression, and externalizing behavior. *Child Development, 78*, 1222–1239. doi:10.1111/j.1467-8624.2007.01062.x

Alleyne, E., & Wood, J. L. (2010). Gang involvement: Psychological and behavioral characteristics of gang members, peripheral youth, and nongang youth. *Aggressive Behavior, 36,* 423–436. doi:10.1002/ab.20360

Alonso-Alberca, N., Vergara, A. I., Fernández-Berrocal, P., Johnson, S. R., & Izard, C. E. (2012). The adaptation and validation of the Emotion Matching Task for preschool children in Spain. *International Journal of Behavioral Development, 36*, 489–494.

Altenhofen, S., Sutherland, K., & Biringen, Z. (2010). Families experiencing divorce: Age at onset of overnight stays, conflict, and emotional availability as predictors of child attachment. *Journal of Divorce & Remarriage, 51*(3), 141–156. doi:10.1080/10502551003597782

Altermatt, E. R., & Pomerantz, E. M. (2003). The development of competence-related and motivational beliefs: An investigation of similarity and influence among friends. *Journal of Educational Psychology, 95*, 111–123. doi:10.1037/0022-0663.95.1.111

Altschul, I., Lee, S. J., & Gershoff, E. T. (2016). Hugs, not hits: Maternal warmth, not spanking, predicts positive child behaviors in the first five years of life. *Journal of Marriage and Family, 78*, 695–714. doi:10.1111/jomf.12306

Altshuler, J. L., Genevaro, J. L., Ruble, D. N., & Bornstein, M. H. (1995). Children's knowledge and use of coping strategies during hospitalization for elective surgery. *Journal of Applied Developmental Psychology, 16*, 53–76. doi:10.1016/0193-3973(95)90016-0

Alwin, D. F. (1984). Trends in parental socialization values: Detroit, 1958–1983. *American Journal of Sociology, 90*, 359–382.

Amano, S., Shrestha, B. P., Chaube, S. S., Higuchi, M., Manandhar, D. S., Osrin, D., . . . Saville, N. (2014). Effectiveness of female community health volunteers in the detection and management of low-birth-weight in Nepal. *Rural and remote health, 14*(1), 2508.

Amaral, D. G., Schumann, C. M., & Nordahl, C. W. (2008). Neuroanatomy of autism. *Trends in Neurosciences, 31*, 137–145. doi:10.1016/j.tins.2007.12.005

Amato, M. S., Moore, C. F., Magzamen, S., Imm, P., Havlena, J. A., Anderson, H. A., & Kanarek, M. S. (2012). Lead exposure and educational proficiency: Moderate lead exposure and educational proficiency on end-of-grade examinations. *Annals of Epidemiology, 22*(10), 738–743.

Amato, P. R. (2001). Children of divorce in the 1990s: An update of the Amato and Keith (1991) meta-analysis. *Journal of Family Psychology, 15,* 355–370. doi:10.1037/0893-3200.15.3.355

Amato, P. R. (2010). Research on divorce: Continuing trends and new developments. *Journal of Marriage and Family, 72*, 650–666. doi:10.1111/j.1741-3737.2010.00723.x

Amato, P. R., & Gilbreth, J. G. (1999). Nonresident fathers and children's well-being: A meta-analysis. *Journal of Marriage and the Family, 61*, 557–573.

Amato, P. R., & Keith, B. (1991). Parental divorce and the well-being of children: A meta-analysis. *Psychological Bulletin, 110*, 26–46.

Amato, P. R., Loomis, L. S., & Booth, A. (1995). Parental divorce, marital conflict, and offspring well-being during early adulthood. *Social Forces, 73*, 895–915. doi:10.1093/sf/73.3.895

American Academy of Child and Adolescent Psychiatry. (2012, July 30). *Policy statement on corporal punishment.* Retrieved from http://www.aacap.org/aacap/policy_statements/2012/

Policy_Statement_on_Corporal_Punishment.aspx

American Academy of Pediatrics. (2016). *Early brain and child development: Building brains, forging futures.* Retrieved May 26, 2016, from https://www.aap.org/en-us/advocacy-and-policy/aap-health-initiatives/EBCD/Pages/default.aspx

American Academy of Pediatrics, American Public Health Association, & National Resource Center for Health and Safety in Child Care and Early Education. (2011). *Caring for our children: National health and safety performance standards guidelines for early care and education programs* (3rd ed.). Elk Grove Village, IL: American Academy of Pediatrics.

American Academy of Pediatrics, Committee on Psychosocial Aspects of Child and Family Health. (1998). Guidance for effective discipline. *Pediatrics, 101*(2, Pt. 1), 723–728.

American Academy of Pediatrics, Council on Communications Media. (2009). Media violence [Policy statement]. *Pediatrics, 124,* 1495–1503. doi:10.1542/peds.2009-2146

American Association of University Women. (2011). *Crossing the line: Sexual harassment at school.* Washington, DC: Author.

American Professional Society on the Abuse of Children. (2016). *APSAC Position Statement on Corporal Punishment of Children.* Retrieved from http://www.apsac.org/

American Psychiatric Association. (1994). *Diagnostic and statistical manual of mental disorders* (4th ed.). Washington, DC: Author.

American Psychiatric Association. (2013). *Diagnostic and statistical manual of mental disorders* (5th ed.). Arlington, VA: American Psychiatric Publishing.

Anda, R. F., Felitti, V. J., Walker, J., Whitfield, C. L., Bremner, J. D., Perry, B. D., . . . Giles, W. H. (2006). The enduring effects of abuse and related adverse experiences in childhood: A convergence of evidence from neurobiology and epidemiology. *European Archives of Psychiatry and Clinical Neurosciences, 56,* 174–186. doi:10.1007/s00406-005-0624-4

Anderson, C. A., Berkowitz, L., Donnerstein, E., Huesmann, L. R., Johnson, J. D., Linz, D., . . . Wartella, E. (2003). The influence of media violence on youth. *Psychological Science in the Public Interest, 4,* 81–110. doi:10.1111/j.1529-1006.2003.pspi_1433.x

Anderson, C. A., & Bushman, B. J. (2001). Effects of violent video games on aggressive behavior, aggressive cognition, aggressive affect, physiological arousal, and prosocial behavior: A meta-analytic review of the scientific literature. *Psychological Science, 12,* 353–359. doi:10.1111/1467-9280.00366

Anderson, E. (1999). *Code of the street: Decency, violence, and the moral life of the inner city.* New York, NY: W. W. Norton.

Anderson, M. E., Johnson, D. C., & Batal, H. A. (2005). Sudden infant death syndrome and prenatal maternal smoking: Rising attributed risk in the Back to Sleep era. *BMC Medicine, 3,* 4. Retrieved from http://www.biomedcentral.com/1741-7015/3/4

Anderson, R. C., Wilson, P. T., & Fielding, L. G. (1988). Growth in reading and how children spend their time outside of school. *Reading Research Quarterly, 23,* 285–303.

Anderson, S. F., Salk, R. H., & Hyde, J. S. (2015). Stress in romantic relationships and adolescent depressive symptoms: Influence of parental support. *Journal of Family Psychology, 29,* 339–348. doi:10.1037/fam0000089

Anderson, V., Godfrey, C., Rosenfeld, J. V., & Catroppa, C. (2012). Predictors of cognitive function and recovery 10 years after traumatic brain injury in young children. *Pediatrics, 129,* e254–e261. Advance online publication. doi:10.1542/peds.2011-0311

Andre, T., Whigham, M., Hendrickson, A., & Chambers, S. (1999). Competency beliefs, positive affect, and gender stereotypes of elementary students and their parents about science versus other school subjects. *Journal of Research in Science Teaching, 36,* 719–747. doi:10.1002/(SICI)1098-2736(199908)36:6<719::AID-TEA8>3.0.CO;2-R

Angier, N. (1999). *Woman: An intimate geography.* Boston, MA: Houghton Mifflin.

Anglin, J. M. (1993). Vocabulary development: A morphological analysis. *Monographs of the Society for Research in Child Development, 58*(10, Serial No. 238).

Angulo-Barroso, R. M., Peciña, S., Lin, X., Li, M., Sturza, J., Shao, J., & Lozoff, B. (2016). Implicit learning and emotional responses in nine-month-old infants. *Cognition and Emotion,* doi:10.1080/02699931.2016.1179624.

Anim-Somuah, M., Smyth, R. M., & Jones, L. (2011). Epidural versus non-epidural or no analgesia in labour. *Cochrane Database Systematic Reviews, 12.* doi:10.1002/14651858.CD000331.pub3

Ansari, D. (2008). Effects of development and enculturation on number representation in the brain. *Nature Reviews Neuroscience, 9,* 278–291. doi:10.1038/nrn2334

Appelhans, B. M., Fitzpatrick, S. L., Li, H., Cail, V., Waring, M. E., Schneider, K. L., . . . Pagoto, S. L. (2014). The home environment and childhood obesity in low-income households: Indirect effects via sleep duration and screen time. *BMC Public Health, 14*(1160). doi:10.1186/1471-2458-14-1160

Aptekar, L., & Ciano-Federoff, L. M. (1999). Street children in Nairobi: Gender differences in mental health. In M. Raffaelli & R. W. Larson (Eds.), *New Directions for Child and Adolescent Development: No. 85. Homeless and working youth around the world: Exploring developmental issues* (Vol. 1999, pp. 35–46). San Francisco, CA: Jossey-Bass.

Aptekar, L., & Stoecklin, D. (2014) *Street children and homeless youth: A cross-cultural perspective.* doi:10.1007/978-94-007-7356-1_2.

Apthorp, H., Randel, B., Cherasaro, T., Clark, T., McKeown, M., & Beck, I. (2012). Effects of a supplemental vocabulary program on word knowledge and passage comprehension. *Journal of Research on Educational Effectiveness, 5*(2), 160–188. doi:10.1080/19345747.2012.660240

Archer, J. (1991). The influence of testosterone on human aggression. *British Journal of Psychology, 82,* 1–28. doi:10.1111/j.2044-8295.1991.tb02379.x

Archer, J. (2004). Sex differences in aggression in real-world settings: A meta-analytic review. *Review of General Psychology, 8,* 291–322. doi:10.1037/1089-2680.8.4.291

Archer, J. (2006). Testosterone and human aggression: An evaluation of the challenge hypothesis. *Neuroscience and Biobehavioral Reviews, 30,* 319–345. doi:10.1016/j.neubiorev.2004.12.007

Archer, J. (2013). Can evolutionary principles explain patterns of family violence? *Psychological Bulletin, 139*(2), 403–440.

Archer, J., & Coyne, S. M. (2005). An integrated review of indirect, relational, and social aggression. *Personality and Social Psychology Review, 9,* 212–230. doi:10.1207/s15327957pspr0903_2

Archer, J., Graham-Kevan, N., & Davies, M. (2005). Testosterone and aggression: A reanalysis of Book, Starzyk, and Quinsey's (2001) study. *Aggression and Violent Behavior, 10,* 241–261. doi:10.1016/j.avb.2004.01.001

Archer, J., & Lloyd, B. B. (2002). *Sex and gender* (2nd ed.). New York, NY: Cambridge University Press.

Ardizzi, M., Martini, F., Umiltà, M. A., Evangelista, V., Ravera, R., & Gallese, V. (2015). Impact of childhood maltreatment on the recognition of facial expressions of emotions. *PloS ONE, 10*(10), e0141732. doi:10.1371/journal.pone.0141732

Arduini, D., Rizzo, G., & Romanini, C. (1995). Fetal behavioral states and behavioral transitions in normal and compromised fetuses. In J.-P. Lecanuet, W. P. Fifer, N. A. Krasnegor, & W. P. Smotherman (Eds.), *Fetal development: A psychobiological perspective* (pp. 83–99). Hillsdale, NJ: Erlbaum.

Arim, R. G., Dahinten, V. S., Marshall, S. K., & Shapka, J. D. (2011). An examination of the reciprocal relations between adolescents' aggressive behaviors and their perceptions of parental nurturance. *Journal of Youth and Adolescence, 40,* 207–220.

Aristotle. (1954). *The Nicomachean ethics* (D. Ross, Trans.). London, England: Oxford University Press.

Arim, R. G., Dahinten, V. S., Marshall, S. K., & Shapka, J. D. (2011). An examination of the reciprocal relationships between adolescents' aggressive behaviors and their perceptions of parental nurturance. *Journal of Youth and Adolescence, 40,* 207–220. doi:10.1007/s10964-009-9493-x

Armenta, B. E., Knight, G. P., Carlo, G., & Jacobson, R. P. (2011). The relation between ethnic group attachment and prosocial tendencies: The mediating role of cultural values. *European Journal of Social Psychology, 41,* 107–115. doi:10.1002/ejsp.742

Armsden, G. C., & Greenberg, M. T. (1987). The inventory of parent and peer attachment: Relationships to well-being in adolescence. *Journal of Youth and Adolescence, 16,* 427–454. doi:10.1007/BF02202939

Arndorfer, C., & Stormshak, E. (2008). Same-sex versus other-sex best friendship in early adolescence: Longitudinal predictors of antisocial behavior throughout adolescence. *Journal of Youth and Adolescence, 37,* 1059–1070. doi:10.1007/s10964-008-9311-x

Arneson, J. J., Sackett, P. R., & Beatty, A. S. (2011). Ability-performance relationships in education and employment settings: Critical tests of the more-is-better and the good-enough hypotheses. *Psychological Science, 22,* 1336–1342. doi:10.1177/0956797611417004

Arnett, J. J. (1999). Adolescent storm and stress, reconsidered. *American Psychologist, 54,* 317–326.

Aronson, E. (2000). *Nobody left to hate: Teaching compassion after Columbine.* New York, NY: Freeman.

Arseneault, L., Moffitt, T. E., Caspi, A., Taylor, A., Rijsdijk, F. V., Jaffee, S. R., . . . Measelle, J. R. (2003). Strong genetic effects on cross-situational antisocial behaviour among 5-year-old children according to mothers, teachers, examiner-observers, and twins' self-reports. *Journal of Child Psychology and Psychiatry, 44,* 832–848. doi:10.1111/1469-7610.00168

Arsenio, W. F., Adams, E., & Gold, J. (2009). Social information processing, moral reasoning, and emotion attributions: Relations with adolescents' reactive and proactive aggression. *Child Development, 80,* 1739–1755. doi:10.1111/j.1467-8624.2009.01365.x

Arterberry, M. E., & Kellman, P. J. (2016). *Development of perception in infancy: The cradle of knowledge revisited.* Oxford, England: Oxford University Press.

Asbury, K., Dunn, J. F., Pike, A., & Plomin, R. (2003). Nonshared environmental influences on individual differences in early behavioral development: A monozygotic twin differences study. *Child Development, 74,* 933–943. doi:10.1111/1467-8624.00577

Asendorpf, J. B. (1990). Development of inhibition during childhood: Evidence for situational specificity and a two-factor model. *Developmental Psychology, 26,* 721–730. doi:10.1037/0012-1649.26.5.721

Asendorpf, J. B., Warkentin, V., & Baudonnière, P.-M. (1996). Self-awareness and other-awareness: II. Mirror self-recognition, social contingency awareness, and synchronic imitation. *Developmental Psychology, 32,* 313–321. doi:10.1037/0012-1649.32.2.313

Ashcraft, M. H., & Ridley, K. S. (2005). Math anxiety and its cognitive consequences. In J. I. D. Campbell (Ed.), *Handbook of mathematical cognition* (pp. 315–327). New York, NY: Psychology Press.

Asher, S. R., & Dodge, K. A. (1986). Identifying children who are rejected by their peers. *Developmental Psychology, 22,* 444–449. doi:10.1037/0012-1649.22.4.444

Asher, S. R., & Paquette, J. A. (2003). Loneliness and peer relations in childhood. *Current Directions in Psychological Science, 12,* 75–78. doi:10.1111/1467-8721.01233

Ashman, S. B., Dawson, G., Panagiotides, H., Yamada, E., & Wilkinson, C. W. (2002). Stress hormone levels of children of depressed mothers. *Development and Psychopathology, 14,* 333–349.

Aslin, R. N. (2012). Questioning the questions that have been asked about the infant brain using near-infrared spectroscopy. *Cognitive Neuropsychology, 29,* 7–33. doi:10.1080/02643294.2012.654773

Aslin, R. N., Saffran, J. R., & Newport, E. L. (1998). Computation of conditional probability statistics by 8-month-old infants. *Psychological Science, 9,* 321–324. doi:10.1111/1467-9280.00063

Association for Pet Obesity Prevention. (2013). 2012 National Pet Obesity Survey Results: Pet Obesity Rates Rise, Cats Heavier than Ever. Retrieved July 6, 2016, from http://petobesityprevention.org/2012-national-pet-obesity-survey-results/

Atladóttir, H. O., Thorsen, P., Østergaard, L., Schendel, D. E., Lemcke, S., Abdallah, M., & Parner, E. T. (2010). Maternal infection requiring hospitalization during pregnancy and autism spectrum disorders. *Journal of Autism and Developmental disorders, 40*(12), 1423–1430.

Atran, S. (1990). *Cognitive foundations of natural history: Towards an anthropology of science.* Cambridge, England: Cambridge University Press.

Atran, S. (2002). Modular and cultural factors in biological understanding: An experimental approach to the cognitive basis of science. In P. Carruthers, S. P. Stich, & M. Siegal (Eds.), *The cognitive basis of science* (pp. 41–72). New York, NY: Cambridge University Press.

Attili, G., Vermigli, P., & Schneider, B. H. (1997). Peer acceptance and friendship patterns among Italian schoolchildren within a cross-cultural perspective. *International Journal of Behavioral Development, 21,* 277–288. doi:10.1080/016502597384866

Auerbach, R. P., Bigda-Peyton, J. S., Eberhart, N. K., Webb, C. A., & Ho, M.-H. R. (2011). Conceptualizing the prospective relationship between social support, stress, and depressive symptoms among adolescents. *Journal of Abnormal Child Psychology, 39,* 475–487.

Austad, S. N. (2015). The human prenatal sex ratio: A major surprise. *Proceedings of the National Academy of Sciences, 112*(16), 4839–4840.

Avenevoli, S., Swendsen, J., He, J., Burstein, M., & Merikangas, K. R. (2015). Major depression in the National Comorbidity Survey—Adolescent Supplement: Prevalence, correlates, and treatment. *Journal of the American Academy of Child and Adolescent Psychiatry, 54,* 37–44.e2

Awong, T., Grusec, J. E., & Sorenson, A. (2008). Respect-based control and anger as determinants of children's socio-emotional development. *Social Development, 17,* 941–959. doi:10.1111/j.1467-9507.2008.00460.x

Ayduk, O., Mendoza-Denton, R., Mischel, W., Downey, G., Peake, P. K., & Rodriguez, M. (2000). Regulating the interpersonal self: Strategic self-regulation for coping with rejection sensitivity. *Journal of Personality and Social Psychology, 79,* 776–792.

Azmitia, M., & Montgomery, R. (1993). Friendship, transactive dialogues, and the development of scientific reasoning. *Social Development, 2,* 202–221. doi:10.1111/j.1467-9507.1993.tb00014.x

Bachman, H. J., Coley, R. L., & Carrano, J. (2011). Maternal relationship instability influences on children's emotional and behavioral functioning in low-income families. *Journal of Abnormal Child Psychology, 39,* 1149–1161. doi:10.1007/s10802-011-9535-1

Bachman, H. J., Coley, R. L., & Carrano, J. (2012). Low-income mothers' patterns of partnership instability and adolescents' socioemotional well-being. *Journal of Family Psychology, 26,* 263–273. doi:10.1037/a0027427

Backscheider, A. G., Shatz, M., & Gelman, S. A. (1993). Preschoolers' ability to distinguish living kinds as a function of regrowth. *Child Development, 64,* 1242–1257. doi:10.1111/j.1467-8624.1993.tb04198.x

Baden, A. L., Treweeke, L. M., & Ahluwalia, M. K. (2012). Reclaiming culture: Reculturation of transracial and international adoptees. *Journal of Counseling and Development, 90,* 387–399.

Bagwell, C. L., Newcomb, A. F., & Bukowski, W. M. (1998). Preadolescent friendship and peer rejection as predictors of adult adjustment. *Child Development, 69,* 140–153. doi:10.1111/j.1467-8624.1998.tb06139.x

Baham, M. E., Weimer, A. A., Braver, S. L., & Fabricius, W. V. (2008). Sibling relationships in blended families. In J. Pryor (Ed.), *The international handbook of stepfamilies: Policy and practice in legal, research, and clinical environments* (pp. 175–207). Hoboken, NJ: Wiley.

Bahrick, H. P., & Phelps, E. (1987). Retention of Spanish vocabulary over 8 years. *Journal of Experimental Psychology: Learning, Memory, and Cognition, 13*(2), 344. doi:10.1037/0278-7393.13.2.344

Bail, A., Morini, G., & Newman, R. S. (2015). Look at the gato! Code-switching in speech to toddlers. *Journal of Child Language, 42*(05), 1073–1101.

Bailey, D. H., Nguyen, T. Jenkins, J. M., Domina, T., Clements, D. H., & Sarama, J. S. (2016). Fadeout in an early mathematics intervention: Constraining content of preexisting differences? *Developmental Psychology, 52*(9), 1457–1469. doi:10.1037/dev0000188

Bailey, D. H., Zhou, X., Zhang, Y., Cui, J., Fuchs, L. S., Jordan, N. C., . . . Siegler, R. S. (2015). Development of fraction concepts and procedures in U.S. and Chinese children. *Journal of Experimental Child Psychology, 129*, 68–83. doi:10.1016/j.jecp.2014.08.006

Bailey, J. M., Bobrow, D., Wolfe, M., & Mikach, S. (1995). Sexual orientation of adult sons of gay fathers. *Developmental Psychology, 31*, 124–129. doi:10.1037/0012-1649.31.1.124

Baillargeon, R. (1987a). Object permanence in 3½- and 4½-month-old infants. *Developmental Psychology, 23*, 655–664.

Baillargeon, R. (1987b). Young infants' reasoning about the physical and spatial properties of a hidden object. *Cognitive Development, 2*, 179–200. doi:10.1016/S0885-2014(87)90043-8

Baillargeon, R. (1993). The object concept revisited: New directions in the investigation of infants' physical knowledge. In C. E. Granrud (Ed.), *Visual perception and cognition in infancy* (Vol. 23, pp. 265–315). Hillsdale, NJ: Erlbaum.

Baillargeon, R. (1998). Infants' understanding of the physical world. In M. Sabourin, F. Craik, & M. Robert (Eds.), *Advances in psychological science: Vol. 2. Biological and cognitive aspects* (pp. 503–529). Hove, England: Psychology Press.

Baillargeon, R. (2004). Infants' physical world. *Current Directions in Psychological Science, 13*(3), 89–94. doi:10.1111/j.0963-7214.2004.00281.x

Baillargeon, R. (2004). Infants' reasoning about hidden objects: Evidence for event-general and event-specific expectations. *Developmental Science, 7*, 391–414. doi:10.1111/j.1467-7687.2004.00357.x

Baillargeon, R., Li, J., Gertner, Y., & Wu, D. (2011). How do infants reason about physical events? *The Wiley-Blackwell handbook of childhood cognitive development* (2nd ed., pp. 11–48). Oxford, England: Wiley-Blackwell.

Baillargeon, R., Needham, A., & Devos, J. (1992). The development of young infants' intuitions about support. *Early Development and Parenting, 1*, 69–78. doi:10.1002/edp.2430010203

Baillargeon, R., Spelke, E. S., & Wasserman, S. (1985). Object permanence in five-month-old infants. *Cognition, 20*, 191–208. doi:10.1016/0010-0277(85)90008-3

Baillargeon, R., Stavans, M., Wu, D., Gertner, Y., Setoh, P., Kittredge, A. K., & Bernard, A. (2012). Object individuation and physical reasoning in infancy: An integrative account. *Language Learning and Development, 8*(1), 4–46.

Baines, E., & Blatchford, P. (2011). Children's games and playground activities in school and their role in development. In A. D. Pellegrini (Ed.) & P. E. Nathan (Series Ed.), *The Oxford Handbook of the Development of Play* (1st ed., pp. 260–283). New York, NY: Oxford University Press.

Baio, J. (2012). Prevalence of autism spectrum disorders: Autism and Developmental Disabilities Monitoring Network, 14 sites, United States, 2008. *Morbidity and Mortality Weekly Report Surveillance Summaries, 61*(3).

Baker, J. K., Fenning, R. M., & Crnic, K. A. (2011). Emotion socialization by mothers and fathers: Coherence among behaviors and associations with parent attitudes and children's social competence. *Social Development, 20*, 412–430. doi:10.1111/j.1467-9507.2010.00585.x

Baker, S. T., Friedman, O., & Leslie, A. M. (2010). The opposites task: Using general rules to test cognitive flexibility in preschoolers. *Journal of Cognition and Development, 11*, 240–254. doi:10.1080/15248371003699944

Baker, S. T., Lubman, D. I., Yücel, M., Allen, N. B., Whittle, S., Fulcher, B. D., . . . Fornito, A. (2015). Developmental changes in brain network hub connectivity in late adolescence. *The Journal of Neuroscience, 35*(24), 9078–9087. doi:10.1523/JNEUROSCI.5043-14.2015

Bakermans-Kranenburg, M. J., Dobrova-Krol, N., & van IJzendoorn, M. (2012). Impact of institutional care on attachment disorganization and insecurity of Ukrainian preschoolers: Protective effect of the long variant of the serotonin transporter gene (5HTT). *International Journal of Behavioral Development, 36*, 11–18. doi:10.1177/0165025411406858

Bakermans-Kranenburg, M. J., & van IJzendoorn, M. H. (2006). Gene-environment interaction of the dopamine D4 receptor (DRD4) and observed maternal insensitivity predicting externalizing behavior in preschoolers. *Developmental Psychobiology, 48*, 406–409. doi:10.1002/dev.20152

Bakermans-Kranenburg, M. J., & van IJzendoorn, M. H. (2007). Research review: Genetic vulnerability or differential susceptibility in child development: The case of attachment. *Journal of Child Psychology and Psychiatry, 48*, 1160–1173. doi:10.1111/j.1469-7610.2007.01801.x

Bakermans-Kranenburg, M. J., & van IJzendoorn, M. H. (2011). Differential susceptibility to rearing environment depending on dopamine-related genes: New evidence and a meta-analysis. *Development and Psychopathology, 23*, 39–52. doi:10.1017/S0954579410000635

Bakermans-Kranenburg, M. J., van IJzendoorn, M. H., & Juffer, F. (2003). Less is more: Meta-analyses of sensitivity and attachment interventions in early childhood. *Psychological Bulletin, 129*, 195–215. doi:10.1037/0033-2909.129.2.195

Baldwin, D. A. (1991). Infants' contribution to the achievement of joint reference. *Child Development, 62*, 874–890. doi:10.1111/j.1467-8624.1991.tb01577.x

Baldwin, D. A. (1993). Early referential understanding: Infants' ability to recognize referential acts for what they are. *Developmental Psychology, 29*, 832–843. doi:10.1037/0012-1649.29.5.832

Balsam, K. E., Molina, Y., Blayney, J. A., Dillworth, T., Zimmerman, L., & Kaysen, D. (2015). Racial/ethnic differences in identity and mental health outcomes among young sexual minority women. *Cultural Diversity and Ethnic Minority Psychology, 21*, 380–390. doi:10.1037/a0038680

Bámaca, M. Y., Umaña-Taylor, A. J., Shin, N., & Alfaro, E. C. (2005). Latino adolescents' perception of parenting behaviors and self-esteem: Examining the role of neighborhood risk. *Family Relations, 54*, 621–632. doi:10.1111/j.1741-3729.2005.00346.x

Bamford, C., & Lagattuta, K. H. (2012). Looking on the bright side: Children's knowledge about the benefits of positive versus negative thinking. *Child Development, 83*, 667–682. doi:10.1111/j.1467-8624.2011.01706.x

Bandura, A. (1965). Influence of models' reinforcement contingencies on the acquisition of imitative responses. *Journal of Personality and Social Psychology, 1*, 589–595. doi:10.1037/h0022070

Bandura, A. (1977). *Social learning theory*. Englewood Cliffs, NJ: Prentice Hall.

Bandura, A. (1986). *Social foundations of thought and action: A social cognitive theory*. Englewood Cliffs, NJ: Prentice-Hall.

Bandura, A., Ross, D., & Ross, S. A. (1963). Imitation of film-mediated aggressive models. *Journal of Abnormal and Social Psychology, 66*, 3–11. doi:10.1037/h0048687

Banerjee, M. (1997). Hidden emotions: Preschoolers' knowledge of appearance-reality and emotion display rules. *Social Cognition, 15*, 107–132. doi:10.1521/soco.1997.15.2.107

Banerjee, R., & Lintern, V. (2000). Boys will be boys: The effect of social evaluation concerns on gender-typing. *Social Development, 9*, 397–408.

Banich, M. T. (1997). *Neuropsychology: The neural bases of mental function*. Boston, MA: Houghton Mifflin.

Banich, M. T., Levine, S. C., Kim, H., & Huttenlocher, P. (1990). The effects of developmental factors on IQ in hemiplegic children. *Neuropsychologia, 28,* 35–47. doi:10.1016/0028-3932(90)90084-2

Banks, M. S., Aslin, R. N., & Letson, R. D. (1975). Sensitive period for the development of human binocular vision. *Science, 190*(4215), 675–677.

Banks, M. S., & Dannemiller, J. L. (1987). Infant visual psychophysics. In P. Salapatek & L. B. Cohen (Eds.), *Handbook of infant perception* (Vol. 1, pp. 115–184). Orlando, FL: Academic Press.

Bar-Haim, Y., Ziv, T., Lamy, D., & Hodes, R. M. (2006). Nature and nurture in own-race face processing. *Psychological Science, 17,* 159–163. doi:10.1111/j.1467-9280.2006.01679.x

Barbaresi, W. J., Katusic, S. K., Colligan, R. C., Weaver, A. L., & Jacobsen, S. J. (2007a). Long-term school outcomes for children with attention-deficit/hyperactivity disorder: A population-based perspective. *Journal of Developmental and Behavioral Pediatrics, 28,* 265–273. doi:10.1097/DBP.0b013e31811ff87d

Barbaresi, W. J., Katusic, S. K., Colligan, R. C., Weaver, A. L., & Jacobsen, S. J. (2007b). Modifiers of long-term school outcomes for children with attention-deficit/hyperactivity disorder: Does treatment with stimulant medication make a difference? Results from a population-based study. *Journal of Developmental and Behavioral Pediatrics, 28,* 274–287. doi:10.1097/DBP.0b013e3180cabc28

Barchia, K., & Bussey, K. (2011). Individual and collective social cognitive influences on peer aggression: Exploring the contribution of aggression efficacy, moral disengagement, and collective efficacy. *Aggressive Behavior, 37,* 107–120. doi:10.1002/ab.20375

Bard, K. A., Todd, B. K., Bernier, C., Love, J., & Leavens, D. A. (2006). Self-awareness in human and chimpanzee infants: What is measured and what is meant by the mark and mirror test? *Infancy, 9,* 191–219. doi:10.1207/s15327078in0902_6

Barden, R. C., Zelko, F. A., Duncan, S. W., & Masters, J. C. (1980). Children's consensual knowledge about the experiential determinants of emotion. *Journal of Personality and Social Psychology, 39,* 968–976.

Barker, E. D., Boivin, M., Brendgen, M., Fontaine, N., Arseneault, L., Vitaro, F., . . . Tremblay, R. E. (2008). Predictive validity and early predictors of peer-victimization trajectories in preschool. *Archives of General Psychiatry, 65,* 1185–1192. doi:10.1001/archpsyc.65.10.1185

Barker, J. E., & Munakata, Y. (2015). Time isn't of the essence: Activating goals rather than imposing delays improves inhibitory control in children. *Psychological Science, 26*(12), 1898–1908. doi:0956797615604625

Barnes, J., Leach, P., Malmberg, L. E., Stein, A., Sylva, K., & The FCCC Team. (2009). Experiences of childcare in England and socio-emotional development at 36 months. *Early Child Development and Care, 180,* 1215–1229. doi:10.1080/03004430902943959

Barnes, J. C., Beaver, K. M., & Miller, J. M. (2010). Estimating the effect of gang membership on nonviolent and violent delinquency: A counterfactual analysis. *Aggressive Behavior, 36,* 437–451. doi:10.1002/ab.20359

Baron-Cohen, S. (1991). The development of a theory of mind in autism: Deviance and delay? *Psychiatric Clinics of North America, 14,* 33–51.

Baron-Cohen, S. (1993). From attention-goal psychology to belief-desire psychology: The development of a theory of mind, and its dysfunction. In S. Baron-Cohen, H. Tager-Flusberg, & D. J. Cohen (Eds.), *Understanding other minds: Perspectives from autism* (pp. 59–82). Oxford, England: Oxford University Press.

Baron-Cohen, S. (1995). *Mindblindness: An essay on autism and theory of mind.* Cambridge, MA: MIT Press.

Barr, C. S. (2012). Temperament in animals. In M. R. Zentner & R. L. Shiner (Eds.), *Handbook of temperament* (pp. 251–272). New York, NY: Guilford Press.

Barr, R., Dowden, A., & Hayne, H. (1996). Developmental changes in deferred imitation by 6- to 24-month-old infants. *Infant Behavior and Development, 19,* 159–170. doi:10.1016/S0163-6383(96)90015-6

Barr, R. G., Quek, V. S. H., Cousineau, D., Oberlander, T. F., Brian, J. A., & Young, S. N. (1994). Effects of intra-oral sucrose on crying, mouthing and hand-mouth contact in newborn and six-week-old infants. *Developmental Medicine and Child Neurology, 36,* 608–618. doi:10.1111/j.1469-8749.1994.tb11898.x

Barr, R. G., Rajabali, F., Aragon, M., Colbourne, M., & Brant, R. (2015). Education about crying in normal infants is associated with a reduction in pediatric emergency room visits for crying complaints. *Journal of Developmental & Behavioral Pediatrics, 36*(4), 252–257.

Barrett, K. C., Zahn-Waxler, C., & Cole, P. M. (1993). Avoiders vs. amenders: Implications for the investigation of guilt and shame during toddlerhood? *Cognition and Emotion, 7,* 481–505.

Barrouillet, P., & Camos, V. (2015). *Working memory: Loss and reconstruction.* New York, NY: Psychology Press.

Barry, R. A., & Kochanska, G. (2010). A longitudinal investigation of the affective environment in families with young children: From infancy to early school age. *Emotion, 10,* 237–249.

Bartlett, N. H., Vasey, P. L., & Bukowski, W. M. (2000). Is gender identity disorder in children a mental disorder? *Sex Roles, 43,* 753–785. doi:10.1023/A:1011004431889

Bartrip, J., Morton, J., & de Schonen, S. (2001). Responses to mother's face in 3-week to 5-month-old infants. *British Journal of Developmental Psychology, 19,* 219–232. doi:10.1348/026151001166047

Bartsch, K., & Wellman, H. M. (1995). *Children talk about the mind.* New York, NY: Oxford University Press.

Bascoe, S. M., Davies, P. T., & Cummings, E. M. (2012). Beyond warmth and conflict: The developmental utility of a boundary conceptualization of sibling relationship processes. *Child Development, 83,* 2121–2138. doi:10.1111/j.1467-8624.2012.01817.x

Bassen, C. R., & Lamb, M. E. (2006). Gender differences in adolescents' self-concepts of assertion and affiliation. *European Journal of Developmental Psychology, 3,* 71–94.

Bates, J. E., Bayles, K., Bennett, D. S., Ridge, B., & Brown, M. M. (1991). Origins of externalizing behavior problems at eight years of age. In D. J. Pepler & K. H. Rubin (Eds.), *The development and treatment of childhood aggression* (pp. 93–120). Hillsdale, NJ: Erlbaum.

Bates, J. E., Schermerhorn, A. C., & Petersen, I. T. (2012). Temperament and parenting in developmental perspective. In M. R. Zentner & R. L. Shiner (Eds.), *Handbook of temperament* (pp. 425–441). New York, NY: Guilford Press.

Bates, L., Luster, T., & Vandenbelt, M. (2003). Factors related to social competence in elementary school among children of adolescent mothers. *Social Development, 12,* 107–124. doi:10.1111/1467-9507.00224

Battistich, V., Schaps, E., Watson, M., Solomon, D., & Lewis, C. (2000). Effects of the Child Development Project on students' drug use and other problem behaviors. *Journal of Primary Prevention, 21,* 75–99. doi:10.1023/A:1007057414994

Battistich, V., Schaps, E., & Wilson, N. (2004). Effects of an elementary school intervention on students' "connectedness" to school and social adjustment during middle school. *Journal of Primary Prevention, 24,* 243–262. doi:10.1023/B:JOPP.0000018048.38517.cd

Battistich, V., Solomon, D., Watson, M., & Schaps, E. (1997). Caring school communities. *Educational Psychologist, 32,* 137–151. doi:10.1207/s15326985ep3203_1

Battistich, V., Watson, M., Solomon, D., Schaps, E., & Solomon, J. (1991). The Child Development Project: A comprehensive program for the development of prosocial character. In W. M. Kurtines & J. L. Gewirtz (Eds.), *Handbook of moral behavior and development: Vol. 3. Application* (pp. 1–34). Hillsdale, NJ: Erlbaum.

Bauer, P. J. (1995). Recalling past events: From infancy to early childhood. In R. Vasta (Ed.), *Annals of child development* (Vol. 11, pp. 25–71). London, England: Jessica Kingsley.

Bauer, P. J. (2002). Long–term recall memory: Behavioral and neuro–developmental changes in the first 2 years of life. *Current Directions in Psychological Science, 11,* 137–141. doi:10.1111/1467-8721.00186

Bauer, P. J. (2007). *Remembering the times of our lives: Memory in infancy and beyond.* Mahwah, NJ: Erlbaum.

Bauer, P. J., Hertsgaard, L. A., Dropik, P., & Daly, B. P. (1998). When even arbitrary order becomes important: Developments in reliable temporal sequencing of arbitrarily ordered events. *Memory, 6*(2), 165–198. doi:10.1080/741942074

Baumeister, R. F. (2005). Self-concept, self-esteem, and identity. In V. Derlega, B. Winstead, & W. Jones (Eds.), *Personality: Contemporary Theory and Research* (3rd ed.), pp. 246–280. San Francisco, CA: Wadsworth.

Baumgartner, H. A., & Oakes, L. M. (2013). Investigating the relation between infants' manual activity with objects and their perception of dynamic events. *Infancy, 18*(6), 983–1006. doi:10.1111/infa.12009

Bauminger, N., Finzi-Dottan, R., Chason, S., & Har-Even, D. (2008). Intimacy in adolescent friendship: The roles of attachment, coherence, and self-disclosure. *Journal of Social and Personal Relationships, 25,* 409–428. doi:10.1177/0265407508090866

Baumrind, D. (1973). The development of instrumental competence through socialization. In A. D. Pick (Ed.), *Minnesota Symposia on Child Psychology* (Vol. 7, pp. 3–46). Minneapolis: University of Minnesota Press.

Baumrind, D. (1991a). The influence of parenting style on adolescent competence and substance use. *Journal of Early Adolescence, 11,* 56–95. doi:10.1177/0272431691111004

Baumrind, D. (1991b). Parenting styles and adolescent development. In R. M. Lerner, A. C. Petersen, & J. Brooks-Gunn (Eds.), *Encyclopedia of adolescence* (pp. 746–758). New York, NY: Garland.

Beach, S. R. H., Lei, M. K., Brody, G. H., Simons, R. L., Cutrona, C., & Philibert, R. A. (2012). Genetic moderation of contextual effects on negative arousal and parenting in African-American parents. *Journal of Family Psychology, 26,* 46–55. doi:10.1037/a0026236

Beardsall, L., & Dunn, J. (1992). Adversities in childhood: Siblings' experiences, and their relations to self-esteem. *Journal of Child Psychology and Psychiatry, 33,* 349–359.

Beauchaine, T. (2001). Vagal tone, development, and Gray's motivational theory: Toward an integrated model of autonomic nervous system functioning in psychopathology. *Development and Psychopathology, 13,* 183–214.

Beck, A. T. (1979). Cognitive therapy of depression. In P. J. Clayton & J. E. Barrett (Eds.), *Treatment of depression: Old controversies and new*

approaches (pp. 265–290). New York, NY: Raven Press.

Becker, M., Weinberger, T., Chandy, A., & Schmukler, S. (2016). Depression during pregnancy and postpartum. *Current Psychiatry Reports, 18*(3), 1–9.

Becker-Stoll, F., Delius, A., & Scheitenberger, S. (2001). Adolescents' nonverbal emotional expressions during negotiation of a disagreement with their mothers: An attachment approach. *International Journal of Behavioral Development, 25,* 344–353.

Beckett, C., Maughan, B., Rutter, M., Castle, J., Colvert, E., Groothues, C., . . . Sonuga-Barke, E. J. (2006). Do the effects of early severe deprivation on cognition persist into early adolescence? Findings from the English and Romanian Adoptees study. *Child Development, 77,* 696–711. doi:10.1111/j.1467-8624.2006.00898.x

Bedard, A.-C., Nichols, S., Barbosa, J. A., Schachar, R., Logan, G. D., & Tannock, R. (2002). The development of selective inhibitory control across the life span. *Developmental Neuropsychology, 21,* 93–111. doi:10.1207/S15326942DN2101_5

Begus, K., Gliga, T., & Southgate, V. (2014). Infants learn what they want to learn: Responding to infant pointing leads to superior learning. *PloS One, 9*(10), e108817.

Behl-Chadha, G. (1996). Basic-level and super-ordinate-like categorical representations in early infancy. *Cognition, 60,* 105–141.

Behne, T., Liszkowski, U., Carpenter, M., & Tomasello, M. (2012). Twelve-month-olds' comprehension and production of pointing. *British Journal of Developmental Psychology, 30,* 359–375. doi:10.1111/j.2044-835X.2011.02043.x

Behnke, A. O., Plunkett, S. W., Sands, T., & Bámaca-Colbert, M. Y. (2011). The relationship between Latino adolescents' perceptions of discrimination, neighborhood risk, and parenting on self-esteem and depressive symptoms. *Journal of Cross-Cultural Psychology, 42,* 1179–1197. doi:10.1177/0022022110383424

Behnke, M., Smith, V. C., Levy, S., Ammerman, S. D., Gonzalez, P. K., Ryan, S. A., . . . Cummings, J. J. (2013). Prenatal substance abuse: Short-and long-term effects on the exposed fetus. *Pediatrics, 131*(3), e1009–e1024.

Behrens, K. Y., Hesse, E., & Main, M. (2007). Mothers' attachment status as determined by the Adult Attachment Interview predicts their 6-year-olds' reunion responses: A study conducted in Japan. *Developmental Psychology, 43,* 1553–1567.

Beier, J. S., & Carey, S. (2014). Contingency is not enough: Social context guides third-party attributions of intentional agency. *Developmental Psychology, 50*(3), 889.

Beijersbergen, M. D., Juffer, F., Bakermans-Kranenburg, M. J., & van IJzendoorn,

M. H. (2012). Remaining or becoming secure: Parental sensitive support predicts attachment continuity from infancy to adolescence in a longitudinal adoption study. *Developmental Psychology, 48,* 1277–1282. doi:10.1037/a0027442

Beilock, S. L., Gunderson, E. A., Ramirez, G., & Levine, S. C. (2010). Female teachers' math anxiety affects girls' math achievement. *Proceedings of the National Academy of Sciences of the United States of America, 107,* 1860–1863.

Beilock, S. L., & Willingham, D. T. (2014, Summer). Math anxiety: Can teachers help students reduce it? American Educator. Retrieved from http://www.aft.org/sites/default/files/periodicals/beilock.pdf

Bell, M. L., & Ebisu, K. (2012). Environmental inequality in exposures to airborne particulate matter components in the United States. Environmental health perspectives, 120(12), 1699. doi:10.1289/ehp.1205201

Bell, S. M., & Ainsworth, M. D. S. (1972). Infant crying and maternal responsiveness. *Child Development, 43*(4), 1171–1190.

Belsky, J. (1986). Infant day care: A cause for concern? *Zero to Three, 7*(1), 1–7.

Belsky, J. (1993). Etiology of child maltreatment: A developmental-ecological analysis. *Psychological Bulletin, 114,* 413–434. doi:10.1037/0033-2909.114.3.413

Belsky, J., Bakermans-Kranenburg, M. J., & van IJzendoorn, M. H. (2007). For better and for worse: Differential susceptibility to environmental influences. *Current Directions in Psychological Science, 16,* 300–304. doi:10.1111/j.1467-8721.2007.00525.x

Belsky, J., Newman, D. A., Widaman, K. F., Rodkin, P., Pluess, M., Fraley, R. C., . . . Roisman, G. I. (2015). Differential susceptibility to effects of maternal sensitivity? A study of candidate plasticity genes. *Development and Psychopathology, 27,* 725–746. doi:10.1017/S0954579414000844

Belsky, J., & Pluess, M. (2009). Beyond diathesis stress: Differential susceptibility to environmental influences. *Psychological Bulletin, 135,* 885–908. doi:10.1037/a0017376

Belsky, J., & Pluess, M. (2012). Differential susceptibility to long-term effects of quality of child care on externalizing behavior in adolescence? *International Journal of Behavioral Development, 36,* 2–10. doi:10.1177/0165025411406855

Belsky, J., & Pluess, M. (2013). Genetic moderation of early child-care effects on social functioning across childhood: A developmental analysis. *Child Development, 84,* 1209–1225. doi:10.1111/cdev.12058

Belsky, J., Rosenberger, K., & Crnic, K. (1995). Maternal personality, marital quality, social support and infant temperament: Their significance for infant–mother attachment in human families. In C. R. Pryce, R. D. Martin, & D. Skuse (Eds.),

Motherhood in human and nonhuman primates: Biosocial determinants (pp. 115–124). Basel, Switzerland: Karger.

Belsky, J., Schlomer, G. L., & Ellis, B. J. (2012). Beyond cumulative risk: Distinguishing harshness and unpredictability as determinants of parenting and early life history strategy. *Developmental Psychology, 48*, 662–673. doi:10.1037/a0024454

Belsky, J., & van Ijzendoorn, M. H. (2015). What works for whom? Genetic moderation of intervention efficacy. *Development and Psychopathology, 27*(01), 1–6.

Belsky, J., Vandell, D. L., Burchinal, M., Clarke-Stewart, K. A., McCartney, K., Owen, M. T., & The NICHD Early Child Care Research Network. (2007). Are there long-term effects of early child care? *Child Development, 78*, 681–701.

Bem, S. L. (1993). *The lenses of gender: Transforming the debate on sexual inequality.* New Haven, CT: Yale University Press.

Benedict, R. (1934). *Patterns of culture.* Boston, MA: Houghton Mifflin.

Benenson, J. (2014). *Warriors and worriers: The survival of the sexes.* New York, NY: Oxford University Press.

Benenson, J. F., & Christakos, A. (2003). The greater fragility of females' versus males' closest same-sex friendships. *Child Development, 74*, 1123–1129. doi:10.1111/1467-8624.00596

Benenson, J. F., Morganstein, T., & Roy, R. (1998). Sex differences in children's investment in peers. *Human Nature, 9*, 369–390. doi:10.1007/s12110-998-1015-0

Benitez, V. L., & Smith, L. B. (2012). Predictable locations aid early object name learning. *Cognition, 125*(3), 339–352.

Benner, A. D., & Kim, S. Y. (2010). Understanding Chinese American adolescents' developmental outcomes: Insights from the family stress model. *Journal of Research on Adolescence, 20*, 1–12. doi:10.1111/j.1532-7795.2009.00629.x

Bennett, D. S., Bendersky, M., & Lewis, M. (2002). Facial expressivity at 4 months: A context by expression analysis. *Infancy, 3*, 97–113.

Bennett, D. S., Bendersky, M., & Lewis, M. (2005). Does the organization of emotional expression change over time? Facial expressivity from 4 to 12 months. *Infancy, 8*, 167–187.

Benson, J. E., Sabbagh, M. A., Carlson, S. M., & Zelazo, P. D. (2013). Individual differences in executive functioning predict preschoolers' improvement from theory-of-mind training. *Developmental Psychology, 49*(9), 1615–1627. doi:10.1037/a0031056

Bereiter, C., & Scardamalia, M. (1982). From conversation to composition: The role of instruction in a developmental process. In R. Glaser (Ed.), *Advances in instructional psychology* (Vol. 2, pp. 1–64). Hillsdale, NJ: Erlbaum.

Berg, C. A. (1989). Knowledge of strategies for dealing with everyday problems from childhood through adolescence. *Developmental Psychology, 25*, 607–618.

Berg, C. A., Strough, J., Calderone, K., Meegan, S. P., & Sansone, C. (1997). Planning to prevent everyday problems from occurring. In S. L. Friedman & E. K. Scholnick (Eds.), *The developmental psychology of planning: Why, how, and when do we plan?* (pp. 209–236). Mahwah, NJ: Erlbaum.

Berg, N. E., & Mussen, P. (1975). The origins and development of concepts of justice. *Journal of Social Issues, 31*, 183–201. doi:10.1111/j.1540-4560.1975.tb01003.x

Bergelson, E., & Swingley, D. (2012). At 6–9 months, human infants know the meanings of many common nouns. *Proceedings of the National Academy of Sciences of the United States of America, 109*, 3253–3258. doi:10.1073/pnas.1113380109

Berger, A. (2011). *Self-regulation: Brain, cognition, and development.* Washington, DC: American Psychological Association.

Berger, L., Brooks-Gunn, J., Paxson, C., & Waldfogel, J. (2008). First-year maternal employment and child outcomes: Differences across racial and ethnic groups. *Children and Youth Services Review, 30*, 365–387. doi:10.1016/j.childyouth.2007.10.010

Berger, L. M., Hill, J., & Waldfogel, J. (2005). Maternity leave, early maternal employment and child health and development in the U.S. *The Economic Journal, 115*, F29–F47.

Berkel, C., Murry, V. M., Hurt, T. R., Chen, Y.-f., Brody, G. H., Simons, R. L., . . . Gibbons, F. X. (2009). It takes a village: Protecting rural African American youth in the context of racism. *Journal of Youth and Adolescence, 38*, 175–188. doi:10.1007/s10964-008-9346-z

Berko, J. (1958). The child's learning of English morphology. *Word, 14*, 150–177.

Berlin, L. J., Ispa, J. M., Fine, M. A., Malone, P. S., Brooks-Gunn, J., Brady-Smith, C., . . . Bai, Y. (2009). Correlates and consequences of spanking and verbal punishment for low-income White, African American, and Mexican American toddlers. *Child Development, 80*, 1403–1420. doi:10.1111/j.1467-8624.2009.01341.x

Berman, J. M. J., Chambers, C. G., & Graham, S. A. (2010). Preschoolers' appreciation of speaker vocal affect as a cue to referential intent. *Journal of Experimental Child Psychology, 107*, 87–99. doi:10.1016/j.jecp.2010.04.012

Bernal, M. E., Knight, G. P., Garza, C. A., Ocampo, K. A., & Cota, M. K. (1990). The development of ethnic identity in Mexican-American children. *Hispanic Journal of Behavioral Sciences, 12*, 3–24. doi:10.1177/07399863900121001

Bernard, K., & Dozier, M. (2010). Examining infants' cortisol responses to laboratory tasks among children varying in attachment disorganization: Stress reactivity or return to baseline? *Developmental Psychology, 46*, 1771–1778. doi:10.1037/a0020660

Bernard, K., Dozier, M., Bick, J., Lewis-Morrarty, E., Lindhiem, O., & Carlson, E. (2012). Enhancing attachment organization among maltreated children: Results of a randomized clinical trial. *Child Development, 83*, 623–636. doi:10.1111/j.1467-8624.2011.01712.x

Bernard, K., Simons, R., & Dozier, M. (2015). Effects of an attachment-based intervention on child protective services-referred mothers' event-related potentials to children's emotions. *Child Development, 86*, 1673–1684. doi:10.111/cdev.12418

Berndt, T. J. (1979). Developmental changes in conformity to peers and parents. *Developmental Psychology, 15*, 608–616. doi:10.1037/0012-1649.15.6.608

Berndt, T. J., Hawkins, J. A., & Jiao, Z. (1999). Influences of friends and friendships on adjustment to junior high school. *Merrill-Palmer Quarterly, 45*, 13–41.

Berninger, V. W., & Richards, T. L. (2002a). *Brain literacy for educators and psychologists.* San Diego, CA: Academic Press.

Berninger, V. W., & Richards, T. L. (2002b). Building a writing brain neurologically. In V. W. Berninger & T. L. Richards (Eds.), *Brain literacy for educators and psychologists* (pp. 247–271). San Diego, CA: Academic Press.

Berteletti, I., Lucangeli, D., Piazza, M., Dehaene, S., & Zorzi, M. (2010). Numerical estimation in preschoolers. *Developmental Psychology, 46*, 545–551. doi:10.1037/a0017887

Bertenthal, B. I. (1993). Infants' perception of biomechanical motions: Intrinsic image and knowledge-based constraints. In C. Granrud (Ed.), *Visual perception and cognition in infancy* (pp. 175–214). Hillsdale, NJ: Erlbaum.

Bertenthal, B. I., Campos, J. J., & Kermoian, R. (1994). An epigenetic perspective on the development of self-produced locomotion and its consequences. *Current Directions in Psychological Science, 3*, 140–145. doi:10.2307/20182292

Bertenthal, B. I., & Clifton, R. K. (1998). Perception and action. In W. Damon (Series Ed.) & D. Kuhn & R. S. Siegler (Vol. Eds.), *Handbook of child psychology: Vol. 2. Cognition, perception, and language* (5th ed., pp. 51–102). New York, NY: Wiley.

Best, D. L. (2010). Gender. In M. H. Bornstein (Ed.), *Handbook of cultural developmental science* (pp. 209–222). New York, NY: Psychology Press.

Best, D. L., & Thomas, J. J. (2004). Cultural diversity and cross-cultural perspectives. In A. H. Eagly, A. E. Beall, & R. J. Sternberg (Eds.), *The psychology of gender* (2nd ed., pp. 296–327). New York, NY: Guilford Press.

Best, D. L., & Williams, J. E. (1993). A cross-cultural viewpoint. In A. E. Beall & R. J. Sternberg (Eds.), *The psychology of gender* (pp. 215–248). New York, NY: Guilford Press.

Best, J. R., & Miller, P. H. (2010). A developmental perspective on executive function. *Child Development, 81*(6), 1641–1660. doi:10.1111/j.1467-8624.2010.01499.x

Beyers, W., & Goossens, L. (2008). Dynamics of perceived parenting and identity formation in late adolescence. *Journal of Adolescence, 31,* 165–184. doi:10.1016/j.adolescence.2007.04.003

Bezdjian, S., Raine, A., Baker, L. A., & Lynam, D. R. (2011). Psychopathic personality in children: Genetic and environmental contributions. *Psychological Medicine, 41,* 589–600. doi:10.1017/S0033291710000966

Bhanot, R., & Jovanovic, J. (2005). Do parents' academic gender stereotypes influence whether they intrude on their children's homework? *Sex Roles, 52,* 597–607. doi:10.1007/s11199-005-3728-4

Bialystok, E. (2000). Symbolic representation across domains in preschool children. *Journal of Experimental Child Psychology, 76,* 173–189.

Bialystok, E. (2015). Bilingualism and the development of executive function: The role of attention. *Child Development Perspectives, 9*(2), 117–121. doi:10.1111/cdep.12116

Bialystok, E., & Craik, F. I. M. (2010). Cognitive and linguistic processing in the bilingual mind. *Current Directions in Psychological Science, 19,* 19–23. doi:10.1177/0963721409358571

Bibok, M. B., Carpendale, J. I., & Müller, U. (2009). Parental scaffolding and the development of executive function. *New Directions for Child and Adolescent Development, 2009*(123), 17–34. doi:10.1002/cd.233

Bick, J., Dozier, M., & Perkins, E. (2012). Convergence between attachment classifications and natural reunion behavior among children and parents in a child care setting. *Attachment & Human Development, 14,* 1–10. doi:10.1080/14616734.2012.636645

Bick, J., Zhu, T., Stamoulis, C., Fox, N. A., Zeanah, C. H., & Nelson, C. A. (2015). Effect on early institutionalization and foster care on long-term white matter development: A randomized clinical trial. *JAMA Pediatrics, 169,* 211–219. doi:10.1001/jamapediatrics.2014.3212

Biederman, J., Petty, C. R., Dolan, C., Hughes, S., Mick, E., Monuteaux, M. C., & Faraone, S. V. (2008). The long-term longitudinal course of oppositional defiant disorder and conduct disorder in ADHD boys: Findings from a controlled 10-year prospective longitudinal follow-up study. *Psychological Medicine, 38,* 1027–1036. doi:10.1017/S0033291707002668

Biederman, J., Rosenbaum, J. F., Hirshfeld, D. R., Faraone, S. V., -Bolduc, E. A., Gersten, M., . . . Reznick, J. S. (1990). Psychiatric correlates of behavioral inhibition in young children of parents with and without psychiatric disorders. *Archives of General Psychiatry, 47,* 21–26.

Biehle, S. N., & Mickelson, K. D. (2012). First-time parents' expectations about the division of childcare and play. *Journal of Family Psychology, 26,* 36–45. doi:10.1037/a0026608

Bierman, K. L., Coie, J. D., Dodge, K. A., Greenberg, M. T., Lochman, J. E., McMahon, R. J., . . . Conduct Problems Prevention Research Group. (2010). The effects of a multi-year universal social–emotional learning program: The role of student and school characteristics. *Journal of Consulting and Clinical Psychology, 78,* 156–168. doi:10.1037/a0018607

Biernat, M. (1991). Gender stereotypes and the relationship between masculinity and femininity: A developmental analysis. *Journal of Personality and Social Psychology, 61,* 351–365. doi:10.1037/0022-3514.61.3.351

Bigelow, B. J. (1977). Children's friendship expectations: A cognitive-developmental study. *Child Development, 48,* 246–253.

Bigler, R. S. (1999). Psychological interventions designed to counter sexism in children: Empirical limitations and theoretical foundations. In J. W. B. Swann, J. H. Langlois, & L. A. Gilbert (Eds.), *Sexism and stereotypes in modern society: The gender science of Janet Taylor Spence* (pp. 129–151). Washington, DC: American Psychological Association.

Bigler, R. S., & Liben, L. S. (1990). The role of attitudes and interventions in gender-schematic processing. *Child Development, 61,* 1440–1452.

Bigler, R. S., & Liben, L. S. (2007). Developmental intergroup theory: Explaining and reducing children's social stereotyping and prejudice. *Current Directions in Psychological Science, 16,* 162–166. doi:10.1111/j.1467-8721.2007.00496.x

Bird, A., Reese, E., & Tripp, G. (2006). Parent–child talk about past emotional events: Associations with child temperament and goodness-of-fit. *Journal of Cognition and Development, 7,* 189–210.

Bjorklund, D. F. (1997). The role of immaturity in human development. *Psychological Bulletin, 122,* 153–169.

Bjorklund, D. F. (2007). *Why youth is not wasted on the young: Immaturity in human development.* Oxford, England: Blackwell.

Bjorklund, D. F., & Pellegrini, A. D. (2002). *The origins of human nature: Evolutionary developmental psychology.* Washington, DC: American Psychological Association.

Björkqvist, K., Österman, K., & Kaukiainen, A. (1992). The development of direct and indirect aggressive strategies in males and females. In K. Björkqvist & P. Niemelä (Eds.), *Of mice and women: Aspects of female aggression* (pp. 51–64). San Diego, CA: Academic Press.

Blackwell, L. S., Trzesniewski, K. H., & Dweck, C. S. (2007). Implicit theories of intelligence predict achievement across an adolescent transition: A longitudinal study and an intervention. *Child Development, 78,* 246–263. doi:10.1111/j.1467-8624.2007.00995.x

Blair, C. (2006). How similar are fluid cognition and general intelligence? A developmental neuroscience perspective on fluid cognition as an aspect of human cognitive ability. *Behavioral and Brain Sciences, 29,* 109–125. doi:10.1017/S0140525X06009034

Blair, C. (2016). Developmental science and executive function. *Current Directions in Psychological Science, 25*(1), 3–7. doi:10.1177/0963721415622634

Blair, C., Gamson, D., Thorne, S., & Baker, D. (2005). Rising mean IQ: Cognitive demand of mathematics education for young children, population exposure to formal schooling, and the neurobiology of the prefrontal cortex. *Intelligence, 33,* 93–106.

Blair, C., Granger, D. A., Kivlighan, K. T., Mills-Koonce, R., Willoughby, M., Greenberg, M. T., . . . Family Life Project Investigators. (2008). Maternal and child contributions to cortisol response to emotional arousal in young children from low-income, rural communities. *Developmental Psychology, 44,* 1095–1109. doi:10.1037/0012-1649.44.4.1095

Blair, C., & Raver, C. C. (2014). Closing the achievement gap through modification of neurocognitive and neuroendocrine function: Results from a cluster randomized controlled trial of an innovative approach to the education of children in kindergarten. *PLOS ONE, 9*(11), e112393. doi:10.1371/journal.pone.0112393

Blair, C., & Raver, C. C. (2015). School readiness and self-regulation: A developmental psychobiological approach. *Annual Review of Psychology, 66,* 711. doi:10.1146/annurev-psych-010814-015221

Blair, C., & Razza, R. P. (2007). Relating effortful control, executive function, and false belief understanding to emerging math and literacy ability in kindergarten. *Child Development, 78,* 647–663. doi:10.1111/j.1467-8624.2007.01019.x

Blair, K. A., Denham, S. A., Kochanoff, A., & Whipple, B. (2004). Playing it cool: Temperament, emotion regulation, and social behavior in preschoolers. *Journal of School Psychology, 42,* 419–443.

Blais, J. J., Craig, W. M., Pepler, D., & Connolly, J. (2008). Adolescents online: The importance of internet activity choices to salient relationships. *Journal of Youth and Adolescence, 37,* 522–536. doi:10.1007/s10964-007-9262-7

Blakemore, J. E. O., Berenbaum, S. A., & Liben, L. S. (2009). *Gender development.* New York, NY: Taylor & Francis.

Blandon, A. Y., Calkins, S. D., Keane, S. P., & O'Brien, M. (2008). Individual differences in trajectories of emotion regulation processes: The effects of maternal depressive symptomatology and children's physiological regulation. *Developmental Psychology, 44,* 1110–1123. doi:10.1037/0012-1649.44.4.1110

Blasi, A. (1980). Bridging moral cognition and moral action: A critical review of the literature. *Psychological Bulletin, 88,* 1–45. doi:10.1037/0033-2909.88.1.1

Blass, E. M., & Camp, C. A. (2003). Biological bases of face preference in 6-week-old infants. *Developmental Science, 6,* 524–536. doi:10.1111/1467-7687.00310

Blass, E. M., & Hoffmeyer, L. B. (1991). Sucrose as an analgesic for newborn infants. *Pediatrics, 87,* 215–218.

Blass, E. M., & Teicher, M. H. (1980, October 3). Suckling. *Science, 210,* 15–22.

Bleeker, M. M., & Jacobs, J. E. (2004). Achievement in math and science: Do mothers' beliefs matter 12 years later? *Journal of Educational Psychology, 96,* 97–109. doi:10.1037/0022-0663.96.1.97

Bleidorn, W., Arslan, R. C., Denissen, J. A., Rentfrow, P. J., Gebauer, J. E., Potter, J., & Gosling, S. D. (2015). Age and gender differences in self-esteem—A cross-cultural window. *Journal of Personality and Social Psychology, 111,* 396–410. doi:10.1037/pspp0000078

Bloom, L. (1973). *One word at a time: The use of single word utterances before syntax.* The Hague, The Netherlands: Mouton.

Bloom, L. (1991). *Language development from two to three.* Cambridge, England: Cambridge University Press.

Bloom, L. (1998). Language acquisition in its developmental context. In W. Damon (Series Ed.) & D. Kuhn & R. S. Siegler (Vol. Eds.), *Handbook of child psychology: Vol. 2. Cognition, perception, and language* (5th ed., pp. 309–370). Hoboken, NJ: Wiley.

Bloom, L., Rocissano, L., & Hood, L. (1976). Adult-child discourse: Developmental interaction between information processing and linguistic knowledge. *Cognitive Psychology, 8,* 521–552. doi:10.1016/0010-0285(76)90017-7

Bloom, L., & Tinker, E. (2001). The intentionality model and language acquisition: Engagement, effort, and the essential tension in development. *Monographs of the Society for Research in Child Development, 66*(4, Serial No. 267).

Bloom, P. (2000). *How children learn the meanings of words.* Cambridge, MA: MIT Press.

Blumberg, M. S. (2015). Developing sensorimotor systems in our sleep. *Current Directions in Psychological Science, 24*(1), 32–37.

Bode, L., Kuhn, L., Kim, H. Y., Hsiao, L., Nissan, C., Sinkala, M., . . . Aldrovandi, G. M. (2012). Human milk oligosaccharide concentration and risk of postnatal transmission of

HIV through breastfeeding. *American Journal of Clinical Nutrition, 96,* 831–839. doi:10.3945/ajcn.112.039503

Boden, J. M., Fergusson, D. M., & Horwood, L. J. (2008). Does adolescent self-esteem predict later life outcomes? A test of the causal role of self-esteem. *Development and Psychopathology, 20,* 319–339. doi:10.1017/S0954579408000151

Boeke, J. D., Church, G., Hessel, A., Kelley, N. J., Arkin, A., Cai, Y., . . . Isaacs, F. J. (2016). The Genome Project-Write. *Science, 353(6295),* 126–127.

Bohlin, G., Hagekull, B., & Rydell, A.-M. (2000). Attachment and social functioning: A longitudinal study from infancy to middle childhood. *Social Development, 9,* 24–39. doi:10.1111/1467-9507.00109

Boiger, M., & Mesquita, B. (2012). The construction of emotion in interactions, relationships, and cultures. *Emotion Review, 4,* 221–229.

Boivin, M., Petitclerc, A., Feng, B., & Barker, E. D. (2010). The developmental trajectories of peer victimization in middle to late childhood and the changing nature of their behavioral correlates. *Merrill-Palmer Quarterly, 56,* 231–260.

Bokhorst, C. L., Bakermans-Kranenburg, M. J., Pasco Fearon, R. M., van IJzendoorn, M. H., Fonagy, P., & Schuengel, C. (2003). The importance of shared environment in mother–infant attachment security: A behavioral genetic study. *Child Development, 74,* 1769–1782. doi:10.1046/j.1467-8624.2003.00637.x

Bokhorst, C. L., Sumter, S. R., & Westenberg, P. M. (2010). Social support from parents, friends, classmates, and teachers in children and adolescents aged 9 to 18 years: Who is perceived as most supportive? *Social Development, 19,* 417–426. doi:10.1111/j.1467-9507.2009.00540.x

Boland, A. M., Haden, C. A., & Ornstein, P. A. (2003). Boosting children's memory by training mothers in the use of an elaborative conversational style as an event unfolds. *Journal of Cognition and Development, 4,* 39–65. doi:10.1080/15248372.2003.9669682

Bolger, K. E., & Scarr, S. (1995). Not so far from home: How family characteristics predict child care quality. *Early Development and Parenting, 4,* 103–112. doi:10.1002/edp.2430040303

Bolkan, C., Sano, Y., De Costa, J., Acock, A. C., & Day, R. D. (2010). Early adolescents' perceptions of mothers' and fathers' parenting styles and problem behavior. *Marriage and Family Review, 46,* 563–579. doi:10.1080/01494929.2010.543040

Bona, K., Blonquist, T. M., Neuberg, D. S., Silverman, L. B., & Wolfe, J. (2016). Impact of socioeconomic status on timing of relapse and overall survival for children treated on Dana-Farber Cancer Institute ALL consortium protocols (2000–2010). *Pediatric Blood & Cancer, 63,* 1012–1018. doi:10.1002/pbc.25928

Bonica, C., Arnold, D. H., Fisher, P. H., Zeljo, A., & Yershova, K. (2003). Relational aggression, relational victimization, and language development in preschoolers. *Social Development, 12,* 551–562. doi:10.1111/1467-9507.00248

Bonner, J. T. (1988). *The evolution of culture in animals.* Princeton, NJ: Princeton University Press.

Book, A. S., Starzyk, K. B., & Quinsey, V. L. (2001). The relationship between testosterone and aggression: A meta-analysis. *Aggression and Violent Behavior, 6,* 579–599. doi:10.1016/S1359-1789(00)00032-X

Booth, A. E., & Waxman, S. R. (2009). A horse of a different color: Specifying with precision infants' mappings of novel nouns and adjectives. *Child Development, 80,* 15–22. doi:10.1111/j.1467-8624.2008.01242.x

Booth, J. L., & Siegler, R. S. (2006). Developmental and individual differences in pure numerical estimation. *Developmental Psychology, 42,* 189–201. doi:10.1037/0012-1649.41.6.189

Booth, J. L., & Siegler, R. S. (2008). Numerical magnitude representations influence arithmetic learning. *Child Development, 79,* 1016–1031. doi:10.1111/j.1467-8624.2008.01173.x

Booth-Laforce, C., Oh, W., Kennedy, A. E., Rubin, K. H., Rose-Krasnor, L., & Laursen, B. (2012). Parent and peer links to trajectories of anxious withdrawal from grades 5 to 8. *Journal of Clinical Child and Adolescent Psychology, 41,* 138–149. doi:10.1080/15374416.2012.651995

Booth-LaForce, C., & Oxford, M. L. (2008). Trajectories of social withdrawal from grades 1 to 6: Prediction from early parenting, attachment, and temperament. *Developmental Psychology, 44,* 1298–1313. doi:10.1037/a0012954

Borelli, J. L., Crowley, M. J., David, D. H., Sbarra, D. A., Anderson, G. M., & Mayes, L. C. (2010). Attachment and emotion in school-aged children. *Emotion, 10,* 475–485. doi:10.1037/a0018490

Borge, A. I. H., Rutter, M., Côté, S., & Tremblay, R. E. (2004). Early childcare and physical aggression: Differentiating social selection and social causation. *Journal of Child Psychology and Psychiatry, 45,* 367–376. doi:10.1111/j.1469-7610.2004.00227.x

Borke, H. (1971). Interpersonal perception of young children: Egocentrism or empathy? *Developmental Psychology, 5,* 263–269.

Bornstein, M. H. (2007). On the significance of social relationships in the development of children's earliest symbolic play: An ecological perspective. In A. Göncü & S. Gaskins (Eds.), *Play and development: Evolutionary, sociocultural, and functional perspectives* (pp. 101–129). New York, NY: Erlbaum.

Bornstein, M. H., & Bradley, R. H. (Eds.). (2003). *Socioeconomic status, parenting, and child development.* Mahwah, NJ: Erlbaum.

Bornstein, M. H., Cote, L. R., Haynes, O. M., Hahn, C.-S., & Park, Y. (2010). Parenting knowledge: Experiential and sociodemographic factors in European American mothers of young children. *Developmental Psychology, 46,* 1677–1693. doi:10.1037/a0020677

Bornstein, M. H., Hahn, C. S., & Suwalsky, J. T. (2013). Physically developed and exploratory young infants contribute to their own long-term academic achievement. *Psychological Science, 24*(10), 1906–1917.

Bornstein, M. H., Hahn, C. S., & Wolke, D. (2013). Systems and cascades in cognitive development and academic achievement. *Child Development, 84*(1), 154–162.

Bornstein, M. H., & Putnick, D. L. (2012). Cognitive and socioemotional caregiving in developing countries. *Child Development, 83,* 46–61. doi:10.1111/j.1467-8624.2011.01673.x

Bornstein, M. H., Putnick, D. L., Bradley, R. H., Deater-Deckard, K., & Lansford, J. E. (2016). Gender in low- and middle-income countries: I. Introduction. *Monographs of the Society for Research in Child Development, 81*(1), 1–144.

Bornstein, M. H., Putnick, D. L., Gartstein, M. A., Hahn, C., Auestad, N., & O'Connor, D. L. (2015). Infant temperament: Stability by age, gender, birth order, term status, and socioeconomic status. *Child Development, 86,* 844–863. doi:10.1111/cdev.12367

Borstelmann, L. J. (1983). Children before psychology: Ideas about children from antiquity to the late 1800s. In P. H. Mussen (Series Ed.) & W. Kessen (Vol. Ed.), *Handbook of child psychology: Vol. 1. History, theory, and methods* (4th ed., pp. 1–40). New York, NY: Wiley.

Bortfeld, H., Fava, E., & Boas, D. A. (2009). Identifying cortical lateralization of speech processing in infants using near-infrared spectroscopy. *Developmental Neuropsychology, 34,* 52–65. doi:10.1080/87565640802564481

Bortfeld, H., Morgan, J. L., Golinkoff, R. M., & Rathbun, K. (2005). Mommy and me: Familiar names help launch babies into speech-stream segmentation. *Psychological Science, 16,* 298–304. doi:10.1111/j.0956-7976.2005.01531.x

Bos, H. M. W., Knox, J. R, van Rijn-van Gelderen, L., & Gatrell, N. K. (2016). Same-sex and different-sex parent households and child health outcomes: Findings from the National Survey of Children's Health. *Journal of Developmental and Behavioral Pediatrics, 37,* 179–187. doi:10.1097/DBP.0000000000000288

Bos, H. M. W., Sandfort, T. G. M., de Bruyn, E. H., & Hakvoort, E. M. (2008). Same-sex attraction, social relationships, psychosocial functioning, and school performance in early adolescence. *Developmental Psychology, 44,* 59–68. doi:10.1037/0012-1649.44.1.59

Bos, H. M. W., & van Balen, F. (2008). Children in planned lesbian families: Stigmatisation, psychological adjustment and protective factors. *Culture, Health and Sexuality, 10,* 221–236. doi:10.1080/13691050701601702

Bosma, H. A., & Kunnen, E. S. (2001). Determinants and mechanisms in ego identity development: A review and synthesis. *Developmental Review, 21,* 39–66. doi:10.1006/drev.2000.0514

Boskey, E. R. (2014). Understanding transgender identity development in childhood and adolescence. *American Journal of Sexuality Education, 9,* 445–463.

Bouchard, T. J., Jr. (2004). Genetic influence on human psychological traits: A survey. *Current Directions in Psychological Science, 13,* 148–151. doi:10.1111/j.0963-7214.2004.00295.x

Bouchard, T. J., Jr., Lykken, D. T., McGue, M., Segal, N. L., & Tellegen, A. (1990, October 12). Sources of human psychological differences: The Minnesota Study of Twins Reared Apart. *Science, 250,* 223–228.

Boukhris, T., Sheehy, O., Mottron, L., & Bérard, A. (2016). Antidepressant use during pregnancy and the risk of autism spectrum disorder in children. *JAMA Pediatrics, 170*(2), 117–124.

Boutwell, B. B., Franklin, C. A., Barnes, J. C., & Beaver, K. M. (2011). Physical punishment and childhood aggression: The role of gender and gene–environment interplay. *Aggressive Behavior, 37,* 559–568. doi:10.1002/ab.20409

Bowker, A., Bukowski, W., Zargarpour, S., & Hoza, B. (1998). A structural and functional analysis of a two-dimensional model of social isolation. *Merrill-Palmer Quarterly, 44,* 447–463. doi:10.2307/23093748

Bowker, J. C., & Raja, R. (2011). Social withdrawal subtypes during early adolescence in India. *Journal of Abnormal Child Psychology, 39,* 201–212. doi:10.1007/s10802-010-9461-7

Bowlby, J. (1953). *Child care and the growth of love* (M. Fry, Ed.). London, England: Penguin Books.

Bowlby, J. (1969). *Attachment and loss: Vol. 1. Attachment.* New York, NY: Basic Books.

Bowlby, J. (1973). *Attachment and loss: Vol. 2. Separation: Anxiety and anger.* New York, NY: Basic Books.

Bowlby, J. (1980). *Attachment and loss: Vol. 3. Loss.* New York, NY: Basic Books.

Boxer, P., Groves, C. L., & Docherty, M. (2015). Video games do indeed influence children and adolescents' aggression, prosocial behavior, and academic performance: A clearer reading of Ferguson (2015). *Perspectives on Psychological Science, 10*(5), 671–673.

Boyce, W. T., & Ellis, B. J. (2005). Biological sensitivity to context: I. An evolutionary-developmental theory of the origins and functions of stress reactivity. *Development and Psychopathology, 17,* 271–301. doi:10.1017/S0954579405050145

Braaksma, M. A. H., Rijlaarsdam, G., Van den Bergh, H., & van Hout-Wolters, B. H. A. M. (2004). Observational learning and its effects on the orchestration of writing processes. *Cognition and Instruction, 22,* 1–36.

Bradbard, M. R., Martin, C. L., Endsley, R. C., & Halverson, C. F. (1986). Influence of sex stereotypes on children's exploration and memory: A competence versus performance distinction. *Developmental Psychology, 22,* 481–486. doi:10.1037/0012-1649.22.4.481

Bradley, R. H., & Caldwell, B. M. (1979). Home observation for measurement of the environment: A revision of the preschool scale. *American Journal of Mental Deficiency, 84,* 235–244.

Bradley, R. H., & Caldwell, B. M. (1984). 174 children: A study of the relationship between home environment and cognitive development during the first 5 years. In A. W. Gottfried (Ed.), *Home environment and early cognitive development* (pp. 5–56). New York, NY: Academic Press.

Bradley, R. H., Convyn, R. F., Burchinal, M., McAdoo, H. P., & García Coll, C. (2001). The home environments of children in the United States: Part II. Relations with behavioral development through age thirteen. *Child Development, 72,* 1868–1886.

Bradley, R. H., Whiteside, L., Mundrom, D. J., Casey, P. H., Kelleher, K. J., & Pope, S. K. (1994). Contribution of early intervention and early caregiving experiences to resilience in low-birthweight, premature children living in poverty. *Journal of Clinical Child Psychology, 23,* 425–434.

Bradshaw, C. P., Waasdorp, T. E., & Leaf, P. J. (2012). Effects of school-wide positive behavioral interventions and supports on child behavior problems. *Pediatrics, 130,* e1136–e1145. doi:10.1542/peds.2012-0243

Braine, M. D. S. (1976). [Review of the book *The acquisition of phonology,* by N. V. Smith]. *Language, 52,* 489–498.

Bramlett, M. D., & Mosher, W. D. (2002). *Vital and health statistics: Series 22. Cohabitation, marriage, divorce, and remarriage in the United States.* Hyattsville, MD: National Center for Health Statistics.

Brannon, E. M., Lutz, D., & Cordes, S. (2006). The development of area discrimination and its implications for number representation in infancy. *Developmental Science, 9,* F59–F64. doi:10.1111/j.1467-7687.2006.00530.x

Brannon, E. M., Suanda, S., & Libertus, K. (2007). Temporal discrimination increases in precision over development and parallels the development of numerosity discrimination. *Developmental Science, 10,* 770–777. doi:10.1111/j.1467-7687.2007.00635.x

Branstetter, S. A., Low, S., & Furman, W. (2011). The influence of parents and friends on adolescent substance use: A multidimensional approach. *Journal of Substance Use, 16*, 150–160. doi:10.3109/14659891.2010.519421

Braungart-Rieker, J. M., Hill-Soderlund, A. L., & Karrass, J. (2010). Fear and anger reactivity trajectories from 4 to 16 months: The roles of temperament, regulation, and maternal sensitivity. *Developmental Psychology, 46*, 791–804. doi:10.1037/a0019673

Braver, S. L., Ellman, I. M., & Fabricius, W. V. (2003). Relocation of children after divorce and children's best interests: New evidence and legal considerations. *Journal of Family Psychology, 17*, 206–219. doi:10.1037/0893-3200.17.2.206

Bray, J. H., Adams, G. J., Getz, J. G., & McQueen, A. (2003). Individuation, peers, and adolescent alcohol use: A latent growth analysis. *Journal of Consulting and Clinical Psychology, 71*, 553–564. doi:10.1037/0022-006X.71.3.553

Bray, J. H., & Berger, S. H. (1993). Developmental issues in StepFamilies Research Project: Family relationships and parent–child interactions. *Journal of Family Psychology, 7*, 76–90. doi:10.1037/0893-3200.7.1.76

Breazeal (Ferrell), C. (1998), Early Experiments using Motivations to Regulate Human-Robot Interaction. In *Proceedings of 1998 AAAI Fall Symposium: Emotional and Intelligent, The Tangled Knot of Cognition*, Orlando, FL. 31–36.

Bremner, J. G. (1978). Spatial errors made by infants: Inadequate spatial cues or evidence of egocentrism? *British Journal of Psychology, 69*, 77–84. doi:10.1111/j.2044-8295.1978.tb01634.x

Bremner, J. G., Knowles, L., & Andreasen, G. (1994). Processes underlying young children's spatial orientation during movement. *Journal of Experimental Child Psychology, 57*, 355–376. doi:10.1006/jecp.1994.1017

Brendgen, M., Boivin, M., Dionne, G., Barker, E. D., Vitaro, F., Girard, A., . . . Pérusse, D. (2011). Gene–environment processes linking aggression, peer victimization, and the teacher–child relationship. *Child Development, 82*, 2021–2036. doi:10.1111/j.1467-8624.2011.01644.x

Brendgen, M., Boivin, M., Vitaro, F., Bukowski, W. M., Dionne, G., Tremblay, R. E., & Pérusse, D. (2008). Linkages between children's and their friends' social and physical aggression: Evidence for a gene–environment interaction? *Child Development, 79*, 13–29. doi:10.1111/j.1467-8624.2007.01108.x

Brendgen, M., Vitaro, F., & Bukowski, W. M. (2000). Deviant friends and early adolescents' emotional and behavioral adjustment. *Journal of Research on Adolescence, 10*, 173–189. doi:10.1207/SJRA1002_3

Brendgen, M., Vitaro, F., Bukowski, W. M., Doyle, A. B., & Markiewicz, D. (2001). Developmental profiles of peer social preference over the course of elementary school: Associations with trajectories of externalizing and internalizing behavior. *Developmental Psychology, 37*, 308–320.

Brennan, P. A., Hammen, C., Katz, A. R., & Le Brocque, R. M. (2002). Maternal depression, paternal psychopathology, and adolescent diagnostic outcomes. *Journal of Consulting and Clinical Psychology, 70*, 1075–1085.

Brenner, E. M., & Salovey, P. (1997). Emotion regulation during childhood: Developmental, interpersonal, and individual considerations. In P. Salovey & D. J. Sluyter (Eds.), *Emotional development and emotional intelligence: Educational implications* (pp. 168–195). New York, NY: Basic Books.

Bretherton, I., & Beeghly, M. (1982). Talking about internal states: The acquisition of an explicit theory of mind. *Developmental Psychology, 18*, 906–921.

Bretherton, I., Golby, B., & Cho, E. (1997). Attachment and the transmission of values. In J. E. Grusec & L. Kuczynski (Eds.), *Parenting and children's internalization of values: A handbook of contemporary theory* (pp. 103–134). Hoboken, NJ: Wiley.

Bretherton, I., & Munholland, K. A. (1999). Internal working models in attachment relationships: A construct revisited. In J. Cassidy & P. R. Shaver (Eds.), *Handbook of attachment: Theory, research, and clinical applications* (pp. 89–111). New York, NY: Guilford Press.

Briars, D. J., & Siegler, R. S. (1984). A featural analysis of preschoolers' counting knowledge. *Developmental Psychology, 20*(4), 607–618. doi:10.1037/0012-1649.20.4.607

Bridges, L. J., & Grolnick, W. S. (1995). The development of emotional self-regulation in infancy and early childhood. In N. Eisenberg (Ed.), *Review of personality and social psychology: Vol. 15. Social development* (pp. 185–211). Thousand Oaks, CA: Sage.

Bril, B., & Sabatier, C. (1986). The cultural context of motor development: Postural manipulations in the daily life of Bambara babies (Mali). *International Journal of Behavioral Development, 9*, 439–453.

Bringewatt, E. H., & Gershoff, E. T. (2010). Falling through the cracks: Gaps and barriers in the mental health system for America's disadvantaged children. *Children and Youth Services Review, 32*, 1291–1299. doi:10.1016/j.childyouth.2010.04.021

Brody, G. H., Stoneman, Z., McCoy, J. K., & Forehand, R. (1992). Contemporaneous and longitudinal associations of sibling conflict with family relationship assessments and family discussions about sibling problems. *Child Development, 63*, 391–400. doi:10.1111/j.1467-8624.1992.tb01635.x

Brody, N. (1992). *Intelligence* (2nd ed.). San Diego, CA: Academic Press.

Broesch, T. L., Callaghan, T., Henrich, J., Murphy, C., & Rochat, P. (2010). Cultural variations in children's mirror self-recognition.

Journal of Cross-Cultural Psychology, 42, 1018–1029. doi:10.1177/0022022110381114

Broidy, L. M., Nagin, D. S., Tremblay, R. E., Bates, J. E., Brame, B., Dodge, K. A., . . . Vitaro, F. (2003). Developmental trajectories of childhood disruptive behaviors and adolescent delinquency: A six-site, cross-national study. *Developmental Psychology, 39*, 222–245. doi:10.1037/0012-1649.39.2.222

Bronfenbrenner, U. (1979). *The ecology of human development: Experiments by nature and design.* Cambridge, MA: Harvard University Press.

Bronfenbrenner, U. (1993). The ecology of cognitive development: Research models and fugitive findings. In R. H. Wozniak & K. W. Fischer (Eds.), *Development in context: Acting and thinking in specific environments* (pp. 3–44). Hillsdale, NJ: Erlbaum.

Bronfenbrenner, U., & Morris, P. A. (1998). The ecology of developmental processes. In W. Damon (Series Ed.) & R. M. Lerner (Vol. Ed.), *Handbook of child psychology: Vol. 1. Theoretical models of human development* (5th ed., pp. 993–1028). New York, NY: Wiley.

Bronfenbrenner, U., & Morris, P. A. (2006). The bioecological model of human development. In R. M. Lerner & W. Damon (Eds.), *Handbook of child psychology* (6th ed.): Vol 1, Theoretical models of human development (pp. 793–828). Hoboken, NJ: John Wiley & Sons.

Bronson, G. W. (1972). Infants' reactions to unfamiliar persons and novel objects. *Monographs of the Society for Research in Child Development, 37*(3, Serial No. 148).

Brooker, I., & Poulin-Dubois, D. (2013). Is a bird an apple? The effect of speaker labeling accuracy on infants' word learning, imitation, and helping behaviors. *Infancy, 18*(s1), E46–E68. doi:10.1111/infa.12027

Brooks, R., & Meltzoff, A. N. (2008). Infant gaze following and pointing predict accelerated vocabulary growth through two years of age: A longitudinal, growth curve modeling study. *Journal of Child Language, 35*, 207–220. doi:10.1017/S030500090700829X

Brooks-Gunn, J., Han, W.-J., & Waldfogel, J. (2010). First-year maternal employment and child development in the first 7 years: III. What distinguishes women who work full-time, part-time, or not at all in the 1st year? *Monographs of the Society for Research in Child Development, 75*(2, Serial No. 296), 35–49.

Brophy-Herb, H. E., Schiffman, R. F., Bocknek, E. L., Dupuis, S. B., Fitzgerald, H. E., Horodynski, M., . . . Hillaker, B. (2011). Toddlers' social-emotional competence in the contexts of maternal emotion socialization and contingent responsiveness in a low-income sample. *Social Development, 20*, 73–92.

Brown, A. L. (1997). Transforming schools into communities of thinking and learning about serious matters. *American Psychologist, 52,* 399–413. doi:10.1037/0003-066X.52.4.399

Brown, A. S., Begg, M. D., Gravenstein, S., Schaefer, C. A., Wyatt, R. J., Bresnahan, M., . . . Susser, E. S. (2004). Serologic evidence of prenatal influenza in the etiology of schizophrenia. *Archives of General Psychiatry, 61,* 774–780. doi:10.1001/archpsyc.61.8.774

Brown, A. S., & Derkits, E. J. (2010). Prenatal infection and schizophrenia: A review of epidemiologic and translational studies. *American Journal of Psychiatry, 167*(3), 261–280.

Brown, B. B. (1990). Peer groups and peer cultures. In S. S. Feldman & G. R. Elliott (Eds.), *At the threshold: The developing adolescent* (pp. 171–196). Cambridge, MA: Harvard University Press.

Brown, B. B. (2004). Adolescents' relationships with peers. In R. M. Lerner & L. Steinberg (Eds.), *Handbook of adolescent psychology* (2nd ed., pp. 363–394). Hoboken, NJ: Wiley.

Brown, B. B., Bank, H., & Steinberg, L. (2008). Smoke in the looking glass: Effects of discordance between self- and peer rated crowd affiliation on adolescent anxiety, depression and self-feelings. *Journal of Youth and Adolescence, 37,* 1163–1177. doi:10.1007/s10964-007-9198-y

Brown, B. B., Clasen, D. R., & Eicher, S. A. (1986). Perceptions of peer pressure, peer conformity dispositions, and self-reported behavior among adolescents. *Developmental Psychology, 22,* 521–530. doi:10.1037/0012-1649.22.4.521

Brown, B. B., & Klute, C. (2003). Friends, cliques, and crowds. In G. R. Adams & M. D. Berzonsky (Eds.), *Blackwell handbook of adolescence* (pp. 330–348). Malden, MA: Blackwell.

Brown, C. S., & Bigler, R. S. (2004). Children's perceptions of gender discrimination. *Developmental Psychology, 40,* 714–726. doi:10.1037/0012-1649.40.5.714

Brown, C. S., & Bigler, R. S. (2005). Children's perceptions of discrimination: A developmental model. *Child Development, 76,* 533–553. doi:10.1111/j.1467-8624.2005.00862.x

Brown, G. L., Mangelsdorf, S. C., & Neff, C. (2012). Father involvement, paternal sensitivity, and father–child attachment security in the first 3 years. *Journal of Family Psychology, 26,* 421–430. doi:10.1037/a0027836

Brown, J. R., & Dunn, J. (1996). Continuities in emotion understanding from three to six years. *Child Development, 67,* 789–802.

Brown, R. (1973). *A first language: The early stages.* Cambridge, MA: Harvard University Press.

Brown, R., & Fraser, C. (1963). The acquisition of syntax. In C. N. Cofer & B. S. Musgrave (Eds.), *Verbal behavior and learning: Problems and processes; proceedings* (pp. 158–196). New York, NY: McGraw-Hill.

Brown, R., & Hanlon, C. (1970). Derivational complexity and order of acquisition in child speech. In J. R. Hayes (Ed.), *Cognition and the development of language* (Vol. 8, pp. 11–53). New York, NY: Wiley.

Brown, R. W. (1957). Linguistic determinism and the part of speech. *Journal of Abnormal Psychology and Social Psychology, 55,* 1–5.

Brownell, C. A., Ramani, G. B., & Zerwas, S. (2006). Becoming a social partner with peers: Cooperation and social understanding in one- and two-year-olds. *Child Development, 77,* 803–821. doi:10.1111/j.1467-8624.2006.t01-1-.x-i1

Brownell, C. A., Zerwas, S., & Ramani, G. B. (2007). "So big": The development of body self-awareness in toddlers. *Child Development, 78,* 1426–1440. doi:10.1111/j.1467-8624.2007.01075.x

Brownell, K. (2004). Overfeeding the future. In A. Heintzman & E. Solomon (Eds.), *Feeding the future: From fat to famine* (pp. 155–190). Toronto, Ontario, Canada: House of Anansi Press.

Brownell, K. D. (2003). Diet, obesity, public policy, and defiance. In R. J. Sternberg (Ed.), *Psychologists defying the crowd: Stories of those who battled the establishment and won* (pp. 47–64). Washington, DC: American Psychological Association.

Bruck, M., Ceci, S. J., & Principe, G. F. (2006). The child and the law. In W. Damon & R. M. Lerner (Series Eds.) & K. A. Renninger & I. E. Sigel (Vol. Eds.), *Handbook of child psychology: Vol. 4. Child psychology in practice* (6th ed., pp. 776–816). Hoboken, NJ: Wiley.

Brumariu, L. E., & Kerns, K. A. (2010). Parent–child attachment and internalizing symptoms in childhood and adolescence: A review of empirical findings and future directions. *Development and Psychopathology, 22,* 177–203. doi:10.1017/S0954579409990344

Brummelman, E., Crocker, J., & Bushman, B. J. (2016). The praise paradox: When and why praise backfires in children with low self-esteem. *Child Development Perspectives, 10,* 111–115. doi:10.1111/cdep.12171

Brummelman, E., Thomaes, S., de Castro, B. O., Overbeek, G., & Bushman, B. J. (2014). "That's not just beautiful—That's incredibly beautiful!" The adverse impact of inflated praise on children with low self-esteem. *Psychological Science, 25,* 728–735. doi:0956797613514251

Brummelte, S., & Galea, L. A. (2016). Postpartum depression: Etiology, treatment and consequences for maternal care. *Hormones and Behavior, 77,* 153–166.

Bruner, J. S. (1973). *Beyond the information given: Studies in the psychology of knowing* (J. M. Anglin, Ed.). New York, NY: Norton.

Bruner, J. S. (1977). Early social interaction and language acquisition. In H. R. Schaffer (Ed.), *Studies in mother–infant interaction* (pp. 271–289). London, England: Academic Press.

Bryan, J. H., & Walbek, N. H. (1970). Preaching and practicing generosity: Children's actions and reactions. *Child Development, 41,* 329–353. doi:10.2307/1127035

Bryant, J. A., Sanders-Jackson, A., & Smallwood, A. M. K. (2006). IMing, text messaging, and adolescent social networks. *Journal of Computer-Mediated Communication, 11,* 577–592.

Bryant, J. B., & Polkosky, M. (2001, April). *Parents responses to pre-schoolers' lexical innovations.* Paper presented at the Biennial Meeting of the Society for Research in Child Development, Minneapolis, MN.

Buchanan, C. M., Maccoby, E. E., & Dornbusch, S. M. (1991). Caught between parents: Adolescents' experience in divorced homes. *Child Development, 62,* 1008–1029. doi:10.1111/j.1467-8624.1991.tb01586.x

Bucchianeri, M. M., Eisenberg, M. E., Wall, M. M., Piran, N., & Neumark-Sztainer, D. (2014). Multiple types of harassment: Associations with emotional well-being and unhealthy behaviors in adolescents. *Journal of Adolescent Health, 54,* 724–729.

Buckley, C. (2015, October 29). China ends one-child policy, allowing families two children. *The New York Times.* Retrieved from http://www .nytimes.com/2015/10/30/world/asia/china-end-one-child-policy.html?_r=0

Buckner, J. C., Bassuk, E. L., Weinreb, L. F., & Brooks, M. G. (1999). Homelessness and its relation to the mental health and behavior of low-income school-age children. *Developmental Psychology, 35,* 246–257. doi:10.1037/0012-1649.35.1.246

Buehler, C., Anthony, C., Krishnakumar, A., Stone, G., Gerard, J., & Pemberton, S. (1997). Interparental conflict and youth problem behaviors: A meta-analysis. *Journal of Child and Family Studies, 6,* 233–247. doi:10.1023/A:1025006909538

Buehler, C., Lange, G., & Franck, K. L. (2007). Adolescents' cognitive and emotional responses to marital hostility. *Child Development, 78,* 775–789. doi:10.1111/j.1467-8624.2007.01032.x

Bugental, D. B., Beaulieu, D. A., & Silbert-Geiger, A. (2010). Increases in parental investment and child health as a result of an early intervention. *Journal of Experimental Child Psychology, 106,* 30–40. doi:10.1016/j.jecp.2009.10.004

Bugental, D. B., Blue, J., & Cruzcosa, M. (1989). Perceived control over caregiving outcomes: Implications for child abuse. *Developmental Psychology, 25,* 532–539. doi:10.1037/0012-1649.25.4.532

Bugental, D. B., Ellerson, P. C., Lin, E. K., Rainey, B., Kokotovic, A., & O'Hara, N. (2002). A cognitive approach to child abuse prevention. *Journal of Family Psychology, 16,* 243–258. doi:10.1037/0893-3200.16.3.243

Bugental, D. B., & Happaney, K. (2004). Predicting infant maltreatment in low-income families: The interactive effects of maternal attributions and child status at birth. *Developmental Psychology, 40,* 234–243.

Bugental, D. B., Martorell, G. A., & Barraza, V. (2003). The hormonal costs of subtle forms of infant maltreatment. *Hormones and Behavior, 43,* 237–244. doi:10.1016/S0018-506X(02)00008-9

Bugental, D. B., & Schwartz, A. (2009). A cognitive approach to child mistreatment prevention among medically at-risk infants. *Developmental Psychology, 45*(1), 284.

Buist, K. L., Paalman, C. H., Branje, S. J., Deković, M., Reitz, E., Verhoeven, M. . . . Hale III, W. W. (2014). Longitudinal effects of sibling relationship quality on adolescent problem behavior: A cross-ethnic comparison. *Cultural Diversity and Ethnic Minority Psychology, 20*(2), 266. doi:10.1037/a0033675

Bukowski, W. M., Cillessen, A. H. N., & Velasquez, A. M. (2012). Peer ratings. In B. Laursen, T. D. Little, & N. A. Card (Eds.), *Handbook of developmental research methods* (pp. 211–230). New York, NY: Guilford Press.

Bukowski, W. M., Gauze, C., Hoza, B., & Newcomb, A. F. (1993). Differences and consistency between same-sex and other-sex peer relationships during early adolescence. *Developmental Psychology, 29,* 255–263. doi:10.1037/0012-1649.29.2.255

Bukowski, W. M., Laursen, B., & Hoza, B. (2010). The snowball effect: Friendship moderates escalations in depressed affect among avoidant and excluded children. *Development and Psychopathology, 22,* 749–757. doi:10.1017/S095457941000043X

Bukowski, W. M., Newcomb, A. F., & Hartup, W. W. (1996). Friendship and its significance in childhood and adolescence: Introduction and comment. In W. M. Bukowski, A. F. Newcomb, & W. W. Hartup (Eds.), *The company they keep: Friendship in childhood and adolescence* (pp. 1–15). Cambridge, England: Cambridge University Press.

Bulf, H., Johnson, S. P., & Valenza, E. (2011). Visual statistical learning in the newborn infant. *Cognition, 121,* 127–132. doi:10.1016/j.cognition.2011.06.010

Bullock, M., & Lütkenhaus, P. (1990). Who am I? Self-understanding in toddlers. *Merrill-Palmer Quarterly, 36,* 217–238.

Bullock, M., & Russell, J. A. (1985). Further evidence on preschoolers' interpretation of facial expressions. *International Journal of Behavioral Development, 8,* 15–38.

Bumpass, L. L., Martin, T. C., & Sweet, J. A. (1991). The impact of family background

and early marital factors on marital disruption. *Journal of Family Issues, 12,* 22–42. doi:10.1177/019251391012001003

Bunge, S. A., & Zelazo, P. D. (2006). A brain-based account of the development of rule use in childhood. *Current Directions in Psychological Science, 15,* 118–121.

Burchinal, M. R., Campbell, F. A., Brayant, D. M., Wasik, B. H., & Ramey, C. T. (1997). Early intervention and mediating processes in cognitive performance of children of low-income African American families. *Child Development, 68,* 935–954.

Burchinal, M. R., & Clarke-Stewart, K. A. (2007). Maternal employment and child cognitive outcomes: The importance of analytic approach. *Developmental Psychology, 43,* 1140–1155. doi:10.1037/0012-1649.43.5.1140

Burgess, K. B., Marshall, P. J., Rubin, K. H., & Fox, N. A. (2003). Infant attachment and temperament as predictors of subsequent externalizing problems and cardiac physiology. *Journal of Child Psychology and Psychiatry, 44,* 819–831. doi:10.1111/1469-7610.00167

Burkam, D. T., Lee, V. E., & Smerdon, B. A. (1997). Gender and science learning early in high school: Subject matter and laboratory experiences. *American Educational Research Journal, 34,* 297–331. doi:10.3102/00028312034002297

Burkam, D. T., Ready, D. D., Lee, V. E., & LoGerfo, L. F. (2004). Social-class differences in summer learning between kindergarten and first grade: Model specification and estimation. *Sociology of Education, 77,* 1–31.

Burmeister, D. (1996). Need fulfillment, interpersonal competence, and the developmental contexts of early adolescent friendship. In W. M. Bukowski, A. F. Newcomb, & W. W. Hartup (Eds), *The company they keep. Friendship in childhood and adolescence* (pp. 66–86). Cambridge, England: Cambridge University Press.

Burnette, M. L., Oshri, A., Lax, R., Richards, D., & Ragbeer, S. N. (2012). Pathways from harsh parenting to adolescent antisocial behavior: A multidomain test of gender moderation. *Development and Psychopathology, 24,* 857–870. doi:10.1017/S0954579412000417

Burnham, D., & Dodd, B. (2004). Auditory–visual speech integration by prelinguistic infants: Perception of an emergent consonant in the McGurk effect. *Developmental Psychobiology, 45*(4), 204–220.

Burt, S. A., Barnes, A. R., McGue, M., & Iacono, W. G. (2008). Parental divorce and adolescent delinquency: Ruling out the impact of common genes. *Developmental Psychology, 44,* 1668–1677. doi:10.1037/a0013477

Burt, S. A., Donnellan, M. B., Iacono, W., & McGue, M. (2011). Age-of-onset or behavioral sub-types? A prospective comparison of two approaches to characterizing the heterogeneity

within antisocial behavior. *Journal of Abnormal Child Psychology, 39,* 633–644. doi:10.1007/s10802-011-9491-9

Burt, S. A., McGue, M., Krueger, R. F., & Iacono, W. G. (2005). How are parent–child conflict and childhood externalizing symptoms related over time? Results from a genetically informative cross-lagged study. *Development and Psychopathology, 17,* 145–165.

Bushnell, E. W., McKenzie, B. E., Lawrence, D. A., & Connell, S. (1995). The spatial coding strategies of one-year-old infants in a locomotor search task. *Child Development, 66,* 937–958.

Bushnell, I. W. R., Sai, F., & Mullin, J. T. (2011). Neonatal recognition of the mother's face. *British Journal of Developmental Psychology, 7,* 3–15. doi:10.1111/j.2044-835X.1989.tb00784.x

Buss, A. T., & Spencer, J. P. (2014). The emergent executive: A dynamic field theory of the development of executive function. *Monographs of the Society for Research in Child Development, 79*(2), vii–103. doi:10.1002/mono.12096

Buss, D. M. (1999). *Evolutionary psychology: The new science of the mind.* Boston, MA: Allyn and Bacon.

Buss, K. A., Davidson, R. J., Kalin, N. H., & Goldsmith, H. H. (2004). Context-specific freezing and associated physiological reactivity as a dysregulated fear response. *Developmental Psychology, 40,* 583–594. doi:10.1037/0012-1649.40.4.583

Buss, K. A., & Kiel, E. J. (2011). Do maternal protective behaviors alleviate toddlers' fearful distress? *International Journal of Behavioral Development, 35,* 136–143. doi:10.1177/0165025410375922

Bussey, K., & Bandura, A. (1999). Social cognitive theory of gender development and differentiation. *Psychological Review, 106,* 676–713.

Bussey, K., & Bandura, A. (2004). Social cognitive theory of gender development and functioning. In A. H. Eagly, A. E. Beall, & R. J. Sternberg (Eds.), *The Psychology of Gender* (2nd ed., pp. 92–119). New York, NY: Guilford Press.

Buttelmann, D., Carpenter, M., Call, J., & Tomasello, M. (2008). Rational tool use and tool choice in human infants and great apes. *Child Development, 79,* 609–626. doi:10.1111/j.1467-8624.2008.01146.x

Butterworth, B. (2010). Foundational numerical capacities and the origins of dyscalculia. *Trends in Cognitive Sciences, 14,* 534–541. doi:10.1016/j.tics.2010.09.007

Byers-Heinlein, K. (2013). Parental language mixing: Its measurement and the relation of mixed input to young bilingual children's vocabulary size. *Bilingualism: Language and Cognition, 16*(01), 32–48.

Byers-Heinlein, K., Burns, T. C., & Werker, J. F. (2010). The roots of bilingualism in newborns. *Psychological Science, 21*, 343–348. doi:10.1177/0956797609360758

Byers-Heinlein, K., & Lew-Williams, C. (2013). Bilingualism in the early years: What the science says. *LEARNing Landscapes, 7*(1), 95–112.

Byers-Heinlein, K., & Werker, J. F. (2009). Monolingual, bilingual, trilingual: Infants' language experience influences the development of a word-learning heuristic. *Developmental Science, 12*, 815–823. doi:10.1111/j.1467-7687.2009.00902.x

Byrnes, J. P., Miller, D. C., & Schafer, W. D. (1999). Gender differences in risk taking: A meta-analysis. *Psychological Bulletin, 125*, 367–383. doi:10.1037/0033-2909.125.3.367

Cahan, S., & Cohen, N. (1989). Age versus schooling effects on intelligence development. *Child Development, 60*, 1239–1249.

Cai, H., Brown, J. D., Deng, C., & Oakes, M. A. (2007). Self-esteem and culture: Differences in cognitive self-evaluations or affective self-regard? *Asian Journal of Social Psychology, 10*, 162–170. doi:10.1111/j.1467-839X.2007.00222.x

Cain, K. M., & Dweck, C. S. (1995). The relation between motivational patterns and achievement cognitions through the elementary school years. *Merrill-Palmer Quarterly, 41*, 25–52. doi:10.2307/23087453

Cairns, R. B., Cairns, B. D., Neckerman, H. J., Ferguson, L. L., & Gariépy, J.-L. (1989). Growth and aggression: I. Childhood to early adolescence. *Developmental Psychology, 25*, 320–330. doi:10.1037/0012-1649.25.2.320

Cairns, R. B., Leung, M.-C., Buchanan, L., & Cairns, B. D. (1995). Friendships and social networks in childhood and adolescence: Fluidity, reliability, and interrelations. *Child Development, 66*, 1330–1345. doi:10.2307/1131650

Calati, R., Pedrini, L., Alighieri, S., Alvarez, M. I., Desideri, L., Durante, D., . . . Pericoli, V. (2011). Is cognitive behavioural therapy an effective complement to antidepressants in adolescents? A meta-analysis. *Acta Neuropsychiatrica, 23*, 263–271.

Caldwell, C. H., Zimmerman, M. A., Bernat, D. H., Sellers, R. M., & Notaro, P. C. (2002). Racial identity, maternal support, and psychological distress among African American adolescents. *Child Development, 73*, 1322–1336. doi:10.1111/1467-8624.00474

Caldwell, M. S., Rudolph, K. D., Troop-Gordon, W., & Kim, D.-Y. (2004). Reciprocal influences among relational self-views, social disengagement, and peer stress during early adolescence. *Child Development, 75*, 1140–1154. doi:10.1111/j.1467-8624.2004.00730.x

Calkins, S. D. (2002). Does aversive behavior during toddlerhood matter? The effects of difficult temperament on maternal perceptions

and behavior. *Infant Mental Health Journal, 23*, 381–402.

Calkins, S. D., & Dedmon, S. E. (2000). Physiological and behavioral regulation in two-year-old children with aggressive/destructive behavior problems. *Journal of Abnormal Child Psychology, 28*, 103–118.

Calkins, S. D., Fox, N. A., & Marshall, T. R. (1996). Behavioral and physiological antecedents of inhibited and uninhibited behavior. *Child Development, 67*, 523–540.

Calkins, S. D., & Keane, S. P. (2004). Cardiac vagal regulation across the preschool period: Stability, continuity, and implications for childhood adjustment. *Developmental Psychobiology, 45*, 101–112. doi:10.1002/dev.20020

Calkins, S. D., & Swingler, M. M. (2012). Psychobiological measures of temperament in childhood. In M. R. Zentner & R. L. Shiner (Eds.), *Handbook of temperament* (pp. 229–247). New York, NY: Guilford Press.

Callaghan, T., Moll, H., Rakoczy, H., Warneken, F., Liszkowski, U., Behne, T., & Tomasello, M. (2011). Early social cognition in three cultural contexts. *Monographs of the Society for Research in Child Development, 76*(2, Serial No. 299), vii–142. doi:10.1111/j.1540-5834.2011.00603.x

Callaghan, T., Rochat, P., Lillard, A., Claux, M. L., Odden, H., Itakura, S., . . . Singh, S. (2005). Synchrony in the onset of mental-state reasoning: Evidence from five cultures. *Psychological Science, 16*, 378–384. doi:10.1111/j.0956-7976.2005.01544.x

Callaghan, T. C. (1999). Early understanding and production of graphic symbols. *Child Development, 70*, 1314–1324. doi:10.1111/1467-8624.00096

Callaghan, T. C., Rochat, P., & Corbit, J. (2012). Young children's knowledge of the representational function of pictorial symbols: Development across the preschool years in three cultures. *Journal of Cognition and Development, 13*(3), 320–353.

Callanan, M. A. (1990). Parents' descriptions of objects: Potential data for children's inferences about category principles. *Cognitive Development, 5*, 101–122. doi:10.1016/0885-2014(90)90015-L

Callanan, M. A., & Sabbagh, M. A. (2004). Multiple labels for objects in conversations with young children: Parents' language and children's developing expectations about word meanings. *Developmental Psychology, 40*, 746–762.

Calvete, E., & Orue, I. (2012). Social information processing as a mediator between cognitive schemas and aggressive behavior in adolescents. *Journal of Abnormal Child Psychology, 40*, 105–117. doi:10.1007/s10802-011-9546-y

Camarena, P. M., Sarigiani, P. A., & Petersen, A. C. (1990). Gender-specific pathways to intimacy in early adolescence. *Journal of Youth and Adolescence, 19*, 19–32. doi:10.1007/BF01539442

Campbell, A., Shirley, L., & Caygill, L. (2002). Sex-typed preferences in three domains:

Do two-year-olds need cognitive variables? *British Journal of Psychology, 93*, 203–217. doi:10.1348/000712602162544

Campbell, F. A., Pungello, E. P., Burchinal, M., Kainz, K., Pan, Y., Wasik, B. H., . . . Ramey, C. T. (2012). Adult outcomes as a function of an early childhood educational program: An Abecedarian Project follow-up. *Developmental Psychology, 48*, 1033–1043.

Campbell, F. A., Pungello, E. P., Miller-Johnson, S., Burchinal, M., & Ramey, C. T. (2001). The development of cognitive and academic abilities: Growth curves from an early childhood educational experiment. *Developmental Psychology, 37*, 231–242.

Campbell, F. A., & Ramey, C. T. (2007, December). *Carolina Abecedarian Project.* Paper presented at the National Invitational Conference of the Early Childhood Research Collaborative on "Critical Issues in Cost Effectiveness in Children's First Decade," Minnesota, MN.

Campbell, S. B., Matestic, P., von Stauffenberg, C., Mohan, R., & Kirchner, T. (2007). Trajectories of maternal depressive symptoms, maternal sensitivity, and children's functioning at school entry. *Developmental Psychology, 43*, 1202–1215. doi:10.1037/0012-1649.43.5.1202

Campbell, S. B., Spieker, S., Vandergrift, N., Belsky, J., Burchinal, M., & NICHD Early Child Care Research Network. (2010). Predictors and sequelae of trajectories of physical aggression in school-age boys and girls. *Development and Psychopathology, 22*, 133–150.

Campos, J. J., Anderson, D. I., Barbu-Roth, M. A., Hubbard, E. M., Hertenstein, M. J., & Witherington, D. (2000). Travel broadens the mind. *Infancy, 1*, 149–219.

Campos, J. J., Frankel, C. B., & Camras, L. (2004). On the nature of emotion regulation. *Child Development, 75*, 377–394. doi:10.1111/j.1467-8624.2004.00681.x

Campos, J. J., Kermoian, R., & Zumbahlen, M. R. (1992). Socioemotional transformations in the family system following infant crawling onset. In N. Eisenberg & R. A. Fabes (Eds.), *New Directions for Child and Adolescent Development: No. 55. Emotion and its regulation in early development* (pp. 25–40). San Francisco, CA: Jossey-Bass.

Campos, J. J., Mumme, D. L., Kermoian, R., & Campos, R. G. (1994). A functionalist perspective on the nature of emotion. *Monographs of the Society for Research in Child Development, 59*(2–3, Serial No. 240), 284–303.

Campos, J. J., Witherington, D., Anderson, D. I., Frankel, C. I., Uchiyama, I., & Barbu-Roth, M. (2008). Rediscovering development in infancy. *Child Development, 79*, 1625–1632. doi:10.1111/j.1467-8624.2008.01212.x

Campos, R. G. (1989). Soothing pain-elicited distress in infants with swaddling and pacifiers. *Child Development, 60*, 781–792.

Camras, L. A. (1992). Expressive development and basic emotions. *Cognition and Emotion, 6,* 269–283.

Camras, L. A. (2011). Differentiation, dynamical integration and functional emotional development. *Emotion Review, 3,* 138–146.

Camras, L. A., Malatesta, C., & Izard, C. E. (1991). The development of facial expressions in infancy. In R. S. Feldman & B. Rimé (Eds.), *Fundamentals of nonverbal behavior* (pp. 73–105). New York, NY: Cambridge University Press.

Camras, L. A., & Shutter, J. M. (2010). Emotional facial expressions in infancy. *Emotion Review, 2,* 120–129.

Canli, T., Omura, K., Haas, B. W., Fallgatter, A., Constable, R. T., & Lesch, K. P. (2005). Beyond affect: A role for genetic variation of the serotonin transporter in neural activation during a cognitive attention task. *Proceedings of the National Academy of Sciences of the United States of America, 102,* 12224–12229.doi:10.1073/pnas.0503880102

Cannon, E. N., & Woodward, A. L. (2012). Infants generate goal-based action predictions. *Developmental Science, 15,* 292–298. doi:10.1111/j.1467-7687.2011.01127.x

Canobi, K. H., Reeve, R. A., & Pattison, P. E. (2002). Young children's understanding of addition concepts. *Educational Psychology, 22,* 513–532.

Cantin, R. H., Gnaedinger, E. K., Gallaway, K. C., Hesson-McInnis, M. S., & Hund, A. M. (2016). Executive functioning predicts reading, mathematics, and theory of mind during the elementary years. *Journal of Experimental Child Psychology, 146,* 66–78. doi:10.1016/j.jecp.2016.01.014

Capizzano, J., Tout, K., & Adams, G. (2000). Child care patterns of school-age children with employed mothers. Retrieved from http://www.urban.org/publications/310283.html

Caputi, M., Lecce, S., Pagnin, A., & Banerjee, R. (2012). Longitudinal effects of theory of mind on later peer relations: The role of prosocial behavior. *Developmental Psychology, 48,* 257–270. doi:10.1037/a0025402

Card, N. A., Stucky, B. D., Sawalani, G. M., & Little, T. D. (2008). Direct and indirect aggression during childhood and adolescence: A meta-analytic review of gender differences, intercorrelations, and relations to maladjustment. *Child Development, 79,* 1185–1229. doi:10.1111/j.1467-8624.2008.01184.x

Cardno, A. G., & Gottesman, I. I. (2000). Twin studies of schizophrenia: From bow-and-arrow concordances to Star Wars Mx and functional genomics. *American Journal of Medical Genetics, 97,* 12–17.

Cardoso, J. B., Padilla, Y. C., & Sampson, M. (2010). Racial and ethnic variation in the predictors of maternal parenting stress. *Journal of Social Service Research, 36,* 429–444. doi:10.1080/01488376.2010.510948

Carey, S. (1985). *Conceptual change in childhood.* Cambridge, MA: MIT Press.

Carey, S. (1999). Sources of conceptual change. In E. K. Scholnick, K. Nelson, S. A. Gelman, & P. H. Miller (Eds.), *Conceptual development: Piaget's legacy* (pp. 293–326). Mahwah, NJ: Erlbaum.

Carey, S. (2009). Where our number concepts come from. *Journal of Philosophy, 106,* 220–254.

Carey, S., & Bartlett, E. (1978). Acquiring a single new word. *Papers and Reports on Child Language Development, 15,* 17–29.

Carlo, G., Knight, G. P., McGinley, M., & Hayes, R. (2011). The roles of parental inductions, moral emotions, and moral cognitions in prosocial tendencies among Mexican American and European American early adolescents. *Journal of Early Adolescence, 31,* 757–781. doi:10.1177/0272431610373100

Carlo, G., Knight, G. P., McGinley, M., Zamboanga, B. L., & Jarvis, L. H. (2010). The multidimensionality of prosocial behaviors and evidence of measurement equivalence in Mexican American and European American early adolescents. *Journal of Research on Adolescence, 20,* 334–358. doi:10.1111/j.1532-7795.2010.00637.x

Carlo, G., Koller, S. H., Eisenberg, N., Da Silva, M. S., & Frohlich, C. B. (1996). A cross-national study on the relations among pro-social moral reasoning, gender role orientations, and prosocial behaviors. *Developmental Psychology, 32,* 231–240. doi:10.1037/0012-1649.32.2.231

Carlo, G., McGinley, M., Roesch, S. C., & Kaminski, J. W. (2008). Measurement invariance in a measure of prosocial moral reasoning to use with adolescents from the USA and Brazil. *Journal of Moral Education, 37,* 485–502. doi:10.1080/03057240802399368

Carlo, G., Mestre, M. V., Samper, P., Tur, A., & Armenta, B. E. (2010). Feelings or cognitions? Moral cognitions and emotions as longitudinal predictors of prosocial and aggressive behaviors. *Personality and Individual Differences, 48,* 872–877. doi:10.1016/j.paid.2010.02.010

Carlson, E. A. (1998). A prospective longitudinal study of attachment disorganization/disorientation. *Child Development, 69,* 1107–1128. doi:10.1111/j.1467-8624.1998.tb06163.x

Carlson, E. A., Sroufe, L. A., & Egeland, B. (2004). The construction of experience: A longitudinal study of representation and behavior. *Child Development, 75,* 66–83. doi:10.1111/j.1467-8624.2004.00654.x

Carlson, S., Hyvärinen, L., & Raninen, A. (1986). Persistent behavioural blindness after early visual deprivation and active visual rehabilitation: A case report. *British Journal of Ophthalmology, 70,* 607–611. doi:10.1136/bjo.70.8.607

Carlson, S. M., Gum, J., Davis, A., & Malloy, A. (2003, June). *Predictors of imaginary companion in early childhood.* Poster session presented at the annual meeting of the Jean Piaget Society, Chicago, IL.

Carlson, S. M., Mandell, D. J., & Williams, L. (2004). Executive function and theory of mind: Stability and prediction from ages 2 to 3. *Developmental Psychology, 40,* 1105–1122. doi:10.1037/0012-1649.40.6.1105

Carlson, S. M., Moses, L. J., & Hix, H. R. (1998). The role of inhibitory processes in young children's difficulties with deception and false belief. *Child Development, 69*(3), 672–691. doi:10.1111/j.1467-8624.1998.tb06236.x

Carlson, W., & Rose, A. J. (2007). The role of reciprocity in romantic relationships in middle childhood and early adolescence. *Merrill-Palmer Quarterly, 53,* 262–290.

Carpenter, M., Nagell, K., & Tomasello, M. (1998). Social cognition, joint attention, and communicative competence from 9 to 15 months of age. *Monographs of the Society for Research in Child Development, 63*(4, Serial No. 255).

Carra, C., Lavelli, M., & Keller, H. (2014). Differences in practices of body stimulation during the first 3 months: Ethnotheories and behaviors of Italian mothers and West African immigrant mothers. *Infant Behavior & Development, 37,* 5–15.

Carroll, J. B. (1993). *Human cognitive abilities: A survey of factor-analytic studies.* New York, NY: Cambridge University Press.

Carroll, J. B. (2005). The three-stratum theory of cognitive abilities. In D. P. Flanagan & P. L. Harrison (Eds.), *Contemporary intellectual assessment: Theories, tests, and issues* (2nd ed., pp. 69–76). New York, NY: Guilford Press.

Carter, D. B., & Patterson, C. J. (1982). Sex roles as social conventions: The development of children's conceptions of sex-role stereotypes. *Developmental Psychology, 18,* 812–824. doi:10.1037/0012-1649.18.6.812

Cartmill, E. A., Armstrong, B. F., Gleitman, L. R., Goldin-Meadow, S., Medina, T. N., & Trueswell, J. C. (2013). Quality of early parent input predicts child vocabulary 3 years later. *Proceedings of the National Academy of Sciences, 110*(28), 11278–11283.

Carver, K., Joyner, K., & Udry, J. R. (2003). National estimates of adolescent romantic relationships. In P. Florsheim (Ed.), *Adolescent romantic relations and sexual behavior: Theory, research, and practical implications* (pp. 23–56). Mahwah, NJ: Erlbaum.

Carver, L. J. (1999). When the event is more than the sum of its parts: 9-month-olds' long-term ordered recall. *Memory, 7,* 147–174. doi:10.1080/741944070

Carver, L. J., Bauer, P. J., & Nelson, C. A. (2000). Associations between infant brain activity and recall memory. *Developmental Science, 3,* 234–246. doi:10.1111/1467-7687.00116

Carver, L. J., & Vaccaro, B. G. (2007). 12-month-old infants allocate increased neural resources to stimuli associated with negative adult emotion. *Developmental Psychology, 43,* 54–69. doi:10.1037/0012-1649.43.1.54

Casasola, M. (2008). The development of infants' spatial categories. *Current Directions in Psychological Science, 17,* 21–25. doi:10.1111/j.1467-8721.2008.00541.x

Case, R. (1998). The development of conceptual structures. In W. Damon (Series Ed.) & D. Kuhn & R. S. Siegler (Vol. Eds.), *Handbook of child psychology: Vol. 2. Cognition, perception, and language* (5th ed., pp. 745–800). New York, NY: Wiley.

Case, R., Griffin, S., & Kelly, W. M. (1999). Socioeconomic gradients in mathematical ability and their responsiveness to intervention during early childhood. In D. P. Keating & C. Hertzman (Eds.), *Developmental health and the wealth of nations: Social, biological, and educational dynamics* (pp. 125–149). New York, NY: Guilford Press.

Casey, B. J. (1999). Brain development, XII: Maturation in brain activation. *American Journal of Psychiatry, 156,* 504.

Casey, B. J., Somerville, L. H., Gotlib, I. H., Ayduk, O., Franklin, N. T., Askren, M. K., . . . Shoda, Y. (2011). Behavioral and neural correlates of delay of gratification 40 years later. *Proceedings of the National Academy of Sciences of the United States of America, 108,* 14998–15003. doi:10.1073/pnas.1108561108

Cashon, C. H., Ha, O. R., Graf Estes, K., Saffran, J. R., & Mervis, C. B. (2016). Infants with Williams syndrome detect statistical regularities in continuous speech. *Cognition, 154,* 165–168.

Casiglia, A. C., Lo Coco, A., & Zappulla, C. (1998). Aspects of social reputation and peer relationships in Italian children: A cross-cultural perspective. *Developmental Psychology, 34,* 723–730. doi:10.1037/0012-1649.34.4.723

Caspi, A. (2000). The child is father of the man: Personality continuities from childhood to adulthood. *Journal of Personality and Social Psychology, 78,* 158–172.

Caspi, A., Harrington, H., Milne, B., Amell, J. W., Theodore, R. F., & Moffitt, T. E. (2003). Children's behavioral styles at age 3 are linked to their adult personality traits at age 26. *Journal of Personality, 71,* 495–514.

Caspi, A., Henry, B., McGee, R. O., Moffitt, T. E., & Silva, P. A. (1995). Temperamental origins of child and adolescent behavior problems: From age three to age fifteen. *Child Development, 66,* 55–68.

Caspi, A., McClay, J., Moffitt, T. E., Mill, J., Martin, J., Craig, I. W., . . . Poulton, R. (2002, August 2). Role of genotype in the cycle of violence in maltreated children. *Science, 297,* 851–854.

Caspi, A., & Silva, P. A. (1995). Temperamental qualities at age three predict personality traits in young adulthood: Longitudinal evidence from a birth cohort. *Child Development, 66,* 486–498.

Caspi, A., Williams, B., Kim-Cohen, J., Craig, I. W., Milne, B. J., Poulton, R., . . . Moffitt, T. E. (2007). Moderation of breastfeeding effects on the IQ by genetic variation in fatty acid metabolism. *Proceedings of the National Academy of Sciences of the United States of America, 104,* 18860–18865. doi:10.1073/pnas.0704292104

Cassidy, J. (1994). Emotion regulation: Influences of attachment relationships. *Monographs of the Society for Research in Child Development, 59*(2–3, Serial No. 240), 228–249.

Cassidy, J., Ziv, Y., Mehta, T. G., & Feeney, B. C. (2003). Feedback seeking in children and adolescents: Associations with self-perceptions, attachment representations, and depression. *Child Development, 74,* 612–628. doi:10.1111/1467-8624.7402019

Casasola, M. (2008). The development of infants' spatial categories. *Current Directions in Psychological Science, 17,* 21–25. doi:10.1111/j.1467-8721.2008.00541.x

Castillo, R., Salguero, J. M., Fernández-Berrocal, P., & Balluerka, N. (2013). Effects of an emotional intelligence intervention on aggression and empathy among adolescents. *Journal of Adolescence, 36,* 883–892. doi:10.1016/j.adolescence.2013.07.001

Castro, D. C., Páez, M. M., Dickinson, D. K., & Frede, E. (2011). Promoting language and literacy in young dual language learners: Research, practice, and policy. *Child Development Perspectives, 5,* 15–21. doi:10.1111/j.1750-8606.2010.00142.x

Cattell, R. B. (1987). *Intelligence: Its structure, growth, and action.* Amsterdam, The Netherlands: North-Holland.

Cavanagh, S. E., & Huston, A. C. (2006). Family instability and children's early behavior problems. *Social Forces, 85,* 551–585. doi:10.1353/sof.2006.0120

Ceballo, R., & McLoyd, V. C. (2002). Social support and parenting in poor, dangerous neighborhoods. *Child Development, 73,* 1310–1321. doi:10.1111/1467-8624.00473

Cecchini, M., Barnoi, E., Di Vito, C., & Lai, C. (2011). Smiling in newborns during communicative wake and active sleep. *Infant Behavior and Development, 34,* 417–423. doi:10.1016/j.infbeh.2011.04.001

Ceci, S. J. (1991). How much does schooling influence general intelligence and its cognitive components? A reassessment of the evidence. *Developmental Psychology, 27,* 703–723.

Ceci, S. J. (1996). *On intelligence: A bioecological treatise on intellectual development.* Cambridge, MA: Harvard University Press.

Ceci, S. J., & Bruck, M. (1998). Children's testimony: Applied and basic issues. In W. Damon (Series Ed.) & I. E. Sigel & K. A. Renninger (Vol. Eds.), *Handbook of child psychology: Vol. 4. Child psychology in practice* (5th ed., pp. 713–774). New York, NY: Wiley.

Celio, C. I., Durlak, J., & Dymnicki, A. (2011). A meta-analysis of the impact of service-learning on students. *Journal of Experiential Education, 34,* 164–181. doi:10.5193/JEE34.2.164

Center for Behavioral Health Statistics and Quality. (2015). *Behavioral health trends in the United States: Results from the 2014 National Survey on Drug Use and Health* (HHS Publication No. SMA 15-4927, NSDUH Series H-50). Retrieved from http://www.samhsa.gov/data/

Centers for Disease Control and Prevention. (2002). 2000 CDC growth charts for the United States: Methods and development. *Vital and Health Statistics, 11.* Retrieved from http://www.cdc.gov/growthcharts/

Centers for Disease Control and Prevention. (2013). Breastfeeding report card 2012. Retrieved from http://www.cdc.gov/breastfeeding/data/reportcard/reportcard2012.htm

Centers for Disease Control and Prevention. (2014). Prevalence of autism spectrum disorder among children aged 8 years—Autism and developmental disabilities monitoring network, 11 sites, United States, 2010. *MMWR. Surveillance Summaries, 63*(SS02), 1–21.

Centers for Disease Control and Prevention, Autism and Developmental Disabilities Monitoring Network Surveillance Year 2008 Principal Investigators. (2012). Prevalence of autism spectrum disorders—Autism and Developmental Disabilities Monitoring Network, 14 sites, United States, 2008. *Morbidity and Mortality Weekly Report Surveillance Summaries, 61*(SS-3), 1–19.

Central Intelligence Agency. (2015). *The world factbook.* Retrieved from https://www.cia.gov/library/publications/the-world-factbook/rankorder/2091rank.html

Chabris, C. F., Lee, J. J., Cesarini, D., Benjamin, D. J., & Laibson, D. I. (2015). The fourth law of behavior genetics. *Current Directions in Psychological Science, 24*(4), 304–312. doi:10.1177/0963721415580430

Chai, X. J., Hirshfeld-Becker, D., Biederman, J., Uchida, M., Doehrmann, O., Leonard, J. A., . . . Whitfield-Gabrieli, S. (2016). Altered intrinsic functional brain architecture in children at familial risk of major depression. *Biological Psychiatry, 80*(11), 849–858, Online first publication. doi:10.1016/j.biopsych.2015.12.003

Chall, J. (1979). The great debate: Ten years later, with a modest proposal for reading stages. In L. B. Resnick & P. A. Weaver (Eds.), *Theory and practice of early reading* (Vol. 1, pp. 29–55). Hillsdale, NJ: Erlbaum.

Chall, J. S. (1983). *Stages of reading development.* New York, NY: McGraw-Hill.

Chalmers, D., & Lawrence, J. A. (1993). Investigating the effects of planning aids on adults' and adolescents' organisation of a complex task. *International Journal of Behavioral Development, 16,* 191–214.

Chan, A., & Poulin, F. (2007). Monthly changes in the composition of friendship networks in early adolescence. *Merrill-Palmer Quarterly, 53,* 578–602.

Chan, R. W., Brooks, R. C., Raboy, B., & Patterson, C. J. (1998). Division of labor among lesbian and heterosexual parents: Associations with children's adjustment. *Journal of Family Psychology, 12,* 402–419. doi:10.1037/0893-3200.12.3.402

Chan, R. W., Raboy, B., & Patterson, C. J. (1998). Psychosocial adjustment among children conceived via donor insemination by lesbian and heterosexual mothers. *Child Development, 69,* 443–457. doi:10.1111/j.1467-8624.1998.tb06201.x

Chandler, M. J., Greenspan, S., & Barenboim, C. (1973). Judgments of intentionality in response to videotaped and verbally presented moral dilemmas: The medium is the message. *Child Development, 44,* 315–320. doi:10.2307/1128053

Chang, L., Lansford, J. E., Schwartz, D., & Farver, J. M. (2004). Marital quality, maternal depressed affect, harsh parenting, and child externalising in Hong Kong Chinese families. *International Journal of Behavioral Development, 28,* 311–318. doi:10.1080/01650250344000523

Chang, Z., Lichtenstein, P., Asherson, P. J., & Larsson, H. (2013). Developmental twin study of attention problems: High heritabilities throughout development. *JAMA Psychiatry, 70*(3), 311–318.

Chao, R. K. (1994). Beyond parental control and authoritarian parenting style: Understanding Chinese parenting through the cultural notion of training. *Child Development, 65,* 1111–1119. doi:10.1111/j.1467-8624.1994.tb00806.x

Chaplin, T. M., & Aldao, A. (2013). Gender differences in emotion expression in children: A meta-analytic review. *Psychological Bulletin, 139*(4), 735–765. doi:10.1037/a0030737

Chase-Lansdale, P. L., Cherlin, A. J., & Kiernan, K. E. (1995). The long-term effects of parental divorce on the mental health of young adults: A developmental perspective. *Child Development, 66,* 1614–1634. doi:10.1111/j.1467-8624.1995.tb00955.x

Chavarria-Siles, I., White, T., De Leeuw, C., Goudriaan, A., Lips, E., Ehrlich, S., . . . Ho, B. C. (2016). Myelination-related genes are associated with decreased white matter integrity in schizophrenia. *European Journal of Human Genetics, 24*(3), 381–386.

Chayer, M.-H., & Bouffard, T. (2010). Relations between impostor feelings and upward and downward identification and contrast among 10- to 12-year-old students. *European Journal of Psychology of Education, 25,* 125–140. doi:10.1007/s10212-009-0004-y

Cheah, C., & Rubin, K. (2004). European American and Mainland Chinese mothers' responses to aggression and social withdrawal in preschoolers. *International Journal of Behavioral Development, 28,* 83–94.

Cheah, C. S. L., Leung, C. Y. Y., Tahseen, M., & Schultz, D. (2009). Authoritative parenting among immigrant Chinese mothers of preschoolers. *Journal of Family Psychology, 23,* 311–320. doi:10.1037/a0015076

Chen, A., Oster, E., & Williams, W. (2016). Why is infant mortality higher in the United States than in Europe? *American Economic Journal: Economic Policy, 8*(2), 89–124.

Chen, E., & Miller, G. E. (2012). "Shift-and-persist" strategies: Why being low in socio-economic status isn't always bad for health. *Perspectives on Psychological Science, 7,* 135–158. doi:10.1177/1745691612436694

Chen, X., Cen, G., Li, D., & He, Y. (2005). Social functioning and adjustment in Chinese children: The imprint of historical time. *Child Development, 76,* 182–195. doi:10.1111/j.1467-8624.2005.00838.x

Chen, X., Chang, L., & He, Y. (2003). The peer group as a context: Mediating and moderating effects on relations between academic achievement and social functioning in Chinese children. *Child Development, 74,* 710–727. doi:10.2307/3696225

Chen, X., Chang, L., He, Y., & Liu, H. (2005). The peer group as a context: Moderating effects on relations between maternal parenting and social and school adjustment in Chinese children. *Child Development, 76,* 417–434. doi:10.1111/j.1467-8624.2005.00854.x

Chen, X., Dong, Q., & Zhou, H. (1997). Authoritative and authoritarian parenting practices and social and school performance in Chinese children. *International Journal of Behavioral Development, 21,* 855–873. doi:10.1080/016502597384703

Chen, X., Rubin, K. H., & Li, B. (1995). Social and school adjustment of shy and aggressive children in China. *Development and Psychopathology, 7,* 337–349. doi:10.1017/S0954579400006544

Chen, X., Rubin, K. H., Li, B.-s., & Li, D. (1999). Adolescent outcomes of social functioning in Chinese children. *International Journal of Behavioral Development, 23,* 199–223. doi:10.1080/016502599384071

Chen, X., Rubin, K. H., & Li, Z.-y. (1995). Social functioning and adjustment in Chinese children: A longitudinal study. *Developmental Psychology, 31,* 531–539. doi:10.1037/0012-1649.31.4.531

Chen, X., Rubin, K. H., & Sun, Y. (1992). Social reputation and peer relationships in Chinese and Canadian children: A cross-cultural study. *Child Development, 63,* 1336–1343. doi:10.1111/j.1467-8624.1992.tb01698.x

Chen, X., Wang, L., & Cao, R. (2011). Shyness-sensitivity and unsociability in rural Chinese children: Relations with social, school, and psychological adjustment. *Child Development, 82,* 1531–1543. doi:10.1111/j.1467-8624.2011.01616.x

Chen, X., Wang, L., & Wang, Z. (2009). Shyness-sensitivity and social, school, and psychological adjustment in rural migrant and urban children in China. *Child Development, 80,* 1499–1513. doi:10.1111/j.1467-8624.2009.01347.x

Chen, Z., Mo, L., & Honomichl, R. (2004). Having the memory of an elephant: Long-term retrieval and the use of analogues in problem solving. *Journal of Experimental Psychology: General, 133,* 415–433.

Chen, Z., & Siegler, R. (2000). Across the great divide: Bridging the gap between understanding of toddlers' and older children's thinking. *Monographs of the Society for Research in Child Development, 65*(2, Serial No. 261).

Cheour, M., Martynova, O., Näätänen, R., Erkkola, R., Sillanpää, M., Kero, P., . . . Hämäläinen, H. (2002, February 7). Speech sounds learned by sleeping newborns. *Nature, 415,* 599–600.

Cherney, I. D., & London, K. (2006). Gender-linked differences in the toys, television shows, computer games, and outdoor activities of 5- to 13-year-old children. *Sex Roles, 54,* 717–726. doi:10.1007/s11199-006-9037-8

Chi, M. T. H., & Ceci, S. J. (1987). Content knowledge: Its role, representation, and restructuring in memory development. In H. W. Reese (Ed.), *Advances in child development and behavior* (Vol. 20, pp. 91–142). San Diego, CA: Academic Press.

Chiandetti, C., & Vallortigara, G. (2011). Chicks like consonant music. *Psychological Science, 22,* 1270–1273. doi:10.1177/0956797611418244

Child Trends. (2012). Mothers who smoke while pregnant. Retrieved from www.childtrendsdatabank.org/?q=node/241

Child Trends Data Bank. (2015). *High school dropout rates: Indicators on children and youth.* Retrieved from http://www.childtrends.org/

Child Trends DataBank. (2015, March). Mothers who smoke while pregnant. Retrieved from http://www.childtrends.org/wp-content/uploads/2014/07/11_Mothers_Who_Smoke_While_Pregnant.pdf

Child Trends Data Bank. (2016). *Children's exposure to violence: Indicators on children and youth.* Retrieved from http://www.childtrends.org/

Chisholm, J. S. (1983). *Navajo infancy: An ethological study of child development.* Hawthorne, NY: Aldine.

Choi, K., & Kirkorian, H. L. (2016). Touch or watch to learn? Toddlers' object retrieval using contingent and noncontingent video. *Psychological Science, 27*(5), 726–736.

Choi, U. S., Sung, Y. W., Hong, S., Chung, J. Y., & Ogawa, S. (2015). Structural and functional plasticity specific to musical training with wind instruments. *Frontiers in Human Neuroscience, 9,* 597. doi:10.3389/fnhum.2015.00597

Chomsky, N. (1957). *Syntactic Structures.* The Hague, Netherlands/Paris, France: Mouton.

Chomsky, N. (1959). A review of B. F. Skinner's *Verbal Behavior. Language, 35,* 26–58.

Chomsky, N. (1988). *Language and problems of knowledge: The Managua lectures (Vol. 16).* Cambridge, MA: MIT press.

Chouinard, M. M. (2007). Children's questions: A mechanism for cognitive development. *Monographs of the Society for Research in Child Development, 72*(1, Serial No. 286).

Christensen, D. L., Baio J., Van Naarden Braun, K., Bilder, D., Charles, J., Constantino, J. N., . . . Centers for Disease Control and Prevention (CDC). (2016). Prevalence and characteristics of autism spectrum disorder among children aged 8 years—Autism and Developmental Disabilities Monitoring Network, 11 sites, United States, 2012 [Abstract]. *MMWR Surveillance Summaries, 65*(3), 1–23.

Christian, R. E., Frick, P. J., Hill, N. L., Tyler, L., & Frazer, D. R. (1997). Psychopathy and conduct problems in children: II. Implications for subtyping children with conduct problems. *Journal of the American Academy of Child and Adolescent Psychiatry, 36,* 233–241. doi:10.1097/00004583-199702000-00014

Chugani, H. T., Behen, M. E., Muzik, O., Juhasz, C., Nagy, F., & Chugani, D. C. (2001). Local brain functional activity following early deprivation: A study of postinstitutionalized Romanian orphans. *Neuroimage, 14,* 1290–1301. doi:10.1006/nimg.2001.0917

Chung, S., & McBride, A. M. (2015). Social and emotional learning in middle school curricula: A service learning model based on positive youth development. *Children and Youth Services Review, 53,* 192–200. doi:10.1016/j.childyouth.2015.04.008

Chung-Hall, J., & Chen, X. (2010). Aggressive and prosocial peer group functioning: Effects on children's social, school, and psychological adjustment. *Social Development, 19,* 659–680. doi:10.1111/j.1467-9507.2009.00556.x

Church, R. B. (1999). Using gesture and speech to capture transitions in learning. *Cognitive Development, 14,* 313–342.

Cianciolo, A. T., Matthew, C., Sternberg, R. J., & Wagner, R. K. (2006). Tacit knowledge, practical intelligence, and expertise. In K. A. Ericsson, N. Charness, P. J. Feltovich, & R. R. Hoffman (Eds.), *The Cambridge handbook of expertise and expert performance* (pp. 613–632). New York, NY: Cambridge University Press.

Cicchetti, D. (2016). Socioemotional and personality development: Insights from normality and atypicality. *Annual Review of Psychology, 67*(1), 23.1–23.25.

Cicchetti, D., & Ng, R. (2014). Emotional development in maltreated children. In K. H. Lagattuta (Ed.) *Children and emotion:*

New insights into developmental affective sciences (pp. 29–41). Basel, Switzerland.: Karger.

Cicchetti, D., & Rogosch, F. A. (1996). Equifinality and multifinality in developmental psychopathology. *Development and Psychopathology, 8,* 597–600. doi:10.1017/S0954579400007318

Cicchetti, D., Rogosch, F. A., & Thibodeau, E. L. (2012). The effects of child maltreatment on early signs of antisocial behavior: Genetic moderation by tryptophan hydroxylase, serotonin transporter, and monoamine oxidase A genes. *Development and Psychopathology, 24,* 907–928.

Cicchetti, D., & Toth, S. L. (2006). Developmental psychopathology and preventive intervention. In W. Damon & R. M. Lerner (Series Eds.) & K. A. Renninger & I. E. Sigel (Vol. Eds.), *Handbook of child psychology: Vol. 4. Child psychology in practice* (6th ed., pp. 497–547). Hoboken, NJ: Wiley.

Cicchetti, D., & Toth, S. L. (2015). Child maltreatment. In R. M. Lerner & M. E. Lamb (Eds.), *Handbook of child psychology and developmental science: Vol. 3 Socioemotional processes,* (7th ed., pp. 515–563). Hoboken, NJ: Wiley.

Cillessen, A. H. N. (2011). Toward a theory of popularity. In A. H. N. Cillessen, D. Schwartz, & L. Mayeux, *Popularity in the peer system* (pp. 273–299). New York, NY: Guilford Press.

Cillessen, A. H. N., & Mayeux, L. (2004). From censure to reinforcement: Developmental changes in the association between aggression and social status. *Child Development, 75,* 147–163. doi:10.2307/3696572

Cimpian, A., & Scott, R. M. (2012). Children expect generic knowledge to be widely shared. *Cognition, 123,* 419–433. doi:10.1016/j.cognition.2012.02.003

Clark, C. A. C., Woodward, L. J., Horwood, L. J., & Moor, S. (2008). Development of emotional and behavioral regulation in children born extremely preterm and very preterm: Biological and social influences. *Child Development, 79,* 1444–1462.

Clark, E. V. (1993). *The lexicon in acquisition.* Cambridge, England: Cambridge University Press.

Clarke-McLean, J. G. (1996). Social networks among incarcerated juvenile offenders. *Social Development, 5,* 203–217. doi:10.1111/j.1467-9507.1996.tb00081.x

Clarke-Stewart, K. A., Vandell, D. L., McCartney, K., Owen, M. T., & Booth, C. (2000). Effects of parental separation and divorce on very young children. *Journal of Family Psychology, 14,* 304–326. doi:10.1037/0893-3200.14.2.304

Clary, E. G., & Miller, J. (1986). Socialization and situational influences on sustained altruism. *Child Development, 57,* 1358–1369. doi:10.2307/1130415

Claxton, L. J., Keen, R., & McCarty, M. E. (2003). Evidence of motor planning in infant

reaching behavior. *Psychological Science, 14,* 354–356. doi:10.1111/1467-9280.24421

Clearfield, M. (2006). A dynamic account of infant looking behavior in small and large number tasks. In M. A. Vanchevsky (Ed.), *Focus on cognitive psychology research* (pp. 59–83). New York, NY: Nova Science.

Clearfield, M. W., Dineva, E., Smith, L. B., Diedrich, F. J., & Thelen, E. (2009). Cue salience and infant perseverative reaching: Tests of the dynamic field theory. *Developmental Science, 12,* 26–40. doi:10.1111/j.1467-7687.2008.00769.x

Clegg, J. M., & Legare, C. H. (2016). A cross-cultural comparison of children's imitative flexibility. *Developmental Psychology, 52*(9), 1435–1444.

Clément, M. E., & Chamberland, C. (2014). Trends in corporal punishment and attitudes in favor of this practice: Toward a change in societal norms. *Canadian Journal of Community Mental Health, 33,* 13–17. doi:10.7870/cjcmh-2014-013

Clifton, R. K., Rochat, P., Litovsky, R. Y., & Perris, E. E. (1991). Object representation guides infants' reaching in the dark. *Journal of Experimental Psychology: Human Perception and Performance, 17,* 323–329. doi:10.1037/0096-1523.17.2.323

Clore, G. (1981). *The wit and wisdom of Benjamin Clore.* Unpublished manuscript.

Cloutier, M. M., Wiley, J., Wang, Z., Grant, A., & Gorin, A. A. (2015). The Early Childhood Obesity Prevention Program (ECHO): An ecologically-based intervention delivered by home visitors for newborns and their mothers. *BMC Public Health, 15*(584). doi:10.1186/s12889-015-1897-9

Coe, C. L., & Lubach, G. R. (2008). Fetal programming: Prenatal origins of health and illness. *Current Directions in Psychological Science, 17,* 36–41. doi:10.1111/j.1467-8721.2008.00544.x

Cohen, D. J. (1980). The pathology of the self in primary childhood autism and Gilles de la Tourette syndrome. *Psychiatric Clinics of North America, 3,* 383–402.

Cohen, J. (1988). *Statistical power analysis for the behavioral sciences* (2nd ed.). Hillsdale, NJ: Erlbaum.

Cohen, L. B., & Cashon, C. H. (2006). Infant cognition. In W. Damon & R. M. Lerner (Series Eds.) & D. Kuhn & R. S. Siegler (Vol. Eds.), *Handbook of child psychology: Vol. 2. Cognition, perception, and language* (6th ed., pp. 214–251). Hoboken, NJ: Wiley.

Coie, J., Terry, R., Lenox, K., Lochman, J., & Hyman, C. (1995). Childhood peer rejection and aggression as predictors of stable patterns of adolescent disorder. *Development and Psychopathology, 7,* 697–713. doi:10.1017/S0954579400006799

Coie, J. D., & Dodge, K. A. (1983). Continuities and changes in children's social status: A five-year longitudinal study. *Merrill-Palmer Quarterly, 29*, 261–282.

Coie, J. D., & Dodge, K. A. (1998). Aggression and antisocial behavior. In W. Damon (Series Ed.) & N. Eisenberg (Vol. Ed.), *Handbook of child psychology: Vol. 3. Social, emotional, and personality development* (5th ed., pp. 779–862). Hoboken, NJ: Wiley.

Coie, J. D., Dodge, K. A., & Kupersmidt, J. B. (1990). Peer group behavior and social status. In S. R. Asher & J. D. Coie (Eds.), *Peer rejection in childhood* (pp. 17–59). New York, NY: Cambridge University Press.

Coie, J. D., Lochman, J. E., Terry, R., & Hyman, C. (1992). Predicting early adolescent disorder from childhood aggression and peer rejection. *Journal of Consulting and Clinical Psychology, 60*, 783–792. doi:10.1037/0022-006X.60.5.783

Coker, T. R., Austin, S. B., & Schuster, M. A. (2010). The health and health care of lesbian, gay, and bisexual adolescents. *Annual Review of Public Health, 31*, 457–477. doi:10.1146/annurev.publhealth.012809.103636

Colby, A., & Kohlberg, L. (1987a). *The measurement of moral judgment* (Vol. 1). New York, NY: Cambridge University Press.

Colby, A., & Kohlberg, L. (1987b). *The measurement of moral judgment* (Vol. 2). New York, NY: Cambridge University Press.

Colby, A., Kohlberg, L., Gibbs, J., Lieberman, M., Fischer, K., & Saltzstein, H. D. (1983). A longitudinal study of moral judgment. *Monographs of the Society for Research in Child Development, 48*(1–2, Serial No. 200), 1–124. doi:10.2307/1165935

Coldwell, J., Pike, A., & Dunn, J. (2008). Maternal differential treatment and child adjustment: A multi-informant approach. *Social Development, 17*, 596–612. doi:10.1111/j.1467-9507.2007.00440.x

Cole, P. M. (1986). Children's spontaneous control of facial expression. *Child Development, 57*, 1309–1321.

Cole, P. M., Bruschi, C. J., & Tamang, B. L. (2002). Cultural differences in children's emotional reactions to difficult situations. *Child Development, 73*, 983–996.

Cole, P. M., & Dennis, T. A. (1998). Variations on a theme: Culture and the meaning of socialization practices and child competence. *Psychological Inquiry, 9*, 276–278.

Cole, P. M., & Tamang, B. L. (1998). Nepali children's ideas about emotional displays in hypothetical challenges. *Developmental Psychology, 34*, 640–646.

Cole, P. M., Tamang, B. L., & Shrestha, S. (2006). Cultural variations in the socialization of young children's anger and

shame. *Child Development, 77*, 1237–1251. doi:10.1111/j.1467-8624.2006.00931.x

Cole, P. M., Tan, P. Z., Hall, S. E., Zhang, Y., Crnic, K. A., Blair, C. B., & Li, R. (2011). Developmental changes in anger expression and attention focus: Learning to wait. *Developmental Psychology, 47*, 1078–1089. doi:10.1037/a0023813

Cole, S. W. (2009). Social regulation of human gene expression. *Current Directions in Psychological Science, 18*, 132–137. doi:10.1111/j.1467-8721.2009.01623.x

Cole, W. G., Lingeman, J. M., & Adolph, K. E. (2012). Go naked: Diapers affect infant walking. *Developmental Science, 15*, 783–790. doi:10.1111/j.1467-7687.2012.01169.x

Coley, J. D. (2000). On the importance of comparative research: The case of folkbiology. *Child Development, 71*, 82–90.

Coley, R. L., & Chase-Lansdale, P. L. (1998). Adolescent pregnancy and parenthood: Recent evidence and future directions. *American Psychologist, 53*, 152–166. doi:10.1037/0003-066X.53.2.152

Coley, R. L., & Lombardi, C. M. (2013). Does maternal employment following childbirth support or inhibit low-income children's long-term development? *Child Development, 84*, 178–197. doi:10.1111/j.1467-8624.2012.01840.x

Coley, R. L., Votruba-Drzal, E., Miller, P. L., & Koury, A. (2013). Timing, extent, and type of child care and children's behavioral functioning in kindergarten. *Developmental Psychology, 49*, 1859–1873. doi:10.1037/a0031251

Collie, R., & Hayne, H. (1999). Deferred imitation by 6-and 9-month-old infants: More evidence for declarative memory. *Developmental Psychobiology, 35*, 83–90.

Collignon, O., Dormal, G., de Heering, A., Lepore, F., Lewis, T. L., & Maurer, D. (2015). Long-lasting crossmodal cortical reorganization triggered by brief postnatal visual deprivation. *Current Biology, 25*(18), 2379–2383.

Collins, K. P., & Cleary, S. D. (2016). Racial and ethnic disparities in parent-reported diagnosis of ADHD. *Journal of Clinical Psychiatry, 77*(1), 52–59.

Collins, N. L., & Feeney, B. C. (2013). Attachment and caregiving in adult close relationships: Normative processes and individual differences. *Attachment & Human Development, 15*(3), 241–245. doi:10.1080/14616734.2013.782652

Collins, W. A. (2003). More than myth: The developmental significance of romantic relationships during adolescence. *Journal of Research on Adolescence, 13*, 1–24. doi:10.1111/1532-7795.1301001

Collins, W. A., Hennighausen, K. C., Schmit, D. T., & Sroufe, L. A. (1997). Developmental precursors of romantic relationships: A longitudinal analysis. In S. Shulman & W. A. Collins (Eds.), *New Directions for Child and Adolescent*

Development: No. 78. Romantic relationships in adolescence: Developmental perspectives (pp. 69–84). San Francisco, CA: Jossey-Bass.

Collins, W. A., & Steinberg, L. (2006). Adolescent development in interpersonal context. In W. Damon & R. M. Lerner (Series Eds.) & N. Eisenberg (Vol. Ed.), *Handbook of child psychology: Vol. 3. Social, emotional, and personality development* (6th ed., pp. 1003–1067). Hoboken, NJ: Wiley.

Collins, W. A., Welsh, D. P., & Furman, W. (2009). Adolescent romantic relationships. *Annual Review of Psychology, 60*, 631–652. doi:10.1146/annurev.psych.60.110707.163459

Colombo, J., & Richman, W. A. (2002). Infant timekeeping: Attention and temporal estimation in 4-month-olds. *Psychological Science, 13*, 475–479.

Colombo, J., Shaddy, D. J., Richman, W. A., Maikranz, J. M., & Blaga, O. M. (2004). The developmental course of habituation in infancy and preschool outcome. *Infancy, 5*, 1–38. doi:10.1207/s15327078in0501_1

Coltrane, S. (1996). *Family man: Fatherhood, housework, and gender equity*. New York, NY: Oxford University Press.

Combs-Ronto, L., Olson, S., Lunkenheimer, E., & Sameroff, A. (2009). Interactions between maternal parenting and children's early disruptive behavior: Bidirectional associations across the transition from preschool to school entry. *Journal of Abnormal Child Psychology, 37*, 1151–1163. doi:10.1007/s10802-009-9332-2

Compas, B. E., Connor-Smith, J. K., Saltzman, H., Thomsen, A. H., & Wadsworth, M. E. (2001). Coping with stress during childhood and adolescence: Problems, progress, and potential in theory and research. *Psychological Bulletin, 127*, 87–127.

Compian, L., Gowen, L. K., & Hayward, C. (2004). Peripubertal girls' romantic and platonic involvement with boys: Associations with body image and depression symptoms. *Journal of Research on Adolescence, 14*, 23–47.

Compton, D. L., Miller, A. C., Elleman, A. M., & Steacy, L. M. (2014). Have we forsaken reading theory in the name of "quick fix" interventions for children with reading disability? *Scientific Studies of Reading, 18*(1), 55–73. doi:10.1080/10888438.2013.836200

Compton, K., Snyder, J., Schrepferman, L., Bank, L., & Shortt, J. W. (2003). The contribution of parents and siblings to antisocial and depressive behavior in adolescents: A double jeopardy coercion model. *Development and Psychopathology, 15*, 163–182. doi:10.1017.S0954579403000099

Conde-Agudelo, A., & Díaz-Rossello, J. L. (2014). Kangaroo mother care to reduce morbidity and mortality in low birthweight infants. *Cochrane Database of Systematic Reviews, 4*,

Art. No.: CD002771. doi:10.1002/14651858.CD002771.pub3

Condry, J. C., & Ross, D. F. (1985). Sex and aggression: The influence of gender label on the perception of aggression in children. *Child Development, 56,* 225–233. doi:10.2307/1130189

Conduct Problems Prevention Research Group. (1999a). Initial impact of the Fast Track prevention trial for conduct problems: I. The high-risk sample. *Journal of Consulting and Clinical Psychology, 67,* 631–647. doi:10.1037/0022-006X.67.5.631

Conduct Problems Prevention Research Group. (1999b). Initial impact of the Fast Track prevention trial for conduct problems: II. Classroom effects. *Journal of Consulting and Clinical Psychology, 67,* 648–657. doi:10.1037/0022-006X.67.5.648

Conduct Problems Prevention Research Group. (2002a). Evaluation of the first 3 years of the Fast Track prevention trial with children at high risk for adolescent conduct problems. *Journal of Abnormal Child Psychology, 30,* 19–35. doi:10.1023/A:1014274914287

Conduct Problems Prevention Research Group. (2002b). Using the Fast Track randomized prevention trial to test the early-starter model of the development of serious conduct problems. *Development and Psychopathology, 14,* 925–943.

Conduct Problems Prevention Research Group. (2002c). The implementation of the Fast Track Program: An example of a large-scale prevention science efficacy trial. *Journal of Abnormal Child Psychology, 30*(1), 1–17.

Conduct Problems Prevention Research Group. (2004). The effects of the Fast Track program on serious problem outcomes at the end of elementary school. *Journal of Clinical Child and Adolescent Psychology, 33,* 650–661. doi:10.1207/s15374424jccp3304_1

Conduct Problems Prevention Research Group. (2007). Fast Track randomized controlled trial to prevent externalizing psychiatric disorders: Findings from grades 3 to 9. *Journal of the American Academy of Child and Adolescent Psychiatry, 46,* 1250–1262. doi:10.1097/chi.0b013e31813e5d39

Conduct Problems Prevention Research Group. (2010). Fast Track intervention effects on youth arrests and delinquency. *Journal of Experimental Criminology, 6,* 131–157. doi:10.1007/s11292-010-9091-7

Conduct Problems Prevention Research Group. (2011). The effects of the Fast Track preventive intervention on the development of conduct disorder across childhood. *Child Development, 82,* 331–345. doi:10.1111/j.1467-8624.2010.01558.x

Conger, R. D., Conger, K. J., & Martin, M. J. (2010). Socioeconomic status, family processes, and individual development. *Journal of Marriage and Family, 72,* 685–704. doi:10.1111/j.1741-3737.2010.00725.x

Conger, R. D., & Ge, X. (1999). Conflict and cohesion in parent–adolescent relations: Changes in emotional expression from early to midadolescence. In M. J. Cox & J. Brooks-Gunn (Eds.), *Conflict and cohesion in families: Causes and consequences* (pp. 185–206). Mahwah, NJ: Erlbaum.

Conger, R. D., Ge, X., Elder, G. H., Jr., Lorenz, F. O., & Simons, R. L. (1994). Economic stress, coercive family process, and developmental problems of adolescents. *Child Development, 65,* 541–561. doi:10.2307/1131401

Conger, R. D., Wallace, L. E., Sun, Y., Simons, R. L., McLoyd, V. C., & Brody, G. H. (2002). Economic pressure in African American families: A replication and extension of the family stress model. *Developmental Psychology, 38,* 179–193. doi:10.1037/0012-1649.38.2.179

Conley, D., Rauscher, E., Dawes, C., Magnusson, P. K., & Siegal, M. L. (2013). Heritability and the equal environments assumption: Evidence from multiple samples of misclassified twins. *Behavior Genetics, 43*(5), 415–426.

Connell, A., Bullock, B., Dishion, T., Shaw, D., Wilson, M., & Gardner, F. (2008). Family intervention effects on co-occurring early childhood behavioral and emotional problems: A latent transition analysis approach. *Journal of Abnormal Child Psychology, 36,* 1211–1225. doi:10.1007/s10802-008-9244-6

Connellan, J., Baron-Cohen, S., Wheelwright, S., Batki, A., & Ahluwalia, J. (2000). Sex differences in human neonatal social perception. *Infant Behavior and Development, 23,* 113–118. doi:10.1016/S0163-6383(00)00032-1

Conner, D. B., Knight, D. K., & Cross, D. R. (1997). Mothers' and fathers' scaffolding of their 2-year-olds during problem-solving and literacy interactions. *British Journal of Developmental Psychology, 15,* 323–338. doi:10.1111/j.2044-835X.1997.tb00524.x

Connolly, E. J., & Beaver, K. M. (2015). Prenatal caloric intake and the development of academic achievement among U.S. children from ages 5 to 14. *Child Development, 86*(6), 1738–1758.

Connolly, J., Craig, W., Goldberg, A., & Pepler, D. (1999). Conceptions of cross-sex friendships and romantic relationships in early adolescence. *Journal of Youth and Adolescence, 28,* 481–494. doi:10.1023/A:1021669024820

Connolly, J., Craig, W., Goldberg, A., & Pepler, D. (2004). Mixed-gender groups, dating, and romantic relationships in early adolescence. *Journal of Research on Adolescence, 14,* 185–207. doi:10.1111/j.1532-7795.2004.01402003.x

Connolly, J. A., & Konarski, R. (1994). Peer self-concept in adolescence: Analysis of factor structure and of associations with peer experience. *Journal of Research on Adolescence, 4,* 385–403. doi:10.1207/s15327795jra0403_3

Conry-Murray, C. (2015). Children's judgments of inequitable distributions that conform to gender norms. *Merrill-Palmer Quarterly, 61,* 319–344.

Conway, C. C., Keenan-Miller, D., Hammen, C., Lind, P. A., Najman, J. M., & Brennan, P. A. (2012). Coaction of stress and serotonin transporter genotype in predicting aggression at the transition to adulthood. *Journal of Clinical Child and Adolescent Psychology, 41,* 53–63. doi:10.1080/15374416.2012.632351

Cooke, M. B., Ford, J., Levine, J., Bourke, C., Newell, L., & Lapidus, G. (2007). The effects of city-wide implementation of "Second Step" on elementary school students' prosocial and aggressive behaviors. *Journal of Primary Prevention, 28,* 93–115. doi:10.1007/s10935-007-0080-1

Cooklin, A. R., Westrupp, E., Strazdins, L., Giallo, R., Martin, A., & Nicholson, J. M. (2015), Mothers' work–family conflict and enrichment: Associations with parenting quality and couple relationship. *Child, 41*(2), 266–277. doi:10.1111/cch.12137

Cooley, C. H. (1902). *Human nature and the social order.* New York, NY: Charles Scribner's Sons.

Cooney, T. M., Pedersen, F. A., Indelicato, S., & Palkovitz, R. (1993). Timing of fatherhood: Is "on-time" optimal? *Journal of Marriage and the Family, 55,* 205–215.

Cooper, C. R., & Grotevant, H. D. (1987). Gender issues in the interface of family experience and adolescents' friendship and dating identity. *Journal of Youth & Adolescence, 16,* 247–264.

Cooper, R. P., & Aslin, R. N. (1994). Developmental differences in infant attention to the spectral properties of infant-directed speech. *Child Development, 65,* 1663–1677.

Cooper, S. M., & McLoyd, V. C. (2011). Racial barrier socialization and the well-being of African American adolescents: The moderating role of mother–adolescent relationship quality. *Journal of Research on Adolescence, 21,* 895–903. doi:10.1111/j.1532-7795.2011.00749.x

Copen, C. E., Daniels, K., Vespa, J., & Mosher, W. D. (2012). *First marriages in the United States: Data from the 2006–2010 National Survey of Family Growth.* (National Health Statistics Reports, 49). Retrieved from Centers for Disease Control and Prevention website: http://www.cdc.gov/nchs/fastats/marriage-divorce.htm

Coplan, R. J., Arbeau, K. A., & Armer, M. (2008). Don't fret, be supportive! Maternal characteristics linking child shyness to psychosocial and school adjustment in kindergarten. *Journal of Abnormal Child Psychology, 36*(3), 359–371. doi:10.1007/s10802-007-9183-7

Coplan, R. J., & Armer, M. (2007). A "multitude" of solitude: A closer look at social withdrawal and nonsocial play in early childhood. *Child Development Perspectives, 1,* 26–32. doi:10.1111/j.1750-8606.2007.00006.x

Coplan, R. J., & Bullock, A. (2012). Temperament and peer relationships. In M. R. Zentner & R. L. Shiner (Eds.), *Handbook of temperament* (pp. 442–461). New York, NY: Guilford Press.

Corballis, M. (1999). The gestural origins of language. *American Scientist, 87,* 138–146. doi:10.1511/1999.2.138

Corbeil, M., Trehub, S. E., & Peretz, I. (2015). Singing delays the onset of infant distress. *Infancy, 21,* 373–391.

Cordes, S., & Brannon, E. M. (2008). Quantitative competencies in infancy. *Developmental Science, 11*(6), 803–808. doi:10.1111/j.1467-7687.2008.00770.x

Cornell, E. H., Heth, C. D., Kneubuhler, Y., & Sehgal, S. (1996). Serial position effects in children's route reversal errors: Implications for police search operations. *Applied Cognitive Psychology, 10,* 301–326.

Costa, A., Hernández, M., & Sebastián-Gallés, N. (2008). Bilingualism aids conflict resolution: Evidence from the ANT task. *Cognition, 106,* 59–86. doi:10.1016/j.cognition.2006.12.013

Costello, D. M., Swendsen, J., Rose, J. S., & Dierker, L. C. (2008). Risk and protective factors associated with trajectories of depressed mood from adolescence to early adulthood. *Journal of Consulting and Clinical Psychology, 76,* 173–183. doi:10.1037/0022-006X.76.2.173

Costello, E. J., Copeland, W., & Angold, A. (2011). Trends in psychopathology across the adolescent years: What changes when children become adolescents, and when adolescents become adults? *Journal of Child Psychology and Psychiatry, 52,* 1015–1025. doi:10.1111/j.1469-7610.2011.02446.x

Costello, E. J., Foley, D. L., & Angold, A. (2006). 10-year research update review: The epidemiology of child and adolescent psychiatric disorders: II. Developmental epidemiology. *Journal of the American Academy of Child and Adolescent Psychiatry, 45,* 8–25.

Côté, S., Zoccolillo, M., Tremblay, R. E., Nagin, D., & Vitaro, F. (2001). Predicting girls' conduct disorder in adolescence from childhood trajectories of disruptive behaviors. *Journal of the American Academy of Child and Adolescent Psychiatry, 40,* 678–684.

Côté, S. M., Borge, A. I., Geoffroy, M.-C., Rutter, M., & Tremblay, R. E. (2008). Nonmaternal care in infancy and emotional/behavioral difficulties at 4 years old: Moderation by family risk characteristics. *Developmental Psychology, 44,* 155–168. doi:10.1037/0012-1649.44.1.155

Côté, S. M., Doyle, O., Petitclerc, A., & Timmins, L. (2013). Child care in infancy and cognitive performance until middle childhood in the Millennium Cohort Study. *Child Development, 84,* 1191–1208. doi:10.1111/cdev.12049

Coulton, C. J., Korbin, J. E., Su, M., & Chow, J. (1995). Community level factors and child maltreatment rates. *Child Development, 66,* 1262–1276. doi:10.2307/1131646

Courage, M. L., Edison, S. C., & Howe, M. L. (2004). Variability in the early development of visual self-recognition. *Infant Behavior and Development, 27,* 509–532. doi:10.1016/j.infbeh.2004.06.001

Courage, M. L., & Howe, M. L. (2002). From infant to child: The dynamics of cognitive change in the second year of life. *Psychological Bulletin, 128,* 250–277.

Court Appointed Special Advocates (CASA) for Children. (2012, September). Rationale and methods for preparing children for success in the courtroom. *The Judges' Page Newsletter,* National CASA Association and the National Council of Juvenile and Family Court Judges. Retrieved from http://www.casaforchildren.org/site/c.mtJSJ7MPIsE/b.8173513/k.1FB7/JP_10_NCAC.htm

Cowan, N. (2016). Working memory maturation: Can we get at the essence of cognitive growth? *Perspectives on Psychological Science, 11*(2), 239–264. doi:10.1177/1745691615621279

Cowan, P. A., Powell, D., & Cowan, C. P. (1998). Parenting interventions: A family systems perspective. In W. Damon (Series Ed.) & I. E. Sigel & K. A. Renninger (Vol. Eds.), *Handbook of child psychology: Vol. 4. Child psychology in practice* (5th ed., pp. 3–72). Hoboken, NJ: Wiley.

Cox, M. J., Owen, M. T., Lewis, J. M., & Henderson, V. K. (1989). Marriage, adult adjustment, and early parenting. *Child Development, 60,* 1015–1024. doi:10.2307/1130775

Cox, S. J., Mezulis, A. H., & Hyde, J. S. (2010). The influence of child gender role and maternal feedback to child stress on the emergence of the gender difference in depressive rumination in adolescence. *Developmental Psychology, 46*(4), 842–852. doi:10.1037/a0019813

Coyle, T. R., Pillow, D. R., Snyder, A. C., & Kochunov, P. (2011). Processing speed mediates the development of general intelligence (g) in adolescence. *Psychological Science, 22,* 1265–1269. doi:10.1177/0956797611418243

Coyne, S. M., & Archer, J. (2005). The relationship between indirect and physical aggression on television and in real life. *Social Development, 14,* 324–338. doi:10.1111/j.1467-9507.2005.00304.x

Coyne, S. M., Archer, J., & Eslea, M. (2004). Cruel intentions on television and in real life: Can viewing indirect aggression increase viewers' subsequent indirect aggression? *Journal of Experimental Child Psychology, 88,* 234–253. doi:10.1016/j.jecp.2004.03.001

Crean, H. F., & Johnson, D. B. (2013). Promoting Alternative Thinking Strategies (PATHS) and elementary school aged children's aggression: Results from a cluster randomized trial. *American Journal of Community Psychology, 52,* 56–72. doi:10.1007/s10464-013-9576-4

Crick, N. R., Casas, J. F., & Mosher, M. (1997). Relational and overt aggression in preschool. *Developmental Psychology, 33,* 579–588. doi:10.1037/0012-1649.33.4.579

Crick, N. R., & Dodge, K. A. (1994). A review and reformulation of social information-processing mechanisms in children's social adjustment. *Psychological Bulletin, 115,* 74–101. doi:10.1037/0033-2909.115.1.74

Crick, N. R., & Dodge, K. A. (1996). Social information-processing mechanisms in reactive and proactive aggression. *Child Development, 67,* 993–1002. doi:10.2307/1131875

Crocetti, E., Rubini, M., Luyckx, K., & Meeus, W. (2008). Identity formation in early and middle adolescents from various ethnic groups: From three dimensions to five statuses. *Journal of Youth and Adolescence, 37,* 983–996. doi:10.1007/s10964-007-9222-2

Crockenberg, S., & Langrock, A. (2001). The role of specific emotions in children's responses to interparental conflict: A test of the model. *Journal of Family Psychology, 15,* 163–182.

Crockett, L., Losoff, M., & Petersen, A. C. (1984). Perceptions of the peer group and friendship in early adolescence. *Journal of Early Adolescence, 4,* 155–181. doi:10.1177/0272431684042004

Croft, A., Schmader, T., Block, K., & Baron, A. S. (2014). The second shift reflected in the second generation: Do parents' gender roles at home predict children's aspirations? *Psychological Science, 25,* 1418–1428.

Crosbie-Burnett, M., & Helmbrecht, L. (1993). A descriptive empirical study of gay male stepfamilies. *Family Relations, 42,* 256–262.

Crosby, D. A., Dowsett, C. J., Gennetian, L. A., & Huston, A. C. (2010). A tale of two methods: Comparing regression and instrumental variables estimates of the effects of preschool child care type on the subsequent externalizing behavior of children in low-income families. *Developmental Psychology, 46,* 1030–1048. doi:10.1037/a0020384

Crosby, K. A., Fireman, G. D., & Clopton, J. R. (2011). Differences between non-aggressive, rejected children and popular children during peer collaboration. *Child & Family Behavior Therapy, 33*(1), 1–19.

Crosnoe, R., Augustine, J. M., & Huston, A. C. (2012). Children's early child care and their mothers' later involvement with schools. *Child Development, 83,* 758–772. doi:10.1111/j.1467-8624.2011.01726.x

Cross, D., Epstein, M., Hearn, L., Slee, P., Shaw, T., & Monks, H. (2011). National Safe Schools Framework: Policy and practice to reduce bullying in Australian schools. *International Journal of Behavioral Development, 35,* 398–404. doi:10.1177/0165025411407456

Cross, D., Shaw, T., Hadwen, K., Cardoso, P., Slee, P., Roberts, C., & Barnes, A. (2016), Longitudinal impact of the Cyber Friendly Schools program on adolescents' cyberbullying behavior. *Aggressive Behavior, 42,* 166–180. doi:10.1002/ab.21609

Cross-Disorder Group of the Psychiatric Genomics Consortium. (2013). Identification of risk loci with shared effects on five major psychiatric disorders: A genome-wide analysis. *The Lancet, 381,* 1371–1379.

Crowley, K., Callanan, M. A., Tenenbaum, H. R., & Allen, E. (2001). Parents explain more often to boys than to girls during shared scientific thinking. *Psychological Science, 12,* 258–261. doi:10.1111/1467-9280.00347

Cruz, J. E., Emery, R. E., & Turkheimer, E. (2012). Peer network drinking predicts increased alcohol use from adolescence to early adulthood after controlling for genetic and shared environmental selection. *Developmental Psychology, 48,* 1390–1402. doi:10.1037/a0027515

Csibra, G., Bíró, S., Koós, O., & Gergely, G. (2003). One-year-old infants use teleological representations of actions productively. *Cognitive Science, 27,* 111–133. doi:10.1016/ S0364-0213(02)00112-X

Csibra, G., & Gergely, G. (2009). Natural pedagogy. *Trends in Cognitive Sciences, 13(4),* 148–153.

Csibra, G., Gergely, G., Bíró, S., Koós, O., & Brockbank, M. (1999). Goal attribution without agency cues: The perception of "pure reason" in infancy. *Cognition, 72,* 237–267.

Cummings, E. M., & Davies, P. T. (2002). Effects of marital conflict on children: Recent advances and emerging themes in process-oriented research. *Journal of Child Psychology and Psychiatry, 43,* 31–63. doi:10.1111/1469-7610.00003

Cunningham, A. E., & Stanovich, K. E. (1997). Early reading acquisition and its relation to reading experience and ability 10 years later. *Developmental Psychology, 33,* 934–945.

Curry, D., Schmitt, M. J., & Waldron, S. (1996). A framework for adult numeracy standards: The mathematical skills and abilities adults need to be equipped for the future. Retrieved from http://shell04.theworld.com/std/anpn// framewk

Curtin, S., Mintz, T. H., & Christiansen, M. H. (2005). Stress changes the representational landscape: Evidence from word segmentation. *Cognition, 96,* 233–262. doi:10.1016/j. cognition.2004.08.005

Curtis, V., De Barra, M., & Aunger, R. (2011). Disgust as an adaptive system for disease avoidance behaviour. *Philosophical Transactions of the Royal Society B: Biological Sciences, 366,* 389–401. doi:10.1098/rstb.2010.0117

Curtiss, S. (1977). *Genie: A psycholinguistic study of a modern-day "wild child."* New York, NY: Academic Press.

Curtiss, S. (1989). The independence and task-specificity of language. In M. H. Bornstein & J. S. Bruner (Eds.), *Interaction in human development* (pp. 105–137). Hillsdale, NJ: Erlbaum.

Cusack, R., Ball, G., Smyser, C. D., & Dehaene-Lambertz, G. (2016), A neural window on the emergence of cognition. *Annals of the New York Academy of Sciences, 1369,* 7–23. doi:10.1111/nyas.13036

Cutrona, C. E., Hessling, R. M., Bacon, P. L., & Russell, D. W. (1998). Predictors and correlates of continuing involvement with the baby's father among adolescent mothers. *Journal of Family Psychology, 12,* 369–387. doi:10.1037/0893-3200.12.3.369

Cyr, C., Euser, E. M., Bakermans-Kranenburg, M. J., & van Ijzendoorn, M. H. (2010). Attachment security and disorganization in maltreating and high-risk families: A series of meta-analyses. *Development & Psychopathology, 22.* 87–108.

D'Ortenzio, E., Matheron, S., de Lamballerie, X., Hubert, B., Piorkowski, G., Maquart, M., . . . Leparc-Goffart, I. (2016). Evidence of sexual transmission of Zika virus. *New England Journal of Medicine, 374,* 2195–2198.

Daly, M., & Wilson, M. I. (1996). Violence against stepchildren. *Current Directions in Psychological Science, 5,* 77–80. doi:10.1111/1467-8721. ep10772793

Damasio, A. R. (1999). *The feeling of what happens: Body and emotion in the making of consciousness.* New York, NY: Harcourt Brace.

Damon, W. (1977). *The social world of the child.* San Francisco, CA: Jossey-Bass.

Damon, W., & Hart, D. (1988). *Self-understanding in childhood and adolescence.* Cambridge, England: Cambridge University Press.

Danese, A., & McEwen, B. S. (2012). Adverse child experiences, allostasis, allostatic load, and age-related disease. *Physiology and Behavior, 106,* 29–39. doi:10.1016/j.physbeh.2011.08.019

Dank, M., Lachman, P., Zweig, J. M., & Yahner, J. (2014). Dating violence experiences of lesbian, gay, bisexual, and transgender youth. *Journal of Youth & Adolescence, 43,* 846–857.

Darling, N., & Steinberg, L. (1993). Parenting style as context: An integrative model. *Psychological Bulletin, 113,* 487–496. doi:10.1037/0033-2909.113.3.487

Darwin, C. (1872). *The expression of the emotions in man and animals.* London, England: J. Murray.

Darwin, C. (1877). A biographical sketch of an infant. *Mind, 2,* 285–294.

Davidson, J., Dunne, R., Eccles, J. S., Engle, A., Greenberg, M., Jennings, P., . . . Roeser, R. W. (2012). Contemplative practices and mental training: Prospects for American education. *Child Development Perspectives, 6(2),* 146–153.

Davidson, R. J. (1994). Asymmetric brain function, affective style, and psychopathology: The role of early experience and plasticity. *Development and Psychopathology, 6,* 741–758.

Davies, P. T., Cicchetti, D., & Martin, M. J. (2012). Toward greater specificity in identifying associations among interparental aggression, child emotional reactivity to conflict, and child problems. *Child Development, 83,* 1789–1804. doi:10.1111/j.1467-8624.2012.01804.x

Davies, P. T., Cummings, E. M., & Winter, M. A. (2004). Pathways between profiles of family functioning, child security in the interparental subsystem, and child psychological problems. *Development and Psychopathology, 16,* 525–550. doi:10.1017/S0954579404004651

Davies, P. T., Sturge-Apple, M. L., Cicchetti, D., Manning, L. G., & Vonhold, S. E. (2012). Pathways and processes of risk in associations among maternal antisocial personality symptoms, interparental aggression, and preschooler's psychopathology. *Development and Psychopathology, 24,* 807–832. doi:10.1017/ S0954579412000387

Davies, P. T., & Windle, M. (2000). Middle adolescents' dating pathways and psychosocial adjustment. *Merrill-Palmer Quarterly, 46,* 90–118. doi:10.2307/23093344

Davis, O. S. P., Haworth, C. M. A., & Plomin, R. (2009). Dramatic increase in heritability of cognitive development from early to middle childhood: An 8-year longitudinal study of 8,700 pairs of twins. *Psychological Science, 20,* 1301–1308. doi:10.1111/j.1467-9280.2009.02433.x

Dawson, G., Rogers, S., Munson, J., Smith, M., Winter, J., Greenson, J., . . . Varley, J. (2010). Randomized, controlled trial of an intervention for toddlers with autism: The Early Start Denver Model. *Pediatrics, 125,* e17–e23. doi:10.1542/ peds.2009-0958

Day, R. D., & Padilla-Walker, L. M. (2009). Mother and father connectedness and involvement during early adolescence. *Journal of Family Psychology, 23,* 900–904. doi:10.1037/ a0016438

de Boysson-Bardies, B. (1999). *How language comes to children: From birth to two years* (M. B. DeBevoise, Trans.). Cambridge, MA: MIT Press. (Original work published 1996)

De Brito, S. A., Hodgins, S., McCrory, E. J. P., Mechelli, A., Wilke, M., Jones, A. P., & Viding, E. (2009). Structural neuroimaging and the antisocial brain: Main findings and methodological challenges. *Criminal Justice and Behavior, 36,* 1173–1186. doi:10.1177/0093854809342883

De Goede, I. H. A., Branje, S. J. T., & Meeus, W. H. J. (2009). Developmental changes and gender differences in adolescents' perceptions of friendships. *Journal of Adolescence, 32,* 1105–1123. doi:10.1016/j.adolescence.2009.03.002

de Guzman, M. R. T., Carlo, G., & Edwards, C. P. (2008). Prosocial behaviors in context: Examining the role of children's social companions. *International Journal of Behavioral Development, 32,* 522–530. doi:10.1177/0165025408095557 de Heering, A., & Maurer, D. (2014). Face memory deficits in patients deprived of early visual input by bilateral congenital cataracts. *Developmental Psychobiology, 56*(1), 96–108.

de Hevia, M. D., & Spelke, E. S. (2010). Number-space mapping in human infants. *Psychological Science, 21,* 653–660. doi:10.1177/0956797610366091

de Rooij, S. R., Wouters, H., Yonker, J. E., Painter, R. C., & Roseboom, T. J. (2010). Prenatal undernutrition and cognitive function in late adulthood. *Proceedings of the National Academy of Sciences of the United States of America, 107,* 16881–16886.

De Snoo, K. (1937). Das trinkende Kind im Uterus [The drinking child in utero]. *Monatsschr. Geburtsh. Gynaekol. [International Monthly Review of Obstretics and Gynaecology], 105,* 88–97.

De Souza, E., Alberman, E., & Morris, J. K. (2009). Down syndrome and paternal age, a new analysis of case–control data collected in the 1960s. *American Journal of Medical Genetics Part A, 149A,* 1205–1208. doi:10.1002/ajmg.a.32850

de Vries, J. I. P., Visser, G. H. A., & Prechtl, H. F. R. (1982). The emergence of fetal behaviour: I. Qualitative aspects. *Early Human Development, 7,* 301–322. doi:10.1016/0378-3782(82)90033-0

de Wied, M., van Boxtel, A., Matthys, W., & Meeus, W. (2012). Verbal, facial and autonomic responses to empathy-eliciting film clips by disruptive male adolescents with high versus low callous-unemotional traits. *Journal of Abnormal Child Psychology, 40,* 211–223. doi:10.1007/s10802-011-9557-8

De Wolff, M. S., & van IJzendoorn, M. H. (1997). Sensitivity and attachment: A meta-analysis on parental antecedents of infant attachment. *Child Development, 68,* 571–591.

Deák, G. O. (2015, August). When and where do infants follow gaze? *2015 Joint IEEE International Conference on Development and Learning and Epigenetic Robotics (ICDL-EpiRob),* Brown University (pp. 182–187). doi:10.1109/DEVLRN.2015.7346138

Deák, G. O., Flom, R. A., & Pick, A. D. (2000). Effects of gesture and target on 12- and 18-month-olds' joint visual attention to objects in front of or behind them. *Developmental Psychology, 36,* 511–523.

DeAnda, S., Hendrickson, K., Zesiger, P., Poulin-Dubois, D., & Friend, M. (2016). Lexical access in the second year: A cross-linguistic study of monolingual and bilingual vocabulary development. *San Diego Linguistic Papers, 6,* 14–28.

Dearing, E., McCartney, K., & Taylor, B. A. (2009). Does higher quality early child care promote low-income children's math and reading achievement in middle childhood? *Child Development, 80,* 1329–1349. doi:10.1111/j.1467-8624.2009.01336.x

Deary, I. J. (2000). *Oxford Psychology Series: No. 34. Looking down on human intelligence:*

From psychometrics to the brain. Oxford, England: Oxford University Press.

Deary, I. J., Strand, S., Smith, P., & Fernandes, C. (2007). Intelligence and educational achievement. *Intelligence, 35,* 13–21.

Deater-Deckard, K. (2000). Parenting and child behavioral adjustment in early childhood: A quantitative genetic approach to studying family processes. *Child Development, 71,* 468–484. doi:10.1111/1467-8624.00158

Deater-Deckard, K., & Dodge, K. A. (1997). Externalizing behavior problems and discipline revisited: Nonlinear effects and variation by culture, context, and gender. *Psychological Inquiry, 8,* 161–175. doi:10.1207/s15327965pli0803_1

Deater-Deckard, K., Dodge, K. A., Bates, J. E., & Pettit, G. S. (1995, April). *Risk factors for the development of externalizing behavior problems: Are there ethnic group differences in process?* Paper presented at the biennial meeting of the Society for Research in Child Development, Indianapolis, IN.

Deater-Deckard, K., Petrill, S. A., & Thompson, L. A. (2007). Anger/frustration, task persistence, and conduct problems in childhood: A behavioral genetic analysis. *Journal of Child Psychology and Psychiatry, 48,* 80–87. doi:10.1111/j.1469-7610.2006.01653.x

Deater-Deckard, K., Pike, A., Petrill, S. A., Cutting, A. L., Hughes, C., & O'Connor, T. G. (2001). Nonshared environmental processes in social-emotional development: An observational study of identical twin differences in the preschool period. *Developmental Science, 4*(2), F1–F6. doi:10.1111/1467-7687.00157

DeCasper, A., & Fifer, W. (1980, June 6). Of human bonding: Newborns prefer their mothers' voices. *Science, 208,* 1174–1176.

DeCasper, A. J., & Spence, M. J. (1986). Prenatal maternal speech influences newborns' perception of speech sounds. *Infant Behavior and Development, 9,* 133–150. doi:10.1016/0163-6383(86)90025-1

DeGarmo, D. S. (2010). Coercive and prosocial fathering, antisocial personality, and growth in children's postdivorce noncompliance. *Child Development, 81,* 503–516. doi:10.1111/j.1467-8624.2009.01410.x

Değirmencioğlu, S. M., Urberg, K. A., Tolson, J. M., & Richard, P. (1998). Adolescent friendship networks: Continuity and change over the school year. *Merrill-Palmer Quarterly, 44,* 313–337.

Dehaene, S., & Brannon, E. (Eds.). (2011). *Space, time and number in the brain: Searching for the foundations of mathematical thought.* San Diego, CA: Academic Press.

Dehaene-Lambertz, G., Dehaene, S., & Hertz-Pannier, L. (2002, December 6). Functional neuroimaging of speech perception in infants. *Science, 298,* 2013–2015.

Del Rey, R., Casas, J. A. and Ortega, R. (2016). Impact of the ConRed program on different

cyberbullying roles. *Aggressive Behavior, 42,* 123–135. doi:10.1002/ab.21608

Delaney, C. (2000). Making babies in a Turkish village. In J. S. DeLoache & A. Gottlieb (Eds.), *A world of babies: Imagined childcare guides for seven societies* (pp. 117–144). New York, NY: Cambridge University Press.

DeLisi, M., Barnes, J. C., Beaver, K. M., & Gibson, C. L. (2009). Delinquent gangs and adolescent victimization revisited: A propensity score matching approach. *Criminal Justice and Behavior, 36,* 808–823. doi:10.1177/0093854809337703

DeLoache, J. S. (1987, December 11). Rapid change in the symbolic functioning of very young children. *Science, 238,* 1556–1557.

DeLoache, J. S. (2002). The symbol-mindedness of young children. In W. W. Hartup & R. A. Weinberg (Eds.), *Minnesota Symposia on Child Psychology: Vol. 32. Child psychology in retrospect and prospect: In celebration of the 75th anniversary of the Institute of Child Development* (pp. 73–101). Mahwah, NJ: Erlbaum.

DeLoache, J. S. (2004). Becoming symbol-minded. *Trends in Cognitive Sciences, 8,* 66–70. doi:10.1016/j.tics.2003.12.004

DeLoache, J. S., Chiong, C., Sherman, K., Islam, N., Vanderborght, M., Troseth, G. L., . . . O'Doherty, K. (2010). Do babies learn from baby media? *Psychological Science, 21,* 1570–1574. doi:10.1177/0956797610384145

DeLoache, J. S., & Marzolf, D. P. (1995). The use of dolls to interview young children: Issues of symbolic representation. *Journal of Experimental Child Psychology, 60,* 155–173.

DeLoache, J. S., Miller, K. F., & Rosengren, K. S. (1997). The credible shrinking room: Very young children's performance with symbolic and nonsymbolic relations. *Psychological Science, 8,* 308–313. doi:10.1111/j.1467-9280.1997.tb00443.x

DeLoache, J. S., Pierroutsakos, S. L., Uttal, D. H., Rosengren, K. S., & Gottlieb, A. (1998). Grasping the nature of pictures. *Psychological Science, 9,* 205–210. doi:10.1111/1467-9280.00039

DeLoache, J. S., Strauss, M. S., & Maynard, J. (1979). Picture perception in infancy. *Infant Behavior and Development, 2,* 77–89. doi:10.1016/S0163-6383(79)80010-7

DeLoache, J. S., Uttal, D. H., & Rosengren, K. S. (2004, May 14). Scale errors offer evidence for a perception-action dissociation early in life. *Science, 304,* 1027–1029.

Delsing, M. J. M. H., ter Bogt, T. F. M., Engels, R. C. M. E., & Meeus, W. H. J. (2007). Adolescents' peer crowd identification in the Netherlands: Structure and associations with problem behaviors. *Journal of Research on Adolescence, 17,* 467–480. doi:10.1111/j.1532-7795.2007.00530.x

Deluty, R. H. (1985). Cognitive mediation of aggressive, assertive, and submissive behavior in children. *International Journal of Behavioral Development, 8*, 355–369. doi:10.1177/016502548500800309

DeMarie-Dreblow, D., & Miller, P. H. (1988). The development of children's strategies for selective attention: Evidence for a transitional period. *Child Development, 59*, 1504–1513.

Dempster, F. N. (1995). Interference and inhibition in cognition: An historical perspective. In F. N. Dempster & C. J. Brainerd (Eds.), *Interference and inhibition in cognition* (pp. 3–16). San Diego, CA: Academic Press.

DeNavas-Walt, C., & Proctor, B. D. (2015). *U.S. Census Bureau, Current Population Reports, P60-252, Income and Poverty in the United States: 2014*. U.S. Government Printing Office, Washington, DC, 2015. Retrieved from https://www.census.gov/newsroom/press-releases/2015/cb15-157.html

DeNavas-Walt, C., Proctor, B. D., & Smith, J. C. (2011). *Income, poverty, and health insurance coverage in the United States: 2009* (Current Population Reports P60-238). Washington, DC: U.S. Government Printing Office.

Denham, S. A. (1986). Social cognition, prosocial behavior, and emotion in preschoolers: Contextual validation. *Child Development, 57*, 194–201.

Denham, S. A. (1998). *Emotional development in young children*. New York, NY: Guilford Press.

Denham, S. A. (2006). The emotional basis of learning and development in early childhood education. In B. Spodek & O. N. Saracho (Eds.), *Handbook of research on the education of young children* (2nd ed., pp. 85–103). Mahwah, NJ: Erlbaum.

Denham, S. A., Blair, K. A., DeMulder, E., Levitas, J., Sawyer, K., Auerbach-Major, S., & Queenan, P. (2003). Preschool emotional competence: Pathway to social competence? *Child Development, 74*, 238–256.

Denham, S. A., & Burton, R. (1996). A social-emotional intervention for at-risk 4-year-olds. *Journal of School Psychology, 34*, 225–245. doi:10.1016/0022-4405(96)00013-1

Denham, S. A., & Couchoud, E. A. (1990). Young preschoolers' understanding of emotions. *Child Study Journal, 20*, 171–192.

Denham, S. A., Warren-Khot, H. K., Bassett, H. H., Wyatt, T., & Perna, A. (2012). Factor structure of self-regulation in preschoolers: Testing models of a field-based assessment for predicting early school readiness. *Journal of Experimental Child Psychology, 111*, 386–404. doi:10.1016/j.jecp.2011.10.002

Denham, S. A., Zoller, D., & Couchoud, E. A. (1994). Socialization of preschoolers' emotion understanding. *Developmental Psychology, 30*, 928–936.

Denison, S., Reed, C., & Xu, F. (2013). The emergence of probabilistic reasoning in very young infants: Evidence from 4.5- and 6-month-olds. *Developmental Psychology, 49*, 243–249. doi:10.1037/a0028278

Denison, S., & Xu, F. (2010). Integrating physical constraints in statistical inference by 11-month-old infants. *Cognitive Science, 34*, 885–908. doi:10.1111/j.1551-6709.2010.01111.x

Denissen, J. J. A., van Aken, M. A. G., & Dubas, J. S. (2009). It takes two to tango: How parents' and adolescents' personalities link to the quality of their mutual relationship. *Developmental Psychology, 45*, 928–941. doi:10.1037/a0016230

Dennis, S. (1992). Stage and structure in the development of children's spatial representations. In R. Case (Ed.), *The mind's staircase: Exploring the conceptual underpinnings of children's thought and knowledge* (pp. 229–245). Hillsdale, NJ: Erlbaum.

Dennis, T., Bendersky, M., Ramsay, D., & Lewis, M. (2006). Reactivity and regulation in children prenatally exposed to cocaine. *Developmental Psychology, 42*, 688–697. doi:10.1037/0012-1649.42.4.688

Dennis, W., & Najarian, P. (1957). Infant development under environmental handicap. *Psychological Monographs: General and Applied, 71*(7, Whole No. 436).

Densley, J. A. (2012). Street gang recruitment. *Social Problems, 59*, 301–321. doi:10.1525/sp.2012.59.3.301

Department of Statistics Singapore. (2016). General Household Survey 2015. Retrieved from http://www.singstat.gov.sg/publications/publications-and-papers/GHS/ghs2015content

Depue, R. A., & Fu, Y. (2012). Neurobiology and neurochemistry of temperament (adults). In M. R. Zentner & R. L. Shiner (Eds.), *Handbook of temperament* (pp. 368–399). New York, NY: Guilford Press.

DeRosier, M. E., Kupersmidt, J. B., & Patterson, C. J. (1994). Children's academic and behavioral adjustment as a function of the chronicity and proximity of peer rejection. *Child Development, 65*, 1799–1813. doi:10.1111/j.1467-8624.1994.tb00850.x

Desjarlais, M., & Willoughby, T. (2010). A longitudinal study of the relation between adolescent boys' and girls' computer use with friends and friendship quality: Support for the social compensation or the rich-get-richer hypothesis? *Computers in Human Behavior, 26*, 896–905. doi:10.1016/j.chb.2010.02.004

Dettling, A. C., Parker, S. W., Lane, S., Sebanc, A., & Gunnar, M. R. (2000). Quality of care and temperament determine changes in cortisol concentrations over the day for young children in childcare. *Psychoneuroendocrinology, 25*, 819–836.

Deutsch, F. M. (2006). Filial piety, patrilineality, and China's one-child policy. *Journal of Family Issues, 27*, 366–389. doi:10.1177/0192513x05283097

Devine, A., Fawcett, K., Szücs, D., & Dowker, A. (2012). Gender differences in mathematics anxiety and the relation to mathematics performance while controlling for test anxiety. *Behavioral and Brain Functions, 8*(33). doi:10.1186/1744-9081-8-33

DeWitt, A. L., Cready, C. M., & Seward, R. R. (2013). Parental role portrayals in twentieth century children's picture books: More egalitarian or ongoing stereotyping? *Sex Roles, 69*, 89–106.

Di Florio, A., Forty, L., Gordon-Smith, K., Heron, J., Jones, L., Craddock, N., & Jones, I. (2013). Perinatal episodes across the mood disorder spectrum. *Journal of the American Medical Association Psychiatry, 70*, 168–175.

Di Giorgio, E., Leo, I., Pascalis, O., & Simion, F. (2012). Is the face-perception system human-specific at birth? *Developmental Psychology, 48*, 1083–1090. doi:10.1037/a0026521

Di Giunta, L., Pastorelli, C., Eisenberg, N., Gerbino, M., Castellani, V., & Bombi, A. (2010). Developmental trajectories of physical aggression: Prediction of overt and covert antisocial behaviors from self- and mothers' reports. *European Child and Adolescent Psychiatry, 19*, 873–882. doi:10.1007/s00787-010-0134-4

Di Martino, A., Yan, C. G., Li, Q., Denio, E., Castellanos, F. X., Alaerts, K., . . . Milham, M. P. (2014). The autism brain imaging data exchange: Towards a large-scale evaluation of the intrinsic brain architecture in autism. *Molecular Psychiatry, 19*(6), 659–667.

Diamond, A. (1985). Development of the ability to use recall to guide action, as indicated by infants' performance on AB⁻. *Child Development, 56*, 868–883. doi:10.2307/1130099

Diamond, A. (2013). Executive functions. *Annual Review of Psychology, 64*, 135–168. doi:10.1146/annurev-psych-113011-143750

Diamond, A., Briand, L., Fossella, J., & Gehlbach, L. (2004). Genetic and neurochemical modulation of prefrontal cognitive functions in children. *American Journal of Psychiatry, 161*, 125–132.

Diamond, A., & Goldman-Rakic, P. S. (1989). Comparison of human infants and rhesus monkeys on Piaget's AB task: Evidence for dependence on dorsolateral prefrontal cortex. *Experimental Brain Research, 74*, 24–40. doi:10.1007/BF00248277

Diamond, A., & Lee, K. (2011, August 19). Interventions shown to aid executive function development in children 4 to 12 years old. *Science, 333*, 959–964.

Diamond, L. M. (2008). Female bisexuality from adolescence to adulthood: Results from a 10-year longitudinal study. *Developmental Psychology, 44*, 5–14. doi:10.1037/0012-1649.44.1.5

Diamond, L. M., Bonner, S. B., & Dickenson, J. (2015). The development of sexuality. In M. E. Lamb (Vol. Ed.) & R. M. Lerner (Editor-in-Chief), *Handbook of Child Psychology and*

Developmental Science (7th ed.), Volume 3: Socio-emotional processes (pp. 888–931). Hoboken, NJ: Wiley.

Diamond, L. M., & Lucas, S. (2004). Sexual-minority and heterosexual youths' peer relationships: Experiences, expectations, and implications for well-being. *Journal of Research on Adolescence, 14,* 313–340. doi:10.1111/j.1532-7795.2004.00077.x

Díaz, R. M., & Berk, L. E. (Eds.). (2014). *Private speech: From social interaction to self-regulation.* New York, NY: Psychology Press.

DiBiase, R., & Waddell, S. (1995). Some effects of homelessness on the psychological functioning of preschoolers. *Journal of Abnormal Child Psychology, 23,* 783–792. doi:10.1007/BF01447477

Dick, D. M., Pagan, J. L., Holliday, C., Viken, R., Pulkkinen, L., Kaprio, J., & Rose, R. J. (2007). Gender differences in friends' influences on adolescent drinking: A genetic epidemiological study. *Alcoholism: Clinical and Experimental Research, 31,* 2012–2019. doi:10.1111/j.1530-0277.2007.00523.x

Dickens, W. T., & Flynn, J. R. (2001). Heritability estimates versus large environmental effects: The IQ paradox resolved. *Psychological Review, 108,* 346–369.

Dickens, W. T., & Flynn, J. R. (2006). Black Americans reduce the racial IQ gap: Evidence from standardization samples. *Psychological Science, 17,* 913–920. doi:10.1111/j.1467-9280.2006.01802.x

Dickinson, D. K. (2011, August 19). Teachers' language practices and academic outcomes of preschool children. *Science, 333,* 964–967.

Dickinson, D. K., & Porche, M. V. (2011). Relation between language experiences in preschool classrooms and children's kindergarten and fourth-grade language and reading abilities. *Child Development, 82,* 870–886. doi:10.1111/j.1467-8624.2011.01576.x

DiCorcia, J. A., Snidman, N., Sravish, A. V., & Tronick, E. (2016). Evaluating the nature of the still-face effect in the double face-to-face still-face paradigm using different comparison groups. *Infancy, 21,* 332–352. doi:10.1111/infa.12123

Diekelmann, S., & Born, J. (2010). The memory function of sleep. *Nature Reviews Neuroscience, 11,* 114–126. doi:10.1038/nrn2762

Diekman, A. B., & Murnen, S. K. (2004). Learning to be little women and little men: The inequitable gender equality of nonsexist children's literature. *Sex Roles, 50,* 373–385. doi:10.1023/B:SERS.0000018892.26527.ea

Diener, M. (2000). Gift from the gods: A Balinese guide to early child rearing. In J. S. DeLoache & A. Gottlieb (Eds.), *A world of babies: Imagined childcare guides for seven societies* (pp. 96–116). New York, NY: Cambridge University Press.

Diener, M. L., & Kim, D.-Y. (2004). Maternal and child predictors of preschool children's social competence. *Journal of Applied Developmental Psychology, 25,* 3–24.

Diener, M. L., & Lucas, R. E. (2004). Adults' desires for children's emotions across 48 countries: Associations with individual and national characteristics. *Journal of Cross-Cultural Psychology, 35,* 525–547. doi:10.1177/0022022104268387

Dijkstra, J. K., Cillessen, A. H. N., & Borch, C. (2013). Popularity and adolescent friendship networks: Selection and influence dynamics. *Developmental Psychology, 49,* 1242–1252. doi:10.1037/a0030098

Dijkstra, J. K., Lindenberg, S., & Veenstra, R. (2008). Beyond the class norm: Bullying behavior of popular adolescents and its relation to peer acceptance and rejection. *Journal of Abnormal Child Psychology, 36,* 1289–1299. doi:10.1007/s10802-008-9251-7

Dillon, M. R., & Spelke, E. S. (2015). Core geometry in perspective. *Developmental Science, 18*(6), 894–908.

Dimidjian, S., & Goodman, S. H. (2014). Preferences and attitudes toward approaches to depression relapse/recurrence prevention among pregnant women. *Behaviour Research and Therapy, 54,* 7–11.

Dimidjian, S., Goodman, S. H., Felder, J. N., Gallop, R., Brown, A. P., & Beck, A. (2016). Staying well during pregnancy and the postpartum: A pilot randomized trial of mindfulness-based cognitive therapy for the prevention of depressive relapse/recurrence. *Journal of Consulting and Clinical Psychology, 84*(2), 134–145.

Dimou, L., & Götz, M. (2014). Glial cells as progenitors and stem cells: New roles in the healthy and diseased brain. *Physiological Reviews, 94*(3), 709–737.

Dinstein, I., Heeger, D. J., Lorenzi, L., Minshew, N. J., Malach, R., & Behrmann, M. (2012). Unreliable evoked respones in autism. *Neuron, 75*(6), 981–991. doi:10.1016/j.neuron.2012.07.026

Dionne, G., Tremblay, R., Boivin, M., Laplante, D., & Pérusse, D. (2003). Physical aggression and expressive vocabulary in 19-month-old twins. *Developmental Psychology, 39,* 261–273. doi:10.1037/0012-1649.39.2.261

DiPietro, J. A. (1981). Rough and tumble play: A function of gender. *Developmental Psychology, 17,* 50.

DiPietro, J. A. (2012). Maternal stress in pregnancy: Considerations for fetal development. *Journal of Adolescent Health, 51*(2, Suppl.), S3–8. doi:10.1016/j.jadohealth.2012.04.008

DiPietro, J. A., Bornstein, M. H., Costigan, K. A., Pressman, E. K., Hahn, C. S., Painter, K., . . . Yi, L. J. (2002). What does fetal movement predict about behavior during the first two years of life? *Developmental Psychobiology, 40,* 358–371.

DiPietro, J. A., Costigan, K. A., Shupe, A. K., Pressman, E. K., & Johnson, T. R. (1998). Fetal neurobehavioral development: Associations with socioeconomic class and fetal sex. *Developmental Psychobiology, 33,* 79–91.

DiPietro, J. A., Costigan, K. A., & Voegtline, K. M. (2015). Studies in fetal behavior: Revisited, renewed and reimagined. *Monographs for the Society of Research in Child Development, 80*(3), vii, 1–94.

DiPietro, J. A., Hilton, S. C., Hawkins, M., Costigan, K. A., & Pressman, E. K. (2002). Maternal stress and affect influence fetal neurobehavioral development. *Developmental Psychology, 38,* 659–668.

DiPietro, J. A., & Voegtline, K. M. (2015). The gestational foundation of sex differences in development and vulnerability. *Neuroscience,* doi:10.1016/j.neuroscience.2015.07.068

Dirks, J., & Gibson, E. (1977). Infants' perception of similarity between live people and their photographs. *Child Development, 48,* 124–130. doi:10.2307/1128890

Dirks, M. A., Persram, R., Recchia, H. E., & Howe, N. (2015). Sibling relationships as sources of risk and resilience in the development and maintenance of internalizing and externalizing problems during childhood and adolescence. *Clinical Psychology Review, 42,* 145–155. doi:10.1016/j.cpr.2015.07.003

Dishion, T. J. (1990). The family ecology of boys' peer relations in middle childhood. *Child Development, 61,* 874–892. doi:10.1111/j.1467-8624.1990.tb02829.x

Dishion, T. J., Andrews, D. W., & Crosby, L. (1995). Antisocial boys and their friends in early adolescence: Relationship characteristics, quality, and interactional process. *Child Development, 66,* 139–151. doi:10.1111/j.1467-8624.1995.tb00861.x

Dishion, T. J., Ha, T., & Véronneau, M.-H. (2012). An ecological analysis of the effects of deviant peer clustering on sexual promiscuity, problem behavior, and childbearing from early adolescence to adulthood: An enhancement of the life history framework. *Developmental Psychology, 48,* 703–717. doi:10.1037/a0027304

Dishion, T. J., Shaw, D., Connell, A., Gardner, F., Weaver, C., & Wilson, M. (2008). The family check-up with high-risk indigent families: Preventing problem behavior by increasing parents' positive behavior support in early childhood. *Child Development, 79,* 1395–1414. doi:10.1111/j.1467-8624.2008.01195.x

Dishion, T. J., & Tipsord, J. M. (2011). Peer contagion in child and adolescent social and emotional development. *Annual Review of Psychology, 62,* 189–214. doi:10.1146/annurev.psych.093008.100412

Dishion, T. J., Véronneau, M.-H., & Myers, M. W. (2010). Cascading peer dynamics underlying the progression from problem behavior to violence in early to late adolescence. *Development and Psychopathology, 22,* 603–619. doi:10.1017/S0954579410000313

DiVitto, B., & Goldberg, S. (1979). The effects of newborn medical status on early parent-infant interaction. In T. Field, A. M. Sostek, S. Goldberg, & H. H. Shuman (Eds.), *Infants born*

at risk: Behavior and development (pp. 311–332). New York, NY: Spectrum.

Dix, T., & Grusec, J. E. (1983). Parental influence techniques: An attributional analysis. *Child Development, 54,* 645–652. doi:10.2307/1130051

Doan, S. N., Fuller-Rowell, T. E., & Evans, G. W. (2012). Cumulative risk and adolescent's internalizing and externalizing problems: The mediating roles of maternal responsiveness and self-regulation. *Developmental Psychology, 48,* 1529–1539. doi:10.1037/a0027815

Doan, S. N., & Wang, Q. (2010). Maternal discussions of mental states and behaviors: Relations to emotion situation knowledge in European American and immigrant Chinese children. *Child Development, 81,* 1490–1503. doi:10.1111/j.1467-8624.2010.01487.x

Dobzhansky, T. (1955). *Evolution, genetics, and man.* New York, NY: Wiley.

Dodge, K. A. (1980). Social cognition and children's aggressive behavior. *Child Development, 51,* 162–170. doi:10.2307/1129603

Dodge, K. A. (1986). A social information processing model of social competence in children. In M. Perlmutter (Ed.), *Minnesota Symposia on Child Psychology: Vol. 18. Cognitive perspectives on children's social and behavioral development* (pp. 77–125). Hillsdale, NJ: Erlbaum.

Dodge, K. A., Dishion, T. J., & Lansford, J. E. (Eds.). (2006). *Deviant peer influences in programs for youth: Problems and solutions.* New York, NY: Guilford Press.

Dodge, K. A., Godwin, J., & Conduct Problems Prevention Research Group. (2013). Social-information-processing patterns mediate the impact of preventive intervention on adolescent antisocial behavior. *Psychological Science, 24*(4), 456–465.

Dodge, K. A., Greenberg, M. T., Malone, P. S., & Conduct Problems Prevention Research Group. (2008). Testing an idealized dynamic cascade model of the development of serious violence in adolescence. *Child Development, 79,* 1907–1927. doi:10.1111/j.1467-8624.2008.01233.x

Dodge, K. A., Lansford, J. E., Burks, V. S., Bates, J. E., Pettit, G. S., Fontaine, R., & Price, J. M. (2003). Peer rejection and social information-processing factors in the development of aggressive behavior problems in children. *Child Development, 74,* 374–393. doi:10.1111/1467-8624.7402004

Dodge, K. A., Lansford, J. E., & Dishion, T. J. (2006). The problem of deviant peer influences in intervention programs. In K. A. Dodge, T. J. Dishion, & J. E. Lansford (Eds.), *Deviant peer influences in programs for youth: Problems and solutions* (pp. 3–13). New York, NY: Guilford Press.

Dodge, K. A., Lochman, J. E., Harnish, J. D., Bates, J. E., & Pettit, G. S. (1997). Reactive and proactive aggression in school children and psychiatrically impaired chronically assaultive youth. *Journal of Abnormal Psychology, 106,* 37–51.

Dodge, K. A., Malone, P. S., Lansford, J. E., Sorbring, E., Skinner, A. T., Tapanya, S., . . . Bacchini, D. (2015). Hostile attributional bias and aggressive behavior in global context. *Proceedings of the National Academy of Sciences, 112*(30), 9310–9315.

Dodge, K. A., Murphy, R. R., & Buchsbaum, K. (1984). The assessment of intention-cue detection skills in children: Implications for developmental psychopathology. *Child Development, 55,* 163–173.

Dodge, K. A., Pettit, G. S., & Bates, J. E. (1994). Socialization mediators of the relation between socioeconomic status and child conduct problems. *Child Development, 65,* 649–665. doi:10.2307/1131407

Dodge, K. A., Pettit, G. S., Bates, J. E., & Valente, E. (1995). Social information-processing patterns partially mediate the effect of early physical abuse on later conduct problems. *Journal of Abnormal Psychology, 104,* 632–643. doi:10.1037/0021-843X.104.4.632

Dodge, K. A., Pettit, G. S., McClaskey, C. L., Brown, M. M., & Gottman, J. M. (1986). Social competence in children. *Monographs of the Society for Research in Child Development, 51*(2, Serial No. 213), i–85. doi:10.2307/1165906

Dogan, S. J., Conger, R. D., Kim, K. J., & Masyn, K. E. (2007). Cognitive and parenting pathways in the transmission of antisocial behavior from parents to adolescents. *Child Development, 78,* 335–349. doi:10.1111/j.1467-8624.2007.01001.x

Doherty, M. J. (2008). *Theory of mind: How children understand others' thoughts and feelings.* New York, NY: Psychology Press. doi:10.4324/9780203929902

Dollard, J., & Miller, N. E. (1950). *Personality and psychotherapy.* New York: McGraw-Hill.

Dombroski, J., & Newman, R. S. (2014). Toddlers' ability to map the meaning of new words in multi-talker environments. *Journal of the Acoustic Society of America, 136*(5), 2807–2815.

Domitrovich, C. E., Bradshaw, C. P., Greenberg, M. T., Embry, D., Poduska, J. M., & Ialongo, N. S. (2010). Integrated models of school-based prevention: Logic and theory. *Psychology in the Schools, 47,* 71–88. doi:10.1002/pits.20452

Domitrovich, C. E., Cortes, R. C., & Greenberg, M. T. (2007). Improving young children's social and emotional competence: A randomized trial of the preschool "PATHS" curriculum. *Journal of Primary Prevention, 28,* 67–91. doi:10.1007/s10935-007-0081-0

Donaldson, S. K., & Westerman, M. A. (1986). Development of children's understanding of ambivalence and causal theories of emotions. *Developmental Psychology, 22,* 655–662.

Donnellan, M. B., Trzesniewski, K. H., Robins, R. W., Moffitt, T. E., & Caspi, A. (2005). Low self-esteem is related to aggression, antisocial behavior, and delinquency. *Psychological Science, 16,* 328–335. doi:10.1111/j.0956-7976.2005.01535.x

Doornwaard, S. M., Branje, S., Meeus, W. H. J., & ter Bogt, T. F. M. (2012). Development of adolescents' peer crowd identification in relation to changes in problem behaviors. *Developmental Psychology, 48,* 1366–1380. doi:10.1037/a0026994

Downey, G., & Coyne, J. C. (1990). Children of depressed parents: An integrative review. *Psychological Bulletin, 108,* 50–76.

Downs, E., & Smith, S. L. (2010). Keeping abreast of hypersexuality: A video game character content analysis. *Sex Roles, 62,* 721–733.

Doyle, A. B., Lawford, H., & Markiewicz, D. (2009). Attachment style with mother, father, best friend, and romantic partner during adolescence. *Journal of Research on Adolescence, 19,* 690–714. doi:10.1111/j.1532-7795.2009.00617.x

Dragowski, E. A., Scharrón-del Río, M. R., & Sandigorsky, A. L. (2011). Childhood gender identity . . . disorder? Developmental, cultural, and diagnostic concerns. *Journal of Counseling & Development, 89,* 360–366.

Drake, K., Belsky, J., & Fearon, R. P. (2014). From early attachment to engagement with learning in school: The role of self-regulation and persistence. *Developmental Psychology, 50,* 1350–1361. doi:10.1037/a0032779

Drevenstedt, G. L., Crimmins, E. M., Vasunilashorn, S., & Finch, C. E. (2008). The rise and fall of excess male infant mortality. *Proceedings of the National Academy of Sciences, 105*(13), 5016–5021.

Driscoll, A. K., Russell, S. T., & Crockett, L. J. (2008). Parenting styles and youth well-being across immigrant generations. *Journal of Family Issues, 29,* 185–209. doi:10.1177/0192513x07307843

Drummond, K. D., Bradley, S. J., Peterson-Badali, M., & Zucker, K. J. (2008). A follow-up study of girls with gender identity disorder. *Developmental Psychology, 44,* 34–45. doi:10.1037/0012-1649.44.1.34

Du, H., Li, X., & Lin, D. (2015). Individualism and sociocultural adaptation: Discrimination and social capital as moderators among rural-to-urban migrants in China. *Asian Journal of Social Psychology 18,* 176–181. doi:10.1111/ajsp.12085

Dubé, E. M., Savin-Williams, R. C., & Diamond, L. M. (2001). Intimacy development, gender, and ethnicity among sexual-minority youths. In A. R. D'Augelli & C. Patterson (Eds.), *Lesbian, gay, and bisexual identities and youth* (pp. 129–152). New York, NY: Oxford University Press.

Dubois, J., Dehaene-Lambertz, G., Kulikova, S., Poupon, C., Hüppi, P. S., & Hertz-Pannier, L. (2014). The early development of brain white matter: A review of imaging studies in fetuses, newborns and infants. *Neuroscience, 276,* 48–71.

Duckworth, A. L., Quinn, P. D., Lynam, D. R., Loeber, R., & Stouthamer-Loeber, M. (2011). Role of test motivation in intelligence testing. *Proceedings of the National Academy of Sciences, 108*(19), 7716–7720. doi:10.1073/pnas.1018601108

Duckworth, A. L., Quinn, P. D., & Tsukayama, E. (2012). What *No Child Left Behind* leaves behind: The roles of IQ and self-control in predicting standardized achievement test scores and report card grades. *Journal of Educational Psychology, 104,* 439–451. doi:10.1037/a0026280

Duff, C. K., & Flattery, J. J. (2014). Developing mirror self awareness in students with autism spectrum disorder. *Journal of Autism and Developmental Disorders, 44,* 1027–1038. doi:10.1007/s10803-013-1954

Duncan, G. J., Dowsett, C. J., Claessens, A., Magnuson, K., Huston, A. C., Klebanov, P., . . . Japel, C. (2007). School readiness and later achievement. *Developmental Psychology, 43,* 1428–1446. doi:10.1037/0012-1649.43.6.1428

Duncan, G. J., Jenkins, J. M., Watts, T. W., Magnuson, K., Clements, D., Sarama, J., . . . Spitler, M. E. (2015). *Preventing preschool fadeout through instructional intervention in kindergarten and first grade.* Society for Research on Educational Effectiveness. Downloaded from http://eric.ed.gov/?id=ED562417

Duncan, G. J., & Murnane, R. J. (2011). *Whither opportunity? Rising inequality, schools, and children's life chances.* New York, NY: Russell Sage Foundation.

Duncan, G. J., & Murnane, R. J. (2014). *Restoring opportunity: The crisis of inequality and the challenge for American education.* Retrieved from http://escholarship.org/uc/item/2v8169pn

Dunfield, K. A., & Kuhlmeier, V. A. (2013). Classifying prosocial behavior: Children's responses to instrumental need, emotional distress, and material desire. *Child Development, 84,* 1766–1776. doi:10.1111/cdev.12075

Dunfield, K., Kuhlmeier, V. A., O'Connell, L., & Kelley, E. (2011). Examining the diversity of prosocial behavior: Helping, sharing, and comforting in infancy. *Infancy, 16,* 227–247. doi:10.1111/j.1532-7078.2010.00041.x

Dunfield, K. A., & Kuhlmeier, V. A. (2010). Intention-mediated selective helping in infancy. *Psychological Science, 21,* 523–527. doi:10.1177/0956797610364119

Dunifon, R., Kalil, A., Crosby, D. A., & Su, J. H. (2013). Mothers' night work and children's behavior problems. *Developmental Psychology, 49,* 1874–1885. doi:10.1037/a0031241

Dunkel, C. S., & Anthis, K. S. (2001). The role of possible selves in identity formation: A short-term longitudinal study. *Journal of Adolescence, 24,* 765–776. doi:10.1006/jado.2001.0433

Dunn, J. (1988). *The beginnings of social understanding.* Cambridge, MA: Harvard University Press.

Dunn, J. (1992). Siblings and development. *Current Directions in Psychological Science, 1,* 6–9. doi:10.1111/1467-8721.ep10767741

Dunn, J. (2004). *Children's friendships: The beginnings of intimacy.* Malden, MA: Blackwell.

Dunn, J., & Brown, J. (1994). Affect expression in the family, children's understanding of emotions, and their interactions with others. *Merrill-Palmer Quarterly, 40,* 120–137.

Dunn, J., Brown, J., & Beardsall, L. (1991). Family talk about feeling states and children's later understanding of others' emotions. *Developmental Psychology, 27,* 448–455.

Dunn, J., Brown, J., Slomkowski, C., Tesla, C., & Youngblade, L. (1991). Young children's understanding of other people's feelings and beliefs: Individual differences and their antecedents. *Child Development, 62,* 1352–1366.

Dunsmore, J. C., & Halberstadt, A. G. (1997). How does family emotional expressiveness affect children's schemas? In K. C. Barrett (Ed.), *New Directions for Child and Adolescent Development: No. 77. The communication of emotion: Current research from diverse perspectives* (pp. 45–68). San Francisco, CA: Jossey-Bass.

Duong, M. T., Schwartz, D., Chang, L., Kelly, B. M., & Tom, S. R. (2009). Associations between maternal physical discipline and peer victimization among Hong Kong Chinese children: The moderating role of child aggression. *Journal of Abnormal Child Psychology, 37,* 957–966. doi:10.1007/s10802-009-9322-4

Durbin, C. E. (2010). Validity of young children's self-reports of their emotion in response to structured laboratory tasks. *Emotion, 10,* 519–535. doi:10.1037/a0019008

Durbin, C. E., Hayden, E. P., Klein, D. N., & Olino, T. M. (2007). Stability of laboratory-assessed temperamental emotionality traits from ages 3 to 7. *Emotion, 7,* 388–399.

Durlak, J. A., Weissberg, R. P., Dymnicki, A. B., Taylor, R. D., & Schellinger, K. B. (2011). The impact of enhancing students' social and emotional learning: A meta-analysis of school-based universal interventions. *Child Development, 82,* 405–432. doi:10.1111/j.1467-8624.2010.01564.x

Durrant, J., Trocmé, N., Fallon, B., Milne, C., Black, T., & Knoke, D. (2006). *Punitive violence against children in Canada* (CECW Information Sheet #41E). Retrieved from University of Toronto, Faculty of Social Work website: http://cwrp.ca/publications/497

Dush, C. M. K., Kotila, L. E., & Schoppe-Sullivan, S. J. (2011). Predictors of supportive coparenting after relationship dissolution among at-risk parents. *Journal of Family Psychology, 25,* 356–365. doi:10.1037/a0023652

Dweck, C. S. (1999). *Self-theories: Their role in motivation, personality, and development.* Philadelphia, PA: Psychology Press.

Dweck, C. S. (2006). *Mindset: The new psychology of success.* New York, NY: Random House.

Dweck, C. S., & Leggett, E. L. (1988). A social-cognitive approach to motivation and personality. *Psychological Review, 95,* 256–273.

Dwyer, K. M., Fredstrom, B. K., Rubin, K. H., Booth-LaForce, C., Rose-Krasnor, L., & Burgess, K. B. (2010). Attachment, social information processing, and friendship quality of early adolescent girls and boys. *Journal of Social and Personal Relationships, 27,* 91–116. doi:10.1177/0265407509346420

East, P. L., Felice, M. E., & Morgan, M. C. (1993). Sisters' and girlfriends' sexual and childbearing behavior: Effects on early adolescent girls' sexual outcomes. *Journal of Marriage and the Family, 55,* 953–963.

East, P. L., & Jacobson, L. J. (2001). The younger siblings of teenage mothers: A follow-up of their pregnancy risk. *Developmental Psychology, 37,* 254–264. doi:10.1037/0012-1649.37.2.254

Eaton, W. O., & Enns, L. R. (1986). Sex differences in human motor activity level. *Psychological Bulletin, 100,* 19–28. doi:10.1037/0033-2909.100.1.19

Eaton, W. O., & Saudino, K. J. (1992). Prenatal activity level as a temperament dimension? Individual differences and developmental functions in fetal movement. *Infant Behavior and Development, 15,* 57–70. doi:10.1016/0163-6383(92)90006-R

Eccles, J. S., Freedman-Doan, C., Frome, P., Jacobs, J., & Yoon, K. S. (2000). Gender-role socialization in the family: A longitudinal approach. In T. Eckes & H. M. Trautner (Eds.), *The developmental social psychology of gender* (pp. 333–360). Mahwah, NJ: Erlbaum.

Eccles, J. S. (2015). Gender socialization of STEM interests in the family. *International Journal of Gender, Science, & Technology, 7,* 116–132.

Eccles, J. S., & Gootman, J. (Eds.). (2002). *Community programs to promote youth development.* Washington, DC: National Academy Press.

Eccles, J. S., & Wigfield, A. (2002). Motivational beliefs, values, and goals. *Annual Review of Psychology, 53,* 109–132. doi:10.1146/annurev.psych.53.100901.135153

Eccles, J. S., Wigfield, A., Flanagan, C. A., Miller, C., Reuman, D. A., & Yee, D. (1989). Self-concepts, domain values, and self-esteem: Relations and changes at early adolescence. *Journal of Personality, 57,* 283–310. doi:10.1111/j.1467-6494.1989.tb00484.x

Eckert, P. (1989). *Jocks and burnouts: Social categories and identity in the high school.* New York, NY: Teachers College Press.

Edelman, G. M. (1987). *Neural Darwinism: The theory of neuronal group selection.* New York, NY: Basic Books.

Eder, D. (1985). The cycle of popularity: Interpersonal relations among female adolescents. *Sociology of Education, 58,* 154–165. doi:10.2307/2112416

Edgin, J. O., Tooley, U., Demara, B., Nyhuis, C., Anand, P., & Spanò, G. (2015). Sleep disturbance and expressive language development in preschool-age children with Down syndrome. *Child Development, 86*(6), 1984–1998. doi:10.1111/cdev.12443

Education Commission of the States. (2016). *High school graduation requirement or credit toward graduation – Service-learning/community service.* Retrieved from http://ecs.force.com/mbdata/mbquest3RTE?Rep=SL1301

Edwards, C. P. (1992). Cross-cultural perspectives on family-peer relations. In R. D. Parke & G. W. Ladd (Eds.), *Family-peer relationships: Modes of linkage* (pp. 285–316). Hillsdale, NJ: Erlbaum.

Edwards, G. D., Bangert, A. W., Cooch, G., Shinfuku, N., Chen, T., Bi, Y., & Rappe, P. (2005). The impact of sibling status on Chinese college students' quality of life. *Social Behavior and Personality, 33,* 227–242.

Egeland, B., & Sroufe, L. A. (1981). Attachment and early maltreatment. *Child Development, 52,* 44–52. doi:10.2307/1129213

Egger, H. L., & Angold, A. (2006), Common emotional and behavioral disorders in preschool children: Presentation, nosology, and epidemiology. *Journal of Child Psychology and Psychiatry, 47,* 313–337. doi:10.1111/j.1469-7610.2006.01618.x

Ehri, L. C. (2014). Orthographic mapping in the acquisition of sight word reading, spelling memory, and vocabulary learning. *Scientific Studies of Reading, 18*(1), 5–21. doi:10.1080/10888443 8.2013.819356

Eiden, R. D., Colder, C., Edwards, E. P., & Leonard, K. E. (2009). A longitudinal study of social competence among children of alcoholic and non-alcoholic parents: Role of parental psychopathology, parental warmth, and self-regulation. *Psychology of Addictive Behaviors, 23,* 36–46.

Eigsti, I. M., Zayas, V., Mischel, W., Shoda, Y., Ayduk, O., Dadlani, M. B., . . . Casey, B. J. (2006). Predicting cognitive control from preschool to late adolescence and young adulthood. *Psychological Science, 17,* 478–484. doi:10.1111/j.1467-9280.2006.01732.x

Eimas, P. D., Siqueland, E. R., Jusczyk, P., & Vigorito, J. (1971, January 22). Speech perception in infants. *Science, 171,* 303–306.

Eisenberg, N. (1986). *Altruistic emotion, cognition, and behavior.* Hillsdale, NJ: Erlbaum.

Eisenberg, N. (2000). Emotion, regulation, and moral development. *Annual Review of Psychology, 51,* 665–697. doi:10.1146/annurev .psych.51.1.665

Eisenberg, N., Boehnke, K., Schuhler, P., & Silbereisen, R. K. (1985). The development of prosocial behavior and cognitions in German children. *Journal of Cross-Cultural Psychology, 16,* 69–82. doi:10.1177/0022002185016001006

Eisenberg, N., Carlo, G., Murphy, B., & van Court, P. (1995). Prosocial development in late adolescence: A longitudinal study. *Child Development, 66,* 1179–1197. doi:10.2307/1131806

Eisenberg, N., Chang, L., Ma, Y., & Huang, X. (2009). Relations of parenting style to Chinese children's effortful control, ego resilience, and maladjustment. *Development and Psychopathology, 21,* 455–477. doi:10.1017/S095457940900025X

Eisenberg, N., Cumberland, A., Guthrie, I. K., Murphy, B. C., & Shepard, S. A. (2005). Age changes in prosocial responding and moral reasoning in adolescence and early adulthood. *Journal of Research on Adolescence, 15,* 235–260. doi:10.1111/j.1532-7795.2005.00095.x

Eisenberg, N., Cumberland, A., & Spinrad, T. L. (1998). Parental socialization of emotion. *Psychological Inquiry, 9,* 241–273.

Eisenberg, N., & Fabes, R. A. (1998). Prosocial development. In W. Damon (Series Ed.) & N. Eisenberg (Vol. Ed.), *Handbook of child psychology: Vol. 3. Social, emotional, and personality development* (5th ed., pp. 701–778). New York, NY: Wiley.

Eisenberg, N., Fabes, R. A., & Murphy, B. C. (1996). Parents' reactions to children's negative emotions: Relations to children's social competence and comforting behavior. *Child Development, 67,* 2227–2247. doi:10.1111/j.1467-8624.1996.tb01854.x

Eisenberg, N., Fabes, R. A., Shepard, S. A., Guthrie, I. K., Murphy, B. C., & Reiser, M. (1999). Parental reactions to children's negative emotions: Longitudinal relations to quality of children's social functioning. *Child Development, 70,* 513–534.

Eisenberg, N., Gershoff, E. T., Fabes, R. A., Shepard, S. A., Cumberland, A. J., Losoya, S. H., . . . Murphy, B. C. (2001). Mothers' emotional expressivity and children's behavior problems and social competence: Mediation through children's regulation. *Developmental Psychology, 37,* 475–490.

Eisenberg, N., Guthrie, I. K., Cumberland, A., Murphy, B. C., Shepard, S. A., Zhou, Q., & Carlo, G. (2002). Prosocial development in early adulthood: A longitudinal study. *Journal of Personality and Social Psychology, 82,* 993–1006. doi:10.1037/0022-3514.82.6.993

Eisenberg, N., Guthrie, I. K., Murphy, B. C., Shepard, S. A., Cumberland, A., & Carlo, G. (1999). Consistency and development of prosocial dispositions: A longitudinal study. *Child Development, 70,* 1360–1372. doi:10.1111/1467-8624.00100

Eisenberg, N., Hofer, C., Spinrad, T. L., Gershoff, E. T., Valiente, C., Losoya, S. H., . . . Maxon, E. (2008). Understanding mother-adolescent conflict discussions: Concurrent and across-time prediction from youths' dispositions and parenting. *Monographs of the Society for Research in Child Development, 73*(2, Serial No. 290). doi:10.1111/j.1540-5834.2008.00470.x

Eisenberg, N., Michalik, N., Spinrad, T. L., Hofer, C., Kupfer, A., Valiente, C., . . . Reiser, M. (2007). The relations of effortful control and impulsivity to children's sympathy: A longitudinal study. *Cognitive Development, 22,* 544–567. doi:10.1016/j.cogdev.2007.08.003

Eisenberg, N., Miller, P. A., Shell, R., McNalley, S., & Shea, C. (1991). Prosocial development in adolescence: A longitudinal study. *Developmental Psychology, 27,* 849–858.

Eisenberg, N., Murphy, B. C., & Shepard, S. (1997). The development of empathic accuracy. In W. J. Ickes (Ed.), *Empathic accuracy* (pp. 73–116). New York, NY: Guilford Press.

Eisenberg, N., & Mussen, P. H. (1989). *The roots of prosocial behavior in children.* Cambridge, England: Cambridge University Press.

Eisenberg, N., Sallquist, J., French, D. C., Purwono, U., Suryanti, T. A., & Pidada, S. (2009). The relations of majority-minority group status and having an other-religion friend to Indonesian youths' socioemotional functioning. *Developmental Psychology, 45,* 248–259. doi:10.1037/a0014028

Eisenberg, N., & Silver, R. C. (2011). Growing up in the shadow of terrorism: Youth in America after 9/11. *American Psychologist, 66,* 468–481. doi:10.1037/a0024619

Eisenberg, N., Spinrad, T. L., & Eggum, N. D. (2010). Emotion-related self-regulation and its relation to children's maladjustment. *Annual Review of Clinical Psychology, 6,* 495–525. doi:10.1146/annurev.clinpsy.121208.131208

Eisenberg, N., Spinrad, T. L., & Knafo-Noam, A. (2015). Prosocial development. In M. E. Lamb (Ed.) & R. M. Lerner (Series Ed.), *Handbook of child psychology and developmental science: Vol. 3* (7the ed., pp. 610–656). Hoboken, NJ: Wiley.

Eisenberg, N., Valiente, C., Spinrad, T. L., Cumberland, A., Liew, J., Reiser, M., . . . Losoya, S. H. (2009). Longitudinal relations of children's effortful control, impulsivity, and negative emotionality to their externalizing, internalizing, and co-occurring behavior problems. *Developmental Psychology, 45,* 988–1008. doi:10.1037/a0016213

Eisenberg, N., Zhou, Q., Spinrad, T. L., Valiente, C., Fabes, R. A., & Liew, J. (2005). Relations among positive parenting, children's effortful control, and externalizing problems: A three-wave longitudinal study. *Child Development, 76,* 1055–1071. doi:10.1111/j.1467-8624.2005.00897.x

Eisenberg-Berg, N., & Geisheker, E. (1979). Content of preachings and power of the model/preacher: The effect on children's generosity. *Developmental Psychology, 15,* 168–175.

Eisenberg-Berg, N., & Hand, M. (1979). The relationship of preschoolers' reasoning about prosocial moral conflicts to prosocial behavior. *Child Development, 50,* 356–363. doi:10.2307/1129410

Eisner, M. P., & Malti, T. (2015). Aggressive and violent behavior. In M. E. Lamb (Ed.) & R. M. Lerner (Series Ed.), *Handbook of child psychology and developmental science: Vol. 3* (7th ed., pp. 794–841). Hoboken, NJ: Wiley.

Ekas, N. V., Lickenbrock, D. M., & Braungart-Rieker, J. (2013). Developmental trajectories of emotion regulation across infancy: Do age and the social partner influence temporal patterns? *Infancy, 18*, 729–754. doi:10.1111/infa.12003

Ekéus, C., Christensson, K., & Hjern, A. (2004). Unintentional and violent injuries among pre-school children of teenage mothers in Sweden: A national cohort study. *Journal of Epidemiology and Community Health, 58*, 680–685. doi:10.1136/jech.2003.015255

Ekins, E. (2014, August 19). *Reason-Rupe poll: 57 percent of Americans say only kids who win should get trophies*. Retrieved from http://reason.com/poll/2014/08/19/57-percent-of-americans-say-only-kids-wh

Ekman, P., & Cordaro, D. (2011). What is meant by calling emotions basic. *Emotion Review, 3*, 364–370. doi:10.1177/1754073911410740

El-Sheikh, M., & Whitson, S. A. (2006). Longitudinal relations between marital conflict and child adjustment: Vagal regulation as a protective factor. *Journal of Family Psychology, 20*, 30–39.

El-Sheikh, M., Harger, J., & Whitson, S. M. (2001). Exposure to interparental conflict and children's adjustment and physical health: The moderating role of vagal tone. *Child Development, 72*, 1617–1636.

Elicker, J., Englund, M., & Sroufe, L. A. (1992). Predicting peer competence and peer relationships in childhood from early parent–child relationships. In R. D. Parke & G. W. Ladd (Eds.), *Family-peer relationships: Modes of linkage* (pp. 77–106). Hillsdale, NJ: Erlbaum.

Elkind, D. (1967). Egocentrism in adolescence. *Child Development, 38*, 1025–1034.

Elledge, L. C., Williford, A., Boulton, A. J., DePaolis, K. J., Little, T. D., & Salmivalli, C. (2013). Individual and contextual predictors of cyberbullying: The influence of children's provictim attitudes and teachers' ability to intervene. *Journal of Youth and Adolescence, 42*, 698–710. doi:10.1007/s10964-013-9920-x

Elliott, D. S. (1994). Serious violent offenders: Onset, developmental course, and termination: The American Society of Criminology 1993 presidential address. *Criminology, 32*, 1–21. doi:10.1111/j.1745-9125.1994.tb01144.x

Ellis, B. J., Bates, J. E., Dodge, K. A., Fergusson, D. M., Horwood, L. J., Pettit, G. S., & Woodward, L. (2003). Does father absence place daughters at special risk for early sexual activity and teenage pregnancy? *Child Development, 74*, 801–821. doi:10.1111/1467-8624.00569

Ellis, R. R., & Simmons, T. (2014). Coresident grandparents and their grandchildren:

2012 (Current Population Reports, P20-576). Washington, DC: U.S. Census Bureau. Retrieved from U.S Census Bureau website: http://www.census.gov/content/dam/Census/library/publications/2014/demo/p20-576.pdf

Ellis, W. E., Crooks, C. V., & Wolfe, D. A. (2009). Relational aggression in peer and dating relationships: Links to psychological and behavioral adjustment. *Social Development, 18*, 253–269. doi:10.1111/j.1467-9507.2008.00468.x

Ellsworth, C. P., Muir, D. W., & Hains, S. M. (1993). Social competence and person-object differentiation: An analysis of the still-face effect. *Developmental Psychology, 29*, 63–73. doi:10.1037/0012-1649.29.1.63

Elman, J. L., Bates, E., Johnson, M. H., Karmiloff-Smith, A., Parisi, D., & Plunkett, K. (1996). *Rethinking innateness: A connectionist perspective on development*. Cambridge, MA: MIT Press.

Else-Quest, N. M., Hyde, J. S., Goldsmith, H. H., & Van Hulle, C. A. (2006). Gender differences in temperament: A meta-analysis. *Psychological Bulletin, 132*, 33–72. doi:10.1037/0033-2909.132.1.33

Else-Quest, N. M., Hyde, J. S., & Linn, M. C. (2010). Cross-national patterns of gender differences in mathematics: A meta-analysis. *Psychological Bulletin, 136*, 103–127. doi:10.1037/a0018053

Ely, R., & McCabe, A. (1994). The language play of kindergarten children. *First Language, 14*, 19–35. doi:10.1177/014272379401404002

Emde, R. N. (1994). Individual meaning and increasing complexity: Contributions of Sigmund Freud and René Spitz to developmental psychology. In R. D. Parke, P. A. Ornstein, J. J. Rieser, & C. Zahn-Waxler (Eds.), *A century of developmental psychology* (pp. 203–231). Washington, DC: American Psychological Association.

Emery, R. E. (1989). Family violence. *American Psychologist, 44*, 321–328. doi:10.1037/0003-066X.44.2.321

Emery, R. E., & Forehand, R. (1996). Parental divorce and children's well-being: A focus on resilience. In R. J. Haggerty, L. R. Sherrod, N. Garmezy, & M. Rutter (Eds.), *Stress, risk, and resilience in children and adolescents: Processes, mechanisms, and interventions* (pp. 64–99). Cambridge, England: Cambridge University Press.

Engle, J. M., & McElwain, N. L. (2011). Parental reactions to toddlers' negative emotions and child negative emotionality as correlates of problem behavior at the age of three. *Social Development, 20*, 251–271.

Engle, J. M., McElwain, N. L., & Lasky, N. (2011). Presence and quality of kindergarten children's friendships: Concurrent and longitudinal associations with child adjustment in the early school years. *Infant and Child Development, 20*, 365–386. doi:10.1002/icd.706

Englund, M. M., Kuo, S. I.-C., Puig, J., & Collins, W. A. (2011). Early roots of adult competence: The significance of close relationships from infancy to early adulthood. *International Journal of Behavioral Development, 35*, 490–496. doi:10.1177/0165025411422994

Ensor, R., & Hughes, C. (2008). Content or connectedness? Mother–child talk and early social understanding. *Child Development, 79*, 201–216.

Eppig, C., Fincher, C. L., & Thornhill, R. (2010). Parasite prevalence and the worldwide distribution of cognitive ability. *Proceedings of the Royal Society B: Biological Sciences, 277*, 3801–3808. doi:10.1098/rspb.2010.0973

Eppler, M. A., Adolph, K. E., & Weiner, T. (1996). The developmental relationship between infants' exploration and action on slanted surfaces. *Infant Behavior and Development, 19*, 259–264. doi:10.1016/S0163-6383(96)90025-9

Erdley, C. A., Nangle, D. W., Newman, J. E., & Carpenter, E. M. (2001). Children's friendship experiences and psychological adjustment: Theory and research. In C. A. Erdley & D. W. Nangle (Eds.), *New Directions for Child and Adolescent Development: No. 91. The role of friendship in psychological adjustment* (Vol. 2001, pp. 5–24). San Francisco, CA: Jossey-Bass.

Erel, O., Margolin, G., & John, R. S. (1998). Observed sibling interaction: Links with the marital and the mother–child relationship. *Developmental Psychology, 34*, 288–298. doi:10.1037/0012-1649.34.2.288

Erel, O., Oberman, Y., & Yirmiya, N. (2000). Maternal versus nonmaternal care and seven domains of children's development. *Psychological Bulletin, 126*, 727–747. doi:10.1037/0033-2909.126.5.727

Erickson, M. F., Sroufe, L. A., & Egeland, B. (1985). The relationship between quality of attachment and behavior problems in preschool in a high-risk sample. *Monographs of the Society for Research in Child Development, 50*(1–2, Serial No. 209), 147–166. doi:10.2307/3333831

Erikson, E. H. (1950). *Childhood and society*. New York, NY: Norton.

Erikson, E. H. (1968). *Identity: Youth and crisis*. New York, NY: Norton.

Erikson, E. H. (1994). *Identity and the life cycle*. New York, NY: Norton. (Original work published 1959)

Erkut, S., Marx, F., Fields, J. P., & Sing, R. (1999). Raising confident and competent girls: One size does not fit all. In L. A. Peplau, S. DeBro, R. Veniegas, & P. Taylor (Eds.), *Gender, culture, and ethnicity: Current research about women and men* (pp. 83–101). Mountain View, CA: Mayfield.

Eron, L. D., Huesmann, L. R., Dubow, E., Romanoff, R., & Yarmel, P. W. (1987). Aggression and its correlates over 22 years. In D. H. Crowell, I. M. Evans, & C. R. O'Donnell (Eds.),

Childhood aggression and violence: Sources of influence, prevention, and control (pp. 249–262). New York, NY: Plenum.

Espelage, D. L., Holt, M. K., & Henkel, R. R. (2003). Examination of peer-group contextual effects on aggression during early adolescence. *Child Development, 74*, 205–220. doi:10.1111/1467-8624.00531

Esposito, G., Yoshida, S., Ohnishi, R., Tsuneoka, Y., Rostagno, M. d. C., Yokota, S., . . . Kuroda, K. O. (2013). Infant calming responses during maternal carrying in humans and mice. *Current Biology, 23*, 739–745. doi:10.1016/j.cub.2013.03.041

Espy, K. A., Sheffield, T. D., Wiebe, S. A., Clark, C. A. C., & Moehr, M. J. (2011). Executive control and dimensions of problem behaviors in preschool children. *Journal of Child Psychology and Psychiatry, 52*, 33–46. doi:10.1111/j.1469-7610.2010.02265.x

Essex, M. J., Thomas Boyce, W., Hertzman, C., Lam, L. L., Armstrong, J. M., Neumann, S. M. A., & Kobor, M. S. (2013). Epigenetic vestiges of early developmental adversity: Childhood stress exposure and DNA methylation in adolescence. *Child Development, 84*, 58–75. doi:10.1111/j.1467-8624.2011.01641.x

Ettinger, A. S., & Wengrovitz, A. G. (2010). Guidelines for the identification and management of lead exposure in pregnant and lactating women. Centers for Disease Control and Prevention. Retrieved from https://www.cdc.gov/nceh/lead/publications/leadandpregnancy2010.pdf

Eurydice Network. (2012). Key Data on Teaching Languages at School in Europe – 2012. Education, Audiovisual and Culture Executive Agency. Retrieved from http://ec.europa.eu/eurostat/documents/3217494/5775673/EC-XA-12-001-EN.PDF/917d3746-886e-456a-8b01-1971013d1cef

Evans, A. B., Banerjee, M., Meyer, R., Aldana, A., Foust, M., & Rowley, S. (2012). Racial socialization as a mechanism for positive development among African American youth. *Child Development Perspectives, 6*, 251–257. doi:10.1111/j.1750-8606.2011.00226.x

Evans, A. D., Xu, F., & Lee, K. (2011). When all signs point to you: Lies told in the face of evidence. *Developmental Psychology, 47*, 39–49.

Evans, E. M. (2008). Conceptual change and evolutionary biology: A developmental analysis. In S. Vosniadou (Ed.), *International handbook of research on conceptual change* (pp. 263–294). New York, NY: Routledge.

Evans, E. M., Legare, C., & Rosengren, K. (2011). Engaging multiple epistemologies: Implications for science education. In R. Taylor & M. Ferrari (Eds.). *Epistemology and science education: Understanding the evolution vs. intelligent design controversy* (pp. 111–139). New York, NY: Routledge.

Evans, G. W. (2004). The environment of childhood poverty. *American Psychologist, 59*, 77–92. doi:10.1037/0003-066X.59.2.77

Evans, G. W., & Cassells, R. C. (2014). Childhood poverty, cumulative risk exposure, and mental health in emerging adults. *Clinical Psychological Science, 2(3)*, 287–296. doi:10.1177/2167702613501496

Evans, G. W., Li, D., & Whipple, S. S. (2013). Cumulative risk and child development. *Psychological Bulletin, 139(6)*, 1342–1396. doi:10.1037/a0031808

Evans, J. L., Saffran, J. R., & Robe-Torres, K. (2009). Statistical learning in children with specific language impairment. *Journal of Speech, Language, and Hearing Research, 52*, 321–335. doi:10.1044/1092-4388(2009/07-0189)

Ewart, C. K., & Suchday, S. (2002). Discovering how urban poverty and violence affect health: Development and validation of a neighborhood stress index. *Health Psychology, 21*, 254–262. doi:10.1037/0278-6133.21.3.254

Ezkurdia, I., Juan, D., Rodriguez, J. M., Frankish, A., Diekhans, M., Harrow, J., . . . Tress, M. L. (2014). Multiple evidence strands suggest that there may be as few as 19,000 human protein-coding genes. *Human Molecular Genetics, 23(22)*, 5866–5878.

Fabes, R. A., & Eisenberg, N. (1992). Young children's coping with interpersonal anger. *Child Development, 63*, 116–128. doi:10.1111/j.1467-8624.1992.tb03600.x

Fabes, R. A., Eisenberg, N., McCormick, S. E., & Wilson, M. S. (1988). Preschoolers' attributions of the situational determinants of others' naturally occurring emotions. *Developmental Psychology, 24*, 376–385.

Fabes, R. A., Eisenberg, N., Nyman, M., & Michealieu, Q. (1991). Young children's appraisals of others' spontaneous emotional reactions. *Developmental Psychology, 27*, 858–866.

Fabes, R. A., Eisenberg, N., Smith, M. C., & Murphy, B. C. (1996). Getting angry at peers: Associations with liking of the provocateur. *Child Development, 67*, 942–956. doi:10.1111/j.1467-8624.1996.tb01775.x

Fabes, R. A., Fultz, J., Eisenberg, N., May-Plumlee, T., & Christopher, F. S. (1989). Effects of rewards on children's prosocial motivation: A socialization study. *Developmental Psychology, 25*, 509–515. doi:10.1037/0012-1649.25.4.509

Fabes, R. A., Martin, C. L., & Hanish, L. D. (2003). Young children's play qualities in same-, other-, and mixed-sex peer groups. *Child Development, 74*, 921–932. doi:10.1111/1467-8624.00576

Fabricius, W. V., & Braver, S. L. (2006). Relocation, parent conflict, and domestic violence: Independent risk factors for children of divorce. *Journal of Child Custody, 3*, 7–27. doi:10.1300/j190v03n03_02

Fagan, J., Bernd, E., & Whiteman, V. (2007). Adolescent fathers' parenting stress, social support, and involvement with infants. *Journal of Research on Adolescence, 17*, 1–22. doi:10.1111/j.1532-7795.2007.00510.x

Fagan, J., & Lee, Y. (2010). Perceptions and satisfaction with father involvement and adolescent mothers' postpartum depressive symptoms. *Journal of Youth and Adolescence, 39*, 1109–1121. doi:10.1007/s10964-009-9444-6

Fagot, B. I. (1977). Consequences of moderate cross-gender behavior in preschool children. *Child Development, 48*, 902–907. doi:10.2307/1128339

Fagot, B. I., & Leinbach, M. D. (1989). The young child's gender schema: Environmental input, internal organization. *Child Development, 60*, 663–672. doi:10.2307/1130731

Falbo, T., & Poston, D. L. (1993). The academic, personality, and physical outcomes of only children in China. *Child Development, 64*, 18–35. doi:10.1111/j.1467-8624.1993.tb02893.x

Falbo, T., Poston, D. L., Ji, G., Jiao, S., Jing, Q., Wang, S., . . . Liu, Y. (1989). Physical, achievement and personality characteristics of Chinese children. *Journal of Biosocial Science, 21*, 483–496. doi:10.1017/S0021932000018228

Falci, C. (2006). Family structure, closeness to residential and nonresidential parents, and psychological distress in early and middle adolescence. *Sociological Quarterly, 47*, 123–146. doi:10.1111/j.1533-8525.2006.00040.x

Fallang, B., Saugstad, O. D., Grogaard, J., & Hadders-Algra, M. (2003). Kinematic quality of reaching movements in preterm infants. *Pediatric Research, 53*, 836–842. doi:10.1203/01.PDR.0000058925.94994.BC

Fan, S. P., Liberman, Z., Keysar, B., & Kinzler, K. D. (2015). The exposure advantage: Early exposure to a multilingual environment promotes effective communication. *Psychological Science, 26(7)*, 1090–1097.

Fanger, S. M., Frankel, L. A., & Hazen, N. (2012). Peer exclusion in preschool children's play: Naturalistic observations in a playground setting. *Merrill-Palmer Quarterly, 58*, 224–254. doi:10.1353/mpq.2012.0007

Fantz, R. L. (1961, May). The origin of form perception. *Scientific American, 204(5)*, 66–72.

Farkas, T., & Leaper, C. (2016). The psychology of boys. In Y. J. Wong, & S. R. Wester. (Eds.), *APA Handbook of Men and Masculinities* (pp. 357–387). Washington, DC: American Psychological Association.

Farmer, T. W., Hall, C. M., Leung, M.-C., Estell, D. B., & Brooks, D. (2011). Social prominence and the heterogeneity of rejected status in late elementary school. *School Psychology Quarterly, 26*, 260–274. doi:10.1037/a0025624

Farr, R. H., Forssell, S. L., & Patterson, C. J. (2010). Parenting and child development in adoptive families: Does parental sexual orientation matter? *Applied Developmental Science, 14,* 164–178. doi:10.1080/10888691.2010.500958

Farr, R. H., & Patterson, C. J. (2013). Coparenting among lesbian, gay, and heterosexual couples: Associations with adopted children's outcomes. *Child Development, 84,* 1226–1240. doi:10.1111/cdev.12046

Farrant, B. M., Devine, T. A. J., Maybery, M. T., & Fletcher, J. (2012). Empathy, perspective taking and prosocial behaviour: The importance of parenting practices. *Infant and Child Development, 21,* 175–188. doi:10.1002/icd.740

Farrant, K., & Reese, E. (2002). *Attachment security and mother-child reminiscing: Reflections on a shared past.* Manuscript submitted for publication.

Farrell, A. D., & White, K. S. (1998). Peer influences and drug use among urban adolescents: Family structure and parent–adolescent relationship as protective factors. *Journal of Consulting and Clinical Psychology, 66,* 248–258. doi:10.1037/0022-006X.66.2.248

Fausey, C. M., Jayaraman, S., & Smith, L. B. (2016). From faces to hands: Changing visual input in the first two years. *Cognition, 152,* 101–107.

Fazio, L. K., DeWolf, M., & Siegler, R. S. (2016). Strategy use and strategy choice in fraction magnitude comparison. *Journal of Experimental Psychology: Learning, Memory, and Cognition, 42,* 1–16. doi:10.1037/xlm0000153

Fearon, R. P., Bakermans-Kranenburg, M. J., van IJzendoorn, M. H., Lapsley, A.-M., & Roisman, G. I. (2010). The significance of insecure attachment and disorganization in the development of children's externalizing behavior: A meta-analytic study. *Child Development, 81,* 435–456. doi:10.1111/j.1467-8624.2009.01405.x

Feddes, A. R., Noack, P., & Rutland, A. (2009). Direct and extended friendship effects on minority and majority children's interethnic attitudes: A longitudinal study. *Child Development, 80,* 377–390. doi:10.1111/j.1467-8624.2009.01266.x

Federal Bureau of Investigation. (n.d.). Innocent images. Retrieved from http://www.fbi.gov/about-us/investigate/vc_majorthefts/innocent

Federal Bureau of Investigation. (2014). *Hate crime statistics report.* Retrieved from https://www.fbi.gov/news/stories/2014/december/latest-hate-crime-statistics-report-released

Federal Interagency Forum on Child and Family Statistics. (2015). *America's children in brief: Key national indicator of well-being, 2015.* Washington, DC: Government Printing Office. Retrieved from http://www.childstats.gov/pdf/ac2015/ac_15.pdf

Feigenson, L., Dehaene, S., & Spelke, E. (2004). Core systems of number. *Trends in cognitive sciences, 8*(7), 307–314. doi:10.1016/j.tics.2004.05.002

Feinberg, M., & Hetherington, E. M. (2001). Differential parenting as a within-family variable. *Journal of Family Psychology, 15,* 22–37. doi:10.1037/0893-3200.15.1.22

Feitelson, D., & Goldstein, Z. (1986). Patterns of book ownership and reading to young children in Israeli school-oriented and nonschool-oriented families. *The Reading Teacher, 39,* 924–930.

Feldman, H., Goldin-Meadow, S., & Gleitman, L. R. (1978). Beyond Herodotus: The creation of language by linguistically deprived deaf children. In A. Lock (Ed.), *Action, symbol, and gesture: The emergence of language* (pp. 351–413). New York, NY: Academic Press.

Feldman, R. (2009). The development of regulatory functions from birth to 5 years: Insights from premature infants. *Child Development, 80,* 544–561. doi:10.1111/j.1467-8624.2009.01278.x

Feldman, R. (2012). Oxytocin and social affiliation in humans. *Hormones and Behavior, 61,* 380–391. doi:10.1016/j.yhbeh.2012.01.008

Feldman, R. (2015). Mutual influences between child emotion regulation and parent–child reciprocity support development across the first 10 years of life: Implications for developmental psychopathology. *Development and Psychopathology, 27,* 1007–1023. doi:10.1017/S0954579415000656

Feldman, R., & Masalha, S. (2007). The role of culture in moderating the links between early ecological risk and young children's adaptation. *Development and Psychopathology, 19,* 1–21. doi:10.1017/S0954579407070010

Feldman, R., & Masalha, S. (2010). Parent–child and triadic antecedents of children's social competence: Cultural specificity, shared process. *Developmental Psychology, 46,* 455–467. doi:10.1037/a0017415

Feldman, R., Masalha, S., & Derdikman-Eiron, R. (2010). Conflict resolution in the parent–child, marital, and peer contexts and children's aggression in the peer group: A process-oriented cultural perspective. *Developmental Psychology, 46,* 310–325. doi:10.1037/a0018286

Feldman, R. S., Philippot, P., & Custrini, R. J. (1991). Social competence and nonverbal behavior. In R. S. Feldman & B. Rimé (Eds.), *Fundamentals of nonverbal behavior* (pp. 329–350). Cambridge, England: Cambridge University Press.

Felsman, J. K., & Vaillant, G. E. (1987). Resilient children as adults: A 40-year study. In E. J. Anthony & B. J. Cohler (Eds.), *The invulnerable child* (pp. 289–314). New York, NY: Guilford Press.

Felson, J. (2014). What can we learn from twin studies? A comprehensive evaluation of the equal environments assumption. *Social Science Research, 43,* 184–199.

Feng, X., Keenan, K., Hipwell, A. E., Henneberger, A. K., Rischall, M. S., Butch, J., . . . Babinski, D. E. (2009). Longitudinal associations between emotion regulation and depression in preadolescent girls: Moderation by the caregiving environment. *Developmental Psychology, 45,* 798–808.

Fenson, L., Dale, P. S., Reznick, J. S., Bates, E., Thal, D. J., & Pethick, S. J. (1994). Variability in early communicative development. *Monographs of the Society for Research in Child Development, 59*(5, Serial No. 242), 1–173.

Ferguson, C. J. (2007). The good, the bad and the ugly: A meta-analytic review of positive and negative effects of violent video games. *Psychiatric Quarterly, 78,* 309–316. doi:10.1007/s11126-007-9056-9

Ferguson, C. J. (2015). Do angry birds make for angry children? A meta-analysis of video game influences on children's and adolescents' aggression, mental health, prosocial behavior, and academic performance. *Perspectives on Psychological Science, 10*(5), 646–666. doi:10.1177/1745691615592234

Fergusson, D. M., Woodward, L. J., & Horwood, L. J. (1999). Childhood peer relationship problems and young people's involvement with deviant peers in adolescence. *Journal of Abnormal Child Psychology, 27,* 357–369. doi:10.1023/A:1021923917494

Fergusson, E., Maughan, B., & Golding, J. (2008). Which children receive grandparental care and what effect does it have? *Journal of Child Psychology and Psychiatry, 49,* 161–169. doi:10.1111/j.1469-7610.2007.01840.x

Fernald, A. (1993). Approval and disapproval: Infant responsiveness to vocal affect in familiar and unfamiliar languages. *Child Development, 64,* 657–674.

Fernald, A., & Marchman, V. A. (2012). Individual differences in lexical processing at 18 months predict vocabulary growth in typically developing and late-talking toddlers. *Child Development, 83,* 203–222. doi:10.1111/j.1467-8624.2011.01692.x

Fernald, A., Perfors, A., & Marchman, V. A. (2006). Picking up speed in understanding: Speech processing efficiency and vocabulary growth across the 2nd year. *Developmental Psychology, 42,* 98–116. doi:10.1037/0012-1649.42.1.98

Fernald, A., Taeschner, T., Dunn, J., Papousek, M., de Boysson-Bardies, B., & Fukui, I. (1989). A cross-language study of prosodic modifications in mothers' and fathers' speech to preverbal infants. *Journal of Child Language, 16,* 477–501.

Ferrari, M., & Chi, M. T. H. (1998). The nature of naïve explanations of natural selection. *International Journal of Science Education, 20*(10), 1231–1256. doi:10.1080/0950069980201005

Ferrari, P. F., Vanderwert, R. E., Paukner, A., Bower, S., Suomi, S. J., & Fox, N. A. (2012). Distinct EEG amplitude suppression to facial gestures as evidence for a mirror mechanism in newborn monkeys. *Journal of Cognitive Neuroscience, 24*(5), 1165–1172.

Ferry, T. R., Fouad, N. A., & Smith, P. L. (2000). The role of family context in a social cognitive model for career-related choice behavior: A math and science perspective. *Journal of Vocational Behavior, 57,* 348–364. doi:10.1006/jvbe.1999.1743

Field, A. E., Austin, S. B., Camargo, C. A., Taylor, C. B., Striegel-Moore, R. H., Loud, K. J., & Colditz, G. A. (2005). Exposure to the mass media, body shape concerns, and use of supplements to improve weight and shape among male and female adolescents. *Pediatrics, 116,* e214–e220. doi:10.1542/peds.2004-2022

Field, D. (1987). A review of preschool conservation training: An analysis of analyses. *Developmental Review, 7,* 210–251. doi:10.1016/0273-2297(87)90013-X

Field, T. (2001). Massage therapy facilitates weight gain in preterm infants. *Current Directions in Psychological Science, 10,* 51–54. doi:10.1111/1467-8721.00113

Field, T., Grizzle, N., Scafidi, F., Abrams, S., Richardson, S., Kuhn, C., & Schanberg, S. (1996). Massage therapy for infants of depressed mothers. *Infant Behavior and Development, 19,* 107–112. doi:10.1016/S0163-6383(96)90048-X

Field, T., Hernandez-Reif, M., & Freedman, J. (2004). Stimulation programs for preterm infants. *Social Policy Report, 28*(1), 1, 3–19.

Fifer, W. P., Byrd, D. L., Kaku, M., Eigsti, I.-M., Isler, J. R., Grose-Fifer, J., . . . Balsam, P. D. (2010). Newborn infants learn during sleep. *Proceedings of the National Academy of Sciences of the United States of America, 107,* 10320–10323. doi:10.1073/pnas.1005061107

Filardo, E. K. (1996). Gender patterns in African American and White adolescents' social interactions in same-race, mixed-gender groups. *Journal of Personality and Social Psychology, 71,* 71–82.

Filippi, C. A., Cannon, E. N., Fox, N. A., Thorpe, S. G., Ferrari, P. F., & Woodward, A. L. (2016). Motor system activation predicts goal imitation in 7-month-old infants. *Psychological Science, 27*(5), 675–684.

Fine, S. E., Izard, C. E., Mostow, A. J., Trentacosta, C. J., & Ackerman, B. P. (2003). First grade emotion knowledge as a predictor of fifth grade self-reported internalizing behaviors in children from economically disadvantaged families. *Development and Psychopathology, 15,* 331–342.

Finkelhor, D., Turner, H., Ormrod, R., Hamby, S., and Kracke, K. (2009). *Children's Exposure to Violence: A Comprehensive National Survey. Bulletin.* Washington, DC: U.S. Department of Justice, Office of Justice Programs, Office of Juvenile Justice and Delinquency Prevention. Retrieved from https://www.ncjrs.gov/pdffiles1/ojjdp/227744.pdf

Finnie, V., & Russell, A. (1988). Preschool children's social status and their mothers' behavior and knowledge in the supervisory role. *Developmental Psychology, 24,* 789–801. doi:10.1037/0012-1649.24.6.789

Fischer, A. R., & Shaw, C. M. (1999). African Americans' mental health and perceptions of racist discrimination: The moderating effects of racial socialization experiences and self-esteem. *Journal of Counseling Psychology, 46,* 395–407. doi:10.1037/0022-0167.46.3.395

Fischer, K. W., & Bidell, T. R. (2006). Dynamic development of action and thought. In W. Damon & R. M. Lerner (Series Eds.) & R. M. Lerner (Vol. Ed.), *Handbook of child psychology: Vol. 1. Theoretical models of human development* (6th ed., pp. 313–399). Hoboken, NJ: Wiley.

Fiser, J., & Aslin, R. N. (2001). Unsupervised statistical learning of higher-order spatial structures from visual scenes. *Psychological Science, 12,* 499–504. doi:10.1111/1467-9280.00392

Fisher, A. V., Godwin, K. E., & Seltman, H. (2014). Visual environment, attention allocation, and learning: When too much of a good thing may be bad. *Psychological Science, 25*(7), 1362–1370. doi:10.1177/0956797614533801

Fisher, C. (1999). From form to meaning: A role for structural alignment in the acquisition of language. *Advances in Child Development and Behavior, 27,* 1–53.

Fisher, C., Gleitman, H., & Gleitman, L. R. (1991). On the semantic content of subcategorization frames. *Cognitive Psychology, 23,* 331–392.

Fisher, P. A., Gunnar, M. R., Chamberlain, P., & Reid, J. B. (2000). Preventive intervention for maltreated preschool children: Impact on children's behavior, neuroendocrine activity, and foster parent functioning. *Journal of the American Academy of Child and Adolescent Psychiatry, 39,* 1356–1364. doi:10.1097/00004583-200011000-00009

Fitzgerald, J. (1992). Variant views about good thinking during composing: Focus on revision. In M. Pressley, K. R. Harris, & J. T. Guthrie (Eds.), *Promoting academic competence and literacy in school* (pp. 337–358). Bingley, England: Emerald Group.

Fivush, R. (1991). The social construction of personal narratives. *Merrill-Palmer Quarterly, 37,* 59–81.

Flavell, J. H. (1986). The development of children's knowledge about the appearance-reality distinction. *American Psychologist, 41,* 418–425.

Fleischer, N. L., Merialdi, M., van Donkelaar, A., Vadillo-Ortega, F., Martin, R. V., Betran, A. P., & Souza, J. P. (2015). Outdoor air pollution, preterm birth, and low birth weight: Analysis of the World Health Organization global survey on maternal and perinatal health. *Environmental Health Perspectives, 22*(4), 425–430.

Fletcher, A. C., Rollins, A., & Nickerson, P. (2004). The extension of school-based inter- and intraracial children's friendships:

Influences on psychosocial well-being. *American Journal of Orthopsychiatry, 74,* 272–285. doi:10.1037/0002-9432.74.3.272

Flook, L., Goldberg, S. B., Pinger, L. J., & Davidson, R. J. (2015). Promoting prosocial behavior and self-regulatory skills in preschool children through a mindfulness-based kindness curriculum. *Developmental Psychology, 51*(1), 44–51.

Floyd, F. J., Stein, T. S., Harter, K. S. M., Allison, A., & Nye, C. L. (1999). Gay, lesbian, and bisexual youths: Separation-individuation, parental attitudes, identity consolidation, and well-being. *Journal of Youth and Adolescence, 28,* 719–739. doi:10.1023/A:1021691601737

Flynn, J. R. (1987). Massive IQ gains in 14 nations: What IQ tests really measure. *Psychological Bulletin, 101,* 171–191.

Flynn, J. R. (2009). *What is intelligence? Beyond the Flynn effect.* Cambridge, England: Cambridge University Press.

Flynn, J. R., & Weiss, L. G. (2007). American IQ gains from 1931 to 2002: The WISC subtests and educational progress. *International Journal of Testing, 7,* 209–224.

Fodor, J. A. (1983). *The modularity of mind: An essay on faculty psychology.* Cambridge, MA: MIT Press.

Fogel, A., Nwokah, E., Dedo, J. Y., Messinger, D., Dickson, K. L., Matusov, E., & Holt, S. A. (1992). Social process theory of emotion: A dynamic systems approach. *Social Development, 1,* 122–142.

Fontaine, R. G., Tanha, M., Yang, C., Dodge, K. A., Bates, J. E., & Pettit, G. S. (2010). Does response evaluation and decision (RED) mediate the relation between hostile attributional style and antisocial behavior in adolescence? *Journal of Abnormal Child Psychology, 38,* 615–626. doi:10.1007/s10802-010-9397-y

Fontaine, R. G., Yang, C., Dodge, K. A., Bates, J. E., & Pettit, G. S. (2008). Testing an individual systems model of response evaluation and decision (RED) and antisocial behavior across adolescence. *Child Development, 79,* 462–475. doi:10.1111/j.1467-8624.2007.01136.x

Fontaine, R. G., Yang, C., Dodge, K. A., Pettit, G. S., & Bates, J. E. (2009). Development of response evaluation and decision (RED) and antisocial behavior in childhood and adolescence. *Developmental Psychology, 45,* 447–459. doi:10.1037/a0014142

Fonteneau, E., & van der Lely, H. K. J. (2008). Electrical brain responses in language-impaired children reveal grammar-specific deficits. *PLoS ONE, 3,* e1832. doi:10.1371/journal.pone.0001832

Fonzi, A., Schneider, B. H., Tani, F., & Tomada, G. (1997). Predicting children's friendship status from their dyadic interaction in structured situations of potential conflict. *Child Development, 68,* 496–506. doi:10.1111/j.1467-8624.1997.tb01954.x

Foorman, B., Beyler, N., Borradaile, K., Coyne, M., Denton, C. A., Dimino, J., . . . Wissel, S. (2016). *Foundational skills to support reading for understanding in kindergarten through 3rd grade* (NCEE 2016-4008). Washington, DC: National Center for Education Evaluation and Regional Assistance (NCEE), Institute of Education Sciences, U.S. Department of Education. Retrieved from http://ies.ed.gov/ncee/wwc/PracticeGuide.aspx?sid=21

Forbes, G. B., Adams-Curtis, L. E., Pakalka, A. H., & White, K. B. (2006). Dating aggression, sexual coercion, and aggression-supporting attitudes among college men as a function of participation in aggressive high school sports. *Violence Against Women, 12,* 441–455. doi:10.1177/1077801206288126

Forbes, L. M., Evans, E. M., Moran, G., & Pederson, D. R. (2007). Change in atypical maternal behavior predicts change in attachment disorganization from 12 to 24 months in a high-risk sample. *Child Development, 78,* 955–971. doi:10.1111/j.1467-8624.2007.01043.x

Fortson, B. L., Klevens, J., Merrick, M. T., Gilbert, L. K., & Alexander, S. P. (2016). *Preventing child abuse and neglect: A technical package for policy, norm, and programmatic activities.* Retrieved from National Center for Injury Prevention and Control, Centers for Disease Control and Prevention website: http://www/cdc/gov/violenceprevention/childmaltreatment/index.html

Foster, E. M., & Jones, D. E. (2007). The economic analysis of prevention: An illustration involving children's behavior problems. *Journal of Mental Health Policy and Economics, 10,* 165–175.

Fox, N. A., & Calkins, S. D. (1993). Pathways to aggression and social withdrawal: Interactions among temperament, attachment, and regulation. In K. H. Rubin & J. B. Asendorpf (Eds.), *Social withdrawal, inhibition, and shyness in childhood* (pp. 81–100). Hillsdale, NJ: Erlbaum.

Fox, N. A., & Field, T. M. (1989). Individual differences in preschool entry behavior. *Journal of Applied Developmental Psychology, 10,* 527–540.

Fox, N. A., & Pine, D. S. (2012). Temperament and the emergence of anxiety disorders. *Journal of the American Academy of Child and Adolescent Psychiatry, 51,* 125–128. doi:10.1016/j.jaac.2011.10.006

Fraga, M. F., Ballestar, E., Paz, M. F., Ropero, S., Setien, F., Ballestar, M. L., . . . Esteller, M. (2005). Epigenetic differences arise during the lifetime of monozygotic twins. *Proceedings of the National Academy of Sciences of the United States of America, 102,* 10604–10609. doi:10.1073/pnas.0500398102

Fraley, R. C., & Spieker, S. J. (2003). Are infant attachment patterns continuously or categorically distributed? A taxometric analysis of Strange Situation Behavior. *Developmental Psychology, 39,* 387–404. doi:10.1037/0012-1649.39.3.387

Frankenhuis, W. E., & de Weerth, C. (2013). Does early-life exposure to stress shape or impair cognition? *Current Directions in Psychological Science, 22,* 407–412. doi:10.1177/0963721413484324

Frazier, B. N., Gelman, S. A., Kaciroti, N., Russell, J. W., & Lumeng, J. C. (2012). I'll have what she's having: The impact of model characteristics on children's food choices. *Developmental Science, 15*(1), 87–98.

Freedman, D. G., & Freedman, N. C. (1969, December 20). Behavioural differences between Chinese-American and European-American newborns. *Nature, 224,* 1227.

Freedner, N., Freed, L. H., Yang, Y. W., & Austin, S. B. (2002). Dating violence among gay, lesbian, and bisexual adolescents: Results from a community survey. *Journal of Adolescent Health, 31,* 469–474. doi:10.1016/S1054-139X(02)00407-X

Freitag, M. K., Belsky, J., Grossmann, K., Grossmann, K. E., & Scheuerer-Englisch, H. (1996). Continuity in parent–child relationships from infancy to middle childhood and relations with friendship competence. *Child Development, 67,* 1437–1454. doi:10.2307/1131710

Freitas, G. V. S., Cais, C. F. S., Stefanello, S., & Botega, N. J. (2008). Psychosocial conditions and suicidal behavior in pregnant teenagers. *European Child and Adolescent Psychiatry, 17,* 336–342. doi:10.1007/s00787-007-0668-2

French, D. C., Pidada, S., Denoma, J., McDonald, K., & Lawton, A. (2005). Reported peer conflicts of children in the United States and Indonesia. *Social Development, 14,* 458–472. doi:10.1111/j.1467-9507.2005.00311.x

French, D. C., Setiono, K., & Eddy, J. M. (1999). Bootstrapping through the cultural comparison minefield: Childhood social status and friendship in the United States and Indonesia. In W. A. Collins & B. Laursen (Eds.), *Minnesota Symposia on Child Psychology: Vol. 30. Relationships as developmental contexts* (pp. 109–131). Mahwah, NJ: Erlbaum.

French, S. E., Seidman, E., Allen, L., & Aber, J. L. (2006). The development of ethnic identity during adolescence. *Developmental Psychology, 42,* 1–10. doi:10.1037/0012-1649.42.1.1

Freud, A., & Dann, S. (1972). An experiment in group upbringing. In U. Bronfenbrenner (Ed.), *Influences on human development* (pp. 127–168). Hinsdale, IL: Dryden Press. (Reprinted from *The Psychoanalytic Study of the Child* (Vol. 6), pp. 127–168, by R. S. Eissler, A. Freud, H. Hartmann, & E. Kris, Eds., 1951, New York, NY: International Universities Press)

Freud, S. (1959). Inhibitions, symptoms and anxiety. In J. Strachey (Ed.), *Standard edition of the complete psychological works of Sigmund Freud: Vol. XX (1925–1926). An autobiographical study, inhibitions, symptoms and anxiety, the question of lay analysis and other works* (pp. 77–175). London, England: The Hogarth Press and the Institute of Psycho-Analysis. (Original work published 1926)

Freud, S. (1964). *New introductory lectures on psychoanalysis: The standard edition* (J. Strachey, Ed. & Trans.). New York, NY: Norton. (Original work published 1933)

Freud, S. (1964). An outline of psycho-analysis. In J. Strachey (Ed. & Trans.), *The standard edition of the complete psychological works of Sigmund Freud* (Vol. 23, pp. 144–207). London, England: Hogarth Press. (Original work published 1940)

Frick, P. J., & Morris, A. S. (2004). Temperament and developmental pathways to conduct problems. *Journal of Clinical Child and Adolescent Psychology, 33,* 54–68. doi:10.1207/S15374424JCCP3301_6

Friedlmeier, W., Corapci, F., & Cole, P. M. (2011). Emotion socialization in cross-cultural perspective. *Social and Personality Psychology Compass, 5,* 410–427.

Friedman, E. M., Karlamangla, A. S., Gruenewald, T., & Seeman, T. E. (2015). Early life adversity and adult biological risk profiles. *Psychosomatic Medicine, 77*(2), 176–185.

Friedman, M. S., Marshal, M. P., Guadamuz, T. E., Wei, C., Wong, C. F., Saewyc, E. M., & Stall, R. (2011). A meta-analysis of disparities in childhood sexual abuse, parental physical abuse, and peer victimization among sexual minority and sexual nonminority individuals. *American Journal of Public Health, 101,* 1481–1494. doi:10.2105/AJPH.2009.190009

Friedman, N. P., Miyake, A., Robinson, J. L., & Hewitt, J. K. (2011). Developmental trajectories in toddlers' self-restraint predict individual differences in executive functions 14 years later: A behavioral genetic analysis. *Developmental Psychology, 47,* 1410–1430.

Friedman, W. J. (1991). The development of children's memory for the time of past events. *Child Development, 62,* 139–155. doi:10.1111/j.1467-8624.1991.tb01520.x

Friedman, W. J. (2000). The development of children's knowledge of the times of future events. *Child Development, 71,* 913–932.

Friedman, W. J. (2003). The development of a differentiated sense of the past and the future. *Advances in Child Development and Behavior, 31,* 229–269.

Friedman, W. J. (2008). Developmental perspectives on the psychology of time. In S. Grondin (Ed.), *Psychology of time* (pp. 345–366). Bingley, England: Emerald.

Friedman, W. J., & Lyon, T. D. (2005). Development of temporal-reconstructive abilities. *Child Development, 76,* 1202–1216. doi:10.1111/j.1467-8624.2005.00845.x

Friedrich, M., Wilhelm, I., Born, J., & Friederici, A. D. (2015). Generalization of word meaning during infant sleep. *Nature Communications, 6,* 1–9. doi:10.1038/ncomms7004

Friend, A., DeFries, J. C., & Olson, R. K. (2008). Parental education moderates genetic influences on reading disability. *Psychological Science, 19,* 1124–1130. doi:10.1111/j.1467-9280.2008.02213.x

Frosch, C. A., Mangelsdorf, S. C., & McHale, J. L. (2000). Marital behavior and the security of preschooler–parent attachment relationships. *Journal of Family Psychology, 14,* 144–161. doi:10.1037/0893-3200.14.1.144

Fry, D. P. (1988). Intercommunity differences in aggression among Zapotec children. *Child Development, 59,* 1008–1019. doi:10.2307/1130267

Frye, D., Braisby, N., Lowe, J., Maroudas, C., & Nicholls, J. (1989). Young children's understanding of counting and cardinality. *Child Development, 60,* 1158–1171.

Frye, D., Zelazo, P. D., Brooks, P. J., & Samuels, M. C. (1996). Inference and action in early causal reasoning. *Developmental Psychology, 32,* 120–131.

Fuchs, I., Eisenberg, N., Hertz-Lazarowitz, R., & Sharabany, R. (1986). Kibbutz, Israeli city, and American children's moral reasoning about prosocial moral conflicts. *Merrill-Palmer Quarterly, 32,* 37–50. doi:10.2307/23086241

Fuchs, L. S., Schumacher, R. F., Long, J., Namkung, J., Hamlett, C. L., Cirino, P. T., . . . Changas, P. (2013). Improving at-risk learners' understanding of fractions. *Journal of Educational Psychology, 105,* 683–700. doi:10.1037/a0032446

Fulcher, M., Sutfin, E. L., & Patterson, C. J. (2008). Individual differences in gender development: Associations with parental sexual orientation, attitudes, and division of labor. *Sex Roles, 58,* 330–341. doi:10.1007/s11199-007-9348-4

Fuligni, A. J. (1998). Authority, autonomy, and parent–adolescent conflict and cohesion: A study of adolescents from Mexican, Chinese, Filipino, and European backgrounds. *Developmental Psychology, 34,* 782–792. doi:10.1037/0012-1649.34.4.782

Fuligni, A. J., Eccles, J. S., Barber, B. L., & Clements, P. (2001). Early adolescent peer orientation and adjustment during high school. *Developmental Psychology, 37,* 28–36. doi:10.1037/0012-1649.37.1.28

Fuligni, A. J., Yip, T., & Tseng, V. (2002). The impact of family obligation on the daily activities and psychological well-being of Chinese American adolescents. *Child Development, 73,* 302–314. doi:10.1111/1467-8624.00407

Fuligni, A. J., & Zhang, W. (2004). Attitudes toward family obligation among adolescents in contemporary urban and rural China. *Child Development, 75,* 180–192. doi:10.1111/j.1467-8624.2004.00662.x

Fung, H. (1999). Becoming a moral child: The socialization of shame among young Chinese children. *Ethos, 27,* 180–209.

Fung, H., & Chen, E. C.-H. (2001). Across time and beyond skin: Self and transgression in the everyday socialization of shame among Taiwanese preschool children. *Social Development, 10,* 419–437.

Furman, W., & Buhrmester, D. (1992). Age and sex differences in perceptions of networks of personal relationships. *Child Development, 63,* 103–115. doi:10.1111/j.1467-8624.1992.tb03599.x

Furman, W., & Rose, A. J. (2015). Friendship, romantic relationships, and peer relationships. In M. E. Lamb & R. M. Lerner (Eds.), *Handbook of Child Psychology and Developmental Science (7th ed.), Vol. 3: Socioemotional Processes* (pp. 932–974). Hoboken, NJ: Wiley.

Furman, W., Simon, V. A., Shaffer, L., & Bouchey, H. A. (2002). Adolescents' working models and styles for relationships with parents, friends, and romantic partners. *Child Development, 73,* 241–255. doi:10.1111/1467-8624.00403

Furnes, B., & Samuelsson, S. (2011). Phonological awareness and rapid automatized naming predicting early development in reading and spelling: Results from a cross-linguistic longitudinal study. *Learning and Individual Differences, 21,* 85–95. doi:10.1016/j.lindif.2010.10.005

Furukawa, E., Tangney, J., & Higashibara, F. (2012). Cross-cultural continuities and discontinuities in shame, guilt, and pride: A study of children residing in Japan, Korea and the USA. *Self and Identity, 11,* 90–113.

Furuya-Kanamori, L., & Doi, S. (May 2016). Angry birds, angry children, and angry meta-analysts: A reanalysis. *Perspectives on Psychological Science, 11*(3), 408–414. doi:10.1177/1745691616635599

Gaddis, A., & Brooks-Gunn, J. (1985). The male experience of pubertal change. *Journal of Youth and Adolescence, 14,* 61–69. doi:10.1007/BF02088647

Gaetz, S., O'Grady, B., Buccieri, K., Karabanow, J., & Marsolais, A. (Eds.). (2013). *Youth Homelessness in Canada: Implications for policy and practice.* Toronto, Canada: Canadian Homelessness Research Network Press.

Gaither, S. E., Pauker, K., & Johnson, S. P. (2012). Biracial and monoracial infant own-race face perception: An eye tracking study. *Developmental Science, 15,* 775–782. doi:10.1111/j.1467-7687.2012.01170.x

Galambos, N., Leadbeater, B., & Barker, E. (2004). Gender differences in and risk factors for depression in adolescence: A 4-year longitudinal study. *International Journal of Behavioral Development, 28,* 16–25.

Galambos, N. L., Almeida, D. M., & Petersen, A. C. (1990). Masculinity, femininity, and sex role attitudes in early adolescence: Exploring gender intensification. *Child Development, 61,* 1905–1914. doi:10.1111/j.1467-8624.1990.tb03574.x

Gallese, V., Fadiga, L., Fogassi, L., & Rizzolatti, G. (1996). Action recognition in the premotor cortex. *Brain, 119,* 593–609. doi:10.1093/brain/119.2.593

Galliher, R. V., Jones, M. D., & Dahl, A. (2011). Concurrent and longitudinal effects of ethnic identity and experiences of discrimination on psychosocial adjustment of Navajo adolescents. *Developmental Psychology, 47,* 509–526. doi:10.1037/a0021061

Galton, F. (1962). *Hereditary genius: An inquiry into its laws and consequences.* Cleveland, OH: World. (Original work published 1869)

Gamble, W. C., Yu, J. J., & Kuehn, E. D. (2011). Adolescent sibling relationship quality and adjustment: Sibling trustworthiness and modeling, as factors directly and indirectly influencing these associations. *Social Development, 20,* 605–623. doi:10.1111/j.1467-9507.2010.00591.x

Gamliel, I., Yirmiya, N., Jaffe, D., Manor, O., & Sigman, M. (2009). Developmental trajectories in siblings of children with autism: Cognition and language from 4 months to 7 years. *Journal of Autism and Developmental Disorders, 39,* 1131–1144. doi:10.1007/s10803-009-0727-2

Gandelman, R. (1992). *The psychobiology of behavioral development.* New York, NY: Oxford University Press.

Ganiban, J. M., Saudino, K. J., Ulbricht, J., Neiderhiser, J. M., & Reiss, D. (2008). Stability and change in temperament during adolescence. *Journal of Personality and Social Psychology, 95,* 222–236.

Ganiban, J. M., Ulbricht, J., Saudino, K. J., Reiss, D., & Neiderhiser, J. M. (2011). Understanding child-based effects on parenting: Temperament as a moderator of genetic and environmental contributions to parenting. *Developmental Psychology, 47,* 676–692.

Ganong, L., Coleman, M., & Jamison, T. (2011). Patterns of stepchild–stepparent relationship development. *Journal of Marriage and Family, 73,* 396–413. doi:10.111/j.1741-3737.2010.00814.x

Ganong, L., Coleman, M., & Russell, L. T. (2015). Children in diverse families. In M. H. Bornstein & T. Leventhal (Vol. Eds.) & R. M. Lerner (Editor in Chief), *Handbook of Child Psychology and Developmental Science, Vol. 4: Ecological settings and processes* (pp. 133–174). Hoboken, NJ: Wiley.

Ganzach, Y., Gotlibobski, C., Greenberg, D., & Pazy, A. (2013). General mental ability and pay: Nonlinear effects. *Intelligence, 41*(5), 631–637. doi:10.1016/j.intell.2013.07.015

Garandeau, C. F., Ahn, H.-J., & Rodkin, P. C. (2011). The social status of aggressive students across contexts: The role of classroom status hierarchy, academic achievement, and grade. *Developmental Psychology, 47,* 1699–1710. doi:10.1037/a0025271

Garbarino, J., & Kostelny, K. (1992). Child maltreatment as a community problem. *Child Abuse and Neglect, 16,* 455–464. doi:10.1016/0145-2134(92)90062-V

Garber, J., & Cole, D. A. (2010). Intergenerational transmission of depression: A launch and grow model of change across adolescence. *Development and Psychopathology, 22,* 819–830. doi:10.1017/S0954579410000489

Garces, E., Duncan, T., & Currie, J. (2002). Longer-term effects of Head Start. *American Economic Review, 92*(4), 999–1012. doi:10.1257/00028280260344560

Gardner, D., Harris, P. L., Ohmoto, M., & Hamazaki, T. (1988). Japanese children's understanding of the distinction between real and apparent emotion. *International Journal of Behavioral Development, 11,* 203–218.

Gardner, H. (1993). *Multiple intelligences: The theory in practice.* New York, NY: Basic Books.

Gardner, H. (1999). *Intelligence reframed: Multiple intelligences for the 21st Century.* New York, NY: Basic Books.

Gardner, H., & Davis, K. (2013). *The app generation: How today's youth navigate identity, intimacy, and imagination in a digital world.* New Haven, CT: Yale University Press.

Gardner, R. A., & Gardner, B. T. (1969, August 15). Teaching sign language to a chimpanzee. *Science, 165,* 664–672.

Gardner, T. W., Dishion, T. J., & Connell, A. M. (2008). Adolescent self-regulation as resilience: Resistance to antisocial behavior within the deviant peer context. *Journal of Abnormal Child Psychology, 36,* 273–284. doi:10.1007/s10802-007-9176-6

Gargus, R. A., Vohr, B. R., Tyson, J. E., High, P., Higgins, R. D., Wrage, L. A., & Poole, K. (2009). Unimpaired outcomes for extremely low birth weight infants at 18 to 22 months. *Pediatrics, 124,* 112–121. doi:10.1542/peds.2008-2742

Garmezy, N. (1983). Stressors of childhood. In N. Garmezy & M. Rutter (Eds.), *Stress, coping, and development in children* (pp. 43–84). New York, NY: McGraw-Hill.

Garrett-Peters, P., Mills-Koonce, R., Adkins, D., Vernon-Feagans, L., Cox, M., & The Family Life Project Key Investigators. (2008). Early environmental correlates of maternal emotion talk. *Parenting, Science and Practice, 8,* 117–152. doi:10.1080/15295190802058900

Garrett-Peters, P., Mills-Koonce, R., Zerwas, S., Cox, M., Vernon-Feagans, L., & The Family Life Project Key Investigators. (2011). Fathers' early emotion talk: Associations with income, ethnicity, and family factors. *Journal of Marriage and Family, 73,* 335–353. doi:10.1111/j.1741-3737.2010.00810.x

Gartrell, N., & Bos, H. (2010). US National Longitudinal Lesbian Family Study: Psychological adjustment of 17-year-old adolescents. *Pediatrics, 126,* 28–36. doi:10.1542/peds.2009-3153

Gartstein, M. A., & Rothbart, M. K. (2003). Studying infant temperament via the Revised Infant Behavior Questionnaire. *Infant Behavior and Development, 26*(1), 64–86.

Gass, K., Jenkins, J., & Dunn, J. (2007). Are sibling relationships protective? A longitudinal study. *Journal of Child Psychology and Psychiatry, 48,* 167–175. doi:10.1111/j.1469-7610.2006.01699.x

Gassman-Pines, A., & Yoshikawa, H. (2006). The effects of antipoverty programs on children's cumulative level of poverty-related risk. *Developmental Psychology, 42,* 981–999. doi:10.1037/0012-1649.42.6.981

Gatzke-Kopp, L. M., Beauchaine, T. P., Shannon, K. E., Chipman, J., Fleming, A. P., Crowell, S. E., . . . Aylward, E. (2009). Neurological correlates of reward responding in adolescents with and without externalizing behavior disorders. *Journal of Abnormal Psychology, 118,* 203–213. doi:10.1037/a0014378

Gauvain, M. (2001). *The social context of cognitive development.* New York, NY: Guilford Press.

Gavin, L. A., & Furman, W. (1989). Age differences in adolescents' perceptions of their peer groups. *Developmental Psychology, 25,* 827–834. doi:10.1037/0012-1649.25.5.827

Gaylord-Harden, N. K., Burrow, A. L., & Cunningham, J. A. (2012). A cultural-asset framework for investigating successful adaptation to stress in African American youth. *Child Development Perspectives, 6,* 264–271. doi:10.1111/j.1750-8606.2012.00236.x

Gazelle, H. (2008). Behavioral profiles of anxious solitary children and heterogeneity in peer relations. *Developmental Psychology, 44,* 1604–1624. doi:10.1037/a0013303

Gazelle, H., & Ladd, G. W. (2003). Anxious solitude and peer exclusion: A diathesis–stress model of internalizing trajectories in childhood. *Child Development, 74,* 257–278. doi:10.1111/1467-8624.00534

Gazzaniga, M. S., Ivry, R., & Mangun, G. R. (2013). *Cognitive Neuroscience: The Biology of Mind, 4th Edition.* New York, NY: W. W. Norton.

Ge, X., Conger, R. D., & Elder, G. H., Jr. (1996). Coming of age too early: Pubertal influences on girls' vulnerability to psychological distress. *Child Development, 67,* 3386–3400.

Ge, X., Kim, I. J., Brody, G. H., Conger, R. D., Simons, R. L., Gibbons, F. X., & Cutrona, C. E. (2003). It's about timing and change: Pubertal transition effects on symptoms of major depression among African American youths. *Developmental Psychology, 39,* 430–439.

Ge, X., Natsuaki, M. N., & Conger, R. D. (2006). Trajectories of depressive symptoms and stressful life events among male and female adolescents in divorced and nondivorced families. *Development and Psychopathology, 18,* 253–273. doi:10.1017/S0954579406060147

Geangu, E., Ichikawa, H., Lao, J., Kanazawa, S., Yamaguchi, M., Caldara, R., & Turati, C. (2016). Culture shapes 7-month-olds' perceptual strategies in discriminating facial expressions of emotion. *Current Biology, 26,* R1–R3.

Geary, D. C. (2004). Mathematics and learning disabilities. *Journal of Learning Disabilities, 37,* 4–15. doi:10.1177/00222194040370010201

Geary, D. C. (2005). *The origin of mind: Evolution of brain, cognition, and general intelligence.* Washington, DC: American Psychological Association.

Geary, D. C. (2006). Development of mathematical understanding. In W. Damon & R. M. Lerner (Series Eds.) & D. Kuhn & R. S. Siegler (Vol. Eds.), *Handbook of child psychology: Vol. 2. Cognition, perception, and language* (6th ed., pp. 777–810). Hoboken, NJ: Wiley.

Geary, D. C. (2009). *Male, female: The evolution of human sex differences* (2nd ed.). Washington, DC: American Psychological Association.

Geary, D. C. (2010). *Male, female: The evolution of human sex differences* (2nd ed.). Washington, DC: American Psychological Association.

Geary, D. C. (2010). Missouri longitudinal study of mathematical development and disability. *British Journal of Educational Psychology Monograph Series II, 7,* 31–49.

Geary, D. C., Berch, D. B., & Mann Koepke, K. (Eds.). (2015). *Evolutionary origins and early development of number processing (Vol. 1, Mathematical Cognition and Learning).* San Diego, CA: Elsevier Academic Press.

Geary, D. C., Hoard, M. K., Byrd-Craven, J., Nugent, L., & Numtee, C. (2007). Cognitive mechanisms underlying achievement deficits in children with mathematical learning disability. *Child Development, 78,* 1343–1359. doi:10.1111/j.1467-8624.2007.01069.x

Geary, D. C., Hoard, M. K., Nugent, L., & Bailey, D. H. (2012). Mathematical cognition deficits in children with learning disabilities and persistent low achievement: A five-year prospective study. *Journal of Educational Psychology, 104,* 206–223. doi:10.1037/a0025398

Geary, D. C., Hoard, M. K., Nugent, L., & Byrd-Craven, J. (2008). Development of number line representations in children with mathematical learning disability. *Developmental Neuropsychology, 33,* 277–299. doi:10.1080/87565640801982361

Gejman, P. V., Sanders, A. R., & Duan, J. (2010). The role of genetics in the etiology of schizophrenia. *Psychiatric Clinics of North America, 33*(1), 35–66. doi:10.1016/j.psc.2009.12.003

Gelman, R., & Gallistel, C. R. (1978). *The child's understanding of number.* Cambridge, MA: Harvard University Press.

Gelman, R., Meck, E., & Merkin, S. (1986). Young children's numerical competence. *Cognitive Development, 1,* 1–29.

Gelman, R., & Williams, E. M. (1998). Enabling constraints for cognitive development and learning: Domain specificity and epigenesis. In W. Damon (Series Ed.) & D. Kuhn & R. S. Siegler (Vol. Eds.), *Handbook of child psychology: Vol. 2: Cognition, perception,* *and language* (5th ed., pp. 575–630). Hoboken, NJ: Wiley.

Gelman, S. A. (2003). *The essential child: Origins of essentialism in everyday thought.* New York, NY: Oxford University Press.

Gelman, S. A., Coley, J. D., Rosengren, K. S., Hartman, E., & Pappas, A. (1998). Beyond labeling: The role of maternal input in the acquisition of richly structured categories. *Monographs of the Society for Research in Child Development, 63*(1, Serial No. 253).

Gelman, S. A., & Kalish, C. W. (2006). Conceptual development. In W. Damon & R. M. Lerner (Series Eds.) & D. Kuhn & R. S. Siegler (Vol. Eds.), *Handbook of child psychology: Vol. 2. Cognition, perception, and language* (6th ed., pp. 687–733). Hoboken, NJ: Wiley.

Gelman, S. A., & Noles, N. S. (2011). Domains and naïve theories. *Wiley Interdisciplinary Reviews: Cognitive Science, 2*(5), 490–502. doi:10.1002/wcs.124

Gentile, B., Grabe, S., Dolan-Pascoe, B., Twenge, J. M., & Wells, B. E. (2009). Gender differences in domain-specific self-esteem: A meta-analysis. *Review of General Psychology, 13,* 34–45. doi:10.1037/a0013689

Gentile, D. A. (2015). What is a good skeptic to do? The case for skepticism in the media violence discussion. *Perspectives on Psychological Science, 10*(5), 674–676.

Gentner, D., & Boroditsky, L. (2001). Individuation, relativity, and early word learning. In M. Bowerman & S. Levinson (Eds.), *Language acquisition and conceptual development* (pp. 215–256). Cambridge, England: Cambridge University Press.

Gerbner, G., Gross, L., Morgan, M., Signorielli, N., & Shanahan, J. (2002). Growing up with television: Cultivation processes. In J. Bryant & D. Zillmann (Eds.), *Media effects: Advances in theory and research* (2nd ed., pp. 43–67). Mahwah, NJ: Erlbaum.

Gerding, A., & Signorielli, N. (2014). Gender roles in tween television programming: A content analysis of two genres. *Sex Roles, 70,* 43–56.

Gergely, G., Bekkering, H., & Kiraly, I. (2002, February 14). Developmental psychology: Rational imitation in preverbal infants. *Nature, 415,* 755.

Gerken, L. (1994). Child phonology: Past research, present questions, future directions. In M. A. Gernsbacher (Ed.), *Handbook of psycholinguistics* (pp. 781–820). San Diego, CA: Academic Press.

Gerken, L., Balcomb, F. K., & Minton, J. L. (2011). Infants avoid "labouring in vain" by attending more to learnable than unlearnable linguistic patterns. *Developmental Science, 14,* 972–979. doi:10.1111/j.1467-7687.2011.01046.x

Gerken, L., Wilson, R., & Lewis, W. (2005). Infants can use distributional cues to form syntactic categories. *Journal of Child Language, 32,* 249–268. doi:10.1017/S0305000904006786

German, T. P., & Nichols, S. (2003). Children's counterfactual inferences about long and short causal chains. *Developmental Science, 6,* 514–523. doi:10.1111/1467-7687.00309

Gernsbacher, M. A., Dawson, M., & Goldsmith, H. H. (2005). Three reasons not to believe in an autism epidemic. *Current Directions in Psychological Science, 14,* 55–58. doi:10.1111/j.0963-7214.2005.00334.x

Gershkoff-Stowe, L., Connell, B., & Smith, L. (2006). Priming overgeneralizations in two- and four-year-old children. *Journal of Child Language, 33,* 461–486. doi:10.1017/S0305000906007562

Gershoff, E. T. (2002). Corporal punishment by parents and associated child behaviors and experiences: A meta-analytic and theoretical review. *Psychological Bulletin, 128,* 539–579.

Gershoff, E. T. (2013). Spanking and child development: We know enough now to stop hitting our children. *Child Development Perspectives, 7,* 133–137. doi:10.1111/cdep.12038

Gershoff, E. T. (2016, in press). Discipline. In M. H. Bornstein, M. Arterberry, K. Fingerman, & J. Lansford (Eds.), *The Sage Encyclopedia of Lifespan Human Development.* Thousand Oaks, CA: Sage.

Gershoff, E. T., Aber, J. L., Raver, C. C., & Lennon, M. C. (2007). Income is not enough: Incorporating material hardship into models of income associations with parent mediators and child outcomes. *Child Development, 78*(1), 70–95. doi:10.1111/j.1467-8624.2007.00986.x

Gershoff, E. T., Aber, J. L., Ware, A., & Kotler, J. (2010). Exposure to 9/11 among youth and their mothers in New York City: Enduring associations with mental health and sociopolitical attitudes. *Child Development, 81,* 1142–1160.

Gershoff, E. T., & Benner, A. D. (2014). Neighborhood and school contexts in the lives of children. In E. T. Gershoff, R. S. Mistry, R. S., & D. A. Crosby (Eds.). *Societal contexts of child development.* New York: Oxford University Press.

Gershoff, E. T., & Grogan-Kaylor, A. (2016a). Corporal punishment by parents and its consequences for children: Old controversies and new meta-analyses. *Journal of Family Psychology, 30,* 453–469. doi:10.1037/fam0000191

Gershoff, E. T., & Grogan-Kaylor, A. (2016b). Cultural normativeness, race, and spanking: Preliminary meta-analytic findings. *Family Relations, 65,* 490–501. doi:10.1111/fare.12205

Gershoff, E. T., Grogan-Kaylor, A., Lansford, J. E., Chang, L., Zelli, A., Deater-Deckard, K., & Dodge, K. A. (2010). Parent discipline practices in an international sample: Associations with child behaviors and moderation by perceived normativeness. *Child Development, 81,* 487–502. doi:10.1111/j.1467-8624.2009.01409.x

Gershoff, E. T., Lansford, J. E., Sexton, H. R., Davis-Kean, P., & Sameroff, A. J. (2012). Longitudinal links between spanking and children's externalizing behaviors in a national sample of White, Black, Hispanic, and Asian American families. *Child Development, 83,* 838–843. doi:10.1111/j.1467-8624.2011.01732.x

Gertner, Y., Fisher, C., & Eisengart, J. (2006). Learning words and rules: Abstract knowledge of word order in early sentence comprehension. *Psychological Science, 17,* 684–691. doi:10.1111/j.1467-9280.2006.01767.x

Gesell, A., & Thompson, H. (1938). *The psychology of early growth, including norms of infant behavior and a method of genetic analysis.* New York, NY: Macmillan.

Gest, S. D., Graham-Bermann, S. A., & Hartup, W. W. (2001). Peer experience: Common and unique features of number of friendships, social network centrality, and sociometric status. *Social Development, 10,* 23–40. doi:10.1111/1467-9507.00146

Gfellner, B. M., & Armstrong, H. D. (2012). Ego development, ego strengths, and ethnic identity among First Nation adolescents. *Journal of Research on Adolescence, 22,* 225–234. doi:10.1111/j.1532-7795.2011.00769.x

Gianino, A., & Tronick, E. Z. (1988). The mutual regulation model: The infant's self and interactive regulation and coping and defensive capacities. In T. M. Field, P. M. McCabe, & N. Schneiderman (Eds.), *Stress and coping across development* (pp. 47–68). Hillsdale, NJ: Erlbaum.

Gibbs, J. C., Basinger, K. S., Grime, R. L., & Snarey, J. R. (2007). Moral judgment development across cultures: Revisiting Kohlberg's universality claims. *Developmental Review, 27,* 443–500. doi:10.1016/j.dr.2007.04.001te

Gibbs, N. (1999, May 3). The Littleton massacre: . . . In sorrow and disbelief. *Time, 153*(17), 20–36.

Gibson, E. J. (1988). Exploratory behavior in the development of perceiving, acting, and the acquiring of knowledge. *Annual Review of Psychology, 39,* 1–42. doi:10.1146/annurev.ps.39.020188.000245

Gibson, E. J., Riccio, G., Schmuckler, M. A., Stoffregen, T. A., Rosenberg, D., & Taormina, J. (1987). Detection of the traversability of surfaces by crawling and walking infants. *Journal of Experimental Psychology: Human Perception and Performance, 13,* 533–544. doi:10.1037/0096-1523.13.4.533

Gibson, E. J., & Schumuckler, M. A. (1989). Going somewhere: An ecological and experimental approach to development of mobility. *Ecological Psychology, 1,* 3–25. doi:10.1207/s15326969eco0101_2

Gibson, E. J., & Walk, R. D. (1960, April). The "visual cliff." *Scientific American, 202*(4), 64–71.

Giedd, J. N., Blumenthal, J., Jeffries, N. O., Castellanos, F. X., Liu, H., Zijdenbos, A., . . . Rapoport, J. L. (1999). Brain development during childhood and adolescence: A longitudinal MRI study. *Nature Neuroscience, 2,* 861–863.

Giles, J. W., & Heyman, G. D. (2005). Young children's beliefs about the relationship between gender and aggressive behavior. *Child Development, 76,* 107–121. doi:10.1111/j.1467-8624.2005.00833.x

Giletta, M., Scholte, R. H., Burk, W. J., Engels, R. C., Larsen, J. K., Prinstein, M. J., & Ciairano, S. (2011). Similarity in depressive symptoms in adolescents' friendship dyads: Selection or socialization? *Developmental Psychology, 47,* 1804–1814. doi:10.1037/a0023872

Gilligan, C. (1982). *In a different voice: Psychological theory and women's development.* Cambridge, MA: Harvard University Press.

Gilligan, C., & Attanucci, J. (1988). Two moral orientations: Gender differences and similarities. *Merrill-Palmer Quarterly, 34,* 223–237. doi:10.2307/23086381

Gitterman, B. A., Flanagan, P. J., Cotton, W. H., Dilley, K. J., Duffee, J. H., Green, A. E., . . . Nelson, J. L. (2016). Poverty and child health in the United States. *Pediatrics, 137*(4), e20160339. doi:10.1542/peds.2016-0339

Gladwell, M. (2008). *Outliers: The story of success.* New York, NY: Little, Brown.

Glasper, E. R., Schoenfeld, T. J., & Gould, E. (2012). Adult neurogenesis: Optimizing hippocampal function to suit the environment. *Behavioural Brain Research, 227,* 380–383. doi:10.1016/j.bbr.2011.05.013

Glass, B. D., Maddox, W. T., & Love, B. C. (2013). Real-time strategy game training: Emergence of a cognitive flexibility trait. *PLoS ONE, 8*(8), Article e70350. Retrieved from http://journals.plos.org/plosone/article?id=10.1371/journal.pone.0070350

Gleason, J. B., & Ely, R. (2002). Gender differences in language development. In A. V. McGillicuddy-De Lisi & R. De Lisi (Eds.), *Biology, society, and behavior: The development of sex differences in cognition* (Vol. 21, pp. 127–154). Westport, CT: Ablex.

Glick, G. C., & Rose, A. J. (2011). Prospective associations between friendship adjustment and social strategies: Friendship as a context for building social skills. *Developmental Psychology, 47,* 1117–1132.

Global Initiative to End All Corporal Punishment of Children. (2016). *States which have prohibited all corporal punishment.* Retrieved from http://www.endcorporalpunishment.org/progress/prohibiting-states/

Gnepp, J., & Hess, D. L. (1986). Children's understanding of verbal and facial display rules. *Developmental Psychology, 22,* 103–108.

Godlee, F., Smith, J., & Marcovitch, H. (2011). Wakefield's article linking MMR vaccine and autism was fraudulent. *BMJ, 342.* doi:10.1136/bmj.c7452

Gogtay, N., Sporn, A., Clasen, L. S., Nugent, T. F., Greenstein, D., Nicolson, R., . . . Rapoport, J. L. (2004). Comparison of progressive cortical gray matter loss in childhood-onset schizophrenia with that in childhood-onset atypical psychoses. *Archives of General Psychiatry, 61,* 17–22. doi:10.1001/archpsyc.61.1.17

Gogtay, N., Giedd, J. N., Lusk, L., Hyashi, K. M., Greenstein, D., Vaituzis, A.C., . . . Thompson, P. M. (2004). Dynamic mapping of human cortical development during childhood through early adulthood. *PNAS, 101*(21), 8174–8179.

Goksan, S., Hartley, C., Emery, F., Cockrill, N., Poorun, R., Moultrie, F., . . . Slater, R. (2015). fMRI reveals neural activity overlap between adult and infant pain. *Elife, 4,* e06356. doi:10.7554/eLife.06356

Goldberg, A. E., Gartrell, N. K., & Gates, G. (2014). *Research report on LGB-parent families.* Retrieved from The Williams Institute, UCLA School of Law website: http://williamsinstitute.law.ucla.edu/wp-content/uploads/lgb-parent-families-july-2014.pdf

Goldfield, B. A., & Reznick, J. S. (1990). Early lexical acquisition: Rate, content, and the vocabulary spurt. Journal of Child Language, *17*(1), 171–183.

Goldin-Meadow, S. (2003). *The resilience of language: What gesture creation in deaf children can tell us about how all children learn language.* New York, NY: Psychology Press.

Goldin-Meadow, S., & Alibali, M. W. (2002). Looking at the hands through time: A microgenetic perspective on learning and instruction. In N. Granott & J. Parziale (Eds.), *Microdevelopment: Transition processes in development and learning* (pp. 80–105). Cambridge, England: Cambridge University Press.

Goldin-Meadow, S., Cook, S. W., & Mitchell, Z. A. (2009). Gesturing gives children new ideas about math. *Psychological Science, 20,* 267–272.

Goldin-Meadow, S., & Mylander, C. (1998, January 15). Spontaneous sign systems created by deaf children in two cultures. *Nature, 391,* 279–281. doi:10.1038/34646

Goldsmith, H. H., Buss, K. A., & Lemery, K. S. (1997). Toddler and childhood temperament: Expanded content, stronger genetic evidence, new evidence for the importance of environment. *Developmental Psychology, 33,* 891–905. doi:10.1037/0012-1649.33.6.891

Goldsmith, H. H., Pollak, S. D., & Davidson, R. J. (2008). Developmental neuroscience perspectives on emotion regulation. *Child Development Perspectives, 2,* 132–140.

Goldstein, M. H., King, A. P., & West, M. J. (2003). Social interaction shapes babbling: Testing parallels between birdsong and speech. *Proceedings of the National Academy of Sciences of the United States of America, 100,* 8030–8035. doi:10.1073/pnas.1332441100

Goldstein, M. H., & Schwade, J. A. (2008). Social feedback to infants' babbling facilitates rapid phonological learning. *Psychological Science, 19,* 515–523. doi:10.1111/j.1467-9280.2008.02117.x

Goldstein, M. H., Schwade, J., Briesch, J., & Syal, S. (2010). Learning while babbling: Prelinguistic object-directed vocalizations indicate a readiness to learn. *Infancy, 15,* 362–391. doi:10.1111/j.1532-7078.2009.00020.x

Goldstein, S. E., Malanchuk, O., Davis-Kean, P. E., & Eccles, J. S. (2007). Risk factors of sexual harassment by peers: A longitudinal investigation of African American and European American adolescents. *Journal of Research on Adolescence, 17,* 285–300. doi:10.1111/j.1532-7795.2007.00523.x

Goldstein, T. R., & Winner, E. (2011). Enhancing empathy and theory of mind. *Journal of Cognition and Development, 13,* 19–37. doi:10.1080/15248372.2011.573514

Goleman, D. (1995). *Emotional intelligence.* New York, NY: Bantam Books.

Golish, T. D. (2003). Stepfamily communication strengths. *Human Communication Research, 29,* 41–80. doi:10.1111/j.1468-2958.2003.tb00831.x

Golombok, S., Perry, B., Burston, A., Murray, C., Mooney-Somers, J., Stevens, M., & Golding, J. (2003). Children with lesbian parents: A community study. *Developmental Psychology, 39,* 20–33. doi:10.1037/0012-1649.39.1.20

Gómez, R. L. (2002). Variability and detection of invariant structure. *Psychological Science, 13,* 431–436.

Gómez, R. L., Bootzin, R. R., & Nadel, L. (2006). Naps promote abstraction in language-learning infants. *Psychological Science, 17,* 670–674. doi:10.1111/j.1467-9280.2006.01764.x

Gómez, R. L., & Edgin, J. O. (2015). Sleep as a window into early neural development: Shifts in sleep-dependent learning effects across early childhood. *Child Development Perspectives, 9*(3), 183–189. doi:10.1111/cdep.12130

Göncü, A. (1993). Development of intersubjectivity in the dyadic play of preschoolers. *Early Childhood Research Quarterly, 8,* 99–116.

Göncü, A., Mistry, J., & Mosier, C. (2000). Cultural variations in the play of toddlers. *International Journal of Behavioral Development, 24,* 321–329. doi:10.1080/016502500501183303

Gonzales, N. A., Pitts, S. C., Hill, N. E., & Roosa, M. W. (2000). A mediational model of the impact of interparental conflict on child adjustment in a multiethnic, low-income sample. *Journal of Family Psychology, 14,* 365–379. doi:10.1037/0893-3200.14.3.365

Good, T. L., & Brophy, J. E. (1996). *Looking in classrooms* (7th ed.). New York, NY: Longman.

Gooden, A. M., & Gooden, M. A. (2001). Gender representation in notable children's picture books: 1995–1999. *Sex Roles, 45,* 89–101. doi:10.1023/A:1013064418674

Goodnight, J. A., Lahey, B. B., Van Hulle, C. A., Rodgers, J. L., Rathouz, P. J., Waldman, I. D., & D'Onofrio, B. M. (2012). A quasi-experimental analysis of the influence of neighborhood disadvantage on child and adolescent conduct problems. *Journal of Abnormal Psychology, 121,* 95–108. doi:10.1037/a0025078

Goodnow, J. J. (1977). *Children drawing.* Cambridge, MA: Harvard University Press.

Goodson, B., Wolf, A., Bell, S., Turner, H., & Finney, P. B. (2010). *The effectiveness of a program to accelerate vocabulary development in kindergarten* (VOCAB) (NCEE 2010-4014). Washington, DC: National Center for Education Evaluation and Regional Assistance, Institute of Education Sciences, U.S. Department of Education. Retrieved from http://eric.ed.gov/?id=ED512900

Gooren, E. M. J. C., van Lier, P. A. C., Stegge, H., Terwogt, M. M., & Koot, H. M. (2011). The development of conduct problems and depressive symptoms in early elementary school children: The role of peer rejection. *Journal of Clinical Child and Adolescent Psychology, 40,* 245–253. doi:10.1080/15374416.2011.546045

Gopnik, A., & Astington, J. W. (1988). Children's understanding of representational change and its relation to the understanding of false belief and the appearance-reality distinction. *Child Development, 59,* 26–37.

Gopnik, A., & Slaughter, V. (1991). Young children's understanding of changes in their mental states. *Child Development, 62,* 98–110. doi:10.1111/j.1467-8624.1991.tb01517.x

Gopnik, A., & Wellman, H. M. (2012). Reconstructing constructivism: Causal models, Bayesian learning mechanisms, and the theory theory. *Psychological Bulletin, 138*(6), 1085–1108. doi:10.1037/a0028044

Gordon, K., Murin, M., Baykaner, O., Roughan, L., Livermore-Hardy, V., Skuse, D., & Mandy, W. (2015). A randomized controlled trial of PEGASUS, a psychoeducational programme for young people with high-functioning autism spectrum disorder. *Journal of Child Psychology and Psychiatry, 56,* 468–476. doi:10/111/jcpp.12304\

Gorin, A. A., Wiley, J., Ohannessian, C. M., Hernandez, D., Grant, A., & Cloutier, M. M. (2014). Steps to growing up healthy: A pediatric primary care based obesity prevention program for young children. *BMC Public Health, 14*(1). doi:10.1186/1471-2458-14-72

Gosselin, J., & David, H. (2007). Risk and resilience factors linked with the psychosocial adjustment of adolescents, stepparents and biological parents. *Journal of Divorce and Remarriage, 48,* 29–53. doi:10.1300/j087v48n01_02

Gottesman, I. I. (with Wolfgram, D. L.). (1991). *Schizophrenia genesis: The origins of madness.* New York, NY: Freeman.

Gottfredson, L. S. (1997). Why g matters: The complexity of everyday life. *Intelligence, 24,* 79–132.

Gottfredson, L. S. (2011). Intelligence and social inequality: Why the biological link. In T. Chamorro-Premuzic, S. von Stumm, & A. Furnham (Eds.), *Handbook of individual differences* (pp. 538–575). Chichester, West Sussex, England: Wiley-Blackwell.

Gottfried, A. E., Gottfried, A. W., Bathurst, K., & Bornstein, M. H. (2002). Maternal and dual-earner employment status and parenting. In M. H. Bornstein (Ed.), *Handbook of parenting: Vol. 2. Biology and ecology of parenting* (2nd ed., pp. 207–229). Mahwah, NJ: Erlbaum.

Gottlieb, A. (2004). *The afterlife is where we come from: The culture of infancy in West Africa.* Chicago, IL: University of Chicago Press.

Gottman, J. M. (1986). The world of coordinated play: Same- and cross-sex friendship in young children. In J. M. Gottman & J. G. Parker (Eds.), *Conversations of friends: Speculations on affective development* (pp. 139–191). New York, NY: Cambridge University Press.

Gottman, J. M., Katz, L. F., & Hooven, C. (1997). *Meta-emotion: How families communicate emotionally.* Mahwah, NJ: Erlbaum.

Gottman, J. M., & Mettetal, G. (1986). Speculations about social and affective development: Friendship and acquaintanceship through adolescence. In J. M. Gottman & J. G. Parker (Eds.), *Conversations of friends: Speculations on affective development* (pp. 192–237). New York, NY: Cambridge University Press.

Gould, E., Beylin, A., Tanapat, P., Reeves, A., & Shors, T. J. (1999). Learning enhances adult neurogenesis in the hippocampal formation. *Nature Neuroscience, 2,* 260–265.

Gould, E., & Cooke, T. (2015, October). High-quality child care is out of reach for working families (Issue Brief No. 404). Washington, DC: Economic Policy Institute. Retrieved from Economic Policy Institute website: http://www.epi.org/publication/child-care-affordability/

Gould, S. J. (1997, June 12). Darwinian fundamentalism. *New York Review of Books, 44,* 34–37.

Govindan, R. B., Wilson, J. D., Murphy, P., Russel, W. A., & Lowery, C. L. (2007). Scaling analysis of paces of fetal breathing, gross body and extremity movements. *Physica A: Statistical Mechanics and Its Applications, 386,* 231–239. doi:10.1016/j.physa.2007.08.021

Gradisar, M., Jackson, K., Spurrier, N. J., Gibson, J., Whitham, J., Williams, A. S., . . . Kennaway, D. J. (2016). Behavioral interventions for infant sleep problems: A randomized controlled trial. *Pediatrics,* e20151486.

Grady, C. L., Mondloch, C. J., Lewis, T. L., & Maurer, D. (2014). Early visual deprivation from congenital cataracts disrupts activity and functional connectivity in the face network. *Neuropsychologia, 57*(May), 122–139. doi:10.1016/j.neuropsychologia.2014.03.005

Graf Estes, K., Evans, J. L., Alibali, M. W., & Saffran, J. R. (2007). Can infants map meaning to newly segmented words? Statistical segmentation and word learning. *Psychological Science, 18*(3), 254–260.

Graf Estes, K., Evans, J. L., & Else-Quest, N. M. (2007). Differences in the nonword repetition performance of children with and without specific language impairment: A meta-analysis. *Journal of Speech, Language, and Hearing Research, 50,* 177–195. doi:10.1044/1092-4388(2007/015)

Graham, S. [Steve], & Harris, K. R. (1996). Self-regulation and strategy instruction for students who find writing and learning challenging. In C. M. Levy & S. Ransdell (Eds.), *The science of writing: Theories, methods, individual differences, and applications* (pp. 347–360). Hillsdale, NJ: Erlbaum.

Graham, S. [Sandra], & Hudley, C. (1994). Attributions of aggressive and nonagressive African-American male early adolescents: A study of construct accessibility. *Developmental Psychology, 30,* 365–373. doi:10.1037/0012-1649.30.3.365

Graham, S., McKeown, D., Kiuhara, S., & Harris, K. R. (2012). A meta-analysis of writing instruction for students in the elementary grades. *Journal of Educational Psychology, 104*(4), 879. doi:10.1037/a0029185

Graham, S. A., & Diesendruck, G. (2010). Fifteen-month-old infants attend to shape over other perceptual properties in an induction task. *Cognitive Development, 25*(2), 111–123.

Graham, S. A., & Fisher, S. E. (2015). Understanding language from a genomic perspective. *Annual Review of Genetics, 49,* 131–160. doi:10.1146/annurev-genet-120213-092236

Graham, S. A., & Poulin-Dubois, D. (1999). Infants' reliance on shape to generalize novel labels to animate and inanimate objects. *Journal of Child Language, 26,* 295–320.

Graham, S. A., Poulin-Dubois, D., & Baker, R. K. (1998). Infants' disambiguation of novel object words. *First Language, 18,* 149–164. doi:10.1177/014272379801805302

Graham-Bermann, S. A., & Brescoll, V. (2000). Gender, power, and violence: Assessing the family stereotypes of the children of batterers. *Journal of Family Psychology, 14,* 600–612. doi:10.1037/0893-3200.14.4.600

Granger, D. A., Serbin, L. A., Schwartzman, A., Lehoux, P., Cooperman, J., & Ikeda, S. (1998). Children's salivary cortisol, internalising behaviour problems, and family environment: Results from the Concordia Longitudinal Risk Project. *International Journal of Behavioral Development, 22,* 707–728.

Granger, D. A., Stansbury, K., & Henker, B. (1994). Preschoolers' behavioral and neuroendocrine responses to social challenge. *Merrill-Palmer Quarterly, 40,* 190–211.

Granier-Deferre, C., Ribeiro, A., Jacquet, A. Y., & Bassereau, S. (2011). Near-term fetuses process temporal features of speech. *Developmental Science, 14,* 336–352.

Granot, D., & Mayseless, O. (2001). Attachment security and adjustment to school in middle childhood. *International Journal of Behavioral Development, 25,* 530–541. doi:10.1080/01650250042000366

Hastings, P. D., Zahn-Waxler, C., & McShane, K. E. (2005). We are, by nature, moral creatures: Biological bases of concern for others. In M. Killen & J. Smetana (Eds.), *Handbook of moral development* (pp. 483–516). Hillsdale, NJ: Erlbaum.

Hastings, P. D., Zahn-Waxler, C., Robinson, J., Usher, B., & Bridges, D. (2000). The development of concern for others in children with behavior problems. *Developmental Psychology, 36,* 531–546. doi:10.1037/0012-1649.36.5.531

Hatano, G. (1990). The nature of everyday science: A brief introduction. *British Journal of Developmental Psychology, 8,* 245–250. doi:10.1111/j.2044-835X.1990.tb00839.x

Hatano, G., & Inagaki, K. (1996). Cognitive and cultural factors in the acquisition of intuitive biology. In D. R. Olson, & N. Torrance (Eds.), *The Handbook of Education and Human Development: New Models of Learning, Teaching and Schooling,* (pp. 683–708). Malden, MA: Blackwell Publishing.

Hatano, G., Siegler, R. S., Richards, D. D., Inagaki, K., Stavy, R., & Wax, N. (1993). The development of biological knowledge: A multinational study. *Cognitive Development, 8,* 47–62. doi:10.1016/0885-2014(93)90004-O

Hatzichristou, C., & Hopf, D. (1996). A multiperspective comparison of peer sociometric status groups in childhood and adolescence. *Child Development, 67,* 1085–1102. doi:10.2307/1131881

Hauck, F. R., Omojokun, O. O., & Siadaty, M. S. (2005). Do pacifiers reduce the risk of sudden infant death syndrome? A meta-analysis. *Pediatrics, 116*(5), e716–e723.

Hauck, F. R., Thompson, J. M., Tanabe, K. O., Moon, R. Y., & Vennemann, M. M. (2011). Breastfeeding and reduced risk of sudden infant death syndrome: A meta-analysis. *Pediatrics, 128,* 103–110. doi:10.1542/peds.2010–3000

Hawkins, D. L., Pepler, D. J., & Craig, W. M. (2001). Naturalistic observations of peer interventions in bullying. *Social Development, 10,* 512–527. doi:10.1111/1467-9507.00178

Hawley, P. H. (2003). Prosocial and coercive configurations of resource control in early adolescence: A case for the well-adapted Machiavellian. *Merrill-Palmer Quarterly, 49,* 279–309.

Hawley, P. H., Little, T. D., & Card, N. A. (2008). The myth of the alpha male: A new look at dominance-related beliefs and behaviors among adolescent males and females. *International Journal of Behavioral Development, 32,* 76–88. doi:10.1177/0165025407084054

Haworth, C. M. A., Wright, M. J., Luciano, M., Martin, N. G., de Geus, E. J. C., van Beijsterveldt, C. E. M., . . . Plomin, R. (2010). The heritability of general cognitive ability increases linearly from childhood to young adulthood. *Molecular Psychiatry, 15,* 1112–1120. doi:10.1038/mp.2009.55

Hay, D. F. (2007). The gradual emergence of sex differences in aggression: Alternative hypotheses. *Psychological Medicine, 37,* 1527–1537. doi:10.1017/S0033291707000165

Hay, D. F., Caplan, M., & Nash, A. (2009). The beginnings of peer relations. In K. H. Rubin, W. M. Bukowski, & B. Laursen (Eds.), *Handbook of peer interactions, relationships, and groups* (pp. 121–142). New York, NY: Guilford Press.

Hay, D. F., Hurst, S.-L., Waters, C. S., & Chadwick, A. (2011). Infants' use of force to defend toys: The origins of instrumental aggression. *Infancy, 16,* 471–489. doi:10.1111/j.1532-7078.2011.00069.x

Hay, D. F., Mundy, L., Roberts, S., Carta, R., Waters, C. S., Perra, O., . . . van Goozen, S. (2011). Known risk factors for violence predict 12-month-old infants' aggressiveness with peers. *Psychological Science, 22,* 1205–1211. doi:10.1177/0956797611419303

Hay, J. F., Graf Estes, K., Wang, T., & Saffran, J. R. (2015). From flexibility to constraint: The contrastive use of lexical tone in early word learning. *Child Development, 86*(1), 10–22.

Hay, J. F., Pelucchi, B., Graf Estes, K., & Saffran, J. R. (2011). Linking sounds to meanings: Infant statistical learning in a natural language. *Cognitive Psychology, 63,* 93–106. doi:10.1016/j.cogpsych.2011.06.002

Hayes, K. J., & Hayes, C. (1951). The intellectual development of a home-raised chimpanzee. *Proceedings of the American Philosophical Society, 95,* 105–109.

Hayne, H., Barr, R., & Herbert, J. (2003). The effect of prior practice on memory reactivation and generalization. *Child Development, 74,* 1615–1627. doi:10.2307/3696293

Hazel, N. A., Oppenheimer, C. W., Technow, J. R., Young, J. F., & Hankin, B. L. (2014). Parent relationship quality buffers against the effect of peer stressors on depressive symptoms from middle childhood to adolescence. *Developmental Psychology, 50,* 2115–2123. doi:10.1037/a0037192

He, M., Walle, E. A., & Campos, J. J. (2015). A cross-national investigation of the relationship between infant walking and language development. *Infancy, 20*(3), 283–305.

Heathcock, J. C., Lobo, M., & Galloway, J. C. (2008). Movement training advances the emergence of reaching in infants born at less than 33 weeks of gestational age: A randomized clinical trial. *Physical Therapy, 88,* 310–322. doi:10.2522/ptj.20070145

Heatherington, L., & Lavner, J. A. (2008). Coming to terms with coming out: Review and recommendations for family systems-focused research. *Journal of Family Psychology, 22,* 329–343. doi:10.1037/0893-3200.22.3.329

Heaven, P., & Ciarrochi, J. (2008). Parental styles, gender and the development of hope and self-esteem. *European Journal of Personality, 22,* 707–724. doi:10.1002/per.699

Hebb, D. O. (1949). *The organization of behavior: A neuropsychological theory.* New York, NY: Wiley.

Hecht, S. A., & Vagi, K. J. (2010). Sources of group and individual differences in emerging fraction skills. *Journal of Educational Psychology, 102,* 843–859. doi:10.1037/a0019824

Heckman, J. J. (2011, Spring). The economics of inequality. *American Educator, 31–35,* 47.

Hedges, L. V., & Nowell, A. (1995, July 7). Sex differences in mental test scores, variability, and numbers of high-scoring individuals. *Science, 269,* 41–45.

Heine, S. J., Lehman, D. R., Markus, H. R., & Kitayama, S. (1999). Is there a universal need for positive self-regard? *Psychological Review, 106,* 766–794.

Held, R., Birch, E., & Gwiazda, J. (1980). Stereoacuity of human infants. *Proceedings of the National Academy of Sciences of the United States of America, 77,* 5572–5574.

Held, R., Ostrovsky, Y., de Gelder, B., Gandhi, T., Ganesh, S., Mathur, U., & Sinha, P. (2011). The newly sighted fail to match seen with felt. *Nature Neuroscience, 14*(5), 551–553.

Helsen, M., Vollebergh, W., & Meeus, W. (2000). Social support from parents and friends and emotional problems in adolescence. *Journal of Youth and Adolescence, 29,* 319–335. doi:10.1023/A:1005147708827

Henry, B., Caspi, A., Moffitt, T. E., & Silva, P. A. (1996). Temperamental and familial predictors of violent and nonviolent criminal convictions: Age 3 to age 18. *Developmental Psychology, 32,* 614–623. doi:10.1037/0012-1649.32.4.614

Henry, C. S., Sager, D. W., & Plunkett, S. W. (1996). Adolescents' perceptions of family system characteristics, parent-adolescent dyadic behaviors, adolescent qualities, and adolescent empathy. *Family Relations, 45,* 283–292. doi:10.2307/585500

Hepper, P. G. (1988). Adaptive fetal learning: Prenatal exposure to garlic affects postnatal preferences. *Animal Behaviour, 36,* 935–936. doi:10.1016/S0003-3472(88)80177-5

Herbers, J. E., Cutuli, J. J., Lafavor, T. L., Vrieze, D., Leibel, C., Obradovic, J., & Masten, A. S. (2011). Direct and indirect effects of parenting on academic functioning of young homeless children. *Early Education and Development, 22,* 77–104. doi:10.1080/10409280903507261

Herbers, J. E., Cutuli, J. J., Supkoff, L. M., Heistad, D., Chan, C.-K., Hinz, E., & Masten, A. S. (2012). Early reading skills and academic achievement trajectories of students facing poverty, homelessness, and high residential mobility. *Educational Researcher, 41*, 366–374. doi:10.3102/0013189X12445320

Herman, M. (2004). Forced to choose: Some determinants of racial identification in multiracial adolescents. *Child Development, 75*, 730–748. doi:10.1111/j.1467-8624.2004.00703.x

Hermans, E. J., Ramsey, N. F., & van Honk, J. (2008). Exogenous testosterone enhances responsiveness to social threat in the neural circuitry of social aggression in humans. *Biological Psychiatry, 63*, 263–270. doi:10.1016/j.biopsych.2007.05.013

Hermer, L., & Spelke, E. (1996). Modularity and development: The case of spatial reorientation. *Cognition, 61*, 195–232.

Hernandez, J. T., & Diclemente, R. J. (1992). Self-control and ego identity development as predictors of unprotected sex in late adolescent males. *Journal of Adolescence, 15*, 437–447. doi:10.1016/0140-1971(92)90073-E

Herold, K., & Akhtar, N. (2014). Two-year-olds' understanding of self-symbols. *British Journal of Developmental Psychology, 32*(3), 262–275.

Herrmann, E., Call, J., Hernàndez-Lloreda, M. V., Hare, B., & Tomasello, M. (2007, September 7). Humans have evolved specialized skills of social cognition: The cultural intelligence hypothesis. *Science, 317*, 1360–1366.

Hertenstein, M. J., & Campos, J. J. (2004). The retention effects of an adult's emotional displays on infant behavior. *Child Development, 75*, 595–613. doi:10.1111/j.1467-8624.2004.00695.x

Hesketh, T., & Ding, Q. J. (2005). Anxiety and depression in adolescents in urban and rural China. *Psychological Reports, 96*, 435–444. doi:10.2466/pr0.96.2.435-444

Hesketh, T., Zheng, Y., Jun, Y. X., Xing, Z. W., Dong, Z. X., & Lu, L. (2011). Behaviour problems in Chinese primary school children. *Social Psychiatry and Psychiatric Epidemiology, 46*, 733–741. doi:10.1007/s00127-010-0240-0

Hespos, S. J., Ferry, A. L., Anderson, E. M., Hollenbeck, E. N., & Rips, L. J. (2016). Five-month-old infants have general knowledge of how nonsolid substances behave and interact. *Psychological Science, 27*(2), 244–256.

Hespos, S. J., & Spelke, E. S. (2004, July 22). Conceptual precursors to language. *Nature, 430*, 453–456. doi:10.1038/nature02634

Hesse, E., & Main, M. (2006). Frightened, threatening, and dissociative parental behavior in low-risk samples: Description, discussion, and interpretations. *Development and Psychopathology, 18*, 309–343.

Hespos, S. J., & vanMarle, K. (2012). Physics for infants: Characterizing the origins of knowledge about objects,

substances, and number. *Wiley Interdisciplinary Reviews: Cognitive Science, 3*(1), 19–27. doi:10.1002/wcs.157

Hetherington, E. M. (1989). Coping with family transitions: Winners, losers, and survivors. *Child Development, 60*, 1–14.

Hetherington, E. M. (1993). An overview of the Virginia Longitudinal Study of Divorce and Remarriage with a focus on early adolescence. *Journal of Family Psychology, 7*, 39–56. doi:10.1037/0893-3200.7.1.39

Hetherington, E. M. (1999). Social capital and the development of youth from nondivorced, divorced and remarried families. In W. A. Collins & B. Laursen (Eds.), *Minnesota Symposia on Child Psychology: Vol. 30. Relationships as developmental contexts* (pp. 177–209). Mahwah, NJ: Erlbaum.

Hetherington, E. M., Bridges, M., & Insabella, G. M. (1998). What matters? What does not? Five perspectives on the association between marital transitions and children's adjustment. *American Psychologist, 53*, 167–184. doi:10.1037/0003-066X.53.2.167

Hetherington, E. M., Henderson, S. H., Reiss, D. (with Anderson, E. R., Bridges, M., Chan, R. W., Insabella, G. M., Jodl, K. M., Kim, J. E., Mitchell, A. S., O'Connor, T. G., Skaggs, M. J., & Taylor, L. C.). (1999). Adolescent siblings in stepfamilies: Family functioning and adolescent adjustment, with commentary by James H. Bray. *Monographs of the Society for Research in Child Development, 64*(4, Serial No. 259), i–209.

Hetherington, E. M., & Stanley-Hagan, M. (2002). Parenting in divorced and remarried families. In M. H. Bornstein (Ed.), *Handbook of parenting: Vol. 3. Being and becoming a parent* (2nd ed., pp. 287–315). Mahwah, NJ: Erlbaum.

Hetherington, E. M., Stanley-Hagan, M., & Anderson, E. R. (1989). Marital transitions: A child's perspective. *American Psychologist, 44*, 303–312. doi:10.1037/0003-066X.44.2.303

Hetherington, E. M., & Stanley-Hagan, M. M. (1995). Parenting in divorced and remarried families. In M. H. Bornstein (Ed.), *Handbook of parenting: Vol. 3. Status and social conditions of parenting* (pp. 233–254). Hillsdale, NJ: Erlbaum.

Hewlett, B. S., Lamb, M. E., Shannon, D., Leyendecker, B., & Scholmerich, A. (1998). Culture and early infancy among central African foragers and farmers. *Developmental Psychology, 34*, 653–661.

Heyman, G. D., Genyue, F., & Lee, K. (2008). Reasoning about the disclosure of success and failure to friends among children in the United States and China. *Developmental Psychology 44*, 908–918.doi:10.1037/0012-1649.44.4.908

Hiatt, S. W., Campos, J. J., & Emde, R. N. (1979). Facial patterning and infant emotional expression: Happiness, surprise, and fear. *Child Development, 50*, 1020–1035.

Hickling, A. K., & Gelman, S. A. (1995). How does your garden grow? Early conceptualization

of seeds and their place in the plant growth cycle. *Child Development, 66*, 856–876. doi:10.1111/j.1467-8624.1995.tb00910.x

Hickman, L. J., Jaycox, L. H., & Aronoff, J. (2004). Dating violence among adolescents: Prevalence, gender distribution, and prevention program effectiveness. *Trauma, Violence, and Abuse, 5*, 123–142. doi:10.1177/1524838003262332

Higgins, E. T. (1991). Development of self-regulatory and self--evaluative processes: Costs, benefits, and tradeoffs. In M. R. Gunnar & L. A. Sroufe (Eds.), *Self processes and development* (pp. 125–165). Hillsdale, NJ: Erlbaum.

High, P. C., Klass, P., Donoghue, E., Glassy, D., DelConte, B., Earls, M., . . . Schulte, E. E. (2014). Literacy promotion: An essential component of primary care pediatric practice. *Pediatrics, 134*(2), 404–409.

Hill, C., & Kearl, H. (2011). Crossing the line: Sexual harassment at school. Washington, DC: AAUW.

Hill, J., Emery, R. E., Harden, K. P., Mendle, J., & Turkheimer, E. (2008). Alcohol use in adolescent twins and affiliation with substance using peers. *Journal of Abnormal Child Psychology, 36*, 81–94. doi:10.1007/s10802-007-9161-0

Hill, J. P. (1988). Adapting to menarche: Familial control and conflict. In M. R. Gunnar & W. A. Collins (Eds.), *Minnesota Symposia on Child Psychology: Vol. 21. Development during the transition to adolescence* (pp. 43–77). Hillsdale, NJ: Erlbaum.

Hill, J. P., & Lynch, M. E. (1983). The intensification of gender-related role expectations during early adolescence. In J. Brooks-Gunn & A. C. Petersen (Eds.), *Girls at puberty: Biological and psychosocial perspectives* (pp. 201–228). New York, NY: Springer.

Hill, S. A., & Sprague, J. (1999). Parenting in black and white families: The interaction of gender with race and class. *Gender and Society, 13*, 480–502. doi:10.1177/089124399013004004

Hilt, L. M., & Nolen-Hoeksema, S. (2009). The emergence of gender differences in depression in adolescence. In S. Nolen-Hoeksema & L. M. Hilt (Eds.), *Handbook of depression in adolescents* (pp. 111–135). New York, NY: Routledge/Taylor & Francis Group.

Hilt, L. M., & Pollak, S. D. (2012). Getting out of rumination: Comparison of three brief interventions in a sample of youth. *Journal of Abnormal Child Psychology, 40*(7), 1157–1165.

Hilton, J. M., & Haldeman, V. A. (1991). Gender differences in the performance of household tasks by adults and children in single-parent and two-parent, two-earner families. *Journal of Family Issues, 12*(1), 114–130.

Hindman, A. H., Wasik, B. A., & Snell, E. K. (2016). Closing the 30 million word gap: Next steps in designing research to inform practice. *Child Development Perspectives, 10*(2), 134–139.

Hinduja, S., & Patchin, J. W. (2015). *Teens use of technology: Weekly activities (11 to 15 year olds).* Cyberbullying Research Center. Retrieved from http://cyberbullying.org/2015-data/teen-tech-use-2015

Hineline, P. N., & Rosales-Ruiz, J. (2012). Behavior in relation to aversive events: Punishment and negative reinforcement. In G. J. Madden, W. V. Dube, T. Hackenberg, G. Hanley, & K. A. Lattal (Eds.), *APA Handbook of Operant Behavior* (pp. 483–512). Washington, DC: American Psychological Association.

Hines, M. (2004). *Brain gender.* Oxford, England: Oxford University Press.

Hines, M. (2013). Sex and sex differences. In P. D. Zelazo (Ed.), *Oxford handbook of developmental psychology* (Vol. 1, pp. 164–201). New York, NY: Oxford University Press.

Hines, M., Fane, B. A., Pasterski, V. L., Mathews, G. A., Conway, G. S., & Brook, C. (2003). Spatial abilities following prenatal androgen abnormality: Targeting and mental rotations performance in individuals with congenital adrenal hyperplasia. *Psychoneuroendocrinology, 28,* 1010–1026. doi:10.1016/S0306-4530(02)00121-X

Hinshaw, S. P. (2015). Developmental psychopathology, ontogenic process models, gene–environment interplay, and brain development: An emerging synthesis. *Journal of Abnormal Psychology, 124*(4), 771–775. doi:10.1037/abn0000110

Hinshaw, S. P., & Arnold, L. E. (2015). Attention-deficit hyperactivity disorder, multimodal treatment, and longitudinal outcome: Evidence, paradox, and challenge. *Wiley Interdisciplinary Reviews: Cognitive Science, 6*(1), 39–52.

Hinshaw, S. P., & Lee, S. S. (2003). Conduct and oppositional defiant disorders. In E. J. Mash & R. A. Barkley (Eds.), *Child psychopathology* (2nd ed., pp. 144–198). New York, NY: Guilford Press.

Hirsh-Pasek, K., Adamson, L. B., Bakeman, R., Owen, M. T., Golinkoff, R. M., Pace, A., .. Suma, K. (2015). The contribution of early communication quality to low-income children's language success. *Psychological Science, 26*(7), 1071–1083.

Hirsh-Pasek, K., & Golinkoff, R. M. (1996). The preferential looking paradigm reveals emerging language comprehension. In D. McDaniel, C. McKee, & H. Cairns (Eds.), *Methods for assessing children's syntax* (pp. 105–124). Cambridge, MA: MIT Press.

Hirsh-Pasek, K., Golinkoff, R. M., Berk, L. E., & Singer, D. G. (2009). *A mandate for playful learning in preschool: Presenting the evidence.* New York, NY: Oxford University Press.

Hirsh-Pasek, K., Zosh, J. M., Golinkoff, R. M., Gray, J. H., Robb, M. B., & Kaufman, J. (2015). Putting education in "educational" apps: Lessons from the science of learning. *Psychological Science in the Public Interest, 16*(1), 3–34.

Hirshfeld-Becker, D. R., Biederman, J., Henin, A., Faraone, S. V., Davis, S., Harrington, K., & Rosenbaum, J. F. (2007). Behavioral inhibition in preschool children at risk is a specific predictor of middle childhood social anxiety: A five-year follow-up. *Journal of Developmental and Behavioral Pediatrics, 28,* 225–233.

Ho, D. Y. F. (1986). Chinese patterns of socialization: A critical review. In M. H. Bond (Ed.), *The psychology of the Chinese people* (pp. 1–37). New York, NY: Oxford University Press.

Hobson, J. A., Harris, R., Garcia-Perez, R., & Hobson, R. P. (2009). Anticipatory concern: A study in autism. *Developmental Science, 12,* 249–263. doi:10.1111/j.1467-7687.2008.00762.x

Hochberg, J., & Brooks, V. (1962). Pictorial recognition as an unlearned ability: A study of one child's performance. *American Journal of Psychology, 75,* 624–628. doi:10.2307/1420286

Hoeve, M., Dubas, J. S., Gerris, J. R. M., van der Laan, P. H., & Smeenk, W. (2011). Maternal and paternal parenting styles: Unique and combined links to adolescent and early adult delinquency. *Journal of Adolescence, 34,* 813–827. doi:10.1016/j.adolescence.2011.02.004

Hoeve, M., Stams, G. J. J. M., Put, C. E., Dubas, J. S., Laan, P. H., & Gerris, J. R. M. (2012). A meta-analysis of attachment to parents and delinquency. *Journal of Abnormal Child Psychology, 40,* 771–785. doi:10.1007/s10802-011-9608-1

Hoff, E. (2001). *Language development* (2nd ed.). Belmont, CA: Wadsworth/Thomson Learning.

Hoff, E. (2003). The specificity of environmental influence: Socioeconomic status affects early vocabulary development via maternal speech. *Child Development, 74,* 1368–1378. doi:10.1111/1467-8624.00612

Hoff, E., Laursen, B., & Tardif, T. (2002). Socioeconomic status and parenting. In M. H. Bornstein (Ed.), *Handbook of parenting: Vol. 2. Biology and ecology of parenting* (2nd ed., pp. 231–252). Mahwah, NJ: Erlbaum.

Hoff, K. E., Reese-Weber, M., Schneider, W. J., & Stagg, J. W. (2009). The association between high status positions and aggressive behavior in early adolescence. *Journal of School Psychology, 47,* 395–426. doi:10.1016/j.jsp.2009.07.003

Hoff-Ginsberg, E., & Tardif, T. (1995). Socioeconomic status and parenting. In M. H. Bornstein (Ed.), *Handbook of parenting, Vol. 2: Biology and ecology of parenting* (pp. 161–188). Hillsdale, NJ: Erlbaum.

Hoffman, H., Li, C., Bainbridge, K., Losonczy, K., Chiu, M., & Rice, M. (2014). Voice, speech, and language problems in the U.S. pediatric population: The 2012 National Health Interview Survey (NHIS). Poster #3852 presented at the IEA 20th World Congress of Epidemiology, Anchorage, AK.

Hoffman, M. L. (1976). Empathy, role-taking, guilt and development of altruistic motives. In T. Lickona (Ed.), *Moral development and behavior: Theory, research, and social issues.* New York: Holt, Rinehart, & Winston.

Hoffman, M. L. (1981). Is altruism part of human nature? *Journal of Personality and Social Psychology, 40,* 121–137. doi:10.1037/0022-3514.40.1.121

Hoffman, M. L. (1982). Development of prosocial motivation: Empathy and guilt. In N. Eisenberg (Ed.), *The development of prosocial behavior* (pp. 281–313). New York, NY: Academic Press.

Hoffman, M. L. (1983). Affective and cognitive processes in moral internalization. In E. T. Higgins, D. N. Ruble, & W. W. Hartup (Eds.), *Social cognition and social development: A sociocultural perspective* (pp. 236–274). Cambridge, England: Cambridge University Press.

Hoffman, M. L. (2000). *Empathy and moral development: Implications for caring and justice.* Cambridge, England: Cambridge University Press.

Hoffner, C. (1993). Children's strategies for coping with stress: Blunting and monitoring. *Motivation and Emotion, 17,* 91–106.

Hofmann, S. G., Asnaani, A., Vonk, I. J. J., Sawyer, A. T., & Fang, A. (2012). The efficacy of cognitive behavioral therapy: A review of meta-analyses. *Cognitive Therapy and Research, 36,* 427–440. doi:10.1007/s10608-013-9595-3

Hofstede, G. (2000). Masculine and feminine cultures. In A. E. Kazdin (Ed.), *Encyclopedia of psychology* (Vol. 5, pp. 115–118). Washington, DC: American Psychological Association.

Hogue, A., & Steinberg, L. (1995). Homophily of internalized distress in adolescent peer groups. *Developmental Psychology, 31,* 897–906. doi:10.1037/0012-1649.31.6.897

Holden, C. (1980, March 21). Identical twins reared apart. *Science, 207,* 1323–1325.

Holder, M. D., & Coleman, B. (2015). Children's friendships and positive well-being. In M. Demir & M. Demir (Eds.), *Friendship and happiness: Across the life-span and cultures* (pp. 81–97). New York, NY: Springer Science + Business Media.

Homae, F., Watanabe, H., Nakano, T., Asakawa, K., & Taga, G. (2006). The right hemisphere of sleeping infant perceives sentential prosody. *Neuroscience Research, 54,* 276–280. doi:10.1016/j.neures.2005.12.006

Hong, H.-Y., & Lin-Siegler, X. (2012). How learning about scientists' struggles influences students' interest and learning in physics. *Journal*

of Educational Psychology, 104(2), 469–484. doi:10.1037/a0026224

Horn, J. L., & McArdle, J. J. (2007). Understanding human intelligence since Spearman. In R. Cudeck & R. C. MacCallum (Eds.), *Factor analysis at 100: Historical developments and future directions* (pp. 205–247). Mahwah, NJ: Erlbaum.

Horn, S. S. (2003). Adolescents' reasoning about exclusion from social groups. *Developmental Psychology, 39,* 71–84. doi:10.1037/0012-1649.39.1.71

Horne, R. S., Parslow, P. M., Ferens, D., Watts, A. M., & Adamson, T. M. (2004). Comparison of evoked arousability in breast and formula fed infants. *Archives of Disease in Childhood, 89,* 22–25.

Houltberg, B. J., Morris, A. S., Cui, L., Henry, C. S., & Criss, M. M. (2014). The role of youth anger in explaining links between parenting and early adolescent prosocial and antisocial behavior. *The Journal of Early Adolescence.* doi:10.1177/0272431614562834.

Houston, D. M., & Miyamoto, R. T. (2010). Effects of early auditory experience on word learning and speech perception in deaf children with cochlear implants: Implications for sensitive periods of language development. *Otology and Neurotology, 31,* 1248–1253.

Howe, M. L., & Courage, M. L. (1997). The emergence and early development of autobiographical memory. *Psychological Review, 104,* 499–523.

Howe, N., Aquan-Assee, J., & Bukowski, W. M. (2001). Predicting sibling relations over time: Synchrony between maternal management styles and sibling relationship quality. *Merrill-Palmer Quarterly, 47,* 121–141.

Howes, C. (1996). The earliest friendships. In W. M. Bukowski, A. F. Newcomb, & W. W. Hartup (Eds.), *The company they keep: Friendship in childhood and adolescence* (pp. 66–86). Cambridge, England: Cambridge University Press.

Howes, C., & Matheson, C. C. (1992). Sequences in the development of competent play with peers: Social and social pretend play. *Developmental Psychology, 28,* 961–974.

Howes, C., & Phillipsen, L. (1998). Continuity in children's relations with peers. *Social Development, 7,* 340–349. doi:10.1111/1467-9507.00071

Howes, D. (2012). Hiccups: A new explanation for the mysterious reflex. *Bioessays, 34,* 451–453. doi:10.1002/bies.201100194

Hoza, B., Molina, B. S. G., Bukowski, W. M., & Sippola, L. K. (1995). Peer variables as predictors of later childhood adjustment. *Development and Psychopathology, 7,* 787–802. doi:10.1017/S0954579400006842

Huang, F. L., & Cornell, D. G. (2015). The impact of definition and question order on the prevalence of bullying victimization using student self-reports. *Psychological Assessment, 27,* 1484–1493. doi:10.1037/pas0000149

Hubbard, F. O. A., & van IJzendoorn, M. H. (1991). Maternal unresponsiveness and infant crying across the first 9 months: A naturalistic longitudinal study. *Infant Behavior and Development, 14,* 299–312. doi:10.1016/0163-6383(91)90024-M

Hubel, D. H., & Wiesel, T. N. (1962). Receptive fields, binocular interaction and functional architecture in the cat's visual cortex. *The Journal of Physiology, 160*(1), 106–154.

Hubel, D. H., & Wiesel, T. N. (1970). The period of susceptibility to the physiological effects of unilateral eye closure in kittens. *The Journal of Physiology, 206*(2), 419.

Huber, A., McMahon, C. A., & Sweller, N. (2015). Efficacy of the 20-week Circle of Security intervention: Changes in caregiver reflective functioning, representations, and child attachment in an Australian clinical sample. *Infant Mental Health Journal, 36,* 556–574. doi:10.1002/imhj.21540

Hudson, J. A., Sosa, B., & Shapiro, L. R. (1997). Scripts and plans: The development of preschool children's event knowledge and event planning. In S. L. Friedman & E. K. Scholnick (Eds.), *The developmental psychology of planning: Why, how, and when do we plan?* (pp. 77–102). Mahwah, NJ: Erlbaum.

Huebner, R. R., & Izard, C. E. (1988). Mothers' responses to infants' facial expressions of sadness, anger, and physical distress. *Motivation and Emotion, 12,* 185–196.

Huffman, L. C., Bryan, Y. E., del Carmen, R., Pedersen, F. A., Doussard-Roosevelt, J. A., & Porges, S. W. (1998). Infant temperament and cardiac vagal tone: Assessments at twelve weeks of age. *Child Development, 69,* 624–635.

Hughes, C., & Dunn, J. (1998). Understanding mind and emotion: Longitudinal associations with mental-state talk between young friends. *Developmental Psychology, 34,* 1026–1037. doi:10.1037/0012-1649.34.5.1026

Hughes, D., Rodriguez, J., Smith, E. P., Johnson, D. J., Stevenson, H. C., & Spicer, P. (2006). Parents' ethnic-racial socialization practices: A review of research and directions for future study. *Developmental Psychology, 42,* 747–770.

Hughes, D., Way, N., & Rivas-Drake, D. (2011). Stability and change in private and public ethnic regard among African American, Puerto Rican, Dominican, and Chinese American early adolescents. *Journal of Research on Adolescence, 21,* 861–870. doi:10.1111/j.1532-7795.2011.00744.x

Huguet, G., Benabou, M., & Bourgeron, T. (2016). The genetics of autism spectrum disorders. In P. Sassone-Corsi & Y. Christen (Eds.) *A Time for Metabolism and Hormones* (pp. 101–129). Heidelberg, Germany; New York, NY; Dordrecht, Netherlands; London, England: Springer International Publishing.

Huizink, A. C. (2008). Prenatal stress exposure and temperament: A review. *International Journal of Developmental Science, 2,* 77–99. doi:10.3233/DEV-2008-21206

Huizink, A. C. (2012). Prenatal factors in temperament: The role of prenatal stress and substance use exposure. In M. R. Zentner & R. L. Shiner (Eds.), *Handbook of temperament* (pp. 297–314). New York, NY: Guilford Press.

Human Rights Campaign. (2012). *Growing up LGBT in America: At home, at school, and in the community.* Washington, DC: Author. Retrieved from from http://www.hrc.org/files/assets/resources/Growing-Up-LGBT-in-America_Report.pdf

Humphreys, L. G. (1989). Intelligence: Three kinds of instability and their consequences for policy. In R. L. Linn (Ed.), *Intelligence* (pp. 193–216). Urbana: University of Illinois Press.

Hunt, J. M. (1961). *Intelligence and experience.* New York, NY: Ronald Press.

Hunter, F. T., & Youniss, J. (1982). Changes in functions of three relations during adolescence. *Developmental Psychology, 18,* 806–811.

Hunziker, U. A., & Barr, R. G. (1986). Increased carrying reduces infant crying: A randomized controlled trial. *Pediatrics, 77,* 641–648.

Hurles, M. (2012). Older males beget more mutations. *Nature Genetics, 44,* 1174–1176.

Hurtado, N., Marchman, V. A., & Fernald, A. (2008). Does input influence uptake? Links between maternal talk, processing speed and vocabulary size in Spanish-learning children. *Developmental Science, 11,* F31–F39. doi:10.1111/j.1467-7687.2008.00768.x

Huston, A. C., & Aronson, S. R. (2005). Mothers' time with infant and time in employment as predictors of mother–child relationships and children's early development. *Child Development, 76,* 467–482. doi:10.1111/j.1467-8624.2005.00857.x

Hutchinson, E. A., De Luca, C. R., Doyle, L. W., Roberts, G., Anderson, P. J., & Victorian Infant Collaborative Study Group. (2013). School-age outcomes of extremely preterm or extremely low birth weight children. *Pediatrics, 131*(4), e1053–e1061.

Huttenlocher, J., Levine, S., & Vevea, J. (1998). Environmental input and cognitive growth: A study using time-period comparisons. *Child Development, 69,* 1012–1029.

Huttenlocher, P. R., & Dabholkar, A. S. (1997). Regional differences in synaptogenesis in human cerebral cortex. *Journal of Comparative Neurology, 387,* 167–178.

Hutton, E. K., Cappelletti, A., Reitsma, A. H., Simioni, J., Horne, J., McGregor, C., & Ahmed, R. J. (2015, December 22). Outcomes associated with planned place of birth among women with low-risk pregnancies. *Canadian Medical Association Journal*, cmaj-150564. doi:10.1503/cmaj.150564.

Hwang, C. P. (1987). The changing role of Swedish fathers. In M. E. Lamb (Ed.), *The father's role: Cross-cultural perspectives* (pp. 115–138). Hillsdale, NJ: Erlbaum.

Hwang, J. M., Cheong, P. H., & Feeley, T. H. (2009). Being young and feeling blue in Taiwan: Examining adolescent depressive mood and online and offline activities. *New Media and Society, 11*, 1101–1121. doi:10.1177/1461444809341699

Hyde, J. S. (2005). The gender similarities hypothesis. *American Psychologist, 60*, 581–592. doi:10.1037/0003-066X.60.6.581

Hyde, J. S., & Linn, M. C. (1988). Gender differences in verbal ability: A meta-analysis. *Psychological Bulletin, 104*, 53–69. doi:10.1037/0033-2909.104.1.53

Hymel, S., Bowker, A., & Woody, E. (1993). Aggressive versus withdrawn unpopular children: Variations in peer and self-perceptions in multiple domains. *Child Development, 64*, 879–896. doi:10.1111/j.1467-8624.1993.tb02949.x

Imperato-McGinley, J., Pichardo, M., Gautier, T., Voyer, D., & Bryden, M. P. (2007). Cognitive abilities in androgen-insensitive subjects: Comparison with control males and females from the same kindred. In G. Einstein (Ed.), *Sex and the brain* (pp. 555–560). Cambridge, MA: The MIT Press. (Reprinted from *Clinical Endocrinology, 34*, pp. 341–347, 1991)

Inagaki, K., & Hatano, G. (1993). Young children's understanding of the mind-body distinction. *Child Development, 64*, 1534–1549.

Inagaki, K., & Hatano, G. (1996). Young children's recognition of commonalities between animals and plants. *Child Development, 67*, 2823–2840. doi:10.1111/j.1467-8624.1996.tb01890.x

Inagaki, K., & Hatano, G. (2002). *Young children's naive thinking about the biological world.* New York, NY: Psychology Press.

Inagaki, K., & Hatano, G. (2008). Conceptual change in naïve biology. In S. Vosniadou (Ed.), *International handbook of research on conceptual change* (pp. 240–262). New York, NY: Routledge/Taylor & Francis.

Inam, A., Tariq, P. N., & Zaman, S. (2015). Cultural adaptation of preschool PATHS (Promoting Alternative Thinking Strategies) curriculum for Pakistani children. *International Journal of Psychology, 50*, 232–239. doi:10.1002/ijop.12090

Ingoldsby, E. M., Shaw, D. S., & Garcia, M. M. (2001). Intrafamily conflict in relation to boys' adjustment at school. *Development and Psychopathology, 13*, 35–52.

Inhelder, B., & Piaget, J. (1958). *The growth of logical thinking from childhood to adolescence: An essay on the construction of formal operational structures.* New York, NY: Basic Books.

Inlow, J. K., & Restifo, L. L. (2004). Molecular and comparative genetics of mental retardation. *Genetics, 166*, 835–881.

Intons-Peterson, M. J. (1988). *Children's concepts of gender.* Norwood, NJ: Ablex.

Idring, S., Magnusson, C., Lundberg, M., Ek, M., Rai, D., Svensson, A. C., . . . Lee, B. K. (2014). Parental age and the risk of autism spectrum disorders: Findings from a Swedish population-based cohort. *International Journal of Epidemiology 43*(1), 107–115.

Isabella, R. A. (1993). Origins of attachment: Maternal interactive behavior across the first year. *Child Development, 64*, 605–621. doi:10.1111/j.1467-8624.1993.tb02931.x

Islami, F., Liu, Y., Jemal, A., Zhou, J., Weiderpass, E., Colditz, G., . . . Weiss, M. (2015). Breastfeeding and breast cancer risk by receptor status—A systematic review and meta-analysis. *Annals of Oncology, 26*(12), 2398–2407.

It Gets Better Project. (n.d.). What is the It Gets Better Project? Los Angeles, CA. Accessed June 14, 2016, from http://www.itgetsbetter.org/pages/about-it-gets-better-project/

Ito, T., Ando, H., Suzuki, T., Ogura, T., Hotta, K., Imamura, Y., . . . Handa, H. (2010, March 12). Identification of a primary target of thalidomide teratogenicity. *Science, 327*, 1345–1350.

Iverson, J. M., & Goldin-Meadow, S. (1998, November 26). Why people gesture when they speak. *Nature, 396*, 228.

Iyer, R. V., Kochenderfer-Ladd, B., Eisenberg, N., & Thompson, M. (2010). Peer victimization and effortful control: Relations to school engagement and academic achievement. *Merrill-Palmer Quarterly, 56*, 361–387.

Izard, C. E. (2007). Basic emotions, natural kinds, emotion schemas, and a new paradigm. *Perspectives on Psychological Science, 2*, 260–280. doi:10.1111/j.1745-6916.2007.00044.x

Izard, C. E. (2010). The many meanings/aspects of emotion: Definitions, functions, activation, and regulation. *Emotion Review, 2*, 363–370.

Izard, C. E. (2011). Forms and functions of emotions: Matters of -emotion–cognition interactions. *Emotion Review, 3*, 371–378.

Izard, C. E., & Dougherty, L. (1980). *A system for identifying affect expressions by holistic judgments (AFFEX).* Newark, DE: University of Delaware, Instructional Resources Center.

Izard, C. E., Fantauzzo, C. A., Castle, J. M., Haynes, O. M., Rayias, M. F., & Putnam, P. H. (1995). The ontogeny and significance of infants' facial expressions in the first 9 months of life. *Developmental Psychology, 31*, 997–1013. doi:10.1037/0012-1649.31.6.997

Izard, C. E., Hembree, E. A., & Huebner, R. R. (1987). Infants' emotion expressions to acute pain: Developmental change and stability of individual differences. *Developmental Psychology, 23*, 105–113. doi:10.1037/0012-1649.23.1.105

Izard, C. E., King, K. A., Trentacosta, C. J., Morgan, J. K., Laurenceau, J. P., Krauthamer-Ewing, E. S., & Finlon, K. J. (2008). Accelerating the development of emotion competence in Head Start children: Effects on adaptive and maladaptive behavior. *Development and Psychopathology, 20*, 369–397. doi:10.1017/S0954579408000175

Izard, C. E., Woodburn, E. M., & Finlon, K. J. (2010). Extending emotion science to the study of discrete emotions in infants. *Emotion Review, 2*, 134–136. doi:10.1177/1754073909355003

Izard, V., Sann, C., Spelke, E. S., & Streri, A. (2009). Newborn infants perceive abstract numbers. *Proceedings of the National Academy of Sciences of the United States of America, 106*, 10382–10385. doi:10.1073/pnas.0812142106

Jaccard, J., Blanton, H., & Dodge, T. (2005). Peer influences on risk behavior: An analysis of the effects of a close friend. *Developmental Psychology, 41*, 135–147.

Jack, R. E., Garrod, O. G., Yu, H., Caldara, R., & Schyns, P. G. (2012). Facial expressions of emotion are not culturally universal. *Proceedings of the National Academy of Sciences, 109*(19), 7241–7244.

Jacobson, J. L., & Jacobson, S. W. (1996). Intellectual impairment in children exposed to polychlorinated biphenyls in utero. *New England Journal of Medicine, 335*, 783–789. doi:10.1056/NEJM199609123351104

Jacobson, J. L., & Jacobson, S. W. (2002). Effects of prenatal alcohol exposure on child development. *Alcohol Research and Health, 26*, 282–286.

Jacobson, J. L., Jacobson, S. W., Padgett, R. J., Brumitt, G. A., & Billings, R. L. (1992). Effects of prenatal PCB exposure on cognitive processing efficiency and sustained attention. *Developmental Psychology, 28*, 297–306.

Jacobson, K. C., & Crockett, L. J. (2000). Parental monitoring and adolescent adjustment: An ecological perspective. *Journal of Research on Adolescence, 10*, 65–97. doi:10.1207/SJRA1001_4

Jaffe, A. C. (2011). Failure to thrive: Current clinical concepts. *Pediatrics in Review, 32*, 100–108. doi:10.1542/pir.32-3-100

Jaffee, S., Caspi, A., Moffitt, T. E., Belsky, J., & Silva, P. (2001). Why are children born to teen mothers at risk for adverse outcomes in young adulthood? Results from a 20-year longitudinal study. *Development and Psychopathology, 13*, 377–397.

Jaffee, S., & Hyde, J. S. (2000). Gender differences in moral orientation: A meta-analysis.

Psychological Bulletin, 126, 703–726. doi:10.1037/0033-2909.126.5.703

Jaffee, S. R. (2002). Pathways to adversity in young adulthood among early childbearers. *Journal of Family Psychology, 16,* 38–49. doi:10.1037/0893-3200.16.1.38

Jaffee, S. R., Caspi, A., Moffitt, T. E., Polo-Tomas, M., Price, T. S., & Taylor, A. (2004a). The limits of child effects: Evidence for genetically mediated child effects on corporal punishment but not on physical maltreatment. *Developmental Psychology, 40,* 1047–1058. doi:10.1037/0012-1649.40.6.1047

Jaffee, S. R., Caspi, A., Moffitt, T. E., & Taylor, A. (2004b). Physical maltreatment victim to antisocial child: Evidence of an environmentally mediated process. *Journal of Abnormal Psychology, 113,* 44–55. doi:10.1037/0021-843X.113.1.44

Jaffee, S. R., & Christian, C. W. (2014). The biological embedding of child abuse and neglect: Implications for policy and practice. *Social Policy Report, 28,* 3–19.

Jaffee, S. R., Hanscombe, K. B., Haworth, C. M. A., Davis, O. S. P., & Plomin, R. (2012). Chaotic homes and children's disruptive behavior: A longitudinal cross-lagged twin study. *Psychological Science, 23,* 643–650. doi:10.1177/0956797611431693

Jaffee, S. R., Moffitt, T. E., Caspi, A., Taylor, A., & Arseneault, L. (2002). Influence of adult domestic violence on children's internalizing and externalizing problems: An environmentally informative twin study. *Journal of the American Academy of Child and Adolescent Psychiatry, 41,* 1095–1103. doi:10.1097/00004583-200209000-00010

Jahromi, L. B., Putnam, S. P., & Stifter, C. A. (2004). Maternal regulation of infant reactivity from 2 to 6 months. *Developmental Psychology, 40,* 477–487. doi:10.1037/0012-1649.40.4.477

Jahromi, L. B., Umana-Taylor, A. J., Updegraff, K. A., & Lara, E. E. (2012). Birth characteristics and developmental outcomes of infants of Mexican-origin adolescent mothers: Risk and promotive factors. *International Journal of Behavioral Development, 36,* 146–156. doi:10.1177/0165025411430777

Jakobson, R. (1968). *Child language. Aphasia and phonological universals* (A. R. Keiler, Trans.). The Hague, The Netherlands: Mouton. (Original work published 1941)

James, D., Pillai, M., & Smoleniec, J. (1995). Neurobehavioral development in the human fetus. In J.-P. Lecanuet, W. P. Fifer, N. A. Krasnegor, & W. P. Smotherman (Eds.), *Fetal development: A psychobiological perspective* (pp. 101–128). Hillsdale, NJ: Erlbaum.

Jansen, P. W., Raat, H., Mackenbach, J. P., Hofman, A., Jaddoe, V. W. V., Bakermans-Kranenburg, M. J., . . . Tiemeier, H. (2012). Early determinants of maternal and paternal harsh discipline: The Generation R Study. *Family Relations, 61,* 253–270. doi:10.1111/j.1741-3729.2011.00691.x

Janssens, J. M. A. M., & Deković, M. (1997). Child rearing, prosocial moral reasoning, and prosocial behaviour. *International Journal of Behavioral Development, 20,* 509–527. doi:10.1080/016502597385252

Jaser, S. S., Champion, J. E., Reeslund, K. L., Keller, G., Merchant, M. J., Benson, M., & Compas, B. E. (2007). Cross-situational coping with peer and family stressors in adolescent offspring of depressed parents. *Journal of Adolescence, 30,* 917–932.

Jaswal, V. K. (2004). Don't believe everything you hear: Preschoolers' sensitivity to speaker intent in category induction. *Child Development, 75,* 1871–1885. doi:10.1111/j.1467-8624.2004.00822.x

Jayaraman, S., Fausey, C. M., & Smith, L. B. (2015). The faces in infant-perspective scenes change over the first year of life. *PloS one, 10*(5), e0123780. doi:10.1371/journal.pone.0123780

Jenkins, J. (1992). Sibling relationships in disharmonious homes: Potential difficulties and protective effects. In F. Boer & J. Dunn (Eds.), *Children's sibling relationships: Developmental and clinical issues* (pp. 125–138). Hillsdale, NJ: Erlbaum.

Jenkins, J. M., & Astington, J. W. (1996). Cognitive factors and family structure associated with theory of mind development in young children. *Developmental Psychology, 32,* 70–78.

Jennings, P. A., & Greenberg, M. T. (2009). The prosocial classroom: Teacher social and emotional competence in relation to student and classroom outcomes. *Review of Educational Research, 79,* 491–525. doi:10.3102/0034654308325693

Jensen, A. R. (1973). *Educability and group differences.* New York, NY: Harper & Row.

Jiang, Y., Ekono, M., & Skinner, C. (2016). Basic facts about low-income children: Children under 18 years, 2014. Retrieved from National Center for Children in Poverty website: http://www.nccp.org/publications/pdf/text_1145.pdf

Jiao, S., Ji, G., & Jing, Q. (1986). Comparative study of behavioral qualities of only children and sibling children. *Child Development, 57,* 357–361.

Jiao, S., Ji, G., & Jing, Q. (1996). Cognitive development of Chinese urban only children and children with siblings. *Child Development, 67,* 387–395. doi:10.1111/j.1467-8624.1996.tb01740.x

Jin, M. K., Jacobvitz, D., Hazen, N., & Jung, S. H. (2012). Maternal sensitivity and infant attachment security in Korea: Cross-cultural validation of the Strange Situation. *Attachment and Human Development, 14,* 33–44. doi:10.1080/14616734.2012.636656

Jirout, J. J., & Newcombe, N. S. (2015). Building blocks for developing spatial skills: Evidence from a large, representative U.S. sample. *Psychological Science, 26*(3), 302–310. doi:10.1177/0956797614563338

Johnson, D. E., & Gunnar, M. R. (2011). IV. Growth failure in institutionalized children. *Monographs of the Society for Research in Child Development, 76*(4, Serial No. 301), 92–126. doi:10.1111/j.1540-5834.2011.00629.x

Johnson, E. K., & Jusczyk, P. W. (2001). Word segmentation by 8-month-olds: When speech cues count more than statistics. *Journal of Memory and Language, 44,* 548–567. doi:10.1006/jmla.2000.2755

Johnson, J., & Martin, C. (1985). Parents' beliefs and home learning environments: Effects on cognitive development. In I. E. Sigel (Ed.), *Parental belief systems: The psychological consequences for children* (pp. 25–49). Hillsdale, NJ: Erlbaum.

Johnson, J. L., McWilliams, K., Goodman, G. S., Shelley, A. E., & Piper, B. (2016). Basic principles of interviewing the child eyewitness. In *Forensic Interviews Regarding Child Sexual Abuse* (pp. 179–195). Springer International Publishing.

Johnson, J. S., & Newport, E. L. (1989). Critical period effects in second language learning: The influence of maturational state on the acquisition of English as a second language. *Cognitive Psychology, 21,* 60–99.

Johnson, K. E., & Mervis, C. B. (1994). Microgenetic analysis of first steps in children's acquisition of expertise on shorebirds. *Developmental Psychology, 30,* 418–435.

Johnson, M. H. (1992). Imprinting and the development of face recognition: From chick to man. *Current Directions in Psychological Science, 1,* 52–55. doi:10.2307/20182129

Johnson, M. H. (2011). Interactive specialization: A domain-general framework for human functional brain development? *Developmental Cognitive Neuroscience, 1*(1), 7–21. doi:10.1016/j.dcn.2010.07.003

Johnson, M. K., Beebe, T., Mortimer, J. T., & Snyder, M. (1998). Volunteerism in adolescence: A process perspective. *Journal of Research on Adolescence, 8,* 309–332. doi:10.1207/s15327795jra0803_2

Johnson, S., & Marlow, N. (2011). Preterm birth and childhood psychiatric disorders. *Pediatric Research, 69,* 11R–18R.

Johnson, S. C., Bolz, M., Carter, E., Mandsanger, J., Teichner, A., & Zettler, P. (2008). Calculating the attentional orientation of an unfamiliar agent in infancy. *Cognitive Development, 23*(1), 24–37.

Johnson, S. C., & Chen, F. S. (2011). Socioemotional information processing in human infants: From genes to subjective construals. *Emotion Review, 3*, 169–178. doi:10.1177/1754073910387945

Johnson, S. C., Dweck, C. S., & Chen, F. S. (2007). Evidence for infants' internal working models of attachment. *Psychological Science, 18*, 501–502. doi:10.1111/j.1467-9280.2007.01929.x

Johnson, S. C., Shimizu, Y. A., & Ok, S. J. (2007). Actors and actions: The role of agent behavior in infants' attribution of goals. *Cognitive Development, 22*(3), 310–322.

Johnson, S. C., & Solomon, G. E. A. (1997). Why dogs have puppies and cats have kittens: The role of birth in young children's understanding of biological origins. *Child Development, 68*, 404–419. doi:10.1111/j.1467-8624.1997.tb01948.x

Johnson, S. P. (Ed.). (2010). *Neoconstructivism: The new science of cognitive development.* New York, NY: Oxford University Press.

Johnson, S. P., Amso, D., & Slemmer, J. A. (2003). Development of object concepts in infancy: Evidence for early learning in an eye-tracking paradigm. *Proceedings of the National Academy of Sciences of the United States of America, 100*, 10568–10573. doi:10.1073/pnas.1630655100

Johnson, S. P., & Aslin, R. N. (1995). Perception of object unity in 2-month-old infants. *Developmental Psychology, 31*, 739–745. doi:10.1037/0012-1649.31.5.739

Johnson, S. P., Davidow, J., Hall-Haro, C., & Frank, M. C. (2008). Development of perceptual completion originates in information acquisition. *Developmental Psychology, 44*, 1214–1224. doi:10.1037/a0013215

Johnson, W., McGue, M., & Iacono, W. G. (2006). Genetic and environmental influences on academic achievement trajectories during adolescence. *Developmental Psychology, 42*, 514–532. doi:10.1037/0012-1649.42.3.514

Johnston, A. M., Barnes, M. A., & Desrochers, A. (2008). Reading comprehension: Developmental processes, individual differences, and interventions. *Canadian Psychology/Psychologie canadienne, 49*(2), 125. doi:10.1037/0708-5591.49.2.125

Jome, L. M., & Tokar, D. M. (1998). Dimensions of masculinity and major choice traditionality. *Journal of Vocational Behavior, 52*, 120–134. doi:10.1006/jvbe.1996.1571

Jones, D. C., Abbey, B. B., & Cumberland, A. (1998). The development of display rule knowledge: Linkages with family expressiveness and social competence. *Child Development, 69*, 1209–1222.

Jones, K. L., & Smith, D. W. (1973, November 3). Recognition of the fetal alcohol syndrome in early infancy. *The Lancet, 302*, 999–1001.

Jones, M. (1990). Children's writing. In R. Grieve & M. Hughes (Eds.), *Understanding*

children: Essays in honour of Margaret Donaldson (pp. 94–120). Cambridge, MA: Basil Blackwell.

Jones, M. C. (1924). A laboratory study of fear: The case of Peter. *Pedagogical Seminary, 31*, 308–315.

Jones, M. D., & Galliher, R. V. (2007). Ethnic identity and psychosocial functioning in Navajo adolescents. *Journal of Research on Adolescence, 17*, 683–696.

Jones, R. M. (1992). Ego identity and adolescent problem behavior. In G. R. Adams, T. P. Gullotta, & R. Montemayor (Eds.), *Advances in adolescent development: Vol. 4. Adolescent identity formation* (pp. 216–233). Thousand Oaks, CA: Sage.

Jones, S., & Myhill, D. (2004). "Troublesome boys" and "compliant girls": Gender identity and perceptions of achievement and underachievement. *British Journal of Sociology of Education, 25*, 547–561. doi:10.2307/4128701

Jones, W., Carr, K., & Klin, A. (2008). Absence of preferential looking to the eyes of approaching adults predicts level of social disability in 2-year-old toddlers with autism spectrum disorder. *Archives of General Psychiatry, 65*, 946–954. doi:10.1001/archpsyc.65.8.946.

Jonson-Reid, M., Kohl, P. L., & Drake, B. (2012). Child and adult outcomes of chronic child maltreatment. *Pediatrics, 129*(5), 839–845.

Joormann, J., Cooney, R. E., Henry, M. L., & Gotlib, I. H. (2012). Neural correlates of automatic mood regulation in girls at high risk for depression. *Journal of Abnormal Psychology, 121*, 61–72. doi:10.1037/a0025294

Jordan, N. C. (2007). Do words count? Connections between mathematics and reading difficulties. In D. B. Berch & M. M. M. Mazzocco (Eds.), *Why is math so hard for some children? The nature and origins of mathematical learning difficulties and disabilities* (pp. 107–120). Baltimore, MD: Paul H. Brookes.

Jordan, N. C., Hansen, N., Fuchs, L. S., Siegler, R. S., Gersten, R., & Micklos, D. (2013). Developmental predictors of fraction concepts and procedures. *Journal of Experimental Child Psychology, 116*, 45–58. doi:10.1016/j.jecp.2013.02.001

Jorgensen, M., Keiding, N., & Skakkebaek, N. E. (1991). Estimation of spermarche from longitudinal spermaturia data. *Biometrics, 47*, 177–193. doi:10.2307/2532505

Joshi, M. S., & MacLean, M. (1994). Indian and English children's understanding of the distinction between real and apparent emotion. *Child Development, 65*, 1372–1384.

Joussemet, M., Vitaro, F., Barker, E. D., Côté, S., Nagin, D. S., Zoccolillo, M., & Tremblay, R. E. (2008). Controlling parenting and physical aggression during elementary school. *Child Development, 79*, 411–425. doi:10.1111/j.1467-8624.2007.01133.x

Jowkar-Baniani, G., & Schmuckler, M. A. (2011). Picture perception in infants: Generalization from two-dimensional to three-dimensional displays. *Infancy, 16*(2), 211–226.

Juel, C. (1988). Learning to read and write: A longitudinal study of 54 children from first through fourth grades. *Journal of Educational Psychology, 80*, 437–447. doi:10.1037/0022-0663.80.4.437

Juel, C. (1994). *Learning to read and write in one elementary school.* New York, NY: Springer-Verlag.

Jung, R. E., & Haier, R. J. (2007). The Parieto-Frontal Integration Theory (P-FIT) of intelligence: Converging neuroimaging evidence. *Behavioral and Brain Sciences, 30*, 135–154. doi:10.1017/S0140525X07001185

Jusczyk, P. W., & Aslin, R. N. (1995). Infants' detection of the sound patterns of words in fluent speech. *Cognitive Psychology, 29*, 1–23. doi:10.1006/cogp.1995.1010

Justice, L. M., Petscher, Y., Schatschneider, C., & Mashburn, A. (2011). Peer effects in preschool classrooms: Is children's language growth associated with their classmates' skills? *Child Development, 82*, 1768–1777. doi:10.1111/j.1467-8624.2011.01665.x

Juvonen, J., Nishina, A., & Graham, S. (2000). Peer harassment, psychological adjustment, and school functioning in early adolescence. *Journal of Educational Psychology, 92*, 349–359. doi:10.1037/0022-0663.92.2.349

Kaas, J. H. (2013). The evolution of brains from early mammals to humans. *Wiley Interdisciplinary Reviews: Cognitive Science, 4*(1), 33–45.

Kabali, H. K., Irigoyen, M. M., Nunez-Davis, R., Budacki, J. G., Mohanty, S. H., Leister, K. P., & Bonner, R. L. (2015). Exposure and use of mobile media devices by young children. *Pediatrics, 136*, 1–7.

Kagan, J. (1976). Emergent themes in human development. *American Scientist, 64*, 186–196.

Kagan, J. (1997). Temperament and the reactions to unfamiliarity. *Child Development, 68*, 139–143.

Kagan, J. (1998). Biology and the child. In W. Damon (Series Ed.) & N. Eisenberg (Vol. Ed.), *Handbook of child psychology: Vol. 3. Social, emotional, and personality development* (5th ed., pp. 177–235). Hoboken, NJ: Wiley.

Kagan, J. (2008). In defense of qualitative changes in development. *Child Development, 79*, 1606–1624. doi:10.1111/j.1467-8624.2008.01211.x

Kagan, J. (2012). The biography of behavioral inhibition. In M. R. Zentner & R. L. Shiner (Eds.), *Handbook of temperament* (pp. 69–82). New York, NY: Guilford Press.

Kagan, J., & Fox, N. A. (2006). Biology, culture, and temperamental biases. In W. Damon &

R. M. Lerner (Series Eds.) & N. Eisenberg (Vol. Ed.), *Handbook of child psychology: Vol. 3. Social, emotional, and personality development* (6th ed., pp. 167–225). Hoboken, NJ: Wiley.

Kagan, J., Kearsley, R. B., & Zelazo, P. R. (1978). *Infancy: Its place in human development.* Cambridge, MA: Harvard University Press.

Kagan, J., Snidman, N., & Arcus, D. (1998). Childhood derivatives of high and low reactivity in infancy. *Child Development, 69,* 1483–1493.

Kagan, J., Snidman, N., Kahn, V., & Towsley, S. (2007). The preservation of two infant temperaments into adolescence. *Monographs of the Society for Research in Child Development, 72*(2, Serial No. 287). doi:10.1111/j.1540-5834.2007.00436.x

Kahen, V., Katz, L. F., & Gottman, J. M. (1994). Linkages between parent–child interaction and conversations of friends. *Social Development, 3,* 238–254. doi:10.1111/j.1467-9507.1994.tb00043.x

Kail, R. (1991). Developmental change in speed of processing during childhood and adolescence. *Psychological Bulletin, 109,* 490–501.

Kail, R. (1997). Processing time, imagery, and spatial memory. *Journal of Experimental Child Psychology, 64,* 67–78. doi:10.1006/jecp.1996.2337

Kail, R. V. (1984). *The development of memory in children* (2nd ed.). New York, NY: Freeman.

Kaiser Family Foundation. (2010, January 20). Generation M2: Media in the lives of 8- to 18-year-olds. Retrieved from http://kff.org/other/report/generation-m2-media-in-the-lives-of-8-to-18-year-olds/

Kaler, S. R., & Kopp, C. B. (1990). Compliance and comprehension in very young toddlers. *Child Development, 61,* 1997–2003.

Kalil, A., Levine, J. A., & Ziol-Guest, K. M. (2005). Following in their parents' footsteps: How characteristics of parental work predict adolescents' interest in parents' jobs. In B. Schneider & L. J. Waite (Eds.), *Being together, working apart: Dual-career families and the work-life balance* (pp. 422–442). New York, NY: Cambridge University Press.

Kalil, A., & Ziol-Guest, K. M. (2005). Single mothers' employment dynamics and adolescent well-being. *Child Development, 76,* 196–211. doi:10.1111/j.1467-8624.2005.00839.x

Kalish, C. (1997). Preschoolers' understanding of mental and bodily reactions to contamination: What you don't know can hurt you, but cannot sadden you. *Developmental Psychology, 33,* 79–91.

Kalish, C. W. (1996). Preschoolers' understanding of germs as invisible mechanisms. *Cognitive Development, 11*(1), 83–106. doi:10.1016/S0885-2014(96)90029-5

Kam, C., Wong, L. W., & Fung, K. M. (2011). Promoting social-emotional learning in Chinese schools: A feasibility study of PATHS implementation in Hong Kong. *The International Journal of Emotional Education, 3,* 30–47.

Kam, C.-M., Greenberg, M. T., Bierman, K. L., Coie, J. D., Dodge, K. A., Foster, M. E., . . . Pinderhughes, E. E. (2011). Maternal depressive symptoms and child social preference during the early school years: Mediation by maternal warmth and child emotion regulation. *Journal of Abnormal Child Psychology, 39,* 365–377. doi:10.1007/s10802-010-9468-0

Kaminski, J., Call, J., & Fischer, J. (2004, June 11). Word learning in a domestic dog: Evidence for "fast mapping." *Science, 304,* 1682–1683.

Kanazawa, S. (2015). Breastfeeding is positively associated with child intelligence even net of parental IQ. *Developmental Psychology, 51*(12), 1683–1689.

Kann, L., Olsen, E. O., McManus, T., Harris, W. A., Shanklin, S. L., Flint, K. H., . . . Zaza, S. (2016, August 12). Sexual identity, sex of sexual contacts, and health-related behaviors among students in grades 9–12—United States and selected sites, 2015. *Surveillance Summaries, 65*(9), 1–202.

Kanner, A. D., Feldman, S. S., Weinberger, D. A., & Ford, M. E. (1987). Uplifts, hassles, and adaptational outcomes in early adolescents. *Journal of Early Adolescence, 7,* 371–394. doi:10.1177/0272431687074002

Kaplan, H., & Dove, H. (1987). Infant development among the Ache of eastern Paraguay. *Developmental Psychology, 23,* 190–198. doi:10.1037/0012-1649.23.2.190

Karasik, L. B., Tamis-LeMonda, C. S., Adolph, K. E., & Bornstein, M. H. (2015). Places and postures: A cross-cultural comparison of sitting in 5-month-olds. *Journal of Cross-Cultural Psychology, 46,* 1023–1038.

Karevold, E., Roysamb, E., Ystrom, E., & Mathiesen, K. S. (2009). Predictors and pathways from infancy to symptoms of anxiety and depression in early adolescence. *Developmental Psychology, 45,* 1051–1060. doi:10.1037/a0016123

Karmiloff-Smith, A., Broadbent, H., Farran, E. K., Longhi, E., D'Souza, D., Metcalfe, K., . . . Sansbury, F. (2012). Social cognition in Williams syndrome: Genotype/phenotype insights from partial deletion patients. *Frontiers in Psychology, 3.* Advance online publication. doi:10.3389/fpsyg.2012.00168

Karriker-Jaffe, K. J., Foshee, V. A., Ennett, S. T., & Suchindran, C. (2008). The development of aggression during adolescence: Sex differences in trajectories of physical and social aggression among youth in rural areas. *Journal of Abnormal Child Psychology, 36,* 1227–1236. doi:10.1007/s10802-008-9245-5

Kärtner, J., Keller, H., & Chaudhary, N. (2010). Cognitive and social influences on early prosocial behavior in two sociocultural contexts. *Developmental Psychology, 46,* 905–914. doi:10.1037/a0019718

Katz, C., Barnetz, Z., & Hershkowitz, I. (2014). The effect of drawing on children's experiences of investigations following alleged child abuse. *Child Abuse & Neglect, 38*(5), 858–867.

Katz, L. F., Hunter, E., & Klowden, A. (2008). Intimate partner violence and children's reaction to peer provocation: The moderating role of emotion coaching. *Journal of Family Psychology, 22,* 614–621. doi:10.1037/a0012793

Katz, L. F., & Low, S. M. (2004). Marital violence, co-parenting, and family-level processes in relation to children's adjustment. *Journal of Family Psychology, 18,* 372–382. doi:10.1037/0893-3200.18.2.372

Katz, L. F., Maliken, A. C., & Stettler, N. M. (2012). Parental meta-emotion philosophy: A review of research and theoretical framework. *Child Development Perspectives, 6,* 417–422. doi:10.1111/j.1750-8606.2012.00244.x

Katz, P. A., & Ksansnak, K. R. (1994). Developmental aspects of gender role flexibility and traditionality in middle childhood and adolescence. *Developmental Psychology, 30,* 272–282. doi:10.1037/0012-1649.30.2.272

Katz, S. J., Conway, C. C., Hammen, C. L., Brennan, P. A., & Najman, J. M. (2011). Childhood social withdrawal, interpersonal impairment, and young adult depression: A mediational model. *Journal of Abnormal Child Psychology, 39,* 1227–1238. doi:10.1007/s10802-011-9537-z

Kaufman, A. S., Raiford, S. E., & Coalson, D. L. (2016). *Intelligence testing with WISC-V.* Hoboken, NJ: Wiley.

Kaul, Y. F., Rosander, K., von Hofsten, C., Brodd, K. S., Holmström, G., Kaul, A., . . . Hellström-Westas, L. (2016). Visual tracking in very preterm infants at 4 mo predicts neurodevelopment at 3 y of age. *Pediatric Research.* doi:10.1038/pr.2016.37

Kavanaugh, R. D., & Engel, S. (1998). The development of pretense and narrative in early childhood. In O. N. Saracho & B. Spodek (Eds.), *Multiple perspectives on play in early childhood education* (pp. 80–99). Albany: State University of New York Press.

Kawabata, Y., & Crick, N. R. (2008). The role of cross-racial/ethnic friendships in social adjustment. *Developmental Psychology, 44,* 1177–1183. doi:10.1037/0012-1649.44.4.1177

Kawabata, Y., & Crick, N. R. (2011). The significance of cross-racial/ethnic friendships: Associations with peer victimization, peer support, sociometric status, and classroom diversity. *Developmental Psychology, 47,* 1763–1775. doi:10.1037/a0025399

Kawabata, Y., Crick, N. R., & Hamaguchi, Y. (2010). Forms of aggression, social-psychological adjustment, and peer victimization in a Japanese sample: The moderating role of positive and negative friendship quality. *Journal of Abnormal Child Psychology, 38,* 471–484. doi:10.1007/s10802-010-9386-1

Kaye, K. L., & Bower, T. G. R. (1994). Learning and intermodal transfer of information in newborns. *Psychological Science, 5,* 286–288. doi:10.1111/j.1467-9280.1994.tb00627.x

Kearins, J. M. (1981). Visual spatial memory in Australian Aboriginal children of desert regions. *Cognitive Psychology, 13,* 434–460.

Kearney, M. S., & Levine, P. B. (2015). *Early childhood education by MOOC: Lessons from Sesame Street* (Report No. w21229). Cambridge, Massachusetts: National Bureau of Economic Research. doi:10.3386/w21229

Keates, J., Graham, S. A., & Ganea, P. A. (2014). Infants transfer nonobvious properties from pictures to real-world objects. *Journal of Experimental Child Psychology, 125,* 35–47.

Keating, D. P., & Clark, L. V. (1980). Development of physical and social reasoning in adolescence. *Developmental Psychology, 16,* 23–30. doi:10.1037/0012-1649.16.1.23

Keen, R. E., & Berthier, N. E. (2004). Continuities and discontinuities in infants' representation of objects and events. In V. K. Robert (Ed.), *Advances in child development and behavior* (Vol. 32, pp. 243–279). San Diego, CA: Elsevier.

Keenan, K., Loeber, R., Zhang, Q., Stouthamer-Loeber, M., & van Kammen, W. B. (1995). The influence of deviant peers on the development of boys' disruptive and delinquent behavior: A temporal analysis. *Development and Psychopathology, 7,* 715–726. doi:10.1017/S0954579400006805

Keenan, K., Wroblewski, K., Hipwell, A., Loeber, R., & Stouthamer-Loeber, M. (2010). Age of onset, symptom threshold, and expansion of the nosology of conduct disorder for girls. *Journal of Abnormal Psychology, 119,* 689–698. doi:10.1037/a0019346

Keil, F. C. (1979). *Semantic and conceptual development: An ontological perspective.* Cambridge, MA: Harvard University Press.

Keil, F. C. (1992). The origins of an autonomous biology. In M. R. Gunnar & M. Maratsos (Eds.), *Minnesota Symposia on Child Psychology: Vol. 25. Modularity and constraints in language and cognition* (pp. 103–137). Hillsdale, NJ: Erlbaum.

Keiley, M. K., Bates, J. E., Dodge, K. A., & Pettit, G. S. (2000). A cross-domain growth analysis: Externalizing and internalizing behaviors during 8 years of childhood. *Journal of Abnormal Child Psychology, 28,* 161–179. doi:10.1023/A:1005122814723

Kelemen, D., & DiYanni, C. (2005). Intuitions about origins: Purpose and intelligent design in children's reasoning about nature. *Journal of Cognition and Development, 6,* 3–31. doi:10.1207/s15327647jcd0601_2

Kelemen, D., Emmons, N. A., Schillaci, R. S., & Ganea, P. A. (2014). Young children can be taught basic natural selection using a picture-storybook intervention. *Psychological Science, 25*(4), 893–902. doi:10.1177/0956797613516009

Kell, H. J., Lubinski, D., & Benbow, C. P. (2013). Who rises to the top? Early indicators. *Psychological Science, 24*(5), 648–659. doi:10.1177/0956797612457784

Keller, P. S., Cummings, E. M., Davies, P. T., & Mitchell, P. M. (2008). Longitudinal relations between parental drinking problems, family functioning, and child adjustment. *Development and Psychopathology, 20,* 195–212. doi:10.1017/S0954579408000096

Kellis, M., Wold, B., Snyder, M. P., Bernstein, B. E., Kundaje, A., Marinov, G. K., . . . Dunham, I. (2014). Defining functional DNA elements in the human genome. *Proceedings of the National Academy of Sciences, 111*(17), 6131–6138.

Kellman, P. J., & Spelke, E. S. (1983). Perception of partly occluded objects in infancy. *Cognitive Psychology, 15,* 483–524. doi:10.1016/0010-0285(83)90017-8

Kelly, D. J., Liu, S., Ge, L., Quinn, P. C., Slater, A. M., Lee, K., . . . Pascalis, O. (2007). Cross-race preferences for same-race faces extend beyond the African versus Caucasian contrast in 3-month-old infants. *Infancy, 11,* 87–95.

Kelly, D. J., Liu, S., Lee, K., Quinn, P. C., Pascalis, O., Slater, A. M., & Ge, L. (2009). Development of the other-race effect during infancy: Evidence toward universality? *Journal of Experimental Child Psychology, 104,* 105–114. doi:10.1016/j.jecp.2009.01.006

Kelly, D. J., Quinn, P. C., Slater, A. M., Lee, K., Ge, L., & Pascalis, O. (2007). The other-race effect develops during infancy: Evidence of perceptual narrowing. *Psychological Science, 18,* 1084–1089. doi:10.1111/j.1467-9280.2007.02029.x

Kelly, D. J., Quinn, P. C., Slater, A. M., Lee, K., Gibson, A., Smith, M., . . . Pascalis, O. (2005). Three-month-olds, but not newborns, prefer own-race faces. *Developmental Science, 8,* F31-F36. doi:10.1111/j.1467-7687.2005.0434a.x

Kennedy, S., & Bumpass, L. (2008). Cohabitation and children's living arrangements: New estimates from the United States. *Demographic Research, 19,* 1663–1692. doi:10.4054/DemRes.2008.19.47

Kenrick, D. T., Trost, M. R., & Sundie, J. M. (2004). Sex roles as adaptations: An evolutionary perspective on gender differences and similarities. In A. H. Eagly, A. E. Beall, & R. J. Sternberg (Eds.), *The psychology of gender* (2nd ed., pp. 65–91). New York, NY: Guilford Press.

Kenyon, D. B., & Koerner, S. S. (2008). Post-divorce maternal disclosure and the father–adolescent relationship: Adolescent emotional autonomy and inter-reactivity as moderators. *Journal of Child and Family Studies, 17,* 791–808. doi:10.1007/s10826-008-9190-5

Kerig, P. K., Chaplo, S. D., Bennett, D. C., & Modrowski, C. A. (2016). "Harm as harm": Gang membership, perpetration trauma, and posttraumatic stress symptoms among youth in the juvenile justice system. *Criminal Justice and Behavior, 43,* 635–652. doi:10.1177/0093854815607307

Kerns, K. A., Abraham, M. M., Schlegelmilch, A., & Morgan, T. A. (2007). Mother–child attachment in later middle childhood: Assessment approaches and associations with mood and emotion regulation. *Attachment and Human Development, 9,* 33–53. doi:10.1080/14616730601151441

Kerns, K. A., Klepac, L., & Cole, A. (1996). Peer relationships and preadolescents' perceptions of security in the child-mother relationship. *Developmental Psychology, 32,* 457–466. doi:10.1037/0012-1649.32.3.457

Kerr, M., Stattin, H., & Özdemir, M. (2012). Perceived parenting style and adolescent adjustment: Revisiting directions of effects and the role of parental knowledge. *Developmental Psychology, 48,* 1540–1553. doi:10.1037/a0027720

Kessels, U. (2015). Bridging the gap by enhancing the fit: How stereotypes about STEM clash with stereotypes about girls. International *Journal of Gender, Science, & Technology, 7,* 280–296.

Kessels, U., & Steinmayr, R. (2013). Macho-man in school: Toward the role of gender role self-concepts and help seeking in school performance. *Learning and Individual Differences, 23,* 234–240.

Kessen, W. (1965). *The child.* New York, NY: Wiley.

Kestenbaum, R., Farber, E. A., & Sroufe, L. A. (1989). Individual differences in empathy among preschoolers: Relation to attachment history. In N. Eisenberg (Ed.), *New Directions for Child and Adolescent Development: No. 44. Empathy and related emotional responses* (pp. 51–64). San Francisco, CA: Jossey-Bass.

Kety, S. S., Wender, P. H., Jacobsen, B., Ingraham, L. J., Jansson, L., Faber, B., & Kinney, D. K. (1994). Mental illness in the biological and adoptive relatives of schizophrenic adoptees: Replication of the Copenhagen Study in the rest of Denmark. *Archives of General Psychiatry, 51,* 442–455.

Keys, T. D., Farkas, G., Burchinal, M. R., Duncan, G. J., Vandell, D. L., Li, W., . . . Howes, C. (2013). Preschool center quality and school readiness: Quality effects and variation by demographic and child characteristics. *Child Development, 84,* 1171–1190. doi:10.1111/cdev.12048

Khaleque, A., & Rohner, R. P. (2012). Pancultural associations between perceived parental acceptance and psychological adjustment of children and adults: A meta-analytic review of worldwide research. *Journal of Cross-Cultural Psychology, 43*(5), 784–800. doi:10.1177/0022022111406120

Kiang, L., & Harter, S. (2008). Do pieces of the self-puzzle fit? Integrated/fragmented selves in biculturally-identified Chinese Americans. *Journal of Research in Personality, 42,* 1657–1662. doi:10.1016/j.jrp.2008.07.010

Kiang, L., Yip, T., & Fuligni, A. J. (2008). Multiple social identities and adjustment in young adults from ethnically diverse backgrounds. *Journal of Research on Adolescence, 18,* 643–670. doi:10.1111/j.1532-7795.2008.00575.x

Kiang, L., Yip, T., Gonzales-Backen, M., Witkow, M., & Fuligni, A. J. (2006). Ethnic identity and the daily psychological well-being of adolescents from Mexican and Chinese backgrounds. *Child Development, 77,* 1338–1350.

Kidd, B. (2013). Sports and masculinity. *Sport in Society, 16,* 553–564.

Kidd, C., Piantadosi, S. T., & Aslin, R. N. (2012). The Goldilocks effect: Human infants allocate attention to visual sequences that are neither too simple nor too complex. *PLoS ONE, 7*(5), e36399. doi:10.1371/journal.pone.0036399

Kidd, C., Piantadosi, S. T., & Aslin, R. N. (2014). The Goldilocks effect in infant auditory attention. *Child Development, 85*(5), 1795–1804.

Kiesner, J., Poulin, F., & Dishion, T. J. (2010). Adolescent substance use with friends: Moderating and mediating effects of parental monitoring and peer activity contexts. *Merrill Palmer Quarterly, 56,* 529–556.

Kiesner, J., Poulin, F., & Nicotra, E. (2003). Peer relations across contexts: Individual-network homophily and network inclusion in and after school. *Child Development, 74,* 1328–1343. doi:10.2307/3696181

Kiff, C. J., Lengua, L. J., & Bush, N. R. (2011). Temperament variation in sensitivity to parenting: Predicting changes in depression and anxiety. *Journal of Abnormal Child Psychology, 39,* 1199–1212. doi:10.1007/s10802-011-9539-x

Kiff, C. J., Lengua, L. J., & Zalewski, M. (2011). Nature and nurturing: Parenting in the context of child temperament. *Clinical Child and Family Psychology Review, 14,* 251–301. doi:10.1007/s10567-011-0093-4

Killen, M. (2007). Children's social and moral reasoning about exclusion. *Current Directions in Psychological Science, 16,* 32–36. doi:10.1111/j.1467-8721.2007.00470.x

Killen, M., & Smetana, J. G. (2015). Origins and development of morality. In M. E. Lamb (Ed.) & R. M. Lerner (Series Ed.), *Handbook of child psychology and developmental science, Vol. 3* (7th ed., pp. 701–749). Hoboken, NJ: Wiley.

Killen, M., & Stangor, C. (2001). Children's social reasoning about inclusion and exclusion in gender and race peer group contexts. *Child Development, 72,* 174–186. doi:10.2307/1132478

Killen, M., & Turiel, E. (1998). Adolescents' and young adults' evaluations of helping and sacrificing for others. *Journal of Research on Adolescence, 8,* 355–375. doi:10.1207/s15327795jra0803_4

Kim, E. Y., & Song, H. J. (2015). Six-month-olds actively predict others' goal-directed actions. *Cognitive Development, 33,* 1–13.

Kim, H. K., Capaldi, D. M., & Stoolmiller, M. (2003). Depressive symptoms across adolescence and young adulthood in men: Predictions from parental and contextual risk factors. *Development and Psychopathology, 15,* 469–495.

Kim, I. K., & Spelke, E. S. (1992). Infants' sensitivity to effects of gravity on visible object motion. *Journal of Experimental Psychology: Human Perception and Performance, 18,* 385–393. doi:10.1037/0096-1523.18.2.385

Kim, J.-Y., McHale, S. M., Wayne Osgood, D., & Crouter, A. C. (2006). Longitudinal course and family correlates of sibling relationships from childhood through adolescence. *Child Development, 77,* 1746–1761. doi:10.1111/j.1467-8624.2006.00971.x

Kim, K. H., Relkin, N. R., Lee, K. M., & Hirsch, J. (1997, July 10). Distinct cortical areas associated with native and second languages. *Nature, 388,* 171–174.

Kim, K. J., Conger, R. D., Lorenz, F. O., & Elder, G. H., Jr. (2001). Parent–adolescent reciprocity in negative affect and its relation to early adult social development. *Developmental Psychology, 37,* 775–790. doi:10.1037/0012-1649.37.6.775

Kim, P., Evans, G. W., Angstadt, M., Ho, S. S., Sripada, C. S., Swain, J. E., . . . Phan, K. L. (2013). Effects of childhood poverty and chronic stress on emotion regulatory brain function in adulthood. *Proceedings of the National Academy of Sciences, 110*(46), 18442–18447. doi:10.1073/pnas.1308240110

Kim, S., Nordling, J. K., Yoon, J. E., Boldt, L. J., & Kochanska, G. (2013). Effortful control in "hot" and "cool" tasks differentially predicts children's behavior problems and academic performance. *Journal of Abnormal Child Psychology, 41*(1), 43–56. doi:10.1007/s10802-012-9661-4

Kindermann, T. A. (2007). Effects of naturally existing peer groups on changes in academic engagement in a cohort of sixth graders. *Child Development, 78,* 1186–1203. doi:10.1111/j.1467-8624.2007.01060.x

King, V. (2007). When children have two mothers: Relationships with nonresident mothers, stepmothers, and fathers. *Journal of Marriage and Family, 69,* 1178–1193. doi:10.1111/j.1741-3737.2007.00440.x

King, V. (2009). Stepfamily formation: Implications for adolescent ties to mothers, nonresident fathers, and stepfathers. *Journal of Marriage and Family, 71,* 954–968. doi:10.1111/j.1741-3737.2009.00646.x

Kingery, J. N., Erdley, C. A., & Marshall, K. C. (2011). Peer acceptance and friendship as predictors of early adolescents' adjustment across the middle school transition. *Merrill-Palmer Quarterly, 57,* 215–243.

Kinzler, K. D., Dupoux, E., & Spelke, E. S. (2007). The native language of social cognition. *Proceedings of the National Academy of Sciences of the United States of America, 104,* 12577–12580. doi:10.1073/pnas.0705345104

Kirkham, N. Z., Slemmer, J. A., & Johnson, S. P. (2002). Visual statistical learning in infancy: Evidence for a domain general learning mechanism. *Cognition, 83,* B35-B42. doi:10.1016/S0010-0277(02)00004-5

Kisilevsky, B. S., Fearon, I., & Muir, D. W. (1998). Fetuses differentiate vibroacoustic stimuli. *Infant Behavior and Development, 21,* 25–46.

Kisilevsky, B. S., Hains, S. M., Lee, K., Xie, X., Huang, H., Ye, H. H., . . . Wang, Z. (2003). Effects of experience on fetal voice recognition. *Psychological Science, 14,* 220–224.

Kiuru, N., Nurmi, J.-E., Aunola, K., & Salmela-Aro, K. (2009). Peer group homogeneity in adolescents' school adjustment varies according to peer group type and gender. *International Journal of Behavioral Development, 33,* 65–76. doi:10.1177/0165025408098014

Klahr, D. (1978). Goal formation, planning, and learning by pre-school problem solvers or: "My socks are in the dryer." In R. Siegler (Ed.), *Children's thinking: What develops?* (pp. 181–212). Hillsdale, NJ: Erlbaum.

Klein, D. N., Kujawa, A. J., Black, S. R., & Pennock, A. T. (2013). Depressive disorders. In T. P. Beauchaine & S. P. Hinshaw (Eds.), *Child and adolescent psychopathology* (2nd ed., pp. 543–575). New York, NY: Wiley.

Klima, T., & Repetti, R. L. (2008). Children's peer relations and their psychological adjustment: Differences between close friendships and the larger peer group. *Merrill-Palmer Quarterly, 54,* 151–178.

Klimes-Dougan, B., Brand, A. E., Zahn-Waxler, C., Usher, B., Hastings, P. D., Kendziora, K., & Garside, R. B. (2007). Parental emotion socialization in adolescence: Differences in sex, age and problem status. *Social Development, 16,* 326–342.

Klimes-Dougan, B., & Kopp, C. B. (1999). Children's conflict tactics with mothers: A longitudinal investigation of the toddler and preschool years. *Merrill-Palmer Quarterly, 45,* 226–241.

Klin, A., Jones, W., Schultz, R., & Volkmar, F. (2004). The enactive mind, or from actions to cognition: Lessons from autism. In U. Frith & E. L. Hill (Eds.), *Autism, mind, and brain* (pp. 127–160). Oxford, England: Oxford University Press.

Knafo, A., & Israel, S. (2010). Genetic and environmental influences on prosocial behavior. In M. Mikulincer & P. R. Shaver (Eds.), *Prosocial motives, emotions, and behavior: The better angels of our nature* (pp. 149–167). Washington, DC: American Psychological Association.

Knafo, A., & Israel, S. (2012). Empathy, prosocial behavior, and other aspects of kindness. In M. R. Zentner & R. L. Shiner (Eds.), *Handbook of temperament* (pp. 168–182). New York, NY: Guilford Press.

Knafo, A., & Jaffee, S. R. (2013). Gene–environment correlation in developmental psychopathology. *Development and Psychopathology, 25*(01), 1–6.

Knafo, A., & Plomin, R. (2006a). Parental discipline and affection and children's prosocial behavior: Genetic and environmental links. *Journal of Personality and Social Psychology, 90,* 147–164. doi:10.1037/0022-3514.90.1.147

Knafo, A., & Plomin, R. (2006b). Prosocial behavior from early to middle childhood: Genetic and environmental influences on stability and change. *Developmental Psychology, 42,* 771–786. doi:10.1037/0012-1649.42.5.771

Knafo, A., Zahn-Waxler, C., Van Hulle, C., Robinson, J. L., & Rhee, S. H. (2008). The developmental origins of a disposition toward empathy: Genetic and environmental contributions. *Emotion, 8,* 737–752. doi:10.1037/a0014179

Knecht, A., Snijders, T. A. B., Baerveldt, C., Steglich, C. E. G., & Raub, W. (2010). Friendship and delinquency: Selection and influence processes in early adolescence. *Social Development, 19,* 494–514. doi:10.1111/j.1467-9507.2009.00564.x

Knecht, A. B., Burk, W. J., Weesie, J., & Steglich, C. (2011). Friendship and alcohol use in early adolescence: A multilevel social network approach. *Journal of Research on Adolescence, 21,* 475–487. doi:10.1111/j.1532-7795.2010.00685.x

Knight, G. P., Cota, M. K., & Bernal, M. E. (1993). The socialization of cooperative, competitive, and individualistic preferences among Mexican American children: The mediating role of ethnic identity. *Hispanic Journal of Behavioral Sciences, 15,* 291–309. doi:10.1177/07399863930153001

Knight, G. P., Fabes, R. A., & Higgins, D. A. (1996). Concerns about drawing causal inferences from meta-analyses: An example in the study of gender differences in aggression. *Psychological Bulletin, 119,* 410–421. doi:10.1037/0033-2909.119.3.410

Knudsen, E. I., Heckman, J. J., Cameron, J. L., & Shonkoff, J. P. (2006). Economic, neurobiological, and behavioral perspectives on building America's future workforce. *Proceedings of the National Academy of Sciences of the United States of America, 103,* 10155–10162. doi:10.1073/pnas.0600888103

Kobasigawa, A., Ransom, C. C., & Holland, C. J. (1980). Children's knowledge about skimming. *Alberta Journal of Educational Research, 26,* 169–182.

Kobiella, A., Grossmann, T., Reid, V. M., & Striano, T. (2008). The discrimination of angry and fearful facial expressions in 7-month-old infants: An event-related potential study. *Cognition and Emotion, 22,* 134–146.

Kochanska, G. (1993). Toward a synthesis of parental socialization and child temperament in early development of conscience. *Child Development, 64,* 325–347. doi:10.2307/1131254

Kochanska, G. (1997). Mutually responsive orientation between mothers and their young children: Implications for early socialization. *Child Development, 68,* 94–112. doi:10.2307/1131928

Kochanska, G. (2001). Emotional development in children with different attachment histories: The first three years. *Child Development, 72,* 474–490.

Kochanska, G. (2002). Committed compliance, moral self, and internalization: A mediational model. *Developmental Psychology, 38,* 339–351. doi:10.1037/0012-1649.38.3.339

Kochanska, G., & Aksan, N. (2006). Children's conscience and self-regulation. *Journal of Personality, 74,* 1587–1618. doi:10.1111/j.1467-6494.2006.00421.x

Kochanska, G., Aksan, N., & Joy, M. E. (2007). Children's fearfulness as a moderator of parenting in early socialization: Two longitudinal studies. *Developmental Psychology, 43,* 222–237. doi:10.1037/0012-1649.43.1.222

Kochanska, G., Aksan, N., Penney, S. J., & Doobay, A. F. (2007). Early positive emotionality as a heterogeneous trait: Implications for children's self-regulation. *Journal of Personality and Social Psychology, 93,* 1054–1066.

Kochanska, G., Barry, R. A., Aksan, N., & Boldt, L. J. (2008). A developmental model of maternal and child contributions to disruptive conduct: The first six years. *Journal of Child Psychology and Psychiatry, 49,* 1220–1227. doi:10.1111/j.1469-7610.2008.01932.x

Kochanska, G., Barry, R. A., Stellern, S. A., & O'Bleness, J. J. (2009). Early attachment organization moderates the parent–child mutually coercive pathway to children's antisocial conduct. *Child Development, 80,* 1288–1300. doi:10.1111/j.1467-8624.2009.01332.x

Kochanska, G., Coy, K. C., & Murray, K. T. (2001). The development of self-regulation in the first four years of life. *Child Development, 72,* 1091–1111.

Kochanska, G., Forman, D. R., Aksan, N., & Dunbar, S. B. (2005). Pathways to conscience: Early mother–child mutually responsive orientation and children's moral emotion, conduct, and cognition. *Journal of Child Psychology and Psychiatry, 46,* 19–34. doi:10.1111/j.1469-7610.2004.00348.x

Kochanska, G., Gross, J. N., Lin, M. H., & Nichols, K. E. (2002). Guilt in young children: Development, determinants, and relations with a broader system of standards. *Child Development, 73,* 461–482. doi:10.1111/1467-8624.00418

Kochanska, G., & Kim, S. (2012). Toward a new understanding of legacy of early attachments for future antisocial trajectories: Evidence from two longitudinal studies. *Development and Psychopathology, 24,* 783–806. doi:10.1017/S0954579412000375

Kochanska, G., & Kim, S. (2013). Early attachment organization with both parents and future behavior problems: From infancy to middle childhood. *Child Development, 84,* 283–296. doi:10.1111/j.1467-8624.2012.01852.x

Kochanska, G., Kim, S., Barry, R. A., & Philibert, R. A. (2011). Children's genotypes interact with maternal responsive care in predicting children's competence: Diathesis–stress or differential susceptibility? *Development and Psychopathology, 23,* 605–616. doi:10.1017/S0954579411000071

Kochanska, G., Koenig, J. L., Barry, R. A., Kim, S., & Yoon, J. E. (2010). Children's conscience during toddler and preschool years, moral self, and a competent, adaptive developmental trajectory. *Developmental Psychology, 46,* 1320–1332. doi:10.1037/a0020381

Kochanska, G., Murray, K. T., & Harlan, E. T. (2000). Effortful control in early childhood: Continuity and change, antecedents, and implications for social development. *Developmental Psychology, 36,* 220–232.

Kochanska, G., Philibert, R. A., & Barry, R. A. (2009). Interplay of genes and early mother–child relationship in the development of self-regulation from toddler to preschool age. *Journal of Child Psychology and Psychiatry, 50,* 1331–1338. doi:10.1111/j.1469-7610.2008.02050.x

Kochel, K. P., Ladd, G. W., & Rudolph, K. D. (2012). Longitudinal associations among youth depressive symptoms, peer victimization, and low peer acceptance: An interpersonal process perspective. *Child Development, 83,* 637–650.

Kochenderfer, B. J., & Ladd, G. W. (1996). Peer victimization: Cause or consequence of school maladjustment? *Child Development, 67,* 1305–1317. doi:10.2307/1131701

Koenig, M. A., & Harris, P. L. (2005). Preschoolers mistrust ignorant and inaccurate speakers. *Child Development, 76,* 1261–1277. doi:10.1111/j.1467-8624.2005.00849.x

Koenig, M. A., & Woodward, A. L. (2010). Sensitivity of 24-month-olds to the prior inaccuracy of the source: Possible mechanisms.

Developmental Psychology, 46, 815–826. doi:10.1037/a0019664

Kohen, D. E., Leventhal, T., Dahinten, V. S., & McIntosh, C. N. (2008). Neighborhood disadvantage: Pathways of effects for young children. *Child Development, 79*, 156–169. doi:10.1111/j.1467-8624.2007.01117.x

Kohlberg, L. (1966). A cognitive-developmental analysis of children's sex-role concepts and attitudes. In E. E. Maccoby (Ed.), *The development of sex differences* (Vol. 5, pp. 82–173). Palo Alto, CA: Stanford University Press.

Kohlberg, L. (1969). Stage and sequence: The cognitive-developmental approach to socialization. In D. A. Goslin (Ed.), *Handbook of socialization theory and research* (pp. 347–480). New York, NY: Rand McNally.

Kohlberg, L. (1976). Moral stages and moralization: The cognitive--developmental approach. In T. Lickona (Ed.), *Moral development and behavior: Theory, research, and social issues* (pp. 31–53). New York, NY: Holt, Rinehart and Winston.

Kohlberg, L. (1978). Revisions in the theory and practice of moral development. In W. Damon (Ed.), *New Directions for Child and Adolescent Development: No. 2. Moral development* (Vol. 1978, pp. 83–87). San Francisco, CA: Jossey-Bass.

Kohlberg, L., & Candee, D. (1984). The relationship of moral judgment to moral action. In W. M. Kurtines & J. L. Gewirtz (Eds.), *Morality, moral behavior, and moral development* (pp. 52–73). New York, NY: Wiley.

Kolb, B. (1995). *Brain plasticity and behavior.* Mahwah, NJ: Erlbaum.

Kolb, B., & Whishaw, I. Q. (1996). *Fundamentals of human neuropsychology* (4th ed.). New York: Freeman.

Koleva, S., Selterman, D., Kang, H., & Graham, J. (2014, August 23). Beyond Kohlberg vs. Gilligan: Empathy and disgust sensitivity mediate gender differences in moral judgments. Retrieved from *Social Science Research Network* website: http://ssrn.com/abstract=2486030 . doi:10.2139/ssrn.2486030

Kopp, C. B. (1989). Regulation of distress and negative emotions: A developmental view. *Developmental Psychology, 25*, 343–354. doi:10.1037/0012-1649.25.3.343

Kopp, C. B. (1990). Risks in infancy: Appraising the research. *Merrill-Palmer Quarterly, 36*, 117–140.

Kopp, C. B. (1992). Emotional distress and control in young children. In R. A. Fabes & N. Eisenberg (Eds.), *New Directions for Child and Adolescent Development: No. 55. Emotion and its regulation in early development* (Vol. 1992, pp. 41–56). San Francisco, CA: Jossey-Bass.

Kopp, C. B. (2001). Self-regulation in childhood. In N. J. Smelser & P. B. Baltes (Eds.), *International encyclopedia of the social and behavioral sciences* (pp. 13862–13866). London, England: Elsevier.

Kopp, C. B., & Kaler, S. R. (1989). Risk in infancy: Origins and implications. *American Psychologist, 44*, 224–230.

Korenman, S., Miller, J. E., & Sjaastad, J. E. (1995). Long-term poverty and child development in the United States: Results from the NLSY [Special Issue on Child Poverty, Public Practices, and Welfare Reform]. *Children and Youth Services Review, 17*, 127–155.

Korner, A. F., & Thoman, E. B. (1970). Visual alertness in neonates as evoked by maternal care. *Journal of Experimental Child Psychology, 10*, 67–78.

Kortenhaus, C. M., & Demarest, J. (1993). Gender role stereotyping in children's literature: An update. *Sex Roles, 28*, 219–232. doi:10.1007/BF00299282

Kouros, C. D., Cummings, E. M., & Davies, P. T. (2010). Early trajectories of interparental conflict and externalizing problems as predictors of social competence in preadolescence. *Development and Psychopathology, 22*, 527–537.

Koutamanis, M., Vossen, H. G. M., Peter, J., & Valkenberg, P. M. (2013). Practice makes perfect: The longitudinal effect of adolescents' instant messaging on their ability to initiate offline friendships. *Computers in Human Behavior, 29*, 2265–2272. doi:10.1016/j.chb.2013.04.033

Kovács, Á. M., & Mehler, J. (2009a). Cognitive gains in 7-month-old bilingual infants. *Proceedings of the National Academy of Sciences of the United States of America, 106*, 6556–6560. doi:10.1073/pnas.0811323106

Kovács, Á. M., & Mehler, J. (2009b, July 31). Flexible learning of multiple speech structures in bilingual infants. *Science, 325*, 611–612.

Kovas, Y., & Plomin, R. (2007). Learning abilities and disabilities: Generalist genes, specialist environments. *Current Directions in Psychological Science, 16*, 284–288. doi:10.1111/j.1467-8721.2007.00521.x

Kovas, Y., Voronin, I., Kaydalov, A., Malykh, S. B., Dale, P. S., & Plomin, R. (2013). Literacy and numeracy are more heritable than intelligence in primary school. *Psychological Science, 24*(10), 2048–2056.

Kowal, A., & Kramer, L. (1997). Children's understanding of parental differential treatment. *Child Development, 68*, 113–126. doi:10.1111/j.1467-8624.1997.tb01929.x

Kowal, A. K., Krull, J. L., & Kramer, L. (2004). How the differential treatment of siblings is linked with parent–child relationship quality. *Journal of Family Psychology, 18*, 658–665. doi:10.1037/0893-3200.18.4.658

Kowalski, R. M., Giumetti, G. W., Schroeder, A. N., & Lattanner, M. R. (2014). Bullying in the digital age: A critical review and meta-analysis of cyberbullying research among youth. *Psychological Bulletin, 140*, 1073–1137. doi:10.1037/a0035618

Kraak, V. I., & Story, M. (2015). Influence of food companies' brand mascots and entertainment companies' cartoon media characters on children's diet and health: A systematic review and research needs. *Obesity Reviews, 16*(2), 107–126.

Kramer, M. S., Aboud, F., Mironova, E., Vanilovich, I., Platt, R. W., Matush, L., . . . Shapiro, S. (2008). Breastfeeding and child cognitive development: New evidence from a large randomized trial. *Archives of General Psychiatry, 65*, 578–584. doi:10.1001/archpsyc.65.5.578

Krapohl, E., & Plomin, R. (2016). Genetic link between family socioeconomic status and children's educational achievement estimated from genome-wide SNPs. *Molecular Psychiatry, 21*(3), 437–443.

Krapohl, E., Rimfeld, K., Shakeshaft, N. G., Trzaskowski, M., McMillan, A., Pingault, J. B., . . . Plomin, R. (2014). The high heritability of educational achievement reflects many genetically influenced traits, not just intelligence. *Proceedings of the National Academy of Sciences, 111*(42), 15273–15278. doi:10.1073/pnas.1408777111

Krascum, R. M., & Andrews, S. (1998). The effects of theories on children's acquisition of family-resemblance categories. *Child Development, 69*, 333–346. doi:10.1111/j.1467-8624.1998.tb06192.x

Kraus, N., & Chandrasekaran, B. (2010). Music training for the development of auditory skills. *Nature Reviews Neuroscience, 11*(8), 599–605.

Kraut, R., Patterson, M., Lundmark, V., Kiesler, S., Mukophadhyay, T., & Scherlis, W. (1998). Internet paradox: A social technology that reduces social involvement and psychological well-being? *American Psychologist, 53*, 1017–1031. doi:10.1037/0003-066X.53.9.1017

Kreager, D. A. (2007). When it's good to be "bad": Violence and adolescent peer acceptance. *Criminology, 45*, 893–923. doi:10.1111/j.1745-9125.2007.00097.x

Kreider, R. M., & Ellis, R. (2011, June). Living arrangements of children: 2009: Household economic studies. *Current Population Reports.* Retrieved from http://www.census.gov/prod/2011pubs/p70-126.pdf

Kreppner, J. M., Rutter, M., Beckett, C., Castle, J., Colvert, E., Groothues, C., . . . Sonuga-Barke, E. J. (2007). Normality and impairment following profound early institutional deprivation: A longitudinal follow-up into early adolescence. *Developmental Psychology, 43,* 931–946. doi:10.1037/0012-1649.43.4.93

Krevans, J., & Gibbs, J. C. (1996). Parents' use of inductive discipline: Relations to children's empathy and prosocial behavior. *Child Development, 67,* 3263–3277. doi:10.1111/j.1467-8624.1996.tb01913.x

Kroger, J. (2006). Identity development during adolescence. In G. R. Adams & M. D. Berzonsky (Eds.), *Blackwell handbook of adolescence.* Oxford, England: Blackwell Publishing Ltd. doi:10.1002/9780470756607.ch10

Kroger, J., Martinussen, M., & Marcia, J. E. (2010). Identity status change during adolescence and young adulthood: A meta-analysis. *Journal of Adolescence, 33,* 683–698. doi:10.1016/j.adolescence.2009.11.002

Kromm, H., Färber, M., & Holodynski, M. (2015). Felt or false smiles? Volitional regulation of emotional expression in 4-, 6-, and 8-year-old children. *Child Development, 86,* 579–597. doi:10.1111/cdev.12315

Krueger, A. B. (1999). Experimental estimates of educational production functions. *Quarterly Journal of Economics, 114,* 497–532.

Krueger, R. F., South, S., Johnson, W., & Iacono, W. (2008). The heritability of personality is not always 50%: Gene-environment interactions and correlations between personality and parenting. *Journal of Personality, 76,* 1485–1522.

Kruger, A. C., & Konner, M. (2010). Who responds to crying? Maternal care and allocare among the !Kung. *Human Nature, 21,* 309–329. doi:10.1007/s12110-010-9095-z

Kruger, D. J., & Nesse, R. M. (2006). An evolutionary life-history framework for understanding sex differences in human mortality rates. *Human Nature, 17,* 74–97.

Kuczaj, S. A., II. (1977). The acquisition of regular and irregular past tense forms. *Journal of Verbal Learning and Verbal Behavior, 16,* 589–600. doi:10.1016/S0022-5371(77)80021-2

Kudo, N., Nonaka, Y., Mizuno, N., Mizuno, K., & Okanoya, K. (2011). On-line statistical segmentation of a non-speech auditory stream in neonates as demonstrated by event-related brain potentials. *Developmental Science, 14,* 1100–1106. doi:10.1111/j.1467-7687.2011.01056.x

Kuhl, P. K., Andruski, J. E., Chistovich, I. A., Chistovich, L. A., Kozhevnikova, E. V., Ryskina, V. L., . . . Lacerda, F. (1997, August 1). Cross-language analysis of phonetic units in language addressed to infants. *Science, 277,* 684–686.

Kuhl, P. K., Conboy, B. T., Coffey-Corina, S., Padden, D., Rivera-Gaxiola, M., & Nelson, T. (2008). Phonetic learning as a pathway to language: New data and native language magnet theory expanded (NLM-e). *Philosophical Transactions of the Royal Society B: Biological Sciences, 363,* 979–1000. doi:10.1098/rstb.2007.2154

Kuhl, P. K., Tsao, F.-M., & Liu, H.-M. (2003). Foreign-language experience in infancy: Effects of short-term exposure and social interaction on phonetic learning. *Proceedings of the National Academy of Sciences of the United States of America, 100,* 9096–9101. doi:10.1073/pnas.1532872100

Kuhl, P. K., Williams, K. A., Lacerda, F., Stevens, K. N., & Lindblom, B. (1992, January 31). Linguistic experience alters phonetic perception in infants by 6 months of age. *Science, 255,* 606–608.

Kuhn, D., & Franklin, S. (2006). The second decade: What develops (and how). In W. Damon & R. M. Lerner (Series Eds.) & D. Kuhn & R. Siegler (Vol. Eds.), *Handbook of child psychology: Vol. 2. Cognition, perception, and language* (6th ed., pp. 953–993). Hoboken, NJ: Wiley.

Kulkofsky, S. C., & Ceci, S. J. (2006). Intelligence, schooling, and occupational success. In J. H. Greenhaus & G. A. Callanan (Eds.), *Encyclopedia of Career Development: Vol. 2* (pp. 390–392). Thousand Oaks, CA: Sage Publications.

Kumru, A., Carlo, G., Mestre, M. V., & Samper, P. (2012). Prosocial moral reasoning and prosocial behavior among Turkish and Spanish adolescents. *Social Behavior and Personality, 40,* 205–214. doi:10.2224/sbp.2012.40.2.205

Kurdek, L. A. (1993). Predicting marital dissolution: A 5-year prospective longitudinal study of newlywed couples. *Journal of Personality and Social Psychology, 64,* 221–242. doi:10.1037/0022-3514.64.2.221

Kurdziel, L., Duclos, K., & Spencer, R. M. (2013). Sleep spindles in midday naps enhance learning in preschool children. *Proceedings of the National Academy of Sciences, 110*(43), 17267–17272. doi:10.1073/pnas.1306418110

Kuryluk, A., Cohen, R., & Audley-Piotrowski, S. (2011). The role of respect in the relation of aggression to popularity. *Social Development, 20,* 703–717. doi:10.1111/j.1467-9507.2011.00613.x

Kuschel, C. (2007). Managing drug withdrawal in the newborn infant. *Seminars in Fetal and Neonatal Medicine, 12,* 127–133. doi:10.1016/j.siny.2007.01.004

Kushnerenko, E., Teinonen, T., Volein, A., & Csibra, G. (2008). Electrophysiological evidence of illusory audiovisual speech percept in human infants. *Proceedings of the National Academy of Sciences, 105*(32), 11442–11445.

Kutnick, P. (1986). The relationship of moral judgment and moral action: Kohlberg's theory, criticism and revision. In S. Modgil & C. Modgil (Eds.), *Lawrence Kohlberg: Consensus and controversy* (pp. 125–148). Philadelphia, PA: Falmer Press.

Kwon, K., Lease, A. M., & Hoffman, L. (2012). The impact of clique membership on children's social behavior and status nominations. *Social Development, 21,* 150–169. doi:10.1111/j.1467-9507.2011.00620.x

Kyratzis, A. (2004). Talk and interaction among children and the co-construction of peer groups and peer culture. *Annual Review of Anthropology, 33,* 625–649.

La Greca, A. M., Prinstein, M. J., & Fetter, M. D. (2001). Adolescent peer crowd affiliation: Linkages with health-risk behaviors and close friendships. *Journal of Pediatric Psychology, 26,* 131–143. doi:10.1093/jpepsy/26.3.131

LaBounty, J., Wellman, H. M., Olson, S., Lagattuta, K., & Liu, D. (2008). Mothers' and fathers' use of internal state talk with their young children. *Social Development, 17,* 757–775.

Lacourse, E., Nagin, D., Tremblay, R. E., Vitaro, F., & Claes, M. (2003). Developmental trajectories of boys' delinquent group membership and facilitation of violent behaviors during adolescence. *Development and Psychopathology, 15,* 183–197. doi:10.1017.S0954579403000105

Ladd, G. W. (1992). Themes and theories: Perspectives on processes in family-peer relationships. In R. D. Parke & G. W. Ladd (Eds.), *Family-peer relationships: Modes of linkage* (pp. 1–34). Hillsdale, NJ: Erlbaum.

Ladd, G. W., & Coleman, C. C. (1997). Children's classroom peer relationships and early school attitudes: Concurrent and longitudinal associations. *Early Education and Development, 8,* 51–66. doi:10.1207/s15566935eed0801_5

Ladd, G. W., & Golter, B. S. (1988). Parents' management of preschooler's peer relations: Is it related to children's social competence? *Developmental Psychology, 24,* 109–117. doi:10.1037/0012-1649.24.1.109

Ladd, G. W., & Hart, C. H. (1992). Creating informal play opportunities: Are parents' and preschoolers' initiations related to children's competence with peers? *Developmental Psychology, 28,* 1179–1187. doi:10.1037/0012-1649.28.6.1179

Ladd, G. W., Herald-Brown, S. L., & Reiser, M. (2008). Does chronic classroom peer rejection predict the development of children's classroom participation during the grade school years? *Child Development, 79,* 1001–1015. doi:10.1111/j.1467-8624.2008.01172.x

Ladd, G. W., Kochenderfer, B. J., & Coleman, C. C. (1996). Friendship quality as a predictor of young children's early school adjustment. *Child Development, 67,* 1103–1118. doi:10.1111/j.1467-8624.1996.tb01785.x

Ladd, G. W., & Troop-Gordon, W. (2003). The role of chronic peer difficulties in the development of children's psychological adjustment problems. *Child Development, 74,* 1344–1367. doi:10.1111/1467-8624.00611

LaFreniere, P. J., & Sroufe, L. A. (1985). Profiles of peer competence in the preschool: Interrelations between measures, influence of social ecology, and relation to attachment history. *Developmental Psychology, 21,* 56–69. doi:10.1037/0012-1649.21.1.56

LaFromboise, T., Coleman, H. L., & Gerton, J. (1993). Psychological impact of biculturalism: Evidence and theory. *Psychological Bulletin, 114,* 395–412. doi:10.1037/0033-2909.114.3.395

Lagattuta, K. H. (2007). Thinking about the future because of the past: Young children's knowledge about the causes of worry and preventative decisions. *Child Development, 78,* 1492–1509.

Lagattuta, K. H., Nucci, L., & Bosacki, S. L. (2010). Bridging theory of mind and the personal domain: Children's reasoning about resistance to parental control. *Child Development, 81,* 616–635. doi:10.1111/j.1467-8624.2009.01419.x

Lagattuta, K. H., & Thompson, R. A. (2007). The development of self-conscious emotions: Cognitive processes and social influences. In J. L. Tracy, R. W. Robins, & J. P. Tangney (Eds.), *The self-conscious emotions: Theory and research* (pp. 91–113). New York, NY: Guilford Press.

Lagattuta, K. H., Wellman, H. M., & Flavell, J. H. (1997). Preschoolers' understanding of the link between thinking and feeling: Cognitive cuing and emotional change. *Child Development, 68,* 1081–1104.

Lagercrantz, H., & Slotkin, T. A. (1986, April). The "stress" of being born. *Scientific American, 254*(4), 100–107.

Laghi, F., Schneider, B. H., Vitoroulis, R. J., Coplan, R. J., & Baiocco, R. (2013). Knowing when not to use the internet: Shyness and adolescents' on-line and off-line interactions with friends. *Computers in Human Behavior, 29,* 51–57. doi:10.1016/j.chb.2012.07.015

Lahey, B. B., Goodman, S. H., Waldman, I. D., Bird, H., Canino, G., Jensen, P., . . . Applegate, B. (1999). Relation of age of onset to the type and severity of child and adolescent conduct problems. *Journal of Abnormal Child Psychology, 27,* 247–260.

Lahey, B. B., Gordon, R. A., Loeber, R., Stouthamer-Loeber, M., & Farrington, D. P. (1999). Boys who join gangs: A prospective study of predictors of first gang entry. *Journal of Abnormal Child Psychology, 27,* 261–276.

Lahey, B. B., Hulle, C. A., Rathouz, P. J., Rodgers, J. L., D'Onofrio, B. M., & Waldman, I. D. (2009). Are oppositional-defiant and hyperactive–inattentive symptoms developmental precursors to conduct problems in late childhood? Genetic and environmental links. *Journal of Abnormal Child Psychology, 37,* 45–58. doi:10.1007/s10802-008-9257-1

Lahey, B. B., Schwab-Stone, M., Goodman, S. H., Waldman, I. D., Canino, G., Rathouz, P. J., . . . Jensen, P. S. (2000). Age and gender differences in oppositional behavior and conduct problems: A cross-sectional household study of middle childhood and adolescence. *Journal of Abnormal Psychology, 109,* 488–503. doi:10.1037/0021-843X.109.3.488

Laible, D., Eye, J., & Carlo, G. (2008). Dimensions of conscience in mid-adolescence: Links with social behavior, parenting, and temperament. *Journal of Youth and Adolescence, 37,* 875–887. doi:10.1007/s10964-008-9277-8

Laible, D. J., & Thompson, R. A. (1998). Attachment and emotional understanding in preschool children. *Developmental Psychology, 34,* 1038–1045. doi:10.1037/0012-1649.34.5.1038

Laird, R. D., Pettit, G. S., Bates, J. E., & Dodge, K. A. (2003). Parents' monitoring-relevant knowledge and adolescents' delinquent behavior: Evidence of correlated developmental changes and reciprocal influences. *Child Development, 74,* 752–768. doi:10.1111/1467-8624.00566

Laird, R. D., Pettit, G. S., Mize, J., Brown, E. G., & Lindsey, E. (1994). Mother–child conversations about peers: Contributions to competence. *Family Relations, 43,* 425–432. doi:10.2307/585374

Lalande, N. M., Hétu, R., & Lambert, J. (1986). Is occupational noise exposure during pregnancy a risk factor of damage to the auditory system of the fetus? *American Journal of Industrial Medicine, 10,* 427–435. doi:10.1002/ajim.4700100410

Lam, C. B., McHale, S. M., & Crouter, A. C. (2012). Parent–child shared time from middle childhood to late adolescence: Developmental course and adjustment correlates. *Child Development, 83,* 2089–2103. doi:10.1111/j.1467-8624.2012.01826.x

Lam, C. B., McHale, S. M., & Crouter, A. C. (2014). Time with peers from middle childhood to late adolescence: Developmental course and adjustment correlates. *Child Development, 85,* 1677–1693. doi:10.1111/cdev.12235

Lam, E. T., Hastie, A., Lin, C., Ehrlich, D., Das, S. K., Austin, M. D., . . . Kwok, P. Y. (2012). Genome mapping on nanochannel arrays for structural variation analysis and sequence assembly. *Nature Biotechnology, 30*(8), 771–776. doi:10.1038/nbt.2303

Lamb, M. E. (1998). Nonparental child care: Context, quality, correlates, and consequences. In W. Damon (Series Ed.) & I. E. Sigel & K. A. Renninger (Vol. Eds.), *Handbook of child psychology: Vol. 4. Child psychology in practice* (5th ed., pp. 135–210). New York, NY: Wiley.

Lamb, M. E., Hershkowitz, I., Orbach, Y., & Esplin, P. W. (2008). *Tell me what happened: Structured investigative interviews of child victims and witnesses.* Hoboken, NJ: Wiley.

Lamb, S., & Zakhireh, B. (1997). Toddlers' attention to the distress of peers in a daycare setting. *Early Education and Development, 8,* 105–118. doi:10.1207/s15566935eed0802_1

Lamborn, S. D., Mounts, N. S., Steinberg, L., & Dornbusch, S. M. (1991). Patterns of competence and adjustment among adolescents from authoritative, authoritarian, indulgent, and neglectful families. *Child Development, 62,* 1049–1065. doi:10.1111/j.1467-8624.1991.tb01588.x

Landau, B., Smith, L., & Jones, S. (1998). Object perception and object naming in early development. *Trends in Cognitive Sciences, 2,* 19–24.

Landau, B., Smith, L. B., & Jones, S. S. (1988). The importance of shape in early lexical learning. *Cognitive Development, 3,* 299–321. doi:10.1016/0885-2014(88)90014-7

Langley, K., Heron, J., Smith, G. D., & Thapar, A. (2012). Maternal and paternal smoking during pregnancy and risk of ADHD symptoms in offspring: Testing for intrauterine effects. *American Journal of Epidemiology, 176*(3), 261–268.

Langlois, J. H., Ritter, J. M., Roggman, L. A., & Vaughn, L. S. (1991). Facial diversity and infant preferences for attractive faces. *Developmental Psychology, 27,* 79–84. doi:10.1037/0012-1649.27.1.79

Langlois, J. H., Roggman, L. A., Casey, R. J., Ritter, J. M., Rieser-Danner, L. A., & Jenkins, V. Y. (1987). Infant preferences for attractive faces: Rudiments of a stereotype? *Developmental Psychology, 23,* 363–369. doi:10.1037/0012-1649.23.3.363

Langlois, J. H., Roggman, L. A., & Rieser-Danner, L. A. (1990). Infants' differential social responses to attractive and unattractive faces. *Developmental Psychology, 26,* 153–159. doi:10.1037/0012-1649.26.1.153

Lansford, J. E., Criss, M. M., Dodge, K. A., Shaw, D. S., Pettit, G. S., & Bates, J. E. (2009). Trajectories of physical discipline: Early childhood antecedents and developmental outcomes. *Child Development, 80,* 1385–1402. doi:10.1111/j.1467-8624.2009.01340.x

Lansford, J. E., Criss, M. M., Laird, R. D., Shaw, D. S., Pettit, G. S., Bates, J. E., & Dodge, K. A. (2011). Reciprocal relations between parents' physical discipline and children's externalizing behavior during middle childhood and adolescence. *Development and Psychopathology, 23,* 225–238. doi:10.1017/S0954579410000751

Lansford, J. E., Malone, P. S., Dodge, K. A., Pettit, G. S., & Bates, J. E. (2010). Developmental cascades of peer rejection, social information processing biases, and aggression during middle childhood. *Development and Psychopathology, 22,* 593–602. doi:10.1017/S0954579410000301

Lansford, J. E., Skinner, A. T., Sorbring, E., Giunta, L. D., Deater-Deckard, K., Dodge, K. A., . . . Chang, L. (2012). Boys' and girls' relational and physical aggression in nine countries. *Aggressive Behavior, 38,* 298–308. doi:10.1002/ab.21433

Lany, J., & Saffran, J. R. (2010). From statistics to meaning: Infants' acquisition of lexical categories. *Psychological Science, 21,* 284–291. doi:10.1177/0956797609358570

Lapsley, D. K. (2006). Moral stage theory. In J. S. Melanie Killen (Ed.), *Handbook of moral development* (pp. 37–66). Mahwah, NJ: Erlbaum.

Larsen, J. K., Hermans, R. C., Sleddens, E. F., Engels, R. C., Fisher, J. O., & Kremers, S. P. (2015). How parental dietary behavior and food parenting practices affect children's dietary behavior. Interacting sources of influence? *Appetite, 89,* 246–257.

Larson, K., Russ, S. A., Nelson, B. B., Olson, L. M., & Halfon, N. (2015). Cognitive ability at kindergarten entry and socioeconomic status. *Pediatrics, 135,* e440–e448. doi:10.1542/peds.2014-0434

Larson, R., & Lampman-Petraitis, C. (1989). Daily emotional states as reported by children and adolescents. *Child Development, 60,* 1250–1260.

Larson, R., & Richards, M. H. (1991). Daily companionship in late childhood and early adolescence: Changing developmental contexts. *Child Development, 62,* 284–300. doi:10.1111/j.1467-8624.1991.tb01531.x

Larson, R. W., Moneta, G., Richards, M. H., & Wilson, S. (2002). Continuity, stability, and change in daily emotional experience across adolescence. *Child Development, 73,* 1151–1165.

Larson, R. W., & Verma, S. (1999). How children and adolescents spend time across the world: Work, play, and developmental opportunities. *Psychological Bulletin, 125,* 701–736. doi:10.1037/0033-2909.125.6.701

Larsson, H., Chang, Z., D'Onofrio, B. M., & Lichtenstein, P. (2014). The heritability of clinically diagnosed attention deficit hyperactivity disorder across the lifespan. *Psychological medicine, 44*(10), 2223–2229.

Laski, E. V., & Siegler, R. S. (2014). Learning from number board games: You learn what you encode. *Developmental Psychology, 50,* 853–864. doi:10.1037/a0034321

Laski, E. V., & Yu, Q. (2014). Number line estimation and mental addition: Examining the potential roles of language and education. *Journal of Experimental Child Psychology, 117,* 29–44. doi:10.1016/j.jecp.2013.08.007

Laughlin, J. (2014). *A child's day: Living arrangements, nativity, and family transitions: 2011* (Current Population Reports, P70–139). Retrieved from U.S. Census Bureau website: https://www.census.gov/content/dam/Census/library/publications/2014/demo/p70-139.pdf

Laughlin, L. (2013). *Who's minding the kids? Child care arrangements: Spring 2011* (Current Population Reports, P70-135). Washington, DC: U.S. Census Bureau. Retrieved from U.S. Census Bureau website: http://www.census.gov/content/dam/Census/library/publications/2013/demo/p70-135.pdf

Laursen, B., Bukowski, W. M., Aunola, K., & Nurmi, J.-E. (2007). Friendship moderates prospective associations between social isolation and adjustment problems in young children. *Child Development, 78,* 1395–1404. doi:10.1111/j.1467-8624.2007.01072.x

Laursen, B., & Collins, W. A. (1994). Interpersonal conflict during adolescence. *Psychological Bulletin, 115,* 197–209. doi:10.1037/0033-2909.115.2.197

Laursen, B., DeLay, D., & Adams, R. E. (2010). Trajectories of perceived support in mother–adolescent relationships: The poor (quality) get poorer. *Developmental Psychology, 46,* 1792–1798. doi:10.1037/a0020679

Laursen, B., Finkelstein, B. D., & Betts, N. T. (2001). A developmental meta-analysis of peer conflict resolution. *Developmental Review, 21,* 423–449. doi:10.1006/drev.2000.0531

Laursen, B., Hafen, C. A., Kerr, M., & Stattin, H. (2012). Friend influence over adolescent problem behaviors as a function of relative peer acceptance: To be liked is to be emulated. *Journal of Abnormal Psychology, 121,* 88–94. doi:10.1037/a0024707

Lavelli, M., & Fogel, A. (2005). Developmental changes in the relationship between the infant's attention and emotion during early face-to-face communication: The 2-month transition. *Developmental Psychology, 41,* 265–280.

Lawford, H., Pratt, M. W., Hunsberger, B., & Pancer, S. M. (2005). Adolescent generativity: A longitudinal study of two possible contexts for learning concern for future generations. *Journal of Research on Adolescence, 15,* 261–273. doi:10.1111/j.1532-7795.2005.00096.x

Lazar, I., Darlington, R., Murray, H., Royce, J., & Snipper, A. (1982). Lasting effects of early education: A report from the Consortium for Longitudinal Studies. *Monographs of the Society for Research in Child Development, 47*(2/3, Serial No. 195).

Lazenby, D. C., Sideridis, G. D., Huntington, N., Prante, M., Dale, P. S., Curtin, S., . . . Akshoomoff, N. (2016). Language differences at 12 months in infants who develop autism spectrum disorder. *Journal of Autism and Developmental Disorders, 46*(3), 899–909.

Le, H.-N. (2000). Never leave your little one alone: Raising an Ifaluk child. In J. S. DeLoache & A. Gottlieb (Eds.), *A world of babies: Imagined childcare guides for seven societies* (pp. 199–220). New York, NY: Cambridge University Press.

Le Corre, M., & Carey, S. (2007). One, two, three, four, nothing more: An investigation of the conceptual sources of the verbal counting principles. *Cognition, 105,* 395–438. doi:10.1016/j.cognition.2006.10.005

Le Corre, M., Van de Walle, G., Brannon, E. M., & Carey, S. (2006). Re-visiting the competence/performance debate in the acquisition of the counting principles. *Cognitive Psychology, 52*(2), 130–169. doi:10.1016/j.cogpsych.2005.07.

Le Grand, R., Mondloch, C. J., Maurer, D., & Brent, H. P. (2001, April 19). Early visual experience and face processing. *Nature, 410,* 890. doi:10.1038/35073749

Le Grand, R., Mondloch, C. J., Maurer, D., & Brent, H. P. (2003). Expert face processing requires visual input to the right hemisphere during infancy. *Nature Neuroscience, 6,* 1108–1112. doi:10.1038/nn1121

Leadbeater, B. J., & Hoglund, W. L. G. (2009). The effects of peer victimization and physical aggression on changes in internalizing from first to third grade. *Child Development, 80,* 843–859. doi:10.1111/j.1467-8624.2009.01301.x

Leaper, C. (1991). Influence and involvement in children's discourse: Age, gender, and partner effects. *Child Development, 62,* 797–811.

Leaper, C. (1994). Exploring the consequences of gender segregation on social relationships: Social relationships in childhood, adolescence and adulthood. In C. Leaper (Ed.), *New Directions for Child and Adolescent Development: No. 65. Childhood gender segregation: Causes and consequences* (pp. 67–86). San Francisco, CA: Jossey-Bass.

Leaper, C. (2000). The social construction and socialization of gender. In P. H. Miller & E. K. Scholnick (Eds.), *Toward a feminist developmental psychology* (pp. 127–152). New York, NY: Routledge Press.

Leaper, C. (2011). More similarities than differences in contemporary theories of social development? A plea for theory bridging. In J. B. Benson (Ed.), *Advances in child development and behavior* (pp. 337–378). San Diego, CA: Elsevier.

Leaper, C. (2013). Gender development during childhood. In P. D. Zelazo (Ed.), *Oxford handbook of developmental psychology: Vol. 2. Self and other* (pp. 326–376). New York, NY: Oxford University Press.

Leaper, C. (2015a). Gender and social-cognitive development. In R. M. Lerner (Series Ed.), L. S. Liben & U. Muller (Vol. Eds.), *Handbook of child psychology and developmental science* (7th ed.), *Vol. 2: Cognitive processes* (pp. 806–853). Hoboken, NJ: Wiley.

Leaper, C. (2015b). Do I belong? Gender, peer groups, and STEM achievement.

International Journal of Gender, Science, & Technology, 7, 166–179.

Leaper, C., & Anderson, K. J. (1997). Gender development and heterosexual romantic relationships during adolescence. In S. Shulman & W. A. Collins (Eds.), *New Directions for Child and Adolescent Development: No. 78. Romantic relationships in adolescence: Developmental perspectives* (pp. 85–103). San Francisco, CA: Jossey-Bass.

Leaper, C., Anderson, K. J., & Sanders, P. (1998). Moderators of gender effects on parents' talk to their children: A meta-analysis. *Developmental Psychology, 34,* 3–27. doi:10.1037/0012-1649.34.1.3

Leaper, C., & Ayres, M. M. (2007). A meta-analytic review of gender variations in adults' language use: Talkativeness, affiliative speech, and assertive speech. *Personality and Social Psychology Review, 11,* 328–363. doi:10.1177/1088868307302221

Leaper, C., & Bigler, R. S. (in press). Gender typing of toys: Consequences for society. In E. S. Weisgram & L. M. Dinella (Eds.), *Gender-typing of children's toys.* Washington, DC: American Psychological Association.

Leaper, C., Breed, L., Hoffman, L., & Perlman, C. A. (2002). Variations in the gender-stereotyped content of children's television cartoons across genres. *Journal of Applied Social Psychology, 32,* 1653–1662. doi:10.1111/j.1559-1816.2002.tb02767.x

Leaper, C., & Brown, C. S. (2008). Perceived experiences with sexism among adolescent girls. *Child Development, 79,* 685–704. doi:10.1111/j.1467-8624.2008.01151.x

Leaper, C., Carson, M., Baker, C., Holliday, H., & Myers, S. (1995). Self-disclosure and listener verbal support in same-gender and cross-gender friends' conversations. *Sex Roles, 33,* 387–404. doi:10.1007/BF01954575

Leaper, C., & Gleason, J. B. (1996). The relationship of play activity and gender to parent and child sex-typed communication. *International Journal of Behavioral Development, 19,* 689–703. doi:10.1177/016502549601900401

Leaper, C., & Holliday, H. (1995). Gossip in same-gender and cross-gender friends' conversations. *Personal Relationships, 2,* 237–246. doi:10.1111/j.1475-6811.1995.tb00089.x

Leaper, C., & Robnett, R. D. (2016). Sexism. In R. J. R. Levesque (Ed.), *Encyclopedia of Adolescence.* New York, NY: Springer.

Leaper, C., & Smith, T. E. (2004). A meta-analytic review of gender variations in children's language use: Talkativeness, affiliative speech, and assertive speech. *Developmental Psychology, 40,* 993–1027. doi:10.1037/0012-1649.40.6.993

Leaper, C., Tenenbaum, H. R., & Shaffer, T. G. (1999). Communication patterns of African American girls and boys from low-income, urban

backgrounds. *Child Development, 70,* 1489–1503. doi:10.1111/1467-8624.00108

Leaper, C., & Van, S. R. (2008). Masculinity ideology, covert sexism, and perceived gender typicality in relation to young men's academic motivation and choices in college. *Psychology of Men and Masculinity, 9,* 139–153. doi:10.1037/1524-9220.9.3.139

Lecanuet, J.-P., Granier-Deferre, C., & Busnel, M. C. (1995). Human fetal auditory perception. In J.-P. Lecanuet, W. P. Fifer, N. A. Krasnegor, & W. P. Smotherman (Eds.), *Fetal development: A psychobiological perspective* (pp. 239–262). Hillsdale, NJ: Erlbaum.

Lecanuet, J.-P., & Jacquet, A.-Y. (2002). Fetal responsiveness to maternal passive swinging in low heart rate variability state: Effects of stimulation direction and duration. *Developmental Psychobiology, 40,* 57–67. doi:10.1002/dev.10013

Lee, B. K., Magnusson, C., Gardner, R. M., Blomström, Å., Newschaffer, C. J., Burstyn, I., . . . Dalman, C. (2015). Maternal hospitalization with infection during pregnancy and risk of autism spectrum disorders. *Brain, Behavior, and Immunity, 44,* 100–105.

Lee, C. C., Jhang, Y., Chen, L. M., Relyea, G., & Oller, D. K. (2016). Subtlety of ambient-language effects in babbling: A study of English-and Chinese-learning infants at 8, 10, and 12 months. *Language Learning and Development.* doi:10.1080/15475441.2016.1180983

Lee, C.-Y. S., Lee, J., & August, G. J. (2011). Financial stress, parental depressive symptoms, parenting practices, and children's externalizing problem behaviors: Underlying processes. *Family Relations, 60,* 476–490. doi:10.1111/j.1741-3729.2011.00656.x

Lee, E. H., Zhou, Q., Eisenberg, N., & Wang, Y. (2013). Bidirectional relations between temperament and parenting styles in Chinese children. *International Journal of Behavioral Development, 37,* 57–67. doi:10.1177/0165025412460795

Lee, K. (2013). Little liars: Development of verbal deception in children. *Child Development Perspectives, 7*(2), 91–96. doi:10.1111/cdep.12023

Lee, K., & Karmiloff-Smith, A. (2002). Macro-and microdevelopmental research: Assumptions, research strategies, constraints, and utilities. In N. Granott & J. Parziale (Eds.), *Microdevelopment: Transition processes in development and learning* (pp. 243–265). Cambridge, England: Cambridge University Press.

Lee, K., & Lee, J. (2012). Self-esteem and delinquency in South Korean adolescents: Latent growth modeling. *School Psychology International, 33,* 54–68. doi:10.1177/0143034311409856

Lee, L., Howes, C., & Chamberlain, B. (2007). Ethnic heterogeneity of social networks and

cross-ethnic friendships of elementary school boys and girls. *Merrill-Palmer Quarterly, 53,* 325–346.

Lee, L. C., & Zhan, G. Q. (1991). Political socialisation and parental values in the People's Republic of China. *International Journal of Behavioral Development, 14,* 337–373. doi:10.1177/016502549101400401

Lee, S. J., Altschul, I., & Gershoff, E. T. (2013). Does warmth moderate longitudinal associations between maternal spanking and child aggression in early childhood? *Developmental Psychology, 49,* 2017–2028. doi:10.1037/a0031630

Lee, S. J., Grogan-Kaylor, A., & Berger, L. M. (2014). Parental spanking of 1-year-old children and subsequent protective services involvement. *Child Abuse & Neglect, 38,* 875–883. doi:10.1016/j.chiabu.2014.01.018

Leerkes, E. M., Parade, S. H., & Gudmundson, J. A. (2011). Mothers' emotional reactions to crying pose risk for subsequent attachment insecurity. *Journal of Family Psychology, 25,* 635–643. doi:10.1037/a0023654

LeFevre, J.-A., Bisanz, J., Daley, K. E., Buffone, L., Greenham, S. L., & Sadesky, G. S. (1996). Multiple routes to solution of single-digit multiplication problems. *Journal of Experimental Psychology: General, 125,* 284–306.

Legare, C. H., & Gelman, S. A. (2008). Bewitchment, biology, or both: The co-existence of natural and supernatural explanatory frameworks across development. *Cognitive Science, 32*(4), 607–642. doi:10.1080/03640210802066766

Legare, C. H., & Gelman, S. A. (2014). Examining explanatory biases in young children's biological reasoning. *Journal of Cognition and Development, 15*(2), 287–303. doi:10.1080/15248372.2012.749480

Legare, C. H., & Nielsen, M. (2015). Imitation and innovation: The dual engines of cultural learning. *Trends in Cognitive Sciences, 19*(11), 688–699.

Leichtman, M. D., Pillemer, D. B., Wang, Q., Koreishi, A., & Han, J. J. (2000). When Baby Maisy came to school: Mothers' interview styles and preschoolers' event memories. *Cognitive Development, 15,* 99–114. doi:10.1016/S0885-2014(00)00019-8

Leigh, J., Dettman, S., Dowell, R., & Briggs, R. (2013). Communication development in children who receive a cochlear implant by 12 months of age. *Otology & Neurotology, 34*(3), 443–450.

Lemaire, P. (2010). Cognitive strategy variations during aging. *Current Directions in Psychological Science, 19,* 363–369. doi:10.1177/0963721410390354

Leman, P. J., Ahmed, S., & Ozarow, L. (2005). Gender, gender relations, and the social dynamics of children's conversations. *Developmental Psychology, 41,* 64–74.

Lemerise, E. A., & Arsenio, W. F. (2000). An integrated model of emotion processes and cognition in social information processing. *Child Development, 71,* 107–118. doi:10.1111/1467-8624.00124

Lemery, K. S., Goldsmith, H. H., Klinnert, M. D., & Mrazek, D. A. (1999). Developmental models of infant and childhood temperament. *Developmental Psychology, 35,* 189–204.

Lemery-Chalfant, K., Kao, K., Swann, G., & Goldsmith, H. H. (2013). Childhood temperament: Passive gene–environment correlation, gene–environment interaction, and the hidden importance of the family environment. *Development and Psychopathology, 25*(1), 51–63. doi:10.1017/S0954579412000892

Lengua, L. J. (2008). Anxiousness, frustration, and effortful control as moderators of the relation between parenting and adjustment in middle-childhood. *Social Development, 17,* 554–577.

Lengua, L. J., Bush, N. R., Long, A. C., Kovacs, E. A., & Trancik, A. M. (2008). Effortful control as a moderator of the relation between contextual risk factors and growth in adjustment problems. *Development and Psychopathology, 20,* 509–528.

Lenhart, A. (2015). *How teens hang out and stay in touch with their closest friends.* Pew Research Center. Retrieved from http://www.pewinternet .org/2015/08/06/chapter-2-how-teens-hang-out-and-stay-in-touch-with-their-closest-friends/

Lenhart, A. (2015). *Teen, social media and technology overview 2015.* Retrieved from Pew Research Center website: http://www.pewinternet.org/files/2015/04/PI_TeensandTech_Update2015_0409151.pdf

Lenhart, A., Smith, A., & Anderson, M. (2015). *Teens, technology and romantic relationships.* Retrieved from Pew Research Center website: http://www.pewinternet.org/files/2015/10/PI_2015-10-01_teens-technology-romance_FINAL.pdf

Leonard, L. B., Ellis Weismer, S., Miller, C. A., Francis, D. J., Tomblin, J. B., & Kail, R. V. (2007). Speed of processing, working memory, and language impairment in children. *Journal of Speech, Language, and Hearing Research, 50,* 408–428. doi:10.1044/1092-4388(2007/029)

Lereya, S. T., Copeland, W. E., Zammit, S., & Wolke, D. (2015). Bully/victims: A longitudinal, population-based cohort study of their mental health. *European Child & Adolescent Psychiatry, 24,* 1461–1471.doi:10.1007/s00787-015-0705-5

Lerner, R. M., & Lerner, J. V., & Colleagues. (2013). *The positive development of youth: Comprehensive findings from the 4-H study of positive youth development.* Retrieved from http://www.4-h.org/about/youth-development-research/positive-youth-development-study/

Lerner, R. M., Lerner, J. V., Almerigi, J. B., Theokas, C., Phelps, E., Gestsdottir, T., . . . von Eye, A. (2005). Positive youth development, participation in community youth development programs, and community contributions of fifth-grade adolescents: Findings from the first wave of the 4-H study of positive youth development. *The Journal of Early Adolescence, 25,* 17–71. doi:10.1177/0272431604272461

Leslie, A. M. (1986). Getting development off the ground: Modularity and the infant's perception of causality. In P. van Geert (Ed.), *Theory building in developmental psychology* (pp. 406–437). New York, NY: Elsevier.

Leslie, A. M. (1995). A theory of agency. In D. Sperber, D. Premack, & A. J. Premack (Eds.), *Causal cognition: A multidisciplinary debate* (pp. 121–141). New York, NY: Oxford University Press. doi:10.1093/acprof:oso/9780198524021.003.0005

Leslie, A. M. (2000). How to acquire a representational theory of mind. In D. Sperber (Ed.), *Metarepresentations: A multidisciplinary perspective* (pp. 197–223). Oxford, England: Oxford University Press.

Leslie, A. M., Friedman, O., & German, T. P. (2004). Core mechanisms in 'theory of mind.' *Trends in Cognitive Sciences, 8*(12), 528–533. doi:10.1016/j.tics.2004.10.001

Lester, B. M., Anderson, L. T., Boukydis, C. F., García Coll, C. T., Vohr, B., & Peucker, M. (1989). Early detection of infants at risk for later handicap through acoustic cry analysis. *Birth Defects: Original Article Series, 25,* 99–118.

Letourneau, N., Tryphonopoulos, P., Giesbrecht, G., Dennis, C., Bhogal, S., & Watson, B. (2015). Narrative and meta-analytic review of interventions aiming to improve maternal-child attachment security. *Infant Mental Health Journal, 36,* 366–387. doi:10.1002/imhj.21525

Leung, F. K. S., Park, K., Shimizu, Y., & Xu, B. (2015). Mathematics education in East Asia. In S. J. Cho (Ed.), *The proceedings of the 12th International Congress on Mathematical Education* (pp. 123–143). New York, NY: Springer. doi:10.1007/978-3-319-12688-3_11

Leung, M.-C. (1996). Social networks and self enhancement in Chinese children: A comparison of self reports and peer reports of group membership. *Social Development, 5,* 146–157. doi:10.1111/j.1467-9507.1996.tb00077.x

Levant, R. F. (2005). The crises of boyhood. In G. E. Good & G. R. Brooks (Eds.), *The new handbook of psychotherapy and counseling with men: A comprehensive guide to settings, problems, and treatment approaches* (Rev. and abridged ed., pp. 161–171). San Francisco, CA: Jossey-Bass.

Leve, L. D., Pears, K. C., & Fisher, P. A. (2002). Competence in early development. In J. B. Reid, G. R. Patterson, & J. Snyder (Eds.), *Antisocial behavior in children and adolescents: A*

developmental analysis and model for intervention (pp. 45–64). Washington, DC: American Psychological Association.

Levin, I. (1982). The nature and development of time concepts in children: The effects of interfering cues. In W. J. Friedman (Ed.), *Developmental psychology of time* (pp. 47–85). New York, NY: Academic Press.

Levin, I., & Aram, D. (2013). Promoting early literacy via practicing invented spelling: A comparison of different mediation routines. *Reading Research Quarterly, 48,* 221–236. doi:10.1002/rrq.48

Levin, I., & Korat, O. (1993). Sensitivity to phonological, morphological, and semantic cues in early reading and writing in Hebrew. *Merrill-Palmer Quarterly, 39,* 213–232.

Levin, I., Siegler, R. S., & Druyan, S. (1990). Misconceptions about motion: Development and training effects. *Child Development, 61,* 1544–1557. doi:10.1111/j.1467-8624.1990.tb02882.x

Levine, M. P., & Smolak, L. (2010). Cultural influences on body image and the eating disorders. In W. S. Agras (Ed.), *The Oxford handbook of eating disorders* (pp. 223–246). New York, NY: Oxford University Press.

LeVine, R. A. (1988). Human parental care: Universal goals, cultural strategies, individual behavior. In R. A. LeVine, P. M. Miller, & M. M. West (Eds.), *New Directions for Child and Adolescent Development: No. 40. Parental behavior in diverse societies* (pp. 3–12). San Francisco, CA: Jossey-Bass.

LeVine, R. A., Dixon, S., LeVine, S., Richman, A., Keefer, C. H., Leiderman, P. H., & Brazelton, T. B. (1996). *Child care and culture: Lessons from Africa.* Cambridge, England: Cambridge University Press.

Levine, S. C., Kraus, R., Alexander, E., Suriyakham, L. W., & Huttenlocher, P. R. (2005). IQ decline following early unilateral brain injury: A longitudinal study. *Brain and Cognition, 59,* 114–123. doi:10.1016/j.bandc.2005.05.008

Levine, S. C., Ratliff, K. R., Huttenlocher, J., & Cannon, J. (2012). Early puzzle play: A predictor of preschoolers' spatial transformation skill. *Developmental Psychology, 48,* 530–542. doi:10.1037/a0025913

Lew, A. R. (2011). Looking beyond the boundaries: Time to put landmarks back on the cognitive map? *Psychological Bulletin, 137,* 484–507. doi:10.1037/a0022315

Lew-Williams, C., & Fernald, A. (2007). Young children learning Spanish make rapid use of grammatical gender in spoken word recognition. *Psychological Science, 18,* 193–198. doi:10.1111/j.1467-9280.2007.01871.x

Lewinsohn, P. M., Joiner, T. E., Jr., & Rohde, P. (2001). Evaluation of cognitive diathesis-stress models in predicting major depressive disorder in adolescents. *Journal of Abnormal Psychology, 110,* 203–215.

Lewis, E. E., Dozier, M., Ackerman, J., & Sepulveda-Kozakowski, S. (2007). The effect of placement instability on adopted children's inhibitory control abilities and oppositional behavior. *Developmental Psychology, 43*, 1415–1427. doi:10.1037/0012-1649.43.6.1415

Lewis, M. (1992). *Shame: The exposed self.* New York, NY: Free Press.

Lewis, M. (1995). Embarrassment: The emotion of self-exposure and evaluation. In J. P. Tangney & K. W. Fischer (Eds.), *Self-conscious emotions: The psychology of shame, guilt, embarrassment, and pride* (pp. 198–218). New York, NY: Guilford Press.

Lewis, M. (1998). Emotional competence and development. In D. Pushkar, W. M. Bukowski, A. E. Schwartzman, D. M. Stack, & D. R. White (Eds.), *Improving competence across the lifespan: Building interventions based on theory and research* (pp. 27–36). New York, NY: Plenum Press.

Lewis, M. (2002). Emotional competence and development. In D. Pushkar, W. M. Bukowski, A. E. Schwartzman, D. M. Stack, & D. R. White (Eds.), *Improving competence across the lifespan* (pp. 27–36). New York, NY: Plenum Press.

Lewis, M. (2011). Problems in the study of infant emotional development. *Emotion Review, 3*, 131–137.

Lewis, M., Alessandri, S. M., & Sullivan, M. W. (1990). Violation of expectancy, loss of control, and anger expressions in young infants. *Developmental Psychology, 26*, 745–751.

Lewis, M., Alessandri, S. M., & Sullivan, M. W. (1992). Differences in shame and pride as a function of children's gender and task difficulty. *Child Development, 63*, 630–638.

Lewis, M., & Brooks-Gunn, J. (1979). *Social cognition and the acquisition of self.* New York, NY: Plenum Press.

Lewis, M., Feiring, C., & Rosenthal, S. (2000). Attachment over time. *Child Development, 71*, 707–720. doi:10.1111/1467-8624.00180

Lewis, M. D. (2005). Bridging emotion theory and neurobiology through dynamic systems modeling. *Behavioral and Brain Sciences, 28*, 169–193.

Lewkowicz, D. J. (2004). Perception of serial order in infants. *Developmental Science, 7*, 175–184.

Lewkowicz, D. J., & Ghazanfar, A. A. (2006). The decline of cross-species intersensory perception in human infants. *Proceedings of the National Academy of Sciences of the United States of America, 103*, 6771–6774. doi:10.1073/pnas.0602027103

Lewkowicz, D. J., & Hansen-Tift, A. M. (2012). Infants deploy selective attention to the mouth of a talking face when learning speech. *Proceedings of the National Academy of Sciences, 109*(5), 1431–1436.

Lewkowicz, D. J., & Minar, N. J. (2014). Infants are not sensitive to synesthetic cross-Modality correspondences: A comment on Walker et al. (2010). *Psychological Science, 25*(3), 832–834.

Lewontin, R. C. (1982). *Human diversity.* New York, NY: Scientific American Library.

Li, R., Montpetit, A., Rousseau, M., Wu, S. Y. M., Greenwood, C. M., Spector, T. D., . . . Richards, J. B. (2014). Somatic point mutations occurring early in development: A monozygotic twin study. *Journal of Medical Genetics, 51*, 28–43. doi:10.1136/jmedgenet-2013-101712

Li, Y., Putallaz, M., & Su, Y. (2011). Interparental conflict styles and parenting behaviors: Associations with overt and relational aggression among Chinese children. *Merrill-Palmer Quarterly, 57*, 402–428.

Liaw, F.-R., & Brooks-Gunn, J. (1993). Patterns of low-birth-weight children's cognitive development. *Developmental Psychology, 29*, 1024–1035. doi:10.1037/0012-1649.29.6.1024

Libbey, J. E., Sweeten, T. L., McMahon, W. M., & Fujinami, R. S. (2005). Autistic disorder and viral infections. *Journal of Neurovirology, 11*, 1–10.

Liben, L. S., & Bigler, R. S. (1987). Children's gender schemata. In L. S. Liben & M. L. Signorella (Eds.), *New Directions for Child and Adolescent Development: No. 38. Children's gender schemata* (Vol. 1987, pp. 89–105). San Francisco, CA: Jossey-Bass.

Liben, L. S., & Bigler, R. S. (2002). The developmental course of gender differentiation: Conceptualizing, measuring, and evaluating constructs and pathways. *Monographs of the Society for Research in Child Development, 67*(2, Serial No. 269), i–183. doi:10.2307/3181530

Liben, L. S., & Myers, L. J. (2007). Developmental changes in children's understanding of maps: What, when, and how. In J. M. Plumert & J. P. Spence (Eds.), *The emerging spatial mind* (pp. 193–218). Oxford, England: Oxford University Press.

Liben, L. S., & Signorella, M. L. (1980). Gender-related schemata and constructive memory in children. *Child Development, 51*, 11–18.

Liben, L. S., & Signorella, M. L. (1993). Gender-schematic processing in children: The role of initial interpretations of stimuli. *Developmental Psychology, 29*, 141–149. doi:10.1037/0012-1649.29.1.141

Liberman, Z., Woodward, A. L., Keysar, B., & Kinzler, K. D. (2016). Exposure to multiple languages enhances

communication skills in infancy. *Developmental Science.* doi:10.1111/desc.12420

Liberman, Z., Woodward, A. L., Sullivan, K., & Kinzler, K. (2016). Early emerging system for reasoning about the social nature of food. *Proceedings of the National Academy of Sciences, 113*(34). doi:10.1073/pnas.1605456113

Libertus, M. E., & Brannon, E. M. (2010). Stable individual differences in number discriminations in infancy. *Developmental Science, 13*(6), 900–906. doi:10.1111/j.1467-7687.2009.00948.x

Libertus, K., Joh, A. S., & Needham, A. W. (2015). Motor training at 3 months affects object exploration 12 months later. *Developmental Science, 19*(6), 1058–1066. doi:10.1111/desc.12370

Libertus, K., & Needham, A. (2010). Teach to reach: The effects of active vs. passive reaching experiences on action and perception. *Vision Research, 50*, 2750–2757. doi:10.1016/j.visres.2010.09.001

Lickliter, R., & Honeycutt, H. (2003). Developmental dynamics: Toward a biologically plausible evolutionary psychology. *Psychological Bulletin, 129*, 819–835. doi:10.1037/0033-2909.129.6.819

Lickona, T. (1976). Research on Piaget's theory of moral development. In T. Lickona (Ed.), *Moral development and behavior: Theory, research, and social issues* (pp. 219–240). New York, NY: Holt, Rinehart and Winston.

Liew, J., Eisenberg, N., Spinrad, T. L., Eggum, N. D., Haugen, R. G., Kupfer, A., . . . Baham, M. E. (2011). Physiological regulation and fearfulness as predictors of young children's empathy-related reactions. *Social Development, 20*, 111–134. doi:10.1111/j.1467-9507.2010.00575.x

Lillard, A. (2007). Guided participation: How mothers structure and children understand pretend play. In A. Göncü & S. Gaskins (Eds.), *Play and development: Evolutionary, sociocultural, and functional perspectives* (pp. 131–154). Mahwah, NJ: Erlbaum.

Lillard, A. S., & Flavell, J. H. (1992). Children's understanding of different mental states. *Developmental Psychology, 28*, 626–634.

Lillard, A. S., Lerner, M. D., Hopkins, E. J., Dore, R. A., Smith, E. D., & Palmquist, C. M. (2013). The impact of pretend play on children's development: A review of the evidence. *Psychological Bulletin, 139*, 1–34. doi:10.1037/a0029321

Lin-Siegler, X., Ahn, J. N., Chen, C., Fang, F.-F. A., & Luna-Lucero, M. (2016). Even Einstein struggled: Effects of learning about great scientists' struggles on high school students' motivation to learn science. *Journal of Educational Psychology, 108*(3), 314–328. doi:10.1037.edu0000092

Linares, L. O., Heeren, T., Bronfman, E., Zuckerman, B., Augustyn, M., & Tronick, E. (2001). A mediational model for the impact of exposure to community violence on early child behavior problems. *Child Development, 72*, 639–652. doi:10.1111/1467-8624.00302

Lindberg, M. (1991). A taxonomy of suggestibility and eyewitness memory: Age, memory process, and focus of analysis. In J. Doris (Ed.), *The suggestibility of children's recollection: Implications for eyewitness memory* (pp. 47–55). Washington, DC: American Psychological Association.

Lindberg, M. A. (1980). Is knowledge base development a necessary and sufficient condition for memory development? *Journal of Experimental Child Psychology, 30,* 401–410. doi:10.1016/0022-0965(80)90046-6

Lindberg, S. M., Hyde, J. S., Petersen, J. L., & Linn, M. C. (2010). New trends in gender and mathematics performance: A meta-analysis. *Psychological Bulletin, 136,* 1123-1135.

Lindquist, K. A., Siegel, E. H., Quigley, K. S., & Barrett, L. F. (2013). The hundred-year emotion war: Are emotions natural kinds or psychological constructions? Comment on Lench, Flores, and Bench (2011). *Psychological Bulletin, 139,* 255–263. doi:10.1037/a0029038

Linkletter, A. (1957). *Kids say the darndest things!* Englewood Cliffs, NJ: Prentice-Hall.

Linn, M. C., & Petersen, A. C. (1985). Emergence and characterization of sex differences in spatial ability: A meta-analysis. *Child Development, 56,* 1479–1498. doi:10.2307/1130467

Lino, M. (2014). *Expenditures on children by families, 2013* (Miscellaneous Publication No. 1528-2013). Retrieved from U.S. Department of Agriculture, Center for Nutrition Policy and Promotion website: http://www.cnpp.usda.gov/ExpendituresonChildrenbyFamilies

Lins-Dyer, M. T., & Nucci, L. (2007). The impact of social class and social cognitive domain on northeastern Brazilian mothers' and daughters' conceptions of parental control. *International Journal of Behavioral Development, 31,* 105–114. doi:10.1177/0165025407073577

Lipman, E. L., Georgiades, K., & Boyle, M. H. (2011). Young adult outcomes of children born to teen mothers: Effects of being born during their teen or later years. *Journal of the American Academy of Child and Adolescent Psychiatry, 50,* 232–241.e4. doi:10.1016/j.jaac.2010.12.007

Lipsitt, L. P. (2003). Crib death: A biobehavioral phenomenon? *Current Directions in Psychological Science, 12,* 164–170. doi:10.1111/1467-8721.01253

Lipton, J. S., & Spelke, E. S. (2003). Origins of number sense large-number discrimination in human infants. *Psychological Science, 14,* 396–401.

Lister-Landman, K. M., Domoff, S. E., & Dubow, E. F. (2015, October 5). The role of compulsive texting in adolescents' academic functioning. *Psychology of Popular Media Culture.* Advance online publication. doi:10.1037/ppm0000100

Litwack, S. D., Wargo Aikins, J., & Cillessen, A. H. N. (2012). The distinct roles of sociometric and perceived popularity in friendship: Implications for adolescent depressive affect

and self-esteem. *Journal of Early Adolescence, 32,* 226–251. doi:10.1177/0272431610387142

Liu, J., Coplan, R. J., Ooi, L. L., Chen, X., & Li, D. (2015). Examining the implications of social anxiety in a community sample of mainland Chinese children. *Journal of Clinical Psychology, 71,* 979–993. doi:10.1002/jclp.22195

Llewellyn, C. H., van Jaarsveld, C. H., Boniface, D., Carnell, S., & Wardle, J. (2008). Eating rate is a heritable phenotype related to weight in children. *American Journal of Clinical Nutrition, 88,* 1560–1566. doi:10.3945/ajcn.2008.26175

Lobo, M. A., Galloway, J. C., & Savelsbergh, G. J. (2004). General and task-related experiences affect early object interaction. *Child Development, 75,* 1268–1281. doi:10.1111/j.1467-8624.2004.00738.x

Lockman, J. J., Ashmead, D. H., & Bushnell, E. W. (1984). The development of anticipatory hand orientation during infancy. *Journal of Experimental Child Psychology, 37,* 176–186. doi:10.1016/0022-0965(84)90065-1

Loeber, R. (1982). The stability of antisocial and delinquent child behavior: A review. *Child Development, 53,* 1431–1446. doi:10.2307/1130070

Loeber, R., & Burke, J. D. (2011). Developmental pathways in juvenile externalizing and internalizing problems. *Journal of Research on Adolescence, 21,* 34–46. doi:10.1111/j.1532-7795.2010.00713.x

Loeber, R., & Schmaling, K. B. (1985). Empirical evidence for overt and covert patterns of antisocial conduct problems: A metaanalysis. *Journal of Abnormal Child Psychology, 13,* 337–353. doi:10.1007/BF00910652

Loeber, R., & Stouthamer-Loeber, M. (1986). Family factors as correlates and predictors of juvenile conduct problems and delinquency. In M. Tonry & N. Morris (Eds.), *Crime and justice* (Vol. 7, pp. 29–149). Chicago, IL: University of Chicago Press.

Loewy, J., Stewart, K., Dassler, A.-M., Telsey, A., & Homel, P. (2013). The effects of music therapy on vital signs, feeding, and sleep in premature infants. *Pediatrics, 131,* 902–918. doi:10.1542/peds.2012-1367

Lofquist, D. (2011). *Same-sex couple households* (American Community Survey Briefs, ACSBR/10-03). Retrieved from U.S. Census Bureau website: https://www.census.gov/prod/2011pubs/acsbr10-03.pdf

Lomas, J., Stough, C., Hansen, K., & Downey, L. A. (2012). Emotional intelligence, victimization, and bullying in adolescents. *Journal of Adolescence, 35,* 207–211. doi:10.1016/j.adolescence.2011.03.002

Lonardo, R. A., Giordano, P. C., Longmore, M. A., & Manning, W. D. (2009). Parents, friends, and romantic partners: Enmeshment in deviant networks and adolescent delinquency

involvement. *Journal of Youth and Adolescence, 38,* 367–383. doi:10.1007/s10964-008-9333-4

Longacre, M. R., Drake, K. M., Titus, L. J., Cleveland, L. P., Langeloh, G., Hendricks, K., & Dalton, M. A. (2016). A toy story: Association between young children's knowledge of fast food toy premiums and their fast food consumption. *Appetite, 96,* 473–480.

Lonigan, C. J. (2015). Early literacy. In R. M. Lerner (Ed.-in-Chief), L. S. Liben, & U. M. Müller (Vol. Eds.), *Handbook of child psychology and developmental science: Vol. 2 Cognitive processes* (7th Ed., pp. 763–805). Hoboken, NJ: Wiley.

Loomis, J. M., Klatzky, R. L., Golledge, R. G., Cicinelli, J. G., Pellegrino, J. W., & Fry, P. A. (1993). Nonvisual navigation by blind and sighted: Assessment of path integration ability. *Journal of Experimental Psychology: General, 122,* 73–91.

Lopez-Duran, N. L., Kuhlman, K. R., George, C., & Kovacs, M. (2013). Facial emotion expression recognition by children at familial risk for depression: High-risk boys are oversensitive to sadness. *Journal of Child Psychology and Psychiatry, 54,* 565–574. doi:10.1111/jcpp.12005

Lorenz, K. (1935). Der Kumpan in der Umwelt des Vogels. Der Artgenosse als auslosendes Moment sozialer Verhaltungsweisen. [The companion in the bird's world. The fellow-member of the species as releasing factor of social behavior.]. *Journal fur Ornithologie. Beiblatt. (Leipzig), 83,* 137–213.

Lorenz, K. (1952). *King Solomon's ring: New light on animal ways.* New York, NY: Crowell.

Lotze, G. M., Ravindran, N., & Myers, B. J. (2010). Moral emotions, emotion self-regulation, callous-unemotional traits, and problem behavior in children of incarcerated mothers. *Journal of Child and Family Studies, 19,* 702–713. doi:10.1007/s10826-010-9358-7

Loukas, A., Prelow, H. M., Suizzo, M.-A., & Allua, S. (2008). Mothering and peer associations mediate cumulative risk effects for Latino youth. *Journal of Marriage and Family, 70,* 76–85. doi:10.1111/j.1741-3737.2007.00462.x

Lourenco, S. F., & Longo, M. R. (2010). General magnitude representation in human infants. *Psychological Science, 21,* 873–881. doi:10.1177/0956797610370158

Love, J. M., Chazan-Cohen, R., & Raikes, H. (2007). Forty years of research knowledge and use: From Head Start to Early Head Start and beyond. In J. L. Aber, S. J. Bishop-Josef, S. M. Jones, K. T. McLearn, & D. A. Phillips (Eds.), *Child development and social policy: Knowledge for action* (pp. 79–95). Washington, DC: American Psychological Association.

Love, J. M., Harrison, L., Sagi-Schwartz, A., van IJzendoorn, M. H., Ross, C., Ungerer, J. A., . . . Chazan-Cohen, R. (2003). Child care quality matters: How conclusions may vary with context. *Child Development, 74,* 1021–1033. doi:10.1111/1467-8624.00584

Lovejoy, M. C., Graczyk, P. A., O'Hare, E., & Neuman, G. (2000). Maternal depression and parenting behavior: A meta-analytic review. *Clinical Psychology Review, 20,* 561–592.

Low, S., Shortt, J. W., & Snyder, J. (2012). Sibling influences on adolescent substance use: The role of modeling, collusion, and conflict. *Development and Psychopathology, 24,* 287–300. doi:10.1017/S0954579411000836

Lubinski, D., Benbow, C. P., & Kell, H. J. (2014). Life paths and accomplishments of mathematically precocious males and females four decades later. *Psychological Science, 25*(12), 2217–2232. doi:10.1177/0956797614551371

Lubinski, D., & Humphreys, L. G. (1997). Incorporating general intelligence into epidemiology and the social sciences. *Intelligence, 24,* 159–201.

Lubinski, D., Webb, R. M., Morelock, M. J., & Benbow, C. P. (2001). Top 1 in 10,000: A 10-year follow-up of the profoundly gifted. *Journal of Applied Psychology, 86,* 718–729.

Luby, J. L. (2010). Preschool depression: The importance of identification of depression early in development. *Current Directions in Psychological Science, 19,* 91–95. doi:10.1177/0963721410364493

Luby, J. L., Belden, A. C., Whalen, D., Harms, M. P., & Barch, D. M. (2016). Breastfeeding and childhood IQ: The mediating role of gray matter volume. *Journal of the American Academy of Child & Adolescent Psychiatry, 55*(5), 367–375.

Lucas-Thompson, R., & Clarke-Stewart, K. A. (2007). Forecasting friendship: How marital quality, maternal mood, and attachment security are linked to children's peer relationships. *Journal of Applied Developmental Psychology, 28,* 499–514. doi:10.1016/j.appdev.2007.06.004

Lucassen, N., Tharner, A., van IJzendoorn, M. H., Bakermans-Kranenburg, M. J., Volling, B. L., Verhulst, F. C., . . . Tiemeier, H. (2011). The association between paternal sensitivity and infant–father attachment security: A meta-analysis of three decades of research. *Journal of Family Psychology, 25,* 986–992. doi:10.1037/a0025855

Luciana, M., & Collins, P. F. (2012). Incentive motivation, cognitive control, and the adolescent brain: Is it time for a paradigm shift? *Child Development Perspectives, 6,* 392–399. doi:10.1111/j.1750-8606.2012.00252.x

Luciana, M., Wahlstrom, D., Porter, J. N., & Collins, P. F. (2012). Dopaminergic modulation of incentive motivation in adolescence: Age-related changes in signaling, individual differences, and implications for the development of self-regulation. *Developmental Psychology, 48,* 844–861. doi:10.1037/a0027432

Luebbe, A. M., Kiel, E. J., & Buss, K. A. (2011). Toddlers' context-varying emotions, maternal responses to emotions, and internalizing behaviors. *Emotion, 11,* 697–703.

Luengo Kanacri, B. P., Pastorelli, C., Eisenberg, N., Zuffianò, A., & Caprara, G. V. (2013). The development of prosociality from adolescence to early adulthood: The role of effortful control. *Journal of Personality, 81,* 302–312. doi:10.1111/jopy.12001

Luijk, M. P. C. M., Saridjan, N., Tharner, A., van IJzendoorn, M. H., Bakermans-Kranenburg, M. J., Jaddoe, V. W. V., . . . Tiemeier, H. (2010). Attachment, depression, and cortisol: Deviant patterns in insecure-resistant and disorganized infants. *Developmental Psychobiology, 52,* 441–452. doi:10.1002/dev.20446

Lumeng, J. C., Taveras, E. M., Birch, L., & Yanovski, S. Z. (2015). Prevention of obesity in infancy and early childhood: A National Institutes of Health workshop. *JAMA Pediatrics, 169*(5), 484–490.

Luna, B., Garver, K. E., Urban, T. A., Lazar, N. A., & Sweeney, J. A. (2004). Maturation of cognitive processes from late childhood to adulthood. *Child Development, 75,* 1357–1372. doi:10.1111/j.1467-8624.2004.00745.x

Lund, T. J. and Dearing, E. (2013). Is growing up affluent risky for adolescents or is the problem growing up in an affluent neighborhood? *Journal of Research on Adolescence, 23,* 274–282.

Lunkenheimer, E. S., Shields, A. M., & Cortina, K. S. (2007). Parental emotion coaching and dismissing in family interaction. *Social Development, 16,* 232–248.

Luntz, B. K., & Widom, C. S. (1994). Antisocial personality disorder in abused and neglected children grown up. *American Journal of Psychiatry, 151,* 670–674.

Luster, T., Rhoades, K., & Haas, B. (1989). The relation between parental values and parenting behavior: A test of the Kohn hypothesis. *Journal of Marriage and the Family, 51,* 139–147.

Lutchmaya, S., & Baron-Cohen, S. (2002). Human sex differences in social and non-social looking preferences, at 12 months of age. *Infant Behavior and Development, 25,* 319–325. doi:10.1016/S0163-6383(02)00095-4

Luthar, S. S., & Barkin, S. H. (2012). Are affluent youth truly "at risk"? Vulnerability and resilience across three diverse samples. *Development and Psychopathology, 24*(02), 429–449.

Luthar, S. S., Barkin, S. H., & Crossman, E. J. (2013). "I can, therefore I must": Fragility in the upper-middle classes [Monograph]. *Development and Psychopathology, 25*(4, Pt. 2), 1529–1549. doi:10.1017/S0954579413000758

Luthar, S. S., & Becker, B. E. (2002). Privileged but pressured? A study of affluent youth. *Child Development, 73,* 1593–1610. doi:10.1111/1467-8624.00492

Luxen, M. F. (2007). Sex differences, evolutionary psychology and biosocial theory: Biosocial theory is no alternative. *Theory and Psychology, 17,* 383–394. doi:10.1177/0959354307077289

Luyckx, K., Goossens, L., & Soenens, B. (2006). A developmental contextual perspective on identity construction in emerging adulthood: Change dynamics in commitment formation and commitment evaluation. *Developmental Psychology, 42,* 366–380. doi:10.1037/0012-1649.42.2.366

Luyckx, K., Goossens, L., Soenens, B., & Beyers, W. (2006). Unpacking commitment and exploration: Preliminary validation of an integrative model of late adolescent identity formation. *Journal of Adolescence, 29,* 361–378. doi:10.1016/j.adolescence.2005.03.008

Luyckx, K., Goossens, L., Soenens, B., Beyers, W., & Vansteenkiste, M. (2005). Identity statuses based on 4 rather than 2 identity dimensions: Extending and refining Marcia's paradigm. *Journal of Youth and Adolescence, 34,* 605–618. doi:10.1007/s10964-005-8949-x

Luyckx, K., Schwartz, S. J., Goossens, L., Soenens, B., & Beyers, W. (2008). Developmental typologies of identity formation and adjustment in female emerging adults: A latent class growth analysis approach. *Journal of Research on Adolescence, 18,* 595–619. doi:10.1111/j.1532-7795.2008.00573.x

Luyckx, K., Soenens, B., & Goossens, L. (2006). The personality-identity interplay in emerging adult women: Convergent findings from complementary analyses. *European Journal of Personality, 20,* 195–215.

Luyckx, K., Soenens, B., Vansteenkiste, M., Goossens, L., & Berzonsky, M. D. (2007). Parental psychological control and dimensions of identity formation in emerging adulthood. *Journal of Family Psychology, 21,* 546–550. doi:10.1037/0893-3200.21.3.546

Lyman, E. L., & Luthar, S. S. (2014). Further evidence on the "costs of privilege": Perfectionism in high-achieving youth at socioeconomic extremes. *Psychology in the Schools, 51*(9), 913–930.

Lynam, D. R. (1996). Early identification of chronic offenders: Who is the fledgling psychopath? *Psychological Bulletin, 120,* 209–234. doi:10.1037/0033-2909.120.2.209

Lynn, R. (2009). What has caused the Flynn effect? Secular increases in the Development Quotients of infants. *Intelligence, 37,* 16–24.

Lyons, I. M., & Ansari, D. (2015). Chapter three: Foundations of children's numerical and mathematical skills: The roles of symbolic and nonsymbolic representations of numerical magnitude. *Advances in Child Development and Behavior, 48,* 93–116. doi:10.1016/bs.acdb.2014.11.003

Lyons, I. M., & Beilock, S. L. (2012). When math hurts: Math anxiety predicts pain network activation in anticipation of doing math. *PLoS ONE, 7,* e48076. doi:10.1371/journal.pone.0048076

Ma, W., Golinkoff, R. M., Houston, D. M., & Hirsh-Pasek, K. (2011). Word learning in infant- and adult-directed speech. *Language Learning and Development, 7,* 185–201. doi:10.1080/15475441.2011.579839

Mabbott, D. J., & Bisanz, J. (2003). Developmental change and individual differences in children's multiplication. *Child Development, 74,* 1091–1107.

MacBrayer, E. K., Milich, R., & Hundley, M. (2003). Attributional biases in aggressive children and their mothers. *Journal of Abnormal Psychology, 112,* 698–708. doi:10.1037/0021-843X.112.4.598

Macchi Cassia, V., Kuefner, D., Westerlund, A., & Nelson, C. A. (2006). A behavioural and ERP investigation of 3-month-olds' face preferences. *Neuropsychologia, 44,* 2113–2125. doi:10.1016/j.neuropsychologia.2005.11.014

Macchi Cassia, V., Turati, C., & Simion, F. (2004). Can a nonspecific bias toward top-heavy patterns explain newborns' face preference? *Psychological Science, 15,* 379–383. doi:10.1111/j.0956-7976.2004.00688.x

Maccoby, E. E. (1998). *The two sexes: Growing up apart, coming together.* Cambridge, MA: Harvard University Press.

Maccoby, E. E. (2000). Perspectives on gender development. *International Journal of Behavioral Development, 24,* 398–406. doi:10.1080/016502500750037946

Maccoby, E. E. (2015). Historical overeiview of socialization research and theory. In J. E. Grusec & P. D. Hastings (Eds.), *Handbook of Socialization: Theory and Research* (pp. 3–32). New York, NY: Guilford.

Maccoby, E. E., & Martin, J. A. (1983). Socialization in the context of the family: Parent–child interaction. In P. H. Mussen (Series Ed.) & E. M. Hetherington (Vol. Ed.), *Handbook of child psychology: Vol. 4. Socialization, personality, and social development* (4th ed., pp. 1–101). New York, NY: Wiley.

MacDonald, G. W., & Cornwall, A. (1995). The relationship between phonological awareness and reading and spelling achievement eleven years later. *Journal of Learning Disabilities, 28,* 523–527.

MacDonald, K., & MacDonald, T. M. (2010). The peptide that binds: A systematic review of oxytocin and its prosocial effects in humans. *Harvard Review of Psychiatry, 18,* 1–21. doi:10.3109/10673220903523615

MacDorman, M. F., Mathews, M. S., & Declercq, E. (2014, March). *Trends in out-of-hospital births in the United States, 1990–2012.* (NCHS Data Brief No. 144). Hyattsville, MD: National Center for Health Statistics.

MacEvoy, J. P., & Asher, S. R. (2012). When friends disappoint: Boys' and girls' responses to transgressions of friendship expectations. *Child Development, 83,* 104–119. doi:10.1111/j.1467-8624.2011.01685.x

Macfarlane, A. (2008). Olfaction in the development of social preferences in the human neonate. In R. Porter & M. O'Connor (Eds.), *Ciba Foundation symposium: No. 3. Parent–infant interaction* (pp. 103–117). Amsterdam, The Netherlands: Elsevier.

MacKenzie, H., Graham, S. A., & Curtin, S. (2011). Twelve-month-olds privilege words over other linguistic sounds in an associative learning task. *Developmental Science, 14,* 249–255.

Mackey, A. P., Finn, A. S., Leonard, J. A., Jacoby-Senghor, D. S., West, M. R., Gabrieli, C. F., & Gabrieli, J. D. (2015). Neuroanatomical correlates of the income-achievement gap. *Psychological Science, 26*(6), 925–933.

Maclean, M., Bryant, P., & Bradley, L. (1987). Rhymes, nursery rhymes, and reading in early childhood. *Merrill-Palmer Quarterly, 33,* 255–281.

Macmillan, R., McMorris, B. J., & Kruttschnitt, C. (2004). Linked lives: Stability and change in maternal circumstances and trajectories of antisocial behavior in children. *Child Development, 75,* 205–220. doi:10.1111/j.1467-8624.2004.00664.x

MacPhee, D., Fritz, J., & Miller-Heyl, J. (1996). Ethnic variations in personal social networks and parenting. *Child Development, 67,* 3278–3295. doi:10.1111/j.1467-8624.1996.tb01914.x

Madigan, S., Brumariu, L. E., Villani, V., Atkinson, L., & Lyons-Ruth, K. (2016). Representational and questionnaire measures of attachment: A meta-analysis of relations to child internalizing and externalizing problems. *Psychological Bulletin, 142*(4), 367–399. doi:10.1037/bul0000029

Madigan, S., Moran, G., & Pederson, D. R. (2006). Unresolved states of mind, disorganized attachment relationships, and disrupted interactions of adolescent mothers and their infants. *Developmental Psychology, 42,* 293–304. doi:10.1037/0012-1649.42.2.293

Madole, K. L., & Oakes, L. M. (1999). Making sense of infant categorization: Stable processes and changing representations. *Developmental Review, 19,* 263–296. doi:10.1006/drev.1998.0481

Maes, H. H., Silberg, J. L., Neale, M. C., & Eaves, L. J. (2007). Genetic and cultural transmission of antisocial behavior: An extended twin parent model. *Twin Research and Human Genetics, 10,* 136–150. doi:10.1375/twin.10.1.136

Mage, D. T., & Donner, E. M. (2014). Is excess male infant mortality from sudden infant death syndrome and other respiratory diseases X- linked? *Acta Paediatrica, 103,* 188–193.

Maguire, M. C., & Dunn, J. (1997). Friendships in early childhood, and social understanding. *International Journal of Behavioral Development, 21,* 669–686. doi:10.1080/016502597384613

Maher, C., Olds, T. S., Eisenmann, J. C., & Dollman, J. (2012). Screen time is more strongly associated than physical activity with overweight and obesity in 9-to 16-year-old Australians. *Acta Pædiatrica, 101*(11), 1170–1174.

Mahy, C. E., Moses, L. J., & Pfeifer, J. H. (2014). How and where: Theory-of-mind in the brain. *Developmental Cognitive Neuroscience, 9,* 68–81. doi:10.1016/j.dcn.2014.01.002

Main, M., & Goldwyn, R. (1998). *Adult attachment interview scoring and classification manual–6th version.* Unpublished manuscript, University of California, Berkeley.

Main, M., & Solomon, J. (1990). Procedures for identifying infants as disorganized/disoriented during the Ainsworth Strange Situation. In M. T. Greenberg, D. Cicchetti, & E. M. Cummings (Eds.), *Attachment in the preschool years: Theory, research, and intervention* (pp. 121–160). Chicago, IL: University of Chicago Press.

Makel, M. C., Kell, H. J., Lubinski, D., Putallaz, M., & Benbow, C. P. (2016). When lightning strikes twice: Profoundly gifted, profoundly accomplished. *Psychological Science, 27*(7), 1004–1018. doi:10.1177/0956797616644735

Malina, R. M., & Bouchard, C. (1991). *Growth, maturation, and physical activity.* Champaign, IL: Human Kinetics.

Malone, P. S., Lansford, J. E., Castellino, D. R., Berlin, L. J., Dodge, K. A., Bates, J. E., & Pettit, G. S. (2004). Divorce and child behavior problems: Applying latent change score models to life event data. *Structural Equation Modeling: A Multidisciplinary Journal, 11,* 401–423. doi:10.1207/s15328007sem1103_6

Maloney, E. A., & Beilock, S. L. (2012). Math anxiety: Who has it, why it develops, and how to guard against it. *Trends in Cognitive Sciences, 16,* 404–406.

Maltz, D. N., & Borker, R. (1982). A cultural approach to male-female miscommunication. In J. J. Gumperz (Ed.), *Language and social identity* (pp. 196–216). Cambridge, England: Cambridge University Press.

Malvaso, C., Delfabbro, P., Proeve, M., & Nobes, G. (2015). Predictors of child injury in biological and stepfamilies. *Journal of Child & Adolescent Trauma, 8*(3), 149–159. doi:10.1111/j.1467-8624.2009.01360.x

Mandel, D. R., Jusczyk, P. W., & Pisoni, D. B. (1995). Infants' recognition of the sound patterns of their own names. *Psychological Science, 6,* 314–317. doi:10.1111/j.1467-9280.1995.tb00517.x

Mandler, J. M., & McDonough, L. (1998). Studies in inductive inference in infancy. *Cognitive Psychology, 37*, 60–96. doi:10.1006/cogp.1998.0691

Manicklal, S., Emery, V. C., Lazzarotto, T., Boppana, S. B., & Gupta, R. K. (2013). The "silent" global burden of congenital cytomegalovirus. *Clinical Microbiology Reviews, 26*(1), 86–102.

Marceau, K., Horwitz, B. N., Narusyte, J., Ganiban, J. M., Spotts, E. L., Reiss, D., & Neiderhiser, J. M. (2013). Gene–environment correlation underlying the association between parental negativity and adolescent externalizing problems. *Child Development. 84*, 2031–2046. doi:10.1111/cdev.12094

Marcia, J. E. (1980). Identity in adolescence. In J. Adelson (Ed.), *Handbook of adolescent psychology* (pp. 159–187). New York, NY: Wiley.

Marcus, D. E., & Overton, W. F. (1978). The development of cognitive gender constancy and sex role preferences. *Child Development, 49*, 434–444. doi:10.2307/1128708

Marcus, G. F. (1996). Why do children say "breaked"? *Current Directions in Psychological Science, 5*, 81–85.

Marcus, G. F. (2004). *The birth of the mind: How a tiny number of genes creates the complexities of human thought.* New York, NY: Basic Books.

Marcus, G. F., Vijayan, S., Bandi Rao, S., & Vishton, P. M. (1999, January 1). Rule learning by seven-month-old infants. *Science, 283*, 77–80.

Mares, M. L., & Pan, Z. (2013). Effects of Sesame Street: A meta-analysis of children's learning in 15 countries. *Journal of Applied Developmental Psychology, 34*(3), 140–151.

Margett, T. E., & Witherington, D. C. (2011). The nature of preschoolers' concept of living and artificial objects. *Child Development, 82*, 2067–2082. doi:10.1111/j.1467-8624.2011.01661.x

Margolin, G., Gordis, E. B., & John, R. S. (2001). Coparenting: A link between marital conflict and parenting in two-parent families. *Journal of Family Psychology, 15*, 3–21. doi:10.1037/0893-3200.15.1.3

Marin, M. M., Rapisardi, G., & Tani, F. (2015). Two-day-old newborn infants recognise their mother by her axillary odour. *Acta Paediatrica, 104*(3), 237–240.

Markman, E. M. (1989). *Categorization and naming in children: Problems of induction.* Cambridge, MA: MIT Press.

Markman, E. M., & Hutchinson, J. E. (1984). Children's sensitivity to constraints on word meaning: Taxonomic versus thematic relations. *Cognitive Psychology, 16*, 1–27. doi:10.1016/0010-0285(84)90002-1

Markman, E. M., & Wachtel, G. F. (1988). Children's use of mutual exclusivity to constrain the meanings of words. *Cognitive Psychology, 20*, 121–157.

Marks, A. K., Patton, F., & García Coll, C. (2011). Being bicultural: A mixed-methods study of adolescents' implicitly and explicitly measured multiethnic identities. *Developmental Psychology, 47*, 270–288. doi:10.1037/a0020730

Markson, L., & Bloom, P. (1997, February 27). Evidence against a dedicated system for word learning in children. *Nature, 385*, 813–815. doi:10.1038/385813a0

Markus, H. R., & Kitayama, S. (1991). Culture and the self: Implications for cognition, emotion, and motivation. *Psychological Review, 98*, 224–253.

Marlier, L., & Schaal, B. (2005). Human newborns prefer human milk: Conspecific milk odor is attractive without postnatal exposure. *Child Development, 76*, 155–168. doi:10.1111/j.1467-8624.2005.00836.x

Marlier, L., Schaal, B., & Soussignan, R. (1998). Neonatal responsiveness to the odor of amniotic and lacteal fluids: A test of perinatal chemosensory continuity. *Child Development, 69*, 611–623.

Marsh, H. W., Craven, R., & Debus, R. (1998). Structure, stability, and development of young children's self-concepts: A multicohort–multioccasion study. *Child Development, 69*, 1030–1053. doi:10.1111/j.1467-8624.1998.tb06159.x

Marshal, M. P., Friedman, M. S., Stall, R., King, K. M., Miles, J., Gold, M. A., . . . Morse, J. Q. (2008). Sexual orientation and adolescent substance use: A meta-analysis and methodological review. *Addiction, 103*, 546–556. doi:10.1111/j.1360-0443.2008.02149.x

Marshall, P. J., & Meltzoff, A. N. (2014). Neural mirroring mechanisms and imitation in human infants. *Philosophical Transactions of the Royal Society of B: Biological Sciences, 369*(1644), doi:10.1098/rstb.2013.0620

Marsiglio, W., Amato, P., Day, R. D., & Lamb, M. E. (2000). Scholarship on fatherhood in the 1990s and beyond. *Journal of Marriage and Family, 62*, 1173–1191. doi:10.1111/j.1741-3737.2000.01173.x

Martin, C. L., & Fabes, R. A. (2001). The stability and consequences of young children's same-sex peer interactions. *Developmental Psychology, 37*, 431–446. doi:10.1037/0012-1649.37.3.431

Martin, C. L., Fabes, R. A., Evans, S. M., & Wyman, H. (1999). Social cognition on the playground: Children's beliefs about playing with girls versus boys and their relations to sex segregated play. *Journal of Social and Personal Relationships, 16*, 751–771. doi:10.1177/0265407599166005

Martin, C. L., & Halverson, C. F., Jr. (1981). A schematic processing model of sex typing and stereotyping in children. *Child Development, 52*, 1119–1134. doi:10.2307/1129498

Martin, C. L., & Halverson, C. F., Jr. (1983). The effects of sex-typing schemas on young children's memory. *Child Development, 54*, 563–574. doi:10.2307/1130043

Martin, C. L., Kornienko, O., Schaefer, D. R., Hanish, L. D., Fabes, R. A., & Goble, P. (2013). The role of sex of peers and gender-typed activities in young children's peer affiliative networks: A longitudinal analysis of selection and influence. *Child Development, 84*, 921–937. doi:10.1111/cdev.12032

Martin, C. L., Ruble, D. N., & Szkrybalo, J. (2002). Cognitive theories of early gender development. *Psychological Bulletin, 128*, 903–933.

Martin, J., & Ross, H. (2005). Sibling aggression: Sex differences and parents' reactions. *International Journal of Behavioral Development, 29*, 129–138. doi:10.1080/01650250444000469

Martin, J. A., Hamilton, B. E., & Osterman, M. J. K. (2015). *Births in the United States, 2014* (National Center for Health Statistics Data Brief No. 216). Retrieved from http://www.cdc.gov/nchs/data/databriefs/db216.pdf

Martin, M. J., Conger, R. D., Schofield, T. J., Dogan, S. J., Widaman, K. F., Donnellan, M. B., & Neppl, T. K. (2010). Evaluation of the interactionist model of socioeconomic status and problem behavior: A developmental cascade across generations. *Development and Psychopathology, 22*, 695–713. doi:10.1017/S0954579410000374

Martin, N. G., Maza, L., McGrath, S. J., & Phelps, A. E. (2014). An examination of referential and affect specificity with five emotions in infancy. *Infant Behavior and Development, 37*, 286–297. doi:10.1016/j.infbeh.2014.04.009

Martin-Biggers, J., Spaccarotella, K., Berhaupt-Glickstein, A., Hongu, N., Worobey, J., & Byrd-Bredbenner, C. (2014). Come and get it! A discussion of family mealtime literature and factors affecting obesity risk. *Advances in Nutrition: An International Review Journal, 5*(3), 235–247.

Martin-Biggers, J., Spaccarotella, K., Delaney, C., Koenings, M., Alleman, G., Hongu, N., . . . Byrd-Bredbenner, C. (2015). Development of the intervention materials for the homestyles obesity prevention program for parents of preschoolers. *Nutrients, 7*(8), 6628–6669.

Martin-Storey, A., & Crosnoe, R. (2012). Sexual minority status, peer harassment, and adolescent depression. *Journal of Adolescence, 35*, 1001–1011. doi:10.1016/j.adolescence.2012.02.006

Martinot, D., Bagès, C., & Désert, M. (2012). French children's awareness of gender stereotypes about mathematics and reading: When girls improve their reputation in math. *Sex Roles, 66*, 210–219. doi:10.1007/s11199-011-0032-3

Martorell, R., Onis, M., Martines, J., Black, M., Onyango, A., & Dewey, K. G. (2006). WHO motor development study: Windows of achievement for six gross motor development milestones. *Acta Paediatrica, 95,* 86–95.

Martos, A. J., Nezhad, S., & Meyer, I. H. (2015). Variations in sexual identity milestones among lesbians, gay men, and bisexuals. *Sexuality Research & Social Policy: A Journal of the NSRC, 12,* 24–33. doi:10.1007/s13178-014-0167-4

Marufu, T. C., Ahankari, A., Coleman, T., & Lewis, S. (2015). Maternal smoking and the risk of still birth: Systematic review and meta-analysis. *BMC Public Health, 15,* 239. doi:10.1186/s12889-015-1552-5

Masataka, N. (1992). Motherese in a signed language. *Infant Behavior and Development, 15,* 453–460. doi:10.1016/0163-6383(92)80013-K

Masataka, N. (1999). Preference for infant-directed singing in 2-day-old hearing infants of deaf parents. *Developmental Psychology, 35,* 1001–1005. doi:10.1037/0012-1649.35.4.1001

Masataka, N. (2006). Preference for consonance over dissonance by hearing newborns of deaf parents and of hearing parents. *Developmental Science, 9,* 46–50. doi:10.1111/j.1467-7687.2005.00462.x

Mascolo, M. F., Fischer, K. W., & Li, J. (2003). Dynamic development of component systems of emotions: Pride, shame, and guilt in China and the United States. In R. J. Davidson, K. R. Scherer, & H. H. Goldsmith (Eds.), *Handbook of affective sciences* (pp. 375–408). Oxford, England: Oxford University Press.

Mason, M. G., & Gibbs, J. C. (1993). Social perspective taking and moral judgment among college students. *Journal of Adolescent Research, 8,* 109–123. doi:10.1177/074355489381008

Masten, A. S. (2007). Resilience in developing systems: Progress and promise as the fourth wave rises. *Development and Psychopathology, 19,* 921–930. doi:10.1017/S0954579407000442

Masten, A. S. (2014). Global perspectives on resilience in children and youth. *Child Development, 85*(1), 6–20. doi:10.1111/cdev.12205

Masten, A. S., Best, K. M., & Garmezy, N. (1990). Resilience and development: Contributions from the study of children who overcome adversity. *Development and Psychopathology, 2,* 425–444. doi:10.1017/S0954579400005812

Masten, A. S., & Cicchetti, D. (2010). Developmental cascades. *Development and Psychopathology, 22,* 491–495. doi:10.1017/S0954579410000222

Masten, A. S., Cutuli, J. J., Herbers, J. E., Hinz, E., Obradović, J., & Wenzel, A. J. (2014). Academic risk and resilience in the context of homelessness. *Child Development Perspectives, 8,* 201–206. doi:10.1111/cdep.12088

Masten, A. S., Herbers, J. E., Desjardins, C. D., Cutuli, J. J., McCormick, C. M., Sapienza, J. K., . . . Zelazo, P. D. (2012). Executive function skills and school success in young children experiencing homelessness. *Educational Researcher, 41,* 375–384. doi:10.3102/0013189X12459883

Matsuba, M. K., & Walker, L. J. (2004). Extraordinary moral commitment: Young adults involved in social organizations. *Journal of Personality, 72,* 413–436. doi:10.1111/j.0022-3506.2004.00267.x

Matsumoto, D. R. (1996). *Unmasking Japan: Myths and realities about the emotions of the Japanese.* Stanford, CA: Stanford University Press.

Matteson, L. K., McGue, M., & Iacono, W. G. (2013). Shared environmental influences on personality: A combined twin and adoption approach. *Behavior Genetics, 43*(6), 491–504.

Matthews, G., Zeidner, M., & Roberts, R. D. (2002). *Emotional intelligence: Science and myth.* Cambridge, MA: MIT Press.

Matuz, T., Govindan, R. B., Preissl, H., Siegel, E. R., Muenssinger, J., Murphy, P., . . . Eswaran, H. (2012). Habituation of visual evoked responses in neonates and fetuses: A MEG study. *Developmental Cognitive Neuroscience, 2*(3), 303–316.

Maughan, B., Collishaw, S., & Stringaris, A. (2013). Depression in childhood and adolescence. *Journal of the Canadian Academy of Child and Adolescent Psychiatry, 22*(1), 35–40.

Maurer, D., & Maurer, C. (1988). *The world of the newborn.* New York, NY: Basic Books.

Maurer, D., & Salapatek, P. (1976). Developmental changes in the scanning of faces by young infants. *Child Development, 47,* 523–527. doi:10.2307/1128813

Maya-Vetencourt, J. F., & Origlia, N. (2012). Visual cortex plasticity: A complex interplay of genetic and environmental influences. *Neural Plasticity, 2012.* doi:10.1155/2012/631965

Mayberry, M. L., & Espelage, D. L. (2007). Associations among empathy, social competence, & reactive/proactive aggression subtypes. *Journal of Youth and Adolescence, 36,* 787–798. doi:10.1007/s10964-006-9113-y

Mayer, J. D., Roberts, R. D., & Barsade, S. G. (2008). Human abilities: Emotional intelligence. *Annual Review of psychology, 59,* 507–537. doi:10.1146/annurev.psych.59.103006.093646

Mayeux, L., & Cillessen, A. H. N. (2008). It's not just being popular, it's knowing it, too: The role of self-perceptions of status in the associations between peer status and aggression. *Social Development, 17,* 871–888. doi:10.1111/j.1467-9507.2008.00474.x

Mayor, J., & Plunkett, K. (2014). Shared understanding and idiosyncratic expression in early vocabularies. *Developmental Science, 17*(3), 412–423.

Mazur, E., & Richards, L. (2011). Adolescents' and emerging adults' social networking online: Homophily or diversity? *Journal of Applied Developmental Psychology, 32,* 180–188. doi:10.1016/j.appdev.2011.03.001

Mazzocco, M. M. M., & Kover, S. T. (2007). A longitudinal assessment of executive function skills and their association with math performance. *Child Neuropsychology, 13,* 18–45.

McAdams, D. P., & Olson, B. D. (2010). Personality development: Continuity and change over the life course. *Annual Review of Psychology, 61,* 517–542. doi:10.1146/annurev.psych.093008.100507

McBride-Chang, C. (2004). *Children's literacy development.* New York, NY: Oxford University Press.

McCabe, A., & Peterson, C. (1991). Getting the story: A longitudinal study of parental styles in eliciting narratives and developing narrative skill. In A. McCabe & C. Peterson (Eds.), *Developing narrative structure* (pp. 217–253). Hillsdale, NJ: Erlbaum.

McCabe, A., Tamis-LeMonda, C. S., Bornstein, M. H., Cates, C. B., Golinkoff, R., Guerra, A. W., . . . Mendelsohn, A. (2013). Multilingual children. *Social Policy Report, 27*(4), 1–21.

McCabe, K. M., Hough, R., Wood, P. A., & Yeh, M. (2001). Childhood and adolescent onset conduct disorder: A test of the developmental taxonomy. *Journal of Abnormal Child Psychology, 29,* 305–316. doi:10.1023/A:1010357812278

McCabe, K. M., Rodgers, C., Yeh, M., & Hough, R. (2004). Gender differences in childhood onset conduct disorder. *Development and Psychopathology, 16,* 179–192. doi:10.1017/S0954579404044463

McCabe, P. C., & Altamura, M. (2011). Empirically valid strategies to improve social and emotional competence of preschool children. *Psychology in the Schools, 48,* 513–540. doi:10.1002/pits.20570

McCall, R. B., van IJzendoorn, M. H., Juffer, F., Groark, C. J., & Groza, V. K. (2011). Children without permanent parents: Research, practice, and policy. *Monographs of the Society for Research in Child Development, 76*(4, Serial No. 301), 1–318.

McCarthy, A., & Lee, K. (2009). Children's knowledge of deceptive gaze cues and its relation to their actual lying behavior. *Journal of Experimental Child Psychology, 103,* 117–134. doi:10.1016/j.jecp.2008.06.005

McCartney, K., Burchinal, M., Clarke-Stewart, A., Bub, K. L., Owen, M. T., & Belsky, J. (2010). Testing a series of causal propositions relating time in child care to children's externalizing behavior. *Developmental Psychology, 46,* 1–17. doi:10.1037/a0017886

McClelland, J. L., McNaughton, B. L., & O'Reilly, R. C. (1995). Why there are complementary learning systems in the hippocampus and neocortex: Insights from the successes and failures of connectionist models of learning and memory. *Psychological Review, 102*(3), 419–457. doi:10.1037/0033-295X.102.3.419

McClintock, M. K., & Herdt, G. (1996). Rethinking puberty: The development of sexual attraction. *Current Directions in Psychological Science, 5*, 178–183. doi:10.1111/1467-8721.ep11512422

McCloskey, M. (2007). Quantitative literacy and developmental dyscalculias. In D. B. Berch & M. M. M. Mazzocco (Eds.), *Why is math so hard for some children? The nature and origins of mathematical learning difficulties and disabilities* (pp. 415–429). Baltimore, MD: Paul H. Brookes.

McConnell, D., Breitkreuz, R., & Savage, A. (2011). From financial hardship to child difficulties: Main and moderating effects of perceived social support. *Child: Care, Health and Development, 37*, 679–691. doi:10.1111/j.1365-2214.2010.01185.x

McCormick, M. C., Brooks-Gunn, J., Buka, S. L., Goldman, J., Yu, J., Salganik, M., . . . Casey, P. H. (2006). Early intervention in low birth weight premature infants: Results at 18 years of age for the Infant Health and Development Program. *Pediatrics, 117*, 771–780. doi:10.1542/peds.2005-1316

McCoy, D. C., & Raver, C. C. (2011). Caregiver emotional expressiveness, child emotion regulation, and child behavior problems among Head Start families. *Social Development, 20*, 741–761.

McCrink, K., & Wynn, K. (2004). Large-number addition and subtraction by 9-month-old infants. *Psychological Science, 15*(11), 776–781. doi:10.1111/j.0956-7976.2004.00755.x

McCrory, E. J., De Brito, S. A., Kelly, P. A., Bird, G., Sebastian, C. L., Mechelli, A., . . . Viding, E. (2013). Amygdala activation in maltreated children during pre-attentive emotional processing. *British Journal of Psychiatry, 202*, 269–276.

McCrory, E. J., & Viding, E. (2015). The theory of latent vulnerability: Reconceptualizing the link between childhood maltreatment and psychiatric disorder. *Development and Psychopathology, 27*(02), 493–505.

McDaniel, M. A. (2005). Big-brained people are smarter: A meta-analysis of the relationship between in vivo brain volume and intelligence. *Intelligence, 33*, 337–346. doi:10.1016/j.intell.2004.11.005

McDonald, K. L., Malti, T., Killen, M., & Rubin, K. H. (2014). Best friends' discussions of social dilemmas. *Journal of Youth and Adolescence, 43*, 233–244. doi:10.1007/s10964-013-9961-1

McDonald, K. L., Putallaz, M., Grimes, C. L., Kupersmidt, J. B., & Coie, J. D. (2007). Girl talk: Gossip, friendship, and sociometric status. *Merrill-Palmer Quarterly, 53*, 381–411.

McDougall, P., & Hymel, S. (2007). Same-gender versus cross-gender friendship conceptions: Similar or different? *Merrill-Palmer Quarterly, 53*, 347–380.

McDowell, D. J., & Parke, R. D. (2009). Parental correlates of children's peer relations: An empirical test of a tripartite model. *Developmental Psychology, 45*, 224–235. doi:10.1037/a0014305

McElwain, N. L., Booth-LaForce, C., & Wu, X. (2011). Infant–mother attachment and children's friendship quality: Maternal mental-state talk as an intervening mechanism. *Developmental Psychology, 47*, 1295–1311. doi:10.1037/a0024094

McFadyen-Ketchum, S. A., Bates, J. E., Dodge, K. A., & Pettit, G. S. (1996). Patterns of change in early childhood aggressive-disruptive behavior: Gender differences in predictions from early coercive and affectionate mother–child interactions. *Child Development, 67*, 2417–2433. doi:10.2307/1131631

McGill, R. K., Way, N., & Hughes, D. (2012). Intra- and interracial best friendships during middle school: Links to social and emotional well-being. *Journal of Research on Adolescence, 22*, 722–738. doi:10.1111/j.1532-7795.2012.00826.x

McGowan, P. O., Sasaki, A., D'Alessio, A. C., Dymov, S., Labonté, B., Szyf, M., . . . Meaney, M. J. (2009). Epigenetic regulation of the glucocorticoid receptor in human brain associates with childhood abuse. *Nature Neuroscience, 12*, 342–348. doi:10.1038/nn.2270

McGraw, M. B. (1943). *The neuromuscular maturation of the human infant.* New York, NY: Columbia University Press.

McGue, M., Bouchard, T. J., Jr., Iacono, W. G., & Lykken, D. T. (1993). Behavioral genetics of cognitive ability: A life-span perspective. In R. Plomin & G. E. McClearn (Eds.), *Nature, nurture and psychology* (pp. 59–76). Washington, DC: American Psychological Association.

McGuigan, F., & Salmon, K. (2004). The time to talk: The influence of the timing of adult–child talk on children's event memory. *Child Development, 75*, 669–686. doi:10.1111/j.1467-8624.2004.00700.x

McGuire, S., McHale, S. M., & Updegraff, K. (1996). Children's perceptions of the sibling relationship in middle childhood: Connections within and between family relationships. *Personal Relationships, 3*, 229–239. doi:10.1111/j.1475-6811.1996.tb00114.x

McGurk, H., & MacDonald, J. (1976, December 23–30). Hearing lips and seeing voices. *Nature, 264*, 746–748.

McHale, J. P., Kazali, C., Rotman, T., Talbot, J., Carleton, M., & Lieberson, R. (2004). The transition to coparenthood: Parents' prebirth expectations and early coparental adjustment at 3 months postpartum. *Development and Psychopathology, 16*, 711–733. doi:10.1017/S0954579404004742

McHale, S. M., Bissell, J., & Kim, J.-Y. (2009). Sibling relationship, family, and genetic factors in sibling similarity in sexual risk. *Journal of Family Psychology, 23*, 562–572. doi:10.1037/a0014982

McHale, S. M., Crouter, A. C., McGuire, S. A., & Updegraff, K. A. (1995). Congruence between mothers' and fathers' differential treatment of siblings: Links with family relations and children's well-being. *Child Development, 66*, 116–128. doi:10.1111/j.1467-8624.1995.tb00859.x

McHale, S. M., Updegraff, K. A., Jackson-Newsom, J., Tucker, C. J., & Crouter, A. C. (2000). When does parents' differential treatment have negative implications for siblings? *Social Development, 9*, 149–172. doi:10.1111/1467-9507.00117

McHale, S. M., Updegraff, K. A., Shanahan, L., Crouter, A. C., & Killoren, S. E. (2005). Siblings' differential treatment in Mexican American families. *Journal of Marriage and Family, 67*, 1259–1274. doi:10.1111/j.1741-3737.2005.00215.x

McHale, S. M., Whiteman, S. D., Kim, J.-Y., & Crouter, A. C. (2007). Characteristics and correlates of sibling relationships in two-parent African American families. *Journal of Family Psychology, 21*, 227–235. doi:10.1037/0893-3200.21.2.227

McMahon, A. W., Iskander, J. K., Haber, P., Braun, M. M., & Ball, R. (2008). Inactivated influenza vaccine (IIV) in children <2 years of age: Examination of selected adverse events reported to the Vaccine Adverse Event Reporting System (VAERS) after thimerosal-free or thimerosal-containing vaccine. *Vaccine, 26*, 427–429. doi:10.1016/j.vaccine.2007.10.071

McMahon, R. J., Witkiewitz, K., & Kotler, J. S. (2010). Predictive validity of callous–unemotional traits measured in early adolescence with respect to multiple antisocial outcomes. *Journal of Abnormal Psychology, 119*, 752–763. doi:10.1037/a0020796

McMahon, S. D., & Washburn, J. J. (2003). Violence prevention: An evaluation of program effects with urban African American students. *Journal of Primary Prevention, 24*, 43–62. doi:10.1023/A:1025075617356

McMaster, L. E., Connolly, J., Pepler, D., & Craig, W. M. (2002). Peer to peer sexual harassment in early adolescence: A developmental perspective. *Development and Psychopathology, 14*, 91–105.

McMillan, B., & Saffran, J. R. (2016). Learning in complex environments: The effects of background speech on early word learning. *Child Development, 87*(6), 1841–1855. doi:10.1111/cdev.12559

McMurray, B. (2007, August 3). Defusing the childhood vocabulary explosion. *Science, 317,* 631.

McMurray, B., Horst, J. S., & Samuelson, L. K. (2012). Word learning emerges from the interaction of online referent selection and slow associative learning. *Psychological Review, 119*(4), 831–877. doi:10.1037/a0029872

McNeil, N. M., Fyfe, E. R., Petersen, L. A., Dunwiddie, A. E., & Brletic-Shipley, H. (2011). Benefits of practicing 4 = 2 + 2: Nontraditional problem formats facilitate children's understanding of mathematical equivalence. *Child Development, 82,* 1620–1633.

McQuaid, N., Bigelow, A. E., McLaughlin, J., & MacLean, K. (2007). Maternal mental state language and preschool children's attachment security: Relation to children's mental state language and expressions of emotional understanding. *Social Development, 17,* 61–83. doi:10.1111/j.1467-9507.2007.00415.x

Meaney, M. J. (2001). Maternal care, gene expression, and the transmission of individual differences in stress reactivity across generations. *Annual Review of Neuroscience, 24,* 1161–1192. doi:10.1146/annurev.neuro.24.1.1161

Meaney, M. J. (2010). Epigenetics and the biological definition of gene × environment interactions. *Child Development, 81,* 41–79.

Meece, J. L., Wigfield, A., & Eccles, J. S. (1990). Predictors of math anxiety and its influence on young adolescents' course enrollment intentions and performance in mathematics. *Journal of Educational Psychology, 82,* 60–70.

Meert, G., Grégoire, J., & Noël, M.-P. (2010). Comparing the magnitude of two fractions with common components: Which representations are used by 10- and 12-year-olds? *Journal of Experimental Child Psychology, 107,* 244–259. doi:10.1016/j.jecp.2010.04.008

Meeus, W. (1996). Studies on identity development in adolescence: An overview of research and some new data. *Journal of Youth and Adolescence, 25,* 569–598. doi:10.1007/BF01537355

Meeus, W. (2011). The study of adolescent identity formation 2000–2010: A review of longitudinal research. *Journal of Research on Adolescence, 21,* 75–94. doi:10.1111/j.1532-7795.2010.00716.x

Meeus, W., Van De Schoot, R., Keijsers, L., Schwartz, S. J., & Branje, S. (2010). On the progression and stability of adolescent identity formation: A five-wave longitudinal study in early-to-middle and middle-to-late adolescence. *Child Development, 81,* 1565–1581. doi:10.1111/j.1467-8624.2010.01492.x

Mehler, J., Jusczyk, P., Lambertz, G., Halsted, N., Bertoncini, J., & Amiel-Tison, C. (1988). A precursor of language acquisition in young infants. *Cognition, 29,* 143–178.

Meier, M. H., Slutske, W. S., Heath, A. C., & Martin, N. G. (2011). Sex differences in the genetic and environmental influences on childhood conduct disorder and adult antisocial behavior. *Journal of Abnormal Psychology, 120,* 377–388. doi:10.1037/a0022303

Meisels, S. J., & Plunkett, J. W. (1988). Developmental consequences of preterm birth: Are there long-term effects? In P. B. Baltes, D. L. Featherman, & R. M. Lerner (Eds.), *Life-span development and behavior* (Vol. 9, pp. 87–128). Hillsdale, NJ: Erlbaum.

Melby, J. N., Conger, R. D., Fang, S., Wickrama, K. A. S., & Conger, K. J. (2008). Adolescent family experiences and educational attainment during early adulthood. *Developmental Psychology, 44,* 1519–1536.

Meltzoff, A. N. (1988a). Imitation of televised models by infants. *Child Development, 59,* 1221–1229.

Meltzoff, A. N. (1988b). Infant imitation and memory: Nine-month-olds in immediate and deferred tests. *Child Development, 59,* 217–225.

Meltzoff, A. N. (1995a). Understanding the intentions of others: Re-enactment of intended acts by 18-month-old children. *Developmental Psychology, 31,* 838–850. doi:10.1037/0012-1649.31.5.838

Meltzoff, A. N. (1995b). What infant memory tells us about infantile amnesia: Long-term recall and deferred imitation. *Journal of Experimental Child Psychology, 59,* 497–515. doi:10.1006/jecp.1995.1023

Meltzoff, A. N., & Borton, R. W. (1979, November 22). Intermodal matching by human neonates. *Nature, 282,* 403–404.

Meltzoff, A. N., & Moore, M. K. (1977, October 7). Imitation of facial and manual gestures by human neonates. *Science, 198,* 75–78.

Meltzoff, A. N., & Moore, M. K. (1983). Newborn infants imitate adult facial gestures. *Child Development, 54,* 702–709.

Mendle, J., Harden, K. P., Brooks-Gunn, J., & Graber, J. A. (2010). Development's tortoise and hare: Pubertal timing, pubertal tempo, and depressive symptoms in boys and girls. *Developmental Psychology, 46,* 1341–1353. doi:10.1037/a0020205

Mendle, J., Harden, K. P., Brooks-Gunn, J., & Graber, J. A. (2012). Peer relationships and depressive symptomatology in boys at puberty. *Developmental Psychology, 48,* 429–435. doi:10.1037/a0026425

Mennella, J. A., Jagnow, C. P., & Beauchamp, G. K. (2001). Prenatal and postnatal flavor learning by human infants. *Pediatrics, 107*(6), e88. doi:10.1542/peds.107.6.e88

Mennella, J. A., Johnson, A., & Beauchamp, G. K. (1995). Garlic ingestion by pregnant women alters the odor of amniotic fluid. *Chemical Senses, 20,* 207–209.

Menon, M., Tobin, D. D., Corby, B. C., Menon, M., Hodges, E. V., & Perry, D. G. (2007). The developmental costs of high self-esteem for antisocial children. *Child Development, 78,* 1627–1639.

Mental Health Parity and Addiction Equity Act, Pub. L. 110-343, div. C, title V, subtitle B (Sec. 511 et seq.) (2008).

Mervis, C. B., & Velleman, S. L. (2011). Children with Williams syndrome: Language, cognitive, and behavioral characteristics and their implications for intervention. *Perspectives on Language Learning and Education, 18,* 98–107. doi:10.1044/lle18.3.98

Mesman, J., Stoel, R., Bakermans-Kranenburg, M. J., van IJzendoorn, M. H., Juffer, F., Koot, H. M., & Alink, L. R. (2009). Predicting growth curves of early childhood externalizing problems: Differential susceptibility of children with difficult temperament. *Journal of Abnormal Child Psychology, 37,* 625–636. doi:10.1007/s10802-009-9298-0

Mesman, J., van IJzendoorn, M. H., & Bakermans-Kranenburg, M. J. (2012). Unequal in opportunity, equal in process: Parental sensitivity promotes positive child development in ethnic minority families. *Child Development Perspectives, 6,* 239–250. doi:10.1111/j.1750-8606.2011.00223.x

Mesquita, B., & Frijda, N. H. (1992). Cultural variations in emotions: A review. *Psychological Bulletin, 112,* 179–204.

Messner, M. (2002). *Taking the field: Women, men, and sports.* Minneapolis, MN: University of Minnesota Press.

Metz, E., & Youniss, J. (2003). A demonstration that school-based required service does not deter—but heightens—volunteerism. *Political Science and Politics, 36,* 281–286. doi:10.1017/S1049096503002221

Meunier, J. C., Boyle, M., O'Connor, T. G., & Jenkins, J. M. (2013). Multilevel mediation: Cumulative contextual risk, maternal differential treatment, and children's behavior within families. *Child Development, 84,* 1594–1615. doi:10.1111/cdev.12066

Michalik, N. M., Eisenberg, N., Spinrad, T. L., Ladd, B., Thompson, M., & Valiente, C. (2007). Longitudinal relations among parental emotional expressivity and sympathy and prosocial behavior in adolescence. *Social Development, 16,* 286–309. doi:10.1111/j.1467-9507.2007.00385.x

Michalson, L., & Lewis, M. (1985). What do children know about emotions and when do they know it? In M. Lewis & L. A. Rosenblum (Series Eds.) & M. Lewis & C. Saarni (Vol. Eds.), *Genesis of behavior: Vol. 5. The socialization of emotions* (pp. 117–139). New York, NY: Plenum Press.

Michl, L. C., McLaughlin, K. A., Shepherd, K., & Nolen-Hoeksema, S. (2013). Rumination as a mechanism linking stressful life events to symptoms of depression and anxiety: Longitudinal evidence in early adolescents and adults. *Journal of Abnormal Psychology, 122*(2), 339–352. doi:10.1037/a0031994

Miell, D., & MacDonald, R. (2000). Children's creative collaborations: The importance of friendship when working together on a musical composition. *Social Development, 9,* 348–369. doi:10.1111/1467-9507.00130

Mikami, A. Y., Szwedo, D. E., Allen, J. P., Evans, M. A., & Hare, A. L. (2010). Adolescent peer relationships and behavior problems predict young adults' communication on social networking websites. *Developmental Psychology, 46,* 46–56. doi:10.1037/a0017420

Miklikowska, M., Duriez, B., & Soenens, B. (2011). Family roots of empathy-related characteristics: The role of perceived maternal and paternal need support in adolescence. *Developmental Psychology, 47,* 1342–1352. doi:10.1037/a0024726

Milewski, A. E. (1976). Infants' discrimination of internal and external pattern elements. *Journal of Experimental Child Psychology, 22,* 229–246. doi:10.1016/0022-0965(76)90004-7

Miller, A. C., & Keenan, J. M. (2009). How word decoding skill impacts text memory: The centrality deficit and how domain knowledge can compensate. *Annals of Dyslexia, 59*(2), 99–113. doi:10.1007/s11881-009-0025-x

Miller, A. L., Clifford, C., Sturza, J., Rosenblum, K., Vazquez, D. M., Kaciroti, N., & Lumeng, J. C. (2013). Blunted cortisol response to stress is associated with higher body mass index in low-income preschool-aged children. *Psychoneuroendocrinology, 38*(11), 2611–2617.

Miller, A. L., Sturza, J., Rosenblum, K., Vazquez, D. M., Kaciroti, N., & Lumeng, J. C. (2015). Salivary alpha amylase diurnal pattern and stress response are associated with body mass index in low-income preschool-aged children. *Psychoneuroendocrinology, 53,* 40–48.

Miller, B. C., Benson, B., & Galbraith, K. A. (2001). Family relationships and adolescent pregnancy risk: A research synthesis. *Developmental Review, 21,* 1–38. doi:10.1006/drev.2000.0513

Miller, D. J., Duka, T., Stimpson, C. D., Schapiro, S. J., Baze, W. B., McArthur, M. J., ... Sherwood, C. C. (2012). Prolonged myelination in human neocortical evolution. *Proceedings of the National Academy of Sciences of the United States of America, 109,* 16480–16485. doi:10.1073/pnas.1117943109

Miller, G. A., & Gildea, P. M. (1987, September). How children learn words. *Scientific American, 257*(3), 94–99.

Miller, G. E., Chen, E., & Parker, K. J. (2011). Psychological stress in childhood and susceptibility to the chronic diseases of aging: Moving toward a model of behavioral and biological mechanisms. *Psychological Bulletin, 137*(6), 959–997.

Miller, J. G., & Bersoff, D. M. (1995). Development in the context of everyday family relationships: Culture, interpersonal morality, and adaptation. In M. Killen & D. Hart (Eds.), *Morality in everyday life: Developmental perspectives* (pp. 259–282). New York, NY: Cambridge University Press.

Miller, J. G., Bersoff, D. M., & Harwood, R. L. (1990). Perceptions of social responsibilities in India and in the United States: Moral imperatives or personal decisions? *Journal of Personality and Social Psychology, 58,* 33–47. doi:10.1037/0022-3514.58.1.33

Miller, J. L. (2014). Effects of familiar contingencies on infants' vocal behavior in new communicative contexts. *Developmental Psychobiology, 56*(7), 1518–1527.

Miller, K. (1984). Child as the measurer of all things: Measurement of procedures and the development of quantitative concepts. In C. Sophian (Ed.), *Origins of cognitive skills: The Eighteenth Annual Carnegie Symposium on Cognition* (pp. 193–228). Hillsdale, NJ: Erlbaum.

Miller, K. F., Smith, C. M., Zhu, J., & Zhang, H. (1995). Preschool origins of cross-national differences in mathematical competence: The role of number-naming systems. *Psychological Science, 6,* 56–60. doi:10.1111/j.1467-9280.1995.tb00305.x

Miller, P., & Sperry, L. L. (1987). The socialization of anger and aggression. *Merrill-Palmer Quarterly, 33,* 1–31.

Miller, P. H. (2002). *Theories of developmental psychology* (4th ed.). New York, NY: Worth.

Miller, P. H. (2011). *Theories of developmental psychology* (5th ed.). New York, NY: Worth.

Miller, P. H., & Coyle, T. R. (1999). Developmental change: Lessons from microgenesis. In E. K. Scholnick, K. Nelson, S. A. Gelman, & P. H. Miller (Eds.), *Conceptual development: Piaget's legacy* (pp. 209–239). Mahwah, NJ: Erlbaum.

Miller, P. H., & Seier, W. L. (1994). Strategy utilization deficiencies in children: When, where, and why. In H. W. Reese (Ed.), *Advances in child development and behavior* (Vol. 25, pp. 108–156). San Diego, CA: Academic Press.

Miller, P. J., & Sperry, L. L. (1988). Early talk about the past: The origins of conversational stories of personal experience. *Journal of Child Language, 15,* 293–315. doi:10.1017/S0305000900012381

Miller, P. M., Danaher, D. L., & Forbes, D. (1986). Sex-related strategies for coping with interpersonal conflict in children aged five and seven. *Developmental Psychology, 22,* 543–548. doi:10.1037/0012-1649.22.4.543

Miller, S., Lansford, J. E., Costanzo, P., Malone, P. S., Golonka, M., & Killeya-Jones, L. A. (2009). Early adolescent romantic partner status, peer standing, and problem behaviors.

Journal of Early Adolescence, 29, 839–861. doi:10.1177/0272431609332665

Miller, S. A. (2012). *Theory of mind: Beyond the preschool years.* New York, NY: Psychology Press.

Miller-Johnson, S., Winn, D.-M. C., Coie, J. D., Malone, P. S., & Lochman, J. (2004). Risk factors for adolescent pregnancy reports among African American males. *Journal of Research on Adolescence, 14,* 471–495. doi:10.1111/j.1532-7795.2004.00083.x

Mindell, J. A., Kuhn, B., Lewin, D. S., Meltzer, L. J., & Sadeh, A. (2006). Behavioral treatment of bedtime problems and night wakings in infants and young children. *Sleep, 29*(10), 1263–1276.

Miner, J. L., & Clarke-Stewart, K. A. (2008). Trajectories of externalizing behavior from age 2 to age 9: Relations with gender, temperament, ethnicity, parenting, and rater. *Developmental Psychology, 44,* 771–786. doi:10.1037/0012-1649.44.3.771

Mirescu, C., & Gould, E. (2006). Stress and adult neurogenesis. *Hippocampus, 16,* 233–238. doi:10.1002/hipo.20155

Mischel, W. (1981). Metacognition and the rules of delay. In J. H. Flavell & L. Ross (Eds.), *Social cognitive development: Frontiers and possible futures* (pp. 240–271). New York, NY: Cambridge University Press.

Mischel, W. (2015). *The marshmallow test: Why self-control is the engine of success.* New York: Little, Brown.

Mischel, W., & Ayduk, O. (2004). Willpower in a cognitive-affective processing system: The dynamics of delay of gratification. In R. F. Baumeister & K. D. Vohs (Eds.), *Handbook of self-regulation: Research, theory, and applications* (pp. 99–129). New York, NY: Guilford Press.

Mischel, W., & Ayduk, O. (2011). Willpower in a cognitive affective processing system: The dynamics of delay of gratification. In K. D. Vohs & R. F. Baumeister (Eds.), *Handbook of self-regulation: Research, theory, and applications* (2nd ed., pp. 99–129). New York, NY: Guilford Press.

Mischel, W., Shoda, Y., & Peake, P. K. (1988). The nature of adolescent competencies predicted by preschool delay of gratification. *Journal of Personality and Social Psychology, 54,* 687–696.

Mitchell, K. J., Ybarra, M. L., & Korchmaros, J. D. (2014). Sexual harassment among adolescents of different sexual orientations and gender identities. *Child Abuse & Neglect, 38,* 280–295.

Miura, I. T., Okamoto, Y., Vlahovic-Stetic, V., Kim, C. C., & Han, J. H. (1999). Language supports for children's understanding of numerical fractions: Cross-national comparisons. *Journal of Experimental Child Psychology, 74*(4), 356–365. doi:10.1006/jecp.1999.2519

Mizuta, I., Zahn-Waxler, C., Cole, P. M., & Hiruma, N. (1996). A cross-cultural study of preschoolers' attachment: Security and sensitivity in Japanese and US dyads. *International Journal of Behavioral Development, 19*, 141–159.

Modecki, K. L., Barber, B. L., & Vernon, L. (2013). Mapping developmental precursors of cyber-aggression: Trajectories of risk predict perpetration and victimization. *Journal of Youth and Adolescence, 42*, 651–661. doi:10.1007/s10964-012-9887-z

Modin, B., Östberg, V., & Almquist, Y. (2011). Childhood peer status and adult susceptibility to anxiety and depression: A 30-year hospital follow-up. *Journal of Abnormal Child Psychology, 39*, 187–199. doi:10.1007/s10802-010-9462-6

Moffitt, T. E. (1993a). Adolescence-limited and life-course-persistent antisocial behavior: A developmental taxonomy. *Psychological Review, 100*, 674–701. doi:10.1037/0033-295X.100.4.674

Moffitt, T. E. (1993b). The neuropsychology of conduct disorder. *Development and Psychopathology, 5*, 135–151. doi:10.1017/S0954579400004302

Moffitt, T. E., Arseneault, L., Belsky, D., Dickson, N., Hancox, R. J., Harrington, H., . . . Caspi, A. (2011). A gradient of childhood self-control predicts health, wealth, and public safety. *Proceedings of the National Academy of Sciences of the United States of America, 108*, 2693–2698. doi:10.1073/pnas.1010076108

Moffitt, T. E., & Caspi, A. (2001). Childhood predictors differentiate life-course persistent and adolescence-limited antisocial pathways among males and females. *Development and Psychopathology, 13*, 355–375.

Moffitt, T. E., Caspi, A., Harrington, H., & Milne, B. J. (2002). Males on the life-course-persistent and adolescence-limited antisocial pathways: Follow-up at age 26 years. *Development and Psychopathology, 14*, 179–207.

Moffitt, T. E., Harrington, H., Caspi, A., Kim-Cohen, J., Goldberg, D., Gregory, A. M., & Poulton, R. (2007). Depression and generalized anxiety disorder: Cumulative and sequential comorbidity in a birth cohort followed prospectively to age 32 years. *Archives of General Psychiatry, 64*, 651–660. doi:10.1001/archpsyc.64.6.651

Moilanen, K. L., Shaw, D. S., Dishion, T. J., Gardner, F., & Wilson, M. (2009). Predictors of longitudinal growth in inhibitory control in early childhood. *Social Development, 19*, 326–347. doi:10.1111/j.1467-9507.2009.00536.x

Möller, E. L., Nickolić, M., Majdandžić, M., & Bögels, S. M. (2016). Associations between maternal and paternal parenting behaviors, anxiety and its precursors in early childhood: A meta-analysis. *Clinical Psychology Review, 45*, 17–33. doi:10.1016/j.cpr.2016.03.002

Monahan, K. C., Steinberg, L., & Cauffman, E. (2009). Affiliation with antisocial peers, susceptibility to peer influence, and antisocial behavior

during the transition to adulthood. *Developmental Psychology, 45*, 1520–1530.

Monahan, K. C., Steinberg, L., Cauffman, E., & Mulvey, E. P. (2009). Trajectories of antisocial behavior and psychosocial maturity from adolescence to young adulthood. *Developmental Psychology, 45*, 1654–1668. doi:10.1037/a0015862

Montag, J. L., Jones, M. N., & Smith, L. B. (2015). The words children hear: Picture books and the statistics for language learning. *Psychological Science, 26*(9), 1489–1496.

Montirosso, R., Peverelli, M., Frigerio, E., Crespi, M., & Borgatti, R. (2010). The development of dynamic facial expression recognition at different intensities in 4-to 18-year-olds. *Social Development, 19*, 71–92.

Moon, C., Cooper, R. P., & Fifer, W. P. (1993). Two-day-olds prefer their native language. *Infant Behavior and Development, 16*, 495–500.

Moon, C., & Fifer, W. (1990, April). *Newborns prefer a prenatal version of mother's voice.* Poster session presented at the Biannual Meeting of the International Society of Infant Studies, Montreal, Canada.

Moon, M., & Hoffman, C. D. (2008). Mothers' and fathers' differential expectancies and behaviors: Parent × child gender effects. *Journal of Genetic Psychology, 169*, 261–280. doi:10.3200/GNTP.169.3.261-280

Moon, R. Y. (2011). SIDS and other sleep-related infant deaths: Expansion of recommendations for a safe infant sleeping environment. *Pediatrics, 128*(5), e1341–e1367.

Moore, A. M., & Ashcraft, M. H. (2013). Emotionality in mathematical problem solving. In C. Mohiyeddini, M. Eysenck, & S. Bauer (Eds.), *Handbook of psychology of emotions: Recent theoretical perspectives and novel empirical findings* (pp. 115–141). Hauppauge, NY: Nova Science Publishers.

Moore, C. (2008). The development of gaze following. *Child Development Perspectives, 2*, 66–70. doi:10.1111/j.1750-8606.2008.00052.x

Moore, C. F. (2003). *Silent scourge: Children, pollution, and why scientists disagree.* New York, NY: Oxford University Press.

Moore, D. R., & Florsheim, P. (2001). Interpersonal processes and psychopathology among expectant and nonexpectant adolescent couples. *Journal of Consulting and Clinical Psychology, 69*, 101–113. doi:10.1037/0022-006X.69.1.101

Moore, K. A., Manlove, J., Glei, D. A., & Morrison, D. R. (1998). Nonmarital school-age motherhood: Family, individual, and school characteristics. *Journal of Adolescent Research, 13*, 433–457. doi:10.1177/0743554898134004

Moore, K. L., & Persaud, T. V. N. (1993). *Before we are born: Essentials of embryology and*

birth defects (4th ed.). Philadelphia, PA: Saunders.

Moore, M. R., & Brooks-Gunn, J. (2002). Adolescent parenthood. In M. H. Bornstein (Ed.), *Handbook of parenting: Vol. 3. Being and becoming a parent* (2nd ed., pp. 173–214). Mahwah, NJ: Erlbaum.

Moors, A., Phoebe C., Ellsworth, P. C., Scherer, K. R., & Frijda, N. H. (2013). Appraisal theories of emotion: State of the art and future development. *Emotion Review, 5*, 119–124. doi:10.1177/1754073912468165

Morales, J. R., & Guerra, N. G. (2006). Effects of multiple context and cumulative stress on urban children's adjustment in elementary school. *Child Development, 77*, 907–923. doi:10.1111/j.1467-8624.2006.00910.x

Moreau, D., Clerc, J., Mansy-Dannay, A., & Guerrien, A. (2012). Enhancing spatial ability through sport practice: Evidence for an effect of motor training on mental rotation performance. *Journal of Individual Differences, 33*, 83–88. doi:10.1027/1614-0001/a000075

Morelen, D., Southam-Gerow, M., & Zeman, J. (2016). Child emotion regulation and peer victimization: The moderating role of child sex. *Journal of Child and Family Studies, 25*, 1941–1953. doi:10.1007/s10826-016-0360-6

Morelen, D., & Suveg, C. (2012). A real-time analysis of parent–child emotion discussions: The interaction is reciprocal. *Journal of Family Psychology, 26*, 998–1003. doi:10.1037/a0030148

Morelli, G. A., Rogoff, B., Oppenheim, D., & Goldsmith, D. (1992). Cultural variation in infants' sleeping arrangements: Questions of independence. *Developmental Psychology, 28*, 604–613. doi:10.1037/0012-1649.28.4.604

Morgan, J., Shaw, D., & Olino, T. (2012). Differential susceptibility effects: The interaction of negative emotionality and sibling relationship quality on childhood internalizing problems and social skills. *Journal of Abnormal Child Psychology, 40*, 885–899. doi:10.1007/s10802-012-9618-7

Morgan, J. K., Izard, C. E., & Hyde, C. (2014). Emotional reactivity and regulation in Head Start children: Links to ecologically valid behaviors and internalizing problems. *Social Development, 23*(2), 250–266. doi:10.1111/sode.12049

Morris, A. S., Silk, J. S., Steinberg, L., Myers, S. S., & Robinson, L. R. (2007). The role of the family context in the development of emotion regulation. *Social Development, 16*, 361–388. doi:10.1111/j.1467-9507.2007.00389.x

Morris, A. S., Silk, J. S., Steinberg, L., Sessa, F. M., Avenevoli, S., & Essex, M. J. (2002). Temperamental vulnerability and negative parenting as interacting predictors of child adjustment. *Journal of Marriage and Family, 64*, 461–471.

Morrissey, T. W. (2009). Multiple child-care arrangements and young children's behavioral outcomes. *Child Development, 80*(1), 59–76. doi:10.1111/j.1467-8624.2008.01246.x

Morrissey, T. W., Dunifon, R. E., & Kalil, A. (2011). Maternal employment, work schedules, and children's body mass index. *Child Development, 82*, 66–81. doi:10.1111/j.1467-8624.2010.01541.x

Moses, L. J., Baldwin, D. A., Rosicky, J. G., & Tidball, G. (2001). Evidence for referential understanding in the emotions domain at twelve and eighteen months. *Child Development, 72*, 718–735.

Moss, E., Cyr, C., & Dubois-Comtois, K. (2004). Attachment at early school age and developmental risk: Examining family contexts and behavior problems of controlling-caregiving, controlling-punitive, and behaviorally disorganized children. *Developmental Psychology, 40*, 519–532. doi:10.1037/0012-1649.40.4.519

Mounts, N. S. (2002). Parental management of adolescent peer relationships in context: The role of parenting style. *Journal of Family Psychology, 16*, 58–69. doi:10.1037/0893-3200.16.1.58

Mounts, N. S., & Steinberg, L. (1995). An ecological analysis of peer influence on adolescent grade point average and drug use. *Developmental Psychology, 31*, 915–922. doi:10.1037/0012-1649.31.6.915

Mouse Genome Sequencing Consortium. (2002, December 5). Initial sequencing and comparative analysis of the mouse genome. *Nature, 420*, 520–562. doi:10.1038/nature01262

Mrug, S., Hoza, B., & Bukowski, W. (2004). Choosing or being chosen by aggressive–disruptive peers: Do they contribute to children's externalizing and internalizing problems? *Journal of Abnormal Child Psychology, 32*, 53–65. doi:10.1023/B:JACP.0000007580.77154.69

Mueller, S. C., Temple, V., Oh, E., VanRyzin, C., Williams, A., Cornwell, B., . . . Merke, D. P. (2008). Early androgen exposure modulates spatial cognition in congenital adrenal hyperplasia (CAH). *Psychoneuroendocrinology, 33*, 973–980. doi:10.1016/j.psyneuen.2008.04.005

Muensinger, J., Matuz, T., Schleger, F., Kiefer-Schmidt, I., Goelz, R., Wacker-Gussmann, A., . . . Preissl, H. (2013). Auditory habituation in the fetus and neonate: An fMEG study. *Developmental Science, 16*(2), 287–295.

Mukherjee, H. B. (2016). *Education for fullness: A study of the educational thought and experiment of Rabindranath Tagore.* New York, NY: Routledge.

Mullally, S. L., & Maguire, E. A. (2014). Learning to remember: The early ontogeny of episodic memory. *Developmental Cognitive Neuroscience, 9*(100), 12–29. doi:10.1016/j.dcn.2013.12.006

Mulvaney, M. K., & Mebert, C. J. (2007). Parental corporal punishment predicts behavior problems in early childhood.

Journal of Family Psychology, 21, 389–397. doi:10.1037/0893-3200.21.3.389

Mumme, D. L., Fernald, A., & Herrera, C. (1996). Infants' responses to facial and vocal emotional signals in a social referencing paradigm. *Child Development, 67*, 3219–3237.

Munakata, Y., & McClelland, J. L. (2003). Connectionist models of development. *Developmental Science, 6*(4), 413–429. doi:10.1111/1467-7687.00296

Munakata, Y., McClelland, J. L., Johnson, M. H., & Siegler, R. S. (1997). Rethinking infant knowledge: Toward an adaptive process account of successes and failures in object permanence tasks. *Psychological Review, 104*, 686–713. doi:10.1037/0033-295X.104.4.686

Munakata, Y., Snyder, H. R., & Chatham, C. H. (2012). Developing cognitive control: Three key transitions. *Current Directions in Psychological Science, 21*, 71–77. doi:10.1177/0963721412436807

Munekata, H., & Ninomiya, K. (1985). The development of prosocial moral judgments. *Japanese Journal of Educational Psychology, 33*, 157–164.

Munroe, R. H., Shimmin, H. S., & Munroe, R. L. (1984). Gender understanding and sex role preference in four cultures. *Developmental Psychology, 20*, 673–682. doi:10.1037/0012-1649.20.4.673

Muraskas, J., Hasson, A., & Besinger, R. E. (2004). A girl with a birth weight of 280 g, now 14 years old. *New England Journal of Medicine, 351*, 836–837. doi:10.1056/NEJM200408193510826

Murphy, B. C., Eisenberg, N., Fabes, R. A., Shepard, S., & Guthrie, I. K. (1999). Consistency and change in children's emotionality and regulation: A longitudinal study. *Merrill-Palmer Quarterly, 45*, 413–444.

Murray, M. M., Lewkowicz, D. J., Amedi, A., & Wallace, M. T. (2016). Multisensory processes: A balancing act across the lifespan. *Trends in Neurosciences.* doi:10.1016/j.tins.2016.05.003

Murray-Close, D., Ostrov, J. M., & Crick, N. R. (2007). A short-term longitudinal study of growth of relational aggression during middle childhood: Associations with gender, friendship intimacy, and internalizing problems. *Development and Psychopathology, 19*, 187–203.

Musolino, J., & Landau, B. (2012). Genes, language, and the nature of scientific explanations: The case of Williams syndrome. *Cognitive Neuropsychology, 29*, 123–148. doi:10.1080/02643294.2012.702103

Mustonen, U., Huurre, T., Kiviruusu, O., Haukkala, A., & Aro, H. (2011). Long-term impact of parental divorce on intimate relationship quality in adulthood and the mediating role of psychosocial resources. *Journal of Family Psychology, 25*, 615–619. doi:10.1037/a0023996

Myers, L. J., LeWitt, R. B., Gallo, R. E., & Maselli, N. M. (2016). Baby FaceTime: Can toddlers learn from online video chat? *Developmental Science.* doi:10.1111/desc.12430

Myowa-Yamakoshi, M., & Takeshita, H. (2006). Do human fetuses anticipate self-oriented actions? A study by four-dimensional (4D) ultrasonography. *Infancy, 10*, 289–301.

Nadig, A. S., & Sedivy, J. C. (2002). Evidence of perspective-taking constraints in children's online reference resolution. *Psychological Science, 13*, 329–336. doi:10.1111/j.0956-7976.2002.00460.x

Naigles, L. (1990). Children use syntax to learn verb meanings. *Journal of Child Language, 17*, 357–374. doi:10.1017/S0305000900013817

Naigles, L. G., & Gelman, S. A. (1995). Overextensions in comprehension and production revisited: Preferential-looking in a study of dog, cat, and cow. *Journal of Child Language, 22*, 19–46.

Nakamoto, J., & Schwartz, D. (2010). Is peer victimization associated with academic achievement? A meta-analytic review. *Social Development, 19*, 221–242. doi:10.1111/j.1467-9507.2009.00539.x

Namy, L. L. (2001). What's in a name when it isn't a word? 17-month-olds' mapping of nonverbal symbols to object categories. *Infancy, 2*, 73–86. doi:10.1207/S15327078IN0201_5

Namy, L. L., & Waxman, S. R. (1998). Words and gestures: Infants' interpretations of different forms of symbolic reference. *Child Development, 69*, 295–308.

Náñez, J. (1988). Perception of impending collision in 3- to 6-week-old human infants. *Infant Behavior & Development, 11*, 447–463.

Nantel-Vivier, A., Kokko, K., Caprara, G. V., Pastorelli, C., Gerbino, M. G., Paciello, M., . . . Tremblay, R. E. (2009). Prosocial development from childhood to adolescence: A multi-informant perspective with Canadian and Italian longitudinal studies. *Journal of Child Psychology and Psychiatry, 50*, 590–598. doi:10.1111/j.1469-7610.2008.02039.x

Naoi, N., Minagawa-Kawai, Y., Kaboyashi, A., Takeuchi, K., Nakamura, K., Yamamoto, J., & Kojima, S. (2012). Cerebral responses to infant-directed speech and the effect of talker familiarity. *NeuroImage, 59*, 1735–1744.

Narusyte, J., Neiderhiser, J. M., D'Onofrio, B. M., Reiss, D., Spotts, E. L., Ganiban, J., & Lichtenstein, P. (2008). Testing different types of genotype-environment correlation: An extended children-of-twins model. *Developmental Psychology, 44*, 1591–1603. doi:10.1037/a0013911

Naterer, A., & Godina, V. (2011). Bomzhji and their subculture: An anthropolitical study of street children subculture in Makeevka, Eastern Ukraine. *Childhood, 18*, 20–38. doi:10.1177/0907568210379924

Naterer, A., & Lavrič, M. (2016). Using social indicators in assessing factors and numbers of street children in the world. *Child Indicators Research, 9*, 21–37. doi:10.1007/s12187-015-9306-6L

Nathanielsz, P. W. (1994). *A time to be born: The life of the unborn child.* Oxford, England: Oxford University Press.

Nation, K. (2008). Learning to read words. *Quarterly Journal of Experimental Psychology, 61,* 1121–1133. doi:10.1080/17470210802034603

National Academies of Sciences, Engineering, and Medicine. (2016). *Parenting Matters: Supporting Parents of Children Ages 0–8.* Washington, DC: The National Academies Press. doi:10.17226/21868

National Alliance to End Homelessness. (2016). *The state of homelessness in America: 2016.* Retrieved from http://www.endhomelessness.org/library/entry/SOH2016

National Association for the Education of Young Children. (1986). *Good teaching practices for 4- and 5-year olds: A position statement of the National Association for the Education of Young Children.* Washington, DC: Author.

National Association for the Education of Young Children. (2011). 2010 NAEYC Standards for Initial & Advanced Early Childhood Professional Preparation Programs. Retrieved from http://www.naeyc.org/ncate/files/ncate/file/faculty/Standards/NAEYC%20Initial%20and%20Advanced%20Standards%203_2012.pdf.

National Association of Pediatric Nurse Practitioners. (2011). NAPNAP Position Statement on Corporal Punishment. *Journal of Pediatric Health Care, 25*, e31–e32. Retrieved from http://www.jpedhc.org/article/S0891-5245(11)00228-8/pdf

National Campaign to Prevent Teen and Unplanned Pregnancy. (2014). *How Does the United States Compare?* Retrieved from http://thenationalcampaign.org/resource/fast-facts-how-does-united-states-compare

National Institutes of Health. (n.d.) Comparative genomics. National Institutes of Health: National Human Genome Research Institute. Retrieved July 14, 2016, from https://www.genome.gov/11509542/comparative-genomics-fact-sheet/

National Poverty Center. (2013). Poverty in the United States: Frequently asked questions. Retrieved from http://npc.umich.edu/poverty/

National Reading Panel. (2000). *Teaching children to read: An evidence-based assessment of the scientific research literature on reading and its implications for reading instruction: Reports of the subgroups* (NIH Publication No. 00–4754). Washington, DC: National Institute of Child Health and Human Development, National Institutes of Health.

National Research Council. (2010). *Student mobility: Exploring the impact of frequent moves on achievement.* Washington, DC: National Academies Press.

National Science Foundation, National Center for Science and Engineering Statistics. (2013). *Women, minorities, and persons with disabilities in science and engineering: 2013* (Special Report NSF 13-304). Arlington, VA: Author.

National Science Foundation, National Center for Science and Engineering Statistics. (2015). *Women, minorities, and persons with disabilities in science and engineering: 2015* (Special Report NSF 15-311). Arlington, VA: Author.

Neal, J. W. (2010). Hanging out: Features of urban children's peer social networks. *Journal of Social and Personal Relationships, 27*, 982–1000. doi:10.1177/0265407510378124

Neale, B. M., Kou, Y., Liu, L., Ma'Ayan, A., Samocha, K. E., Sabo, A., . . . Polak, P. (2012). Patterns and rates of exonic de novo mutations in autism spectrum disorders. *Nature, 485*(7397), 242–245.

Neblett, E. W., Rivas-Drake, D., & Umaña-Taylor, A. J. (2012). The promise of racial and ethnic protective factors in promoting ethnic minority youth development. *Child Development Perspectives, 6*, 295–303. doi:10.1111/j.1750-8606.2012.00239.x

Neblett, E. W., White, R. L., Ford, K. R., Philip, C. L., Nguyên, H. X., & Sellers, R. M. (2008). Patterns of racial socialization and psychological adjustment: Can parental communications about race reduce the impact of racial discrimination? *Journal of Research on Adolescence, 18*, 477–515. doi:10.1111/j.1532-7795.2008.00568.x

Neckerman, H. J. (1996). The stability of social groups in childhood and adolescence: The role of the classroom social environment. *Social Development, 5*, 131–145. doi:10.1111/j.1467-9507.1996.tb00076.x

Nederhof, E., Belsky, J., Ormel, J., & Oldehinkel, A. J. (2012). Effects of divorce on Dutch boys' and girls' externalizing behavior in Gene × Environment perspective: Diathesis stress or differential susceptibility in the Dutch Tracking Adolescents' Individual Lives Survey study? *Development and Psychopathology, 24*, 929–939. doi:10.1017/S0954579412000454

Needham, A. (1997). Factors affecting infants' use of featural information in object segregation. *Current Directions in Psychological Science, 6*, 26–33. doi:10.2307/20182439

Needham, A., & Baillargeon, R. (1993). Intuitions about support in 4.5-month-old infants. *Cognition, 47*, 121–148. doi:10.1016/0010-0277(93)90002-D

Needham, A., & Baillargeon, R. (1997). Object segregation in 8-month-old infants. *Cognition, 62*, 121–149. doi:10.1016/S0010-0277(96)00727-5

Needham, A., & Baillargeon, R. (1998). Effects of prior experience on 4.5-month old infants' object segregation. *Infant Behavior and Development, 21*, 1–24. doi:10.1016/S0163-6383(98)90052-2

Needham, A., Barrett, T., & Peterman, K. (2002). A pick-me-up for infants' exploratory skills: Early simulated experiences reaching for objects using 'sticky mittens' enhances young infants' object exploration skills. *Infant Behavior and Development, 25*, 279–295. doi:10.1016/S0163-6383(02)00097-8

Needham, A. W. (2016). *Learning about objects in infancy* (1st ed.). New York, NY: Routledge.

Negriff, S., & Susman, E. J. (2011). Pubertal timing, depression, and externalizing problems: A framework, review, and examination of gender differences. *Journal of Research on Adolescence, 21*, 717–746.

Neiderhiser, J. M., Reiss, D., Pedersen, N. L., Lichtenstein, P., Spotts, E. L., Hansson, K., . . . Elthammer, O. (2004). Genetic and environmental influences on mothering of adolescents: A comparison of two samples. *Developmental Psychology, 40*, 335–351. doi:10.1037/0012-1649.40.3.335

Nelson, C. A., III, Bos, K., Gunnar, M. R., & Sonuga-Barke, E. J. S. (2011). The neurobiological toll of early human deprivation. *Monographs of the Society for Research in Child Development, 76*(4, Serial No. 301), 127–146. doi:10.1111/j.1540-5834.2011.00630.x

Nelson, C. A., III, Thomas, K. M., & de Haan, M. (2006). Neural bases of cognitive development. In W. Damon & R. M. Lerner (Series Eds.) & D. Kuhn & R. S. Siegler (Vol. Eds.), *Handbook of child psychology: Vol. 2. Cognition, perception, and language* (6th ed., pp. 3–57). Hoboken, NJ: Wiley.

Nelson, C. A., III, Zeanah, C. H., Fox, N. A., Marshall, P. J., Smyke, A. T., & Guthrie, D. (2007, December 21). Cognitive recovery in socially deprived young children: The Bucharest Early Intervention Project. *Science, 318*, 1937–1940.

Nelson, D. A., Mitchell, C., & Yang, C. (2008). Intent attributions and aggression: A study of children and their parents. *Journal of Abnormal Child Psychology, 36*, 793–806. doi:10.1007/s10802-007-9211-7

Nelson, D. A., Robinson, C. C., Hart, C. H., Albano, A. D., & Marshall, S. J. (2010). Italian preschoolers' peer-status linkages with sociability and subtypes of aggression and victimization. *Social Development, 19*, 698–720. doi:10.1111/j.1467-9507.2009.00551.x

Nelson, E. A., Schiefenhoevel, W., & Haimerl, F. (2000). Child care practices in nonindustrialized societies. *Pediatrics, 105*, e75. doi:10.1542/peds.105.6.e75

Nelson, J. K. (2005). Interference resolution in the left inferior frontal gyrus. *Dissertation*

Abstracts International: Section B: The Sciences and Engineering, 66(10), 5703.

Nelson, K. (1973). Structure and strategy in learning to talk. *Monographs of the Society for Research in Child Development, 38*(1–2, Serial No. 149).

Nelson, K. (1993). The psychological and social origins of autobiographical memory. *Psychological Science, 4,* 7–14. doi:10.1111/j.1467-9280.1993.tb00548.x

Nelson, K., & Fivush, R. (2000). Socialization of memory. In E. Tulving & F. I. M. Craik (Eds.), *The Oxford handbook of memory* (pp. 283–295). Oxford, England: Oxford University Press.

Nelson, K., & Fivush, R. (2004). The emergence of autobiographical memory: A social cultural developmental theory. *Psychological Review, 111,* 486–511. doi:10.1037/0033-295X.111.2.486

Nesdale, D. (2007). Children's perceptions of social groups. In J. A. Zebrowski (Ed.), *New research on social perception* (pp. 1–45). Hauppauge, NY: Nova Science.

Neuman, S. B., Kaefer, T., Pinkham, A., & Strouse, G. (2014). Can babies learn to read? A randomized trial of baby media. *Journal of Educational Psychology, 106*(3), 815.

Neville, B., & Parke, R. D. (1997). Waiting for paternity: Interpersonal and contextual implications of the timing of fatherhood. *Sex Roles, 37,* 45–59. doi:10.1023/A:1025636619455

Newcomb, A. F., & Bukowski, W. M. (1984). A longitudinal study of the utility of social preference and social impact sociometric classification schemes. *Child Development, 55,* 1434–1447. doi:10.2307/1130013

Newcomb, A. F., Bukowski, W. M., & Pattee, L. (1993). Children's peer relations: A meta-analytic review of popular, rejected, neglected, controversial, and average sociometric status. *Psychological Bulletin, 113,* 99–128.

Newcombe, N., & Huttenlocher, J. (2000). *Making space: The development of spatial representation and reasoning.* Cambridge, MA: MIT Press.

Newcombe, N., Huttenlocher, J., Drummey, A. B., & Wiley, J. G. (1998). The development of spatial location coding: Place learning and dead reckoning in the second and third years. *Cognitive Development, 13,* 185–200. doi:10.1016/S0885-2014(98)90038-7

Newcombe, N. S., & Huttenlocher, J. (2006). Development of spatial cognition. In W. Damon & R. M. Lerner (Series Eds.) & D. Kuhn & R. S. Siegler (Vol. Eds.), *Handbook of child psychology: Vol. 2. Cognition, perception, and language* (6th ed., pp. 734–776). Hoboken, NJ: Wiley.

Newcombe, N. S., Levine, S. C., & Mix, K. (2015). Thinking about quantity: The intertwined development of spatial and numerical cognition. *Wiley Interdisciplinary Reviews: Cognitive Science, 6,* 491–505. doi:10.1002/wcs.1369

Newcombe, N. S., & Ratliff, K. R. (2007). Explaining the development of spatial reorientation. In J. M. Plumert & J. P. Spencer (Eds.), *The emerging spatial mind* (pp. 53–76). New York, NY: Oxford University Press.

Newell, K. M., Scully, D. M., McDonald, P. V., & Baillargeon, R. (1989). Task constraints and infant grip configurations. *Developmental Psychobiology, 22,* 817–831. doi:10.1002/dev.420220806

Newheiser, A. K., & Olson, K. R. (2012). White and Black American children's implicit intergroup bias. *Journal of Experimental Social Psychology, 48*(1), 264–270.

Newman, R. S. (2005). The cocktail party effect in infants revisited: Listening to one's name in noise. *Developmental Psychology, 41,* 352–362.

Newman, S. D., Carpenter, P. A., Varma, S., & Just, M. A. (2003). Frontal and parietal participation in problem solving in the Tower of London: fMRI and computational modeling of planning and high-level perception. *Neuropsychologia, 41,* 1668–1682.

Newport, E., Gleitman, H., & Gleitman, L. (1977). Mother, I'd rather do it myself: Some effects and non-effects of maternal speech style. In C. E. Snow & C. A. Ferguson (Eds.), *Talking to children: Language input and acquisition* (pp. 109–150). Cambridge, England: Cambridge University Press.

Newport, E. L. (1990). Maturational constraints on language learning. *Cognitive Science, 14,* 11–28.

Newton, E. K., Laible, D., Carlo, G., Steele, J. S., & McGinley, M. (2014). Do sensitive parents foster kind children, or vice versa? Bidirectional influences between children's prosocial behavior and parental sensitivity. *Developmental Psychology, 50,* 1808–1816. doi:10.1037/a0036495

Ngun, T. C., & Vilain, E. (2014). The biological basis of human sexual orientation: Is there a role for epigenetics? *Advances in Genetics, 86,* 167–184. doi:10.1016/B978-0-12-800222-3.00008-5

Nguyen, S. P., & Gelman, S. A. (2002). Four and 6-year olds' biological concept of death: The case of plants. *British Journal of Developmental Psychology, 20,* 495–513. doi:10.1348/026151002760390918

NICHD Early Child Care Research Network. (1997). Familial factors associated with the characteristics of nonmaternal care for infants. *Journal of Marriage and the Family, 59,* 389–408.

NICHD Early Child Care Research Network. (1998a). Early child care and self-control, compliance, and problem behavior at twenty-four and thirty-six months. *Child Development, 69,* 1145–1170.

NICHD Early Child Care Research Network. (1998b, April–May). *When child care classrooms meet recommended guidelines for quality.* Paper presented at the meeting, "Child Care in the New Policy Context," U.S. Department of Health and Human Services, Bethesda, MD.

NICHD Early Child Care Research Network. (2000a). Factors associated with fathers' caregiving activities and sensitivity with young children. *Journal of Family Psychology 14,* 200–219.

NICHD Early Child Care Research Network. (2000b). The relation of child care to cognitive and language development. *Child Development, 71,* 960–980.

NICHD Early Child Care Research Network. (2001). Child-care and family predictors of preschool attachment and stability from infancy. *Developmental Psychology, 37,* 847–862, doi:10.1037//0012-1649.37.6.847

NICHD Early Child Care Research Network. (2002). Early child care and children's development prior to school entry: Results from the NICHD Study of Early Child Care. *American Educational Research Journal, 39,* 133–164.

NICHD Early Child Care Research Network. (2003). Social functioning in first grade: Associations with earlier home and child care predictors and with current classroom experiences. *Child Development, 74,* 1639–1662.

NICHD Early Child Care Research Network. (2004). Trajectories of physical aggression from toddlerhood to middle childhood: Predictors, correlates, and outcomes. *Monographs of the Society for Research in Child Development, 69*(4, Serial No. 278), i–143. doi:10.2307/3701390

NICHD Early Child Care Research Network. (2006). Child-care effect sizes for the NICHD Study of Early Child Care and Youth Development. *American Psychologist, 61,* 99–116. doi:10.1037/0003-066X.61.2.99

NICHD Early Child Care Research Network, & Duncan, G. J. (2003). Modeling the impacts of child care quality on children's preschool cognitive development. *Child Development, 74,* 1454–1475. doi:10.1111/1467-8624.00617

Nicholson, T. (1999). Reading comprehension processes. In G. B. Thompson & T. Nicholson (Eds.), *Learning to read: Beyond phonics and whole language* (pp. 127–149). Newark, DE: International Reading Association.

Nicolopoulou, A. (2007). The interplay of play and narrative in children's development: Theoretical reflections and concrete examples. In A. Göncü & S. Gaskins (Eds.), *Play and development: Evolutionary, sociocultural, and functional perspectives* (pp. 247–273). New York, NY: Erlbaum.

NIDA Substance Use in Women Report. (2015). Retrieved from https://www.drugabuse.gov/sites/default/files/substanceuseinwomen_final_02182016.pdf

Nieder, A. (2012). Supramodal numerosity selectivity of neurons in primate prefrontal and posterior parietal cortices. *Proceedings of the National Academy of Sciences of the United States of America, 109,* 11860–11865. doi:10.1073/pnas.1204580109

Nieder, A., & Dehaene, S. (2009). Representation of number in the brain. *Annual Review of Neuroscience, 32,* 185–208. doi:10.1146/annurev.neuro.051508.135550

Nielsen, J. A., Zielinski, B. A., Ferguson, M. A., Lainhart, J. E., & Anderson, J. S. (2013). An evaluation of the left-brain vs. right-brain hypothesis with resting state functional connectivity magnetic resonance imaging. *PloS One, 8*(8), e71275.

Nielsen, M., Suddendorf, T., & Slaughter, V. (2006). Mirror self–recognition beyond the face. *Child Development, 77,* 176–185. doi:10.1111/j.1467-8624.2006.00863.x

Nievar, M. A., & Becker, B. J. (2008). Sensitivity as a privileged predictor of attachment: A second perspective on De Wolff and van IJzendoorn's meta-analysis. *Social Development, 17,* 102–114.

Nigg, J. T. (2012). Future directions in ADHD etiology research. *Journal of Clinical Child & Adolescent Psychology, 41*(4), 524–533.

Nigg, J. T., Elmore, A. L., Natarajan, N., Friderici, K. H., & Nikolas, M. A. (2016). Variation in an iron metabolism gene moderates the association between blood lead levels and attention-deficit/hyperactivity disorder in children. *Psychological Science, 27,* 257–269.

Nigg, J. T., Lewis, K., Edinger, T., & Falk, M. (2012). Meta-analysis of attention-deficit/hyperactivity disorder or attention-deficit/hyperactivity disorder symptoms, restriction diet, and synthetic food color additives. *Journal of the American Academy of Child and Adolescent Psychiatry, 51,* 86–97, e88.

Nilsen, E. S., & Graham, S. A. (2009). The relations between children's communicative perspective-taking and executive functioning. *Cognitive Psychology, 58,* 220–249. doi:10.1016/j.cogpsych.2008.07.002

Nisan, M., & Kohlberg, L. (1982). Universality and variation in moral judgment: A longitudinal and cross-sectional study in Turkey. *Child Development, 53,* 865–876. doi:10.2307/1129123

Nisbett, R. E., Aronson, J., Blair, C., Dickens, W., Flynn, J., Halpern, D. F., & Turkheimer, E. (2012). Intelligence: New findings and theoretical developments. *American Psychologist, 67,* 130–159. doi:10.1037/a0026699

Nisbett, R. E., & Miyamoto, Y. (2005). The influence of culture: Holistic versus analytic perception. *Trends in Cognitive Sciences, 9*(10), 467–473.

Nishina, A., Bellmore, A., Witkow, M. R., & Nylund-Gibson, K. (2010). Longitudinal consistency of adolescent ethnic identification across varying school ethnic contexts. *Developmental Psychology, 46,* 1389–1401. doi:10.1037/a0020728

Nobes, G., Panagiotaki, G., & Pawson, C. (2009). The influence of negligence, intention, and outcome on children's moral judgments. *Journal of Experimental Child Psychology, 104,* 382–397. doi:10.1016/j.jecp.2009.08.001

Noble, K. G., Houston, S. M., Brito, N. H., Bartsch, H., Kan, E., Kuperman, J. M., . . . Sowell, E. R. (2015). Family income, parental education and brain structure in children and adolescents. *Nature Neuroscience, 18*(5), 773–778. doi:10.1038/nn.3983

Nolen-Hoeksema, S. (2012). Emotion regulation and psychopathology: The role of gender. *Annual Review of Clinical Psychology, 8,* 161–187. doi:10.1146/annurev-clinpsy-032511-143109

Nolen-Hoeksema, S., Larson, J., & Grayson, C. (1999). Explaining the gender difference in depressive symptoms. *Journal of Personality and Social Psychology, 77,* 1061–1072.

Nolen-Hoeksema, S., Stice, E., Wade, E., & Bohon, C. (2007). Reciprocal relations between rumination and bulimic, substance abuse, and depressive symptoms in female adolescents. *Journal of Abnormal Psychology, 116,* 198–207.

Nordenström, A., Servin, A., Bohlin, G., Larsson, A., & Wedell, A. (2002). Sex-typed toy play behavior correlates with the degree of prenatal androgen exposure assessed by CYP21 genotype in girls with congenital adrenal hyperplasia. *Journal of Clinical Endocrinology and Metabolism, 87,* 5119–5124. doi:10.1210/jc.2001-011531

Nordhov, S. M., Rønning, J. A., Ulvund, S. E., Dahl, L. B., & Kaaresen, P. I. (2012). Early intervention improves behavioral outcomes for preterm infants: Randomized controlled trial. *Pediatrics, 129*(1). doi:10.1542/peds.2011-0248

Nosek, B. A., & Banaji, M. R. (2009). Implicit attitude. In T. Bayne, A. Cleeremans, & P. Wilken (Eds.), *The Oxford companion to consciousness* (pp. 84–85). Oxford, England: Oxford University Press.

Novin, S., Banerjee, R., Dadkhah, A., & Rieffe, C. (2009). Self-reported use of emotional display rules in the Netherlands and Iran: Evidence for sociocultural influence. *Social Development, 18,* 397–411. doi:10.1111/j.1467-9507.2008.00485.x

Nowell, A., & Hedges, L. V. (1998). Trends in gender differences in academic achievement from 1960 to 1994: An analysis of differences in mean, variance, and extreme scores. *Sex Roles, 39,* 21–43. doi:10.1023/A:1018873615316

Nucci, L. (1981). Conceptions of personal issues: A domain distinct from moral or societal concepts. *Child Development, 52,* 114–121. doi:10.2307/1129220

Nucci, L. (1997). Culture, universals, and the personal. In H. D. Saltzstein (Ed.), *New Directions for Child and Adolescent Development: No. 76. Culture as a context for moral development: New perspectives on the particular and the universal* (Vol. 1997, pp. 5–22). San Francisco, CA: Jossey-Bass.

Nucci, L. P., & Gingo, M. (2011). The development of moral reasoning. In U. Goswami (Ed.), *The Wiley-Blackwell handbook of childhood cognitive development* (2nd ed., pp. 420–445). Oxford, England: Wiley-Blackwell.

Nurmi, J.-E. (2004). Socialization and self-development: Channeling, selection, adjustment, and reflection. In R. M. Lerner & L. D. Steinberg (Eds.), *Handbook of adolescent psychology* (2nd ed., pp. 85–124). Hoboken, NJ: Wiley.

Nylund, K., Bellmore, A., Nishina, A., & Graham, S. (2007). Subtypes, severity, and structural stability of peer victimization: What does latent class analysis say? *Child Development, 78,* 1706–1722. doi:10.1111/j.1467-8624.2007.01097.x

Obergefell v. Hodges, 135 S. Ct. 2071 (2015).

O'Connor, A., & Boag, S. (2010). Do stepparents experience more parental antagonism than biological parents? A test of evolutionary and socialization perspectives. *Journal of Divorce and Remarriage, 51,* 508–525. doi:10.1080/10502556.2010.504101

O'Connor, T. G., Heron, J., Golding, J., Beveridge, M., & Glover, V. (2002). Maternal antenatal anxiety and children's behavioural/emotional problems at 4 years. Report from the Avon Longitudinal Study of Parents and Children. *British Journal of Psychiatry, 180,* 502–508.

O'Doherty, K., Troseth, G. L., Shimpi, P. M., Goldenberg, E., Akhtar, N., & Saylor, M. M. (2011). Third-party social interaction and word learning from video. *Child Development, 82,* 902–915. doi:10.1111/j.1467-8624.2011.01579.x

O'Leary, K. D., Slep, A. M. S., Avery-Leaf, S., & Cascardi, M. (2008). Gender differences in dating aggression among multiethnic high school students. *Journal of Adolescent Health, 42,* 473–479. doi:10.1016/j.jadohealth.2007.09.012

O'Rourke, J. A., Scharf, J. M., Yu, D., & Pauls, D. L. (2009). The genetics of Tourette syndrome: A review. *Journal of Psychosomatic Research, 67,* 533–545.

Oakes, L. M., & Cohen, L. B. (1995). Infant causal perception. In L. P. Lipsitt & C. K. Rovee-Collier (Eds.), *Advances in infancy research* (Vol. 9, pp. 1–54). Norwood, NJ: Ablex.

Oakhill, J., & Cain, K. (2000). Children's difficulties in text comprehension: Assessing causal issues. *Journal of Deaf Studies and Deaf Education, 5,* 51–59. doi:10.1093/deafed/5.1.51

Oakhill, J. V., & Cain, K. (2012). The precursors of reading ability in young readers: Evidence from a four-year longitudinal study. *Scientific*

Studies of Reading, 16(2), 91–121. doi:10.1080/10 888438.2010.529219

Oberlander, T. F., Weinberg, J., Papsdorf, M., Grunau, R., Misri, S., & Devlin, A. M. (2008). Prenatal exposure to maternal depression, neonatal methylation of human glucocorticoid receptor gene (NR3C1) and infant cortisol stress responses. *Epigenetics, 3,* 97–106.

Obradović, J. (2010). Effortful control and adaptive functioning of homeless children: Variable-focused and person-focused analyses. *Journal of Applied Developmental Psychology, 31,* 109–117. doi:10.1016/j.appdev.2009.09.004

Obradović, J., Bush, N. R., Stamperdahl, J., Adler, N. E., & Boyce, W. T. (2010). Biological sensitivity to context: The interactive effects of stress reactivity and family adversity on socio-emotional behavior and school readiness. *Child Development, 81,* 270–289.

Obradović, J., & Hipwell, A. (2010). Psycho-pathology and social competence during the transition to adolescence: The role of family adversity and pubertal development. *Development and Psychopathology, 22,* 621–634. doi:10.1017/S0954579410000325

Ocampo, K. A., Bernal, M. E., & Knight, G. P. (1993). Gender race and ethnicity: The sequencing of social constancies. In M. E. Bernal & G. P. Knight (Eds.), *Ethnic identity: Formation and transmission among Hispanics and other minorities* (pp. 11–30). Albany: State University of New York Press.

Ocampo, K. A., Knight, G. P., & Bernal, M. E. (1997). The development of cognitive abilities and social identities in children: The case of ethnic identity. *International Journal of Behavioral Development, 21,* 479–500. doi:10.1080/016502597384758

Odgers, C. L., Caspi, A., Russell, M. A., Sampson, R. J., Arseneault, L., & Moffitt, T. E. (2012). Supportive parenting mediates neighborhood socioeconomic disparities in children's antisocial behavior from ages 5 to 12. *Development and Psychopathology, 24,* 705–721. doi:10.1017/S0954579412000326

OECD Family Database. (2016). *Key characteristics of parental leave systems.* Retrieved from https://www.oecd.org/els/soc/PF2_1_Parental_leave_systems.pdf

Office of Head Start. (2015). History of Head Start. Office of Head Start, An Office of the Administrator for Children & Families. Washington, D.C. Accessed August 14, 2016, from http://www.acf.hhs.gov/programs/ohs/about/history-of-head-start

Office of the Mayor of New York City. (2014). *Ready to Launch: New York City's Implementation Plan for Free, High-Quality, Full-Day Universal Pre-Kindergarten.* Retrieved from http://www1.nyc.gov/office-of-the-mayor/news/038-14/city-releases-implementation-plan-free-high-quality-full-day-universal-pre-kindergarten#/0

Offord, D. R., Alder, R. J., & Boyle, M. H. (1986). Prevalence and sociodemographic correlates of conduct disorder. *American Journal of Social Psychiatry, 6,* 272–278.

Ogbu, J. U. (1981). Origins of human competence: A cultural-ecological perspective. *Child Development, 52,* 413–429. doi:10.2307/1129158

Ogden, C. L., Carroll, M. D., Lawman, H. G., Fryar, C. D., Kruszon-Moran, D., Kit, B. K., & Flegal, K. M. (2016). Trends in obesity prevalence among children and adolescents in the United States, 1988–1994 through 2013–2014. *Journal of the American Medical Association, 315*(21), 2292–2299.

Oh, W., Rubin, K., Bowker, J., Booth-LaForce, C., Rose-Krasnor, L., & Laursen, B. (2008). Trajectories of social withdrawal from middle childhood to early adolescence. *Journal of Abnormal Child Psychology, 36,* 553–566. doi:10.1007/s10802-007-9199-z

Ohayon, M. M., Carskadon, M. A., Guilleminault, C., & Vitiello, M. V. (2004). Meta-analysis of quantitative sleep parameters from childhood to old age in healthy individuals: Developing normative sleep values across the human lifespan. Sleep, *27,* 1255–1274.

Olfson, M., Druss, B. G., & Marcus, S. C. (2015). Trends in mental health care among children and adolescents. *The New England Journal of Medicine, 372,* 2029–2038. doi:10.1056/NEJMsa1413512

Oliner, S. P., & Oliner, P. M. (1988). *The altruistic personality: Rescuers of Jews in Nazi Europe.* New York, NY: Free Press.

Oliver, B., Dale, P. S., & Plomin, R. (2004). Verbal and nonverbal predictors of early language problems: An analysis of twins in early childhood back to infancy. *Journal of Child Language, 31,* 609–631.

Ollendick, T. H., Weist, M. D., Borden, M. C., & Greene, R. W. (1992). Sociometric status and academic, behavioral, and psychological adjustment: A five-year longitudinal study. *Journal of Consulting and Clinical Psychology, 60,* 80–87. doi:10.1037/0022-006X.60.1.80

Oller, D. K., & Eilers, R. E. (1988). The role of audition in infant babbling. *Child Development, 59,* 441–449.

Oller, D. K., & Pearson, B. Z. (2002). Assessing the effects of bilingualism: A background. In D. K. Oller & R. E. Eilers (Eds.), *Language and literacy in bilingual children* (pp. 3–21). Clevedon, England: Multilingual Matters.

Olson, R. K., Keenan, J. M., Byrne, B., & Samuelsson, S. (2014). Why do children differ in their development of reading and related skills? *Scientific Studies of Reading, 18*(1), 38–54. doi:10.1080/10888438.2013.800521

Olson, S. L., Bates, J. E., & Kaskie, B. (1992). Caregiver–infant interaction antecedents of children's school-age cognitive ability. *Merrill-Palmer Quarterly, 38,* 309–330.

Olson, S. L., Bates, J. E., Sandy, J. M., & Lanthier, R. (2000). Early developmental precursors of externalizing behavior in middle childhood and adolescence. *Journal of Abnormal Child Psychology, 28,* 119–133. doi:10.1023/A:1005166629744

Olson, S. L., Lopez-Duran, N., Lunkenheimer, E. S., Chang, H., & Sameroff, A. J. (2011). Individual differences in the development of early peer aggression: Integrating contributions of self-regulation, theory of mind, and parenting. *Development and Psychopathology, 23,* 253–266. doi:10.1017/S0954579410000775

Olson, S. L., Tardif, T. Z., Miller, A., Felt, B., Grabell, A. S., Kessler, D., . . . Hirabayashi, H. (2011). Inhibitory control and harsh discipline as predictors of externalizing problems in young children: A comparative study of US, Chinese, and Japanese preschoolers. *Journal of Abnormal Child Psychology, 39,* 1163–1175.

Olweus, D. (1994). Bullying at school: Basic facts and effects of a school based intervention program. *Journal of Child Psychology and Psychiatry, 35,* 1171–1190. doi:10.1111/j.1469-7610.1994.tb01229.x

Onishi, K. H., & Baillargeon, R. (2005, April 8). Do 15-month-old infants understand false beliefs? *Science, 308,* 255–258.

Oostenbroek, J., Suddendorf, T., Nielsen, M., Redshaw, J., Kennedy-Costantini, S., Davis, J., . . . Slaughter, V. (2016). Comprehensive longitudinal study challenges the existence of neonatal imitation in humans. *Current Biology, 26*(10), 1334–1338.

Opfer, J. E., & Gelman, S. A. (2001). Children's and adults' models for predicting teleological action: The development of a biology-based model. *Child Development, 72,* 1367–1381.

Opfer, J. E., & Siegler, R. S. (2004). Revisiting preschoolers' *living things* concept: A microgenetic analysis of conceptual change in basic biology. *Cognitive Psychology, 49,* 301–332. doi:10.1016/j.cogpsych.2004.01.002

Oppliger, P. A. (2007). Effects of gender stereotyping on socialization. In R. W. Preiss, B. M. Gayle, N. Burrell, M. Allen, & J. Bryant (Eds.), *Mass media effects research: Advances through meta-analysis* (pp. 199–214). Mahwah, NJ: Erlbaum.

Oriña, M. M., Collins, W. A., Simpson, J. A., Salvatore, J. E., Haydon, K. C., & Kim, J. S. (2011). Developmental and dyadic perspectives on commitment in adult romantic relationships. *Psychological Science, 22,* 908–915. doi:10.1177/0956797611410573

Orth, U., & Robins, R. W. (2014). The development of self-esteem. *Current Directions in Psychological Science, 23,* 381–387. doi:10.1177/0963721414547414

Orth, U., Robins, R. W., & Roberts, B. W. (2008). Low self-esteem prospectively predicts depression in adolescence and young adulthood. *Journal of Personality and Social Psychology, 95,* 695–708. doi:10.1037/0022-3514.95.3.695

Orzack, S. H., Stubblefield, J. W., Akmaev, V. R., Colls, P., Munné, S., Scholl, T., . . . Zuckerman, J. E. (2015). The human sex ratio from conception to birth. *Proceedings of the National Academy of Sciences, 112*(16), E2102–E2111.

Osborne, C., & McLanahan, S. (2007). Partnership instability and child well-being. *Journal of Marriage and Family, 69,* 1065–1083. doi:10.1111/j.1741-3737.2007.00431.x

Osborne, L. R., & Mervis, C. B. (2007). Rearrangements of the Williams-Beuren syndrome locus: Molecular basis and implications for speech and language development. *Expert Reviews in Molecular Medicine, 9,* 1–16. doi:10.1017/S146239940700035X

Oster, H., Hegley, D., & Nagel, L. (1992). Adult judgments and fine-grained analysis of infant facial expressions: Testing the validity of a priori coding formulas. *Developmental Psychology, 28,* 1115–1131.

Ostrov, J. M., Ries, E. E., Stauffacher, K., Godleski, S. A., & Mullins, A. D. (2008). Relational aggression, physical aggression and deception during early childhood: A multimethod, multi-informant short-term longitudinal study. *Journal of Clinical Child and Adolescent Psychology, 37,* 664–675. doi:10.1080/15374410802148137

Otake, M., & Schull, W. J. (1984). In utero exposure to A-bomb radiation and mental retardation: A reassessment. *British Journal of Radiology, 57,* 409–414.

Oveis, C., Cohen, A. B., Gruber, J., Shiota, M. N., Haidt, J., & Keltner, D. (2009). Resting respiratory sinus arrhythmia is associated with tonic positive emotionality. *Emotion, 9,* 265–270. doi:10.1037/a0015383

Overman, W., Pate, B. J., Moore, K., & Peuster, A. (1996). Ontogeny of place learning in children as measured in the Radial Arm Maze, Morris Search Task, and Open Field Task. *Behavioral Neuroscience, 110,* 1205–1228.

Oyserman, D., Elmore, K., & Smith, G. (2012). Self, self-concept, and identity. In M. R. Leary & J. P. Tangney (Eds.), *Handbook of self and identity,* 2nd ed. (pp. 69–104). New York, NY: Guilford.

Ozonoff, S., Cook, I., Coon, H., Dawson, G., Joseph, R. M., Klin, A., . . . Wrathall, D. (2004). Performance on Cambridge Neuropsychological Test Automated Battery subtests sensitive to frontal lobe function in people with autistic disorder: Evidence from the Collaborative Programs of Excellence in Autism Network. *Journal of Autism and Developmental Disorders, 34,* 139–150. doi:10.1023/B:JADD.0000022605.81989.cc

Padilla-Walker, L. M., Carlo, G., Christensen, K. J., & Yorgason, J. B. (2012).

Bidirectional relations between authoritative parenting and adolescents' prosocial behaviors. *Journal of Research on Adolescence, 22,* 400–408. doi:10.1111/j.1532-7795.2012.00807.x

Padilla-Walker, L. M., & Christensen, K. J. (2011). Empathy and self-regulation as mediators between parenting and adolescents' prosocial behavior toward strangers, friends, and family. *Journal of Research on Adolescence, 21,* 545–551. doi:10.1111/j.1532-7795.2010.00695.x

Padilla-Walker, L. M., Harper, J. M., & Jensen, A. C. (2010). Self-regulation as a mediator between sibling relationship quality and early adolescents' positive and negative outcomes. *Journal of Family Psychology, 24,* 419–428. doi:10.1037/a0020387

Padilla-Walker, L. M., & Nelson, L. J. (2010). Parenting and adolescents' values and behaviour: The moderating role of temperament. *Journal of Moral Education, 39,* 491–509. doi:10.1080/0305 7240.2010.521385

Paik, J. H., & Mix, K. S. (2003). U.S. and Korean children's comprehension of fraction names: A re-examination of cross-national differences. *Child Development, 74,* 144–154. doi:10.1111/1467-8624.t01-1-00526

Pakulak, E., & Neville, H. J. (2011). Maturational constraints on the recruitment of early processes for syntactic processing. *Journal of Cognitive Neuroscience, 23,* 2752–2765. doi:10.1162/jocn.2010.21586

Paley, V. G. (1981). *Wally's stories.* Cambridge, MA: Harvard University Press.

Palincsar, A. S., & Magnusson, S. J. (2001). The interplay of first-hand and second-hand investigations to model and support the development of scientific knowledge and reasoning. In S. M. Carver & D. Klahr (Eds.), *Cognition and instruction: Twenty-five years of progress* (pp. 151–187). Mahwah, NJ: Erlbaum.

Palladino, B. E., Nocentini, A., & Menesini, E. (2016). Evidence-based intervention against bullying and cyberbullying: Evaluation of the NoTrap! program in two independent trials. *Aggressive Behavior, 42,* 194–206. doi:10.1002/ab.21636

Pallini, S., Baiocco, R., Schneider, B. H., Madigan, S., & Atkinson, L. (2014). Early child–parent attachment and peer relations: A meta-analysis of recent research. *Journal of Family Psychology, 28,* 118–123. doi:10.1037/a0035736

Palmen, H., Vermande, M. M., Deković, M., & van Aken, M. A. G. (2011). Competence, problem behavior, and the effects of having no friends, aggressive friends, or nonaggressive friends: A four-year longitudinal study. *Merrill-Palmer Quarterly, 57,* 186–213.

Palmer, S. B., Fais, L., Golinkoff, R. M., & Werker, J. F. (2012). Perceptual narrowing of linguistic sign occurs in the 1st year

of life. *Child Development, 83,* 543–553. doi:10.1111/j.1467-8624.2011.01715.x

Panfile, T. M., & Laible, D. J. (2012). Attachment security and child's empathy: The mediating role of emotion regulation. *Merrill-Palmer Quarterly, 58,* 1–21.

Papastergiou, M. (2008). Are computer science and information technology still masculine fields? High school students' perceptions and career choices. *Computers & Education, 51,* 594–608.

Papini, D. R., & Sebby, R. A. (1988). Variations in conflictual family issues by adolescent pubertal status, gender, and family member. *Journal of Early Adolescence, 8,* 1–15. doi:10.1177/0272431688081001

Pardini, D. A., & Byrd, A. L. (2012). Perceptions of aggressive conflicts and others' distress in children with callous-unemotional traits: 'I'll show you who's boss, even if you suffer and I get in trouble.' *Journal of Child Psychology and Psychiatry, 53,* 283–291. doi:10.1111/j.1469-7610.2011.02487.x

Parke, R. D., & Buriel, R. (1998). Socialization in the family: Ethnic and ecological perspectives. In W. Damon (Series Ed.) & N. Eisenberg (Vol. Ed.), *Handbook of child psychology: Vol. 3. Social, emotional, and personality development* (5th ed., pp. 463–552). New York, NY: Wiley.

Parke, R. D., & Buriel, R. (2006). Socialization in the family: Ethnic and ecological perspectives. In W. Damon & R. M. Lerner (Series Eds.) & N. Eisenberg (Vol. Ed.), *Handbook of child psychology: Vol. 3. Social, emotional, and personality development* (6th ed., pp. 429–504). Hoboken, NJ: Wiley.

Parke, R. D., Coltrane, S., Duffy, S., Buriel, R., Dennis, J., Powers, J., . . . Widaman, K. F. (2004). Economic stress, parenting, and child adjustment in Mexican American and European American families. *Child Development, 75,* 1632–1656. doi:10.1111/j.1467-8624.2004.00807.x

Parke, R. D., O'Neil, R., Spitzer, S., Isley, S., Welsh, M., Wang, S., . . . Cupp, R. (1997). A longitudinal assessment of sociometric stability and the behavioral correlates of children's social acceptance. *Merrill-Palmer Quarterly, 43,* 635–662. doi:10.2307/23093363

Parker, J. G., & Asher, S. R. (1987). Peer relations and later personal adjustment: Are low-accepted children at risk? *Psychological Bulletin, 102,* 357–389. doi:10.1037/0033-2909.102.3.357

Parker, J. G., & Asher, S. R. (1993). Friendship and friendship quality in middle childhood: Links with peer group acceptance and feelings of loneliness and social dissatisfaction. *Developmental Psychology, 29,* 611–621.

Parker, J. G., Rubin, K. H., Price, J. M., & DeRosier, M. E. (1995). Peer relationships, child development, and adjustment: A developmental psychopathology perspective. In D. Cicchetti & D. J. Cohen (Eds.), *Developmental*

psychopathology: Vol. 2. Risk, disorder, and adaptation (pp. 96–161). New York, NY: Wiley.

Parker, K. J., & Maestripieri, D. (2011). Identifying key features of early stressful experiences that produce stress vulnerability and resilience in primates. *Neuroscience & Biobehavioral Reviews, 35*(7), 1466-1483.

Partanen, E., Kujala, T., Näätänen, R., Liitola, A., Sambeth, A., & Huotilainen, M. (2013). Learning-induced neural plasticity of speech processing before birth. *Proceedings of the National Academy of Sciences, 110*(37), 15145–15150.

Partners United in the Fight Against Poverty. (2015). Towards the end of child poverty [Web log post]. Retrieved from https://blogs.unicef .org/blog/a-joint-vision-to-end-child-poverty/

Pas, E. T., & Bradshaw, C. P. (2012). Examining the association between implementation and outcomes: State-wide scale-up of school-wide Positive Behavior Intervention and Supports. *Journal of Behavioral Health Services & Research, 39*, 417–433. doi:10.1007/ s11414-012-9290-2

Pascalis, O., de Haan, M., & Nelson, C. A. (2002, May 17). Is face processing species-specific during the first year of life? *Science, 296*, 1321–1323.

Paschall, M. J., & Hubbard, M. L. (1998). Effects of neighborhood and family stressors on African American male adolescents' self-worth and propensity for violent behavior. *Journal of Consulting and Clinical Psychology, 66*, 825–831. doi:10.1037/0022-006X.66.5.825

Pastorelli, C., Lansford, J. E., Luengo Kanacri, B. P., Malone, P. S., Di Giunta, L., Bacchini, D., . . . Sorbring, E. (2016). Positive parenting and children's prosocial behavior in eight countries. *Journal of Child Psychology and Psychiatry, 57*, 824–834. doi:10.1111/jcpp.12477

Patient Protection and Affordable Care Act, 42 U.S.C. § 18001 (2010).

Patterson, C. J. (1995). Families of the baby boom: Parents' division of labor and children's adjustment. *Developmental Psychology, 31*, 115–123. doi:10.1037/0012-1649.31.1.115

Patterson, C. J., Griesler, P. C., Vaden, N. A., & Kupersmidt, J. B. (1992). Family economic circumstances, life transitions, and children's peer relations. In R. D. Parke & G. W. Ladd (Eds.), *Family–peer relationships: Modes of linkage* (pp. 385–424). Hillsdale, NJ: Erlbaum.

Patterson, F., & Linden, E. (1981). *The education of Koko*. New York, NY: Holt, Rinehart, and Winston.

Patterson, G. R. (1982). *Coercive family process*. Eugene, OR: Castalia.

Patterson, G. R. (1995). Coercion as a basis for early age of onset for arrest. In J. McCord (Ed.), *Coercion and punishment in long-term perspectives* (pp. 81–105). New York, NY: Cambridge University Press.

Patterson, G. R., Capaldi, D., & Bank, L. (1991). An early starter model for predicting delinquency. In D. J. Pepler & K. H. Rubin (Eds.), *The development and treatment of childhood aggression* (pp. 139–168). Hillsdale, NJ: Erlbaum.

Patton, D. U., Eschmann, R. D., Elsaesser, C., & Bocanegra, E. (2016). Sticks, stones and Facebook accounts: What violence outreach workers know about social media and urban-based gang violence in Chicago. *Computers in Human Behavior, 65*, 591–600. doi:10.1016/j. chb.2016.05.052

Paulson, S. E. (1996). Maternal employment and adolescent achievement revisited: An ecological perspective. *Family Relations, 45*, 201–208.

Paus, T. (2010). Growth of white matter in the adolescent brain: Myelin or axon? *Brain and Cognition, 72*, 26–35. doi:10.1016/j. bandc.2009.06.002

Peacock, J. L., Marston, L., Marlow, N., Calvert, S. A., & Greenough, A. (2012). Neonatal and infant outcome in boys and girls born very prematurely. *Pediatric Research, 71*(3), 305–310.

Peake, P. K., Hebl, M., & Mischel, W. (2002). Strategic attention deployment for delay of gratification in working and waiting situations. *Developmental Psychology, 38*, 313–326. doi:10.1037/0012-1649.38.2.313

Peake, P. K., & Mischel, W. (2000). *Adult correlates of preschool delay of gratification*. Unpublished data. Smith College, Northampton, MA.

Pearson, D., Rouse, H., Doswell, S., Ainsworth, C., Dawson, O., Simms, K., . . . Faulconbridge, J. (2001). Prevalence of imaginary companions in a normal child population. *Child: Care, Health and Development, 27*(1), 13–22. doi:10.1046/j.1365-2214.2001.00167.x

Pedersen, P. E., & Blass, E. M. (1982). Prenatal and postnatal determinants of the 1st suckling episode in albino rats. *Developmental Psychobiology, 15*, 349–355. doi:10.1002/dev.420150407

Pedersen, S., Vitaro, F., Barker, E. D., & Borge, A. I. H. (2007). The timing of middle-childhood peer rejection and friendship: Linking early behavior to early-adolescent adjustment. *Child Development, 78*, 1037–1051. doi:10.1111/j. 1467-8624.2007.01051.x

Pederson, D. R., & Moran, G. (1996). Expressions of the attachment relationship outside of the Strange Situation. *Child Development, 67*, 915–927.

Peets, K., Pöyhönen, V., Junvonen, J., & Salmivalli, C. (2015). Classroom norms of bullying alter the degree to which children defend in response to their affective empathy and power. *Developmental Psychology, 51*, 913–920. doi:10.1037/a0039287

Pegg, J. E., Werker, J. F., & McLeod, P. J. (1992). Preference for infant-directed over adult-directed speech: Evidence from 7-week-old infants. *Infant Behavior and Development, 15*, 325–345. doi:10.1016/0163-6383(92)80003-D

Peisner-Feinberg, E. S., Burchinal, M. R., Clifford, R. M., Culkin, M. L., Howes, C., Kagan, S. L., & Yazejian, N. (2001). The relation of preschool child-care quality to children's cognitive and social developmental trajectories through second grade. *Child Development, 72*, 1534–1553. doi:10.1111/1467-8624.00364

Peláez-Nogueras, M., Field, T. M., Hossain, Z., & Pickens, J. (1996). Depressed mothers' touching increases infants' positive affect and attention in still-face interactions. *Child Development, 67*, 1780–1792.

Pellegrini, A. D. (2009). *The role of play in human development*. New York, NY: Oxford University Press.

Pellegrini, A. D., Long, J. D., Roseth, C. J., Bohn, C. M., & Van Ryzin, M. (2007). A short-term longitudinal study of preschoolers' (homo sapiens) sex segregation: The role of physical activity, sex, and time. *Journal of Comparative Psychology, 121*, 282–289.

Pellegrino, J. W., Chudowsky, N., & Glaser, R. (Eds.). (2001). *Knowing what students know: The science and design of educational assessment*. Washington, DC: National Academy Press.

Pellizzoni, S., Siegal, M., & Surian, L. (2009). Foreknowledge, caring, and the side-effect effect in young children. *Developmental Psychology, 45*, 289–295. doi:10.1037/a0014165

Pelucchi, B., Hay, J. F., & Saffran, J. R. (2009). Statistical learning in a natural language by 8-month-old infants. *Child Development, 80*, 674–685. doi:10.1111/j.1467-8624.2009.01290.x

Pena, M., Maki, A., Kovacic, D., Dehaene-Lambertz, G., Koizumi, H., Bouquet, F., & Mehler, J. (2003). Sounds and silence: An optical topography study of language recognition at birth. *Proceedings of the National Academy of Sciences of the United States of America, 100*, 11702–11705. doi:10.1073/pnas.1934290100

Penman-Aguilar, A., Carter, M., Snead, M. C., & Kourtis, A. P. (2013). Socioeconomic disadvantage as a social determinant of teen childbearing in the U.S. *Public Health Reports, 128*, 5–22. Retrieved from http://www.jstor.org/stable/23646793

Pepperberg, I. M. (2009). *The Alex studies: Cognitive and communicative abilities of grey parrots*. Cambridge, MA: Harvard University Press.

Perani, D., Saccuman, M. C., Scifo, P., Anwander, A., Spada, D., Baldoli, C., . . . Friederici, A. D. (2011). Neural language networks at birth. *Proceedings of the National Academy of Sciences of the United States of America, 108*, 16056–16061. doi:10.1073/pnas.1102991108

Pereira, A. F., Smith, L. B., & Yu, C. (2014). A bottom-up view of toddler word learning. *Psychonomic Bulletin & Review, 21*(1), 178–185.

Perfetti, C., & Stafura, J. (2014). Word knowledge in a theory of reading comprehension.

Scientific Studies of Reading, 18(1), 22–37. doi:10.1080/10888438.2013.827687

Perlman, S. B., Kalish, C. W., & Pollak, S. D. (2008). The role of maltreatment experience in children's understanding of the antecedents of emotion. *Cognition and Emotion, 22,* 651–670. doi:10.1080/02699930701461154

Perou, R., Bitsko, R. H., Blumberg, S. J., Pastor, P., Ghandour, R. M., Gfroerer, J. C., . . . Huang, L. N. (2013, May 17). Mental health surveillance among children—United States, 2005–2011. *Morbidity and Mortality Weekly Report, 62*(02), 1–35. Retrieved May 26, 2016, from http://www.cdc.gov/mmwr/preview/mmwrhtml/su6202a1.htm?s_cid=su6202a1_w#Ta7

Perris, E. E., & Clifton, R. K. (1988). Reaching in the dark toward sound as a measure of auditory localization in infants. *Infant Behavior and Development, 11,* 473–491. doi:10.1016/0163-6383(88)90007-0

Perry, D. G., Bussey, K., & Freiberg, K. (1981). Impact of adults' appeals for sharing on the development of altruistic dispositions in children. *Journal of Experimental Child Psychology, 32,* 127–138. doi:10.1016/0022-0965(81)90098-9

Perry, D. G., Perry, L. C., & Rasmussen, P. (1986). Cognitive social learning mediators of aggression. *Child Development, 57,* 700–711. doi:10.2307/1130347

Perry, D. G., Perry, L. C., & Weiss, R. J. (1989). Sex differences in the consequences that children anticipate for aggression. *Developmental Psychology, 25,* 312–319. doi:10.1037/0012-1649.25.2.312

Perry, L. K., Samuelson, L. K., & Burdinie, J. B. (2014). Highchair philosophers: The impact of seating context-dependent exploration on children's naming biases. *Developmental Science, 17*(5), 757–765.

Petanjek, Z., Judaš, M., Šimić, G., Rašin, M. R., Uylings, H. B., Rakic, P., & Kostović, I. (2011). Extraordinary neoteny of synaptic spines in the human prefrontal cortex. *Proceedings of the National Academy of Sciences, 108*(32), 13281–13286.

Peter, J., Valkenburg, P. M., & Schouten, A. P. (2005). Developing a model of adolescent friendship formation on the internet. *Cyberpsychology and Behavior, 8,* 423–430. doi:10.1089/cpb.2005.8.423

Peterson, C., & McCabe, A. (1988). The connective "and" as discourse glue. *First Language, 8,* 19–28. doi:10.1177/014272378800802202

Peterson, C. C., Wellman, H. M., & Liu, D. (2005). Steps in theory-of-mind development for children with deafness or autism. *Child Development, 76,* 502–517. doi:10.1111/j.1467-8624.2005.00859.x

Petitto, L. A., Holowka, S., Sergio, L. E., & Ostry, D. (2001, September 6). Language rhythms in baby hand movements. *Nature, 413,* 35–36. doi:10.1038/35092613

Petitto, L. A., & Marentette, P. F. (1991, March 22). Babbling in the manual mode: Evidence for the ontogeny of language. *Science, 251,* 1493–1496.

Petrides, K. V., Sangareau, Y., Furnham, A., & Frederickson, N. (2006). Trait emotional intelligence and children's peer relations at school. *Social Development, 15,* 537e547. doi:10.1111/j.1467-9507.2006.00355.x

Petrill, S. A., Deater-Deckard, K., Schatschneider, C., & Davis, C. (2005). Measured environmental influences on early reading: Evidence from an adoption study. *Scientific Studies of Reading, 9,* 237–259.

Petrill, S. A., Deater-Deckard, K., Thompson, L. A., Schatschneider, C., Dethorne, L. S., & Vandenbergh, D. J. (2007). Longitudinal genetic analysis of early reading: The Western Reserve Reading Project. *Reading and Writing, 20,* 127–146. doi:10.1007/s11145-006-9021-2

Petrill, S. A., Lipton, P. A., Hewitt, J. K., Plomin, R., Cherny, S. S., Corley, R., & DeFries, J. C. (2004). Genetic and environmental contributions to general cognitive ability through the first 16 years of life. *Developmental Psychology, 40,* 805–812. doi:10.1037/0012-1649.40.5.805

Pettit, G. S., Brown, E. G., Mize, J., & Lindsey, E. (1998). Mothers' and fathers' socializing behaviors in three contexts: Links with children's peer competence. *Merrill-Palmer Quarterly, 44,* 173–193. doi:10.2307/23093665

Pettit, G. S., Lansford, J. E., Malone, P. S., Dodge, K. A., & Bates, J. E. (2010). Domain specificity in relationship history, social information processing, and violent behavior in early adulthood. *Journal of Personality and Social Psychology, 98*(2), 190–200.

Pew Research Center. (2015). *Parenting in America.* Retrieved from http://www.pewsocialtrends.org/2015/12/17/1-the-american-family-today/

Pew Research Center. (2015, December 17). Parenting in America: Outlook, worries, aspirations are strongly linked to financial situation. Retrieved from http://www.pewsocialtrends.org/files/2015/12/2015-12-17_parenting-in-america_FINAL.pdf

Pew Research Center. (2016, January 7). Parents, teens and digital monitoring. Retrieved from http://www.pewinternet.org/files/2016/01/PI_2016-01-07_Parents-Teens-Digital-Monitoring_FINAL.pdf

Phillips, A. T., Wellman, H. M., & Spelke, E. S. (2002). Infants' ability to connect gaze and emotional expression to intentional action. *Cognition, 85,* 53–78.

Phinney, J. S. (1993). Multiple group identities: Differentiation, conflict, and integration. In J. Kroger (Ed.), *Discussions on ego identity* (pp. 47–73). Hillsdale, NJ: Erlbaum.

Phipps, M. G., Blume, J. D., & DeMonner, S. M. (2002). Young maternal age associated with increased risk of postneonatal death. *Obstetrics and Gynecology, 100,* 481–486.

Piaget, J. (1926). *The language and thought of the child* (M. Warden, Trans.). New York, NY: Harcourt Brace & Company. (Original work published 1923)

Piaget, J. (1951). *Play, dreams, and imitation in childhood* (C. Gattegno & F. M. Hodgson, Trans.). New York, NY: Norton.

Piaget, J. (1952a). *The child's concept of number* (C. Gattegno & F. M. Hodgson, Trans.). London, England: Routledge.

Piaget, J. (1952b). *The origins of intelligence in children* (M. Cook, Trans.). Oxford, England: International Universities Press.

Piaget, J. (1954). *The construction of reality in the child* (M. Cook, Trans.). New York, NY: Basic Books.

Piaget, J. (1964). Development and learning. In R. E. Ripple & V. N. Rockcastle (Eds.), *Piaget rediscovered* (pp. 7–20). Ithaca, NY: Cornell University.

Piaget, J. (1965). *The moral judgment of the child* (M. Gabain, Trans.). New York, NY: Free Press. (Original work published 1932)

Piaget, J. (1969). *The child's conception of time* (A. J. Pomerans, Trans.). London, England: Routledge & K. Paul.

Piaget, J. (1971). *The construction of reality in the child* (M. Cook, Trans.). New York, NY: Ballantine. (Original work published 1954)

Piaget, J. (1972). *Psychology and epistemology: Towards a theory of knowledge* (P. A. Wells, Trans.). Harmondsworth, England: Penguin.

Piaget, J., & Inhelder, B. (1977). The child's conception of space. In H. E. Gruber & J. J. Vonèche (Eds.), *The essential Piaget* (pp. 576–642). New York, NY: Basic Books. (Reprinted from *The child's conception of space* by Piaget, J., & Inhelder, B. (F. J. Langdon & J. L. Lunzer, Trans.), 1956, London, England: Routledge & K. Paul)

Piasta, S. B., & Wagner, R. K. (2010). Developing early literacy skills: A meta-analysis of alphabet learning and instruction. *Reading Research Quarterly, 45,* 8–38. doi:10.1598/RRQ.45.1.2

Piazza, M. (2011). Neurocognitive start-up tools for symbolic number representations. In S. Dehaene & E. Brannon (Eds.), *Space, time, and number in the brain: Searching for the foundations of mathematical thought* (pp. 267–285). London: Elsevier.

Piehler, T. F., & Dishion, T. J. (2007). Interpersonal dynamics within adolescent friendships:

Dyadic mutuality, deviant talk, and patterns of antisocial behavior. *Child Development, 78*, 1611–1624. doi:10.1111/j.1467-8624.2007.01086.x

Pierce, K., Marinero, S., Hazin, R., McKenna, B., Barnes, C. C., & Malige, A. (2016). Eye tracking reveals abnormal visual preference for geometric images as an early biomarker of an autism spectrum disorder subtype associated with increased symptom severity. *Biological Psychiatry, 79*(8), 657–666.

Pierce, T. (2009). Social anxiety and technology: Face-to-face communication versus technological communication among teens. *Computers in Human Behavior, 25*, 1367–1372. doi:10.1016/j.chb.2009.06.003

Pierroutsakos, S. L., & DeLoache, J. S. (2003). Infants' manual exploration of pictorial objects varying in realism. *Infancy, 4*, 141–156. doi:10.1207/S15327078IN0401_7

Pietschnig, J., & Voracek, M. (2015). One century of global IQ gains: A formal meta-analysis of the Flynn effect (1909–2013). *Perspectives on Psychological Science, 10*(3), 282–306. doi:10.1177/1745691615577701

Pilgrim, C., Luo, Q., Urberg, K. A., & Fang, X. (1999). Influence of peers, parents, and individual characteristics on adolescent drug use in two cultures. *Merrill-Palmer Quarterly, 45*, 85–107. doi:10.2307/23093315

Pillow, B. H. (1988). The development of children's beliefs about the mental world. *Merrill-Palmer Quarterly, 34*, 1–32.

Pinderhughes, E. E., Dodge, K. A., Bates, J. E., Pettit, G. S., & Zelli, A. (2000). Discipline responses: Influences of parents' socioeconomic status, ethnicity, beliefs about parenting, stress, and cognitive-emotional processes. *Journal of Family Psychology, 14*, 380–400. doi:10.1037/0893-3200.14.3.380

Pinker, S. (1994). *The language instinct: The new science of language and mind.* Harmondsworth, Middlesex, England: Allen Lane, The Penguin Press.

Pinquart, M., Feussner, C., & Ahnert, L. (2013). Meta-analytic evidence for stability in attachments from infancy to early adulthood. *Attachment & Human Development, 15*, 189–218. doi:10.1080/14616734.2013.746257

Planalp, E. M., & Braungart-Rieker, J. M. (2015). Trajectories of regulatory behaviors in early infancy: Determinants of infant self-distraction and self-comforting. *Infancy, 20*(2), 129–159. doi:10.1111/infa.12068

Plante, I., Théorêt, M., & Favreau, O. E. (2009). Student gender stereotypes: Contrasting the perceived maleness and femaleness of mathematics and language. *Educational Psychology, 29*, 385–405.

Plato. (1961). The laws. In E. Hamilton & H. Cairns (Eds.), *The collected dialogues of Plato.* Princeton, NJ: Princeton University Press.

Plato. (1980). *The laws of Plato* (T. L. Pangle, Trans.). New York, NY: Basic Books.

Plomin, R. (1990). *Nature and nurture: An introduction to human behavioral genetics.* Pacific Grove, CA: Brooks/Cole.

Plomin, R. (2004). Genetics and developmental psychology. *Merrill-Palmer Quarterly, 50*, 341–352.

Plomin, R. (2014). Genotype–environment correlation in the era of DNA. *Behavior Genetics, 44*(6), 629–638.

Plomin, R., & Daniels, D. (2011). Why are children in the same family so different from one another? *International Journal of Epidemiology, 40*(3), 563–582. doi:10.1093/ije/dyq148

Plomin, R., & Deary, I. J. (2015). Genetics and intelligence differences: Five special findings. *Molecular Psychiatry, 20*(1), 98–108.

Plomin, R., DeFries, J. C., Knopik, V. S., & Neiderhiser, J. M. (2012). *Behavioral genetics: A primer* (6th ed.). New York, NY: Worth.

Plomin, R., DeFries, J. C., Knopik, V. S., & Neiderhiser, J. M. (2016). Top 10 replicated findings from behavioral genetics. *Perspectives on Psychological Science, 11*(1), 3–23.

Plomin, R., Fulker, D. W., Corley, R., & DeFries, J. C. (1997). Nature, nurture, and cognitive development from 1 to 16 years: A parent-offspring adoption study. *Psychological Science, 8*, 442–447.

Pluess, M., & Belsky, J. (2010). Differential susceptibility to parenting and quality child care. *Developmental Psychology, 46*, 379–390. doi:10.1037/a0015203

Pluess, M., & Belsky, J. (2012). Vantage sensitivity: Individual differences in response to positive experiences. *Psychological Bulletin.* Advance online publication. doi:10.1037/a0030196

Plumert, J. M. (1995). Relations between children's overestimation of their physical abilities and accident proneness. *Developmental Psychology, 31*, 866–876.

Plumert, J. M., Kearney, J. K., & Cremer, J. F. (2004). Children's perception of gap affordances: Bicycling across traffic-filled intersections in an immersive virtual environment. *Child Development, 75*, 1243–1253.

Polanczyk, G. V., Salum, G. A., Sugaya, L. S., Caye, A., & Rohde, L. A. (2015). Annual research review: A meta-analysis of the worldwide prevalence of mental disorders in children and adolescents. *Journal of Child Psychology and Psychiatry, 56*, 345–365. doi:10.1111/jcpp.12381

Polderman, T. J., Benyamin, B., De Leeuw, C. A., Sullivan, P. F., Van Bochoven, A., Visscher, P. M., & Posthuma, D. (2015). Meta-analysis of the heritability of human traits based on fifty years of twin studies. *Nature Genetics, 47*, 702–709.

Polka, L., & Werker, J. F. (1994). Developmental changes in perception of nonnative vowel contrasts. *Journal of Experimental Psychology: Human Perception and Performance, 20*, 421–435.

Pollak, S. D., Cicchetti, D., Hornung, K., & Reed, A. (2000). Recognizing emotion in faces: Developmental effects of child abuse and neglect. *Developmental Psychology, 36*, 679–688.

Pollak, S. D., Messner, M., Kistler, D. J., & Cohn, J. F. (2009). Development of perceptual expertise in emotion recognition. *Cognition, 110*, 242–247. doi:10.1016/j.cognition.2008.10.010

Pollak, S. D., Nelson, C. A., Schlaak, M. F., Roeber, B. J., Wewerka, S. S., Wiik, K. L., . . . Gunnar, M. R. (2010). Neurodevelopmental effects of early deprivation in postinstitutionalized children. *Child Development, 81*(1), 224–236. doi:10.1111/j.1467-8624.2009.01391.x

Pollak, S. D., Vardi, S., Putzer Bechner, A. M., & Curtin, J. J. (2005). Physically abused children's regulation of attention in response to hostility. *Child Development, 76*, 968–977. doi:10.1111/j.1467-8624.2005.00890.x

Pomerantz, E. M., & Kempner, S. G. (2013). Mothers' daily person and process praise: Implications for children's theory of intelligence and motivation. *Developmental Psychology, 49*, 2040–2046. doi:10.1037/a0031840

Pomerleau, A., Bolduc, D., Malcuit, G., & Cossette, L. (1990). Pink or blue: Environmental gender stereotypes in the first two years of life. *Sex Roles, 22*, 359–367. doi:10.1007/BF00288339

Ponitz, C. C., McClelland, M. M., Matthews, J. S., & Morrison, F. J. (2009). A structured observation of behavioral self-regulation and its contribution to kindergarten outcomes. *Developmental Psychology, 45*, 605–619.

Pons, F., Bosch, L., & Lewkowicz, D. J. (2015). Bilingualism modulates infants' selective attention to the mouth of a talking face. *Psychological Science, 26*(4), 490–498.

Pons, F., & Harris, P. (2005). Longitudinal change and longitudinal stability of individual differences in children's emotion understanding. *Cognition and Emotion, 19*, 1158–1174.

Pons, F., Lewkowicz, D. J., Soto-Faraco, S., & Sebastián-Gallés, N. (2009). Narrowing of intersensory speech perception in infancy. *Proceedings of the National Academy of Sciences of the United States of America, 106*, 10598–10602. doi:10.1073/pnas.0904134106

Poole, D. A., Bruck, M., & Pipe, M. E. (2011). Forensic interviewing aids: Do props help children answer questions about touching? *Current Directions in Psychological Science, 20*, 11–15. doi:10.1177/0963721410388804

Popp, D., Laursen, B., Kerr, M., Stattin, H., & Burk, W. K. (2008). Modeling homophily over time with an actor-partner interdependence model. *Developmental Psychology, 44*, 1028–1039. doi:10.1037/0012-1649.44.4.1028

Porges, S. W. (2007). The polyvagal perspective. *Biological Psychology, 74,* 116–143. doi:10.1016/j.biopsycho.2006.06.009

Porges, S. W., Doussard-Roosevelt, J. A., & Maiti, A. K. (1994). Vagal tone and the physiological regulation of emotion. *Monographs of the Society for Research in Child Development, 59*(2–3, Serial No. 240), 167–186.

Posada, G., Lu, T., Trumbell, J., Trudel, M., Plata, S. J., Peña, P. P., . . . & Lay, K. (2013). Is the secure base phenomenon evident here, there, and anywhere? A cross-cultural study of child behavior and experts' definitions. *Child Development, 84,* 1896–1905. doi:10.111/cdev.12084

Posada, G., Trumbell, J., Noblega, M., Plata, S., Peña, P., Carbonell, O. A., & Lu, T. (2016). Maternal sensitivity and child secure base use in early childhood: Studies in different cultural contexts. *Child Development, 87,* 297–311. doi:10.111/cdev.12454

Posner, M. I., Rothbart, M. K., & Sheese, B. E. (2007). Attention genes. *Developmental Science, 10,* 24–29.

Poston, D. L., Jr., & Falbo, T. (1990). Academic performance and personality traits of Chinese children: "Onlies" versus others. *American Journal of Sociology, 96,* 433–451.

Potter, D. (2010). Psychosocial well-being and the relationship between divorce and children's academic achievement. *Journal of Marriage and Family, 72,* 933–946. doi:10.1111/j.1741-3737.2010.00740.x

Potter, D. (2012). Same-sex parent families and children's academic achievement. *Journal of Marriage & Family, 74,* 556–571. doi:10.1111/j.1741-3737.2012.00966.x

Poulin, F., Kiesner, J., Pedersen, S., & Dishion, T. J. (2011). A short-term longitudinal analysis of friendship selection on early adolescent substance use. *Journal of Adolescence, 34,* 249–256. doi:10.1016/j.adolescence.2010.05.006

Poulin, F., & Pedersen, S. (2007). Developmental changes in gender composition of friendship networks in adolescent girls and boys. *Developmental Psychology, 43,* 1484–1496. doi:10.1037/0012-1649.43.6.1484

Poulin-Dubois, D. (1999). Infants' distinction between animate and inanimate objects: The origins of naive psychology. In P. Rochat (Ed.), *Early social cognition: Understanding others in the first months of life* (pp. 257–280). Mahwah, NJ: Erlbaum.

Poulin-Dubois, D., Blaye, A., Coutya, J., & Bialystok, E. (2011). The effects of bilingualism on toddlers' executive functioning. *Journal of Experimental Child Psychology, 108,* 567–579. doi:10.1016/j.jecp.2010.10.009

Poulin-Dubois, D., & Brosseau-Liard, P. (2016). The developmental origins of selective social learning. *Current Directions in Psychological Science, 25*(1), 60–64. doi:10.1177/0963721415613962

Poulin-Dubois, D., Serbin, L. A., Eichstedt, J. A., Sen, M. G., & Beissel, C. F. (2002). Men don't put on make-up: Toddlers' knowledge of the gender stereotyping of household activities. *Social Development, 11,* 166–181. doi:10.1111/1467-9507.00193

Powell, B., Cooper, G., Hoffman, K., & Marvin, B. (2014). *The Circle of Security Intervention: Enhancing attachment in early parent–child relationships.* New York, NY: Guilford Press.

Power, T. G. (2004). Stress and coping in childhood: The parents' role. *Parenting: Science and Practice, 4,* 271–317.

Powers, K. L., Brooks, P. J., Aldrich, N. J., Palladino, M. A., & Alfieri, L. (2013). Effects of video-game play on information processing: A meta-analytic investigation. *Psychonomic Bulletin & Review, 20,* 1055–1079. doi:10.3758/s13423-013-0418-z

Powlishta, K. K. (1995). Intergroup processes in childhood: Social categorization and sex role development. *Developmental Psychology, 31,* 781–788. doi:10.1037/0012-1649.31.5.781

Pratt, M. W., Hunsberger, B., Pancer, S. M., & Alisat, S. (2003). A longitudinal analysis of personal values socialization: Correlates of a moral self- ideal in late adolescence. *Social Development, 12,* 563–585. doi:10.1111/1467-9507.00249

Pressley, M., & Hilden, K. (2006). Cognitive strategies: Production deficiencies and successful strategy instruction everywhere. In W. Damon & R. M. Lerner (Series Eds.) & D. Kuhn & R. S. Siegler (Vol. Eds.), *Handbook of child psychology: Vol. 2. Cognition, perception, and language* (6th ed., pp. 511–556). Hoboken, NJ: Wiley.

Pressley, M., Levin, J. R., & McDaniel, M. A. (1987). Remembering versus inferring what a word means: Mnemonic and contextual approaches. In M. G. McKeown & M. E. Curtis (Eds.), *The nature of vocabulary acquisition* (pp. 107–127). Hillsdale, NJ: Erlbaum.

Preves, S. E. (2003). *Intersex and identity: The contested self.* New Brunswick, NJ: Rutgers University Press.

Price, C. S., Thompson, W. W., Goodson, B., Weintraub, E. S., Croen, L. A., Hinrichsen, V. L., . . . DeStefano, F. (2010). Prenatal and infant exposure to thimerosal from vaccines and immunoglobulins and risk of autism. *Pediatrics, 126,* 656–664. doi:10.1542/peds.2010-0309

Price, M., Hides, L., Cockshaw, W., Staneva, A. A., & Stoyanov, S. R. (2016). Young love: Romantic concerns and associated mental health issues among adolescent help-seekers. *Behavioral Sciences, 6*(2), 9. doi:10.3390/bs6020009

Prinstein, M. J., Brechwald, W. A., & Cohen, G. L. (2011). Susceptibility to peer influence: Using a performance-based measure to identify adolescent males at heightened risk for deviant peer socialization. *Developmental Psychology, 47,* 1167–1172.

Prinstein, M. J., & Cillessen, A. H. N. (2003). Forms and functions of adolescent peer aggression associated with high levels of peer status. *Merrill-Palmer Quarterly, 49,* 310–342. doi:10.2307/23096058

Prinz, R. J., Sanders, M. R., Shapiro, C. J., Whitaker, D. J., & Lutzker, J. R. (2009). Population-based prevention of child maltreatment: The US Triple P System population trial. *Prevention Science, 10,* 1–12. doi:10.1007/s11121-009-0123-3

Proctor, B. D., Semega, J. L., & Kollar, M. A. (2016). *Income and poverty in the United States: 2015* (U.S. Census Bureau, Current Population Reports, P60-256). Washington, DC: Government Printing Office. Retrieved from U.S. Census Bureau website: http://www.census.gov/library/publications/2016/demo/p60-256.html

Puig, J., Englund, M. M., Simpson, J. A., & Collins, W. A. (2013). Predicting adult physical illness from infant attachment: A prospective longitudinal study. *Health Psychology, 32*(4), 409–417. doi:10.1037/a0028889

Puma, M., Bell, S., Cook, R., Heid, C., Broene, P., Jenkins, F., . Downer, J. T. (2012). *Third grade follow-up to the Head Start impact study: Final report* [Executive summary] (OPRE Report 2012-45b). Washington, DC: U.S. Administration for Children and Families, Office of Planning, Research and Evaluation. Retrieved from http://eric.ed.gov/?id=ED539264

Punamäki, R.-L., Wallenius, M., Hölttö, H., Nygård, C.-H., & Rimpelä, A. (2009). The associations between information and communication technology (ICT) and peer and parent relations in early adolescence. *International Journal of Behavioral Development, 33,* 556–564. doi:10.1177/0165025409343828

Putnam, S. P., Gartstein, M. A., & Rothbart, M. K. (2006). Measurement of fine-grained aspects of toddler temperament: The Early Childhood Behavior Questionnaire. *Infant Behavior and Development, 29,* 386–401.

Puzzanchera, C. (2009, April). Juvenile arrests 2007. *Juvenile Justice Bulletin.* Retrieved from https://www.ncjrs.gov/pdffiles1/ojjdp/225344.pdf

Puzzanchera, C. (2014). Juvenile arrests 2012. *Juvenile Offenders and Victims: National Report Series.* Retrieved from http://www.ojjdp.gov/pubs/248513.pdf

Pyrooz, D. C., Moule, R. K., & Decker, S. H. (2014). The contribution of gang membership to the victim–offender overlap. *Journal of Research in Crime & Delinquency, 51,* 315–348. doi:10.1177/0022427813516128

Qin, D. B. (2009). Being "good" or being "popular": Gender and ethnic identity negotiations of Chinese immigrant adolescents. *Journal of Adolescent Research, 24,* 37–66. doi:10.1177/0743558408326912

Quiggle, N. L., Garber, J., Panak, W. F., & Dodge, K. A. (1992). Social information processing in aggressive and depressed children. *Child Development, 63,* 1305–1320. doi:10.2307/1131557

Quine, W. V. O. (1960). *Word and object.* Cambridge, MA: Technology Press of the Massachusetts Institute of Technology.

Quinn, G. E., Shin, C. H., Maguire, M. G., & Stone, R. A. (1999, May 1). Myopia and ambient lighting at night. *Nature, 399,* 113–114.

Quinn, M., & Hennessy, E. (2010). Peer relationships across the preschool to school transition. *Early Education and Development, 21,* 825–842. doi:10.1080/10409280903329013

Quinn, P. C. (2005). Developmental constraints on the representation of spatial relation information: Evidence from preverbal infants. In L. Carlson & E. van der Zee (Eds.), *Functional features in language and space: Insights from perception, categorization, and development* (pp. 293–309). New York, NY: Oxford University Press.

Quinn, P. C., & Eimas, P. D. (1996). Perceptual organization and categorization in young infants. In C. Rovee-Collier & L. P. Lipsitt (Eds.), *Advances in infancy research* (Vol. 10, pp. 1–36). Westport, CT: Ablex.

Quinn, P. C., Yahr, J., Kuhn, A., Slater, A. M., & Pascalis, O. (2002). Representation of the gender of human faces by infants: A preference for female. *Perception, 31,* 1109–1121.

Raby, K. L., Cicchetti, D., Carlson, E. A., Egeland, B., & Collins, W. A. (2013). Genetic contributions to continuity and change in attachment security: A prospective, longitudinal investigation from infancy to young adulthood. *Journal of Child Psychology and Psychiatry, 54,* 1223–1230. doi:10.111/jcpp.12093

Radesky, J. S., Kistin, C. J., Zuckerman, B., Nitzberg, K., Gross, J., Kaplan-Sanoff, M., . . . Silverstein, M. (2014). Patterns of mobile device use by caregivers and children during meals in fast food restaurants. *Pediatrics, 133*(4), e843–e849.

Radke-Yarrow, M., & Kochanska, G. (1990). Anger in young children. In N. L. Stein, B. Leventhal, & T. Trabasso (Eds.), *Psychological and biological approaches to emotion* (pp. 297–310). Hillsdale, NJ: Erlbaum.

Radke-Yarrow, M., & Zahn-Waxler, C. (1984). Roots, motives, and patterns in children's prosocial behavior. In E. Staub, D. Bar-Tal, J. Karylowski, & J. Reykowski (Eds.), *Development and maintenance of prosocial behavior: International perspectives on positive behavior* (pp. 81–99). New York, NY: Plenum Press.

Raffan, E., Dennis, R. J., O'Donovan, C. J., Becker, J. M., Scott, R. A., Smith, S. P., . . . Summers, K. M. (2016). A deletion in the canine POMC gene is associated with weight and appetite in obesity-prone labrador retriever dogs. *Cell Metabolism, 23*(5), 893–900.

Rafferty, Y., & Shinn, M. (1991). The impact of homelessness on children. *American Psychologist, 46,* 1170–1179. doi:10.1037/0003-066X.46.11.1170

Raghubar, K. P., Barnes, M. A., & Hecht, S. A. (2010). Working memory and mathematics: A review of developmental, individual difference, and cognitive approaches. *Learning and Individual Differences, 20,* 110–122. doi:10.1016/j.lindif.2009.10.005

Ragozin, A. S., Basham, R. B., Crnic, K. A., Greenberg, M. T., & Robinson, N. M. (1982). Effects of maternal age on parenting role. *Developmental Psychology, 18,* 627–634. doi:10.1037/0012-1649.18.4.627

Rai, R., & Regan, L. (2006, August 12). Recurrent miscarriage. *The Lancet, 368,* 601–611. doi:10.1016/S0140-6736(06)69204-0

Raikes, H. A., & Thompson, R. A. (2006). Family emotional climate, attachment security and young children's emotion knowledge in a high risk sample. *British Journal of Developmental Psychology, 24,* 89–104.

Raikes, H. A., & Thompson, R. A. (2008). Attachment security and parenting quality predict children's problem-solving, attributions, and loneliness with peers. *Attachment and Human Development, 10,* 319–344. doi:10.1080/14616730802113620

Rakison, D. H., & Derringer, J. (2008). Do infants possess an evolved spider-detection mechanism? *Cognition, 107,* 381–393. doi:10.1016/j.cognition.2007.07.022

Rakison, D. H., & Krogh, L. (2012). Does causal action facilitate causal perception in infants younger than 6 months of age? *Developmental Science, 15*(1), 43–54. doi:10.1111/j.1467-7687.2011.01096.x

Rakison, D. H., & Lupyan, G. (2008). Developing object concepts in infancy: An associative learning perspective. *Monographs of the Society for Research in Child Development, 73*(1). doi:10.1111/j.1540-5834.2008.00454.x

Rakison, D. H., & Lupyan, G. (2008). The development of modeling or the modeling of development? *Behavioral and Brain Sciences, 31*(6), 726. doi:10.1017/S0140525X0800602X

Rakison, D. H., & Poulin-Dubois, D. (2001). Developmental origin of the animate-inanimate distinction. *Psychological Bulletin, 127,* 209–228.

Rakison, D. H., & Woodward, A. L. (2008). New perspectives on the effects of action on perceptual and cognitive development. *Developmental Psychology, 44*(5), 1209–1213. doi:10.1037/a0012999

Ramani, G. B., & Siegler, R. S. (2008). Promoting broad and stable improvements in low-income children's numerical knowledge through playing number board games. *Child Development, 79,* 375–394. doi:10.1111/j.1467-8624.2007.01131.x

Ramenzoni, V. C., & Liszkowski, U. (2016). The social reach: 8-month-olds reach for unobtainable objects in the presence of another person. *Psychological Science, 27*(9), 1278–1285. doi:10.1177/0956797616659938.

Ramey, C. T., & Campbell, F. A. (1991). Poverty, early childhood education, and academic competence: The Abecedarian experiment. In A. C. Huston (Ed.), *Children in poverty: Child development and public policy* (pp. 190–221). Port Chester, NY: Cambridge University Press.

Ramey, C. T., Campbell, F. A., Burchinal, M., Skinner, M. L., Gardner, D. M., & Ramey, S. L. (2000). Persistent effects of early childhood education on high-risk children and their mothers. *Applied Developmental Science, 4,* 2–14.

Ramey, C. T., & Ramey, S. L. (2004). Early learning and school readiness: Can early intervention make a difference? *Merrill-Palmer Quarterly, 50,* 471–491.

Ramirez, G., & Beilock, S. L. (2011, January 14). Writing about testing worries boosts exam performance in the classroom. *Science, 331,* 211–213.

Ramirez, G., Gunderson, E. A., Levine, S. C., & Beilock, S. L. (2012). Spatial anxiety relates to spatial abilities as a function of working memory in children. *Quarterly Journal of Experimental Psychology, 65,* 474–487. doi:10.1080/17470218.2011.616214

Rao, N., & Stewart, S. M. (1999). Cultural influences on sharer and recipient behavior: Sharing in Chinese and Indian preschool children. *Journal of Cross-Cultural Psychology, 30,* 219–241. doi:10.1177/0022022199030002005

Rasbash, J., Jenkins, J., O'Connor, T. G., Tackett, J., & Reiss, D. (2011). A social relations model of observed family negativity and positivity using a genetically informative sample. *Journal of Personality and Social Psychology, 100,* 474–491. doi:10.1037/a0020931

Rasmussen, S. (2011). 31% believe in ghosts. *Rasmussen Reports.* Retrieved from http://www.rasmussenreports.com/public_content/-lifestyle/-holidays/october_2011/31_believe_in_ghosts

Rasmussen, S. A. (2012). Human teratogens update 2011: Can we ensure safety during pregnancy? *Birth Defects Research Part A: Clinical and Molecular Teratology, 94,* 123–128. doi:10.1002/bdra.22887

Ratner, N., & Bruner, J. (1978). Games, social exchange and the acquisition of language. *Journal of Child Language, 5,* 391–401.

Rattan, A., Good, C., & Dweck, C. S. (2012). "It's ok—Not everyone can be good at math": Instructors with an entity theory comfort (and demotivate) students. *Journal of Experimental*

Social Psychology, 48, 731–737. doi:10.1016/j.jesp.2011.12.012

Rauer, A. J., Pettit, G. S., Lansford, J. E., Bates, J. E., & Dodge, K. A. (2013). Romantic relationship patterns in young adulthood and their developmental antecedents. *Developmental Psychology*. Advance online publication. doi:10.1037/a0031845

Raval, V. V., & Martini, T. S. (2009). Maternal socialization of children's anger, sadness, and physical pain in two communities in Gujarat, India. *International Journal of Behavioral Development, 33*, 215–229.

Raval, V. V., & Martini, T. S. (2011). "Making the child understand": Socialization of emotion in urban India. *Journal of Family Psychology, 25*, 847–856. doi:10.1037/a0025240

Raver, C. C., Jones, S. M., Li-Grining, C., Zhai, F., Bub, K., & Pressler, E. (2011). CSRP's Impact on low-income preschoolers' preacademic skills: Self-regulation as a mediating mechanism. *Child Development, 82*, 362–378. doi:10.1111/j.1467-8624.2010.01561.x

Rayner, K., Foorman, B. R., Perfetti, C. A., Pesetsky, D., & Seidenberg, M. S. (2001). How psychological science informs the teaching of reading. *Psychological Science in the Public Interest, 2*, 31–74.

Raznahan, A., Shaw, P. W., Lerch, J. P., Clasen, L. S., Greenstein, D., Berman, R., . . . Giedd, J. N. (2014). Longitudinal four-dimensional mapping of subcortical anatomy in human development. *Proceedings of the National Academy of Sciences, 111*(4), 1592–1597.

Recchia, H. E., Wainryb, C., Bourne, S., & Pasupathi, M. (2015), Children's and adolescents' accounts of helping and hurting others: Lessons about the development of moral agency. *Child Development, 86*, 864–876. doi:10.1111/cdev.12349

Reeb-Sutherland, B. C., Fifer, W. P., Byrd, D. L., Hammock, E. A., Levitt, P., & Fox, N. A. (2011). One-month-old human infants learn about the social world while they sleep. *Developmental Science, 14*(5), 1134–1141.

Reed, J. M., & Squire, L. R. (1998). Retrograde amnesia for facts and events: Findings from four new cases. *Journal of Neuroscience, 18*, 3943–3954.

Reese, E., & Fivush, R. (1993). Parental styles of talking about the past. *Developmental Psychology, 29*, 596–606.

Regan, P. C., & Joshi, A. (2003). Ideal partner preferences among adolescents. *Social Behavior and Personality: An International Journal, 31*, 13–20. doi:10.2224/sbp.2003.31.1.13

Reich, S. M., Subrahmanyam, K., & Espinoza, G. (2012). Friending, IMing, and hanging out face-to-face: Overlap in adolescents' online and offline social networks. *Developmental Psychology, 48*, 356–368. doi:10.1037/a0026980

Reijntjes, A., Thomaes, S., Kamphuis, J. H., Bushman, B. J., de Castro, B. O., & Telch, M. J. (2011). Explaining the paradoxical rejection-aggression link: The mediating effects of hostile intent attributions, anger, and decreases in state self-esteem on peer rejection-induced aggression in youth. *Personality and Social Psychology Bulletin, 37*, 955–963. doi:10.1177/0146167211410247

Reilly, D. (2012). Gender, culture, and sex-typed cognitive abilities. *PLoS ONE, 7*(7).

Reis, H. T., Lin, Y.-C., Bennett, M. E., & Nezlek, J. B. (1993). Change and consistency in social participation during early adulthood. *Developmental Psychology, 29*, 633–645. doi:10.1037/0012-1649.29.4.633

Reiss, D. (2010). Genetic thinking in the study of social relationships: Five points of entry. *Perspectives on Psychological Science, 5*, 502–515.

Reissland, N. (1985). The development of concepts of simultaneity in children's understanding of emotions. *Journal of Child Psychology and Psychiatry, 26*, 811–824.

Reissland, N., & Shepherd, J. (2006). The effect of maternal depressed mood on infant emotional reaction in a surprise-eliciting situation. *Infant Mental Health Journal, 27*, 173–187. doi:10.1002/imhj.20087

Relier, J. P. (2001). Influence of maternal stress on fetal behavior and brain development. *Biology of the Neonate, 79*, 168–171. doi:10.1159/000047086

Ren, A., Qiu, X., Jin, L., Ma, J., Li, Z., Zhang, L., . . . Zhu, T. (2011). Association of selected persistent organic pollutants in the placenta with the risk of neural tube defects. *Proceedings of the National Academy of Sciences of the United States of America, 108*, 12770–12775. doi:10.1073/pnas.1105209108

Rende, R., & Plomin, R. (1995). Nature, nurture, and the development of psychopathology. In D. Cicchetti & D. J. Cohen (Eds.), *Developmental psychopathology: Vol. 1. Theory and methods* (pp. 291–314). New York, NY: Wiley.

Renken, B., Egeland, B., Marvinney, D., Mangelsdorf, S., & Sroufe, L. A. (1989). Early childhood antecedents of aggression and passive-withdrawal in early elementary school. *Journal of Personality, 57*, 257–281. doi:10.1111/j.1467-6494.1989.tb00483.x

Renold, E. (2001). 'Square-girls,' femininity and the negotiation of academic success in the primary school. *British Educational Research Journal, 27*, 577–588. doi:10.1080/01411920120095753

Rest, J. (1983). Morality. In P. H. Mussen (Series Ed.) & J. Flavell & E. Markman (Vol. Eds.), *Handbook of child psychology: Vol. 3. Cognitive development* (4th ed., pp. 556–629). New York, NY: Wiley.

Rest, J. R. (1979). *Development in judging moral issues.* Minneapolis: University of Minnesota Press.

Resurrección, D., Salguero, J., & Ruiz-Aranda, D. (2014). Emotional intelligence and psychological maladjustment in adolescence: A systematic review. *Journal of Adolescence, 37*, 461–472. doi:10.1016/j.adolescence.2014.03.012

Reynolds, A. J., Temple, J. A., & Ou, S. R. (2010). Preschool education, educational attainment, and crime prevention: Contributions of cognitive and non-cognitive skills. *Children and Youth Services Review, 32*(8), 1054–1063. doi:10.1016/j.childyouth.2009.10.019

Reynolds, A. J., Temple, J. A., Robertson, D. L., & Mann, E. A. (2001). Long-term effects of an early childhood intervention on educational achievement and juvenile arrest: A 15-year follow-up of low-income children in public schools. *JAMA: Journal of the American Medical Association, 285*(18), 2339–2346. doi:10.1001/jama.285.18.2339

Rhee, S. H., & Waldman, I. D. (2002). Genetic and environmental influences on antisocial behavior: A meta-analysis of twin and adoption studies. *Psychological Bulletin, 128*, 490–529. doi:10.1037/0033-2909.128.3.490

Rheingold, H. L., & Eckerman, C. O. (1970, April 3). The infant separates himself from his mother. *Science, 168*, 78–83.

Rhoades, K. A. (2008). Children's responses to interparental conflict: A meta-analysis of their associations with child adjustment. *Child Development, 79*, 1942–1956. doi:10.1111/j.1467-8624.2008.01235.x

Rhoades, K. A., Leve, L. D., Harold, G. T., Neiderhiser, J. M., Shaw, D. S., & Reiss, D. (2011). Longitudinal pathways from marital hostility to child anger during toddlerhood: Genetic susceptibility and indirect effects via harsh parenting. *Journal of Family Psychology, 25*, 282–291. doi:10.1037/a0022886

Rhodes, M., & Wellman, H. (2013). Constructing a new theory from old ideas and new evidence. *Cognitive Science, 37*(3), 592–604. doi:10.1111/cogs.12031

Ricard, M., & Allard, L. (1993). The reaction of 9- to 10-month-old infants to an unfamiliar animal. *Journal of Genetic Psychology, 154*, 5–16. doi:10.1080/00221325.1993.9914716

Rice, E., Petering, R., Rhoades, H., Winetrobe, H., Goldbach, J., Plant, A., . . . Kordic, T. (2015). Cyberbullying perpetration and victimization among middle-school students. *American Journal of Public Health, 105*, e66–e72. doi:10.2015/AJPH.2014.302393

Rice, F., Harold, G. T., Boivin, J., Van den Bree, M., Hay, D. F., & Thapar, A. (2010). The links between prenatal stress and offspring development and psychopathology: Disentangling environmental and inherited influences. *Psychological Medicine, 40*(02), 335–345.

Rice, M. L. (2004). Growth models of developmental language disorders. In M. L. Rice & S. F.

Warren (Eds.), *Developmental language disorders: From phenotypes to etiologies* (pp. 207–240). Mahwah, NJ: Erlbaum.

Richards, M. H., Crowe, P. A., Larson, R., & Swarr, A. (1998). Developmental patterns and gender differences in the experience of peer companionship during adolescence. *Child Development, 69,* 154–163. doi:10.2307/1132077

Richman, C. L., Berry, C., Bittle, M., & Himan, M. (1988). Factors related to helping behavior in preschool-age children. *Journal of Applied Developmental Psychology, 9,* 151–165.

Rideout, V. (2012). *Social media, social life: How teens view their digital lives.* Retrieved from Common Sense Media website: https://www.commonsensemedia.org/research/social-media-social-life-how-teens-view-their-digital-lives

Rideout, V. (2014). *Learning at home: Families' educational media use in America.* New York, NY: Joan Ganz Cooney Center.

Rideout, V. (2015). *The Common Sense census: Media use by tweens and teens.* Retrieved from Common Sense Media website: https://www.commonsensemedia.org/research/the-common-sense-census-media-use-by-tweens-and-teens

Rideout V. J., Foehr, U. G., Roberts, D. F. (2010). Generation M²: Media in the lives of 8–18 year-olds. Menlo Park, CA: Kaiser Family Foundation. Available at: http://www.kff.org/entmedia/upload/8010.pdf.

Ridge, K. E., Weisberg, D. S., Ilgaz, H., Hirsh-Pasek, K. A., & Golinkoff, R. M. (2015). Supermarket speak: Increasing talk among low-socioeconomic status families. *Mind, Brain, and Education, 9*(3), 127–135.

Ridolfo, H., Chepp, V., & Milkie, M. A. (2013). Race and girls' self-evaluations: How mothering matters. *Sex Roles, 68,* 496–509. doi:10.1007/s11199-013-0259-2

Riegle-Crumb, C., & Humphries, M. (2012). Exploring bias in math teachers' perceptions of students' ability by gender and race/ethnicity. *Gender & Society, 26,* 290–322.

Riegle-Crumb, C., & Moore, C. (2014). The gender gap in high school physics: Considering the local communities. *Social Science Quarterly, 95,* 253–268.

Rieser, J. J., Garing, A. E., & Young, M. F. (1994). Imagery, action, and young children's spatial orientation: It's not being there that counts, it's what one has in mind. *Child Development, 65,* 1262–1278.

Rietveld, C. A., Medland, S. E., Derringer, J., Yang, J., Esko, T., Martin, N. W., . . . Albrecht, E. (2013). GWAS of 126,559 individuals identifies genetic variants associated with educational attainment. *Science, 340*(6139), 1467–1471.

Riggs, N. R., Greenberg, M. T., Kusché, C. A., & Pentz, M. A. (2006). The mediational role of neurocognition in the behavioral outcomes of a social-emotional prevention program in elementary school students: Effects of the PATHS Curriculum. *Prevention Science, 7,* 91–102. doi:10.1007/s11121-005-0022-1

Riley, E. A., Sitharthan, G., Clemson, L., & Diamond, M. (2013). Recognising the needs of gender-variant children and their parents. *Sex Education, 13,* 644–659.

Rimm-Kaufman, S. E., Curby, T. W., Grimm, K. J., Nathanson, L., & Brock, L. L. (2009). The contribution of children's self-regulation and classroom quality to children's adaptive behaviors in the kindergarten classroom. *Developmental Psychology, 45,* 958–972.

Rinaldi, C. M., & Howe, N. (2012). Mothers' and fathers' parenting styles and associations with toddlers' externalizing, internalizing, and adaptive behaviors. *Early Childhood Research Quarterly, 27,* 266–273. doi:10.1016/j.ecresq.2011.08.001

Rioux, C., Castellanos-Ryan, N., Parent, S., & Séguin, J. R. (2016a). The interaction between temperament and the family environment in adolescent substance use and externalizing behaviors: Support for diathesis-stress or differential susceptibility? *Developmental Review.* Advance online publication. doi:10.1016/j.dr.2016.03.003.0273-2297

Rioux, C., Castellanos-Ryan, N., Parent, S., Vitaro, F., Tremblay, R. E., & Séguin, J. R. (2016b). Differential susceptibility to environmental influences: Interaction between child temperament and parenting in adolescent alcohol use. *Development and Psychopathology, 28,* 265–275. doi:10.1017/S0954579415000437.

Ritchie, S. J., Bates, T. C., & Deary, I. J. (2015). Is education associated with improvements in general cognitive ability, or in specific skills? *Developmental Psychology, 51*(5), 573. doi:10.1037/a0038981

Riva Crugnola, C., Tambelli, R., Spinelli, M., Gazzotti, S., Caprin, C., & Albizzati, A. (2011). Attachment patterns and emotion regulation strategies in the second year. *Infant Behavior and Development, 34,* 136–151. doi:10.1016/j.infbeh.2010.11.002

Rivers, S. E., Brackett, M. A., Reyes, M. R., Elbertson, N. A., & Salovey, P. (2012). Improving the social and emotional climate of classrooms: A clustered randomized controlled trial testing the RULER approach. *Prevention Science, 14,* 77–87. doi:10.1007/s11121-012-0305-2

Rizzolatti, G., & Craighero, L. (2004). The mirror-neuron system. *Annual Review of Neuroscience, 27,* 169–192. doi:10.1146/annurev.neuro.27.070203.144230

Roberts, B. W., & DelVecchio, W. F. (2000). The rank-order consistency of personality traits from childhood to old age: A quantitative review of longitudinal studies. *Psychological Bulletin, 126,* 3–25. doi:10.1037/0033-2909.126.1.3

Roberts, B. W., Kuncel, N. R., Shiner, R., Caspi, A., & Goldberg, L. R. (2007). The power of personality: The comparative validity of personality traits, socioeconomic status, and cognitive ability for predicting important life outcomes. *Perspectives on Psychological Science, 2,* 313–345.

Roberts, S., Wilsnack, S. C., Foster, D. G., & Delucchi, K. L. (2014). Alcohol use before and during unwanted pregnancy. *Alcoholism: Clinical and Experimental Research, 38*(11), 2844–2852.

Robertson, D. L., Farmer, T. W., Fraser, M. W., Day, S. H., Duncan, T., Crowther, A., & Dadisman, K. A. (2010). Interpersonal competence configurations and peer relations in early elementary classrooms: Perceived popular and unpopular aggressive subtypes. *International Journal of Behavioral Development, 34,* 73–87. doi:10.1177/0165025409345074

Robertson, J., & Robertson, J. (Directors). (1971). *Young children in brief separation: Thomas, 2 years 4 months, in foster care for 10 days* [Motion picture]. England: Tavistock Institute of Human Relations.

Robertson, L. A., McAnally, H. M., & Hancox, R. J. (2013). Childhood and adolescent television viewing and antisocial behavior in early adulthood. *Pediatrics, 131*(3), 439–446.

Robertson, S. S. (1990). Temporal organization in fetal and newborn movement. In H. Bloch & B. Bertenthal (Eds.), *Sensory-motor organizations and development in infancy and early childhood* (pp. 105–122). Dordrecht, The Netherlands: Kluwer Academic.

Robin, D. J., Berthier, N. E., & Clifton, R. K. (1996). Infants' predictive reaching for moving objects in the dark. *Developmental Psychology, 32,* 824–835. doi:10.1037/0012-1649.32.5.824

Robinson, M., Mattes, E., Oddy, W. H., Pennell, C. E., van Eekelen, A., McLean, N. J., . . . Newnham, J. P. (2011). Prenatal stress and risk of behavioral morbidity from age 2 to 14 years: The influence of the number, type, and timing of stressful life events. *Development and Psychopathology, 23,* 507–520. doi:10.1017/S0954579411000241

Robinson, N. M., & Robinson, H. (1992). The use of standardized tests with young gifted children. In P. S. Klein & A. J. Tannenbaum (Eds.), *To be young and gifted* (pp. 141–170). Westport, CT: Ablex.

Robinson, T. N. (2003). Television viewing and childhood obesity. *Pediatric Clinics of North America, 48,* 1017–1025. doi:10.1016/S0031-3955(05)70354-0

Robnett, R. D., & Leaper, C. (2013). Friendship groups, personal motivation, and gender in relation to high school students' STEM career interest. *Journal of Research on Adolescence, 23,* 652–664.

Rochat, P. (2009). *Others in mind: Social origins of self-consciousness.* New York, NY: Cambridge University Press.

Roche, K. M., Ghazarian, S. R., Little, T. D., & Leventhal, T. (2011). Understanding links between punitive parenting and adolescent adjustment: The relevance of context and reciprocal associations. *Journal of Research on Adolescence, 21*, 448–460. doi:10.1111/j.1532-7795.2010.00681.x

Rochman, D. (2011, December 12). Incredibly, world's tiniest preterm babies are doing fust fine. *Time.* Retrieved July 19, 2016, from http://healthland.time.com/2011/12/12/worlds-tiniest-preterm-babies-are-doing-just-fine/

Rodgers, B., Power, C., & Hope, S. (1997). Parental divorce and adult psychological distress: Evidence from a national birth cohort: A research note. *Journal of Child Psychology and Psychiatry, 38*, 867–872. doi:10.1111/j.1469-7610.1997.tb01605.x

Rodkin, P. C., Espelage, D. L., & Hanish, L. D. (2015). A relational framework for understanding bullying: Developmental antecedents and outcomes. *American Psychologist, 70*, 311–321. doi:10.1037/a0038658

Rodkin, P. C., Farmer, T. W., Pearl, R., & Van Acker, R. (2000). Heterogeneity of popular boys: Antisocial and prosocial configurations. *Developmental Psychology, 36*, 14–24. doi:10.1037/0012-1649.36.1.14

Rodkin, P. C., Farmer, T. W., Pearl, R., & Van Acker, R. (2006). They're cool: Social status and peer group supports for aggressive boys and girls. *Social Development, 15*, 175–204. doi:10.1046/j.1467-9507.2006.00336.x

Rodriguez, M. L., Mischel, W., & Shoda, Y. (1989). Cognitive person variables in the delay of gratification of older children at risk. *Journal of Personality and Social Psychology, 57*, 358–367.

Roffwarg, H. P., Muzio, J. N., & Dement, W. C. (1966, April 29). Ontogenetic development of the human sleep-dream cycle. *Science, 152*, 604–619.

Rogers, F. (1996). *Dear Mister Rogers: Does it ever rain in your neighborhood? Letters to Mister Rogers.* New York, NY: Penguin Books.

Rogers, S. J., Vismara, L., Wagner, A. L., McCormick, C., Young, G., & Ozonoff, S. (2014). Autism treatment in the first year of life: A pilot study of infant start, a parent-implemented intervention for symptomatic infants. *Journal of Autism and Developmental Disorders, 44*(12), 2981–2995. doi:10.1007/s10803-014-2202-y

Rogers, T. T., & McClelland, J. L. (2004). *Semantic cognition: A parallel distributed processing approach.* Cambridge, MA: MIT Press.

Rogoff, B. (2003). *The cultural nature of human development.* Oxford, England: Oxford University Press.

Roisman, G. I., & Fraley, R. C. (2006). The limits of genetic influence: A behavior-genetic analysis of infant–caregiver relationship quality and temperament. *Child Development, 77*, 1656–1667. doi:10.1111/j.1467-8624.2006.00965.x

Roisman, G. I., Monahan, K. C., Campbell, S. B., Steinberg, L., & Cauffman, E. (2010). Is adolescence-onset antisocial behavior developmentally normative? *Development and Psychopathology, 22*, 295–311. doi:10.1017/S0954579410000076

Romens, S. E., McDonald, J., Svaren, J., & Pollak, S. D. (2015). Associations between early life stress and gene methylation in children. *Child Development, 86*(1), 303–309.

Ronald, A., & Hoekstra, R. A. (2011). Autism spectrum disorders and autistic traits: A decade of new twin studies. *American Journal of Medical Genetics Part B: Neuropsychiatric Genetics, 156*, 255–274. doi:10.1002/ajmg.b.31159

Roopnarine, J. L., & Hossain, Z. (1992). Parent–child interactions in urban Indian families in New Delhi: Are they changing? In J. L. Roopnarine & D. B. Carter (Eds.), *Parent–child socialization in diverse cultures* (Vol. 5, pp. 1–16). Norwood, NJ: Ablex.

Roopnarine, J. L., Lu, M. W., & Ahmeduzzaman, M. (1989). Parental reports of early patterns of caregiving, play and discipline in India and Malaysia. *Early Child Development and Care, 50*, 109–120. doi:10.1080/0300443890500109

Rosander, K. (2007). Visual tracking and its relationship to cortical development. *Progress in Brain Research, 164*, 105–122.

Rosch, E., Mervis, C. B., Gray, W. D., Johnson, D. M., & Boyes-Braem, P. (1976). Basic objects in natural categories. *Cognitive Psychology, 8*, 382–439. doi:10.1016/0010-0285(76)90013-X

Rose, A. J. (2002). Co-rumination in the friendships of girls and boys. *Child Development, 73*, 1830–1843.

Rose, A. J., Carlson, W., & Waller, E. M. (2007). Prospective associations of co-rumination with friendship and emotional adjustment: Considering the socioemotional trade-offs of co-rumination. *Developmental Psychology, 43*, 1019–1031. doi:10.1037/0012-1649.43.4.1019

Rose, A. J., & Rudolph, K. D. (2006). A review of sex differences in peer relationship processes: Potential trade-offs for the emotional and behavioral development of girls and boys. *Psychological Bulletin, 132*, 98–131. doi:10.1037/0033-2909.132.1.98

Rose, A. J., Swenson, L. P., & Carlson, W. (2004). Friendships of aggressive youth: Considering the influences of being disliked and of being perceived as popular. *Journal of Experimental Child Psychology, 88*, 25–45. doi:10.1016/j.jecp.2004.02.005

Rose, A. J., Swenson, L. P., & Waller, E. M. (2004). Overt and relational aggression and perceived popularity: Developmental differences in concurrent and prospective relations. *Developmental Psychology, 40*, 378–387. doi:10.1037/0012-1649.40.3.378

Rose, N. C., & Dolan, S. M. (2012). Newborn screening and the obstetrician. *Obstetrics and Gynecology, 120*(4), 908–917.

Rose, S. A., & Feldman, J. F. (1997). Memory and speed: Their role in the relation of infant information processing to later IQ. *Child Development, 68*, 630–641. doi:10.2307/1132115

Rose, S. A., Feldman, J. F., & Jankowski, J. J. (2011). Modeling a cascade of effects: The role of speed and executive functioning in preterm/full-term differences in academic achievement. *Developmental Science, 14*, 1161–1175. doi:10.1111/j.1467-7687.2011.01068.x

Roseberry, S., Hirsh-Pasek, K., & Golinkoff, R. M. (2014). Skype me! Socially contingent interactions help toddlers learn language. *Child Development, 85*(3), 956–970.

Roseberry, S., Richie, R., Hirsh-Pasek, K., Golinkoff, R. M., & Shipley, T. F. (2011). Babies catch a break: 7- to 9-month-olds track statistical probabilities in continuous dynamic events. *Psychological Science, 22*, 1422–1424. doi:10.1177/0956797611422074

Rosen, A. (2015, May 15). Jurors rejected key elements of defense case. *The Boston Globe.* Retrieved from http://www.bostonglobe.com/metro/2015/05/15/dzhokhar-tsarnaev-jurors-rejected-key-elements-defense-case/42sbaezSA7WXaFmB23LOCP/story.html

Rosen, L. H., Underwood, M. K., & Beron, K. J. (2011). Peer victimization as a mediator of the relation between facial attractiveness and internalizing problems. *Merrill-Palmer Quarterly, 57*, 319–347.

Rosenberg, E. (2016, July 7). Why Finland's newborns sleep in cardboard cribs. *The New York Times.* Retrieved July 19, 2016, from http://www.nytimes.com/2016/07/07/world/what-in-the-world/finland-baby-box.html?smid=nytcore-ipad-share&smprod=nytcore-ipad&_r=0

Rosengren, K. S., Gelman, S. A., Kalish, C. W., & McCormick, M. (1991). As time goes by: Children's early understanding of growth in animals. *Child Development, 62*, 1302–1320. doi:10.1111/j.1467-8624.1991.tb01607.x

Rosengren, K. S., & Hickling, A. K. (2000). Metamorphosis and magic: The development of children's thinking about possible events and plausible mechanisms. In K. S. Rosengren, C. N. Johnson, & P. L. Harris (Eds.), *Imagining the impossible: Magical, scientific, and religious thinking in children* (pp. 75–98). Cambridge, England: Cambridge University Press.

Rosenshine, B., & Meister, C. (1994). Reciprocal teaching: A review of the research. *Review of Educational Research, 64*, 479–530. doi:10.3102/00346543064004479

Ross, H. S., & Lazinski, M. J. (2014). Parent mediation empowers sibling conflict resolution.

Early Education and Development, 25(2), 259–275. doi:10.1080/10409289.2013.788425

Ross, J., Yilmaz, M., Dale, R., Cassidy, R., Yildirim, I., & Zeedyk, M. S. (2016). Cultural differences in self-recognition: The early development of autonomous and related selves? *Developmental Science.* Advance online publication. doi:10.1111/desc.12387

Ross, N., Medin, D., Coley, J. D., & Atran, S. (2003). Cultural and experiential differences in the development of folk biological induction. *Cognitive Development, 18,* 25–47. doi:10.1016/S0885-2014(02)00142-9

Rotenberg, K. J., & Eisenberg, N. (1997). Developmental differences in the understanding of and reaction to others' inhibition of emotional expression. *Developmental Psychology, 33,* 526–537.

Roth, G., Assor, A., Niemiec, C. P., Ryan, R. M., & Deci, E. L. (2009). The emotional and academic consequences of parental conditional regard: Comparing conditional positive regard, conditional negative regard, and autonomy support as parenting practices. *Developmental Psychology, 45,* 1119–1142. doi:10.1037/a0015272

Roth-Hanania, R., Davidov, M., & Zahn-Waxler, C. (2011). Empathy development from 8 to 16 months: Early signs of concern for others. *Infant Behavior and Development, 34,* 447–458. doi:10.1016/j.infbeh.2011.04.007

Rothbart, M. K. (2011). *Becoming who we are: Temperament and personality in development.* New York, NY: Guilford Press.

Rothbart, M. K., Ahadi, S. A., Hershey, K. L., & Fisher, P. (2001). Investigations of temperament at 3–7 years: The Children's Behavior Questionnaire. *Child Development, 72,* 1394–1408.

Rothbart, M. K., Derryberry, D., & Hershey, K. (2000). Stability of temperament in childhood: Laboratory infant assessment to parent report at seven years. In V. J. Molfese & D. L. Molfese (Eds.), *Temperament and personality development across the life span* (pp. 85–119). Mahwah, NJ: Erlbaum.

Rothbart, M. K., Sheese, B. E., & Posner, M. I. (2007). Executive attention and effortful control: Linking temperament, brain networks, and genes. *Child Development Perspectives, 1,* 2–7. doi:10.1111/j.1750-8606.2007.00002.x

Rothbaum, F., Pott, M., Azuma, H., Miyake, K., & Weisz, J. (2000). The development of close relationships in Japan and the United States: Paths of symbiotic harmony and generative tension. *Child Development, 71,* 1121–1142.

Rothstein, H. R., & Bushman, B. J. (2015). Methodological and reporting errors in meta-analytic reviews make other meta-analysts angry: A commentary on Ferguson (2015). *Perspectives on Psychological Science, 10*(5), 677–679.

Rovee-Collier, C. (1997). Dissociations in infant memory: Rethinking the development of implicit and explicit memory. *Psychological Review, 104,* 467–498. doi:10.1037/0033-295X.104.3.467

Rovee-Collier, C. (1999). The development of infant memory. *Current Directions in Psychological Science, 8,* 80–85. doi:10.1111/1467-8721.00019

Rowe, D. C., Jacobson, K. C., & Van den Oord, E. J. (1999). Genetic and environmental influences on vocabulary IQ: Parental education level as moderator. *Child Development, 70,* 1151–1162.

Rowe, D. W. (2008). Social contracts for writing: Negotiating shared understandings about text in the preschool years. *Reading Research Quarterly, 43,* 66–95.

Rowe, M. L. (2008). Child-directed speech: Relation to socioeconomic status, knowledge of child development and child vocabulary skill. *Journal of Child Language, 35*(01), 185–205.

Rowe, M. L., & Goldin-Meadow, S. (2009, February 13). Differences in early gesture explain SES disparities in child vocabulary size at school entry. *Science, 323,* 951–953.

Rowe, M. L., Ozcaliskan, S., & Goldin-Meadow, S. (2008). Learning words by hand: Gesture's role in predicting vocabulary development. *First Language, 28,* 182–199. doi:10.1177/0142723707088310

Rowe, R., Costello, E. J., Angold, A., Copeland, W. E., & Maughan, B. (2010). Developmental pathways in oppositional defiant disorder and conduct disorder. *Journal of Abnormal Psychology, 119,* 726–738. doi:10.1037/a0020798

Rowe, R., Maughan, B., Costello, E. J., & Angold, A. (2005). Defining oppositional defiant disorder. *Journal of Child Psychology and Psychiatry, 46,* 1309–1316. doi:10.1111/j.1469-7610.2005.01420.x

Rowley, S. J., Kurtz-Costes, B., Mistry, R., & Feagans, L. (2007). Social status as a predictor of race and gender stereotypes in late childhood and early adolescence. *Social Development, 16,* 150–168. doi:10.1111/j.1467-9507.2007.00376.x

Roy, B. C., Frank, M. C., DeCamp, P., Miller, M., & Roy, D. (2015). Predicting the birth of a spoken word. *Proceedings of the National Academy of Sciences, 112*(41), 12663–12668.

Rubenstein, A. J., Kalakanis, L., & Langlois, J. H. (1999). Infant preferences for attractive faces: A cognitive explanation. *Developmental Psychology, 35,* 848–855. doi:10.1037/0012-1649.35.3.848

Rubin, K. H., Bukowski, W., & Parker, J. G. (1998). Peer interactions, relationships, and groups. In W. Damon (Series Ed.) & N. Eisenberg (Vol. Ed.), *Handbook of child psychology: Vol. 3. Social, emotional, and personality development* (5th ed., pp. 619–700). Hoboken, NJ: Wiley.

Rubin, K. H., Bukowski, W. M., & Bowker, J. C. (2015). Children in peer groups. In M. H. Bornstein & T. Leventhal (Vol. Eds.) & R. M. Lerner (Ed. in Chief), *Handbook of child psychology and developmental science* (7th ed., pp. 175–222). Hoboken, NJ: Wiley.

Rubin, K. H., Bukowski, W. M., & Parker, J. G. (2006). Peer interactions, relationships, and groups. In W. Damon & R. M. Lerner (Series Eds.) & N. Eisenberg (Vol. Ed.), *Handbook of child psychology: Vol. 3. Social, emotional, and personality development* (6th ed., pp. 571–645). Hoboken, NJ: Wiley.

Rubin, K. H., Coplan, R. J., & Bowker, J. C. (2009). Social withdrawal in childhood. *Annual Review of Psychology, 60,* 141–171. doi:10.1146/annurev.psych.60.110707.163642

Rubin, K. H., Fein, G. G., & Vandenberg, B. (1983). Play. In P. H. Mussen (Series Ed.) & E. M. Hetherington (Vol. Ed.), *Handbook of child psychology: Vol. 4. Socialization, personality, and social development* (4th ed., pp. 693–774). New York, NY: Wiley.

Rubin, K. H., Lynch, D., Coplan, R., Rose-Krasnor, L., & Booth, C. L. (1994). "Birds of a feather . . .": Behavioral concordances and preferential personal attraction in children. *Child Development, 65,* 1778–1785. doi:10.1111/j.1467-8624.1994.tb00848.x

Ruble, D. N., Grosovsky, E. H., Frey, K. S., & Cohen, R. (1992). Developmental changes in competence assessment. In A. K. Boggiano & T. S. Pittman (Eds.), *Achievement and motivation: A social-developmental perspective* (pp. 138–164). New York, NY: Cambridge University Press.

Ruble, D. N., Martin, C. L., & Berenbaum, S. A. (2006). Gender development. In W. Damon & R. M. Lerner (Series Eds.) & N. Eisenberg (Vol. Ed.), *Handbook of child psychology: Vol. 3. Social, emotional, and personality development* (6th ed., pp. 858–932). Hoboken, NJ: Wiley.

Rudolph, K. D., Dennig, M. D., & Weisz, J. R. (1995). Determinants and consequences of children's coping in the medical setting: Conceptualization, review, and critique. *Psychological Bulletin, 118,* 328–328.

Rudolph, K. D., & Flynn, M. (2007). Childhood adversity and youth depression: Influence of gender and pubertal status. *Development and Psychopathology, 19,* 497–521. doi:10.1017/S0954579407070241

Rudolph, K. D., Lambert, S. F., Clark, A. G., & Kurlakowsky, K. D. (2001). Negotiating the transition to middle school: The role of self-regulatory processes. *Child Development, 72,* 929–946.

Rudolph, K. D., Lansford, J. E., Agoston, A. M., Sugimura, N., Schwartz, D., Dodge, K. A., . . . Bates, J. E. (2013). Peer victimization and social alienation: Predicting deviant peer affiliation in middle school. *Child Development.* Advance online publication. doi:10.1111/cdev.12112

Rueda, M. R., Posner, M. I., & Rothbart, M. K. (2011). Attentional control and self-regulation. In K. D. Vohs & R. F. Baumeister (Eds.), *Handbook of self-regulation: Research, theory, and applications* (2nd ed., pp. 284–299). New York, NY: Guilford Press.

Rueda, M. R., Rothbart, M. K., McCandliss, B. D., Saccomanno, L., & Posner, M. I. (2005). Training, maturation, and genetic influences on the development of executive attention. *Proceedings of the National Academy of Sciences of the United States of America, 102,* 14931–14936. doi:10.1073/pnas.0506897102

Rueter, M. A., & Conger, R. D. (1998). Reciprocal influences between parenting and adolescent problem-solving behavior. *Developmental Psychology, 34,* 1470–1482. doi:10.1037/0012-1649.34.6.1470

Ruff, H. A., & Capozzoli, M. C. (2003). Development of attention and distractibility in the first 4 years of life. *Developmental Psychology, 39,* 877–890.

Ruffman, T., Slade, L., & Crowe, E. (2002). The relation between children's and mothers' mental state language and theory-of-mind understanding. *Child Development, 73,* 734–751. doi:10.1111/1467-8624.00435

Rumelhart, D. E., & McClelland, J. L. (1986). On learning the past tense of English verbs. In J. L. McClelland, D. E. Rumelhart, & PDP Research Group (Eds.), *Parallel distributed processing: Explorations in the microstructure of cognition: Vol. 2. Psychological and biological models* (pp. 170–215). Cambridge, MA: MIT Press.

Russell, A., & Finnie, V. (1990). Preschool children's social status and maternal instructions to assist group entry. *Developmental Psychology, 26,* 603–611. doi:10.1037/0012-1649.26.4.603

Russell, J. A., & Bullock, M. (1986). On the dimensions preschoolers use to interpret facial expressions of emotion. *Developmental Psychology, 22,* 97–102.

Russell, J. A., & Widen, S. C. (2002). A label superiority effect in children's categorization of facial expressions. *Social Development, 11,* 30–52.

Rutgers, S. G., & Meyers, S. (2015). Skin-to-skin contact. *Journal of Alternative Medicine Research, 7*(3), 185.

Rutten, B. P., & Mill, J. (2009). Epigenetic mediation of environmental influences in major psychotic disorders. *Schizophrenia Bulletin, 35,* 1045–1056. doi:10.1093/schbul/sbp104

Rutter, M. (1979). Protective factors in children's responses to stress and disadvantage. In M. W. Kent & J. E. Rolf (Eds.), *Primary Prevention of Psychopathology: Vol. 3. Social competence in children* (pp. 49–74). Hanover, NH: University Press of New England.

Rutter, M., Beckett, C., Castle, J., Kreppner, J., Stevens, S., & Sonuga-Barke, E. (2009). *Policy and practice implications from the English and Romanian adoptees (ERA) study: Forty-five key questions.* London: British Association for Adoption & Fostering.

Rutter, M., O'Connor, T. G., & The English and Romanian Adoptees (ERA) Study Team. (2004). Are there biological programming effects for psychological development? Findings from a study of Romanian adoptees. *Developmental Psychology, 40,* 81–94.

Rutter, M., Sonuga-Barke, E. J., Beckett, C., Castle, J., Kreppner, J., Kumsta, R., . . . Gunnar, M. R. (2010). Deprivation-specific psychological patterns: Effects of institutional deprivation. *Monographs of the Society for Research in Child Development, 75*(1, Serial No. 295), 1–252.

Ruvolo, P., Messinger, D., & Movellan, J. (2015). Infants time their smiles to make their moms smile. *PLoS ONE 10*(9), e0136492. doi:10.1371/journal.pone.0136492

Ryan, C., Huebner, D., Diaz, R. M., & Sanchez, J. (2009). Family rejection as a predictor of negative health outcomes in white and Latino lesbian, gay, and bisexual young adults. *Pediatrics, 123,* 346–352. doi:10.1542/peds.2007-3524

Rymer, R. (1993). *Genie: An abused child's flight from silence.* New York, NY: HarperCollins.

Saarni, C. (1979). Children's understanding of display rules for expressive behavior. *Developmental Psychology, 15,* 424–429.

Saarni, C. (1984). An observational study of children's attempts to monitor their expressive behavior. *Child Development, 55,* 1504–1513.

Saarni, C., Campos, J. J., Camras, L. A., & Witherington, D. (2006). Emotional development: Action, communication, and understanding. In W. Damon & R. L. Lerner (Series Eds.) & N. Eisenberg (Vol. Ed.), *Handbook of child psychology: Vol. 3. Social, emotional, and personality development* (6th ed., pp. 226–299). Hoboken, NJ: Wiley.

Saarni, C., Mumme, D. L., & Campos, J. J. (1998). Emotional development: Action, communication, and understanding. In W. Damon (Series Ed.) & N. Eisenberg (Vol. Ed.), *Handbook of child psychology: Vol. 3. Social, emotional, and personality development* (5th ed., pp. 237–309). Hoboken, NJ: Wiley.

Sabbagh, M. A., & Shafman, D. (2009). How children block learning from ignorant speakers. *Cognition, 112,* 415–422.

Sabbagh, M. A., Xu, F., Carlson, S. M., Moses, L. J., & Lee, K. (2006). The development of executive functioning and theory of mind: A comparison of Chinese and U.S. preschoolers. *Psychological Science, 17,* 74–81. doi:10.1111/j.1467-9280.2005.01667.x

Sabongui, A. G., Bukowski, W. M., & Newcomb, A. F. (1998). The peer ecology of popularity: The network embeddedness of a child's friend predicts the child's subsequent popularity. In W. M. Bukowski & A. H. Cillessen (Eds.), *New Directions for Child and Adolescent Development: No. 80. Sociometry then and now: Building on 6 decades of measuring children's experiences with the peer group* (pp. 83–91). San Francisco, CA: Jossey-Bass.

Sackett, P. R., Borneman, M. J., & Connelly, B. S. (2008). High stakes testing in higher education and employment: Appraising the evidence for validity and fairness. *American Psychologist, 63,* 215–227. doi:10.1037/0003-066X.63.4.215

Sackett, P. R., Schmitt, N., Ellingson, J. E., & Kabin, M. B. (2001). High-stakes testing in employment, credentialing, and higher education. *American Psychologist, 56,* 302–318.

Sadeh, A., Hen-Gal, S., & Tikotzky, L. (2008). Young children's reactions to war-related stress: A survey and assessment of an innovative intervention. *Pediatrics, 121*(1), 46–53. doi:10.1542/peds.2007-1348

Saewyc, E. M. (2011). Research on adolescent sexual orientation: Development, health disparities, stigma, and resilience. *Journal of Research on Adolescence, 21,* 256–272. doi:10.1111/j.1532-7795.2010.00727.x

Saffran, J., Hauser, M., Seibel, R., Kapfhamer, J., Tsao, F., & Cushman, F. (2008). Grammatical pattern learning by human infants and cotton-top tamarin monkeys. *Cognition, 107,* 479–500. doi:10.1016/j.cognition.2007.10.010

Saffran, J. R., Aslin, R. N., & Newport, E. L. (1996, December 13). Statistical learning by 8-month-old infants. *Science, 274,* 1926–1928.

Saffran, J. R., & Griepentrog, G. J. (2001). Absolute pitch in infant auditory learning: Evidence for developmental reorganization. *Developmental Psychology, 37,* 74–85. doi:10.1037/0012-1649.37.1.74

Saffran, J. R., Johnson, E. K., Aslin, R. N., & Newport, E. L. (1999). Statistical learning of tone sequences by human infants and adults. *Cognition, 70,* 27–52. doi:10.1016/S0010-0277(98)00075-4

Sagi, A., Koren-Karie, N., Gini, M., Ziv, Y., & Joels, T. (2002). Shedding further light on the effects of various types and quality of early child care on infant–mother attachment relationship: The Haifa Study of Early Child Care. *Child Development, 73,* 1166–1186. doi:10.1111/1467-8624.00465

Sainio, M., Veenstra, R., Huitsing, G., & Salmivalli, C. (2011). Victims and their defenders: A dyadic approach. *International Journal of Behavioral Development, 35,* 144–151. doi:10.1177/0165025410378068

Saint Augustine (2002). The confessions of Saint Augustine. Translator: E. B. Pusey (Edward Bouverie). Accessed August 3, 2016, from Project Gutenberg website: http://www.gutenberg.org/files/3296/3296-h/3296-h.htm

Sakai, T., Mikami, A., Tomonaga, M., Matsui, M., Suzuki, J., Hamada, Y., . . . Matsuzawa, T. (2011). Differential prefrontal white matter development in chimpanzees and humans. *Current Biology, 21,* 1397–1402.

Sale, A., Berardi, N., & Maffei, L. (2009). Enrich the environment to empower the brain. *Trends in Neurosciences, 32,* 233–239. doi:10.1016/j.tins.2008.12.004

Salguero, J. M., Palomera, R., & Fernández-Berrocal, P. (2012). Perceived emotional intelligence as predictor of psychological adjustment in adolescents: A 1-year prospective study. *European Journal of Psychology of Education, 27,* 21e34. doi:10.1007/s10212-011-0063-8

Salihovic, S., Kerr, M., Özdemir, M., & Pakalniskiene, V. (2012). Directions of effects between adolescent psychopathic traits and parental behavior. *Journal of Abnormal Child Psychology, 40,* 957–969. doi:10.1007/s10802-012-9623-x

Sallquist, J., Eisenberg, N., Spinrad, T. L., Gaertner, B. M., Eggum, N. D., & Zhou, N. (2010). Mothers' and children's positive emotion: Relations and trajectories across four years. *Social Development, 19,* 799–821. doi:10.1111/j.1467-9507.2009.00565.x

Sallquist, J. V., Eisenberg, N., Spinrad, T. L., Reiser, M., Hofer, C., Zhou, Q., . . . Eggum, N. (2009). Positive and negative emotionality: Trajectories across six years and relations with social competence. *Emotion, 9,* 15–28. doi:10.1037/a0013970

Salmivalli, C., Kärnä, A., & Poskiparta, E. (2011). Counteracting bullying in Finland: The KiVa program and its effects on different forms of being bullied. *International Journal of Behavioral Development, 35,* 405–411. doi:10.1177/0165025411407457

Salmivalli, C., & Voeten, M. (2004). Connections between attitudes, group norms, and behaviour in bullying situations. *International Journal of Behavioral Development, 28,* 246–258. doi:10.1080/01650250344000488

Salthouse, T. A. (2009). Decomposing age correlations on neuropsychological and cognitive variables. *Journal of the International Neuropsychological Society, 15,* 650–661. doi:10.1017/S1355617709990385

Salvadori, E., Blazsekova, T., Volein, A., Karap, Z., Tatone, D., Mascaro, O., & Csibra, G. (2015). Probing the strength of infants' preference for Helpers over Hinderers: Two replication attempts of Hamlin and Wynn (2011). *PloS One, 10*(11), e0140570.

Salvas, M.-C., Vitaro, F., Brendgen, M., Lacourse, É., Boivin, M., & Tremblay, R. E. (2011). Interplay between friends' aggression and friendship quality in the development of child aggression during the early

school years. *Social Development, 20,* 645–663. doi:10.1111/j.1467-9507.2010.00592.x

Salvatore, J. E., Kuo, S. I.-C., Steele, R. D., Simpson, J. A., & Collins, W. A. (2011). Recovering from conflict in romantic relationships: A developmental perspective. *Psychological Science, 22,* 376–383. doi:10.1177/0956797610397055

Sameroff, A. J. (1998). Environmental risk factors in infancy. In J. G. Warhol (Ed.), *New perspectives in early emotional development* (pp. 159–171). Calverton, NY: Johnson & Johnson Pediatric Institute.

Sameroff, A. J., Seifer, R., Baldwin, A., & Baldwin, C. (1993). Stability of intelligence from preschool to adolescence: The influence of social and family risk factors. *Child Development, 64,* 80–97.

Samuelson, L. K. (2002). Statistical regularities in vocabulary guide language acquisition in connectionist models and 15–20-month-olds. *Developmental Psychology, 38,* 1016–1037.

Samuelson, L. K., & Horst, J. S. (2008). Confronting complexity: Insights from the details of behavior over multiple timescales. *Developmental Science, 11,* 209–215. doi:10.1111/j.1467-7687.2007.00667.x

Samuelson, L. K., & Smith, L. B. (2005). They call it like they see it: Spontaneous naming and attention to shape. *Developmental Science, 8,* 182–198. doi:10.1111/j.1467-7687.2005.00405.x

Samuelson, L. K., Smith, L. B., Perry, L. K., & Spencer, J. P. (2011). Grounding word learning in space. *PLoS ONE, 6*(12), e28095. doi:10.1371/journal.pone.0028095

Sanders, J., & Munford, R. (2014). Youth-centered practice: Positive youth development practices and pathways to better outcomes for vulnerable youth. *Children and Youth Services Review, 46,* 160–167. doi:10.1016/j.childyouth.2014.08.020

Sandin, S., Hultman, C. M., Kolevzon, A., Gross, R., MacCabe, J. H., & Reichenberg, A. (2012). Advancing maternal age is associated with increasing risk for autism: A review and meta-analysis. *Journal of the American Academy of Child & Adolescent Psychiatry, 51*(5), 477–486.

Sandler, W., Meir, I., Padden, C., & Aronoff, M. (2005). The emergence of grammar: Systematic structure in a new language. *Proceedings of the National Academy of Sciences of the United States of America, 102,* 2661–2665. doi:10.1073/pnas.0405448102

Sanger, K. L., & Dorjee, D. (2015). Mindfulness training for adolescents: A neurodevelopmental perspective on investigating modifications in attention and emotion regulation using event-related brain potentials. *Cognitive, Affective, & Behavioral Neuroscience, 15*(3), 1–16.

Sanson, A., Hemphill, S. A., Yagmuriu, B., & McClowry, S. (2014). Temperament and social

development. In P. K. Smith & C. H. Hart (Eds.), *The Wiley Handbook of Childhood Social Development* (2nd ed.). Hoboken, NJ: Wiley.

Saraswati, T. S., & Dutta, R. (1988). *Invisible boundaries, grooming for adult roles: A descriptive study of socialization in a poor rural and urban slum setting in Gujarat.* New Delhi, India: Northern Book Centre.

Saudino, K. J., & Wang, M. (2012). Quantitative and molecular genetic studies of temperament. In M. R. Zentner & R. L. Shiner (Eds.), *Handbook of temperament* (pp. 315–346). New York, NY: Guilford Press.

Saul, J., Valle, L. A., Mercy, J. A., Turner, S., Kaufmann, R., & Popovic, T. (2014). CDC grand rounds: Creating a healthier future through prevention of child maltreatment. *Morbidity and Mortality Weekly Report, 63,* 260–263. PMID: 24670927

Saunders, B. E., Berliner, L., & Hanson, R. F. (2004). *Child physical and sexual abuse: Guidelines for treatment* (revised report: April 26, 2004). Charleston, SC: National Crime Victims Research and Treatment Center.

Sauter, D. A., Eisner F., Ekman P., & Scott S. K. (2010). Cross-cultural recognition of basic emotions through nonverbal emotional vocalizations. *Proceedings of the National Academy of Sciences, USA, 107,* 2408–2412. doi:10.1073/pnas.0908239106

Savage-Rumbaugh, E. S., Murphy, J., Sevcik, R. A., Brakke, K. E., Williams, S. L., & Rumbaugh, D. M. (1993). Language comprehension in ape and child. *Monographs of the Society for Research in Child Development, 58*(3–4, Serial No. 233).

Savin-Williams, R. C. (1989a). Coming out to parents and self-esteem among gay and lesbian youths. *Journal of Homosexuality, 18,* 1–35. doi:10.1300/j082v18n01_01

Savin-Williams, R. C. (1989b). Parental influences on the self-esteem of gay and lesbian youths: A reflected appraisals model. *Journal of Homosexuality, 17,* 93–109. doi:10.1300/j082v17n01_04

Savin-Williams, R. C. (1998a). ". . . And then I became gay": Young men's stories. New York, NY: Routledge.

Savin-Williams, R. C. (1998b). The disclosure to families of same-sex attractions by lesbian, gay, and bisexual youths. *Journal of Research on Adolescence, 8,* 49–68. doi:10.1207/s15327795jra0801_3

Savin-Williams, R. C. (2001). A critique of research on sexual-minority youths. *Journal of Adolescence, 24,* 5–13. doi:10.1006/jado.2000.0369

Savin-Williams, R. C., & Cohen, K. M. (2004). Homoerotic development during childhood and adolescence. *Child and Adolescent Psychiatric Clinics of North America, 13,* 529–549.

Savin-Williams, R. C., & Cohen, K. M. (2007). Development of same-sex attracted youth. In

I. H. Meyer & M. E. Northridge (Eds.), *The health of sexual minorities: Public health perspectives on lesbian, gay, bisexual and transgender populations* (pp. 27–47). New York, NY: Springer.

Savin-Williams, R. C., & Ream, G. L. (2003). Sex variations in the disclosure to parents of same-sex attractions. *Journal of Family Psychology, 17,* 429–438. doi:10.1037/0893-3200.17.3.429

Savin-Williams, R. C., & Ream, G. L. (2007). Prevalence and stability of sexual orientation components during adolescence and young adulthood. *Archives of Sexual Behavior, 36,* 385–394. doi:10.1007/s10508-006-9088-5

Sawaya, A. L., Dallal, G., Solymos, G., de Sousa, M. H., Ventura, M. L., Roberts, S. B., & Sigulem, D. M. (1995). Obesity and malnutrition in a shantytown population in the city of São Paulo, Brazil. *Obesity Research, 3*(Suppl. 2), 107s-115s. doi:10.1002/j.1550-8528.1995.tb00453.x

Saxe, R., & Powell, L. J. (2006). It's the thought that counts: Specific brain regions for one component of theory of mind. *Psychological Science, 17,* 692–699. doi:10.1111/j.1467-9280.2006.01768.x

Sayfan, L., & Lagattuta, K. H. (2009). Scaring the monster away: What children know about managing fears of real and imaginary creatures. *Child Development, 80,* 1756–1774.

Scaramella, L. V., Conger, R. D., Simons, R. L., & Whitbeck, L. B. (1998). Predicting risk for pregnancy by late adolescence: A social contextual perspective. *Developmental Psychology, 34,* 1233–1245. doi:10.1037/0012-1649.34.6.1233

Scaramella, L. V., Conger, R. D., Spoth, R., & Simons, R. L. (2002). Evaluation of a social contextual model of delinquency: A cross-study replication. *Child Development, 73,* 175–195. doi:10.1111/1467-8624.00399

Scaramella, L. V., Neppl, T. K., Ontai, L. L., & Conger, R. D. (2008). Consequences of socioeconomic disadvantage across three generations: Parenting behavior and child externalizing problems. *Journal of Family Psychology, 22,* 725–733. doi:10.1037/a0013190

Scarf, D., Imuta, K., Colombo, M., & Hayne, H. (2012). Social evaluation or simple association? Simple associations may explain moral reasoning in infants. *PloS One, 7*(8), e42698. doi:10.1371/journal.pone.0042698

Scarpa, A., Haden, S. C., & Tanaka, A. (2010). Being hot-tempered: Autonomic, emotional, and behavioral distinctions between childhood reactive and proactive aggression. *Biological Psychology, 84,* 488–496. doi:10.1016/j.biopsycho.2009.11.006

Scarr, S. (1992). Developmental theories for the 1990s: Development and individual differences. *Child Development, 63,* 1–19.

Scarr, S., & McCartney, K. (1983). How people make their own environments: A theory of

genotype greater than environment effects. *Child Development, 54,* 424–435.

Schaal, B., Marlier, L., & Soussignan, R. (2000). Human foetuses learn odours from their pregnant mother's diet. *Chemical Senses, 25,* 729–737. doi:10.1093/chemse/25.6.729

Schaal, B., Orgeur, P., & Rognon, C. (1995). Odor sensing in the human fetus: Anatomical, functional and chemo-ecological bases. In J.-P. Lecanuet, W. P. Fifer, N. A. Krasnegor, & W. P. Smotherman (Eds.), *Fetal development: A psychobiological perspective* (pp. 205–237). Hillsdale, NJ: Erlbuam.

Schaefer, D. R., Simpkins, S. D., Vest, A. E., & Price, C. D. (2011). The contribution of extracurricular activities to adolescent friendships: New insights through social network analysis. *Developmental Psychology, 47,* 1141–1152. doi:10.1037/a0024091

Schaeffer, C. M., Petras, H., Ialongo, N., Poduska, J., & Kellam, S. (2003). Modeling growth in boys' aggressive behavior across elementary school: Links to later criminal involvement, conduct disorder, and antisocial personality disorder. *Developmental Psychology, 39,* 1020–1035. doi:10.1037/0012-1649.39.6.1020

Scharrer, E. L. (2013). Representations of gender in the media. *The Oxford handbook of media psychology* (pp. 267–284). New York, NY: Oxford University Press.

Schellenberg, E. G., & Trehub, S. E. (1996). Natural musical intervals: Evidence from infant listeners. *Psychological Science, 7,* 272–277. doi:10.2307/40062961

Schenck, C., Braver, S., Wolchik, S., Saenz, D., Cookston, J., & Fabricius, W. (2009). Relations between mattering to step- and nonresidential fathers and adolescent mental health. *Fathering, 7,* 70–90. doi:10.3149/fth.0701.70

Schieffelin, B. B., & Ochs, E. (Eds.). (1987). *Studies in the social and cultural foundations of language: No. 3. Language socialization across cultures.* New York, NY: Cambridge University Press.

Schlaggar, B. L., & Church, J. A. (2009). Functional neuroimaging insights into the development of skilled reading. *Current Directions in Psychological Science, 18,* 21–26.

Schleger, F., Landerl, K., Muenssinger, J., Draganova, R., Reinl, M., Kiefer-Schmidt, I., . . . Preissl, H. (2014). Magnetoencephalographic signatures of numerosity discrimination in fetuses and neonates. *Developmental Neuropsychology, 39*(4), 316–329.

Schmidt, F. L., & Hunter, J. (2004). General mental ability in the world of work: Occupational attainment and job performance. *Journal of Personality and Social Psychology, 86,* 162–173. doi:10.1037/0022-3514.86.1.162

Schmidt, J. A., Shumow, L., & Kackar, H. (2007). Adolescents' participation in service activities and its impact on academic, behavioral,

and civic outcomes. *Journal of Youth and Adolescence, 36,* 127–140. doi:10.1007/s10964-006-9119-5

Schmidt, M. E., & Bagwell, C. L. (2007). The protective role of friendships in overtly and relationally victimized boys and girls. *Merrill-Palmer Quarterly, 53,* 439–460.

Schmidt, M. E., Pempek, T. A., Kirkorian, H. L., Lund, A. F., & Anderson, D. R. (2008). The effects of background television on the toy play behavior of very young children. *Child Development, 79,* 1137–1151.

Schmit, S. (2011). Early Head Start participants, programs, families and staff in 2010 [Fact sheet]. Retrieved from http://www.clasp.org/admin/site/publications/files/EHS-PIR-2010-Fact-Sheet.pdf

Schneider, B. H. (2016). *Childhood friendships and peer relations: Friends and enemies* (2nd ed.). New York, NY: Routledge.

Schneider, B. H., Atkinson, L., & Tardif, C. (2001). Child–parent attachment and children's peer relations: A quantitative review. *Developmental Psychology, 37,* 86–100. doi:10.1037/0012-1649.37.1.86

Schneider, W. (1998). Performance prediction in young children: Effects of skill, metacognition and wishful thinking. *Developmental Science, 1,* 291–297. doi:10.1111/1467-7687.00044

Schneider, W. (2015). *Memory development from early childhood through emerging adulthood.* New York, NY: Springer.

Schneider, W., Körkel, J., & Weinert, F. E. (1989). Domain-specific knowledge and memory performance: A comparison of high- and low-aptitude children. *Journal of Educational Psychology, 81,* 306–312.

Schneider, W., & Ornstein, P. A. (2015). The development of children's memory. *Child Development Perspectives, 9*(3): 190–195. doi:10.1111/cdep.12129

Schober-Peterson, D., & Johnson, C. J. (1991). Non-dialogue speech during preschool interactions. *Journal of Child Language, 18,* 153–170.

Schofield, T. J., Martin, M. J., Conger, K. J., Neppl, T. M., Donnellan, M. B., & Conger, R. D. (2011). Intergenerational transmission of adaptive functioning: A test of the interactionist model of SES and human development. *Child Development, 82,* 33–47. doi:10.1111/j.1467-8624.2010.01539.x

Scholl, B. J., & Leslie, A. M. (2001). Minds, modules, and meta-analysis. *Child Development, 72,* 696–701. doi:10.1111/1467-8624.00308

Scholte, R. H. J., Poelen, E. A. P., Willemsen, G., Boomsma, D. I., & Engels, R. C. M. E. (2008). Relative risks of adolescent and young adult alcohol use: The role of drinking fathers, mothers, siblings, and friends. *Addictive Behaviors, 33,* 1–14. doi:10.1016/j.addbeh.2007.04.015

Schoppe-Sullivan, S. J., Brown, G. L., Cannon, E. A., Mangelsdorf, S. C., & Sokolowski, M. S. (2008). Maternal gatekeeping, coparenting quality, and fathering behavior in families with infants. *Journal of Family Psychology, 22*, 389–398. doi:10.1037/0893-3200.22.3.389

Schulenberg, J., Maggs, J. L., Dielman, T. E., Sharon, L. L., Kloska, D. D., Shope, J. T., & Laetz, V. B. (1999). On peer influences to get drunk: A panel study of young adolescents. *Merrill-Palmer Quarterly, 45*, 108–142. doi:10.2307/23093317

Schult, C. A., & Wellman, H. M. (1997). Explaining human movements and actions: Children's understanding of the limits of psychological explanation. *Cognition, 62*, 291–324.

Schultz, D., Izard, C. E., Ackerman, B. P., & Youngstrom, E. A. (2001). Emotion knowledge in economically disadvantaged children: Self-regulatory antecedents and relations to social difficulties and withdrawal. *Development and Psychopathology, 13*, 53–67.

Schultze-Krumbholz, A., Schultze, M., Zagorscak, P., Wölfer, R., & Scheithauer, H. (2016). Feeling cybervictims' pain—The effect of empathy training on cyberbullying. *Aggressive Behavior, 42*, 147–156. doi:10.1002/ab.21613

Schulz, L. (2012). The origins of inquiry: Inductive inference and exploration in early childhood. *Trends in Cognitive Sciences, 16*, 382–389.

Schulz, L. C. (2010). The Dutch Hunger Winter and the developmental origins of health and disease. *Proceedings of the National Academy of Sciences, 107*(39), 16757–16758.

Schulz, L. E., & Sommerville, J. (2006). God does not play dice: Causal determinism and preschoolers' causal inferences. *Child Development, 77*, 427–442. doi:10.1111/j.1467-8624.2006.00880.x

Schutte, A. R., Spencer, J. P., & Schöner, G. (2003). Testing the dynamic field theory: Working memory for locations becomes more spatially precise over development. *Child Development, 74*, 1393–1417.

Schwartz, D., McFadyen-Ketchum, S. A., Dodge, K. A., Pettit, G. S., & Bates, J. E. (1998). Peer group victimization as a predictor of children's behavior problems at home and in school. *Development and Psychopathology, 10*, 87–99.

Schwartz, D., Tom, S. R., Chang, L., Xu, Y., Duong, M. T., & Kelly, B. M. (2010). Popularity and acceptance as distinct dimensions of social standing for Chinese children in Hong Kong. *Social Development, 19*, 681–697. doi:10.1111/j.1467-9507.2009.00558.x

Schwartz, O. S., Dudgeon, P., Sheeber, L. B., Yap, M. B., Simmons, J. G., & Allen, N. B. (2012). Parental behaviors during family interactions predict changes in depression and anxiety symptoms during adolescence.

Journal of Abnormal Child Psychology, 40, 59–71. doi:10.1007/s10802-011-9542-2

Schwartz, P. D., Maynard, A. M., & Uzelac, S. M. (2008). Adolescent egocentrism: A contemporary view. *Adolescence, 43*, 441–448.

Schwartz, S., & Johnson, J. H. (1985). *Psychopathology of childhood: A clinical-experimental approach* (2nd ed.). New York, NY: Pergamon Press.

Schwartz, S. J., Mason, C. A., Pantin, H., & Szapocznik, J. (2009). Longitudinal relationships between family functioning and identity development in Hispanic adolescents: Continuity and change. *Journal of Early Adolescence, 29*, 177–211. doi:10.1177/0272431608317605

Schwartz-Mette, R. A., & Rose, A. J. (2012). Co-rumination mediates contagion of internalizing symptoms within youths' friendships. *Developmental Psychology, 48*, 1355–1365. doi:10.1037/a0027484

Schwarz, B., Mayer, B., Trommsdorff, G., Ben-Arieh, A., Friedlmeier, M., Lubiewska, K., . . . Peltzer, K. (2012). Does the importance of parent and peer relationships for adolescents' life satisfaction vary across cultures? *Journal of Early Adolescence, 32*, 55–80. doi:10.1177/0272431611419508

Scott, K. M., Smith, D. R., & Ellis, P. M. (2010). Prospectively ascertained child maltreatment and its association with DSM-IV mental disorders in young adults. *Archives of General Psychiatry, 67*, 712–719. doi:10.1001/archgenpsychiatry.2010.71

Scott, R. M., & Baillargeon, R. (2013). Do infants really expect agents to act efficiently? A critical test of the rationality principle. *Psychological Science, 24*(4), 466–474.

Sears, M. S., Repetti, R. L., Reynolds, B. M., & Sperling, J. B. (2014). A naturalistic observational study of children's expressions of anger in the family context. *Emotion, 14*(2), 272–283. doi:10.1037/a0034753

Seaton, E. K., Caldwell, C. H., Sellers, R. M., & Jackson, J. S. (2008). The prevalence of perceived discrimination among African American and Caribbean Black youth. *Developmental Psychology, 44*, 1288–1297. doi:10.1037/a0012747

Seaton, E. K., Yip, T., & Sellers, R. M. (2009). A longitudinal examination of racial identity and racial discrimination among African American adolescents. *Child Development, 80*, 406–417. doi:10.1111/j.1467-8624.2009.01268.x

Sebanc, A. M., Kearns, K. T., Hernandez, M. D., & Galvin, K. B. (2007). Predicting having a best friend in young children: Individual characteristics and friendship features. *Journal of Genetic Psychology, 168*, 81–96. doi:10.3200/GNTP.168.1.81-96

Sebastián-Gallés, N., Albareda-Castellot, B., Weikum, W. M., & Werker, J. F. (2012). A bilingual advantage in visual language

discrimination in infancy. *Psychological Science, 23*, 994–999. doi:10.1177/0956797612436817

Seehagen, S., & Herbert, J. S. (2011). Infant imitation from televised peer and adult models. *Infancy, 16*, 113–136. doi:10.1111/j.1532-7078.2010.00045.x

Segal, N. L., McGuire, S. A., Havlena, J., Gill, P., & Hershberger, S. L. (2007). Intellectual similarity of virtual twin pairs: Developmental trends. *Personality and Individual Differences, 42*, 1209–1219. doi:10.1016/j.paid.2006.09.028

Segal, N. L., Stohs, J. H., & Evans, K. (2011). Chinese twin children reared apart and reunited: First prospective study of co-twin reunions. *Adoption Quarterly, 14*(1), 61–78.

Seidenberg, M. S. (2005). Connectionist models of word reading. *Current Directions in Psychological Science, 14*(5), 238–242. doi:10.1111/j.0963-7214.2005.00372.x

Seidman, E., Allen, L., Aber, J. L., Mitchell, C., & Feinman, J. (1994). The impact of school transitions in early adolescence on the self-system and perceived social context of poor urban youth. *Child Development, 65*, 507–522. doi:10.1111/j.1467-8624.1994.tb00766.x

Seiffge-Krenke, I., Overbeek, G., & Vermulst, A. (2010). Parent–child relationship trajectories during adolescence: Longitudinal associations with romantic outcomes in emerging adulthood. *Journal of Adolescence, 33*, 159–171. doi:10.1016/j.adolescence.2009.04.001

Sekar, A., Bialas, A. R., de Rivera, H., Davis, A., Hammond, T. R., Kamitaki, N., . . . Genovese, G. (2016). Schizophrenia risk from complex variation of complement component 4. *Nature, 530*(7589), 177–183.

Selfe, L. (1995). Nadia reconsidered. In C. Golomb (Ed.), *The development of artistically gifted children* (pp. 197–237). Hillsdale, NJ: Erlbaum.

Selfhout, M. H. W., Branje, S. J. T., Delsing, M., ter Bogt, T. F. M., & Meeus, W. H. J. (2009). Different types of Internet use, depression, and social anxiety: The role of perceived friendship quality. *Journal of Adolescence, 32*, 819–833. doi:10.1016/j.adolescence.2008.10.011

Selfhout, M. H. W., Branje, S. J. T., & Meeus, W. H. J. (2008). The development of delinquency and perceived friendship quality in adolescent best friendship dyads. *Journal of Abnormal Child Psychology, 36*, 471–485. doi:10.1007/s10802-007-9193-5

Selman, R. L. (1980). *The growth of interpersonal understanding: Developmental and clinical analyses.* New York, NY: Academic Press.

Senghas, A., & Coppola, M. (2001). Children creating language: How Nicaraguan sign language acquired a spatial grammar. *Psychological Science, 12*, 323–328.

Senju, A., & Csibra, G. (2008). Gaze following in human infants depends on communicative signals. *Current Biology, 18*(9), 668–671.

Sentse, M., & Laird, R. D. (2010). Parent–child relationships and dyadic friendship experiences as predictors of behavior problems in early adolescence. *Journal of Clinical Child and Adolescent Psychology, 39*, 873–884. doi:10.1080/15374416. 2010.517160

Serbin, L. A., Poulin-Dubois, D., Colburne, K. A., Sen, M. G., & Eichstedt, J. A. (2001). Gender stereotyping in infancy: Visual preferences for and knowledge of gender-stereotyped toys in the second year. *International Journal of Behavioral Development, 25*, 7–15. doi:10.1080/01650250042000078

Serbin, L. A., Powlishta, K. K., & Gulko, J. (1993). The development of sex typing in middle childhood. *Monographs of the Society for Research in Child Development, 58*(2, Serial No. 232), i-95. doi:10.2307/1166118

Sevy, A. B. G., Bortfeld, H., Huppert, T. J., Beauchamp, M. S., Tonini, R. E., & Oghalai, J. S. (2010). Neuroimaging with near-infrared spectroscopy demonstrates speech-evoked activity in the auditory cortex of deaf children following cochlear implantation. *Hearing Research, 270*, 39–47. doi:10.1016/j.heares.2010.09.010

Seyfarth, R. M., & Cheney, D. L. (1993). Meaning, reference, and intentionality in the natural vocalizations of monkeys. In H. L. Roitblat, L. M. Herman, & P. E. Nachtigall (Eds.), *Language and communication: Comparative perspectives* (pp. 195–220). Hillsdale, NJ: Erlbaum.

Shackman, J. E., & Pollak, S. D. (2014). Impact of physical maltreatment on the regulation of negative affect and aggression. *Development and Psychopathology, 26*, 1021–1033.

Shalev, R. S. (2007). Prevalence of developmental dyscalculia. In D. B. Berch & M. M. M. Mazzocco (Eds.), *Why is math so hard for some children? The nature and origins of mathematical learning difficulties and disabilities* (pp. 49–60). Baltimore, MD: Paul H. Brookes.

Shanahan, L., McHale, S. M., Crouter, A. C., & Osgood, D. W. (2007). Warmth with mothers and fathers from middle childhood to late adolescence: Within- and between-families comparisons. *Developmental Psychology, 43*, 551–563. doi:10.1037/0012-1649.43.3.551

Shanahan, L., McHale, S. M., Crouter, A. C., & Osgood, D. W. (2008). Linkages between parents' differential treatment, youth depressive symptoms, and sibling relationships. *Journal of Marriage and Family, 70*, 480–494. doi:10.1111/j.1741-3737.2008.00495.x

Shantz, C. U. (1987). Conflicts between children. *Child Development, 58*, 283–305. doi:10.2307/1130507

Shapiro, D. N., & Stewart, A. J. (2011). Parenting stress, perceived child regard, and depressive symptoms among stepmothers and biological mothers. *Family Relations, 60*, 533–544. doi:10.1111/j.1741-3729.2011.00665.x

Shapiro, L. R., & Hudson, J. A. (1991). Tell me a make-believe story: Coherence and cohesion in young children's picture-elicited narratives. *Developmental Psychology, 27*, 960–974.

Share, D. L. (2004). Knowing letter names and learning letter sounds: A causal connection. *Journal of Experimental Child Psychology, 88*, 213–233. doi:10.1016/j.jecp.2004.03.005

Shaw, D. S., Criss, M. M., Schonberg, M. A., & Beck, J. E. (2004). The development of family hierarchies and their relation to children's conduct problems. *Development and Psychopathology, 16*, 483–500. doi:10.1017/S0954579404004638

Shaw, D. S., Gilliom, M., Ingoldsby, E. M., & Nagin, D. S. (2003). Trajectories leading to school-age conduct problems. *Developmental Psychology, 39*, 189–200. doi:10.1037/0012-1649. 39.2.189

Shaw, J. A. (2003). Children exposed to war/terrorism. *Clinical Child and Family Psychology Review, 6*, 237–246. doi:10.1023/B:CCFP.0000006291.10180.bd

Shaywitz, S. E., Mody, M., & Shaywitz, B. A. (2006). Neural mechanisms in dyslexia. *Current Directions in Psychological Science, 15*, 278–281.

Sheehan, M. J., & Watson, M. W. (2008). Reciprocal influences between maternal discipline techniques and aggression in children and adolescents. *Aggressive Behavior, 34*, 245–255. doi:10.1002/ab.20241

Sheese, B. E., Voelker, P. M., Rothbart, M. K., & Posner, M. I. (2007). Parenting quality interacts with genetic variation in dopamine receptor D4 to influence temperament in early childhood. *Development and Psychopathology, 19*, 1039–1046. doi:10.1017/S0954579407000521

Shell, R., & Eisenberg, N. (1990). The role of peers' gender in children's naturally occurring interest in toys. *International Journal of Behavioral Development, 13*, 373–388. doi:10.1177/016502549001300309

Sheridan, C. J., Matuz, T., Draganova, R., Eswaran, H., & Preissl, H. (2010). Fetal magnetoencephalography—Achievements and challenges in the study of prenatal and early postnatal brain responses: A review. *Infant and Child Development, 19*, 80–93. doi:10.1002/icd.657

Sheridan, M. A., Fox, N. A., Zeanah, C. H., McLaughlin, K. A., & Nelson, C. A. (2012). Variation in neural development as a result of exposure to institutionalization early in childhood. *Proceedings of the National Academy of Sciences, 109*(32), 12927–12932.

Shetty, P. (2006). Achieving the goal of halving global hunger by 2015. *Proceedings of the Nutrition Society, 65*, 7–18. doi:10.1079/PNS2005479

Shiell, M. M., Champoux, F., & Zatorre, R. J. (2016). The right hemisphere planum temporale supports enhanced visual motion detection ability in deaf people: Evidence from cortical thickness. *Neural Plasticity.* doi:10.1155/2016/7217630

Shiell, M. M., & Zatorre, R. J. (2016). White matter structure in the right planum temporale region correlates with visual motion detection thresholds in deaf people. *Hearing Research.* doi:10.1016/j.heares.2016.06.011

Shiller, V. M., Izard, C. E., & Hembree, E. A. (1986). Patterns of emotion expression during separation in the strange-situation procedure. *Developmental Psychology, 22*, 378–382. doi:10.1037/0012-1649.22.3.378

Shin, M. (2010). Peeking at the relationship world of infant friends and caregivers. *Journal of Early Childhood Research, 8*, 294–302. doi:10.1177/1476718x10366777

Shiner, R. L., Buss, K. A., McClowry, S. G., Putnam, S. P., Saudino, K. J., & Zentner, M. (2012). What is temperament now? Assessing progress in temperament research on the twenty-fifth anniversary of Goldsmith et al. *Child Development Perspectives, 6*, 436–444.

Shirtcliff, E. A., Coe, C. L., & Pollak, S. D. (2009). Early childhood stress is associated with elevated antibody levels to Herpes Simplex Virus Type 1. *Proceedings of the National Academy of Sciences, 106*, 2963–2967.

Shirtcliff, E. A., Granger, D. A., Booth, A., & Johnson, D. (2005). Low salivary cortisol levels and externalizing behavior problems in youth. *Development and Psychopathology, 17*, 167–184.

Shoal, G. D., Giancola, P. R., & Kirillova, G. P. (2003). Salivary cortisol, personality, and aggressive behavior in adolescent boys: A 5-year longitudinal study. *Journal of the American Academy of Child and Adolescent Psychiatry, 42*, 1101–1107. doi:10.1097/01. CHI.0000070246.24125.6D

Shoda, Y., Mischel, W., & Peake, P. K. (1990). Predicting adolescent cognitive and self–regulatory competencies from preschool delay of gratification. *Development Psychology, 26*, 978–986. doi:10.1037/0012-1649.26.6.978

Shomaker, L. B., & Furman, W. (2009). Parent—adolescent relationship qualities, internal working models, and attachment styles as predictors of adolescents' interactions with friends. *Journal of Social and Personal Relationships, 26*, 579–603. doi:10.1177/0265407509354441

Shonkoff, J. P., Boyce, W. T., & McEwen, B. S. (2009). Neuroscience, molecular biology, and the childhood roots of health disparities: Building a new framework for health promotion and disease prevention. *JAMA, 301*(21), 2252–2259. doi:10.1001/jama.2009.754

Shonkoff, J. P., Garner, A. S., & the Committee on Psychosocial Aspects of Child and Family Health, Committee on Early Childhood,

Adoption, and Dependent Care, and Section on Developmental and Behavioral Pediatrics. (2012). The lifelong effects of early childhood adversity and toxic stress. *Pediatrics, 129,* e232–e246. doi:10.1542/peds.2011-2663

Short, J. F., Jr. (1996). Personal, gang, and community careers. In C. R. Huff (Ed.), *Gangs in America* (2nd ed., pp. 221–240). Thousand Oaks, CA: Sage.

Shrum, W., & Cheek, N. H., Jr. (1987). Social structure during the school years: Onset of the degrouping process. *American Sociological Review, 52,* 218–223. doi:10.2307/2095450

Shutts, K., Kinzler, K. D., & DeJesus, J. M. (2013). Understanding infants' and children's social learning about foods: Previous research and new prospects. *Developmental Psychology, 49*(3), 419.

Shutts, K., Kinzler, K. D., McKee, C. B., & Spelke, E. S. (2009). Social information guides infants' selection of foods. *Journal of Cognition and Development, 10,* 1–17.

Shweder, R. A., Mahapatra, M., & Miller, J. G. (1987). Culture and moral development. In J. Kagan & S. Lamb (Eds.), *The emergence of morality in young children* (pp. 1–83). Chicago, IL: University of Chicago Press.

Sickmund, M., & Puzzanchera, C. (Eds.). (2014). *Juvenile Offenders and Victims: 2014 National Report.* Pittsburgh, PA: National Center for Juvenile Justice. Retrieved from http://www.ncjj.org/nr2014/downloads/NR2014.pdf

Siegel, B. S., Perrin, E. C., & Committee on psychosocial aspects of child and family health. (2013). Promoting the well-being of children whose parents are gay or lesbian. *Pediatrics, 131*(4), 827–830. doi:10.1542/peds.2013-0376

Siegel, L. S. (1993). The cognitive basis of dyslexia. In M. L. Howe & R. Pasnak (Eds.), *Emerging themes in cognitive development: Vol. 2. Competencies* (pp. 33–52). New York, NY: Springer-Verlag.

Siegler, R. S. (1976). The effects of simple necessity and sufficiency relationships on children's causal inferences. *Child Development, 47,* 1058–1063.

Siegler, R. S. (1986). Unities in strategy choices across domains. In M. Perlmutter (Ed.), *Minnesota Symposia on Child Psychology: Vol. 19. Perspectives on intellectual development* (pp. 1–48). Hillsdale, NJ: Erlbaum.

Siegler, R. S. (1987). The perils of averaging data over strategies: An example from children's addition. *Journal of Experimental Psychology: General, 116,* 250–264.

Siegler, R. S. (1995). How does change occur: A microgenetic study of number conservation. *Cognitive Psychology, 28,* 225–273. doi:10.1006/cogp.1995.1006

Siegler, R. S. (1996). *Emerging minds: The process of change in children's thinking.* New York, NY: Oxford University Press.

Siegler, R. S. (2006). Microgenetic analyses of learning. In W. Damon & R. M. Lerner (Series Eds.) & D. Kuhn & R. S. Siegler (Vol. Eds.), *Handbook of child psychology: Vol. 2. Cognition, perception, and language* (6th ed., pp. 464–510). Hoboken, NJ: Wiley.

Siegler, R. S. (2016). Magnitude knowledge: The common core of numerical development. *Developmental Science, 19,* 341–361. doi:10.1111/desc.12395

Siegler, R. S., & Araya, R. (2005). A computational model of conscious and unconscious strategy discovery. In R. V. Kail (Ed.), *Advances in child development and behavior* (Vol. 33, pp. 1–42). Oxford, England: Elsevier.

Siegler, R. S., & Booth, J. L. (2004). Development of numerical estimation in young children. *Child Development, 75,* 428–444. doi:10.1111/j.1467-8624.2004.00684.x

Siegler, R. S., & Braithwaite, D. W. (in press). Numerical development. *Annual Review of Psychology.*

Siegler, R. S., & Jenkins, E. (1989). *How children discover new strategies.* Hillsdale, NJ: Erlbaum.

Siegler, R. S., & Mu, Y. (2008). Chinese children excel on novel mathematics problems even before elementary school. *Psychological Science, 19,* 759–763. doi:10.1111/j.1467-9280.2008.02153.x

Siegler, R. S., & Opfer, J. E. (2003). The development of numerical estimation evidence for multiple representations of numerical quantity. *Psychological Science, 14,* 237–250.

Siegler, R. S., & Pyke, A. A. (2013). Developmental and individual differences in understanding of fractions. *Developmental Psychology, 49,* 1994–2004. doi:10.1037/a0031200

Siegler, R. S., & Ramani, G. B. (2009). Playing linear number board games—but not circular ones—improves low-income preschoolers' numerical understanding. *Journal of Educational Psychology, 101,* 545–560. doi:10.1037/a0014239

Siegler, R. S., Thompson, C. A., & Schneider, M. (2011). An integrated theory of whole number and fractions development. *Cognitive Psychology, 62,* 273–296. doi:10.1016/j.cogpsych.2011.03.001

Sigman, M., & Ruskin, E. (1999). Continuity and change in the social competence of children with autism, Down syndrome, and developmental delays. *Monographs of the Society for Research in Child Development, 64*(1, Serial No. 256).

Signorella, M. L., Bigler, R. S., & Liben, L. S. (1997). A meta-analysis of children's memories for own-sex and other-sex information. *Journal of Applied Developmental Psychology, 18,* 429–445. doi:10.1016/S0193-3973(97)80009-3

Signorielli, N. (2012). Television's gender-role images and contribution to stereotyping: Past, present, future. *Handbook of children and the media* (2nd ed., pp. 321–339). Thousand Oaks, CA: Sage Publications.

Sijtsema, J. J., Veenstra, R., Lindenberg, S., & Salmivalli, C. (2009). Empirical test of bullies' status goals: Assessing direct goals, aggression, and prestige. *Aggressive Behavior, 35,* 57–67. doi:10.1002/ab.20282

Silk, J. S., Steinberg, L., & Morris, A. S. (2003). Adolescents' emotion regulation in daily life: Links to depressive symptoms and problem behavior. *Child Development, 74,* 1869–1880.

Silk, J. S., Tan, P. Z., Ladouceur, C. D., Meller, S., Siegle, G. J., McMakin, D. L., . . . Ryan, N. D. (2016). A randomized clinical trial comparing individual cognitive behavioral therapy and child-centered therapy for child anxiety disorders. *Journal of Clinical Child & Adolescent Psychology.* Advance online publication. doi:10.1080/15374416.2016.1138408

Silverman, W. K., La Greca, A. M., & Wasserstein, S. (1995). What do children worry about? Worries and their relation to anxiety. *Child Development, 66,* 671–686.

Simion, F., Valenza, E., Macchi Cassia, V., Turati, C., & Umiltà, C. (2002). Newborns' preference for up–down asymmetrical configurations. *Developmental Science, 5,* 427–434. doi:10.1111/1467-7687.00237

Simon, T. J., & Klahr, D. (1995). A computational theory of children's learning about number conservation. In T. J. Simon & G. S. Halford (Eds.), *Developing cognitive competence: New approaches to process modeling* (pp. 315–353). Hillsdale, NJ: Erlbaum.

Simon, T. J., & Rivera, S. M. (2007). Neuroanatomical approaches to the study of mathematical ability and disability. In D. B. Berch & M. M. M. Mazzocco (Eds.), *Why is math so hard for some children? The nature and origins of mathematical learning difficulties and disabilities* (pp. 283–305). Baltimore, MD: Paul H. Brookes.

Simon, V. A., Aikins, J. W., & Prinstein, M. J. (2008). Romantic partner selection and socialization during early adolescence. *Child Development, 79,* 1676–1692. doi:10.1111/j.1467-8624.2008.01218.x

Simons, K. D., & Klein, J. D. (2007). The impact of scaffolding and student achievement levels in a problem-based learning environment. *Instructional Science, 35*(1), 41–72. doi:10.1007/s11251-006-9002-5

Simons, R. L., Lei, M. K., Beach, S. R., Brody, G. H., Philibert, R. A., & Gibbons, F. X. (2011). Social environmental variation, plasticity genes, and aggression: Evidence for the differential susceptibility hypothesis. *American Sociological Review, 76,* 833–912. doi:10.1177/0003122411427580

Simons, R. L., Lei, M. K., Stewart, E. A., Brody, G. H., Beach, S. R., Philibert, R. A., & Gibbons, F. X. (2012). Social adversity, genetic variation, street code, and aggression: A genetically informed model of violent behavior. *Youth Violence and Juvenile Justice, 10,* 3–24. doi:10.1177/1541204011422087

Simpkins, S. D., Eccles, J. S., & Becnel, J. N. (2008). The mediational role of adolescents' friends in relations between activity breadth and adjustment. *Developmental Psychology, 44,* 1081–1094.

Simpkins, S. D., Fredricks, J. A., & Eccles, J. S. (2015). The role of parents in the ontogeny of achievement-related motivation and behavioral choices. *Monographs of the Society for Research in Child Development, 80*(2), 1–151.

Simpson, E. A., Murray, L., Paukner, A., & Ferrari, P. F. (2014). The mirror neuron system as revealed through neonatal imitation: Presence from birth, predictive power and evidence of plasticity. *Philosophical Transactions of the Royal Society B: Biological Sciences, 369*(1644). doi:10.1098/rstb.2013.0289

Simpson, J. A., Collins, W. A., Tran, S., & Haydon, K. C. (2007). Attachment and the experience and expression of emotions in romantic relationships: A developmental perspective. *Journal of Personality and Social Psychology, 92,* 355–367. doi:10.1037/0022-3514.92.2.355

Sims, M., Hutchins, T., & Taylor, M. (1998). Gender segregation in young children's conflict behavior in child care settings. *Child Study Journal, 28,* 1–16.

Singh, L., Fu, C. S., Rahman, A. A., Hameed, W. B., Sanmugam, S., Agarwal, P., . . . Rifkin-Graboi, A. (2015). Back to basics: A bilingual advantage in infant visual habituation. *Child Development, 86*(1), 294–302.

Singh, L., Morgan, J. L., & Best, C. T. (2002). Infants' listening preferences: Baby talk or happy talk? *Infancy, 3,* 365–394. doi:10.1207/S15327078IN0303_5

Singh, L., Nestor, S., Parikh, C., & Yull, A. (2009). Influences of infant-directed speech on early word recognition. *Infancy, 14,* 654–666. doi:10.1080/15250000903263973

Singleton, J. L., & Newport, E. L. (2004). When learners surpass their models: The acquisition of American Sign Language from inconsistent input. *Cognitive Psychology, 49,* 370–407. doi:10.1016/j.cogpsych.2004.05.001

Sinopoli, K. J., Schachar, R., & Dennis, M. (2011). Reward improves cancellation and restraint inhibition across childhood and adolescence. *Developmental Psychology, 47,* 1479–1489. doi:10.1037/a0024440

Siqueland, E. R., & DeLucia, C. A. (1969, September 12). Visual reinforcement of nonnutritive sucking in human infants. *Science, 165,* 1144–1146.

Siqueland, E. R., & Lipsitt, L. P. (1966). Conditioned head-turning in human newborns. *Journal of Experimental Child Psychology, 3,* 356–376.

Skerry, A. E., Carey, S. E., & Spelke, E. S. (2013). First-person action experience reveals sensitivity to action efficiency in prereaching infants. *Proceedings of the National Academy of Sciences, 110*(46), 18728–18733.

Skinner, B. F. (1953). *Science and human behavior.* New York, NY: Macmillan.

Skinner, B. F. (1957). *Verbal behavior.* New York, NY: Appleton-Century-Crofts.

Skinner, B. F. (1971). *Beyond freedom and dignity.* New York, NY: Knopf.

Skinner, E. A. (1985). Determinants of mother sensitive and contingent-responsive behavior: The role of childrearing beliefs and socioeconomic status. In I. E. Sigel (Ed.), *Parental belief systems: The psychological consequences for children* (pp. 51–82). Hillsdale, NJ: Erlbaum.

Skoe, E. E. (1998). The ethic of care: Issues in moral development. In E. Skoe & A. von der Lippe (Eds.), *Personality development in adolescence: A cross national and life span perspective* (pp. 143–171). New York, NY: Routledge.

Skwerer, D. P., & Tager-Flusberg, H. (2011). Williams syndrome: Overview and recent advances in research. In P. Howlin, T. Charman, & M. Ghaziuddin (Eds.), *The SAGE handbook of developmental disorders* (pp. 81–106). Newbury Park, CA: Sage.

Slaby, R. G., & Frey, K. S. (1975). Development of gender constancy and selective attention to same-sex models. *Child Development, 46,* 849–856. doi:10.2307/1128389

Slaby, R. G., & Guerra, N. G. (1988). Cognitive mediators of aggression in adolescent offenders: I. Assessment. *Developmental Psychology, 24,* 580–588. doi:10.1037/0012-1649.24.4.580

Slater, A., Bremner, G., Johnson, S. P., Sherwood, P., Hayes, R., & Brown, E. (2000). Newborn infants' preference for attractive faces: The role of internal and external facial features. *Infancy, 1,* 265–274. doi:10.1207/S15327078IN0102_8

Slater, A., Johnson, S. P., Brown, E., & Badenoch, M. (1996). Newborn infant's perception of partly occluded objects. *Infant Behavior and Development, 19,* 145–148. doi:10.1016/S0163-6383(96)90052-1

Slater, A., Mattock, A., & Brown, E. (1990). Size constancy at birth: Newborn infants' responses to retinal and real size. *Journal of Experimental Child Psychology, 49,* 314–322. doi:10.1016/0022-0965(90)90061-C

Slater, A., Morison, V., & Rose, D. (1984). New-born infants' perception of similarities and differences between two- and three-dimensional stimuli. *British Journal of Developmental Psychology, 2,* 287–294. doi:10.1111/j.2044-835X.1984.tb00936.x

Slater, A., Von der Schulenburg, C., Brown, E., Badenoch, M., Butterworth, G., Parsons, S., & Samuels, C. (1998). Newborn infants prefer attractive faces. *Infant Behavior and Development, 21,* 345–354. doi:10.1016/S0163-6383(98)90011-X

Slater, M. E., Haughwout, S. P., & Castle, I. J. P. (2015). *Trends in substance use among reproductive-age females in the United States, 2002–2013* (Surveillance Report No. 103). Retrieved from NIH website: http://pubs.niaaa.nih.gov/publications/surveillance103/SUBST01.pdf

Slaughter, V., Jaakkola, R., & Carey, S. (1999). Constructing a coherent theory: Children's biological understanding of life and death. In M. Siegal & C. C. Peterson (Eds.), *Children's understanding of biology and health* (pp. 71–96). Cambridge, England: Cambridge University Press.

Slavich, G. M., & Cole, S. W. (2013). The emerging field of human social genomics. *Clinical Psychological Science, 1*(3), 331–348. doi:10.1177/2167702613478594

Slone, M., & Mann, S. (2016). Effects of war, terrorism and armed conflict on young children: A systematic review. *Child Psychiatry and Human Development.* Advance online publication. doi:10.1007/s10578-016-0626-7

Slough, N. M., McMahon, R. J., & The Conduct Problems Prevention Research Group. (2008). Preventing serious conduct problems in school-age youth: The Fast Track Program. *Cognitive and Behavioral Practice, 15,* 3–17. doi:10.1016/j.cbpra.2007.04.002

Sloutsky, V. M. (2010). From perceptual categories to concepts: What develops? *Cognitive Science, 34,* 1244–1286. doi:10.1111/j.1551-6709.2010.01129.x

Slutske, W. S., Moffitt, T. E., Poulton, R., & Caspi, A. (2012). Undercontrolled temperament at age 3 predicts disordered gambling at age 32: A longitudinal study of a complete birth cohort. *Psychological Science, 23,* 510–516.

Sluzenski, J., Newcombe, N. S., & Satlow, E. (2004). Knowing where things are in the second year of life: Implications for hippocampal development. *Journal of Cognitive Neuroscience, 16,* 1443–1451. doi:10.1162/0898929042304804

Smahel, D., & Wright, M. F. (Eds.). (2014). *The meaning of online problematic situations for children: Results of qualitative cross-cultural investigation in nine European countries.* London, England: EU Kids Online, London School of Economics and Political Science.

Smetana, J. G. (1988). Adolescents' and parents' conceptions of parental authority. *Child Development, 59,* 321–335. doi:10.2307/1130313

Smetana, J. G., & Asquith, P. (1994). Adolescents' and parents' conceptions of parental authority and personal autonomy. *Child Development, 65,* 1147–1162. doi:10.2307/1131311

Smetana, J. G., & Braeges, J. L. (1990). The development of toddlers' moral and conventional judgments. *Merrill-Palmer Quarterly, 36,* 329–346. doi:10.2307/23087284

Smetana, J. G., Rote, W. M., Jambon, M., Tasopoulos-Chan, M., Villalobos, M., & Comer, J. (2012). Developmental changes and individual differences in young children's moral judgments. *Child Development, 83,* 683–696. doi:10.1111/j.1467-8624.2011.01714.x

Smider, N., Essex, M., Kalin, N., Buss, K., Klein, M., Davidson, R., & Goldsmith, H. (2002). Salivary cortisol as a predictor of socioemotional adjustment during kindergarten: A prospective study. *Child Development, 73,* 75–92.

Smiler, A. P., Frankel, L. B. W., & Savin-Williams, R. C. (2011). From kissing to coitus? Sex-of-partner differences in the sexual milestone achievement of young men. *Journal of Adolescence, 34,* 727–735. doi:10.1016/j.adolescence.2010.08.009

Smiley, P. A., & Dweck, C. S. (1994). Individual differences in achievement goals among young children. *Child Development, 65,* 1723–1743. doi:10.1111/j.1467-8624.1994.tb00845.x

Smith, B. A., & Blass, E. M. (1996). Taste-mediated calming in premature, preterm, and full-term human infants. *Developmental Psychology, 32,* 1084–1089.

Smith, C. L., Calkins, S. D., Keane, S. P., Anastopoulos, A. D., & Shelton, T. L. (2004). Predicting stability and change in toddler behavior problems: Contributions of maternal behavior and child gender. *Developmental Psychology, 40,* 29–42. doi:10.1037/0012-1649.40.1.29

Smith, C. L., Diaz, A., Day, K. L., & Bell, M. A. (2016). Infant frontal electroencephalogram asymmetry and negative emotional reactivity as predictors of toddlerhood effortful control. *Journal of Experimental Child Psychology, 142,* 262–273. doi:10.1016/j.jecp.2015.09.031

Smith, E. D., & Lillard, A. S. (2011). Play on: Retrospective reports of the persistence of pretend play into middle childhood. *Journal of Cognition and Development, 13,* 524–549. doi:10.1080/15248372.2011.608199

Smith, H. J., Sheikh, H. I., Dyson, M. W., Olino, T. M., Laptook, R. S., Durbin, C. E., . . . Klein, D. N. (2012). Parenting and child DRD4 genotype interact to predict children's early emerging effortful control. *Child Development, 83,* 1932–1944. doi:10.1111/j.1467-8624.2012.01818.x

Smith, J. S. (1992). Women in charge: Politeness and directives in the speech of Japanese women. *Language in Society, 21,* 59–82.

Smith, L., & Yu, C. (2008). Infants rapidly learn word-referent mappings via cross-situational statistics. *Cognition, 106,* 1558–1568. doi:10.1016/j.cognition.2007.06.010

Smith, L. B. (2003). Learning to recognize objects. *Psychological Science, 14,* 244–250.

Smith, L. B. (2005). Action alters shape categories. *Cognitive Science, 29,* 665–679. doi:10.1207/s15516709cog0000_13

Smith, L. B., Jones, S. S., & Landau, B. (1992). Count nouns, adjectives, and perceptual properties in children's novel word interpretations. *Developmental Psychology, 28,* 273–286.

Smith, L. B., Thelen, E., Titzer, R., & McLin, D. (1999). Knowing in the context of acting: The task dynamics of the A-not-B error. *Psychological Review, 106,* 235–260.

Smith, R. L., & Rose, A. J. (2011). The "cost of caring" in youths' friendships: Considering associations among social perspective taking, co-rumination, and empathetic distress. *Developmental Psychology, 47,* 1792–1803. doi:10.1037/a0025309

Smith, S. L., Choueiti, M., Prescott, A., & Pieper, K. (2013a). *Gender roles and occupations: A look at character attributes and job-related aspirations in film and television.* Executive Report, Geena Davis Institute on Gender in Media. Retrieved from http://seejane.org/wp-content/uploads/full-study-gender-roles-and-occupations-v2.pdf

Smith, S. L., Choueiti, M., Prescott, A., & Pieper, K. (2013b). *Occupational aspirations: What are G-rated films teaching children about the world of work?* Executive Report, Geena Davis Institute on Gender in Media. Retrieved from http://seejane.org/wp-content/uploads/key-findings-occupational-aspirations-2013.pdf

Smotherman, W. P., & Robinson, S. R. (1987). Psychobiology of fetal experience in the rat. In N. A. Krasnegor, M. A. Hofer, W. P. Smotherman, & E. M. Blass (Eds.), *Perinatal development: A psychobiological perspective* (pp. 39–60). Orlando, FL: Academic Press.

Snarey, J. R. (1985). Cross-cultural universality of social-moral development: A critical review of Kohlbergian research. *Psychological Bulletin, 97,* 202–232. doi:10.1037/0033-2909.97.2.202

Snow, C. E. (1990). Building memories: The ontogeny of autobiography. In D. Cicchetti & M. Beeghly (Eds.), *The self in transition: Infancy to childhood* (pp. 213–242). Chicago, IL: University of Chicago Press.

Snow, C. E. (1999). Social perspectives on the emergence of language. In B. MacWhinney (Ed.), *The emergence of language* (pp. 257–276). Mahwah, NJ: Erlbaum.

Snyder, J., Brooker, M., Patrick, M. R., Snyder, A., Schrepferman, L., & Stoolmiller, M. (2003). Observed peer victimization during early elementary school: Continuity, growth, and relation to risk for child antisocial and depressive behavior. *Child Development, 74,* 1881–1898. doi:10.1046/j.1467-8624.2003.00644.x

Snyder, J., Cramer, A., Afrank, J., & Patterson, G. R. (2005). The contributions of ineffective discipline and parental hostile attributions of child misbehavior to the development of conduct problems at home and school. *Developmental Psychology, 41,* 30–41. doi:10.1037/0012-1649.41.1.30

Snyder, J., Reid, J., & Patterson, G. (2003). A social learning model of child and adolescent antisocial behavior. In B. B. Lahey, T. E. Moffitt, & A. Caspi (Eds.), *Causes of conduct disorder and juvenile delinquency* (pp. 27–48). New York, NY: Guilford Press.

Snyder, J., Schrepferman, L., McEachern, A., Barner, S., Johnson, K., & Provines, J. (2008). Peer deviancy training and peer coercion: Dual processes associated with early-onset conduct problems. *Child Development, 79,* 252–268. doi:10.1111/j.1467-8624.2007.01124.x

Snyder, J., Stoolmiller, M., Wilson, M., & Yamamoto, M. (2003). Child anger regulation, parental responses to children's anger displays, and early child antisocial behavior. *Social Development, 12,* 335–360.

Snyder, J. J., Schrepferman, L. P., Bullard, L., McEachern, A. D., & Patterson, G. R. (2012). Covert antisocial behavior, peer deviancy training, parenting processes, and sex differences in the development of antisocial behavior during childhood. *Development and Psychopathology, 24,* 1117–1138. doi:10.1017/S0954579412000570

Snyder, T. D., & Dillow, S. A. (2010). *Digest of education statistics, 2009* (NCES 2010–013). Washington, DC: National Center for Education Statistics.

Sobel, D. M., & Kirkham, N. Z. (2006). Blickets and babies: The development of causal reasoning in toddlers and infants. *Developmental Psychology, 42,* 1103–1115. doi:10.1037/0012-1649.42.6.1103

Soderstrom, M. (2007). Beyond babytalk: Reevaluating the nature and content of speech input to preverbal infants. *Developmental Review, 27,* 501–532.

Solheim, E., Wichstrøm, L., Belsky, J., & Berg-Nielsen, T. S. (2013). Do time in child care and peer group exposure predict poor socioemotional adjustment in Norway? *Child Development, 84,* 1701–1715. doi:10.1111/cdev.12071

Solis, M., Ciullo, S., Vaughn, S., Pyle, N., Hassaram, B., & Leroux, A. (2012). Reading comprehension interventions for middle school students with learning disabilities: A synthesis of 30 years of research. *Journal of Learning Disabilities, 45*(4), 327–340. doi:10.1177/0022219411402691

Solmeyer, A. R., Killoren, S. E., McHale, S. M., & Updegraff, K. A. (2011). Coparenting around siblings' differential treatment in Mexican-origin families. *Journal of Family Psychology, 25,* 251–260. doi:10.1037/a0023201

Solomon, D., Battistich, V., & Watson, M. (1993, March). *A longitudinal investigation of the effects of a school intervention program on children's*

social development. Paper presented at the biennial meeting of the Society for Research in Child Development, New Orleans, LA.

Solomon, D., Battistich, V., Watson, M., Schaps, E., & Lewis, C. (2000). A six-district study of educational change: Direct and mediated effects of the Child Development Project. *Social Psychology of Education, 4,* 3–51. doi:10.1023/A:1009609606692

Solomon, D., Watson, M. S., Delucchi, K. L., Schaps, E., & Battistich, V. (1988). Enhancing children's prosocial behavior in the classroom. *American Educational Research Journal, 25,* 527–554. doi:10.3102/00028312025004527

Solomon, G. E., Johnson, S. C., Zaitchik, D., & Carey, S. (1996). Like father, like son: Young children's understanding of how and why offspring resemble their parents. *Child Development, 67,* 151–171.

Solomon, J., & George, C. (1999). The measurement of attachment security in infancy and childhood. In J. Cassidy & P. R. Shaver (Eds.), *Handbook of attachment: Theory, research, and clinical applications* (pp. 287–316). New York, NY: Guilford Press.

Solomon, J., George, C., & De Jong, A. (1995). Children classified as controlling at age six: Evidence of disorganized representational strategies and aggression at home and at school. *Development and Psychopathology, 7,* 447–463. doi:10.1017/S0954579400006623

Sommerville, J. A., & Crane, C. C. (2009). Ten-month-old infants use prior information to identify an actor's goal. *Developmental Science, 12,* 314–325. doi:10.1111/j.1467-7687.2008.00787.x

Sommerville, J. A., Woodward, A. L., & Needham, A. (2005). Action experience alters 3-month-old infants' perception of others' actions. *Cognition, 96,* B1–B11. doi:10.1016/j.cognition.2004.07.004

Song, C., Benin, M., & Glick, J. (2012). Dropping out of high school: The effects of family structure and family transitions. *Journal of Divorce and Remarriage, 53,* 18–33. doi:10.1080/1050255 6.2012.635964

Sosa, A. V. (2016). Association of the type of toy used during play with the quantity and quality of parent–infant communication. *JAMA Pediatrics, 170*(2), 132–137.

Sosinsky, L. S., Lord, H., & Zigler, E. (2007). For-profit/nonprofit differences in center-based child care quality: Results from the National Institute of Child Health and Human Development Study of Early Child Care and Youth Development. *Journal of Applied Developmental Psychology, 28,* 390–410.

Soska, K. C., Adolph, K. E., & Johnson, S. P. (2010). Systems in development: Motor skill acquisition facilitates three-dimensional object completion. *Developmental Psychology, 46,* 129–138. doi:10.1037/a0014618

Southgate, V., & Vernetti, A. (2014). Belief-based action prediction in preverbal infants. *Cognition, 130*(1), 1–10.

Sowislo, J. F., & Orth, U. (2013). Does low self-esteem predict depression and anxiety? A meta-analysis of longitudinal studies. *Psychological Bulletin, 139,* 213–240. doi:10.1037/a0028931

Spearman, C. E. (1927). *The abilities of man, their nature and measurement.* New York, NY: Macmillan.

Spector, F., & Maurer, D. (2009). Synesthesia: A new approach to understanding the development of perception. *Developmental Psychology, 45*(1), 175.

Spelke, E. S. (1976). Infants' intermodal perception of events. *Cognitive Psychology, 8,* 553–560.

Spelke, E. S. (1979). Perceiving bimodally specified events in infancy. *Developmental Psychology, 15,* 626–636. doi:10.1037/0012-1649.15.6.626

Spelke, E. S. (2003). What makes us smart? Core knowledge and natural language. In D. Gentner & S. Goldin-Meadow (Eds.), *Language in mind: Advances in the study of language and thought* (pp. 277–311). Cambridge, MA: MIT Press.

Spelke, E. S. (2004). Core knowledge. In N. Kanwisher & J. Duncan (Eds.), *Attention and performance: Functional neuroimaging of visual cognition* (Vol. 20, pp. 29–56). Oxford, England: Oxford University Press.

Spelke, E. S. (2011). Core systems and the growth of human knowledge: Natural geometry. In A. M. Battro, S. Dehaene, & W. J. Singer (Eds.), *The proceedings of the Working Group on Human Neuroplasticity and Education: Vol. 117. Human neuroplasticity and education* (pp. 73–99). Vatican City: Pontifical Academy of Sciences.

Spelke, E. S., & Kinzler, K. D. (2007). Core knowledge. *Developmental Science, 10,* 89–96. doi:10.1111/j.1467-7687.2007.00569.x

Speltz, M. L., DeKlyen, M., Calderon, R., Greenberg, M. T., & Fisher, P. A. (1999). Neuropsychological characteristics and test behaviors of boys with early onset conduct problems. *Journal of Abnormal Psychology, 108,* 315–325. doi:10.1037/0021-843X.108.2.315

Spence, I., & Feng, J. (2010). Video games and spatial cognition. *Review of General Psychology, 14,* 92–104. doi:10.1037/a0019491

Spence, M. J., & Freeman, M. S. (1996). Newborn infants prefer the maternal low-pass filtered voice, but not the maternal whispered voice. *Infant Behavior and Development, 19,* 199–212. doi:10.1016/S0163-6383(96)90019-3

Spencer, J. P., Clearfield, M., Corbetta, D., Ulrich, B., Buchanan, P., & Schöner, G. (2006). Moving toward a grand theory of development: In memory of Esther Thelen. *Child Development, 77,* 1521–1538. doi:10.1111/j.1467-8624.2006.00955.x

Spencer, M. B., & Markstrom-Adams, C. (1990). Identity processes among racial and ethnic minority children in America. *Child Development, 61,* 290–310.

Spencer-Rodgers, J., Peng, K., Wang, L., & Hou, Y. (2004). Dialectical self-esteem and East-West differences in psychological well-being. *Personality and Social Psychology Bulletin, 30,* 1416–1432. doi:10.1177/0146167204264243

Spitz, R. A. (1945). Hospitalism: An inquiry into the genesis of psychiatric conditions in early childhood. *The Psychoanalytic Study of the Child, 1,* 53–74.

Spitz, R. A. (1946). Hospitalism: A follow-up report. *The Psychoanalytic Study of the Child, 2,* 113–117.

Spitz, R. A. (1949). The role of ecological factors in emotional development in infancy. *Child Development, 20,* 145–155.

Spivak, A. L., & Howes, C. (2011). Social and relational factors in early education and prosocial actions of children of diverse ethnocultural communities. *Merrill-Palmer Quarterly, 57,* 1–24.

Sprenger-Charolles, L. (2004). Linguistic processes in reading and spelling: The case of alphabetic writing systems: English, French, German and Spanish. In T. Nunes & P. Bryant (Eds.), *Handbook of children's literacy* (pp. 43–65). Dordrecht, The Netherlands: Kluwer.

Springer, K. (1996). Young children's understanding of a biological basis for parent–offspring relations. *Child Development, 67*(6), 2841–2856. doi:10.1111/j.1467-8624.1996.tb01891.x

Springer, K., & Keil, F. C. (1991). Early differentiation of causal mechanisms appropriate to biological and nonbiological kinds. *Child Development, 62,* 767–781. doi:10.1111/j.1467-8624.1991.tb01568.x

Springer, K., Ngyuen, T., & Samaniego, R. (1996). Early understanding of age- and environment-related noxiousness in biological kinds: Evidence for a naive theory. *Cognitive Development, 11,* 65–82. doi:10.1016/ S0885-2014(96)90028-3

SRCD Governing Council. (2007). SRCD ethical standards for research with children. Retrieved from http://www.srcd.org/about-us/ ethical-standards-research

Srinivasan, M., & Carey, S. (2010). The long and the short of it: On the nature and origin of functional overlap between representations of space and time. *Cognition, 116,* 217–241. doi:10.1016/j.cognition.2010.05.005

Sroufe, L. A. (1979). Socioemotional development. In J. D. Osofsky (Ed.), *Handbook of infant development* (pp. 462–516). New York, NY: Wiley.

Sroufe, L. A. (1995). *Emotional development: The organization of emotional life in the early years.* Cambridge, England: Cambridge University Press.

Sroufe, L. A., Bennett, C., Englund, M., Urban, J., & Shulman, S. (1993). The significance of gender boundaries in preadolescence: Contemporary correlates and antecedents of boundary violation and maintenance. *Child Development, 64,* 455–466. doi:10.2307/1131262

St James-Roberts, I., Conroy, S., & Wilsher, C. (1998). Stability and outcome of persistent infant crying. *Infant Behavior and Development, 21,* 411–435. doi:10.1016/S0163-6383(98)90017-0

Stack, D. M., & Arnold, S. L. (1998). Changes in mothers' touch and hand gestures influence infant behavior during face-to-face interchanges. *Infant Behavior and Development, 21,* 451–468. doi:10.1016/S0163-6383(98)90019-4

Stack, D. M., & Muir, D. W. (1990). Tactile stimulation as a component of social interchange: New interpretations for the still-face effect. *British Journal of Developmental Psychology, 8,* 131–145. doi:10.1111/j.2044-835X.1990.tb00828.x

Stack, D. M., & Muir, D. W. (1992). Adult tactile stimulation during face-to-face interactions modulates five-month-olds' affect and attention. *Child Development, 63,* 1509–1525. doi:10.1111/j.1467-8624.1992.tb01711.x

Stack, D. M., Muir, D. W., Sherriff, F., & Roman, J. (1989). Development of infant reaching in the dark to luminous objects and 'invisible sounds.' *Perception, 18,* 69–82.

Stahl, A. E., & Feigenson, L. (2015). Observing the unexpected enhances infants' learning and exploration. *Science, 348*(6230), 91–94.

Stake, J. E., & Mares, K. R. (2005). Evaluating the impact of science-enrichment programs on adolescents' science motivation and confidence: The splashdown effect. *Journal of Research in Science Teaching, 42,* 359–375.

Stams, G. J., Brugman, D., Deković, M., van Rosmalen, L., van der Laan, P., & Gibbs, J. C. (2006). The moral judgment of juvenile delinquents: A meta-analysis. *Journal of Abnormal Child Psychology, 34,* 692–708. doi:10.1007/s10802-006-9056-5

State of Michigan, Governor's Task Force on Child Abuse and Neglect and Department of Human Services. (2011). *Forensic interviewing protocol* (3rd ed.). Retrieved from http://www.michigan.gov/documents/dhs/DHS-PUB-0779_211637_7.pdf

Stecher, B. M., McCaffrey, D. F., & Bugliari, D. (2003, November 10). The relationship between exposure to class size reduction and student achievement in California. *Education Policy Analysis Archives, 11*(40). Retrieved June 2, 2005, from http://epaa.asu.edu/epaa/v11n40/.

Steele, H., Steele, M., & Croft, C. (2008). Early attachment predicts emotion recognition at 6 and 11 years old. *Attachment and Human Development, 10,* 379–393. doi:10.1080/14616730802461409

Steenbeek, H., & van Geert, P. (2008). An empirical validation of a dynamic systems model of interaction: Do children of different sociometric statuses differ in their dyadic play? *Developmental Science, 11,* 253–281. doi:10.1111/j.1467-7687.2007.00655.x

Stein, N. L. (1988). The development of children's storytelling skill. In M. B. Franklin & S. S. Barten (Eds.), *Child language: A reader* (pp. 282–297). New York, NY: Oxford University Press.

Steinberg, L. (1987). Impact of puberty on family relations: Effects of pubertal status and pubertal timing. *Developmental Psychology, 23,* 451–460. doi:10.1037/0012-1649.23.3.451

Steinberg, L. (1988). Reciprocal relation between parent–child distance and pubertal maturation. *Developmental Psychology, 24,* 122–128. doi:10.1037/0012-1649.24.1.122

Steinberg, L. (1990). Autonomy, conflict, and harmony in the family relationship. In S. S. Feldman & G. R. Elliott (Eds.), *At the threshold: The developing adolescent* (pp. 255–276). Cambridge, MA: Harvard University Press.

Steinberg, L. (2008). A social neuroscience perspective on adolescent risk-taking. *Developmental Review, 28*(1), 78–106. doi:10.1016/j.dr.2007.08.002

Steinberg, L. (2010). A dual systems model of adolescent risk-taking. *Developmental Psychobiology, 52,* 216–224. doi:10.1002/dev.20445

Steinberg, L., Lamborn, S. D., Darling, N., Mounts, N. S., & Dornbusch, S. M. (1994). Over-time changes in adjustment and competence among adolescents from authoritative, authoritarian, indulgent, and neglectful families. *Child Development, 65,* 754–770. doi:10.1111/j.1467-8624.1994.tb00781.x

Steinberg, L., & Morris, A. S. (2001). Adolescent development. *Journal of Cognitive Education and Psychology, 2,* 55–87.

Steinberg, L., & Silverberg, S. B. (1986). The vicissitudes of autonomy in early adolescence. *Child Development, 57,* 841–851. doi:10.2307/1130361

Steinmayr, R., & Spinath, B. (2009). What explains boys' stronger confidence in their intelligence? *Sex Roles, 61,* 736–749. doi:10.1007/s11199-009-9675-8

Stenberg, G. (2013). Do 12-month-old infants trust a competent adult? *Infancy, 18,* 873–904. doi:10.1111/infa.12011

Stern, D. N. (1985). *The interpersonal world of the infant: A view from psychoanalysis and developmental psychology.* New York, NY: Basic Books.

Sternberg, R. J. (1999). The theory of successful intelligence. *Review of General Psychology, 3,* 292–316. doi:10.1037/1089-2680.3.4.292

Sternberg, R. J. (2003). A broad view of intelligence: The theory of successful intelligence. *Consulting Psychology Journal: Practice and Research, 55,* 139–154. doi:10.1037/1061-4087.55.3.139

Sternberg, R. J. (2004). Culture and intelligence. *American Psychologist, 59,* 325–338.

Sternberg, R. J. (2007). *Wisdom, intelligence, and creativity synthesized.* New York, NY: Cambridge University Press.

Sternberg, R. J. (2008). g, g's, or Jeez: Which is the best model for developing abilities, competencies, and expertise? In P. C. Kyllonen, R. D. Roberts, & L. Stankov (Eds.), *Extending intelligence: Enhancement and new constructs* (pp. 225–266). New York, NY: Erlbaum.

Sterrett, E. M., Jones, D. J., McKee, L. G., & Kincaid, C. (2011). Supportive non-parental adults and adolescent psychosocial functioning: Using social support as a theoretical framework. *American Journal of Community Psychology, 48,* 284–295. doi:10.1007/s10464-011-9429-y

Stevens, T., Wang, K., Olivárez, A., Jr., & Hamman, D. (2007). Use of self-perspectives and their sources to predict the mathematics enrollment intentions of girls and boys. *Sex Roles, 56,* 351–363. doi:10.1007/s11199-006-9180-2

Stevenson, H. W. (1991). The development of prosocial behavior in large-scale collective societies: China and Japan. In R. A. Hinde & J. Groebel (Eds.), *Cooperation and prosocial behaviour* (pp. 89–105). Cambridge, England: Cambridge University Press.

Stifter, C. A., Bono, M., & Spinrad, T. (2003). Parent characteristics and conceptualizations associated with the emergence of infant colic. *Journal of Reproductive and Infant Psychology, 21,* 309–322. doi:10.1080/0264683031000 1622123

Stifter, C. A., & Braungart, J. (1992). Infant colic: A transient condition with no apparent effects. *Journal of Applied Developmental Psychology, 13,* 447–462. doi:10.1016/0193-3973(92)90012-7

Stiles, J., & Jernigan, T. L. (2010). The basics of brain development. *Neuropsychology Review, 20*(4), 327–348.

Stipek, D. J., Gralinski, J. H., & Kopp, C. B. (1990). Self-concept development in the toddler years. *Developmental Psychology, 26,* 972–977. doi:10.1037/0012-1649.26.6.972

Stipek, D. J., Roberts, T. A., & Sanborn, M. E. (1984). Preschool-age children's performance expectations for themselves and another child as a function of the incentive value of success and the salience of past performance. *Child Development, 55,* 1983–1989.

Stocker, C. M., & Richmond, M. K. (2007). Longitudinal associations between hostility in adolescents' family relationships and friendships and hostility in their romantic relationships. *Journal of Family Psychology, 21,* 490–497.

Stocker, C. M., Richmond, M. K., Rhoades, G. K., & Kiang, L. (2007). Family emotional processes and adolescents' adjustment. *Social Development, 16,* 310–325.

Stoddart, T., & Turiel, E. (1985). Children's concepts of cross-gender activities. *Child Development, 56,* 1241–1252. doi:10.2307/1130239

Stone, L. B., Hankin, B. L., Gibb, B. E., & Abela, J. R. Z. (2011). Co-rumination predicts the onset of depressive disorders during adolescence. *Journal of Abnormal Psychology, 120,* 752–757. doi:10.1037/a0023384

Stone, L. J., & Church, J. (1957). *Childhood and adolescence: A psychology of the growing person.* New York, NY: Random House.

Stone, W. L., & Yoder, P. J. (2001). Predicting spoken language level in children with autism spectrum disorders. *Autism, 5,* 341–361.

Stouthamer-Loeber, M., Loeber, R., Wei, E., Farrington, D. P., & Wikström, P.-O. H. (2002). Risk and promotive effects in the explanation of persistent serious delinquency in boys. *Journal of Consulting and Clinical Psychology, 70,* 111–123. doi:10.1037/0022-006X.70.1.111

Stover, C. S., Connell, C. M., Leve, L. D., Neiderhiser, J. M., Shaw, D. S., Scaramella, L. V., . . . Reiss, D. (2012). Fathering and mothering in the family system: Linking marital hostility and aggression in adopted toddlers. *Journal of Child Psychology and Psychiatry, 53,* 401–409. doi:10.1111/j.1469-7610.2011.02510.x

Strand-Brodd, K., Ewald, U., Grönqvist, H., Holmström, G., Strömberg, B., Grönqvist, E., . . . Rosander, K. (2011). Development of smooth pursuit eye movements in very preterm infants: 1. General aspects. *Acta Paediatrica, 100,* 983–991. doi:10.1111/j.1651-2227.2011.02218.x

Strasburger, V. C., Jordan, A. B., & Donnerstein, E. (2010). Health effects of media on children and adolescents. *Pediatrics, 125*(4), 756–767. doi:10.1542/peds.2009-2563

Strayer, J. (1986). Children's attributions regarding the situational determinants of emotion in self and others. *Developmental Psychology, 22,* 649–654.

Strazdins, L., O'Brien, L., Lucas, N., & Rodgers, B. (2013). Combining work and family: Rewards or risks for children's mental health? *Social Science and Medicine, 87,* 99–107. doi:10.1016/j.socscimed.2013.03.030

Streeter, L. A. (1976, January 1). Language perception of 2-month-old infants shows effects of both innate mechanisms and experience. *Nature, 259,* 39–41.

Streissguth, A. P. (2001). Recent advances in fetal alcohol syndrome and alcohol use in pregnancy. In Dharam Agarwal & H. K. Seitz (Eds.), *Alcohol in health and disease* (pp. 303–324). New York, NY: Marcel Dekker.

Streissguth, A. P., Aase, J. M., Clarren, S. K., Randels, S. P., LaDue, R. A., & Smith, D. F. (1991, April 17). Fetal alcohol syndrome in adolescents and adults. *Journal of the American Medical Association, 265,* 1961–1967.

Streissguth, A. P., Bookstein, F. L., Barr, H. M., & Sampson, P. D. (1993). *The enduring effects of prenatal alcohol exposure on child development: Birth through seven years, a partial least squares solution.* Ann Arbor: University of Michigan Press.

Striepens, N., Kendrick, K. M., Maier, W., & Hurlemann, R. (2011). Prosocial effects of oxytocin and clinical evidence for its therapeutic potential. *Frontiers in Neuroendocrinology, 32,* 426–450. doi:10.1016/j.yfrne.2011.07.001

Stronach, E. P., Toth, S. L., Rogosch, F., Oshri, A., Manly, J. T., & Cicchetti, D. (2011). Child maltreatment, attachment security, and internal representations of mother and mother–child relationships. *Child Maltreatment, 16,* 137–145. doi:10.1177/1077559511398294

Strong, D. D., Bean, R. A., & Feinauer, L. L. (2010). Trauma, attachment, and family therapy with grandfamilies: A model for treatment. *Children and Youth Services Review, 32*(1), 44–50. doi:10.1016/j.childyouth.2009.06.015

Strough, J., & Berg, C. A. (2000). Goals as a mediator of gender differences in high-affiliation dyadic conversations. *Developmental Psychology, 36,* 117–125. doi:10.1037/0012-1649.36.1.117

Strough, J., & Covatto, A. M. (2002). Context and age differences in same- and other-gender peer preferences. *Social Development, 11,* 346–361. doi:10.1111/1467-9507.00204

Stuewig, J., Tangney, J. P., Heigel, C., Harty, L., & McCloskey, L. (2010). Shaming, blaming, and maiming: Functional links among the moral emotions, externalization of blame, and aggression. *Journal of Research in Personality, 44,* 91–102. doi:10.1016/j.jrp.2009.12.005

Stukas, A. A., Snyder, M., & Clary, E. G. (1999). The effects of "mandatory volunteerism" on intentions to volunteer. *Psychological Science, 10,* 59–64. doi:10.2307/40063378

Stukas, A. A., Switzer, G. E., Dew, M. A., Goycoolea, J. M., & Simmons, R. G. (1999). Parental helping models, gender, and service-learning. *Journal of Prevention and Intervention in the Community, 18,* 5–18. doi:10.1300/j005v18n01_02

Sturaro, C., van Lier, P. A. C., Cuijpers, P., & Koot, H. M. (2011). The role of peer relationships in the development of early school-age externalizing problems. *Child Development, 82,* 758–765. doi:10.1111/j.1467-8624.2010.01532.x

Subbotsky, E. (1994). Early rationality and magical thinking in preschoolers: Space and time. *British Journal of Developmental Psychology, 12,* 97–108. doi:10.1111/j.2044-835X.1994.tb00621.x

Subbotsky, E. (2005). The permanence of mental objects: Testing magical thinking on perceived and imaginary realities. *Developmental Psychology, 41,* 301–318. doi:10.1037/0012-1649.41.2.301

Subbotsky, E. V. (1993). *Foundations of the mind: Children's understanding of reality.* Cambridge, MA: Harvard University Press.

Substance Abuse and Mental Health Services Administration. (2015). *Behavioral Health Barometer: United States, 2014.* HHS Publication No. SMA–15–4895. Retrieved May 26, 2016, from http://www.samhsa.gov/data/sites/default/files/National_BHBarometer_2014.pdf

Suess, P. E., Porges, S. W., & Plude, D. J. (1994). Cardiac vagal tone and sustained attention in school-age children. *Psychophysiology, 31,* 17–22.

Sugai, G., & Horner, R. R. (2006). A promising approach for expanding and sustaining school-wide positive behavior support. *School Psychology Review, 35,* 245–259.

Sugden, N. A., Mohamed-Ali, M. I., & Moulson, M. C. (2014). I spy with my little eye: Typical, daily exposure to faces documented from a first-person infant perspective. *Developmental Psychobiology, 56*(2), 249–261.

Sugimoto, T., Kobayashi, H., Nobuyoshi, N., Kiriyama, Y., Takeshita, H., Nakamura, T., & Hashiya, K. (2010). Preference for consonant music over dissonant music by an infant chimpanzee. *Primates, 51,* 7–12. doi:10.1007/s10329-009-0160-3

Sullivan, K., & Winner, E. (1993). Three-year-olds' understanding of mental states: The influence of trickery. *Journal of Experimental Child Psychology, 56,* 135–148. doi:10.1006/jecp.1993.1029

Sullivan, M. W., & Lewis, M. (2003). Contextual determinants of anger and other negative expressions in young infants. *Developmental Psychology, 39,* 693–705.

Sun, Y., & Li, Y. (2011). Effects of family structure type and stability on children's academic performance trajectories. *Journal of Marriage and Family, 73,* 541–556. doi:10.1111/j.1741-3737.2011.00825.x

Sundara, M., Polka, L., & Molnar, M. (2008). Development of coronal stop perception: Bilingual infants keep pace with their monolingual peers. *Cognition, 108,* 232–242. doi:10.1016/j.cognition.2007.12.013

Super, C. M., & Harkness, S. (1986). The developmental niche: A conceptualization at the interface of child and culture. *International Journal of Behavioral Development, 9,* 545–569. doi:10.1177/016502548600900409

Suskind, D. L., Leffel, K. R., Graf, E., Hernandez, M. W., Gunderson, E. A., Sapolich, S. G., . . . Levine, S. C. (2015). A parent-directed language intervention for children of low socioeconomic status: A randomized controlled pilot study. *Journal of Child Language, 43*(02), 366–406.

Susman, E. J. (2006). Psychobiology of persistent antisocial behavior: Stress, early vulnerabilities and the attenuation hypothesis. *Neuroscience and Biobehavioral Reviews, 30*, 376–389. doi:10.1016/j.neubiorev.2005.08.002

Susman, E. J., Schmeelk, K. H., Ponirakis, A., & Gariepy, J. L. (2001). Maternal prenatal, postpartum, and concurrent stressors and temperament in 3-year-olds: A person and variable analysis. *Development and Psychopathology, 13*, 629–652.

Sutherland, K. E., Altenhofen, S., & Biringen, Z. (2012). Emotional availability during mother–child interactions in divorcing and intact married families. *Journal of Divorce and Remarriage, 53*, 126–141. doi:10.1080/10502556.2011.651974

Sutherland, S. L., & Friedman, O. (2012). Preschoolers acquire general knowledge by sharing in pretense. *Child Development, 83*, 1064–1071. doi:10.1111/j.1467-8624.2012.01748.x

Sutton, J. E., Joanisse, M. F., & Newcombe, N. S. (2010). Spinning in the scanner: Neural correlates of virtual reorientation. *Journal of Experimental Psychology: Learning, Memory, and Cognition, 36*, 1097–1107. doi:10.1037/a0019938

Suzuki, L. A., & Valencia, R. R. (1997). Race-ethnicity and measured intelligence: Educational implications. *American Psychologist, 52*, 1103–1114.

Suzuki, L. K., Davis, H. M., & Greenfield, P. M. (2008). Self-enhancement and self-effacement in reaction to praise and criticism: The case of multiethnic youth. *Ethos, 36*, 78–97. doi:10.1111/j.1548-1352.2008.00005.x

Swagerman, S. C., van Bergen, E., Dolan, C., de Geus, E. J., Koenis, M. M., Pol, H. E. H., & Boomsma, D. I. (2016). Genetic transmission of reading ability. *Brain and Language.* doi:10.1016/j.bandl.2015.07.008

Swahn, M. H., Simon, T. R., Arias, I., & Bossarte, R. M. (2008). Measuring sex differences in violence victimization and perpetration within date and same-sex peer relationships. *Journal of Interpersonal Violence, 23*, 1120–1138. doi:10.1177/0886260508314086

Swearer, S. M., & Hymel, S. (2015). Understanding the psychology of bullying: Moving toward a social-ecological diathesis-stress model. *American Psychologist, 70*, 344–353. doi:10.1037/a0038929

Swingley, D., & Aslin, R. N. (2000). Spoken word recognition and lexical representation in very young children. *Cognition, 76*, 147–166.

Szalacha, L. A., Erkut, S., García Coll, C., Alarcón, O., Fields, J. P., & Ceder, I. (2003). Discrimination and Puerto Rican children's and adolescents' mental health. *Cultural Diversity and Ethnic Minority Psychology, 9*, 141–155. doi:10.1037/1099-9809.9.2.141

Szatmari, P., Bryson, S. E., Boyle, M. H., Streiner, D. L., & Duku, E. (2003). Predictors of outcome among high functioning children with autism and Asperger syndrome. *Journal of Child Psychology and Psychiatry, 44*, 520–528. doi:10.1111/1469-7610.00141

Tager-Flusberg, H. (2007). Evaluating the theory-of-mind hypothesis of autism. *Current Directions in Psychological Science, 16*, 311–315. doi:10.1111/j.1467-8721.2007.00527.x

Tager-Flusberg, H., & Joseph, R. M. (2005). How language facilitates the acquisition of false-belief understanding in children with autism. In J. W. Astington & J. A. Baird (Eds.), *Why language matters for theory of mind* (pp. 298–318). New York, NY: Oxford University Press.

Tajfel, H., & Turner, J. C. (1979). An integrative theory of intergroup conflict. In W. G. Austin & S. Worchel (Eds.), *The social psychology of intergroup relations* (pp. 33–47). Monterey, CA: Brooks/Cole.

Takahashi, K. (1986). Examining the strange-situation procedure with Japanese mothers and 12-month-old infants. *Developmental Psychology, 22*, 265–270. doi:10.1037/0012-1649.22.2.265

Tamis-LeMonda, C. S., Kuchirko, Y., & Song, L. (2014). Why is infant language learning facilitated by parental responsiveness? *Current Directions in Psychological Science, 23*(2), 121–126.

Tan, C. H., Denny, C. H., Cheal, N. E., Sniezek, J. E., & Kanny, D. (2015). Alcohol use and binge drinking among women of childbearing age—United States, 2011–2013. *Morbidity & Mortality Weekly Report (CDC), 64*(37), 1042–1046.

Tanaka, H., Black, J. M., Hulme, C., Stanley, L. M., Kesler, S. R., Whitfield-Gabrieli, S., . . . Hoeft, F. (2011). The brain basis of the phonological deficit in dyslexia is independent of IQ. *Psychological Science, 22*, 1442–1451.

Tandon, P. S., Zhou, C., & Christakis, D. A. (2012). Frequency of parent-supervised outdoor play of US preschool-aged children. *Archives of Pediatrics and Adolescent Medicine, 166*, 707–712. doi:10.1001/-archpediatrics.2011.1835

Tang, H., Hammack, C., Ogden, S. C., Wen, Z., Qian, X., Li, Y., . . . Christian, K. M. (2016). Zika virus infects human cortical neural progenitors and attenuates their growth. *Cell Stem Cell, 18*(5), 587–590.

Tangney, J. P., & Dearing, R. L. (2002). *Shame and guilt.* New York, NY: Guilford Press.

Tangney, J. P., Stuewig, J., & Mashek, D. J. (2007). Moral emotions and moral behavior. *Annual Review of Psychology, 58*, 345–372. doi:10.1146/annurev.psych.56.091103.070145

Tanner, J. M. (1961). *Education and physical growth: Implications of the study of children's growth for educational theory and practice.* London, England: University of London Press.

Tardif, T., Fletcher, P., Liang, W., Zhang, Z., Kaciroti, N., & Marchman, V. A. (2008). Baby's first 10 words. *Developmental Psychology, 44*, 929–938. doi:10.1037/0012-1649.44.4.929

Tarullo, A. R., Mliner, S., & Gunnar, M. R. (2011). Inhibition and exuberance in preschool classrooms: Associations with peer social experiences and changes in cortisol across the preschool year. *Developmental Psychology, 47*, 1374–1388. doi:10.1037/a0024093

Task Force on Sudden Infant Death Syndrome. (2011). SIDS and other sleep-related infant deaths: Expansion of recommendations for a safe infant sleeping environment. *Pediatrics, 128*(5), e1341-e1367. doi:10.1542/peds.2011-2285

Tasker, F., & Golombok, S. (1995). Adults raised as children in lesbian families. *American Journal of Orthopsychiatry, 65*, 203–215. doi:10.1037/h0079615

Taumoepeau, M., & Ruffman, T. (2006). Mother and infant talk about mental states relates to desire language and emotion understanding. *Child Development, 77*, 465–481.

Taumoepeau, M., & Ruffman, T. (2008). Stepping stones to others' minds: Maternal talk relates to child mental state language and emotion understanding at 15, 24, and 33 months. *Child Development, 79*, 284–302.

Taylor, B. L., Cavanagh, K., & Strauss, C. (2016). The effectiveness of mindfulness-based interventions in the perinatal period: A systematic review and meta-analysis. *PloS One, 11*(5), e0155720.

Taylor, J., Iacono, W. G., & McGue, M. (2000). Evidence for a genetic etiology of early-onset delinquency. *Journal of Abnormal Psychology, 109*, 634–643. doi:10.1037/0021-843X.109.4.634

Taylor, M. (1999). *Imaginary companions and the children who create them.* New York, NY: Oxford University Press.

Taylor, M., & Carlson, S. M. (1997). The relation between individual differences in fantasy and theory of mind. *Child Development, 68*, 436–455. doi:10.1111/j.1467-8624.1997.tb01950.x

Taylor, M., Carlson, S. M., Maring, B. L., Gerow, L., & Charley, C. M. (2004). The characteristics and correlates of fantasy in school-age children: Imaginary companions, impersonation, and social understanding. *Developmental Psychology, 40*, 1173–1187. doi:10.1037/0012-1649.40.6.1173

Taylor, M., Hulette, A. C., & Dishion, T. J. (2010). Longitudinal outcomes of young high-risk adolescents with imaginary companions. *Developmental Psychology, 46*(6), 1632–1636. doi:10.1037/a0019815

Taylor, M., & Mannering, A. M. (2007). Of Hobbes and Harvey: The imaginary companions created by children and adults. In A. Göncü & S. Gaskins (Eds.), *Play and development: Evolutionary, sociocultural, and functional perspectives* (pp. 227–246). New York, NY: Erlbaum.

Taylor, M. G. (1993). *Children's beliefs about the biological and social origins of gender differences* (Unpublished doctoral dissertation). University of Michigan, Ann Arbor.

Taylor, R. (2011). Kin support and parenting practices among low-income African American mothers: Moderating effects of mothers' psychological adjustment. *Journal of Black Psychology, 37,* 3–23. doi:10.1177/0095798410372623

Teglas, E., Girotto, V., Gonzalez, M., & Bonatti, L. L. (2007). Intuitions of probabilities shape expectations about the future at 12 months and beyond. *Proceedings of the National Academy of Sciences of the United States of America, 104,* 19156–19159. doi:10.1073/pnas.0700271104

Teglas, E., Vul, E., Girotto, V., Gonzalez, M., Tenenbaum, J. B., & Bonatti, L. L. (2011, May 27). Pure reasoning in 12-month-old infants as probabilistic inference. *Science, 332,* 1054–1059.

Teicher, M. H., Anderson. C. M., & Polcari, A. (2012). Childhood maltreatment is associated with reduced volume in the hippocampal subfields CA3, dentate gyrus, and subiculum. *Proceedings of the National Academy of Sciences, 109,* E563–E572. doi:10.1073/pnas.1115396109

Teinonen, T., Fellman, V., Näätänen, R., Alku, P., & Huotilainen, M. (2009). Statistical language learning in neonates revealed by event-related brain potentials. *BMC Neuroscience, 10,* 1–8. doi:10.1186/1471-2202-10-21

Tempelmann, S., Kaminski, J., & Tomasello, M. (2014). Do domestic dogs learn words based on humans' referential behaviour? *PloS One, 9*(3), e91014. doi:10.1371/journal.pone.0091014

Tenenbaum, H. R., & Leaper, C. (2002). Are parents' gender schemas related to their children's gender-related cognitions? A meta-analysis. *Developmental Psychology, 38,* 615–630.

Tenenbaum, H. R., & Leaper, C. (2003). Parent–child conversations about science: The socialization of gender inequities? *Developmental Psychology, 39,* 34–47. doi:10.1037/0012-1649.39.1.34

Teoh, S., Chin, L., Menon, V., Ng, M., Peat, N., Raper, M., . . . Savage, J. (2006).World records in obstetrics and gynaecology. *Journal of Obstetrics and Gynaecology, 26*(7), 607–611.

Terrace, H. S., Petitto, L.-A., Sanders, R. J., & Bever, T. G. (1979, November 23). Can an ape create a sentence? *Science, 206,* 891–902.

Teunissen, H. A., Adelman, C. B., Prinstein, M. J., Spijkerman, R., Poelen, E. A. P., Engels, R. C. M. E., & Scholte, R. H. J. (2011). The interaction between pubertal timing and peer popularity for boys and girls: An integration of biological and interpersonal perspectives on adolescent depression. *Journal of Abnormal Child Psychology, 39,* 413–423.

Thamotharan, S., Lange, K., Zale, E. L., Huffhines, L., & Fields, S. (2013). The role of impulsivity in pediatric obesity and weight status. A meta-analytic review. *Clinical Psychology Review, 33*(2), 253–262.

Thanh, N. X., Jonsson, E., Salmon, A., & Sebastianski, M. (2014). Incidence and prevalence of fetal alcohol spectrum disorder by sex and age group in Alberta, Canada. *Journal of Population Therapeutics and Clinical Pharmacology, 21*(3), e395–404.

Thapar, A., Cooper, M., Eyre, O., & Langley, K. (2013). Practitioner review: What have we learnt about the causes of ADHD? *Journal of Child Psychology and Psychiatry, 54*(1), 3–16.

Thelen, E. (1986). Treadmill-elicited stepping in seven-month-old infants. *Child Development, 57,* 1498–1506. doi:10.2307/1130427

Thelen, E. (1995). Motor development: A new synthesis. *American Psychologist, 50,* 79–95. doi:10.1037/0003-066X.50.2.79

Thelen, E. (2001). Dynamic mechanisms of change in early perceptual-motor development. In J. L. McClelland & R. Siegler (Eds.), *Mechanisms of cognitive development: Behavioral and neural perspectives* (pp. 161–184). Mahwah, NJ: Erlbaum.

Thelen, E., & Corbetta, D. (1994). Exploration and selection in the early acquisition of skill. *International Review of Neurobiology, 37,* 75–102.

Thelen, E., & Fisher, D. M. (1982). Newborn stepping: An explanation for a "disappearing" reflex. *Developmental Psychology, 18,* 760–775. doi:10.1037/0012-1649.18.5.760

Thelen, E., Fisher, D. M., & Ridley-Johnson, R. (1984). The relationship between physical growth and a newborn reflex. *Infant Behavior and Development, 7,* 479–493. doi:10.1016/S0163-6383(84)80007-7

Thelen, E., & Smith, L. B. (1998). Dynamic systems theories. In W. Damon (Series Ed.) & R. M. Lerner (Vol. Ed.), *Handbook of child psychology: Vol. 1. Theoretical models of human development* (5th ed., pp. 563–634). Hoboken, NJ: Wiley.

Thelen, E., & Smith, L. B. (2006). Dynamic systems theories. In W. Damon & R. M. Lerner (Series Eds.) & R. M. Lerner (Vol. Ed.), *Handbook of child psychology: Vol. 1. Theoretical models of human development* (6th ed., pp. 258–312). Hoboken, NJ: Wiley.

Thiessen, E. D., Hill, E. A., & Saffran, J. R. (2005). Infant-directed speech facilitates word segmentation. *Infancy, 7,* 53–71. doi:10.1207/s15327078in0701_5

Thiessen, E. D., & Pavlik, P. I. (2013). iMinerva: A mathematical model of distributional statistical learning. *Cognitive Science, 37*(2), 310–343. doi:10.1111/cogs.12011

Thiessen, E. D., & Saffran, J. R. (2003). When cues collide: Statistical and stress cues in infant word segmentation. *Developmental Psychology, 39,* 706–716.

Thinus-Blanc, C., & Gaunet, F. (1997). Representation of space in blind persons: Vision as a spatial sense? *Psychological Bulletin, 121,* 20–42.

Thomaes, S., Bushman, B. J., Stegge, H., & Olthof, T. (2008). Trumping shame by blasts of noise: Narcissism, self-esteem, shame, and aggression in young adolescents. *Child Development, 79,* 1792–1801. doi:10.1111/j.1467-8624.2008.01226.x

Thomas, A., & Chess, S. (1977). *Temperament and development.* New York, NY: Brunner/Mazel.

Thomas, A., Chess, S., & Birch, H. G. (1968). *Temperament and behavior disorders in children.* New York, NY: New York University Press.

Thomas, J. R., & French, K. E. (1985). Gender differences across age in motor performance: A meta-analysis. *Psychological Bulletin, 98,* 260–282. doi:10.1037/0033-2909.98.2.260

Thompson, C. A., & Opfer, J. E. (2010). How 15 hundred is like 15 cherries: Effect of progressive alignment on representational changes in numerical cognition. *Child Development, 81,* 1768–1786. doi:10.1111/j.1467-8624.2010.01509.x

Thompson, R. A. (1998). Early sociopersonality development. In W. Damon (Series Ed.) & N. Eisenberg (Vol. Ed.), *Handbook of child psychology: Vol. 3. Social, emotional, and personality development* (5th ed., pp. 25–104). Hoboken, NJ: Wiley.

Thompson, R. A. (2006). The development of the person: Social understanding, relationships, conscience, self. In W. Damon & R. M. Lerner (Series Eds.) & N. Eisenberg (Vol. Ed.), *Handbook of child psychology: Vol. 3. Social, emotional, and personality development* (6th ed., pp. 24–98). Hoboken, NJ: Wiley.

Thompson, R. A. (2008). Early attachment and later development: Familiar questions, new answers. In J. Cassidy & P. R. Shaver (Eds.), *Handbook of attachment: Theory, research, and clinical applications* (2nd ed., pp. 348–365). New York, NY: Guilford Press.

Thompson, R. A. (2012). Whither the preconventional child? Toward a life-span moral development theory. *Child Development Perspectives, 6,* 423–429. doi:10.1111/j.1750-8606.2012.00245.x

Thompson, R. A. (2015). Relationships, regulation, and early development. In M. E. Lamb & R. M. Lerner (Eds.), *Handbook of child psychology and developmental science* (7th ed., pp. 201–246). Hoboken, NJ: Wiley.

Thompson, R. A., Lewis, M. D., & Calkins, S. D. (2008). Reassessing emotion regulation. *Child Development Perspectives, 2,* 124–131.

Thompson, R. A., & Newton, E. K. (2010). Emotion in early conscience. In W. F. Arsenio & E. A. Lemerise (Eds.), *Emotions, aggression, and morality in children: Bridging development and psychopathology* (pp. 13–31). Washington, DC: American Psychological Association.

Thornberry, T. P., Freeman-Gallant, A., Lizotte, A. J., Krohn, M. D., & Smith, C. A. (2003).

Linked lives: The intergenerational transmission of antisocial behavior. *Journal of Abnormal Child Psychology, 31,* 171–184. doi:10.1023/A: 1022574208366

Thornberry, T. P., Lizotte, A. J., Krohn, M. D., Farnworth, M., & Jang, S. J. (1994). Delinquent peers, beliefs, and delinquent behavior: A longitudinal test of interactional theory. *Criminology, 32,* 47–83. doi:10.1111/j.1745-9125.1994. tb01146.x

Thorne, B. (1992). Girls and boys together . . . but mostly apart: Gender arrangements in elementary schools. In W. W. Hartup & Z. Rubin (Eds.), *Relationships and development* (pp. 167–184). Hillsdale, NJ: Erlbaum.

Thorne, B. (1993). *Gender play: Girls and boys in school.* New Brunswick, NJ: Rutgers University Press.

Thorne, B., & Luria, Z. (1986). Sexuality and gender in children's daily worlds. *Social Problems, 33,* 176–190. doi:10.2307/800703

Thurstone, L. L. (1938). *Primary mental abilities.* Chicago, IL: The University of Chicago Press.

Tiedemann, J. (2000). Parents' gender stereotypes and teachers' beliefs as predictors of children's concept of their mathematical ability in elementary school. *Journal of Educational Psychology, 92,* 144–151. doi:10.1037/0022-0663. 92.1.144

Tienari, P., Wahlberg, K.-E., & Wynne, L. C. (2006). Finnish adoption study of schizophrenia: Implications for family interventions. *-Families, Systems, and Health, 24,* 442–451. doi:10.1037/1091-7527.24.4.442

Tietjen, A. M. (1986). Prosocial reasoning among children and adults in a Papua New Guinea society. *Developmental Psychology, 22,* 861–868. doi:10.1037/0012-1649.22.6.861

Tincoff, R., & Jusczyk, P. W. (1999). Some beginnings of word comprehension in 6-month-olds. *Psychological Science, 10,* 172–175. doi:10.1111/1467-9280.00127

Tobin, K., & Murphy, J. (2013). Addressing the challenges of child and family homelessness. *Journal of Applied Research on Children: Informing Policy for Children at Risk, 4*(1), Article 9. Retrieved from http://digitalcommons.library. tmc.edu/childrenatrisk/vol4/iss1/9

Tognoli, J., Pullen, J., & Lieber, J. (1994). The privilege of place: Domestic and work locations of characters in children's books. *Children's Environments, 11,* 272–280. doi:10.2307/41514948

Tolan, P. H., Gorman-Smith, D., & Henry, D. B. (2003). The developmental ecology of urban males' youth violence. *Developmental Psychology, 39,* 274–291. doi:10.1037/0012-1649.39.2.274

Tolchinsky, L. (2003). *The cradle of culture and what children know about writing and numbers before being taught.* Mahwah, NJ: Erlbaum.

Tolman, D. L., & McClelland, S. I. (2011). Normative sexuality development in

adolescence: A decade in review, 2000–2009. *Journal of Research on Adolescence, 21,* 242–255. doi:10.1111/j.1532-7795.2010.00726.x

Tom, S. R., Schwartz, D., Chang, L., Farver, J. A. M., & Xu, Y. (2010). Correlates of victimization in Hong Kong children's peer groups. *Journal of Applied Developmental Psychology, 31,* 27–37. doi:10.1016/j.appdev.2009.06.002

Tomada, G., & Schneider, B. H. (1997). Relational aggression, gender, and peer acceptance: Invariance across culture, stability over time, and concordance among informants. *Developmental Psychology, 33,* 601–609. doi:10.1037/0012-1649.33.4.601

Tomasello, M. (1994). Can an ape understand a sentence? [Review of the monograph *Language comprehension in ape and child,* by E. S. Savage-Rumbaugh et al.]. *Language and Communication, 14,* 377–390.

Tomasello, M. (2001). Perceiving intentions and learning words in the second year of life. In M. Bowerman & S. C. Levinson (Eds.), *Language acquisition and conceptual development* (pp. 132–158). Cambridge, England: Cambridge University Press.

Tomasello, M. (2003). *Constructing a language: A usage-based theory of language acquisition.* Cambridge, MA: Harvard University Press.

Tomasello, M. (2008). *Origins of human communication.* Cambridge, MA: MIT Press.

Tomasello, M. (2009). *The cultural origins of human cognition.* Cambridge, MA: Harvard University Press.

Tomasello, M. (2009). *Why we cooperate.* Cambridge, MA: MIT Press.

Tomasello, M. (2014). *A natural history of human thinking.* Cambridge, MA: Harvard University Press.

Tomasello, M., & Barton, M. E. (1994). Learning words in nonostensive contexts. *Developmental Psychology, 30,* 639–650. doi:10.1037/0012-1649. 30.5.639

Tomasello, M., Strosberg, R., & Akhtar, N. (1996). Eighteen-month-old children learn words in non-ostensive contexts. *Journal of Child Language, 23,* 157–176. doi:10.1017/ S0305000900010138

Tomasello, M., & Vaish, A. (2013). Origins of human cooperation and morality. *Annual Review of Psychology, 64,* 231–255. doi:10.1146/ annurev-psych-113011-143812

Tomblin, J. B., Mainela-Arnold, E., & Zhang, X. (2007). Procedural learning in adolescents with and without specific language impairment. *Language Learning and Development, 3,* 269–293. doi:10.1080/15475440701377477

Tomkins, S. S., & Karon, B. P. (1962). *Affect, imagery, consciousness: Vol. 1. The positive affects.* New York, NY: Springer.

Tomlinson, H. B. (2009). Developmentally appropriate practice in the kindergarten

year—Ages 5–6: An overview. In C. Copple & S. Bredekamp (Eds.), *Developmentally appropriate practice in early childhood programs serving children from birth through age 8* (3rd ed., pp. 187–216). Washington, DC: National Association for the Education of Young Children.

Tooby, J., & Cosmides, L. (2005). Conceptual foundations of evolutionary psychology. In D. M. Buss (Ed.), *The handbook of evolutionary psychology* (pp. 5–67). Hoboken, NJ: Wiley.

Tooley, G. A., Karakis, M., Stokes, M., & Ozanne-Smith, J. (2006). Generalising the Cinderella Effect to unintentional childhood fatalities. *Evolution and Human Behavior, 27,* 224–230.

Toomey, R. B., Ryan, C., Diaz, R. M., Card, N. A., & Russell, S. T. (2010). Gender-nonconforming lesbian, gay, bisexual, and transgender youth: School victimization and young adult psychosocial adjustment. *Developmental Psychology, 46,* 1580–1589. doi:10.1037/a0020705

Torassa, U. (2000, March 8). Leave it on: Study says night lighting won't harm children's eyesight. Retrieved from http://edition.cnn. com/2000/HEALTH/children/03/08/light .myopia.wmd/index.html

Torbeyns, J., Schneider, M., Xin, Z., & Siegler, R. S. (2015). Bridging the gap: Fraction understanding is central to mathematics achievement in students from three different continents. *Learning and Instruction, 37,* 5–13. doi:10.1016/ j.learninstruc. 2014.03.002

Tornello, S. L., Farr, R. H., & Patterson, C. J. (2011). Predictors of parenting stress among gay adoptive fathers in the United States. *Journal of Family Psychology, 25,* 591–600. doi:10.1037/ a0024480

Totsika, V., & Sylva, K. (2004). The home observation for measurement of the environment revisited. *Child and Adolescent Mental Health, 9*(1), 25–35. doi:10.1046/j.1475-357X.2003.00073.x

Tottenham, N., Hare, T. A., Quinn, B. T., McCarry, T. W., Nurse, M., Gilhooly, T., . . . Casey, B. J. (2010). Prolonged institutional rearing is associated with atypically large amygdala volume and difficulties in emotion regulation. *Developmental Science, 13,* 46–61. doi: 10.1111/j.1467-7687.2009.00852.x.

Trainor, L. J. (1996). Infant preferences for infant-directed versus noninfant-directed playsongs and lullabies. *Infant Behavior and Development, 19,* 83–92. doi:10.1016/ S0163-6383(96)90046-6

Trainor, L. J., & Heinmiller, B. M. (1998). The development of evaluative responses to music: Infants prefer to listen to consonance over dissonance. *Infant Behavior and Development, 21,* 77–88. doi:10.1016/S0163-6383 (98)90055-8

Trainor, L. J., & Trehub, S. E. (1992). A comparison of infants' and adults'

sensitivity to Western musical structure. *Journal of Experimental Psychology: Human Perception and Performance, 18*, 394–402. doi:10.1037/0096-1523.18.2.394

Trainor, L. J., & Trehub, S. E. (1994). Key membership and implied harmony in Western tonal music: Developmental perspectives. *Perception and Psychophysics, 56*, 125–132.

Tran, C. V., Cole, D. A., & Weiss, B. (2012). Testing reciprocal longitudinal relations between peer victimization and depressive symptoms in young adolescents. *Journal of Clinical Child & Adolescent Psychology, 41*, 353–360. doi:10.1080/15374416.2012.662674

Tran, U. S., & Voracek, M. (2015). Evidence of sex-linked familial transmission of lateral preferences for hand, foot, eye, ear, and overall sidedness in a latent variable analysis. *Behavior Genetics, 45*(5), 537–546.

Trehub, S. E., Plantinga, J., & Russo, F. A. (2015). Maternal vocal interactions with infants: Reciprocal visual influences. *Social Development, 25*, 665–683. doi:10.1111/sode.12164

Trehub, S. E., & Schellenberg, E. G. (1995). Music: Its relevance to infants. In R. Vasta (Ed.), *Annals of child development* (Vol. 11, pp. 1–24). London, England: Jessica Kingsley Publishers.

Treiman, R., Hompluem, L., Gordon, J., Decker, K., & Markson, L. (2016). Young children's knowledge of the symbolic nature of writing. *Child Development, 87*(2), 583–592.

Treiman, R., & Yin, L. (2011). Early differentiation between drawing and writing in Chinese children. *Journal of Experimental Child Psychology, 108*(4), 786–801.

Tremblay, R. E., Pihl, R. O., Vitaro, F., & Dobkin, P. L. (1994). Predicting early onset of male antisocial behavior from preschool behavior. *Archives of General Psychiatry, 51*, 732–739. doi:10.1001/archpsyc.1994.03950090064009

Trentacosta, C. J., Hyde, L. W., Shaw, D. S., Dishion, T. J., Gardner, F., & Wilson, M. (2008). The relations among cumulative risk, parenting, and behavior problems during early childhood. *Journal of Child Psychology and Psychiatry, 49*, 1211–1219. doi:10.1111/j.1469-7610.2008.01941.x

Trivers, R. L. (1972). Parental investment and sexual selection, 1871–1971. In B. Campbell (Ed.), *Sexual selection and the descent of man* (pp. 136–179). Chicago, IL: Aldine.

Trivers, R. L. (1983). The evolution of cooperation. In D. Bridgeman (Ed.), *The nature of prosocial development* (pp. 95–112). New York, NY: Academic Press.

Trommsdorff, G., Friedlmeier, W., & Mayer, B. (2007). Sympathy, distress, and prosocial behavior of preschool children in four cultures. *International Journal of Behavioral Development, 31*, 284–293. doi:10.1177/0165025407076441

Tronick, E. Z., Als, H., Adamson, L., Wise, S., & Brazelton, T. B. (1978). The infant's response to entrapment between contradictory messages in face-to-face interaction. *Journal of American Academy of Child Psychiatry, 17*, 1–13. doi:10.1016/s0002-7138(09)62273-1

Tronick, E. Z., Thomas, R. B., & Daltabuit, M. (1994). The Quechua manta pouch: A caretaking practice for buffering the Peruvian infant against the multiple stressors of high altitude. *Child Development, 65*, 1005–1013.

Tryphonopoulos, P. D., Letourneau, N., & Ditommaso, E. (2014). Attachment and caregiver–infant interaction: A review of observational-assessment tools. *Infant Mental Health Journal, 35*, 642–656. doi:10.1002/imhj.21461

Trzaskowski, M., Yang, J., Visscher, P. M., & Plomin, R. (2014). DNA evidence for strong genetic stability and increasing heritability of intelligence from age 7 to 12. *Molecular Psychiatry, 19*(3), 380–384.

Trzesniewski, K. H., Donnellan, M. B., Moffitt, T. E., Robins, R. W., Poulton, R., & Caspi, A. (2006). Low self-esteem during adolescence predicts poor health, criminal behavior, and limited economic prospects during adulthood. *Developmental Psychology, 42*, 381–390. doi:10.1037/0012-1649.42.2.381

Trzesniewski, K. H., Kinal, M. P.-A., & Donnellan, M. B. (2010). Self-enhancement and self-protection in a developmental context. In M. D. Alicke & C. Sedikides (Eds.), *The handbook of self-enhancement and self-protection* (pp. 341–357). New York, NY: Guilford Press.

Tsao, F.-M., Liu, H.-M., & Kuhl, P. K. (2004). Speech perception in infancy predicts language development in the second year of life: A longitudinal study. *Child Development, 75*, 1067–1084. doi:10.1111/j.1467-8624.2004.00726.x

Ttofi, M. M., & Farrington, D. P. (2011). Effectiveness of school-based programs to reduce bullying: A systematic and meta-analytic review. *Journal of Experimental Criminology, 7*, 27–56. doi:10.1007/s11292-010-9109-1

Tucker-Drob, E. M., & Bates, T. C. (2016). Large cross-national differences in gene × socioeconomic status interaction on intelligence. *Psychological Science, 27*(2), 138–149. doi:10.1177/0956797615612727

Tucker-Drob, E. M., Rhemtulla, M., Harden, K. P., Turkheimer, E., & Fask, D. (2011). Emergence of a gene × socioeconomic status interaction on infant mental ability between 10 months and 2 years. *Psychological Science, 22*, 125–133. doi:10.1177/0956797610392926

Tummeltshammer, K. S., Wu, R., Sobel, D. M., & Kirkham, N. Z. (2014). Infants track the reliability of potential informants. *Psychological Science, 25*(9), 1730–1738. doi:10.1177/0956797614540178

Tung, Y. L., Yeo, G. S., O'Rahilly, S., & Coll, A. P. (2014). Obesity and FTO: Changing focus at a complex locus. *Cell Metabolism, 20*(5), 710–718.

Turiel, E. (1987). Potential relations between the development of social reasoning and childhood aggression. In D. H. Crowell, I. M. Evans, & C. R. O'Donnell (Eds.), *Childhood aggression and violence: Sources of influence, prevention, and control* (pp. 95–114). New York, NY: Plenum Press.

Turiel, E. (1998). Moral development. In W. Damon (Series Ed.) & R. M. Lerner & N. Eisenberg (Vol. Eds.), *Handbook of child psychology: Vol. 3. Social, emotional, and personality development* (pp. 863–932). New York, NY: Wiley.

Turiel, E. (2006). The development of morality. In W. Damon & R. M. Lerner (Series Eds.) & N. Eisenberg (Vol. Ed.), *Handbook of child psychology: Vol. 3. Social, emotional, and personality development* (6th ed., pp. 789–857). Hoboken, NJ: Wiley.

Turiel, E. (2008). Thought about actions in social domains: Morality, social conventions, and social interactions. *Cognitive Development, 23*, 136–154. doi:10.1016/j.cogdev.2007.04.001

Turiel, E. (2014). Morality: Epistemology, development, and social opposition. In M. Killen and J. G. Smetana (Eds.), *Handbook of moral development* (2nd ed., pp. 3–22). New York, NY: Psychology Press.

Turkheimer, E. (2000). Three laws of behavior genetics and what they mean. *Current Directions in Psychological Science, 9*, 160–164. doi:10.1111/1467-8721.00084

Turkheimer, E., Haley, A., Waldron, M., D'Onofrio, B., & Gottesman, I. I. (2003). Socioeconomic status modifies heritability of IQ in young children. *Psychological Science, 14*, 623–628.

Turley, R. N. L. (2003). When do neighborhoods matter? The role of race and neighborhood peers. *Social Science Research, 32*, 61–79.

Turner, C. M., & Barrett, P. M. (2003). Does age play a role in structure of anxiety and depression in children and youths? An investigation of the tripartite model in three age cohorts. *Journal of Consulting and Clinical Psychology, 71*, 826–833.

Turner-Bowker, D. M. (1996). Gender stereotyped descriptors in children's picture books: Does "curious Jane" exist in the literature? *Sex Roles, 35*, 461–488. doi:10.1007/BF01544132

Tuvblad, C., Raine, A., Zheng, M., & Baker, L. A. (2009). Genetic and environmental stability differs in reactive and proactive aggression. *Aggressive Behavior, 35*, 437–452. doi:10.1002/ab.20319

Twenge, J. M., & Crocker, J. (2002). Race and self-esteem: Meta-analyses comparing Whites, Blacks, Hispanics, Asians, and American Indians and comment on Gray-Little and Hafdahl (2000).

Psychological Bulletin, 128, 371–408. doi:10.1037/0033-2909.128.3.371

Twenge, J. M., & Nolen-Hoeksema, S. (2002). Age, gender, race, socioeconomic status, and birth cohort differences on the children's depression inventory: A meta-analysis. *Journal of Abnormal Psychology, 111,* 578–588.

Twyman, K., Saylor, C., Taylor, L. A., & Comeaux, C. (2010). Comparing children and adolescents engaged in cyberbullying to matched peers. *Cyberpsychology, Behavior and Social Networking, 13,* 195–199.

Tynes, B. M., Umaña-Taylor, A. J., Rose, C. A., Lin, J., & Anderson, C. J. (2012). Online racial discrimination and the protective function of ethnic identity and self-esteem for African American adolescents. *Developmental Psychology, 48*(2), 343–355. doi:10.1037/a0027032

Tyrka, A. R., Graber, J. A., & Brooks-Gunn, J. (2000). The development of disordered eating. In A. J. Sameroff, M. Lewis, & S. M. Miller (Eds.), *Handbook of developmental psychopathology* (pp. 607–624). New York, NY: Springer.

U.S. Census Bureau. (2007). POV04. Families by age of householder, number of children, and family structure. Retrieved from http://www.census.gov/hhes/www/cpstables/macro/032007/pov/new04_050.htm

U.S. Census Bureau. (2011, November). *Child poverty in the United States 2009 and 2010: Selected race groups and Hispanic origin* (American Community Survey Briefs ACSBR/10-05). Washington, DC: Author.

U.S. Census Bureau. (2015). *America's families and living arrangements: 2015: Children (C table series).* Retrieved from http://www.census.gov/hhes/families/data/cps2015C.html

U.S. Census Bureau. (2015). Detailed Languages Spoken at Home and Ability to Speak English for the Population 5 Years and Over: 2009–2013. Retrieved from http://www.census.gov/data/tables/2013/demo/2009-2013-lang-tables.html

U.S. Department of Education. (2015). *Student reports of bullying and cyber-bullying: Results from the 2013 School Crime Supplement to the National Crime Victimization Survey* (NCES 2015-056). Retrieved from http://nces.ed.gov/pubs2015/2015056.pdf

U.S. Department of Education. (2016). Supporting the success of homeless children and youths. Retrieved from http://www2.ed.gov/policy/elsec/leg/essa/160315ehcyfactsheet072716.pdf

U.S. Department of Health and Human Services, Administration for Children and Families. (2010). Head Start impact study: Final report, executive summary. Retrieved from http://www.acf.hhs.gov/sites/default/files/opre/executive_summary_final.pdf

U.S. Department of Health and Human Services, Administration for Children and Families, Office of Planning, Research and Evaluation. (2008). *Head Start Family and Child Experiences Survey (FACES): 2003 cohort [United States]* (ICPSR22580-v6). Ann Arbor, MI: Inter-university Consortium for Political and Social Research.

U.S. Department of Health and Human Services, Administration for Children and Families, Office of Planning, Research and Evaluation. (2016). *Child maltreatment 2014.* Retrieved from http://www.acf.hhs.gov/programs/cb/research-data-technology/statistics-research/child-maltreatment

U.S. Department of Health and Human Services, Health Resources and Services Administration, Maternal and Child Health Bureau. (2006). Child health USA 2006: Population characteristics: Working mothers and child care. Retrieved from http://www.mchb.hrsa.gov/chusa_06/popchar/0206wmcc.htm

U.S. Department of Health and Human Services, Health Resources and Services Administration, Maternal and Child Health Bureau. (2013). Child health USA 2012. Retrieved from http://mchb.hrsa.gov/chusa12/pc/pc.html

U.S. Department of Justice. (2015). Child Pornography. Retrieved from https://www.justice.gov/criminal-ceos/child-pornography

U.S. Department of Labor. (2016). Mothers and families. Retrieved from https://www.dol.gov/wb/stats/mother_families.htm

Uddin, M., Tammimies, K., Pellecchia, G., Alipanahi, B., Hu, P., Wang, Z., . . . Scherer, S. W. (2014). Brain-expressed exons under purifying selection are enriched for de novo mutations in autism spectrum disorder. *Nature Genetics, 46,* 742–747. doi:10.1038/ng.2980.

Uhlhaas, P. J., Roux, F., Rodriguez, E., Rotarska-Jagiela, A., & Singer, W. (2010). Neural synchrony and the development of cortical networks. *Trends in Cognitive Sciences, 14*(2), 72–80. doi:10.1016/j.tics.2009.12.002

Umaña-Taylor, A. J. (2011). Ethnic identity. In S. J. Schwartz, K. Luyckx, & V. L. Vignoles (Eds.), *Handbook of identity theory and research* (pp. 791–809). New York, NY: Springer.

Umaña-Taylor, A. J., Bhanot, R., & Shin, N. (2006). Ethnic identity formation during adolescence: The critical role of families. *Journal of Family Issues, 27,* 390–414. doi:10.1177/0192513x05282960

Umaña-Taylor, A. J., Diversi, M., & Fine, M. A. (2002). Ethnic identity and self-esteem of Latino adolescents: Distinctions among the Latino populations. *Journal of Adolescent Research, 17,* 303–327. doi:10.1177/0743558402173005

Umaña-Taylor, A. J., & Guimond, A. B. (2010). A longitudinal examination of parenting behaviors and perceived discrimination predicting Latino adolescents' ethnic identity. *Developmental Psychology, 46,* 636–650. doi:10.1037/a0019376

Umaña-Taylor, A. J., Quintana, S. M., Lee, R. M., Cross, W. E., Rivas-Drake, D., Schwartz, S. J., . . . Seaton, E. (2014). Ethnic and racial identity during adolescence and into young adulthood: An integrated conceptualization. *Child Development, 85*(1), 21–39. doi:10.1111/cdev.12196

Underwood, B., & Moore, B. (1982). Perspective-taking and altruism. *Psychological Bulletin, 91,* 143–173. doi:10.1037/0033-2909.91.1.143

Underwood, M. K. (2003). *Social aggression among girls.* New York, NY: Guilford Press.

UNICEF. (2012). *The State of the World's Children 2012: Children in an urban world.* Retrieved from www.unicef.org/sowc2012/

UNICEF. (2013). *Improving child nutrition: The achievable imperative for global progress.* New York, NY: United Nations Children's Fund. Retrieved from http://data.unicef.org/corecode/uploads/document6/uploaded_pdfs/corecode/NutritionReport_April2013_Final_29.pdf

UNICEF. (2016). *Undernutrition contributes to nearly half of all deaths in children under 5 and is widespread in Asia and Africa.* Retrieved July 6, 2016, from http://data.unicef.org/nutrition/malnutrition.html

UNICEF Innocenti Research Centre. (2012). *Measuring child poverty: New league tables of child poverty in the world's richest countries* (Innocenti Report Card 10). Florence, Italy: Author. Retrieved from https://www.unicef-irc.org/publications/pdf/rc10_eng.pdf

United Nations, Committee on the Rights of the Child. (2006). *General Comment No. 8 (2006): The right of the child to protection from corporal punishment and or cruel or degrading forms of punishment* (articles 1, 28(2), and 37, inter alia) (CRC/C/GC/8). Geneva, Switzerland: United Nations.

United Nations, Department of Economic and Social Affairs, Population Division. (2015). *World population prospects: The 2015 revision.* Retrieved from https://esa.un.org/unpd/wpp/Download/Standard/Population/

United Nations Population Division. (n.d.) Adolescent fertility rate (births per 1,000 women ages 15–19). United Nations Population Division, World Populations Prospects. Accessed June 22, 2016, from World Bank website: http://data.worldbank.org/indicator/SP.ADO.TFRT

Unsworth, N., Redick, T. S., McMillan, B. D., Hambrick, D. Z., Kane, M. J., & Engle, R. W. (2015). Is playing video games related to cognitive abilities? *Psychological Science, 26*(6), 759–774. doi:10.1177/0956797615570367

Updegraff, K. A., Kim, J.-Y., Killoren, S. E., & Thayer, S. M. (2010). Mexican American parents' involvement in adolescents' peer relationships: Exploring the role of culture and adolescents' peer experiences. *Journal of Research on Adolescence, 20,* 65–87. doi:10.1111/j.1532-7795.2009.00625.x

Updegraff, K. A., McHale, S. M., & Crouter, A. C. (1996). Gender roles in marriage: What do they mean for girls' and boys' school achievement? *Journal of Youth and Adolescence, 25,* 73–88. doi:10.1007/BF01537381

Urberg, K. A., Değirmencioğlu, S. M., & Pilgrim, C. (1997). Close friend and group influence on adolescent cigarette smoking and alcohol use. *Developmental Psychology, 33,* 834–844.

Uttal, D. H., Meadow, N. G., Tipton, E., Hand, L. L., Alden, A. R., Warren, C., & Newcombe, N. S. (2013). The malleability of spatial skills: A meta-analysis of training studies. *Psychological Bulletin, 139,* 352–402.

Uttal, D. H., O'Doherty, K., Newland, R., Hand, L. L., & DeLoache, J. (2009). Dual representation and the linking of concrete and symbolic representations. *Child Development Perspectives, 3*(3), 156–159.

Uttal, D. H., & Yuan, L. (2014). Using symbols: Developmental perspectives. *Wiley Interdisciplinary Reviews: Cognitive Science, 5*(3), 295–304.

Vaillancourt, T., Brendgen, M., Boivin, M., & Tremblay, R. E. (2003). A longitudinal confirmatory factor analysis of indirect and physical aggression: Evidence of two factors over time? *Child Development, 74,* 1628–1638. doi:10.1046/j.1467-8624.2003.00628.x

Vaillant-Molina, M., & Bahrick, L. E. (2012). The role of intersensory redundancy in the emergence of social referencing in 5½-month-old infants. *Developmental Psychology, 48,* 1–9.

Vainio, A. (2011). Religious conviction, morality and social convention among Finnish adolescents. *Journal of Moral Education, 40,* 73–87. doi:10.1080/03057240.2010.521390

Vaish, A., Carpenter, M., & Tomasello, M. (2009). Sympathy through affective perspective taking and its relation to prosocial behavior in toddlers. *Developmental Psychology, 45,* 534–543. doi:10.1037/a0014322

Vaish, A., Carpenter, M., & Tomasello, M. (2010). Young children selectively avoid helping people with harmful intentions. *Child Development, 81,* 1661–1669. doi:10.1111/j.1467-8624.2010.01500.x

Vaish, A., & Striano, T. (2004). Is visual reference necessary? Contributions of facial versus vocal cues in 12-month-olds' social referencing behavior. *Developmental Science, 7,* 261–269.

Valentino, K., Toth, S. L., & Cicchetti, D. (2009). Autobiographical memory functioning among abused, neglected, and nonmaltreated children: The overgeneral memory effect. *Journal of Child Psychology and Psychiatry, 50*(8), 1029–1038.

Valenzuela, M. (1997). Maternal sensitivity in a developing society: The context of urban poverty and infant chronic undernutrition. *Developmental Psychology, 33,* 845–855. doi:10.1037/0012-1649.33.5.845

Valeski, T. N., & Stipek, D. J. (2001). Young children's feelings about school. *Child Development, 72,* 1198–1213.

Valiente, C., Eisenberg, N., Fabes, R. A., Shepard, S. A., Cumberland, A., & Losoya, S. H. (2004). Prediction of children's empathy-related responding from their effortful control and parents' expressivity. *Developmental Psychology, 40,* 911–926.

Valkenburg, P. M. (2015). The limited informativeness of meta-analyses of media effects. *Perspectives on Psychological Science, 10*(5), 680–682.

Valkenburg, P. M., & Peter, J. (2007). Preadolescents' and adolescents' online communication and their closeness to friends. *Developmental Psychology, 43,* 267–277. doi:10.1037/0012-1649.43.2.267

Valkenburg, P. M., & Peter, J. (2009). The effects of instant messaging on the quality of adolescents' existing friendships: A longitudinal study. *Journal of Communication, 59,* 79–97. doi:10.1111/j.1460-2466.2008.01405.x

Valkenburg, P. M., & Peter, J. (2011). Online communication among adolescents: An integrated model of its attraction, opportunities, and risks. *Journal of Adolescent Health, 48,* 121–127. doi:10.1016/j.jadohealth.2010.08.020

Van Beek, Y., Van Dolderen, M. S. M., & Demon Dubas, J. J. S. (2006). Gender-specific development of nonverbal behaviours and mild depression in adolescence. *Journal of Child Psychology and Psychiatry, 47,* 1272–1283. doi:10.1111/j.1469-7610.2006.01663.x

Van de Gaer, E., Pustjens, H., Van Damme, J., & De Munter, A. (2006). Tracking and the effects of school-related attitudes on the language achievement of boys and girls. *British Journal of Sociology of Education, 27,* 293–309. doi:10.1080/01425690600750478

van den Boom, D. C., & Hoeksma, J. B. (1994). The effect of infant irritability on mother–infant interaction: A growth-curve analysis. *Developmental Psychology, 30,* 581–590.

van den Eijnden, R. J. J. M., Meerkerk, G.-J., Vermulst, A. A., Spijkerman, R., & Engels, R. C. M. E. (2008). Online communication, compulsive internet use, and psychosocial well-being among adolescents: A longitudinal study. *Developmental Psychology, 44,* 655–665. doi:10.1037/0012-1649.44.3.655

Van den Oord, E. J. C. G., Boomsma, D. I., & Verhulst, F. C. (2000). A study of genetic and environmental effects on the co-occurrence of problem behaviors in three-year-old-twins. *Journal of Abnormal Psychology, 109,* 360–372. doi:10.1037/0021-843X.109.3.360

Van der Ven, S. H., Boom, J., Kroesbergen, E. H., & Leseman, P. P. (2012). Microgenetic patterns of children's multiplication learning: Confirming the overlapping waves model by latent growth modeling. *Journal of Experimental Child Psychology, 113*(1), 1–19. doi:10.1016/j.jecp.2012.02.001

van der Zee, E., Zulch, H., & Mills, D. (2012). Word generalization by a dog (Canis familiaris): Is shape important?. *PloS One, 7*(11), e49382. doi:10.1371/journal.pone.0049382

Van Doorn, M. D., Branje, S. J. T., & Meeus, W. H. J. (2008). Conflict resolution in parent-adolescent relationships and adolescent delinquency. *Journal of Early Adolescence, 28,* 503–527. doi:10.1177/0272431608317608

Van Doorn, M. D., Branje, S. J. T., & Meeus, W. H. J. (2011). Developmental changes in conflict resolution styles in parent–adolescent relationships: A four-wave longitudinal study. *Journal of Youth and Adolescence, 40,* 97–107. doi:10.1007/s10964-010-9516-7

Van Heugten, M., & Shi, R. (2009). French-learning toddlers use gender information on determiners during word recognition. *Developmental Science, 12,* 419–425. doi:10.1111/j.1467-7687.2008.00788.x

Van Houtte, M. (2004). Why boys achieve less at school than girls: The difference between boys' and girls' academic culture. *Educational Studies, 30,* 159–173. doi:10.1080/0305569032000159804

van IJzendoorn, M. H. (1995). Adult attachment representations, parental responsiveness, and infant attachment: A meta-analysis on the predictive validity of the Adult Attachment Interview. *Psychological Bulletin, 117,* 387–403.

van IJzendoorn, M. H., & Bakermans-Kranenburg, M. J. (2010). Invariance of adult attachment across gender, age, culture, and socioeconomic status? *Journal of Social and Personal Relationships, 27,* 200–208.

van IJzendoorn, M. H., Bakermans-Kranenburg, M. J., & Ebstein, R. P. (2011). Methylation matters in child development: Toward developmental behavioral epigenetics. *Child Development Perspectives, 5,* 305–310. doi:10.1111/j.1750-8606.2011.00202.x

van IJzendoorn, M. H., & De Wolff, M. S. (1997). In search of the absent father—Meta-analyses of infant-father attachment: A rejoinder to our discussants. *Child Development, 68,* 604–609. doi:10.1111/j.1467-8624.1997.tb04223.x

van IJzendoorn, M. H., Juffer, F., & Duyvesteyn, M. G. C. (1995). Breaking the intergenerational cycle of insecure attachment: A review of the effects of attachment-based interventions on maternal sensitivity and infant security. *Journal of Child Psychology and Psychiatry, 36,* 225–248. doi:10.1111/j.1469-7610.1995.tb01822.x

van IJzendoorn, M. H., & Sagi, A. (1999). Cross-cultural patterns of attachment: Universal and contextual dimensions. In J. Cassidy & P. R. Shaver (Eds.), *Handbook of attachment: Theory, research, and clinical applications* (pp. 713–734). New York, NY: Guilford Press.

van IJzendoorn, M. H., & Sagi-Schwartz, A. (2008). Cross-cultural patterns of attachment: Universal and contextual dimensions. In J. Cassidy & P. R. Shaver (Eds.), *Handbook of attachment: Theory, research, and clinical applications* (2nd ed., pp. 880–905). New York, NY: Guilford Press.

van IJzendoorn, M. H., Schuengel, C., & Bakermans-Kranenburg, M. J. (1999). Disorganized attachment in early childhood: Meta-analysis of precursors, concomitants, and sequelae. *Development and Psychopathology, 11,* 225–249.

van IJzendoorn, M. H., Vereijken, C. M., Bakermans-Kranenburg, M. J., & Riksen-Walraven, J. M. (2004). Assessing attachment security with the Attachment Q Sort: Meta-analytic evidence for the validity of the observer AQS. *Child Development, 75,* 1188–1213. doi:10.1111/j.1467-8624.2004.00733.x

van Lier, P. A. C., van der Ende, J., Koot, H. M., & Verhulst, F. C. (2007). Which better predicts conduct problems? The relationship of trajectories of conduct problems with ODD and ADHD symptoms from childhood into adolescence. *Journal of Child Psychology and Psychiatry, 48,* 601–608. doi:10.1111/j.1469-7610.2006.01724.x

van Lier, P. A. C., Vitaro, F., Barker, E. D., Brendgen, M., Tremblay, R. E., & Boivin, M. (2012). Peer victimization, poor academic achievement, and the link between childhood externalizing and internalizing problems. *Child Development, 83,* 1775–1788. doi:10.1111/j.1467-8624.2012.01802.x

Van Ryzin, M. J., & Dishion, T. J. (2012). The impact of a family-centered intervention on the ecology of adolescent antisocial behavior: Modeling developmental sequelae and trajectories during adolescence. *Development and Psychopathology, 24,* 1139–1155. doi:10.1017/S0954579412000582

van Wermeskerken, M., van der Kamp, J., Savelsbergh, G. J., & von Hofsten, C. (2013). Getting the closer object? An information-based dissociation between vision for perception and vision for movement in early infancy. *Developmental Science, 16,* 91–100. doi:10.1111/desc.12006

Van Zalk, M. H., Kerr, M., Branje, S. J., Stattin, H., & Meeus, W. H. (2010). It takes three: Selection, influence, and de-selection processes of depression in adolescent friendship networks. *Developmental Psychology, 46,* 927–938.

Van Zalk, N., Van Zalk, M., Kerr, M., & Stattin, H. (2011). Social anxiety as a basis for friendship selection and socialization in adolescents' social networks. *Journal of Personality, 79,* 499–525. doi:10.1111/j.1467-6494.2011.00682.x

Vandell, D. L., Belsky, J., Burchinal, M., Steinberg, L., Vandergrift, N., & NICHD Early Child Care Research Network. (2010). Do effects of early child care extend to age 15 years? Results from the NICHD Study of Early Child Care and Youth Development. *Child Development, 81,* 737–756. doi:10.1111/j.1467-8624.2010.01431.x

Vanfossen, B., Brown, C. H., Kellam, S., Sokoloff, N., & Doering, S. (2010). Neighborhood context and the development of aggression in boys and girls. *Journal of Community Psychology, 38,* 329–349. doi:10.1002/jcop.20367

Vannatta, K., Gartstein, M. A., Zeller, M., & Noll, R. B. (2009). Peer acceptance and social behavior during childhood and adolescence: How important are appearance, athleticism, and academic competence? *International Journal of Behavioral Development, 33,* 303–311. doi:10.1177/0165025408101275

Vaquera, E., & Kao, G. (2008). Do you like me as much as I like you? Friendship reciprocity and its effects on school outcomes among adolescents. *Social Science Research, 37,* 55–72. doi:10.1016/j.ssresearch.2006.11.002

Varendi, H., Porter, R. H., & Winberg, J. (2002). The effect of labor on olfactory exposure learning within the first postnatal hour. *Behavioral Neuroscience, 116,* 206–211.

Vasek, M. E. (1986). Lying as a skill: The development of deception in children. In R. W. Mitchell & N. S. Thompson (Eds.), *Deception: Perspectives on human and non-human deceit* (pp. 271–292). New York, NY: SUNY Press.

Vaughan, C. C. (1996). *How life begins: The science of life in the womb.* New York, NY: Times Books.

Vaughn, B. E., Vollenweider, M., Bost, K. K., Azria-Evans, M. R., & Snider, J. B. (2003). Negative interactions and social competence for preschool children in two samples: Reconsidering the interpretation of aggressive behavior for young children. *Merrill-Palmer Quarterly, 49,* 245–278.

Vellutino, F. R., & Scanlon, D. M. (1987). Phonological coding, phonological awareness, and reading ability: Evidence from a longitudinal and experimental study. *Merrill-Palmer Quarterly, 33,* 321–363.

Venker, C. E., Haebig, E., Edwards, J., Saffran, J. R., & Weismer, S. E. (2016). Brief report: Early lexical comprehension in young children with ASD: Comparing eye-gaze methodology and parent report. *Journal of Autism and Developmental Disorders, 46*(6), 2260–2266.

Ventura, A. K., & Worobey, J. (2013). Early influences on the development of food preferences. *Current Biology, 23*(9), R401–R408.

Vera, E. M., & Quintana, S. M. (2004). Ethnic identity development in Chicana/o youth. In R. J. Velasquez, L. M. Arellano, & B. W. McNeill (Eds.), *The handbook of Chicana/o psychology and mental health* (pp. 43–59). Mahwah, NJ: Erlbaum.

Veríssimo, M., Santos, A. J., Vaughn, B. E., Torres, N., Monteiro, L., & Santos, O. (2011). Quality of attachment to father and mother and number of reciprocal friends. *Early Child Development and Care, 181,* 27–38. doi:10.1080/03004430903211208

Verma, S. (1999). Socialization for survival: Developmental issues among working street children in India. In M. Raffaelli & R. W. Larson (Eds.), *New Directions for Child and Adolescent Development: No. 85. Homeless and working youth around the world: Exploring developmental issues* (Vol. 1999, pp. 5–18). San Francisco, CA: Jossey-Bass.

Vernon, P. A., Wickett, J. C., Bazana, P. G., & Stelmack, R. M. (2000). The neuropsychology and psychophysiology of human intelligence. In R. J. Sternberg (Ed.), *Handbook of intelligence* (pp. 245–266). Cambridge, England: Cambridge University Press.

Véronneau, M.-H., Vitaro, F., Brendgen, M., Dishion, T. J., & Tremblay, R. E. (2010). Transactional analysis of the reciprocal links between peer experiences and academic achievement from middle childhood to early adolescence. *Developmental Psychology, 46,* 773–790. doi:10.1037/a0019816

Verschueren, K., Marcoen, A., & Schoefs, V. (1996). The internal working model of the self, attachment, and competence in five-year-olds. *Child Development, 67,* 2493–2511. doi:10.1111/j.1467-8624.1996.tb01870.x

Victora, C. G., Bahl, R., Barros, A. J., França, G. V., Horton, S., Krasevec, J., . . . Lancet Breastfeeding Series Group. (2016). Breastfeeding in the 21st century: Epidemiology, mechanisms, and lifelong effect. *The Lancet, 387*(10017), 475–490.

Viding, E., & McCrory, E. J. (2012). Genetic and neurocognitive contributions to the development of psychopathy. *Development and Psychopathology, 24,* 969–983.

Vikan, A., & Clausen, S. E. (1993). Freud, Piaget, or neither? Beliefs in controlling others by wishful thinking and magical behavior in young children. *Journal of Genetic Psychology, 154,* 297–314. doi:10.1080/00221325.1993.10532183

Vitaro, F., Barker, E. D., Boivin, M., Brendgen, M., & Tremblay, R. E. (2006). Do early difficult temperament and harsh parenting differentially predict reactive and proactive aggression? *Journal of Abnormal Child Psychology, 34,* 681–691. doi:10.1007/s10802-006-9055-6

Vitaro, F., Pedersen, S., & Brendgen, M. (2007). Children's disruptiveness, peer rejection, friends' deviancy, and delinquent behaviors: A process-oriented approach. *Development and Psychopathology, 19,* 433–453. doi:10.1017/S0954579407070216

Viteri, O. A., Soto, E. E., Bahado-Singh, R. O., Christensen, C. W., Chauhan, S. P., & Sibai, B. M. (2015). Fetal anomalies and long-term effects associated with substance abuse in pregnancy: A literature review. *American Journal of Perinatology, 32(5),* 405–416.

Vitoroulis, I., Schneider, B. H., Vasquez, C. C., Soteras de Toro, M. P., & Gonzales, Y. S. (2012). Perceived parental and peer support in relation to Canadian, Cuban, and Spanish adolescents' valuing of academics and intrinsic academic motivation. *Journal of Cross-Cultural Psychology 43,* 704–722. doi:10.1177/0022022111405657

Voegtline, K. M., Costigan, K. A., Pater, H. A., & DiPietro, J. A. (2013). Near-term fetal response to maternal spoken voice. *Infant Behavior and Development, 36*(4), 526–533.

Vohr, B. R., & Garcia Coll, C. T. (1988). Follow-up studies of high risk low-birthweight infants: Changing trends. In H. E. Fitzgerald, B. M. Lester, & M. H. Yogman (Eds.), *Theory and research in behavioral pediatrics* (Vol. 4, pp. 1–65). New York, NY: Plenum.

Volbrecht, M. M., Lemery-Chalfant, K., Aksan, N., Zahn-Waxler, C., & Goldsmith, H. H. (2007). Examining the familial link between positive affect and empathy development in the second year. *Journal of Genetic Psychology, 168,* 105–130. doi:10.3200/GNTP.168.2.105-130

Volling, B. L., & Belsky, J. (1991). Multiple determinants of father involvement during infancy in dual-earner and single-earner families. *Journal of Marriage and the Family, 53,* 461–474.

Volling, B. L., Mahoney, A., & Rauer, A. J. (2009). Sanctification of parenting, moral socialization, and young children's conscience development. *Psychology of Religion and Spirituality, 1,* 53–68. doi:10.1037/a0014958

von Bartheld, C. S., Bahney, J., & Herculano-Houzel, S. (2016). The search for true numbers of neurons and glial cells in the human brain: A review of 150 years of cell counting. *Journal of Comparative Neurology, 524*(18), 3865–3895. doi:10.1002/cne.24040

von der Lippe, A. L. (1999). The impact of maternal schooling and occupation on child-rearing attitudes and behaviours in low income neighbourhoods in Cairo, Egypt. *International Journal of Behavioral Development, 23,* 703–729. doi:10.1080/016502599383766

von Hofsten, C. (2004). An action perspective on motor development. *Trends in Cognitive Sciences, 8,* 266–272. doi:10.1016/j.tics.2004.04.002

von Hofsten, C. (2007). Action in development. *Developmental Science, 10,* 54–60. doi:10.1111/j.1467-7687.2007.00564.x

von Hofsten, C., Dahlström, E., & Fredriksson, Y. (2005). 12-month-old infants' perception of attention direction in static video images. *Infancy, 8,* 217–231. doi:10.1207/s15327078in0803_2

von Hofsten, C., Vishton, P., Spelke, E. S., Feng, Q., & Rosander, K. (1998). Predictive action in infancy: Tracking and reaching for moving objects. *Cognition, 67,* 255–285. doi:10.1016/S0010-0277(98)00029-8

von Stumm, S., Hell, B., & Chamorro-Premuzic, T. (2011). The hungry mind: Intellectual curiosity is the third pillar of academic performance. *Perspectives on Psychological Science, 6,* 574–588.

von Stumm, S., & Plomin, R. (2015). Breastfeeding and IQ growth from toddlerhood through adolescence. *PLoS ONE, 10*(9), e0138676. doi:10.1371/journal.pone.0138676

Vondra, J. I., Shaw, D. S., Swearingen, L., Cohen, M., & Owens, E. B. (2001). Attachment stability and emotional and behavioral regulation from infancy to preschool age. *Development and Psychopathology, 13,* 13–33.

Voos, A. C., Pelphrey, K. A., Tirrell, J., Bolling, D. Z., Vander Wyk, B., Kaiser, M. D., . . . Ventola, P. (2013). Neural mechanisms of improvements in social motivation after pivotal response treatment: Two case studies. *Journal of Autism and Developmental Disorders, 43,* 1–10. doi:10.1007/s10803-012-1683-9

Voss, W., Jungmann, T., Wachtendorf, M., & Neubauer, A. P. (2012). Long-term cognitive outcomes of extremely low-birth-weight infants: The influence of the maternal educational background. *Acta Paediatrica, 101*(6), 569–573.

Votruba-Drzal, E., Coley, R. L., & Chase-Lansdale, P. L. (2004). Child care and low-income children's development: Direct and moderated effects. *Child Development, 75,* 296–312. doi:10.1111/j.1467-8624.2004.00670.x

Vouloumanos, A., Hauser, M. D., Werker, J. F., & Martin, A. (2010). The tuning of human neonates' preference for speech. *Child Development, 81,* 517–527. doi:10.1111/j.1467-8624.2009.01412.x

Vouloumanos, A., & Werker, J. F. (2009). Infants' learning of novel words in a stochastic environment. *Developmental Psychology, 45,* 1611–1617.

Voyer, D., & Voyer, S. D. (2014). Gender differences in scholastic achievement: A meta-analysis. *Psychological Bulletin, 140,* 1174–1204.

Voyer, D., Voyer, S., & Bryden, M. P. (1995). Magnitude of sex differences in spatial abilities: A meta-analysis and consideration of critical variables. *Psychological Bulletin, 117,* 250–270.

Vukasović, T., & Bratko, D. (2015). Heritability of personality: A meta-analysis of behavior genetic studies. *Psychological Bulletin, 141*(4), 769.

Vukovic, R. K., Fuchs, L. S., Geary, D. C., Jordan, N. C., Gersten, R., & Siegler, R. S. (2014). Sources of individual differences in children's understanding of fractions. *Child Development, 85*(4), 1461–1476. doi:10.1111/cdev.12218

Vygotsky, L. S. (1962). *Thought and language* (E. Hanfmann & G. Vakar, Trans.). Cambridge, MA: MIT Press. (Original work published 1934)

Vygotsky, L. S. (1978). *Mind in society: The development of higher psychological processes* (M. Cole, V. John-Steiner, S. Scribner, & E. Souberman, Eds.). Cambridge, MA: Harvard University Press.

Wade, T. J., Cairney, J., & Pevalin, D. (2002). Emergence of gender differences in depression during adolescence: National panel results from three countries. *Journal of the American Academy of Child and Adolescent Psychiatry, 41,* 190–198. doi:10.1097/00004583-200202000-00013

Wadsworth, S. J., Corley, R., Plomin, R., Hewitt, J. K., & De Fries, J. C. (2006). Genetic and environment influences on continuity and change in reading achievement in the Colorado adoption project. In A. C. Huston & M. N. Ripke (Eds.), *Developmental contexts in middle childhood: Bridges to adolescence and adulthood* (pp. 87–106). New York, NY: Cambridge University Press

Wai, J., Lubinski, D., Benbow, C. P., & Steiger, J. H. (2010). Accomplishment in science, technology, engineering, and mathematics (STEM) and its relation to STEM educational dose: A 25-year longitudinal study. *Journal of Educational Psychology, 102,* 860–871. doi:10.1037/a0019454

Wai, J., Putallaz, M., & Makel, M. C. (2012). Studying intellectual outliers: Are there sex differences, and are the smart getting smarter? *Current Directions in Psychological Science, 21,* 382–390. doi:10.1177/0963721412455052

Wainryb, C., & Recchia, H. (2014). Moral lives across cultures: Heterogeneity and conflict. In M. Killen and J. G. Smetana (Eds.), *Handbook of moral development* (2nd ed., pp. 259–278). New York, NY: Psychology Press.

Wainright, J. L., & Patterson, C. J. (2006). Delinquency, victimization, and substance use among adolescents with female same-sex parents. *Journal of Family Psychology, 20,* 526–530. doi:10.1037/0893-3200.20.3.526

Wainright, J. L., & Patterson, C. J. (2008). Peer relations among adolescents with female same-sex parents. *Developmental Psychology, 44,* 117–126. doi:10.1037/0012-1649.44.1.117

Wainright, J. L., Russell, S. T., & Patterson, C. J. (2004). Psychosocial adjustment, school outcomes, and romantic relationships of adolescents with same-sex parents. *Child Development, 75,* 1886–1898. doi:10.1111/j.1467-8624.2004.00823.x

Wainryb, C., & Turiel, E. (1995). Diversity in social development: Between or within cultures? In M. Killen & D. Hart (Eds.), *Morality in everyday life: Developmental perspectives* (pp. 283–313). New York, NY: Cambridge University Press.

Wakefield, A. J., Murch, S. H., Anthony, A., Linnell, J., Casson, D. M., Malik, M., . . . Walker-Smith, J. A. (1998, February 28). Ileal-lymphoid-nodular hyperplasia, non-specific colitis, and pervasive developmental disorder in children. *The Lancet, 351,* 637–641. doi:10.1016/S0140-6736(97)11096-0 (Retraction published February 6, 2010, *The Lancet, 375,* p. 445)

Wakschlag, L. S., Gordon, R. A., Lahey, B. B., Loeber, R., Green, S. M., & Leventhal, B. L. (2000). Maternal age at first birth and boys' risk for conduct disorder. *Journal of Research on Adolescence, 10,* 417–441. doi:10.1207/SJRA1004_03

Waldman, I. D., Tackett, J. L., Van Hulle, C. A., Applegate, B., Pardini, D., Frick, P. J., & Lahey, B. B. (2011). Child and adolescent conduct disorder substantially shares genetic influences with three socioemotional dispositions. *Journal of Abnormal Psychology, 120,* 57–70. doi:10.1037/a0021351

Waldrip, A. M., Malcolm, K. T., & Jensen-Campbell, L. A. (2008). With a little help from your friends: The importance of high-quality friendships on early adolescent adjustment. *Social Development, 17,* 832–852. doi:10.1111/j.1467-9507.2008.00476.x

Walker, C. H. (1987). Relative importance of domain knowledge and overall aptitude on acquisition of domain-related information. *Cognition and Instruction, 4*(1), 25–42. doi:10.1207/s1532690xci0401_2

Walker, C. M., Walker, L. B., & Ganea, P. A. (2013). The role of symbol-based experience in early learning and transfer from pictures: Evidence from Tanzania. *Developmental Psychology, 49,* 1315–1324. doi:10.1037/a0029483

Walker, K., Taylor, E., McElroy, A., Phillip, D.-A., & Wilson, M. N. (1995). Familial and ecological correlates of self-esteem in African American children. In M. N. Wilson (Ed.), *New Directions for Child and Adolescent Development: No. 68. African American family life: Its structural and ecological aspects* (Vol. 1995, pp. 23–34). San Francisco, CA: Jossey-Bass.

Walker, P., Bremner, J. G., Mason, U., Spring, J., Mattock, K., Slater, A., & Johnson, S. P. (2010). Preverbal infants' sensitivity to synaesthetic cross-modality correspondences. *Psychological Science, 21,* 21–25.

Walker, S. (2009). Sociometric stability and the behavioral correlates of peer acceptance in early childhood. *Journal of Genetic Psychology, 170,* 339–358. doi:10.1080/00221320903218364

Walker-Andrews, A. S., & Dickson, L. R. (1997). Infants' understanding of affect. In S. Hala (Ed.), *The development of social cognition* (pp. 161–186). Hove, East Sussex, England: Psychology Press.

Wall, J. A., Power, T. G., & Arbona, C. (1993). Susceptibility to antisocial peer pressure and its relation to acculturation in Mexican–American adolescents. *Journal of Adolescent Research, 8,* 403–418. doi:10.1177/074355489384004

Walle, E. A., & Campos, J. J. (2014). The development of infant detection of inauthentic emotion. *Emotion, 14,* 488–503. doi:10.1037/a0035305

Wallerstein, J., & Lewis, J. M. (2007). Sibling outcomes and disparate parenting and step-parenting after divorce: Report from a 10-year longitudinal study. *Psychoanalytic Psychology, 24,* 445–458. doi:10.1037/0736-9735.24.3.445

Wallman, J. (1992). *Aping language.* Cambridge, England: Cambridge University Press.

Wang, D., Kato, N., Inaba, Y., Tango, T., Yoshida, Y., Kusaka, Y., . . . Zhang, Q. (2000). Physical and personality traits of preschool children in Fuzhou, China: Only child vs sibling. *Child: Care, Health and Development, 26,* 49–60. doi:10.1046/j.1365-2214.2000.00143.x

Wang, J.-L., Jackson, L. A., & Zhang, D.-J. (2011). The mediator role of self-disclosure and moderator roles of gender and social anxiety in the relationship between Chinese adolescents' online communication and their real-world social relationships. *Computers in Human Behavior, 27,* 2161–2168. doi:10.1016/j.chb.2011.06.010

Wang, M.-T., & Huguley, J. P. (2012). Parental racial socialization as a moderator of the effects of racial discrimination on educational success among African American adolescents. *Child Development, 83,* 1716–1731. doi:10.1111/j.1467-8624.2012.01808.x

Wang, Q. (2004). The emergence of cultural self-constructs: Autobiographical memory and self-description in European American and Chinese children. *Developmental Psychology, 40,* 3–15. doi:10.1037/0012-1649.40.1.3

Wang, Q. (2006). Earliest recollections of self and others in European American and Taiwanese young adults. *Psychological Science, 17,* 708–714. doi:10.1111/j.1467-9280.2006.01770.x

Wang, Q. (2013). *The autobiographical self in time and culture.* New York, NY: Oxford University Press.

Wang, Q., & Fivush, R. (2005). Mother–child conversations of emotionally salient events: Exploring the functions of emotional reminiscing in European-American and Chinese families. *Social Development, 14,* 473–495.

Wang, S., & Baillargeon, R. (2008). Can infants be "taught" to attend to a new physical variable in an event category? The case of height in covering events. *Cognitive Psychology, 56,* 284–326.

Wang, X., Chen, C., Wang, L., Chen, D., Guang, W., & French, J. (2003). Conception, early pregnancy loss, and time to clinical pregnancy: A population-based prospective study. *Fertility and Sterility, 79,* 577–584.

Ware, E. A., Uttal, D. H., Wetter, E. K., & DeLoache, J. S. (2006). Young children make scale errors when playing with dolls. *Developmental Science, 9,* 40–45. doi:10.1111/j.1467-7687.2005.00461.x

Warneken, F., Chen, F., & Tomasello, M. (2006). Cooperative activities in young children and chimpanzees. *Child Development, 77,* 640–663. doi:10.2307/3696552

Warneken, F., & Tomasello, M. (2007). Helping and cooperation at 14 months of age. *Infancy, 11,* 271–294. doi:10.1111/j.1532-7078.2007.tb00227.x

Warneken, F., & Tomasello, M. (2008). Extrinsic rewards undermine altruistic tendencies in 20-month-olds. *Developmental Psychology, 44,* 1785–1788. doi:10.1037/a0013860

Wassenaer-Leemhuis, A. G., Jeukens-Visser, M., Hus, J. W., Meijssen, D., Wolf, M. J., Kok, J. H., . . . Koldewijn, K. (2016). Rethinking preventive post-discharge intervention programmes for very preterm infants and their parents. *Developmental Medicine & Child Neurology, 58*(S4), 67–73.

Waterman, A. S. (1999). Issues of identity formation revisited: United States and The Netherlands. *Developmental Review, 19,* 462–479. doi:10.1006/drev.1999.0488

Waters, E., & Cummings, E. M. (2000). A secure base from which to explore close relationships. *Child Development, 71,* 164–172. doi:10.1111/1467-8624.00130

Waters, E., & Deane, K. E. (1985). Defining and assessing individual differences in attachment relationships: Q-methodology and the organization of behavior in infancy and early childhood. *Monographs of the Society for Research in Child Development, 50,* 41–65.

Waters, E., Merrick, S., Treboux, D., Crowell, J., & Albersheim, L. (2000). Attachment security in infancy and early adulthood: A twenty-year longitudinal study. *Child Development, 71,* 684–689.

Waters, H. S. (1980). "Class news": A single-subject longitudinal study of prose production and schema formation during childhood. *Journal of Verbal Learning and Verbal Behavior, 19,* 152–167.

Waters, H. S. (1989, April). *Problem-solving at two: A year-long naturalistic study of two children.* Paper presented at the biennial meeting of the Society for Research in Child Development, Kansas City, MO.

Watson, J. B. (1924). *Behaviorism.* New York, NY: Norton.

Watson, J. B. (1928). *Psychological care of infant and child.* New York, NY: Norton.

Watson, J. B., & Rayner, R. (1920). Conditioned emotional reactions. *Journal of Experimental Psychology, 3,* 1–14. doi:10.1037/h0069608

Watson-Gegeo, K. A., & Gegeo, D. W. (1986). Calling-out and repeating routines in Kwara'ae children's language socialization. In B. B. Schieffelin & E. Ochs (Eds.), *Studies in the social and cultural foundations of language: No. 3. Language socialization across cultures* (pp. 17–50). New York, NY: Cambridge University Press.

Watt, H. M. G. (2006). The role of motivation in gendered educational and occupational trajectories related to maths. *Educational Research and Evaluation, 12,* 305–322. doi:10.1080/13803610600765562

Watts, T. W., Duncan, G. J., Chen, M., Claessens, A., Davis-Kean, P. E., Duckworth, P., . . . Susperreguy, M. I. (2015). The role of mediators in the development of longitudinal mathematics achievement associations. *Child Development, 86*(6), 1892–1907, doi:10.1111/cdev.12416

Waxman, S. R. (1990). Linguistic biases and the establishment of conceptual hierarchies: Evidence from preschool children. *Cognitive Development, 5,* 123–150. doi:10.1016/0885-2014(90)90023-M

Waxman, S. R., Fu, X., Ferguson, B., Geraghty, K., Leddon, E., Liang, J., & Zhao, M. F. (2016). How early is infants' attention to objects and actions shaped by culture? New evidence from 24-month-olds raised in the U.S. and China. *Frontiers in Psychology, 7,* 97. doi:10.3389/fpsyg.2016.00097

Waxman, S. R., & Hall, D. G. (1993). The development of a linkage between count nouns and object categories: Evidence from fifteen- to twenty-one-month-old infants. *Child Development, 64,* 1224–1241. doi:10.1111/j.1467-8624.1993.tb04197.x

Waxman, S. R., & Markow, D. B. (1995). Words as invitations to form categories: Evidence from 12- to 13-month-old infants. *Cognitive Psychology, 29,* 257–302. doi:10.1006/cogp.1995.1016

Waxman, S. R., & Markow, D. B. (1998). Object properties and object kind: Twenty-one-month-old infants' extension of novel adjectives. *Child Development, 69,* 1313–1329.

Waxman, S. R., & Senghas, A. (1992). Relations among word meanings in early lexical development. *Developmental Psychology, 28,* 862–873.

Way, N., & Greene, M. L. (2006). Trajectories of perceived friendship quality during adolescence: The patterns and contextual predictors. *Journal of Research on Adolescence, 16,* 293–320. doi:10.1111/j.1532-7795.2006.00133.x

Webster-Stratton, C. (1998). Preventing conduct problems in Head Start children: Strengthening parenting competencies. *Journal of Consulting and Clinical Psychology, 66,* 715–730. doi:10.1037/0022-006X.66.5.715

Weems, C. F., & Silverman, W. K. (2013). Anxiety disorders. In T. P. Beauchaine &

S. P. Hinshaw (Eds.). *Child and adolescent psychopathology* (2nd ed., pp. 513–541). Hoboken, NJ: Wiley.

Weems, C. F., Taylor, L. K., Cannon, M. F., Marino, R. C., Romano, D. M., Scott, B. G., . . . Triplett, V. (2010). Post traumatic stress, context, and the lingering effects of the Hurricane Katrina disaster among ethnic minority youth. *Journal of Abnormal Child Psychology, 38,* 49–56. doi:10.1007/s10802-009-9352-y

Wegge, D., Vandebosch, H., Eggermont, S., & Pabian, S. (2016). Popularity through online harm: The longitudinal associations between cyberbullying and sociometric status in early adolescence. *Journal of Early Adolescence, 36,* 86–107. doi:10.1177/0272431614556351

Weigelt, S., Koldewyn, K., & Kanwisher, N. (2013). Face recognition deficits in autism spectrum disorders are both domain specific and process specific. *PloS One, 8*(9), e74541. doi:10.1371/journal.pone.0074541

Weinberg, M. K., & Tronick, E. Z. (1994). Beyond the face: An empirical study of infant affective configurations of facial, vocal, gestural, and regulatory behaviors. *Child Development, 65,* 1503–1515.

Weinburgh, M. (1995). Gender differences in student attitudes toward science: A meta-analysis of the literature from 1970 to 1991. *Journal of Research in Science Teaching, 32,* 387–398.

Weinraub, M., Bender, R. H., Friedman, S. L., Susman, E. J., Knoke, B., Bradley, R., . . . Williams, J. (2012). Patterns of developmental change in infants' nighttime sleep awakenings from 6 through 36 months of age. *Developmental Psychology, 48*(6), 1511–1528.

Weinstein, S. M., Mermelstein, R. J., Hankin, B. L., Hedeker, D., & Flay, B. R. (2007). Longitudinal patterns of daily affect and global mood during adolescence. *Journal of Research on Adolescence, 17,* 587–600. doi:10.1111/j.1532-7795.2007.00536.x

Weis, R., & Cerankosky, B. C. (2010). Effects of video-game ownership on young boys' academic and behavioral functioning: A randomized, controlled study. *Psychological Science, 21,* 463–470. doi:10.1177/0956797610362670

Weisleder, A., & Fernald, A. (2013). Talking to children matters: Early language experience strengthens processing and builds vocabulary. *Psychological Science, 24*(11), 2143–2152.

Weiss, B., Dodge, K. A., Bates, J. E., & Pettit, G. S. (1992). Some consequences of early harsh discipline: Child aggression and a maladaptive social information processing style. *Child Development, 63,* 1321–1335. doi:10.2307/1131558

Weissman, M. D., & Kalish, C. W. (1999). The inheritance of desired characteristics: Children's view of the role of intention in parent–offspring resemblance. *Journal of Experimental Child Psychology, 73,* 245–265. doi:10.1006/jecp.1999.2505

Wellman, H. M., Cross, D., & Watson, J. (2001). Meta-analysis of theory-of-mind development: The truth about false belief. *Child Development, 72,* 655–684. doi:10.1111/1467-8624.00304

Wellman, H. M., & Gelman, S. A. (1998). Knowledge acquisition in foundational domains. In W. Damon (Series Ed.) & D. Kuhn & R. S. Siegler (Vol. Eds.), *Handbook of child psychology: Vol. 2. Cognition, perception, and language* (5th ed., pp. 523–573). Hoboken, NJ: Wiley.

Wentzel, K. R. (2003). Sociometric status and adjustment in middle school: A longitudinal study. *Journal of Early Adolescence, 23,* 5–28. doi:10.1177/0272431602239128

Wentzel, K. R. (2009). Peers and academic functioning at school. In K. H. Rubin, W. M. Bukowski, & B. Laursen (Eds.), *Handbook of peer interactions, relationships, and groups* (pp. 531–547). New York, NY: Guilford Press.

Wentzel, K. R., & Asher, S. R. (1995). The academic lives of neglected, rejected, popular, and controversial children. *Child Development, 66,* 754–763. doi:10.2307/1131948

Wentzel, K. R., & Caldwell, K. (1997). Friendships, peer acceptance, and group membership: Relations to academic achievement in middle school. *Child Development, 68,* 1198–1209. doi:10.1111/j.1467-8624.1997.tb01994.x

Werchan, D. M., & Gómez, R. L. (2014). Wakefulness (not sleep) promotes generalization of word learning in 2.5-year-old children. *Child Development, 85*(2), 429–436. doi:10.1111/cdev.12149

Werker, J. F. (1989, January-February). Becoming a native listener. *American Scientist, 77,* 54–59.

Werker, J. F., & Lalonde, C. E. (1988). Cross-language speech perception: Initial capabilities and developmental change. *Developmental Psychology, 24,* 672–683.

Werker, J. F., Pegg, J. E., & McLeod, P. J. (1994). A cross-language investigation of infant preference for infant-directed communication. *Infant Behavior and Development, 17,* 323–333. doi:10.1016/0163-6383(94)90012-4

Werker, J. F., & Tees, R. C. (1984). Cross-language speech perception: Evidence for perceptual reorganization during the first year of life. *Infant Behavior and Development, 7,* 49–63. doi:10.1016/S0163-6383(84)80022-3

Werner, E. (2005). Resilience and recovery: Findings from the Kauai longitudinal study. *Focal Point: Research, Policy, and Practice in Children's Mental Health: Resilience and Recovery, 19*(1), 11–14. Retrieved from http://www.pathwaysrtc.pdx.edu/publications?terms=Werner%2C+Resilience+and+recovery&transition=on&author=&year1=&year2=&pubtype=&hide=hide

Werner, E. E. (1989, April). Children of the Garden Island. *Scientific American, 260*(4), 106–108, 108D, 110–111.

Werner, N. E., & Crick, N. R. (2004). Maladaptive peer relationships and the development of relational and physical aggression during middle childhood. *Social Development, 13,* 495–514. doi:10.1111/j.1467-9507.2004.00280.x

Werner, N. E., & Hill, L. G. (2010). Individual and peer group normative beliefs about relational aggression. *Child Development, 81,* 826–836. doi:10.1111/j.1467-8624.2010.01436.x

West, J., Denton, K., & Germino-Hausken, E. (2000). *America's kindergartners* (NCES 2000-070). Washington, DC: U.S. Department of Education, National Center for Education Statistics.

West, M. J., & Rheingold, H. L. (1978). Infant stimulation of maternal instruction. *Infant Behavior and Development, 1,* 205–215. doi:10.1016/S0163-6383(78)80031-9

Westinghouse Learning Corporation. (1969). *The impact of Head Start: An evaluation of the effects of Head Start on children's cognitive and affective development.* Springfield, VA: Clearing house for Federal Scientific & Technical Information.

Wethington, H., Pan, L., & Sherry, B. (2013). The association of screen time, television in the bedroom, and obesity among school-aged youth: 2007 National Survey of Children's Health. *Journal of School Health, 83*(8), 573–581.

White, B. L. (1985). *The first three years of life* (Rev. ed.). New York, NY: Prentice-Hall.

White, E. B. (1952). *Charlotte's web.* New York, NY: Harper & Brothers.

White, L. K., Lamm, C., Helfinstein, S. M., & Fox, N. A. (2012). Neurobiology and neurochemistry of temperament in children. In M. R. Zentner & R. L. Shiner (Eds.), *Handbook of temperament* (pp. 347–367). New York, NY: Guilford Press.

The White House, Office of the White House Press Secretary. (2015). *Remarks by the President in State of the Union Address: January 20, 2015.* Retrieved from https://www.whitehouse.gov/the-press-office/2015/01/20/remarks-president-state-union-address-january-20-2015

Whitehurst, G. J., & Lonigan, C. J. (1998). Child development and emergent literacy. *Child Development, 69,* 848–872.

Whitehurst, G. J., Zevenbergen, A. A., Crone, D. A., Schultz, M. D., Velting, O. N., & Fischel, J. E. (1999). Outcomes of an emergent literacy intervention from Head Start through second grade. *Journal of Educational Psychology, 91,* 261–272.

Whitesell, N. R., & Harter, S. (1996). The interpersonal context of emotion: Anger with close friends and classmates. *Child Development, 67,* 1345–1359.

Whiteside, M. F., & Becker, B. J. (2000). Parental factors and the young child's postdivorce adjustment: A meta-analysis with implications for parenting arrangements. *Journal of Family Psychology, 14,* 5–26. doi:10.1037/0893-3200.14.1.5

Whiting, B. B., & Edwards, C. P. (1988). *Children of different worlds: The formation of social behavior.* Cambridge, MA: Harvard University Press.

Whiting, B. B., & Whiting, J. W. (1975). *Children of six cultures: A psycho-cultural analysis.* Cambridge, MA: Harvard University Press.

Whitley, B. E. (1997). Gender differences in computer-related attitudes and behavior: A meta-analysis. Computers in *Human Behavior, 13,* 1–22. doi:10.1016/S0747-5632(96)00026-X

Whitney, M. P., & Thoman, E. B. (1994). Sleep in premature and fullterm infants from 24-hour home recordings. *Infant Behavior and Development, 17,* 223–234. doi:10.1016/0163-6383(94)90001-9

Wichstrom, L. (1999). The emergence of gender difference in depressed mood during adolescence: The role of intensified gender socialization. *Developmental Psychology, 35,* 232–245.

Widen, S. C., & Naab, P. (2012). Can an anger face also be scared? Malleability of facial expressions. *Emotion, 12,* 919–925.

Widen, S. C., & Russell, J. A. (2003). A closer look at preschoolers' freely produced labels for facial expressions. *Developmental Psychology, 39,* 114–127.

Widen, S. C., & Russell, J. A. (2010a). Children's scripts for social emotions: Causes and consequences are more central than are facial expressions. *British Journal of Developmental Psychology, 28,* 565–581.

Widen, S. C., & Russell, J. A. (2010b). Descriptive and prescriptive definitions of emotion. *Emotion Review, 2,* 377–378.

Widen, S. C., & Russell, J. A. (2013). Children's recognition of disgust in others. *Psychological Bulletin, 139,* 271–299. doi:10.1037/a0031640

Wiesel, T. N., & Hubel, D. H. (1963). Single-cell responses in striate cortex of kittens deprived of vision in one eye. *Journal of Neurophysiology, 26*(6), 1003–1017.

Wiesen, S. E., Watkins, R. M., & Needham, A. W. (2016). Active motor training has long-term effects on infants' object exploration. *Frontiers in Psychology, 7,* 599. doi:10.3389/fpsyg.2016.00599

Wiesenfeld, A. R., Malatesta, C. Z., & Deloach, L. L. (1981). Differential parental response to familiar and unfamiliar infant distress signals. *Infant Behavior and Development, 4,* 281–295.

Wigfield, A., Eccles, J. S., Schiefele, U., Rosser, R. W., & Davis-Kean, P. (2006). Development of achievement motivation. In W. Damon & R. M. Lerner (Series Eds.) & N. Eisenberg (Vol. Ed.), *Handbook of child psychology: Vol. 3. Social, emotional, and personality development* (6th ed., pp. 933–1002). Hoboken, NJ: Wiley.

Wilgenbusch, T., & Merrell, K. W. (1999). Gender differences in self-concept among children and adolescents: A meta-analysis of multidimensional studies. *School Psychology Quarterly, 14,* 101–120. doi:10.1037/h0089000

Wilk, S. L., Desmarais, L. B., & Sackett, P. R. (1995). Gravitation of jobs commensurate with ability: Longitudinal and cross-sectional tests. *Journal of Applied Psychology, 80,* 79–85.

Williams, T., Connolly, J., Pepler, D., & Craig, W. (2005). Peer victimization, social support, and psychosocial adjustment of sexual minority adolescents. *Journal of Youth and Adolescence, 34,* 471–482. doi:10.1007/s10964-005-7264-x

Willinger, M. (1995). SIDS prevention. *Pediatric Annals, 24,* 358–364.

Willis, C. (2009). *Teaching infants, toddlers, and twos with special needs.* Beltsville, MD: Gryphon House.

Wilson, B. J. (2008). Media violence and aggression in youth. In S. Calvert & B. Wilson (Eds.), *The handbook of children, media, and development* (pp. 237–267). West Sussex, England: Blackwell.

Wilson, B. J., Kunkel, D., Linz, D., Potter, J., Donnerstein, E., Smith, S., . . . Gray, T. (1997). Television violence and its context: University of California, Santa Barbara study. In J. Federman (Ed.), *National television violence study* (Vol. 1, pp. 3–268). Thousand Oaks, CA: Sage.

Wilson, E. O. (1975). *Sociobiology: The new synthesis.* Cambridge, MA: Belknap Press of Harvard University Press.

Wilson, M., & Brooks-Gunn, J. (2001). Health status and behaviors of unwed fathers. *Children and Youth Services Review, 23,* 377–401. doi:10.1016/S0190-7409(01)00138-4

Wilson, T. D., & Dunn, E. W. (2004). Self-knowledge: Its limits, value, and potential for improvement. *Annual Review of Psychology, 55,* 493–518. doi:10.1146/annurev. psych.55.090902.141954

Winner, E. (1996). *Gifted children: Myths and realities.* New York, NY: Basic Books.

Winsler, A., De Leon, J. R., Wallace, B. A., Carlton, M. P., & Willson-Quayle, A. (2003). Private speech in preschool children: Developmental stability and change, across-task consistency, and relations with classroom behaviour. *Journal of Child Language, 30,* 583–608.

Winter, T. F. (2010, May 10). The government should stop kids from buying violent video games. *U.S. News and World Report.* Retrieved from http://www.usnews.com/opinion/articles/2010/05/10/7twotakesprocopy

Wismer Fries, A. B., Shirtcliff, E. A., & Pollak, S. D. (2008). Neuroendocrine dysregulation following early social deprivation in children. *Developmental Psychobiology, 50,* 588–599.

Wismer Fries, A. B., Ziegler, T. E., Kurian, J. R., Jacoris, S., & Pollak, S. D. (2005). Early experience in humans is associated with changes in neuropeptides critical for regulating social behavior. *Proceedings of the National Academy of Sciences, 102*(47), 17237–17240.

Witherington, D. C., Campos, J. J., Harriger, J. A., Bryan, C., & Margett, T. E. (2010). Emotion and its development in infancy. In J. G. Bremner & T. D. Wachs (Eds.), *The Wiley-Blackwell Handbook of Infant Development* (2nd edition, Vol. 1, pp. 569–591). Malden, MA: Blackwell.

Witherington, D. C., Campos, J. J., & Hertenstein, M. J. (2008). Principles of emotion and its development in infancy. In J. G. Bremner & A. Fogel (Eds.), *Blackwell handbook of infant development* (pp. 427–464). Malden, MA: Blackwell.

Witherington, D. C., & Crichton, J. A. (2007). Frameworks for understanding emotions and their development: Functionalist and dynamic systems approaches. *Emotion, 7*, 628–637. doi:10.1037/1528-3542.7.3.628

Witherspoon, D., Schotland, M., Way, N., & Hughes, D. (2009). Connecting the dots: How connectedness to multiple contexts influences the psychological and academic adjustment of urban youth. *Applied Developmental Science, 13*, 199–216. doi:10.1080/10888690903288755

Witkowska, E., & Gådin, K. G. (2005). Have you been sexually harassed in school? What female high school students regard as harassment. *International Journal of Adolescent Medicine and Health, 17*, 391–406. doi:10.1515/IJAMH.2005.17.4.391

Witt, S. D. (2000). The influence of peers on children's socialization to gender roles. *Early Child Development & Care, 162*, 1–7.

Witt, W. P., Wisk, L. E., Cheng, E. R., Mandell, K., Chatterjee, D., Wakeel, F., . . . Zarak, D. (2015). Determinants of cesarean delivery in the U.S.: A lifecourse approach. *Maternal and Child Health Journal, 19*(1), 84–93.

Wittmann, B. C., Daw, N. D., Seymour, B., & Dolan, R. J. (2008). Striatal activity underlies novelty-based choice in humans. *Neuron, 58*, 967–973. doi:10.1016/j.neuron.2008.04.027

Witvliet, M., Brendgen, M., van Lier, P. A., Koot, H. M., & Vitaro, F. (2010). Early adolescent depressive symptoms: Prediction from clique isolation, loneliness, and perceived social acceptance. *Journal of Abnormal Child Psychology, 38*, 1045–1056. doi:10.1007/s10802-010-9426-x

Witvliet, M., Olthof, T., Hoeksma, J. B., Goossens, F. A., Smits, M. S. I., & Koot, H. M. (2010). Peer group affiliation of children: The role of perceived popularity, likeability, and behavioral similarity in bullying. *Social Development, 19*, 285–303. doi:10.1111/j.1467-9507.2009.00544.x

Wolitzky-Taylor, K. B., Ruggiero, K. J., Danielson, C. K., Resnick, H. S., Hanson, R. F., Smith, D. W., . . . Kilpatrick, D. G. (2008). Prevalence and correlates of dating violence in a national sample of adolescents. *Journal of the American Academy of Child and Adolescent Psychiatry, 47*, 755–762. doi:10.1097/CHI.0b013e318172ef5f

Wolpert, L. (1991). *The triumph of the embryo.* Oxford, England: Oxford University Press.

Wong, C. F., Clark, L. F., & Marlotte, L. (2016). The impact of specific and complex trauma on the mental health of homeless youth. *Journal of Interpersonal Violence, 31*, 831–854. doi:10.1177/0886260514556770

Wong, P. C., Skoe, E., Russo, N. M., Dees, T., & Kraus, N. (2007). Musical experience shapes human brainstem encoding of linguistic pitch patterns. *Nature Neuroscience, 10*(4), 420–422.

Wood, D., Bruner, J. S., & Ross, G. (1976). The role of tutoring in problem solving. *Journal of Child Psychology and Psychiatry, and Allied Disciplines, 17*, 89–100.

Wood, W., & Eagly, A. H. (2002). A cross-cultural analysis of the behavior of women and men: Implications for the origins of sex differences. *Psychological Bulletin, 128*, 699–727. doi:10.1037/0033-2909.128.5.699

Wood, W., & Eagly, A. H. (2012). Biosocial constructions of sex differences and similarities in behavior. In J. M. Olson & M. P. Zanna (Eds.), *Advances in experimental social psychology* (Vol. 46, pp. 55–123). San Diego, CA: Academic Press.

Woodhouse, S. S., Dykas, M. J., & Cassidy, J. (2012). Loneliness and peer relations in adolescence. *Social Development, 21*, 273–293. doi:10.1111/j.1467-9507.2011.00611.x

Woodward, A. L. (1998). Infants selectively encode the goal object of an actor's reach. *Cognition, 69*, 1–34. doi:10.1016/S0010-0277(98)00058-4

Woodward, A. L., & Hoyne, K. L. (1999). Infants' learning about words and sounds in relation to objects. *Child Development, 70*, 65–77.

Woodward, A. L., & Markman, E. M. (1998). Early word learning. In W. Damon (Series Ed.) & D. Kuhn & R. S. Siegler (Vol. Eds.), *Handbook of child psychology: Vol. 2. Cognition, perception, and language* (5th ed., pp. 371–420). Hoboken, NJ: Wiley.

Woodward, L. J., & Fergusson, D. M. (1999). Childhood peer relationship problems and psychosocial adjustment in late adolescence. *Journal of Abnormal Child Psychology, 27*, 87–104. doi:10.1023/A:1022618608802

Woolley, J. D. (1997). Thinking about fantasy: Are children fundamentally different thinkers and believers from adults? *Child Development, 68*, 991–1011. doi:10.1111/j.1467-8624.1997.tb01975.x

Woolley, J. D., Cornelius, C. A., & Lacy, W. (2011). Developmental changes in the use of supernatural explanations for unusual events. *Journal of Cognition and Culture, 11*(3–4), 311–337. doi:10.1163/156853711X591279

Woolley, J. D., & Phelps, K. E. (1994). Young children's practical reasoning about imagination. *British Journal of Developmental Psychology, 12*, 53–67. doi:10.1111/j.2044-835X.1994.tb00618.x

World Health Organization. (2014). Commission on ending childhood obesity: Facts and figures on childhood obesity. Retrieved July 6, 2016, from http://www.who.int/end-childhood-obesity/facts/en/

World Health Organization. (2016). Media center fact sheet: Obesity and overweight. Retrieved July 6, 2016, from http://www.who.int/mediacentre/factsheets/fs311/en/

Worobey, J., & Worobey, H. S. (2014). Body-size stigmatization by preschool girls: In a doll's world, it is good to be "Barbie." *Body image, 11*(2), 171–174.

Wynn, K. (1992, August 27). Addition and subtraction by human infants. *Nature, 358*, 749–750. doi:10.1038/358749a0

Wynn, K. (2008). Some innate foundations of social and moral cognition. In P. Carruthers, S. Laurence, & S. Stich (Eds.), *The innate mind: Foundations and the future* (pp. 330–347). Oxford, England: Oxford University Press.

Xie, H., Drabick, D. A. G., & Chen, D. (2011). Developmental trajectories of aggression from late childhood through adolescence: Similarities and differences across gender. *Aggressive Behavior, 37*, 387–404. doi:10.1002/ab.20404

Xu, F., & Arriaga, R. I. (2007). Number discrimination in 10-month-old infants. *British Journal of Developmental Psychology, 25*, 103–108.

Xu, F., & Denison, S. (2009). Statistical inference and sensitivity to sampling in 11-month-old infants. *Cognition, 112*, 97–104. doi:10.1016/j.cognition.2009.04.006

Xu, F., & Garcia, V. (2008). Intuitive statistics by 8-month-old infants. *Proceedings of the National Academy of Sciences of the United States of America, 105*, 5012–5015. doi:10.1073/pnas.0704450105

Xu, F., & Kushnir, T. (2013). Infants are rational constructivist learners. *Current Directions in Psychological Science, 22*, 28–32. doi:10.1177/0963721412469396

Xu, F., & Pinker, S. (1995). Weird past tense forms. *Journal of Child Language, 22*, 531–556.

Xu, F., & Spelke, E. S. (2000). Large number discrimination in 6-month-old infants. *Cognition, 74*, B1-B11.

Xu, Y., Farver, J. A. M., Schwartz, D., & Chang, L. (2004). Social networks and aggressive behaviour in Chinese children. *International Journal of Behavioral Development, 28*, 401–410. doi:10.1080/01650250444000090

Xu, Y., Farver, J. A. M., & Zhang, Z. (2009). Temperament, harsh and indulgent parenting, and Chinese children's proactive and reactive aggression. *Child Development, 80,* 244–258. doi:10.1111/j.1467-8624.2008.01257.x

Xue, Y., & Meisels, S. J. (2004). Early literacy instruction and learning in kindergarten: Evidence from the Early Childhood Longitudinal Study—Kindergarten Class of 1998–1999. *American Educational Research Journal, 41,* 191–229.

Yamada, H. (2009). Japanese children's reasoning about conflicts with parents. *Social Development, 18,* 962–977. doi:10.1111/j.1467-9507.2008.00492.x

Yamagata, K. (1997). Representational activity during mother–child interaction: The scribbling stage of drawing. *British Journal of Developmental Psychology, 15,* 355–366. doi:10.1111/j.2044-835X.1997.tb00526.x

Yaman, A., Mesman, J., van IJzendoorn, M. H., & Bakermans–Kranenburg, M. J. (2010). Parenting and toddler aggression in second-generation immigrant families: The moderating role of child temperament. *Journal of Family Psychology, 24,* 208–211. doi:10.1037/a0019100

Yang, J., Kanazawa, S., Yamaguchi, M. K., & Kuriki, I. (2016). Cortical response to categorical color perception in infants investigated by near-infrared spectroscopy. *Proceedings of the National Academy of Sciences, 113*(9), 2370–2375.

Yang, S.-J., Stewart, R., Kim, J.-M., Kim, S.-W., Shin, I.-S., Dewey, M., . . . Yoon, J.-S. (2013). Differences in predictors of traditional and cyber-bullying: A 2-year longitudinal study in Korean school children. *European Child and Adolescent Psychiatry, 22,* 309–318. doi:10.1007/s00787-012-0374-6

Yang, Y. T., Mello, M. M., Subramanian, S. V., & Studdert, D. M. (2009). Relationship between malpractice litigation pressure and rates of cesarean section and vaginal birth after cesarean section. *Medical Care, 47,* 234–242. doi:10.1097/MLR.0b013e31818475de

Yarrow, M. R., Scott, P. M., & Zahn-Waxler, C. Z. (1973). Learning concern for others. *Developmental Psychology, 8,* 240–260. doi:10.1037/h0034159

Yates, M., & Youniss, J. (1996). A developmental perspective on community service in adolescence. *Social Development, 5,* 85–111. doi:10.1111/j.1467-9507.1996.tb00073.x

Yau, J., Smetana, J. G., & Metzger, A. (2009). Young Chinese children's authority concepts. *Social Development, 18,* 210–229. doi:10.1111/j.1467-9507.2008.00463.x

Yavorsky, J. E., Kamp Dush, C. M., & Schoppe-Sullivan, S. J. (2015). The production of inequality: The gender division of labor across the transition to parenthood. *Journal of Marriage and Family, 77*(3), 662–679. doi:10.1111/jomf.12189

Ybarra, M. L., & Mitchell, K. J. (2007). Prevalence and frequency of internet harassment instigation: Implications for adolescent health. *Journal of Adolescent Health, 41,* 189–195. doi:10.1016/j.jadohealth.2007.03.005

Yeager, D. S., Miu, A. S., Powers, J., & Dweck, C. S. (2013). Implicit theories of personality and attributions of hostile intent: A meta-analysis, an experiment, and a longitudinal intervention. *Child Development, 84,* 1651–1667. doi:10.1111/cdev.12062

Yeates, K. O., & Selman, R. L. (1989). Social competence in the schools: Toward an integrative developmental model for intervention. *Developmental Review, 9,* 64–100. doi:10.1016/0273-2297(89)90024-5

Yonas, A., Cleaves, W. T., & Pettersen, L. (1978). Development of sensitivity to pictorial depth. *Science, 200,* 77–79.

Yonas, A., Elieff, C. A., & Arterberry, M. E. (2002). Emergence of sensitivity to pictorial depth cues: Charting development in individual infants. *Infant Behavior and Development, 25,* 495–514. doi:10.1016/S0163-6383(02)00147-9

Yonkers, K. A., Blackwell, K. A., Glover, J., & Forray, A. (2014). Antidepressant use in pregnant and postpartum women. *Annual Review of Clinical Psychology, 10,* 369–392.

Yoshikawa, H., Aber, J. L., & Beardslee, W. R. (2012). The effects of poverty on the mental, emotional, and behavioral health of children and youth: Implications for prevention. *American Psychologist, 67*(4), 272–284. doi:10.1037/a0028015

Young, C. B., Wu, S. S., & Menon, V. (2012). The neurodevelopmental basis of math anxiety. *Psychological Science, 23,* 492–501. doi:10.1177/0956797611429134

Young, S. K., Fox, N. A., & Zahn-Waxler, C. (1999). The relations between temperament and empathy in 2-year-olds. *Developmental Psychology, 35,* 1189–1197. doi:10.1037/0012-1649.35.5.1189

Youngblade, L. M., & Belsky, J. (1992). Parent–child antecedents of 5-year-olds' close friendships: A longitudinal analysis. *Developmental Psychology, 28,* 700–713. doi:10.1037/0012-1649.28.4.700

Youngblade, L. M., & Dunn, J. (1995). Individual differences in young children's pretend play with mother and sibling: Links to relationships and understanding of other people's feelings and beliefs. *Child Development, 66,* 1472–1492. doi:10.1111/j.1467-8624.1995.tb00946.x

Youniss, J., & Smollar, J. (1985). *Adolescent relations with mothers, fathers, and friends.* Chicago, IL: University of Chicago Press.

Yuan, S., & Fisher, C. (2009). "Really? She blicked the baby?": Two-year-olds learn combinatorial facts about verbs by listening. *Psychological Science, 20,* 619–626. doi:10.1111/j.1467-9280.2009.02341.x

Yuill, N., & Perner, J. (1988). Intentionality and knowledge in children's judgments of actor's responsibility and recipient's emotional reaction. *Developmental Psychology, 24,* 358–365. doi:10.1037/0012-1649.24.3.358

Zachrisson, H. D., Dearing, E., Lekhal, R., & Toppelberg, C. O. (2013). Little evidence that time in child care causes externalizing problems during early childhood in Norway. *Child Development, 84,* 1152–1170. doi:10.1111/cdev.12040

Zadnik, K., Jones, L. A., Irvin, B. C., Kleinstein, R. N., Manny, R. E., Shin, J. A., & Mutti, D. O. (2000, March 9). Myopia and ambient night-time lighting. *Nature, 404,* 143–144. doi:10.1038/35004661

Zahn-Waxler, C., Friedman, R. J., Cole, P. M., Mizuta, I., & Hiruma, N. (1996). Japanese and United States preschool children's responses to conflict and distress. *Child Development, 67,* 2462–2477.

Zahn-Waxler, C., Radke-Yarrow, M., & King, R. A. (1979). Child rearing and children's prosocial initiations toward victims of distress. *Child Development, 50,* 319–330. doi:10.2307/1129406

Zahn-Waxler, C., Radke-Yarrow, M., Wagner, E., & Chapman, M. (1992). Development of concern for others. *Developmental Psychology, 28,* 126–136. doi:10.1037/0012-1649.28.1.126

Zahn-Waxler, C., & Robinson, J. (1995). Empathy and guilt: Early origins of feelings of responsibility. In J. P. Tangney & K. W. Fischer (Eds.), *Self-conscious emotions: The psychology of shame, guilt, embarrassment, and pride* (pp. 143–173). New York, NY: Guilford Press.

Zakay, D. (1992). The role of attention in children's time perception. *Journal of Experimental Child Psychology, 54,* 355–371.

Zakay, D. (1993). The roles of non-temporal information processing load and temporal expectations in children's prospective time estimation. *Acta Psychologica, 84,* 271–280.

Zani, B. (1991). Male and female patterns in the discovery of sexuality during adolescence. *Journal of Adolescence, 14,* 163–178. doi:10.1016/0140-1971(91)90029-Q

Zarbatany, L., McDougall, P., & Hymel, S. (2000). Gender-differentiated experience in the peer culture: Links to intimacy in pre-adolescence. *Social Development, 9,* 62–79. doi:10.1111/1467-9507.00111

Zatorre, R. J., & Belin, P. (2001). Spectral and temporal processing in human auditory cortex. *Cerebral Cortex, 11,* 946–953.

Zatorre, R. J., Belin, P., & Penhune, V. B. (2002). Structure and function of auditory cortex: Music and speech. *Trends in Cognitive Sciences, 6,* 37–46.

Zatorre, R. J., Evans, A. C., Meyer, E., & Gjedde, A. (1992, May 8). Lateralization of phonetic and pitch discrimination in speech processing. *Science, 256,* 846–849.

Zelazo, P. D., & Carlson, S. M. (2012). Hot and cool executive function in childhood and adolescence: Development and plasticity. *Child Development Perspectives, 6*(4), 354–360. doi:10.1111/j.1750-8606.2012.00246.x

Zelazo, P. D., Reznick, J. S., & Spinazzola, J. (1998). Representational flexibility and response control in a multistep multilocation search task. *Developmental Psychology, 34,* 203–214.

Zelazo, P. R., Zelazo, N. A., & Kolb, S. (1972, April 21). "Walking" in the newborn. *Science, 176,* 314–315.

Zeman, J., & Garber, J. (1996). Display rules for anger, sadness, and pain: It depends on who is watching. *Child Development, 67,* 957–973.

Zentner, M. R., & Kagan, J. (1996, September 5). Perception of music by infants [Letter to the editor]. *Nature, 383,* 29. doi:10.1038/383029a0

Zentner, M. R., & Kagan, J. (1998). Infants' perception of consonance and dissonance in music. *Infant Behavior and Development, 21,* 483–492. doi:10.1016/S0163-6383(98)90021-2

Zevalkink, J., Riksen-Walraven, J. M., & Van Lieshout, C. F. (1999). Attachment in the Indonesian caregiving context. *Social Development, 8,* 21–40.

Zevenbergen, A. A., & Whitehurst, G. J. (2003). Dialogic reading: A shared picture book reading intervention for preschoolers. In A. van Kleeck, S. A. Stahl, & E. B. Bauer (Eds.), *On reading books to children: Parents and teachers* (pp. 177–200). Mahwah, NJ: Erlbaum.

Zevin, J. D., Datta, H., & Skipper, J. I. (2012). Sensitive periods for language and recovery from stroke: Conceptual and practical parallels. *Developmental Psychobiology, 54,* 332–342. doi:10.1002/dev.20626

Zhai, F., Brooks-Gunn, J., & Waldfogel, J. (2011). Head Start and urban children's school readiness: A birth cohort study in 18 cities. *Developmental Psychology, 47,* 134–152. doi:10.1037/a0020784

Zhang, S. (1997). Investigation of behavior problem of only child in kindergarten children in a Beijing urban area. *International Medical Journal, 4,* 117–118.

Zhang, T.-Y., & Meaney, M. J. (2010). Epigenetics and the environmental regulation of the genome and its function. *Annual Review of Psychology, 61,* 439–466. doi:10.1146/annurev.psych.60.110707.163625

Zhao, T. C., & Kuhl, P. K. (2016). Musical intervention enhances infants' neural processing of temporal structure in music and speech. *Proceedings of the National Academy of Sciences, 113*(19), 5212–5217.

Zhou, Q., Eisenberg, N., Wang, Y., & Reiser, M. (2004). Chinese children's effortful control and dispositional anger/frustration: Relations to parenting styles and children's social functioning. *Developmental Psychology, 40,* 352–366. doi:10.1037/0012-1649.40.3.352

Zhou, Q., Wang, Y., Deng, X., Eisenberg, N., Wolchik, S. A., & Tein, J.-Y. (2008). Relations of parenting and temperament to Chinese children's experience of negative life events, coping efficacy, and externalizing problems. *Child Development, 79,* 493–513. doi:10.1111/j.1467-8624.2008.01139.x

Zhu, J. L., Olsen, J., Liew, Z., Li, J., Niclasen, J., & Obel, C. (2014). Parental smoking during pregnancy and ADHD in children: The Danish national birth cohort. *Pediatrics, 134*(2), e382–e388.

Ziegler, J. C., Pech-Georgel, C., George, F., Alario, F.-X., & Lorenzi, C. (2005). Deficits in speech perception predict language learning impairment. *Proceedings of the National Academy of Sciences of the United States of America, 102,* 14110–14115. doi:10.1073/pnas.0504446102

Ziemer, C. J., Plumert, J. M., & Pick, A. D. (2012). To grasp or not to grasp: Infants' actions toward objects and pictures. *Infancy, 17*(5), 479–497.

Zigler, E., & Styfco, S. J. (2004). The wisdom of a federal effort on behalf of impoverished children and their families. In E. Zigler & S. J. Styfco (Eds.), *The Head Start debates* (pp. 221–249). Baltimore, MD: Paul H. Brookes.

Zimmer, E. Z., Chao, C. R., Guy, G. P., Marks, F., & Fifer, W. P. (1993). Vibroacoustic stimulation evokes human fetal micturition. *Obstetrics and Gynecology, 81,* 178–180.

Zimmer-Gembeck, M. J., Siebenbruner, J., & Collins, W. A. (2001). Diverse aspects of dating: Associations with psychosocial functioning from early to middle adolescence. *Journal of Adolescence, 24,* 313–336. doi:10.1006/jado.2001.0410

Zimmer-Gembeck, M. J., Siebenbruner, J., & Collins, W. A. (2004). A prospective study of intraindividual and peer influences on adolescents' heterosexual romantic and sexual behavior. *Archives of Sexual Behavior, 33,* 381–394. doi:10.1023/B:ASEB.0000028891.16654.2c

Zimmer-Gembeck, M. J., & Skinner, E. A. (2011). Review: The development of coping across childhood and adolescence: An integrative review and critique of research. *International Journal of Behavioral Development, 35,* 1–17. doi:10.1177/0165025410384923

Zimmermann, P., Maier, M. A., Winter, M., & Grossmann, K. E. (2001). Attachment and adolescents' emotion regulation during a joint problem-solving task with a friend. *International Journal of Behavioral Development, 25,* 331–343.

Zisenwine, T., Kaplan, M., Kushnir, J., & Sadeh, A. (2013). Nighttime fears and fantasy-reality differentiation in preschool children. *Child Psychiatry and Human Development, 44,* 186–199. doi:10.1007/s10578-012-0318-x

Zolotor, A. J., Robinson, T. W., Runyan, D. K., Barr, R. G., & Murphy, R. A. (2011). The emergence of spanking among a representative sample of children under 2 years of age in North Carolina. *Frontiers in Psychiatry, 2,* 1–8. doi:10.2289/fpsyt.2011.00036

Zucker, K. J. (2006). Commentary on Langer and Martin's (2004) "How dresses can make you mentally ill: Examining gender identity disorder in children." *Child and Adolescent Social Work Journal, 23,* 533–555. doi:10.1007/s10560-006-0074-5

Zucker, K. J., & Bradley, S. J. (1995). Gender identity disorder and psychosexual problems in children and adolescents. New York, NY: Guilford Press.

Name Index

Subject Index

Page numbers in **bold** indicate definitions.